D. H. LAWRENCE

A Reference Companion

PAUL POPLAWSKI

With a Biography by
JOHN WORTHEN

GREENWOOD PRESS
Westport, Connecticut • London

Library of Congress Cataloging-in-Publication Data

Poplawski, Paul.
    D. H. Lawrence : a reference companion / Paul Poplawski ; with a
biography by John Worthen.
        p.   cm.
    Includes bibliographical references and index.
    ISBN 0–313–28637–X (alk. paper)
    1. Lawrence, D. H. (David Herbert), 1885–1930—Bibliography.
I. Worthen, John. II. Title.
Z8490.5.P67   1996
[PR6023.A93]
016.823'912—dc20   95–38654

British Library Cataloguing in Publication Data is available.

Library of Congress Catalog Card Number: 95–38654
ISBN: 0–313–28637–X

First published in 1996

Greenwood Press, 88 Post Road West, Westport, CT 06881
An imprint of Greenwood Publishing Group, Inc.

Printed in the United States of America

The paper used in this book complies with the
Permanent Paper Standard issued by the National
Information Standards Organization (Z39.48–1984).

10 9 8 7 6 5 4 3 2 1

D. H. LAWRENCE

D. H. Lawrence
Basia Wilamowska, 1995. Pencil and colored chalk.

TO ANGIE

Contents

Preface: How to Use This Book

This book provides a comprehensive but easy-to-use reference guide to the life, works, and critical reception of D. H. Lawrence. It contains perhaps a wider range of detailed information on Lawrence than any other single book currently available and will therefore serve as an invaluable reference tool for the specialist; but it has also been organized to be readily accessible to the beginning student and casual reader. The volume has been systematically structured to convey a coherent, overall sense of Lawrence's achievement and critical reputation, but I have kept constantly before me the needs of a hypothetical ''average reader,'' who may be interested in only one aspect of Lawrence's career, or only one of his novels or stories, and who will want to find relevant information quickly and easily without having to read large parts of the rest of the text.

Information provides the main focus of the book, for although it certainly contains some interpretation and critical commentary, it has been designed, first and foremost, as a *reference* work. To the extent that it does aim to do more than simply provide information, it aims to clear the ground for future critical scholarship on Lawrence by taking comprehensive stock of what we now know of his life and works and of what has been said and thought of him throughout the twentieth century to the present day. In this sense, it seeks to be both a retrospective survey of information and scholarship and a prospectus for future scholarship.

There are five major parts to the book:

I. Life

II. Works

III. Critical Reception

IV. Reference Bibliographies

V. Indexes

The first three parts are divided into sections and chapters, and interspersed throughout these are ninety-eight specialized bibliographies and seven chronologies dealing in summary form with various aspects of Lawrence's life, works, and criticism. Each of these parts can be referred to largely independently of the others; but there are inherent connections between them, and they have been ordered and internally sectionalized to give maximum potential for sequential reading either in their entirety or along selected ''pathways'' of the reader's own choosing. Part V is functionally related to the other parts of the book in obvious ways; and while Part IV can be referred to in its own right as a comprehensive checklist of books, pamphlets, and journals devoted to Lawrence and as a checklist of Lawrence's own major publications, it also has an important cross-referencing function in relation to author-date citations to be found throughout the first three parts of the book. Although I have endeavored to keep to an absolute minimum the use of any sort of abbreviation and (for reasons already suggested) to provide full and usable information, including *full* bibliographical references, at the point of use, constraints of space have inevitably dictated some compromises. Thus, it is important to note that full details of all author-date citations in the book (e.g., Moore 1951) can be found in Bibliography 96 (''Master Bibliography of Books and Pamphlets on Lawrence''). The only abbreviation used in the book is *DHL* for *D. H. Lawrence* within bibliographies and chronologies. Apart from these points, Parts IV and V of the book are self-explanatory.

   Part I of the book contains:

1. a complete narrative biography of Lawrence by John Worthen, along with a chronology of Lawrence's life and works;

2. a comprehensive bibliography of biographical scholarship and criticism on Lawrence, including collections of his letters;

3. two chronologies on aspects of Lawrence's sociohistoric background that were crucial not only in determining the kind of person and writer he became but also in providing him with a major source of subject matter for his writing, namely, a chronology of the development of state education in Britain (virtually nonexistent before Lawrence's time) and a chronology charting key developments in the history of coal mining and the labor movement, along with related social reforms (Lawrence's father was a coal miner, and Lawrence grew up within a working-class culture still acutely aware of its need to ''organize, educate, and agitate'' for workers' rights);

4. a travel chronology of Lawrence's life, and a series of locational maps indicating places associated with his life and works.

Each chapter of John Worthen's biography deals with a clearly defined period in Lawrence's life so that, with careful use of the table of contents and/or indexes, the chapters can be easily correlated to other parts of the book to make relevant connections. For example, at the end of a particular chapter of the biography, the reader might like to pause to find out more about the works Lawrence wrote in that period by looking up the relevant entries for those works in Part II. Or, by consulting the maps and the travel chronology, he or she might wish to clarify Lawrence's movements for that period.

The maps contained in this part of the book are intended for cross-referencing not only with the biography of Lawrence but also with the places mentioned in relation to his works in the next part of the book—hence, their positioning at the end of Part I, where they can also be conveniently consulted from Part II.

Part II contains a separate entry on almost every single text that Lawrence produced (the main exceptions being individual poems and paintings). Works in this part are organized first by genre (novels, short fiction, poetry, plays, other works) and then, within each genre section, chronologically. All entries provide information on the *composition* and *publication* of a work—(1) first publication, (2) scholarly Cambridge edition, where applicable, and, in some entries, (3) other significant editions—and a comprehensive bibliography listing of the criticism that has been devoted to it. All entries under the sections for the novels and short fiction provide, in addition, a *who's who* of characters embedded within a critical *summary* of the work (the names of characters are highlighted on first significant reference) and details of its *setting*. In the bibliographies for each work, the main list of full citations contains *all* studies that are devoted specifically to that work (including books and pamphlets, even if these are listed in the master bibliography); however, books that appear in the master bibliography and that contain material on the work without being entirely devoted to it are given at the end of the main list and abbreviated to author-date citations. Entries are set out as in the following (abbreviated) example:

"THINGS"

WRITTEN

May 1927. . . .

PUBLISHED

Bookman 67 (August 1928): 632–37. . . .

WHO'S WHO AND SUMMARY

This comic critique of idealism is executed by means of a superbly controlled satirical presentation of the story's two central characters, the New England idealists, *Erasmus* and *Valerie Melville* . . .

SETTING

The story follows the Melvilles from home to home around the world as follows . . .

BIBLIOGRAPHY 58

Cushman, Keith. "The Serious Comedy of 'Things.' " *Etudes Lawrenciennes* 6 (1991): 83–94. . . .

See also Draper (1969): 25–28.

In the bibliographies for the novels and some of the longer short fictions, *two* groups of author-date citations are given, one of criticism published before 1979 and one of criticism published between 1980 and 1994. This has been done to provide readers with a quick checklist of the most recent criticism on a particular work (as many readers will already be familiar with older criticism), though without neglecting older works. In all bibliographies, where a short item has been published, *after* initial publication, in one of the books listed in the master bibliography, this secondary information is given with an author-date citation for that book. In all bibliographies, also, "op. cit." is used only to refer the reader to works already listed within the *same* bibliography.

Part III maps out the means to a detailed understanding of Lawrence's changing critical and popular reputation throughout this century, as well as to indicate something of the range of modes and methods that have been adopted by critics in exploring his works. It is organized in three sections. Section A provides a general bibliographical guide to the essential sources in Lawrentian scholarship, along with a chronological listing of criticism since the start of his writing career (Chronology 5 contains a complete but abbreviated list of all books and pamphlets, while Chronology 6 lists a selection of essays and articles). Section B contains seven separate bibliographies differentiated according to type of critical approach (e.g., psychoanalytic approaches, myth criticism, feminist approaches). Section C presents two essays by Nigel Morris that address the question of Lawrence's popular image as represented by screen mediations of his life and works. After reconsidering received opinion as to Lawrence's own attitudes toward popular media such as film, Morris looks in detail at specific film adaptations and, perhaps most important, establishes some systematic principles in the analysis of literary adaptation for the screen. As Lawrence's life coincided almost exactly with the initial flowering of the film industry, these essays are consolidated later in the section by Nigel Morris's chronology of cinema and broadcasting. The section also contains a bibliography of "Lawrence and Film" that is probably the most comprehensive listing available both of film adaptations of Lawrence and of criticism relating to these.

I would like to thank my collaborators, John Worthen and Nigel Morris, for the meticulous care with which they carried out their parts of this work, for their enthusiasm for the project, and for the marvelous support they have both given me throughout its duration: John in thousands of practical ways to do with the substance of the book, and Nigel in almost daily doses of reassurance and encouragement. For his superb maps and for the care and effort he put into their production, I would also like to express my gratitude to Trevor Harris.

I am indebted to Marilyn Brownstein, formerly of Greenwood Press, for asking me to produce this book in the first place and to George Butler, my present editor, for his continued enthusiasm for the project and for being ''the pattern of all patience'' in the face of several delays in the submission of the manuscript.

I am grateful for their help to the members of staff of several libraries, but particularly those at Trinity College Carmarthen, Swansea University College, and the Nottinghamshire County Library. Trinity College Carmarthen has provided financial help to enable me to undertake several research trips to the British Library and has supported the writing of this book in other material and practical ways. I wish also to thank my colleague, Conway Davies, for the loan of books and for generously agreeing to check and comment on Chronologies 2 and 3.

I would like to express my love and thanks to all the members of my family— Dad, Jan, Alina, Barbara, Peter, and their respective families, not forgetting Emily, of course, and Freiga—for their forbearance in the face of ''the book.'' The greatest forbearance, however, has been shown by my partner, Angie, who has helped and supported me in every conceivable way through all the stages of the book's development. Indeed, parts of it are as much hers as mine—and I dedicate all of it, with all my love, to her.

PART I

LIFE

SECTION A

A BIOGRAPHY, BY JOHN WORTHEN

Full details of the works and letters of Lawrence cited here can be found in the reference bibliography of works by Lawrence at the end of this book. The works are referred to in the text by their main titles or shortened versions thereof. The letters are referred to simply as *Letters,* followed by the appropriate volume number, except in the case of the Huxley edition, which is referred to as *Letters* 1932.

References to other works are made using the author-date citation system, and full details of all such references can be found in Bibliography 1 ("Biographies, Memoirs, Letters, and Related Materials") immediately following this biography.

Chapters 1 and 2 are indebted throughout to the work cited as Worthen 1991 (John Worthen. *D. H. Lawrence: The Early Years 1885–1912.* Cambridge: Cambridge University Press, 1991); in the absence of other information, it should be assumed that sources will be found there.

CHRONOLOGY 1: THE LIFE AND MAJOR WORKS OF D. H. LAWRENCE

1885	David Herbert Richards Lawrence (hereafter, DHL) born in Eastwood, Nottinghamshire, the fourth child of Arthur John Lawrence, collier, and Lydia, née Beardsall, daughter of a pensioned-off engine fitter.
1891–98	Attends Beauvale Board School.

1898–1901   Becomes first boy from Eastwood to win a County Council schol-
             arship to Nottingham High School, which he attends until July 1901.

1901   Three months as a clerk at Haywood's surgical appliances factory in
             Nottingham; severe attack of pneumonia.

1902   Begins frequent visits to the Chambers family at Haggs Farm, Un-
             derwood, and starts his friendship with Jessie Chambers.

1902–5   Pupil-teacher at the British School, Eastwood; sits the King's Schol-
             arship exam in December 1904 and is placed in the first division of
             the first class.

1905–6   Works as uncertificated teacher at the British School; writes his first
             poems and starts his first novel, *Laetitia* (later, *The White Peacock,*
             1911).

1906–8   Student at Nottingham University College following the Normal
             course leading to a teachers' certificate; qualifies in July 1908. Also
             wins *Nottinghamshire Guardian* Christmas 1907 short story compe-
             tition with "A Prelude" (submitted under name of Jessie Chambers);
             writes second version of *Laetitia.*

1908–11   Elementary teacher at Davidson Road School, Croydon.

1909   Meets Ford Madox Hueffer, who begins to publish his poems and
             stories in the *English Review* and recommends rewritten version of
             The White Peacock to William Heinemann; DHL writes *A Collier's
             Friday Night* (1934) and first version of "Odour of Chrysanthe-
             mums" (1911); friendship with Agnes Holt.

1910   Writes *The Saga of Siegmund* (first version of *The Trespasser,* 1912),
             based on the experiences of his friend the Croydon teacher Helen
             Corke; starts affair with Jessie Chambers; writes first version of *The
             Widowing of Mrs. Holroyd* (1914); ends affair with Jessie Chambers
             but continues friendship; starts to write *Paul Morel* (later, *Sons and
             Lovers,* 1913); death of Lydia Lawrence in December; gets engaged
             to his old friend Louie Burrows.

1911   Fails to finish *Paul Morel;* strongly attracted to Helen Corke; starts
             affair with Alice Dax, wife of an Eastwood chemist; meets Edward
             Garnett, publisher's reader for Duckworth, who advises him on writ-
             ing and publication. In November, falls seriously ill with pneumonia
             and has to give up schoolteaching; *The Saga* accepted by Duckworth;
             DHL commences its revision as *The Trespasser.*

1912   Convalesces in Bournemouth. Breaks off engagement to Louie; re-
             turns to Eastwood; works on *Paul Morel;* in March, meets Frieda
             Weekley, wife of Ernest, Professor of Modern Languages at Notting-
             ham; ends affair with Alice Dax; goes to Germany on a visit to his
             relations on 3 May; travels, however, with Frieda to Metz. After
             many vicissitudes (some memorialized in *Look! We Have Come
             Through!,* 1917), Frieda gives up her marriage and her children for
             DHL. In August, they journey over the Alps to Italy and settle at
             Gargnano, where DHL writes the final version of *Sons and Lovers.*

1913	*Love Poems* published. Writes *The Daughter-in-Law* (1965) and 200 pages of *The Insurrection of Miss Houghton* (abandoned); begins *The Sisters,* eventually to be split into *The Rainbow* (1915) and *Women in Love* (1920). DHL and Frieda spend some days at San Gaudenzio, then stay at Irschenhausen in Bavaria; DHL writes first versions of ''The Prussian Officer'' and ''The Thorn in the Flesh'' (1914). *Sons and Lovers* published in May. DHL and Frieda return to England in June, meet John Middleton Murry and Katherine Mansfield. They return to Italy (Fiascherino, near La Spezia) in September; DHL revises *The Widowing of Mrs. Holroyd,* resumes work on *The Sisters.*
1914	Rewrites *The Sisters* (now called *The Wedding Ring*) yet again; agrees for Methuen to publish it; takes J. B. Pinker as agent. DHL and Frieda return to England in June, marry on 13 July 1914. DHL meets Catherine Carswell and S. S. Koteliansky; compiles short story collection *The Prussian Officer* (1914). Outbreak of war prevents DHL and Frieda returning to Italy; at Chesham he first writes ''Study of Thomas Hardy'' (1936) and then begins *The Rainbow;* starts important friendships with Ottoline Morrell, Cynthia Asquith, Bertrand Russell, and E. M. Forster; grows increasingly desperate and angry about the war.
1915	Finishes *The Rainbow* in Greatham in March; plans lecture course with Russell; quarrels in June. DHL and Frieda move to Hampstead in August; he and Murry publish *The Signature* (magazine, three issues only). *The Rainbow* published by Methuen in September, suppressed at end of October, prosecuted and banned in November. DHL meets painters Dorothy Brett and Mark Gertler; he and Frieda plan to leave England for Florida; decide to move to Cornwall instead.
1916	Writes *Women in Love* between April and October; publishes *Twilight in Italy* and *Amores.*
1917	*Women in Love* rejected by publishers; DHL continues to revise it. Makes unsuccessful attempts to go to America. Begins *Studies in Classic American Literature* (1923); publishes *Look! We Have Come Through!* In October, he and Frieda evicted from Cornwall on suspicion of spying; in London, he begins *Aaron's Rod* (1922).
1918	DHL and Frieda move to Hermitage, Berkshire, then to Middleton-by-Wirksworth: he publishes *New Poems,* writes *Movements in European History* (1921), *Touch and Go* (1920), first version of *The Fox* (1920).
1919	Seriously ill with influenza; moves back to Hermitage; publishes *New Poems.* In the autumn, Frieda goes to Germany and then joins DHL in Florence; they visit Picinisco and settle in Capri.
1920	Writes *Psychoanalysis and the Unconscious* (1921). He and Frieda move to Taormina, Sicily; DHL writes *The Lost Girl* (1920), *Mr Noon* (1984), continues with *Aaron's Rod;* on summer visit to Florence, has affair with Rosalind Baynes, writes many poems from *Birds, Beasts and Flowers* (1923). *Women in Love* published.

1921   DHL and Frieda visit Sardinia, and he writes *Sea and Sardinia* (1921); meets Earl and Achsah Brewster; finishes *Aaron's Rod* in the summer and writes *Fantasia of the Unconscious* (1922) and *The Captain's Doll* (1923); plans to leave Europe and visit United States; puts together collection of stories *England, My England* (1922) and group of short novels *The Ladybird, The Fox, The Captain's Doll* (1923).

1922   DHL and Frieda leave for Ceylon, stay with Brewsters, then travel to Australia; he translates Verga. In western Australia, meets Mollie Skinner. In Thirroul, near Sydney, he writes *Kangaroo* (1923) in six weeks. August–September, he and Frieda travel to California via South Sea islands and meet Witter Bynner and Willard Johnson; settle in Taos, New Mexico, at invitation of Mabel Dodge (later, Luhan). In December, move up to Del Monte ranch, near Taos; DHL rewrites *Studies in Classic American Literature.*

1923   Finishes *Birds, Beasts and Flowers.* He and Frieda spend summer at Chapala in Mexico, where he writes *Quetzalcoatl* (first version of *The Plumed Serpent*, 1926). Frieda returns to Europe in August after serious quarrel with DHL; he journeys in United States and Mexico, rewrites Mollie Skinner's ''The House of Ellis'' as *The Boy in the Bush* (1924); arrives back in England in December.

1924   At dinner in Café Royal, DHL invites his friends to come to New Mexico; Dorothy Brett accepts and accompanies him and Frieda in March. Mabel Luhan gives Lobo (later renamed Kiowa) ranch to Frieda; DHL gives her *Sons and Lovers* manuscript in return. During summer on the ranch, he writes *St. Mawr* (1925), ''The Woman Who Rode Away'' (1925), and ''The Princess'' (1925). In August, suffers his first bronchial hemorrhage. His father dies in September. In October, he, Frieda, and Brett move to Oaxaca, Mexico, where he starts *The Plumed Serpent* and writes most of *Mornings in Mexico* (1927).

1925   Finishes *The Plumed Serpent,* falls ill, and almost dies of typhoid and pneumonia in February; in March, diagnosed as suffering from tuberculosis. Recuperates at Kiowa ranch, writes *David* (1926) and compiles *Reflections on the Death of a Porcupine* (1925). He and Frieda return to Europe in September, spend a month in England, and settle at Spotorno, Italy; DHL writes first version of *Sun* (1926); Frieda meets Angelo Ravagli.

1926   Writes *The Virgin and the Gipsy* (1930); serious quarrel with Frieda during visit from DHL's sister Ada. DHL visits Brewsters and Brett, has affair with Brett. Reconciled, DHL and Frieda move to Villa Mirenda, near Florence, in May and visit England (his last visit) in late summer. On return to Italy in October, he writes first version of *Lady Chatterley's Lover* (1944), starts second version in November. Friendship with Aldous and Maria Huxley; DHL starts to create paintings.

1927	Finishes second version of *Lady Chatterley's Lover* (1972), visits Etruscan sites with Earl Brewster, writes *Sketches of Etruscan Places* (1932) and the first part of *The Escaped Cock* (1928). In November, after meetings with Michael Arlen and Norman Douglas, works out scheme for private publication with Pino Orioli and starts final version of *Lady Chatterley's Lover* (1928).
1928	Finishes *Lady Chatterley's Lover* and arranges for its printing and publication in Florence; fights many battles to ensure its dispatch to subscribers in Britain and United States. In June, writes second part of *The Escaped Cock* (1929). He and Frieda travel to Switzerland (Gsteig) and the island of Port Cros; then settle in Bandol, in the south of France. He writes many of the poems in *Pansies* (1929). *Lady Chatterley's Lover* pirated in Europe and United States.
1929	Visits Paris to arrange for cheap edition of *Lady Chatterley's Lover* (1929); unexpurgated typescript of *Pansies* seized by police; exhibition of his paintings in London raided by police. He and Frieda visit Majorca, France, and Bavaria, returning to Bandol for the winter. He writes *Nettles* (1930), *Apocalypse* (1931), and *Last Poems* (1932); sees much of Brewsters and Huxleys.
1930	Goes into Ad Astra sanatorium in Vence at start of February; discharges himself on 1 March, dies at Villa Robermond, Vence, on Sunday, 2 March, is buried on 4 March.
1935	Frieda sends Angelo Ravagli (now living with her at Kiowa ranch; they marry in 1950) to Vence to have DHL exhumed and cremated and his ashes brought back to the ranch.
1956	Frieda dies and is buried at Kiowa ranch.

1 Background and Youth: 1885–1908

I.

D. H. Lawrence (1885–1930) was born on 11 September 1885 in the small house that is now 8a Victoria Street, Eastwood, Nottinghamshire. Eastwood was a growing colliery village of around 5,000 inhabitants: there were ten pits within easy walking distance, and a massive majority of the male population were colliers (Lawrence's father and all three paternal uncles worked down the pit). The district had grown and prospered because of the rewards offered by the industry; the very house where Lawrence was born had been built by the largest of the local colliery companies, Barber Walker & Co. But by the mid-1880s, the great coal boom was over; and though Eastwood continued to grow, the only future it seemed to offer was in the coal industry itself. A tight-knit community of men whose lives depended on each other also supported wives, few of whom had jobs, and children, who mostly could not wait until they were— at fourteen—able themselves to start as colliers. It was not a promising background for a man who would make his life's work writing about the fulfilled relationships of men and women, and the crucial relationship between human beings and the natural world, although such things were remarkable in his background by their very absence.

Lawrence was the fourth child of Arthur Lawrence (1846–1924) and Lydia Beardsall (1851–1910) and their first to have been born in Eastwood. Ever since their marriage in 1875, the couple had been on the move: Arthur's job as a miner had taken them where the best-paid work had been during the boom years of the 1870s, and they had lived in a succession of small and recently built grimy colliery villages all over Nottinghamshire. But when they moved to East-wood in 1883, it was to a place where they would remain for the rest of their lives; the move seems to have marked a watershed in their early history.

For one thing, they were settling down: Arthur Lawrence would work at Brinsley colliery until he retired in 1912. For another, they now had three small children—George (1876–1967), Ernest (1878–1901), and Emily (1882–1962)—and Lydia may have wanted to give them the kind of continuity in schooling they had never previously had. It was also the case that, when they came to Eastwood, they took a house with a shop window, and Lydia ran a small clothes shop, presumably to supplement their income, but also perhaps because she felt she could do it in addition to raising their children. It seems possible that, getting on badly with her husband as she did, she imagined that further children were out of the question. Taking on the shop may have marked her own bid for independence.

She certainly needed to stand up for herself. Arthur's parents—John (1815–1901) and Louisa (1818–98)—and his brother George (1853–1929) lived less than a mile away, down in Brinsley, where his brother James (1851–80) had been killed at work, three years earlier, while his youngest brother, Walter (1856–1904), lived only 100 yards away from them in another company house, in Princes Street. When the family moved to Eastwood, Arthur Lawrence was coming back to his own family's center; one of the reasons, for sure, that they stayed there.

Lydia Lawrence probably felt, on the other hand, more as if she were digging in for a siege. Eastwood may have been home to Arthur Lawrence, but to Lydia it was just another grimy colliery village that she never liked very much and where she never felt either much at home or properly accepted. Her family originally came from Nottingham, but she had been brought up in Sheerness, and her Kent accent doubtless made Midlands people feel that she put on airs. Her grandfather lived not far off, but the rest of her family were all still in Nottingham, twelve miles away. Her father, George Beardsall (1825–99), was a pensioned-off engine fitter who had been injured at work in Sheerness back in 1870 and who had never worked since. The family had come back to Not-tingham, and her mother, Lydia (1830–1900), had somehow contrived that they should survive on his tiny pension and on what the children of the family had been able to bring in. Lydia the daughter had originally had ambitions to be a teacher and was always bookish and interested in intellectual matters; but fol-lowing her family's financial disaster, like her sisters, she had had to fall back on the humiliations of lace-drawing—one of the sweated home-working jobs that Nottingham's lace industry created. George and Lydia Beardsall probably became a little better off, as their children grew up and married; but it also seems probable that their daughter Lydia's marriage to a collier in 1875 created a great deal of tension in the family. She married beneath her, her parents would have said. No matter their own poverty: Lydia had married, for love, a man who worked with his hands (and came home black)—and the Beardsalls had a cherished and legendary family history in which they had owned factories and had (once) even married into the aristocracy. They felt themselves to be gentlefolk even while everything about their circumstances ensured that they were not.

Arthur Lawrence was a butty—that is, a man responsible for the working of a small section of coal-face along with the team of workmen he organized—and it seems possible that, when he married Lydia, he had not told her that he himself worked underground. The loss of her own family, her disillusionment with her husband, and her anger at the ease with which—after early promises—he slipped back into the male world of evenings spent drinking with his mates, her dissatisfaction with her own roles as wife and mother in the succession of—to her—alien villages in which they had lived, all this had created in Lydia Lawrence both depression and a great deal of anger. Finding herself pregnant again in the early months of 1885 cannot have helped. The Victoria Street shop had not done well (Lydia was probably not an engaging saleswoman), and a new baby born in September 1885—they called him Bert—for whom she had to care signaled, perhaps, the end of her attempt to be independent that the shop had marked. In 1887, shortly after the family had moved down into a larger company house in "the Breach"—and the Breach, if well built, was notoriously common, even by Eastwood standards—she had another baby, Lettice Ada (1887–1948): another link in the chain she felt binding her down.

Home life for the Lawrence children became polarized between loyalty to their mother as she struggled to do her best for them, in scrimping and saving and encouraging them in taking their education seriously, and a rather troubled love for their father, who was increasingly treated by his wife as a drunken ne'er-do-well and who drank to escape the tensions he (as a consequence) experienced at home. Lydia Lawrence consciously alienated the children from their father and told them stories of her early married life (like the episode when Arthur locked her out of the house at night), which they never forgot or forgave their father for. All the children, apart from the eldest son, George, grew up with an abiding love for their mother and various kinds of dislike for their father. Arthur Lawrence, for his part, unhappy at the lack of respect and love shown him and the way in which his male privilege as head of the household was constantly being breached, reacted by drinking and deliberately irritating and alienating his family. It seems quite likely that, for long periods of their childhood, his drinking and staying out in the evenings, until his tipsy return would lead to a row, effectively dominated the children's experience. His behavior—and his spending of a portion of the family income on drink—caused all the major quarrels between the parents, divided the children's loves and loyalties, and left Bert with a profound hatred of his father and an anxious, sympathetic love for his mother. The young Paul Morel lying in bed at night praying, "Let him be killed at pit" (*Sons and Lovers* 85) is probably a true memory of the young Bert Lawrence, lying in bed waiting for his father's return home at night.

This matter should be kept in perspective. Arthur Lawrence never left his family (though he may have threatened to); he never seems to have had to miss work because of his drinking; his earnings were never so diverted into drink as to leave his family seriously hard up; he was rarely, if ever, violent; and it is probably wrong to think of him simply as an alcoholic. As always, the problems with the marriage did not stem from the behavior of only one of the partners. Lydia Lawrence certainly played her part in alienating the children from their father and in setting the agenda for their behavior. They were *not* to look forward to becoming colliers, like their uncles and their father and like the vast majority of their contemporaries at school. They would take the teetotal pledge; they would treat school and its possibilities very seriously; they would go to Sunday school and chapel; they would become clerks and teachers; they would not grow up believing that men should boss women about; they would have ambitions to rise, if possible, into the middle classes. All this, of course, still further alienated and angered Arthur Lawrence. But, in short, the Lawrence children would conform to the Beardsall family's image of itself rather than to Arthur Lawrence's; and they would grow up to do the things and take the chances that their mother would have liked to have done and taken.

All Lydia Lawrence had to look forward to, in the long term, was the growth of her children, especially her sons, into adulthood and independence. Both literally and metaphorically, she always seems to have looked forward to some kind of painful struggle back up the hill into respectability. In 1891, the family managed the literal move when they moved up to a bay-windowed house in Walker Street commanding a magnificent view over the valley and beyond; and, the same year, the eldest son, George, left school and started work. Her favorite child, however, was her second son, Ernest, who was the cleverest of all her children at school (Bert was delicate in health and missed too much school when young to do particularly well). Ernest left Beauvale school in 1893 and quickly found work as a clerk; and his mother's hopes became bound up with his success. George was always rather a problem to his mother: he ran away to join the army in 1895, and his mother had to buy him out; and then, in 1897, he had to marry his pregnant girlfriend, Ada Wilson (1876–1938). Altogether, he probably seemed (to his mother and to his siblings) rather too much like his father, of whom he always thought very highly. But Ernest went from strength to strength, through a succession of relatively well paid jobs. As well as working, he studied in the evenings, read widely, taught shorthand at the local night school, and also gave private lessons. He ended up, at the age of twenty-one, getting a job in London at £120 a year. Arthur Lawrence, even in a good year, would not have earned as much as that and would normally have earned considerably less.

The family dynamics changed with George's and Ernest's leaving home. The eldest daughter, Emily, was not especially good at school and had always done a great deal of caring for her younger siblings (they never forgot the stories she would tell them); she would remain living at home until her marriage to a local man, Sam King (1880–1965), in 1904. Bert was, however, starting to flourish: a sickly child who had been bullied as ''mard-arsed''—soft—when young and who had preferred the company of girls to boys and of books to either, cardinal sins in a male-dominated society. But he was doing better and better at school: he won a scholarship to Nottingham High School in 1898, his last year at the Board School in Beauvale he had been attending since he was seven; the County Council was sponsoring the children of the poor to allow them access to such institutions. Bert Lawrence was only the second miner's son ever to go to the High School in Nottingham. Having never been a normal, games-playing, and colliery-directed Eastwood boy, he was now going to be a distinctly abnormal one, with his high collar and dark suit and the books under his arm.

His performance at Nottingham, however, was only briefly distinguished and bottomed out badly at the end of his second year. He turned out to be even more of a fish out of water in an almost completely middle-class school than he had been in Eastwood. Events in March 1900 must have contributed to making things worse still. His uncle Walter Lawrence (now living in Ilkeston, three miles away, just over the border into Derbyshire) was arrested for killing his son by throwing the carving steel at him during a row and was committed for trial at the Derby assizes. The story was splashed over the local newspapers, and Bert Lawrence's performance at school that summer was his worst yet. He left at the age of sixteen, in the summer of 1901, with almost nothing to show for his three years there: years that (in spite of the scholarship) had cost the family a good deal of money.

It was now imperative that he get a job. Although his Nottingham High School training had equipped him to start as a pupil-teacher in a local school—if he could get a place—it seemed more important that he should start earning than that his long-term future should be considered. Accordingly, in the early autumn, like his brother Ernest, he started work as a clerk. He acquired a position in a Nottingham surgical goods factory and warehouse, at last doing something to offset the railway fares and the cost of the clothes out of which he was now fast growing. Having always been a small child, he was now getting lanky.

While he was at work in Nottingham, at Haywoods, the great tragedy of the family occurred. Ernest was still working in London and had recently become engaged to a London stenographer, Louisa "Gipsy" Dennis. He had been home for the traditional October Nottinghamshire holiday, known as the Wakes, but had fallen ill with erysipelas on his return to his south London lodgings. His landlady sent a telegram to Eastwood, and Lydia Lawrence braved the trains and the suburbs to go to him and nurse him. She found him unconscious and dangerously ill when she arrived; doctors could do nothing (the disease commonly led very quickly to blood poisoning, high fever, and pneumonia), and he died within a day of her arrival.

Of all the possible disasters in Lydia's disappointed life, this must have been the worst. She took little interest in her family that autumn; and when Bert himself fell ill, just before Christmas, it came only as a dull shock to his mother. But the work in the factory and the strain of the long day (twelve hours at work and two more hours traveling), combined, doubtless, with the fact that his mother was effectively ignoring him, weakened him, and Bert developed double pneumonia. His mother nearly lost him, too. Release from the emotional traumas of the autumn and Bert's recovery led her to identify her hopes and emotions with her youngest son to an extent that she had never done before; he came back to a new and very significant kind of intimacy with his mother. He would now be carrying the weight of her hopes and expectations—and of her love, a love to which he instinctively responded and never forgot.

II.

Something else Lawrence came back to after his illness—he never returned to Haywoods—was a new awareness of the country around his home. For all its griminess and ugliness, Eastwood was set in a surprisingly rural landscape; Arthur Lawrence could gather mushrooms on his morning's walk across the fields and at work would chew grass stems picked on the same walk. Lawrence's new relationship with the countryside was largely gleaned from visits to the Haggs farm, two miles north of Eastwood. The Chambers family and the Lawrence family had gone to the same chapel in Eastwood, and Mrs. Ann Chambers (1859–1937)—another stranger in Eastwood—had struck up a friendship with Lydia Lawrence. In 1898, the Chambers family had gone to live and work at the farm; and Bert Lawrence had first visited them there, with his mother, during his last summer at Nottingham High School. Now, the walk to the farm and the life he could share there became an important part of his convalescence. We may suspect, too, that he found the tensions and outbursts of a very different family from his own more bearable than the sometimes stiflingly moralizing and emotionally constrained atmosphere of home. He became friends with the two younger boys first and then with the eldest son, Alan (1882–1946), three years older than himself. The elder daughter, May (1883–1955), was in the process of an adolescent extraction of herself from the family toils; but the younger daughter, Jessie (1887–1944), seems to have worshiped Lawrence from the start. His relationship with her developed into the most significant of his young life.

For one thing, she was already fascinated by poetry and fiction; and in her, Lawrence found the willing companion in reading and discussing who was so significantly lacking at home. Lydia Lawrence always read a good deal, but only novels; and although at times she wrote poetry, she regarded such things as merely the diversions of a busy life lived to other and more significant ends. But Jessie and the young Lawrence—who had always read a good deal, the natural occupation of a rather withdrawn but clever child—now devoured books, lived through them, lost themselves in them. Lawrence found that, in their discussions, he could express himself to Jessie as to no one else.

During the spring and early summer, he got better; he had a month's convalescence at Skegness, at a boardinghouse run by his maternal aunt Nellie (1855–1908). He had to work, too: his aptitude for mathematics got him a job doing the accounts for a local pork butcher in the evenings. But that autumn, too, he embarked on a new career. A place had been found for him at last as a pupil-teacher in the British Schools in Eastwood; he received his own lessons from the headmaster, George Holderness, for an hour before school started, then spent most of the rest of his time teaching the collier lads who only a couple of years earlier would have jeered at him for being a softy. But being a pupil-teacher was the natural way forward to gaining (in the end) a teacher's certificate and to becoming the teacher that both Lawrence and his mother now recognized as his natural vocation. The work was taxing, but Lawrence impressed Holderness with his dedication and his intelligence. The pupil-teachers also spent some time each week at a pupil-teacher center in Ilkeston, rather to their headmaster's annoyance, because he lost valuable teachers while they were away; and here Lawrence met with a whole group of other men and women in his situation (he also thoroughly impressed the head). Jessie Chambers started to attend the center the year after Lawrence began, for example; so did Lawrence's younger sister Ada.

After two years as a pupil-teacher in Eastwood, paying visits to the new center in Ilkeston, furiously reading, going out to the Haggs farm and talking to Jessie, Lawrence sat the competitive King's Scholarship examination in December 1904. Now, for the first time, he emerged as a real star. He was placed in the first class of the first division; his name was printed in the local papers, and he had to send an account of himself and his working methods (with a photograph) to the magazine *The Schoolmaster.* The question remained of how he would actually study for his teacher's certificate. This could be done either full-time at an institution and sitting final examinations or by fitting the study into spare time and taking the examinations externally. It was decided that Bert Lawrence would go to college: Nottingham University College. This would be yet another strain on the family finances, to which Lawrence had, as yet, contributed almost nothing; it was decided that he would spend a year (this time, in full-time teaching) at the British Schools, earning fifty pounds, before going.

III.

The interval between taking the King's Scholarship examination and going to college in September 1906 proved to be perhaps the most significant period of Lawrence's life so far. In the first place, in the spring of 1905, he started to write. It was, perhaps, the most natural outcome of the years he had spent reading and discussing literature; yet, he began writing with a strong sense of the oddity of his ambition. "What will the others say? That I'm a fool. A collier's son a poet!" he remarked, scathingly, to Jessie Chambers. It was poetry that he began with. "I remember the slightly self-conscious Sunday afternoon, when . . . I 'composed' my first two 'poems.' One was to *Guelder-roses,* and one to *Campions,* and most young ladies would have done better: at least I hope so. But I thought the effusions very nice, and so did Miriam'' (Worthen 1991:

130–31). For perhaps a year, he wrote poetry. Then, at Easter 1906, he started the greatest experiment of his early life: he began to write a novel, which he called *Laetitia,* the first version of *The White Peacock.*

But other feelings also came to a head at Easter 1906. For four years, he and Jessie had accompanied each other's intellectual and literary development; they had progressed from the delighted sharing of novels to the serious work of reading Carlyle, Schopenhauer, and Emerson. Lawrence had helped answer her need for intense involvement in matters apart from the everyday life of the farm girl. Jessie had been not only the audience for all of Lawrence's fledgling work but, in many ways, its nurse, too: fiercely possessive of it, demanding its creation, loving it when she saw it. She and Lawrence had continued to see all they could of each other. But to other people—in particular, to Lawrence's mother, Lydia, and his sisters Emily and Ada—the relationship with Jessie must have seemed to have been growing positively unhealthy. Lawrence was out at all hours with her, walking and talking and reading; to a loving and possessive mother confronting his college career and all that depended on it, the time he spent with Jessie, like his writing, must have seemed a dangerous waste. Emily—now a married woman—thought her brother and Jessie must be lovers and wanted them to behave more respectably. Even Ada resented the way Jessie monopolized her brother. Lawrence was confronted with an ultimatum from his family. He should either become formally engaged to Jessie or stop seeing so much of her. It was explained to him that he was damaging her chances of getting to know other men: spoiling her chances of marriage.

Lawrence gauchely told Jessie what he felt he must, that he did not love her enough to want to marry her and that he must see less of her. She was horribly hurt, especially as her own feelings for him had grown more and more like love, over the years. They agreed to see less of each other and, if possible, only when a third person was there. But it was a savage blow to Jessie: the ending of her first, implicit, unexpressed belief that she and Lawrence were destined to spend their lives together. The Lawrence family, however, must have felt that they had foreseen a dangerous and distracting influence in Jessie.

That September, Lawrence brought his teaching in Eastwood to an end with some regrets. Holderness, a tough disciplinarian, had clearly valued him and protected him against the toughest of his pupils, while the pupils seem to have liked him as much as he liked them. But Lawrence had to start at college in Nottingham: another break with the old days. He acquired a new group of friends, among them a girl from Cossall he had first met at the Ilkeston Center, Louie Burrows (1888–1962), and moved into new worlds intellectually, eventually spending a good deal of his time with socialist and freethinking companions. Emily recalled ''a psychological set at the University, who ridiculed religion'' (Worthen 1991: 178). He also spent a lot of time writing; for example, he finished the first draft of his novel toward the end of his first year in college and wrote a second draft during his second year. This seems to have been his main achievement at Nottingham; he found the course stultifying and the teachers too often patronizing toward students working only for teacher's certificates rather than for degrees. His mother seems to have been keen on the idea of his transferring to a degree course or continuing studying part-time for a degree after he had obtained his teacher's certificate; but Lawrence seems to have done what he had to do, and no more. In spite of this, he came out with the best marks of any of the men in his final year, 1908.

But the two years at Nottingham, which he later felt had been largely wasted (he strongly advised Jessie Chambers to take her certificate as an external student), were actually another crucial opportunity for his development. He had more time for his writing than ever before. Not only did he continue to write *Laetitia,* but he worked hard at his poetry and, in the autumn of 1907, started to write short stories. This was originally because Jessie and Alan Chambers had challenged him to enter the annual *Nottinghamshire Guardian* competition, which had three categories for stories with a local setting. Lawrence determined to enter all three categories: he employed Jessie and Louie Burrows to submit entries for him, and he himself entered the story he thought had the best chance—an early version of "A Fragment of Stained Glass." As it turned out, the sentimental story entered by Jessie, "A Prelude"—containing re-creations of the Haggs and her family—won the category for the best story of a happy Christmas and was printed in the *Nottinghamshire Guardian.* Jessie's father, Edmund (1863–1946), cashed the three-pound check for Lawrence. He rewrote both the other stories eventually (Louie's being an early version of "The White Stocking") and wrote at least one other story ("The Vicar's Garden") around the same time. He also submitted some work—probably an essay—to the essayist and novelist G. K. Chesterton (1874–1936) at the *Daily News* but, to his irritation, had it returned and (according to Jessie) resolved to "try no more" (Worthen 1991: 191). He may well have sent a version of the essay "Art and the Individual," which he wrote to deliver at a debating society at the house of Willie (1862–1951) and Sallie (1867–1922) Hopkin (noted socialists both, who would stay his friends for years) in Eastwood, in the spring of 1908. Socialism mattered to him a lot, at the time: he joined a Society for the Study of Social Questions at college.

That last fact suggests, once again, his development during college away from his adolescent acceptance of the values of his mother and her world. In the first place, although he continued to live at home during his college years, he moved further away from the conditioning and expectations of home than he had ever done before. Although he was training to work as a teacher, his writing, reading, and thinking became increasingly important to him. He started to rebel against chapel; his friends were astonished one night in 1908 when, walking home to the Haggs with the Chambers family, he launched into a savage denunciation of the minister, the Reverend Robert Reid (1865–1955). Only the previous year, he had engaged in a scholarly dispute with Reid over contemporary objections to Christianity (*Letters* I: 36–37, 39–41), and Reid had chosen to deliver a series of sermons in the Eastwood Congregational Chapel specifically aimed at

Lawrence and his increasingly freethinking friends. Lawrence had been reading Schopenhauer, Haeckel, and William James since before going to college but now moved decisively against Christianity and eventually (under the influence of one of his teachers at college) declared himself to be a pragmatist of the William James sort: agnostic, not atheist.

But his immediate problem, after the exams that concluded his college career, was getting a job. Some of his college friends quickly assumed teaching posts (e.g., Louie Burrows had begun teaching in Leicester as soon as her college exams were over, probably to help pay for the expense of her years of study). But Lawrence was determined to hold out for a decent salary and to move out of Nottinghamshire if possible, and his family was obviously able to support him. He spent the summer helping with work on the Haggs farm, writing and reading and applying for jobs, eventually being interviewed at the end of September in Stockport but failing to get the job. But he was interviewed in the south London suburb of Croydon a few days later and was offered a post as assistant master at the Davidson Road Boys' School, starting 12 October. He was twenty-three-years-and-one-month-old: a committed poet and prose writer who had been published only once, a man who was steeped in the life and characters of his particular background and who (in one sense) would never leave the place in which he had grown up but whose taste for literature, contemporary thought, art, and music marked him as an oddity and exception in it. His move to London would, however, be decisive in his career, and after numerous farewells to old Nottinghamshire friends, he traveled down to Croydon on Sunday, 11 October, to start work the following day.

2   London and First Publication: 1908–12

I.

Lawrence found Croydon in October 1908 quite a shock. For the first time in his life (apart from holidays), he was away from home, in lodgings; he was a long way from family and friends and missed them badly; he was living in a fast-developing and rather squalid suburb of a suburb; and he was teaching full-time in a school very different (and much tougher) from any he had so far experienced. He wrote a letter "like a howl of terror" (*Letters* I: 82) to Jessie Chambers on his second day in Croydon: all his life, he later confessed, he had found new places and experiences upsetting—"Very rarely have I been able to enjoy the first weeks of anything, even a holiday" (*Letters* I: 106)—and Croydon took a great deal of getting used to, especially as he found himself working under a headmaster, Philip Smith (1866–1961), who was not (like George Holderness) concerned to protect him. The sons of colliers in Nottinghamshire, however rude they had been to the snuffly-nosed mard-arsed young Bert Lawrence, had been (by Eastwood standards) not badly off. But now Lawrence was teaching boys from institutions and from the really poor and deprived. He had very bad discipline problems; the account of Ursula's horrendous experiences at school in *The Rainbow* probably stemmed from Lawrence's own problems in his first weeks in Croydon, and—like Ursula's—his problems seemed to have been solved only by the eventual, self-brutalizing use of the cane.

Living in Croydon did offer, however, a new set of landscapes (he explored far and wide on his bicycle); and, in London itself, he went to plays and operas and explored art galleries and secondhand bookshops. But he found little intellectual stimulus in Croydon itself, and its lack of diversion offered him time to write. During his first year in Croydon, his social life was probably confined to occasional visits to pubs with his landlord, John William Jones (1868–1956); his evenings were spent marking or writing or helping Mrs. Marie Jones (1869–1950) with the children. He signaled the end of his mother's idea that he should study for a degree by symbolically turning two partly used Nottingham University College notebooks into storehouses for completed poems and poem drafts; as late as 1918, he would be still drawing upon drafts of poems first written down there. During his first year in Croydon, too, he managed a complete revision of *Laetitia:* "I am astonished to find how maudlin is the latter. It needed to come out here to toughen me off a bit; I am a fearful, sickly sentimentalist" (*Letters* I: 106). His reading broadened to include French poets like Charles Baudelaire (1821–67) and Paul Verlaine (1844–96); he was also lucky in having a sympathetic colleague at school—Arthur McLeod (1885–1956)—with a love of books and an extensive library.

His poetry led to his first significant break into print. He had continued sending all his writing to Jessie Chambers for her to read and comment on; and, in June 1909, she sent some of his poems to the editor of the *English Review,* the critic and novelist Ford Madox Hueffer (1873–1939). She and Lawrence had both admired the magazine when it started publication at the end of 1908; it had quickly established itself as one of the major journals. Hueffer was at the heart of the London literary scene: he had worked with Joseph Conrad (1857–1924), corresponded with Henry James (1843–1916), knew W. B. Yeats (1865–1939) and H. G. Wells (1866–1946) and (of the new generation of writers) Ezra Pound (1885–1972). Hueffer was struck by Lawrence and his poetry—by the facts of Lawrence's upbringing, perhaps, as much as by the poetry itself. The *English Review* saw itself as a radical journal with left-wing sympathies, and "a collier's son a poet" must have seemed heaven-sent. At all events, while the Lawrences were away on a family holiday on the Isle of Wight at the start of August 1909, Hueffer not only wrote to Jessie saying that he had decided to print some of the poems but asked to see Lawrence and—even more to the point—"says he will be glad to read any of the work I like to send him" (*Letters* I: 138). In order to produce a clean draft of *Laetitia* to replace the patched together and rewritten draft of 1908–9, as soon as he was back in Croydon, Lawrence commandeered his friends to help him: a rather older fellow teacher at Davidson School, Agnes Mason (1871–1950), and a new, younger schoolteacher acquaintance, Agnes Holt (1883–1971), whom he found very attractive. His poems came out in the November number of the *English Review,* and Agnes Holt made a fair copy of them into his second poetry notebook: to celebrate his success, to mark the start of the second notebook, and—doubtless—to show her own response to the successful young schoolteacher to whom she, too, was drawn. Success followed success; by the start of November, with the help of his friends, Lawrence had also got the new, clean manuscript of *Laetitia* into Hueffer's hands and, during December, made his first appearances in London literary society, introduced by Hueffer and his mistress Violet Hunt (1866–1942). He visited Wells, met Yeats, and stayed with Pound, all the time conscious of his socially unpresentable boots and shabby schoolmaster's suit.

At a stroke, he had been catapulted into the heart of contemporary literary intellectual circles. Yet, in 1909, just as he would for the rest of his life, Lawrence felt distinctly uncomfortable. He did not fit easily in that world—"I am no Society man—it bores me" (*Letters* I: 156); he was too aware of its pretensions, of its self-conscious artistry, of his own kinds of difference. He never became a popular author, nor an author much involved in contemporary writers' circles. A good deal of his life, he lived and worked a long way from the metropolis, cast himself in the role of an outsider, and remained on the outside. He would eventually become closer, in London, to practicing psychoanalysts than to literary folk; he visited a small circle of friends and relatively rarely moved beyond it.

It can hardly be an accident, however, that Lawrence's writing about his own background in the mining community started at exactly the time when Hueffer was a great influence upon him. He had completed his play *A Collier's Friday Night* by the end of November 1909, had a draft of "Odour of Chrysanthemums" finished by December, and would write the first version of his play *The Widowing of Mrs. Holroyd* early in the spring of 1910: all three of them probably responses to Hueffer's suggestion that he should write about " 'the other half'—though we might as well have said the other ninety-nine hundredths" (Worthen 1991: 216)—of which he had such intimate knowledge. Although Lawrence later described *A Collier's Friday Night* as "most horribly green," it remains eminently actable, negotiating as it does the difficult waters of the *Sons and Lovers* family situation without the aid of a pilot-narrator; the audience's sympathies are beautifully controlled as they swing from mother to son to father.

It was, however, his major fiction that Lawrence still thought most highly of—as he was right to do, if he was thinking of making a career of his writing. With a letter from Hueffer recommending it, he placed the manuscript of his novel *Laetitia* in the hands of the publisher William Heinemann (1863–1920) in mid-December. Heinemann took just a month to accept it, returning the manuscript in mid-January with requests for cuts and some changes, all of which Lawrence was happy to make. He worked on it during the early spring with a new friend, Helen Corke (1882–1978), a teacher in another Croydon school whom he had met through his fellow-teacher Agnes Mason. Helen Corke was still recovering from an appalling experience suffered the previous summer. On the Isle of Wight (by coincidence, at the same time as, but never meeting, the Lawrence family party), she had gone through five days of extraordinarily mixed feelings of love, liking, sexual repulsion, admiration, and astonished response to the natural world, in the company of a married music teacher and violinist in his late thirties, Herbert Macartney (1870–1909), who had persuaded her to go on holiday with him. On their return to south London, her lover—after two days back with his family—had killed himself. Helen herself was still coming

to terms with what had happened, and part of her therapy for herself was a long
diary letter to her dead lover; she had also written a diary of her five days on
the island. Lawrence became closely involved with her; listened to, sympathized
with, and analyzed her experiences; found himself intensely imagining the man's
own version of events; and began to work out his own version of the story.
Doing this while revising *Laetitia,* he accidentally incorporated one of the names
belonging to the other story in his first novel, thus betraying the power of the
new story on his imagination; and as soon as he had finished the revision of
Laetitia (now to be called *The White Peacock*), he turned to writing a novel
based on Helen Corke's story. *The White Peacock* had, up to this point, taken
him over four years to write; the new novel he wrote between March and August
1910. He called it *The Saga of Siegmund,* Siegmund being the Wagnerian name
given by Helen Corke to her lover (he called her Sieglinde). It suited Lawrence,
too, and the tragic kind of novel he himself was writing, with its use of motifs
and its Wagnerian ambience.

His experiences in Croydon during the autumn of 1909, followed by his
growing involvement with Helen Corke, seem to have triggered his attempts at
establishing a new kind of relationship, too. He had thought of an engagement
to Agnes Holt but had broken off from her when she resisted his attempts to
make the relationship sexual. A week or so later, at Christmas 1909, he had
ended his eight years or so of purely intellectual companionship with Jessie
Chambers by suggesting that they should become lovers. Jessie, who had loved
him for years, agreed that they would—later. Back in Croydon, increasingly
attracted to Helen Corke, Lawrence finished his revision of *The White Peacock*
(about the tragedy of a man who marries the wrong woman) and sketched out
in *The Saga of Siegmund* what happens to a man in love with a woman who
does not respond to him sexually; and then, in the Whitsun holidays, after getting
a good way into the writing of *The Saga,* he started his affair with Jessie. It
seems to have been desperately unhappy and unsuccessful from the start: as
Jessie wrote, later, "The times of our coming together, under conditions both
difficult and irksome, and with Lawrence's earnest injunction to me not to try
to hold him, would not exhaust the fingers of one hand" (Worthen 1991: 251).
Lawrence finished the final revisions of *The White Peacock* and went on working at *The Saga,* with a sense that he was in danger of badly messing up his
life, as well as Jessie's life. Come August 1910, within a week of finishing the
novel, he resolved on a complete break with Jessie, perhaps the cruelest thing
of all the cruel things he ever did to her.

His family would, however, have been both pleased and relieved; a few
months later, Lawrence confessed that his mother "hated J.—and would have
risen from the grave to prevent my marrying her" (*Letters* I: 197). It must have
been with an extraordinary sense of the way in which her own influence had
worked on her son, that—only a fortnight after Lawrence had told her of his
break with Jessie—Lydia Lawrence, on holiday in Leicester, herself collapsed
from the cancer that was going to kill her. It was as if her guard had finally

dropped. Lawrence, too, seems to have been struck by the coincidence. Within a month, he was at work on an autobiographical novel, which was going to go deep into the nature of his parents' marriage and the influences that had been at work on him; the novel would, too, investigate what had happened to its hero's relationships with women and with a woman drawn closely from Jessie Chambers in particular. Lawrence had the unerring sense, as an artist, that what troubled him most deeply in his own life was also the substance of much contemporary anxiety and that the divisions from which he suffered could become the central subject of major works of fiction.

All that autumn, with his mother slowly dying and in increasing pain and Lawrence making regular (though exhausting) weekend visits, he tried to work on the novel; but he managed to write only 100 pages or so. Cut off from Jessie, he was increasingly lonely, and it was with relief that he started to see more of his old friend Louie Burrows, who was still living near Leicester and who was also doing her best to care for Lydia Lawrence. Unintellectual, unneurotic, undamaged by experience, but warm and generous-hearted and always fond of Lawrence without ever knowing him very well, Louie was a good companion at such a time: "Someone to rest with—you perhaps don't know what a deep longing that may be," he told her (*Letters* I: 198). At the start of December, Lawrence proposed to her: marriage to Louie suddenly seemed a brilliant answer to his problems. He had already discussed the idea with his mother, as if the news might comfort her and her fears for him, and Lydia had, a little grudgingly, accepted the idea. Louie accepted at once. The day before proposing to Louie, he had put into his mother's hands the first, specially bound copy of *The White Peacock,* but she had hardly responded (*Letters* I: 194). The book symbolized the side of her son she associated with Jessie and with his potential abandonment of a proper professional career, as well as with his independence—intellectual and moral—of her.

On 9 December, Lydia Lawrence died; they buried her on the twelfth, and Lawrence went back to Croydon to work—he described it as "[t]he desert of Sahara" (*Letters* I: 202). But now he had the thought of Louie helping to sustain him; writing her a letter from school as it grew dark one December afternoon, he remarked, "I've had the gas lighted. I wish I might light myself at your abundant life" (*Letters* I: 202). Family Christmas back in Eastwood was an unbearably gloomy prospect; Lawrence and Ada went to Brighton to get away.

II.

It is too easy to dismiss Lawrence's engagement to Louie as an aberration. It was exceedingly important to him at the time, a break with the past and with the gloomy emotional ties binding him to his mother and (in a different way) to Jessie. Though he ended up very critical of Louie—there was so much of his life that she, a more conventional person than he was, could not share—he always retained a good feeling for her and for the support she gave him in the winter of 1910–11 and into the spring. But the year 1911 was, all the same, a very difficult one for him. *The White Peacock* came out in January and should have been an occasion for great cheerfulness, but its links with his dying mother inhibited any such celebration. The conflict between the demands of school, the demands of the engagement, and Lawrence's desire to build upon his early success in order to become a full-time writer grew increasingly problematic. He wanted to write and to be published and did not have the time he really needed to concentrate and work. Ford Madox Hueffer had, too, been damning about *The Saga of Siegmund;* and its links with the life of Helen Corke made it, anyway, a dubious prospect for publication. The matter was effectively settled by the attitude of the publisher of *The White Peacock,* Heinemann, who found Lawrence's second novel tedious and not very good. Throughout the spring and early summer of 1911, Lawrence accordingly struggled with his third novel, *Paul Morel:* this was the book that would have to cement his reputation. But it went very slowly, and he ended up in July with it only just over half written and no desire to go on with it. He had continued to write poems and produced a number of short stories, and the *English Review* continued to print small quantities of his work; but he had no sense of a breakthrough. All the time, his renewed attraction to Helen Corke meant that he felt guilty about Louie. Helen, however, refused to sleep with him, so that he felt frustrated and hurt as well as guilty, and he soon lost the companionship and shared intellectual life that Helen offered. It seems likely that, at around this point, he started an affair with a married woman, Alice Dax (1878–1959), an old Eastwood friend now living in Shirebrook, who had loved him for years; but he could see her only rarely (she seems to have visited London once). In the summer, Louie went on holiday with him and Ada, but the holiday seems to have been an unhappy affair; and return to school for the autumn term did not lift his spirits. Only a new contact with a literary mentor—the publisher's reader Edward Garnett (1868–1937)— seemed to hold out any prospects of future publishing success. A chance meeting with Jessie Chambers in October led, however, to his doing what he had always done in the old days: sending her the whole unfinished manuscript of *Paul Morel* for her comments. She offered to write what she remembered of their early days, so perhaps he would be able to get the novel back on track.

But the relationship with Louie now did little more than weigh on him and his sense of guilt, while offering him no relief and no sense of a future; and the whole of the autumn seems to have followed the pattern of a complex slide into depression and bad health, unrelieved by a new determination to restart *Paul Morel* in November. When he finally collapsed with pneumonia later that month, after getting wet at Garnett's and not changing his clothes, it seemed an almost inevitable outcome to the year since his mother's death.

III.

He was very seriously ill and nearly died. Ada went down to Croydon to nurse him; Louie was kept away, at his earnest request. After almost a month lying on his back, he began to struggle back to life (and to writing) in mid-December.

Helen and Jessie both paid him visits; and, after seeing the latter, he wrote an anguished, nostalgic account of his break with her and with the Haggs farm, the story that eventually became "The Shades of Spring." Louie finally joined the Croydon party for Christmas—Ada had her Eastwood fiancé Eddie Clark (1889–1964) with her, too—but early in January, Lawrence had to go to Bournemouth for a month's convalescence. What for many people would have been a month relieved of all thoughts of work was, for Lawrence, a heaven-sent opportunity to take firm hold of the literary career that was now being forced upon him; he had been advised not to go back to work as a teacher. Edward Garnett had cheered him immensely by saying that *The Saga of Siegmund* was nowhere near as bad as Hueffer or Heinemann had suggested and that Lawrence needed only to knock it into shape to get it published; Garnett supplied notes, and Lawrence took the manuscript with him to Bournemouth, to help rebuild his literary career.

During January, in the intervals of going for lengthy walks and eating enormous meals to build up his strength, he rewrote a good deal of it and revised the rest. It may have been good for his recovery and his career to do this (it gave him a novel to follow up the relative success of *The White Peacock,* and Garnett's firm of Duckworth would take it); but thinking about the tragedy of Siegmund was nothing but a disaster for his relationship with Louie. He ended the month knowing that he would have to break his engagement to her; and this he did at the start of February, greatly to her distress. She believed that there must be another woman in his life, and there was, of course—more than one—though that was not the reason for his break with her.

On 9 February 1912, Lawrence returned to Eastwood, feeling he had unexpectedly been given (and had grasped at) a whole new set of chances. He had left home in 1908 to start work as a professional man and had almost settled down to conventional marriage of the kind of which his mother would certainly have approved; he now returned to start a new kind of life, in which he would have to live by his writing. He no longer needed to placate the two women (Lydia Lawrence and Louie Burrows) for whose sake he had stuck at working to earn a decent salary; but his prospects were fairly bleak, all the same. He thought of going abroad but knew that first he must finish that third novel, *Paul Morel,* due to Heinemann for more than a year now.

Jessie Chambers had made the notes she had promised to make; and she read the new draft of the novel as he wrote it, very fast. It was one of the turning points of his career, this creation of the revised *Paul Morel* in the Eastwood house he was sharing with his sisters and his father, while showing the manuscript to Jessie, the representative of his past life. He was surrounded by the past but, for the first time, was trying to get it into real perspective and to understand what had really happened between his parents and to himself when young. He was also looking with profound skepticism at his relationship with Jessie Chambers; the fictional arena gave him a chance to work out what kind of a self-conscious and ruthless prig he had been, but also how incapable she, too, had been of a balanced relationship. He wrote the novel at white heat and to her lasting terror and distress. She would later blame his continuing love for Lydia Lawrence for the way in which he dismissed both the fictional Miriam and the real-life Jessie; but the resolution of the novel seems, rather, to have been one of those breakthroughs into understanding and hard, intellectual clarity of which Lawrence was capable, often to his own dismay, certainly to that of his friends. By the end of March, the novel was done, all but a last revision; but another symbolic miracle had occurred. He had been writing to free himself of the past and had now discovered something of his future: he had met Frieda Weekley.

3   Frieda and the Escape Abroad: 1912–14

I.

Emma Maria Frieda Johanna Weekley (1879–1956) was the thirty-three-year-old wife of Ernest Weekley (1865–1959), Professor of Modern Languages at the University of Nottingham. Daughter of Anna (1851–1930) and Baron Friedrich von Richthofen (1845–1915), minor German aristocrats, she had grown up in Metz, where her father had a desk job in the Prussian army of occupation; at the age of nineteen, she had married Weekley and since 1899 had lived the life of a professor's wife in a sequence of superior Nottingham suburbs. It seems possible that Lawrence had seen her before, either when he was going to his brother George's Nottingham house for lunch while a student at the High School (George lived in the street opposite the Weekleys at that time) or while at University College, when he was taught French by Weekley: the professor's handsome young wife may well have been pointed out to him. The Weekleys had three children, Monty (1900–82), aged almost twelve, Elsa (1902–85), aged nine, and Barby (b. 1904), aged seven.

But now in March 1912 (probably on the third: Worthen 1991: 562–63), Lawrence went to lunch at the Weekleys; he wanted advice from Weekley about the chance of getting a teaching job abroad; he had cousins in Germany and was contemplating a visit to them later in the spring. He and Frieda talked briefly before lunch, however, and found themselves strongly attracted to each other. Extramarital relationships were something Frieda specialized in; we know of at least three men in Germany and one in England with whom she had had affairs over the previous six years (she had the habit of making lengthy visits to Germany most summers to see her family). She probably thought of Lawrence simply as another man she very much liked and wanted and imagined that an affair with him would (as usual) do nothing to upset her life as a wife and mother. Lawrence was struck rather differently. ''You are the most wonderful woman in all England,'' he wrote to her within a few days (*Letters* I: 376). Over the next eight weeks, they saw each other fairly often; they went to the theater in Nottingham, and Frieda had the excuse of taking her children out; they visited the farm run by Jessie Chambers's sister May (1883–1955) and her husband, Will Holbrook (1884–1960), for example. The differences between Lawrence and Frieda also became very obvious; Lawrence was shocked when he arrived at the Weekley house for an afternoon with Frieda when the maid had been given the afternoon off and found that she didn't even know how to light the gas to make tea. But her beauty, her directness, her foreignness, her spontaneity and carelessness fascinated him. For her part, she quickly became a reader of *Paul Morel;* she was deeply impressed by Lawrence's background and the way it fed into his work as a writer—and by his insistence that she was throwing away her life in her comfortable Nottingham surroundings.

As a consequence of meeting her, Lawrence broke off from his affair with Alice Dax and devoted himself to creating as much of a relationship with Frieda as he could manage. He went to London in April, and she was able to go with him; Edward Garnett was happy to take the illicit couple into his house in Kent for a couple of days. By now even Frieda was getting disturbingly involved with Lawrence; but she still failed to do the one thing Lawrence was urging her to do, which was tell Weekley that she was leaving him. What was possible, however, was a trip to Germany together; Lawrence was due to see his cousins the Krenkows in May, and Frieda was going to see her family. Again Lawrence insisted that Frieda tell Weekley about him; again Frieda failed to do so, though she did tell Weekley about two earlier affairs just before she left, leaving him in a state of great alarm about her. She left her children with her parents-in-law in London, as usual when she went away; and on Friday, 3 May 1912, Frieda and Lawrence met in London to catch the boat train; they arrived in Metz just after six o'clock on Saturday morning.

But what might have looked like their best chance yet of enjoying their affair turned out very differently. Over the next three days, they hardly saw each other. Lawrence was briefly introduced to Frieda's mother and her sisters but could not be allowed to meet her father, who—in spite of having an illegitimate son of his own—believed strongly in morality and respectability. Lawrence found lodgings in a strict, religious hotel, which cost more than he could afford, while Frieda was staying with her parents about a mile away. They saw each other briefly on Sunday and then not at all on Monday, apart from a glimpse in a crowded fair: Frieda's father had enjoyed fifty years' service in the Prussian army, and celebrations public and private dominated the day. Lawrence spent his time exploring Metz and its environs and growing angry with Frieda for continuing to pretend that he was just an English visitor whom she knew slightly. By Tuesday, he was desperate: "Now I can't stand it any longer, I cant. . . . I've tried so hard to work—but I cant. . . . But no, I won't utter or act or willingly let you utter or act, another single lie in the business" (*Letters* I: 392–93). Weekley had sent a telegram saying that he suspected Frieda of having a man with her; he also apparently wrote wildly to her father about her. Frieda, on the advice of her mother and sisters, temporized with Weekley, saying that she would write. She was obviously trying to retain her chances of going back to him and of keeping her children; her family was totally opposed to her abandoning her marriage and her children for the love of a penniless writer.

But Lawrence loved her and was determined not to let her take the compromising way out. On Tuesday the seventh, he drafted a letter for her to send to Weekley, explaining what was happening. She failed to send it, so on Wednesday he himself wrote to Weekley: "I love your wife and she loves me" (*Letters* I: 392). Weekley got the letter on Friday the tenth and immediately wrote to Frieda, asking her to agree to a divorce; there was no doubt in his mind that she should never be allowed to see her children again. In Metz, meanwhile, events had taken a comic turn; on Wednesday, at last spending a few hours together and carelessly wandering into a military area, Lawrence and Frieda had been questioned by a military policeman, and their names were taken: Lawrence was suspected of spying. Frieda's father was able to get Lawrence out of trouble but demanded to meet him; that afternoon, they saw each other for the first and only time. The baron clearly had his suspicions, and it was suggested to Lawrence that he had better leave Metz; he took the train to Trier, eighty miles away and farther from Frieda than ever. But this time, he knew that his letter was winging its way to Weekley and that Frieda would no longer be able to back away from commitment to him. Anyway, Trier was far more attractive than the garrison town of Metz, where there had been soldiers on every street corner. Frieda came to visit him in Trier on Friday, albeit for only half a day (her father demanded her return to Metz that night), bringing with her a telegram from Weekley. Lawrence ensured that she sent a direct answer. On Saturday, he had to go on to his cousins in the Rhineland; but at last he felt secure of Frieda and on the journey wrote one of his most beautiful love poems to her, "Bei Hennef": "At last I know my love for you is here" (*Complete Poems* 203).

His relations lived in what was then a remote village, and he spent the next fortnight peacefully going on trips around Waldbröl, his cousin Hannah Krenkow (b. 1881) apparently starting to fall in love with him, while he applied himself to learning German and doing a final revision of *Paul Morel:* he would, in the future, have to support himself and Frieda with what he could earn. But all the time he was hearing from Frieda how wretched her life in Metz now was, as her parents accused her of behaving stupidly and as they tried to repair the damage with Weekley. Frieda appealed to Lawrence to come and rescue her, but he insisted that they must come together again only when they were really ready for each other; he wanted to leave behind the emotional crevasses of Metz and now saw their relationship as, in effect, a marriage. In desperation, she fled to Munich, to her sister Else Jaffe (1874–1973), who knew exactly what it was to have escaped from a marriage but to have kept her children: for some years, although remaining married to a university professor, Edgar Jaffe (1866–1921), she had been having an affair with the economist Alfred Weber (1868–1958). The marriages of all three von Richthofen daughters, including that of Johanna (1882–1971) with Max von Schreibershofen (1864–1944), had proved failures; Frieda's was only the most recent to do so.

To Munich Lawrence at last traveled, at the end of May; he and Frieda had a marvelous week together in an old inn in Beuerberg and then moved into the flat in Icking that Weber rented; they could have this until August, rent-free, important to them now that they were living on Lawrence's meager literary earnings. In the Icking flat, the final revisions to *Paul Morel* were done, and Lawrence triumphantly posted it off to Heinemann on 8 June. It was that novel—begun as his mother was dying, linked with the unhappy engagement to Louie, marked by the final break with Jessie Chambers—that he now hoped would support Frieda and him.

To his distress, the novel came back from Heinemann almost immediately: it was too overtly sexual, the degradation of Mrs. Morel through living in the working class was impossible, it was badly structured, and Heinemann was turning it down flat. Lawrence was only lucky in having Edward Garnett and the firm of Duckworth waiting in the wings; Garnett read the manuscript, recommended its acceptance, and made many suggestions for one final revision. Lawrence does not seem to have been too upset; he may have recognized that he now really wanted to include in it something of his new experience with Frieda.

At the start of August, they had to return Weber his flat. Else had suggested that—while England was effectively barred to them—they go to Italy, where living was cheap. They set off, with all their belongings sent ahead in trunks, before dawn on Monday, 5 August, on what turned out to be one of the memorable adventures of their lives. A combination of walking and train took them through the rain and past the wayside crucifixes to Bad Tölz on the first evening; the second day saw them walking all day and getting high up into the border country between Bavaria and Austria; a shortcut went both disastrously wrong and marvelously right, as they ended up at nightfall with a choice to make between a hayhut and a tiny wooden chapel to sleep in. Lawrence fancied the chapel, with its candles and its dry wooden floor; but Frieda had always wanted to sleep in a hayhut. So they did and tossed and turned all night; and in the morning they found that the snow had almost come down to their level. A tiny breakfast of a single roll and another five miles' walking and scrambling brought them down to a main road and a house where they took a room, dried their clothes, and got some sleep until midafternoon (and Lawrence apparently began to write his account of the journey). Pouring rain persuaded them to take a horse-drawn post-omnibus across the Austrian border and on to the Achensee, under dark mountains, where their tramplike appearance barred them from the hotel but not from a farmhouse. On Thursday, they set out to recover their trunks from customs at Kufstein, fifteen miles up the Inn Valley; here, again, a train journey helped. They slept a night in Kufstein, having raided their trunks for fresh clothes, and sent on the trunks again to Mayrhofen, where a further day's walk and train got them by Friday night. Here they took a room for a fortnight and spent their time walking and exploring. Lawrence wrote; they recovered.

After a week, they were joined by English friends, Garnett's son David (1892–1981) and a friend of his, Harold Hobson (1891–1974). Trunks were eventually again dispatched, to Bozen, and the group of four set out over the Pfitscherjoch Pass. One night in a hayhut (now under the tutelage of the outdoor expert Garnett) and a night at the Dominicushütte mountain hut brought them on the third day over the pass and down the far side into the Pfitscher Valley to an inn. These days of walking had been especially exhausting, and on the fourth day Lawrence and Frieda ambled down to Sterzing, while Garnett and Hobson hurried on to catch a train back to the north.

Things never recovered their joy after this. Their days in Sterzing were boring; and Lawrence miscalculated how long it would take them to walk up to the next pass, the Jaufen. They ended up exhausted, with night falling, a bitter wind, and great steep slopes still to climb—and then Frieda told Lawrence that she had slept with Hobson two days ago, at the Dominicushütte. It was the first time Frieda had been unfaithful to Lawrence and doubtless had something to do with her assertion to him (and to herself) that she was not giving up her independence even if she had decided to cross the Alps with him and thus give up her marriage and her children for him. But it would not be the last time she had an affair; and if Lawrence wanted her to stay with him, then he would simply have to accept that she would, by no means, always stay faithful.

They struggled on up, at last found the mountain hut, and spent the whole of the next day walking, believing that they were finally on the road down to Meran. In fact, they were taking the direct road back to Sterzing and only realized it at four in the afternoon. For all their shortness of money, they took a train that night to Bozen. But they didn't much like it and went on to Trento, where attempts to find a place to stay led to filthy rooms and doors slammed in their faces. Near despair was overcome by taking a final train down to Riva on the shores of Lake Garda (they had seen a poster at the station).

This was the warm south they had been looking for. In spite of their even more bedraggled appearance, they got a room and waited for their trunks to arrive, so that they could appear presentable; they remained desperately short of money until fifty pounds for—of all novels—*The Trespasser* arrived. Lawrence started to work again, on *Paul Morel:* always a sign of settled living. They stayed in Riva only a fortnight—it was a little expensive—but farther down the lake they found a room in Villa, next to Gargnano, just over the Italian border. There they would stay until the spring; the money would carry them that far. Now, with Frieda criticizing and making suggestions, in two months

Lawrence rewrote *Paul Morel* into the *Sons and Lovers* we know, in one of
those great bursts of creative energy typical of him. He took only one break,
and in those three days contrived to write a play about Frieda's marital status
called *The Fight for Barbara*. The novel was finished in mid-November and
sent off to Garnett; and another part of their joint future seemed thus financed,
as Lawrence's own past was symbolically put behind him. Garnett's insistence
that the book was still far too long and that he would cut it—he did, by one-
tenth—made Lawrence (he told Garnett) "wither up" (*Letters* I: 481), but the
important thing was that the novel was done.

Lawrence now cast around for his next subject; experience of the money for
The Trespasser suggested that novels were by far his best bet for financing his
career. He started at least two (getting 200 pages into one before breaking off)—
and dashed off another play, *The Daughter-in-Law,* his best, wholly in the dialect he had left so far behind him—before settling to write a novel he called
The Sisters. This really would incorporate his experience of Frieda; it began as
a light, easy-to-write book but, over the next three years, it turned into both *The
Rainbow* and *Women in Love*. He was starting to write about marriage, his main
subject for the immediate future. After writing a first draft of the novel, he and
Frieda set out for a visit first to Germany (where Lawrence wrote the marvelous
story that became known as "The Prussian Officer") and then back to England;
Frieda was desperate to see her children, one way or another, and Lawrence
wanted to attend his sister Ada's wedding in August. They arrived three weeks
after *Sons and Lovers* had been published and in the glory of the excellent
reviews it got, but they were, of course, homeless. Lawrence could not introduce
the not-even-divorced, let alone unmarried, Frieda to his family. Garnett—responsible for so much that sustained them at this time—again came to their
rescue and put them up until they could find lodgings in Kingsgate, on the Kent
coast. Lawrence was able to revise and get typed some of the short stories he
had been compiling over the past two years. Garnett was still advising him on
his career, on what to try to publish and where. Here, too, for the first time,
they could see friends. Katherine Mansfield (1888–1923) and John Middleton
Murry (1889–1957), both leading the literary life in London and also unmarried,
whom they had got to know the previous month, came down on a visit; a
friendship grew among the four of them. Frieda enlisted Katherine's help in
trying to waylay and see her children on their way to school, foreshadowing the
way, the following year, she attempted an entry into the house in Chiswick
where the children now lived with Weekley's parents, Charles (1834–1918) and
Agnes (1840–1926); a court order was threatened in consequence, and Frieda
did not get to see her children legally until 1915. The literary patron Edward
Marsh (1872–1953) had got to know Lawrence via Murry and introduced them
to the Asquith family (also on holiday in Kent); Cynthia Asquith (1887–1960),
daughter-in-law to the prime minister, was the first genuine aristocrat Lawrence
had ever met, and he and Frieda both got on well with her. Lawrence went to
see his sister married at the start of August—without Frieda, of course—and

then, after a reasonably productive seven weeks, they returned to Germany, on the way back to Italy, and here Lawrence wrote the first hundred pages of a revised second version of *The Sisters* before they set off for Italy. This time they went where Else's husband, Edgar Jaffe (1866–1921), used to go with a mistress, the northwest coast, on the gulf of Spezia. A cottage in the fishing hamlet of Fiascherino was quickly found; and they settled to their second year abroad.

II.

Lawrence's first job before going on with *The Sisters* was to prepare for publication his play *The Widowing of Mrs. Holroyd;* Garnett had got it accepted by the American publisher Mitchell Kennerley (1878–1950). Lawrence revised it heavily, in accord with his new thinking about marriage. "It seems to me that the chief thing about a woman—who is much of a woman—is that in the long run she is not to be had" (*Letters* II: 94), he remarked in a letter he wrote in October; that idea of independence probably also suggests the direction of *The Sisters,* which in its autumn 1913 revision grew long and complex as it charted the emotional and sexual relationships of Ella and Gudrun Brangwen; he finished only its first half (now called *The Wedding Ring,* which suggests that the point of marriage was being reached) in January 1914 and sent it to Garnett. Garnett was, however, severely critical, finding some episodes badly handled and the central character incoherent; he also apparently remarked that the artistic side was "in the background." A second letter was even more critical. Lawrence tended to agree with the criticisms, though not with Garnett's (to him) rather patronizing attitude and his apparently fundamental objection to the book's method. Shortly afterward, Lawrence embarked on yet another rewriting, which went far faster and this time (to him) more satisfactorily.

But the novel's future at this point starts to be affected by the fact that Lawrence, in the aftermath of *Sons and Lovers,* was, for the first time in his life, being wooed by publishers and (in particular) by the agent J. B. Pinker (1863–1922), who was signing up novelists for lucrative three-volume contracts with the publisher Methuen. Lawrence was strongly attracted by the thought of financial security, and Garnett's attitude to his recent work did not help. He had the new draft of *The Wedding Ring* typed in two copies while he was still writing it, a sign of his confidence with it before Garnett read it and probably suggesting that he thought of placing it in the hands of publishers other than Duckworth for their consideration.

Crucially, Garnett turned out to object strongly to this new version, too, saying that it was "shaky" and that the "psychology was wrong" (*Letters* II: 182–83). Lawrence must have felt he had got to the end of the road of Garnett's helpfulness; when he arrived back in England at the end of June, he was determined to try to get the novel away from Duckworth, unless the latter was prepared to make an offer as high as Methuen's. It turned out that Duckworth either would not or could not match Methuen's £300, so, on 30 June 1914, Lawrence signed the contract with Pinker and immediately acquired an advance of £100 (*Letters* II: 189, 211). For the moment, he seemed set up as a promising young author, living in London and making acquaintances among the intelligentsia; they were sharing a house with Murry and Katherine Mansfield, and Lawrence shortly afterward made the acquaintance of the writer and reviewer Catherine Jackson, later Carswell (1879–1946), and a whole group of intellectuals (including Freudians) in Hampstead, while, at the end of July, he would meet for the first time the Russian translator S. S. Koteliansky (1882–1955), who remained his friend all his life.

Also in July came a symbolic moment for the author of *The Wedding Ring*. Frieda's divorce had been completed at the end of April, and Lawrence—"with neuralgia in my left eye and my heart in my boots" (*Letters* II: 196)—married her in a south London registry office on 14 July 1914. The two-year exile was at an end, and they could live where and how they wanted to—but that probably meant back in Italy, which they both loved.

The summer's changes had effectively marked the end of Lawrence's working relationship with Edward Garnett, though Duckworth would bring out one more book of his—a volume of short stories—which he revised during July but which would, much to his annoyance, be called (by Garnett) *The Prussian Officer* when it came out. However, that—only five months later—would be another world away: a world at war, with Lawrence and Frieda's life irrevocably changed once more.

4 War: 1914–19

I.

The Lawrences (as they can now be called) did not return to Italy until 1919. Lawrence was on a walking tour in Westmoreland with three men friends (including Koteliansky) at the start of August when they came down to Barrow on Furness to find that war had been declared. "The War finished me," Lawrence said later; "it was the spear through the side of all sorrows and hopes" (*Letters* II: 268). Not just his hopes of returning to Italy or living happily with Frieda or having his novel published—though all these things were indeed affected by the war—but, more profoundly, the making certain that his belief in the potential progress (in sorrows and hopes) of civilization was dead and finished. Ever since 1908, he had nursed a Whitmanesque belief in an "eternal progression," in a sense that "the great procession is marching, on the whole, in the right direction" and that "I am sure I can help the march if I like" (*Letters* I: 57). His early writing had been based on the unspoken assumption that what he wrote was a "help" because it addressed the deepest needs of people; as he wrote early in 1913, "I think, do you know, I have inside me a sort of answer to the *want* of today: to the real, deep want of the English people" (*Letters* I: 511). Every now and then, he would articulate this feeling, as in 1912, when he angrily remarked of English people that "I should like to bludgeon them into realizing their own selves" (*Letters* I: 424), or in 1913, when, more blithely, he remarked, "I do write because I want folk—English folk—to alter, and have more sense" (*Letters* I: 544). What the war took away was his confidence that this was possible. At a stroke, the country's energies redirected themselves into barbarous opposition, hatred, and a relapse into communal—not individual—emotion; and the writer who believed in the progress and development of "the great racial or human consciousness, a little of which is in me" and who wanted people to read his fictions and "be made alert and active" (*Letters* II: 302), to alter their relationships, to realize their own hearts and desires, felt himself utterly displaced.

There were other, more practical, consequences for him as well. In August, Methuen returned to him the manuscript of *The Wedding Ring*. There was some doubt about the explicit nature of some of its sexual scenes, which he was asked to tone down; and (anyway) the war meant an immediate cutback in what they would publish. He was asked to resubmit the book, revised, in six months but was thus deprived of the money, due on its publication, on which he was relying. Returning to what was now their home in Italy also became impossible, and the cheapness (and happiness) of living they had found there, especially in Fiascherino, was denied them. "What is going to become of us?" Lawrence wrote to Pinker (*Letters* II: 206). All they could do was rent as cheap a place as they could find, near friends like Murry and Katherine Mansfield, in the country outside London—and wait.

Lawrence had one small project to be going on with: a 15,000-word book on the novelist Thomas Hardy (1840–1928) in a series "Writers of the Day," which had been commissioned from him in July. Down in Chesham in a tiny cottage, twenty miles from London, and helped enormously by a wedding present from Edward Marsh of a complete set of Hardy's books, he spent the autumn working on it, though his current state of mind led to his turning it away from Hardy and into an expression of his own personal philosophy, "a sort of Confessions of my Heart" (*Letters* II: 235). It was never published in the series; it seems doubtful whether Lawrence even submitted it. But it did give Lawrence a new understanding of abiding human dualities, which he would employ directly in his revision of *The Wedding Ring* for Methuen.

This final rewriting, between November 1914 and March 1915, changed both the novel and Lawrence's career irrevocably. For one thing, the novel split: the material that had been accumulating round the original "Sisters" of the title had become too long for one volume. The new novel—to be called *The Rainbow*—would consist of the story of the sisters' grandparents, Tom and Lydia Brangwen, their parents, Will and Anna Brangwen, and the early life of one of the sisters (now called Ursula), including her first—and unsuccessful—love affair. The second book would show the subsequent relationships of both Ursula and Gudrun Brangwen and how those relationships finally worked out: Ursula's successfully, Gudrun's unhappily. But *The Rainbow* also apparently became even more sexually overt in this revision, not less so; and the things that Methuen had been troubled by in the summer of 1914 became still more worrying. This would have unimaginable consequences.

For the moment, Lawrence was simply happy to have a new novel to be involved with and to take his mind off the war. He was also starting to meet people who impressed him and whom he impressed. The old friendship with David Garnett had brought him, during the winter of 1914, to meet Lady Ottoline Morrell (1873–1938), a great hostess for artists, writers, and other intelligentsia; and dining with Ottoline had brought him into contact with both the novelist E. M. Forster (1879–1970) and the philosopher and mathematician Bertrand Russell (1872–1970). He also got to know the young painters Mark Gertler (1892–1939) and Dorothy Brett (1883–1977) and kept their friendship while his meeting with Cynthia Asquith in 1913 had also developed into a steady friendship, in spite of the pressures of the war on her (her husband was already on active service). Many of these friends came to see Lawrence and Frieda in Sussex in the spring of 1915; they had moved down there in January, overcome by the cold and damp of the Chesham cottage. Lawrence felt himself taken seriously by all of them, while Frieda seems to have relished the fact that she was now moving in the higher echelons of English intellectual society and was the friend of two titled ladies. For his part, Bertrand Russell was at first enormously impressed, seeing Lawrence as "infallible. He is like Ezekiel or some other Old Testament prophet . . . he sees everything and is always right" (Ottoline 1963: 273), though the two men quarreled later in the summer, and their plans for a joint lecture course (Russell on Society, Lawrence on Eternity) never materialized. But Lawrence's letters of the winter of 1914 and the spring of 1915 are among the most remarkable he ever wrote. They chart his developing ideas about how to understand and symbolize the historical development of human consciousness, society, and self-responsibility: how it came to be the fact that "one is not only a little individual living a little individual life, but that one is in oneself the whole of mankind, and ones fate is the fate of the whole of mankind, and ones charge is the charge of the whole of mankind" (*Letters* II: 302). This philosophy grew to be at the heart of *The Rainbow*. He finished the novel, triumphantly, on 2 March: "bended it and set it firm. Now off and away to find the pots of gold at its feet" (*Letters* II: 299), and he immediately turned back to the rewriting into a new form of the philosophy that had taken over his Hardy book.

He had not, however, finally finished with *The Rainbow;* the typescript needed (he found) extensive revision, and the proofs, later in the summer, needed still further work. In between work on the novel, he wrote away at his philosophy, with occasional breaks—as for the first version of his story "England, My England," which he wrote in June and which summed up his sense of why men were so eager to fight. Its central character, a failure in his marriage, gives up on "love and the creative side of life. . . . He had a right to his own satisfaction. He was a destructive spirit entering into destruction" (*England, My England* 225). In such ways Lawrence expressed his fundamental opposition to the war and to the spirit of war.

With a sense, however, of being too much on the fringes of life (and also perhaps so that Frieda could resume her attempts to see her children), in August, Frieda and he moved back to London, to Hampstead, where they had a circle of friends; the imminent publication of *The Rainbow* meant that he would at last be paid his final advance. He had other plans, too: a small magazine, which he and Murry would edit and which would say the kinds of things he thought needed saying to the public at large in wartime, and a series of small public meetings, advertised in the magazine, which might perhaps draw together a body of sympathetic people. It was characteristic of Lawrence at this stage of his career that he should be doing so much to make contact with people and to change their ideas, through his writing, his magazine, and the meetings. He was, in spite of the war, still a believer in his own capacity to make people "alert and active," as he had put it in March (*Letters* II: 302).

But the autumn of 1915 turned out to be a sequence of failures and disasters. First, the magazine (called *The Signature*) failed to pay its way, in spite of Murry and Lawrence sending subscription forms to all their friends, old and new; they managed to produce only three numbers rather than the six they had originally planned for, so that only three parts of Lawrence's new philosophical writing, "The Crown," got into print. The public meetings, too, turned out to be a complete failure: only two, apparently, were ever held. But by far the worst blow was the fate of *The Rainbow*. It was savagely attacked by nearly all its reviewers on publication, and at least two called for it to be suppressed. It was not adopted by the public libraries or bookstalls, and early in November, the police moved in on it, collecting all the undistributed copies from Methuen. On 13 November 1915, the Bow Street magistrates heard a prosecution under the Obscene Publications Act of 1857, which Methuen failed to defend, saying, instead, that "they regretted having published it" (*The Rainbow* 1); the book was ordered to be destroyed. All Lawrence could do was sit on the sidelines and watch as the book he was so proud of, together with his reputation and his earning power as a professional writer, was destroyed. Having the matter raised in Parliament by Ottoline Morrell's MP husband Philip (1870–1943) got nowhere, and none of Lawrence's literary friends was (it turned out) prepared to argue for the book, only against the idea of censorship; even friends as close as Murry and Katherine Mansfield thoroughly disliked the book itself.

During October—following the failure of *The Signature* and even before the suppression order—Lawrence had been thinking of trying to go abroad. America, still out of the war but a place where an English writer could publish, seemed the obvious place; for two months Lawrence and Frieda tried to get passports and to encourage their friends to come with them and form a kind of colony in Florida (a move that seemed even more urgent after the novel's suppression). But matters came to a head on 12 December, when Lawrence—in order to get a passport—had to stand in line to "attest": that is, to enroll himself as ready for military service when called up, something in which he absolutely did not believe. He went down to Battersea Town Hall, over the river from Westminster and Parliament, to do it: "But I hated it so much, after waiting nearly two hours, that I came away" (*Letters* II: 474). If they could not go to America, Lawrence and Frieda would do the next best thing and go down to

Cornwall, as far from warmongering London as possible. The novelist J. D. Beresford (1873–1947), a friend of Murry, had a cottage in Cornwall, which he was prepared to lend; after a Christmas visit to the Midlands, on the penultimate day of the old year Lawrence and Frieda traveled down to Porthcothan, on the Cornish north coast, not knowing anymore what they would live on or what they would do in the long run; but, Lawrence felt, it was "like being at the window and looking out of England to the beyond. This is my first move outwards, to a new life" (*Letters* II: 491).

II.

He had, fortunately, one more book on the stocks, its publication arranged before *The Rainbow* had been suppressed; his Italian essays, heavily revised, some of them first drafted beside the Lago di Garda in 1913, were being published as *Twilight in Italy.* That brought in a little money. Duckworth was also prepared to publish a volume of his poems, and, in the early months of 1916, he worked at his old University College notebooks, digging out and rewriting poetry. He also wrote a story, this time nothing to do with the war, an early version of "The Horse-Dealer's Daughter." He developed a plan for the private publication of *The Rainbow,* by subscription, and he was ill in bed a good deal of the time.

But he and Frieda both liked Cornwall: the rocks, the sea, the sense of being almost out of England. It became their plan to bring down congenial friends. They had visitors during January, including the musician Philip Heseltine (1894–1930), his mistress "Puma" (Minnie Channing, b. 1894), and his friend the writer Dikran Kouyoumdjian (1895–1956); but, in the long term, the idea of living together with Middleton Murry and Katherine Mansfield remained the dominant one. At the start of March, the Lawrences went down to Zennor, in the far west of Cornwall, and found there two houses side by side, "just under the moors, on the edge of the few rough stony fields that go to the sea" (*Letters* II: 563), which they decided immediately were meant for the Murrys and for themselves. The rent was very little; they decorated, moved in, began to buy secondhand furniture, and waited for their friends. Frieda wrote to them that "we are *friends* and we wont bother anymore about the *deep* things, they are all right, just let's live like the lilies in the field" (*Letters* II: 571). It was an impossible dream; Katherine hated the place, Frieda felt herself squeezed out by the literary talk of the other three, Lawrence found Murry oppressive, at times Murry found Lawrence dangerously unstable. They lived in adjacent cottages for only about eight weeks, until mid-June.

There had remained for Lawrence, of course, the problem of what he was going to do as a novelist, because he *was* a novelist—a magistrate's decision could not alter that—and purely commercial considerations did not have much to do with his desire to go on re-creating and reinterpreting the society and the consciousness of the contemporary human being that fascinated him. His mind had at first gone back to those 200 pages of manuscript, left in Germany in 1913, when he had abandoned that particular novel to write "The Sisters." Could he do something with them? But getting the manuscript out of Germany in wartime proved an insuperable problem; and sometime in April he went back to the material left over from *The Sisters* when he had carved out *The Rainbow* the previous year and between April and July created his most extraordinary work yet, the novel that became *Women in Love*. The tensions of life with the Murrys, something of the sense of small, brightly colored figures moving against a large landscape, the details of house furnishing, Lawrence's profound desire to work out a way of life away from the industrial and cosmopolitan centers, his tragic sense of a society and individuals driven by (and riven by) the passions of war—all these got into it. He went on working on it for months, first typing the first half himself, revising it as he went, and then, in the early autumn, writing it out by hand; on 31 October, he sent the last of it to Pinker. "It is a terrible and horrible and wonderful novel. You will hate it and nobody will publish it. But there, these things are beyond us" (*Letters* II: 669). He proceeded to revise it massively in the typescript copies, so that when it finally began to make the rounds of publishers in December, one asked if it really *was* complete.

It met with universal rejection; he was obliged by the terms of his contract to offer it first to Methuen, and (naturally) they refused it, but even the faithful Duckworth turned it down, along with three or four other publishers to whom Pinker offered it. Another novel by the author of *The Rainbow* was commercially quite unacceptable. It was no more than Lawrence had feared; but it was, still, a nasty indication of his potential future as a writer. The circulation of one of the two typescript copies among his friends had also led to the end of his friendship with Ottoline Morrell, who detected in the character of Hermione a portrait of herself. Lawrence vehemently rejected the connection, but it meant the loss of a good, supportive friend. His thoughts turned again to the possibility of leaving for America, "that far-off retreat, which is the future to me" (*Letters* III: 75), a dream encouraged by a new friendship with two young Americans, Esther Andrews and Robert Mountsier (1888–1972). But this plan, too, came to nothing; his application for passports was refused. All he and Frieda could do was sit tight in Cornwall, and Lawrence could research and flesh out his American dream by starting to write the essays that became *Studies in Classic American Literature,* a pioneering study. They also became something he could publish, in these barren years, along with yet another version of his philosophy, this time called (in direct opposition to the war) "The Reality of Peace." *The English Review* continued to support him, printing both the American essays and part of the philosophy, but, that apart, his publishing had almost come to a standstill. Almost all he could do was grow vegetables in his garden, help in the neighboring farm, read, and occasionally add revisions to the typescript of *Women in Love*. His only publishing in 1917 was a small volume of poems, *Look! We Have Come Through!,* the old sequence of poems written 1912–17, centered on his relationship with Frieda and now wholly revised and made coherent.

The year 1917 passed like 1916, with Lawrence, making just one brief journey away from Cornwall, to see his relatives in the Midlands, but this time with the possibility of military conscription just a little closer. He had been rejected on health grounds in June 1916 and then again in June 1917, but some local people were clearly not happy with having this odd, antiwar individual with a German wife in their midst. The usual wartime rumors developed: there was a stock of petrol for German submarines at the bottom of the cliffs near the Lawrences' cottage; the patterns on the Lawrences' chimney were a signal for patrolling submarines (the main Atlantic convoy route lay along the nearby coast). Individuals clearly spied on them and heard the singing of German songs in the cottage. They were stopped on one occasion by a military patrol, and their shopping was searched (a square loaf of bread was seized on as a camera). Things were made worse by the presence on the same coast of other nonconscripted, artistic individuals. Heseltine had a house nearby, and the musician Cecil Gray (1895–1951) also lived in the neighborhood; he and Lawrence discussed the nature of a revolution in the state, much as Lawrence had discussed it with Russell in 1915, and all three of them (doubtless also overheard) sang the Hebridean songs that were a recent musical discovery. In September, Gray was summoned for letting a light show in his house after dark in a seaward-facing window•and was fined punitively. In the end, it was easier for the authorities to act than to spend time finding out whether there was anything in the rumors. The Lawrences' cottage was searched while they were out one afternoon, and some papers were taken away (probably the texts of Hebridean songs: clearly coded messages). The following day, they were served with a military exclusion order, forbidding them to reside in Cornwall; they had to be out within three days.

III.

It was a financial disaster, as well as a moral blow; the cottage was cheap, and the rent was paid, and they had no money to rent other accommodations. They were taken in by friends in London and moved from room to room for a couple of months; the poet H. D. (1886–1961) was especially helpful, and Cecil Gray's mother also provided them with a room. *Look! We Have Come Through!* came out at the end of November, an ironic reminder of those prewar days in Icking and beside the Lago di Garda, when the building of a new relationship was the most important thing in the world. Lawrence now published those poems as a salute to the past and perhaps also as an acknowledgment that it was over; as a thinker and writer, Lawrence was now less interested in mutual love and marriage than in what happens within a loving relationship and in how the male struggles to escape what he now called ''the devouring mother'': ''I do think a woman must yield some sort of precedence to a man, and he must take this precedence'' (*Letters* III: 302). Frieda disagreed with him, calling him ''antediluvian,'' and it was around this time that she probably had a brief affair with Gray, as if to prove her point.

But in this new spirit, in London in the autumn of 1917, Lawrence started yet another novel, always a sign in him that his new thinking had to meet the test of experience and actuality. But the new book about a man who walks out on his destructive relationship with his wife, to find a new life—one day to be *Aaron's Rod*—did not get very far; shifting from one friend's property to another was hardly conducive to the writing of large-scale fiction. They were finally rescued by their friend the poet Dolly Radford (1864–1920), who let them have a cottage in Berkshire when she wasn't using it; this became one of their two main homes during the next two years. The only writing Lawrence could do was yet another version of the American essays, which had become both a new version of his philosophy and pioneering essays of literary criticism, and yet another small collection of poems, to be called *Bay.* Fiction from him was no longer acceptable; essays and poetry were all he could expect to be published.

By February 1918, they were desperately hard up, with barely a penny for bread and margarine, as Lawrence told his agent (*Letters* III: 211). Pinker helped out with a loan, as did other friends; and Lawrence's sister Ada assisted by renting a house for them, for a year, back in the Midlands, at Middleton-by-Wirksworth. They moved up there at the start of May, feeling ''lost and exiled,'' with Lawrence ''queer and desolate in my soul—like Ovid in Thrace'' (*Letters* III: 242). They saw more of his family and of old Eastwood friends than for years. He finished his American essays, and he put together yet another little book of poems out of the old notebooks, misleadingly called *New Poems,* this time for a new young publisher, Martin Secker (1882–1978), who would one day become very important to his career. But there was no change to his prospects as a man or a writer. The war went on, in spite of rumors of its ending; visitors came and went; and Lawrence grew steadily more desperate as he watched the months go by: ''there must be a change'' (*Letters* III: 283).

There was. On 11 September, his thirty-third birthday, he received his third notice of medical examination for call-up; by this stage of the war, almost no one was rejected. He was classed as Grade 3 (''conscripted for light non-military duties''). The decision maddened him: ''from this day I take a new line. I've done with society and humanity. . . . Henceforth it is for myself, my own life, I live'' (*Letters* III: 288). This was perhaps the culmination of his long redirection of his energies away from a belief in society and its well-being, to a concentration on the life of the individual. As it turned out, he was never actually called up for service. But his ejection from Cornwall and this final attempt to conscript him were perhaps his breaking points. Some of the profound problems of his work during the rest of his career derived from the peculiar kind of isolation to which he deliberately subjected himself, from 1918 onward.

His next pieces of writing summed up the problems of his career. He wrote, very quickly, a play in November 1918: *Touch and Go,* drawing, in part, upon still unpublished *Women in Love* material but concentrating upon the current industrial unrest into which living in the Midlands had given him an insight. Yet, it was most unlikely to be published or performed, and, in spite of some dramatic moments of confrontation, it suffers from a kind of slackness of construction very unusual in his writing; it needed a revision, which it never got. The other piece of writing, which he did with gritted teeth, marked the only time in his whole career when he did a piece of work almost entirely for money: he wrote a brief history for schools, entitled *Movements in European History.* In one way, it fitted rather well into reading he had already done earlier in 1918, when he had gone through Gibbon's *Decline and Fall of the Roman Empire,* thinking of the parallels with modern times. He took the school-history job seriously and did quite a lot of reading for it; but, apart from a few moments of pleasure seeing it fall into shape, mostly he hated it ''like poison'' (*Letters* III: 322, 309). The only things he was able to put his heart into were some short stories he wrote in November, including ''The Blind Man'' and ''Tickets Please'' and the first version of his short novel *The Fox.* His most immediate hopes of earning any money lay with these (*Letters* III: 299), but, for the moment, Pinker was able to place only the weakest of them, ''Tickets Please.''

As a culmination of his desperation and in a kind of response to the ''vile sick winter,'' in February 1919, he came down with influenza, during the wave of illness that swept Europe that spring. He was seriously ill for six weeks; for two days, he told Koteliansky, the doctor ''feared I should not pull through'' (*Letters* III: 347, 337). Friends rallied round with presents of wine and decent food, but the spring never seemed to come, with snow still lying round the cottage late in March (*Letters* III: 340). The year in Derbyshire, which, on almost all counts, had been a depressing failure, was coming to an end, rather to his relief. At the end of April, he first finished the history book—rejoicing, ''I am a free man'' (*Letters* III: 352)—and then he and Frieda traveled back down to Berkshire, to Dolly Radford's cottage. He had to do something to reestablish himself as a writer; the only book he would publish during 1919 was the tiny book of poems *Bay.* Pinker suggested that short stories might be sold to an American magazine, and—like a proper professional writer—Lawrence promised to write nothing but short stories for six weeks, ''if the short stories will come'' (*Letters* III: 355). They did, of course: ''Fannie and Annie,'' ''Monkey Nuts,'' ''Hadrian'' (published as ''You Touched Me''). But the best news, in July, was that *The Fox* had been accepted for publication; Lawrence's reputation was, little by little, being rebuilt, and a publisher also decided to take the play *Touch and Go.*

But Lawrence himself had made the contact that led to the latter success; and he was increasingly wondering whether it was sensible for him to continue with Pinker as his agent. He had certainly never made his agent much money. He had once previously broached the idea of leaving Pinker, back in November 1918; but now, in the latter half of 1919, he became increasingly disillusioned with what Pinker was doing for him, especially in the American market. Things came to a head with the publication of *Women in Love*. It turned out that Pinker had never even sent Benjamin Huebsch (1876–1964), who had published all Lawrence's works in America since 1914, a copy of the typescript of the novel; Lawrence discovered this only when he had arranged (again, without Pinker's assistance) for the American publisher Thomas Seltzer (1875–1943) to take the novel. His bitterness toward England over its treatment of *The Rainbow* made American publication particularly appealing to him (*Letters* III: 391). He revised the novel slightly in September for Seltzer and wrote it a Preface, while—in England—Martin Secker had expressed interest in it.

During the summer, spent in Berkshire, Lawrence and Frieda made friends with Rosalind Baynes (1891–1973), among others; she was recently separated from her husband, the psychoanalyst Godwin Baynes (1882–1943), and also longed to get away to Italy. Lawrence and Frieda were now both itching to get away from the England they had felt trapped in for the past five years. Frieda wanted to see her German family—her father had died in 1915, but she had, of course, not been able to go across; Lawrence wanted to go back to Italy and would actually go to prospect a house in the Abruzzi that Rosalind Baynes knew about and was considering for herself and her children. They had to wait till October for passports to come, but Frieda left as soon as she got hers, on the fifteenth. Lawrence stayed a month longer, arranging his affairs with magazines and publishers, not wanting to go to Germany "so soon after the war" (Frieda Lawrence 1935: 91). At last, on 14 November 1919, he sailed for the Continent. At least twice, he reproduced in fictional form his feelings on leaving behind the white cliffs of Dover: the version in his novel *The Lost Girl* contains a vision of England haunting in its power: "England, beyond the water, rising with ash-grey, corpse-grey cliffs, and streaks of snow on the downs above. England, like a long, ash-grey coffin slowly submerging. . . . It seemed to re- pudiate the sunshine, to remain unilluminated, long and ash-grey and dead, with streaks of snow like cerements. That was England!" (*The Lost Girl* 294). The war years had brought Lawrence to a deliberate exile that would, in one form or another, last for the rest of his life.

5 Exile: 1919–22

Lawrence had left England for the Continent where he was once again a stranger and (once again) a poor one; this time he had nine pounds in his pocket, rather than the eleven pounds he had had in 1912. He stopped in Turin for a couple of nights on the way, using a contact he had made in England; his host, the diplomat Sir Walter Becker (1855–1927), later remembered the arrival at the door of ''a homespun-clad figure, carrying some sort of travelling bag.'' Gentlemen don't carry their own bags, of course, or have shabby overcoats, but Lawrence wasn't a gentleman. Becker also recalled having ''a good deal of conversation with him . . . we appeared to be on terms of friendship and sympathy'' (Nehls 1958: 12). But Lawrence had never found the rich English abroad very sympathetic and remembered ''a sincere half-mocking argument, he for security and bank-balance and power, I for naked liberty'' (*Letters* III: 417). Sir Walter would later find a lengthy re-creation of his house and the conversations there in Lawrence's novel *Aaron's Rod* and strongly objected to them. But it was also characteristic of Lawrence to find his material as a novelist in such a place and to have no scruple in using it; it had long been his practice to take what he wanted of real-life situations and people and to re-create them in whatever form he wanted. What he could create as his art mattered more to him than the sensibilities of those who got caught up in the process or his liking for them. Frieda once remarked that ''I like people more than he does'' (Bynner 1951: 62), while he commented in 1920 that ''I don't like people—truly I don't'' (*Letters* III: 491); in consequence, perhaps, he was prepared to be quite ruthless in using in fiction the "secrets of my heart," which Faith (1888–1960), the wife of the novelist Compton Mackenzie (1883–1972), for example, regretted ever allowing him access to (Nehls 1959: 35).

He made, however, no attempt to go back and recover the experience of living in the Italian places he had known before the war. All he did was spend one night in La Spezia, near the place Frieda and he had left five years earlier, and that, perhaps, only because his train went that way. He was going on to somewhere new, even if he did not know exactly where it was yet; but he knew he was pausing in Florence, to meet Frieda. In Florence, his raffish old acquaintance the novelist and essayist Norman Douglas (1868–1952) turned out to be a good deal more sympathetic than the inhabitants of the house in Turin had been, and Lawrence also met there Douglas's friend the minor American writer Maurice Magnus (1876–1920), who would become the subject of one of Lawrence's greatest pieces of writing, the "Introduction" to Magnus's *Memoirs of the Foreign Legion*. But for the moment, Lawrence simply enjoyed being out of England in the company of congenial people, even if money was scarce. Italy remained a magical place, and Florence, in particular, had "a certain perfection" for him (*Letters* III: 450). When Frieda arrived in Florence, he met her train at four o'clock in the morning and immediately took her for a drive: " 'I must show you this town.' We went in an open carriage, I saw the pale crouching Duomo and in the thick moonmist the Giotto tower disappearing at the top into the sky" (Frieda Lawrence 1935: 92). But they stayed only briefly; they were headed for the wildest part of the Abruzzi mountains, where Rosalind Baynes had her potential house and where they would stay to see what the house was like.

It turned out to be an extraordinary journey into the wilds, which (again) Lawrence re-created at length in *The Lost Girl,* the novel he would shortly write. After hours of traveling, they arrived well after dark in a house "staggeringly primitive" even for them: "Everything must be cooked gipsy-fashion in the chimney over a wood fire. The chickens wander in, the ass is tied to the doorpost and makes his droppings on the doorstep, and brays his head off" (*Letters* III: 432). The Lawrences could rough it when required, but after ten days, nearly getting snowed in just before Christmas, Lawrence sent a strong recommendation to Rosalind never to bring the children there, and the Lawrences escaped back over the mountains to Capri, where Compton Mackenzie—whom they had known since before the war—had promised to find them a room if ever they needed it.

Yet another new Italy awaited them: this time an expatriate colony, "the uttermost uttermost limit for spiteful scandal" (*Letters* III: 444), which Lawrence observed with as much relish as he observed everything else: "All the world's a stage etc." (*Letters* III: 447). But Frieda didn't like it, and it was not a good place for writing; and Lawrence was further hampered by the Italian postal strike, which stopped him getting hold of the 200-page, 1913 novel fragment "The Insurrection of Miss Houghton," which he had tried to recover in

1916 and which he still wanted to work on again. He desperately needed to write and publish, to recover from the wartime slump in his work's reputation, and to reestablish himself. Without an English agent—he had broken with Pinker at the end of 1919—he entered negotiations with the publisher Secker for the publication of *Women in Love* (and perhaps the republication of *The Rainbow*) in England, while Seltzer would be bringing out *Women in Love* in America before the end of the year, and Robert Mountsier had agreed to act as Lawrence's American agent for the future.

But all he wrote in Capri at this stage was the first draft of *Psychoanalysis and the Unconscious.* Finally, the old novel manuscript arrived, and Lawrence set to work. Yet—although he may have taken from it the starting date and the central character's situation—typically, he rewrote and reconceived it completely. During February, Frieda and he started house-hunting seriously, this time, almost as far south in Europe as they could go, in Taormina in Sicily. Here Lawrence discovered the Fontana Vecchia, a house standing away from the town, by itself among fields and gardens, looking over the Ionian Sea. Just as in 1912, they had at last found the southern place where they could live happily and cheaply, away from the threat of the north, "with one's back on Europe forever" (*Letters* III: 491), and now had to remain until Lawrence had earned enough for them to travel on again. But it was also a place they came to love deeply, where Lawrence felt at home "in the garden and up the hills among the goats" (*Letters* III: 491) and where he wrote some of his best poems about the natural world, including "Snake."

Through the spring and early summer, Lawrence worked energetically away at *The Lost Girl,* which was what the old 1913 manuscript had turned into; and almost as soon as he had finished it, he started another novel, *Mr Noon,* the first part also set in a re-created English Midlands, but this time using his own early history with Frieda as the basis for its continuation. It was, however, a sign of how far he had moved as a novelist, partner, and thinker that the experience of delighted partnership and love of eight years earlier should now be subjected to such wicked sarcasm and detached irony. But just as he used the experience of others, so he would use his own experience as a way of going beyond it, something in which he always believed. As he would shortly write in his Magnus "Introduction": "We have got to realize. And then we can surpass" (*Phoenix II* 358). Not only did he have *Mr Noon* under way from the summer of 1920, but he also went back to *Aaron's Rod,* though not yet to finish it. Together with *The Lost Girl,* the three novels comprise a kind of comic trilogy of disillusionment with English society, with marriage, with love itself: a process also sharply defined in a number of poems written in the sequence *Birds, Beasts and Flowers* around this time, such as many of the "Fruits" poems and the "Tortoise" sequence.

Perhaps as part of this process of change, in the summer of 1920, while staying in Florence again in the summer, away from the heat of the Sicilian summer and while Frieda was in Germany, Lawrence had a brief affair with

Rosalind Baynes, who had moved to a villa just outside Florence. In no way does the relationship seem to have deflected him from his commitment to his marriage, anymore than the relationship of Aaron with the Marchesa in *Aaron's Rod* deflects his sense of being married: "women will only have lovers now, and never a husband. Well, I am a husband, if I am anything. And I shall never be a lover again, not while I live" (*Aaron's Rod* 266). The affair seems, though, to have been a confirmation of his own independence within marriage. He does not seem to have seen Rosalind Baynes again, but some of the writing about Constance Chatterley in *Lady Chatterley's Lover* six years later drew on her background and her appearance.

He and Frieda met in Venice and were back in Sicily by mid-October; and, shortly, copies of *The Lost Girl* arrived, along with proofs of the English edition of *Women in Love*. But then, characteristically, things went wrong with his publications in England; the libraries refused to take *The Lost Girl* as it stood and Secker wrote, imploring for changes. Lawrence made one big one, and Secker added three others of his own. Then, Secker asked for changes in *Women in Love* and warned Lawrence that he would be getting an advance of only seventy-five pounds on the book, as Secker was so sure it would not be taken by the libraries. These things naturally combined with Lawrence's existing sense of the pusillanimity of England and of the literary establishment in general and got into his attack on critics in *Mr Noon*, which he was still working on:

So, darling, don't *look* at the nasty book any more: don't you then: there, there, don't cry, my pretty.

No one really takes more trouble soothing and patting his critics on the back than I. But alas, all my critics are troubled with wind. (*Mr Noon* 142)

He and Frieda spent the winter of 1920 and the first quarter of 1921 in a very similar way to how they had spent the year before, securely at home, with Lawrence doing a great deal of writing, interrupted only by a flying visit to Sardinia in January 1921, partly with the idea of looking for a house there and partly so that Lawrence could get a travel book out of it. The latter he succeeded in doing; a whole book was finished by the start of March and—with illustrations by the artist Jan Juta (b. 1897)—came out as *Sea and Sardinia* in 1923. At this point, Lawrence decided to ask the agent Curtis Brown (1866–1945) to act for him in England; the effort of doing all his own work in the placing of his books had, with his new productivity (and the interest taken in his work), become too much for him, and much as he liked the idea of working as a kind of independent spirit, there were practical drawbacks.

In mid-April 1921, he and Frieda left Sicily to go north, this year before the heat really struck; in Capri they met an American couple, Earl (1878–1957) and Achsah (1878–1945) Brewster, who would be good friends to them for the rest of the decade. In Germany, where he had gone with Frieda on her visit to her mother, writing away in the woods, Lawrence at last managed to finish *Aaron's*

Rod, the novel he had been struggling with since the winter of 1917. It became, like all his novels, the final statement (for the moment) of how he saw relationship and marriage. The individual must stand apart, married or unmarried, must admit subordination only to a being he or she knows to be superior. It was not a position Lawrence would remain with; but it was what he believed, for the moment. It was a position that he further developed in the second of his psychoanalysis books, *Fantasia of the Unconscious,* which he also drafted in the woods in Germany that summer, the theory growing (as he always said it did) out of the passional experience of fiction, both a confirmation of it and a development away from it.

After their time in Germany, he and Frieda went to visit her sister Johanna in Austria, where she was with her children and the banker Emil von Krug (1870–1944), who would be her new husband. This visit provided the background for the second part of Lawrence's short novel *The Captain's Doll,* another work concerned with a marriage abandoned and a new relationship, without love, attempted. Back in Florence, Lawrence wrote poems, including "Bat" and "Man and Bat," before he and Frieda traveled on to Sicily, and Lawrence experienced a renewed onrush of love for the place: "But how lovely it is here! . . . the great window of the eastern sky, seaward, I like it much the best of any place in Italy" (*Letters* IV: 90). But Europe itself continued to annoy him: "[M]y heart—and my soul are broken, in Europe." He found, for example, that Secker, the English publisher of *Women in Love,* which had come out in June, had capitulated to threats of a libel action from Philip Heseltine and needed the descriptions of Halliday and the Pussum in the novel altered. With very bad grace, Lawrence made the changes he was asked to, and the novel went back on sale. But such things confirmed his prejudice that his novels would never do very well in England; and he was well aware that he was now almost wholly dependent on America for his living (*Letters* IV: 114). Once again, he was convinced that America was his land of the future. He had lost hope in Europe and was tired of it (*Letters* IV: 141). During the autumn and winter of 1921, he made continual inquiries about places to live in America; and a letter from the American society hostess and patron of the arts Mabel Dodge Sterne (1879–1962), inviting him to Taos in New Mexico, effectively settled the matter. That was where he would go first, at any rate.

But committing himself to America—something he had been trying to do for six or seven years—was not as easy as it had looked; he had a strong sense that America would be barbaric and that he would hate it. Even Taos had a colony of artists—"Evil everywhere. But I want to go—to try" (*Letters* IV: 151). During the winter of 1921–22, he wavered between going to Taos and following his friends the Brewsters to Ceylon, where Earl would be studying at a Buddhist temple. He finally resolved the dilemma by deciding to do both; to go first to Ceylon and thence to America.

He was very conscious of the significance and the pain of leaving Europe (*Letters* IV: 191). To leave Europe was, in a way, finally to demonstrate the abandonment of his *belief* in things—in society's progress and especially in himself as a writer who could make some significant difference to his society. ''But I want to go.'' He readied himself by getting all the short pieces he could finish into a final state and posted off to Curtis Brown; out of this burst of work came the final version of *Fantasia of the Unconscious,* his book of short stories *England, My England,* and the short novel collection *The Fox, The Ladybird, and The Captain's Doll.*

With his European work behind him, he could leave. He was 36½, a moderately successful writer but fundamentally disillusioned with the literary world and eager for experience of what lay outside the Europe he had written about for so long. Writing for him was inevitably linked with his sense of place, of what a particular place could bring him, what it was like to live in, and how it might be seen to symbolize the lives of the human beings who inhabited it. He was going away to write, not just to travel: to find the place that was satisfying to live in, as a writer. But he was also going to see if he could find a place where he wanted to live, where he could find a way of living that would satisfy his complex nature and needs. Frieda and he sailed away from Europe for Ceylon on 26 February 1922: a symbolic move if ever they made one.

6   Round the World and Back Again: Ceylon, Australia, America, Mexico, Europe, America: 1922–24

I.

The journey to Ceylon and Ceylon itself were, however, to play almost no part in Lawrence's subsequent writing. The journey he and Frieda loved: a letter written in the course of it is among his most beautiful, as it describes their passage through Egypt and the Suez Canal (*Letters* IV: 208–12). They made friends with some Australian people on the boat; but, ever the professional writer, Lawrence was still working, even if only at translating a novel—*Mastro-Don Gesualdo*—by the Italian author Giovanni Verga (1840–1922). Almost as soon as they arrived in Ceylon, they watched the Pera-Hera, when Edward Prince of Wales (1894–1972) visited Kandy and there was, at night, a procession of dancers, chiefs, and elephants. This remained marvelously memorable: Lawrence described it in a number of letters, as well as in his poem "Elephant."

But although Kandy was "lovely to look at," they were overwhelmed by "the terrific sun that makes like a bell-jar of heat, like a prison over you" (*Letters* IV: 214, 227) and by a continual unease. The Brewsters' bungalow was very near the forest, and Lawrence unhappily described "the thick, choky feel of tropical forest" and "the horrid noises of the birds and creatures" (*Letters* IV: 225). They slept badly, and, though the Brewsters were kind and helpful, Lawrence remained ill at ease and disoriented (*Letters* IV: 216). He also picked up a stomach bug early on and remained sick his whole time in Ceylon; this certainly colored and narrowed his responses—"I don't like the silly dark people or their swarming billions or their hideous little Buddha temples." He did some more Verga translation but (apart from the poem) no creative work at all, which was thoroughly unusual for him in a new place. "I don't believe I shall ever work here" (*Letters* IV: 221, 217), he remarked. Ceylon was thus most certainly not a place in which to stop for long, on an extremely expensive journey that depended, in part, on Lawrence earning money as he traveled. After only six weeks, he and Frieda moved on—but still not yet to America. They headed first toward Australia, to take up invitations received from shipboard acquaintances on the journey out to Colombo, but not with any particular expectation: "[O]ne may as well move on, once one has started" (*Letters* IV: 220). Having cut loose, loose he would now remain.

They landed in Perth on 4 May 1922 but stayed in Western Australia only a fortnight before taking the next boat on to Sydney. They were a little overwhelmed by the hospitality of their friends, though the place and the atmosphere of a late Australian autumn were a great relief after Ceylon: "Air beautiful and pure and sky fresh, high" (*Letters* IV: 235). The best thing in Western Australia was the bush, "hoary and unending, no noise, still . . . somewhat like a dream, a twilight forest that has not yet seen a day" (*Letters* IV: 238); the contrast with Ceylon's noisy forest could not have been clearer. Lawrence's most significant meeting was with the writer Mollie Skinner (1878–1955): it was her manuscript that, the following year, he would transform into *The Boy in the Bush.*

But their tickets took them on to Sydney, and, on 18 May, they were off again. Frieda was starting to want to stay somewhere a few months, and Lawrence was prepared to try New South Wales, to see if he liked it and could write there. Sydney itself turned out too expensive, however; they retreated down the coast forty miles to Thirroul and took a bungalow for a month "with the Pacific in the garden" (*Letters* IV: 253). They knew no one, and their neighbors (unlike neighbors in Italy) did not cross-examine them, much to Lawrence's relief. For all Lawrence's forebodings, he started a novel and found himself able to write at something over 3,000 words a day for six weeks, with only a short break in the middle. Ceylon should have been marvelous, but he had written nothing. They had expected little of Australia; but here Lawrence was, writing furiously.

Kangaroo was, in effect, a progress report from a European in the middle of his travels; it took the European problems that had always interested Lawrence (how society can be changed and who is to rule it, how individuals can both remain themselves and have relationships like marriage) and explored them in a context that allowed Lawrence to make them both usefully diagrammatic. Socialism could be set politically against authoritarianism, love against separateness; and, as in any novel, they could be sustained (and subverted) fictively. The invented figure of Kangaroo himself, the lawyer Ben Cooley, the representative of the idea of love, is far more than a cardboard figure. His appeals to Richard Lovatt Somers, his emotionalism, his rhetorical power are the kinds of things that only a man—and a writer—who had been deeply committed to such things at one stage of his life could now create (and reject). To that extent, Lawrence was once again revisiting his own past and rejecting it, at a cost he was all too well aware of. The central character, Somers, ends up feeling that the past is a mere "decomposed body . . . whirling and choking us, language, love, and meaning" (*Kangaroo* 333): a depressing enough conclusion for a writer. Lawrence also used the socialists and fascists he had seen in Italy and the ideas of socialism that he had brought forward from his youth in Eastwood; he set them in the haunting, new/old world of Australia, where every issue seemed clearer. The marriage of Somers and Harriett is even less of a loving partnership than the marriage of Tanny and Lilly in *Aaron's Rod* had been; the marriage exists in continual flux, among the possibilities of love, of lordship, of companionship.

Through *Kangaroo* goes the small figure of Somers, pulled in all directions, but finally—for all the claims of the past, with all its old ideas of rootedness in love, in marriage, and with mankind—coming down on the side of lonely individualism, even within marriage, and asserting a belief in the nonhuman world as a crucial context for human beings' sense of themselves. Australia offered a superb context for this way of thinking: "The soft, blue, humanless sky of Australia, the pale, white unwritten atmosphere of Australia. Tabula rasa. The world a new leaf. . . . Without a mark, without a record" (*Kangaroo* 332). Lawrence had found Australia fascinating: "But for the remains of a fighting conscience, I would stay" (*Letters* IV: 275).

He seems to have done very little in Australia apart from think, look, and write; but the novel was a real achievement and remains one of the crucial twentieth-century perceptions of the country. As soon as he realized he could finish it, however, he and Frieda booked their tickets for leaving; and Lawrence posted his manuscript ahead to his American agent Mountsier as soon as he had finished it. On 11 August 1922, Frieda's forty-third birthday, they sailed for San Francisco; the moment for going to America could no longer be put off, even though Lawrence had so managed things that at least he would not be arriving in the North American industrial heartland.

II.

They stopped briefly in New Zealand on the way, as well as at a number of the Pacific islands, and, on 4 September 1922, landed in San Francisco, which Lawrence found noisy and expensive. They took the train to Santa Fe and then on to Lamy junction, where Mabel Sterne met them, took them by car to Taos, and installed them in a new adobe house.

Now, Lawrence could genuinely experience the America he had been thinking of for so long. Everyone was extremely kind, he found—in Santa Fe he met the poet Witter Bynner (1881–1968) and the journalist Willard Johnson (1897–1968), and in Taos they met two Danish painters, Kai Götzsche (b. 1886) and Knud Merrild (1894–1954), whom they liked very much. Tony Luhan (d. 1963), Mabel Sterne's Indian lover, was a more difficult person to get on with; but Mabel herself exerted every effort to give her new guests an interesting time.

More than anything else, the place was marvelously, compellingly beautiful. Lawrence celebrated it famously in an essay on New Mexico he wrote six years later: "I think New Mexico was the greatest experience from the outside world that I have ever had . . . the moment I saw the brilliant, proud morning shine high up over the deserts of Santa Fe, something stood still in my soul, and I started to attend"; he wrote how the person who lives there "above the great proud world of desert will know, almost unbearably how beautiful it is, how clear and unquestioned is the might of the day" (*Phoenix* 142–43). A new world it was, where (too) he experienced for the first time an old world religion in the Red Indians both in Taos and in reservations and dances in Arizona, where Mabel took her guests only three days after they reached Taos.

Lawrence was also at last able to do some sustained work: he added a new last chapter to *Kangaroo* and revised the whole novel, as well as writing some poems and some essays and journalism about New Mexico. Most significantly, however, he turned again to his old essays on American literature and started to give them a thoroughgoing revision, in a new, hard-hitting style that he seems to have considered peculiarly North American. They were his first work for America: a sign of his new relationship with it. The England where he had first created them seemed very far away, though he was poignantly reminded of it with the death of his old Eastwood friend Sallie Hopkin; he wrote a touching and loving letter to Hopkin when he heard the news (*Letters* IV: 327). And he wrote a poem, "Spirits Summoned West," starting from the last phrase of the letter ("England seems full of graves to me"), which explicitly linked the death of his mother with the death of Sallie Hopkin.

Life with Mabel and in Taos had its disadvantages, however: the Eden of the high American desert contained the usual snakes. Having invited Lawrence to New Mexico, Mabel wanted him to write for her, to advise her on her own novel, to show him off, to talk to her for hours, to fit in with her plans and imaginings. "I don't think I can bear to be here very long," Lawrence confessed to his agent after six weeks, "too much on Mabel Sterne's ground." They solved the problem by moving out of Taos, up to a ranch on nearby Lobo mountain, where they could be properly independent (*Letters* IV: 330, 333). Here, with the two Danish painters as companions (very necessary on a ranch 8,000 feet up in winter), they lived till the spring. And Lawrence was able to work hard again: he finished the revision of the American essays, giving them the proud declaration "Lobo" at the end; he revised some of his Verga translations; and he wrote a number of poems, bringing them together and revising them for the volume he would publish as *Birds, Beasts and Flowers* later in 1923. His American publisher Seltzer and his agent Mountsier both came to visit in December; Mountsier stayed on in Taos, but his relations with Lawrence became progressively more strained. Mountsier had not liked *Aaron's Rod* and had also objected to *Kangaroo;* Lawrence was finding him awkward as an agent, particularly in his relations with Seltzer, upon whom Lawrence was depending more and more for his publication (and income) in North America. He finally broke with Mountsier in February 1923 and put his American business (like his English) in the hands of the Curtis Brown agency.

With the spring, toward the end of his first six months in America, Lawrence decided to go to Mexico; he had been wondering about writing a novel in America, but nothing (apart from an abortive effort to help with Mabel's novel) had so far suggested itself. The American novel would have to become a Mexican novel. Lawrence and Frieda traveled to Mexico in March and there met Bynner and Johnson, whom they had suggested might make the trip, too. After a month based in Mexico City, visiting outlying places, the party moved to Chapala; Lawrence had prospected for a place for them all to live and had telegraphed back: "Chapala paradise. Take evening train" (*Letters* IV: 435). Here, beside the lake, he was once more able to write a novel, as he had written *Sons and Lovers* beside the Lago di Garda, *The Sisters* beside the sea in Fiascherino, *Women in Love* high above the ocean in Cornwall, *The Lost Girl* and *Mr Noon* overlooking the sea in Taormina, and *Kangaroo* beside the sea in Australia. The habit of living and writing somewhere above, looking out and over, was one he retained all his life (Worthen 1991: 460). The novel he now wrote he called *Quetzalcoatl* and formed the first version of *The Plumed Serpent:* "It interests me, means more to me than any other novel of mine. This is my real novel of America" (*Letters* IV: 457). It was a real fantasy novel, in which an Englishwoman visiting Mexico experiences, firsthand, a religious revolution there, in which a new structure of society is created: one based on a revival of old Mexican religion, a structure of nonhuman belief that finally evades and supersedes the Christian context. The novel thus attempted to answer the despairs about the individual and society into which *Kangaroo* had led him; it was characteristic of Lawrence's writing that one novel should address the problems the previous novel had thrown up. But he also knew that what he was writing was only a first draft; for the first time since 1914, the novel he was writing would have to be radically recast before he would want to publish it. He could now, however, afford this luxury; Seltzer was bringing out a string of books and (for the first time since 1914) making him a good income. He could thus afford the luxury of prolonged revision and rethinking.

III.

He finished the novel—or at last reached a suitable resting point—in Chapala at the end of June; and he and Frieda reentered the United States and traveled slowly to New York, where Seltzer had offered to find them somewhere to live (and where Lawrence could work, mostly on his proofs) before they went back to Europe. Although they both wanted to return to the ranch in Taos, in the long run, they were not keen on spending another winter at altitude; Frieda had been away from her German family for nearly two years and wanted to go back; and her son Monty and daughter Elsa were both now twenty-one and could make up their own minds about seeing their mother. Middleton Murry was also starting a new magazine (the *Adelphi*) in England and wanted Lawrence's contributions and help.

But, a fortnight before the boat left, Lawrence refused to sail; he and Frieda seem to have had a massive and wounding quarrel and effectively separated, with Frieda going to London (and thence to Germany) and Lawrence returning to travel through America, across to Chicago and thence to the West Coast, finally retreating to Mexico. He seems to have accused Frieda of wanting to go back (in every sense): of "chasing . . . those Weekley children" (something he felt "I can't stomach"), while he himself, when it came to it, could not bear the thought of "England and home and my people" or even of the Fontana Vecchia, which he had loved so much. He felt caught between "the old world which I loved" (but now used the past tense about) and the new world, "which means nothing to me"; the situation of Richard Lovatt Somers had become very real to him, and simply returning to Europe was not going to change that.

There followed a few, fairly miserable months of travel for Lawrence, some of it once again in the company of the Danish painters; he felt, at one point, "as if I should wander over the brink of existence" (*Letters* IV: 507). He was in fact, to begin with, expecting Frieda to come back at any time. But she didn't. What he succeeded in writing (and also turning into the next stage of his thinking about relationships) was a completely new version of Molly Skinner's Australian novel; he gradually turned it into *The Boy in the Bush* and developed the idea of a hero refusing ties and obligations but going his own way, doing what he wants. Jack marries but feels that, if he wants two wives, he should have them; he also believes that his wife "knows she can't get past me. Therefore, in one corner of her, she hates me, like a scorpion lurking" (*The Boy in the Bush* 334). Jack also fantasizes about turning into a kind of patriarch, with wives and cattle and land. Molly Skinner was astonished (and hurt) to see what Lawrence had made of her book, but it was what he currently wanted to write and to work his thinking through.

He ended up in Mexico in November with Kai Götzsche, finishing the novel and with a sense that his marriage was probably at an end; he wrote to Frieda, making an offer of "a regular arrangement for you to have an income, if you wish" (*Letters* IV: 529). But Frieda kept asking him to go back, as did other friends, and it was not as if his experience of the months spent traveling on his own had been very satisfying. On 21 November, after almost exactly three months on his own, he reluctantly went back: "I suppose it is the next move in the battle which never ends and in which I never win" (*Letters* IV: 541). He was committed to struggle, in writing and in living, and made both a point of principle. But, in this case, he was prepared to see if he and Frieda were able to journey on together. He could not simply give up all ties to the old life. Götzsche and he sailed from Vera Cruz; in his unfinished novel "The Flying-Fish," Lawrence re-created the voyage and his experience of watching flying fish and porpoises from the bows, and it was again the mesmerizing power of the nonhuman world he watched in the speeding, playful fish:

This is sheer joy—and men have lost it, or never accomplished it. The cleverest sports-men in the world are owls beside these fish. And the togetherness of love is nothing to the spinning unison of dolphins playing under-sea. It would be wonderful to know joy as these fish know it. The life of the deep waters is ahead of us, it contains sheer togetherness and sheer joy. We have never got there— (*St. Mawr* 221–22)

IV.

England could hardly have been more of a contrast. His first reaction, after four years away, was to "loathe London—hate England—feel like an animal in a trap" (*Letters* IV: 542). He came down with a cold and retreated to bed: "I don't belong over here any more. It's like being among the dead of one's pre-vious existence" (*Letters* IV: 545). He wrote some essays for Murry's *Adelphi* (including the caustic "On Coming Home," which proved too caustic for Murry) and visited his Midlands family for a few days over New Year; but as soon as he could decently manage it, he laid plans for going back to the ranch for the summer. But, this time, it was with a strong sense of saying good-bye to England forever; and he would have liked to keep certain people with him, if he was giving up England. Now had come the moment for him to appeal to people to do what he had fantasized about for ten years but now had found a place for. He proposed getting a group of people to live together, dedicated to earning little and living sensibly; above all, they would live away from the industrial world he hated so much. Accordingly, at a dinner arranged for many of his London friends at the Café Royal—Catherine Carswell and her husband, Donald (1882–1940), Mary Cannan (1867–1950), Murry, Koteliansky, and the painters Dorothy Brett and Mark Gertler—he publicly asked which of them would come to New Mexico. Various excuses were made, and various reasons were given; only Dorothy Brett absolutely committed herself to coming. Murry, in spite of his frequent professions of friendship and love, said that he would come, clearly meaning not to. He had, however, recently ended an affair with Dorothy Brett (which Lawrence did not know about), and Frieda had—before Lawrence returned to England—invited Murry to become her lover: both strong reasons inhibiting him from making up such a foursome. He would also be getting married again the following May. Koteliansky made a speech of love and devotion to Lawrence, breaking glasses to celebrate every sentence end; but he would not leave the London that was now his home. What Lawrence drank made him violently sick over the tablecloth; the evening turned out a disaster, and its outcome—Brett's coming back to the ranch with them—was perhaps unexpected. But Brett, always willing to give her devotion as she had given it to Murry and would now give it to Lawrence, was a surprisingly independent person who would paint and could also type and would (Lawrence hoped) not

only give Frieda some company but might act as a buffer in the marriage relationship. Her deafness (she used an ear trumpet they called ''Toby'') might
not be altogether a disadvantage. They would have to find out.

In the new year, Lawrence and Frieda stayed in London, Lawrence writing
journalism and starting some stories—Murry would figure comically in a number of them, such as ''Jimmy and the Desperate Woman,'' ''The Last Laugh,''
and ''The Border Line''—before they went to Germany to see Frieda's mother.
They also spent some time in Paris, where Lawrence wrote his extraordinarily
prescient ''Letter from Germany'' about the breakdown of the old values and
the rise of a new commitment to destruction, with ''queer gangs of *Young Socialists*'': a country ''[W]hirling to the ghost of the old Middle Ages of Europe''
(*Phoenix* 109–10). Back briefly in London to collect Dorothy Brett and her
painting things, the three of them set sail for America on 5 March 1924.

After months of silence, which had started to worry Lawrence, Thomas Seltzer met them in New York and was as friendly as ever; but there was no
disguising the fact that his business was in serious trouble. (It would, in fact,
shortly collapse, taking with it the bulk of Lawrence's American earnings; but
that was still a few months away.) After a fortnight of snow and sun, they took
the train south, to have a second attempt at living in Mabel's orbit in Taos—
the balance of relationships changed, anyway, by the presence of Brett.
Lawrence set to work, this time on his essays ''Indians and Entertainment'' and
''The Dance of the Sprouting Corn'': both of them attempts to say what it was
about Indian culture that was so important, both of them ways of thinking
through what he would want in the end to say in his novel.

But this time, after only a few days of relative harmony, Mabel—now Mabel
Luhan, having married Tony the previous year—presented Frieda with a ranch
on Lobo about two miles farther up from the Del Monte ranch where they had
lived with the Danes, and they started making plans to go back to it. Lawrence,
hating the obligation of a gift, insisted in giving Mabel something in return and
wrote to Europe for the original manuscript of *Sons and Lovers,* which he, in
turn, presented to her: a gift whose value certainly outweighed what he and
Frieda had received. After having some preliminary work on the buildings done,
on 5 May they moved up to the three-cabin ranch for the summer, Lawrence
and Frieda sharing one cabin and Brett taking a smaller one nearby.

This would be Lawrence's most creative and fulfilled summer for some while;
it is worth taking some time to look at his life on the ranch, in the first half of
the next chapter, and to examine how his fiction emerged out of the isolation
of his life there.

7   Ranch Life and the Return to Mexico: 1924–25

Work on repairing and rebuilding the ranch went on for five weeks, throughout May and into June; the big, three-room cabin had to be repaired, its chimney rebuilt with adobe bricks, and all three cabins restored and reroofed. Lawrence worked with three Indian laborers and a Mexican carpenter; he made no difference between the amount of heavy or difficult work he expected them to do and what he did himself. When it came to someone's having to crawl along inside the main cabin's tin roof on a hot day, with a wet handkerchief over mouth and nose, to clear out the old rats' nests, then he did it. Brett, too, "was amazing for the hard work she would do" (Frieda Lawrence 1935: 137). Mabel and Tony stayed up at the ranch for some of the time, sleeping in a big tepee up on the hillside, as the Indians did; at night, they would eat together, the Indians would sing, plans for the next day's work would be made. While building the house, Lawrence did almost no writing, though he does seem to have finished his essay "Pan in America." The old tensions among Lawrence, Frieda, and Mabel seem to have continued, with (now) the added complication of Brett; but, for a good deal of May, there was no time for quarreling, simply the day-to-day work. They took just a couple of trips away; in the course of a journey back to Taos on horseback, for example, Mabel and Tony took them to the cave at Arroyo Seco, which Lawrence would use as the setting for his story "The Woman Who Rode Away" the following month.

But what was Lawrence doing, spending five weeks rebuilding a run-down ranch on which he would (in the end) spend only five months in the summer of 1924 and five months the following year, in a country where he would never live more than seven months at a time? Although he was a professional writer, his books never sold in very large numbers, so he depended on publishing a great deal—and so on writing a great deal, too. The place was punishingly remote and (what is more) could never be inhabited in winter.

But there was, to begin with, the huge pleasure for Lawrence and Frieda of having their own place at last. Frieda had been pining for a farm or something equivalent since Australia in May 1922, and at the back of Lawrence's mind was the memory of his days at the Haggs farm between 1902 and 1908. The ranch (first called Lobo, later Kiowa) was the first place they had ever inhabited where they could really do what they wanted and that they were not beholden to others for or paying rent for or looking after for someone else. Lawrence had always strongly resisted owning property. But now they had acquired it, in the most extraordinary of all the places that he and Frieda had visited since 1912. Lawrence threw himself into the work, which offered him a new challenge, a wholly new field to explore and master.

It was the most beautiful, if also the most soul-destroyingly difficult and destructive place in which they had ever lived. "One doesn't talk any more about being happy. . . . But I do like having the big unbroken spaces round me" (*Letters* V: 47), Lawrence wrote to Catherine Carswell. But he told Murry very early on how hard and trying it was, too. The animal life (rats, in particular) could nearly defeat human occupation, gnawing through and eating almost anything left unattended. Furniture had to be slung up to the ceiling on ropes when they went away, for example; rats bounced on the roofs at nights "like hippopotamuses" (*St. Mawr* 148); black ants swarmed into the kitchen. Everyday life was always hard, with water having to be carried from the spring (they only got the water flowing through pipes the following year), horses that needed to be fed and cared for, wood that had to be chopped; and every evening there were milk and mail (and sometimes butter and eggs) to be ridden for, two miles down to the Del Monte ranch, where the Hawk family lived and worked, and back just before dark. And always there was unremitting hard physical work, even when the main work of restoration was done: making shelves and cupboards, baking bread, catching horses (*Letters* V: 75). Frieda knitted, cooked, made butter, and (in 1925) looked after the chickens. Animals would fall ill; there was "the underlying rat-dirt, the everlasting bristling tussle of the wild life" (*St. Mawr* 150). The nearest shop for provisions or supplies was half a day's journey away, seventeen miles down in Taos.

Yet, the place was quite extraordinary. "The landscape lived, and lived as the world of the gods, unsullied and unconcerned. The great circling landscape lived its own life, sumptuous and uncaring," Lawrence would write in *St. Mawr* (*St. Mawr* 146). They could see down to the desert 1,000 feet below, the houses of a pueblo looking like crystals, and away for thirty miles to where the Rio Grande Canyon wound its way and then beyond that to the distant mountains, "like icebergs showing up from an outer sea." Lawrence wrote to his German mother-in-law how, here, one sensed "something wild and untamed . . . that really is America. But not the America of the whites" (*Letters* V: 63). Unlike Mexico, which had offered him a human world that was different, the Kiowa ranch gave him a life with nature almost untrammeled and beyond the merely beautiful: "something savage unbreakable in the spirit of place out here" (*Letters* V: 47). That brought out for him, always, a strong sense of what human beings really needed in their lives, the "aboriginal quality" (*Letters* V: 75). It was this very special quality of the ranch that Lawrence celebrated in his short novel *St. Mawr,* which starts in England but ends up in a re-creation of the ranch itself. He wrote this over the summer, between June and August; it was his second novel of North America. Over and over again, we can see how it conveyed something of his own feeling for the place, as when, for example, the fictional Lou of the story first sees the ranch against a backdrop of "blue balsam pines, the round hills, the solid uprise of the mountain flank": "In an instant, her heart sprang to it . . . she looked across the purple and gold of the clearing. . . . '*This is the place,*' she said to herself" (*St. Mawr* 140). More than anything else, the Kiowa ranch offered the chance to live "circumstantially, from day to day, with the hills and the trees" (*Letters* V: 79). It was the ideal ordinariness of the place, as a context for human lives, that mattered as much as its spectacular views. Human beings could struggle, work, get tired, live simply, do what they wanted and always in the eye of nature, "living up against these savage Rockies" (*Letters* V: 148).

Lawrence had prefaced writing *St. Mawr* with another North American story that he had perhaps been thinking about during the three weeks since Arroyo Seco, "The Woman Who Rode Away." He wrote this very fast and showed it to Mabel Luhan in Taos at the end of June. These were his first two North American fictions: both, strikingly, about the danger, the destructiveness for twentieth-century white consciousness, of America, both attempts to suggest that the challenge of another kind of consciousness is what can and should confront modern men and women. "The Woman Who Rode Away" describes a white woman who unthinkingly decides to see Indians and blindly gives herself up to them; the story conveyed something of what Lawrence must have felt as he saw Mabel's marrying herself to Tony, the pueblo Indian. But whereas Tony was something of an outcast from the pueblo for what he had done, the woman of Lawrence's story is seized upon as a sacrifice by the Indians; the story reveals just how opposed to white civilization Lawrence felt Indians were, how much they hated it and would do it down if they could. Yet, they reminded him of what the white races lack, too; it is a story (like *St. Mawr*) that is thoroughly ambivalent about the opposition of cultures it reveals.

Being sent a copy of *A Passage to India* by E. M. Forster in July must have added to his sense of the efforts that other writers, too, were making to confront their European characters with alien worlds (*Letters* V: 77). But it was now possible to live quietly from day to day, and the writing of *St. Mawr* flowed through the summer. He finally ended it around the middle of August, tired but able to pronounce it "a corker" (*Letters* V: 91).

A disturbing moment had come, however, early in August. Lawrence had been remarkably well for months, but the ranch was at 8,600 feet, and around 2 August, coming down with a cold, he began to spit blood. He was actually (as he admitted eighteen months later) suffering a bronchial hemorrhage. To his rage, Frieda had a doctor come up to the ranch to see him; but the doctor declared that it was simply a bit of bronchial trouble, to be dealt with by mustard plasters. This treatment seems to have worked, in the short run; but the attack may also have marked the first real onset of the tuberculosis that would, in some ways, dominate the last five years of his life.

For the moment, he was well enough to be up and about in a few days, to finish *St. Mawr,* and to prepare for a visit with Mabel and Tony (but without Brett) to Santa Fe and thence to Hotevilla to see the Hopi Indians' Snake Dance. His reactions are beautifully set out in the two quite different pieces he wrote about it. One, which thoroughly annoyed Mabel Luhan—"I had not taken him to the Snake Dance to have him describe it in this fashion" (Luhan 1934: 268)— called "Just Back from the Snake Dance—Tired Out" and written four days after the dance, views the whole occasion as a white man's opportunity for a bit of a show: "The south-west is the great playground of the white America" (*Letters* 1932: 609). The other, "The Hopi Snake Dance," written eight days after the dance, is one of the profoundest of all Lawrence's writings about America. The jeering, satirical, and philosophical sides of his nature could hardly be better illustrated than by these two essays.

They had only a month left at the ranch before leaving for the winter; Lawrence had long planned to go back to Mexico to write the final version of his *Quetzalcoatl* novel. Then, out of the blue, came news from England he had not expected: his father had died, very suddenly, at the age of seventy-eight, the day before Lawrence's thirty-ninth birthday. "It is better to be gone than lingering on half helpless and half alive," he wrote to his sister Emily, obviously thinking of the protracted dying of his mother during the autumn of 1910; "But it upsets one, nevertheless: makes a strange break" (*Letters* V: 124). He wrote more elegiacally in a letter to Murry three weeks later, linking the death with the coming of autumn: "The country here is very lovely at the moment, aspens high on the mountains like a fleece of gold. . . . Did I tell you my father died on Sept. 10th. . . . The autumn always gets me badly, as it breaks into colours" (*Letters* V: 143). The autumn breaking into colors doubtless also linked in his mind with the autumn of his mother dying, back in 1910.

He wrote just one more highly significant piece, to complete his major writings of this summer: the short story "The Princess," in which a white woman again goes out to explore the American southwest but in which her peculiar reluctance in the face of experience is brutally challenged. He would not have written it, perhaps, without knowing Brett, though in no sense is the central character a portrait of her, but the essential experience described in it is also his own.

He looked back at the summer as one when he had written relatively little, but it had been extraordinarily creative in many ways, if a little ominous, too. He had, however, successfully answered the question he had been asking since 1913: he had found where he wanted to live, at least in the summer. But now it was time to go. On 11 October, Brett, Frieda, and he went to Taos; by 23 October, they were in Mexico City.

II.

It is significant that Lawrence felt he wanted to be in Mexico in order to rewrite *Quetzalcoatl*. He had not felt he needed to be in Australia to write a new last chapter for *Kangaroo* or to write any of *The Boy in the Bush;* he had written *Sons and Lovers, The Lost Girl, Aaron's Rod,* and *Mr Noon* while out of England. But *The Plumed Serpent*—as it would now become—was to be instilled with a social atmosphere and with a cast of characters that he had to create especially for the novel, and he clearly wanted day-to-day and firsthand experience of Mexico to do it. But he did not go back to Chapala. He wanted somewhere less touristy, more real, he said (*Letters* V: 163); and Oaxaca, where the British consul had a brother—a priest, Edward Rickards (1879–1941)—and which he recommended as "very nice," with "a perfect climate," sounded ideal. After a fortnight in Mexico City, Lawrence, Frieda, and Brett traveled south and after a short while in a hotel, the Lawrences moved into a wing of Rickards's house, Brett staying in a nearby hotel.

On 19 November, Lawrence started to work on his novel again. He had the experience of the three white women heroines of the three pieces of fiction he had written during the summer to use as a background for the character of Kate Leslie; while the place he was now living in (a far more indigenous place than Chapala had been) felt politically even more unsure than Chapala had been in 1923. He was working on a book about political and religious revolution and change; although he was thoroughly unsure about America as a place to live and work, he recognized the opportunities Mexico would give him for his vision of a new society. He worked almost unremittingly from mid-November to the end of January, with a break only in mid-December to write four pieces about life in Oaxaca, which later formed the central part of *Mornings in Mexico*. The novel proved exhausting to conceive and to write: much of it went against the grain. Just before starting, he felt "a bit sick of the American continent," "put out by the vibration of this rather malevolent continent" (*Letters* V: 174, 170). Oaxaca turned out almost tropical in climate and vegetation, disturbing Lawrence and making him uncomfortable in ways reminiscent of Ceylon (*Letters* V: 192). In spite of such feelings, he went on working tremendously hard: "wrote at home and got run down" (Frieda Lawrence 1935: 140). The novel grew enormously, ending up almost twice as long as *Quetzalcoatl;* Lawrence noted, "It is good, but scares me a bit, also" (*Letters* V: 196). He was following through the ambivalent logic of his own feelings suggested in a story like "The Woman Who Rode Away": the execution of the prisoners of Quetzalcoatl is, for example, one of the most unpleasant pieces of writing he ever did, and it would be natural for him to be scared by it. He quoted Macbeth at a friend: "*I dare do all that may become a man,* said somebody. It's the becoming" (*Letters* V: 199). To add to the problems, Frieda had finally get fed up with Brett, who "came every day and I thought she was becoming too much part of our lives and I resented it." She told Lawrence, and they quarreled about it; Lawrence "said I was a jealous fool" (Frieda Lawrence 1935: 140). But things got more and more tense; finally, Lawrence told Brett that she would have to leave. Obediently, she did, going back to the Hawks' Del Monte ranch, leaving Lawrence with a final ten days' work on the novel still to do.

It cannot have been a coincidence that, when he stopped, he collapsed into illness. It was as if the onset had been delayed by the fevered excitement of the writing and his total involvement with it and through the pressure of the quarrel with Frieda. On 29 January, he finished the book. A week later, he was almost dead, with a combination of typhoid, malaria, and influenza; his tuberculosis took a great leap forward; and then there was an earthquake. He was moved back into the hotel; and toward the end of February, he and Frieda traveled back to Mexico City, with the plan of sailing from Vera Cruz for Europe, as he had done with Götzsche in 1923. But he suffered a relapse and was unable to travel further for almost another month. During this bout of illness, a doctor said straight out that Lawrence was suffering from tuberculosis and advised Frieda to take him back to the ranch; he was given a year or two at most to live.

During this second bout of illness, he started the unfinished novel "The Flying Fish" and dictated its first few pages to Frieda (something unique in his writing career; he must very badly have wanted it written). It started with its central figure ill in Mexico; it used material from the 1923 trip with Götzsche, and it created, most beautifully, the sense of a "greater day" surrounding the human being. But, too, it was haunted by a sense of return to England. It had been a long time since Lawrence had used the English Midlands in his fiction. But now—like Gethin Day himself—"he was sick from the soul outwards, and the common day had cracked for him, and the uncommon day was showing him its immensity, he felt that home was the place" (*St. Mawr* 210).

But all their plans to return to Europe were blown to atoms by the advice of the doctor to go back to the ranch, and they put off the journey till the end of the summer. Lawrence gradually recovered a semblance of health during March, and at the end of the month they traveled north again. But they had terrible troubles at the border at El Paso, as the American doctor initially refused Lawrence permission to enter the United States (presumably observing in him the symptoms of tuberculosis). They finally were allowed in, with Lawrence permitted to stay for just six months in the country (Nehls 1959: 150); they struggled to Santa Fe, where the actress Ida Rauh (1877–1970)—whom they had got to know in 1924—took care of them; and early in April, they got back to the Del Monte ranch, where Brett was waiting for them.

It had not been the return they had been expecting. Lawrence was still desperately weak and ill; but as soon as possible, they went up the final two miles to their own Kiowa ranch (this time leaving Brett down at Del Monte); and Lawrence, sleeping much of the time, began to recover his strength. It says a good deal for their belief in the recuperative powers of the place that they should have struggled back up to it; a place such as the ranch was hardly for a convalescent. But for a while they had a young Indian couple, Trinidad and Ruffina, to look after them, and Frieda clearly did more household work than usual, announcing that she was "developping [*sic*] into a 'chef' " (*Letters* V: 233).

And, amazingly, Lawrence got well again and typically celebrated his recovery by starting to write. At last he created the play he had been promising Ida Rauh and tinkering with for months; he wrote *David*—a play in which modern man develops out of the ruins of the preflood consciousness and religious self. He himself—David Herbert—was both David, articulate and intelligent, and Saul, the representative of the older world that he was trying, in work after work now, to re-create or perhaps, with the help of myth and legend, to create as a kind of alternative myth to the version of human progress and development that had so dominated his early thinking.

By early May, the play was done; and life at the ranch continued its old pattern. The differences this year were that they managed to get the running water working, to irrigate the field, and that, early in June, they acquired chickens (which Frieda cared for) and a cow, Susan, Lawrence's responsibility. This saved them the daily journeys for milk down to Del Monte, where Brett continued to live and to type for Lawrence; though Lawrence then had to spend an inordinate amount of time chasing his cow, to milk her. They had relatively few visitors, seeing even less of Mabel this year than the last, though Frieda's German nephew Friedel Jaffe (b. 1903) came and stayed for a couple of months and was able to help with the everyday chores, and Ida Rauh came, to hear Lawrence read the whole of *David* out loud. Lawrence compiled a book of essays, using some old material (including a much revised version of "The Crown" from 1915), which became *Reflections on the Death of a Porcupine*. Brett typed and came up occasionally; Frieda continued her war against her. And Lawrence was sent the typescript of *The Plumed Serpent* but could hardly bear to look at it for the memories of Mexico (*Letters* V: 254). When he finally went through it and corrected it, he felt about it as he had about *The Trespasser* and *Women in Love:* it meant more to him than any other book, and he hated the thought of having to send it out for publication (*Letters* V: 260).

The months meandered away, the only excitements being the perpetual looking for Susan and rides in the buggy down to San Cristobal, when Lawrence remembered the remark made by the magazine editor Austin Harrison (1873–1928) in a letter to Lydia Lawrence back in 1910:

"By the time he is forty, he will be riding in his carriage." . . . And sitting in my cor-
duroy trousers and blue shirt calling: "Get up Aaron! *Ambrose!*" then I thought of Austin
Harrison's prophecy. . . . "Get up, Ambrose!" Bump! went the buggy over a rock, and
the pine-needles slashed my face! See him driving in his carriage, at forty!—driving it
pretty badly too! Put the brake on! (*Phoenix* II 260–61)

He points the irony beautifully between the kind of prosperous professional
writer he might have become—it is natural to think of the novelist Arnold
Bennett (1867–1931)—and the outsider and maverick, just about making his
living but writing exactly what he wanted to, which he had actually become.
He was forty on 11 September 1925, just after they left the ranch: "lovely
autumn, pity to go" (*Letters* V: 296). But the six months allowed to him were
up. He and Frieda traveled via Denver to New York and by 21 September were
on the SS *Resolute*, bound for Europe.

It was as symbolic a journey as when they had left for Ceylon in 1922. Their
American adventure was over. Lawrence had always wanted to come; he had
written extensively about it, had explored through his writing what it meant to
be there, and had found an extraordinary place to live. But it took too much out
of him, and his illness meant that he would probably never again be able to live
there as he would have liked. At forty, he was coming back to Europe, as it
turned out, for good. He never saw America again.

8   Europe Once More: 1925–28

I.

They had come back to Europe for very different reasons from those that had brought them back in 1923. Then, Frieda had wanted to see her family, and Lawrence had come most reluctantly to join her and had gone for as short a time to the Midlands as possible. This time, obliged to leave the United States, Lawrence wanted to come as much as Frieda and, drawn by the "hopeless attraction" of his native land, it was England he wanted (*Letters* V: 312). He had not been back since his father died, and he wanted to see his sisters. Frieda's youngest daughter, Barby, was now also twenty-one and could choose to see her mother. After a week in a London hotel, Lawrence and Frieda spent nearly a fortnight in the Midlands (with Barby coming to visit them there) and then another week in London before traveling on to see Frieda's mother. Both England and the Midlands, however, depressed him thoroughly—he was in bed with a cold as soon as he reached Nottingham and complaining about both place and weather (*Letters* V: 316). Their original plan of staying for a month or so, so that Frieda could see her children, quickly turned into a decision to go south, first to Germany and then back to Italy. Martin Secker's wife, Rina (1896–1969), had her family living in Spotorno, and that was where they would head. Before they left the Midlands, however, the weather improved, and they toured around a bit; but even that was painful—"England just depresses me, like a long funeral" (*Letters* V: 322). All he was writing were a few book reviews.

They stayed a fortnight in Baden-Baden, where Lawrence wrote a couple of essays on books, and Frieda had her hair fashionably bobbed. But he was happy to move on to Spotorno, where, within three days, they had rented the Villa Bernarda for four months. Set above the village, they once again had a view, over "the eternal Mediterranean" (*Letters* V: 337). It became the setting for one of his first three post-America pieces of fiction—his first prose fiction since finishing *The Plumed Serpent* in Oaxaca, in fact. One was the tiny short story "Smile," a tailpiece to his three anti-Murry stories of 1923–24; one (*Glad Ghosts*) was a commissioned ghost story for Cynthia Asquith. But *Sun* grew straight out of the situation in Spotorno, where a woman suffering from nerves and with a small child goes to live and to take sunbaths—until her gray-suited husband comes out to her. Secker's wife, Rina, nervous and with an eighteen-month-old son, was waiting for her publisher husband to come out from England; and Lawrence used that situation in a re-creation of the situation of the Fontana Vecchia in Sicily, in another of those stories exploring the relationship between the human being and the circumambient universe, but this time a story in which they eventually get into a better and more creative relationship. In one way, it seems extraordinary that Lawrence should have written so directly and so closely about a situation in front of him as he wrote (Martin/Maurice arrived early in December, and Lawrence sent the story off for typing on the twelfth), but it was what he had always done. The creation of the experience of the sun paved the way for the writing, in these last years of his creativity, of that theme of the relationship between person, sun, and universe over and over again; it is in *The Escaped Cock,* in *Sketches of Etruscan Places,* in *Lady Chatterley's Lover,* in *Apocalypse.*

Another significant event was in their meeting their landlord: a married officer in the Italian Bersaglieri, Angelo Ravagli (1891–1976), a striking figure in uniform and a cheerful, immensely practical one when out of it. Frieda made sure he was out of it fairly soon. She started an affair with him that continued at intervals over the next four years. He took English lessons from Lawrence and also helped Lawrence fix a smoking chimney; Lawrence remarked to Frieda afterward, "That is a man who would be useful to have at the Kiowa ranch" (Nehls 1959: 18). In 1931, Angelo would leave his wife and family and accompany Frieda back to the ranch and would live with her there until her death in 1956.

For the moment, it was simply one of those affairs Frieda had had all her life. Lawrence certainly knew about them—it seems possible that Frieda actually told him about them, as she had told him about Hobson in 1912 and had also discussed Gray with him in 1917. Her affairs seem to have made no difference to her dependence on Lawrence or to her fundamental belief in him as *the* extraordinary man in her life, one whose sheer understanding of her and of the world surpassed that of anyone else she knew. The worst quarrels of their lives did not occur over her affairs (or his, for that matter) but over other people altogether, people he insisted on bringing into their lives, like Ottoline or Mabel or Brett or—at other times—his sister Ada or Frieda's daughters or (at times) almost anyone with whom one of the two felt the other was siding, against him or her. Those who invaded their living space mattered, not those who briefly occupied their beds. His friends were the people she tended to hate, because when they were present (and being singled out for special attention), she felt ignored or slighted. She seems, in fact, to have been far more jealous of his nonsexual relationships than he was of her sexual ones; but, then, she had reason to be alarmed. As a writer, he was financially independent and could live where and how he wished. He might conceivably leave her, not (probably) for another woman, but just leave her, as had nearly happened in August 1923, to go his own way. But she could not leave him, as she pointed out, for purely practical reasons: "how could I earn a living? I was never taught anything which might earn me a living . . . I am helpless. I am caught" (Bynner 1951: 62). But, crucially, she also did not *want* to leave him: "I wish to be caught. We love each other" (Bynner 1951: 62). *She* certainly loved *him.* For his part, Lawrence may well have regarded her affairs as the price he had to pay for so often going his own way regardless, in ideas and relationships (though not in sexual ones), as well as for her opposition to him and his opposition to her. This was something marvelously important and useful to him, and this she knew very well. She told Bynner that "he quotes me and often what he quotes from me is attacking what he himself says and in the book he lets me have the best of it. . . . He knows that I'm useful. He likes to have me oppose him in ideas, even while he scolds me for it" (Bynner 1951: 62).

The relationship with Angelo Ravagli did nothing to come between them. Frieda's children, of whom Lawrence often disapproved, were another matter, as was Lawrence's sister Ada. Barby was staying in Alassio, quite near, during the winter of 1925–26, and they all saw a good deal of each other. This led to the usual quarrels, with Frieda telling Lawrence that (according to Barby) "now I was with her at last, he was to keep out of our relationship and not interfere" (Nehls 1959: 21). Anyone who came between Lawrence and Frieda and their complex need of each other (and need for space between them, too) was likely to become a focus for quarrels.

Things grew calmer for a while when Elsa Weekley also came, and Barby remembered, "Unlike me, she hated 'rows.' At the Bernarda she lectured Frieda about them, being concerned to see, after one of their quarrels, that Lawrence had tears in his eyes . . . a rare thing for him" (Nehls 1959: 26). Lawrence talked to both girls about their upbringing, especially about their father, and about life with their father's clergyman brother in Essex and their aunt and grandmother, and these conversations were the direct source of the short novel he almost immediately began to write, *The Virgin and the Gipsy.* This gave him the chance to bring together a good deal of his hatred of the strength of the female will (such as he had seen in a woman like Mabel Luhan) with the real-life situation of the Weekley girls and his own recent observations of the Midlands; the story used some of the landscapes he had seen in October 1925. When he had finished it, however, he decided not to publish it, feeling that it would be unfair to the girls and their father. (After he died, Frieda had no such compunction and published it at once.)

In her new role as mother—early this spring—Frieda also briefly became the author of the household when she translated Lawrence's play *David* into German (*Letters* V: 388). Early in February, however, Lawrence suffered another bronchial hemorrhage, worse than the one at the ranch (*Letters* V: 390), an ominous prelude to an intensely disturbed period following. Lawrence's sister Ada (together with a friend) was coming to stay with them abroad for the first time in their marriage, and Frieda would have her daughters staying in a nearby hotel; the weather was dreadful, and everyone seems to have got on the others' nerves. Lawrence declared that he felt ''absolutely swamped out'' and needed to get away by himself for a while; there had been another ''bust-up,'' and Frieda had gone to stay in the hotel (*Letters* V: 394, 401). The casual words conceal quite how savage and serious the quarrel had been; Lawrence went to Nice and Monte Carlo with Ada, and when she left, he didn't return to Spotorno but went to see the Brewsters and Brett, all of whom were now in Capri. Again there seemed to have been a real possibility that Lawrence and Frieda would not get together again; and it can hardly have been a coincidence that, at this juncture, Lawrence twice went to bed (rather unhappily and unsuccessfully) with Brett (Brett 1974: II–IV). But nothing came of that; and after about a month, Frieda wrote to Lawrence suggesting that they ''must live more with other people'' and not cut themselves off so much (*Letters* V: 406). Her daughters had been giving her good advice, doubtless. It was certainly the case that the Lawrences' most serious rows always seemed to be provoked by the presence (or threat) of other people intruding into their relationship; if they could find a way of living less exclusively for and with each other, so that the ''other people'' did not divide their loyalties so violently, that would have been all to the good.

That, at least, is what they tried. Lawrence went back to Spotorno after being away for seven weeks and found Frieda happy to see him, though he confessed to feeling some anger still (*Letters* V: 413–14). After a brief time back together in Spotorno (the term of their house rent was almost up), they all went to Florence for a while; and then the girls went back to London, leaving Lawrence and Frieda to find somewhere to live. Lawrence opted for Tuscany and very quickly found an old villa where they could rent the top floor very cheaply. The moment for making a decision about America had come and gone. Brett, indeed, had gone back to her cabin at the Del Monte ranch, having successfully applied for immigrant status and doubtless hoping that Lawrence would be back soon; but Lawrence decided not to go. It was a crucial moment. He was not going to apply to live in America for good so in all likelihood would be allowed only six months there, as before—and would then have to travel on. There was, too, the enormous journey, which, in his run-down state, he could not easily face; even the ranch itself now seemed too strenuous an effort to contemplate (*Letters* V: 429). He was a man consciously starting to conserve his energy, and this is a clear indication of it. He concluded that he really did not want to go to

America, that he was becoming weary of the outside world: "I want the world from the inside, not from the outside" (*Letters* V: 437). It was probably with an equally strong sense of his own condition that he wrote this; the ranch demanded more physical effort (as well as the "strain" of combating the place) than he could afford. There was also the unspoken problem of his health, which had almost prevented his readmission to the United States at El Paso in March 1925; there remained a possibility that he would, humiliatingly, actually be refused entry. But there was a signal, too, of the kind of writing in which he would be engaged during the final years of his writing career: "the world from the inside, not from the outside."

II.

The Villa Mirenda was ten miles from Florence and, of course, like all the Lawrences' houses, on a hill with a view, this time over the valley of the Arno (*Letters* V: 448). An English family, the Wilkinsons, lived nearby; but the villa was the center of a whole peasant community, too, and the Lawrences got to know their neighbors well. This was doubtless following their decision to live more closely with other people (*Letters* V: 406). Unlike the ranch, the Villa Mirenda not only had no responsibilities but was rented "with service" (Nehls 1959: 59): they had a local woman, Giulia Pini, as housekeeper. The Mirenda would be the Lawrences' base for just over two years.

But always "base" or "pied-à-terre," not home. It was very barely furnished, and they didn't spend much money on it; and they were away a good deal. They spent just a couple of months there now, apart from a visit to the English aristocrats Sir George (1860–1943) and Lady Ida Sitwell at their castle outside Florence (they had probably met in Florence). Lawrence was now properly back at work, typing and revising Frieda's translation of *David,* writing essays about Florence, and producing two pieces of work provoked by conversation—in Capri back in March—with Compton Mackenzie's wife, Faith (1888–1960) (*Letters* V: 403). "Two Blue Birds" was a skit and no more, but "The Man Who Loved Islands" was one of Lawrence's great works: a profound and tragic study of the temperament that—like his own—seeks out isolation from the world and lives to itself if possible. Lawrence was also planning a book on the Etruscans and doing a lot of preliminary reading for it (something he had started back in the spring).

But by the end of June, it was getting hot; on 12 July, they left for Baden-Baden, spent a fortnight there, and, by the end of the month, were in London, in a borrowed flat. Lawrence wanted to see the early rehearsals of his play *David,* which the Stage Society was supposed to be putting on, while Frieda wanted to see her children. Lawrence very soon made a visit to Scotland, to see Millicent Beveridge (1871–1955), a Scottish painter he had got to know in Sicily in 1921 and who had then painted his portrait and whom he had met again in Capri in the spring, "One of Lorenzo's old maids," Frieda would doubtless have said, knowing his "weakness for these English spinsters" (Nehls 1959: 278).

On the way back from Scotland, Lawrence visited his family on the coast in Lincolnshire; and this stay beside the sea in the Midlands again turned out to bring him unexpected pleasure. He recalled 1901, when he had first visited the sea here, and felt once more at home and in touch with his native land (*Letters* V: 522, 534). After he had spent a week with his family, Frieda joined him; and they stayed together there for another fortnight, waiting for the Stage Society to sort out their plans for *David,* with Lawrence (by himself) visiting his sister Ada in Ripley. Here, however, he was depressed by the effects of the continuing miners' strike, which he wrote about shortly afterward in the essay later entitled "Return to Bestwood." Back in London, it turned out that there was, in fact, no point in waiting for the play, which had been postponed; so after lunching with the intended director and now anxious to be back at the Mirenda for the harvest, Lawrence and Frieda left on 28 September and were back at the Mirenda by 4 October. Although they had enjoyed it, it had been a tiring and rather expensive trip; Lawrence was becoming very aware of how little he was currently earning, with the drying up of the money Seltzer had made for him in America and his own failure to write very much over the previous couple of years (he had not started a new novel since April 1923, but his experience in finishing *The Plumed Serpent* certainly inhibited him from beginning another). He felt he might never write another novel, he told his sister-in-law Else on 18 October (*Letters* V: 559). In spite of this—and with his new sense of England as a place he could feel at home in and might write about again—around 22 October, he started a new work of fiction, a long short story. This had altogether unexpected consequences, for it became *Lady Chatterley's Lover.*

III.

The *Lady Chatterley's Lover* novels would occupy Lawrence from October 1926 to the publication of the third version in the summer of 1928—and beyond, as he would go to Paris primarily to arrange the publication of a cheap edition in the spring of 1929. The book changed his career and has, in many ways, completely altered his reputation. From being the author of a number of books, not particularly well known, he became—for the next sixty years—primarily the author of *Lady Chatterley's Lover.* It made him more money than he had ever made in his life, and this (as it turned out) came just when he needed it, when his own strength did not allow him to write very much, when he was ill and needed doctors and a sanatorium, and when Frieda would have to live on without him but supported by his earnings.

The book began as a long short story, however, of the kind he had frequently written during the past three years, but it grew to around 95,000 words: almost half as long again as *St. Mawr* had been. It used an idea that lay behind the as yet unpublished *The Virgin and the Gipsy*—the middle- or upperclass woman awakening into a new life because of a relationship with an outsider, a man from outside even the working class. But whereas *The Virgin and the Gipsy* and even the first version of *Lady Chatterley's Lover* are aware enough of the constrictions of class not to show the relationship turning into a marriage, by the time Lawrence wrote the third version of the novel, he was being idealistic enough (with some adjustments to the character of the gamekeeper) to make this possible.

But the book changed enormously while being written. Two years after starting it, Lawrence made a remark to the writer Brigit Patmore (1882–1965) that suggests one of the motivations that lay behind its development from a short story about class to a novel about sex. He remarked to her of the sadness he felt "When you think you have something in your life which makes up for everything, and then find you haven't got it. . . . Two years ago I found this out" (Nehls 1959: 258). The novel, which did more than anything else to seal Lawrence's reputation as an erotic writer, was written by a man deeply nostalgic about the life of the body, which—for him—had always culminated in sexual desire. He wrote a number of poems about this, for example, "After all the tragedies are over," where the beach that can do nothing about the ebbing sea becomes a metaphor for the man who can do nothing about his ebbing desire (*Complete Poems* 509).

But what Lawrence could do was write; and after finishing the novel's first version, probably in late November, he started the second; and this one would become the first sexually explicit book he had ever written. It took him much longer; he was still working on it early in March 1927. His other new occupation this first winter at the Mirenda was painting. He had always painted, had made innumerable copies as a boy, had continued making copies of paintings and done occasional originals, all his life. But in November 1926, Maria Huxley (1898–1955)—he had met her and her husband, the writer Aldous Huxley (1894–1963), in London in August, and they began a lasting friendship in Italy in the autumn—had presented him with four blank canvases. He had started to produce a series of paintings—all originals, this time—and many of them also sexual. Coincidentally with the end of the first *Lady Chatterley's Lover,* for example, he had created his *Boccaccio Story,* with its half-naked gardener and bevy of startled nuns. He created a series of striking images, not very skillfully handled but frequently symbolic and oddly powerful.

In the spring of 1927, he finished the second *Lady Chatterley's Lover—* "verbally terribly improper" (*Letters* V: 655)—and did not know what to do with it: it was quite unpublishable as it stood. All he could do was let it stand. He badly needed to publish, however; the cheapness of the Mirenda did not make up for a lack of earnings, and he had spent the winter writing the novel drafts and—apart from that—writing only book reviews and some poems. With the novel out of the way, however, he wrote at least one short story—"The Lovely Lady"—and went back to his idea of a book about the Etruscans; this would allow him to pursue his interest in an older civilization that could speak to the twentieth century, but in a form that would not plunge him into the morasses of *The Plumed Serpent.* He had not been particularly well that winter, but, together with Earl Brewster, he toured Etruscan sites in April and, during the next three months, wrote a number of essays about the Etruscans, some of which were taken by magazines; but he never finished the book, the fragments of which were published only posthumously. It took up, nevertheless, a good deal of his time and energy in research that he wanted to do for it and in obtaining pictures for it. It gave him the chance, which for several years he had been looking for, to re-create a primitive society that would model some of the things he felt the modern world had lost. He had tried this, to some extent, in *The Plumed Serpent* and again in the play fragment *Noah's Flood,* written shortly afterward, and then again at length in *David.* But this was his best chance yet; and he wanted to reach a wide audience with it, telling Secker, ''I want this book—which will be a bit expensive to you, owing to illustrations—to be as popular as I can make it'' (*Letters* VI: 93).

An equally significant thing that he started, however, was a new story, at this stage a short work called ''The Escaped Cock.'' Just as *Lady Chatterley's Lover* had broken sexual taboos, this would infringe on religious ones, as it described Jesus, after the Resurrection, coming back neither as the son of God nor to his mission as a teacher or healer nor to ascension (in the biblical sense) but to the life of the body; it was another of these works exploring the sense of the individual's relationship not with society or even with another person but with the marvelous and extraordinary phenomenon of being alive in the body—and thus inhabiting not just the inner world of everyday experience but, like Gethin Day, possessing a strong sense of the ''Greater Day,'' too: his version of Wordsworth's ''active universe.''

This, he was able to publish, even though its publication caused something of a storm for the magazine involved, the *Forum.* During the early summer, he kept busy with short essays and some new short stories, ''None of That!'' and ''Things,'' drawing on acquaintances as diverse as Mabel Luhan, the painter Dora Carrington (1893–1932), and the Brewsters; but (having not felt well for some days), on 11 July, he suffered his third and then a series of bronchial hemorrhages, the most serious yet; it took him three weeks or so to get back on his feet. It was clearly time he started going to places purely for his health's sake; the weather was going to be uncomfortably hot at the Mirenda from now onward. As soon as he could comfortably travel, he and Frieda went to stay with her sister Johanna at Villach in Austria; and ''I feel a different creature here in the cool''—''It is such a mercy to be able to breathe and move'' (*Letters* VI: 119, 120). He was doing almost no writing, just some further translations of Verga, which always seem to have been his regular standby when he did not feel he could concentrate properly on his writing. After Austria, he and Frieda went on to their long-planned return to Bavaria, to stay in Else's (once Edgar Jaffe's) house in Irschenhausen, which they had last inhabited in 1913 and where Lawrence had written ''The Prussian Officer'': a small wooden house of the kind Lawrence always liked living in, "with forest behind, looking across a wide valley at the blue mountains." "I like it very much—there is no time, and no event—only the sun shines with that pleasant hotness of autumn, and in the shadow it is chill" (*Letters* VI: 154, 139). Again, he did very little writing apart from his translations—"I am glad when I don't work—I have worked too much" (*Letters* VI: 151); but they had a good, quiet, social life, being visited by all kinds of friends, including their 1912 Icking landlady. And Lawrence was fairly well, even allowing himself to be examined by the poet-doctor Hans Carossa (1878–1956), who specialized in tuberculosis and who commented afterward to a friend: "An average man with those lungs would have died long ago. But with a real artist no normal prognosis is ever sure. There are other forces involved" (Nehls 1959: 160).

In many ways, Lawrence would have liked to have stayed in Bavaria; but Frieda wanted to go back to Italy; so, via Baden-Baden, they went, with Lawrence taking an inhalation cure in passing. Once at the Mirenda, Lawrence set to work on two projects: a new volume of short stories and a collection of his poems, which Secker had asked for—"means typing them out and arranging and doing" (*Letters* VI: 195). But in Florence, after talking with the bookseller Guiseppe "Pino" Orioli (1884–1942), with Norman Douglas, and with the successful popular novelist Michael Arlen (the transformed Dikran Kouyoumdjian), he realized that there was—after all—a way, if a slightly risky way, of publishing *Lady Chatterley's Lover*: privately, printed in Florence, and distributed by himself. The enterprise filled him with enthusiasm; it is not overstating the case to say that it probably added months, if not years, to his life. The first thing he did was to rewrite the novel—an astonishing feat in itself, for someone who had been as run-down as he had been. He wrote up to 4,000 words a day for a period of about six weeks, between late November 1927 and early January 1928, and transformed a novel that had been about class barriers and the hopelessness of England to one in which the gamekeeper can, shockingly, become an appropriate future partner for Constance Chatterley. The sexual explicitness remained (and was, indeed, enhanced), but the novel acquired a new, simpler, hard-hitting quality that went with its new task: asserting its outrageousness in public. Clifford became a far less sympathetic character, for one thing; he was now treated with the kinds of savage irony and satire that Lawrence had used about a character like Rico in *St. Mawr*. And the novel acquired an exemplary tone: this is how to live and to love, it says.

IV.

With the book finished, Lawrence embarked on the fascinating business of publishing and distributing it himself. It was already being typed, though one typist cried off because of the explicitness of the book; part of the manuscript had to be sent to London for typing, and it seemed an age before Lawrence had it all back; Maria Huxley also lent a hand. There were a printer to find and a binder and publicity leaflets to print and distribute: "D. H. Lawrence / Will publish in unexpurgated form his new novel / LADY CHATTERLEY'S LOVER / OR / JOHN THOMAS and LADY JANE / limited edition of 1000 copies, numbered and signed / at £2.0.0. net (of which 500 copies for America / at $10 net). / Ready May 15th 1928." Lawrence thought he had better tell the printer, who had no English, what it was he was handling; the printer apparently smiled broadly and said, "But we do it every day!" It was a small printing shop; they had only enough type to set up half the book at a time. The first half was printed and proofread, and 1,200 copies were printed (1,000 for the first edition, 200 in reserve); the type was then distributed, and the same done to the second half. Advance orders started to come in; it became clear that Lawrence was not going to lose on the venture.

But the specially ordered, handmade paper was late in coming, and thus the printing was delayed; the book was still at the printers during the previously announced date of publication; and not until 28 June did Lawrence have a copy in his hands, by which time he had escaped the summer heat of Florence and was up in the mountains in Switzerland. Orioli was left in charge of receiving the subscriptions and posting the copies.

While in Switzerland waiting for the book to come out, Lawrence—in a way most unusual for him—wrote a second part to his previously finished and published story *The Escaped Cock,* to make it a fitting partner to the enterprise of the novel; the man who had died is now not only a man who has given up his mission to live within the Greater Day but one who finds a new relationship with a woman, too; Christ is also Osiris, restored, made whole, revivified, resurrected to the Father in sexual desire. "I think it's lovely," he wrote of it, but "somehow I don't want to let it go out of my hands" (*Letters* VI: 469). In so many ways it now mirrored his sense of all that, bodily, he was not (and could no longer be) himself. He always tended to think of his illness as corresponding to his state of mind: "that's why I too am ill. The hurts, and the bitternesses sink in, however much one may reject them with one's spirit" (*Letters* VI: 409). But the writer of fiction could still make a world that the person could no longer inhabit. As he had written in 1925 about novel writing, "[O]ne can live so intensely with one's characters and the experience, one creates or records, it is a life in itself, far better than the vulgar thing people *call* life" (*Letters* V: 293).

9 Last Years: 1928–30

I.

"Here I am, forty-two, with rather bad health: and a wife who is by no means the soul of patience . . . a stray individual with not much health and not much money" (*Letters* VI: 419). Thus Lawrence characterized himself and Frieda in June 1928 to an American acquaintance threatening a visit. The only thing that would actually change for the better was the money. While his formal English publication was down to a trickle—his only prose books in the last three years had been *David* in 1926, *Mornings in Mexico* in 1927, and *The Woman Who Rode Away* in 1928, hardly enough to make his living—*Lady Chatterley's Lover* would earn him more than he had ever made in his life. It would also make him a household name, and he found that popular newspapers and magazines were now happy to commission topical articles from him. He rather enjoyed writing these, finding that he could write them out in a single morning and earn more from them than a long and serious story would ever bring in. As a result, although the novel was (much to his annoyance) widely pirated, his last two years were, to an extent, cushioned by his ability to work as much or as little as he chose, to live in hotels as often as he liked, where he liked, and to pay for medical treatment.

But, in early June 1928, he still did not know how successful the novel would be. For the summer, his only plan was to go somewhere reasonably cheap, cool, and at altitude, where he believed he would feel better (as at the ranch); for the first time, the places where he and Frieda would live were being dictated almost entirely by his state of health. There were problems, nonetheless. One hotel in

Switzerland turned him out "because I coughed. They said they didn't have anybody who coughed" (*Letters* VI: 428). They ended up in the village of Gsteig by Gstaad and took a small chalet, "quite high up, 4000 ft. and more— the upper world, rather lovely—has a bit of the Greater Day atmosphere" (*Letters* VI: 452), he told the Brewsters, to whom he had read "The Flying-Fish." But Lawrence was condemned to the chalet and the area immediately around it because the extreme steepness of the nearby hills made walking practically impossible for him. He nevertheless spent three months there, believing it was doing him good. He was doing quite a lot of painting—and was actually starting to think of exhibiting his paintings; but he was also writing essays, reviews, a short story ("The Blue Moccasins") and doing his best via a voluminous correspondence to ensure that copies of *Lady Chatterley's Lover* got distributed safely, in spite of increasing action against the book by bookshops, the police, and customs.

At the end of August, his sister Emily and niece Margaret (b. 1909) came to stay, the first time he had seen any of his family since his 1926 trip to England. For once, the visit seems to have caused hardly any tensions between him and Frieda—but Frieda would not have found Emily as possessive as Ada had been, and Lawrence himself was forcibly struck by the distance that had opened up between him and his family. He felt how far they were "from my active life. . . . And I have to hide *Lady C.* like a skeleton in my cupboard" (*Letters* VI: 533). After spending the summer in Switzerland, he and Frieda went to stay in Baden-Baden for ten days, and while there they finally decided to give up the Villa Mirenda. Although they had enjoyed living there, it had been only a flat, with annoying neighbors downstairs; they wanted more space for themselves, and Florence was distant from the friends whom they now depended on a great deal, in particular, Earl and Achsah Brewster, and Maria and Aldous Huxley. The Mirenda was also linked in Lawrence's mind with the last of his dreadful hemorrhages. Frieda went back to see to the packing up of their things and also seems to have taken the chance to spend some time with Angelo Ravagli; Lawrence ended up in Toulon, waiting for her to accompany him across to the island of Port Cros, where Richard Aldington, his mistress Arabella Yorke (b. 1892), and—as it would turn out—his new mistress Brigit Patmore had invited them to stay, in a borrowed house at the top of the island, another place with the most extraordinary view. Once again, when they got there, although Lawrence liked the place and liked the people, his health meant that he could not do very much, could not accompany the others when they went out or went swimming, for example. And Frieda had come back from Italy with a cold, which (of course) he instantly caught. He spent a good deal of time in bed in the mornings, writing; he was starting to compose clusters of the new, short satirical poems that he called "Pensées" and they would become the collection *Pansies:* "he was intensely happy and proud of the *Pansies;* he would read out the newest ones with delight" (Nehls 1959: 274), and he was also doing a new translation from the Italian of the Renaissance writer Lasca's *The Story of Dr. Manente.*

II.

His chronic poor health, in one sense, dominated him during the last eighteen months of his life—and yet, all the same, it would be wrong to make too much of it. He lived, so far as he could, as if illness was simply a necessary but relatively unimportant part of his existence, something "superimposed" and "extraneous" to him: "I feel so strongly as if my illness weren't really me— I feel perfectly well and all right, *in myself*" (*Letters* VII: 546). This was his attitude partly because he believed strongly in *not* being ill; he had advised his Eastwood friend and exact contemporary Gertrude Cooper (1885–1942), just after she had been admitted to a sanatorium in 1926: "The great thing is to have the courage of life. Have the courage to live, and live well" (*Letters* V: 545). His pride and independence hated the subjection of illness: "He did so hate admitting he was ill" (Nehls 1959: 206), noted a visitor to Florence when Lawrence had to take a rest in the middle of the day. But it was also because being ill had always been a particular problem in his relationship with Frieda. People often said she was a bad nurse (the Huxleys were especially shocked during his last illness in 1930), and in a conventional sense that was true. Yet, it was also the case that she could, in the most extraordinary way, revive and arouse him when he was really ill and depressed; more than one person noticed her talent for this (Hilton 1993: 53–54), and she consciously exercised it: "I roused him into the determination to accept the challenge of my virility, he was not going to succumb" (Crotch 1975: 7). The real trouble was, as she herself knew, that "When Lorenzo feels ill, it infuriates him to have me well" (Bynner 1951: 61). Her radiant vitality could easily become a kind of living reproach to him: in the winter of 1929–30, he told her daughter Barby, "Your mother is repelled by the death in me" (Nehls 1959: 428). He regularly made a point, in his letters, of noting when Frieda (for a change) was ill, and his periods of illness always tended to increase the tension between them. After his influenza attack in the spring of 1919, Lawrence had written one of his nastiest denunciations of her: "I am not going to be left to Frieda's tender mercies until I am well again. She really is a devil—and I feel as if I would part from her for ever. . . . For it is true, I have been bullied by her long enough" (*Letters* III: 337). His illness always gave her a kind of effortless upper hand over him—and that he could not bear. This was certainly one of the reasons for his refusal to admit to serious illness during his last years or (in a normal sense) to be a patient. There was clearly some complicity with Frieda in this: Frieda, toward the end of her life, for example, actually remarked that "I never heard him complain about his health" (Frieda Lawrence 1961: 11). He went on working and writing when in bed, "propped up . . . with many pillows, knees bent up with a writing pad on the uplifted legs, allowing him to write" (Hilton 1993: 53). His friends all collaborated in the fiction of his not really being ill; Brigit Patmore recalled how, at Port Cros in the autumn of 1928, "it was against the rules to suggest that anything was wrong" (Nehls 1959: 255). There was also a great deal of courage in his behavior, as he nursed his ailing body: "he knew so well what was good for him, what he needed, by an unfailing instinct, or he would have died many years ago" (Frieda Lawrence 1935: 271).

There can easily be another point of view on the matter. There exists an agonized letter from Aldous Huxley about what he saw as Lawrence's total irresponsibility in refusing to face up to the fact of his tuberculosis or to consult a proper doctor (*Letters* VII: 9). Yet, Huxley was perhaps too sanguine about the possibilities of treatment. We know that at least one specialist doctor who examined Lawrence, Hans Carossa, believed as early as 1927 that "no medical treatment can really save him" (Nehls 1959: 160); and Frieda's sister, Else Jaffe, a highly intelligent woman, believed that "he and my sister had come to a rational way of dealing with his illness—everyone must live and die according to his own precept" (Nehls 1959: 426). Lawrence had known extremely well, from childhood on, what happened to the diagnosed tubercular patient who submitted to treatment: restricted months in a sanatorium, perhaps surgery (Gertrude Cooper had had a lung removed in 1926) that did no real good, and never any certainty of cure, perhaps just a slower decline. Lawrence was not going to let that happen to him; he intended to work as he wanted and to lead his own life, terribly diminished though that eventually came to be. "Somewhere I am not ill," he wrote wistfully in December 1929 (*Letters* VII: 595). He knew the crucial role played by the attitude and feelings of the ill person and insisted that his illness was as much chagrin as anything else—"The body has a strange will of its own, and nurses its own chagrin" (*Letters* VII: 623). And at times he still lived and wrote vividly: his writing of *Lady Chatterley's Lover* in the winter of 1927–28 was almost miraculous. But even if he could no longer be nursed back to health, staying self-responsible and his own person, in an active relationship with Frieda, was far more important to Lawrence than putting himself into the hands of doctors. Noli me tangere, indeed.

III.

After Port Cros, it seemed sensible for the Lawrences to stay on the Mediterranean coast for the winter, where they could think about where they really wanted to live—a question to which there was really no answer, so long as Lawrence was ill. Frieda would actually have liked to go back to the ranch, but, for Lawrence, traveling there and probably having to come back after six months were really not a possibility. All the same, "it seems like losing one's youth and glamour of freedom, to part with Lobo" (*Letters* VII: 288); they didn't want to give it up completely. But it turned out that Bandol was small, warm, and attractive; the hotel Beau-Rivage was nice, the food good, Lawrence felt able to work at his *Pansies* and at the newspaper articles that were currently providing him with a decent small income, and—as usual—because his health was not actually any worse, they stayed. Having expected to spend a fortnight there, they stayed the next five months.

Lawrence had no major project on his hands except for the still-unfinished Etruscan book, which Secker wanted as his next "Lawrence book" for autumn 1929; one possibility was to go back to Italy to finish it. But friends came to Bandol to stay; Rhys Davies (1903–78), the young Welsh writer, came; even Lawrence's sister Ada came, without (this time) any kind of row or repercussions. The weeks went by; "it's sunny here all the time, and quiet and very pleasant: the people are all very nice: why should one hurry away to something worse!" (*Letters* VII: 41). The money from *Lady Chatterley's Lover* meant that he did not have to bother about a new book, even if Secker wanted one. The only problem was that—as usual—Frieda wanted a place of her own; while staying in a hotel she had, unlike Lawrence, nothing to do. They had had the idea of trying Spain for a couple of years now and decided to go to Majorca in the spring; but before that, Lawrence wanted to go to Paris, to arrange for the republication of *Lady Chatterley's Lover* there in a cheap edition, to undercut the pirates. He could stay with the Huxleys, who were currently living nearby, which made the whole enterprise easier; and Frieda joined him there. Having made the arrangements for the book's publication, he and Frieda set off for Majorca, where they would spend two generally happy months.

Majorca reminded them of Sicily, "but not nearly so beautiful as Taormina, just much quieter, the quietest place I've ever known, seems rather boring, but I like it and it certainly is good for my health" (*Letters* VII: 253–54). He wasn't sure he could work much while there; but the success of the unexpurgated *Lady Chatterley's Lover* had probably already given him the idea for his next project, an unexpurgated edition of his volume of poems *Pansies,* which Secker would be bringing out in the normal way that summer (but with a number of poems missing). The fact that, back in January, a copy of the typescript had been seized by the police in London made him still more determined to put the whole book before the public. A London publisher and friend, Charles Lahr (1885–1971), would take care of the unexpurgated *Pansies.* Lawrence also wrote the second of his articles about censorship, "Pornography and Obscenity" (he had written a brief introduction on the subject for the Paris *Lady Chatterley's Lover* earlier in the year), and he continued to write poems along the lines of the *Pansies* collection. But probably the main excitement of life was the edition of his paintings that was currently being photographed—the volume to be published around the time of an exhibition of the paintings put on in London in the summer.

He and Frieda left Majorca just as it was getting hot, in mid-June, Frieda to travel to England to see the paintings exhibition, Lawrence to stay first with the Huxleys in Italy and then with Orioli in Florence, where (once again) he was seriously ill. While Frieda was in London, however, the Warren gallery (where Lawrence's paintings were exhibited) was raided by the police, and thirteen pictures—all those showing pubic hair or traces of it—were removed; a case was heard at Bow Street magistrates court as to why they should not be destroyed. By promising that they would not again be exhibited in England, the gallery was able to prevent their destruction. But the episode left Lawrence feeling newly outraged; he wrote a whole new series of poems (to be called *Nettles*—stinging plants, this time) about it. Frieda came back to Italy when she heard how ill Lawrence was; but after a few days, they both went to Baden-Baden for the seventy-seventh birthday of Frieda's mother.

Lawrence's previous visits to Baden-Baden had been happy ones; but, this time, his increasing debility and illness led to new tensions. He found the baroness unbearable, the climate bad for him, the place horrible, the holiday-makers dreadful; and a stay at the Kurhaus Plättig (at a higher altitude) no better: "though it's supposed to be good for me, I really hate it" (*Letters* VII: 393). A return to Baden-Baden made things better; but he was happy to leave. They had very much liked being back in Bavaria in the autumn of 1927, and Lawrence had felt well there; they had accepted an invitation from the German doctor-writer Max Mohr (1891–1944) to stay in Rottach-am-Tegernsee, among the mountains, from the end of August. But here, unfortunately, Lawrence felt that the altitude was wrong for him, and the medical advice he took while there did him no good at all; one doctor told him that "in a few weeks, with diet and a bit of breathing, I ought to be well" (*Letters* VII: 466), and another prescribed him arsenic and phosphorous. The Lawrences decided to go back south again, probably to Italy: "I feel I am really fed up with moving about, and would be glad to have a place of my own" (*Letters* VII: 473–74). He could not forget having been relatively well at Bandol the previous winter; whereas previously in his life he had been reluctant to revisit places once he had left them and had always preferred to travel on to a new place, they returned to Bandol and, after a few days at the old hotel, rented a villa, and so—especially to Frieda's relief—were in their own place for the first time in more than a year.

IV.

Lawrence had not written much for months except some more *Pansies* and *Nettles* (and would, in fact, write no more fiction, in spite of hoping to do so); but, although he continued to write poems—the bulk of his *Last Poems* date from this second period in Bandol, and he prepared *Nettles* for publication—in Bandol he also began to write concentratedly once again, doing another couple of articles and turning his first introduction to the French *Lady Chatterley's Lover* into the essay *A Propos of "Lady Chatterley's Lover."* Most significant of all, he began reading for what would be his last book, *Apocalypse*. The artist and astrologer Frederick Carter (1883–1967)—whom he had first met early in 1924—had written a book about primitive religious symbolism, and Lawrence, having promised only an introduction for Carter's book, found its turning into a work in its own right; he wrote Carter a separate introduction and followed his own work through to its conclusion. It took him from late October to the end of December and began with a renewal of his old excitement at a vision of the "pre-Christian heavens," of the old world that he had sketched in his Etruscan essays. What he wanted to do was make this "old, pagan vision" something that modern people would recognize as lacking in their own experience; Lawrence's would be a book offering modern people a kind of psychic recovery of their connections with the old world:

my individualism is really an illusion. I am a part of the great whole, and I can never escape. But I *can* deny my connections, break them, and become a fragment. Then I am wretched.

What we want is to destroy our false, inorganic connections . . . and re-establish the living organic connections, with the cosmos, the sun and the earth, with mankind and nation and family. Start with the sun, and the rest will slowly, slowly happen. (*Apocalypse* 149)

He wrote this beside the sea, in the sun of Bandol, where he could still go for short walks; he watched the first new flowers coming out, early in December. But he was spending an increasing amount of time in bed; and the English tuberculosis specialist Andrew Morland (1896–1957)—who had been asked by Gertler and Koteliansky to see Lawrence—advised him to go into a sanatorium. Failing that, Morland insisted that he give up work of all kinds for two months and see nobody, simply lie and rest.

This, Lawrence tried and felt worse than ever. "The weather is sunny, the almond trees are all in blossom, but I am not allowed any more to go out and see them" (*Letters* VII: 633). Not being allowed to work was perhaps the most difficult—and the most damaging—part of the treatment, though it seems that he did, in fact, keep working at some things: Achsah Brewster saw him at the start of February "propped up in bed, galley sheets piled thick about him, correcting proofs of his *Nettles*" (Brewster and Brewster 1934: 310). But he was not getting any better. In despair, he agreed to try a sanatorium. On 6 February 1930, he was admitted into one with the ominous name Ad Astra, in Vence; and that, it turned out, was the beginning of the end.

V.

Mollie Skinner's brother Jack (one of the inspirations for *The Boy in the Bush*) had died at the age of forty-four in 1925. When he heard about the death—a few months after learning of his own tuberculosis—Lawrence wrote Mollie a note of sympathy in which he celebrates the fullness of Jack's life and says, "Death's not sad, when one has lived" (*Letters* V: 292–93). A poem like "Nothing to Save" in *Last Poems* suggests a little of what it was like for Lawrence during the last months of his life, feeling almost given up to illness and death—and yet, somewhere, at the "tiny core of stillness" in himself, still miraculously alive (*Complete Poems* 658). That was what living meant, to him.

He could not bear the kind of living in the fear of death and struggling for
health he believed he had observed in Frieda's mother the previous year in
Baden-Baden, when he had exclaimed: "May god preserve me from ever sinking so low. I never felt so cruelly humiliated" (*Letters* VII: 398). He could not
bear to humiliate himself; he would live every moment he could. A friend commented: "he kept his work and his life free from morbidity, from any sort of
unhealthy resentment. He never accepted defeat. He proved to be *fort comme
la mort,* strong as death—or even strong as life. He lived and died as a real
man" (Schoenberner 1946: 290). We can, for example, observe him offering
marvelously compassionate advice only a month before his own death to Caresse
Crosby, following her husband's dreadful joint suicide with a mistress: "don't
you try to recover yourself too soon—it is much better to be a little blind and
stunned for a time longer. . . . Work is the best, and a certain numbness, a mer-
ciful numbness. It was too dreadful a blow—and it was wrong" (*Letters* VII:
634).

Finally, he had tried to follow his own extraordinary advice, given to Mabel
Luhan in January 1930: "Lie still and gradually let your body come to its own
life, free at last of your own will" (*Letters* VII: 625). But he was too ill for
that to happen again, as it had happened at the ranch in the spring of 1925. At
the Ad Astra, he continued to lose weight and, for the first time in the whole
wretched illness, grew deeply unhappy. His response was characteristic. He
would move on, as he had always moved on. He discharged himself from the
sanatorium; he would live (or die) on his own terms, where he chose, in yet
another rented house. Frieda found the Villa Robermond in Vence and a nurse;
on Saturday, 1 March, he was taken by taxi to the new house. On Sunday, as
usual, he "got up, washed and brushed his teeth" (Nehls 1959: 435); he had
lunch, he sat up in bed and read a biography of Columbus. But in the afternoon,
he began to suffer dreadfully and admitted that he needed morphine. A doctor
was found who gave it to him; but he died that evening, in the company of
Frieda, Barby, and Maria Huxley. Frieda's account of these last weeks and days
is, quite simply, the most moving thing she ever wrote, and it would not do to
emulate it; I simply quote its ending.

Then we buried him, very simply, like a bird we put him away, a few of us who loved
him. We put flowers into his grave and all I said was: "Good-bye, Lorenzo," as his
friends and I put lots and lots of mimosa on his coffin. Then he was covered over with
earth while the sun came out on to his small grave in the little cemetery of Vence which
looks over the Mediterranean that he cared for so much. (Frieda Lawrence 1935: 276)

10   Versions of Lawrence: 1885–1993

I.

The difficulty of creating a reliable biography of Lawrence can be illustrated simply by considering what he looked like. This would seem to be an uncontroversial matter; but experience shows that it is not. We need do no more than compare the drawing Lawrence did of himself in Majorca in June 1929 with two studio photographs taken of him the same month. The photographs show a man whose pale, narrow face is calm, gentle, almost ethereal; his collar and tie (because he has grown so thin) hang loosely on him. The drawing shows a man with a broad, intense, angry face and wild, staring eyes; the same collar and tie fit him perfectly. Lawrence remarked that the drawing was "*basically* like me. But my wife thinks it is awful—chiefly because she doesn't understand" (*Letters* VII: 333). Which might be said to be the "real" Lawrence? It depends on what one understands by "real."

If, however, we draw simply upon memoirs written of Lawrence by people who knew him, some extraordinary divergences can be observed. His Croydon headmaster, who met him in 1908, remembered him as having "a shock of dark hair" (Nehls 1957: 85), and at least one other person who knew him when young referred to him as "dark-haired" (Worthen 1991: 95). Helen Corke, however, who first saw him in 1909, recalled "fair hair," as did Ford Madox Hueffer and Violet Hunt, first seeing him late in 1909, who remembered "sunshot tawny hair" and "yellow hair" (Nehls 1957: 95, 111, 127). In 1917, Esther Andrews noted "ash-coloured hair," while a Berkshire friend, Cecily Lambert, the following year, saw "mousey blonde hair" (Nehls 1957: 416, 463). In 1923,

Dorothy Brett saw "dark, gold hair" (Nehls 1958: 304); three years later, Montague Weekley thought Lawrence "sandy-haired" (Nehls 1957: 161). David Garnett, however, who met him in 1912, recalled his hair tint as "bright mud-colour, with a streak of red in it"; Catherine Carswell remembered "thick dust-coloured hair" in 1914, and Richard Aldington, who also met him in 1914, remembered his "bright red hair" (Nehls 1957: 173, 227, 236). Ottoline Morrell (from 1915) remembered a "mass of red hair," though the writer Douglas Goldring (1887–1960) recalled only "a reddish 'quiff' "; but Compton Mackenzie (who saw him in 1914 and again in 1920) thought he had "wavy reddish hair" (Nehls 1957: 271, 490, 248), and Rebecca West (1892–1983) described his hair in 1921 as "pale luminous red" (Nehls 1958: 63). Lawrence himself once remarked that his hair had "got no particular colour at all" (*Phoenix II* 310), but he also responded to someone who remarked that—with red hair like his—of course he would have a temper, "announcing that his hair was not red, that it used to be pure yellow gold and now was brown; his beard might be red, but his hair was golden brown!" (Brewster and Brewster 1934: 266–67).

His hair probably got browner as he got older. He never dyed it, though at least one person thought he did: "one day [Maurice Magnus] said to me at table: 'How lovely your hair is—such a lovely colour! What do you dye it with?' " (*Phoenix II* 310). But in those descriptions we can, over and over again, observe people seeing in Lawrence what they wanted to see. In each case, the person describing Lawrence is actually describing the power and significance of his or her own reaction to him. The spectrum of colors indicates how striking and unusual people thought Lawrence was and suggests how they attempted, in their recollections of him, to ensure that the extraordinariness of knowing him might somehow be conveyed. Those who saw him as red-haired, in particular, were likely to be thinking of him as some kind of an outsider: as hot-tempered, badly behaved, and very probably working-class. This was exactly how he struck a number of people: "He was the weedy runt you find in every gang of workmen: the one who keeps the other men laughing all the time," "a man sitting in the corner of a third-class compartment . . . that sort of working man, you know" (Nehls 1957: 173, 217); "I found standing at the gate a man something between a reddish-bearded, able-bodied seaman and a handy man at the back door!" (Nehls 1958: 133). Others who remembered Lawrence as strikingly red-haired tended themselves to be middle- or upper-class and were clearly more struck by the color of his beard (which everyone agrees was red) than by the color of his hair.

With this kind of disagreement about something that might seem incontrovertible, it is not surprising that we should find people disagreeing even more comprehensively about what Lawrence was like as a person. He was, according to Willie Hopkin's daughter Enid Hilton (1896–1991), a "kind, fun-loving man" (Hilton 1993: 65), and David Garnett never forgot how his "courage, his high spirits, his perpetual nagging mockery, kept us all gay" (Nehls 1957: 177). On the contrary, the American poet Jean Untermeyer (1886–1970) "was left

feeling overwhelmed by a type of arrogance that I was unable to deal with''
(Nehls 1959: 104), while William Gerhardi (1895–1977) wrote how there was
"something superfluous, something gawky and left-handed about Lawrence. His
humour was defective. Yet, like so many people whose humour is poor, he
prided himself on his tremendous sense of fun'' (Gerhardi 1931: 228–29). For
Norman Douglas, Lawrence—"being inwardly consumed and tormented''—
"had neither poise nor reserve. Nor had he a trace of humour'' (Nehls 1958:
14). Yet, Thomas Seltzer actually singled him out for "extraordinary poise''
(Nehls 1958: 210), and Earl Brewster recalled how "gay and free . . . were our
hours together'' (Nehls 1959: 135). Catherine Carswell thought him "an over-
whelmingly attractive human being'' (Carswell 1932: 213), but the American
author Carleton Beals (b. 1893) remarked, "As did most persons—except neu-
rotic females seeking restless freedom—I soon detested him personally'' (Nehls
1958: 288). Esther Andrews described him as "the gentlest, kindest person in
all human relations that anyone could be on this earth,'' and Dollie Radford
described him as "a sweet man, so simple and kind'' (Nehls 1957: 417, 292).
On the other hand, Witter Bynner thought he was "a bad baby masquerading
as a good Mephistopheles'' (Bynner 1951: 2), Cecil Gray described him as "in
the rôle of lover or friend or anything else . . . a lamentable failure'' (Nehls
1957: 437), and Faith Compton Mackenzie wrote: "He did great harm to the
people who adored him. I suppose no genius has left such a trail of malice in
the hearts of those who professed to love him'' (Mackenzie 1940: 35).

What can a biographer do? Which is the real Lawrence? Or—to be exact—
is there a real Lawrence, rather than a perpetually re-created version of him,
mysteriously colored by the needs and desires of the particular observer? A
biographer cannot simply amalgamate accounts as different as those just given,
which is one reason that Edward Nehls's three-volume work *D. H. Lawrence:
A Composite Biography,* published in the late 1950s, was such an intelligent
way of creating a biography of Lawrence. Nehls did not have to choose between
the details of conflicting accounts; he presented all of them, cheek by jowl, and
excluded his own commentating voice except in the endnotes. This means that
his work is still very much alive nearly forty years after it was done, while other
biographies from the 1950s—like Richard Aldington's *Portrait of an Artist,
But . . .* of 1950 and Harry T. Moore's two biographies *The Life and Works of
D. H. Lawrence* (1951) and *The Intelligent Heart* (1955)—are today interesting
only for representing the fashions of the period to students of Lawrence biography.

II.

There remains, however, the question as to why Lawrence gave rise to such a
conflict of versions of himself. To a considerable extent, the version of Lawrence
we possess today was created in the early 1930s by a significant succession of
publications; and most of the memoirs so far cited were actually written in the

1930s, 1940s, and 1950s, rather than in Lawrence's lifetime. Toward the end of Lawrence's life, critical assessments of his writings had started to appear, beginning with Herbert J. Seligmann's *D. H. Lawrence, An American Interpretation* in 1924, Aldington's pamphlet of 1927, and Stephen Potter's book of 1930. But—with its contract signed in September 1930—Murry's *Son of Woman,* which came out in April 1931, only thirteen months after Lawrence's death, was a new kind of book, which, although outwardly a critical book, was also an attempt at a kind of spiritual biography. It purported to explain what was fundamentally wrong with Lawrence the person, not just what was wrong with his books. (Only Rebecca West's 1930 pamphlet about Lawrence could have been called strictly biographical, up to that point.)

At the start of 1932, the real biographical books began to come out, the first, published in Florence in January 1932, being Ada Lawrence's *Young Lorenzo* (published in England the following November), which contained a brief memoir of Lawrence's family and early life and some letters and postcards from throughout his career. In February 1932 came Mabel Luhan's *Lorenzo in Taos*—which dealt with only two of Lawrence's three periods in the American Southwest, 1922–23 and 1924. In June 1922 was published Catherine Carswell's *The Savage Pilgrimage,* a kind of answer to the reminiscences of Lawrence that Murry had been publishing in the *New Adelphi* from 1931 onward and the first attempt at a full-length biography drawing on material from outside the writer's actual knowledge of her subject. *The Savage Pilgrimage* had, however, to be withdrawn after threats of legal action from Murry, who objected to the way he himself was presented; the book was reissued by another publisher in December 1932. Frederick Carter's book *D. H. Lawrence and the Body Mystical* and Anaïs Nin's *D. H. Lawrence: An Unprofessional Study* (neither of them primarily biographical) also came out in 1932; but probably the most significant of all the publications was Huxley's edition of Lawrence's *Letters,* which came out at the end of September 1932. Then, in January 1933, hard on the heels of the reissued *Savage Pilgrimage* came Murry's own collected *Reminiscences of D. H. Lawrence,* his response to Catherine Carswell's book; it dealt only with the period during which Murry had known Lawrence, between 1913 and 1924, but also contained a collection of the reviews of Lawrence's work Murry had written over the years. Later in 1933 came Dorothy Brett's *Lawrence and Brett: A Friendship,* which dealt (again) only with the periods during which Brett had known Lawrence (1915 and then 1923–26); the same year came two more primarily nonbiographical books, Helen Corke's *Lawrence and Apocalypse* and Horace Gregory's *Pilgrim of the Apocalypse.* Three more major biographical works were to come: Earl and Achsah Brewster's *D. H. Lawrence, Reminiscences and Correspondence* in February 1934, Frieda Lawrence's *"Not I, But the Wind . . . "* in July 1934 (1935 in England), and Jessie Chambers's *D. H. Lawrence: A Personal Record* in May 1935. The Brewsters' memoirs were tactful, respectful, and noncontroversial and described Lawrence between 1921 and 1930; Frieda's book described his life from 1912 to 1930; Jessie Chambers was concerned only with the period up to 1912.

Only the first and last books in this sequence—Ada Lawrence and Jessie Chambers—described much of Lawrence's life before the 1920s; even Catherine Carswell and Murry knew him only from just before the First World War. The overwhelming picture given was inevitably that of a man wandering the world in the company of quarreling, possessive, and adoring women. It was also clear that the books by Carswell, Murry, Luhan, Brett, and Chambers were all, in their different ways, attempt to repossess Lawrence: attempts to be the book written by the one true friend who understood him where none of the other friends (or partners) did. Coming out when it did, even Frieda's book took on the appearance of a slightly sanctimonious volume, designed to repossess him; it tended to play down the painful extremes of his life. A friend heard her giving a very different account of life with him in the autumn of 1930 and observed that the person who came to write *"Not I, But the Wind..."* "was not the same Frieda I knew . . . but someone who must have been born again" (Crotch 1975: 6).

The end result of this sequence of memoirs was that Lawrence seemed caught emotionally among friends, sexual partners, and lovers, the vacillations in his loyalty to one or the other of them apparently being of a piece with the wide range and apparent randomness of his travels. To those who had known Lawrence, the stream of books—all claiming to offer the real truth about him—was a painful and rather shameful experience. How he would have hated it! But it became the standard by which he would be judged. Faith Compton Mackenzie, writing at the end of the decade in 1940, summed up: "For Lawrence to allow himself to be surrounded by a corps of infatuated women was perfectly natural. It is the sport of genius; their antics have a tonic effect, and even the exasperation to which Lawrence was occasionally driven, and of which we read in the copious reminiscences that his death produced, was stimulating enough to be worthwhile" (Mackenzie 1940: 32–33).

The idea that there might be a rather tough, fiercely private, lonely, very self-reliant, determined, and highly intellectual man behind the vacillating and almost wholly emotional being created by these biographies was almost impossible to conceive. Instead, the tone was set for the appreciation of Lawrence as a weak, muddled, and emotional man incapable of choosing his friends well and wholly the victim of his instincts. A final book from the 1930s, this time a critical one, William York Tindall's *D. H. Lawrence and Susan His Cow* of 1939, took advantage of the previously created portrait of a confused man to mount a satirical demolition of the work as well, concentrating on what Tindall significantly described as "Lawrence's vague transcendentalism and inner confusion" (Tindall 1939: 205).

The 1930s version of Lawrence, to some extent, remains current to this day, the publicity surrounding the publication in America and England of *Lady Chatterley's Lover* in 1959 and 1960 tending to confirm once again the portrait of

Lawrence as a man helplessly enslaved to the writing of instinctive truths about bodily experience and never thinking about such things carefully or seeing beyond them. The title *The Priest of Love,* which Harry T. Moore gave as late as 1974 to his reissued biography of Lawrence, added its own confirmation of the idea of Lawrence as a man who had made a religion out of his emotions; and in 1990, Jeffrey Meyers's biography *D. H. Lawrence,* in spite of a wealth of new material unavailable to Moore, was happy to maintain the overall picture of Lawrence as a man obsessed with following the dictates of his instincts; his account of *Women in Love,* for example, reads the novel simply as its author's exercise in anal homoerotics (Meyers 1990: 216–21). The present writer's first volume of the Cambridge biography of Lawrence, *D. H. Lawrence: The Early Years 1885–1912,* was, I believe, the first attempt to do justice to Lawrence as a man with an intellectual history; it presented him as an exceptionally thoughtful, coolly judging, and reflective individual, whose concern with the instinctive and the physical was, to some extent, an attempt to overcome serious tendencies toward ratiocination and spirituality within himself.

III.

The 1930 versions of Lawrence were, however, not altogether supported by Huxley's first collection of his letters, which gave to those who liked Lawrence a chance to point out just how different he was from the person contemporary memoirs and biographies made him—even if Huxley's Introduction was, in its own way, just as possessive of its own version of Lawrence as any of the other books. (Huxley's Lawrence was the extraordinary, natural savant, the man who instinctively and always knew what was true and right, who never revised his books but got them right first time, every time.) But at least Huxley's edition of the letters allowed Lawrence to speak in his own voice; and that voice turned out to be alluringly sensitive, thoughtful, understanding, and witty, if at times desperate.

This was the more so because, of course, Huxley had to exert a certain degree of censorship over what he printed; many of the people who had known Lawrence and to whom he referred were still alive. Accordingly, the version of Lawrence's correspondence that Huxley's collection created was distinctly biased toward the sweet-tempered and the appreciative and, to this extent, collaborated with what was, in general, Lawrence's own extremely controlled written relationships. Only occasionally would the conflicting evidence of a surviving letter and an unwitting memoir reveal how polite (or two-faced) and kindly (or hypocritical) a letter from Lawrence could be, given what he obviously actually thought of the person to whom he was writing. This became clearer in the subsequent, uncensored publications of his letters. But it should also make us aware of how controlled Lawrence's letters are. They are not the simple outpourings of genius; they are deliberate, carefully aimed missives, saying things that Lawrence thinks a particular person needs to hear. It is natural that this should be so; they are the work of a major writer. But one must not be misled into thinking that they simply reveal the man behind them. They do so only in complicated ways.

IV.

What links this habit of Lawrence as a writer with the oddly varied accounts of him that have survived is, of course, the fact that he always presented himself in strikingly different ways to different people. Jan Juta found it impossible to paint him in 1921—not because he was difficult to paint but because ''I could not make up my mind which of the facets of his personality I felt most representative.'' It was, Juta went on, ''this complexity which baffled so many'' (Nehls 1958: 85). Added to that innate complexity and contradictoriness was the fact that he was, to some extent, both an actor and an impersonator, in life and in his writing. His skill at mimicry is well known; David Garnett, for example, said that Lawrence

was the only great mimic I have ever known; he had a genius for ''taking people off'' and could reproduce voice and manner exactly. He told you that he had once seen Yeats or Ezra Pound for half an hour in a drawing-room, and straightway Yeats or Pound appeared before you. (Garnett 1953: 245)

All his life, Lawrence not only imitated people but also presented polished and, at times, complex comic turns to his friends; report after report of such occasions survives in the biographical record. As late as 1927, he was still doing his turn of Florence Farr reciting W. B. Yeats to the minimal music of the psaltery (Nehls 1959: 138) that David Garnett had seen back in 1912 and that Lawrence had probably first witnessed—and performed—in 1909.

But David Garnett also noticed of the mimicry and the charades that ''the person whom Lawrence most constantly made fun of was himself.''

He mimicked himself ruthlessly and continually and, as he told a story, acted ridiculous versions of a shy and gawky Lawrence being patronized by literary lions, of a winsome Lawrence charming his landlady, of a bad-tempered whining Lawrence picking a quarrel with Frieda over nothing. There was more than a little of Charlie Chaplin in his acting: but bitterer, less sentimental. (Garnett 1953: 245)

Lawrence knew very well how many people he himself was. To some extent—and nearly always in his letters—he controlled the version of himself that he presented and by which he would be remembered. He was clearly a radically different person to, say, Catherine Carswell than the person he was to someone like Norman Douglas. Hence, in part, the utter divergence of opinion of him seen in the writing of people like Catherine Carswell and Norman Douglas quoted earlier.

It is also easier to see in his *Letters* than in memoirs of him the charming, outgoing person he was, because that is the sense of self he so often projected in his letters. Frieda knew this, too, telling Witter Bynner that

I like people more than he does and he doesn't want me to like them more than he does. He does things for people, Hal, because he's soft in some ways. He writes interesting letters all the time to people he doesn't really like, which is not what I would do. (Bynner 1951: 62)

Lawrence regularly seems to have created relationships and then to have continued them in his correspondence, from which he also wanted to escape. This is especially visible in his lengthy correspondences with Dorothy Brett and Mabel Luhan in the middle and late 1920s. We can observe, at times, a deliberate (and perhaps necessary) forcing of himself into sympathy with other people, which he carried through in his letter writing and which frequently makes his letters so attractive; but we can understand this as, to some extent, making up for the rather colder feelings he had in reality. It is possible to obtain an unreasonably attractive notion of Lawrence from his letters. Mostly, they do not reproduce the kinds of anger and bitterness to which he subjected, at some time or other, almost all those to whom he was close and that almost every person who met him reported. The written version is nearly always milder than what he would say when actually face-to-face with people; would say, that is, unless they were sensitive souls like Catherine Carswell, who never got more than a warning knock of the paw in everyday relationships.

Just occasionally, however, the underlying asperity of so many of his relationships breaks through into his correspondence. The letter about Frieda written after influenza in 1919, quoted earlier (*Letters* III: 337), is an example; and in 1920 he wrote savage letters to Katherine Mansfield and Middleton Murry, one of which (that to Murry) survives. Murry had returned some articles Lawrence had written for Murry's magazine *The Athenaeum,* and Lawrence was furious: "I have no doubt you 'didn't like them.' . . . But as a matter of fact, what it amounts to is that you are a dirty little worm, and you take the ways of a dirty little worm" (*Letters* III: 467–68). Associating Katherine Mansfield with what Murry had done, he wrote something equally savage to her around the same time, remarking (in her own memory of the letter): "I loathe you, you revolt me stewing in your consumption. . . . The Italians were quite right to have nothing to do with you" (*Letters* III: 470). In those letters, just for once, we hear what Lawrence's speaking voice and manner were probably like when he was really angry. As Frieda remembered, "he made no concession to the ordinary conventions, and that's what upset people" (Frieda Lawrence 1961: 12). He would, according to a number of people, say the most extraordinarily bitter and vicious things when irritated, though especially and most often to Frieda; and even Frieda, late in life, when she was doing her very best to re-create an image of Lawrence as a marvelously intelligent, warm, and understanding person, could not help confessing that "he had a very nasty temper" (Frieda Lawrence 1961: 12) and that he was "bad tempered and never sorry" (Bynner 1951: 62).

If it is true that his letters, in general, reveal a rather more kindly person than he probably was, day to day, then that perhaps helps explain why he wrote to Koteliansky about Frieda and to the Murrys about themselves so savagely. Just for a moment, thoroughly angry with people he knew very well, his guard was down; he was normally more in control of himself when he wrote (letters or anything else) than he generally chose to be, or probably thought it healthy to be, person-to-person (he once remarked that he believed in self-discipline but not in self-control). But in those three letters we find, just for once, the uncensored version of life with Lawrence. That might also help explain why both Murrys forgave him for what he had written, too, and how he went on living with Frieda. Lawrence's friends knew this tone, this language. It wasn't as final or unforgivable as it would have been from someone else. He did not hold or bear a grudge; he was regularly forgiven and, in his turn, forgave.

But there is, all the same, a great deal of evidence that, in everyday life, Lawrence could be extremely aggravating: questioning, demanding, unrelenting, contradicting—though never so much as toward himself. He clearly gave himself a very hard time. Illness, of course, preyed on him; late in life, he remarked irritably, "I have had bronchitis since I was a fortnight old" (Worthen 1991: 6). But he drove himself frighteningly hard, for a man as ill as he was. And, always, he questioned. One of our earliest memories of him comes from his first headmaster: "young Bert was a note of interrogation—he was always wanting to know why" (Nehls 1957: 74). Frieda recalled that when she disagreed with him about his writing, "he worried me about the why. I wouldn't always know the why, but he insisted, and I didn't like so much insistence" (Frieda Lawrence 1961: 12). It was Lawrence's profoundest need to question, to explore, to understand, to know; and that drove him into extraordinary demands and, at times, into extreme assertiveness. Frieda once confessed that "Lawrence wasn't a comfortable person to be with. . . . He worried things out in his own soul. 'You're like a dog with a bone,' I would tell him. But once he had worried a question out to his own satisfaction he stuck to the result" (Frieda Lawrence 1961: 133). Another friend remarked of a particular problem that "[h]e challenged it as he challenged everything" and that "he had the sense of strife always upon his thought" (Nehls 1958: 316, 318).

Oppositions were, then, both natural to him and a conscious choice. He once remarked, about his choice of Frieda as a partner, "She is the one possible woman for me, for I must have opposition—something to fight"; in contrast, he knew he could never have married Jessie Chambers, for "[i]t would have been a fatal step, I should have had too easy a life, nearly everything my own way" (Nehls 1957: 71). A habit of conscious opposition, though, made everyday life exhausting. "When Lorenzo feels ill, it infuriates him to have me feel well. When his nerves are carrying him too fast, he cannot bear to have me feel tired" (Bynner 1951: 61). Frieda herself doubted whether "if any other woman would live with him . . . I sometimes wonder if I myself can live with him'' (Bynner 1951: 62).

But the habit of never being simple or single, but of being fascinated and, more often than not, opposed, means that Lawrence offers us many more biographical riddles than most people, and often, only the conflicting versions of him and of his thinking confront us. A biography should not endeavor to iron these out, only to clarify them. A habit of mind rooted in opposition accounts for some, at least, of his physical restlessness and rootlessness. Frieda commented about it in Chapala in 1923: ''He does not dislike it here or the people. He just thinks some other place or some other people might be better. It's all inside him. And I wish it weren't. *Ach,* how I'd like to settle down somewhere, to stop this wandering. I want a home'' (Bynner 1951: 63). She never had that until Lawrence died. But to be awkward, to be contrary, to keep hammering away at problems, to keep questioning, never to be satisfied because ''it's all inside him,'' and to keep traveling on, even when the place he had found was wonderful—he once ''tried to explain his wanderings by saying that he intensely longed to visit remote lands and there to live and recreate himself anew'' (Nehls 1958: 134)—this was Lawrence as a man and as a writer. The fact of his writing itself was rooted in opposition; he once remarked to a friend, ''If there weren't so many lies in the world . . . I wouldn't write at all'' (Nehls 1959: 293).

Frieda was the only person who accepted all of this in him, though it made her life very difficult at times. But when desperately ill at one of the extremes they had reached, Oaxaca in 1925, he said to her, ''remember . . . whatever happens, nothing has mattered but you'' (Frieda Lawrence 1961: 11–12); and when he was dying in 1930, he told her—after yet another quarrel—''Don't mind, you know I want nothing but you, but sometimes something is stronger in me'' (Nehls 1959: 442). She was the one person to whom he was absolutely committed. Although ''at times they loathed each other'' (Crotch 1975: 6), he knew from 1913 that life with her was ''the best I have known, or ever shall know'' (*Letters* I: 553). The French painter Edgar Dégas (1834–1917) remarked that one can either love or have a life's work, but that one only has one heart. Lawrence seems to contradict that, as he contradicted so much; in forty-four years he managed an extraordinary life, an extraordinary love, and an extraordinary life's work.

SECTION B

BIOGRAPHICAL SCHOLARSHIP AND CRITICISM

BIBLIOGRAPHY 1: BIOGRAPHIES, MEMOIRS, LETTERS, AND RELATED MATERIALS

The three-volume Cambridge Biography of D. H. Lawrence (see entry for Worthen [1991] in the second section to follow) promises to be the most complete, authoritative, and scholarly account of Lawrence's life yet produced, and this will almost certainly become the standard reference work in the field for many years to come. However, apart from the fact that only the first volume, covering the early years to 1912, has been published so far, it is likely that most nonspecialists will continue to need shorter and somewhat less detailed overviews of Lawrence's life as an aid and supplement to their reading of his works. Hopefully, the biography by John Worthen contained in this book will cater more than adequately to this need (and see his last chapter for further comment on many of the biographies listed here); but, as the number of entries in the following bibliography indicates, there are plenty of additional sources to choose from. Indeed, for students and readers new to Lawrence studies (and even for many not so new to them), the amount of biographical material on the author must appear almost overwhelming, and for this reason, among others, I have divided the following list into five sections that map out the field in what I hope will be a helpful way for Lawrentian specialists and nonspecialists alike.

The first section contains biographies that aim to provide full general accounts of Lawrence's life—that is, they aim to cover the whole of the life, rather than one particular phase or period of it, and they aim to do so from a general point of view, rather than from one that focuses on some area of special interest in Lawrence's life. Following logically from this, the second section contains precisely those works that provide "partial" biographical accounts—either of a limited period of the life or from a particular perspective on that life; and priority is given here to books and longer works (though there are a few exceptions to this, as explained at the start of the section). The third section lists shorter memoirs and biographical pieces, along with memoirs, biographies, and autobiographies that are not primarily devoted to Lawrence but that contain material on him. The fourth section contains works of critical metacommentary on Lawrentian biography and memoirs, as well as works that, without necessarily dealing in depth with Lawrence himself, provide various forms of background information relevant to our understanding of his life.

The fifth section is essentially a bibliography of Lawrence's letters and of scholarship relating to them. This is included here on the grounds that the letters themselves tell their own story of Lawrence's life and are thus a form of indirect autobiography and that the different editions, collections, and selections of the letters, along with the critical introductions and commentaries that invariably accompany them, almost inevitably constitute biographical reconstructions of Lawrence in their own right.

In addition to this broad subdivision of biographical material, at the head of each of the first three sections I make brief critical comments that may serve as further guidance to reading and research—again with the primary aim being to help the reader new to Lawrence studies to pick a manageable path through the mass of works available. A general point that can be made here is that many of the memoirs listed in the second and third sections are, by their nature, highly subjective; they primarily provide "human interest" to the story of Lawrence's life and will be of only marginal value to most readers (though they can, of course, be interesting and entertaining in their own right as anecdotal discourse and may often provide useful snippets of information or insight). Accordingly, the nonspecialist reader can quite safely ignore the whole of the third section and a large part of the second section without fear of missing any important biographical information relevant to an understanding of Lawrence's art.

GENERAL BIOGRAPHIES

Of the book-length accounts listed here, Moore's second work is still the most detailed general biography available, even though it is now inevitably showing its age somewhat, despite revisions. Sagar's two books are perhaps the most immediately useful in illuminating the works of Lawrence from a biographical perspective—and Moore's 1951 work is also still useful for the same reason that it systematically interrelates the life and the works (Schneider's "intellectual" biography, too—listed under the second section—provides a helpfully focused and sustained connection between life and works). Aldington's book is unique in being the only complete biography of Lawrence written by someone who knew him, and, although it is inevitably compromised, to some degree, by that personal involvement in the subject, it largely avoids the crass one-sidedness of many of the memoirs of others who knew Lawrence. The biographies of Burgess and Meyers are more punchy and popular in their approach than most of the others listed here, and, though sometimes sacrificing accuracy and academic rigor because of this, they remain useful and readable (Burgess—himself a major creative writer, of course—eminently so). The perfunctory and unsympathetic biography by Kingsmill seems to have been almost entirely commercially motivated and is of little value; it relies heavily on previously published matter and is frequently factually misleading (e.g., in the first chapter, where large parts of *Sons and Lovers* are simplistically transposed into "factual" biographical evidence). Trease's book is a simple account of Lawrence's life told partly through a fictional re-creation of events.

The shorter accounts listed here—those of Draper, Littlewood, Pinion, Salgādo, Schorer, and West—all provide reliable and accessible overviews of the whole life, ranging from chapter-length summaries (Draper and Littlewood) to short, book-length treatments (e.g., Schorer). They are all somewhat dated now, however, and are superseded, really, by John Worthen's biography in the present book.

Finally, I include here the unique *Composite Biography* compiled by Edward Nehls, which, though not a conventional narrative biography like the other works in this list, does systematically cover the whole of Lawrence's life from a nonspecialized point of view—or rather from multiple points of view, given that the three volumes are made up of a variety of materials (including extracts from published and unpublished memoirs, correspondence, and Lawrence's own writings) and from an extremely wide variety of sources. Nehls also comprehensively documents his sources and, in detailed endnotes, provides extensive supplementary information on Lawrence's life and on the background of the various contributors. (As in most of the other bibliographies in this book, "D. H. Lawrence" is abbreviated to DHL throughout.)

Aldington, Richard. *Portrait of a Genius, But . . . The Life of DHL.* London: Heinemann, 1950.

Burgess, Anthony. *Flame into Being: The Life and Work of DHL.* London: Heinemann; New York: Arbor House, 1985.

Draper, R. P. *DHL.* New York: Twayne, 1964, pp. 17–29. (Reprinted, London: Macmillan, 1976. See also the biographical section of his *DHL.* London: Routledge and Kegan Paul; New York: Humanities Press, 1969.)

Kingsmill, Hugh (H. K. Lunn). *DHL.* London: Methuen, 1938.

Littlewood, J.C.F. *DHL I: 1885–1914.* Harlow, Essex: Longman, 1976. (Begins with a general biography, pp. 7–14, before concentrating on the period of the title.)

Meyers, Jeffrey. *DHL: A Biography.* New York: Alfred A. Knopf, 1990.

Moore, Harry T. *The Life and Works of DHL.* London: Allen and Unwin; New York: Twayne, 1951. (Revised as *DHL: His Life and Works.* New York: Twayne, 1964.)

————. *The Intelligent Heart: The Story of DHL.* New York: Farrar, Straus, and Young, 1954; London: Heinemann, 1955. (Revised as *The Priest of Love: A Life of DHL.* Carbondale: Southern Illinois University Press; London: Heinemann, 1974. Further revised, Harmondsworth: Penguin, 1976.)

Nehls, Edward, ed. *DHL: A Composite Biography.* 3 vols. Madison: University of Wisconsin Press, 1957, 1958, 1959.

Pinion, F. B. *A DHL Companion: Life, Thought, and Works.* London: Macmillan, 1978; New York: Barnes and Noble, 1979, pp. 1–64.

Sagar, Keith. *DHL: Life into Art.* Harmondsworth: Penguin; New York: Viking, 1985a.

————. *The Life of DHL.* London: Methuen, 1985b.

Salgādo, Gāmini. *A Preface to Lawrence.* London: Longman, 1982, pp. 9–62.

Schorer, Mark. "The Life of DHL." In *DHL [An Anthology].* Edited by Mark Schorer. New York: Dell, 1968, pp. 3–106.

Trease, Geoffrey. *DHL: The Phoenix and the Flame.* London: Macmillan; New York: Viking, 1973.

West, Anthony. *DHL.* London: Barker; Denver: Alan Swallow, 1950.

MAJOR BIOGRAPHIES AND MEMOIRS DEALING WITH SPECIFIC PERIODS, PLACES, OR THEMES IN LAWRENCE'S LIFE

Apart from those listed in the previous section, no other full-length works cover the whole of Lawrence's life from a general perspective, though many devote themselves to a limited period of Lawrence's life, to a particular place associated with him, or to a particular thematic concern such as marriage, literary finances, or the influence of a specific relationship. Into this group fall most of the personal memoirs by Lawrence's friends and acquaintances, that is, the works of Brett (1933), Brewster and Brewster (1934), Bynner (1951), Carswell (1932), Carter (1932), Chambers (1935), Corke (1965), Foster (1972), Hilton (1993), Lawrence and Gelder (1932), Luhan (1932), Merrild (1938), Murry (1931 and 1933), Neville (1981), West (1930). While all of these works give us some valuable insights into, and information about, Lawrence's life and works, many, if not all, of them are critically undisciplined and represent highly subjective points of view on Lawrence; a few are almost wholly vitiated by an all too evident desire on the part of the writers to rationalize, retrospectively, their own particular involvements with Lawrence (the works of Brett, Luhan, and Murry are perhaps the most notorious of these—see Meyers [1981], listed in the fourth section, for detailed discussion of the memoirs of the 1930s). Many of these works provide little reward to the reader primarily interested in Lawrence's art, and time could be spent far more profitably with the selection of materials collected by Nehls (see under the previous section), much of it extracted from these books.

Of most use to serious Lawrentian scholarship have been the works of Jessie Chambers and Helen Corke for the insights they offer into Lawrence's early formation as a writer and artist, particularly in relation to *Sons and Lovers* and

The Trespasser. Indeed, Jessie Chambers's 1935 memoir, though clearly partisan in many details, remains an important exception to what I have just said, and it is a work that any serious student of Lawrence—and of the early novels, stories, and poems in particular—will find helpful to read.

Some of the other biographies included here, by people who did not know Lawrence, also suffer from the same lack of critical discipline as those just mentioned—even while they remain useful in other ways to the biographical picture of Lawrence. Such works include those by Fay (1955) and Hahn (1975) and, for different reasons, Miller (1980) (which is unashamedly a "passionate" appreciation).

In terms of period biographies, the early life has clearly provided a popular focus, with nine full-scale works devoted to it—Callow (1975), Chambers (1935), Corke (1965), Delavenay (1969), Hilton (1993), Lawrence and Gelder (1932), Neville (1981), Spencer (1980), and Worthen (1991). Of these, Worthen's book, as has already been suggested, provides the most reliable, scholarly, and up-to-date account; prior to the publication of this work, Delavenay's was probably the standard scholarly reference work to Lawrence's early life, and this remains an important and highly detailed source of information and insight. Apart from these two works and that of Callow (a straightforward and readable account of Lawrence's life to 1919) and Spencer (a useful background guide), the others in this category are mainly memoirs, about which I have already commented.

Lawrence's own avid interest in "the spirit of place" makes it unsurprising that there are also a great many studies of his life focused on particular locales as well as on his far-flung travels. These range from invaluable general information guides, such as those of Cooke (1980), Moore (1956), Preston (1994), Sagar (1979 and 1982), and Spencer (1980), to more detailed and specialized discursive works, such as those of Davis (1989), Darroch (1981), Fay (1972), Hamalian (1982), Hilton (1993), and Stevens (1988) (all useful in their own ways, depending on one's interests, but none absolutely essential to the non-specialist). (Other, shorter works on Lawrence places can be found in the third section.)

Works with a specialized focus include those by Delany (1979—an intensive study of Lawrence in the war years), Delavenay (1971—on putative connections between Lawrence and Edward Carpenter), Feinstein (1993—along with Hahn [1975] and Maddox [1994], concentrating on Lawrence's love life), Joost and Sullivan (1970—on Lawrence's involvement with the *Dial* magazine), Lea (1985—on Lawrence's relationship with John Middleton Murry), and Worthen (1989—on Lawrence's day-to-day career as a professional writer). With these, again, readers will obviously be guided by their own particular interests, but the studies of Delany, Maddox, and Worthen are fairly essential reading for the serious student of Lawrence.

Although most of the works in this list are full-scale biographies or memoirs, I include several shorter items where it has seemed logical to do so (e.g., where an author has written both a book and a related article), and some items that are strictly background material rather than direct biography (again, mostly where there seems a close relation between such material and other work by a particular author).

Finally, I also include here, for obvious reasons, biographies and memoir material relating to Frieda Lawrence—see under Byrne (1995), Crotch (1975), Green (1974), Jackson (1994), Lucas (1973), Moore and Montague (1981), and the items under Frieda Lawrence.

Brett, Dorothy. *Lawrence and Brett: A Friendship.* Philadelphia: Lippincott, 1933. (Reprinted, with additional material: Edited by John Manchester. Santa Fe, N. Mex.: Sunstone, 1974. Covers period 1915–26.)
———. "Autobiography: My Long and Beautiful Journey." *South Dakota Review* 5 (Summer 1967): 11–71.
Brewster, Earl, and Achsah Brewster. *DHL: Reminiscences and Correspondence.* London: Secker, 1934.
Bynner, Witter. *Journey with Genius: Recollections and Reflections concerning the DHLs.* New York: Day, 1951; London: Nevill, 1953.
———. *Witter Bynner's Photographs of DHL.* Santa Fe, N. Mex.: Great Southwest Books, 1981.
Byrne, Janet. *A Genius for Living: A Biography of Frieda Lawrence.* London: Bloomsbury, 1995.
Callow, Philip. *Son and Lover: The Younger DHL.* London: Bodley Head; New York: Stein and Day, 1975.
Carswell, Catherine. *The Savage Pilgrimage: A Narrative of DHL.* London: Chatto and Windus; New York: Harcourt, Brace, 1932.
Carter, Frederick. *DHL and the Body Mystical.* London: Archer, 1932. (Reprinted, New York: Haskell House, 1972.)
Chambers, Jessie ("E.T."). *DHL: A Personal Record.* London: Jonathan Cape, 1935; New York: Knight, 1936. (Reprinted, Cambridge: Cambridge University Press, 1980. Second edition—with additional material by J. D. Chambers, May Holbrook [excerpts from a memoir originally in Nehls 1959, op. cit.], Helen Corke, and J. A. Bramley [reprint of 1960 article cited earlier]—London: Cass; New York: Barnes and Noble, 1965.)
———. *The Collected Letters of Jessie Chambers.* Edited by George J. Zytaruk. *DHL Review* 12, nos. 1–2, special double issue (1983).
Chambers, Jonathan David. "Memories of DHL." *Renaissance and Modern Studies* 16 (1972): 5–17.
Cooke, Sheila M. *DHL and Nottinghamshire, 1885–1910.* Nottingham: Nottinghamshire County Library Service, 1980. (Dossier of photographs, documents, background information, early works.)
Corke, Helen. *Lawrence and Apocalypse.* London: Heinemann, 1933. (Included in Corke 1965, pp. 57–132.)
———. *DHL's "Princess": A Memory of Jessie Chambers.* London: Thames Ditton, Merle Press, 1951. (Included in Corke 1965.)
———. "DHL As I Saw Him." *Renaissance and Modern Studies* 4 (1960): 5–13.

———. "Portrait of DHL, 1909–1910." *Texas Quarterly* 5 (Spring 1962): 168–77. (Included in Corke 1965.)

———. "An Introductory Note: 'Muriel' and David." In Chambers 1965, op. cit., pp. xix–xxiv.

———. *DHL: The Croydon Years.* Austin: University of Texas Press, 1965.

———. "The Dreaming Woman." *Listener* 80 (25 July 1968): 104–7.

———. "DHL: The Early Stage." *DHL Review* 4 (Summer 1971): 111–21.

———. *In Our Infancy.* Cambridge: Cambridge University Press, 1975.

Crotch, Martha Gordon. *Memories of Frieda Lawrence.* Edinburgh: Tragara Press, 1975.

Darroch, Robert. *DHL in Australia.* Melbourne: Macmillan, 1981.

Davis, Joseph. *DHL at Thirroul.* Sydney: Collins, 1989.

Delany, Paul. *DHL's Nightmare: The Writer and His Circle in the Years of the Great War.* New York: Basic Books, 1978; Sussex: Harvester, 1979.

Delavenay, Emile. *DHL: L'Homme and La Genèse de son Oeuvre: Les Années de Formation: 1885–1919.* 2 vols. Paris: Libraire C. Klincksieck, 1969. (Shorter English edition, translated by Katherine M. Delavenay, *DHL: The Man and His Work: The Formative Years: 1885–1919.* London: Heinemann; Carbondale: Southern Illinois University Press, 1972.)

———. *DHL and Edward Carpenter: A Study in Edwardian Transition.* London: Heinemann, 1971.

Fay, Eliot. *Lorenzo in Search of the Sun: DHL in Italy, Mexico, and the American Southwest.* New York: Bookman, 1953; London: Vision, 1955.

Feinstein, Elaine. *Lawrence's Women: The Intimate Life of DHL.* London: HarperCollins, 1993.

Foster, Joseph. *DHL in Taos.* Albuquerque: University of New Mexico Press, 1972. (A semifictionalized account; see also Mark Schorer's review, "A Book So Bad It Was Impossible to Put Down." *New York Times Book Review* [16 January 1972].)

Green, Martin. *The von Richthofen Sisters: The Triumphant and the Tragic Modes of Love: Else and Frieda von Richthofen, Otto Gross, Max Weber, and DHL, in the Years 1870–1970.* London: Weidenfeld and Nicolson, 1974.

Hahn, Emily. *Lorenzo; DHL and the Women Who Loved Him.* Philadelphia and New York: Lippincott, 1975.

———. "Lawrence in Taos." In her *Mabel: A Biography of Mabel Dodge Luhan.* Boston: Houghton Mifflin, 1977, pp. 157–218.

Hamalian, Leo. *DHL in Italy.* New York: Tapligen, 1982.

Hilton, Enid Hopkin. *More than One Life: A Nottinghamshire Childhood with DHL.* Stroud, Gloucestershire: Alan Sutton, 1993.

Jackson, Rosie. *Frieda Lawrence.* London: Pandora, 1994.

Joost, Nicholas, and Alvin Sullivan. *DHL and "The Dial."* Carbondale and Edwardsville: Southern Illinois University Press; London and Amsterdam: Feffer and Simons, 1970.

Lavrin, Nora. *DHL: Nottingham Connections.* Nottingham: Astra Press, 1986.

Lawrence, Ada, and G. Stuart Gelder. *The Early Life of DHL Together with Hitherto Unpublished Letters and Articles.* London: Secker, 1932.

Lawrence, Frieda. *"Not I, But the Wind..."* Santa Fe, N. Mex.: Rydal Press; New York: Viking, 1934; London: Heinemann, 1935. (Reprinted, Carbondale: Southern Illinois University Press; London: Feffer and Simons, 1974.)

———. *Frieda Lawrence: The Memoirs and Correspondence.* Edited by E. W. Tedlock, Jr. London: Heinemann, 1961; New York: Knopf, 1964.

———. "Introduction." In *Look! We Have Come Through!* by DHL. Dulverton: Ark Press, 1971.

Lea, F. A. *Lawrence and Murry: A Twofold Vision.* London: Brentham Press, 1985.

Lucas, Robert. *Frieda Lawrence: The Story of Frieda von Richthofen and DHL.* Translated from the German original by Geoffrey Skelton. London: Secker and Warburg, 1973; New York: Viking, 1974.

Luhan, Mabel Dodge. *Lorenzo in Taos.* New York: Knopf, 1932; London: Secker, 1933.

Merrild, Knud. *A Poet and Two Painters: A Memoir of DHL.* London: Routledge, 1938. (Reprinted as *With DHL in New Mexico: A Memoir of DHL.* London: Routledge and Kegan Paul, 1964.)

Murry, John Middleton. *Son of Woman: The Story of DHL.* London: Cape; New York: Cape and Smith, 1931.

———. *Reminiscences of DHL.* London: Cape, 1933.

———. *Between Two Worlds: An Autobiography.* London: Cape, 1935; New York: Julian Messner, 1936, pp. 261–429.

Needham, Margaret. "DHL Remembered, by His Niece Margaret Needham." Tape recording, 1988.

Neville, George. "The Early Days of DHL." *London Mercury* 23 (March 1931): 477–80.

———. *A Memoir of DHL (The Betrayal).* Edited by Carl Baron. Cambridge: Cambridge University Press, 1981. (Introduction by Baron, pp. 1–31, deals with Neville's life and friendship with Lawrence.)

Maddox, Brenda. *The Married Man: A Life of DHL.* London: Sinclair-Stevenson, 1994.

Miller, Henry. *The World of DHL: A Passionate Appreciation.* Edited with an Introduction and Notes by Evelyn J. Hinz and John J. Teunissen. Santa Barbara, Calif.: Capra Press, 1980.

Moore, Harry T. *Poste Restante: A Lawrence Travel Calendar.* Berkeley and Los Angeles: University of California Press, 1956.

Moore, Harry T., and Warren Roberts. *DHL and His World.* New York: Viking; London: Thames and Hudson, 1966.

Moore, Harry T., and Dale B. Montague, eds. *Frieda Lawrence and Her Circle: Letters from, to and about Frieda Lawrence.* London: Macmillan; Hamden, Conn.: Shoe String, 1981.

Page, Norman, ed. *DHL: Interviews and Recollections.* 2 vols. London: Macmillan; Totowa, N.J.: Barnes and Noble, 1981.

Philippron, Guy. *DHL: The Man Struggling for Love, 1885–1912.* Belgium: Centre Permanent de Documentation et de Formation Loveral, 1985.

Preston, Peter. *A DHL Chronology.* London: Macmillan, 1994.

Sagar, Keith. "A Lawrence Travel Calendar." In *A DHL Handbook.* Edited by Keith Sagar. Manchester: Manchester University Press; New York: Barnes and Noble, 1982, pp. 229–38.

———. *DHL: A Calendar of His Works.* Manchester: Manchester University Press, 1979. (This incorporates full details of Lawrence's whereabouts and travels at any particular time.)

Schneider, Daniel J. *The Consciousness of DHL: An Intellectual Biography.* Lawrence: University Press of Kansas, 1986.

Spencer, Roy. *DHL Country: A Portrait of His Early Life and Background with Illustrations, Maps and Guides.* London: Cecil Woolf, 1980.

Stevens, C. J. *Lawrence at Tregerthen.* Troy, N.Y.: Whitston, 1988.

West, Rebecca. *DHL: An Elegy.* London: Secker, 1930.

Worthen, John. *DHL: A Literary Life.* London: Macmillan, 1989.

―――. *DHL: The Early Years 1885–1912.* Cambridge: Cambridge University Press, 1991. (First of a three-volume biography, by Worthen, Mark Kinkead-Weekes, and David Ellis, to accompany the Cambridge Edition of the Works and Letters of DHL. Vols. 2 and 3 forthcoming.)

SHORTER MEMOIRS AND BIOGRAPHICAL PIECES

This section includes shorter memoirs and biographical pieces on Lawrence and memoirs and biographies not primarily related to Lawrence but including material on him. While many items listed here contain some useful information about Lawrence's life and background, most of them—and the memoirs in particular—provide little more than cameo snapshots of Lawrence at a particular time and place and from a particular, often highly subjective, point of view; they can be safely ignored by anyone wanting to learn only the main details of Lawrence's life and those details that are most pertinent to an understanding of his works. Of relative importance, however, are the memoirs and biographies of the people most closely involved with Lawrence's writing and with key moments in his career: people such as the Asquiths, Ford Maddox Ford, David Garnett (and Edward Garnett, of course—see under Heilbrun), Aldous Huxley, Katherine Mansfield, Edward Marsh, Ottoline Morrell, John Middleton Murry, Brigit Patmore, Bertrand Russell, Mollie Skinner.

Agg, Howard. *A Cypress in Sicily: A Personal Adventure.* Edinburgh: Blackwood, 1967, pp. 34–41 and passim.

Aldington, Richard. *Life for Life's Sake: A Book of Reminiscences.* New York: Viking, 1941, pp. 228–34, 301–9, 329–34 and passim.

Allott, Kenneth, and Miriam Allott. "DHL and Blanche Jennings." *Review of English Literature* 1 (July 1960): 57–76.

Alpers, Antony. *Katherine Mansfield: A Biography.* New York: Knopf, 1953; London: Cape, 1954, pp. 188–226 and passim.

―――. *The Life of Katherine Mansfield.* New York: Viking; London: Cape, 1980, passim.

Asquith, Lady Cynthia. "DHL As I Knew Him." *Listener* 42 (15 September 1949): 441–42.

―――. "DHL." In her *Remember and Be Glad.* New York: Charles Scribner's Sons, 1952, pp. 133–50.

―――. *Diaries: 1915–1918.* London: Hutchinson, 1968.

Asquith, Herbert H. "A Poet in Revolt." In his *Moments of Memory: Recollections and Impressions.* London: Hutchinson, 1937, pp. 182–92.

Atkins, A. R. "New Lawrences." *Cambridge Quarterly* 22, no. 2 (1993): 210–16. (Review essay on Worthen [1991], op. cit. in second section.)

Barr, Barbara. "I Look Back: About Frieda Lawrence." *Twentieth Century* 165 (March 1959): 254–61.

———. "Step-Daughter to Lawrence." *London Magazine* 33 (August–September 1993): 23–33.

———. "Step-Daughter to Lawrence, II." *London Magazine* 33 (October–November 1993): 12–23.

Bedford, Sybille. *Aldous Huxley: A Biography.* Vol. 1, 1894–1939. London: Chatto and Windus, 1973; New York: Knopf, 1974, passim.

Bell, Quentin. *Bloomsbury.* London: Weidenfeld and Nicolson; New York: Basic Books, 1968, pp. 70–78.

Bragg, Melvyn. "Celebrations in the Country of My Heart." *Sunday Times Magazine* (30 December 1984): 28–33.

———. "DHL—The Country of His Heart." In Cooper 1985, op. cit., pp. 39–50.

Bramley, J. A. "DHL and Miriam." *Cornhill Magazine* 1024 (Summer 1960): 241–49.

Brooks, Emily Potter. "DHL: A Day in the Country and a Poem in Autograph." *DHL Review* 9 (Summer 1976): 278–82. (Memoir of a day in 1909; the poem is "Cherry Robbers.")

Carrington, Dora. *Carrington: Letters and Extracts from Her Diaries.* Edited by David Garnett. New York: Holt, Rinehart, and Winston, 1971, passim.

Chambers, Maria Cristina. "Afternoons in Italy with DHL." *Texas Quarterly* 7 (Winter 1964): 114–20.

Clark, L. D. "The Continent of the Afterwards: Lawrence and New Mexico." In Cooper 1985, op. cit., pp. 51–62. (Adapted from Clark 1980.)

Clark, Ronald. *The Huxleys.* New York: McGraw-Hill, 1968, pp. 228–31.

Clark, R. W. *The Life of Bertrand Russell.* London: Jonathan Cape, 1975, pp. 259–76.

Collier, Peter. "The Man Who Died." *Ramparts* 6 (January 1968): 12–14. (Memoir of Lawrence in Taos.)

Conrad, Peter. "Lawrence in New Mexico." In his *Imagining America.* New York: Oxford University Press, 1980, pp. 159–93.

Cooper, Andrew, ed. *DHL: 1885–1930: A Celebration.* Nottingham: DHL Society, 1985. (Centennial issue of *Journal of the DHL Society* containing a variety of relevant items; the main ones are cited separately in this bibliography.)

Crone, Nora. *A Portrait of Katherine Mansfield.* Devon: Stockwell, 1985. ("Meeting with DHL," pp. 128–40.)

Damon, S. Foster. *Amy Lowell, A Chronicle.* Boston and New York: Houghton Mifflin, 1935.

Darroch, Sandra Jobson. *Ottoline.* New York: Coward, McCann, and Geoghegan, 1975; London: Chatto and Windus, 1976, passim.

Davies, Rhys. "DHL in Bandol." *Horizon* 2 (October 1940): 192–208.

———. *Print of a Hare's Foot.* London: Heinemann; New York: Dodd, Mead, 1969, pp. 136–48.

Delavenay, Emile. "DHL and Jessie Chambers: The Traumatic Experiment." *DHL Review* 12 (1979): 305–25.

DHL Review 2 (Spring 1969): "John Middleton Murry Special Number." (seven articles on Murry; see especially, Griffin and Lea [both 1969], op. cit.)

Douglas, Norman. "Chapters from an Autobiography: Memories of DHL, Rupert Brooke, Frank Harris." *American Bookman* 76 (February 1933): 105–13.

————. "Mr. DHL." In his *Looking Back*. London: Chatto and Windus, 1934, pp. 344–56.

Enser, A.G.S. "DHL in Sussex." *Sussex Life* 4 (May 1968): 46–47.

Fabricant, Noah D. "The Lingering Cough of DHL." In his *Thirteen Famous Patients*. Philadelphia: Chilton, 1960, pp. 116–27.

Farjeon, Eleanor. "Springtime with DHL." *London Magazine* 2 (April 1955): 50–57.

Firchow, Peter E. "Rico and Julia: The Hilda Doolittle—DHL Affair Reconsidered." *Journal of Modern Literature* 8 (1980): 51–76.

Ford, Ford Madox. *Return to Yesterday*. London: Gollancz, 1931.

————. "DHL." *American Mercury* 38 (June 1936): 167–79. (Reprinted in his *Portraits from Life*. Boston: Houghton Mifflin, 1937, pp. 70–89.)

————. "DHL." In his *Mightier than the Sword*. London: Allen, 1938, pp. 98–122.

Ford, George. "Jessie Chambers' Last Tape on DHL." *Mosaic* 6 (Spring 1973): 1–12.

Fraser, Grace Lovat. *In the Days of My Youth*. London: Cassell, 1970, pp. 133–52.

Furbank, P. N. *E. M. Forster: A Life*. Vol. 2. London: Secker and Warburg, 1978, pp. 4–13 and passim.

Fussell, Paul. "The Places of DHL." In his *Abroad: British Literary Traveling between the Wars*. New York: Oxford University Press, 1980, pp. 141–64.

Gardiner, R. "Meetings with Lawrence, August 1926, and February 1928." *Letters from Springhead*, 4th series, no. 2 (Christmas 1959): 48–54.

Garnett, David. *The Golden Echo*. London: Chatto and Windus, 1953, passim.

————. *The Flowers of the Forest*. London: Chatto and Windus, 1955, passim.

————. "DHL and Frieda." In his *Great Friends: Portraits of Seventeen Writers*. London: Macmillan, 1979; New York: Atheneum, 1980, pp. 74–93.

Gerhardi, William A. *Memoirs of a Polyglot*. London: Duckworth; New York: Knopf, 1931, pp. 224–29.

Ghiselin, Brewster. "DHL in Bandol: A Memoir." *Western Humanities Review* 12 (Autumn 1958): 293–305.

Goldring, Douglas. *Odd Man Out: The Autobiography of a "Propaganda Novelist."* London: Chapman and Hall, 1935, pp. 249–66 and passim. (Memoir reprinted in his *Life Interests*. London: MacDonald, 1948, pp. 83–108.)

Gosling, Roy. "Orgies and Abortions: Lawrence and 'Place.'" In Cooper 1985, op. cit., pp. 45–50.

Gray, Cecil. *Peter Warlock: A Memoir of Philip Heseltine*. London: Cape, 1934, pp. 85–122.

————. *Musical Chairs, or between Two Stools*. London: Home and Van Thal, 1948, pp. 114–15, 120, 126–42.

Grey, A. "Up the Rough Deserted Pasture . . . The Country of My Heart." *In Britain* 29 (April 1974): 15–18.

Griffin, Ernest G. "The Circular and the Linear: The Middleton Murry—DHL Affair." *DHL Review* 2 (Spring 1969): 76–92.

————. *John Middleton Murry*. New York: Twayne, 1969, pp. 121–40.

Heilbrun, Carolyn G. *The Garnett Family: The History of a Literary Family*. New York: Macmillan, 1961, pp. 142–62 and passim.

Hobman, J. B., ed. *David Eder: Memoirs of a Modern Pioneer*. London: Gollancz, 1945.

Holroyd, Michael. *Lytton Strachey: A Critical Biography*. 2 vols. London: Heinemann, 1968: vol. 1, pp. 126–27; vol. 2, pp 158–64.

Howard, Ann Chambers. "Memories of Haggs Farm." In Cooper 1985, op. cit., pp. 117–20. (By the niece of Jessie Chambers.)

Innes-Smith, B. " ' . . . like Ovid in Thrace': DHL at Middleton-by-Wirksworth." *Derbyshire Life and Countryside* 43 (June 1978): 40–41.

Jarrett, James L. "DHL and Bertrand Russell." In *A DHL Miscellany.* Edited by Harry T. Moore. Carbondale: Southern Illinois University Press, 1959, pp. 168–87.

Juta, Jan. "Portrait in Shadow: DHL." *Columbia Library Columns* 18, no. 3 (1969): 3–16.

Keith, W. J. "Spirit of Place and *Genius Loci:* DHL and Rolf Gardiner." *DHL Review* 7 (Summer 1974): 127–38. (See subsequent exchange between Delavenay and Keith [1974], op. cit. in fourth section.)

Keynes, John Maynard. *Two Memoirs: Dr. Melchoir: A Defeated Enemy, and My Early Beliefs.* London: Hart-Davis, 1949, pp. 78–103.

Lea, F. A. *The Life of John Middleton Murry.* London: Methuen, 1959.

———. "Murry and Marriage." *DHL Review* 2 (Spring 1969): 1–21.

Lesemann, Maurice. "DHL in New Mexico." *Bookman* 59 (1924): 29–32.

Lewis, D., and M. Holloway. "DHL in Cornwall." *Cornish Review* 3 (Autumn 1949): 71–76.

McDonald, Marguerite. "An Evening with the Lawrences." *DHL Review* 5 (1972): 63–66. (By the wife of Edward D. McDonald, Lawrence's first bibliographer.)

McGuffie, Duncan. "DHL and Nonconformity." In Cooper 1985, op. cit., pp. 31–38.

Mackenzie, Compton. "Memories of DHL." In *On Moral Courage.* London: Collins, 1962, pp. 104–19.

———. *My Life and Times: Octave Four.* London: Chatto and Windus, 1965, pp. 224–25 and passim.

———. *My Life and Times: Octave Five.* London: Chatto and Windus, 1966, pp. 164–73.

Mackenzie, Faith Compton. *More Than I Should.* London: Collins, 1940, pp. 32–35.

Mansfield, Katherine. *Journal of Katherine Mansfield.* Edited by John Middleton Murry. London: Constable; New York: Knopf, 1923, passim. (Rev. ed., London: Constable, 1954.)

———. *Katherine Mansfield's Letters to John Middleton Murry.* London: Constable, 1951.

———. *The Collected Letters of Katherine Mansfield: Volume One 1903–1917.* Edited by Vincent O'Sullivan and Margaret Scott. Oxford: Clarendon, 1984, passim.

———. *The Collected Letters of Katherine Mansfield: Volume Two 1918–1919.* Edited by Vincent O'Sullivan and Margaret Scott. Oxford: Clarendon, 1987, passim.

Marsh, Edward. "DHL." In his *A Number of People: A Book of Reminiscences.* London: Heinemann, 1939, pp. 227–34.

Mayer, Elizabeth. "An Afternoon with DHL." In *A DHL Miscellany.* Edited by Harry T. Moore. Carbondale: Southern Illinois University Press, 1959, pp. 141–43.

Meckier, Jerome. *Aldous Huxley: Satire and Structure.* London: Chatto and Windus, 1969, pp. 78–123.

Mehl, Dieter. "DHL in Waldbröl." *Notes and Queries* 31 (March 1984): 78–81.

Meyers, Jeffrey. "DHL and Katherine Mansfield." *London Magazine,* new series, 18 (May 1978a): 32–54.

———. *Katherine Mansfield: A Biography.* London: Hamilton, 1978b, pp. 78–104. ("Friendship with DHL, 1913–1923.")

Middleton, Victoria. "Happy Birthday Mrs. Lawrence." In Cooper 1985, op. cit., pp. 8–16.

———. "In the 'Woman's Corner': The World of Lydia Lawrence." *Journal of Modern Literature* 13 (1986): 267–88.

Mizener, Arthur. *The Saddest Story: A Biography of Ford Madox Ford.* London: Bodley Head; New York: World, 1971, pp. 168–73 and passim.

Moore, Harry T. "Introduction: DHL and the 'Censor-Morons.' " In *Sex, Literature and Censorship: Essays.* Edited by Harry T. Moore. New York: Twayne, 1953, pp. 9–30. (Enlarged, and with revised introduction, London: Heinemann, 1955.)

Morrell, Ottoline. *Ottoline: The Early Memoirs of Lady Ottoline Morrell.* Edited by Robert Gathorne-Hardy. London: Faber and Faber, 1963.

———. *Ottoline at Garsington: Memoirs of Lady Ottoline Morrell 1915–1918.* Edited by Robert Gathorne-Hardy. London: Faber and Faber, 1974.

———. *Lady Ottoline's Album.* London: Michael Joseph, 1976.

Mori, Haruhide, ed. *A Conversation on DHL.* Los Angeles: Friends of the UCLA Library, 1974. (Discussion among L. C. Powell, Frieda Lawrence Ravagli, Aldous Huxley, and Dorothy G. Mitchell, held on 7 March 1952.)

Morrill, Claire. "Taos Echoes of DHL." *Southwest Review* 47 (Spring 1962): 150–56.

———. "Three Women of Taos: Frieda Lawrence, Mabel Luhan, and Dorothy Brett." *South Dakota Review* 2 (Spring 1965): 3–22.

Moynahan, Julian. "Lawrence and Sicily: The Place of Places." *Mosaic: A Journal for the Interdisciplinary Study of Literature* 19 (Spring 1986): 69–84.

Orioli, Giuseppe. *Adventures of a Bookseller.* Florence: Privately printed, 1937; London: Chatto and Windus, 1938.

Owen, F. R., and David Lindley. "Lawrentian Places." *Human World* 11 (May 1973): 39–54. (On the Tyrol and Eastwood.)

Palmer, P. R. "DHL and the 'Q. B.' in Sardinia." *Columbia Library Columns* 18 (November 1968): 3–9.

Panichas, George A. "The End of the Lamplight." *Modern Age* 14 (1970): 65–74. (On DHL in Lady Cynthia Asquith's memoirs.)

Patmore, Brigit. "Conversations with DHL." *London Magazine* 4 (June 1957): 31–45.

———. "A Memoir of Frieda Lawrence." In *A DHL Miscellany.* Edited by Harry T. Moore. Carbondale: Southern Illinois University Press, 1959, pp. 137–40.

Patmore, Derek. "A Child's Memories of DHL." In *A DHL Miscellany.* Edited by Harry T. Moore. Carbondale: Southern Illinois University Press, 1959, pp. 134–36.

———. *DHL and the Dominant Male.* London: Covent Garden, 1970.

Prichard, Katherine S. "Lawrence in Australia." *Meanjin* 9 (1950): 252–59.

Rhys, Ernest. *Everyman Remembers.* London: Dent, 1931, pp. 251–57.

Robinson, Janice S. *H. D.: The Life and Work of an American Poet.* Boston: Houghton Mifflin, 1982, passim. (Pp. 132–41 deal with the period at the end of 1917 when the Lawrences lived in Hilda Doolittle's flat at 44 Mecklenburgh Square, London—she was then married to Richard Aldington—and with her roman à clef, *Bid Me to Live: A Madrigal* [New York: Grove, 1960], which re-creates the Lawrence of that time as "Rico"; see also the chapter "DHL Everywhere," pp. 286–91.)

Rowse, A. L. *The English Past: Evocations of Persons and Places.* London: Macmillan, 1951, pp. 212–15, 217–37. ("DHL and Nottingham," "DHL at Eastwood." Reissued as *Times, Persons, Places.* London: Macmillan, 1965.)

Russell, Bertrand. "Portraits from Memory III: DHL." *Harper's Magazine* 206 (February 1953): 93–95. (From a BBC radio broadcast of 1952.)

———. "DHL." In his *Portraits from Memory and Other Essays.* London: Allen and Unwin; New York: Simon and Schuster, 1956, pp. 104–8.

———. "Autobiography: 1914–1918." *Harper's Magazine* 236 (January 1968a): 31–39.

———. *The Autobiography of Bertrand Russell.* Vol. 2. London: Allen and Unwin, 1968b, pp. 20–24.

Sagar, Keith. "Lawrence and the Wilkinsons." *Review of English Literature* 3 (October 1962): 62–75.

Schoenberner, Franz. *Confessions of a European Intellectual.* New York: Macmillan, 1946, pp. 284–90. (A shorter version of this memoir was published as "When DHL Was Shocked" in *Saturday Review of Literature* 29 [23 February 1946]: 18–19.)

Schorer, Mark. "Two Houses, Two Ways: The Florentine Villas of Lewis and Lawrence, Respectively." *New World Writing,* no. 4 (October 1953): 136–54.

———. *Lawrence in the War Years.* Stanford, Calif.: Stanford University, 1968. (fifteen-page pamphlet based on a short talk.)

Sheldon, P. "DHL and Nottinghamshire." *Nottinghamshire Countryside* 12 (October 1950): 12–14.

Sitwell, Edith. "A Man with Red Hair." In her *Taken Care Of: An Autobiography.* London: Hutchinson; New York: Atheneum, 1965, pp. 107–11.

Sitwell, Osbert. "Portrait of Lawrence." In his *Penny Foolish.* London: Macmillan, 1935, pp. 293–97.

Skinner, Mollie L. *The Fifth Sparrow: An Autobiography.* Sydney: Sydney University Press, 1972, pp. 109–18, 121–33, 136–53 and passim.

Spolton, L. "The Spirit of Place: DHL and the East Midlands." *East Midland Geographer* 5, nos. 1–2 (1970): 88–96.

Thody, Philip. *Aldous Huxley.* New York: Scribners, 1973, pp. 33–36 and passim.

Thurber, James. "My Memories of DHL." In his *Let Your Mind Alone! And Other More or Less Inspirational Pieces.* New York: Harper; London: Hamilton, 1937, pp. 103–6. (A parody of Lawrence memoirs: Thurber never met Lawrence. Reprinted in Hoffman and Moore [1953]: 88–90.)

Tolchard, C. "DHL in Australia." *Walkabout* 33 (November 1967): 29–31.

Tytell, John. *Passionate Lives: DHL, F. Scott Fitzgerald, Henry Miller, Dylan Thomas, Sylvia Plath—In Love.* New York: Birch Lane Press, 1991.

Villiers, B. (pseudonym of Willard Johnson). "DHL in Mexico." *Southwest Review* 15 (1930): 425–33.

Wade, John Stevens. "DHL in Cornwall: An Interview with Stanley Hocking." *DHL Review* 6 (Fall 1973): 237–83.

Waterfield, Lina. "The Fortress of Aulla and DHL." In her *Castle in Italy: An Autobiography.* New York: Murray, 1961, pp. 119–43.

Weintraub, S. "DHL." In his *Reggie: A Portrait of Reginald Turner.* New York: Braziler, 1965, pp. 193–205.

Wickham, Anna. "The Spirit of the Lawrence Women: A Posthumous Memoir." *Texas Quarterly* 9 (Fall 1966): 31–50.

Woodeson, J. *Mark Gertler: Biography of a Painter, 1891–1939.* London: Sidgwick and Jackson, 1972, passim.

Worthen, John. "DHL and Louie Burrows." *DHL Review* 4 (Fall 1971): 253–62.
———. "Short Story and Autobiography: Kinds of Detachment in DHL's Early Fiction." *Renaissance and Modern Studies* 29 (1985): 1–15.
———. "Lawrence and Eastwood." In *DHL: Centenary Studies*. Edited by Mara Kalnins. Bristol: Bristol Classical Press, 1986, pp. 1–20.
———. "New Materials in the Biography of DHL—II: Catalogue of the Papers of Louie Burrows Relating to DHL." *DHL Review* 21 (1989): 47–53.
———. "A Lawrence Biographer in Nottinghamshire." In *DHL: The Centre and the Circles*. Edited by Peter Preston. Nottingham: University of Nottingham DHL Centre, 1992, pp. 11–29.
———. "Orts and Slarts: Two Biographical Pieces on DHL." *Review of English Studies* 46, no. 181 (February 1995): 26–40.
———. *Cold Hearts and Coronets: Lawrence, the von Richthofens and the Weekleys*. Nottingham: D. H. Lawrence Centre, 1995. (Worthen's inaugural lecture as Professor of D. H. Lawrence Studies at Nottingham.)
Young, Jessica Brett. *Francis Brett Young: A Biography*. London: Heinemann, 1962, passim.
Zytaruk, George, ed. "Dorothy Brett's Letters to S. S. Koteliansky." *DHL Review* 7 (Fall 1974): 240–74.

BACKGROUND MATERIAL AND CRITICAL METACOMMENTARY

Listed here is a small selection of two types of material: works that provide us with general information or insights into the background of Lawrence's life (but that are not directly biographical) and works that comment critically on the biographical criticism itself. (Bibliographies 88 and 89 in Part III should be consulted for additional items of direct relevance to the former category; while Bibliography 86 in Part III should be consulted for items of relevance to the latter category.)

Bennett, Michael. *A Visitor's Guide to Eastwood and the Countryside of DHL*. Nottingham: Nottinghamshire County Library Service, 1979.
Carrier, J. "DHL: A Literary Causerie." *Nottinghamshire Countryside* 16 (October 1954): 3–6.
Christian, Roy. "Lawrence's Country Revisited: The Erewash Valley." *Country Life* 152 (6 July 1972): 19–21.
Cobau, William W. "A View from Eastwood: Conversations with Mrs. O. L. Hopkin." *DHL Review* 9 (Spring 1976): 126–36. (See response by Delavenay [1976], op. cit.)
Coleman, Arthur. *Eastwood through Bygone Ages: A Brief History of the Parish of Eastwood*. Eastwood: Eastwood Historical Society, 1971. (Pp. 107–13 deal specifically with Lawrence.)
Delavenay, Emile. " 'Making Another Lawrence': Frieda and the Lawrence Legend." *DHL Review* 8 (Spring 1975): 80–98. (Review essay on Green [1974], Lucas [1973]—see under second section—and Moore [1974]—see under first section.)

————. "Sandals and Scholarship." *DHL Review* 9 (Fall 1976): 409–17. (Response to Cobau and Sagar [both 1976], op. cit.)

Delavenay, Emile, and W. J. Keith. "Mr. Rolf Gardiner, 'The English Neo-Nazi': An Exchange." *DHL Review* 7 (Fall 1974): 291–94. (Response to Keith [1974]; see under third section.)

Every, G. "Nottinghamshire Notabilities: DHL." *Southwell Review* 2 (June 1951): 12–15.

Fraser, Keith. "Norman Douglas and DHL: A Sideshow in Modern Memoirs." *DHL Review* 9 (Summer 1976): 283–95.

Hardy, George, and Nathaniel Harris. *A DHL Album*. Ashbourne, Derbyshire: Moorland, 1985; New York: Franklin Watts, 1986.

Harris, Nathaniel. *The Lawrences*. London: Dent, 1976.

Hughes, Glyn. "The Roots of DHL." *Illustrated London News* 273 (September 1985): 33–35.

Martin, Adam. "DHL's Eastwood." *Nottingham Topic* (June 1978): 16–18; (July 1978): 10–12; (August 1978): 6–9; (September 1978): 12–13.

————. "DHL's Eastwood." Nottinghamshire: Broxtowe Borough Council, 1980–81. (A useful series of short article-guides in leaflet form providing background information on Lawrence, Eastwood and the surrounding area, and itineraries for walks and tours.)

Meyers, Jeffrey. "Memoirs of DHL: A Genre of the Thirties." *DHL Review* 14 (1981): 1–32.

Pugh, Bridget. *The Country of My Heart: A Local Guide to DHL*. 3d ed. Nottingham: Broxtowe Borough Council, 1991.

Sagar, Keith. "Lawrence and Frieda: The Alternative Story." *DHL Review* 9 (Spring 1976): 117–25. (See response by Delavenay [1976], op. cit.)

Storer, Ronald W. *Some Aspects of Brinsley Colliery and the Lawrence Connection*. Selston, Nottinghamshire: Ronald W. Storer, 1985. (A part of this book appeared also in Cooper [1985], op. cit. in third section as "Arthur Lawrence: A Day in the Life: 1885," pp. 17–30.)

Taylor, J. Clement Phillips. "Boys of the Beauvale Breed." *Eastwood and Kimberley Advertiser* (30 December 1960–17 August 1962). (Series of articles by a contemporary schoolmate of Lawrence's.)

Waldron, Philip J. "The Education of DHL." *Journal of Australasian Universities Language and Literature Association,* no. 24 (November 1965): 239–52.

White, V. "Frieda and the Lawrence Legend." *Southwest Review* 50 (Fall 1965): 388–97.

Widmer, Kingsley. "Profiling an Erotic Prophet: Recent Lawrence Biographies." *Studies in the Novel* 8 (Summer 1976): 234–43.

Zytaruk, George J. "The Chambers' Memoirs of DHL—Which Chambers?" *Renaissance and Modern Studies* 17 (1973): 5–37.

LAWRENCE'S LETTERS AND RELATED CRITICISM

This list is divided into two parts, the first citing major collections of Lawrence's letters in chronological order of publication and the second, arranged in alphabetical order, citing other publications of Lawrence's letters, along with criticism on the letters.

Major Collections of Lawrence's Letters

The Letters of DHL. Edited by Aldous Huxley. London: Heinemann, 1932. (Introduction by Huxley, pp. ix–xxxiv.)

DHL's Letters to Bertrand Russell. Edited by Harry T. Moore. New York: Gotham Book Mart, 1948. (Introduction by Moore, pp. 1–26.)

DHL: Letters. Selected by Richard Aldington. Harmondsworth: Penguin, 1950. (Introduction by Aldous Huxley, pp. 5–31.)

Eight Letters by DHL to Rachel Annand Taylor. Edited by Majl Ewing. Pasadena, Calif.: Castle Press, 1956. (Foreword by Ewing, pp. 3–5.)

The Selected Letters of DHL. Edited by Diana Trilling. New York: Farrar, Straus, and Cudahy, 1958. (Introduction by Trilling, pp. xi–xxxvii.)

The Collected Letters of DHL. 2 vols. Edited by Harry T. Moore. London: Heinemann; New York: Viking, 1962. (Introduction by Moore, pp. ix–xxvii.)

Lawrence in Love: Letters to Louie Burrows. Edited by James T. Boulton. Nottingham: University of Nottingham, 1968. (Introduction by Boulton, pp. vii–xxviii.)

The Quest for Rananim: DHL's Letters to S. S. Koteliansky, 1914–1930. Edited by George J. Zytaruk. Montreal: McGill-Queens University Press, 1970. (Introduction by Zytaruk, pp. xi–xxxvi.)

Letters from DHL to Martin Secker 1911–1930. Edited by Martin Secker. Bridgefoot, Iver, Bucks, England: Privately published, 1970. (See also Martin Secker's *Letters from a Publisher: Martin Secker to DHL and Others, 1911–1929.* London: Enitharmon Press, 1970. Contains forty letters to or about Lawrence.)

The Centaur Letters. Edited by F. Warren Roberts. Austin: Humanities Research Center, University of Texas, 1970. (Thirty letters to Edward D. McDonald and Harold T. Mason of the Centaur Book Shop, Philadelphia, which published McDonald's bibliography of Lawrence in 1925, as well as Lawrence's *Reflections on the Death of a Porcupine* in the same year.)

Letters to Thomas and Adele Seltzer. Edited by Gerald M. Lacy. Santa Barbara, Calif.: Black Sparrow Press, 1976.

The Letters of DHL, Vol. 1: September 1901–May 1913. Edited by James T. Boulton. Cambridge: Cambridge University Press, 1979. (Introduction by Boulton, pp. 1–20.)

The Letters of DHL, Vol. 2: June 1913–October 1916. Edited by George J. Zytaruk and James T. Boulton. Cambridge: Cambridge University Press, 1982. (Introduction by the editors, pp. 1–18.)

The Letters of DHL, Vol. 3: October 1916–June 1921. Edited by James T. Boulton and Andrew Robertson. Cambridge: Cambridge University Press, 1984. (Introduction by the editors, pp. 1–17.)

The Letters of DHL and Amy Lowell 1914–1925. Edited by Claire Healey and Keith Cushman. Santa Barbara, Calif.: Black Sparrow Press, 1985.

The Letters of DHL, Vol. 4: June 1921–March 1924. Edited by Warren Roberts, James T. Boulton, and Elizabeth Mansfield. Cambridge: Cambridge University Press, 1987. (Introduction by the editors, pp. 1–21.)

The Letters of DHL, Vol. 5: March 1924–March 1927. Edited by James T. Boulton and
    Lindeth Vasey. Cambridge: Cambridge University Press, 1989. (Introduction by
    the editors, pp. 1–14.)
The Letters of DHL, Vol. 6: March 1927–November 1928. Edited by James T. Boulton
    and Margaret H. Boulton with Gerald Lacy. Cambridge: Cambridge University
    Press, 1991. (Introduction by the editors, pp. 1–19.)
The Letters of DHL, Vol. 7: November 1928–February 1930. Edited by Keith Sagar and
    James T. Boulton. Cambridge: Cambridge University Press, 1993. (Introduction
    by the editors, pp. 1–15.)
The Letters of DHL, Vol. 8: Index. Edited by James T. Boulton. Cambridge: Cambridge
    University Press, forthcoming.

Other Publications of Lawrence's Letters and Criticism
on the Letters

(The volumes just listed are referred to in abbreviated form in all the following
items.)

Arnold, Armin. "The German Letters of DHL." *Comparative Literature Studies* (Uni-
    versity of Maryland) 3 (1966): 285–98.
Beirne, Raymond M. "Lawrence's Night-Letter on Censorship and Obscenity." *DHL
    Review* 7 (Fall 1974): 321–22.
Boulton, James T. "The Cambridge University Press Edition of Lawrence's Letters, Part
    4." In Partlow and Moore (1980), op. cit., pp. 223–28.
———. "DHL: Letter-Writer." *Renaissance and Modern Studies* 29 (1985): 86–100.
———. "DHL as a Letter-Writer." *Studies in English Language and Literature* 29
    (1989): 1–12.
Cazamian, Louis. "DHL and Katherine Mansfield as Letter Writers." *University of To-
    ronto Quarterly* 3 (April 1934): 286–307.
Cushman, Keith. "DHL and Nancy Henry: Two Unpublished Letters and a Lost Rela-
    tionship." *DHL Review* 6 (Spring 1973): 21–32.
———. "DHL in Chapala: An Unpublished Letter to Thomas Seltzer and Its Context."
    DHL Review 18 (1985–86): 25–31.
Delany, Paul. "Letters of the Artist as a Young Man." *New York Times Book Review* 9
    (September 1979): 3, 44–45. (Review of Cambridge *Letters* 1.)
———, ed. "DHL: Twelve Letters." *DHL Review* 2 (Fall 1969): 195–209.
Donoghue, Denis. " 'Till the Fight Is Finished': DHL in His Letters." In *DHL: Novelist,
    Poet, Prophet.* Edited by Stephen Spender. London: Weidenfeld and Nicolson;
    New York: Harper and Row, 1973, pp. 197–209.
Ellis, David. "Lawrence as Travelling Correspondent." *Meridian: The La Trobe Uni-
    versity English Review* (Australia) 7 (October 1988a): 175–78. (Review of Cam-
    bridge *Letters* 4.)
———. "Lawrence in His Letters." *Etudes Lawrenciennes* 3 (1988b): 41–49.
Farmer, David. "The Cambridge University Press Edition of *The Letters of DHL:*
    Sources for the Edition." In Partlow and Moore (1980), op. cit., pp. 239–41.
Gomme, Andor. "Fortunatus's Purse." *English,* no. 135 (Autumn 1980): 261–66. (Re-
    view of Cambridge *Letters* 1.)

Gordon, Lyndall. "More Pitting against Than Pitying." *Times Literary Supplement* (16 October 1987): 1142. (Review of Cambridge *Letters* 4.)

Gransden, K. W. "Rananim: DHL's Letters to S. S. Koteliansky." *Twentieth Century* 159 (January–June 1955): 22–32.

Henzy, Karl. "Lawrence and Van Gogh in Their Letters." *DHL Review* 24 (Fall 1992a): 145–60.

———. "[Review of Cambridge *Letters* 7]." *DHL Review* 24 (Fall 1992b): 271–75.

Iida, Takeo. "Lawrence's 21 April 1917 Letter to Robert Nichols." *DHL Review* 20 (Spring 1988): 69–70.

Irvine, Peter L., and Anne Kiley, eds. "DHL: Letters to Gordon and Beatrice Campbell." *DHL Review* 6 (Spring 1973): 1–20.

———. "DHL and Frieda Lawrence: Letters to Dorothy Brett." *DHL Review* 9 (Spring 1976): 1–116.

Kermode, Frank. "Lawrence in His Letters." *New Statesman and Nation* (23 March 1962): 422–23. (Review of *Collected Letters* [1962].)

Lacy, Gerald M. "The Case for an Edition of the Letters of DHL." In Partlow and Moore (1980), op. cit., pp. 229–33.

Lawrence, D. H. "Nine Letters (1918–1919) to Katherine Mansfield." *New Adelphi* 3 (June–August 1930): 276–85.

———. *Letter to Charles Lahr.* London: Blue Moon Press, 1930.

———. *A Letter from Cornwall.* San Francisco: Yerba Buena Press, 1931. (Letter to J. D. Beresford, 5 January 1916.)

———. "Briefe an Max Mohr." *Neue Rundschau* 44 (April 1933): 527–40. (Published in English as "The Unpublished Letters of DHL to Max Mohr [I and II]." *T'ien Hsia Monthly* 1 [August 1935]: 21–36; 1 [September 1935]: 166–79.)

———. "A Letter from Germany." *New Statesman and Nation* (Autumn Books Supplement) (13 October 1934): 481–82.

———. *Letter to the "Laughing Horse."* Privately printed [San Francisco: Yerba Buena Press], 1936. (This "letter," actually a review of Ben Hecht's *Fantazius Mallare,* originally appeared in *Laughing Horse,* no. 4 [1922].)

———. "DHL's Letters to Catherine Carswell." *Yale University Library Gazette* 49 (January 1975): 253–60.

Leavis, F. R. " 'Lawrence Scholarship' and Lawrence." *Sewanee Review* 71 (Winter 1963): 25–35. (Critical review of *Collected Letters* [1962]. Reprinted in his *Anna Karenina and Other Essays.* London: Chatto and Windus, 1967, pp. 167–76. See reply by Moore in *Sewanee Review* 71 [Spring 1963]: 347–48.)

Levin, Alexandra L., and Lawrence L. Levin. "The Seltzers and DHL: A Biographical Narrative." In *Letters to Thomas and Adele Seltzer* (1976), pp. 171–201.

MacNiven, Ian S. "[Review of *The Letters of DHL and Amy Lowell* (1985)]." *DHL Review* 19 (Spring 1987): 12–14.

Mason, H. A. "Lawrence in Love." *Cambridge Quarterly* 4 (Spring 1969): 181–200. (On Lawrence, 1906–12, and his relationship to Louie Burrows in particular; partly a review of *Letters to Louie Burrows* [1968].)

Moore, Harry T. "DHL's Letters to Bertrand Russell." *Atlantic Monthly* 182 (December 1948): 92–102.

———. "DHL to Henry Savage: An Introductory Note." *Yale Library Gazette* 33 (July 1959): 24–33.

———. "Some New Volumes of Lawrence's Letters." *DHL Review* 4 (Spring 1971):

61–71. (Review essay on three volumes of letters—those to Burrows [1968], Koteliansky [1970], and Secker [1970].)

Munro, Craig. "The DHL—P. R. Stephensen Letters." *Australian Literary Studies* 11 (1984): 291–315.

Owen, Frederick I. "DHL and Max Mohr: A Late Friendship and Correspondence." *DHL Review* 9 (Spring 1976): 137–56.

Panichas, George A. "DHL: The Hero-Poet as Letter Writer." In *The Spirit of DHL: Centenary Studies*. Edited by Gāmini Salgādo and G. K. Das. London: Macmillan; Totowa, N.J.: Barnes and Noble, 1988, pp. 248–65.

———. "DHL's War Letters." *Texas Studies in Literature and Language* 5 (Fall 1963): 398–409.

Partlow, Robert B., Jr., and Harry T. Moore, eds. *DHL: The Man Who Lived.* Carbondale: Southern Illinois University Press, 1980. ("The Textual Edition of Lawrence's Letters," pp. 221–43: four essays cited separately, by Boulton, Lacy, Zytaruk, and Farmer.)

Pinto, Vivian de Sola. "DHL, Letter-Writer and Craftsman in Verse: Some Hitherto Unpublished Material." *Renaissance and Modern Studies* 1 (1957): 5–34.

———. "Lawrence and Frieda." *English* 14 (Spring 1963): 135–39. (Partly a review of the *Collected Letters* [1962].)

Pollak, Paulina S. "The Letters of DHL to Sallie and Willie Hopkin." *Journal of Modern Literature* 3 (1973): 24–34.

Putt, S. Gorley. "A Packet of Bloomsbury Letters: The Forgotten H. O. Meredith." *Encounter* 59 (November 1982): 77–84.

Ross, Charles L. "[Review of Cambridge *Letters* 4]." *DHL Review* 20 (Fall 1988): 344–46.

Sagar, Keith. "Three Separate Ways: Unpublished DHL Letters to Francis Brett Young." *Review of English Literature* 6 (July 1965): 93–105.

Salgādo, Gāmini. "[Review of Cambridge *Letters* 2]." *Modern Language Review* 79 (1984): 169–70.

Schneider, Daniel J. "[Review of Cambridge *Letters* 3]." *DHL Review* 17 (1984): 251–56.

Schorer, Mark. "I Will Send Address: Unpublished Letters of DHL." *London Magazine* 3 (February 1956): 44–67.

Spender, Stephen. "DHL: Letters to S. S. Koteliansky." *Encounter* 1 (December 1953): 29–35.

Squires, Michael. "Two Newly Discovered Letters to DHL." *DHL Review* 23 (1991): 31–35.

Storey, Richard. "Letters of DHL." *Notes and Queries* 27 (1980): 531.

Troy, William. "Review of *The Letters of DHL.*" *Symposium* 4 (1933): 85–94. (Reprinted as "DHL as Hero" in *William Troy: Selected Essays*. Edited by Stanley Edgar Hyman. New Brunswick, N.J.: Rutgers University Press, 1967, pp. 110–19.)

Wilding, Michael. "DHL in Australia: Some Recently Published Letters." *Australian Literary Studies* 9 (1980): 372–77.

Woodman, Leonora. " 'The Big Old Pagan Vision': The Letters of DHL to Frederick Carter." *Library Chronicle of the University of Texas at Austin,* new series, 34 (1986): 38–51.

Zytaruk, George J., ed. "DHL: Letters to Koteliansky." *Malahat Review* 1 (January 1967): 17–40.

————. "The Last Days of DHL: Hitherto Unpublished Letters of Dr. Andrew Morland." *DHL Review* 1 (Spring 1968): 44–50.

————. "Editing Lawrence's Letters: The Strategy of Volume Division." In Partlow and Moore (1980), op. cit., pp. 234–38.

See also Arnold (1963): 61–64; Cowan (1970): 5–8, passim; Gregory (1933): 87–97; Panichas (1964): 62–94.

SECTION C

SOCIAL CONTEXT: EDUCATION, COAL MINING, REFORM

CHRONOLOGY 2: THE DEVELOPMENT OF STATE EDUCATION IN ENGLAND AND WALES TO 1926

1846 Introduction of pupil-teacher system. Scheme drawn up by Kay-Shuttleworth to foster the training of teachers and put in place by Committee of Council on Education. Stipends to be offered to selected boys and girls indentured as pupil-teachers for a five-year apprenticeship, from the age of thirteen to eighteen. Grants to be made to the schools that train them, and pupil-teachers to be examined annually by Her Majesty's inspectors. Pupil-teachers to receive seven and a half hours' instruction each week, before or after school hours, and to be occupied for five and a half hours every day in teaching of some kind. At end of apprenticeship, pupil-teachers to compete for Queen's Scholarships to be held at a training college; unsuccessful candidates to be given preferential claim for minor appointment in civil service. Annual grant to be made to training colleges in respect of each ex-pupil-teacher in training. At end of three-year course at training, college students to qualify as certificated teachers. College-trained teachers to receive proficiency grants from the government, in addition to salary; also to receive a pension after at least fifteen years' service. (By 1861 there were 13,871 pupil-teachers.)

1851 The Great Exhibition, held at the Crystal Palace, Hyde Park, London (an exhibition of manufactured products and inventions from around the world), draws attention to the fact that, in applied science, Britain is losing its technological lead and, to some extent, falling behind other nations. This realization results in a demand for the technical instruction of workers and a development of the teaching of science, in order to improve the development and use of technology in manufacturing.

1858	Royal Commission recommends national system of girls' secondary schools for middle classes.
1867	Foundation of university extension courses.
1868	Noncollegiate students admitted at Oxford (''unattached'' students living in licensed lodgings).
1870	Forster's Education Act lays the foundation of a national system of elementary education providing instruction in reading, writing, and arithmetic for all children between the ages of five and thirteen. (It would require several further acts—those of 1876, 1880, and 1891 most notably—before a universally available, free, and compulsory elementary education system actually came into being; but this act is generally regarded as a crucial turning point in the progression toward such a system.) Under the act, directly elected local school boards are to determine spending on schools, with the money to be drawn from local rates.
	National Union of (Elementary) Teachers founded.
1871	The University Tests Act removes the last of the religious tests at Oxford and Cambridge. Nonconformists now admitted to both universities on the same terms as Anglicans; university posts thrown open to men of all religious persuasions.
1876	Elementary Education Act (Sandon)—a further step toward free and, in particular, compulsory primary education. Minimum age of employment fixed at ten, and parents obliged to secure elementary schooling for their children. (These provisions were later strengthened by the 1880 Education Act to make attendance at elementary school virtually compulsory for all.)
	First university chairs of education established at Edinburgh and St. Andrew's (Scotland).
1877	Maria Grey Training College founded (at Brondesbury, a suburb of London). First training college for women teachers (secondary). (At least until the 1890s, professional training for secondary education remained largely a women's movement, male secondary teachers being regarded as sufficiently well educated already.)
1880	Attendance at elementary school becomes compulsory for children between five and ten years of age. Great efforts made by the authorities to ensure that children attend regularly. Parents can be fined if their children stay away, and school board inspectors are appointed to seek out nonattenders. The continued charging of fees remains an obstacle, but increasing proportions of children attend school through

the 1880s and 1890s, and by 1900 virtually all children under eleven are attending regularly.

London University admits women to degrees. Regent Street Polytechnic (London) opens.

1884   Central Technical College founded by the City and Guilds of London Institute.

Pupil-teacher centers set up. Pupil-teachers not required to teach for more than half-time in their schools, the other half of the time to be given over to daytime study in these centers. (After 1902, it became more common for pupils to attend secondary school before apprenticeship, rather than to be trained in specialized pupil-teacher centers, many of which themselves became secondary schools.)

1888   Local Government Act brings into being the County and County Borough Councils—the foundation for the Local Education Authorities (the backbone of state provision of education in Britain to this day).

1889   First annual treasury grant to universities.

Royal Commission endorses proposal that University of London should become a teaching as well as an examining institution.

1890   Institution of "University Day Training Colleges" gives prospective elementary school teachers a chance to read for degrees concurrently with their teacher training.

1891   Free Education Act finally makes elementary education virtually (though, in fact, still not universally) free for the majority of children by replacing fees with a special fee-grant, paid to all public elementary schools, of ten shillings per head of the average attendance of children over three and under fifteen years of age.

1893   School Attendance Act enforces eleven as the school-leaving age and as the minimum age of employment.

University of Wales founded.

1895   Royal Commission on Secondary Education recommends a unified central authority to supervise the secondary education of the country.

1899   Education Act of 1893 amended to raise the school-leaving age to twelve.

Board of Education Act passed, putting into effect the recommendations of the Royal Commission on Secondary Education (1895).

Ruskin College, Oxford, opened—an independent workingmen's college that became, in its early years, an influential center for the development of socialist ideas and policies.

1902   Balfour Education Act. School boards are replaced by Local Education Authorities (LEAs) within the County Councils to bring education directly under uniform local government control. All the former board schools and most of the "British" and nonconformist voluntary schools to be transferred to the local education authorities as "provided" schools and under the direct control of LEAs. LEAs also to fund from the rates and to have partial control over "nonprovided" denominational church schools. A state system of secondary schooling now established in the country but separated from elementary schooling and not freely available to all. (A free and compulsory secondary education system was established only with the Butler Act of 1944.)

1903   Workers' Educational Association (WEA) founded by Albert Mansbridge, aiming to give workingmen and workingwomen opportunities of pursuing studies of a university type, under the direction of university teachers. Helps to develop adult education as an integral part of the national system.

1904   Education (Local Authorities' Default) Act passed to force Local Authorities to make grants to voluntary secondary schools.

Elementary School Code lays down the foundations for an entirely new philosophy behind the education of the working classes (child-centered rather than based on the needs of industry).

1905   Education (Provision of Meals) Act allows LEAs to supply meals to children "unable, through lack of food, to profit by the education given in a public elementary school."

Grants made available for "day technical classes" for pupils who have completed their elementary education.

1906   Trades Union Congress demands secondary education for all: "for all children to be full-time day pupils to the age of sixteen."

Government offers to pay three-quarters of the cost of new undenominational teacher training colleges to be provided by the LEAs. Twenty-two LEA teacher training colleges founded.

1907   Education (Administrative) Provisions Act gives LEAs duties with regard to the health and physical condition of children educated in public elementary schools. "Free-place" system started—all grant-aided secondary schools now to admit at least 25 percent of pupils as free-place scholars; these pupils to have spent at least two years at a public elementary school.

Teachers' Registration Council established as a response to a perceived need to control standards of professional efficiency in all educational institutions, including universities; those admitted to appear on an approved list.

Establishment by Royal Charter of the Imperial College of Science and Technology.

Pupils in secondary schools intending to teach allowed to remain there up to the age of seventeen or eighteen as "bursars" and then to proceed directly to a training college; or to become "student teachers," spending half-time in actual practice in an elementary school and continuing studies in secondary school during the other half.

| 1908 | Binet and Simon produce scale for mental testing of children, partly aiming to provide a scientific foundation for the theory that human intelligence is hereditary, not acquired. |

1908   Binet and Simon produce scale for mental testing of children, partly aiming to provide a scientific foundation for the theory that human intelligence is hereditary, not acquired.

1909   Central Labour College movement founded as an independent and militant working-class institution aiming to educate workers throughout the country at a local level.

1910   Education (Choice of Employment) Act enables LEAs to give advice about choice of employment for school leavers.

1911   Institution of grant-earning university places for intending teachers. Four-year teacher training introduced—intending teachers free to study for a degree for the first three years and to devote the fourth year entirely to training.

1913   Junior Technical Schools established, providing a course lasting two or three years from the age of thirteen.

1914   Rachel McMillan opens Rachel McMillan College, Deptford, providing teacher training for nursery school work.

            Average salary for a certificated assistant teacher is £129 for a man and £96 for a woman.

1915   Women's Institutes started, providing classes in cultural and recreational subjects.

1917   Secondary Schools Examination Council set up. Herbert Fisher, president of the Board of Education, obtains increased Exchequer contribution toward the cost of teachers' salaries.

1918   Fisher Education Act lays foundation for modern education provision in allowing for the following measures:

            —abolition of fees in elementary schools

            —establishment of public nursery education

            —provision of facilities for social and physical training during the day or in the evening

            —banning of the employment of children under twelve

            —strict regulation of employment of children over twelve

            —extension of medical inspection to secondary and continuing education

            —raising of upper age limit of compulsory full-time school attendance to fifteen

            —institution of day continuation schools, to be available without fees for children who have left school and made compulsory for 320 hours per year.

1919   Burnham Committee set up to provide salary scales for elementary school teachers on a national basis.

            University Grants Committee set up to allocate and distribute the treasury grant for universities.

Group testing first used in the selection of children for secondary education (Bradford Education Authority, Yorkshire).

1920   Oxford University admits women to degrees.

State scholarships instituted to increase the opportunities for pupils in grant-aided secondary grammar schools to proceed to universities and institutions of higher education (awarded on results of secondary school examinations).

1921   National Council of Labour Colleges founded to provide national coordination for the Labour College movement.

1926   Joint Examining Boards for training of teachers instituted.

The Hadow Report recommends reorganization of education into primary and secondary; transfer at the age of eleven to depend on selective criteria—either to an "academic grammar school or to a more realistic and practical modern school" with a possible transference at thirteen from modern school to junior technical school. Selection to be by written and oral examination.

CHRONOLOGY 3: COAL MINING, THE LABOR MOVEMENT, AND SOCIAL REFORM IN BRITAIN TO 1930

c. 1530–   Enclosure movement helps to promote large-scale colliery enterprises
1700   as mineral property is increasingly transferred from small farmers and from Church possession following the Reformation and Henry VIII's Dissolution of the Monasteries from around 1529. Enclosure continues in various parts of the country until the last quarter of the nineteenth century.

1601   Poor Relief Act makes each parish responsible for the maintenance of its own poor—creates a vast but inefficient system of social welfare.

1620   Coke tried and approved in the smelting of copper, tin, and lead.

1679   Habeas Corpus Act limits government's powers of detention and imprisonment.

1689   Bill of Rights limits powers of the monarchy, establishes sovereignty of Parliament, and legally enshrines many basic democratic rights.

1700   England the largest coal-producing and -consuming country in Europe, though demand still relatively small: coal mined mainly for domestic heating and primarily for town dwellers. Industrial use of coal begins to accelerate from this date.

1705   Thomas Newcomen's "fire" engine first built—enables the development of deeper and larger-scale mining.

1709	Abraham Darby I succeeds in smelting iron with coke in Coalbrook-dale Furnace, Shropshire.
1750s	The process of smelting iron using coke becomes widespread in Britain.
1751	The Sankey Brook Canal built in Lancashire—the first modern canal in Britain.
1761	The Bridgewater Canal opens in Lancashire. Built by James Brindley to connect the Duke of Bridgewater's collieries at Worsley to Manchester (a distance of eight miles), the canal leads to a halving in the price of coal in Manchester and greatly encourages further canal construction for the transportation of coal and for industrial use generally. The development of canal systems continues in Britain until railways begin to dominate from around 1840.
1775	There are approximately fourteen small-scale collieries along the Erewash Valley on the Nottinghamshire–Derbyshire border (where Eastwood lies).
1801–1901	Population of Eastwood grows from 735 to 4,815 as coal mining becomes the staple industry of the area. Rapid expansion in the first half of the century results from widening markets and increased competitiveness brought about by the development of the canals and, later, the railways. Erewash Valley coal sales increase by 169 percent between 1803 and 1849 and by 442 percent between 1849 and 1869, with some 2 million tons of coal being produced annually by this last date. The output of Barber, Walker and Co., the main mine owners around Eastwood, increases from about 150,000 tons a year in the 1850s to over a million tons in the 1890s (Lawrence's father [1846–1924] spent much of his working life—starting at the age of seven—at the company's Brinsley pit). In 1851, almost 20 percent of Eastwood males over the age of ten are employed by the mines; this figure approximately doubles by the 1900s.
1811–12	Luddite riots in Nottinghamshire and Yorkshire (lead to machine breaking being made punishable by death).
1815	Production of miners' Safety Lamp (Davy).
	Corn Law sets artificially high price on wheat in the interests of the landowners—consequent increase in the price of bread creates hardship for the masses.
1816–17	Start of economic slump and of working-class and radical agitation for reform in response to low wages, poor factory conditions, growing unemployment, heavy taxation, and the Corn Law. The Spa Fields Reform Meetings of 1816, the Blanketeers' march of 1817, and other disturbances lead to increasingly repressive governmental measures, including the suspension of habeas corpus in 1817.
1819	Peterloo massacre: a mass reform meeting on St. Peter's Field, Manchester, is broken up by troops who kill eleven people, including two women and a child, and seriously wound 400 others.

Working hours for children in cotton mills limited to twelve.

1824   Reform of penal code by Robert Peel, home secretary, drastically reduces the number of offenses punishable by death; also improves conditions in many prisons.

Repeal of Combination Acts (an act of 1799 forbidding workers to combine together to campaign for better pay and conditions) effectively legalizes trade unions. Rapid spread of unions and strikes leads to an Amending Act in 1825, which reintroduces some constraints on union activities and makes strike action more difficult.

1825   Stockton and Darlington Railway opens—first public railway on which steam locomotives are used (though they do not operate on the whole of the track).

1830   Liverpool and Manchester Railway opens—the first public railway to be worked throughout by locomotives: sparks rapid growth of railways across Britain (from 69 miles of track in 1830 to 6,621 miles in 1850).

1832   The Great Reform Act extends the franchise. Though by no means bringing about real democracy—the electorate was increased by only about 200,000, and five out of six adult males still had no vote—the act significantly advanced progress toward that end by weakening the power of the old landowning classes and paving the way for further reforms (see 1835, 1867, 1884, 1918, and 1928).

1832–33   First cholera outbreak in Britain.

1833   Factory Act passed. The first effective measure of its kind: labor by children under nine prohibited; forty-eight-hour week for children nine to thirteen years of age, with some daily schooling made compulsory; sixty-nine-hour week for persons under eighteen; paid factory inspectors appointed to enforce legislation.

1834   Poor Law Amendment Act.

Robert Owen founds the giant Grand National Consolidated Trades Union (GNCTU), comprising some half a million workers, with the ultimate aim of bringing about a new cooperative social system to replace capitalism (some leaders favoring a general strike as a first step). Government alarm at this development leads to the "Tolpuddle Martyrs"—six men of Tolpuddle, in Dorset—being prosecuted for taking secret oaths when forming a local branch of the Friendly Society of Agricultural Labourers (affiliated with the GNCTU). Such oaths, although illegal, are the usual practice of all unions at this time. All six men are found guilty and sentenced to seven years' transportation to a convict colony in Australia; partly as a result of this, the GNCTU movement collapses.

1835   Municipal Corporations Reform Act rationalizes local government of towns.

1836   Formation of the London Working Men's Association, the starting point for the Chartist movement.

1837	Compulsory registration for births, marriages, and deaths. Accurate statistics lay foundations for later public health measures. Birth certificates make it possible to apply Factory and Education Acts more rigorously.
1838	The Chartist movement for parliamentary reform launches the "People's Charter": it demands votes for all adult males, a secret ballot, annual elections, abolition of the property qualification for Members of Parliament (MPs), payment of MPs, and equal electoral districts. A national "convention" is set up in 1839 to organize a mass petition for the charter. Following a period of political agitation, the charter is finally debated by Parliament in July 1839 and overwhelmingly rejected. Considerable social unrest follows, but the Chartist movement collapses in 1840 due to vigorous government action, confused leadership, and middle-class hostility.
1839	Anti-Corn Law League founded.
1840	Introduction of the penny post makes postage affordable by all.
	Commission on Child Labour in the Mines. Revelations of long hours worked in brutal conditions results in the Mines Act of 1842, abolishing all female labor in the mines, together with that of boys under ten. (E.g., the commission had found that children as young as five were working for an average of fourteen hours per day in Derbyshire mines.)
1842	Mines Act—no female labor underground; no boys under ten; no butty system; Government inspectors.
	First Public Health Act.
1844	Factory Act—reduces working hours for women to twelve hours per day, children to be allowed into the mills at eight instead of nine, but working hours reduced from 9 to 6½ a day.
	First successful consumers' Co-operative Society launched in Rochdale by the "Rochdale Pioneers."
1845	Irish Potato Famine. Mass starvation and privation in Ireland lead to mass immigration into England, Scotland, and Wales.
1846	Corn Laws abolished.
1848	Public Health Act sets up a Board of Health—reveals appalling conditions in towns.
1850–55	Tonnage of coal carried into London increases twentyfold.
1850	Grey's Factory Act introduces 10½-hour day for all employees in the textile mills.
	Coal Mines Inspection Act.
1851	Royal School of Mines founded to train inspectors.
	Amalgamated Society of Engineers founded. A turning point in the history of the trade union movement: this the first *national* union,

formed to bargain with employers for increased wages and better conditions nationally.

Sheffield Women's Political Association petitions Parliament for women's enfranchisement.

Legalization of cooperatives.

1855   Mines Act establishes safety standards for each pit: "General Rules" and "Special Rules."

Women's committee petitions Parliament for a Married Women's Property Bill. Transforms itself into the Society for the Employment of Women (the *Englishwoman's Journal* its magazine).

Abolition of stamp duty on newspapers.

1855–1913   Over fourfold increase in coal output during this period. British per capita consumption of coal greater than four tons by 1900: this remains the highest in the world until 1914. Nearly two-thirds of coal entering world trade between 1870 and 1913 is mined in Britain, with South Wales the major producer and exporter (and particularly important in supplying the demand created by steamships). 287 million tons of coal produced in 1913.

1857–82   Married Women's Property Acts extend women's rights in marriage.

1858   Property qualification for Members of Parliament removed.

1860   Mines Act. Boys ten to twelve to work underground only if they have achieved a certificate of literacy.

1861   Repeal of the tax on paper (the "tax on knowledge").

1863   Co-operative Wholesale Society established.

1864   First chain machine produced to cut coal at the coal face, but mechanization depends on size and condition of the seam. In the Midlands, by 1913, still only 4.5 percent of coal mechanically cut.

1866   Petition to Parliament by Women's Petition Committee, presented by John Stuart Mill and Henry Fawcett, arguing for enfranchisement without distinction of sex—begins concerted campaign for women's suffrage.

1867   Second Parliamentary Reform Act doubles the existing electorate mainly by extending the franchise to all town householders, thus allowing many working-class men to vote for the first time.

Women's Petition Committee succeeded by London National Society for Women's Suffrage, and similar societies are set up in Manchester and elsewhere.

1868   First Trades Union Congress (TUC) meets to consider the general policy of the unions. Arbitration develops as a method of settling disputes, and while the Trade Union Act of 1871 is being planned, the congress uses its influence on Members of Parliament.

1869	John Stuart Mill's *On the Subjection of Women:* classic statement of women's rights, with massive influence on emerging women's movements worldwide.
1870–78	Private members' bills for women's suffrage put to Parliament annually; also from 1884 onward (except for 1899 and 1901). Majorities gained in 1870, 1884, 1897, 1904, 1908—but never acted on.
1871	The Trade Union Act gives unions legal rights, enabling them to hold property and to have the protection of the courts. However, the Criminal Law Amendment Act makes organizing a strike or picketing an offense open to prosecution.
1872	Secret ballot introduced in place of open voting at the hustings. Main effect is to discourage bribery, which still persisted at elections. First union of unskilled workers—the Agricultural Labourers Union—succeeds in obtaining an increase in pay from farmers. However, union collapses due to great agricultural depression of 1874–75. Coal Mines Regulation Act passed as a result of pressure from Trade Union. Increase in General Rules. Mine managers to hold certificate of competency. Mines Inspectorate strengthened.
1874	Factory Act introduces the ten-hour day (Monday to Friday), six hours on Saturdays.
	A women's trade union, the Women's Protective and Provident League, set up by Emma Paterson, Charles Kingsley, and Harriet Martineau and others. Gains admission to the TUC in 1876.
1875	Conspiracy and Protection of Property Act legalizes "peaceful picketing" and declares that any group of strikers might commit any act that is lawful for one person to commit. This considerably increases the power of the unions to organize strikes.
	Beginnings of major agricultural depression.
1880	Democratic Federation founded by H. M. Hyndman (William Morris one of its members, but he leaves to found the Socialist League shortly afterward).
1881	Electric lighting first used underground at Earnock Colliery, Hamilton, Scotland.
1883	Women's Co-operative Guild formed: largely an urban, working-class movement working for reform and the practical self-betterment of women. Combines elements of the cooperative, feminist, and labor movements. (Lawrence's mother was an active member of her local guild—as is Mrs. Morel in *Sons and Lovers.*)
1884	Third Parliamentary Reform Act gives all householders in the countryside the right to vote and redistributes parliamentary seats to bring about a greater standardization in the size of constituencies.
	Fabian Society founded (well-known members include H. G. Wells, G. B. Shaw, and the Webbs).

The Democratic Federation becomes the Social Democratic Federation as it adopts a Marxist socialist program.

1886–87   Demonstrations of unemployed in London.

1888   Local Government Act establishes elected County Councils, rationalizing and democratizing local government in the counties.

1888–89   Outbreak of strikes and demonstrations. There are 500 strikes in 1888, but the most important is the London dockers' strike of 1889.

The dockers demand a minimum of sixpence an hour (the "dockers' tanner") and a minimum of four hours' work at a time.

Subscriptions for their aid flow in from all over Britain, Australia, and Europe to enable them to defeat the employers. Strike arouses public concern over labor issues and speeds the development of trade unions for unskilled workers.

1889   First international congress of miners held in Paris, with the second in Jolimont in Belgium in 1890. Delegates unanimously agree that one day's work should not exceed eight hours in any twenty-four; international strike in support of this resolution considered.

Miners' Federation of Great Britain formed.

Women's Trade Union League set up as a federation of all trade unions admitting women.

Women's Franchise League founded.

1890–1900   Electrification of tramways.

1891   *The Clarion,* one of the most popular radical labour newspapers of the period, launched by Robert Blatchford.

National Union of Shop Assistants formed.

1892   Three independent Labour candidates, including Keir Hardie, the Scottish miners' leader, elected to Parliament.

Committee of inquiry into shop working finds scandalous conditions—some shop assistants (mostly women) working eighty-five hours per week, for example (see also under 1911).

Publication of Charles Booth's pioneering survey *Life and Labour of the People in London* (twelve volumes): this suggests that 35 percent of the population of London are living in poverty. B. S. Rowntree's later *Poverty: A Study of Town Life* (1901) suggests a similar percentage for York. Both studies influential in promoting social reforms.

1893   Independent Labour Party founded with Keir Hardie its first leader.

Mine owners' attempt to reduce wages by 10 percent results in fifteen-week miners' lockout—two miners killed by soldiers called out to keep the peace.

1897   Thirty-week strike by Engineering Union ends in defeat.

National Union of Women's Suffrage Societies federates 16 different suffrage societies (70 member societies by 1909; over 400 by 1913).

1900	Labour Representation Committee set up to promote a distinct Labour group in Parliament, with J. Ramsay MacDonald as secretary (to become the Labour Party in 1906). The trade unions (which by this time have some 2 million members) agree to pay one penny per member per annum to finance candidates who would form a distinct Labour group in Parliament.
1903	Foundation of the Women's Social and Political Union (WSPU), a militant branch of the women's suffrage movement.
1905	Start of suffragette agitation.
1906	Twenty-six Labour MPs elected to the Commons for the first time. Labour Party constituted.
	Women's Labour League set up as a branch of the Labour Party. National Anti-Sweating League formed to campaign for improved conditions in the "sweated" trades—tailoring, lace-making, and the like, predominantly carried out at home by women. Pressure leads to a Parliamentary Select Committee inquiry and report in 1908 and the Trade Boards Act of 1909, which introduces Wage Boards to set minimum rates of pay.
1908	Old Age Pensions introduced by Liberal government. Five shillings a week to be paid to those of seventy years of age and over if their income from other sources is less than eight shillings a week.
	Coal Mines Regulation Act limits underground working to eight hours per day.
1909	First labor exchanges set up to assist in placing men in suitable employment.
1910	No reduction achieved in absolute numbers of deaths due to accidents in mines: 1,000 per year in 1870s and 1,100 in 1910.
	Rates probably higher in East Midlands than elsewhere in England. Accident death rates at this time between four and five times as high for coal mining as for any other occupation.
	South Wales miners' strike. Winston Churchill, the home secretary, sends troops to Tonypandy to quell supposed rioting—hundreds are injured, and one killed, "needlessly," as the general in charge later wrote.
	Eastwood pit strike, June to November.
	Life of Parliament reduced from seven to five years.
1911	Parliament decides MPs to be paid a salary of £400 per year (one of the original Chartists' demands): any male person can now become an MP regardless of personal income.
	National Insurance Act introduces workers' sickness benefit comprising free treatment and medicines from a general medical practitioner, plus weekly payment during absence from work—though neither extended to the families of insured. Act also provides for

unemployment benefit for workers in building, engineering, and ship-building.

Coal miners form 7 percent of total employed population.

Shops Act establishes sixty-hour week and half-day holidays for shop workers.

Suffragette riots in London.

London dockers strike.

Major railway strike paralyzes much of the country.

1912   Nationwide strike of miners, involving over 1 million men, lasts for over a month before the principle of a national minimum wage officially recognized.

The *Daily Herald,* "The Labour Daily Newspaper," launched.

Women's Franchise Bill rejected by the House of Commons.

1913   Trades Union Act legalizes trade union expenditure for political purposes, provided this is approved by a special ballot of members and that any member can decline to contribute. This allows for continued trade union support for the growing Labour Party.

Miners, together with railwaymen and transport workers, initiate the Triple Alliance, potentially the strongest union association in Europe.

Sylvia Pankhurst forms the East London Federation for Working Class Suffragettes—a reaction to the methods and upper-class dominance of the WSPU.

1914   28 June 1914—First World War begins.

1915   Defence of Realm Act.

1916   State takes control of all output and distribution of all mines in the U.K. (reversed in peacetime).

Strike of Clydeside munitions workers.

Labour Party Conference votes against conscription.

Conscription introduced.

Government takes over South Wales coal field under Defence of Realm Act—because of strikes.

1917   Russian Revolution (March).

Co-Operative Congress decides to organize as a Co-Operative Party (one Member of Parliament elected in 1918); informally and later formally allied to the Labour Party.

1918   End of First World War.

Fourth Parliamentary Reform Bill gives the vote to all men over twenty-one and women over thirty (so long as they are ratepayers or the wives of ratepayers).

Membership of Trade Unions peaks at 8,300,000.

Labour Party adopts a new socialist constitution and reorganizes to provide for local constituency party organizations. Individual membership of women, in particular, increases drastically (there are 150,000 women members by 1924, probably a majority of the membership).

1919   Nancy Astor becomes first woman Member of Parliament in Great Britain.

There are over 1,000 strikes between 1919 and 1920, the coal industry being the worst hit.

Sankey Coal Commission leads to Coal Act limiting underground working to seven hours per day (this to be raised to eight hours again in 1926).

1920   Unemployment Insurance Act—all employees earning up to £250 a year covered except for farmworkers and domestic servants.

London dockers, supported by the trade union movement, refuse to load ship *Jolly George* with arms believed to be for use against the Soviet government. This effectively ends British intervention in the Russian Revolution.

Communist Party of Great Britain founded. (Its request for affiliation to the Labour Party is turned down in 1921 and subsequent years, and individual membership of the Labour Party is prohibited to its members from 1924.)

1921   Economic slump: substantial losses in trade on world market lead to nearly 2 million unemployed. A period of widespread and continuous unemployment—which was to last, on and off, up to the start of the Second World War—enables employers to force wages down and hours up, while unions are forced to abandon fight for better conditions in order to limit the cuts in pay and increases in hours.

1922   Triple Alliance of unions fails on "Black Friday" (15 April), when the railwaymen and transport workers refuse, at the last minute, to strike in support of the miners striking against a proposed decrease in wages. After a lockout of several months, the miners are defeated.

Unemployment in Britain stands at 2 million.

Following the general election, the Labour Party forms the official opposition for the first time.

1923   Margaret Bondfield, an ex-shop worker and assistant secretary of the Shop Workers' Union, becomes first woman elected to the chair of the General Council of the TUC.

1924   First short-lived Labour government in Britain under Ramsay Macdonald. Margaret Bondfield first woman junior minister (later, in the 1929 Labour government, also the first woman Cabinet member).

London tram strike.

1925	A new Pensions Act extends national health insurance scheme to allow for old-age pensions at sixty-five years of age.
	Guardianship of Infants Act gives women equal rights to guardianship of their children.
1926	The General Strike—workers in all sections of British industry called out in support of the mine workers, who are facing demands from their employers for a longer working day and less pay: "not a minute on the day, not a penny off the pay" (miners' slogan). Strike lasts for nine days before collapsing in failure. Mine workers stay out for a further six months, before being forced to accept longer hours (eight-hour underground shifts restored) and lower wages.
1927	Trade Disputes and Trade Union Act, government response to General Strike, makes general strikes illegal, forbids Civil Service Trade Unions to belong to the TUC, and reverses the Trade Union Act of 1913.
1928	Minimum voting age for women in Britain reduced to twenty-one from thirty years.
1929	General Election victory for the Labour Party.
1930	Coal Mines Act reduces underground working to 7½ hours per day.

WORKS CONSULTED FOR CHRONOLOGIES 2 AND 3

Barnard, H. C. *A History of English Education from 1760.* 2d ed. London: University of London Press, 1961.

Bédarida, François. *A Social History of England 1851–1975.* Translated by A. S. Forster. London and New York: Methuen, 1979.

Buxton, Neil K. *The Economic Development of the British Coal Industry from the Industrial Revolution to the Present Day.* London: Batsford Academic, 1978.

Castleden, Rodney. *World History: A Chronological Dictionary of Dates.* London: Parragon, 1994.

Chronicle of the 20th Century. London: Longman, 1988.

Church, Roy. *The History of the British Coal Industry. Volume 3: 1830–1913.* Oxford: Clarendon Press, 1986.

A Dictionary of British History. London: Secker and Warburg, 1981.

Evans, Eric J., ed. *Social Policy 1830–1914: Individualism, Collectivism and the Origins of the Welfare State.* London: Routledge and Kegan Paul, 1978.

Evans, Richard J. *The Feminists: Women's Emancipation Movements in Europe, America and Australasia 1840–1920.* Rev. ed. London and Sydney: Croom Helm; Totowa, N.J.: Barnes and Noble, 1979. (Originally published 1977.)

Griffin, A. R., and C. P. Griffin. "A Social and Economic History of Eastwood and the Nottinghamshire Mining Country." In *A DHL Handbook.* Edited by Keith Sagar. Manchester: Manchester University Press; New York: Barnes and Noble, 1982, pp. 127–63.

Hopkins, Eric. *A Social History of the English Working Classes 1815–1945.* London: Edward Arnold, 1979.

Labour Party. *A Pictorial History of the Labour Party 1900–1975.* London: Labour Party, 1975.

Pelling, Henry. *A History of British Trade Unionism.* Harmondsworth: Penguin, 1963.

Pugh, Martin. *Women and the Women's Movement in Britain 1914–1959.* London: Macmillan, 1992.

Richards, Denis, and J. W. Hunt. *An Illustrated History of Modern Britain 1783–1964.* 2d ed. London: Longmans, Green, 1965.

Simon, Brian. *Studies in the History of Education 1780–1870.* London: Lawrence and Wishart, 1960.

———. *Education and the Labour Movement 1870–1920.* London: Lawrence and Wishart, 1965.

Williams, Neville. *Chronology of the Modern World, 1763 to the Present Time.* Rev. ed. London: Barrie and Rockliff, 1969. (Originally published 1966.)

SECTION D

GEOGRAPHICAL CONTEXT: TRAVELS AND PLACES

CHRONOLOGY 4: A LAWRENCE TRAVEL CHRONOLOGY

The vast amount of research carried out into Lawrence's life, works, and letters—especially since the start of the Cambridge Edition project—means that it is now possible to trace Lawrence's movements throughout his life with great precision (and almost day by day for the last fifteen or so years of his life). The seven Cambridge volumes of Lawrence's letters are perhaps the main primary source for detailed information of this sort—in the letters themselves, of course, but also in the chronologies, introductions, and annotations that accompany each volume. In addition to the many biographies of Lawrence (see Bibliography 1, which includes details of the Cambridge letters, too), several secondary works provide fully detailed accounts of his travels. Four works, in particular, stand out for their focused and comprehensive coverage and for their systematic listing of information:

Moore, Harry T. *Post Restante: A Lawrence Travel Calendar.* Los Angeles and Berkeley: University of California Press, 1956. (Superseded by the following works but still useful and largely accurate.)

Sagar, Keith. *DHL: A Calendar of His Works.* Manchester: Manchester University Press, 1979. (The headnotes to each main entry—on the composition of Lawrence's works—provide details of Lawrence's whereabouts for the period specified: these form the basis for the following item.)

———. "A Lawrence Travel Calendar." In *A DHL Handbook.* Edited by Keith Sagar. Manchester: Manchester University Press, 1982, pp. 229–38. (Obviously the most concentrated of the calendars listed here but also the fullest and, to its date, most accurate short chronology of Lawrence's travels—still almost entirely reliable.)

Preston, Peter. *A DHL Chronology.* Basingstoke and London: Macmillan; New York: St. Martin's Press, 1994. (Drawing on the Cambridge edition of Lawrence's letters, this currently provides the most complete, up-to-date, and precise account of Lawrence's travels.)

For Lawrence scholars and specialists, the preceding works and the Cambridge *Letters* are undoubtedly invaluable research tools. However, with the possible exception of Sagar's 1982 calendar, they are probably all too long and involved to be of ready use to the nonspecialist or to the casual reader who wants only a general outline of the author's movements. With such readers in mind, therefore, the following chronology has been designed primarily to provide a succinct general overview of Lawrence's travels—it ignores most minor journeys, for example, and only occasionally adds information to simple statements of location—though it aims also to be sufficiently full and detailed to be of use to specialists for general reference purposes. For quick reference, I provide a short summary of the main movements and places in Lawrence's life before the main chronology. (Most of the places mentioned in this chronology can be found on the maps provided at the end of this section.)

SUMMARY

1885–1908	Eastwood.
1908–11	Croydon.
January–May 1912	Croydon—Bournemouth—Eastwood.
May 1912–June 1913	Germany—Italy.
June–August 1913	England: Kent—London—Eastwood.
August 1913–June 1914	Germany—Switzerland—Italy.
June 1914–December 1915	England: London—Chesham, Buckinghamshire—Greatham, Sussex.
December 1915–October 1917	Cornwall.
October 1917–November 1919	London—Hermitage, Berkshire—Middleton-by-Wirksworth, Derbyshire.
November 1919–April 1921	Italy—Taormina, Sicily—(January 1921, visit to Sardinia).
April–September 1921	Germany—Austria—Italy.
September 1921–February 1922	Taormina, Sicily.
March–August 1922	Ceylon—Australia.
September 1922–November 1923	United States—Mexico.

December 1923–February 1924	London—Paris—Baden-Baden, Germany.
March 1924–September 1925	United States—Mexico.
October–November 1925	England—Germany.
November 1925–June 1928	Italy—(visits to Germany, England, Scotland, Switzerland).
June–September 1928	France—Switzerland—Germany.
October 1928–June 1929	Bandol, France—Mallorca, Balearic Islands.
June–September 1929	Italy—Germany.
October 1929–March 1930	France: Bandol—Vence.
1885–87	Born and lives at 8a Victoria Street, Eastwood, Nottinghamshire, England.
1887–91	57 (later 28) Garden Road, the Breach, Eastwood.
1891–1905	3 (later 8) Walker Street, Eastwood.
1905–8	97 Lynn Croft, Eastwood.
October 1908–September 1911	Lodges at 12 Colworth Road, Croydon, Surrey, while teaching at Davidson Road Boys' School, Croydon. Most holidays spent at Eastwood; frequent visits to Quorn, Leicestershire, to the home of Louie Burrows.
September 1911–January 1912	Lodging at 16 Colworth Road, Croydon.
January–February 1912	Bournemouth, Dorset, recuperating after illness.
February–May 1912	Mainly at Eastwood (though making several visits, including two to Edward Garnett's house, the Cearne, Edenbridge, Kent).
May 1912	Germany: Metz (now in France)—Trier—Waldbröl—Beuerberg.
June–August 1912	Mainly at Icking, near Munich in Bavaria, Germany.
August–September 1912	From Icking to Gargnano on Lake Garda, Italy, via Mayrhofen, Sterzing, Bolzano, Trento, and Riva (all then in Austria).
September 1912–March 1913	Villa Igea, Gargnano, Italy.
April–June 1913	Mainly at Irschenhausen, near Munich, Germany.
June–August 1913	England: mainly at the Cearne, Edenbridge, Kent, and Riley House, 28 Percy Avenue, Broadstairs, Kent, with visits to London and Eastwood.
August–September 1913	Irschenhausen, near Munich, Germany
September 1913	From Constance, across Switzerland via Zurich and Lucerne, to Como, Milan, and Lerici, Italy.
October 1913–June 1914	Villino Ettore Gambrosier, Lerici per Fiascherino, Golfo della Spezia, Italy.

June 1914	To London via Switzerland and Germany.
June–July 1914	Mainly at 9 Selwood Terrace, South Kensington, London.
August 1914–January 1915	The Triangle, near Chesham, Buckinghamshire, England.
January–July 1915	Mainly at Greatham, Pulborough, Sussex.
August–December 1915	Mainly at 1 Byron Villas, Vale-of-Heath, Hampstead, London.
December 1915–February 1916	Porthcothan, St. Merryn, Padstow, Cornwall.
February 1916	The Tinner's Arms, Zennor, Cornwall.
February 1916–October 1917	Higher Tregerthen, Zennor, Cornwall.
October–November 1917	44 Mecklenburgh Square, London.
December 1918	13b Earl's Court Square, London—Chapel Farm Cottage, Hermitage, near Newbury, Berkshire— Ripley, Derbyshire.
January–April 1918	Chapel Farm Cottage, Hermitage, Berkshire.
May–August 1918	Mountain Cottage, Middleton-by-Wirksworth, Derbyshire.
August 1918	London—Mersea, Essex—Hermitage, Berkshire —Upper Lydbrook in the Forest of Dean.
September–October 1918	Mountain Cottage, Middleton-by-Wirksworth, Derbyshire.
October–November 1918	Hampstead, London—Hermitage, Berkshire.
November 1918–April 1919	Mainly at Mountain Cottage, Middleton-by-Wirksworth, Derbyshire. (15 February–17 March 1919, at the home of his sister in Ripley, Derbyshire, while suffering from influenza.)
April–July 1919	Chapel Farm Cottage, Hermitage, Berkshire.
July–August 1919	Myrtle Cottage, Pangbourne, Berkshire.
August–September 1919	Grimsbury Farm, near Newbury, Berkshire.
September–November 1919	Mainly at Chapel Farm Cottage, Hermitage, Berkshire.
November 1919	To Italy via London and Paris: Turin—Lerici— Florence.
December 1919	Italy: Florence—Rome—Picinisco—Capri.
January–February 1920	Mainly at Palazzo Ferraro, Capri. Then to Sicily.
March–July 1920	Mainly at Fontana Vecchia, Taormina, Sicily, Lawrence's home until February 1922. (17–28 May 1920, trip to Malta.)
August–October 1920	Italy: Montecassino—Rome—Florence—Milan —Lakes Como, Iseo, and Garda—Verona— Venice—Florence—Venice.

October 1920–April 1921	Mainly at Fontana Vecchia, Taormina, Sicily. (5–13 January, trip to Sardinia: Cagliari—Mandas—Sorgono—Nuoro—Terranova.)
April 1921	To Baden-Baden, Germany, via Palermo, Capri, Rome, Florence, and Switzerland.
April 1921–July 1921	Hotel Krone, Ebersteinburg, Baden-Baden, Germany. To Zell-am-See, Austria, via Constance, Switzerland.
July–August 1921	Villa Alpensee, Thumersbach, Zell-am-See, Austria.
August–September 1921	Florence, Italy.
September 1921–February 1922	Fontana Vecchia, Taormina, Sicily. February–March, to Ceylon (now Sri Lanka).
March–April 1922	Ardnaree, Lake View Estate, Kandy, Ceylon. April–May, to Australia.
May 1922	Australia: Fremantle—Perth—"Leithdale," Darlington—Sydney—"Wyewurk," Thirroul, New South Wales.
June–August 1922	"Wyewurk," Thirroul, New South Wales. August–September 1922, to United States, via Wellington, New Zealand; Raratonga, Cook Islands; Papeete, Tahiti.
September 1922	United States: San Francisco—Lamy—Santa Fe—Taos, New Mexico.
October–November 1922	Taos, New Mexico.
December 1922–March 1923	Del Monte Ranch, Questa, in the foothills of the Rocky Mountains, some seventeen miles above Taos, New Mexico.
March–April 1923	Mainly at Hotel Monte Carlo, Mexico City.
May–July 1923	Calle Zaragoza 4, Chapala, Mexico. 9–19 July, to New York City via Laredo, San Antonio, New Orleans, and Washington, D.C.
July–August 1923	"Birkindele," Union Hill, Morris Plains, New Jersey (Thomas Seltzer's house).
August 1923	To Buffalo and then, via Chicago and Omaha, to Los Angeles.
September 1923	Santa Monica, California—Los Angeles (12–25). To Guaymas, Sonora, Mexico, via Palm Springs.
October 1923	Mexico: Navajoa, Sonora—Minas Nuevas, Alamos, Sonora—Mazatlan, Sinaloa—Tepic, Nayarit. Via Ixtlan, La Quemada, and Etzalan to Guadalajara.
November 1923	Hotel Garcia, Guadalajara. 17–22 November, to Mexico City and Vera Cruz. 22 November–12 December, to Plymouth, England.

December 1923–January 1924   Mainly at 110 Heath Street, Hampstead, London. (31 December–3 January, visits family in Nottingham and Derby; 3–5 January, visits Frederick Carter in Pontesbury, Shropshire.)

January–February 1924   Hôtel de Versailles, Boulevard Montparnasse, Paris (until 6 February and 21–25 February). 6–20 February, Ludwig-Wilhelmstift, Baden-Baden, Germany.

February–March 1924   Garland's Hotel, Pall Mall, London.

March 1924   Sails from Southampton to New York (5–11). To Taos via Chicago and Santa Fe (18–22).

March–May 1924   Taos, New Mexico.

May–October 1924   Mainly at Lobo Ranch, Questa, above Taos, about two miles from the Del Monte ranch. (Lobo ranch renamed ''Kiowa'' in August. 14–23 August, visits Hopi country.)

October 1924   To Mexico City via Santa Fe and El Paso (16–23).

October–November 1924   Hotel Francis, Oaxaca, Mexico.

November 1924–February 1925   Avenida Pino Suarez 43, Oaxaca, Mexico.

February–March 1925   Seriously ill, Lawrence taken to Hotel Francia, Oaxaca, and then to the Imperial Hotel, Mexico City, before traveling back (25–31 March) to the Del Monte ranch, Questa, New Mexico.

April–September 1925   Kiowa Ranch, Questa, New Mexico.

September 1925   New York City. Sails for Southampton, England (21–30).

October 1925   Garland's Hotel, Pall Mall, London—Buckinghamshire—Nottingham—Ripley, Derbyshire—London. To Baden-Baden, Germany, via Strasbourg at end of the month.

November 1925   Ludwig-Wilhelmstift, Baden-Baden—Kastanienbaum, near Lucerne, Switzerland—Spotorno, Italy.

November 1925–April 1926   Mainly at Villa Bernarda, Spotorno, Italy. (22 February–3 April 1926, visits Monte Carlo, Nice, France, and then travels around Italy: Ventimiglia, Rome, Capri, Ravello, Rome, Assisi, Perugia, Florence, Ravenna.)

April–May 1926   Pensione Lucchesi, Florence, Italy.

May 1926–June 1928   Mainly at Villa Mirenda, San Paolo Mosciano, Scandicci, near Florence. (13 July–28 September 1926: Baden-Baden, Germany—Chelsea, Lon-

	don—Inverness, Scotland [including a trip to Fort William, Mallaig, and the Isle of Skye, 16–18 August]—Mablethorpe and Sutton-on-Sea, Lincolnshire—Hampstead, London. 6–11 April 1927, tours Etruscan sites. 5 August–18 October 1927: Villach, Austria—Irschenhausen and Baden-Baden, Germany. 21 January–6 March 1928, at Château Beau Site, Les Diablerets, Vaud, Switzerland.)
June 1928	Italy: Pisa—Genoa—Turin. France: Chambéry—Aix-les-Bains—Grenoble.
June–July 1928	Switzerland: Grand Hotel, Chexbres-sur-Vevey—Hotel National, Gstaad.
July–September 1928	Kesselmatte, Gsteig bei Gstaad, Bern, Switzerland.
September 1928	Hotel Löwen, Lichtenthal, Baden-Baden, Germany.
October 1928–March 1929	South of France (Var): Grand Hôtel, Le Lavendou—La Vigie, Ile de Port-Cros—Hôtel Beau Rivage, Bandol.
March–April 1929	Mainly at the Hôtel de Versailles, Paris. 7–16 April, to Mallorca via Orleans, Lyons, Carcassonne, Perpignan, and Barcelona.
April–June 1929	Palma de Mallorca, Mallorca, Balearic Islands, Spain. 18–22 June, en route to Lucca, Italy.
June–July 1929	Forte dei Marmi, Lucca, Italy—Florence, Italy.
July–September 1929	Germany: Lichtenthal, Baden-Baden—Kurhaus Plättig, bei Bühl—Kaffee Angermeier, Rottach-am-Tegernsee, near Munich. 18–23, to Bandol, south of France, via Munich and Marseilles.
October 1929–February 1930	Villa Beau Soleil, Bandol, Var, France.
6 February–1 March 1930	Ad Astra Sanatorium, Vence, Alpes-Maritimes, France.
1–2 March 1930	Villa Robermond, Vence.

MAPS: PLACES ASSOCIATED WITH LAWRENCE'S LIFE AND WORKS

The following maps indicate the locations of almost all the places mentioned in this book that are significantly associated with Lawrence's life and works. The word ''locations'' is the operative one here, for these are primarily locational maps, the aim of which is to specify, for general reference purposes, the *posi-*

tions of places in their local, regional, national, or international contexts. The maps, that is, say little or nothing about, for example, the physical nature or size of the places marked or about their social, economic, or political importance (though countries and counties are clearly distinguished from cities, towns, and villages by lettering size, and some rough distinctions of size are also indicated in the contrast between capitalized and lowercase lettering for cities, towns, and villages in the first two maps). Neither are these historical maps, and all borders and boundaries are indicated as they stand today: this is particularly important to note with Map 3, as certain European borders changed quite drastically during the course of Lawrence's lifetime and have changed again since. (Changes in the borders between France and Germany and between Austria and Italy might impinge most directly on our understanding of Lawrence's travel experiences. For the borders as they were in Lawrence's day, see the maps in the Cambridge volumes of Lawrence's *Letters*.)

In cases where it has not proved practical to mark certain places on the maps, I have generally, when referring to such places in the text, specified proximate locations that give a rough indication of their position (e.g., "Questa [not marked], near Taos [marked]"). On the other hand, not *all* places marked on the maps are of relevance to Lawrence (though the majority are); some places he never visited are included simply for general orientation purposes or to provide a general sense of perspective (he never visited Ireland or Cardiff on Map 2, for example, or any of the Eastern European countries marked on Map 3).

Although the maps are intended to be cross-referenced with the text of this book (and especially with Parts I and II), I hope that readers will also find them informative and interesting in their own right as a sort of spatial construction of Lawrence's life and as a suggestive insight into the geographical and cultural wellsprings of his creative imagination. His abiding fascination with what he termed "the spirit of place" is well attested, of course; but, taken together, these maps show very strikingly how far this fascination was fueled—in a relatively short life—by a remarkable range and regularity of movement from place to place and by an extraordinarily energetic willingness on the author's part constantly to reposition the place of his own spirit in the world.

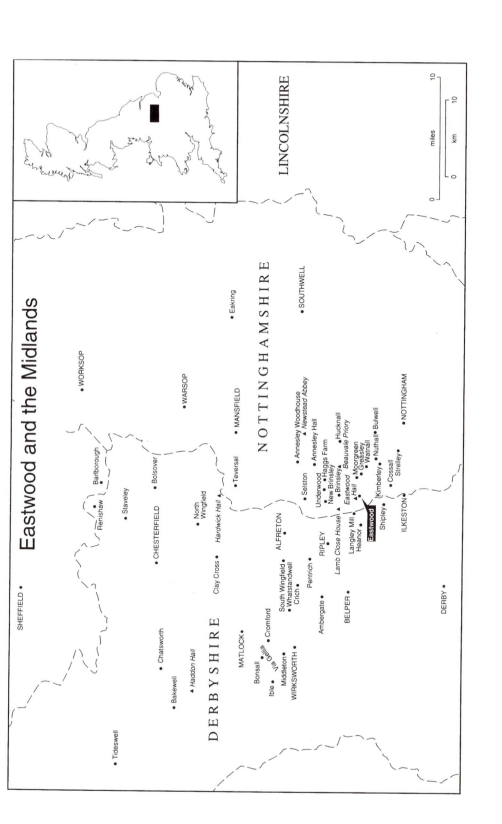

Eastwood and the Midlands

Britain

Key to Counties
1 North Yorkshire
2 West Yorkshire
3 South Yorkshire
4 Derbyshire
5 Nottinghamshire
6 Lincolnshire
7 Oxfordshire
8 Wiltshire
9 Berkshire
10 Hampshire
11 West Sussex
12 East Sussex
13 Kent
14 Cornwall

Hebrides or Western Isles

Isle of Skye

INVERNESS

MALLAIG
FORT WILLIAM

SCOTLAND

EDINBURGH

North

Sea

IRELAND

Irish

Sea

Robin Hood's Bay
SCARBOROUGH
BARROW
Flamborough
LANCASTER YORK
1
BLACKPOOL 2
LEEDS
DONCASTER
PRESTATYN
SHEFFIELD 3
Theddlethorpe
Mablethorpe
Renishaw
Sutton on Sea
6
Middleton 4 Ripley 5 LINCOLN Skegness
Ilkeston Eastwood
DERBY NOTTINGHAM
SHREWSBURY Quorn YARMOUTH
Pontesbury LEICESTER

ENGLAND

CAMBRIDGE

WALES

Upper Lydbrook 7
Forest of OXFORD Chesham
Dean Garsington Hampstead
Pangbourne LONDON
Hermitage
CARDIFF NEWBURY 9 Ewell CROYDON
PURLEY 13
8 10 Edenbridge DOVER
FOLKESTONE
SOUTHAMPTON Pulborough 11 12
BRIGHTON
BOURNEMOUTH Littlehampton FRANCE
Freshwater SHANKLIN
Padstow 14 Isle of
Porthcothan BODMIN Wight
Redruth
Tregerthen TRURO English Channel
Zennor
Lands End
Penzance

Isles of Scilly

Channel Islands

0   miles   50

0   km   80

144

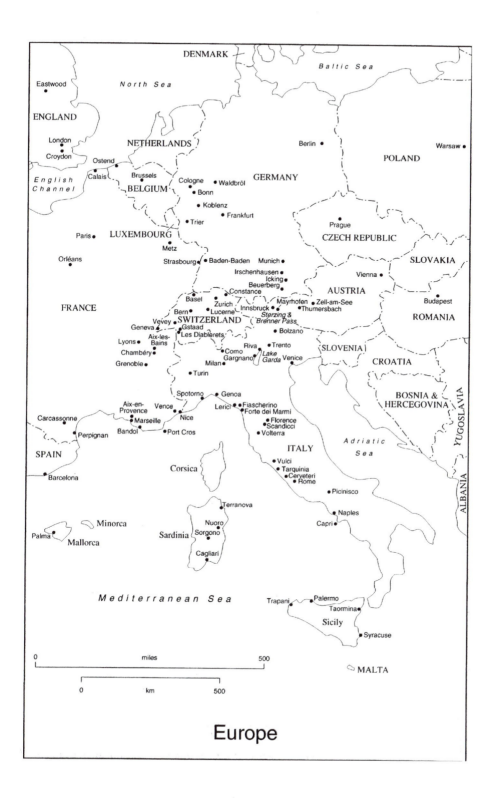

Europe

145

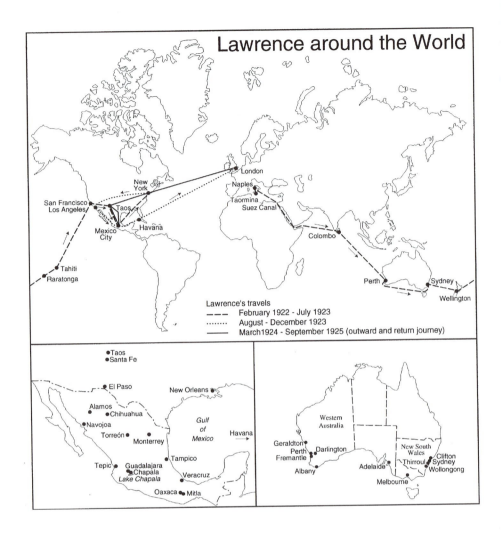

Lawrence around the World

London
New York
Naples
San Francisco
Los Angeles
Taormina
Taos
Suez Canal
Havana
Mexico City
Colombo
Tahiti
Raratonga
Perth
Sydney
Wellington

Lawrence's travels
- - - - February 1922 - July 1923
.... August - December 1923
———— March 1924 - September 1925 (outward and return journey)

Taos
Santa Fe
El Paso
New Orleans
Alamos
Chihuahua
Navojoa
Gulf of Mexico
Havana
Torreón
Monterrey
Tepic
Tampico
Guadalajara
Chapala
Lake Chapala
Veracruz
Oaxaca Mitla

Western Australia
Geraldton
Perth
Darlington
Fremantle
New South Wales
Clifton
Thirroul Sydney
Wollongong
Albany
Adelaide
Melbourne

146

PART II

WORKS

SECTION A

NOVELS

BIBLIOGRAPHY 2: GENERAL CRITICISM OF THE NOVELS

Works listed here deal with all, or a substantial number, of Lawrence's novels together. For ease of reference, the list has been divided between works that look at the novels from a broad perspective designed to provide a general overview and works that pursue a more specialized line of analysis designed to explore a particular dimension to the novels.

GENERAL SURVEYS

Beal, Anthony. *DHL*. Edinburgh: Oliver and Boyd; New York: Grove, 1961.

Becker, George J. *DHL*. New York: Ungar, 1980.

Black, Michael. *DHL: The Early Fiction: A Commentary*. London: Macmillan, 1986.

Daleski, H. M. *The Forked Flame: A Study of DHL*. London: Faber, 1965.

Draper, R. P. *DHL*. New York: Twayne, 1964. (English Authors Series. Reprinted, London: Macmillan, 1976.)

———. *DHL*. London: Routledge and Kegan Paul; New York: Humanities Press, 1969. (Profiles in Literature Series.)

Ford, George H. *Double Measure: A Study of the Novels and Stories of DHL*. New York: Holt, Rinehart, and Winston, 1965.

Hobsbaum, Philip. *A Reader's Guide to Lawrence*. London: Thames and Hudson, 1981.

Holderness, Graham. *DHL: Life, Work, and Criticism*. Fredricton, N.B., Canada: York Press, 1988.

Hough, Graham. *The Dark Sun: A Study of DHL.* London: Gerald Duckworth, 1956.

Hyde, G.M. *DHL.* London: Macmillan, 1990.

Kermode, Frank. *Lawrence.* Suffolk: Collins Fontana, 1973.

Leavis, F. R. *DHL: Novelist.* London: Chatto and Windus, 1955.

Moore, Harry T. *The Life and Works of DHL.* London: Allen and Unwin; New York: Twayne, 1951. (Revised as *DHL: His Life and Works.* New York: Twayne, 1964.)

Moynahan, Julian. *The Deed of Life: The Novels and Tales of DHL.* Princeton: Princeton University Press, 1963.

Niven, Alastair. *DHL: The Novels.* Cambridge: Cambridge University Press, 1978.

———. *DHL: The Writer and His Work.* Harlow, Essex: Longman, 1980.

Pinion, F.B. *A DHL Companion: Life, Thought, and Works.* London: Macmillan, 1978; New York: Barnes and Noble, 1979.

Prasad, Madhusudan. *DHL: A Study of His Novels.* Bereilly, India: Prakesh Book Depot, 1980.

Sagar, Keith. *The Art of DHL.* Cambridge: Cambridge University Press, 1966.

Sanders, Scott. *DHL: The World of the Major Novels.* London: Vision, 1973.

Slade, Tony. *DHL.* London: Evans Brothers, 1969.

Stewart, J.I.M. *Eight Modern Writers* (Oxford History of English Literature, vol. 12). Oxford and New York: Oxford University Press, 1963, pp. 484–593. (Reissued as *Writers of the Early Twentieth Century: Hardy to Lawrence.* Oxford and New York: Oxford University Press, 1990.)

Tedlock, E.W., Jr. *DHL: Artist and Rebel: A Study of Lawrence's Fiction.* Albuquerque: University of New Mexico Press, 1963.

Tripathy, Biyot K. *The Major Novels of DHL: An Approach to His Art and Ideas.* Bhubaneshwar: Pothi, 1973.

Vivas, Eliseo. *DHL: The Failure and the Triumph of Art.* London: George Allen and Unwin, 1960.

West, Anthony. *DHL.* London: Barker; Denver: Alan Swallow, 1950.

Worthen, John. *DHL and the Idea of the Novel.* London: Macmillan; Totowa, N.J.: Rowman, 1979.

———. *DHL.* London: Edward Arnold, 1991. (Modern Fiction Series.)

Young, Kenneth. *DHL.* London, New York, Toronto: Longmans, Green, 1952. (Writers and Their Work Series.)

Yudhishtar. *Conflict in the Novels of DHL.* Edinburgh: Oliver and Boyd; New York: Barnes and Noble, 1969.

SPECIALIZED APPROACHES

Bell, Michael. *DHL: Language and Being.* Cambridge: Cambridge University Press, 1992.

Ben-Ephraim, Gavriel. *The Moon's Dominion: Narrative Dichotomy and Female Dominance in Lawrence's Earlier Novels.* London and Toronto: Associated University Presses, 1981.

Buckley, Margaret, and Brian Buckley. *Challenge and Renewal: Lawrence and the Thematic Novel.* Kenilworth, Warwickshire: Chrysalis Press, 1993.

Cavitch, David. *DHL and the New World.* New York and London: Oxford University Press, 1969.

Clark, L. D. *The Minoan Distance: The Symbolism of Travel in DHL.* Tucson: University of Arizona Press, 1980.

Cowan, James C. *DHL's American Journey: A Study in Literature and Myth.* Cleveland, Ohio, and London: Press of the Case Western Reserve University, 1970.

Dorbad, Leo J. *Sexually Balanced Relationships in the Novels of DHL.* New York: Peter Lang, 1991.

Goodheart, Eugene. *The Utopian Vision of DHL.* Chicago and London: University of Chicago Press, 1963.

Gregory, Horace. *Pilgrim of the Apocalypse: A Critical Study of DHL.* New York: Viking, 1933; London: Secker, 1934. (Revised as *DHL: Pilgrim of the Apocalypse.* New York: Grove, 1957.)

Hochman, Baruch. *Another Ego: The Changing View of Self and Society in the Work of DHL.* Columbia: University of South Carolina Press, 1970.

Holderness, Graham. *DHL: History, Ideology and Fiction.* Dublin: Gill and Macmillan, 1982.

Howe, Marguerite Beede. *The Art of the Self in DHL.* Athens: University of Ohio Press, 1977.

Humma, John B. *Metaphor and Meaning in DHL's Later Novels.* Columbia: University of Missouri Press, 1990.

MacLeod, Sheila. *Lawrence's Men and Women.* London: Heinemann, 1985; London: Grafton Books, 1987.

Miko, Stephen J. *Toward "Women in Love": The Emergence of a Lawrentian Aesthetic.* New Haven, Conn., and London: Yale University Press, 1971.

Nahal, Chaman. *DHL: An Eastern View.* South Brunswick and New York: Barnes, 1970.

Padhi, Bibhu. *DHL: Modes of Fictional Style.* Troy, N.Y.: Whitston, 1989.

Pinkney, Tony. *DHL.* Hemel Hempstead: Harvester Wheatsheaf, 1990. (Published in the United States as *DHL and Modernism.* Iowa City: University of Iowa Press, 1990.)

Prasad, Suman Prabha. *Thomas Hardy and DHL: A Study of the Tragic Vision in Their Novels.* New Delhi, India: Arnold-Heinemann, 1976.

Pritchard, R. E. *DHL: Body of Darkness.* London: Hutchinson University Library, 1971.

Ruderman, Judith. *DHL and the Devouring Mother: The Search for a Patriarchal Ideal of Leadership.* Durham, N.C.: Duke University Press, 1984.

Sagar, Keith. *DHL: Life into Art.* Harmondsworth: Penguin; New York: Viking, 1985.

Scheckner, Peter. *Class, Politics, and the Individual: A Study of the Major Works of DHL.* London and Toronto: Associated University Presses, 1985.

Schneider, Daniel J. *DHL: The Artist as Psychologist.* Lawrence: University Press of Kansas, 1984.

Spilka, Mark. *The Love Ethic of DHL.* London: Dennis Dobson, 1958.

Stoll, John E. *The Novels of DHL: A Search for Integration.* Columbia: University of Missouri Press, 1971.

Storch, Margaret. *Sons and Adversaries: Women in William Blake and DHL.* Knoxville: University of Tennessee Press, 1990.

Templeton, Wayne. *States of Estrangement: The Novels of DHL, 1912–1917.* Troy, N.Y.: Whitston, 1989.

Verhoeven, W. M. *DHL's Duality Concept: Its Development in the Novels of the Early and Major Phase.* Groningen, the Netherlands: Phoenix, 1987.

Weiss, Daniel. *Oedipus in Nottingham: DHL.* Seattle: University of Washington Press, 1962.

11   *The White Peacock*

WRITTEN

Easter 1906–September 1910. Drafts: 1. "Laetitia" I, Easter 1906–June 1907. 2. "Laetitia" II, July 1907–April 1908. 3. "Nethermere" I, Autumn 1908–November 1909. 4. "Nethermere" II, January–April 1910. Proof revision of *The White Peacock,* August–September, 1910, with some late changes for the British edition in December.

PUBLISHED

1. New York: Duffield, 19 January 1911. London: Heinemann, 20 January 1911.
2. Edited by Andrew Robertson. Cambridge: Cambridge University Press, 1983.
3. See also under Moore (1966) and Worthen (1982) in the following bibliography.

WHO'S WHO AND SUMMARY

MAIN CHARACTERS: Lettice (Lettie) Beardsall, George Saxton, Leslie Tempest; Cyril Beardsall, Emily Saxton; Frank Annable

Cyril Beardsall, the young first-person narrator of the novel. Though directly involved in the story, he remains ill defined and insubstantial as a character. Indeed, his self-conscious questioning of his own identity and his attendant sense of alienation and loss determine the wistful, melancholic mood of the novel. He and his sister, *Lettie,* have had a genteel, middle-class upbringing at Nethermere; they are cultivated, articulate, and sensitive to both art and nature. But a dissatisfaction with their lives gradually makes itself felt, and at the end of the novel neither of them finds fulfillment in love. Cyril is ineffectual in his courtship of Emily Saxton, who eventually marries someone else. Lettie, prone to snobbishness and affectation, ultimately resists her passionate physical attraction to the farmer's son, George Saxton, in order to marry the socially more eligible Leslie Tempest, with whom she has a comfortable but limited life of conventional domesticity.

George Saxton, a laborer on his father's farm: strong, dark, and full of instinctive animal vitality, he is frequently shown working in harmony with the rhythms of nature. At the same time, he initially appears—especially to Lettie, despite her strong attraction to him—uneducated and insensitive, even crude; but through his friendship with Cyril and his love for Lettie, he develops a more refined sensibility as the novel progresses. Following his rejection by Lettie, however, he strikes up a relationship with the sensuous *Meg*—the publican's daughter at the Ram Inn—whom he then marries. Though physically fulfilling to begin with, the marriage rapidly deteriorates as George laments what he has lost in Lettie. He loses his vitality, drifts into alcoholism, and ends in a physically dissipated state.

Emily Saxton, George's sister, a schoolteacher and, to begin with, Cyril's girlfriend. She is emotional and instinctive like her brother, but more refined. Somewhat unsure of herself and intensely serious, she appears to Cyril as a brooding, sorrowful, Pre-Raphaelite type of woman, with troubled shadows always in her eyes. However, toward the end of the novel, some ten years after the main period dealt with, Cyril meets her again; she has gained greatly in self-confidence and seems freer and at ease with herself. She is also engaged to be married to *Tom Renshaw,* an ex-soldier and now a farmer.

Leslie Tempest, the urbane, rich son of a local mine-owning family (loosely based on the actual Barber family of Eastwood who lived at Lambclose House: Tempest, Warrall and Co. is a re-creation of Barber, Walker and Co.). His slightly mannered courtship of Lettie seems in jeopardy once George comes on the scene, but, despite suggestions of incompatibility between them, Leslie and Lettie do finally marry.

Frank Annable, the gamekeeper of the Nethermere estate and a somewhat crude early Lawrentian spokesman for the natural life of the body and the instincts. Following his failed marriage to the socially superior *Lady Crystabel,* he hates anything to do with culture and civilization (he had earlier been a student at Cambridge and then a parson) and lives in isolation in the woods with his second wife and an unruly brood of children, *Billy, Jack, Sam,* and *Sarah Anne.* Annable is hated by the locals, who see him as "a devil of the woods," but Cyril befriends him, drawn by his great vitality and his "magnificent physique." A few days after their meeting in the churchyard when they witness the white peacock on the headstone (Part 2, Ch. 2), Cyril finds Annable dead at the bottom of a quarry; the death seems to have been caused by an accidental rockfall, but there are suggestions that it may have been some sort of revenge killing by one of the locals. Annable's funeral is described in terms of a joyous celebration of nature.

Other Characters

Mrs. Beardsall, the mother of Cyril and Lettie. *Mr. Frank Beardsall,* their father: he had abandoned the family when the children were infants, and he reappears briefly, physically wasted, in disguise and under a false name (*French Carlin,* Part I, Ch 4)—he dies shortly afterward at his gloomy lodgings, *Mrs. May*'s "Yew Cottage." *Rebecca,* the Beardsalls' maid.

Mr. Saxton, the head of the Saxton family, a large, good-natured, and jovial farmer. His wife, *Mrs. Saxton,* small, soft-spoken, and motherly. Their two younger children, *Mollie,* aged twelve, and the infant, *David.* (The Saxton family is largely modeled on the family of Jessie Chambers, the intimate friend of Lawrence's youth—see Chapters 1 and 2 of the biography in this book and, for brief details of the Chambers family, under the Who's Who for *Sons and Lovers* under the Leivers family.) *Annie,* maid to the Saxton family.

Marie Tempest, Leslie's sister, a neat, "charming little maid," gentle and serious. *Hilda Slaighter,* a garrulous spinster, acquaintance of the Beardsalls. *Alice Gall,* friend to the Beardsalls and Saxtons and popular at social gatherings for her liveliness; though often outrageous in her behavior, she is "upright" at heart and eventually marries the pious *Percival Charles. Tom Mayhew,* the son of a bankrupt, horse-dealing family to whose house George goes drinking and gambling when his marriage starts to fail. *Maud Mayhew,* Tom's sister. Meg's *Grandmother* at the Ram. *Arthur Renshaw,* brother of Tom Renshaw, who marries Emily.

Guests at Lettie's twenty-first birthday party (Part I, Ch. 9): *Will Bancroft,* a singer and an old college friend of Lettie's; *Tom Smith,* a scientist; *Madie Howitt.* Leslie Tempest's elegant wedding guests who picnic in the Strelley hayfields (Part II, Ch. 9): *Freddy Cresswell,* Leslie's best man; *Agnes D'Arcy, Louis Denys, Hilda Seconde.*

SETTING

The setting of the novel is based on the Nottinghamshire countryside around Lawrence's hometown, Eastwood ("Eberwich" in the novel): the area he called "the country of my heart." The novel focuses specifically on the area just north of Eastwood near to the Haggs farm, Underwood ("Selsby"), home of the Chambers family, who, in the form of the Saxtons, have been transplanted to "Strelley Mill Farm," which is modeled on Felley Mill farm, just to the East of the Haggs farm. "Nethermere" is a re-creation of Moorgreen Reservoir,

"Highclose" of Lambclose House, "The Hall" of Annesley Hall, "The Abbey" of Beauvale Priory, and "Woodside" of Beauvale Lodge. "Graymede" is based on Greasley, just to the east of Eastwood. Nottingham and its environs are described in detail. "Norwood," a suburb of South London, to which Cyril moves in Part III of the novel, is presumably based on Croydon, where Lawrence lived between October 1908 and January 1912. Central London features in more detail in Chapter 5 of Part III, when George Saxton meets up with Cyril there, and they go to dinner in Hampstead with Lettie and Leslie Tempest.

BIBLIOGRAPHY 3

Ben-Ephraim, Gavriel. "The Pastoral Fallacy: Tale and Teller in DHL's *The White Peacock.*" *Literary Review* 19 (Summer 1976): 406–31. (Reprinted in Ben-Ephraim [1981]: 31–60.)

Black, Michael. "A Bit of Both: George Eliot and DHL." *Critical Review* (Canberra) 29 (1989): 89–109.

Brown, Christopher. "As Cyril Likes It: Pastoral Reality and Illusion in *The White Peacock.*" *Essays in Literature* 6 (1979): 187–93.

Corke, Helen. "Concerning *The White Peacock.*" *Texas Quarterly* 2 (Winter 1959): 186–90. (Reprinted in Corke [1965]: 47–55.)

Daleski, H. M. "Lawrence and George Eliot: The Genesis of *The White Peacock.*" In *DHL and Tradition.* Edited by Jeffrey Meyers. London: Athlone, 1985, pp. 51–68.

Gajdusek, Robert E. "A Reading of *The White Peacock.*" In *A DHL Miscellany.* Edited by Harry T. Moore. Carbondale: Southern Illinois University Press, 1959, pp. 188–203.

———. "A Reading of 'A Poem of Friendship,' a Chapter in Lawrence's *The White Peacock.*" *DHL Review* 3 (Spring 1970): 47–62.

Gu, Ming Dong. "Lawrence's Childhood Traumas and the Problematic Form of *The White Peacock.*" *DHL Review* 24 (1992): 127–44.

Hinz, Evelyn J. "Juno and *The White Peacock:* Lawrence's English Epic." *DHL Review* 3 (Summer 1970): 115–35.

Keith, W. J. "DHL's *The White Peacock:* An Essay in Criticism." *University of Toronto Quarterly* 37 (April 1968): 230–47.

McCurdy, Harold G. "Literature and Personality: Analysis of the Novels of DHL." *Character and Personality* 8 (March, June 1940): 181–203, 311–22 (182–90).

Mason, H. A. "DHL and *The White Peacock.*" *Cambridge Quarterly* 7, no 3 (1977): 216–31.

Miliaras, Barbara Langell. "Fashion, Art and the Leisure Class in D. H. Lawrence's *The White Peacock.*" *The Journal of the D. H. Lawrence Society* (1994–95): 67–81.

Modiano, Marko. "Symbolism, Characterization, and Setting in *The White Peacock,* by DHL." *Moderna Språk* (Stockholm) 77 (1983): 345–52.

Moore, Harry T. "Introduction." *The White Peacock* by DHL. Edited by Harry T. Moore. Carbondale: Southern Illinois University Press, 1966, pp. v–viii.

Morrison, Kristin. "Lawrence, Beardsley, Wilde: *The White Peacock* and Sexual Ambiguity." *Western Humanities Review* 30 (1976): 241–48.

Orr, Christopher. "DHL and E. M. Forster: From *The White Peacock* to *Maurice.*" *West Virginia Association of College English Teachers Bulletin* 2 (Fall 1975): 22–28.

Osgerby, J. R. "Set Books: DHL's *The White Peacock.*" *Use of English* 13 (Summer 1962): 256–61.

Parker, David. "*The White Peacock:* Young Lawrence." *Meridian: The La Trobe University English Review* (Australia) 7 (1988): 116–28.

Richards, Bernard. "A Botanical Mistake in Lawrence's *The White Peacock.*" *Notes and Queries* 36 (June 1989): 202.

Robertson, Andrew. "Introduction." *The White Peacock* by DHL. Edited by Andrew Robertson. Cambridge: Cambridge University Press, 1983, pp. xv–xlix.

Schneider, Daniel J. "Psychology and Art in *The White Peacock* and *The Trespasser.*" In *DHL: Modern Critical Views.* Edited by Harold Bloom. New York: Chelsea, 1986, pp. 275–96.

Sepčić, Višnja. "*The White Peacock* Reconsidered." *Studia Romanica et Anglica Zagrabiensia* 38 (December 1974): 105–14.

Sproles, Karyn Z. "DHL and the Schizoid State: Reading *Sons and Lovers* through *The White Peacock.*" *Paunch* 63–64 (December 1990): 39–70.

Squires, Michael. "Lawrence's *The White Peacock:* A Mutation of Pastoral." *Texas Studies in Literature and Language* 12 (Summer 1970): 263–83. (Reprinted in Squires [1974]: 174–95.)

Stanford, Raney. "Thomas Hardy and Lawrence's *The White Peacock.*" *Modern Fiction Studies* 5 (1959): 19–28.

Storch, Margaret. "The Lacerated Male: Ambivalent Images of Women in *The White Peacock.*" *DHL Review* 21 (1989): 17–36.

Utz, Joachim. "Dante Gabriel Rossetti's 'The Blessed Damozel.' " *Archiv für das Studium der Neueren Sprachen und Literaturen* 218 (1981): 59–75.

Worthen, John. "Introduction." *The White Peacock* by DHL. Edited by Alan Newton. Harmondsworth: Penguin, 1982, pp. 11–33.

See also (1980–94) Bell (1992): 14–24. Black (1986): 41–77. Burns (1980): 30–35. Ebbatson (1980): 44–60. Hardy and Harris (1985): 138–41. Herzinger (1982): 32–33, 76–86. Holderness (1982): 95–115. Hyde (1990): 21–23. Ingram (1990): 27–34. Kiely (1980): 150–56. Kushigian (1990): 9–33. MacLeod (1985–87): 118–35. Miliaras (1987): 33–93. Milton (1987): 1–18, 22–35, 68–74. Modiano (1987): 51–56. Montgomery (1994): 43–72. Niven (1980): 23–27. Padhi (1989): 11–15, 17–25. Pinkney (1990): 12–27. Poplawski (1993): 55–57. Prasad (1980): 6–21. Robinson (1992): 128–30. Schneider (1984): 111–19. Siegel (1991): 56–65. Simpson (1982): 25–26, 51–53. Storch (1990): 45–64. Suter (1987): 49–57. Verhoeven (1987): 5–27. Worthen (1991a): 7–13. Worthen (1991b): 224–29, passim.

See also (to 1979) Albright (1978): 34–39, 59–63. Alcorn (1977): 78–81. Alldritt (1971): 4–15. Beal (1961): 4–11. Brunsdale (1978): 165–77. Coombes (1973): 62–63. Daleski (1965): 312–15. Draper (1970): 33–43; (1976): 30–33. Ford (1965): 47–55, 57–60. Freeman (1955): 20–29. Hough (1956): 23–34. Inniss (1971): 108–16. Littlewood (1976): 20–27. Meyers (1975): 46–52. Moore (1951): 38–49, passim. Moynahan (1963): 5–12.

Murfin (1978): 187–98. Murry (1931): 22–30. Nahal (1970): 55–76. Niven (1978): 1–26. Pinion (1978): 127–34. Prasad (1976): 126–36. Stewart (1963): 487–92. Stoll (1971): 16–41. Tedlock (1963): 40–49. West (1950): 106–111. Worthen (1979): 1–14. Yudhishtar (1969): 58–73.

12   The Trespasser

WRITTEN

March 1910–February 1912. Proofs corrected in April 1912.
Draft versions: 1. ''The Saga of Siegmund,'' March–August 1910. 2. *The Trespasser,* 30 December–February 1912.

PUBLISHED

1. London: Duckworth; New York: Kennerley, May 1912.
2. Edited by Elizabeth Mansfield. Cambridge: Cambridge University Press, 1981.
3. See also under Turner (1994) in the following bibliography.

WHO'S WHO AND SUMMARY

MAIN CHARACTERS: Helena Verden, Siegmund MacNair; Cecil Byrne
   Siegmund MacNair, a music teacher and violinist with a London orchestra. He is married to *Beatrice,* and they have five children, *Frank, Vera, Irene, Marjory,* and *Gwen.* Unhappy in his marriage, however, he has begun a relationship with one of his pupils, *Helena Verden,* and the main part of the novel deals with their week's holiday together on the Isle of Wight. This is only partially successful, as Helena finds herself unable fully to reciprocate Siegmund's physical passion for her: she belongs, apparently, to that class of ''dreaming woman'' for whom passion is exhausted at the mouth, in a kiss.

Nevertheless, Siegmund experiences a vitalizing intensification of his life with Helena, a brief but passionate ecstasy that prevents him from accepting any simple return to the mundane routines of his previous life and of his loveless marriage. On his return, he despairs of the future and, unable to resolve the conflicting pressures of his love for Helena and his sense of duty to his family, he hangs himself. Beatrice is horrified at this, but, partly for the children and partly for her own self-defense against "the accusation of the dead," she tries to avoid the full impact of the event: she controls her grief, avoids thinking of Siegmund, and allows his memory to fade quickly. Helena, on the other hand, becomes obsessed with Siegmund's memory and seems unable or unwilling to escape from the experience of their romantic island idyll. She feels totally forlorn by his loss and as if, within herself, she, too, has died or come to some sort of psychic standstill. At the start of the novel, in February, six months after the trip to the Isle of Wight, and again at the end, in the following July, *Cecil Byrne,* Helena's friend and would-be lover, is still trying to rouse her from this state of morbid emotional arrest—an arrest symbolized by the uncanny persistence of her sunburn from the year before.

(The character of Helena is based on Helen Corke [1882–1978], a schoolteacher Lawrence became intimate with while he was teaching in Croydon between October 1908 and November 1911. The novel is largely based on her real-life affair with Herbert Baldwin Macartney [1870–1909], a violinist with the Covent Garden Orchestra and Helen Corke's music teacher and was first inspired by Lawrence's reading of her account of the affair in her "Freshwater Diary," printed as an appendix in her *In Our Infancy,* as well as in the Cambridge and the 1994 Penguin editions of the text.)

Other Characters

Louisa and *Olive,* Helena's friends. *Mrs. Curtiss,* the landlady of the holiday cottage on the Isle of Wight. *Hampson,* a past musical acquaintance of Siegmund's whom he bumps into on the Isle of Wight (Ch. 13): they talk about love and life, and Hampson seems strangely to give expression to Siegmund's deepest feelings, so that he later describes Hampson to Helena as "a sort of Doppelgänger." *Mr. Allport, Mr. Holiday,* and *Mr. MacWhirter* are all boarders at the lodging house Beatrice establishes after Siegmund's death. *Mr. and Mrs. Verden,* Helena's parents. *Mr. and Mrs. Walton,* Beatrice's parents.

SETTING

The main part of the novel is set around Freshwater on the Isle of Wight and is framed at either end by scenes in London and its suburbs (Siegmund lives at Wimbledon, and Helena at Croydon, both in South London; at the end of the novel, Siegmund's wife, Beatrice, moves with the family to Highgate in North London). After her trip with Siegmund, Helena briefly goes on holiday with two women friends to Tintagel in Cornwall, and the first half of Chapter 29 is set there.

BIBLIOGRAPHY 4

Atkins, A. R. "Recognising the 'Stranger' in DHL's *The Trespasser.*" *Cambridge Quarterly* 20 (1991): 1–20.

———. "Textual Influences on DHL's 'The Saga of Siegmund.' " *DHL Review* 24 (1992): 7–26 (includes two appendixes from Helen Corke's "The Freshwater Diary," pp. 17–26).

Blissett, William. "DHL, D'Annunzio, Wagner." *Wisconsin Studies in Contemporary Literature* 7 (Winter–Spring 1966): 21–46.

Corke, Helen. *DHL: The Croydon Years.* Austin: University of Texas Press, 1965.

———. "DHL and the Dreaming Woman." *Listener* 80 (25 July 1968): 104–7. (Summary of the transcript of a BBC television interview with Malcolm Muggeridge, July 1967.)

———. "DHL: The Early Stage." *DHL Review* 4 (Summer 1971): 111–21.

———. "The Writing of *The Trespasser.*" *DHL Review* 7 (Fall 1974): 227–39.

———. *In Our Infancy.* Cambridge: Cambridge University Press, 1975.

Digaetani, John Louis. "Situational Myths: Richard Wagner and DHL." In his *Richard Wagner and the Modern British Novel.* Rutherford, N.J.: Fairleigh Dickinson University Press; London: Associated University Presses, 1978, pp. 58–89 (66–77).

Furness, Raymond. "Wagner and Myth." In his *Wagner and Literature.* Manchester: Manchester University Press; New York: St. Martin's Press, 1982, pp. 79–107.

Gurko, Leo. "*The Trespasser:* DHL's Neglected Novel." *College English* 24 (October 1962): 29–35.

Heath, Jane. "Helen Corke and DHL: Sexual Identity and Literary Relations." *Feminist Studies* 11 (Summer 1985): 317–42.

Hinz, Evelyn J. "*The Trespasser:* Lawrence's Wagnerian Tragedy and Divine Comedy." *DHL Review* 4 (Summer 1971): 122–41.

Howarth, Herbert. "DHL from Island to Glacier." *University of Toronto Quarterly* 37 (April 1968): 215–29.

Kestner, Joseph. "The Literary Wagnerism of DHL's *The Trespasser.*" *Modern British Literature* 2 (Fall 1977): 123–38.

Mansfield, Elizabeth. "Introduction." *The Trespasser* by DHL. Edited by Elizabeth Mansfield. Cambridge: Cambridge University Press, 1981, pp. 3–37.

Millett, Robert. "Greater Expectations: DHL's *The Trespasser.*" In *Twenty-Seven to One.* Edited by Bradford D. Broughton. Ogdensburg, N.Y.: Ryan Press, 1970, pp. 125–32.

Nielsen, Inge Padkaer, and Karsten Hvidtfelt Nielsen. "The Modernism of DHL and the Discourses of Decadence: Sexuality and Tradition in *The Trespasser, Fantasia of the Unconscious,* and *Aaron's Rod.*" *Arcadia* 25, no. 3 (1990): 270–86.

Schneider, Daniel J. "Psychology and Art in *The White Peacock* and *The Trespasser.*" In *DHL: Modern Critical Views.* Edited by Harold Bloom. New York: Chelsea, 1986, pp. 275–96.

Sepčić, Višnja. "A Link between DHL's *The Trespasser* and *The Rainbow.*" *Studia Romanica et Anglica,* no. 24 (December 1967): 113–26.

Sharpe, Michael C. "The Genesis of DHL's *The Trespasser.*" *Essays in Criticism* 11 (January 1961): 34–39.

Steele, Bruce. "The Manuscript of DHL's *Saga of Siegmund.*" *Studies in Bibliography* 33 (1980): 193–205.

Trotter, David. "Edwardian Sex Novels." *Critical Quarterly* 31 (1989): 92–106.

Turner, John. "Introduction." *The Trespasser* by DHL. Edited by Elizabeth Mansfield. Harmondsworth: Penguin, 1994, pp. 11–36.

Van der Veen, Berend Klass. *The Development of DHL's Prose Themes, 1906–1915.* Groningen, Netherlands: University of Groningen, 1983.

Wright, Louise. "Lawrence's *The Trespasser:* Its Debt to Reality." *Texas Studies in Literature and Language* 20 (Summer 1978): 230–48.

Zuckerman, Elliott. "Wagnerizing on the Isle of Wight." In his *The First Hundred Years of Wagner's Tristan.* New York and London: Columbia University Press, 1964, pp. 124–27, and passim.

See also (1980–94) Bell (1992): 25–36. Ben-Ephraim (1981): 61–83. Black (1986): 78–110. Ebbatson (1980): 60–66. Herzinger (1982): passim. Hobsbaum (1981): 45–46. Holderness (1982): 116–29. Hyde (1990): 25–30. Kiely (1980): 18–20, 23–29. Niven (1980): 27–32. Pinkney (1990): 54–60. Poplawski (1993): 59–63. Prasad (1980): 21–30. Schneider (1984): 119–32. Simpson (1982): 53–54, 152–54. Suter (1987): 57–59. Templeton (1989): 15–57. Verhoeven (1987): 29–47. Worthen (1991a): 13–18. Worthen (1991b): 253–62, 332–34, passim.

See also (to 1979) Beal (1961): 11–14. Brunsdale (1978): 241–53. Clark (1980): 20–23. Draper (1964): 33–37. Draper (1970): 44–50. Eisenstein (1974): 32–42. Freeman (1955): 30–35. Hough (1956): 34–35. Littlewood (1976): 27–30. Miko (1971): 35–58. Moore (1951): 82–87. Niven (1978): 27–36. Pinion (1978): 134–39. Prasad (1976): 137–46. Stoll (1971): 42–61. Tedlock (1963): 49–54. Worthen (1979): 15–25. Yudishtar (1969): 73–82.

13   Sons and Lovers

WRITTEN

October 1910–November 1912. Proofs, February–March 1913. Draft versions (first three as "Paul Morel"): 1. October 1910–November 1910. 2. March 1911–July 1911. 3. November 1911–June 1912. 4. July 1912–November 1912.

PUBLISHED

1. London: Duckworth, May 1913. New York: Kennerley, September 1913.
2. Edited by Carl and Helen Baron. Cambridge: Cambridge University Press, 1992.
3. *DHL: "Sons and Lovers": A Facsimile of the Manuscript.* Edited by Mark Schorer. Berkeley, Los Angeles, London: University of California Press, 1977. See also under Baron and Baron (1994), Daly (1994), Sagar (1981), and Trotter (1995) in the following bibliography.

WHO'S WHO AND SUMMARY

MAIN CHARACTERS: Walter and Gertrude Morel, Paul Morel, Miriam Leivers, Clara Dawes

Paul Morel provides, eventually, the novel's main focus of interest as we trace in detail his intellectual, emotional, and sexual formation from childhood to the age of about twenty-five—though this personal focus is strongly contextualized in terms of both the other members of his family (the life and relationship of his parents in particular) and the working-class society and natural environment of the Nottinghamshire mining country. The first part of the novel—roughly a third of it—is devoted to a largely naturalistic re-creation of this society and environment, with the early married life of the Morels and the day-to-day routines of the Morel household, in general, providing the specific focus.

As a young man, *Walter Morel* is a handsome, exuberant figure, full of life and fun, and popular in the local community for his cheerful and friendly spontaneity and for his reputation as a good dancer (he had run a dancing class for five years before marrying Gertrude). *Gertrude Morel,* who has been brought up by a stern, high-minded, and puritanical father, *George Coppard,* an engineer from an old lace-manufacturing family, is initially attracted (when she is twenty-three, and Walter twenty-seven) by his natural warmth of manner and his physical vigor and vitality, his "sensuous flame of life." However, Walter had begun work down the pit when he was ten years old and has received little formal education. His wife, by contrast, has had a good education and likes nothing more than intellectual converse on matters of religion, philosophy, or politics. Beyond their original physical passion for one another, she soon realizes that there can be no "finer intimacy" between them; added to their constantly straitened circumstances and cramped living conditions, this leads her to feel she has married beneath her. Moreover, within Walter's easy spontaneity there lies also a streak of reckless irresponsibility, manifested by his mocking attitude to his managers at the pit (which contributes to his losing some of the better "stalls"), but most damagingly by his return to drink (he had briefly become a teetotaler) and his increasingly ill-tempered and bullying treatment of his wife and children. He has violent quarrels both with his wife and, later, with his sons. Eventually, Gertrude "casts off" Walter and possessively "takes on," as types of substitute "lover," first her eldest boy child, William and, after William's untimely death, her second son, Paul. She tries to ensure that their lives will be better than her husband's, and she pushes them to escape their working-class environment through education and professional work. Inevitably, too, this turns her sons against their father and creates further tensions in the household as Walter feels himself being marginalized in his own home. Although the narrative seems largely to take the part of Gertrude in the conflict with her husband, a sense of balance emerges as we become aware of her rigid and often harshly moralistic attitude toward Walter—"she was almost a fanatic with him"—as well as her emotionally manipulative and self-serving use of the children. There are moments of renewed tenderness between husband and wife and between father and children, but these become fewer as the novel progresses and as the focus shifts decisively from the unhappy domestic drama to a largely psychological exploration of the early life and experiences of Paul Morel.

Paul Morel is a sensitive but sickly child who develops a strong bond with his mother when, immediately after the death of his brother, he, too, nearly dies, when he is sixteen. After this, his mother becomes the dominant influence in his life, and, in many ways, the novel centers on the inevitable problems this gives rise to in his development as he enters into relationships with other women and as he later has to face up to an independent life separate from his mother. He does well at school and develops a talent for painting that later leads to a determination to become an artist. When he leaves school at fourteen, however, he finds employment as a clerk at Jordan's Surgical Appliance Factory in Nottingham, and he continues to work here for the remainder of the novel.

The major relationship explored in the novel, apart from that of Paul and his mother, is that between Paul and *Miriam Leivers.* Paul meets Miriam first when he is sixteen, and they find themselves drawn together by a mutual interest in art, literature, and ideas. Their intimacy develops into a romantic one, and they become sweethearts. However, the movement toward a full sexual relationship is fraught with tension: Paul seems unable to relate to Miriam sexually in any unequivocal way—his powerful allegiance to his mother will not allow him to give Miriam his soul *and* body, but his respect for Miriam will not allow him (at first) to offer his body *without* his soul; while, for her part, Miriam seems sexually repressed and, in any case, reluctant to risk sex before marriage. Paul does force the issue eventually, and Miriam does "sacrifice" herself to his sexual desire; but the experience simply confirms his sense of their sexual incompatibility, and, quite callously, he decides to end their relationship almost immediately. Paul now throws himself more fully into his developing relationship with *Clara Dawes,* an older married woman who works with him at Jordan's. With her, he feels less constrained by any soul-attachment, and through their passionate lovemaking he at last discovers a more integrated sense of his sexual self. However, this affair ends when Clara is reconciled with her husband; and, with the death of Paul's mother at the end of the novel, Paul is left alone and desolate, once more disoriented as to his place in the universe—in "the vastness and terror of the immense night"—and as to his own inner meaning, for he feels "at the core a nothingness." Yet, though unable at present to assimilate these fully, he has made genuine advances and discoveries in each of his three primary relationships, and these sustain him in his turn from the dark of the night to the light (and life) of the town, for, finally, he is "not nothing."

Miriam Leivers, Paul's boyhood sweetheart, soul-companion, and, later, briefly, his lover, lives on a farm with her family but is constantly imagining a more elevated and romantic life for herself. She finds escape from the common drudgery of her daily life through art and literature and through the new ideas and feelings she explores in her relationship with Paul. Although extremely sensitive, idealistic, and spiritual and apparently somewhat repressed sexually, partly as a result of her mother's puritanical attitudes, she develops into a beautiful and sexually alluring woman who, in many ways, belies Paul's defensive attempts at categorizing her as an asexual "nun" who cannot accept *his* sexual being. Miriam later succeeds in her ambition of becoming independent and earning her own living as a teacher.

Clara Dawes, a confident, forthright woman who has recently become estranged from her rough blacksmith husband, Baxter Dawes, and who is active in the suffragette movement when Paul first meets her. Where Miriam is physically quite small and dark and temperamentally shy, spiritual, and romantic, Clara is large, blonde, bluntly assertive, and down-to-earth; sensuous and sexually unconstrained, she appeals to Paul's bodily desire where Miriam appeals to his artist's soul.

Although, at first, *Baxter Dawes* is presented as a surly and aggressive man with few redeeming features, Paul later strikes up a strangely sympathetic relationship with him, and we then see a more tender and more vulnerable side to his character. He is the opposite of Paul, and, as an uneducated laboring man, he, in some ways, represents a mirror image of Walter Morel. Paul's fight with him and their subsequent friendship can thus be seen as a symbolic working out and realignment of Paul's attitudes to his own father; when he then brings Clara to be reunited with Baxter, this, too, can be seen as a symbolic reinstatement of the father as the mother's true lover.

Other Characters

William, the eldest Morel child, becomes his mother's pride and joy and her main source of hope in life as her marriage starts to fail. Lively, athletic, popular, intelligent, and hardworking, he "gets on" rapidly in his career, starting as a clerk at the Bestwood Co-Operative Society office (and continuing to study and to tutor students at home), moving on to a situation in Nottingham, then, at twenty, to a well-paid post in a lawyer's office in London. However, here he begins to overstretch himself, in work and study, in social life—trying to keep up with the "swanky" set he becomes involved with—and in love. He becomes engaged to a beautiful but shallow "lady"—*Louisa Lily Denys Western,* or "Gipsy." Empty-headed, vain, and affected, she soon starts to grate on his nerves. He twice brings her home from London on holiday, and she treats the Morel family in a condescending, "queenly" manner. William comes, in some ways, to hate her, and he complains about her bitterly to his mother—who is her exact opposite—but in other ways he seems to need her, and he cannot bring himself to break off the engagement. Worn down by work and by his emotional turmoil over Lily, he succumbs to pneumonia and a complicating disease, erysipelas, and dies at the age of twenty-three. He proves prophetic in his suggestion that Lily would forget him within three months if he died.

Annie, the second Morel child, five years older than Paul and his main playmate and protector when young. She becomes a teacher at the local Board School and later moves to Sheffield when she marries *Leonard.* She nurses the dying Mrs. Morel together with Paul and supports him in his decision to put their mother out of misery by giving her extra morphine.

The youngest Morel child, *Arthur,* is the only one to have a positive relationship with his father, probably because he takes after him in his vigorous but careless manner and in his fiery temper. He is a spoiled and often peevish child and a hot-headed, restless, and reckless youth; he joins the army on impulse, for example, and regrets it and later gets his girlfriend, the teasing and flirtatious *Beatrice Wyld,* into trouble. He becomes steadier in early adulthood after he has married Beatrice and settled to looking after his own family.

John Field was Gertrude Morel's first love, the college-educated son of a prosperous tradesman. He had given Gertrude a Bible, which she preserves all her life. His father had been ruined, and he had become a teacher; to Gertrude's great chagrin and disillusion, he had then married his landlady, apparently for her property. *Mr. Heaton* is the local Congregationalist minister who comes regularly to the Morel home to talk with Mrs. Morel. *Mrs. Kirk* is the next-door neighbor to the Morels; she helps with the birth of Paul. *Mrs. Bower,* a bossy neighbor who also helps out with Mrs. Morel's child-labors. *Mrs. Dakin,* the Morels' next-door neighbor in Scargill Street. *Billy Pillins,* or Philips, *Eddie Dakin, Alice,* and *Emmie Limb* are all childhood friends of the Morel children in Scargill Street. *Alfred Anthony* is the boy whose collar the young William pulls off in an argument: his mother, *Mrs. Anthony,* comes to complain to Mrs. Morel of William's behavior. *Dr. Jameson* is the doctor who attends Mrs. Morel in her illness.

The Leivers family: *Mr. and Mrs. Leivers, Agatha* (Miriam's older sister, a schoolteacher), *Edgar* (Miriam's older brother with whom Paul develops a special relationship—he is eighteen when Paul first goes to Willey farm), *Geoffrey, Maurice,* and *Hubert* Leivers. (The Leivers are modeled on the Chambers family, tenants of Haggs farm from 1898 to 1910: the parents, Sarah Ann Chambers [1859–1937] and Edmund Chambers [1863–1946], and children, Alan Aubrey [1882–1946], Muriel May Chambers Holbrook [1883–1955], Jessie [1887–1944], Hubert [1888–?], Bernard [1890–?], Mollie [1896–?], Jonathan David [1898–1970]. In the novel, only six Leivers children are mentioned—Mollie Chambers has no fictional counterpart here—but at one point Mrs. Morel refers to the Leivers as having seven children [p. 149].)

Alfred Charlesworth, the colliery manager whom Walter mocks and who then bears a grudge against Walter and gives him harder "stalls" to work in the pit. *Jerry Purdy,* the friend with whom Walter Morel goes on his jaunt to Nottingham in the first chapter. *Mr. Braithwaite,* chief cashier of the colliery company; he pays out the wages to the men along with his assistant, *Mr. Winterbottom. Israel Barker,* Walter's fellow butty. *Bill Hodgkisson,* Walter Morel's friend— he gives him the coconut from the Wakes Fair at the start of the novel.

Thomas Jordan, the proprietorial owner of the factory where Paul works as a clerk. *Mr. Pappleworth,* Paul's immediate superior at Jordan's. *Connie, Polly, Emma, Fanny* are all machinists at Jordan's Surgical Appliance Factory, as is *Louie Travers,* who becomes the mistress of Baxter Dawes. *Mr. Melling,* an old clerk at Jordan's.

Mrs. Radford, Clara's mother: sixty years old and somewhat severe, she does "sweated" home labor as a lace-worker.

Newton, a teacher, is the friend with whom Paul goes on holiday to Blackpool at Whitsuntide just before his mother's illness. Paul's other friends, *Jessop,* from the art school, and *Swain,* a chemistry demonstrator at the university, are briefly mentioned earlier (Ch. 11).

SETTING

Sons and Lovers is a semiautobiographical novel, and the settings are therefore very closely modeled on Lawrence's native Eastwood ("Bestwood" in the novel) and the surrounding Nottinghamshire mining countryside. Parts of Derbyshire and Lincolnshire also feature prominently. The Morel family and their homes are clearly based on the Lawrence family and their homes: 8a Victoria Street (1883–87), 28 Garden Road, the Breach (1887–91—the "Bottoms" in the novel), 3 Walker Street (1891–1905—"Scargill Street"), and 97 Lynn Croft (1905–11—the Morels move to a house near the Scargill Street one shortly after the death of William [see Ch. 7]). The farm of the Chambers family, the Haggs at Underwood, is re-created, along with its surroundings as "Willey Farm." "Nethermere," as in *The White Peacock,* is based on Moor Green Reservoir. The various coal mines that feature in the novel are easily identifiable as actual mines of the time (e.g., "Beggarlee" is Brinsley pit, and "Minton" is Moor Green colliery). Other fictional re-creations of local places are "Aldersley" (Annesley), "Keston" (Kimberley), "Lethley Bridge" (Langley Mill), and "Shepstone" (Shipley). Actual place-names of many other places in Nottinghamshire and Derbyshire are used, for example, Nottingham and Derby themselves, Ripley, Heanor, Ilkeston, Southwell, Crich, Whatstandwell, Ambergate. Further afield, Sheffield, Lincoln, and, on the Lincolnshire coast, Skegness, Mablethorpe, and Theddlethorpe appear, as do, more briefly, the Isle of Wight and London.

BIBLIOGRAPHY 5

Adamowski, T. H. "Intimacy at a Distance: Sexuality and Orality in *Sons and Lovers.*" *Mosaic* 13, no. 2 (1979): 71–89.

———. "Play, Creativity and Matricide: The Implications of Lawrence's 'Smashed Doll' Episode." *Mosaic* 14, no. 3 (1981a): 81–94.

———. "The Father of All Things: The Oral and the Oedipal in *Sons and Lovers.*" *Mosaic* 14, no. 4 (1981b): 69–88.

Alinei, Tamara. "Three Times Morel: Recurrent Structure in *Sons and Lovers.*" *Dutch Quarterly Review* 5 (1975): 39–53.

———. "DHL's Natural Imagery: A Non-Vitalist Reading." *Dutch Quarterly Review* 6 (1976): 116–38 (116–31).

Allen, C. N., and K. Curtis. "A Sociogrammatic Study of Oedipus Complex Formation: DHL's *Sons and Lovers.*" *Sociometry* 2 (1939): 37–51.

Arcana, Judith. "I Remember Mama: Mother-Blaming in *Sons and Lovers* Criticism." *DHL Review* 21 (Spring 1989): 137–51.

Atkins, A. R. "The New *Sons and Lovers.*" *Cambridge Quarterly* 22, no. 4 (1993): 416–21. (On the new Cambridge edition of the novel.)

Balbert, Peter H. "Forging and Feminism: *Sons and Lovers* and the Phallic Imagination." *DHL Review* 11 (Summer 1978): 93–113.

Banerjee, A. "*Sons and Lovers* and Its Editors." *London Magazine* 33 (August–September 1993): 90–95.

Baron, Carl, and Helen Baron. "Introduction." *Sons and Lovers* by DHL. Edited by Carl and Helen Baron. Cambridge: Cambridge University Press, 1992, pp. xxi–lxxxi.

———. "Introduction." *Sons and Lovers* by DHL. Edited by Carl and Helen Baron. Harmondsworth: Penguin, 1994, pp. xv–xli.

Baron, Helen V. "Mrs. Morel Ironing." *Journal of the DHL Society* (1984): 2–12.

———. "Jessie Chambers' Plea for Justice to 'Miriam.' " *Archiv für das Studium der Neueren Sprachen und Literaturen* 222, no. 1 (1985a): 63–84.

———. "*Sons and Lovers:* The Surviving Manuscripts from Three Drafts Dated by Paper Analysis." *Studies in Bibliography* 38 (1985b): 289–328.

———. "Editing *Sons and Lovers.*" *The Journal of the D. H. Lawrence Society* (1994–95): 8–20.

Bazin, Nancy Topping. "The Moment of Revelation in *Martha Quest* and Comparable Moments by Two Modernists." *Modern Fiction Studies* 26 (1980): 87–98. (Lawrence and Joyce.)

Beards, Richard D. "*Sons and Lovers* as Bildungsroman." *College Literature* 1 (Fall 1974): 204–17.

Beebe, Maurice. "Lawrence's Sacred Fount: The Artist Theme of *Sons and Lovers.*" *Texas Studies in Literature and Language* 4 (Winter 1963): 539–52. (Reprinted in his *Ivory Towers and Sacred Founts.* New York: New York University Press, 1964, pp. 101–13. Also in Salgãdo [1969], op. cit.)

Benway, Ann M. Baribault. "Oedipus Abroad: Hardy's Clym Yeobright and Lawrence's Paul Morel." *Thomas Hardy Yearbook* 13 (1986): 51–57.

Bergonzi, B. *The Myth of Modernism and Twentieth Century Literature.* Brighton, Sussex: Harvester, 1986, pp. 22–29.

Betsky, Seymour. "Rhythm and Theme: DHL's *Sons and Lovers.*" In *The Achievement of DHL.* Edited by Frederick J. Hoffman and Harry T. Moore. Norman: University of Oklahoma Press, 1953, pp. 131–43.

Black, Michael. *DHL: "Sons and Lovers."* Cambridge: Cambridge University Press, 1992.

Bloom, Harold, ed. *DHL's "Sons and Lovers."* New York: Chelsea House, 1988. (Modern Critical Interpretations. Nine previously published essays.)

Bonds, Diane S. "Miriam, the Narrator, and the Reader of *Sons and Lovers.*" *DHL Review* 14 (1981): 143–55.

Bramley, J. A. "DHL and 'Miriam.' " *Cornhill* 171 (Summer 1960): 241–49.

———. "DHL's Sternest Critic." *Hibbert Journal* 63 (Spring 1965): 109–11.

Brewster, Dorothy, and Angus Burrell. "DHL: *Sons and Lovers.*" In their *Modern Fiction.* New York: Columbia University Press, 1934, pp. 137–54.

Buckley, Jerome H. *Season of Youth: The Bildungsroman from Dickens to Golding.* Cambridge: Harvard University Press, 1974, pp. 204–24.

Burden, Robert. "Libidinal Structure and the Representation of Desire in *Sons and Lovers.*" *Journal of the D. H. Lawrence Society* (1994–95): 21–38.

Burwell, Rose Marie. "Schopenhauer, Hardy and Lawrence: Toward a New Understanding of *Sons and Lovers.*" *Western Humanities Review* 28 (Spring 1974): 105–17.

Butler, Lance St. John. *York Notes on DHL's "Sons and Lovers."* London: Longman, 1980.

Campbell, Elizabeth A. "Metonymy and Character: *Sons and Lovers* and the Metaphysics of Self." *DHL Review* 20 (Spring 1988): 221–32.

Cardy, Michael. "Beyond Documentation: Emile Zola and DHL." *Neohelicon* 14, no. 2 (1987): 225–31.

Chatterji, Arindam. "*Sons and Lovers:* Dynamic Sanity." *Panjab University Research Bulletin* 16, no. 2 (October 1985): 3–21.

Daiches, David. *The Novel and the Modern World.* Rev. ed. Chicago: University of Chicago Press, 1960, pp. 143–47.

Daly, Macdonald. "Introduction." *Sons and Lovers.* Edited by Macdonald Daly. London: Dent, 1994, pp. xix–xxx.

D'Avanzo, Mario L. "On the Naming of Paul Morel and the Ending of *Sons and Lovers.*" *Southern Review* (Adelaide) 12 (1979): 103–7.

Delany, Paul. "*Sons and Lovers:* The Morel Marriage as a War of Position." *DHL Review* 21 (1989): 153–65.

Delavenay, Emile. "Lawrence's Major Work." In *DHL: The Man Who Lived.* Edited by Robert B. Partlow, Jr., and Harry T. Moore. Carbondale: Southern Illinois University Press, 1980, pp. 139–42.

Dervin, Daniel. "Play, Creativity and Matricide: The Implications of Lawrence's 'Smashed Doll' Episode." *Mosaic* 14, no. 3 (1981): 81–94.

Deva, Som. *A Critical Study of "Sons and Lovers."* 2d ed. Beharipur, Bareilly: Literary Publication Bureau, 1969.

Dietz, Susan. "Miriam." *Recovering Literature: A Journal of Contextualist Criticism* 6, no. 3 (1978): 15–22.

DiMaggio, Richard. "A Note on *Sons and Lovers* and Emerson's 'Experience.'" *DHL Review* 6 (Summer 1973): 214–16. (See also Wise [1972] op. cit.)

Doheny, John. "The Novel Is the Book of Life: DHL and a Revised Version of Polymorphous Perversity." *Paunch* 26 (April 1966): 40–59.

Doherty, Gerald. "The Dialectic of Space in DHL's *Sons and Lovers.*" *Modern Fiction Studies* 39 (Summer 1993): 327–43.

Draper, R. P. *"Sons and Lovers" by DHL.* London and Basingstoke: Macmillan, 1986. (Macmillan Master Guides series.)

Eagleton, Terry. *Exiles and Emigrés: Studies in Modern Literature.* London: Chatto and Windus; New York: Schocken, 1970, pp. 192–200.

Eggert, Paul. "Edward Garnett's *Sons and Lovers.*" *Critical Quarterly* 28, no. 4 (1986): 51–62.

———. "Opening Up the Text: The Case of *Sons and Lovers.*" In *Rethinking Lawrence.* Edited by Keith Brown. Milton Keynes and Philadelphia: Open University Press, 1990, pp. 38–52.

Eichrodt, John M. "Doctrine and Dogma in *Sons and Lovers.*" *Connecticut Review* 4 (1970): 18–32.

Farr, Judith, ed. *Twentieth Century Interpretations of "Sons and Lovers": A Collection of Critical Essays.* Englewood Cliffs, N.J.: Prentice-Hall, 1970.

Fielding, M. L. *Notes on DHL's "Sons and Lovers."* London: Methuen, 1975. (Study guide.)

Finney, Brian. *DHL: "Sons and Lovers."* Harmondsworth: Penguin, 1990. (Penguin Critical Studies series.)

Fleishman, Avrom. "The Fictions of Autobiographical Fiction." *Genre* 9 (1976): 73–86 (82–86).

———. *"Sons and Lovers:* A Prophet in the Making." In his *Figures of Autobiography: The Language of Self-Writing in Victorian and Modern England.* Berkeley: University of California Press, 1983, pp. 395–410.

Fowler, Roger. *Linguistics and the Novel.* London: Methuen, 1977, pp. 113–22.

Fraiberg, Louis. "The Unattainable Self: DHL's *Sons and Lovers.*" In *Twelve Original Essays on Great English Novels.* Edited by Charles Shapiro. Detroit: Wayne State University Press, 1960, pp. 175–201. (Reprinted in Tedlock [1965] op. cit.)

Galbraith, Mary. "Feeling Moments in the Work of DHL." *Paunch* 63–64 (1990): 15–38 (18–23).

Gavin, Adrienne E. "Miriam's Mirror: Reflections on the Labelling of Miriam Leivers." *DHL Review* 24 (Fall 1992): 27–41.

Gilbert, Sandra M. *DHL's "Sons and Lovers," "The Rainbow," "Women in Love," "The Plumed Serpent."* New York: Monarch Press, 1965. (Study guide.)

Gillespie, Michael Patrick. "Lawrence's *Sons and Lovers.*" *Explicator* 40, no 4 (1982): 36–38.

Gomme, Andor H. "Jessie Chambers and Miriam Leivers—An Essay on *Sons and Lovers.*" In *DHL: A Critical Study of the Major Novels and Other Writings.* Edited by Andor H. Gomme. Sussex: Harvester Press; New York: Barnes and Noble, 1978, pp. 30–52.

Gose, Elliott B., Jr. "An Expense of Spirit." *New Mexico Quarterly* 25 (Winter 1955–56): 358–63.

Hampson, Carolyn. "The Morels and the Gants: Sexual Conflict as a Universal Theme." *Thomas Wolfe Review* 8 (Spring 1984): 27–40.

Handley, Graham. *Notes on DHL "Sons and Lovers."* Bath: J. Brodie, 1967.

Hanson, Christopher. *Sons and Lovers.* Oxford: Basil Blackwell, 1966. (Notes on English Literature Series.)

Hardy, Barbara. *The Appropriate Form: An Essay on the Novel.* London: Athlone Press, 1964, pp. 135–46.

Hardy, John Edward. *Man in the Modern Novel.* Seattle: University of Washington Press, 1964, pp. 52–66.

Harvey, Geoffrey. *Sons and Lovers.* London: Macmillan; Atlantic Highlands, N.J.: Humanities, 1987. (Critics Debate Series.)

Heywood, Christopher. "Olive Schreiner's *The Story of an African Farm:* Prototype of Lawrence's Early Novels." *English Language Notes* 14 (September 1976): 44–50.

Hillman, Rodney. *DHL, "Sons and Lovers."* London: British Council, 1976. (Notes on Literature, no. 161.)

Hilton, Enid. "Alice Dax: DHL's Clara in *Sons and Lovers.*" *DHL Review* 22 (Fall 1990): 275–85.

Hinz, Evelyn J. *"Sons and Lovers:* The Archetypal Dimensions of Lawrence's Oedipal Tragedy." *DHL Review* 5 (Spring 1972): 26–53.

Hinz, Evelyn J., and John J. Teunissen. " 'They Thought of *Sons and Lovers':* DHL and Thomas Wolfe." *Southern Quarterly* 29, no. 3 (Spring 1991): 77–89.

Holliday, R. "The Challenge of Lawrence's Fiction." *Journal of the DHL Society* 2 (1979): 7–12.

Idema, James M. "The Hawk and the Plover: 'The Polarity of Life' in the 'Jungle Aviary' of DHL's Mind in *Sons and Lovers* and *The Rainbow." Forum* (Houston) 3 (Summer 1961): 11–14.

Jeffries, C. "Metaphor in *Sons and Lovers." Personalist* 29 (July 1948): 287–92.

Joffe, Phil. *"Sons and Lovers:* The Growth of Paul Morel." *CRUX: A Journal on the Teaching of English* 20, no. 3 (1986): 49–62.

Karl, Frederick R., and Marvin Magalaner. *A Reader's Guide to Great Twentieth-Century English Novels.* New York: Noonday; London: Thames and Hudson, 1959, pp. 156–71.

Kay, Wallace G. "Two Printer's Errors in *Sons and Lovers." DHL Review* 19 (Summer 1987): 185–87. (See also Ross [1988] op. cit.)

Kazin, Alfred. "Sons, Lovers and Mothers." *Partisan Review* 29 (Spring 1962): 373–85. (Reprinted as introduction to the novel, New York: Random House, 1962, and in Tedlock [1965], op. cit., pp. 238–50.)

Kern, Stephen. *The Culture of Love: Victorians to Moderns.* Cambridge: Harvard University Press, 1992, pp. 253–56 and passim.

Kuttner, Alfred Booth. *"Sons and Lovers:* A Freudian Appreciation." *Psychoanalytic Review* 3 (July 1916): 295–317. (Reprinted in Tedlock [1965], op. cit., pp. 76–100, and Salgãdo [1969], op. cit., pp. 69–94.)

Levy, Nancy R. "Values Education through DHL's *Sons and Lovers." English Journal* 73, no. 6 (1984): 48–50.

Littlewood, J.F.C. "Son and Lover." *Cambridge Quarterly* (Autumn–Winter 1969–70): 323–61.

Longmire, Samual E. "Lawrence's *Sons and Lovers." Explicator* 42, no. 3 (Spring 1984): 2–4.

Martz, Louis L. "Portrait of Miriam: A Study in the Design of *Sons and Lovers."* In *Imagined Worlds: Essays on Some English Novels and Novelists in Honour of John Butt.* Edited by Maynard Mack and Ian Gregor. London: Methuen, 1968, pp. 343–69. (Reprinted in Jackson and Jackson [1988]: 47–68.)

Maxwell-Mahon, W. D. "A Note on *Sons and Lovers." Crux* 10 (1976): 17–20.

Melchiori, Barbara. " 'Objects in the Powerful Light of Emotion.' " *Ariel* (Leeds) 1 (January 1970): 21–30.

Mitchell, Giles R. *"Sons and Lovers* and the Oedipal Project." *DHL Review* 13 (Fall 1980): 209–19.

Mortland, Donald E. "The Conclusion of *Sons and Lovers:* A Reconsideration." *Studies in the Novel* 3 (Fall 1971): 305–15.

Moseley, Edwin M. *Pseudonyms of Christ in the Modern World: Motifs and Methods.* Pittsburgh: University of Pittsburgh Press, 1963, pp. 69–91.

Moynahan, Julian, ed. *"Sons and Lovers": Text, Background, and Criticism.* New York: Viking Press, 1968.

Muggeridge, Malcolm. "Lawrence's *Sons and Lovers." New Statesman and Nation* 49 (23 April 1955): 581–82.

Murfin, Ross C. *"Sons and Lovers": A Novel of Division and Desire.* Boston: Twayne, 1987.

Nadel, Ira Bruce. "From Fathers and Sons to *Sons and Lovers.*" *Dalhousie Review* 59 (1979): 221–38.

Nash, Thomas. " 'Bleeding at the Roots': The Folklore of Plants in *Sons and Lovers.*" *Kentucky Folklore Record* 27, nos. 1–2 (1981): 20–32.

New, William H. "Character as Symbol: Annie's Role in *Sons and Lovers.*" *DHL Review* 1 (Spring 1968): 31–43.

Newmarch, David. " 'Death of a Young Man in London': Ernest Lawrence and William Morel in *Sons and Lovers.*" *Durham University Journal* 76 (1983): 73–79.

O'Connor, Frank. "DHL: *Sons and Lovers.*" In his *The Mirror in the Roadway.* London: Hamilton, 1955, pp. 270–79.

Padhi, Bibhu. "Man, Nature and Motions of the Spirit: Symbolic Scenes in DHL's *Sons and Lovers.*" *Wascana Review* 19, no. 2 (1984): 53–67.

Pandit, M. L. "The Family Relationship in *Sons and Lovers:* Gertrude and Walter Morel." In *Essays on DHL.* Edited by T. R. Sharma. Meerut, India: Shalabh Book House, 1987, pp. 89–94.

Panken, Shirley. "Some Psychodynamics in *Sons and Lovers:* A New Look at the Oedipal Theme." *Psychoanalytic Review* 61 (1974–75): 571–89.

Pascal, Roy. "The Autobiographical Novel and the Autobiography." *Essays in Criticism* 9 (April 1959): 134–50. (Brontë's *Villette, Sons and Lovers,* and Joyce's *Portrait of the Artist as a Young Man.*)

Perez, Carlos A. "Husbands and Wives, Sons and Lovers, Intimate Conflict in the Fiction of DHL." In *The Aching Hearth: Family Violence in Life and Literature.* Edited by Sara Munson Deats and Lagretta Tallent Lenker. New York: Plenum, 1991, pp. 175–87.

Phillips, Danna. "Lawrence's Understanding of Miriam through Sue." *Recovering Literature* 7, no. 1 (1979): 46–56.

Pinsker, Sanford. " 'Once Again, the Flowers': A Note on *Sons and Lovers.*" *Modern British Literature* 1 (Fall 1976): 91–92.

Pittock, Malcolm. "*Sons and Lovers:* The Price of Betrayal." *Essays in Criticism* 36, no. 3 (1986): 235–54. (Reprinted in Brown [1990]: 120–32.)

Poynter, John S. "Miner and Mineowner at the Time of Lawrence's Setting for *Sons and Lovers.*" *Journal of the DHL Society* 2, no. 3 (1981): 13–23.

Prakesh, Om. *"Sons and Lovers": A Critical Study.* Bareilly: Prakesh Book Depot, 1972.

Prakesh, Ravendra. *DHL: "Sons and Lovers": A Critical Study.* Agra: Lakshmi Narain Agarwal, 1972.

Pratt, Annis. "Women and Nature in Modern Fiction." *Contemporary Literature* 13 (Fall 1972): 481–83.

Pullin, Faith. "Lawrence's Treatment of Women in *Sons and Lovers.*" In *Lawrence and Women.* Edited by Anne Smith. London: Vision, 1978, pp. 49–73.

Raizada, Harish. "Paul Morel: Architect of His Own Tragedy." *Aligarh Journal of English Studies* 10, no. 2 (1985): 122–40.

Reddick, Bryan. "*Sons and Lovers:* The Omniscient Narrator." *Thoth* 7 (Spring 1966): 68–76.

Richards, Bernard. "Lawrence's *Sons and Lovers.*" *Explicator* 46, no. 3 (1988): 32–35.

Ross, Charles L. " 'Let Him Be Killed' or 'Let Him Not Be Killed': A Reply to Wallace G. Kay." *DHL Review* 20 (Spring 1988): 65–68.

Rossman, Charles. "The Gospel according to DHL: Religion in *Sons and Lovers.*" *DHL Review* 3 (Spring 1970): 31–41.

Rothkopf, C. Z. *"Sons and Lovers": A Critical Commentary.* New York: American R.D.M. Corporation, 1969.

Sagar, Keith. "How Edward Garnett Made Lawrence's Novels Fit for Public Consumption." *Times Higher Education Supplement* (11 January 1980): 10.

———. "Introduction." *Sons and Lovers* by DHL. Edited by Keith Sagar. Harmondsworth: Penguin, 1981, pp. 11–28.

Saje, Natasha. "Hamlet, D. H. Lawrence and *Sons and Lovers.*" *Dalhousie Review* 71 (Fall 1991): 334–47.

Salgādo, Gāmini. *DHL: "Sons and Lovers."* London: Edward Arnold, 1966.

———, ed. *DHL: "Sons and Lovers": A Selection of Critical Essays.* London: Macmillan, 1969. (Published in America as *DHL: "Sons and Lovers," A Casebook.* Nashville, Tenn.: Aurora, 1970.)

Saxena, H. S. "A Study of the Facsimile of the Ms. of *Sons and Lovers.*" In *Essays on DHL.* Edited by T. R. Sharma. Meerut, India: Shalabh Book House, 1987, pp. 79–88.

Schapiro, Barbara. "Maternal Bonds and the Boundaries of Self: DHL and Virginia Woolf." *Soundings* 69 (1986): 347–65.

Scherr, Barry J. "The 'Dark Fire of Desire' in DHL's *Sons and Lovers.*" *Recovering Literature: A Journal of Contextualist Criticism* 16 (1988): 37–67.

Schorer, Mark. "Technique as Discovery." *Hudson Review* 1 (Spring 1948): 67–87. (Excerpt reprinted in Tedlock [1965]: 164–69, Salgādo [1969]: 106–11, and Farr [1970]: 97–99, all op. cit.)

———. "Introduction." *DHL: "Sons and Lovers": A Facsimile of the Manuscript.* Edited by Mark Schorer. Berkeley, Los Angeles, London: University of California Press, 1977, pp. 1–9.

Schwartz, Daniel R. "Speaking of Paul Morel: Voice, Unity, and Meaning in *Sons and Lovers.*" *Studies in the Novel* 8 (Fall 1976): 255–77.

Sexton, Mark S. "Lawrence, Garnett and *Sons and Lovers:* An Exploration of Author–Editor Relationship." *Studies in Bibliography: Papers of the Bibliographical Society of the University of Virginia* 43 (1990): 208–22.

Sharma, Shruti. *DHL: "Sons and Lovers": A Critical Study.* Karnal, India: Natraj Publishing House, 1990.

Shaw, Rita Granger. *Notes on DHL's "Sons and Lovers."* Lincoln, Nebr.: Cliff's Notes, 1965. (Study Guide.)

Shealy, Ann. "The Epiphany Theme in Modern Fiction: E. M. Forster's *Howard's End* and DHL's *Sons and Lovers.*" In her *The Passionate Mind.* Philadelphia: Dorrance, 1976, pp. 1–27.

Shrivastava, K. C. "DHL's *Sons and Lovers* as a Proletarian Novel." In *Essays on DHL.* Edited by T. R. Sharma. Meerut, India: Shalabh Book House, 1987, pp. 104–8.

Shrubb, E. P. "Reading *Sons and Lovers.*" *Sydney Studies in English* 6 (1980–81): 87–104.

Sloan, Gary. "An Emersonian Source for the Title *Sons and Lovers.*" *American Notes and Queries* 16 (1978): 160–61.

Smith, G., Jr. "The Doll-Burners: DHL and Louisa Alcott." *Modern Language Quarterly* 19 (March 1958): 28–32.

Spacks, Patricia Meyers. *The Adolescent Idea: Myths of Youth and the Adult Imagination.* New York: Basic Books, 1981, pp. 243–51.

Spector, Judith. "Taking Care of Mom: Erotic Degradation, Dalliances, and Dichotomies in the Works of Just About Everyone." *Sphinx: A Magazine of Literature and Society* 4 (1984): 184–201.

Spilka, Mark. "The Floral Pattern in *Sons and Lovers.*" *New Mexico Quarterly* 25 (Spring 1955): 44–56.

———. "For Mark Schorer with Combative Love: The *Sons and Lovers* Manuscript." *Review* 3 (1981): 129–47. (Rev. version in Balbert and Marcus [1985]: 29–44, and Spilka [1992]: 27–46.)

Sproles, Karyn Z. "Teaching Sons and Teaching Lovers: Using Lawrence in Freshman English." *DHL Review* 19 (Fall 1987): 330–36.

———. "DHL and the Schizoid State: Reading *Sons and Lovers* through *The White Peacock.*" *Paunch* 63–64 (December 1990): 39–70.

Stoll, John E. *DHL's "Sons and Lovers": Self-Encounter and the Unknown Self.* Muncie, Ind.: Ball State University, 1968.

Stovel, Nora Foster. "DHL and 'The Dignity of Death': Tragic Recognition in 'Odour of Chrysanthemums,' *The Widowing of Mrs. Holroyd,* and *Sons and Lovers.*" *DHL Review* 16 (1983): 59–82.

———. "DHL from Playwright to Novelist: 'Strife in Love' in *A Collier's Friday Night* and *Sons and Lovers.*" *English Studies in Canada* 13, no. 4 (1987): 451–67.

Taylor, John A. "The Greatness of *Sons and Lovers.*" *Modern Philology* 71 (May 1974): 380–87.

Tedlock, E. W., Jr., ed. *DHL and "Sons and Lovers": Sources and Criticism.* New York: New York University Press, 1965; London: London University Press, 1966.

Templeton, Wayne. "The Drift towards Life: Paul Morel's Search for a Place." *DHL Review* 15 (1982): 177–94. (Reprinted in Templeton [1989]: 58–106.)

———. "The *Sons and Lovers* Manuscript." *Studies in Bibliography* 37 (1984): 234–43.

Tilak, Raghukul. *DHL, "Sons and Lovers."* New Delhi: Aarti Book Centre, 1968.

Tomlinson, T. B. "Lawrence and Modern Life: *Sons and Lovers, Women in Love.*" *Critical Review* (Melbourne), no. 8 (1965): 3–18.

———. "DHL: *Sons and Lovers, Women in Love.*" In his *The English Middle-Class Novel.* London: Macmillan; New York: Harper and Row, 1976, pp. 185–98.

Tripathy, Akhilesh Kumar. "DHL's *Sons and Lovers* and *A [sic] Captain's Doll:* A Study in Thematic Link." In *Essays on DHL.* Edited by T. R. Sharma. Meerut, India: Shalabh Book House, 1987, pp. 95–103.

Trotter, David. "Edwardian Sex Novels." *Critical Quarterly* 31 (1989): 92–106.

———. "Introduction." *Sons and Lovers* by DHL. Oxford: Oxford University Press, 1995, pp. vii–xxix.

Unrue, Darlene Harbour. "The Symbolism of Names in *Sons and Lovers.*" *Names* 28 (1980): 131–40.

Van Ghent, Dorothy. "On *Sons and Lovers.*" In her *The English Novel: Form and Function.* New York: Holt, Rinehart, and Winston, 1953, pp. 245–61. (Rev. version in Tedlock [1965]: 170–87, and Salgādo [1969]: 112–29, both op. cit.)

Van Tassel, Daniel E. "The Search for Manhood in DHL's *Sons and Lovers.*" *Costerus* 3 (1972): 197–210.

Vredenburgh, Joseph L. "Further Contributions to a Study of the Incest Object." *American Imago* 16 (Fall 1959): 263–68. (Miriam and Clara as incest objects.)

Weiss, Daniel. "Oedipus in Nottinghamshire." *Literature and Psychology* 7 (August 1957): 33–42.

―――――. *Oedipus in Nottingham: DHL.* Seattle: University of Washington Press, 1962, pp. 3–67 and passim.

―――――. "DHL's Great Circle: From *Sons and Lovers* to *Lady Chatterley's Lover.*" *Psychoanalytic Review* 50 (Fall 1963): 112–38. (Revision of Ch. 4 of *Oedipus in Nottingham,* preceding ref.)

Whiteley, Patrick J. "The Stable Ego: Psychological Realism in *Sons and Lovers.*" In his *Knowledge and Experimental Realism in Conrad, Lawrence, and Woolf.* Baton Rouge: Louisiana State University Press, 1987, pp. 108–24.

Wickham, Anna. "The Spirit of the Lawrence Women." *Texas Quarterly* 9 (Autumn 1966): 31–50. (Reprinted in *The Writings of Anna Wickham.* Edited by R. D. Smith. London, 1984, pp. 355–72.)

Wilson, Raymond J., III. "Paul Morel and Stephen Dedalus: Rebellion and Reconciliation." *Platte Valley Review* 11 (Spring 1983): 27–33.

Wise, James, N. "Emerson's 'Experience' and *Sons and Lovers.*" *Costerus* 6 (1972): 179–221. (See also DiMaggio [1973] op. cit.)

Wolf, Howard R. "British Fathers and Sons, 1773–1913: From Filial Submissiveness to Creativity." *Psychoanalytic Review* 52 (Summer 1965): 53–70.

Worthen, John. "Lawrence's Autobiographies." In *The Spirit of DHL: Centenary Studies.* Edited by Gāmini Salgādo and G. K. Das. London: Macmillan; Totowa, N.J.: Barnes, 1988, pp. 1–15.

See also (1980–94) Alden (1986): 100–13. Becker (1980): 25–42. Bell (1992): 36–50. Ben-Ephraim (1981): 84–128. Black (1986): 150–87. Bonds (1987): 29–52. Burns (1980): 39–45. Clark (1980): 57–61, 67–69. Dix (1980): 29–34, 84–86. Dorbad (1991): 43–58. Gutierrez (1987): 64, 67–68, passim. Hardy and Harris (1985): passim. Herzinger (1982): passim. Hobsbaum (1981): 46–51. Holderness (1982): 130–58. Hyde (1990): 30–36. Ingram (1990): 20–25, 34–44, 81–85. Kelsey (1991): 71–120. Kiely (1980): 61–64. Kushigian (1990): 35–71. MacLeod (1985/87): 99–105. Miliaras (1987): 95–163. Milton (1987): passim. Modiano (1987): 76–85. Niven (1980): 32–42. Padhi (1989): 95–108, 149–57. Pinkney (1990): 27–51. Poplawski (1993): 55–57. Prasad (1980): 30–56. Robinson (1992): 120–23. Sagar (1985a): 75–101. Salgado (1982): 99–107. Scheckner (1985): 23–69. Schneider (1984): 132–43. Siegel (1991): passim. Simpson (1982): 26–37. Sklenicka (1991): 36–55, passim. Spilka (1992): 27–46. Storch (1990): 101–7, passim. Suter (1987): 59–69. Verhoeven (1987): 49–95. Worthen (1991a): 21–31. Worthen (1991b): passim.

See also (to 1979) Albright (1978): 78–85, passim. Alcorn (1977): 82–86, passim. Alldritt (1971): 16–42. Beal (1961): 14–21. Bedient (1972): 117–25. Boadella (1956/78): 79–84. Brunsdale (1978): 254–63. Cavitch (1969): 21–29, passim. Daleski (1965): 42–73. Delavenay (1972): passim. Draper (1964): 37–53. Draper (1970): 58–80. Ford (1965): 28–47. Gregory (1933): 17–28. Hochman (1970): 29–35, passim. Hough (1956): 35–53, passim. Howe (1977): 13–15, passim. Littlewood (1976): 31–41. Maes-Jelinek (1970): 25–40. Michaels-Tonks (1976): 78–84. Miko (1971): 59–107. Millett (1970): 245–57. Moore (1951): 78–90, 285–305. Moynahan (1963): 13–31. Murry (1931): 5–22. Nahal (1970): 130–37. Niven (1978): 36–58. Pinion (1978): 139–48. Prasad (1976): 147–62.

Pritchard (1971): 32–43. Sagar (1966): 19–36. Sale (1973): 22–39. Sanders (1973): 21–59. Sinzelle (1964): passim. Slade (1970): 39–54, passim. Spilka (1955): 39–89. Stewart (1963): 492–98. Stoll (1971): 62–150. Swigg (1972): 44–57. Tedlock (1963): 54–69. Vivas (1960): 173–99. Worthen (1979): 26–44. Yudhishtar (1969): 82–113.

14   *The Rainbow*

WRITTEN

March 1913–August 1915. Revisions and corrections, March–August 1915. Draft versions: 1. "The Sisters," March–June 1913. 2. "The Sisters," August 1913–January 1914. 3. "The Wedding Ring," February–May 1914. 4. *The Rainbow*, November 1914–March 1915. The period between the third and final versions saw Lawrence compiling and revising the stories in *The Prussian Officer* and writing "Study of Thomas Hardy": both projects seem to have significantly influenced the final writing of *The Rainbow*. Proofs for the novel were corrected in July and August 1915.

PUBLISHED

1. London: Methuen, September 1915. New York: Huebsch, November 1915.
2. Edited by Mark Kinkead-Weekes. Cambridge: Cambridge University Press, 1989.
3. See also under Fernihough (1995), Hewitt (1993), and Worthen (1981) in the following bibliography.

WHO'S WHO AND SUMMARY

MAIN CHARACTERS: Tom and Lydia Brangwen; Will and Anna Brangwen; Ursula Brangwen; Anton Skrebensky
   Although it develops into a modernistic exploration of the questing conscious-

ness of Ursula Brangwen, the novel at first appears in the guise of a traditional family saga, and we are only gradually introduced into the main psychosexual focus of the novel alongside and through a social history of the Brangwen family from its immemorial beginnings in the agrarian traditions of old England, through the upheavals of the Industrial Revolution, and into the modern world of the early twentieth century. Another way of putting this, in the novel's own terms, is that we witness a movement "from the heated, blind intercourse of farm-life, to the spoken world beyond."

Following a generalized account of the centuries-old traditional way of life of the Midlands farming family, the emphasis settles on the period of "about 1840." We then hear of the childhood and youth of *Tom Brangwen* until he inherits the patrimony of Marsh farm himself and marries the Polish exile, *Lydia Lensky,* when he is twenty-eight, and she is thirty-four (in the year 1867). The novel explores their married relationship in all its unspoken emotional and psychological complexities and in its erratic swings from love to hate and back again. Although it was precisely her foreign "otherness" that had drawn Tom to Lydia, in marriage he finds this a frustrating barrier to his feeling at one with her—and this is not merely a matter of her being Polish but also that she is more articulate and cultured than he is. However, through their struggle with one another and in a way because of it, they finally break through into "another circle of existence" in which they achieve a "complete confirmation" of their love. Like a pillar of cloud and a pillar of fire meeting together, they now form a complete arch beneath which their daughter, Anna, can play in full security.

The focus now shifts to *Anna Brangwen* (Lydia's daughter by her first marriage to a Polish intellectual and revolutionary, *Paul Lensky,* who had died in London after their flight from Poland). We follow her childhood and adolescent experiences until she is courted by, and eventually married to, her half-cousin, *Will Brangwen,* son of Tom's brother Alfred. As with the previous generation, we witness in detail the vicissitudes of their married life until they achieve some degree of balance and stability together. However, here, the alternation of love and conflict, the unconscious "unknown battle" between Will and Anna, is much more violent and destructive than that involving Tom and Lydia; and where with the older Brangwens the resolution of differences represents a mutually fulfilling consummation of the marriage, the resolution here is more in the nature of a stalemate, with both partners acknowledging the relationship's inherent limitations and turning elsewhere for their further fulfillment (Anna to her childbearing, and Will to his "purposive activity" in the world of work). The crux of their conflict lies in their different attitudes toward religion and religious experience and in how these influence their attitudes to one another. Simply, Will is something of a Christian mystic, striving for spiritual consummation in conventional notions of the eternal, the immortal, and the absolute; while Anna has a diametrically opposed "pagan" reverence for the temporal world of nature and the spontaneous life of the body. In a visit to Lincoln Cathedral (Ch. 7), Anna effectively undermines Will's "transports and ecstasies,'' his ''blind passion'' for the abstractions of traditional Christianity, by drawing attention to the leering carved faces that seem to insist on all the worldly things the church has left out in its pretense of being absolute. Anna thus destroys an important part of Will's life and throws him back on himself to realize ''the limitation of his being.'' However, the very fact of that limitation also prevents him from providing Anna with any further possibilities of development in their relationship together: hence, the stalemate—he has lost his ''vital illusions,'' but she has gained only the satisfaction of being ''Anna Victrix.''

The bulk of the novel is then taken up with the story of *Ursula Brangwen,* the eldest daughter of Will and Anna, and her search for self-understanding and self-fulfillment. From an early age, Ursula is acutely aware of having inherited full responsibility for the shape and nature of her own life, and the question that underlies and informs her life and her narrative is the question of ''how to become oneself,'' how to create and fulfill one's own unique self from the undefined and unfixed ''something-nothing'' one starts out as. We follow Ursula's experiences as a young girl questioning the conventions of the Christian faith she has been brought up in; as a young woman exploring her sexuality, first with the young soldier *Anton Skrebensky* and then with her bisexual teacher *Winifred Inger* (who later marries Ursula's *Uncle Tom Brangwen* [son of Tom and Lydia], Winifred's partner in ''bitter-sweet corruption'' and worship of the machine); as an idealistic utopian critic of industrialized society (most vividly embodied by the amorphous mass of Wiggiston and by Uncle Tom's mechanized colliery there); as a student teacher struggling to make her way in ''the man's world'' of work in a rough and overcrowded school; as a college student working for a degree; and finally as a woman of twenty-two involved once more in a relationship with Anton Skrebensky, now returned from active service in South Africa.

Ursula becomes engaged to Anton but soon senses an inner emptiness and weakness within him: he seems unable to live independently of his social role or to assert himself as a self-responsible individual. Indeed, to Ursula, his whole life seems devoted precisely to the surrender of self and self-responsibility for the sake of conventional institutions and abstractions—the army, the nation, society, duty, self-sacrifice. Making love with Skrebensky by the sea on the Lincolnshire coast and with the moon, as always in the novel, urging her to her deepest self-awareness, Ursula finally realizes that his soul ''could not contain her in its waves of strength.'' The next day she breaks off the engagement and leaves him. Shortly afterward, Skrebensky, unknown to Ursula, marries his colonel's daughter and takes her with him to his new posting in India. Meanwhile, Ursula has found that she is pregnant, and, succumbing to feelings of guilt at her own pride and arrogance in asking too much of life (''wanting the moon'' for her own), she writes to Skrebensky and offers to marry him after all. While awaiting his reply, however, she falls ill following a traumatic encounter with some horses near her home. During her illness, in a sort of delirium, she comes to the realization that she must abide by her original quest for complete self-fulfillment. As she experiences a miscarriage of her child, she simultaneously experiences her own rebirth into a newly confident self and into a new reality that seems absolutely alien to the "unreal" world of Skrebensky and the past. When she then hears of Skrebensky's marriage, she feels glad that she has been prevented from setting the seal on her own "nullity." She recognizes that she cannot create her own man but must wait for the man "created by God" who will come out of Eternity to her. As she emerges from her illness, she has a vision of a new reality for the rest of society, too, embodied in the rainbow that promises "a new germination" and "a new growth" that will crack the coffin-like shell of the old industrial order.

Other Characters

Other members of the Brangwen family: *Alfred, Sr.,* the head of the household at the start of the novel (1840s). *Alfred, Jr.,* brother of Tom and father of Will: he becomes a draftsman in a Nottingham lace factory and marries the daughter of a chemist; he later takes a mistress, the elegant and cultured *Mrs. Forbes,* who also exerts an influence on Tom Brangwen. *Frank,* the third son of Alfred, Sr.: he later works as a butcher. *Alice and Effie,* sisters of Alfred and Tom. *Gudrun, Theresa, Catherine, Billy, Cassandra, Rosalind, Dora*—children to Will and Anna, siblings of Ursula (a ninth child dies of diphtheria). *Fred,* son of Tom: he inherits the Marsh farm and marries *Laura.*

   Dr. Frankstone, Ursula's materialist science lecturer at University College: her suggestion that life is merely a matter of physical and chemical activities reinforces her name's allusion to Mary Shelley's doctor, though it merely precipitates Ursula's opposing vision of life as a sacred and unfathomable mystery. *Miss Grey,* headmistress at Ursula's grammar school. *Mr. Harby,* the authoritarian headmaster of St. Philips, the Brinsley Street school where Ursula works. *Miss Violet Harby,* his daughter and Ursula's fellow teacher. Mr. Brunt, a teacher at Brinsley Street school. *Maggie Schofield,* Ursula's colleague and friend at Brinsley Street school. *Anthony Schofield,* her brother: the Schofields live behind the dilapidated Belcote Hall as farmers, caretakers, gamekeepers, and gardeners. Anthony is the eldest son at twenty-six and a market-gardener. He courts Ursula for a while and proposes to her, though she cannot accept him. *Dorothy Russell,* Ursula's suffragette college friend—an active member of the Women's Social and Political Union. *Baron Skrebensky,* a Polish exile who is now a clergyman in Yorkshire. *Baroness Skrebensky,* his noble, proud Polish wife who dies when he is about forty. He remarries, three years later, *Millicent Maud Pearse:* Anton Skrebensky is their son. *Tilly,* the housekeeper at Marsh farm. *Mr. Wiggington,* landlord of the George Inn at Derby. *Miss Coates,* Anna's teacher at Cossethay school. *Mrs. Hardy,* the squire's lady at Shelly Hall near Cossethay. *Lord William Bentley,* her friend and the local Member of Parliament. *Jennie,* the girl Will picks up at the music hall in Nottingham (Ch. 8). *Mr. Loverseed,* vicar of Cossethay. *Clem, Billy, Walter,* and *Eddie Anthony* Phillips

(Pillins), childhood friends of Ursula and her sisters. *Staples, Wright, Hill,* boys in Ursula's class at Brinsley Street school. *Vernon Williams,* the boy she canes. *Mrs. Williams,* his mother.

SETTING

"Cossethay," the main focus of the novel's setting, is based on Cossall, a village situated on the border between Nottinghamshire and Derbyshire, a mile or so east from Ilkeston and some three miles south of Eastwood ("Beldover" in the novel). The Brangwens' family home, Marsh farmhouse, situated beside the "Erewash Canal," is based on a real house that used to stand beside the embankment and the old Nottingham Canal at Cossall Marsh. The cottage next to the church where Will and Anna Brangwen set up home is based on Church Cottage in Cossall, the home of Louie Burrows (1888–1962), Lawrence's fiancée from 3 December 1910 to 4 February 1912 and one of the inspirations for the character of Ursula Brangwen (the Burrows family generally provided many of the surface details for the second and third generations of the Brangwens). "Belcote Hall," mentioned in Chapter 14, behind which Maggie Schofield and her family live, would seem to be based on Annesley Hall; and "Willey Green," to which Will Brangwen and the family remove in the same chapter, is based on Moor Green: both places are just to the northwest of Eastwood. Apart from Ilkeston, many other places in Derbyshire and Nottinghamshire appear with their actual names: Nottingham, Derby, Matlock, Bakewell, Ambergate, Wirksworth, Southwell, Sawley. Lincoln and its cathedral feature prominently in Chapter 7 ("The Cathedral"), of course; and the house party near the end of Chapter 15 takes place on the Lincolnshire coast. Earlier in that chapter, Ursula and Skrebensky attend a country house party somewhere near Oxford; they also stay with Ursula's college friend, Dorothy Russell, at her cottage on the Sussex Downs (based on Viola Meynall's cottage near Greatham, Pulborough, Sussex, where Lawrence lived between January and August 1915 while he was finishing the novel); and they go on an Easter vacation to London, Paris, and Rouen. The scene returns to London when Ursula goes to sit her final degree examinations at the University of London. "Wiggiston," in Yorkshire, where Ursula goes with Winifred Inger in Chapter 12 to visit Uncle Tom Brangwen, the manager of a big "new" colliery, would seem to be based on Bentley, near Doncaster, forty-eight miles north of Eastwood, for it was here that the Eastwood company of mine owners, Barber, Walker and Co., sank a new mine between 1906 and 1908.

BIBLIOGRAPHY 6

Adam, Ian. "Lawrence's Anti-Symbol: The Ending of *The Rainbow.*" *Journal of Narrative Technique* 3 (May 1973): 77–84.

Adamowski, T. H. "*The Rainbow* and 'Otherness.' " *DHL Review* 7 (Spring 1974): 58–77.

Adelman, Gary. *Snow of Fire: Symbolic Meaning in "The Rainbow" and "Women in Love."* New York and London: Garland, 1991, pp. 17–50.

Alinei, Tamara. "Imagery and Meaning in DHL's *The Rainbow.*" *Yearbook of English Studies* 2 (1972): 205–11.

———. "The Beginning of *The Rainbow:* Novel within a Novel?" *Lingua e Stile* (Bologna) 12 (March 1977): 161–66.

Aylwin, A. M. *Notes on DHL's "The Rainbow."* London: Methuen, 1977.

Balbert, Peter. *DHL and the Psychology of Rhythm: The Meaning of Form in "The Rainbow."* The Hague: Mouton, 1974.

———. " 'Logic of the Soul': Prothalamic Pattern in *The Rainbow.*" *Papers on Language and Literature* 29 (1983): 309–25. (Rev. versions in Balbert and Marcus [1985]: 45–66, and Balbert [1989]: 56–84.)

Baldanza, Frank. "DHL's 'Song of Songs.' " *Modern Fiction Studies* 7 (Summer 1961): 106–14.

Bell, Elizabeth S. "Slang Associations of DHL's Image Patterns in *The Rainbow.*" *Modernist Studies* 4 (1982): 77–86.

Berthoud, Jacques. "*The Rainbow* as Experimental Novel." In *DHL: A Critical Study of the Major Novels and Other Writings.* Edited by A. H. Gomme. New York: Barnes and Noble; Sussex: Harvester, 1978, pp. 53–69.

Bi, Bingbin. "The Era and *The Rainbow.*" *Foreign Literary Studies* (China) 30 (1985): 70–75.

Blanchard, Lydia. "Mothers and Daughters in DHL: *The Rainbow* and Selected Shorter Works." In *Lawrence and Women.* Edited by Anne Smith. London: Vision, 1978, pp. 75–100.

Brandabur, A. M. "The Ritual Corn Harvest Scene in *The Rainbow.*" *DHL Review* 6 (Fall 1973): 284–302.

Brookesmith, Peter. "The Future of the Individual: Ursula Brangwen and Kate Millett's *Sexual Politics.*" *Human World* (Swansea) 10 (1973): 42–65.

Brown, Ashley. "Prose into Poetry: DHL's *The Rainbow.*" In *Order in Variety.* Edited by R. W. Crump. Newark: University of Delaware Press, 1991, pp. 133–42.

Brown, Homer O. " 'The Passionate Struggle into Conscious Being': DHL's *The Rainbow.*" *DHL Review* 7 (Fall 1974): 275–90.

Buckley, Margaret, and Brian Buckley. *Challenge and Renewal: Lawrence and the Thematic Novel.* Kenilworth, Warwickshire: Chrysalis Press, 1993, pp. 1–76.

Bunnell, W. S. *Brodie's Notes on DHL's "The Rainbow."* London: Pan Books, 1978. (Rev. ed., London: Macmillan, 1993.)

Burns, Robert. "The Novel as a Metaphysical Statement: Lawrence's *The Rainbow.*" *Southern Review* (Adelaide) 4 (1970): 139–60.

Butler, Gerald J. "Sexual Experience in DHL's *The Rainbow.*" *Recovering Literature* 2 (1973): 1–92.

———. *This Is Carbon: A Defense of DHL's "The Rainbow" against His Admirers.* Seattle: Genitron Press, 1986.

Carter, John. "*The Rainbow* Prosecution." *Times Literary Supplement* (27 February 1969): 216. (See also subsequent correspondence: 17 April, p. 414; 24 April, p. 440; and 4 September, p. 979.)

Chapple, J.A.V. *Documentary and Imaginative Literature 1880–1920.* London: Blandford Press, 1970, pp. 72–79.

Chavis, Geraldine G. "Ursula Brangwen: Toward Self and Selflessness." *Thoth* 12 (1971): 18–28.

Chrisman, Reva Wells. "Ursula Brangwen in the University: DHL's Rejection of Authority in *The Rainbow.*" *Kentucky Philological Association Bulletin* (1974): 9–16.

Christensen, Peter G. "Problems in Characterization in DHL's *The Rainbow.*" *Journal of the Australasian Universities Language and Literature Association* 77 (May 1992): 78–96.

Clarke, Colin, ed. *DHL: "The Rainbow" and "Women in Love": A Casebook.* London: Macmillan, 1969; Nashville, Tenn.: Aurora, 1970.

Clements, A. L. "The Quest for the Self: DHL's *The Rainbow.*" *Thoth* 3 (Spring 1962): 90–100.

Cockshut, A.O.J. *Man and Woman: A Study of Love and the Novel, 1740–1940.* New York: Oxford University Press, 1978, pp. 152–60.

Core, Deborah. " 'The Closed Door': Love between Women in the Works of DHL." *DHL Review* 11 (Summer 1978): 114–31.

Cross, Barbara. "Lawrence and the Unbroken Circle." *Perspective* 11 (Summer 1959): 81–89.

Cushman, Keith. " 'I am going through a transition stage': *The Prussian Officer* and *The Rainbow.*" *DHL Review* 8 (Summer 1975): 176–97.

Daiches, David. *The Novel and the Modern World.* Rev. ed. Chicago: University of Chicago Press, 1960, pp. 152–66.

Davies, Alistair. "Contexts of Reading: The Reception of DHL's *The Rainbow* and *Women in Love.*" In *The Theory of Reading.* Edited by Frank Gloversmith. Sussex: Harvester, 1984, pp. 199–222.

Davis, E. "DHL, *The Rainbow* and *Women in Love.*" In his *Readings in Modern Fiction.* Cape Town, South Africa: Simondium, 1964, pp. 258–81.

Delany, Paul. "Lawrence and E. M. Forster: Two Rainbows." *DHL Review* 8 (Spring 1975): 54–62.

DeVille, Peter. "In or Out of the Camp Fire: Lawrence and Jack London's Dogs." *Notes and Queries* 38 (1991): 339–41.

DiBattista, Maria. "Angelic Lawrence: *The Rainbow.*" In her *First Love: The Affections of Modern Fiction.* Chicago and London: University of Chicago Press, 1991, pp. 113–39.

Diethe, C. "Expressionism in Lawrence's *The Rainbow* and *Women in Love.*" In *Gedenkschrift for Victor Poznanski.* Edited by C.A.M. Noble. Bern: Peter Lang, 1981, pp. 147–57.

Ditsky, John M. " 'Dark, Darker than Fire': Thematic Parallels in Lawrence and Faulkner." *Southern Humanities Review* 8 (Fall 1974): 497–505.

Doherty, Gerald. "White Mythologies: DHL and the Deconstructive Turn." *Criticism* 29 (Fall 1987): 477–96.

———. "The Metaphorical Imperative: From Trope to Narrative in *The Rainbow.*" *South Central Review* 6 (Spring 1989): 46–62.

Draper, R. P. "*The Rainbow.*" *Critical Quarterly* 20 (Autumn 1978): 49–64.

Eagleton, Terry. *Exiles and Emigrés: Studies in Modern Literature.* London: Chatto and Windus; New York: Schocken, 1970, pp. 200–208.

Ebbatson, Roger. "The Opening of *The Rainbow:* Language and Self." *Osmania Journal of English Studies* 21 (1985): 30–38. (Also in Cooper and Hughes [1985]: 72–76.)

Edwards, Duane. *"The Rainbow": A Search for New Life.* Boston: Twayne, 1990.

Efron, Arthur. "Toward a Dialectic of Sensuality and Work." *Paunch* 44–45 (May 1976): 152–70. ("Sex and Work in Marx and *The Rainbow*," pp. 165–70.)

Eggert, Paul. "The Half-Structured *Rainbow*." *Critical Review* (Melbourne) 23 (1981): 89–97.

Engelberg, Edward. "Escape from the Circles of Experience: DHL's *The Rainbow* as a Modern *Bildungsroman*." *PMLA* 78 (March 1963): 103–13.

Fernihough, Anne. "Introduction." *The Rainbow* by DHL. Edited by Mark Kinkead-Weekes. Harmondsworth: Penguin, 1995, pp. xiii–xxxiv.

Ford, George H. "The Eternal Moment: DHL's *The Rainbow* and *Women in Love*." In *The Study of Time III.* Edited by J. T. Fraser, N. Lawrence, and D. Park. New York: Springer, 1978, pp. 512–36.

Friedman, Alan. *The Turn of the Novel.* New York: Oxford University Press, 1966, pp. 139–51.

Gamache, Lawrence B. "The Making of an Ugly Technocrat: Character and Structure in Lawrence's *The Rainbow*." *Mosaic* 12 (Autumn 1978): 61–78.

———. "Husband Father: DHL's Use of Character in Structuring a Narrative." *Modernist Studies* 4 (1982): 36–52.

Garrett, Peter K. *Scene and Symbol from George Eliot to James Joyce.* New Haven, Conn.: Yale University Press, 1969, pp. 189–98.

Gibbons, Thomas. " 'Allotropic States' and 'Fiddlebow': DHL's Occult Sources." *Notes and Queries* 35, no. 3 (1988): 338–40.

Gilbert, Sandra M. *DHL's "Sons and Lovers," "The Rainbow," "Women in Love," "The Plumed Serpent."* New York: Monarch Press, 1965. (Study Guide.)

Goldberg, S. L. "*The Rainbow:* Fiddle-Bow and Sand." *Essays in Criticism* 11 (October 1961): 418–34.

Greeves, Richard Lynn. "Ursula's Struggle for Independence." *Collection of Articles and Essays* 20 (1987): 279–81.

Gregor, Ian. "What Kind of Fiction Did Hardy Write?" *Essays in Criticism* 16 (July 1966): 290–308. (*The Rainbow* picks up where *Jude the Obscure* left off.)

Haegert, John. "Lawrence's World Elsewhere: Elegy and History in *The Rainbow*." *Clio* 15, no. 2 (1986): 115–35.

Harding, Adrian. "Self-Parody and Ethical Satire in *The Rainbow*." *Etudes Lawrenciennes* 6 (1991): 31–38.

Hayles, Nancy Katherine. "Evasion: The Field of the Unconscious in DHL." In her *The Cosmic Web: Scientific Field Models and Literary Strategies in the Twentieth Century.* Ithaca, N.Y.: Cornell University Press, 1984, pp. 90–95.

Heldt, Lucia Henning. "Lawrence on Love: The Courtship and Marriage of Tom Brangwen and Lydia Lensky." *DHL Review* 8 (Fall 1975): 358–70.

Hewitt, Jan. "Introduction." *The Rainbow* by DHL. London: Dent, 1993, pp. xv–xxvi.

Heywood, Christopher. "Olive Schreiner's *The Story of an African Farm:* Prototype of Lawrence's Early Novels." *English Language Notes* 14 (September 1976): 44–50.

Hildick, Wallace. *Word for Word: A Study of Author's Alterations.* New York: Norton, 1965, pp. 65–69.

Hill, Ordelle G., and Potter Woodbery. "Ursula Brangwen of *The Rainbow:* Christian Saint or Pagan Goddess?" *DHL Review* 4 (Fall 1971): 274–79.

Hinchcliffe, Peter. "*The Rainbow* and *Women in Love:* From George Eliot to Thomas Hardy as Formal Models." In *DHL's "Women in Love": Contexts and Criticism.* Edited by Michael Ballin. Waterloo, Ontario: Wilfrid Laurier University, 1980, pp. 34–46.

Hinz, Evelyn J. "*The Rainbow:* Ursula's 'Liberation.'" *Contemporary Literature* 17 (Winter 1976): 24–43.

———. "*Ancient Art and Ritual* and *The Rainbow.*" *Dalhousie Review* 58 (1979): 617–37.

Hinz, Evelyn J., and John J. Teunissen. "Odysseus, Ulysses, and Ursula: The Context of Lawrence's *Rainbow.*" In *The Modernists: Studies in a Literary Phenomenon: Essays in Honor of Harry T. Moore.* Rutherford, N.J.: Fairleigh Dickinson University Press, 1987, pp. 171–91.

Hoerner, Dennis. "Ursula, Anton, and the 'Sons of God': Armor and Core in *The Rainbow's* Third Generation." *Paunch* 63–64 (1990): 173–98.

Hortmann, Wilhelm. "The Nail and the Novel: Some Remarks on Style and the Unconscious in *The Rainbow.*" In *Theorie und Praxis im Erzählen des 19. und 20. Jahrhunderts: Studien zur englischen und amerikanischen Literatur zu Ehren von Willi Erzgräber.* Edited by Winfried Herget, Klaus Peter Jochum, and Ingeborg Weber. Tübingen: Narr, 1986, pp. 167–79.

Hughs, Richard. "The Brangwen Inheritance: The Archetype in DHL's *The Rainbow.*" *Greyfriar* 17 (1976): 33–40.

Hyde, Virginia. "Will Brangwen and Paradisal Vision in *The Rainbow* and *Women in Love.*" *DHL Review* 8 (Fall 1975): 346–57.

———. "Toward 'The Earth's New Architecture': Triads, Arches, and Angles in *The Rainbow.*" *Modernist Studies* 4 (1982): 7–35.

Idema, James M. "The Hawk and the Plover: 'The Polarity of Life' in the 'Jungle Aviary' of DHL's Mind in *Sons and Lovers* and *The Rainbow.*" *Forum* (Houston) 3 (Summer 1961): 11–14.

Ingersoll, Earl G. "*The Rainbow's* Winifred Inger." *DHL Review* 17 (1984): 67–69.

———. "Lawrence's *The Rainbow.*" *Explicator* 47 (1989): 46–50.

Janik, Del Ivan. "A Cumbrian *Rainbow:* Melvyn Bragg's Tallentire Trilogy." In *DHL's Literary Inheritors.* New York: St. Martin's Press, 1991, pp. 73–88.

Kaplan, Harold J. *The Passive Voice: An Approach to Modern Fiction.* Athens: Ohio University Press, 1966, pp. 169–73, 175–80.

Karl, Frederick R., and Marvin Magalaner. *A Reader's Guide to Great Twentieth-Century English Novels.* New York: Noonday; London: Thames and Hudson, 1959, pp. 171–85.

Kay, Wallace G. "Lawrence and *The Rainbow:* Apollo and Dionysus in Conflict." *Southern Quarterly* 10 (April 1972): 209–22.

Kennedy, Andrew. "After Not So Strange Gods in *The Rainbow.*" *English Studies* 63 (1982): 220–30.

Kern, Stephen. *The Culture of Love: Victorians to Moderns.* Cambridge: Harvard University Press, 1992, pp. 326–30 and passim.

Kettle, Arnold. "DHL: *The Rainbow.*" In his *An Introduction to the English Novel.* Vol. 2, 2d ed. London: Hutchinson, 1967, pp. 100–120 (1st ed., 1951, pp. 111–34).

Kiberd, Declan. "DHL: The New Man as Prophet." In his *Men and Feminism in Modern Literature*. New York: St. Martin's Press, 1985, pp. 136–67.

Kinkead-Weekes, Mark. "The Marble and the Statue: The Exploratory Imagination of DHL." In *Imagined Worlds: Essays on Some English Novels and Novelists in Honour of John Butt*. Edited by Maynard Mack and Ian Gregor. London: Methuen, 1968, pp. 371–418.

———. "The Marriage of Opposites in *The Rainbow*." In *DHL: Centenary Essays*. Edited by Mara Kalnins. Bristol: Bristol Classical Press, 1986, pp. 21–40.

———. "Introduction." *The Rainbow* by DHL. Edited by Mark Kinkead-Weekes. Cambridge: Cambridge University Press, 1989a, pp. xvii–lxxvi.

———. "The Sense of History in *The Rainbow*." In *DHL in the Modern World*. Edited by Peter Preston and Peter Hoare. London: Macmillan, 1989b, pp. 121–38.

———, ed. *Twentieth Century Interpretations of "The Rainbow."* Englewood Cliffs, N.J.: Prentice-Hall, 1971.

Klein, Robert C. "I, Thou and You in Three Lawrencian Relationships." *Paunch*, no. 31 (April 1968): 52–70.

Knapp, James F. "The Self in Lawrence: Languages of History or Myth." In his *Literary Modernism and the Transformation of Work*. Evanston, Ill. Northwestern University Press, 1988, pp. 75–91.

Kondo, Kyoko. "*The Rainbow* in Focus: A Study of the Form of *The Rainbow* by DHL." *Studies in English Literature—Japan* (1985): 53–69.

Kuo, Carol Haseley. "Lawrence's *The Rainbow*." *Explicator* 19 (June 1961), item 70. (On Ursula's connection to St. Ursula.)

Lainoff, Seymour. "*The Rainbow:* The Shaping of Modern Man." *Modern Fiction Studies* 1 (November 1955): 23–27.

Langland, Elizabeth. "Society as Other in *The Rainbow*." In her *Society in the Novel*. Chapel Hill: University of North Carolina Press, 1984, pp. 104–14.

Latta, William. "Lawrence's Debt to Rudolph, Baron Von Hube." *DHL Review* 1 (Spring 1968): 60–62.

Leavis, F. R. "The Novel as Dramatic Poem (VII): *The Rainbow* I–III." *Scrutiny* 18 (Winter 1951–52): 197–210; 18 (June 1952): 273–87; 19 (October 1952): 15–30.

Langbaum, Robert. "Reconstitution of Self: Lawrence and the Religion of Love." In his *Mysteries of Identity: A Theme in Modern Literature*. New York: Oxford University Press, 1977, pp. 251–353.

———. "Lawrence and Hardy." In *DHL and Tradition*. Edited by Jeffrey Meyers. London: Athlone, 1985, pp. 69–90 (passim).

Lenz, William E. "The 'Organic Connexion' of *The Rainbow* with *Women in Love*." *South Atlantic Bulletin* 43 (1978): 5–18.

Lerner, Laurence. *Love and Marriage: Literature and Its Social Context*. New York: St. Martin's Press, 1979, pp. 153–64.

Makolkina, Anna. "The Dance of Dionysos in H. Khodkevych and DHL." *Journal of Ukrainian Studies* 15 (1990): 31–38.

McLaughlin, Ann L. "The Clenched and Knotted Horses in *The Rainbow*." *DHL Review* 13 (1980): 179–86.

Mahalanobis, Shanta. "Pre-War Feminism in Lawrence's *The Rainbow*." *Journal of the Department of English* (Calcutta University) 21 (1986–87): 30–41.

Manicom, David. "An Approach to the Imagery: A Study of Selected Biblical Analogues in DHL's *The Rainbow.*" *English Studies in Canada* 11 (December 1985): 474–83.

Martin, Graham. *DHL's "The Rainbow."* Milton Keynes: Open University Press, 1971.

Meyers, Jeffrey. "*The Rainbow* and Fra Angelico." *DHL Review* 7 (Summer 1974): 139–55. (Reprinted in Meyers [1975]: 53–64.)

Miliaras, Barbara A. "The Collapse of Agrarian Order and the Death of Thomas Brangwen in DHL's *The Rainbow.*" *Etudes Lawrenciennes* 3 (1988): 65–77.

Monell, Siv. "On the Role of Case, Aspect and Valency in the Narrative Technique of *The Rainbow.*" In *Papers from the Second Scandinavian Symposium on Syntactic Variation, Stockholm, May 15–16, 1982.* Edited by Sven Jacobson. Stockholm: Almqvist and Wiksell, 1983, pp. 153–68.

Mori, Haruhide. "Lawrence's Imagistic Development in *The Rainbow* and *Women in Love.*" *Journal of English Literary History* 31 (December 1964): 460–81.

Mudrick, Marvin. "The Originality of *The Rainbow.*" In *A DHL Miscellany.* Edited by Harry T. Moore. Carbondale: Southern Illinois University Press, 1959, pp. 56–82. (Also in *Spectrum* 3 [Winter 1959]: 3–28, and Kinkead-Weekes [1971], op. cit., pp. 11–32.)

Mueller, W. R. "The Paradisal Quest." In his *The Celebration of Life.* New York: Sheed and Ward, 1972, pp. 144–68.

Nabarro, Serry van Mierop. "Of Time and Timelessness in *The Rainbow.*" *Journal of the DHL Society* (1984): 31–37.

Nassar, Eugene Paul. "Stylistic Discontinuity in DHL's *The Rainbow.*" In his *Essays Critical and Metacritical.* Rutherford, N.J.: Fairleigh Dickinson University Press, 1983, pp. 65–83.

Nixon, Cornelia. "To Procreate Oneself: Ursula's Horses in *The Rainbow.*" *English Literary History* 49 (1982): 123–42. (Reprinted in Nixon [1986]: 88–98, 106–12.)

Obler, Paul. "DHL's World of *The Rainbow.*" *Drew University Studies,* no. 8 (December 1957): 1–19.

O'Connell, Adelyn. "The Concept of Person in DHL's *The Rainbow.*" In *Literature and Religion: Views on DHL.* Edited by Charles A Huttar. Holland, Mich.: Hope College, 1968. (Articles independently paginated from 1.)

Orr, John. "Lawrence: Passion and Its Dissolution." In his *The Making of the Twentieth-Century Novel: Lawrence, Joyce, Faulkner and Beyond.* Basingstoke and London: Macmillan, 1987, pp. 20–43.

Otte, George. "The Loss of History in the Modern Novel: The Case of *The Rainbow.*" *Pacific Coast Philology* 16, no. 1 (1981): 67–76.

Padhi, Bibhu. "Lawrence's Idea of Language." *Modernist Studies* 4 (1982): 65–76.

Paul, S. L. "The Meaning of *The Rainbow.*" In *Essays on DHL.* Edited by T. R. Sharma. Meerut, India: Shalabh Book House, 1987, pp. 147–52.

Raddatz, Volher. "Lyrical Elements in DHL's *The Rainbow.*" *Revue des Langues Vivantes* 40, no. 3 (1974): 235–42.

Raina, M. L. "The Wheel and the Centre: An Approach to *The Rainbow.*" *Literary Criterion* (Mysore) 9 (Summer 1970): 41–55.

Robins, Ross. " 'By this he knew she wept': A Note on Lawrence and Meredith." *Review of English Studies* 44 (August 1993): 3889–92.

Rosenzweig, Paul. "A Defense of the Second Half of *The Rainbow:* Its Structure and Characterization." *DHL Review* 13 (1980): 150–60.

————. "The Making of Ursula Brangwen's Identity: The Pattern of the Ritual Scenes in *The Rainbow.*" *University of Mississippi Studies in English* 6 (1988): 206–27.

Ross, C. L. "The Revision of the Second Generation in *The Rainbow.*" *Review of English Studies* 27 (1976): 277–95.

————. "DHL's Use of Greek Tragedy: Euripedes and Ritual." *DHL Review* 10 (Spring 1977): 1–19.

————. *The Composition of "The Rainbow" and "Women in Love": A History.* Charlottesville: University Press of Virginia, 1979.

Ross, Michael L. " 'More or Less a Sequel': Continuity and Discontinuity in Lawrence's Brangwensaga." *DHL Review* 14 (1981): 263–88.

Rossman, Charles. "The Cambridge *Rainbow.*" *DHL Review* 21 (1988): 179–86.

Ruffolo, Lara R. "Lawrence's Borrowed Bird: The Flight of Bede's Sparrow throughout *The Rainbow.*" *Antigonish Review* 53 (1983): 127–32.

Ruthven, K. K. "The Savage God: Conrad and Lawrence." In *Word in the Desert.* Edited by C. B. Cox and A. E. Dyson. Oxford: Oxford University Press, 1968, pp. 39–54.

Sagar, Keith. "The Genesis of *The Rainbow* and *Women in Love.*" *DHL Review* 1 (Fall 1968): 179–99.

Sale, Roger. "The Narrative Technique of *The Rainbow.*" *Modern Fiction Studies* 5 (Spring 1959): 29–38.

Salgādo, Gāmini. *DHL: "Sea and Sardinia"; "The Rainbow."* London: British Council, 1969. (Notes on Literature no. 100.)

————. *DHL: "The Rainbow."* London: British Council, 1976. (Notes on Literature no. 162.)

Scherr, Barry J. "Two Essays on D. H. Lawrence's 'Darkness'; I: The 'Fecund Darkness' of *The Rainbow;* II: The 'Body of Darkness' in *Women in Love.*" *Recovering Literature: A Journal of Contextualist Criticism* 18 (1991–92): 8–40.

Schleifer, Ronald. "Lawrence's Rhetoric of Vision: The Ending of *The Rainbow.*" *DHL Review* 13 (Summer 1980): 161–78.

Schnitzer, Deborah. *The Pictorial in Modernist Fiction from Stephen Crane to Ernest Hemingway.* Ann Arbor, Mich. UMI Research Press, 1988, pp. 138–58 (143–57).

Schwarz, Daniel R. "Lawrence's Quest in *The Rainbow.*" *Ariel* 11, no. 3 (1980): 43–66.

Selby, Keith. "DHL's *The Rainbow.*" *Explicator* 46 (1987): 41–43.

Sepčić, Višnja. "A Link between DHL's *The Trespasser* and *The Rainbow.*" *Studia Romanica et Anglica,* no. 24 (December 1967): 113–26.

Sharma, R. S. *"The Rainbow": A Study of Symbolic Mode in DHL's Primitivism.* Hyderabad, India: Trust, 1981.

Sipple, James B. "Laughter in the Cathedral: Religious Affirmation and Ridicule in the Writings of DHL." In *The Philosophical Reflection of Man in Literature: Selected Papers from Several Conferences Held by the International Society for Phenomenology and Literature in Cambridge, Massachusetts.* Edited by Anna-Teresa Tymieniecka. Boston: Reidel, 1982, pp. 213–44.

Smith, Frank Glover. *DHL: "The Rainbow."* London: Edward Arnold, 1971.

Spano, Joseph. "A Study of Ursula and H. M. Daleski's Commentary." *Paunch,* no. 33 (December 1968): 21–33.

Spear, Hilda D. *York Notes on DHL's "The Rainbow."* London: Longman, 1991.

Spilka, Mark. "The Shape of an Arch: A Study of Lawrence's *The Rainbow*." *Modern Fiction Studies* 1 (May 1955): 30–38.

Squires, Michael. "Recurrence as a Narrative Technique in *The Rainbow*." *Modern Fiction Studies* 21 (Summer 1975a): 230–36.

———. "Scenic Construction and Rhetorical Signals in Hardy and Lawrence." *DHL Review* 8 (Summer 1975b): 125–46.

Stewart, Jack F. "Expressionism in *The Rainbow*." *Novel* 13 (1979–80): 296–315. (Reprinted in Jackson and Jackson [1988]: 72–92.)

Stoll, John E. "Common Womb Imagery in Joyce and Lawrence." *Ball State University Forum* 11 (Spring 1970): 10–24.

Thickstun, William R. "*The Rainbow* and the Flood of Consciousness." In his *Visionary Closure in the Modern Novel*. New York: St. Martin's Press, 1988, pp. 52–76.

Thomas, Marlin. "Somewhere under *The Rainbow*: DHL and the Typology of Hermeneutics." *Mid-Hudson Language Studies* 6 (1983): 57–65.

Tilak, Raghukul. *DHL, "The Rainbow."* New Delhi: Aarti Book Centre, 1971.

Tobin, Patricia Drechsel. "The Cycle Dance: DHL, *The Rainbow*." In her *Time and the Novel: The Genealogical Imperative*. Princeton: Princeton University Press, 1978, pp. 81–106.

Tripathy, B. D. "*The Rainbow*: Unfamiliar Quest." *Aligarh Journal of English Studies* 10, no. 2 (1985): 141–55.

Trotter, David. "Edwardian Sex Novels." *Critical Quarterly* 31 (1989): 92–106.

Twitchell, James. "Lawrence's Lamias: Predatory Women in *The Rainbow* and *Women in Love*." *Studies in the Novel* 11 (1979): 23–42.

Unrue, Darlene H. "Lawrence's Vision of Evil: The Power-Spirit in *The Rainbow* and *Women in Love*." *Dalhousie Review* 55 (Winter 1975–76): 643–54.

Van der Veen, Berend Klass. *The Development of DHL's Prose Themes, 1906–1915*. Groningen, Netherlands: University of Groningen, 1983.

Verleun, Jan. "The Inadequate Male in DHL's *The Rainbow*." *Neophilologus* 72 (January 1988): 116–35.

Wah, Pun Tzoh. "*The Rainbow* and Lawrence's Vision of a New World." *Southeast Asian Review of English* 12–13 (1986): 97–106.

Walsh, William. "The Writer and the Child." In his *The Use of the Imagination: Educational Thought and the Literary Mind*. London: Chatto and Windus, 1959, pp. 163–74. (On Ursula.)

Wasson, R. "Comedy and History in *The Rainbow*." *Modern Fiction Studies* 13 (Winter 1967–68): 465–77.

Whelan, P. T. *DHL: Myth and Metaphysic in "The Rainbow" and "Women in Love."* Ann Arbor, Mich., and London: UMI Research Press, 1988.

Whiteley, Patrick J. *Knowledge and Experimental Realism in Conrad, Lawrence, and Woolf*. Baton Rouge: Louisiana State University Press, 1987, pp. 86–96, 124–27.

Wilding, Michael. "*The Rainbow*: 'smashing the great machine.' " In his *Political Fictions*. Boston: Routledge and Kegan Paul, 1980, pp. 150–91.

Worthen, John. "Introduction." *The Rainbow* by DHL. Edited by John Worthen. Harmondsworth: Penguin, 1981, pp. 11–33.

Wright, Terence. "Rhythm in the Novel." *Modern Language Review* 80 (1985): 1–15.

Wussow, Helen M. "Lawrence's *The Rainbow*." *Explicator* 41 (1982): 44–45.

Young, Richard O. " 'Where Even the Trees Come and Go': DHL and the Fourth Dimension." *DHL Review* 13 (Spring 1980): 30–44.

Zytaruk, George J. "DHL's *The Rainbow* and Leo Tolstoy's *Anna Karenina:* An Instance of Literary 'Clinamen.' " *Germano-Slavica* 5 (1987): 197–209.

See also (1980–94) Alden (1986): 114–26. Becker (1980): 43–60. Bell (1992): 51–102, passim. Ben-Ephraim (1981): 129–78. Bonds (1987): 53–75. Burns (1980): 46–71. Clark (1980): 97–105. Dix (1980): 34–40. Dorbad (1991): 59–89. Ebbatson (1982): 76–95. Herzinger (1982): 91–99, passim. Hobsbaum (1981): 52–61. Holderness (1982): 174–89. Hyde (1990): 37–57. Hyde (1992): 73–99, passim. Ingram (1990): 21–24, 98–102, 119–37. Kelsey (1991): 121–40. Kiely (1980): 103–19. Kushigian (1990): 75–150. MacLeod (1985/87): 107–18. Miliaras (1987): 165–228. Milton (1987): 34–51, passim. Modiano (1987): 89–96. Niven (1980): 42–49. Nixon (1986): 88–98, 106–12. Padhi (1989): 108–36. Pinkney (1990): 60–78. Poplawski (1993): 79–114. Prasad (1980): 57–67. Robinson (1992): 8–31. Sagar (1985a): 102–46. Salgādo (1982): 108–21. Scheckner (1985): 23–69. Schneider (1984): 145–69. Siegel (1991): passim. Simpson (1982): 37–42, passim. Sipple (1992): 65–89. Sklenicka (1991): 56–145. Suter (1987): 69–87. Templeton (1989): 107–65. Urang (1983): 11–31. Verhoeven (1987): 97–160. Widmer (1992): 17–21, passim. Williams (1993): 138–47. Worthen (1991a): 43–49.

See also (to 1979) Albright (1978): 84–88, passim. Alldritt (1971): 45–138. Beal (1961): 23–40. Bedient (1972): 124–35. Boadella (1956/78): 84–90, passim. Cavitch (1969): 37–57. Clarke (1969): 45–69. Daleski (1965): 74–125. Delany (1978): passim. Delavenay (1971): 27–33, 132–35, passim. Delavenay (1972): 344–85. Draper (1964): 54–75. Draper (1970): 84–109. Ford (1965): 115–68. Goodheart (1963): 25–31, 115–20, passim. Gregory (1933): 34–43. Hochman (1970): 35–44. Hough (1956): 54–67, passim. Howe (1977): 28–51. Inniss (1971): 118–36. Jarrett-Kerr (1951): 19–28. Kermode (1973): 40–49. Leavis (1955): 28–31, 96–145. Leavis (1976): 122–46. Maes-Jelinek (1970): 40–51, passim. Miko (1971): 108–85. Miles (1969): 34–36, passim. Millett (1970): 257–62. Moore (1951): 134–44. Moynahan (1963): 42–72. Murfin (1978): 198–207. Murry (1931): 59–75. Nahal (1970): 137–73, passim. Nin (1932): 14–19, 26–28, passim. Niven (1978): 59–113. Pinion (1978): 148–63. Prasad (1976): 163–89. Pritchard (1971): 66–78, passim. Sagar (1966): 41–72. Sale (1973): 52–76. Sanders (1973): 60–93. Slade (1970): 55–67. Spilka (1955): 93–120. Stewart (1963): 498–510. Stoll (1971): 106–50. Swigg (1972): 81–131. Tedlock (1963): 86–96. Vivas (1960): 201–23. Worthen (1979): 45–82. Yudhishtar (1969): 113–57.

15   *Women in Love*

WRITTEN

March 1913–October 1921. The composition of *Women in Love* is inextricably linked with that of *The Rainbow,* as both novels grew from what was initially a single project entitled "The Sisters." There were three full draft versions of "The Sisters" before Lawrence decided, in early January 1915, to divide the novel into two separate volumes. Drafts: 1. "The Sisters," March–June 1913. 2. "The Sisters," August 1913–January 1914. 3. "The Wedding Ring," February–May 1914. 4. (a) *The Rainbow,* November 1914–March 1915; (b) "The Sisters III," April–June 1916. 5. *Women in Love,* July 1916–January 1917. 6. *Women in Love,* March 1917–September 1919. Proofs for the first American edition were corrected between August and October 1920, while corrections and changes for the Secker edition continued until February 1921 for the first publication in June 1921, with Lawrence having to make yet more alterations in September–October, following threats of a lawsuit from Philip Heseltine (Peter Warlock), who thought himself and his wife to have been libeled by the portraits of Halliday and "Pussum" (changed to Minette) Darrington, for a second printing in November 1921. The story of the textual transmission of this novel is extremely complex, and readers should consult the introduction of the Cambridge edition for full details.

The "Foreword to *Women in Love*" was written on 12 September 1919 and first published as an advertising leaflet by Seltzer in the autumn of 1920. Two abandoned chapters, the "Prologue to *Women in Love*" and "The Wedding," were probably written in April 1916 at draft stage 4 (b) (see earlier) and intended as the two opening chapters of the novel at that stage; they were first published separately in 1963 and 1964, respectively (see under Ford in the following bibliography) and are printed as Appendix II in the Cambridge edition of the novel (pp. 487–518).

PUBLISHED

1. New York: privately printed, for subscribers only, 9 November 1920. London: Secker, 10 June 1921.
2. Edited by David Farmer, Lindeth Vasey, and John Worthen. Cambridge: Cambridge University Press, 1987.
3. See also under Ross (1982) and Williams ("Introduction," 1993) in the following bibliography.

WHO'S WHO AND SUMMARY

MAIN CHARACTERS: Rupert Birkin, Ursula Brangwen, Gudrun Brangwen, Gerald Crich

Women in Love, progressing by means of a series of dramatic scenes connected more by principles of contrast and comparison than by any strong sequential order of events, presents an intensive exploration of a complex set of relationships, first and foremost among the four main characters.

Ursula Brangwen, the same character on the surface as the Ursula Brangwen of *The Rainbow* (though she has a somewhat different personality here), now aged twenty-six and a schoolteacher in a grammar school; she becomes the lover and, eventually, wife of Birkin; her "very beautiful" sister, *Gudrun Brangwen,* aged twenty-five and recently returned from art school, teaches in the same school; a confident, forceful character, she is always brightly dressed and wears brilliantly colored stockings that stand out against the drabness of the colliery town of Beldover (the Brangwen family had moved here at the end of *The Rainbow*). *Rupert Birkin,* a highly articulate and independent-minded school inspector, also independent in terms of having a private income. Gudrun's lover, *Gerald Crich,* a handsome, athletic, blond man of about thirty, the son of a wealthy mine owner and responsible for the running of the mines—energetic and commanding in his work and almost obsessive in his desire for efficient production, he is personally insecure, with little sense of any inner meaning to his life; his affair with Gudrun fails largely because of this inner weakness, which seeks self-confirmation from, rather than consummation with, his lover.

The exploration of these characters and relationships has two broad aims: to test, through both dialogue and dramatic interaction, different forms and principles of relationship between man and woman and man and man; and to present, through this testing, a critique of modern industrial society (the context of the First World War clearly provides a sharp edge to this critique for, as Lawrence said in his foreword, "the bitterness of the war may be taken for granted in the characters''). Two central ideas can be seen to provide a structuring focus for the novel—the idea of a creative state of relationship, "star-equilibrium," and the idea of a destructive "flux of corruption": both are given explicit formulation by Rupert Birkin, who himself provides the novel's primary center of consciousness.

Rupert Birkin is an intellectual with unconventional ideas about the nature of love, relationships, and society. Thoroughly disillusioned with the modern industrial world and, at times, despairing of humanity altogether, he nevertheless avoids cynicism and remains full of vitality in himself; he continues to believe in the possibility of personal fulfillment through balanced relationships with others and sees the formation of such relationships as the only hope for the salvation of society. He advocates a doctrine of "star-equilibrium," where two lovers are in balanced polar conjunction with one another like two stars, both perfectly free and single, having achieved their own "integral individuality," but linked together indissolubly within a mutually fulfilling constellation: "a pure balance of two single beings." Birkin's other major theory is expressed in terms of the "flux of corruption" and the "flux of creation": there are cycles of life and history in which humanity can be either progressing creatively, in an organically integrated form, or falling destructively into a process of disintegration and dissolution where life becomes unbalanced, fragmentary, and mechanical. The world for Birkin is currently in a cycle of the latter sort, where, in particular, there has been a crippling fracture between the mind and the senses, between abstract, rational understanding and direct sensual experience. Both individuals and whole cultures now suffer from the imbalance caused by this fracture, being able to experience things only in one mode or the other, but never integrally "knowing in full." For Birkin, the southern dark races have fallen from "integral being" into a process of dissolution through purely mindless, sensual experience; while the northern white races are undergoing "a mystery of ice-destructive knowledge, snow-abstract annihilation." Equally, in the novel itself, we witness various permutations of abstraction and sensuality within individuals and within their relationships with one another. Most obviously, the relationship at the start of the novel between Birkin and *Hermione Roddice,* the society hostess and baronet's daughter, is vitiated by its almost wholly cerebral nature (Hermione—"a medium for the culture of ideas"—being an embodiment of the potential willfulness and sterility of the abstract intellect); while the relationship between Gerald and Gudrun never develops beyond a purely sensual one. Both extremes are shown to be destructive: Hermione nearly fractures Birkin's skull with a paperweight, while Gerald, at the end, attempts to strangle Gudrun before climbing further into the Alpine snows to his own self-willed death.

But as the latter example suggests, the novel does not present this abstraction-sensuality opposition in any simple schematic way; Gerald is limited by his senses in one realm of life, but he is a "demon from the north" in most others (in his Viking-like looks apart from anything else). In particular, when he takes over the colliery company from his father, *Mr. Thomas Crich,* who had run the mines paternalistically on benevolent Christian principles, he institutes a new regime based purely on instrumental reason and principles of maximum efficiency with no regard for the social and human consequences. He is thus aptly characterized at one point as a type of machine himself, made up of ''a million wheels and cogs and axles.'' Similarly, Gudrun's sensual corruption also has an abstract, self-conscious aspect to it, as we see when, having exhausted the possibilities of purely physical, outward experience with Gerald, she turns to explore sensation ''within the ego,'' with the ultimate ''creature,'' the elfin German sculptor, *Herr Loerke,* who lurks, ''like a rat, in the river of corruption,'' in the furthest recesses of humanity's ''diabolic'' disintegration. Together, in rarefied intellectual discussion (in three languages), Gudrun and Loerke exult, first, in asserting art's total divorce from life (in an extreme version of ''art for art's sake'') and then in ''mocking imaginations'' of the destruction of the world.

Moreover, Birkin and his views do not go unchallenged, for they are often fiercely disputed by Ursula. For example, she asks whether, in practice, his concept of star-equilibrium will not simply mean that she becomes his ''satellite'' rather than his equal; and she frequently debunks his more sententious utterances, referring mockingly to his ''Salvator Mundi touch'' (and Ursula is also skeptical of Birkin's rationalizations for desiring a further *male* relationship with Gerald). But perhaps most exhilarating of all to contemporary readers, in this wordy novel of ideas, she particularly distrusts his self-contradictory tendency to try to verbalize and rationalize profound desires and feelings that are by their very nature (and by his own admission) nonverbal and nonrational. Ursula distrusts ''mere word-force'' and considers language as ''but a gesture we make'' toward meaning, and in doing so she both criticizes Birkin and dialogizes the novel's own linguistic attempts at diagnosing the ills of over-cerebral modern society. In drawing attention to the nature and status of language, she points us not only to a crucial, if complex, underlying theme in the novel but also to what has been one of the twentieth century's major philosophical preoccupations. She also prevents her relationship with Birkin being swallowed up in a mere flood of words, for eventually they do achieve a ''perfected relation'' that enables them to be ''free together'': they resign from their jobs, get married, and ''flit'' to the Continent, where the success of their relationship becomes further defined by the failure of the relationship between Gerald and Gudrun in the Austrian Tyrol.

Other Characters

Anna and *Will Brangwen,* the parents of Ursula and Gudrun, as in *The Rainbow,* though they appear only briefly here: *Dora, Rosalind, Billy Brangwen* are their other children. *Palmer,* Gudrun's companion for a time, a gentleman electrician who seems to like Ursula but strikes up a relationship with Gudrun instead—but he is too cold, impersonal, and egotistic "to care really for women."

The Crich family and related characters: *Mrs. Christiana Crich,* Gerald's mother—an eccentric, at times crazy, character who has had an antagonistic relationship with her husband because of her antidemocratic opposition to his philanthropic efforts. Other Crich children are *Basil, Laura, Lottie, Diana* (who drowns in the lake at the water party), and *Winifred. Lupton* marries Laura Crich in the first chapter. *Mademoiselle,* Winifred Crich's governess. *Marshall,* the husband of Lottie Crich. *Mrs. Kirk,* ex-nursery governess for the Crich family: Ursula and Gudrun call at her cottage at Willey Green to buy honey and hear about how she used to pinch Gerald's bottom.

Julius Halliday, a wealthy but dissolute young artist living a mock-bohemian life in London. He has been having an affair with an acquaintance of Birkin's, an artist's model, *Pussum* ("Minette" in pre-Cambridge English editions of the novel) *Darrington,* a vapid, lisping woman whom he has tried to send away to the country because she has become pregnant by him—she has returned unexpectedly, however, and later sleeps with Gerald in Halliday's flat. *Hasan,* Halliday's manservant. *Maxim Libidnikov,* a Russian friend of Halliday and Pussum.

Alexander Roddice, Hermione's bachelor brother and a liberal member of Parliament. *Fräulein März,* Hermione's secretary. Guests at Breadalby: *Sir Joshua Malleson* ("Mattheson" in pre-Cambridge English editions of the novel), an eminent sociologist; *Contessa Palestra. Miss Bradley,* a guest at Breadalby and fitness enthusiast.

Leitner, friend and, apparently, lover of Loerke.

SETTING

Most of the novel up to Chapter 28 is set in the English Midlands in the Lawrence country around his hometown of Eastwood, here called "Beldover." "Willey Green" and "Willey Water" are based on Moorgreen and Moorgreen Reservoir, respectively. The Crich family is modeled on the Eastwood mine owners, the Barbers of Barber, Walker and Co., and "Shortlands" is a re-creation of their estate, Lambclose House. Hermione Roddice's "Breadalby" seems to be based physically on Kedleston Hall in Derbyshire, but the scenes created around it seem rather to reflect the social milieu of Lady Ottoline Morrell's Garsington Manor in Oxfordshire (where Lawrence visited in June 1915). Worksop and Southwell, north of Nottingham, feature in the car journey taken by Birkin and Ursula in Chapter 23, and Chapters 6 and 7 are set in London. After Chapter 28 (set in London), the scene shifts to Europe, as Ursula and Birkin journey via Dover, Ostend, Brussels, Luxembourg, Metz, Basel, and Zürich, to Innsbruck and then to the mountain resort of "Hohenhausen" (based on Mayrhofen in the Austrian Tyrol where Lawrence had stayed in August 1912).

BIBLIOGRAPHY 7

Adamowski, T. H. "Being Perfect: Lawrence, Sartre, and *Women in Love*." *Critical Inquiry* 2 (Winter 1975): 345–68.

Adelman, Gary. *Snow of Fire: Symbolic Meaning in "The Rainbow" and "Women in Love."* New York and London: Garland, 1991.

Ansari, A. "*Women in Love:* Search for Integrated Being." *Aligarh Journal of English Studies* 10 (1985): 156–77.

Balbert, Peter. "Ursula Brangwen and 'The Essential Criticism': The Female Corrective in *Women in Love*." *Studies in the Novel* 17 (1985): 267–85.

Ballin, Michael, ed. *DHL's "Women in Love": Contexts and Criticism.* Waterloo, Ontario: Wilfrid Laurier University, 1980. (Seven essays cited separately.)

———. "DHL's Esotericism: William Blake in Lawrence's *Women in Love*. In Ballin (1980) op. cit., pp. 70–87.

Barber, David S. "Can a Radical Interpretation of *Women in Love* Be Adequate?" *DHL Review* 3 (Summer 1970): 168–74. (Response to Briscoe and Vicinus [1970] op. cit.)

———. "Community in *Women in Love*." *Novel* 5 (Fall 1971): 32–41.

Bassoff, Bruce. "Mimetic Desire in *Women in Love*." In his *The Secret Sharers: Studies in Contemporary Fictions*. New York: AMS, 1983, pp. 125–33.

Bayley, John. *The Uses of Division: Unity and Disharmony in Literature*. New York: Viking, 1976, pp. 25–42.

Becket, Fiona. " 'Star-Equilibrium' and the Language of Love in *Women in Love*." *Etudes Lawrenciennes* 11 (1995): 85–106.

Beker, Miroslav. " 'The Crown,' 'The Reality of Peace,' and *Women in Love*." *DHL Review* 2 (Fall 1969): 254–64.

Bersani, Leo. "Lawrentian Stillness." *Yale Review* 65 (October 1975): 38–60. (Also in his *A Future for Astyanax: Character and Desire in Literature*. Boston and Toronto: Little, Brown, 1976, pp. 156–85.)

Bertocci, Angelo P. "Symbolism in *Women in Love*." In *A DHL Miscellany*. Edited by Harry T. Moore. Carbondale: Southern Illinois University Press, 1959, pp. 83–102.

Bickerton, Derek. "The Language of *Women in Love*." *Review of English Studies* (Leeds) 8 (April 1967): 56–67.

Blanchard, Lydia. "The 'Real Quartet' of *Women in Love:* Lawrence on Brothers and Sisters." In *DHL: The Man Who Lived*. Edited by Robert B. Partlow, Jr., and Harry T. Moore. Carbondale: Southern Illinois University Press, 1980, pp. 199–206.

———. "*Women in Love:* Mourning Becomes Narcissism." *Mosaic* 15 (1982): 105–18.

Bloom, Harold, ed. *DHL's "Women in Love."* New York: Chelsea House, 1988. (Eight previously published essays.)

Bonds, Diane S. "Going into the Abyss: Literalization in *Women in Love*." *Essays in Literature* 8 (1981): 189–202. (Revised as Ch. 4 of Bonds [1987]: 77–91.)

Bradshaw, Graham. " 'Lapsing Out' in *Women in Love*." *English* 32 (1983): 17–32.

Branda, Eldon S. "Textual Changes in *Women in Love.*" *Texas Studies in Language and Literature* 6 (Autumn 1964): 306–21.

Briscoe, Mary Louise, and Martha Vicinus. "Lawrence among the Radicals: MMLA, 1969: An Exchange." *DHL Review* 3 (Spring 1970): 63–69. (On a workshop, "Radical Approaches to Literature: DHL's *Women in Love,*" held at the Midwest Modern Language Association, 1969. See also under Barber [1970] op. cit.)

Brown, Julia Prewitt. "Jane Austen's England." *Persuasions: Journal of the Jane Austen Society of North America* 10 (1988): 53–58.

Buckley, Margaret, and Brian Buckley. *Challenge and Renewal: Lawrence and the Thematic Novel.* Kenilworth, Warwickshire: Chrysalis Press, 1993, pp. 1–76.

Burgan, Mary. "Androgynous Fatherhood in *Ulysses* and *Women in Love.*" *Modern Language Quarterly* 44 (June 1983): 178–97.

Cain, William E. "Lawrence's 'Purely Destructive' Art in *Women in Love.*" *South Carolina Review* 13 (1980): 38–47.

Chamberlain, Robert L. "Pussum, Minette, and the Afro-Nordic Symbol in Lawrence's *Women in Love.*" *PMLA* 78 (September 1963): 407–16.

Clark, L. D. "Lawrence, *Women in Love:* The Contravened Knot." In *Approaches to the Twentieth Century Novel.* Edited by John Unterecker. New York: Crowell, 1965, pp. 51–78.

Clarke, Bruce. "Birkin in Love: Corrupt Sublimity in DHL's Representation of Soul." *Thought: A Review of Culture and Idea* 59 (1984): 449–61.

Clarke, Colin. " 'Living Disintegration': A Scene from *Women in Love* Reinterpreted." In Clarke (1969), pp. 219–34. (The scene is "Moony.")

———, ed. *DHL: "The Rainbow" and "Women in Love": A Casebook.* London: Macmillan, 1969; Nashville, Tenn.: Aurora, 1970. (Essays previously published, except for the above item by Clarke.)

Clayton, Jay. *Romantic Vision and the Novel.* Cambridge: Cambridge University Press, 1987, pp. 175–94.

Coates, Paul. "The Dialectics of Enlightenment: *Elective Affinities* and *Women in Love.*" In his *The Realist Fantasy: Fiction and Reality since "Clarissa."* London: Macmillan, 1983, pp. 88–96.

Cockshut, A.O.J. *Man and Woman: A Study of Love and the Novel 1740–1940.* New York: Oxford University Press, 1978, pp. 152–60.

Cohan, Steven. *Violation and Repair in the English Novel: The Paradigm of Experience from Richardson to Woolf.* Detroit, Mich.: Wayne State University Press, 1986, pp. 187–95.

Collins, Joseph. *The Doctor Looks at Literature: Psychological Studies of Life and Letters.* New York: Doran; London: Allen and Unwin, 1923, pp. 276–84.

Cooney, Seamus. "The First Edition of Lawrence's Foreword to *Women in Love.*" *Library Chronicle* (University of Texas), new series, no. 7 (Spring 1974): 71–79.

Cooper, Annabel. "Lawrence's *Women in Love.*" *Meridian: The La Trobe University English Review* (Australia) 7, no. 2 (1988): 179–84. (Review essay on the Cambridge *Women in Love.*)

Craig, David. "Fiction and the Rising Industrial Classes." *Essays in Criticism* 17 (January 1967): 64–74.

———. "Lawrence and Democracy." In his *The Real Foundations: Literature and Social Change.* London: Chatto and Windus, 1973; New York: Oxford University Press, 1974, pp. 143–67. (Mainly on "The Industrial Magnate" chapter.)

Daiches, David. *The Novel and the Modern World.* Rev. ed. Chicago: University of Chicago Press, 1960, pp. 166–71.

Davies, Alistair. "Contexts of Reading: The Reception of DHL's *The Rainbow* and *Women in Love.*" In *The Theory of Reading.* Edited by Frank Gloversmith. Sussex: Harvester, 1984, pp. 199–222.

Davis, E. "DHL, *The Rainbow* and *Women in Love.*" In his *Readings in Modern Fiction.* Cape Town, South Africa: Simondium, 1964, pp. 258–81.

Davis, Herbert. "*Women in Love:* A Corrected Typescript." *University of Toronto Quarterly* 27 (October 1957): 34–53.

Davis, William A. "Mountains, Metaphors, and Other Entanglements: Sexual Representation in the Prologue to *Women in Love.*" *DHL Review* 22 (Spring 1990): 69–76.

Delany, Paul, ed. "Halliday's Progress: Letters of Philip Heseltine, 1915–21." *DHL Review* 13 (1980): 119–33.

DeVille, Peter. "The City and the New Ego: Lawrence and Lewis." *Quaderno* 2 (1987): 129–42.

DiBattista, Maria. "*Women in Love:* DHL's Judgement Book." In *DHL: A Centenary Consideration.* Edited by Peter Balbert and Philip L. Marcus. Ithaca, N.Y., and London: Cornell University Press, 1985, pp. 67–90. (Also in her *First Love: The Affections of Modern Fiction.* Chicago and London: University of Chicago Press, 1991, pp. 141–64.)

Diethe, C. "Expressionism in Lawrence's *The Rainbow* and *Women in Love.*" In *Gedenkschrift for Victor Poznanski.* Edited by C.A.M. Noble. Bern: Peter Lang, 1981, pp. 147–57.

Dillon, Martin C. "Love in *Women in Love:* A Phenomenological Analysis." *Philosophy and Literature* 2 (Fall 1978): 190–208.

Doherty, Gerald. "The Salvator Mundi Touch: Messianic Typology in DHL's *Women in Love.*" *Ariel* 13, no. 3 (1982): 53–71.

———. "The Darkest Source: DHL; Tantric Yoga, and *Women in Love.*" *Essays in Literature* 11 (1984): 211–22.

———. "White Mythologies: DHL and the Deconstructive Turn." *Criticism* 29 (Fall 1987): 477–96.

———. "The Art of Leaping: Metaphor Unbound in DHL's *Women in Love.*" *Style* 26 (Spring 1992): 50–65.

Donaldson, George. " 'Men in Love'? DHL, Rupert Birkin and Gerald Crich." In *DHL: Centenary Essays.* Edited by Mara Kalnins. Bristol: Bristol Classical Press, 1986, pp. 41–68.

Drain, Richard. "*Women in Love.*" In *DHL: A Critical Study of the Major Novels.* Edited by A. H. Gomme. Sussex: Harvester; New York: Barnes and Noble, 1978, pp. 70–93.

Draper, R. P. "Review of DHL's *Women in Love* edited by David Farmer, Lindeth Vasey, and John Worthen." *DHL Review* 20 (Fall 1988): 337–39.

Drew, Elizabeth. *The Novel: A Modern Guide to Fifteen English Masterpieces.* New York: Norton, 1963, pp. 208–23.

Eagleton, Terry. *Exiles and Emigrés: Studies in Modern Literature.* London: Chatto and Windus; New York: Schocken, 1970, pp. 208–14 and passim.

Eastman, Donald R. "Myth and Fate in the Characters of *Women in Love.*" *DHL Review* 9 (Summer 1976): 177–93.

Ege, Ufuk. *Fusion of Philosophy with Fiction in DHL's "Women in Love."* Lancaster: Lancaster University Central Print Unit, 1990. (Pamphlet, ten pages.)

Eggert, Paul. "The Reviewing of the Cambridge Edition of *Women in Love.*" *DHL Review* 20 (Fall 1988): 297–303. (See also, in the same journal, "From Paul Eggert [Laurentiana]," 22 (1990): 209–46; and related items under Ross [1990] op. cit.)

Eldred, Janet M. "Plot and Subplot in *Women in Love.*" *Journal of Narrative Technique* 20 (Fall 1990): 284–95.

Erlich, Richard D. "Catastrophism and Coition: Universal and Individual Development in *Women in Love.*" *Texas Studies in Language and Literature* 9 (Spring 1967): 117–28.

Farber, Lauren. "An Assemblage of Christians and Heathens: An Exploration into DHL's Sources for *Women in Love.*" *Cresset* 40 (September–October 1977): 10–14.

Farmer, David. "*Women in Love:* A Textual History and Premise for a Critical Edition." In *Editing British and American Literature, 1880–1920.* Edited by Eric Domville. New York: Garland, 1976, pp. 77–92.

Farmer, David, Lindeth Vasey, and John Worthen. "Introduction." *Women in Love* by DHL. Edited by David Farmer, Lindeth Vasey, and John Worthen. Cambridge: Cambridge University Press, 1987, pp. xix–lxi.

Fleishman, Avrom. "Lawrence and Bakhtin: Where Pluralism Ends and Dialogism Begins." In *Rethinking Lawrence.* Edited by Keith Brown. Milton Keynes and Philadelphia: Open University Press, 1990, pp. 109–19 (113–16).

Ford, George H. "Shelley or Schiller? A Note on DHL at Work." *Texas Studies in Literature and Language* 4 (Summer 1962): 154–56.

———. "An Introductory Note to DHL's Prologue to *Women in Love.*" *Texas Quarterly* 6 (Spring 1963): 92–97. (Previously unpublished "Prologue" follows, pp. 98–111.)

———. " 'The Wedding' Chapter of DHL's *Women in Love.*" *Texas Studies in Literature and Language* 6 (Summer 1964): 134–47. (An early version of the opening of the novel.)

———. "The Eternal Moment: DHL's *The Rainbow* and *Women in Love.*" In *The Study of Time III.* Edited by J. T. Fraser, N. Lawrence, and D. Park. New York: Springer, 1978, pp. 512–36.

French, A. L. " 'The Whole Pulse of Social England': *Women in Love.*" *Critical Review* (Melbourne) 21 (1979): 57–71.

Friedman, Alan. *The Turn of the Novel.* New York: Oxford University Press, 1966, pp. 152–59.

Galbraith, Mary. "Feeling Moments in the Work of DHL." *Paunch* 63–64 (1990): 15–38 (27–38).

Garrett, Peter K. *Scene and Symbol from George Eliot to James Joyce.* New Haven, Conn.: Yale University Press, 1969, pp. 198–213.

Gerber, Stephen. "Character, Language and Experience in 'Water Party.' " *Paunch* 36–37 (April 1973): 3–29.

Gilbert, Sandra M. *DHL's "Sons and Lovers," "The Rainbow," "Women in Love," "The Plumed Serpent."* New York: Monarch Press, 1965.

Gill, Stephen. "Lawrence and Gerald Crich." *Essays in Criticism* 27 (July 1977): 231–47.

Gillie, Christopher. *Character in English Literature.* New York: Barnes and Noble, 1965, pp. 187–202.

Goonetilleke, D.C.R.A. *Developing Countries in British Fiction.* London and Basingstoke: Macmillan; Totowa, N.J.: Rowman and Littlefield, 1977, pp. 39–40, 171–73 and passim.

Gordon, David J. ''*Women in Love* and the Lawrencean Aesthetic.'' In Miko (1969), op. cit., pp. 50–60.

———. ''Sex and Language in DHL.'' *Twentieth Century Literature* 27 (1981): 362–75 (364–69).

Gordon, Lyndall. ''More Pitting against than Pitying.'' *Times Literary Supplement* (16 October 1987): 1142. (Review of Cambridge *Women in Love.*)

Gorton, Mark. ''Some Say in Ice: The Apocalyptic Fear of *Women in Love.*'' *Foundation* 28 (1983): 56–60.

Gray, Ronald. ''English Resistance to German Literature from Coleridge to DHL.'' In his *The German Tradition in Literature 1871–1945.* Cambridge: Cambridge University Press, 1965, pp. 327–54. (Mainly on *Women in Love.*)

Gregor, Ian. ''Towards a Christian Literary Criticism.'' *Month* 33 (April 1965): 239–49. (Compares the novel with Iris Murdoch's *A Severed Head.*)

Grimes, Linda S. ''Lawrence's *Women in Love.*'' *Explicator* 46, no. 2 (1988): 24–27.

Haegert, John W. ''DHL and the Ways of Eros.'' *DHL Review* 11 (Fall 1978): 199–233 (219–31).

Hall, William F. ''The Image of the Wolf in Chapter 30 of DHL's *Women in Love.*'' *DHL Review* 2 (Fall 1969): 272–74.

Hardy, Barbara. *The Appropriate Form: An Essay on the Novel.* London: Athlone Press, 1964, pp. 146–61.

Harper, Howard M., Jr. ''*Fantasia* and the Psychodynamics of *Women in Love.*'' *The Classic British Novel.* Edited by Howard M. Harper, Jr., and Charles Edge. Athens: University of Georgia Press, 1972, pp. 202–19.

Hayles, Nancy Katherine. ''The Ambivalent Approach: DHL and the New Physics.'' *Mosaic* 15 (September 1982): 89–108.

———. ''Evasion: The Field of the Unconscious in DHL.'' In her *The Cosmic Web: Scientific Field Models and Literary Strategies in the Twentieth Century.* Ithaca, N.Y.: Cornell University Press, 1984, pp. 85–110 (*Women in Love,* pp. 96–102).

Heywood, Christopher. ''Olive Schreiner's *The Story of an African Farm:* Prototype of Lawrence's Early Novels.'' *English Language Notes* 14 (September 1976): 44–50.

———. ''The Image of Africa in *Women in Love.*'' *DHL: The Journal of the DHL Society* 4 (1986): 13–21.

Hibbard, George. ''Places and People in the Writings of DHL.'' In Ballin (1980), op. cit., pp. 1–16.

Hinchcliffe, Peter. ''*The Rainbow* and *Women in Love:* From George Eliot to Thomas Hardy as Formal Models.'' In Ballin (1980), op. cit., pp. 34–46.

Hinz, Evelyn J., and John J. Teunissen. ''*Women in Love* and the Myth of Eros and Psyche.'' In *DHL: The Man Who Lived.* Edited by Robert B. Partlow, Jr., and Harry T. Moore. Carbondale: Southern Illinois University Press, 1980, pp. 207–20.

Holderness, Graham. *Women in Love.* Milton Keynes and Philadelphia: Open University Press, 1986. (Open Guides to Literature Series.)

Humma, John B. "Lawrence in Another Light: *Women in Love* and Existentialism." *Studies in the Novel* 24 (Winter 1992): 392–409.

Hyde, Virginia. "Will Brangwen and Paradisal Vision in *The Rainbow* and *Women in Love*." *DHL Review* 8 (Fall 1975): 346–57.

———. "Architectural Monuments: Centers of Worship in *Women in Love*." *Mosaic* 17, no. 4 (1984): 73–92.

Ingersoll, Earl G. "The Failure of Bloodbrotherhood in Melville's *Moby-Dick* and Lawrence's *Women in Love*." *Midwest Quarterly* 30 (1989): 458–77.

———. "Lawrence in the Tyrol: Psychic Geography in *Women in Love* and *Mr Noon*." *Forum for Modern Language Studies* 26 (1990): 1–12.

———. "Staging the Gaze in DHL's *Women in Love*." *Studies in the Novel* 26, no. 2 (Fall 1994): 268–80.

Jacobson, Dan. "*Women in Love* and the Death of the Will." *Grand Street* 7 (1987): 130–39.

Jacobson, Sibyl. "The Paradox of Fulfillment: A Discussion of *Women in Love*." *Journal of Narrative Technique* 3 (January 1973): 53–65.

Jacquin, Bernard. "Mark Rampion: A Huxleyan Avatar of DHL." *Etudes Lawrenciennes* 7 (1992): 119–27. (Considers Huxley's *Point Counter Point* and its Rampion-version of Lawrence as inspired largely by *Women in Love* and Rupert Birkin.)

Journet, Debra. "Symbol and Allegory in *Women in Love*." *South Atlantic Review* 49, no. 2 (1984): 42–60.

Kane, Richard. "From Loins of Darkness to Loins of Pork: Body Imagery in Lawrence, Eliot, and Joyce." *Recovering Literature: A Journal of Contextualist Criticism* 17 (1989–90): 5–18.

Karl, Frederick R., and Marvin Magalaner. *A Reader's Guide to Great Twentieth-Century English Novels*. New York: Noonday; London: Thames and Hudson, 1959, pp. 186–97.

Kay, Wallace G. "*Women in Love* and *The Man Who Died*: Resolving Apollo and Dionysus." *Southern Quarterly* 10 (July 1972): 325–39. (See also his "Lawrence and *The Rainbow*: Apollo and Dionysus in Conflict." *Southern Quarterly* 10 [April 1972]: 209–22.)

Keith, W. J. "Another Way of Looking: Lawrence and the Rural." In Ballin (1980), op. cit., pp. 17–33.

Kern, Stephen. *The Culture of Love: Victorians to Moderns*. Cambridge: Harvard University Press, 1992, pp. 48–49, 247–48, and passim.

Kestner, Joseph. "Sculptural Character in Lawrence's *Women in Love*." *Modern Fiction Studies* 21 (1975–76): 543–53.

Kiberd, Declan. "DHL: The New Man as Prophet." In his *Men and Feminism in Modern Literature*. New York: St. Martin's Press, 1985, pp. 136–67.

Kiely, Robert. "Accident and Purpose: 'Bad Form' in Lawrence's Fiction." In *DHL: A Centenary Consideration*. Edited by Peter Balbert and Phillip L. Marcus. Ithaca, N.Y., and London: Cornell University Press, 1985, pp. 91–107.

Kim, Sung Ryol. "The Vampire Lust in DHL." *Studies in the Novel* 25, no. 4 (Winter 1993): 436–48.

Kinkead-Weekes, Mark. "The Marble and the Statue: The Exploratory Imagination of DHL." In *Imagined Worlds: Essays on Some English Novels and Novelists in Honour of John Butt*. Edited by Maynard Mack and Ian Gregor. London: Methuen, 1968, pp. 371–418.

———. "Eros and Metaphor: Sexual Relationship in the Fiction of DHL." *Twentieth Century Studies* 1 (November 1969): 3–19 (11–14). (Reprinted in Smith [1978]: 111–14. Mainly on the "Moony" chapter.)

———. "DHL and the Dance." *DHL: The Journal of the DHL Society* (1992–93): 44–62 (54–56).

Klawitter, George. "Impressionist Characterization in *Women in Love.*" *University of Dayton Review* 17, no. 3 (1985–86): 49–55.

Knapp, James F. "The Self in Lawrence: Languages of History or Myth." In his *Literary Modernism and the Transformation of Work*. Evanston, Ill.: Northwestern University Press, 1988, pp. 75–91.

Knight, G. Wilson. "Lawrence, Joyce and Powys." *Essays in Criticism* 11 (October 1961): 403–17.

Krieger, Murray. *The Tragic Vision: Variations on a Theme in Literary Interpretation*. New York: Holt, Rinehart, and Winston, 1960, pp. 37–49 and passim.

Kumar, P. Shiv. "Live and Let Die: Qualified Misanthropy in *Women in Love.*" *Osmania Journal of English Studies* 21 (1985): 39–52.

Langbaum, Robert. "Reconstitution of Self: Lawrence and the Religion of Love." In his *Mysteries of Identity: A Theme in Modern Literature*. New York: Oxford University Press, 1977, pp. 251–353.

———. "Lawrence and Hardy." In *DHL and Tradition*. Edited by Jeffrey Meyers. London: Athlone, 1985, pp. 69–90 (passim).

Langman, F. H. "*Women in Love.*" *Essays in Criticism* 17 (April 1967): 183–206.

Leavis, F. R. "The Novel as Dramatic Poem (V): *Women in Love* (I–III)." *Scrutiny* 17 (Autumn 1950): 203–20; 17 (March 1951): 318–30; 18 (June 1951): 18–31.

Lee, Robin. "Darkness and 'A Heavy Gold Glamour': Lawrence's *Women in Love.*" *Theoria* 42 (1974): 57–64.

Lenz, William E. "The 'Organic Connexion' of *The Rainbow* with *Women in Love.*" *South Atlantic Bulletin* 43 (1978): 5–18.

Levenson, Michael. " 'The Passion of Opposition' in *Women in Love:* None, One, Two, Few, Many." *Modern Language Studies* 17 (Spring 1987): 22–36.

Levy, Eric P. "Lawrence's Psychology of Void and Center in *Women in Love.*" *DHL Review* 23 (Spring 1991): 5–19.

Little, Judy. "Imagining Marriage." In *Portraits of Marriage in Literature*. Macomber, Ill.: Essays in Literature, 1984, pp. 171–84.

Lodge, David. "Metaphor and Metonymy in Modern Fiction." *Critical Quarterly* 17 (Spring 1975): 75–93 (86–88).

Lucente, Gregory L. "*Women in Love* and *The Man Who Died:* From Realism to the Mythopoeia of Passion and Rebirth." In his *The Narrative of Realism and Myth: Verga, Lawrence, Faulkner, Pavese*. Baltimore: Johns Hopkins University Press, 1981, pp. 107–23.

MacKillop, Ian. "*Women in Love*, Class War and School Inspectors." In *DHL: New Studies*. Edited by Christopher Heywood. London: Macmillan; New York: St. Martin's Press, 1987, pp. 46–58.

McLean, Celia. "The Entropic Artist: Loerke's Theories of Art in *Women in Love.*" *DHL Review* 20 (Fall 1988): 275–86.

Mann, F. Maureen. "On Reading *Women in Love* in Light of Brontë's *Shirley.*" In Ballin (1980), op. cit., pp. 47–69.

Martin, W. R. " 'Freedom Together' in DHL's *Women in Love.*" *English Studies in Africa* (Johannesburg) 8 (September 1965): 111–20.

Matsudaira, Youko. "Hermione Roddice in *Women in Love.*" *Shoin Literary Review* 18 (1984): 1–18.

Meyers, Jeffrey. "DHL, Katherine Mansfield and *Women in Love.*" *London Magazine* 18, no. 2 (1978): 32–54.

Miko, Stephen J. *Toward "Women in Love": The Emergence of a Lawrentian Aesthetic.* New Haven, Conn., and London: Yale University Press, 1971.

———, ed. *Twentieth Century Interpretations of "Women in Love."* Englewood Cliffs, N.J.: Prentice-Hall, 1969. (Previously published essays by Ford, Friedman, Moynahan, Spilka, and Vivas, with other material and one previously unpublished essay by Gordon [1969], op. cit.)

Miles, Thomas H. "Birkin's Electro-Mystical Body of Reality: DHL's Use of Kundalini." *DHL Review* 9 (Summer 1976): 194–212.

Mills, Howard W. "Stylistic Revision of *Women in Love.*" *Etudes Lawrencienne* 3 (1988): 99–108.

Molam, Rosemary. "Lawrence's Use of Symbolism in *Women in Love.*" *Opus,* 2d series, 4 (1979): 31–34.

Moody, H.L.B. "African Sculpture Symbols in a Novel by DHL." *Ibadan* 26 (1969): 73–77.

Mori, Haruhide. "Lawrence's Imagistic Development in *The Rainbow* and *Women in Love.*" *Journal of English Literary History* 31 (December 1964): 460–81.

Morris, Inez R. "African Sculpture Symbols in *Women in Love.*" *Publications of the Mississippi Philological Association* 1 (1982): 8–17. (Reprinted in *DHL Review* 16 [1983]: 25–43; and in *College Language Association Journal* 28 [1985]: 263–80.)

Mudrick, Marvin. *The Man in the Machine.* New York: Horizon Press, 1977, pp. 25–27, 44–48.

New, Peter G. *Fiction and Purpose in "Utopia," "Rasselas," "The Mill on the Floss" and "Women in Love."* London: Macmillan; New York: St. Martin's Press, 1985, pp. 231–302.

Nichols, Marianna da Vinci. "Reining the Imaginary Horse." *International Journal of Symbology* 8 (1977): 47–64.

Oates, Joyce Carol. "Lawrence's Götterdämmerung: The Tragic Vision of *Women in Love.*" *Critical Inquiry* 4 (Spring 1978): 559–78. (Reprinted in her *Contraries: Essays.* New York: Oxford University Press, 1981, pp. 141–70.)

O'Hara, Daniel. "The Power of Nothing in *Women in Love.*" *Bucknell Review* 28, no. 2 (1983): 151–64. (Reprinted in Widdowson [1992]: 146–59.)

Orr, John. "Lawrence: Passion and Its Dissolution." In his *The Making of the Twentieth-Century Novel: Lawrence, Joyce, Faulkner and Beyond.* Basingstoke and London: Macmillan, 1987, pp. 20–43.

Ort, Daniel. "Lawrence's *Women in Love.*" *Explicator* 27 (January 1969): item 38. (On Gudrun's dance before the sterile cattle.)

Paccaud-Huguet, Josiane. "*Women in Love*": de la tentation perverse à l'écriture. Grenoble: Ellug, 1991.

———. "Narrative as a Symbolic Act: The Historicity of Lawrence's Modernity." *Etudes Lawrenciennes* 9 (1993): 75–94. (Mainly on *Women in Love.*)

Padhi, Bibhu. "Lawrence's Idea of Language." *Modernist Studies* 4 (1982): 65–76.

Parker, David. "Into the Ideological Unknown: *Women in Love.*" *Critical Review* 30 (1990): 3–24.

Perkins, Wendy. "Reading Lawrence's Frames: Chapter Division in *Women in Love.*" *DHL Review* 24 (Fall 1992): 229–46.

Pichardie, Jean-Paul. "*Women in Love:* Structures." *Etudes Lawrenciennes* 4 (1989): 7–19.

Pitre, David. "The Mystical Lawrence: Rupert Birkin's Taoist Quest." *Studies in Mystical Literature* 3 (1983): 43–64.

Pluto, Anne Elezabeth. "Blutbrüderschaft." *Paunch* 63–64 (1990): 85–118 (89–97).

Pollak, Paulina S. "Anti-Semitism in the Works of DHL: Search for and Rejection of the Faith." *Literature and Psychology* 32 (1986): 19–29.

Preston, Peter. " 'Under the Same Banner'?: DHL and Catherine Carswell's *Open the Door!*" *Etudes Lawrenciennes* 9 (1993): 111–26. (Considers the the degree of affinity between *Women in Love* and Carswell's novel.)

Price, Martin. "Lawrence: Levels of Consciousness." In his *Forms of Life: Character and Moral Imagination in the Novel.* New Haven, Conn., and London: Yale University Press, 1983, pp. 267–94 (267–72, 282–94).

Pritchard, William H. *Seeing through Everything: English Writers 1918–1940.* London: Faber and Faber, 1977, pp. 73–78 and passim.

Procopiow, Norma. "The Narrator's Stratagem in *Women in Love.*" *College Literature* 5 (Spring 1978): 114–24.

Procter, Margaret. "Possibilities of Completion: The Endings of *A Passage to India* and *Women in Love.*" *English Literature in Transition* 34, no. 3 (1991): 261–80.

Rachman, Shalom. "Art and Value in DHL's *Women in Love.*" *DHL Review* 5 (Spring 1972): 1–25.

Radrum, Alan. "Philosophical Implications in Lawrence's *Women in Love.*" *Dalhousie Review* 51 (Summer 1971): 240–50.

Ragussis, Michael. "DHL: The New Vocabulary of *Women in Love:* Speech and Art Speech." In his *The Subterfuge of Art: Language and the Romantic Tradition.* Baltimore and London: Johns Hopkins University Press, 1978, pp. 172–225.

Raskin, Jonah. *The Mythology of Imperialism: Rudyard Kipling, Joseph Conrad, E. M. Forster, DHL and Joyce Cary.* New York: Random House, 1971, pp. 200–203, 252–56.

Reddick, Bryan D. "Point of View and Narrative Tone in *Women in Love:* The Portrayal of Interpsychic Space." *DHL Review* 7 (Summer 1974): 156–71.

———. "Tension at the Heart of *Women in Love.*" *English Literature in Transition* 19 (1976): 73–86.

Remsbury, John. "*Women in Love* as a Novel of Change." *DHL Review* 6 (Summer 1973): 149–72.

Roberts, Neil. "Lawrence's Tragic Lovers: The Story and the Tale in *Women in Love.*" In *DHL: New Studies.* Edited by Christopher Heywood. London: Macmillan; New York: St. Martin's Press, 1987, pp. 34–45.

Robson, W. W. "DHL and *Women in Love.*" In *The Pelican Guide to English Literature, Volume 7: The Modern Age.* 3d ed. Edited by Boris Ford. Harmondsworth: Penguin, 1973, pp. 298–318.

Romanski, Philippe. " 'Europe Is a Lost Name': Entropy in the First Two Chapters of *Women in Love.*" *Etudes Lawrenciennes* 9 (1993): 51–60.

Ross, Charles L. "A Problem of Textual Transmission in the Typescripts of *Women in Love.*" *The Library,* series 5, 29 (1974): 197–205.

———. "The Composition of *Women in Love:* A History, 1913–1916." *DHL Review* 8 (Summer 1975): 198–212.

———. *The Composition of "The Rainbow" and "Women in Love": A History.* Charlottesville: University Press of Virginia, 1979.

———. "Homoerotic Feeling in *Women in Love:* Lawrence's 'Struggle for Verbal Consciousness' in the Manuscripts." In *DHL: The Man Who Lived.* Edited by Robert B. Partlow, Jr., and Harry T. Moore. Carbondale: Southern Illinois University Press, 1980, pp. 168–82.

———. "Introduction." *Women in Love* by DHL. Edited by Charles L. Ross. Harmondsworth: Penguin, 1982, pp. 13–48.

———. "The Cambridge Lawrence." *Essays in Criticism* 38 (1988): 342–51.

———. "Editorial Principles in the Penguin and Cambridge Editions of *Women in Love:* A Reply to Paul Eggert." *DHL Review* 21 (1989): 223–26.

———. "Rejoinder: The Cambridge *Women in Love* Again." *Essays in Criticism* 40 (1990): 95–97. (See also preceding two items by Ross and Worthen and Vasey [1989], Eggert [1988], Rossman [1989], and Eggert [1990] all op. cit.)

———. *"Women in Love": A Novel of Mythic Realism.* Boston: Twayne, 1991.

Ross, Charles L., and George J. Zytaruk. "*Goats and Compasses* and/or *Women in Love:* An Exchange." *DHL Review* 6 (Spring 1973): 33–46. (See Zytaruk [1971] and Sagar [1973] op. cit.)

Rossman, Charles. "DHL, Women, and *Women in Love.*" *Cahiers Victoriens et Edouardiens,* no. 8 (1979): 93–115.

———. "A Metacommentary on the Rhetoric of Reviewing the Reviewers: Paul Eggert on the New Editions of *Ulysses* and *Women in Love.*" *DHL Review* 21 (1989): 219–22.

Rowley, Stephen. "The Death of Our Phallic Being: Melville's *Moby Dick* as a Warning Which Leads to *Women in Love.*" *Etudes Lawrenciennes* 7 (1992): 93–105.

Sabin, Margery. *The Dialect of the Tribe: Speech and Community in Modern Fiction.* Oxford: Oxford University Press, 1987, pp. 106–38.

Sagar, Keith. "The Genesis of *The Rainbow* and *Women in Love.*" *DHL Review* 1 (Fall 1968): 179–99.

———. "*Goats and Compasses* and *Women in Love* Again." *DHL Review* 6 (Fall 1973): 303–8. (See Zytaruk [1971] and Ross [1973], op. cit.)

Salgādo, Gāmini. "Taking a Nail for a Walk: On Reading *Women in Love.*" In *The Modern English Novel: The Reader, The Writer, and The Work.* Edited by Gabriel Josipovici. London: Open Books, 1976; New York: Barnes and Noble, 1977, pp. 95–112.

Scherr, Barry J. "Lawrence, Keats, and *Tender Is the Night:* Loss of Self and 'Love Battle' Motifs." *Recovering Literature* 14 (1986): 7–17.

———. "Lawrence's 'Dark Flood': A Platonic Interpretation of 'Excurse.' " *Paunch* 63–64 (1990): 209–46.

———. "Two Essays on D. H. Lawrence's 'Darkness'; I: The 'Fecund Darkness' of *The Rainbow;* II: The 'Body of Darkness' in *Women in Love.*" *Recovering Literature: A Journal of Contextualist Criticism* 18 (1991–92): 8–40.

Schneider, Daniel J. "The Laws of Action and Reaction in *Women in Love.*" *DHL Review* 14 (1981): 238–62.

Schorer, Mark. *"Women in Love* and Death.*" Hudson Review* 6 (Spring 1953): 34–47. (Reprinted in Hoffman and Moore [1953]: 163–77; in Spilka [1963]: 50–60; and in Schorer's *The World We Imagine.* New York: Farrar, Straus, and Giroux, 1968, pp. 107–21.)

Schwartz, Daniel R. " 'I Was the World in Which I Walked': The Transformation of the British Novel.*" University of Toronto Quarterly* 51 (1982): 279–97.

Scott, James F. " 'Continental': The Germanic Dimension of *Women in Love.*" *Litera-ture in Wissenschaft und Unterricht* (Kiel) 12 (1979): 117–34.

Sepčić, Višnja. "Notes on the Structure of *Women in Love.*" *Studia Romanica et Anglica Zagrabiensia* 21–22 (1966): 289–304.

———. *"Women in Love* and Expressionism.*" Studia Romanica et Anglica Zagrabien-sia* 26 (1981): 397–443; 27 (1982): 2–64.

Sharma, Radhe Shyam. "The Symbol as Archetype: A Study of Symbolic Mode in DHL's *Women in Love.*" *Osmania Journal of English Studies* (Hyderabad) 8, no. 2 (1971): 31–53. (See also his "Towards a Definition of Modern Literary Prim-itivism.*" Osmania Journal of English Studies* 14, no. 1 [1978]: 23–28.)

Singh, Vishnudat. *"Women in Love:* A Textual Note.*" Notes and Queries* 17 (December 1970): 466.

Smailes, T. A. "The Mythical Bases of *Women in Love.*" *DHL Review* 1 (Summer 1968): 129–36.

———. "Plato's 'Great Lie of Ideals': Function in *Women in Love.*" In *Generous Con-verse: English Essays in Memory of Edward Davis.* Edited by Brian Green. Cape Town: Oxford University Press, 1980, pp. 133–35.

Solecki, Sam. *"Women in Love* and Ideology.*"* In Ballin (1980), op. cit., pp. 88–107.

Spanier, Sandra Whipple. "Two Foursomes in *The Blithedale Romance* and *Women in Love.*" *Comparative Literature Studies* 16 (1979): 58–69.

Spilka, Mark. "Star-Equilibrium in *Women in Love.*" *College English* 17 (November 1955): 79–83.

———. "Lawrence Up-Tight, or the Anal Phase Once Over.*" Novel: A Forum on Fiction* 4 (Spring 1971): 252–67.

Spilka, Mark, with Colin Clarke, George Ford, and Frank Kermode. "Critical Exchange: On 'Lawrence Up-Tight': Four Tail-Pieces.*" Novel: A Forum on Fiction* 5 (Fall 1971): 54–70.

Stewart, Garrett. "Lawrence, 'Being,' and the Allotropic Style.*" Novel* 9 (1975–76): 217–42.

Stewart, Jack F. "Primitivism in *Women in Love.*" *DHL Review* 13 (Spring 1980a): 45–62.

———. "Rhetoric and Image in Lawrence's 'Moony.' " *Studies in the Humanities* 8 (1980b): 33–37.

———. "Dialectics of Knowing in *Women in Love.*" *Twentieth Century Literature* 37 (Spring 1991): 59–75.

Stoll, John E. "Common Womb Imagery in Joyce and Lawrence.*" Ball State University Forum* 11 (Spring 1970): 10–24.

Stroupe, John H. "Ruskin, Lawrence and Gothic Naturalism.*" Forum* 11 (Spring 1970): 3–9. (The influence of Ruskin's "The Nature of Gothic.")

Swift, John N. "Repetition, Consummation, and 'This Eternal Unrelief.' " In *The Chal-lenge of DHL.* Edited by Michael Squires and Keith Cushman. Madison: Uni-versity of Wisconsin Press, 1990, pp. 121–28.

Tatar, Maria Magdalene. *Spellbound: Studies in Mesmerism and Literature.* Princeton: Princeton University Press, 1978, pp. 243–55.

Thompson, Leslie M. "A Lawrence-Huxley Parallel: *Women in Love* and *Point Counterpoint.*" *Notes and Queries* 15 (February 1968): 58–59.

Tomlinson, T. B. "Lawrence and Modern Life: *Sons and Lovers, Women in Love.*" *Critical Review* (Melbourne), no. 8 (1965): 3–18.

———. "DHL: *Sons and Lovers, Women in Love.*" In his *The English Middle-Class Novel.* London: Macmillan; New York: Harper and Row, 1976, pp. 185–98.

Torgovnick, Marianna. "Pictorial Elements in *Women in Love:* The Uses of Insinuation and Visual Rhyme." *Contemporary Literature* 21 (1980): 420–34.

———. "Closure and the Shape of Fictions: The Example of *Women in Love.*" In *The Study of Time IV.* Edited by J. T. Fraser. New York: Springer, 1981, pp. 147–58.

———. "Encoding the Taboo in *Women in Love.*" In her *The Visual Arts, Pictorialism, and the Novel: James, Lawrence, and Woolf.* Princeton: Princeton University Press, 1985, pp. 192–213.

Tristram, Philippa. "Eros and Death (Lawrence, Freud, and Women)." In *Lawrence and Women.* Edited by Anne Smith. London: Vision; New York: Barnes and Noble, 1978, pp. 136–55 (142–50).

Trotter, David. "Modernism and Empire: Reading *The Waste Land.*" *Critical Quarterly* 28 (Spring–Summer 1986): 143–53. (Discusses *Women in Love.*)

Tuck, Susan. "Electricity Is God Now: DHL and O'Neill." *Eugene O'Neill Newsletter* 5, no. 2 (1981): 10–15.

Twitchell, James. "Lawrence's Lamias: Predatory Women in *The Rainbow* and *Women in Love.*" *Studies in the Novel* 11 (1979): 23–42.

Unrue, Darlene H. "Lawrence's Vision of Evil: The Power-Spirit in *The Rainbow* and *Women in Love.*" *Dalhousie Review* 55 (Winter 1975–76): 643–54.

Vitoux, Pierre. "The Chapter 'Excurse' in *Women in Love:* Its Genesis and the Critical Problem." *Texas Studies in Literature and Language* 17 (Winter 1976): 821–36.

———. "*Women in Love:* From Typescripts into Print." *Texas Studies in Literature and Language* 23 (1981): 577–93.

Waller, Gary F. "The 'Open Act': DHL and the Prophetic Deferral of Meaning." In Ballin (1980), op. cit., pp. 108–26.

Walsh, Sylvia. "*Women in Love.*" *Soundings* 65 (1982): 352–68.

Weinstein, Philip M. " 'The Trembling Instability' of *Women in Love.*" In his *The Semantics of Desire: Changing Models of Identity from Dickens to Joyce.* Princeton: Princeton University Press, 1984, pp. 204–24.

Whelan, P. T. *DHL: Myth and Metaphysic in "The Rainbow" and "Women in Love."* Ann Arbor, Mich., and London: UMI Research Press, 1988.

Whiteley, Patrick J. *Knowledge and Experimental Realism in Conrad, Lawrence, and Woolf.* Baton Rouge: Louisiana State University Press, 1987, pp. 89–108, 124–43.

Williams, Linda Ruth. "Introduction." *Women in Love* by DHL. London: Dent, 1993, pp. xxi–xxxv.

Williams, Raymond. "Tolstoy, Lawrence, and Tragedy." *Kenyon Review* 25 (Autumn 1963): 633–50. (Reprinted as "Social and Personal Tragedy: Tolstoy and Lawrence" in his *Modern Tragedy.* London: Chatto and Windus; Stanford, Calif.: Stanford University Press, 1966, pp. 121–38.)

Worthen, John. "Sanity, Madness and *Women in Love.*" *Trivium* 10 (May 1975): 125–36.

———. "Reading *Women in Love.*" *DHL: The Journal of the DHL Society* 4 (1986): 5–12.

———. "The Restoration of *Women in Love.*" In *DHL in the Modern World.* Edited by Peter Preston and Peter Hoare. London: Macmillan, 1989, pp. 7–26.

———, and Lindeth Vasey. "Rejoinder: The Cambridge *Women in Love.*" *Essays in Criticism* 39 (1989): 176–84. (See Ross [1990] op. cit. for related items.)

Wright, Anne. *Literature of Crisis, 1910–1922: "Howard's End," "Heartbreak House," "Women in Love" and "The Wasteland."* London: Macmillan; New York: St. Martin's Press, 1984, pp. 113–57.

Yetman, Michael G. "The Failure of the Un-Romantic Imagination in *Women in Love.*" *Mosaic* 9 (Spring 1976): 83–96.

Zapf, Herbert. "Taylorism in DHL's *Women in Love.*" *DHL Review* 15 (1982): 129–39.

Zhao, Yonghui. "A Fire Burning on Ice: On Lawrence and His 'Women in Love.'" *Foreign Literary Studies* (China) 37, no. 3 (1987): 32–36.

Zytaruk, George J. "What Happened to DHL's *Goats and Compasses?*" *DHL Review* 4 (Fall 1971): 280–86. (This lost philosophical work as a possible early version of the novel. On this, see also Ross and Zytaruk [1973] and Sagar [1973] op. cit.)

See also (1980–94) Becker (1980): 61–78. Bell (1992): 97–132, passim. Ben-Ephraim (1981): 179–240. Bonds (1987): 77–109. Burns (1980): 71–100. Clark (1980): 145–79. Cowan (1990): 60–70. Dix (1980): 41–43, 71–73, 97–100. Dorbad (1991): 89–112. Ebbatson (1982): 96–112. Fernihough (1993): 25–29, 49–54, 145–53, passim. Fjagesund (1991): 31–42, passim. Hardy and Harris (1985): 140–43, passim. Hobsbaum (1981): 60–71. Holderness (1982): 174–76, 190–219. Hostettler (1985): 41–61, 117–36. Hyde (1990): 58–75. Hyde (1992): 101–18, passim. Ingram (1990): 61–65, 109–18. Kelsey (1991): 141–80. Kiely (1980): 156–68. MacLeod (1985/87): 43–57, 118–36. Mensch (1991): 71–118, passim. Miliaras (1987): 229–91. Milton (1987): 148–56, passim. Modiano (1987): 96–107. Montgomery (1994): 111–31, passim. Niven (1980): 49–56. Nixon (1986): passim. Padhi (1989): 131–46, 163–85. Pinkney (1990): 79–99. Prasad (1980): 67–76. Robinson (1992): 99–105. Sagar (1985a): 147–93. Scheckner (1985): 23–69. Schneider (1984): 171–90. Siegel (1991): passim. Sipple (1992): 91–114. Sklenicka (1991): 146–53. Spilka (1992): 59–65, 100–109, 147–51. Storch (1990): 97–130. Suter (1987): 87–98. Templeton (1989): 166–305. Urang (1983): 33–67. Verhoeven (1987): 161–216. Widmer (1992): 21–28, 45–48, passim. Williams (1993): 48–57, 79–94, passim. Worthen (1991a): 50–56.

See also (to 1979) Albright (1978): 84–90, passim. Alcorn (1977): 93–100, passim. Alldritt (1971): 162–218. Beal (1961): 41–58. Bedient (1972): 137–47. Boadella (1956/78): 90–94, passim. Cavitch (1969): 60–77, passim. Clarke (1969): 70–110, passim. Cornwell (1962): 215–19, passim. Daleski (1965): 126–87. Delany (1978): passim. Delavenay (1971): 89–97, 100–110, passim. Draper (1964): 76–87. Draper (1970): 157–72. Eisenstein (1974): 51–55, passim. Ford (1965): 160–222. Goodheart (1963): 120–28, passim. Gregory (1933): 43–50. Hochman (1970): 36–44, 101–17, passim. Hough (1956): 72–90, passim. Howe (1977): 52–78. Inniss (1971): 137–58. Jarrett-Kerr (1951): 28–37.

Kermode (1973): 53–78. Leavis (1955): 146–96. Leavis (1976): 62–91. Lerner (1967): 191–205. Maes-Jelinek (1970): 51–66, passim. Miles (1969): 14–22, 36–39, passim. Millett (1970): 262–69. Moore (1951): 157–67. Moynahan (1963): 72–91. Murry (1933): 218–27. Nahal (1970): 140–48, passim. Nin (1932): 97–112. Niven (1978): 59–113. Panichas (1964): 151–79. Pinion (1978): 163–77. Potter (1930): 60–68. Prasad (1976): 190–209. Pritchard (1971): 85–106, passim. Sagar (1966): 78–98. Sale (1973): 79–105. Sanders (1973): 94–135. Seligmann (1924): 8–15. Slade (1970): 67–78, passim. Spilka (1955): 121–73. Stewart (1963): 510–34. Stoll (1971): 151–97. Swigg (1972): 132–86, passim. Tedlock (1963): 96–106. Tenenbaum (1978): 82–103. Vivas (1960): 225–72. Worthen (1979): 83–104. Yudhishtar (1969): 160–200.

16   *The Lost Girl*

WRITTEN

December 1912–October 1920. Drafts: 1. "Elsa Culverwell," December 1912–
January 1913 (abandoned after twenty pages). 2. "The Insurrection of Miss
Houghton," January–March 1913. 3. *The Lost Girl,* February–May 1920. Re-
visions and corrections, June, August, October 1920.

PUBLISHED

1. London: Secker, 25 November 1920; New York: Seltzer, 28 January 1921.
2. Edited by John Worthen. Cambridge: Cambridge University Press, 1981.

WHO'S WHO AND SUMMARY

MAIN CHARACTERS: Alvina Houghton, Ciccio (Francesco Marasca), James
Houghton

Alvina Houghton, the daughter of a well-to-do family of tradespeople in the
Midlands mining town of Woodhouse, is the "lost girl" of the title whose life
we follow from the age of twenty-three to the age of thirty-two (1906–15), with
the main emphasis falling on the last two years. From being, at the start of the
novel, a "lost" girl "destined to join the ranks of the old maids" of Woodhouse, she becomes a different type of "lost girl" by the end of the novel,
having rebelled against her bourgeois upbringing and the petty provincial attitudes of her hometown. The first sign of rebellion against the genteel life

planned and hoped for her by her governess, Miss Frost, comes with her impulsive decision to become engaged to an Australian doctor and to plan to move to Australia with him. She is eventually talked out of this but then insists on carrying out her next impulsive decision: to become a maternity nurse. She goes to train in Islington for six months, where she witnesses much hardship and poverty in the slum areas she has to visit and where she has also constantly to fend off the amorous advances of the young doctors. On her return to Woodhouse as a qualified nurse and a more worldly woman, she finds that few locals are willing to pay for her services, and her nursing career comes to an abrupt end for the time being. She is briefly tempted into marrying Albert Witham from South Africa, for his money and for the adventure of travel the marriage would bring, but his fishlike "dishumanness" prevents her from taking the path of this "ordinary" fate; she holds out for an extraordinary fate. At thirty, she becomes enthusiastically involved with her father's cinema and variety show, playing the piano accompaniments to the features, and this leads to her involvement with the Natcha-Kee-Tawara traveling theater troupe, which she goes to join after her father's death. She becomes strongly drawn to the dark, sensual *Ciccio,* an Italian member of this troupe; he seems to exert a power over her body and her unconscious self, though, as with other of her suitors, her conscious, rational self resists him and sees him as, in some ways, simply vulgar and even stupid. She decides to leave the troupe, and she becomes a maternity nurse once more, this time in Lancaster, where she becomes engaged, briefly, to a rich old doctor. However, she flees this engagement, marries Ciccio, and goes away with him to the isolated mountain village of "Pescocalascio" in Italy. The novel ends when Ciccio is called up for military service, and Alvina, pregnant, faces the prospect of bearing her child alone, "lost" in the alien and "annihilating" environment of the Abruzzi.

Although Alvina provides the central focus overall, the first part of the novel presents a more general picture of Woodhouse life and deals, in particular, with the various entrepreneurial endeavors of her father, *James Houghton.* As an elegant and dandyish young man of twenty-eight with a fanciful and poetic cast of mind, he inherits the family's flourishing fabrics and draperies business in Woodhouse and sets about turning it into a type of "commercial poem," a fantasy of commerce in his new building (and home), Manchester House (the business deals in "Manchester goods"—cottons). Unfortunately, his fineries are not much in demand in the down-to-earth colliery villages of the district, and, through a steady stream of enforced bargain sales, the business slowly but surely fails. As the business fails, so *Clariss Houghton,* James's wife, sickens and fails, too; she becomes a reclusive invalid and dies when Alvina is twenty-five. James meanwhile becomes even more fantastical in "the gamut of his creations," and the business becomes something of a local joke. Eventually, he is forced to sell parts of it, to open less frequently, and, under the saving supervision of Miss Pinnegar, to diversify into the manufacture of more ordinary but more salable items. His entrepreneurial energies still undimmed, James then also ventures briefly into the manufacture of bricks with the Klondyke brickyard and into coal mining with the opening of his Throttle-Ha'penny pit; inevitably, both ventures fail, and, for a while, James is chastened and downcast. Halfheartedly, he toys with the idea of starting up an ice rink and of converting Manchester House into a hotel; but after three or so fallow years, he has one more great endeavor up his sleeve: Houghton's Pleasure Palace (nicknamed Houghton's Endeavour), a cinema and variety hall. This pays its way for a short time but soon starts to go the way of all James's ventures. Worn down by this last of his endeavors, James Houghton collapses and dies, leaving Alvina nothing but the task of selling off all the family's assets to pay his debts.

Other Characters

Miss Frost, Alvina's protective, high-minded, and influential governess for the first twenty-five years of the heroine's life. She is "straightforward, good-humoured, and a little earnest," and Alvina lives very much under her shadow. Miss Frost strongly disapproves of James Houghton's commercial fantasies and sees it as her role in life to maintain the reputation of Manchester House. After the decline of the business, she stays on in the home without payment: indeed, she gives music lessons in the local mining villages and actually contributes to the income of the household from her earnings. When she dies, aged fifty-four, following a brief late love affair with an insurance agent and in the same year as Alvina's mother, when Alvina is twenty-five, the spirit of the house dies, too.

Alexander Graham, an Australian studying for a medical degree and practicing with old *Dr. Fordham* for a few months at Woodhouse before returning to Australia. He is a small, dark man for whom Alvina has ambivalent feelings: rationally she agrees with everyone else that he is her inferior and possibly untrustworthy, even "creepy," but, physically, she also finds him fascinating. They become engaged (when Alvina is twenty-three), but, partly influenced by pressure from Miss Frost and her parents, Alvina eventually decides not to follow him to Australia as planned (Ch. 2).

Miss Pinnegar, the live-in manageress of the working girls in Manchester House. Short, stout, blunt, and evidently "not a lady," she is suffered unwillingly by Alvina, Miss Frost, and Clariss Houghton. However, she is practically minded and commercially shrewd and comes to have—luckily for him—strong sway over James Houghton in the running of the business. She is, moreover, in her own way, as loyal and unselfish in her allegiance to the family as Miss Frost, and, when the latter lady dies, Miss Pinnegar largely takes over from her as the moral guardian of Manchester House.

Miss Cassie Allsop, the forty-two-year-old daughter of the builder engaged by James Houghton to make alterations to turn Manchester House into a hotel; she comes to warn Alvina of the potential expense of the scheme, and Alvina is taken aback by Miss Allsop's implied placing of her on the shelf "among the old maids" (Ch. 5).

Lottie, a socially aspiring, slightly shrewish woman of thirty-five, and her husband, *Arthur Witham* the plumber, attempt to make a match between Alvina and *Albert Witham,* Arthur's thirty-two-year-old brother, who has returned temporarily from South Africa to take a degree at Oxford. Though Albert is approved of as a suitor by James Houghton and Miss Pinnegar, Alvina finds him wholly unattractive and soon cuts short his attempted courtship of her (Ch. 5).

Mr. May, the drifting, Americanized music hall agent who becomes manager of Houghton's Endeavour. Plump, pink, and perky like a little robin, he affects an honest-to-goodness innocence but actually has a "natural unscrupulousness" in business matters. He seems to have abandoned his wife and children, though he talks ostentatiously about continuing to support them.

Madame Rochard, the leader of the Natcha-Kee-Tawara theater troupe, which, along with Ciccio, consists of the Swiss-French *Louis,* the Swiss-German *Max,* and *Geoffrey,* a Frenchman and Ciccio's close friend.

Dr. Mitchell, a rich and eligible bachelor of fifty-four who becomes Alvina's fiancé in Lancaster (Ch. 11). He is pompous, self-regarding, and affected; he behaves condescendingly to both his patients and Alvina and reveals a nasty streak of temper when he becomes almost hysterical at the thought of Alvina's rejecting his proposal. She does not love him at all—indeed, she actually finds him repulsive as a potential lover—but temporarily succumbs to the temptation of a respectable match and the promise of domestic comfort and security. Deep down she knows she will not marry him, and she eventually runs away from him to Scarborough.

Effie and Tommy Tuke, friends of Alvina's when she is nursing in Lancaster—she stays at their house to nurse Effie through her confinement. Ciccio comes to serenade Alvina outside the Tukes' house (Ch. 12).

Dr. Headley, Dr. James, Dr. Young, Alvina's ardent admirers at the maternity hospital in Islington, all of whom make amorous approaches to her. *Mrs. Rollings,* a widow and servant at Manchester House who now sometimes puts up the performers who come to Houghton's Endeavour—the Natcha-Kee-Tawara troupe stay with her on their first visit. *Mr. Beeby,* the lawyer who deals with James Houghton's affairs after his death. *Giuseppe,* Ciccio's cousin in London; he owns a restaurant there and is married to *Gemma,* with whom he has four children (Ch. 13). *Mr. Calladine,* caretaker of Woodhouse Chapel. *Pancrazio* and *Giovanni,* Ciccio's uncles in Italy.

SETTING

The initial focus of the novel is the town of "Woodhouse" and the surrounding area: a re-creation of Lawrence's own native Eastwood and the Nottinghamshire-Derbyshire countryside around it. "Lumley," where James Houghton sets up his cinema, is based on Langley Mill, a mile or so from Eastwood; "Hathersedge," "Rapton," and "Knarborough" are based on Heanor, Ripley, and Nottingham, respectively. Alfreton, Mansfield, Sheffield, Doncaster, Leeds,

Scarborough, and Lancaster all appear under their actual names. Early in the book, Alvina trains to become a maternity nurse in Islington in London; and later Ciccio takes her to London again, to Battersea, to stay at his cousin's restaurant while they prepare to leave for Italy. They then travel to and through Italy, via Genoa, Pisa, and Rome, to Picinisco (''Pescocalascio'') in the Abruzzi, where the novel ends.

BIBLIOGRAPHY 8

Cowan, James C. ''Lawrence and the Movies: *The Lost Girl* and After.'' In his *DHL and the Trembling Balance.* University Park: Pennsylvania State University Press, 1990, pp. 95–114 (96–101).

Delbaere-Garant, J. ''The Call of the South.'' *Revue des Langues Vivantes* (1963): 336–57.

Gurko, Leo. ''*The Lost Girl:* DHL as a 'Dickens of the Midlands.' '' *PMLA* 78 (December 1963): 601–5.

Fowler, Roger. ''*The Lost Girl:* Discourse and Focalization.'' In *Rethinking Lawrence.* Edited by Keith Brown. Milton Keynes and Philadelphia: Open University Press, 1990, pp. 53–66.

Hafley, J. ''*The Lost Girl*—Lawrence Really Real.'' *Arizona Quarterly* 10 (1954): 312–22.

Herring, Phillip. ''Caliban in Nottingham: DHL's *The Lost Girl.*'' *Mosaic* 12 (1979): 9–19.

Heywood, Christopher. ''DHL's *The Lost Girl* and Its Antecedents by George Moore and Arnold Bennett.'' *English Studies* 47, no. 2 (1966): 131–34.

Ruderman, Judith. ''Rekindling the 'Father-Spark': Lawrence's Ideal of Leadership in *The Lost Girl* and *The Plumed Serpent.*'' *DHL Review* 13 (Fall 1980): 239–59.

Russell, John. ''DHL: *The Lost Girl, Kangaroo.*'' In his *Style in Modern British Fiction: Studies in Joyce, Lawrence, Forster, Lewis and Green.* Baltimore: Johns Hopkins University Press, 1975, pp. 43–88.

Stovel, Nora Foster. '' 'A Great Kick at Misery': Lawrence's and Drabble's Rebellion against the Fatalism of Bennett.'' In *DHL's Literary Inheritors.* Edited by Keith Cushman and Dennis Jackson. New York: St. Martin's Press; London: Macmillan, 1991, pp. 131–54. (Discusses *The Lost Girl, Anna of the Five Towns,* and Margaret Drabble's *Jerusalem the Golden.*)

Wiener, Gary A. ''Lawrence's 'Little Girl Lost.' '' *DHL Review* 19 (Fall 1987): 243–53.

Worthen, John. ''Introduction.'' *The Lost Girl* by DHL. Edited by John Worthen. Cambridge: Cambridge University Press, 1981, pp. xvii–liv.

See also (1980–94) Becker (1980): 97–101. Bell (1992): 136–69. Clark (1980): 214–22. Cowan (1990): 96–101. Dix (1980): 43–46. Hardy and Harris (1985): 67–77, passim. Hobsbaum (1981): 72–75. Hostettler (1985): 136–41. Hyde (1990): 76–88. Kiely (1980): 209–12. MacLeod (1985/87): 105–7. Meyers (1982): 94–104. Niven (1980): 56–60. Prasad (1980): 67–76. Ruderman (1984): 37–47, passim. Siegel (1991): passim. Simpson (1982): 73–78. Suter (1987): 99–101. Widmer (1992): 28–30. Williams (1993): 11–13. Worthen (1991a): 57–62.

See also (to 1979) Albright (1978): 62–67. Beal (1961): 59–64. Draper (1964): 89–92. Eisenstein (1974): 43–76. Freeman (1955): 117–20. Hough (1956): 90–103, passim. Jarrett-Kerr (1951): 41–45. Kermode (1973): 102–4. Moynahan (1963): 117–40. Murry (1931): 125–33. Murry (1933): 214–18. Niven (1978): 114–32. Pinion (1978): 177–82. Pritchard (1971): 129–32. Rees (1958): 73–88. Sagar (1966): 36–38, 114–15. Tedlock (1963): 132–42. Worthen (1979): 105–17. Yudhishtar (1969): 200–212.

17 Mr Noon

WRITTEN

7 May 1920–6 October 1922. These dates indicate the first and last known references to the novel in Lawrence's correspondence rather than a period of sustained attention to the work. The bulk of the writing was done between November 1920 and February 1921, after which date little or no work seems to have been done on the novel. Plans to complete it were finally abandoned altogether in October 1922. It is not known for certain why Lawrence never finished this work.

Lawrence decided to divide the novel into parts in early 1921 so that Part I could be published separately, and he revised a typescript of this in February for that purpose. However, provisional plans for its publication later that year fell through, and it was never published in his lifetime. A typescript was made of a substantial portion of Part II of the novel, but Lawrence did not revise this; the ribbon copy of the typescript of Part I, the carbon copy of the incomplete typescript of Part II, and the five original manuscript notebooks containing both parts of the novel were then effectively lost for fifty years until they reappeared at an auction in 1972. (The carbon copy of the first typescript was used for the 1934 publication of Part I; the ribbon copy of the Part II typescript remains unlocated.)

PUBLISHED

1. *Mr Noon* Part I. In *A Modern Lover*. London: Secker; New York: Viking, October 1934.

2. *Mr Noon* Part I and Part II (unfinished). Edited by Lindeth Vasey. Cambridge: Cambridge University Press, 1984.

WHO'S WHO AND SUMMARY

PART I—MAIN CHARACTERS: Gilbert Noon, Patty and Lewie Goddard, Emmie Bostock

Gilbert Noon, about twenty-six, and currently the science master at Haysfall Technical School, five miles from his industrial hometown of Whetstone in Nottinghamshire. He began his career as an elementary school teacher but proved to be an outstanding scholar in mathematics, music, and science and went on to Cambridge. There, he gained such an outstanding reputation as a mathematician that he might have been awarded a fellowship if he had stayed and worked a little harder. However, this was not to his raffish taste, and he decided to return to his old carousing way of life in Whetstone. This part of the novel then tells of Gilbert's sentimental lovemaking, or "spooning," with Emmie Bostock; of how they are caught together in the greenhouse by her father; and of how Gilbert is subsequently forced to resign his teaching post because of the supposed pregnancy of Emmie. These events provide the pretext for a comic satire on petty provincial life and morality, on hypocritical and stultifying conventions of courtship and marriage, and on idealized notions of romantic love more generally.

Patty and *Lewie Goddard* are Gilbert's friends in Woodhouse. They are socialists and vegetarians; she is forty, an independent, modern woman and a suffragette, and he is forty-five and a member of the Independent Labor Party. Patty seems attracted to Gilbert, and, when they walk together in the park, Gilbert's desire is aroused by the "soft, full, strange, unmated Aphrodite of forty." Though the possibility of any further development in their relationship is cut short by the arrival of an aggressive cow and, later, by the scandal with Emmie, Gilbert's recognition of the older woman's allure and of a type of desire deeper than that represented by "the spoon" seems to prepare the ground somewhat for his later relationship—in Part II—with the sexually experienced Johanna. *Mrs. Prince,* housekeeper to the Goddards.

Emmie Bostock, twenty-three, and a schoolteacher also. She is the daughter of a railwayman and engaged to *Walter George Whiffen,* a young bank clerk. She is willful, sharp-tongued, and flirtatious—she has been engaged several times already—but with an underlying common sense, demonstrated clearly when she determines to marry Walter George as soon as she suspects being pregnant. *Alf Bostock,* Emmie's puritanical, "sermon-imbibing" father. *Jinny Bostock,* her easygoing mother. The *younger Bostock children*—"Fra-Angelico-faced girls" and "long-nosed sons"—appear briefly together at the chapel. When Emmie is diagnosed as having "neuralgia of the stomach," and she can no longer tolerate her father's bad-tempered disapproval of her at home, she runs away to her married sister, *Fanny,* who lives at the schoolhouse at Eakrast with her teacher husband, *Harold Wagstaff,* and newborn baby.

Other Characters

Agatha Sharp, Emmie's friend and confidante and also a schoolteacher. She has a boyfriend named *Freddy,* who appears briefly. *Alvina Houghton* makes a brief guest appearance from *The Lost Girl* as a member of the Woodhouse chapel choir along with Emmie and Agatha—but Alvina disapproves of Emmie and gives her stern looks for talking and passing notes to Agatha. *Cissie Gittens,* another choir girl. The minister of the chapel, *Norman "Daddy" Dixon,* is usually good-natured and indulgent, but he loses his patience with the choirgirls when Emmie and Agatha persist in exchanging notes and causing a disturbance. *Mrs. Slater,* Walter's Victorian-seeming landlady at Warsop. *Gilbert's father* owns a woodyard in Whetstone and is "comfortably well off, but stingy." There seems little love lost between Gilbert and his father, and this is not helped by Gilbert's (unsuccessful) appeal for money just before he leaves for Germany. *Minnie Britten* is the secretary of the County Education Committee, which interviews Gilbert about his "criminal commerce" with Emmie. She writes pamphlets on education and rather likes Gilbert because of his Cambridge pedigree, but she cannot save him from the other "lobsters" of the committee.

PART II—MAIN CHARACTERS: Gilbert Noon, Johanna Keighley

In this part of the novel, we follow Gilbert's picaresque wanderings about Germany, the development of his love affair with a married woman, Johanna Keighley, his wranglings with her family to accept their "true" marriage, and their eventual elopement over the Alps into Italy. Gilbert himself seems a somewhat different character from that of Part I, and where *that* Gilbert is often assumed to be based on a close friend of Lawrence's youth, George Henry Neville (1886–1959), *this* Gilbert is usually taken to be more of a re-creation of Lawrence himself; however, Gilbert does find himself in a totally new environment and in a sense liberated from his old English self—he is, we are told, "unEnglished" as he stands in the Isar Valley surrounded by the vast and majestic Alps—so that one can see this change as a thematically intended "rebirth" of self.

Johanna Keighley, née von Hebenitz, thirty-two and married for twelve years to *Dr. Everard Keighley,* an English academic. They have lived in America for most of their married life, in Boston, and have two children. Everard has an idealized love for Johanna and worships her as his pure white "snowflower"—but she refuses to be worshiped as an ideal abstraction and believes in the sacredness, rather, of the physical senses and of sexual love; thus, she has had many lovers and takes Gilbert straight to bed on the very first night she meets him. *Professor Alfred Kramer,* her cousin, a small, fussy, sensitive soul of fifty-three, in whose flat Gilbert is staying at the start of this part of the novel (he seems to be living off the professor but also helping him a little with the writing of a book). Johanna's "school-sister," *Louise,* is Kramer's wife. Gilbert and Kramer visit her at her *baroness* mother's house on the Starnbergersee, where she has come with her lover *Professor Ludwig Sartorius. Lotte,* Johanna's sister: "a handsome, ultra-fashionable woman" who looks like "a cocotte." *Baron and Baroness von Hebenitz,* Johanna's parents. Her lovers: *Berry,* an American businessman; *Eberhard,* a Viennese psychiatrist and philosopher, advocate of free love and apparently a drug addict; and *Rudolf von Daumling,* a wistful Prussian cavalry officer of thirty-eight (Rudolf is the only one actually to appear in the novel).

Terry and *Stanley,* two young men who briefly join Gilbert and Johanna on their walk across the Alps toward the end of the novel. Terry, an old London friend of Gilbert's, is twenty-one, a Fabian and botanist, cultured and amiable. Stanley, an American acquaintance of Johanna's, English-educated and an engineer by training. He confides in Johanna and makes love with her in a hayhut in the mountains while Gilbert is walking with Terry.

Other, minor characters who appear are *Julie,* Professor Kramer's maidservant; *Marta,* the handsome maid who fascinates Gilbert in the baroness's home on the Starnbergersee; the *Swiss manageress* of the family hotel at Detsch where Gilbert stays; *Fritz,* the young and inquisitive landlord of Grünwald Gasthaus in Trier; *Joseph and Ulma Heysers,* friends of Gilbert who put him up at Wensdorf; *Frau and Herr Breitgau,* shopkeepers below the flat of Gilbert and Johanna in Ommerbach.

SETTING

Part I of the novel is set in Nottinghamshire, in and around Eastwood ("Woodhouse" in the novel), Nottingham ("Knarborough"), Eakring ("Eakrast"), ten miles west of Mansfield, and Warsop, five miles northwest of Mansfield. "Haysfall Technical School," where Gilbert Noon teaches, may be based on a school in Mansfield.

In Part II, the scene shifts to Germany as Gilbert is transformed into a semiautobiographical character, and his experiences and travels begin to reflect those of Lawrence himself in the period May–September 1912. This part of the novel begins in Munich, Bavaria. From Munich, Gilbert takes a day trip to Ebenhausen ("Ommerhausen" in the novel) down the Isar Valley with Professor Alfred Kramer. Chapter 16 takes place in Metz ("Detsch"), where Gilbert has gone to meet Johanna. From here he moves on alone to Trier and thence along the Mosel Valley via Koblenz and Cologne to Waldbröl ("Wensdorf") and then back again to Munich. Here he meets up again with Johanna, and they go up into the mountains to her sister at Wolfratshausen ("Schloss Wolfratsberg") and then on to Beuerberg ("Kloster Schaeftlarn") and, after six days, to Icking ("Ommerbach"). After some time here, they set off to walk over the Austrian Tyrol into Italy. They break their journey at Mayrhofen ("Eckershofen"), before continuing, with various setbacks, via Sterzing, Bozen, and Trento, to Riva on the Lago di Garda, where the novel ends.

BIBLIOGRAPHY 9

Balbert, Peter. "Silver Spoon to Devil's Fork: Diana Trilling and the Sexual Ethics of *Mr. Noon.*" *DHL Review* 20 (Summer 1988): 237–50.
Bell, Michael. "Review of *Mr. Noon* by DHL." *Modern Language Review* 83 (1988): 176–77.
Black, Michael. "DHL and Gilbert Noon." *London Review of Books* (4–17 October 1984): 10, 12.
———. "Gilbert Noon, DHL, and the Gentle Reader." *DHL Review* 20 (Summer 1988): 153–78.
Blanchard, Lydia. "Review of *Mr. Noon* by DHL." *DHL Review* 17 (Summer 1984): 153–59.
———. "DHL and His 'Gentle Reader': The New Audience of *Mr. Noon.*" *DHL Review* 20 (Summer 1988a): 223–35.
———. " 'Reading Out' a 'New Novel': Lawrence's Experiments with Story and Discourse in *Mr. Noon.*" In *Critical Essays on DHL.* Edited by Dennis Jackson and Fleda Brown Jackson. Boston: G. K. Hall, 1988b, pp. 110–18.
"Briefly Noted." *New Yorker* (28 January 1985): 97. (Review.)
Carey, John. "Lawrence at War." *Sunday Times* (2 December 1984): 43. (Review.)
Christensen, Peter S. "*Mr. Noon:* Some Problems in a New Text." *Studies in the Novel* 18 (Winter 1986): 414–26.
Condren, Edward. [On *Mr. Noon*]. *Los Angeles Times/The Book Review* (4 November 1984): 3, 11. (Review.)
Delany, Paul. "*Mr. Noon* and Modern Paganism." *DHL Review* 20 (Summer 1988): 251–61.
Dodsworth, Martin. "Lawrence, Sex and Class." *English* 24 (1985): 69–80. (Review essay.)
Eggert, Paul. "DHL and His Audience: The Case of *Mr. Noon.*" *Southern Review: Literary and Interdisciplinary Essays* 18 (1985): 298–307.
Einersen, Dorrit. "*Mr. Noon:* DHL's Newly Published Picaresque Romance." *Angles on the English Speaking World* (Copenhagen University) 1 (Autumn 1986): 2–6.
———. "Life and Fiction in DHL's *Mr. Noon* and the Novel's Place within the Lawrence Canon." *Orbis Litterarum: International Review of Literary Studies* (Denmark) 42, no. 2 (1987): 97–117.
Fenton, James. "Bing, Bang, Bump Factions." *London Times* (13 September 1984): 13. (Review.)
Ferreira, Maria Aline. "*Mr. Noon:* The Reader in the Text." *DHL Review* 20 (Summer 1988): 209–21.
Fuller, Cynthia. "Cracking the Womb: DHL's *Mr. Noon.*" *Stand Magazine* 26, no. 4 (Autumn 1985): 25–30.
Gray, Paul. "Men and Women in Love." *Time* (15 October 1984): 101. (Review.)
Gross, John. "Books of the Times." *New York Times* (24 October 1984): 24. (Review.)

Haltrecht, Monty. "Fight and Flight." *Times Educational Supplement* (21 September 1984): 36. (Review.)

Hawtree, Christopher. "The Crawling Snail." *Spectator* (15 September 1984): 30–31. (Review.)

Heilbut, Anthony. "All Mixed Up." *Nation* (9 February 1985): 152–55. (Review.)

Holbrook, David. "Sons and Mothers: DHL and *Mr. Noon.*" *Encounter* 70, no. 3 (March 1988): 44–54.

Hough, Graham. "From Spooning to the Real Thing." *Times Literary Supplement* (14 September 1984): 1028. (Review.)

Ingersoll, Earl. "The Pursuit of 'True Marriage': DHL's *Mr. Noon* and *Lady Chatterley's Lover.*" *Studies in the Humanities* 14 (1987): 32–45.

———. "The Progress towards Marriage in DHL's *Mr. Noon.*" *Dutch Quarterly Review* 19 (1989): 294–306.

———. "DHL's *Mr. Noon* as a Postmodern Text." *Modern Language Review* 85 (1990a): 304–9.

———. "Lawrence in the Tyrol: Psychic Geography in *Women in Love* and *Mr. Noon.*" *Forum for Modern Language Studies* 26 (1990b): 1–12.

———. "The Theme of Friendship and the Genesis of DHL's *Mr. Noon.*" *Durham University Journal* 83 (1991): 69–74.

Ingoldby, Grace. "Fall Out." *New Statesman* (14 September 1984): 32. (Review.)

Jackson, Dennis, and Lydia Blanchard, eds. *DHL Review* 20 (Summer 1988a). ("Special Issue: *Mr. Noon.*")

———. "*Mr. Noon*'s Critical Reception 1984–1988." *DHL Review* 20 (Summer 1988): 133–52.

Lawrence, D. H. "*Mr. Noon*: The Lost Novel." *Times* (28 July 1984): 8. (Extract, with two short accompanying items, "A Novel Lost and Found" and brief "Who's Who in *Mr. Noon.*")

Lodge, David. "Comedy of Eros." *New Republic* (10 December 1984): 96–100. (Review.)

———. "Lawrence, Dostoevsky, Bakhtin: DHL and Dialogic Fiction." *Renaissance and Modern Studies* 29 (1985): 16–32. (Reprinted in his *After Bakhtin.* London and New York: Routledge, 1990, pp. 57–74, and in Brown [1990]: 92–108.)

Meyers, Jeffrey. "Lawrence's *Mr. Noon.*" *Modern Fiction Studies* 31 (1985): 710–15.

"*Mr. Noon.*" *Publishers Weekly* (21 September 1984): 89. (Review.)

Mittleman, Leslie B. "*Mr. Noon.*" *Magill's Literary Annual.* Vol. 2. Englewood Cliffs, N.J.: Salem Press, 1985, pp. 619–23.

Neville, George. *A Memoir of DHL.* Edited by Carl Baron. Cambridge: Cambridge University Press, 1981.

"The New Novel by DHL: *Mr. Noon.*" *Books and Bookmen* (September 1984): 19–21. (Review and extract.)

Niven, Alastair. [On *Mr. Noon*]. *British Book News* (October 1984): 618. (Review.)

Oates, Quentin. "Critics Crowner: *Mr. Noon,* by DHL." *Bookseller* (22 September 1984): 1359–60. (Review.)

Parker, Peter. [On *Mr. Noon*]. *London Magazine,* new series, 24, no. 7 (October 1984): 107–10. (Review.)

Poole, Michael. "Noon's Day." *Listener* (13 September 1984): 24. (Review.)

Preston, Peter. "Lawrence and *Mr. Noon.*" In *DHL 1885–1930: A Celebration.* Edited by Andrew Cooper and Glyn Hughes. Nottingham: DHL Society, 1985, pp. 77–88. (Special issue of the *Journal of the DHL Society.*)

———. "*Mr. Noon* and Lawrence's Quarrel with Tolstoy." *Etudes Lawrencienne* 3 (1988): 109–23.

Pritchett, V. S. "His Angry Way." *New York Review of Books* (25 October 1984): 18. (Review.)

Sicker, Philip. "Surgery for the Novel: Lawrence's *Mr. Noon* and the 'Gentle Reader.' " *DHL Review* 20 (Summer 1988): 191–207.

Trilling, Diana. "Lawrence in Love." *New York Times Book Review* (16 December 1984): 3, 24–25. (Review.)

Tucker, M. [On *Mr. Noon*]. *Choice* (March 1985): 990. (Review.)

Vasey, Lindeth. "Introduction." *Mr. Noon* by DHL. Edited by Lindeth Vasey. Cambridge: Cambridge University Press, 1984, pp. xix–xli.

Vasey, Lindeth, and John Worthen. "*Mr. Noon*/Mr. Noon." *DHL Review* 20 (Summer 1988): 179–89.

Walker, Ronald G. "Lawrence's *Mr. Noon.*" *English Literature in Transition* 28, no. 4 (1985): 425–29.

Weinstein, Philip M. "Just-Discovered Work by DHL." *Philadelphia Inquirer* (16 December 1984): 5. (Review.)

Williams, Raymond. "Feeling the Draft." *Guardian* (13 September 1984): 20. (Review.)

See also Bell (1992): 135–36. Hyde (1990): 86–91. MacLeod (1985/87): 212–23. Pinion (1978): 249–50. Worthen (1979): 119–20, 127–29. Worthen (1991a): 62–67.

18   *Aaron's Rod*

WRITTEN

October 1917–November 1921. There were three main phases of (fitful) composition: 1. October 1917; February–March 1918; June 1919. 2. July–December 1920. 3. May–June 1921. Revisions and corrections, July–August, October 1921, with some slight changes possibly made in January 1922. Lawrence seems not to have seen proofs.

PUBLISHED

1. New York: Seltzer, 14 April 1922. London: Secker, June 1922. Part of Chapter 14 had been previously published as ''An Episode'' in *Dial* 72 (February 1922): 143–46.
2. Edited by Mara Kalnins. Cambridge: Cambridge University Press, 1988.

WHO'S WHO AND SUMMARY

MAIN CHARACTERS: Aaron Sisson; Rawdon Lilly
   The novel presents the picaresque adventures of *Aaron Sisson* in London and Italy after he gives up his job and leaves his wife and family in the Midlands after twelve years of marriage. Aaron is, at the start, a miners' checkweighman (one, employed by the miners, who checks that their coal tubs are accurately weighed by the mine owners) and secretary of the Miners' Union for his colliery. He is thirty-three and a proficient musician on the flute and piccolo. He had

originally trained to be a teacher but after three years had decided to go to the pit instead; and, though an educated man, he prefers to appear otherwise. His mother had left him a substantial amount of money when she died, and this enables him to leave his family provided for when he leaves. However, his wife, *Lottie,* is left alone to look after three children, *Marjory* and *Millicent* and a baby of nine months—and she is understandably bitter and angry at his abandonment of her. For his part, Aaron is unclear at first why he has suddenly decided to leave, except "to have a bit of free room . . . to loose myself." Later, he realizes that he left to escape the "forcing" of love within marriage and to try to find his own sheer "perfected singleness."

In London, he finds work in an orchestra and falls in with a bohemian set of artists and intellectuals some of whom he had first met on the Christmas Eve of his departure from Beldover at the home of the local colliery owner, *Alfred Bricknell.* Among the London Bricknell set are two characters of particular importance to Aaron's story: Josephine Ford and Rawdon Lilly. *Josephine Ford,* twenty-five and an artist, has recently broken off her engagement to Jim Bricknell, Alfred's son. Like her ex-fiancé, she is a somewhat ineffectual socialist and revolutionary, but she seems mainly concerned with her own sense of emptiness. She becomes friendly with Aaron in London and eventually succeeds in seducing him. This has a devastating effect on Aaron, for he feels that he has betrayed the very principle of singleness that had motivated his leaving of Lottie. Filled with guilt and self-loathing, he falls into a profound depression and then succumbs to a severe illness (ostensibly influenza). He is taken in and nursed back to health by Rawdon Lilly. Small, thin, and dark, *Rawdon Lilly* is a writer with a sharp intellect who can be both silent and withdrawn *and* overbearingly assertive. A "freak and outsider," "a peculiar bird," he can often seem objectionable to others, sometimes because of his aloof indifference and sometimes because of his candid arrogance and contrariness; but he always appears wholly self-assured and self-sufficient. In fact, he seems to possess exactly that finished singleness that Aaron desires, and the two men immediately recognize an affinity with one another—they have "an almost uncanny understanding," like brothers. But, as we have seen, Aaron's understanding of his own actions and motives has so far been only semiconscious; what Lilly offers him (and the reader) is a more articulate expression of his instinctive feelings, and, in his comments on individuality and singleness, he helps to clarify for Aaron the nature of both his inner yearning and his outer quest. Part of Lilly's clarifying function is to confirm for Aaron his sense of revulsion at modern marriage and at what he considers to be the dominance of women in marriage. But, following the visit of *Captain Herbertson,* a traumatized army officer who talks without stopping about the horrors of the battlefield (Ch. 10), a note of hostility enters the discussion when Aaron senses a desire on Lilly's part to dominate *him.* They begin to quarrel, and Lilly finally asks Aaron to leave.

Later in the year, following a brief and acrimonious return to see Lottie, Aaron makes his way to Italy in response to an invitation from Lilly. In Italy, Aaron falls briefly under the spell of the *Marchesa del Torre* and has a passionate love affair with her. She is the American wife of the *Marchese (Manfredi) del Torre,* a gnomelike ex-cavalry officer in the Italian army. She is about forty, very elegant and handsome, and she exerts an almost "occult" erotic force over Aaron. She revives in him the experience of "unalloyed desire," and, for a time, he glimpses a possible liberation of his soul through her. But once more he recoils from the experience of union with a woman, feeling that it "blasted his own central life," and, remembering Lilly's words about the need to be alone "in possession of oneself," he decides to end the affair. Almost immediately after his last lovemaking with the marchesa, he experiences a real blast, when an anarchist's bomb goes off in a café, and Aaron's rod, his flute—the center of his life—is destroyed. The only thing he has left now is "a thread of destiny attaching him to Lilly," and Aaron now seems ready to make his submission to the "heroic soul" of this "greater man." The novel ends with Lilly's once again articulating systematically what Aaron has realized vaguely and intuitively: that the "love-urge" has been exhausted by civilization, and the creative urge now is that of power, not a bullying sort of power, but the power that urges spontaneously from the deepest realms of the soul.

Other Characters

Occupants of *Mrs. Housely*'s parlor in the Royal Oak in Beldover (Ch. 2): *Tom Kirk, Brewitt, Dr. Sherardy* (the Indian doctor), and *Old Bob.*

The Bricknell set (Chs. 3 and 6): *Jim Bricknell,* the son of Alfred Bricknell, the colliery owner: a large man of thirty-eight, an ex-army officer, and a socialist, he seems absurdly obsessed by the idea of love—he believes he is "losing life" because nobody loves him, and he tries to prevent the loss by eating as much bread as he can! *Julia Cunningham,* Jim Bricknell's sister: "an English beauty" of thirty-two, she is married to *Robert Cunningham,* a sculptor, but on the verge of leaving him for *Cyril Scott,* a young composer. *Mrs. Clariss Browning,* an elegant Irishwoman. *Struthers,* a painter. *Tanny Lilly,* Rawdon Lilly's half-Norwegian wife.

The Franks set (Ch. 12): *Sir William Franks,* a wealthy self-made man at whose luxurious villa Aaron stays on his arrival in Italy. *Lady Franks,* his wife—she reminds Aaron of Queen Victoria. *The Colonel,* a stout, rubicund man with a boyish gallantry. *The Major,* an earnest, Oxford-looking man with a patch over one eye; he is accompanied by his tall, handsome, but frail wife. *Arthur,* a sort of son-in-law to Sir William because married to *Sybil,* an ex-lady's companion to Lady Franks.

The Florence set: *Angus Guest* and *Francis Dekker,* two upper-middle-class dilettante painters who meet Aaron on the way to Florence and who introduce him to the expatriate community there. *James Argyle,* a middle-aged writer and friend of Angus and Francis. *Algy Constable,* a rich, frail old man. *Signor di Lanti,* an old Italian "elegant." *Louis Mee,* another rich old man, over seventy-five and tiny, with the look of an innocent little boy. *Walter Rosen. Mr. ffrench,* a snobbish elderly man of letters who lives in Venice. *Corinna Wade,* a famous elderly English authoress from the 1870s. *Levison,* a socialist who discusses politics fervently with Lilly, Aaron, and Argyle just before the anarchist's bomb goes off (Ch. 20).

SETTING

The novel begins in the English Midlands at ''Beldover,'' based closely on Eastwood. Aaron's house was modeled on the house next door to the Lawrence family home at Lynn Croft (1905–11): the Lawrences lived at number 97, and the Cooper family at number 99. Aaron is partly modeled on Thomas Cooper (1855–1918), the Lawrences' landlord at Lynn Croft: like Aaron, he was a miners' checkweighman and played the flute and piccolo (but see also Rees [1985] in the following bibliography). The scene then shifts to London, largely centering on Covent Garden, with one chapter (8) taking place in a cottage in Hampshire (based on one of Lawrence's main homes for the period December 1917–November 1919, Chapel Farm Cottage, Hermitage, Berkshire). Following a brief return to Beldover in Chapter 11, the scene moves to Italy. Paralleling a journey Lawrence himself made in November and December 1919, Aaron goes to Turin (''Novara'' in the novel: this is the name of an actual town some thirty miles west of Milan) and then, via Milan, to Florence, where the last third or so of the novel takes place (Chs. 16–21).

BIBLIOGRAPHY 10

Aronson, Alex. ''DHL's Anti-Wagnerian Novel *Aaron's Rod.*'' In his *Music and the Novel: A Study in Twentieth Century Fiction.* Totowa, N.J.: Rowman and Little-field, 1980, pp. 96–98.

Baker, Paul G. ''Profile of an Anti-Hero: Aaron Sisson Reconsidered.'' *DHL Review* 10 (Summer 1977): 182–92.

———. *A Reassessment of DHL's ''Aaron's Rod.''* Ann Arbor, Mich. UMI Research Press, 1983.

Barr, William R. ''*Aaron's Rod* as DHL's Picaresque Novel.'' *DHL Review* 9 (Summer 1976): 213–25.

Burnett, Gary. ''H. D. and Lawrence: Two Allusions.'' *H. D. Newsletter* 1 (Spring 1987): 32–35.

Canby, Henry Siedel. *Definitions: Essays in Contemporary Criticism.* 2d series. New York: Harcourt, 1924, pp. 117–20.

Cunliffe, J. W. *English Literature in the Twentieth Century.* New York: Macmillan, 1933, 219–22.

Garcia, Leroy. ''The Quest for Paradise in the Novels of DHL.'' *DHL Review* 3 (Summer 1970): 93–114.

Hoffmann, C. G., and A. C. Hoffmann. ''Re-Echoes of the Jazz Age: Archetypal Women in the Novels of 1922." *Journal of Modern Literature* 7 (1979): 62–86. (Includes *Aaron's Rod*.)

Hyde, Virginia. "*Aaron's Rod:* DHL's Revisionist Typology." *Mosaic* 20 (1987): 111–26.

Kalnins, Mara. "Introduction." *Aaron's Rod* by DHL. Edited by Mara Kalnins. Cambridge: Cambridge University Press, 1988, pp. xvii–xliv.

Macy, John. *The Critical Game.* New York: Boni and Liveright, 1922, pp. 331–34.

Miller, Henry. *Notes on "Aaron's Rod" and Other Notes on Lawrence from the Paris Notebooks.* Edited by Seamus Cooney. Santa Barbara, Calif.: Black Sparrow Press, 1980.

Myers, Neil. "Lawrence and the War." *Criticism* 4 (Winter 1962): 44–58.

Nielsen, Inge Padkaer, and Karsten Hvidtfelt Nielsen. "The Modernism of DHL and the Discourses of Decadence: Sexuality and Tradition in *The Trespasser, Fantasia of the Unconscious,* and *Aaron's Rod.*" *Arcadia 25,* no. 3 (1990): 270–86.

Orr, Christopher. "Lawrence after the Deluge: The Political Ambiguity of *Aaron's Rod.*" *West Virginia Association of College English Teachers Bulletin* 1 (Fall 1974): 1–14.

Parker, Hershel. "Review of DHL's *Aaron's Rod* edited by Mara Kalnins." *DHL Review* 20 (1988): 339–41.

Pluto, Anne Elezabeth. "Blutbrüderschaft." *Paunch* 63–64 (1990): 85–118 (98–102).

Rees, Tony. "William Hopkin and Joseph Birkin: Local Models for Lawrence's Fiction." In *Lawrence and the Real England.* Edited by Donald Measham. Matlock, Derbyshire: Arc and Throttle Press, 1985, pp. 63–66.

Schneider, Daniel J. " 'Strange Wisdom': Leo Frobenius and DHL." *DHL Review* 16 (1983): 183–93.

Scott, Nathan A. *Rehearsals of Discomposure: Alienation and Reconciliation in Modern Literature.* London: John Lehmann, 1952, pp. 164–67.

Tristram, Philippa. "Eros and Death (Lawrence, Freud and Women)." In *Lawrence and Women.* Edited by Anne Smith. London: Vision; Totowa, N.J.: Barnes and Noble, 1978, pp. 136–55 (150–55).

See also (1980–94) Becker (1980): 101–4. Bell (1992): 139–46. Clark (1980): 224–34. Dix (1980): 111–17. Dorbad (1991): 115–19. Hobsbaum (1981): 75–77. Humma (1990): 7–15. Hyde (1990): 92–97. Hyde (1992): 119–41, passim. Kiely (1980): 66–68. Mensch (1991): 119–70. Meyers (1982): 112–16. Mohanty (1993): 29–32, 54–58, 92–96. Pinkney (1990): 106–23. Prasad (1980): 85–94. Ruderman (1984): 90–103. Scheckner (1985): 89–136. Schneider (1984): 194–210. Simpson (1982): 105–18 and passim. Suter (1987): 101–5. Worthen (1991a): 67–74.

See also (to 1979) Alcorn (1977): 100–105. Alldritt (1971): 221–240. Beal (1961): 64–69. Bedient (1972): 162–65. Cavitch (1969): 108–15. Daiches (1960): 173–76. Daleski (1965): 188–213. Eisenstein (1974): 77–86. Gregory (1933): 51–59. Hough (1956): 90–103, passim. Howe (1977): 79–91. Jarrett-Kerr (1951): 46–50. Kermode (1973): 81–86. Leavis (1955): 30–44, 47–50. Meyers (1977): 149–55. Millett (1970): 269–80. Moore (1951): 194–98. Moynahan (1963): 95–101. Murry (1931): 180–204. Murry (1933): 230–

35. Nahal (1970): 173–82. Niven (1978): 133–42. Panichas (1964): 41–44. Pinion (1978): 182–89. Potter (1930): 71–78. Pritchard (1971): 113–19. Sagar (1966): 102–14. Stewart (1963): 536–42. Stoll (1971): 198–201. Tedlock (1963): 142–54. Vivas (1960): 21–36. Worthen (1979): 118–35. Yudhishtar (1969): 210–32.

19 *Kangaroo*

WRITTEN

Early June–15 July 1922. Revisions and corrections, including new ending, October 1922; further corrections, January–February, and (proofs) July 1923.

PUBLISHED

1. London: Secker, 13 September 1923. New York: Seltzer, 17 September 1923.
   The two editions have different endings—there are 375 words more in
   the Secker ending.
2. Edited by Bruce Steele. Cambridge: Cambridge University Press, 1994.

WHO'S WHO AND SUMMARY

MAIN CHARACTERS: Richard Lovatt Somers, Harriett Somers; Jack and Victoria Callcott; William James Trewhella (Jaz); Benjamin Cooley (Kangaroo); Willie Struthers

Richard Lovatt Somers, a small, pale, dark-bearded poet and essayist who, with his wife, *Harriett,* has come to Australia "to start a new life and flutter with a new hope" after becoming disillusioned with Europe. Their neighbors in Sydney are *Jack* and *Victoria Callcott.* Jack turns out to be a senior member of a semisecret paramilitary organization of ex-servicemen committed to seizing political power by military force. (The organization has a legitimate front in the form of the Digger Clubs, which are sporting and social clubs for ex-servicemen.) He offers Somers the opportunity of joining the organization and takes him to see the charismatic leader of the movement, *Benjamin Cooley,* known as *Kangaroo*—an ex-army officer and a lawyer by profession, about forty years old, he has sloping shoulders and a large stomach that make him look like a kangaroo. He advocates a churchlike state of Australia based on ideals of universal love and brotherhood, but he also sees this in terms of a strictly hierarchical system of government controlled by an all-powerful leader. This leader will be a type of pope-figure, a wise patriarch who will rule with a "*generous* power" based on his sensitive divination of "life's ever-strange new imperatives" coming from the deepest promptings of the soul. Kangaroo's vision is essentially that of a benevolent dictatorship. Somers is, at first, drawn to Kangaroo's generosity and warmth of spirit and to his apparently disinterested love of humanity and of the sacredness and mystery of life. But he remains skeptical of Kangaroo's abstract idealism and will not commit himself unequivocally to the movement. At the same time, however, Somers has himself been hankering after major social change, and he has been wanting to engage in "*some* living fellowship with other men": thus he is genuinely tempted by Kangaroo's offer. This creates tensions between Somers and Harriett, for she resents the fact that she is not enough for Somers and that he feels the need to go beyond their relationship for his fulfillment. She resents even more furiously his attempts to use his newfound sense of male camaraderie to justify his assertions of superiority over her; she simply will not accept his little "lord and master" fantasy.

William James Trewhella (Jaz) is Jack's brother-in-law and another member of the Diggers, though he seems to be involved "for the sake of the spree" rather than for any real ideological commitment to the cause. As the secretary of the coal-and-timber-merchants union, Jaz also has some involvement with the labor movement, and he takes Richard to see the leader of the Labor Party, *Willie Struthers,* who, like Kangaroo, also invites him to join his cause, this time by editing a socialist newspaper. Again, Richard is interested and tempted by the offer, particularly as he is from the working classes himself, but, as with Kangaroo, he remains skeptical of yet another abstract idealist vision of Love. Kangaroo's type of love is based on power; Struthers's type of love is based on submission and sacrifice to the general good; but, for Somers, neither type of love seems to speak convincingly to the individual.

Matters come to a head at a labor rally where the Diggers disrupt the meeting by "counting out" the speaker, Struthers. A violent fight ensues, and Somers witnesses what Kangaroo's "generous power" actually means in practice—he also later hears Jack Callcott gloating over the fact of having killed three men in the fight. Kangaroo himself is wounded, and, when Somers goes to see him, Kangaroo asks him to declare his love and allegiance unequivocally. But, even more than before, Somers feels unable to commit himself to a "love" that, he now realizes clearly, is actually a form of bullying. Kangaroo dies, and Somers and Harriett make arrangements to leave for America. The novel ends with a sense of "a plague on both your houses" in terms of the political options Somers has been offered. But Somers does commit himself to something before he leaves: to the mystery of wild nature as represented by the Australian bush—to the "non-human Gods, non-human human being."

Other Characters

The *Buryans—John Thomas, Arthur, Uncle James, Ann,* and her sister—are a family of farmers, neighbors to Richard and Harriett in Cornwall (Ch. 12). Richard becomes close friends with John Thomas.

Rose Trewhella, Jaz's wife and Jack's sister. *Gladys Trewhella,* daughter of Rose and her first husband, Alfred John Trewhella, Jaz's deceased brother.

Dug, a workmate of Jack Calcott who appears briefly at the start of the novel, grinning at the "comical-looking bloke" who turns out to be Somers. *Mr. Evans,* a Welshman who has been in Australia for sixteen years (he talks to the Somerses on the train (Ch. 7)). *Mr. Monsell,* one of two American friends who visit Somers in Cornwall (Ch. 12). He is later arrested in London as a spy. (Lawrence was visited at Christmas 1916 by two journalists, Robert Mountsier, later to become his American agent, and Esther Andrews.) *Mrs. Hattie Redburn,* a staunch old friend of the Somerses who puts them up in London after their expulsion from Cornwall and later rents them her cottage in Oxfordshire. (This character is based on Dollie Radford [1864–1920], with whom the Lawrences had stayed in Hampstead in October 1912. The cottage she actually rented them, later, was Chapel Farm Cottage at Hermitage, Berkshire.) *James Sharpe,* a Scottish neighbor of the Somerses in Cornwall. He is "half an artist" and interested in music. (The character is based on the composer and music critic Cecil Gray [1895–1951].)

SETTING

The novel is set on the South Coast of New South Wales, mainly in and around Sydney and Thirroul ("Mullumbimby" in the novel). Chapter 12, "The Nightmare," is a flashback to Somers's wartime experiences in Cornwall, based closely on Lawrence's experiences while at Higher Tregerthen near Zennor between March 1916 and October 1917 (the Buryans of the novel are based on the Hocking family, who farmed Tregerthen farm next to Lawrence's cottage here.) The Lawrences had moved to Cornwall at the end of December 1915, but Lawrence omits the first two months of their stay from his fictional account. Places in Cornwall that appear under their actual names are Bodmin, Penzance, and Truro. Derby and Nottingham also figure briefly in this chapter.

BIBLIOGRAPHY 11

Alexander, John. "DHL's *Kangaroo:* Fantasy, Fact or Fiction." *Meanjin* 24 (1965): 179–95.

Anantha Murthy, U. R. "DHL's *Kangaroo* as an Australian Novel." *ACLALS Bulletin* (Mysore, India) 4 (1976): 43–49.

Atkinson, Curtis. "Was There Fact in DHL's *Kangaroo?" Meanjin* 29 (September 1965): 358–59.

Bentley, Eric R. *A Century of Hero-Worship.* Philadelphia: Lippincott, 1944, pp. 234–39.

Bradbrook, M. C. *Literature in Action: Studies in Continental and Commonwealth Society.* London: Chatto and Windus, 1972, pp. 133–35.

Cross, Gustav. "Little Magazines in Australia." *Review of English Literature* 5 (October 1964): 20–28. (Lawrence's use of the *Bulletin.*)

Dalton, Jack P. "A Note on DHL." *Papers of the Bibliographic Society of America* 61 (Third Quarter 1967): 269.

Darroch, Robert. "The Mystery of *Kangaroo* and the Secret Army." *Australian* (15 May 1976).

———. "So Many of the Best People Join Secret Armies." *Australian* (15 January 1977): 21, 76.

———. *DHL in Australia.* Melbourne: Macmillan, 1981.

———. "Lawrence in Australia: The Plot Thickens as the Clues Emerge." *Bulletin* (20 May 1986): 82–85.

———. "The Man Who Was Kangaroo." *Quadrant* (September 1987): 56–60.

———. "More on Lawrence in Australia." *DHL Review* 20 (1988): 39–60.

Davis, Joseph. *DHL at Thirroul.* Sydney: Collins, 1989. (See especially pp. 183–99 for a discussion of the critical reputation of the novel.)

Draper, Ronald P. "Authority and the Individual: A Study of DHL's *Kangaroo." Critical Quarterly* 1 (Autumn 1959): 208–15. (Also, in shortened form, in his *DHL.* New York: Twayne, 1964, pp. 96–101 [reissued, 1976].)

Eggert, Paul. "Lawrence, the Secret Army and the West Australian Connexion." *Westerly* 26 (1982): 122–26.

Ellis, David. "Lawrence in Australia: The Darroch Controversy." *DHL Review* 21 (1989): 167–74.

Foster, John Burt, Jr. "Dostoevsky versus Nietzsche in Modernist Fiction: Lawrence's *Kangaroo* and Malraux's *La Condition Humaine." Stanford Literature Review* 2 (1985): 47–83.

Friederich, Werner P. *Australia in Western Imaginative Prose Writings 1600–1960.* Chapel Hill: University of North Carolina Press, 1967, pp. 226–33.

Garcia, Reloy. "The Quest for Paradise in the Novels of DHL." *DHL Review* 33 (Summer 1970): 93–114 (106–9).

Goonetilleke, D.C.R.A. "DHL: Primitivism?" In his *Developing Countries in British Fiction.* London and Basingstoke: Macmillan; Totowa, N.J.: Rowman and Littlefield, 1977, pp. 170–98 (171, 185–86, 193).

Gurko, Leo. "*Kangaroo:* DHL in Transit." *Modern Fiction Studies* 10 (Winter 1964–45): 349–58.

Haegert, John W. "Brothers and Lovers: DHL and the Theme of Friendship." *Southern Review* 8 (March 1975): 39–50.

Heuzenroeder, John. "DHL's Australia." *Australian Literary Studies* (University of Tasmania) 4 (October 1970): 319–33.

Hogan, Robert. "The Amorous Whale: A Study in the Symbolism of DHL." *Modern Fiction Studies* 5 (Spring 1959): 39–46.

Hope, A. D. "DHL's *Kangaroo:* How It Looks to an Australian." In *The Australian Experience: Critical Essays on Australian Novels.* Edited by W. S. Ramson. Canberra: Australian National University, 1974, pp. 157–73.

Humma, John B. "Of Bits, Beasts and Bush: The Interior Wilderness in DHL's *Kangaroo.*" *South Atlantic Review* 51 (1986): 83–100. (Reprinted as Ch. 4 of Humma [1990]: 29–44.)

Jarvis, F. P. "A Textual Comparison of the First British and American Editions of DHL's *Kangaroo.*" *Papers of the Bibliographical Society of America* (Fourth Quarter, 1965): 400–424.

Lee, Robert. "DHL and the Australian Ethos." *Southerly* 33 (1973): 144–51.

Lowe, John. "Judas in for the Spree? The Role of Jaz in *Kangaroo.*" *DHL: The Journal of the DHL Society* 4 (1986): 30–34.

McCormick, John. *Catastrophe and Imagination: An Interpretation of the Recent English and American Novel.* London and New York: Longman, Green, 1957, 244–48.

Martin, Murray S. "*Kangaroo* Revisited." *DHL Review* 18 (1985–86): 201–15.

Maud, Ralph. "The Politics in *Kangaroo.*" *Southerly* 17 (1956): 67–71.

Moore, Andrew. "The Historian as Detective: Pursing the Darroch Thesis and DHL's Secret Army." *Overland* 113 (December 1988): 39–44.

Morgan, Patrick. "Hard Work and Idle Dissipation: The Dual Australian Personality." *Meanjin* 41 (April 1982): 130–37.

———. "Getting Away from It All." *Kunapipi* 5, no. 1 (1983): 73–87.

Peek, Andrew. "Captain Ahab, Moby Dick and a Critical Note on DHL's *Kangaroo.*" *Journal of the DHL Society* 2 (1979a): 4–7.

———. "The Sydney *Bulletin* and DHL's *Kangaroo.*" *Notes and Queries* 26 (1979b): 337–38.

———. "Tim Burstall's *Kangaroo.*" *Westerly* 25 (1980): 39–42. (On the flm version.)

———. "The Sydney *Bulletin, Moby Dick* and the Allusiveness of *Kangaroo.*" In *DHL: New Studies.* Edited by Christopher Heywood. London: Macmillan; New York: St. Martin's Press, 1987, pp. 84–89.

Pluto, Anne Elezabeth. "Blutbrüderschaft." *Paunch* 63–64 (1990): 85–118 (102–7).

Pollak, Paulina S. "Anti-Semitism in the Works of DHL: Search for and Rejection of the Faith." *Literature and Psychology* 32 (1986): 19–29.

Riemer, A. P. "Jumping to Conclusions about the Right-Wing Army of *Kangaroo.*" *Sydney Morning Herald* (9 December 1989): 72. (Review of Davis [1989] op. cit.)

Ross, Harris. "*Kangaroo:* Australian Filmmakers Watching Lawrence Watching Australia." *DHL Review* 19 (Spring 1987): 93–101.

Russell, John. "DHL: *The Lost Girl, Kangaroo.*" In his *Style in Modern British Fiction:*

Studies in Joyce, Lawrence, Forster, Lewis and Green. Baltimore: Johns Hopkins University Press, 1975, pp. 43–88.

St. John, Edward. "DHL and Australia's Secret Army." *Quadrant* 26 (June 1982): 53–57.

Samuels, Marilyn Schauer. "Water, Ships and the Sea: Unifying Symbols in Lawrence's *Kangaroo.*" *University Review* (Kansas City) 37 (October 1970): 46–57.

Schneider, Daniel J. "Psychology and Art in Lawrence's *Kangaroo.*" *DHL Review* 14 (1981): 156–71.

Sepčić, Višnja. "The Category of Landscape in DHL's *Kangaroo.*" *Studia Romanica et Anglica,* nos. 27–28 (July–December 1969): 129–52.

Singh, Vishnudat. "Lawrence's Use of 'Pecker.' " *Papers of the Bibliographical Society of America* 64 (1970): 355.

Steele, Bruce. "*Kangaroo:* Fact and Fiction." *Meridian* 10 (May 1991): 19–34.

———. "Introduction." *Kangaroo* by DHL. Edited by Bruce Steele. Cambridge: Cambridge University Press, 1994, pp. xvii–lvi.

Stevens, C. J. *Lawrence at Tregerthen.* Troy, N.Y.: Whitston, 1988.

Tolchard, C. "DHL in Australia." *Walkabout* 33 (November 1967): 29–31.

Van Herk, Aritha. "CrowB(e)ars and Kangaroos of the Future: The Post-Colonial Ga(s)p." *World Literature Written in English* 30 (Autumn 1990): 42–54. (Discusses *Kangaroo* along with three works by Faulkner, David Ireland, and Robert Kroetsch.)

Vohra, S. K. "*Kangaroo:* Search for Viable Alternatives." In *Essays on DHL.* Edited by T. R. Sharma. Meerut, India: Shalabh Book House, 1987, pp. 109–15.

Wade, John Stevens. "DHL in Cornwall: An Interview with Stanley Hocking." *DHL Review* 6 (1973): 237–83.

Watson-Williams, Helen. "Land into Literature: The Western Australian Bush Seen by Some Early Writers and DHL." *Westerly* 25 (1980): 59–72.

Wilding, Michael. 'A New Show' ": The Politics of *Kangaroo.*" *Southerly* 30 (1969): 20–40. (See also "*Kangaroo:* 'A New Show' " in his *Political Fictions.* Boston: Routledge and Kegan Paul, 1980, pp. 150–91.)

———. "Between Scylla and Charybdis: *Kangaroo* and the Form of the Political Novel." *Australian Literary Studies* (University of Tasmania) 4 (October 1970): 334–48.

Zwicky, Fay. "Speeches and Silences." *Quadrant* 27 (May 1983): 40–46.

See also (1980–94) Bell (1992): 146–61, passim. Clark (1980): 258–65. Delany (1978): passim. Dorbad (1991): 119–23. Hobsbaum (1981): 78–80. Humma (1990): 29–44. Hyde (1990): 15–17, 97–99. MacLeod (1985/87): 63–75. Mensch (1991): 171–206. Meyers (1982): 116–23. Mohanty (1993): 33–39, 58–68, 96–99. Padhi (1989): 31–36. Pinkney (1990): 112–23. Prasad (1980): 94–112. Ruderman (1984): 104–14, passim. Scheckner (1985): 89–136. Schneider (1984): 90–94, 210–23. Siegel (1991): passim. Simpson (1982): 108–15, passim. Suter (1987): 110–15. Worthen (1991): 78–84, passim.

See also (to 1979) Alldritt (1971): 221–40. Beal (1961): 69–77. Cavitch (1969): 132–35. Eisenstein (1974): 87–113. Freeman (1955): 158–76. Harrison (1966): 181–84. Hochman (1970): 180–83. Hough (1956): 103–17, passim. Howe (1977): 92–105. Inniss (1971): 163–68. Jarrett-Kerr (1951): 59–66. Kermode (1973): 105–9. Leavis (1955): 44–

47, 52–56, 64–67. Maes-Jelinek (1970): 72–81. Millett (1970): 280–83. Moore (1951): 211–20, passim. Moynahan (1963): 101–7. Murry (1931): 218–39. Nahal (1970): 117–25. Nin (1932): 59–66, 116–29. Niven (1978): 143–65. Panichas (1964): 84–88. Pinion (1978): 189–95. Potter (1930): 79–86. Pritchard (1971): 150–54. Sagar (1966): 131–37. Slade (1970): 82–87. Stewart (1963): 542–50. Stoll (1971): 201–10. Tedlock (1963): 161–66. Vivas (1960): 37–63. West (1950): 124–27. Worthen (1979): 136–51. Yudishtar (1969): 232–50.

20 *The Boy in the Bush*

WRITTEN

September 1923–May 1924. September–November 1923; January 1924. Proofs, April–May 1924.

The Boy in the Bush was the result of a collaboration between Lawrence and Mollie L. Skinner and therefore bears both names on the title page. However, the precise degree of their respective responsibilities for the published text remains difficult to ascertain because of the disappearance of Skinner's original manuscripts and typescripts of the novel (the dates listed refer only to Lawrence's part in the writing). Lawrence had met Mollie Skinner in Australia in 1922 and had suggested that she write a novel about the early Western Australian settlers, using her own brother as a model for the hero. She took up his suggestion and in 1923 sent him a typescript entitled "The House of Ellis." Lawrence read this in August 1923 and then offered to rework it for publication. Though evidently following the typescript draft closely, Lawrence actually rewrote the whole novel in his own hand, revising and recasting it extensively as he went, and this rewritten version was eventually published in 1924. With the subsequent loss of Skinner's original material, the difficulties of objectively assessing the precise nature and degree of this rewriting are self-evident. However, both authors have given partial (though often unreliable) accounts of their collaboration in letters and memoirs, and various other pieces of evidence exist to guide informed judgments and speculation as to the balance of responsibility for the novel. (See Paul Eggert's introduction to the Cambridge edition of the novel for a fully detailed discussion. Most other items in the bibliography to this chapter also address the question in one way or another.) In general terms, it now seems certain that Lawrence's reworking of the novel was much more radical than previously suspected—it was a matter not just of stylistic polishing, but of fundamental changes to plot, character, and theme. We know that Lawrence definitely added a new ending to Skinner's original story (that, in fact, the final six chapters of the novel were composed almost entirely by him), that he introduced many of the major plot developments, and that, unsurprisingly, he redirected much of the thematic interest toward questions of sexual relationship and the "dark god" of the instincts and toward a critique of bourgeois values. The frequently noted zest and vitality of the writing, though more difficult to attribute with certainty to Lawrence, also undoubtedly reflect his characteristic style.

PUBLISHED

1. London: Secker, August 1924. New York: Seltzer, September 1924.
2. Edited by Paul Eggert. Cambridge: Cambridge University Press, 1990.
3. See also under Moore (1971) in the following bibliography.

WHO'S WHO AND SUMMARY

MAIN CHARACTER: Jack Grant

The Boy in the Bush is probably the closest Lawrence ever came to writing a novel of action and adventure. It centers almost exclusively on just one individual, Jack Grant, although the cast of supporting characters is very large, and their interrelationships are not always easy to remember. We follow the life of Jack Grant from his arrival in Western Australia in 1882 at the age of eighteen as a sort of remittance man (he has been expelled from school and agricultural college in Bedford for various misdemeanors), through his adjustment to farming life with his kinsfolk, the Ellis family at Wandoo, his experiences in the outback and in the Northwest with Tom Ellis (on a sheep station and elsewhere), to his establishment as a successful gold miner and a wealthy farm owner at the age of about twenty-two. Jack Grant ends up feeling like a mixture of "goldminer, a gentleman settler, and a bandit chief."

Perhaps the most important element in Jack's character, something emphasized by the narrator and the sequence of events from the very start, is his inherent predisposition to resist and rebel against social convention: "as far as the world went, he was a sinner, born condemned." In this, Jack follows in the footsteps of his mother, *Katie Grant,* née Reid, rather than those of his "good" military-gentleman father, *General Grant.* Katie Grant had been born and bred in Western Australia, and even in England she remained a "real colonial," "a wild, sweet animal" with a "jolly sensuousness" and an easy indifference to the "rail-fences" of convention: her motto was always that nothing mattered "so long as you were good inside yourself." This motto—and varia-

tions on it such as Gran Ellis's "a man's own true self is God in him"—
becomes Jack's credo, too, and it manifests itself most notably at the end of the
novel when he becomes determined to have *both* of the women in his life—
Monica Ellis and Mary Rath—as wives (and when he also contemplates adding
a third wife, Hilda Blessington).

Other Characters

The Ellis family at Wandoo: *Gran Ellis,* the "presiding deity" of the house.
Jacob Ellis, Gran's son and father and head of the family. *Ma Ellis,* his second
wife. *Tom Ellis,* Jacob's eldest son, but by his first marriage. Tom is the pivot
of the household and becomes head of the family after Jacob's death. He becomes Jack's bosom friend: on their two-year trip to the Northwest he goes
through some sort of makeshift wedding ceremony with *Miss Lucy Snook* (Ch.
17), a barmaid in what seems to be a shantytown, "Honeysuckle"—he is
haunted by the memory forever after. *Monica Ellis* is the twin sister of *Grace
Ellis* (who later marries *Alec Rice*). She is tawny and pantherlike, with a rare
vitality and queenly quality. She is drawn instinctively to Jack, but first his
reticence and then her withdrawal into herself after the death of her father prevent them from coming together before Jack goes away to the Never-Never with
Tom. When he returns, he learns that, pregnant with Red Easu's child, she has
gone to live in Albany with *Percy Pink-eye* (Hal Stockley), a young Queens-
lander friend of the Ellises. She has another child with Percy before he leaves
her to go to Melbourne. After killing Easu, Jack goes to Albany and marries
Monica: he takes her gold prospecting with him to the Northwest. There, Percy's
baby dies, Easu's child, *Jane,* flourishes, and Monica becomes pregnant again
with Jack's child. *Lennie Ellis,* a "cheeky" boy who loves riding, laughing, and
boasting—he marries at seventeen, having made his girlfriend pregnant. The
younger members of the family are *Og and Magog,* twin boys, *Harry, Katie,*
and *Ellie.*

    Dr. Rackett, an Oxford-educated English doctor who tutors Lennie and is
often at Wandoo; he seems to use some sort of drug, possibly opium. *Ruth
Blogg* is a daughter of Gran Ellis: her husband, *Uncle Blogg,* is a Methodist
preacher. The *Misses Ellis* are maiden aunts who turn up at the deathbed of
Gran Ellis.

    Mr. George, the "rumbustical" old lawyer who has been assigned to look
after Jack on his arrival in Australia. He had known Jack's mother before she
left Australia, and Jack has heard many stories about this "hearty colonial hero"
as a child; the actual man seems a little more shabby and provincial than he
had expected, but he is kindly and hospitable, and he gives Jack advice about
life in the colony. He appears at fairly regular intervals throughout the novel
both in his professional role and as a sort of uncle-guardian figure to Jack. *Aunt
Matilda* (Mrs. Watson), the sister of Mr. George and guardian of Mary Rath: a

large, stout woman, ostentatious with gold chains and diamond-ringed hands, she, at first, finds the lamblike Jack quite charming. Later, however, she greets the outback-hardened Jack and his unconventional morals with an outraged "Queen Victoria statue pose." *Mary Rath,* a dark and quietly confident young girl who quickly establishes a "blood-connexion" with Jack. He, at first, considers her somewhat repulsive but is won round by her heavy kind of beauty, and he develops a "strange, blind passion" for her. At the governor's dance (Ch. 18), he urges her not to accept a marriage proposal from Boyd Blessington and to wait for him to come back for her when he has made his fortune and can afford his own farm. However, when he does come back, he is married to Monica, and Mary will not contemplate his bigamous plans for her. From his point of view, she is too tied to social convention; she thinks he "must really be mad."

John Grant, son of Jack's mother's elder sister and of George Rath, Mary Rath's father; he is therefore Jack's uncle and Mary's half-brother. He is liable to bouts of insanity, though he has made a success of his farm. *Amos and Emma Lewis* are his servants at the Coney Hatch farm, which Jack eventually inherits.

The Red Ellises: *Red Easu Ellis,* the oldest brother and head of the "rough crowd of men and youths" that makes up the Red Ellis clan, the sons of Jacob Ellis's twin brother, Easu, and neighboring farmers to the Wandoo Ellises. Red Easu is about thirty and becomes Jack's enemy almost on sight; he is also his bitter rival for the love of Monica Ellis. He later fathers her illegitimate child but marries the heiress *Sarah Ann,* a "grisly" and vulgar "scorpion" of a woman. Jack is eventually forced to kill Easu in self-defense. The other Red brothers are *Ross, Alan,* and *Herbert* (whom Jack nurses after an accident in Ch. 5).

Characters at the "jamboree" wedding party at Paddy's Crossing (Chs. 13 and 14): *Danny Mackinnon,* father of the bride. *Patrick O'Burk Tracy,* the groom. *Paddy O'Burk Tracy,* father of the groom. *Father Prendy,* the old mission priest. *Long-armed Jake,* with whom Jack briefly brawls after Jake's girl, *Deirdre,* makes passes at Jack; she later seduces him anyway—Jack's sexual initiation.

Boyd Blessington, a widower of thirty-seven with five children; he becomes a suitor to Mary Rath. *Hilda Blessington,* daughter of Boyd, is fascinated by Jack Grant and his unconventional ways. She herself would like to live an independent life—she does not want to marry, at least not conventionally, and seems uninterested in men anyway. However, she has been taken by Jack's suggestion to Mary Rath that he might have more than one wife, and, at the end of the novel, she offers to join him and Monica in the Northwest.

Mr. Swallow and *Mr. Bell,* friends of Mr. George. *Grey,* the Fremantle-to-Albany coachman who, talking all the while, drives Jack to Wandoo for the first time. *Joshua Jenkins,* among other things, the undertaker at York. *Jimmie Short,* Tom Ellis's cousin.

SETTING

The novel is set in Western Australia, primarily in the area around Darlington, inland from Fremantle and Perth and near to York, where Lawrence and Frieda stayed for a fortnight, between 4 and 18 May 1922, at Mollie Skinner's guest-house, "Leithdale." Several sections of the book take place in the outback—the "Never-Never"—in the Northwest of the colony, Geraldton on the coast being a point of arrival and departure here. Brief scenes take place in Albany, where Monica goes to live with Pink-eye Percy after becoming pregnant by Red Easu.

BIBLIOGRAPHY 12

Bartlett, Norman. "Mollie Skinner and *The Boy in the Bush*." *Quadrant* 28 (July–August 1984): 73–75.

Eggert, Paul. "Introduction." *The Boy in the Bush* by DHL. Cambridge: Cambridge University Press, 1990, pp. xxi–lxiii.

———. "Document or Process as the Site of Authority: Establishing Chronology of Revision in Competing Typescripts of Lawrence's *The Boy in the Bush*." *Studies in Bibliography* 44 (1991): 364–76.

Faulkner, Thomas C. "Review Essay on DHL and M. L. Skinner, *The Boy in the Bush*. Edited by Paul Eggert. Cambridge: Cambridge University Press, 1990." *DHL Review* 23 (Summer–Fall 1991): 205–9.

Gay, Harriet. "Mollie Skinner: DHL Australian Catalyst." *Biography* 3 (1980): 331–47.

Heuzenroeder, John. "DHL's Australia." *Australian Literary Studies* (University of Tasmania) 4 (October 1970): 319–33.

Moore, Harry T. "Preface." *The Boy in the Bush* by DHL and M. L. Skinner. Carbondale and Edwardsville: Southern Illinois University Press; London and Amsterdam: Feffer and Simons, 1971, pp. vii–xxviii.

Porter, Peter. "Collaborations." *New Statesman* (16 November 1973): 741–42.

Prichard, Katherine Susannah. "Lawrence in Australia." *Meanjin* 9 (Summer 1950): 252–59. (Reprinted in Nehls [1957–59], vol. 2, pp. 274–78.)

Rees, Marjorie. "Mollie Skinner and DHL." *Westerly* 1 (March 1964): 41–49.

Rossman, Charles. "*The Boy in the Bush* in the Lawrence Canon." In *DHL: The Man Who Lived.* Edited by Robert B. Partlow, Jr., and Harry T. Moore. Carbondale: Southern Illinois University Press, 1980, pp. 185–94.

Skinner, Mollie L. "DHL and *The Boy in the Bush*." *Meanjin* 9 (Summer 1950): 260–63. (Reprinted in Nehls [1957–59], vol. 2, pp. 271–74.)

———. "Correspondence: DHL." *Southerly* 13 (1952): 233–35.

———. *The Fifth Sparrow: An Autobiography.* Sydney: Sydney University Press, 1972; London: Angus and Robertson, 1973, pp. 138–44.

Stacy, Paul H. "Lawrence and Movies: A Postscript." *Literature/Film Quarterly* 2 (Winter 1974): 93–95. (Comments on the novel's filmlike style.)

Watson-Williams, Helen. "Land into Literature: The Western Australian Bush Seen by Some Early Writers and DHL." *Westerly* 25 (1980): 59–72.

See also (1980–94) Clark (1980): 293–99. Hyde (1992): 174–77, passim. Ruderman (1984): 115–26, passim. Suter (1987): 105–10. Worthen (1991a): 84–86.

See also (to 1979) Draper (1970): 232–42. Ford (1965): 65–66. Hobsbaum (1981): 80–81. Kermode (1973): 110–12. Moore (1951): 209–11. Murry (1931): 240–47. Sagar (1966): 137–41. Tedlock (1963): 167–70.

21   *The Plumed Serpent (Quetzalcoatl)*

WRITTEN

May 1923–February 1925. Revisions, June 1925; proof corrections, October 1925. Draft versions: 1. "Quetzalcoatl," May–June 1923. 2. November 1924–February 1925.

PUBLISHED

1. London: Secker, January 1926. New York: Knopf, February 1926.
2. Edited by L. D. Clark. Cambridge: Cambridge University Press, 1987.
3. *Quetzalcoatl.* Edited by Louis Martz. Redding Ridge, Conn.: Black Swan Books, 1995. See also Walker (1983) in following bibliography.

WHO'S WHO AND SUMMARY

MAIN CHARACTERS: Kate Leslie; Don Ramón Carrasco (Quetzalcoatl), Don Cipriano (General Viedma and later Huitzilopochtli)

The Plumed Serpent tells the story of *Kate Leslie*'s ambivalent involvement with a religious revolutionary movement in Mexico led by the charismatic figure of *Don Ramón Carrasco* and his military second-in-command, *Don Cipriano.* One of the main aims of the movement is to revive the ancient gods and rituals of pre-Christian times (Aztec and before) and to institute a new-old national religion of Quetzalcoatl—the name of a legendary god, half-bird (Quetzal) and half-serpent (Coatl)—in place of Catholicism. Partly for this reason, the leaders of the organization take on the names of the old gods, though later there is also a suggestion that they somehow take on the *nature* of those gods, too; thus, Don Ramón becomes Quetzalcoatl, and Don Cipriano becomes the red Huitzilopochtli. Kate, an Irish widow of forty, is at first fascinated by the revolutionaries—her recently deceased second husband, *James Joachim Leslie,* had also been an ardent political leader; she is impressed by the cultured nobility of the eminent historian and archaeologist Don Ramón (also a wealthy landowner) and instinctively attracted by the dark vitality of Don Cipriano. But as she moves gradually closer to the center of the movement and becomes introduced herself into the pantheon of gods as the green-clad Malintzi, her rational European mind starts to question the fanatical mysticism of Quetzalcoatl and to recoil from its half-hidden barbarity. The novel then tracks Kate's fluctuating feelings while simultaneously charting the progress of the revolution on the broader political stage. Cipriano, in his official guise as General Viedma, commands the Western division of the national Mexican army, and he starts to use his forces in support of the Quetzalcoatl cause. Eventually, *Socrates Tomás Montes,* the Labor president of Mexico, is forced to ally himself with Quetzalcoatl and to declare it the state religion. Ramón and Cipriano gain in confidence and support and soon control large parts of the country. But now the underlying brutality of the Quetzalcoatl movement starts to reveal itself more clearly to Kate. First, she witnesses Ramón's callous disregard of his wife's suffering and death during a ritual desecration of a Catholic church (Ch. 21)—*Doña Carlota,* his wife, has retained an ardent allegiance to the Catholic Church and fiercely opposes Ramón's crusade. Kate then looks on in horror at Cipriano's savage execution of prisoners—some have their necks broken by guards, and some are stabbed to death by him (Ch. 23). Yet, some part of Kate's consciousness remains in thrall to the movement, or at least to "the old, twilit Pan-power" of the "god-devil" Cipriano. For, despite her conscious revulsion from some of his actions and ideas, and despite her recognition that submission to him will mean the death of her individual self, Kate seems unable to resist the spell of Cipriano's "demon-power," and she first agrees to become his ritual, mystic bride, Malintzi, and then agrees also to marry him legally. Right to the end of the novel, however, her ambivalence about Quetzalcoatl and about her submission to it in the guise of Cipriano, remains—"she was aware of a duality in herself." Even as she decides finally to submit to Cipriano, she qualifies her decision with "as far as I need, and no further."

Other Characters

Owen Rhys, Kate's American cousin: a poet and a socialist, he accompanies her to the bullfight at the start of the novel, along with another American friend, *Bud Villiers.* Both men are portrayed as shallow sensation-seekers, though Villiers more so than Rhys.

Mrs. Norris, an elderly archaeologist, the widow of an English ambassador to Mexico, with an old house in the village of Tlacolulan, just outside Mexico City. Guests at her tea party in Chapter 2 include the irascible old *Judge Burlap* and his baby-faced, faded wife, *Mrs. Burlap; Mr. and Mrs. Henry; Major Law*, an American military attaché.

Doña Isabel, Don Ramón's aunt: she acts as hostess at the dinner party at his home that Kate attends in Chapter 3. Other guests are *Julio Toussaint*, a sententious and didactic old man who presents some dubious theories about racial purity and inherited racial characteristics; *Garcia*, a Mexican university professor of about twenty-eight and a socialist; *Mirabal*, an intense, pale young man, a zealous acolyte of Ramón and the Quetzalcoatl movement.

Juana, Kate's limping and untidy Mexican-Indian housekeeper in Sayula. Her children are *Jesús*, a large, lumbering odd-job man; *Ezequiel*, finer and prouder than his elder half-brother, he later joins the Quetzalcoatl revival; *Concha*, a heavy, "barbaric" girl of fourteen; and *Maria*, eleven, thin and birdlike. *Felipa*, Juana's sixteen-year-old niece. *Julio*, Juana's cousin and a bricklayer, and *Maria del Carmen*, his wife. *Don Antonio*, Kate's landlord at Sayula; he is a fascist ally of the Knights of Cortés, who oppose Quetzalcoatl.

Pedro and *Cyprian* are Don Ramón's young sons; they resent their father for his involvement with Quetzalcoatl and for his antagonism toward their mother and the Catholic faith.

Teresa, Don Ramón's second wife. She is twenty-eight and the daughter of *Don Tomás*, a staunch old friend and supporter of Ramón since Teresa was a child. *Martin*, Ramón's manservant—killed in the assassination attempt on Ramón's hacienda (Ch. 19). *Daniel*, another of Ramón's servants. *Pablo*, the soldier/doctor who attends to Ramón after the assassination attempt. *Guillermo*, one of the rebels who attack Ramón's hacienda. *Maruca*, Guillermo's lover—she helps the assassins gain entry into the hacienda. Guillermo and Maruca are later executed by Cipriano.

SETTING

Mexico: the first four chapters are set in and around Mexico City; the rest of the novel is set in and around Chapala on Lake Chapala ("Sayula" and "Lake Sayula" in the novel), northwest of Mexico City and just south of Guadalajara. Lawrence and Frieda were in Mexico City between 23 March and 27 April 1923 and lived at Chapala from May to July of the same year. Lawrence returned to Mexico with Kai Götzsche in September, traveling there until November. He and Frieda went back again in October 1924 and stayed in Oaxaca in the South between November 1924 and February 1925.

BIBLIOGRAPHY 13

Apter, T. E. "Let's Hear What the Male Chauvinist Is Saying: *The Plumed Serpent.*" In *Lawrence and Women*. Edited by Anne Smith. Totowa, N.J.: Barnes and Noble; London: Vision, 1978, pp. 156–77.

Baldwin, Alice. "The Structure of the Coatl Symbol in *The Plumed Serpent*." *Style* 5 (Spring 1971): 138–50.

Ballin, Michael. "Lewis Spence and the Myth of Quetzalcoatl in DHL's *The Plumed Serpent*." *DHL Review* 13 (Spring 1980): 63–78.

Baron, C. E. "Forster on Lawrence." In *E. M. Forster: A Human Exploration/Centenary Essays*. Edited by G. K. Das and John Beer. New York: New York University Press, 1979, pp. 186–95.

Beckley, Betty. "Finding Meaning in Style: A Computerized Statistical Approach to the Linguistic Analysis of Form." *SECOL Review: Southeastern Conference on Linguistics* 9 (Summer 1985): 143–60.

Brotherston, J. G. "Revolution and the Ancient Literature of Mexico, for DHL and Antonin Artaud." *Twentieth Century Literature* 18 (July 1972): 181–89.

Christensen, Peter G. "The 'Dark Gods' and Modern Society: *Maiden Castle* and *The Plumed Serpent*." In *In the Spirit of Powys: New Essays*. Lewisburg, Pa.: Bucknell University Press; London: Associated University Presses, 1990, pp. 157–79.

———. "Katherine Ann Porter's 'Flowering Judas' and DHL's *The Plumed Serpent*: Contradicting Visions of Women in the Mexican Revolution." *South Atlantic Review* 56 (1991): 35–46.

Clark, L. D. "The Habitat of *The Plumed Serpent*." *Texas Quarterly* 5 (Spring 1962): 162–67.

———. *Dark Night of the Body: DHL's "The Plumed Serpent."* Austin: University of Texas Press, 1964.

———. "The Symbolic Structure of *The Plumed Serpent*." *Tulane Studies in English* 14 (1965): 75–96.

———. "DHL and the American Indian." *DHL Review* 9 (Fall 1976a): 305–72 (350–51, 361–69).

———. "The Making of a Novel: The Search for the Definitive Text of DHL's *The Plumed Serpent*." In *Voices from the Southwest*. Edited by Donald C. Dickinson, W. David Laird, and Margaret F. Maxwell. Flagstaff, Ariz. Northland, 1976b, pp. 113–30.

———. "Introduction." *The Plumed Serpent (Quetzalcoatl)* by DHL. Edited by L. D. Clark. Cambridge: Cambridge University Press, 1987, pp. xvii–xlvii.

———. "Reading Lawrence's American Novel: *The Plumed Serpent*." In *Critical Essays on DHL*. Edited by Dennis Jackson and Fleda Brown Jackson. Boston: G. K. Hall, 1988, pp. 118–28.

Clarke, Bruce. "The Eye and the Soul: A Moment of Clairvoyance in *The Plumed Serpent*." *Southern Review* 19 (1983): 289–301.

Cowan, James C. "The Symbolic Structure of *The Plumed Serpent*." *Tulane Studies in English* 14 (1965): 75–96.

Doherty, Gerald. "The Throes of Aphrodite: The Sexual Dimension in DHL's *The Plumed Serpent*." *Studies in the Humanities* 12 (1985): 67–78.

Edwards, Duane. "Erich Neumann and the Shadow Problem in *The Plumed Serpent*." *DHL Review* 23 (1991): 129–41.

Eliot, T. S. "Le roman anglais contemporain." *La Nouvelle Revue Française* 28 (1 May 1927): 669–75.

———. *After Strange Gods: A Primer of Modern Heresy*. London: Faber and Faber, 1934.

Galea, Ileana. "DHL: The Value of Myth." *Cahiers Roumains d'Etudes Litteraires* 3 (1987): 72–78.

Garcia, Reloy. "The Quest for Paradise in the Novels of DHL." *DHL Review* 3 (Summer 1970): 93–114.

Gilbert, Sandra M. *DHL's "Sons and Lovers," "The Rainbow," "Women in Love," "The Plumed Serpent."* New York: Monarch Press, 1965. (Study Guide.)

Glicksberg, Charles I. "Myth in Lawrence's Fiction." In his *Modern Literary Perspectivism.* Dallas: Southern Methodist University, 1970, pp. 139–48 (144–46).

Goonetilleke, D.C.R.A. "DHL: Primitivism?" In his *Developing Countries in British Fiction.* London and Basingstoke: Macmillan; Totowa, N.J.: Rowman and Littlefield, 1977, pp. 170–98 (*The Plumed Serpent,* 184–93).

Harbison, Robert. *Deliberate Regression.* New York: Knopf, 1980, pp. 193–98.

Harris, Janice. "The Moulting of *The Plumed Serpent:* A Study of the Relationship between the Novel and Three Contemporary Tales." *Modern Language Quarterly* 39 (June 1978): 154–68.

Humma, John B. "The Imagery of *The Plumed Serpent:* The Going Under of Organicism." *DHL Review* 15 (1982): 197–218. (Reprinted in Humma [1990]: 62–76.)

Jones, Keith. "Two Morning Stars." *Western Review* 17 (Autumn 1952): 15–25.

Kessler, Jascha. "Descent in Darkness: The Myth of *The Plumed Serpent.*" In *A DHL Miscellany.* Edited by Harry T. Moore. Carbondale: Southern Illinois University Press, 1959, pp. 239–61.

———. "DHL's Primitivism." *Texas Studies in Literature and Language* 5 (1964): 467–88.

Lewis, Wyndham. "Paleface; or, 'Love? What ho! Smelling Strangeness.' " *The Enemy* 2 (September 1927): 3–112. (Expanded as *Paleface: The Philosophy of the "Melting Pot."* London: Chatto and Windus, 1929.)

Linebarger, Jim, and Lad Kirsten. "[Dylan] Thomas's 'Shall Gods Be Said to Thump the Clouds.' " *Explicator* 48 (Spring 1990): 212–16.

Lok, Chua Cheng. "The European Participant and the Third-World Revolution: André Malraux's *Les Conquerants* and DHL's *The Plumed Serpent.*" In *Discharging the Canon: Cross-Cultural Readings in Literature.* Edited by Peter Hyland. Singapore: Singapore University Press, 1986, pp. 101–11.

MacDonald, Robert H. " 'The Two Principles': A Theory of the Sexual and Psychological Symbolism of DHL's Later Fiction." *DHL Review* 11 (Summer 1978): 132–55.

Martz, Louis L. "*Quetzalcoatl:* The Early Version of *The Plumed Serpent.*" *DHL Review* 22 (Fall 1990): 286–98.

———. "Introduction" to *Quetzalcoatl* by DHL. Edited by Louis Martz. Redding Ridge, Conn.: Black Swan Books, 1995.

Mayers, Ozzie. "The Child as Jungian Hero in DHL's *The Plumed Serpent.*" *Journal of Evolutionary Psychology* 8 (1987): 306–17.

Meyers, Jeffrey. "*The Plumed Serpent* and the Mexican Revolution." *Journal of Modern Literature* 4 (September 1974): 55–72.

Michener, Richard L. "Apocalyptic Mexico: *The Plumed Serpent* and *The Power and the Glory.*" *University Review* (Kansas) 34 (June 1968): 313–16.

Moore, Harry T. "*The Plumed Serpent:* Vision and Language." In *DHL: A Collection of Critical Essays.* Edited by Mark Spilka. Englewood Cliffs, N.J.: Prentice-Hall, 1963, pp. 61–71.

Parmenter, Ross. "How *The Plumed Serpent* Was Changed in Oaxaca." In his *Lawrence in Oaxaca: A Quest for the Novelist in Mexico.* Salt Lake City: Smith, 1984, pp. 273–315.

Powell, Lawrence Clark. "Southwest Classics Reread: *The Plumed Serpent* by DHL." *Westways* 63, no. 11 (November 1971): 18–20, 46–49. (Reprinted as "*The Plumed Serpent*" in his *Southwest Classics.* Los Angeles: Ward Ritchie Press, 1974, pp. 81–92.)

Prasad, Kameshwar. "Evil in DHL's *The Plumed Serpent:* The Collapse of Vision and Art." In *Modern Studies and Other Essays in Honour of Dr. R. K. Sinha.* Edited by R. C. Prasad and A. K. Sharma. New Delhi: Vikas, 1987, pp. 49–59.

Ramey, Frederick. "Words in the Service of Silence: Preverbal Language in Lawrence's *The Plumed Serpent.*" *Modern Fiction Studies* 27 (Winter 1981–82): 613–21.

Ruderman, Judith G. "Rekindling the 'Father-Spark': Lawrence's Ideal of Leadership in *The Lost Girl* and *The Plumed Serpent.*" *DHL Review* 13 (Fall 1980): 239–59.

Rudnick, Lois P. "DHL's New World Heroine: Mabel Dodge Luhan." *DHL Review* 14 (Spring 1981): 85–111.

Sicker, Philip. "Lawrence's Auto da fe: *The Grand Inquisitor* in *The Plumed Serpent.*" *Comparative Literature Studies* 29 (1992): 417–40.

Sommers, Joseph. *After the Storm: Landmarks of the Modern Mexican Novel.* Albuquerque: University of New Mexico Press, 1968, pp. 128–32. (The influence of the novel on Carlos Fuentes.)

Talbot, Lynn K. "Did Baroja Influence Lawrence? A Reading of *César o Nada* and *The Plumed Serpent.*" *DHL Review* 22 (Spring 1990): 39–51.

Tindall, William York. *DHL and Susan His Cow.* New York: Columbia University Press, 1939, pp. 113–18, passim. (Section reprinted in Hoffman and Moore [1953]: 178–84.)

Veitch, Douglas W. "DHL's Elusive Mexico." In his *Lawrence, Greene and Lowry: The Fictional Landscape of Mexico.* Waterloo, Ontario: Wilfrid Laurier University Press, 1978, pp. 14–57.

Vickery, John B. "*The Plumed Serpent* and the Eternal Paradox." *Criticism* 5 (Spring 1963): 119–34.

———. "*The Plumed Serpent* and the Reviving God." *Journal of Modern Literature* 2 (November 1972): 505–32.

———. *Myths and Texts: Strategies of Incorporation and Displacement.* Baton Rouge: Louisiana State University Press, 1983, pp. 104–31.

Walker, Ronald G. *Infernal Paradise: Mexico and the Modern English Novel.* Berkeley, Los Angeles, and London: University of California Press, 1978, pp. 28–104 ("*The Plumed Serpent:* Lawrence's Mexican Nightmare," pp. 79–104).

———. "Introduction." *The Plumed Serpent* by DHL. Edited by Ronald G. Walker. Harmondsworth: Penguin, 1983, 7–33.

Waters, Frank. "Quetzalcoatl Versus DHL's *Plumed Serpent.*" *Western American Literature* 3 (1968): 103–13.

Woodcock, George. "Mexico and the English Novelist." *Western Review* 21 (Fall 1956): 21–32. (Lawrence, Huxley, and Greene.)

Woodman, Leonora. "DHL and the Hermetic Tradition." *Cauda Pavonis: Studies in Hermeticism* 8 (Fall 1989): 1–6.

See also (1980–94) Becker (1980): 107–12. Bell (1992): 165–207. Buckley and Buckley (1993): 24–25, 69–74. Clark (1980): 288–92, 321–32. Cowan (1990): 178–211. Dix

(1980): 46–49, 64–66. Dorbad (1991): 123–27. Fay (1953): passim. Fjagesund (1991): 129–44. Hobsbaum (1981): 81–82. Humma (1990): 62–76. Hyde (1990): 100–103. Hyde (1992): 177–95, passim. Kiely (1980): 212–21. MacLeod (1985/87): 85–91, 146–56. Mensch (1991): 207–52. Meyers (1982): 124–29. Mohanty (1993): 40–43, 99–110. Montgomery (1994): 194–97, 199–207. Niven (1980): 69–74. Padhi (1989): 196–200. Pinkney (1990): 147–62. Prasad (1980): 112–14. Robinson (1992): 125–27. Ruderman (1984): 142–53. Scheckner (1985): 89–136. Schneider (1984): 225–37. Siegel (1991): passim. Simpson (1982): 113–17, passim. Spilka (1992): 215–19, 225–30, passim. Storch (1990): 157–78. Suter (1987): 115–22. Urang (1983): 69–92. Widmer (1992): 58–60. Williams (1993): 36–43, 75–79. Worthen (1991a): 90–99.

See also (to 1979) Albright (1978): 67–71. Alldritt (1971): 221–40. Beal (1961): 77–83. Bedient (1972): 147–53, 168–70. Boadella (1956/78): 114–18. Cavitch (1969): 182–89, passim. Clarke (1969): 143–47. Cowan (1970): 99–121, passim. Daleski (1965): 213–57. Draper (1964): 103–9. Draper (1970): 263–71. Freeman (1955): 177–88. Goodheart (1963): 140–46. Gregory (1933): 60–76. Harrison (1966): 184–86, passim. Hochman (1970): 230–54. Hough (1956): 118–48, passim. Howe (1977): 105–32. Inniss (1971): 176–88. Jarrett-Kerr (1951): 67–77. John (1974): 259–75. Kermode (1973): 113–18. Leavis (1955): 65–69. Leavis (1976): 34–61. Lerner (1967): 172–80. Maes-Jelinek (1970): 81–87. Miles (1969): 22–24, 43–48, 58–59. Millett (1970): 283–85. Moore (1951): 232–39. Moynahan (1963): 107–11, passim. Murry (1931): 282–302. Murry (1933): 252–56. Nahal (1970): 218–23, passim. Niven (1978): 166–74. Pinion (1978): 195–205. Potter (1930): 87–92. Pritchard (1971): 171–77, passim. Sagar (1966): 159–68. Sanders (1973): 136–71. Slade (1970): 87–88, passim. Spilka (1955): 205–19. Stewart (1963): 551–59. Stoll (1971): 210–22. Vivas (1960): 65–91, passim. West (1950): 127–31. Worthen (1979): 152–67. Yudhishtar (1969): 250–66.

22   Lady Chatterley's Lover

WRITTEN

October 1926–January 1928. Lawrence wrote three complete versions of the novel, each of which was subsequently published. 1. October–December 1926 (*The First Lady Chatterley*). 2. December 1926–February 1927 (*John Thomas and Lady Jane*). 3. December 1927–January 1928 (*Lady Chatterley's Lover*).

Realizing that the novel had little chance of commercial publication, Lawrence worked on an expurgated version through February and March 1928. But even this was unacceptable to his publishers, Secker and Knopf, who waited until 1932 before publishing their own, more extensively expurgated versions. Between February and June 1928, Lawrence corrected the typescripts and proofs of the version that was privately printed in July 1928.

PUBLISHED

1. a. *Lady Chatterley's Lover.* Florence: Privately printed, July 1928. Author's unabridged "Popular Edition" (with the introduction, "My Skirmish with Jolly Roger"), Paris: Privately printed, May 1929. First authorized expurgated editions: London: Secker, February 1932; New York: Alfred A. Knopf, September 1932. First authorized unexpurgated editions: New York: Grove Press, May 1959; Harmondsworth: Penguin, 1960 (twelve copies were handed to the police on 16 August; the famous trial then took place between 20 October and 2 November, and, following the failure of the prosecution case, copies were released to the public on 10 November 1960).

    b. *The First Lady Chatterley.* New York: Dial Press, 1944. London: Heine-
      mann, 1972. Harmondsworth: Penguin, 1973.

    c. *John Thomas and Lady Jane.* London: Heinemann; New York: Viking,
      1972. Harmondsworth: Penguin 1973. First published, in Italian, as *La
      Seconda Lady Chatterley* in *Le Tre "Lady Chatterley."* Translated by
      Carlo Izzo. Italy: Mondadori, 1954.

2. *Lady Chatterley's Lover [and] A Propos of "Lady Chatterley's Lover."* Edited by Michael Squires. Cambridge: Cambridge University Press, 1993.

3. See also under Squires (1994) in the following bibliography.

WHO'S WHO AND SUMMARY

MAIN CHARACTERS: Lady Constance (Connie) Chatterley, Sir Clifford Chatterley, Oliver Mellors

    Connie Chatterley, née Reid, is brought up "between artists and cultured
socialists": her father, *Sir Malcolm Reid,* is a well-known Royal Academician,
and her mother is a Fabian socialist. Connie is allowed to travel freely in Europe
and has an unconventional and independent early life. She and her elder sister,
Hilda, two years older than Connie, both have love affairs by the time they are
eighteen—in Dresden, Germany, just before the war—but sex seems little more
than a "sex-thrill," a passing sensation. They return home at the start of the
war and settle for a time in London. Here they mix with a young Cambridge
group representing "a well-bred sort of emotional anarchy." Hilda marries, and
Connie becomes close to *Clifford Chatterley,* an upper-class young man of
twenty-two. Though more "society" than Connie, he is "more provincial and
more timid," shy and nervous when outside his known milieu in the landed
aristocracy. He had been to Cambridge and had been studying coal mining in
Germany when the war broke out. Connie marries him in 1917, when he comes
home on leave, and they have a month's honeymoon. Sex seems unimportant
to Clifford, we are told, and Connie seems to enjoy their intimacy "beyond
sex." Six months later, Clifford is badly wounded and almost dies. After two
precarious years of treatment, however, he pulls through but is paralyzed from
the hips down. His elder brother, *Herbert,* had died in the war, in 1916, and
Clifford is now the heir to the family seat, Wragby Hall. Following the death
of his father, *Sir Geoffrey Chatterley,* in 1918, Connie and Clifford take up
residence there in the autumn of 1920.

    Life for Connie as Lady Chatterley soon becomes empty and meaningless.
As an invalid, Clifford retreats further from the world. He has "fits of vacant
depression" as if not only his body but also his psyche were profoundly
wounded. He becomes almost totally dependent on Connie. Eventually, he takes
up writing, and for a while Connie enjoys helping him in this—they come to
live in a world of ideas, words, and books. Then Clifford starts to make a name
for himself as a successful writer. He has his old Cambridge friends and other

artists and intellectuals to visit, and Connie plays hostess to them. Otherwise, her life seems a void, a ''non-existence,'' and she becomes increasingly restless from the lack of vitality in the house—all seems old, decrepit, and lifeless, from the ancient parlor maid to the endless rooms. She suffers in particular from her sense of ''disconnection.'' She has a desultory sort of affair with *Michaelis,* a young Irish playwright who has made his fortune in America, but this, too, peters out in ''a foreboding of hopelessness,'' and Connie simply becomes thinner and more forlorn.

Then, when she is about twenty-seven (1924), she sees the gamekeeper, *Mellors,* having a strip-wash in the woods, and the sight of his nakedness is a ''visionary experience,'' an epiphany of ''the warm white flame'' of life that shocks her own failing life-flow back into circulation. This ''shock of vision in her womb'' marks the beginnings of a gradual process of fuller ''reawakening'' for her: a reawakening to the wonder of the natural world and the wonder of her own natural bodily desires. For she and Mellors now become lovers and together rediscover a sense of tender, sensuous connectedness with the phenomenal world and with their own inner selves.

Mellors has received a good grammar school education, has been an office clerk, and, during the war, an officer; but he has rejected his middle-class identity and reverted purposely to the working-class life and ways of his blacksmith father by becoming a blacksmith himself for a while, shoeing horses, before becoming Sir Clifford's gamekeeper. Thus, while he is a cultured man who can engage in intellectual and literary discourse and speak in a refined way, he now usually prefers to project an image of working-class bluffness and often speaks in broad Derbyshire dialect. As with Connie, Mellors's life, too, has become empty and disconnected. He lives a self-contained and isolated life in his cottage in the woods. Having experienced the war and witnessed class conflict in the mines and elsewhere, as well as the despoliation of nature by industrialism, he has become cynical about social and political progress in what he now sees as a self-destructive world. Moreover, after several traumatic relationships with women—with a literary and repressed daughter of a schoolmaster, with a sexless but clinging older woman, a teacher, and, most important, with his sexually rampant and domineering estranged wife, *Bertha Coutts*—he has become wholly disillusioned with love, too, and has resigned himself to living a solitary and sexless life. His wood has become for him a sort of last refuge from the world. However, now, Connie renews his hope in the possibility of a better world— she is prepared, after all, to forsake her upper-class lifestyle and the interests of her mine-owning husband—and rekindles his desire for ''warmhearted'' love and relationship.

Slowly, through several secret encounters in the now magical-seeming greenwood, Connie and Mellors gain ''the courage of their own tenderness'' in lovemaking until, at the end, with Connie pregnant and both of them awaiting divorces to allow them to live on a farm together away from the ''Cliffords and

Berthas, colliery companies and governments and money-mass of people," they feel finally that they have truly "fucked a flame into being."

Other Characters

Emma Chatterley is Clifford's sister: she is ten years older than Clifford and feels that Clifford's marrying of Connie is a "desertion and betrayal" of her.

Ivy Bolton, the widow of a miner killed in an underground explosion who becomes Clifford's nurse and later a type of surrogate mother figure for him. Her close contact with the local mining community provides Clifford with an insight into the lives of the working classes and inspires him to take an interest once more in his mines. She gradually establishes a dominance over Clifford.

Clifford's intellectual and artist set: *Tommy Dukes,* a brigadier general who has stayed in the army after the war; although he mouths many of the positive values of the novel, partly as expressed later by Mellors, he is a self-confessed "mental-lifer," and "cerebrating machine." *Charles May,* an Irish scientist who writes about the stars; *Arnold B. Hammond,* a writer; *Berry,* the shy friend of Tommy Dukes—"they all believed in the life of the mind."

Other visitors to Wragby Hall: *Leslie Winter,* Clifford's godfather, a rich mine owner. *Lady Eva Bennerley,* Clifford's aunt. *Jack* and *Olive Strangeways. Harry Winterslow.*

Duncan Forbes, artist friend and admirer of Connie, who goes to Venice with her and Hilda; he offers to pose as the father of Connie's child to make her pregnancy (by Mellors) more palatable to Sir Clifford.

Connie Mellors, daughter to Mellors and Bertha Coutts. *Mrs. Betts,* housekeeper at Wragby Hall. *Field,* manservant at Wragby Hall. *Mrs. Flint,* farmer's wife and tenant on the Wragby estate with daughter, *Josephine. Mr. Linley,* Clifford's colliery manager. *Reverend Ashby,* rector of Tevershall. *Mrs. Weedon,* Mrs. Bolton's friend. *Miss Bentley* runs a tearoom in Uthwaite. *Giovanni,* gondolier to Connie in Venice, and *Daniele,* his assistant.

SETTING

Eastwood, Mansfield, Worksop (all Nottinghamshire), Sheffield (South Yorkshire), and Chesterfield (Derbyshire) provide the main coordinates for the setting of *Lady Chatterley's Lover.* The Chatterley's Wragby Estate seems to be a re-created mixture of two actual estates: Lambclose House and Renishaw House. Lambclose House at Moorgreen, near Eastwood, was the home of the Barber family, one of the area's two most important mine-owning families, who together formed Barber, Walker and Co. This was probably the model for the Chatterleys' colliery company in the novel. The secretary of the real-life company between 1918 and 1931 was George Chatterley (1861–1940), one of whose daughters was named Constance. Lambclose House is also re-created in *Women in Love* and *The White Peacock,* as Shortlands and Highclose, respectively.

Renishaw Hall near Eckington in North Derbyshire, just northeast of Chester-field ("Uthwaite" in the novel, though Chesterfield is also mentioned by name), was the home of the Sitwell family. Lawrence visited here in September 1926, a month or so before writing the first version of the novel.

The name "Wragby" may have been taken from a village of that name near Lincoln. "Tevershall" seems to be based partly on Eckington and partly on Eastwood (the name is taken from Teversal, a village west of Mansfield and a few miles from Hardwick Hall, which appears in the novel as "Chadwick Hall"). Connie's journey from Wragby into "Uthwaite" and back again in Chapter 11 would seem to follow a real-life route as follows: from Eckington (though the description here is clearly based on Eastwood), past Bolsover Castle ("Warsop Castle" in the novel), through Stavely ("Stacks Gate") and into Chesterfield; then home again via Barlborough Hall ("Shipley Hall"), some four miles east of Eckington, where Connie stops to visit Squire Winter (though the description of the hall itself also reflects elements of Rufford Abbey, just northeast of Mansfield, and Melbourne Hall, southeast of Derby).

Most of Chapter 17 is set in Venice. On the journey there, Connie stops over at London and Paris. She returns to London in Chapter 18. In Chapter 19, she returns briefly to Wragby before going to Scotland with her sister.

BIBLIOGRAPHY 14

Criticism relating to the filmed versions of the novel can be found in the "Lawrence and Film" bibliography (Part III, Section C) and are not repeated here. (See also Chapter 41 under *A Propos of "Lady Chatterley's Lover"* and *Pornography and Obscenity.*)

Adamowski, T. H. "The Natural Flowering of Life: The Ego, Sex, and Existentialism." In Squires and Jackson (1985), op. cit., pp. 36–57.

Adams, Elsie B. "A 'Lawrentian' Novel by Bernard Shaw." *DHL Review* 2 (Fall 1969): 245–53. (Shaw's *Cashel Byron's Profession* as anticipation of *Lady Chatterley's Lover.*)

Ansari, Iqbal A. "*Lady Chatterley's Lover:* Pattern of Contrast and Conflict." *Aligarh Journal of English Studies* 10 (1985): 178–87.

Balakian, Nona. "The Prophetic Vogue of the Anti-Heroine." *Southwest Review* 47 (Spring 1962): 134–41.

Balbert, Peter. "The Loving of Lady Chatterley: DHL and the Phallic Imagination." In *DHL: The Man Who Died.* Edited by Robert B. Partlow, Jr., and Harry T. Moore. Carbondale: Southern Illinois University Press, 1980, pp. 143–58.

———. "From *Lady Chatterley's Lover* to *The Deer Park:* Lawrence, Mailer, and the Dialectic of Erotic Risk." *Studies in the Novel* 22 (1990): 67–81.

Baruch, Elaine Hoffman. "The Feminine Bildungsroman: Education through Marriage." *Massachusetts Review* 22 (1981): 335–57 (353–56).

Battye, Louis. "The Chatterley Syndrome." In *Stigma: The Experience of Disability.* Edited by P. Hunt. London: Chapman, 1966, pp. 1–16.

Bedient, Calvin. "The Radicalism of *Lady Chatterley's Lover*." *Hudson Review* 19 (Autumn 1966): 407–16.

Ben-Ephraim, Gavriel. "The Achievement of Balance in *Lady Chatterley's Lover*." In Squires and Jackson (1985), op. cit., pp. 136–57.

Bevan, D. G. "The Sensual and the Cerebral: The Mating of DHL and André Malraux." *Canadian Review of Comparative Literature* 9 (1982): 200–207.

Black, Michael. "Sexuality in Literature: *Lady Chatterley's Lover*." In his *The Literature of Fidelity*. London: Chatto and Windus; New York: Barnes and Noble: 1975, pp. 169–211.

Blanchard, Lydia. "Women Look at *Lady Chatterley's Lover*: Feminine Views of the Novel." *DHL Review* 11 (Fall 1978): 246–59.

———. "Lawrence, Foucault, and the Language of Sexuality." In Squires and Jackson (1985), op. cit., pp. 17–35.

Bowen, Zack. "*Lady Chatterley's Lover* and *Ulysses*." In Squires and Jackson (1985), op. cit., pp. 116–35.

Bowlby, Rachel. " 'But She Would Learn Something from Lady Chatterley': The Obscene Side of the Canon." In *Decolonizing Tradition: New Views of Twentieth-Century "British" Literary Canons*. Edited by Karen R. Lawrence. Urbana: University of Illinois Press, 1992, pp. 113–35.

Britton, Derek. "Henry Moat, Lady Ida Sitwell, and *John Thomas and Lady Jane*." *DHL Review* 15 (1982): 69–76.

———. *Lady Chatterley's Lover: The Making of the Novel*. London: Unwin Hyman, 1988.

Brophy, Brigid. "The British Museum and Solitary Vice." *London Magazine* 2 (March 1963): 55–58. (Also in her *Don't Never Forget*. New York: Holt, Rinehart, and Winston, 1967, pp. 101–5.)

Brophy, Brigid, Michael Levey, and Charles Osborne. *Fifty Works of English and American Literature We Could Do Without*. New York: Stein and Day, 1968, pp. 133–34.

Brown, Richard. " 'Perhaps She Had Not Told Him All the Story . . . ': Observations on the Topic of Adultery in Some Modern Fiction." In *Joyce, Modernity, and Its Mediation*. Edited by Christine van Boheemen. Amsterdam: Rodopi, 1989, pp. 99–111.

Buckley, William K. *Senses' Tender: Recovering the Novel for the Reader*. New York: Lang, 1989.

Burns, Wayne. "*Lady Chatterley's Lover: A Pilgrim's Progress* for Our Time." *Paunch*, no. 26 (April 1966): 16–33.

Caffrey, Raymond. "*Lady Chatterley's Lover*: The Grove Press Publication of the Unexpurgated Text." *Courier* 20 (Spring 1985): 49–79.

Campion, Sidney R. "A Suppressed Masterpiece." *John O'London's* 2 (12 May 1960): 562.

Charney, Maurice. "Sexuality and the Life Force: *Lady Chatterley's Lover* and *Tropic of Cancer*." In his *Sexual Fiction*. New York: Methuen, 1981, pp. 93–112.

Chen, Yi. "Deceptive Equivalence or Expressive Identity? The Chinese Translation of *Lady Chatterley's Lover*." *The Journal of the D. H. Lawrence Society* (1994–95): 47–66.

Clausson, Nils. "*Lady Chatterley's Lover* and the Condition-of-England Novel." *English Studies in Canada* 8 (1982): 296–310.

Coetzee, J. M. "The Taint of the Pornographic: Defending (against) *Lady Chatterley's Lover.*" *Mosaic* 21 (1988): 1–11.

Conquest, Robert. "*Lady Chatterley's Lover* in the Light of Durfian Psychology." *New Statesman* (22 and 29 December 1978): 863–64.

Cowan, James C. "Lawrence, Joyce, and the Epiphanies of *Lady Chatterley's Lover.*" In Squires and Jackson (1985), op. cit., pp. 91–115. (Reprinted in Cowan [1990]: 212–36.)

Cox, C. B. et al. "Symposium: Pornography and Obscenity." *Critical Quarterly* 3 (Summer 1961): 99–122. (Views from St. John-Stevas, Davie, Jarrett-Kerr, and Lewis, cited separately.)

Craig, G. Armour. "DHL on Thinghood and Selfhood." *Massachusetts Review* 1 (October 1959): 56–60.

Croft, B. "Is This Lady Chatterley's Village?" *Derbyshire Life* (July 1967): 26–27, 42.

Cunningham, J. S. "Lady Chatterley's Husband." *Literary Half-Yearly* 3 (July 1962): 20–27.

Cushman, Keith. "*The Virgin and the Gipsy* and the Lady and the Gamekeeper." In Squires and Jackson (1985), op. cit., pp. 154–69.

Davie, Donald. "Literature and Morality." In Cox (1961), op. cit., pp. 109–13.

Davies, Rosemary Reeves. "The Eighth Love Scene: The Real Climax of *Lady Chatterley's Lover.*" *DHL Review* 15 (1982): 167–76.

Doheny, John. "Lady Chatterley and Her Lover." *West Coast Review* 8 (1974): 51–56. (On *John Thomas and Lady Jane.*)

Doherty, Gerald. "Connie and the Chakras: Yogic Patterns in DHL's *Lady Chatterley's Lover.*" *DHL Review* 13 (1980): 79–93.

Dollimore, Jonathan. "The Challenge of Sexuality." In *Society and Literature 1945–1970.* Edited by Alan Sinfield. London: Methuen, 1983, pp. 51–85 (52–61). (The importance of the novel and the trial for modern constructions of "sexuality.")

Donald, D. R. "The First and Final Versions of *Lady Chatterley's Lover.*" *Theoria,* no. 22 (1964): 85–97.

Durrell, Lawrence. "Preface." *Lady Chatterley's Lover* by DHL. New York: Bantam Books, 1968, pp. vii–xi.

Ebbatson, J. R. "Thomas Hardy and Lady Chatterley." *Ariel* 8 (1977): 85–95.

Edwards, Duane. "Mr. Mellors' Lover: A Study of *Lady Chatterley.*" *Southern Humanities Review* 19 (1985): 117–31.

Efron, Arthur. "Lady Chatterley's Lecher?" *Paunch,* no. 26 (April 1966).

———. " 'The Way Our Sympathy Flows and Recoils': Lawrence's Last Theory of the Novel." *Paunch* 63–64 (1990): 71–84.

Fjagesund, Peter. "DHL, Knut Hamsun and Pan." *English Studies* (Netherlands) 72, no. 5 (October 1991): 421–25.

Friedland, Ronald. "Introduction." *Lady Chatterley's Lover* by DHL. New York: Bantam Books, 1968, pp. xiii–xxiv.

Gertzman, Jay A. *A Descriptive Bibliography of "Lady Chatterley's Lover": With Essays toward a Publishing History of the Novel.* Westport, Conn.: Greenwood, 1989.

———. "Legitimizing *Lady Chatterley's Lover:* The Grove Press Strategy, 1959." *Paunch* 63–64 (1990): 1–14.

———. "Erotic Novel, Liberal Lawyer, and 'Censor-Moron': 'Sex for Its Own Sake' and Some Literary Censorship Adjudications of the 1930s." *DHL Review* 24 (1992): 217–27.

Gill, Richard. *Happy Rural Seat: The English Country House and the Literary Imagination* New Haven, Conn.: Yale University Press, 1972, pp. 151–55.

Gill, Stephen. "The Composite World: Two Versions of *Lady Chatterley's Lover*." *Essays in Criticism* 21 (October 1971): 347–64.

Gordon, David J. "Sex and Language in DHL." *Twentieth Century Literature* 27 (1981): 362–75 (369–72).

Gregor, Ian, and Brian Nicholas. "The Novel as Prophecy: *Lady Chatterley's Lover*." In their *The Moral and the Story*. London: Faber and Faber, 1962, pp. 217–48.

Gutierrez, Donald. "The Hylozoistic Vision of *Lady Chatterley's Lover*." *North America Mentor Magazine* 19 (1981): 25–34.

———. " 'The Impossible Notation': The Sodomy Scene in *Lady Chatterley's Lover*." *Sphinx: A Magazine of Literature and Society* 4 (1982); 109–25. (Reprinted in his *The Maze in the Mind and the World: Labyrinths in Modern Literature*. Troy, N.Y.: Whitston, 1985, pp. 55–74.)

Haegert, John W. "DHL and the Ways of Eros." *DHL Review* 11 (Fall 1978): 199–233 (201–18).

Hall, Roland. "DHL and A. N. Whitehead." *Notes and Queries* 9 (May 1962): 188.

Hall, Stuart. "*Lady Chatterley's Lover*: The Novel and Its Relationship to Lawrence's Work." *New Left Review*, no. 6 (November–December 1960): 32–35.

Harding, D. W. "Lawrence's Evils." *Spectator* (11 November 1960): 735–36. (Review.)

Hardy, Barbara. *The Appropriate Form: An Essay on the Novel*. London: Athlone Press, 1964, pp. 162–72.

Hartogue, Renatus. "Intercourse with Lady Chatterley." *Four Letter Word Games: The Psychology of Obscenity*. New York: M. Evans/Delacorte Press, 1967, pp. 11–24.

Henry, G. B. Mck. "Carrying On: *Lady Chatterley's Lover*." *Critical Review* (Melbourne) 10 (1967): 46–62. (Also in Andrews [1971]: 89–104.)

Higdon, David Leon. "*John Thomas and Lady Jane*: 'The Line of Fulfillment.' " In his *Time and English Fiction*. Totowa, N.J.: Rowman and Littlefield, 1977, pp. 23–29.

———. "Bertha Coutts and Bertha Mason: A Speculative Note." *DHL Review* (Fall 1978): 294–96. (See also his *Shadows of the Past in Contemporary British Fiction*. Athens: University of Georgia Press, 1984, pp. 30, 101–3.)

Hinz, Evelyn J. "Pornography, Novel, Mythic Narrative: The Three Versions of *Lady Chatterley's Lover*." *Modernist Studies* 3 (1979): 35–47.

Hinz, Evelyn J., and John J. Teunissen. "War, Love, and Industrialism: The Ares/Aphrodite/Hephaestus Complex in *Lady Chatterley's Lover*." In Squires and Jackson (1985), op. cit., pp. 197–221.

Hoerner, Dennis. "Connie Chatterley: A Case of Spontaneous Therapy." *Energy and Character: Journal of Bioenergetic Research* 12 (1981): 48–55.

Hoyt, C. A. "DHL: The Courage of Human Contact." *English Record* 14 (April 1964): 8–15.

Humma, John B. "The Interpenetrating Metaphor: Nature and Myth in *Lady Chatterley's Lover*." *PMLA* 98 (1983): 77–86. (Reprinted in Humma [1990]: 85–99.)

Hyde, H. Montgomery, ed. *The "Lady Chatterley's Lover" Trial: Regina v. Penguin Books Limited*. London: Bodley Head, 1990. (Verbatim transcript, with an introduction by Hyde.)

Ingersoll, Earl. "The Pursuit of 'True Marriage': DHL's *Mr. Noon* and *Lady Chatterley's Lover.*" *Studies in the Humanities* 14 (1987): 32–45.

———. "*Lady Chatterley's Lover:* 'The Bastard Offspring of This Signifying Concatenation.' " *Studies in Psychoanalytic Theory* 1 (1992): 59–65.

Jackson, Dennis. "The 'Old Pagan Vision': Myth and Ritual in *Lady Chatterley's Lover.*" *DHL Review* 11 (Fall 1978): 260–71. (Expanded version in Jackson and Jackson [1988]: 128–44.)

———. "Lady Chatterley's Color." *Interpretations* 15 (1983): 39–52.

———. "Literary Allusions in *Lady Chatterley's Lover.*" In Squires and Jackson (1985), op. cit., pp. 170–96.

———. "*Lady Chatterley's Lover:* Lawrence's Response to *Ulysses?*" *Philological Quarterly* 66 (1987): 410–16.

———. "Chapter Making in *Lady Chatterley's Lover.*" *Texas Studies in Literature and Language* 35 (Fall 1993): 363–83.

Jarrett-Kerr, Martin. "A Christian View." In Cox (1961), op. cit., pp. 113–18.

Jewinski, Ed. "The Phallus in DHL and Jacques Lacan." *DHL Review* 21 (1989): 7–24.

Jones, Bernard. "The Three Ladies Chatterley." *Books and Bookmen* 19 (March 1974): 46–50. (Review essay on the three versions.)

Journet, Debra. "Patrick White and DHL: Sexuality and the Wilderness in *A Fringe of Leaves* and *Lady Chatterley's Lover.*" *South Central Review* 5 (1988): 62–71.

Kain, Richard M. "*Lady Chatterley's Lover.*" *London Times Literary Supplement* 8 (January 1970): 34.

Kauffman, Stanley. "Lady Chatterley at Last." *New Republic* (25 May 1959): 13–16.

Kazin, Alfred. "Lady Chatterley in America." *Atlantic Monthly* 204 (July 1959): 34–36. (Also in his *Contemporaries.* Boston: Little, Brown, 1962, pp. 105–12.)

Kermode, Frank. "Everybody's Read Chatterley." *Listener* 95 (8 January 1976): 27.

Kern, Stephen. *The Culture of Love: Victorians to Moderns.* Cambridge: Harvard University Press, 1992, passim.

Kernan, Alvin. "*Lady Chatterley* and 'Mere Chatter about Shelley': The University Asked to Define Literature." In his *The Death of Literature.* New Haven, Conn.: Yale University Press, 1990, pp. 32–59.

Kim, Dong-son. "DHL: *Lady Chatterley's Lover:* Phallic Tenderness vs. Industrialism." *Phoenix* (Seoul) 23 (1981): 101–19.

King, Debra W. "Just Can't Find the Words: How Expression Is Achieved." *Philosophy and Rhetoric* 24, no. 1 (1991): 54–72.

King, Dixie. "The Influence of Forster's *Maurice* on *Lady Chatterley's Lover.*" *Contemporary Literature* 23 (1982): 65–82.

Kinkead-Weekes, Mark. "Eros and Metaphor: Sexual Relationship in the Fiction of DHL." *Twentieth Century Studies* 1 (November 1969): 3–19. (Reprinted in Smith [1978]: 101–21.)

Klein, Robert C. "I, Thou and You in Three Lawrencian Relationships." *Paunch,* no. 31 (April 1968): 52–70.

Knight, G. Wilson. "Lawrence, Joyce and Powys." *Essays in Criticism* 11 (1961): 403–17. (Also in his *Neglected Powers.* London: Routledge; New York: Barnes and Noble, 1971, pp. 142–55. See also ensuing debate in *Essays in Criticism:* John Peter, "The Bottom of the Well," 12 [April 1962]: 226–27. John Peter, "Lady Chatterley Again," 12 [October 1962]: 445–47. William Empson, "Lady Chatterley Again,'' 13 [April 1963]: 202–5. John Peter, 13 [July 1963]: 301–2 [with rejoinder by John Sparrow, 303].)

Knoepflmacher, U. C. ''The Rival Ladies: Mrs. Ward's *Lady Connie* and Lawrence's *Lady Chatterley's Lover.''* *Victorian Studies* 4 (Winter 1960): 141–58.

Lauter, Paul. ''Lady Chatterley with Love and Money.'' *New Leader* 42 (31 August 1959): 23–24.

Lawrence, Frieda. ''Foreword.'' In *The First Lady Chatterley* by DHL. New York: Dial Press, 1944, pp. v–xiii. (Also in the Heinemann [1972] and Penguin [1973] editions.)

Lerner, Laurence. *Love and Marriage: Literature and Its Social Context.* New York: St. Martin's Press, 1979, pp. 153–64.

Levine, George. ''Epilogue: Lawrence, *Frankenstein,* and the Reversal of Realism.'' In his *The Realistic Imagination: English Fiction from ''Frankenstein'' to ''Lady Chatterley.''* Chicago: University of Chicago Press, 1981, pp. 317–28 (323–28).

Lewis, C. S. ''Four-Letter Words.'' In Cox (1961), op. cit., pp. 118–22.

McCurdy, Harold G. ''Literature and Personality: Analysis of the Novels of DHL.'' *Character and Personality* 8 (March, June 1940): 181–203, 311–322 (191–97).

McDowell, Frederick P. W. '' 'Moments of Emergence and of a New Splendour': DHL and E. M. Forster in Their Fiction.'' In Squires and Jackson (1985), op. cit., pp. 58–90.

McIntosh, Angus, and M.A.K. Halliday. ''A Four-Letter Word in *Lady Chatterley's Lover.''* In their *Patterns of Language: Papers in General, Descriptive, and Applied Linguistics.* London: Longman, 1966; Bloomington: Indiana University Press, 1967, pp. 151–64.

MacLeish, Archibald. ''Preface: Letter from Archibald MacLeish.'' *Lady Chatterley's Lover* by DHL. New York: Grove Press, 1959, pp. v–vii.

Malcolm, Donald. ''Books: The Prophet and the Poet.'' *New Yorker* 35 (12 September 1959): 193–94, 196–98. (Review.)

Malraux, André. ''Preface to the French translation of *Lady Chatterley's Lover.''* *Criterion* 12 (1933): 215–19.

———. ''DHL and Eroticism.'' In *From the N.R.F.: An Image of the Twentieth Century from the Pages of the Nouvelle Revue Française.* New York: Farrar, Straus, and Cudahy, 1958, pp. 194–98. (Originally published as ''DHL et l'éroticisme: à propos de *L'Amant de Lady Chatterley''* in *La Nouvelle Revue Française* 38 [January 1932]: 136–40.)

Mandel, Jerome. ''Medieval Romance and *Lady Chatterley's Lover.''* *DHL Review* 10 (Spring 1977): 20–33.

Mandel, Oscar. ''Ignorance and Privacy.'' *American Scholar* 29 (Autumn 1960): 509–19. (See also J. Giles, ''Reply to Mandels's 'Ignorance and Privacy.' '' *American Scholar* 30 ((Summer 1961): 454.)

Marcuse, Ludwig. *Obscene: The History of an Indignation.* Translated by Karen Gershon. London: MacGibbon and Kee, 1965, pp. 215–54.

Martin, Graham. '' 'History' and 'Myth' in DHL's Chatterley Novels.'' In *The British Working-Class Novel in the Twentieth Century.* Edited by Jeremy Hawthorn. London: Edward Arnold, 1984, pp. 63–76.

Martin, W. R. ''GBS, DHL, and TEL: Mainly *Lady Chatterley* and *Too True.''* *Shaw: The Annual of Shaw Studies* 4 (1984): 107–12.

Martin, W. R., and Warren U. Ober. "Lawrence and Hemingway: The Cancelled Great Words." *Arizona Quarterly* 41 (1985): 357–61.

Martz, Louis L. "The Second Lady Chatterley." In *The Spirit of DHL: Centenary Studies*. Edited by Gāmini Salgādo and G. K. Das. London: Macmillan; Totowa, N.J.: Barnes and Noble, 1988, pp. 206–24.

Maxwell, J. C. "*Lady Chatterley's Lover:* A Correction." *Notes and Queries* 8 (March 1961): 110. (See also M. T. Tudsbery, "Reply to Maxwell's '*Lady Chatterley's Lover:* A Correction.' " *Notes and Queries* 8 [1961]: 149.)

Moore, Harry T. "Love as a Serious and Sacred Theme." *New York Times Book Review* (Section 7) (3 May 1959): 5. (Reprinted as "*Lady Chatterley's Lover* as Romance" in Moore [1959]: 262–64.

———. "Afterword: *Lady Chatterley's Lover:* The Novel as Ritual." In *Lady Chatterley's Lover* by DHL. New York: Signet, 1962, pp. 285–99.

———. "John Thomas and Lady Jane." *New York Times Book Review* (27 August 1972): 7. (Review.)

Muir, Kenneth. "The Three Lady Chatterleys." *Literary Half-Yearly* 2 (January 1961): 18–25.

Munro, Craig. "*Lady Chatterley* in London: The Secret Third Edition." In Squires and Jackson (1985), op. cit., pp. 222–35.

Newton, Frances J. "Venice, Pope, T. S. Eliot and DHL." *Notes and Queries* 5 (March 1958): 119–20.

Nimitz, Cheryl. "Lawrence and Kundera—'Disturbing.' " *Recovering Literature* 17 (1989–90): 43–51.

Ober, William B. "Lady Chatterley's *What?*" *Academy of Medicine of New Jersey Bulletin* 15 (March 1969): 41–65. (Reprinted in his *Boswell's Clap and Other Essays: Medical Analyses of Literary Men's Afflictions*. Carbondale: Southern Illinois University Press, 1979, pp. 89–117.)

Parker, David. "Lawrence and Lady Chatterley: The Teller and the Tale." *Critical Review* (Australia) 20 (1978): 21–41.

Pearce, T. M. "The Unpublished *Lady Chatterley's Lover.*" *New Mexico Quarterly* 8 (1938): 171–79.

Peters, Joan D. "The Living and the Dead: Lawrence's Theory of the Novel and the Structure of *Lady Chatterley's Lover.*" *DHL Review* 20 (Spring 1988): 2–20.

Polhemus, Robert M. "The Prophet of Love and the Resurrection of the Body: DHL's *Lady Chatterley's Lover* (1928)." In his *Erotic Faith: Being in Love from Jane Austen to DHL*. Chicago: University of Chicago Press, 1990, pp. 279–306.

Pollinger, Gerald J. "*Lady Chatterley's Lover:* A View from Lawrence's Literary Executor." In Squires and Jackson (1985), op. cit., pp. 236–41.

Porter, Katherine Anne. "A Wreath for the Gamekeeper." *Shenandoah* 11 (Autumn 1959): 3–12. (Also in *Encounter* 14 [February 1960]: 69–77. See reply by Richard Aldington, "A Wreath for Lawrence?" *Encounter* 14 [April 1960]: 51–54.)

Purdy, Strother B. "On the Psychology of Erotic Literature." *Literature and Psychology* 20 (1970): 23–29.

Quennell, Peter. "The Later Period of DHL." In *Scrutinies II*. Edited by Edgell Rickword. London: Wishart, 1931, pp. 126–29.

Radford, F. L. "The Educative Sequel: *Lady Chatterley's Second Husband* and *Mrs. Warren's Daughter.*" *Shaw Review* 23 (1980): 57–62.

Ramadoss, Haripriya. "The Creative Evolution of *Lady Chatterley's Lover:* A Study of

Some Key Changes in the Novel.'' *Dutch Quarterly Review of Anglo-American Letters* 15, no. 1 (1985): 25–35.

Rascoe, Burton. *Prometheans: Ancient and Modern.* New York: Putnam's, 1933, pp. 233–37.

Rees, Richard. "Miss Jessel and Lady Chatterley." In his *For Love or Money: Studies in Personality and Essence.* Carbondale: Southern Illinois University Press, 1961, pp. 115–24.

Rembar, Charles. *The End of Obscenity: The Trials of Lady Chatterley, Tropic of Cancer, and Fanny Hill.* New York: Random House, 1968, pp. 59–160. (On 1959 trial.)

Resina, Joan Ramon. "The Word and the Deed in *Lady Chatterley's Lover.*" *Forum for Modern Language Studies* 23 (1987): 351–65.

Rolph, C. H. (pseudonym of C. R. Hewitt), ed. *The Trial of Lady Chatterley: Regina v. Penguin Books Limited: The Transcript of the Trial.* Harmondsworth: Penguin, 1961. (Reprinted, with a new foreword by Geoffrey Robinson, 1990.)

Ross, Michael L. " 'Carrying on the Human Heritage': From *Lady Chatterley's Lover* to *Nineteen Eighty-Four.*" *DHL Review* 17 (1984): 5–28.

Rowley, Stephen. "The Sight-Touch Metaphor in *Lady Chatterley's Lover.*" *Etudes Lawrenciennes* 3 (1988): 179–88.

Rudikoff, Sonya. "DHL and Our Life Today: Re-reading *Lady Chatterley's Lover.*" *Commentary* 28 (November 1959): 408–13.

St. John-Stevas, Norman. "The English Morality Laws." In Cox (1961), op. cit., pp. 103–9.

Sanders, Scott R. "Lady Chatterley's Loving and the Annihilation Impulse." In Squires and Jackson (1985), op. cit., pp. 1–16.

Sarvan, Charles, and Liebetraut Sarvan. "*God's Stepchildren* [Sarah Gertrude Millin] and *Lady Chatterley's Lover:* Failure and Triumph." *Journal of Commonwealth Literature* 14 (1979): 53–57.

Schorer, Mark. "On *Lady Chatterley's Lover.*" *Evergreen Review* 1 (1957): 149–78. (Reprinted as "Introduction" to the 1959 Grove Press edition of the novel, pp. ix–xxxix; in *"A Propos of Lady Chatterley's Lover" and Other Essays* by DHL. Harmondsworth: Penguin, 1961, pp. 127–57; and in Schorer's *The World We Imagine.* New York: Farrar, Straus, and Giroux, 1968, pp. 122–46.)

Schotz, Myra Glazer. "For the Sexes: Blake's Hermaphrodite in *Lady Chatterley's Lover.*" *Bucknell Review* 24 (1978): 17–26.

Sepčić, Višnja. "The Dialogue of *Lady Chatterley's Lover.*" *Studia Romanica et Anglica Zagrebiensia,* nos. 29–32 (1970–71): 461–80.

Sheerin, Daniel J. "John Thomas and the King of Glory: Two Analogues to DHL's Use of Psalm 24:7 in Chapter 14 of *Lady Chatterley's Lover.*" *DHL Review* 11 (Fall 1978): 297–300.

Shonfield, Andrew. "Lawrence's Other Censor." *Encounter* 17 (September 1961): 63–64.

Sparrow, John. "Regina v. Penguin Books Ltd: An Undisclosed Element in the Case." *Encounter* 18 (February 1962): 35–43. (The undisclosed element referred to is buggery. See rebuttal by Colin MacInnes, *Encounter* 18 [March 1962]: 63–65, 94–96. See also letters in *Encounter* 18 [April 1962]: 93–95; "Regina vs. Sparrow." *Encounter* 18 [May 1962]: 91–94; and Sparrow's "After Thoughts on Regina v. Penguin Books Ltd." *Encounter* 18 [June 1962]: 83–88.)

Spilka, Mark. "Lawrence Up-Tight, or the Anal Phase Once Over." *Novel: A Forum on Fiction* 4 (Spring 1971): 252–67.

———. "Critical Exchange: On 'Lawrence Up-Tight': Four Tail-Pieces." *Novel: A Forum on Fiction* 5 (Fall 1971): 54–70. (With Colin Clarke, George Ford, and Frank Kermode.)

———. "On Lawrence's Hostility to Wilful Women: The Chatterley Solution." In *Lawrence and Women.* Edited by Anne Smith. London: Vision; Totowa, N.J.: Barnes and Noble, 1978, pp. 189–211. (Reprinted in Spilka [1992]: 147–70.)

———. "Lawrence versus Peeperkorn on Abdication; or What Happens to a Pagan Vitalist When the Juice Runs Out?" In *DHL: The Man Who Died.* Edited by Robert B. Partlow, Jr., and Harry T. Moore. Carbondale: Southern Illinois University Press, 1980, pp. 105–20. (Also in Spilka [1992]: 70–95.)

———. "Lawrence and the Clitoris." In *The Challenge of DHL.* Edited by Michael Squires and Keith Cushman. Madison: University of Wisconsin Press, 1990, 176–86. (Reprinted in Spilka [1992]: 171–90.)

Sproles, Karen Z. "DHL and the Pre-Raphaelites: Love among the Ruins." *DHL Review* 22 (Fall 1990): 290–305.

Squires, Michael. "Pastoral Patterns and Pastoral Variants in *Lady Chatterley's Lover.*" *English Literary History* 34 (1972): 129–46. (Reprinted in Squires [1974]: 196–212.)

———. "New Light on the Gamekeeper in *Lady Chatterley's Lover.*" *DHL Review* 11 (Fall 1978): 234–45.

———. "Editing *Lady Chatterley's Lover.*" In *DHL: The Man Who Died.* Edited by Robert B. Partlow, Jr., and Harry T. Moore. Carbondale: Southern Illinois University Press, 1980, pp. 62–70.

———. *The Creation of "Lady Chatterley's Lover."* Baltimore: Johns Hopkins University Press, 1983.

———. "Introduction." *Lady Chatterley's Lover [and] A Propos of "Lady Chatterley's Lover"* by DHL. Edited by Michael Squires. Cambridge: Cambridge University Press, 1993, pp. xvii–lx.

———. "Introduction." *Lady Chatterley's Lover [and] A Propos of "Lady Chatterley's Lover"* by DHL. Edited by Michael Squires. Harmondsworth: Penguin, 1994, pp. xiii–xxxii.

Squires, Michael, and Dennis Jackson, eds. *DHL's "Lady": A New Look at "Lady Chatterley's Lover."* Athens: University of Georgia Press, 1985.

Stanley, F. R. "The Artist as Pornographer (The Evaluation of DHL's Genius)." *Literary Half-Yearly* 4 (January 1963): 14–27.

Strickland, G. R. "The First *Lady Chatterley's Lover.*" *Encounter* 36 (January 1971): 44–52. (Reprinted in Gomme [1978]: 159–74.)

Sullivan, J. P. "Lady Chatterley in Rome." *Pacific Coast Philology* 15 (1980): 53–62.

Swift, Jennifer. "The Body and Transcendence of Two Wastelands; *Lady Chatterley's Lover* and *The Waste Land.*" *Paunch* 63–64 (1990): 141–71.

Taube, Myron. "Fanny and the Lady: The Treatment of Sex in *Fanny Hill* and *Lady Chatterley's Lover.*" *Lock Haven Review,* no. 15 (1974): 37–40.

Teunissen, John J. "The Serial Collaboration of DHL and Walker Percy." *Southern Humanities Review* 21 (1987): 101–15.

Tibbets, Robert A. "Addendum to Roberts: Another Piracy of *Lady Chatterley's Lover.*" *Serif* 11 (1974): 58.

Tripathy, Biyot Kesh. "*Lady Chatterley's Lover:* A Trembling Balance." *Bulletin of the Department of English* (Calcutta) 7 (1971–72): 75–89.

Verduin, Kathleen. "Lady Chatterley and *The Secret Garden:* Lawrence's Homage to Mrs. Hodgson Burnett." *DHL Review* 17 (1984): 61–66.

Voelker, Joseph C. "The Spirit of No-Place: Elements of the Classical Ironic Utopia in DHL's *Lady Chatterley's Lover.*" *Modern Fiction Studies* 25 (Summer 1979): 223–39.

Way, Brian. "Sex and Language: Obscene Words in DHL and Henry Miller." *New Left Review,* no. 27 (September–October 1964): 66–80.

Weinstein, Philip M. "Choosing between the Quick and the Dead: Three Versions of *Lady Chatterley's Lover.*" In his *The Semantics of Desire: Changing Models of Identity from Dickens to Joyce.* Princeton: Princeton University Press, 1984, pp. 224–51.

Weiss, Daniel. "DHL's Great Circle: From *Sons and Lovers* to *Lady Chatterley's Lover.*" *Psychoanalytic Review* 50 (Fall 1963): 112–38. (Revision of Ch. 4 of his *Oedipus in Nottingham: DHL.* Seattle: University of Washington Press, 1962.)

Welch, Colin. "Black Magic, White Lies." *Encounter* 16 (February 1961): 75–79. (Review of Rolph [1961], op. cit. See also reply by Rebecca West et al., " 'Chatterley,' the Witnesses, and the Law." *Encounter* 16 [March 1961]: 52–56; and letters by Welch and E. L. Mascall, *Encounter* 16 [April 1961]: 85.)

Welker, Robert H. "Advocate for Eros: Notes on DHL." *American Scholar* 30 (Spring 1961): 191–202.

Whelan, P. T., Mary Herron, Julia Marlowe, and Calvin Trowbridge. "Apollo and Lady Chatterley." *Notes and Queries* 31 (1984): 518–19.

Whitehouse, Carol Sue. "DHL's 'The First Lady Chatterley': Conservation Treatment of a Twentieth-Century Bound Manuscript." *Library Chronicle of the University of Texas* 44–45 (1989): 40–55.

Widmer, Kingsley. "The Pertinence of Modern Pastoral: The Three Versions of *Lady Chatterley's Lover.*" *Studies in the Novel* 5 (1973): 298–313. (Rewritten as "Problems of Desire in *Lady Chatterley's Lover*" in Widmer [1992]: 70–99.)

Wilson, Colin. "Literature and Pornography." In *The Sexual Dimension in Literature.* Edited by Alan Bold. London: Vision; Totowa, N.J.: Barnes and Noble, 1982, pp. 202–19.

Yoshida, Tetsuo. "The Broken Balance and the Negative Victory in *Lady Chatterley's Lover.*" *Studies in English Literature* (Kyushu, Japan) 24 (1974): 117–29.

See also (1980–94) Balbert (1989): 133–87. Becker (1980): 79–92. Bell (1992): 208–25. Buckley and Buckley (1993): 24–25, 69–74. Burns (1980): 101–11. Clark (1980): 361–77. Cowan (1990): 212–36, 74–81. Dervin (1984): 138–47. Dix (1980): 49–53. Dorbad (1991): 129–39. Fjagesund (1991): 146–58. Hardy and Harris (1985): 144–47. Hobsbaum (1981): 82–86. Holderness (1982): 223–27. Hostettler (1985): 150–66. Humma (1990): 85–99. Hyde (1990): 104–13. MacLeod (1985/87): 178–90, 223–49. Meyers (1982): 156–64. Niven (1980): 69–74. Pinkney (1990): 134–47. Prasad (1980): 115–25. Robinson (1992): 106–16. Ruderman (1984): 159–64, passim. Scheckner (1985): 137–70. Schneider (1984): 237–43. Simpson (1982): 130–40, passim. Spilka (1992): 9–13, 63–95, 147–90, passim. Squires (1974): 196–212, passim. Storch (1990): 179–90. Suter (1987): 122–24. Urang (1983): 93–121. Widmer (1992): 70–99, 132–44, 195–206, passim. Williams (1993): 96–100, 102–11. Worthen (1991a): 100–101, 110–20.

See also (to 1979) Beal (1961): 84–97. Bedient (1972): 172–82. Boadella (1956/78): 119–31. Cavitch (1969): 194–201. Clarke (1969): 136–43. Daleski (1965): 258–311. Draper (1964): 109–18. Freeman (1955): 215–23. Gregory (1933): 77–88. Hochman (1970): 221–28. Holbrook (1965): 192–333. Hough (1956): 148–66, passim. Howe (1977): 133–40. Inniss (1971): 163–68. Jarrett-Kerr (1951): 77–89. Kermode (1973): 131–43. Maes-Jelinek (1970): 87–95. Miles (1969): 26–31, 51–53. Millett (1970): 237–45. Moore (1951): 258–69. Moynahan (1963): 117–20, 140–72. Murry (1931): 339–49. Murry (1933): 269–76. Nahal (1970): 267–78. Nin (1932): 141–46, passim. Niven (1978): 175–86. Pinion (1978): 205–17. Prasad (1976): 210–23. Pritchard (1971): 189–95. Sagar (1966): 179–98. Sanders (1973): 172–205. Slade (1970): 88–94. Spilka (1955): 177–204. Stewart (1963): 560–66. Stoll (1971): 223–50. Tedlock (1963): 20–27, 277–316. Vivas (1960): 119–51. West (1950): 131–34. Worthen (1979): 168–82. Yudhishtar (1960): 266–87, 298–301.

SECTION B

SHORT FICTION

23   Introduction

In his lifetime, Lawrence published three collections of short stories and, in three separate volumes, six short novels or novellas. He also had many short stories published individually either in journals or as separate publications, and he wrote several short fictions that were never published in his lifetime. I deal with the individual stories in eight separate groups under the following headings:

Love Among the Haystacks and Other Stories

The Prussian Officer and Other Stories

England, My England and Other Stories

The Fox, The Captain's Doll, The Ladybird (in three separate chapters)

St. Mawr and Other Stories

The Woman Who Rode Away and Other Stories

The Virgin and the Gipsy

The Escaped Cock and Other Stories

This order reflects the order of composition of the stories as far as possible; and the titles and groupings of the first six headings correspond to texts published in the Cambridge Edition of the Works of DHL, which themselves follow, wherever possible, the titles and groupings of texts published in Lawrence's lifetime (uncollected or previously unpublished stories are added to the Cambridge volumes according to chronological affinity). *The Virgin and the Gipsy* is a substantial short novel that was published only posthumously and warrants individual attention, while the last heading groups together Lawrence's last completed fictional writings.

The full range of Lawrence's short fiction has been available for some time in a variety of editions—most notably those of Heinemann and Penguin—and, especially as all the stories have not yet been published in the Cambridge scholarly edition of Lawrence's works, I provide details of some other major collections and selections.

The Complete Short Novels. Edited by Keith Sagar and Melissa Partridge. Harmondsworth: Penguin, 1982.

The Complete Short Stories of DHL. 3 vol. London: Heinemann, 1955; New York: Viking, Compass, 1961; in one volume as *The Collected Short Stories of DHL,* London: Heinemann, 1974; New York: Penguin, 1976.

DHL: Short Stories. Selected and introduced by Stephen Gill. London: Dent, 1992.

Four Short Novels. New York: Viking, 1965; New York: Penguin, 1976.

Full Score: Twenty Tales. London: Reprint Society, 1943.

Love Among the Haystacks and Other Pieces. London: Nonesuch Press, 1930; London: Secker; New York: Viking, 1933. (A different collection from the Cambridge edition.)

Love Among the Haystacks and Other Stories. Harmondsworth: Penguin, 1960. (A different collection from the preceding item and from the Cambridge edition.)

The Lovely Lady and Other Stories. London: Secker, January 1933; New York: Viking, February 1933.

A Modern Lover. London: Secker; New York: Viking, 1934.

The Mortal Coil and Other Stories. Edited by Keith Sagar. Harmondsworth: Penguin 1971.

The Portable DHL. Edited by Diana Trilling. New York: Viking, 1947; New York: Penguin, 1977.

The Princess and Other Stories. Edited by Keith Sagar. Harmondsworth: Penguin, 1971.

Selected Short Stories. Edited by Brian Finney. Harmondsworth and New York: Penguin, 1982.

Selected Tales. London: Heinemann, 1963.

The Short Novels. 2 vols. London: Heinemann, 1956.

The Tales of DHL. London: Secker, 1934.

BIBLIOGRAPHY 15: GENERAL CRITICISM OF THE SHORT FICTION

The following is a list of works wholly or substantially devoted to a range of Lawrence's short fiction. These are not cited again in the bibliographies for each group of stories nor in those for the individual stories except in one or two cases.

Allen, Walter. *The Short Story in English.* Oxford: Clarendon Press, 1981, pp. 99–109.

Amon, Frank. "DHL and the Short Story." In *The Achievement of DHL.* Edited by Frederick J. Hoffman and Harry T. Moore. Norman: University of Oklahoma Press, 1953, pp. 222–34.

Ashworth, Clive. *Notes on DHL's Poems and Stories.* London: Methuen, 1981.

Bates, H. E. "Lawrence and the Writers of Today." In his *The Modern Short Story: A Critical Survey.* London and New York: Nelson, 1941, pp. 194–213.

Black, Michael. *DHL: The Early Fiction: A Commentary.* London: Macmillan, 1986, pp. 111–49, 188–256.

Blanchard, Lydia. "DHL." In *Critical Survey of Short Fiction.* Vol. 5. Edited by Frank N. Magill. Englewood Cliffs, N.J.: Salem Press, 1981, pp. 1788–94.

———. "Lawrence on the Firing Line: Changes in Form of the Post-War Short Fiction." *DHL Review* 16 (1983): 235–46.

Brunsdale, Mitzi M. *The German Effect on DHL and His Works, 1885–1912.* Berne: Peter Lang, 1978.

Cowan, James C. *DHL and the Trembling Balance.* University Park: Pennsylvania State University Press, 1990.

Cox, James. "Pollyanalytics and Pedagogy: Teaching Lawrence's Short Stories." *DHL Review* 8 (Spring 1975): 74–77.

Cushman, Keith. *DHL at Work: The Emergence of the "Prussian Officer" Stories.* Sussex: Harvester, 1978a.

———. "The Young Lawrence and the Short Story." *Modern British Literature* 3 (1978b): 101–12.

Doherty, Gerald. "The Third Encounter: Paradigms of Courtship in DHL's Shorter Fiction." *DHL Review* 17 (1984): 135–51. ("The White Stocking," "The Daughters of the Vicar," *The Fox, The Virgin and the Gipsy.*)

Draper, R. P. "Satire as a Form of Sympathy: DHL as a Satirist." In *Renaissance and Modern Essays Presented to Vivian de Sola Pinto in Celebration of His Seventieth Birthday.* Edited by G. R. Hibbard. London: Routledge and Kegan Paul, 1966, pp. 189–97.

Engel, Monroe. "The Continuity of Lawrence's Short Novels." *Hudson Review* 11 (Summer 1958): 201–9. (Reprinted in Spilka [1963]: 93–100.)

Finney, Brian. "Introduction." *DHL: Selected Short Stories.* Edited by Brian Finney. Harmondsworth and New York: Penguin, 1982, pp. 11–31.

Ford, George H. *Double Measure: A Study of the Novels and Stories of DHL.* New York: Holt, Rinehart, and Winston, 1965.

Garcia, Reloy, and James Karabatsos, eds. *A Concordance to the Short Fiction of DHL.* Lincoln: University of Nebraska Press, 1972.

Harris, Janice Hubbard. "Insight and Experiment in DHL's Early Short Fiction." *Philological Quarterly* 55 (1976): 418–35.

———. *The Short Fiction of DHL.* New Brunswick, N.J.: Rutgers University Press, 1984.

Hirsch, Gordon D. "The Laurentian Double: Images of DHL in the Stories." *DHL Review* 10 (Fall 1977): 270–76.

Hobsbaum, Philip. *A Reader's Guide to DHL.* London: Thames and Hudson, 1981, pp. 23–41, 104–30.

Joost, Nicholas, and Alvin Sullivan. *DHL and "The Dial."* Carbondale and Edwardsville: Southern Illinois University Press; London and Amsterdam: Feffer and Simons, 1970.

Kim, Jungmai. *Themes and Techniques in the Novellas of DHL.* Seoul, Korea: Hanshin, 1986.

Krishnamurthi, M. G. *DHL: Tale as Medium.* Mysore: Rao and Raghavan, 1970.

Laird, Holly. "The Short Fiction of DHL." *Papers on Language and Literature* 24 (1988): 103–8.

Lakshmi, Vijaya. "Dialectic of Consciousness in the Short Fiction of DHL." In *Essays on DHL.* Edited by T. R. Sharma. Meerut: Shalabh Book House, 1987, pp. 125–33.

Leavis, F. R. *DHL: Novelist.* London: Chatto and Windus, 1955.

Modiano, Marko. *Domestic Disharmony and Industrialization in DHL's Early Fiction.* Uppsala, Sweden: Uppsala University, 1987.

Moore, Harry T. *The Life and Works of DHL.* London: Allen and Unwin; New York: Twayne, 1951. (Revised as *DHL: His Life and Works.* New York: Twayne, 1964.)

Moynahan, Julian. *The Deed of Life: The Novels and Tales of DHL.* Princeton: Princeton University Press, 1963.

Mizener, Arthur, "DHL." *Handbook to "Modern Short Stories: The Uses of Imagination."* New York: Norton, 1967, pp. 93–106.

O'Connor, Frank. *The Lonely Voice: A Study of the Short Story.* Cleveland: World, 1963, pp. 147–55.

Padhi, Bibhu. *DHL: Modes of Fictional Style.* Troy, N.Y.: Whitston, 1989.

Piccolo, Anthony. "Ritual Strategy: Concealed Form in the Short Stories of DHL." *Mid-Hudson Language Studies* 2 (1979): 88–99.

Pinion, F. B. *A DHL Companion: Life, Thought, and Works.* London: Macmillan, 1978; New York: Barnes and Noble, 1979, pp. 218–48.

Poynter, John S. "The Early Short Stories of Lawrence." In *DHL: The Man Who Lived.* Edited by Robert B. Partlow, Jr., and Harry T. Moore. Carbondale: Southern Illinois University Press, 1980, pp. 39–41.

Robinson, Jeremy. *The Passion of DHL.* Kidderminster, England: Crescent Moon, 1992, pp. 60–72.

Rose, Shirley. "Physical Trauma in DHL's Short Fiction." *Contemporary Literature* 16 (Winter 1975): 73–83.

Sagar, Keith, and Melissa Partridge. "Introduction." *The Complete Short Novels of DHL.* Edited by Keith Sagar and Melissa Partridge. Harmondsworth: Penguin, 1982, pp. 11–45.

Scott, James F. "DHL's *Germania:* Ethnic Psychology and Cultural Crisis in the Shorter Fiction." *DHL Review* 10 (1977): 142–64.

Sharma, Susheel Kumar. "Antifeminism in DHL's Short Stories." In *Essays on DHL.* Edited by T. R. Sharma. Meerut, India: Shalabh Book House, 1987, pp. 139–46.

Shaw, Valerie. *The Short Story: A Critical Introduction.* London and New York: Longman, 1983, passim.

Tedlock, E. W., Jr. *DHL: Artist and Rebel: A Study of Lawrence's Fiction.* Albuquerque: University of New Mexico Press, 1963.

Thornton, Weldon. "DHL." In *The English Short Story, 1880–1945: A Critical History.* Edited by Joseph M. Flora. Boston: Twayne, 1985, pp. 39–56.

———. *D. H. Lawrence: A Study of the Short Fiction.* New York: Twayne, 1993.

Trebisz, Małgorzata. *The Novella in England at the Turn of the XIX and XX Centuries: H. James, J. Conrad, DHL.* Wrocław, Poland: Wydawnictwo Uniwersytetu Wrocławskiego, 1992. ("DHL's Novellas," pp. 53–64: *The Fox, St. Mawr, The Man Who Died.*)

Van Spanckeren, Kathryn. "Lawrence and the Use of Story." *DHL Review* 18 (1985–86): 291–300.

Vickery, J. B. "Myth and Ritual in the Shorter Fiction of DHL." *Modern Fiction Studies* 5 (Spring 1959): 65–82. (Reprinted in revised form in his *The Literary Impact of the Golden Bough.* Princeton: Princeton University Press, 1973, pp. 294–325.)

Viinikka, Anja. *From Persephone to Pan: DHL's Mythopoeic Vision of the Integrated Personality.* Turku, Finland: Turun Yliopisto Julkaisuja, 1988.

West, Anthony. "The Short Stories." In *The Achievement of DHL.* Edited by Frederick J. Hoffman and Harry T. Moore. Norman: University of Oklahoma Press, 1953, pp. 216–21.

Widmer, Kingsley. *The Art of Perversity: DHL's Shorter Fictions.* Seattle: University of Washington Press, 1962.

Worthen, John. "Short Story and Autobiography: Kinds of Detachment in DHL's Early Fiction." *Renaissance and Modern Studies* 29 (1985): 1–15.

24   *Love Among the Haystacks and Other Stories*

Relatively little criticism has been written on this collection of stories, and, therefore, rather than providing separate lists at the end of each entry, I have compiled just one master bibliography at the end of this chapter to cover both general criticism and criticism of the individual stories.

WRITTEN

Collection

This volume in the Cambridge Edition of the Works of DHL collects all his early short fiction, written between 1907 and 1913, that was either unpublished or uncollected in his lifetime. Many of these stories share their genesis with those of *The Prussian Officer* collection, and the two can be seen as companion volumes. The stories in the volume are "A Prelude," "A Lesson on a Tortoise," "Lessford's Rabbits," "A Modern Lover," "The Fly in the Ointment," "The Witch à la Mode," "The Old Adam," "Love Among the Haystacks," "The Miner at Home," "Her Turn," "Strike-Pay," "Delilah and Mr. Bircumshaw," "Once—!" and "New Eve and Old Adam." The previously unpublished fragments of two unfinished works are also included here as appendixes, one of a story, "Two Schools," and one of the so-called "Burns Novel."

PUBLISHED

Collection

1. This collection was never published in Lawrence's lifetime (it was first published in the Cambridge edition as follows in 2), but two different collections with this same title have been published—one in 1930 (see following section) and one by Penguin in 1960—and these should not be confused with the present one.
2. Edited by John Worthen. Cambridge: Cambridge University Press, 1990.

Individual Stories

"A Modern Lover," "The Old Adam," "Her Turn," "Strike-Pay," "The Witch à la Mode," and "New Eve and Old Adam" were first posthumously collected in *A Modern Lover* (London: Secker; New York: Viking, October 1934). "Love Among the Haystacks" and "Once—!" were first posthumously collected in *Love Among the Haystacks and Other Pieces* (London: Nonesuch Press, November 1930; London: Secker; New York: Viking, 1933). "A Prelude," "A Lesson on a Tortoise," "Lessford's Rabbits," and "Delilah and Mr. Bircumshaw" were first posthumously collected in *Phoenix II: Uncollected, Unpublished and Other Prose Works by DHL,* edited by Warren Roberts and Harry T. Moore (London: Heinemann, 1968).

"A PRELUDE"

WRITTEN

October–November 1907. The story was first published under the name of Jessie Chambers, who sent it in on Lawrence's behalf to the *Nottinghamshire Guardian* 1907 Christmas short story competition. It was Lawrence's first publication.

PUBLISHED

Nottinghamshire Guardian (7 December 1907): 17. Also published separately as follows: *A Prelude, by DHL.* Surrey: Merle Press, Thames Ditton, 1949; reprinted in the *Nottinghamshire Guardian* (10 December 1949): 9, 12.

WHO'S WHO AND SUMMARY

It is Christmas Eve, and the unnamed *mother* and *father* of the small farm in which the story begins and ends recall that they have now been married for twenty-seven years; though they have worked hard to maintain the farm, it still only just provides them with a living, and, we are told, the previous year has been an unlucky one. She is small and gray-haired and has been brooding over their straitened circumstances—in particular, over the future prospects of her three sons; he is large and worn from heavy work, but jovial. *Fred,* their eldest boy, is twenty-five years old and a laborer on the farm. *Henry* and *Arthur,* Fred's two younger brothers, are miners in a local colliery.

Miss Ellen (Nellie) Wycherley is the mistress, following the death of her father, of the neighboring Ramsley Mill, a large and prosperous farm. As a child, before her father had made his fortune in cattle dealing, she had been close to Fred and his family—indeed, until fairly recently, she has been Fred's sweetheart, but her inheritance seems to have created a social distance between them, and they have not seen each other for several months. A recent instance of Nellie's new manner toward her old friends is recounted by Henry, who describes her looking down at him from her trap on the road and haughtily requesting some holly—not long ago, he suggests, she would not have hesitated to come directly to their home to ask.

The three young men decide to go ''guysering'' at Ramsley Mill, that is, to go as mummers or masqueraders to perform the traditional Christmas play of St. George. Before they set off, Fred goes out in the dark and collects some holly to take for Nellie. At Ramsley Mill, however, their performance is not very successful and meets with a cool reception. Nellie and her friend *Blanche,* who is visiting for Christmas, make critical and mocking comments, and when Nellie throws a half-crown coin for them, *Preston,* the live-in farm manager, complains at the waste of money. This is the last straw for Fred, who, besides feeling ridiculous in his disguise, now also feels humiliated in front of his scornful ex-lover. He prevents the others from picking up the money, apologizes for troubling the household, and leads his brothers out. Almost as soon as they have gone, and despite the laughter of Blanche, Nellie regrets her affected behavior. When *Betty,* Preston's daughter, then comes in from the scullery with the richly berried holly that Fred had brought, she feels even worse and begins to cry, lamenting the fact of her inheritance and the rift it has opened between her and Fred. Blanche suggests that they should repay the visit to try to make amends, and Nellie eagerly agrees. In the meantime, Fred has gone into the barn at home to brood over what has happened, so that when the two girls arrive, approaching the kitchen door at the back of the farmhouse, he is able to hear everything they say, particularly Nellie's profession of love for him. The two girls sing a carol as a pretext for the visit, and then Nellie also sings a love song; when the mother opens the door to welcome them, Fred comes forward and takes Nellie in his arms, while Blanche goes into the kitchen with the mother. The two lovers then come in also, and the story ends happily on a note of seasonal cheer in the cozy farmhouse kitchen, where Nellie ''already'' feels at home.

SETTING

The story is set in two neighboring farmhouses somewhere in the region of Nottingham: one is clearly a close re-creation of Haggs farm at Underwood, 2 miles northeast of Eastwood, and the home of the intimate friend of Lawrence's youth, Jessie Chambers. Her parents and elder brother are also re-created in the story (see Who's Who for *Sons and Lovers*). The other farm, Ramsley Mill, is presumably modeled on Felley Mill farm, a few fields east of the Haggs.

"A LESSON ON A TORTOISE"

WRITTEN

Winter 1909. Unpublished in Lawrence's lifetime.

WHO'S WHO AND SUMMARY

This short sketch describes the lesson referred to in the title. The *teacher,* the first-person narrator (and Lawrence-persona), has brought in a tortoise, Joey, for his *Standard VI boys* to sketch as a form of nature study. It is the last lesson on Friday afternoon, and he has planned the activity as a pleasant end to the week. However, no sooner has the lesson begun, than a confrontation between teacher and boys develops over the apparent theft of some erasers. The teacher makes the mistake of accusing boys arbitrarily, and they then bristle with ex- aggerated moral indignation at being unjustly implicated in the crime. This is particularly the case with the Gordon Home boys (waifs and strays), whom the teacher predictably challenges first and who react angrily with the familiar re- frain "you're always picking on us." The crime is eventually solved when, at the suggestion of one of the boys themselves, the teacher distributes a piece of paper to all the boys and asks them to write down the name of the person they believe is guilty. The culprit turns out to be the teacher's trusted assistant- monitor, Ségar, one of the oldest and most respectable-looking of the boys (from a home for the children of actors). After dealing with the boy and depriving him of his position, the teacher goes home feeling tired and wretched.

SETTING

This story and the following one are both semiautobiographical and based on Lawrence's experiences as a teacher at Davidson Road School, Croydon, where he taught from October 1908 to November 1911. Lawrence fell ill with pneu- monia in November 1911 and never taught again, though he did not formally resign his post until February 1912; he remained in Croydon until January 1912.

The two "homes" referred to in the story are based on the Croydon Gordon Boys' Home and a home in Croydon run by the Actors' Orphanage Fund for the orphans and illegitimate children of actors and actresses.

"LESSFORD'S RABBITS"

WRITTEN

Winter 1909. Unpublished in Lawrence's lifetime.

WHO'S WHO AND SUMMARY

This is a breezily narrated anecdote about two errant but enterprising schoolboys, *Lessford* and *Halket. Lessford* is a furtive, slightly surly, but robust young boy who is caught by the *teacher-narrator* taking bread from the free school breakfasts provided for needy pupils. He takes the bread, it later emerges, in order to fatten up the rabbits he breeds with his friend. Halket is brighter and less sulky than Lessford, but equally mischievous; he is the one who sells the rabbits to greengrocers for eightpence each so that the two partners can frequent the "Empire." The full details of this little moneymaking scheme are revealed only at the end of the story when Lessford arrives late for school one afternoon to announce, in great despair, "My rabbits has all gone!"—they have been stolen, apparently. (*Miss Culloch,* an awesome schoolmistress who usually oversees the breakfasts, is memorably described in the story, though she does not appear in person.)

SETTING

See under "A Lesson on a Tortoise." This story is set in the woodwork room of the school where the free breakfasts are served.

"A MODERN LOVER"

WRITTEN

Written as "The Virtuous" and revised as "A Modern Lover," late December 1909–Spring 1910. Unpublished in Lawrence's lifetime. First published posthumously in *Life and Letters* 9 (September–November 1933): 257–86.

WHO'S WHO AND SUMMARY

Cyril Mersham is a young man of twenty-six returning to the Midlands after two years in the south of England and going to visit the girlfriend of his youth, *Muriel,* and her family at Crossleigh Bank farm. It is just after Christmas. Cyril is making his visit without having forewarned the family in the hope that this will make it as natural and familiar as when he used to visit regularly. However, when he arrives, he is not greeted with "the fine broad glow of welcome" he had always received in the past, and, although hospitality is offered freely, the atmosphere in the house is clearly strained because of his presence. After tea, Cyril and Muriel go into the parlor and talk. They discuss their past relationship, and eventually Cyril indicates that he would like to become her lover again, even though he had been responsible for ending their affair originally. However, whereas, in the past, their relationship revolved largely around "speculating and poetising together," he suggests that now it might become a more physical affair, too—though his meaning is not clearly understood by Muriel. At that moment, *Tom Vickers* arrives. He is an electrician at a local colliery and, she now tells Cyril, Muriel's present lover. The three make desultory conversation, with the two men clearly jockeying for position in Muriel's affections. Tom is vigorous, handsome, and well mannered, but somewhat plodding in discussion and clearly no match for the sharp (though affected) intelligence and wit of Mersham, who becomes increasingly confident of winning Muriel over again. Indeed, when Tom leaves, Muriel walks part of the way home with Cyril and expresses her love for him. Gratified by this, he now returns to the question of sex, making his meaning quite clear this time; he cannot afford to marry her as yet, but that, he suggests, should not prevent them from consummating their love "just naturally." Muriel becomes defensive at this and raises some obvious practical objections. Cyril now loses his temper at what he considers to be her cowardly and mistrustful response. She is quietly reproachful of his manner (possibly thinking, like H. T. Moore [1951: 123], that his name suits him— "mere sham"). Their parting, like their meeting at the start of the evening, is strained: without a kiss and without any further discussion, Cyril dispiritedly shouts good-bye and informs Muriel of his departure again at the end of the week. She does not say good-bye.

SETTING

The story is set on and around Crossleigh Bank, the farm of Muriel and her family in the Midlands mining countryside; the farm is based on the Haggs farm at Underwood, two miles northeast of Eastwood, and the family is another re-creation of Jessie Chambers's family (see Who's Who for *Sons and Lovers*). The events of the story re-create aspects of Lawrence's relationship with Jessie Chambers in the period between December 1909 and the spring of 1910—the

later story, "The Shades of Spring," provides a similar but different treatment
of the same situation.

"THE FLY IN THE OINTMENT"

WRITTEN

April 1910 as "The Blot." Revised June 1912 and as "The Fly in the Ointment," June–July 1913.

PUBLISHED

New Statesman (16 August 1913): 595–97. First posthumous publication in
Young Lorenzo: Early Life of DHL by Ada Lawrence and G. Stuart
Gelder. Florence: Orioli, January 1932, pp. 211–30.

WHO'S WHO AND SUMMARY

The first-person narrator is *a teacher* lodging in a London house. He has that
day received a letter from his girlfriend, *Muriel,* along with some flowers. On
his return from school in the evening, the flowers remind him of her and of all
their pleasant times together in the Midlands countryside at home. His memories
distract him from his schoolwork, and he eventually turns to writing a reply to
Muriel. Afterward, he goes into the kitchen and disturbs a "rickety" and grimy
youth of about nineteen in the process of stealing some boots. They have a brief
altercation, and then the narrator allows the youth to go. But the pinched and
pathetic figure of the burglar and the background of crime and poverty he has
conjured up are like "a blot" on the narrator's mind now, and this dissipates
the mood of serenity created by Muriel and her flowers, leaving the narrator
feeling lonely and wretched.

SETTING

The London lodging of the narrator is based on Lawrence's own lodgings at
Colworth Road, Croydon, South London, where he lived with Mr. and Mrs.
Jones between October 1908 and January 1912 while he was a teacher at Da-
vidson Road School.

"THE WITCH À LA MODE"

WRITTEN

By 10 September 1911, but probably drafted in March or April 1911, as "Intimacy." Revised July 1913 as "The White Woman" and then "The Witch à

la Mode.'' Unpublished in Lawrence's lifetime. First published posthumously in *Lovat Dickson's Magazine* 2 (June 1934): 697–718.

WHO'S WHO AND SUMMARY

Bernard Coutts is on his way home from the Continent to his fiancé in Yorkshire. He decides to break his journey at South London, where he has friends in Purley and Croydon. He goes first to Purley, to the house of *Mrs. Laura Braithwaite,* a young widow. *Mr. Cleveland,* her father, is there. *Winifred Varley,* Bernard's ex-lover, and *Miss Syfurt,* a ''winsome'' German lady, arrive, and the party spend the evening talking and playing music. Bernard and the two other guests leave together, and Bernard goes back with Winifred to her house in Croydon. The underlying passion they feel for one another eventually erupts in a passionate kiss just as Coutts is deciding to leave. However, Winifred's apparently characteristic withholding of herself at times like this angers and frustrates Coutts, who recklessly kicks out at the oil lamp, which smashes on the floor and starts a small fire. He carries Winifred from the room, puts out the flames that have caught her dress, and throws a heavy rug over the fire; he then runs off into the night with both literally and symbolically burned fingers.

SETTING

South London: Croydon and Purley. The story re-creates places and people Lawrence knew during his time as a teacher in Croydon: in particular, the homes of Helen Corke (''Winifred'') and Laura MacCartney (''Mrs. Braithwaite''), sister of H. B. MacCartney, Helen Corke's ex-lover and the model for ''Siegmund'' in *The Trespasser.*

''THE OLD ADAM''

WRITTEN

June 1911. Possibly revised in July 1911 and July 1913. Unpublished in Lawrence's lifetime.

WHO'S WHO AND SUMMARY

Edward Severn is a lodger in the house of *Mr. and Mrs. Thomas,* in a London suburb. He is twenty-seven, tall, thin, and graceful in movement; cultured, quick-witted, and sensitive, he often has a diffident and ironic manner. One evening, he is alone with Mrs. Thomas and her three-year-old daughter, *Mary.* He plays with the little girl and helps to put her to bed. An electrical storm gathers, and this symbolically suggests the tension of subconscious sexual attraction between Severn (who is still "quite chaste") and Mrs. Thomas, who is thirty-four, handsome, "full-bosomed and ripe." Mr. Thomas returns home late from the office. He is forty, thickly built, and with an aggressive, thrusting manner. He is usually friendly with Severn, but the two men are sometimes hostile to one another; this seems to be one of these occasions. Following some inconsequential banter with his wife, Thomas makes a comment in opposition to the Woman's Bill (a suffrage bill was passed, though not enacted, in May 1911). Severn springs to its defense, and an argument ensues. It becomes more and more heated as Thomas finds himself constantly outwitted by the younger man. Severn clearly wins the argument and, following a brief silence, prepares for bed. Mrs. Thomas asks him if he would first help her husband down with the maid's box (*Kate,* the young maid, is leaving the following day, apparently because she has been too "insolent" to Mrs. Thomas). The large and heavy trunk is at the top of the house, and the two men struggle down the stairs with it, Mr. Thomas taking the brunt of the weight at the front end. As they near the bottom, Severn slips, and Thomas is thrown back against a banister post, banging his head. Thinking that Severn had acted intentionally, he attacks him, landing two heavy blows in his face (he had been brought up "among the roughs of Swansea" and had been a footballer and boxer in his youth). Severn is enraged, but, having "no instinct for fisticuffs," he leaps at Thomas and brings him crashing to the floor; he begins to strangle him, pushing his head over the edge of the stairs. Kate then appears and shocks Severn out of his frenzy. He is grief-stricken to see what he has done, and, with Kate, he revives Mr. Thomas and leads him to his bed. Mrs. Thomas has been dazed at the brutality shown by the men and by Severn in particular, and she behaves coldly toward him while comforting her husband. The next day, Severn and Thomas apologize to each other, and Severn says, "I didn't know we were such essential brutes." The two men remain close friends to the end of their acquaintance, we are told; Mrs. Thomas henceforth treats Severn as a stranger. (The title of the story is a biblical reference, see Romans vi. 6, though also a slang phrase for the penis. Lawrence often uses the phrase to suggest a bodily or "phallic" consciousness antithetic to spiritual or idealistic abstraction.)

SETTING

The story is based on Lawrence's time in Croydon (1908–12) when he lodged with Mr. and Mrs. Jones at 12 (and later, 16) Colworth Road.

"LOVE AMONG THE HAYSTACKS"

WRITTEN

October–November 1911. Revised July 1913 and possibly again in July 1914. Unpublished in Lawrence's lifetime.

WHO'S WHO AND SUMMARY

The story centers on a Nottinghamshire farming family, *the Wookeys,* and in particular on the two younger sons, *Geoffrey* and *Maurice,* though *Henry,* their elder brother, also features briefly, along with their father, *Mr. Wookey,* and his two laborers, *Bill* and *Jim.*

Geoffrey, a morbidly self-conscious, "heavy, hulking fellow," is twenty-two, a year older than his lighter, more carefree, "debonnair" brother. Overprotected by their mother, they have had little or no experience with women thus far and are "tormented" by the fact. However, they have both recently become fascinated by *Paula Jablonowsky,* an exuberant Polish-German governess at Greasley Vicarage next to the fields where the Wookeys are making hay; she is twenty, "swift and light as a wild cat," with blond hair and blue eyes.

On the night before the day on which the story begins, Maurice had slept out in the field to keep watch over the haystacks, and it seems as if, during the evening, he had courted Paula and struck up an intimacy with her. For, now, as the two brothers wait on the haystack for the next load of hay, he brags about his experience and teases Geoffrey about it. Geoffrey feels intensely jealous but also mortified at seeing his younger brother get a leg up on him in their sexual development. As they begin work, Geoffrey antagonizes Maurice by purposely throwing the hay out of his reach; eventually there is an ill-tempered skirmish that ends with Geoffrey's accidentally pushing his brother over the side of the stack. For a moment, it looks as if Maurice may have been badly injured or even killed, but he has simply been winded and recovers quickly. Having witnessed the fight, Paula has rushed out to help, and, much to his delight as he comes round, she holds Maurice's head in her lap and nurses him lovingly; it is clear now that "they were mated."

Work resumes for a short while before they all break for dinner. As they eat, a seedy and disreputable-looking tramp (*Bredon*) approaches and asks for work. Henry and his father refuse him, but they invite him to share some food, despite his unsavory appearance. When he has eaten his fill, a young woman (*Lydia Bredon*) emerges from the lane and addresses him. She is evidently his wife, though she is neat, clean, and respectable-looking. She has been waiting for him in the lane and is incensed to find that, meanwhile, he has been sharing in the haymakers' dinner. She is clearly an embittered woman and contemptuous of her husband. When she exchanges glances with Geoffrey, there seems to be "a sort of kinship" between them—they are both at odds with the world. The Wookeys offer her some food, but she is too angry and too proud to accept, and she turns away in silence.

Later, Maurice once more stays in the field when the others have left, ostensibly to look after the stack but, in fact, because he wants to continue his courtship of Paula. She comes out to him in the moonlit night; laughing, they race across the field and then ride bareback on a horse together. When they return to the haystack, it begins to rain, and they climb up the ladder to cover the stack with a cloth. Meanwhile, Geoffrey has arrived to help Maurice with the cloth. As he approaches the stack, he hears something fall—the ladder has slipped to the ground—and then he hears the voices of the two lovers. They, too, have heard something fall, and Maurice, realizing it is the ladder, tells Paula that they must either stay there now or call out to the vicarage for help; she says she would rather stay there. On hearing this, Geoffrey, jealous and disconsolate, returns to the little shed where they normally sleep when staying in the field and where they keep tools and provisions. He throws himself down on the hay bed and broods over his failure to attract Paula or, indeed, any other woman. Someone then enters the hut, and he challenges the intruder; it is Lydia Bredon, the downtrodden wife of the tramp, in search of her husband. She is sodden with the rain, cold, hungry, and tired. Geoffrey gives her food and a blanket and tries to make her comfortable. They talk in the dark, and he discovers her true feelings of hate for her neglectful and untrustworthy husband. When she continues to complain about the cold, he comes to warm her, and they fall into an embrace and spend the night together. In the morning, Geoffrey urges her to leave her husband and to come with him to Canada. She seems inclined to do so but cautiously suggests that they both reflect on it for two months, during which time she will find some domestic work through her sister who lives locally and who will put her up until she finds work. They make arrangements to write to one another.

Geoffrey goes out to replace the stack-ladder. When Maurice tells Paula that it is back in place, she assumes that he must have lied to her about it the previous evening, and she becomes extremely angry with him. He descends the ladder, but she refuses to come with him. Coming round the haystack, Maurice finds Geoffrey there and discovers what has happened—and Geoffrey proudly tells him about Lydia, too. They go to prepare some breakfast. While Maurice is looking for twigs for the fire, Paula comes down from the haystack and over to the shed, where she also hears the truth about the ladder from Geoffrey. Over breakfast, Paula is tenderly repentant toward Maurice, and he, though affecting indignation, remains essentially gentle toward her. They are engaged before the week is out, we hear, and Geoffrey and Lydia, too, ''kept faith'' with one another.

SETTING

All the place-names in the story are actual ones. The story is set during harvest time in some fields at Greasley next to the Vicarage there, and, we are told, four miles from the home farm of the Wookey family (the Wookey family are modeled on the actual Chambers family [see Who's Who for *Sons and Lovers*], whose farm at Underwood, the Haggs, lay two miles northeast of Eastwood and about the same distance northwest of Greasley, a mile and half east of Eastwood). The high road from Alfreton to Nottingham runs at the foot of the fields.

Other places mentioned are Bulwell, Nottingham, Crich, Langley Mill, Ambergate, and Chesterfield.

"THE MINER AT HOME"

WRITTEN

February 1912. Proof corrections March 1912.

PUBLISHED

Nation 10 (16 March 1912): 981–82. First posthumous publication in *Phoenix: The Posthumous Papers of DHL.* Edited by Edward D. McDonald. New York: Viking, October 1936; London: Heinemann, November 1936, pp. 775–79.

WHO'S WHO AND SUMMARY

Bower is a miner at home after a day's work and with something clearly on his mind. *Gertie Bower,* his wife, is tired and irritable at the end of a long day with the children and housework and now also with her husband to see to. Their *three children* include a baby in arms and Jack, a fat boy of six years. Following the miner's dinner and bath, he finally broaches the subject of an impending strike that has been called in support of a minimum wage. He clearly favors the strike and supports the union's position, but she strongly opposes both and reacts angrily to the prospect of what will be the third strike since their marriage. As she mocks his arguments, he, too, becomes angry and finally decides to go out, leaving her vexed and worn and alone with the children.

SETTING

The setting is the interior of the Bowers' home in Eastwood.

"HER TURN"

WRITTEN

March 1912 as "The Collier's Wife Scores." Revised July 1913 as "Her Turn." Proofs possibly corrected in August 1913.

PUBLISHED

"Strike Pay I, Her Turn." *Westminster Gazette* (6 September 1913): 2; *Saturday
    Westminster Gazette* (6 September 1913): 9.

WHO'S WHO AND SUMMARY

Radford is a miner out on strike for the second time in eighteen months. *Mrs.
Radford* is his second wife. On the whole, they have a good relationship, but,
during the first strike, Mrs. Radford was unable to wrest any strike pay from
her husband, as he argued that she had enough of her own money. This time,
therefore, she is prepared for action, and, when he again refuses to share the
strike money, she goes out and spends all her own money on new household
goods—although he is angry at first, this forces Radford to accept his responsibility for his wife, and the following week he pays up "without a word."

Minor characters in the story are the *landlady* at the "Golden Horn"; *Frederick Pinnock's daughter,* who is courting the landlady's son, *Willy; Mr. Allcock,*
keeper of the "furnisher-and-upholsterer's shop"; and the *carter,* who brings
the goods from Allcock's to the Radfords' house.

SETTING

Although the name is not mentioned, the setting would seem to be modeled on
Eastwood. The dialect suggests as much, apart from other details—of the strike,
the public house, the shopkeeper—that can be traced to Lawrence's hometown
at the time of writing. "Stony Ford," where Miss Pinnock comes from, suggests
Stoneyford, a hamlet two miles northwest of Eastwood. The colliery company,
"Bryan and Wentworth," is based on the real-life Eastwood owners Barber,
Walker and Co.

"STRIKE-PAY"

WRITTEN

March 1912. Revised July 1913. Proofs possibly corrected in August 1913.

PUBLISHED

"Strike Pay II, Ephraims's Half-Sovereign." *Westminster Gazette* (13 Septem-
    ber 1913): 2; *Saturday Westminster Gazette* (13 September 1913): 9.

WHO'S WHO AND SUMMARY

The story opens with *Ben Townsend,* the union agent, paying out strike pay to a large group of miners, including *Joseph (Joe) Grooby, Thomas (Tom) Sedgwick, John Merfin* (also a local choirmaster), *Sam Coutts, Chris Smitheringale.* The last two, along with *John Wharmby,* decide to walk together to Nottingham to watch the football match between Notts County and Aston Villa, and they persuade *Ephraim Wharmby* to join them, despite the fact that he is newly married and that his wife, *Maud,* is expecting him home with his strike pay. On the way to Nottingham, he and Sam Coutts entertain the others by catching and riding some pit ponies, but when Ephraim overreaches himself and falls off his horse, he also loses his half-sovereign strike pay. When he returns home later that evening, his widowed mother-in-law, the domineering *Mrs. Marriott,* harangues him for keeping her daughter waiting all day as well as for apparently having spent the strike pay. Though at first on the defensive because of his misfortune, he eventually loses his temper and stands up to the old woman, whereupon his wife, who has so far remained silent, asserts her own will and makes clear her allegiance to Ephraim by offering to cook his dinner; the mother storms out of the house.

SETTING

The story begins in "Bestwood," clearly a re-creation of Eastwood, and the miners walk from there to Nottingham via Kimberly Top and Bulwell.

"DELILAH AND MR. BIRCUMSHAW"

WRITTEN

January 1910. Rewritten June 1912. Unpublished in Lawrence's lifetime. First published posthumously in *Virginia Quarterly Review* 16 (Spring 1940): 257–66.

WHO'S WHO AND SUMMARY

Mrs. Ethel Bircumshaw, a former schoolteacher, has been married for four years to *Harry Bircumshaw,* a bank clerk and son of a country clergyman. She is small and sharp-witted, with vivacious brown eyes; he is large and muscular but somewhat listless and sullen in manner; he seems to have little purpose in his life, and because, as a consequence, he lacks true self-esteem, he has become something of a tyrant, bullying his wife—and beating their three-year-old daughter—in order to *assert* a respected position in the home. The story, however, shows this churlish Samson having his locks clipped by his wife and her friend,

Mrs. Gillatt, a slightly superior, older woman whom Harry has previously admired. In his presence, they discuss his performance in a church pageant, making fun of his appearance as one of the "Three Wise Men." He is silent and surly at this—he can cow his wife alone, but "he was afraid of *two* women"—and eventually leaves the room annoyed. The two women know that he will continue to listen to their conversation outside the room, and they now try to mollify his hurt pride by making flattering comments about him. But when they hear him going to bed still in a sulk, they go off to the kitchen where they can talk unheard. Here Mrs. Gillatt expresses surprise at Harry's "brutish" behavior, as previously she had seen only the "gentlemanly," public side of him: Ethel feels satisfied that she has made her husband look a fool in front of "this spoiled, arrogant, generous woman." Before she leaves, Mrs. Gillatt tells Ethel not to take Harry any supper. But Ethel knows she will have to continue to live with Harry, and, when she goes to bed, she brings Harry some milk and sandwiches. He pretends to be asleep, but she makes it clear she knows this so that "another lock fell from his strength." Only when he believes his wife to be asleep does Harry throw the last of his pride to the wind and succumb to his hunger; but his wife watches him devour the food like a "strange animal," and she laughs to herself—before "a real scorn hardened her lips." (For the biblical story of Samson and Delilah, see Judges xvi. For Lawrence's variation on the theme, see the story "Samson and Delilah.")

SETTING

The interior domestic setting of the story makes it difficult to identify any specific location, though the name "Bircumshaw" is a common Eastwood name.

"ONCE—!"

WRITTEN

June–July and August–September 1912. Possibly revised July and October 1913. Unpublished in Lawrence's lifetime.

WHO'S WHO AND SUMMARY

The unnamed first-person *narrator* has been in the Tyrol for the past ten days with his lover, *Anita.* He has loved her since he was boy, he tells us, but only recently has she accepted him as a lover. She is the daughter of a German aristocrat and wife of an army officer whom she married when she was eighteen. Her husband treated her badly, however, and she soon began to take lovers; the narrator seems to be her thirty-first, but he has hopes of being more than just another of her "pocket-editions," a hope that she encourages a little at the end of the story when she admits that there has always been something missing in her affairs. Apart from describing the two characters trying hats on in their bedroom—the narrator naked with his silk hat and Anita seminaked with her enormous, feathered confection—the story mainly presents Anita's happy reminiscence of a brief love affair in Dresden with another young army officer. (Lawrence also uses the name of Anita in "A Chapel among the Mountains" and "A Hay-Hut among the Mountains" for a character with many of the features of his wife, Frieda. The background details of the character here, though, are drawn from the life of Frieda's sister, Johanna von Richthofen [1882–1971], who was married to a German officer stationed in Berlin and whose first child, born in 1901, was named Anita.)

SETTING

The setting is a bedroom somewhere in Germany. The view described at first suggests Bavaria and specifically the area around Icking, south of Munich, where the Lawrences had lived between June and August 1912. We are told, however, that the characters are in the Tyrol, and this might suggest that the setting is based on Mayrhofen in the Austrian Tyrol, where the Lawrences moved in August 1912. Anita has an elegant flat in Berlin after her marriage, and the city of Dresden is the setting for the affair she describes.

"NEW EVE AND OLD ADAM"

WRITTEN

May–June 1913 as "Eve and the Old Adam." Revised July 1913 as "New Eve and Old Adam" and possibly again in July 1914. Unpublished in Lawrence's lifetime.

WHO'S WHO AND SUMMARY

Peter Moest and his wife, *Paula,* have been married for one year and are experiencing difficulties in their relationship. A telegram addressed to "Moest" with an invitation to the theater arrives, signed by "Richard." Peter immediately jumps to the conclusion that this is from a lover of Paula's, and he takes himself off to a hotel for the night. The next day, Paula discovers the true source of the telegram: there is another *Mr. Moest,* a young German, coincidentally living in the same block of flats as the Moests; he is cousin to a *Richard Moest,* who lives in Hampstead, and the latter's telegram message to his German cousin was mistakenly delivered to the apartment of Peter and Paula. Paula sends a message to Peter to come back, and she introduces him to the other Moest. Although the couple are somewhat reconciled to one another after this misunderstanding, the story still finishes with their apparent separation.

SETTING

Central London provides the setting for this story. Most of the action takes place in the apartment of the Moests.

"TWO SCHOOLS" (FRAGMENT)

WRITTEN

An unfinished fragment, probably written sometime between 1909 and 1910. Unpublished in Lawrence's lifetime.

WHO'S WHO AND SUMMARY

Mr. Sturgess is the headmaster of the National School in High Park. He is forty-eight years old, reserved, conservative in educational matters, of "the British Bull-dog type," and mostly friendless among the local community, though courteous to everyone. *Mr. Culverwell,* bachelor headmaster of the British School and native of the town, is a younger and more popular man, though "of the same type" as Mr. Sturgess and, in fact, something of a bully in his teaching as in his social life. *Miss Fanny Sturgess,* the daughter of Mr. Sturgess, is a teaching assistant at the British School, though not particularly effective at her job. She feels antagonized by Culverwell's bullying ways, though it seems as if he is attracted to her, for at the end of the fragment he has just determined "to show her the nice side of him."

SETTING

The mining village of High Park would seem fairly obviously to be a fictional re-creation of Lawrence's native Eastwood. High Park was actually the name of a local colliery.

"BURNS NOVEL" (FRAGMENTS)

WRITTEN

Fragments of an unfinished novel, begun and apparently abandoned in December 1912. Unpublished in Lawrence's lifetime.

WHO'S WHO AND SUMMARY

Mary Renshaw, an eighteen-year-old girl, is out gathering sticks with her neighbor at the start of the story. She has been listening to the whistling of a man in the distance. A donkey is grazing nearby, and, shortly after the whistling stops, Mary hears the man calling out "Bill," presumably to the donkey. She calls back, "He's here!" The man who comes for the donkey is *Jack* (John and, in one or two places, Jock) *Haseldine,* presumably intended to be the Robert Burns character. He is a dark, "limber" youth of twenty, with eyes "full of fire and laughter." He talks to Mary and asks where she is from. Later, after supper with his family (*mother and father* and *Alfred,* his elder brother), he walks over to Mary Renshaw's cottage and courts her at the garden gate; they kiss and express love for one another. He then goes to a local inn where he seems to be well known and well liked for his singing and fiddling. (The fragment ends here.)

SETTING

Actual place-names are used that identify the setting as being around Underwood, two miles northeast of Eastwood. The story begins on common land—presumably the area known as "the Friezeland"—not far from the Haggs farm, where Jack lives (and the home of Jessie Chambers' family in Lawrence's time), and he later walks through Underwood to Jacksdale, two miles northwest of Underwood, to see Mary again. Alfreton and Selston are also mentioned.

BIBLIOGRAPHY 16: *LOVE AMONG THE HAYSTACKS AND OTHER STORIES*

GENERAL CRITICISM

Greenhalgh, Michael John. *Lawrence's Uncollected Stories, 1907–13: A Critical Commentary.* Ruislip: M. J. Greenhalgh, 1988.
Worthen, John. "Introduction." *Love Among the Haystacks and Other Stories.* Edited by John Worthen. Cambridge: Cambridge University Press, 1990, pp. xix–xlix.

CRITICISM OF INDIVIDUAL STORIES

"The Fly in the Ointment"

Cushman, Keith. "A Note on Lawrence's 'The Fly in the Ointment.' " *English Language Notes* 15 (1977): 47–51.

"Love Among the Haystacks"

Draper, R. P. "The Sense of Reality in the Work of DHL." *Revue des Langues Vivantes* 33 (1967): 461–70 (464–66).

Gross, Theodore, and Norman Kelvin. *An Introduction to Literature: Fiction.* New York: Random House, 1967, pp. 205–10.

Holloway, John. *Narrative and Structure.* Cambridge: Cambridge University Press, 1979, pp. 57–62, 67–73.

Padhi, Bibhu. " 'Love Among the Haystacks': Lawrence's Neglected Story." *Osmania Journal of English Studies* 21 (1985): 71–81.

Vause, L. Mikel. "The Death Instinct Reflected in DHL's 'Love Among the Haystacks.' " *Journal of Evolutionary Psychology* 9 (1988): 187–89.

Wilson, Colin. *The Strength to Dream.* Boston: Houghton Mifflin, 1962, pp. 185–86.

"A Modern Lover"

Sagar, Keith. " 'The Best I Have Known': DHL's 'A Modern Lover' and 'The Shades of Spring.' " *Studies in Short Fiction* 4 (Winter 1967): 143–51.

See also Holderness (1982): 16–18.

"New Eve and Old Adam"

See Delavenay (1972): 151–52, 190–92. Schneider (1986): 110–12.

"The Old Adam"

Cushman, Keith. "Domestic Life in the Suburbs: Lawrence, the Joneses, and 'The Old Adam.' " *DHL Review* 16 (1983): 221–34.

See also Weiss (1962): 84–88.

"The Witch à la Mode"

Digaetani, John Louis. *Richard Wagner and the Modern British Novel.* Rutherford, N.J.: Fairleigh Dickinson University Press; London: Associated University Presses, 1978, pp. 64–65.

25   *The Prussian Officer and Other Stories*

WRITTEN

Collection

The twelve stories of *The Prussian Officer* volume, Lawrence's first collection, were written between autumn 1907 and June 1913. All but one (''Daughters of the Vicar'') had been previously published in various periodicals (often under different titles), but they were all extensively revised or rewritten for book publication in June, July, and October 1914. (See individual entries for initial composition and publication details for each of the stories. Full details can be found in the Cambridge edition of *The Prussian Officer* cited below.) The stories in the collection are ''The Prussian Officer'' (''Honour and Arms''), ''The Thorn in the Flesh'' (''Vin Ordinaire''), ''Daughters of the Vicar,'' ''A Fragment of Stained Glass,'' ''The Shades of Spring'' (''The Soiled Rose''), ''Second-Best,'' ''The Shadow in the Rose Garden,'' ''Goose Fair,'' ''The White Stocking,'' ''A Sick Collier,'' ''The Christening,'' ''Odour of Chrysanthemums.''

PUBLISHED

Collection

1. London: Duckworth, November 1914. New York, Huebsch, 1916.
2. Edited by John Worthen. Cambridge: Cambridge University Press, 1983.

BIBLIOGRAPHY 17: GENERAL CRITICISM

Crick, Brian. *The Story of the "Prussian Officer" Revisions: Littlewood Amongst the Lawrence Scholars.* Retford, Nottinghamshire: Brynmill Press, 1983.

Cushman, Keith. " 'I am going through a transition stage': *The Prussian Officer* and *The Rainbow.*" *DHL Review* 8 (Summer 1975): 176–97.

———. *DHL at Work: The Emergence of the "Prussian Officer" Stories.* Sussex: Harvester, 1978.

Finney, Brian H. "DHL's Progress to Maturity: From Holograph Manuscript to Final Publication of *The Prussian Officer and Other Stories.*" *Studies in Bibliography* 28 (1975): 321–32.

———. "Introduction." *The Prussian Officer and Other Stories* by DHL. Edited by John Worthen. Harmondsworth: Penguin, 1995, pp. xiii–xxxiii.

Grmelová, Anna. "Thematic and Structural Diversification of DHL's Short Story in the Wake of World War I." *Litteraria Pragensia: Studies in Literature and Culture* 2, no. 4 (1992): 58–69.

Littlewood, J.C.F. "DHL's Early Tales." *Cambridge Quarterly* 1 (Spring 1966): 107–24.

Worthen, John. "Introduction." *The Prussian Officer and Other Stories* by DHL. Edited by John Worthen. Cambridge: Cambridge University Press, 1983, pp. xix–li.

See also Pritchard (1971): 60–66.

PUBLISHED

Individual Stories

The dates for revisions and corrections undertaken for the book collection–June, July, and October 1914—are not repeated for each individual entry but should be borne in mind for any consideration of a story's overall evolution. There is not always clear evidence for the dating of proof corrections for periodical publication of the stories, and, in one or two cases, Lawrence may not have seen proofs at all, but generally these can be assumed to have taken place usually in the month immediately prior to publication.

"THE PRUSSIAN OFFICER" ("HONOUR AND ARMS")

WRITTEN

May–June 1913. Revisions and corrections July or October 1913; July 1914 (proofs for *English Review*). "Honour and Arms" was Lawrence's preferred title, and the story was published as that in its two periodical appearances. The title was changed, without Lawrence's permission (and to his great annoyance), at the proof stage of the book collection by Edward Garnett, Lawrence's early mentor and literary adviser to Duckworth (he was also responsible for its use as head title for the volume).

PUBLISHED

English Review 18 (August 1914): 24–43. *Metropolitan* 41 (November 1914): 12–14, 61–63.

WHO'S WHO AND SUMMARY

A masterpiece of psychological symbolism, one finds taut and concentrated in this story the essential motifs of much of Lawrence's other writing.

The Captain (''Herr Hauptmann''), the officer of the title, is forty years old, graying slightly, but with stiff reddish hair, and with a bristly moustache over a ''brutal'' mouth and steely blue eyes that flash ''with cold fire.'' The son of a Prussian aristocrat and a Polish countess, outwardly assured, authoritative, often arrogant and overbearing, he is nevertheless in a state of inner nervous tension, maintaining a ''stiffened discipline'' of his nature through conscious control and suppression of his feelings. His *orderly,* the other main character of the story, is a dark-skinned, black-haired youth of about twenty-two, with dark eyes that blaze and flare with hot passion when aroused. He has an easy, sensuous spontaneity that is entirely unself-conscious, and this natural, unthinking, unseeing quality in the youth seems to both fascinate and infuriate the officer: ''the blind, instinctive sureness of movement of an unhampered young animal.'' After an initial period of purely formal, impersonal contact between the officer and orderly, there comes a moment of powerful emotional interchange when the officer flies at the youth for overturning a bottle of red wine; henceforth, the two men become locked in a subconscious psychological embrace whose contradictory impulses of love and hate, attraction and repulsion, sadism and masochism lead inevitably to mutual destruction. The officer becomes strangely obsessed by the orderly and cannot leave him alone. The orderly, on the other hand, tries to withdraw and abstract himself from any intimate contact with his superior, though he cannot totally suppress his growing hate for him, and this further antagonizes the captain, spurring him on to provoke the orderly into some form of consciousness. When he learns that the orderly has a sweetheart, he purposely keeps him on duty in the evenings to prevent him from seeing her. He starts to bully the orderly, and this comes to a sadistic climax when, on a trivial pretext, he viciously kicks the orderly around the legs and thighs, leaving the young man severely bruised and shaken.

The next day, maneuvers involve a long route march in the hot sun, and, though the orderly suppresses the signs of it, he suffers great pain because of his bruises. When the company halts for a break, the officer orders the youth to bring him some food from the inn to a secluded spot in the shade away from the main contingent of men. Here, the seething hate that has been fermenting within the orderly all day finally erupts, and he attacks the officer. In an almost sexual ecstasy, the orderly throttles him to death, watching in horror, but also with deep satisfaction, as the blood streams out of the officer's nostrils and down toward the whites of his eyes—somewhat like the gushing red wine that had initially bound the two men into their strange dance of death. The orderly then takes the officer's horse and rides out of the sun-filled valley and into the darkness of the woods. He lies down beneath the trees and loses consciousness in a delirium. He later stumbles onward for a while, but his hold on reality slips away, and he never regains clarity of consciousness again. He experiences his last hours as a sort of phantasmagoria of dark shadows momentarily lit by flashes of light and tantalizing visions of the cool mountains in their ''wonderlight'' in the distance. During the night there is a storm, and a literal phantasmagoria of thunder and lightning reflects the delirium of the orderly. In the morning, he awakes with the sun ''drilling'' down on him again, and, as he strains his eyes toward the mountain lights, toward ''that which was lost in him,'' his eyes go black. The other soldiers find him lying in the glaring sun, and he dies later that night without regaining sight. In the mortuary, the two antagonists are laid out together, the one white and rigid, the other supple and with the flush of life still showing.

SETTING

Although no specific locations are named, the landscape is recognizably that of the Loisach and Isar Valleys of Bavaria in southern Germany, where Lawrence first wrote the story. He lived at Irschenhausen between April and June 1913, and he had also been in this area, at Beuerberg and Icking, between May and August 1912. Despite the title, the uniforms of the soldiers in the story are based on those of the Bavarian Infantry Regiments of the time.

BIBLIOGRAPHY 18

Adelman, Gary. ''Beyond the Pleasure Principle: An Analysis of DHL's 'The Prussian Officer.' '' *Studies in Short Fiction* 1 (Fall 1963): 8–15.

Anderson, Walter E. '' 'The Prussian Officer': Lawrence's Version of the Fall of Man Legend.'' *Essays in Literature* 12 (Fall 1985): 215–23.

Cushman, Keith. ''The Making of 'The Prussian Officer': A Correction.'' *DHL Review* 4 (Fall 1971): 263–73.

Dataller, Roger. ''Mr. Lawrence and Mrs. Woolf.'' *Essays in Criticism* 8 (January 1958): 48–59 (50–53).

Davies, Rosemary Reeves. ''From Heat to Radiance: The Language of 'The Prussian Officer.' '' *Studies in Short Fiction* 21 (1984): 269–71.

Englander, Ann. '' 'The Prussian Officer': The Self Divided.'' *Sewanee Review* 71 (October–December 1963): 605–19.

Haegert, John W. "DHL and the Aesthetics of Transgression." *Modern Philology* 88 (1990): 2–25.

Howard, Daniel F. " 'The Prussian Officer.' " In his *A Manual to Accompany the Modern Tradition: An Anthology of Short Stories.* Boston: Little, Brown, 1968, pp. 10–11.

Humma, John B. "Melville's *Billy Budd* and Lawrence's 'The Prussian Officer': Old Adam and New." *Essays in Literature* (Western Illinois University) 1 (1974): 83–88.

Kaplan, Harold. *The Passive Voice: An Approach to Modern Fiction.* Athens: Ohio University Press, 1966, pp. 163–67.

Scherr, Barry. " 'The Prussian Officer': A Lawrentian Allegory." *Recovering Literature* 17 (1989–90): 33–42.

Stewart, Jack. "Expressionism in 'The Prussian Officer.' " *DHL Review* 18 (1985–86): 275–89.

Widmer, Kingsley. "DHL and the Art of Nihilism." *Kenyon Review* 20 (1958): 604–16 (604–10).

Wilson, Colin. *The Strength to Dream.* Boston: Houghton Mifflin, 1962, pp. 183–84.

See also Draper (1964): 123–24. Panichas (1964): 75–78. Pritchard (1971): 64–65. Sale (1973): 44–47 and passim. Weiss (1962): 91–93, 95–97.

"THE THORN IN THE FLESH" ("VIN ORDINAIRE")

WRITTEN

May–June 1913. Possibly revised in October 1913. Proofs for magazine publication, possibly May 1914. Published in the *English Review* as "Vin Ordinaire." Lawrence changed the title for the book collection and suggested it as a title for the whole volume (it derives from St. Paul, 2 Corinthians xii. 7: "There was given to me a thorn in the flesh, the messenger of Satan to buffet me, lest I should be exalted above measure").

PUBLISHED

English Review 17 (June 1914): 298–315.

WHO'S WHO AND SUMMARY

Bachmann, a healthy, sensitive, and well-bred young man from rich farming stock, is serving as a private in the Bavarian army and is stationed with his unit in the garrison town of Metz (ceded to Germany by France following the Franco-Prussian War of July 1870–February 1871). He bears himself with pride and dignity, but, during drill one morning, he is paralyzed by fear and unable to go on as he nears the top of some ramparts on a scaling exercise; he wets himself and feels deeply ashamed. He is yanked brutally to the top by his aggressive superior, *Sergeant Huber.* Huber shouts at him, and Bachmann instinctively hits out at the sergeant, who falls over the ramparts into the moat below. Bachmann flees in a panic and makes straight for the home of his sweetheart, *Emilie,* who works as a maidservant for a *baron* and *baroness.* Once there, he explains his predicament and his plan to try to escape over the border to France that night. Emilie, a foundling child taken in by the family, feels compromised by his presence and is unsure what to do, but the nursery governess, *Fräulein Ida Hesse,* suggests that he hides in Emilie's room until after dark. Emilie comes back to her room in the evening and they make love; Bachmann's self-esteem is restored, and Emilie, too, feels reassured and confirmed in their love for one another. Emilie and Ida then go to see Ida's lover, *Franz Brand,* a local forester, to arrange for him to leave his bicycle for Bachmann to use for his escape. As they leave, Bachmann gives Emilie a postcard to mail to his mother. The bicycle is broken, however, and Bachmann has to wait until the following day. He sleeps with Emilie, and they make love again, again experiencing a fulfillment that seems to liberate them from their previous submission to the demands of social authority and duty. The next day, however, soldiers, led to him by the card posted by Emilie the previous night, come to take him away. No longer cowed by superficial authority, Bachmann is defiant and proud in his arrest, and Emilie, too, proudly stands her ground in the face of her employer's embarrassed fury at being caught apparently harboring a deserter (he himself is a veteran of the Franco-Prussian War). After the soldiers leave with their prisoner, though, the baron instinctively recognizes the integrity of the young couple's subversive love, and the story finishes with the suggestion that he will help to arrange things for Bachmann.

SETTING

The garrison town of Metz and the surrounding countryside. The descriptions of Metz are drawn from Lawrence's own experience of the town in May 1912. He had gone there with Frieda, whose parents lived just south of Metz at Montigny. Her father, Baron Friedrich von Richthofen, was a senior administrative officer in Metz, and he and his home (the French grange where Emilie works) are re-created in the story.

BIBLIOGRAPHY 19

Cowan, James C. ''Phobia and Psychological Development in DHL's 'The Thorn in the Flesh.' '' In *The Modernists: Studies in a Literary Phenomenon: Essays in Honor of Harry T. Moore.* Edited by Lawrence B. Gamache and Ian S. MacNiven.

London and Toronto: Associated University Presses, 1987, pp. 163–70. (Reprinted in Cowan [1990]: 156–66.)

Cushman, Keith. "DHL at Work: 'Vin Ordinaire' into 'The Thorn in the Flesh.' " *Journal of Modern Literature 5* (February 1976): 46–58. (Revised and reprinted in Cushman [1978]: 167–69, 173–89.)

Dataller, Roger. "Mr. Lawrence and Mrs. Woolf." *Essays in Criticism* 8 (January 1958): 48–59 (53–58).

See also Hyde (1992): 50–53. Worthen (1991a): 34–41.

"DAUGHTERS OF THE VICAR"

WRITTEN

July 1911, as "Two Marriages." Revised October 1911 and rewritten as "Daughters of the Vicar," July 1913. Further revised, July and October 1914. Unpublished separately in Lawrence's lifetime. An incomplete early version of "Two Marriages" was published in the Supplement to *Time and Tide* 15 (24 March 1934): 393–99.

WHO'S WHO AND SUMMARY

Rev. Ernest Lindley is the impoverished and embittered vicar of Aldecross, a small mining village in the Midlands. Coming from a country curacy in Suffolk where he and *Mrs. Lindley* had been treated like gentry by the agricultural workers, the Lindleys had expected similar treatment from the collier population at Aldecross when they first came to the parish twenty years ago. However, the miners and their families had little use for the vicar's religion and even less for his and his wife's social airs and graces; when they were not treated with outright contempt, the Lindleys found themselves largely ignored by the mining community. To make matters worse, they had only a relatively modest stipend to live on and no private means—so they were not particularly well received by the local tradespeople either. Slowly but surely, the Lindleys' indignation against the community turned to resentment and hatred and then to an inner rage against circumstances generally. Clinging to their shabby-genteel superiority, they kept their children separate from the locals and educated them at home in the manners and values of the upper classes.

Although other children are referred to, the two elder daughters, *Mary* and *Louisa,* provide the main focus for the story. When they are first introduced in earnest, Mary is twenty and Louisa nineteen. Mary is tall and elegant, but with the look of "submission to a high fate." Louisa, by contrast, is short and plump and "obstinate looking," with "more enemies than ideals." Mary acts as governess for a few of the daughters of tradespeople; Louisa helps with her father's parish work and gives piano lessons to colliers' daughters.

One day, on his parish rounds, the vicar visits the Durants—*John Durant* is a gruff, slothful, old tailor; *Mrs. Durant,* a blunt but slightly peevish woman, runs a haberdashery shop. Mrs. Durant is deeply upset because her youngest and favorite son, *Alfred,* who is twenty, has left his job as a miner and run away to sea. The vicar thinks this is for the best, as the Durants are notorious for their drinking, and this may keep Alfred out of trouble, but Mrs. Durant is peevish, indeed, almost abusive with him for suggesting as much. When the vicar returns home and passes this news on to the family, Louisa reacts more like Mrs. Durant than her father—it becomes clear that she has harbored warm feelings for Alfred and is upset to hear that he has gone away for such a long time.

Three years later, Rev. Lindley falls ill, and his duties are to be taken over temporarily by an Oxford graduate, *Mr. Edward Massy,* who has three months free before taking up a comfortable living in Northamptonshire. He is twenty-seven, a bachelor, and has private means; Mrs. Lindley and her daughters look forward to his arrival with anticipation, as eligible suitors for the two girls have so far been unforthcoming. When he arrives, however, there is general disappointment in the household, not only at his unprepossessing physical appearance—he is a small, puny man, "scarcely larger than a boy of twelve"—but also at his almost total lack of social graces; unable to engage in "normal human relationship," he nevertheless has a coldly logical, opinionated, and often sneering manner in discussion of abstract moral or philosophical matters. Despite all this and despite considering him "a little abortion," Mrs. Lindley still sees him as a desirable son-in-law for his income. Moreover, as his powerful Christian sense of duty emerges, Mary begins to see it as *her* duty to honor and respect him. She accompanies him on his parish rounds and becomes protective of him in the face of unspoken criticism from the parishioners and spoken criticism from Louisa.

Six months later, Mary, out of her strong sense of Christian duty and in defiance of her emotional and physical feelings of revulsion for him, marries Mr. Massy and goes to live with him in Northamptonshire. Mary has made a type of bargain: she has sold her body and its feelings for material freedom and devotion to high-minded living; and, though in her marriage she sometimes vaguely realizes that she has "murdered" herself, she keeps to the bargain. She becomes a "slave-like" wife to Massy, bears him two children, and drifts into an "amorphous, purposeless" existence without "real being." Louisa is furious with her sister and cannot forgive her for allowing her body to be degraded for the sake of her "high spirituality." Neither can she forgive her parents for pushing Mary to sacrifice her true self for the sake of financial security. Louisa insists that *she* will marry for love and for love alone. The remainder of the story deals mainly with Louisa's gradual coming together with Alfred Durant.

Since Alfred Durant left for the navy, she has seen him only once, at the funeral of his father just before Mary's marriage. On that occasion she had been dismayed to find a sense of "steel-plate separation" between them, caused partly by his submission to the military discipline of the navy and partly by his now apparently heightened awareness of their class difference: he did not treat her as a person but as an abstraction. Now, having served his ten years in the navy, Alfred is living at home and working down the mine again. It is Christmas, and Mary and her family are visiting Aldecross. Louisa becomes frustrated by the atmosphere created by Mr. Massy and goes out for a walk in the snow. She decides to call on Mrs. Durant and finds her sitting in the frozen garden in pain; she has injured herself internally after pulling too hard on some vegetables. Louisa helps her indoors and sends a message for a doctor. She carries Mrs. Durant upstairs to her bed. The doctor arrives and tells Louisa that Mrs. Durant has a tumor and may die at any moment. Louisa stays to nurse the old woman and to give Alfred his dinner when he returns from work. After his dinner, he has the miner's customary strip-bath by the hearth and Louisa helps to wash his back. Up to this point, Louisa has felt uneasy and alienated in this working-class cottage and cut off from Alfred; this physical contact enables her to break through these feelings of separateness, and it once more galvanizes her long-suppressed love for Alfred. She offers to stay the night to look after Mrs. Durant, and Alfred goes to the vicarage to give the message and to collect some things for her. His feelings, too, are in a tumultuous state, his profound misery at the prospect of losing his mother (on whom he has always depended emotionally) being mixed up with his excitement at the new intimacy with Louisa. The next day, Mrs. Durant dies. Alfred feels totally lost and empty now, and he thinks of emigrating to Canada. A week after Mrs. Durant's funeral, Louisa invites him to supper at the vicarage at Mary's suggestion, but the occasion is a failure; although Louisa does her best to make him feel at ease, he has nothing in common with the Lindleys, and they treat him with condescension—he is merely encouraged in his resolve to emigrate. Two evenings later, Louisa goes to his home to apologize for the evening. They talk inconsequentially for a while and, with a sinking heart, she learns of his intention to emigrate. Receiving no encouragement from him to stay, she picks up her hat to leave, but, on an impulse "like lightning," she asks him, challengingly, almost fiercely, if he would like her to stay with him for the evening. Unable to speak and after some moments of tortured hesitation, Alfred finally responds by means of a passionate embrace. Their love for one another is confirmed, and the next day Alfred comes to the vicarage to announce their intention to marry. At first, thinking wholly of themselves and the further erosion of their prestige in the community, the vicar and his wife respond with hostility, but they soon see the futility of op-posing the match and suggest, as a compromise, that the couple may marry but only if they do so away from Aldecross. Durant has no strong objection to this, as it falls in with his inclination to emigrate. Louisa sees Durant to the gate and apologizes for her parents; they kiss and plan to marry immediately.

SETTING

The main action of the story takes place in and around "Aldecross" in Nottinghamshire. The Durants' cottage, "Quarry Cottage," is based on Lawrence's grandfather's cottage of that name at Brinsley near to Brinsley Colliery, a mile north of Eastwood. This, along with other details, indicates that "Aldecross," the main setting for the story, is a fictional version of Brinsley. "Old Aldecross" thus also corresponds to Old Brinsley; and the reference to "Greymeed" at the start of the story suggests Greasley to the east of Eastwood. Nottingham is also mentioned in the story, and the "Barford" at the end of the story would appear to refer to Basford, a suburb of Nottingham. After her marriage to Mr. Massy, Mary Lindley goes to live with him in Northamptonshire.

BIBLIOGRAPHY 20

Earl, G. A. "Correspondence." *Cambridge Quarterly* 1 (Summer 1966): 273–75.
Kalnins, Mara. "DHL's 'Two Marriages' and 'Daughters of the Vicar.' " *Ariel* 7 (January 1976): 32–49.
Leavis, F. R. "Lawrence and Class: 'The Daughters of the Vicar.' " *Sewanee Review* 62 (1954): 535–62. (Reprinted in Leavis [1955]: 73–95, 100–107.)
Littlewood, J.C.F. *DHL I: 1885–1914.* Harlow, Essex: Longman, 1976, pp. 45–49.
Sabin, Margery. "The Life of English Idiom, the Laws of French Cliché." Part I. *Raritan 1,* no. 2 (1981): 70–89.
Travis, Leigh. "DHL: The Blood-Conscious Artist." *American Imago* 25 (Summer 1968): 163–90 (177–82).

See also Draper (1964): 122–23. Green (1974): 25–27. Littlewood (1976): 45–49. Pritchard (1972): 60–62. Slade (1970): 101–3. Stewart (1963): 567–68. Vivas (1960): 165–67. Weiss (1962): 88–92.

"A FRAGMENT OF STAINED GLASS"

WRITTEN

Autumn 1907 as, variously, "Legend," "A Page from the Annals of Gresleia," and "Ruby Glass." Revised March–April 1911 as "The Hole in the Window" and then "A Fragment of Stained Glass." Proofs for *English Review,* July 1911; for collection, July and October 1914.

PUBLISHED

English Review 9 (September 1911): 242–51.

WHO'S WHO AND SUMMARY

Mr. Colbran, the vicar of "Beauvale" and an archaeologist, tells the *narrator* that he has found a fifteenth-century fragment in the records of Beauvale Abbey about an occasion when the monks believed that the Devil had broken a window in their Abbey. The fragment then explains that the Devil was, however, frightened away by their patron saint, who had come down to defend them, as evidenced by their discovery, the next morning, of the fallen statue of their patron saint lying in the snow with the blood of the Devil clearly visible in its path from the broken glass down to the white snow. To explain this occurrence in nonsupernatural ways, the vicar has written a story about a local serf. This involves *the serf*'s flight from his masters at "Newthorpe Manor," following his beating for the killing of a horse and his subsequent firing of the stables as revenge. He takes refuge first in the pig shed of the local miller whose daughter, *Martha,* he has been courting. She brings him some provisions and agrees to run away with him. As they go, they come upon the Abbey Church, which, in darkness and under snow, they do not recognize as such. They imagine it to be a place of fairy magic and marvel at the lights created by its stained glass. The serf climbs up the wall (standing, unbeknownst to him, on a statue of the Abbey's patron saint) to take a piece of the glass, and, as he pulls, the statue gives way beneath him, and he falls back with a fragment of the glass, cutting himself as he does so. He and Martha then run away with the glass, and, according to the vicar, "live happily ever after."

SETTING

The Cistercian abbey of the story is modeled on the Carthusian Beauvale Priory near Moorgreen, northeast of Eastwood. The "Beauvale" of the story is a recreation of Greasley, a mile or so to the east of Eastwood. The three mining villages referred to in the story as being within the parish of "Beauvale" would correspond to the towns of Eastwood, Kimberley, and Watnall; and the three collieries to High Park, Moorgreen, and Watnall. Lawrence may have derived the name for "Newthorpe Manor" from the real Newthorpe Grange, a quarter of a mile from Eastwood.

BIBLIOGRAPHY 21

Baim, Joseph. "Past and Present in DHL's 'A Fragment of Stained Glass.' " *Studies in Short Fiction* 8 (Spring 1971): 323–26.

Baker, P. G. "By the Help of Certain Notes: A Source for DHL's 'A Fragment of Stained Glass.' " *Studies in Short Fiction* 17 (1980): 317–26.

"THE SHADES OF SPRING" ("THE SOILED ROSE")

WRITTEN

December 1911 as "The Harassed Angel" and then "The Right Thing to Do/ The Only Thing to Be Done." Revised March 1912 as "The Soiled Rose" (periodical publication was under this title). Revised as "The Dead Rose" in July 1914 and as "The Shades of Spring" in October 1914.

PUBLISHED

Forum 49 (March 1913): 324–40.
Blue Review 1 (May 1913): 6–23.

WHO'S WHO AND SUMMARY

John Adderley Syson returns for a visit to his native area and goes to see his old sweetheart, *Hilda Millership.* They are now both twenty-nine; he is married, and she is courting with *Arthur Pilbeam,* a gamekeeper. On the way to her farm, Syson bumps into Pilbeam, and the latter is relieved to hear of Syson's marriage, though he is still uneasy at Syson's possible effect on Hilda. Her family, the parents and four brothers, greet Syson cordially but not as warmly as in the past. Hilda and Syson walk through the woods toward the gamekeeper's hut and talk over their past and the reasons for their incompatibility. Hilda intro- duces Pilbeam to Syson formally, and then Syson leaves. As he is walking along the edge of the woods, he overhears Hilda reassuring Pilbeam that she no longer feels any love for Syson and sees them kiss and profess their love for one another. Hilda agrees to marry the gamekeeper, but not immediately, and, as Pilbeam leaves for home, Syson watches her waiting at the gate but looking at the countryside rather than at her departing lover. He does not leave until she does.

SETTING

"Willeywater farm" and its surroundings provide the setting for the story. As in *Sons and Lovers,* "A Modern Lover," and several other stories and novels, Lawrence here re-creates the family of Jessie Chambers and their home the Haggs farm at Underwood, two miles northeast of Eastwood (see Who's Who for *Sons and Lovers*). "Nuttall" in the story thus corresponds to Under- wood, though there is also an actual place, Nuthall, three miles southeast of Eastwood.

BIBLIOGRAPHY 22

Appleman, Philip. "One of DHL's 'Autobiographical Characters.'" *Modern Fiction Studies* 2 (Winter 1956–57): 237–38.

Cushman, Keith. "Lawrence's Use of Hardy in 'The Shades of Spring.'" *Studies in Short Fiction* 9 (Fall 1972): 402–4.

Davis, Robert Gorham. *Instructor's Manual for "Ten Modern Masters: An Anthology of the Short Story."* New York: Harcourt, Brace, and World, 1953, pp. 49–50.

Delavenay, Emile. "DHL and Sacher-Masoch." *DHL Review* 6 (Summer 1973): 119–48 (131–36, 138–42).

Simonson, Harold P. *Instructor's Manual to Accompany "Trio: A Book of Stories, Plays, and Poems."* New York: Harper and Row, 1965, pp. 5–6.

See also Weiss (1962): 80–84.

"SECOND-BEST"

WRITTEN

August 1911. Proof corrections for periodical publication, January 1912.

PUBLISHED

English Review 10 (February 1912): 461–69.

WHO'S WHO AND SUMMARY

Frances, twenty-three, is sitting by a hedge in the country with her younger sister, *Anne,* who is fourteen. Frances is tired and unhappy because she has just returned from Liverpool, where *Jimmy Barrass,* her "first" choice, whom she has loved for five years, has just become engaged to another girl. As they talk, a mole appears, and Anne picks it up. As moles are considered to be pests, she wraps it in her handkerchief to take home for her father to kill, as neither of the sisters is prepared to do this herself. Their conversation comes round to Jimmy Barrass, and Frances tells Anne about his engagement. At this moment the mole escapes from the handkerchief, and Anne tries to poke it back with her finger; it bites her, and, in her anger at it, she strikes it dead with her sister's walking cane. They move off into another field and come across *Tom Smedley,* a robust local farmer who is a year older than Frances; he has always cared for Frances and would have courted her long ago if she had encouraged him. For her part, Frances has paid only casual attention to Tom in the past, but now she thinks that if she cannot have the best—Jimmy—she will settle for second-best—Tom, who is natural, easy-going, and good-humored. They talk together, and Tom soon notices the mole Anne has killed. As he comments on it, he slips into dialect, and Frances complains that it is not "nice" to talk like that; but this seems to be an automatic snobbish remark influenced partly by her thinking of Jimmy at that moment—for she admits that she does not really care how Tom speaks (in any case, Tom can use standard speech in a cultivated way when he wants to). They argue briefly about the need to kill moles; he insists on the need because of the damage they do, and she eventually agrees to think about it the next time she sees one. As their eyes meet, he feels triumphant, and she smiles. The next day, Frances hunts out a mole and kills it. In the evening she presents it to Tom when he comes to visit, and she laughs with "the recklessness of desire." This gives Tom his cue to ask her to go out with him and she agrees—in a "dead" voice, but with "a thrill of pleasure."

SETTING

The countryside setting is not precisely specified, but the reference to Ollerton, sixteen or so miles northeast of Eastwood, makes it almost certain that Lawrence is once again re-creating the countryside he knew best around the Haggs farm at Underwood.

"THE SHADOW IN THE ROSE GARDEN"

WRITTEN

Late 1907 as "The Vicar's Garden." Revised, possibly in August 1911 and then, with change of title, July 1913.

PUBLISHED

Smart Set 42 (March 1914): 71–77.

WHO'S WHO AND SUMMARY

Frank, a colliery electrician, has come on holiday to a seaside resort with *his wife.* Before she married Frank, his wife had been engaged to *Archie,* a local rector's son. She believes that he had died while on active service in Africa some years ago, and, when she goes from the boardinghouse, without her husband, to pay a sentimental visit to the rose garden of the rectory, she can hardly believe her eyes when Archie comes and sits down beside her. However, she soon realizes that he is deranged and can no longer recognize her. On her return to the hotel, Frank insists on hearing what is troubling her, and he thus learns for the first time of her relationship with Archie. He is clearly upset to hear of the intensity of her previous love affair, but his anger is forestalled somewhat by the news of Archie's present condition; Frank then leaves the room.

SETTING

No specific location is mentioned, but the description of the rose garden seems to tally with one that Jessie Chambers remembered from her holiday with Lawrence and his family at Robin Hood's Bay on the North Yorkshire coast in August 1907 (see Worthen's note on p. 263 of the Cambridge edition of *The Prussian Officer and Other Stories*).

BIBLIOGRAPHY 23

Barrows, Herbert. *Suggestions for Teaching "15 Stories."* Boston: Heath, 1950, pp. 19–31.

Chua, Cheng Lok. "Lawrence's 'The Shadow in the Rose Garden.'" *Explicator* 1 (1978): 23–24.

Cushman, Keith. "DHL at Work: 'The Shadow in the Rose Garden.'" *DHL Review* 8 (Spring 1975): 31–46.

Eliot, T. S. *After Strange Gods.* London: Faber, 1934, pp. 36–37.

Martz, Louis L. *The Poem of the Mind.* New York: Oxford University Press, 1966, pp. 111–13.

Rideout, Walter B. *Instructor's Manual for "The Experience of Prose."* New York: Crowell, 1960, pp. 21–22.

Sale, William, James Hall, and Martin Steinmann. *Critical Discussions for Teachers Using "Short Stories: Tradition and Direction."* Norfolk: New Directions, 1949, pp. 28–30.

Seidl, Frances. "Lawrence's 'The Shadow in the Rose Garden.'" *Explicator* 32 (October 1973): Item 9.

Spender, Stephen. *The Destructive Element: A Study of Modern Writers and Beliefs.* London: Cape, 1935; Boston: Houghton Mifflin, 1936, pp. 168–69.

"GOOSE FAIR"

WRITTEN

July–November 1909 (jointly written with Louie Burrows). *English Review* proofs revised January 1910.

PUBLISHED

English Review 4 (February 1910): 399–408.

WHO'S WHO AND SUMMARY

The story begins with a description of a poor country *goose girl* making her way to the poultry market on the first day of Nottingham Goose Fair. She walks past the charred remains of a lace factory and thinks about the poor state of trade at the moment. The scene then switches to another part of town and to a very different type of girl, one "of superior culture." *Lois Saxton* is the daughter of *Mr. Saxton,* a large lace manufacturer. She has been eagerly awaiting her suitor, *Will Selby* (the son of another lace manufacturer), whom she is expecting for dinner, but she is bitterly disappointed when he arrives only to tell her that he must go and keep watch over his father's lace factory because of the apparent threat of arson from the restless hands. Later that night, Lois is roused by a commotion in the house; it turns out that Selby's factory has, indeed, been set on fire. Lois's father, Mr. Saxton, has gone to the fire to check that his own factory is safe. Worried about the safety of Will, Lois dresses and also makes her way to the factory. When she sees her father, she rushes over and anxiously asks about Will; her father dismisses the inquiry peremptorily and chides her for coming there; he orders her home with *Sampson,* his elderly manager. She feels indignant about his dismissive treatment of her and of her lover. On the way home, however, Sampson suggest that Will Selby is suspected of having started the fire himself (this is a period of economic slump for the lace trade, as was made clear in the opening scene, and many owners have already tried to avoid the consequences of collapse by having their factories "accidentally" burned down); Lois is upset at this thought, and it eats away at her all through the night. The next morning, however, she goes into the town with *Lucy,* the parlor maid, and they bump into Will and her brother, *Jack,* both of them in a highly disheveled state and Will with a black eye as well. It eventually emerges that Will had not been watching over his father's factory at all but had been out reveling with Jack and some friends. They had become involved with the goose girl introduced at the start of the story, teasing her and playing pranks with her geese. It seems as if Will had been somewhat forward with her, too. She had eventually asked some other men to help her retrieve her geese, and a fight had ensued, in the course of which the goose girl had given Will his black eye. Lois receives all this information stonily and then, in revenge, delivers "her blow" by telling Will what has been suspected of him. Despite this antagonism, however, the two lovers walk on side by side "as if they belonged to each other."

SETTING

The places mentioned in the story are actual places in Nottingham where Goose Fair still takes place each year in October. The Lace Market, Hollow Stone, and the Poultry are all in the center of the city; Sneinton is a suburb. The story is set in the 1870s.

"THE WHITE STOCKING"

WRITTEN

Autumn 1907. Rewritten January 1910. Revised March–April 1911; August 1913.

PUBLISHED

Smart Set 44 (October 1914): 97–108.

WHO'S WHO AND SUMMARY

Sam Adams, a bachelor of forty, is the owner of a lace factory in which both *Elsie Whiston* and her husband, *Ted Whiston,* had worked before their marriage two years ago. On each Valentine's Day since their wedding, Elsie has received presents from Adams, first a brooch and then some pearl earrings wrapped in a white stocking, which Elsie had dropped while dancing with Adams at his Christmas dance two years previously (she had taken the stocking with her by mistake, thinking it was a handkerchief). These gifts eventually give rise to an angry confrontation between Ted and Elsie, and this ends with Ted's hitting her on the mouth, making it bleed; but this action seems to jolt him out of his blind anger, and the situation is then quickly resolved as he fetches the brooch and earrings, posts them back to Adams, and then takes Elsie in his arms once more as they reaffirm their love for one another.

SETTING

Though it is not mentioned by name, references to the lace factory, to the Castle and boulevard, and to the Royal (café) identify the location here as Nottingham.

BIBLIOGRAPHY 24

Bassein, Beth Ann. *Women and Death: Linkages in Western Thought and Literature.* Westport, Conn.: Greenwood Press, 1984, pp. 155–57.
Cushman, Keith. "The Making of DHL's 'The White Stocking.' " *Studies in Short Fiction* 10 (Winter 1973): 51–65. (Reprinted in Cushman [1978]: 148–66.)

"A SICK COLLIER"

WRITTEN

March 1912. Revised July 1913; periodical proofs, August–September 1913.

PUBLISHED

New Statesman 1 (13 September 1913): 722–24.

WHO'S WHO AND SUMMARY

Willie Horsepool, the collier of the title, is an energetic, hardworking, and proud man, "without much intelligence" but with "a physical brightness." He marries a quiet, fair, refined girl, *Lucy,* when he is nineteen and she twenty. They live happily for a year, and then he is injured in a pit accident that tears his bladder. He is nursed at home by his wife for six weeks, periodically suffering bouts of apparently excruciating pain. However, as time goes on, the doctors are unsure what is wrong with him anymore—he can eat and has regained his strength, but the pain seems to continue, and he can hardly walk. There is a national miners' strike (there was an actual one between February and April 1912), and Willie sits at his window longing to be with the men lounging and playing marbles in the street. Some of the men start to organize a party to go to Nottingham to see a football match, and this rouses Willie to a frenzy; he insists that he will go to the match, too, and when Lucy tries to calm him, he turns on her, shouting, "Kill her" and blaming her for his pain. Lucy enlists the help of a neighbor, *Ethel Mellor,* and they eventually calm him. The story finishes with Lucy's worrying that Willie's compensation payments may be stopped if the authorities suspect he has lost his mind.

SETTING

Although the name is not given, the Midlands mining town near Nottingham that provides the setting for this story is clearly based on Eastwood, as suggested by the reference to Scargill Street, among other things.

"THE CHRISTENING"

WRITTEN

June 1912 as "A Bag of Cakes" and then "Pat-a-Cake, Pat-a-Cake, Baker's Man." Revised as "The Christening," July 1913.

PUBLISHED

Smart Set 42 (February 1914): 81–85.

WHO'S WHO AND SUMMARY

This is the semicomic description of the christening of an illegitimate child in the Rowbotham family and of the various underlying tensions in the family that are brought out by the occasion. *Hilda Rowbotham,* a college-educated school-mistress in the local British School, is approaching thirty; she is small, thin, and pinched with a heart disease, but she is "the lady of the family" and suffers from the shame of her sister as she returns home from school. *Bertha Rowbotham* is her younger sister of twenty-eight; she is, appropriately, the god-mother to the child, as she seems to care for it more than its mother. *Emma Rowbotham,* the youngest sister, is the mother of the child whose christening we witness. She seems confused and resentful at the experience of motherhood, exhibiting mixed feelings for the child and bitterness toward its father. *Mr. Rowbotham* is the father of the family and a crippled ex-miner. He has been a domineering figure in the household and has weighed heavily on the lives of his children so that they are now "only half-individuals." His loud and sanc-timonious praying provides a moment of comedy both in itself and when it leads to his rebellious miner son, *Laurie,* disrupting it by bursting a paper bag in the scullery. Laurie also has some fun at his sister Emma's expense, because the burst paper bag was from the baker's shop where the baby's father works as a baker's man, and he now starts singing, "Pat-a-cake, pat-a-cake baker's man." The *clergyman* who comes to conduct the christening is somewhat nervous and vague, but kindly and tactful. The baby is, ironically, called *Joseph William* after the elder Mr. Rowbotham, thus underlining the father's continuing influence.

   (The Rowbotham family are based on the Winterbottom family, who lived at the actual [and still standing] Woodbine Cottage, 8 Walker Street, Eastwood, near to the Lawrences' family home [1891–1905] at 3 Walker Street. Joseph Winterbottom also had three daughters, two of whom were teachers. Lawrence used the name of Joseph Winterbottom for the cashier's clerk who gives Paul Morel his father's wages in Chapter 4 of *Sons and Lovers* [94–96]—though that character is based on Alfred Wyld, the assistant cashier Lawrence actually dealt with as a boy when collecting his father's wages from the offices of Barber, Walker and Co.)

SETTING

Although unnamed, the mining town of the story is based on Eastwood, as the descriptive details of Hilda Rowbotham's walk home from her work at "the British School" indicate. Lawrence himself taught at the British Schools, Albert Street, Eastwood, from October 1902 to July 1905 as a pupil-teacher and from August 1905 to September 1906 as an uncertificated assistant teacher. "Wood-bine Cottage," the home of the Rowbothams, provides the setting for the main action of the story.

BIBLIOGRAPHY 25

Baldeshwiler, Eileen. "The Lyric Short Story: The Sketch of a History." *Studies in Short Fiction* 6 (Summer 1969): 443–53.

Cushman, Keith. " 'A Bastard Begot': The Origins of DHL's 'The Christening.' " *Modern Philology* 70 (November 1972): 146–48. (Reprinted in revised form in Cushman [1978]: 216–23.)

See also Delavenay (1972): 186–87. Weiss (1962): 77–79.

"ODOUR OF CHRYSANTHEMUMS"

WRITTEN

Autumn 1909. Revisions and corrections March 1910, July–August 1910, March–April 1911; proofs for *English Review,* May 1911.

PUBLISHED

English Review 8 (June 1911): 415–33.

WHO'S WHO AND SUMMARY

Elizabeth Bates provides the main focus for the story. She is a careworn but determined miner's wife, struggling against straitened circumstances to raise her two young children, *John* and *Annie,* and to maintain a respectable home. Proud and slightly superior, she has clearly become impatient with her increasingly neglectful and thriftless husband (*Walter*), who now regularly indulges in drinking bouts (his latest reported at the start of the story by *Elizabeth's father,* an engine driver) and who now often returns late from work. On the day of the story, he is late once again, and she angrily assumes he has stopped at the public house. The longer he fails to return, however, the more anxious she and the children become, and her anger becomes tinged with fear for his safety. After putting the children to bed, she calls on some neighbors, the *Rigleys,* to see if *Jack Rigley,* one of her husband's workmates, knows what has happened to Walter. Jack uneasily relates that he and another miner (*Bower*) had left Walter working below ground, though they had assumed he would be following just behind them. He offers to go and make further inquiries, but he escorts Elizabeth home first. An hour or so later, the distraught elder *Mrs. Bates,* Walter's mother, comes to the cottage bearing the bad news that Elizabeth had feared—Walter has had an accident down the mine. Shortly afterward, news arrives that Walter has, in fact, been killed, asphyxiated by a fall of coal. The body is brought in by *Matthews,* the pit manager, and some other colliers, then laid out and washed by the two women. The story ends with an extended examination of Elizabeth's inner turmoil and her complex reaction to the tragedy.

SETTING

Actual place-names in the vicinity of Eastwood are used. The Bates' cottage is by the railway crossing at Brinsley, a mile north of Eastwood and south of Underwood and Selston Colliery, which are also mentioned in the story. Like the Durants' cottage in "Daughters of the Vicar" (see earlier in this chapter), the cottage here is based on Quarry Cottage, Lawrence's grandfather's cottage, later his uncle's, at Brinsley; and the death of Walter Bates, like that of Holroyd in *The Widowing of Mrs. Holroyd,* is based on the death of Lawrence's uncle, James Lawrence (b. 1851), in a fall of coal at Brinsley Colliery on 17 February 1880.

BIBLIOGRAPHY 26

Barry, Peter. "Stylistics and the Logic of Intuition; or, How Not to Pick a Chrysanthemum." *Critical Quarterly* 27 (Winter 1985): 51–58. (Critique of Nash [1982], op. cit.)

Boulton, James, T. "DHL's 'Odour of Chrysanthemums': An Early Version." *Renaissance and Modern Studies* 13 (1969): 5–11.

Cushman, Keith. "DHL at Work: The Making of 'Odour of Chrysanthemums.' " *Journal of Modern Literature* 2 (Winter 1971–72): 367–92. (Reprinted in Cushman [1978]: 47–76.)

Donoghue, Denis. "Action Is Eloquence." *Lugano Review* 1, nos. 3–4 (1965): 147–54. (Reprinted in his *The Ordinary Universe: Soundings in Modern Literature.* New York: Macmillan, 1968, pp. 169–79.)

Ford, Ford Madox. "DHL." In his *Portraits from Life.* Boston: Houghton Mifflin, 1937, pp. 70–89 (70–75).

Gettman, Royal A., and Bruce Harkness. *Teacher's Manual for "A Book of Short Stories."* New York: Rinehart, 1955, pp. 18–21.

Havighurst, Walter. *Instructor's Manual for "Masters of the Modern Short Story."* New York: Harcourt, Brace, 1955a, pp. 25–27.

———. "Symbolism and the Student." *College English* 16 (1955b): 433–34.

Hildick, Wallace. *Word for Word: A Study of Author's Alterations.* New York: Norton, 1965, pp. 63–65.

Hodges, Karen. "Language and Litter-ature: Style as Process." *SECOL Review: Southeastern Conference on Linguistics* 6, no. 2 (1982): 98–109.

Hudspeth, Robert N. "Lawrence's 'Odour of Chrysanthemums': Isolation and Paradox." *Studies in Short Fiction* 6 (1969): 630–36.

Jenkins, Stephen. "The Relevance of DHL Today: A Study of 'Odour of Chrysanthemums.' " *DHL: The Journal of the DHL Society* 2, no. 1 (1979): 15–16.

Kalnins, Mara. "DHL's 'Odour of Chrysanthemums': The Three Endings." *Studies in Short Fiction* 13 (1976): 471–79.

Littlewood, J.C.F. "DHL's Early Tales." *Cambridge Quarterly* (Spring 1966): 107–24 (119–24).

McCabe, T. H. "The Otherness of DHL's 'Odour of Chrysanthemums.' " *DHL Review* 19 (Spring 1987): 149–56.

McGinnis, Wayne D. "Lawrence's 'Odour of Chrysanthemums' and Blake." *Research Studies* (Washington State University) 44 (1976): 251–52.

Nash, Walter. "On a Passage from Lawrence's 'Odour of Chrysanthemums.' " In *Language and Literature: An Introductory Reader in Stylistics.* Edited by Ronald Carter. London: George Allen and Unwin, 1982, pp. 101–20.

Schulz, Volker. "DHL's Early Masterpiece of Short Fiction: 'Odour of Chrysanthemums.' " *Studies in Short Fiction* 28 (Summer 1991): 363–96.

Stovel, Nora Foster. "DHL and 'The Dignity of Death': Tragic Recognition in 'Odour of Chrysanthemums,' *The Widowing of Mrs. Holroyd,* and *Sons and Lovers.*" *DHL Review* 16 (1983): 59–82.

Wulff, Ute-Christel. "Hebel, Hofmannsthal and Lawrence's 'Odour of Chrysanthemums.' " *DHL Review* 20 (Fall 1988): 287–96.

See also Draper (1964): 120–22. Littlewood (1976): 15–20. Pritchard (1971): 62–64. Sagar (1966): 14–15. Salgādo (1982): 125–29. Slade (1970): 98–101.

26 *England, My England and Other Stories*

WRITTEN

Collection

July 1913–July 1919. Revision and correction of all the stories for book publication, October–December 1921. All but one of the stories (''The Primrose Path'') had been previously published in various periodicals between 1915 and 1922. (See individual entries. See also the Cambridge edition of the work for full details of the textual history of each individual story.) The stories in the volume are ''England, My England,'' ''Tickets Please,'' ''The Blind Man,'' ''Monkey Nuts,'' ''Wintry Peacock,'' ''You Touched Me,'' ''Samson and Delilah,'' ''The Primrose Path,'' ''The Horse-Dealer's Daughter,'' ''Fanny and Annie.'' Four other stories from the same period that were not included in the original collection and remained uncollected in Lawrence's lifetime are included in the Cambridge edition of *England, My England* and are therefore also dealt with here: ''The Mortal Coil,'' ''The Thimble,'' ''Adolf,'' and ''Rex.''

PUBLISHED

Collection

1. New York: Seltzer, October, 1922. London: Secker, January 1924.
2. Edited by Bruce Steele. Cambridge: Cambridge University Press, 1990.

BIBLIOGRAPHY 27: GENERAL CRITICISM

Cushman, Keith. "The Achievement of *England, My England and Other Stories*." In
    DHL: The Man Who Lived. Edited by Robert B. Partlow, Jr., and Harry T. Moore.
    Carbondale: Southern Illinois University Press, 1980, pp. 27–38.
Mackenzie, D. Kenneth M. "Ennui and Energy in *England, My England*." In *DHL: A
    Critical Study of the Major Novels and Other Writings.* Edited by Andor Gomme.
    Sussex: Harvester Press; New York: Barnes and Noble, 1978, pp. 120–41.
Smith, Duane. "*England, My England* as Fragmentary Novel." *DHL Review* 24 (Fall
    1992): 247–55.
Steele, Bruce. "Introduction." *England, My England and Other Stories.* Edited by Bruce
    Steele. Cambridge: Cambridge University Press, 1990, pp. xvii–li.
Thornton, Weldon. [Review of Cambridge edition of *England, My England.*] *DHL Re-
    view* 22 (Fall 1990): 321–25.

See also Draper (1970): 188–90.

PUBLISHED

Individual Stories

As noted earlier, all the stories were revised for book publication between October and December 1921. This information is not repeated in each individual
entry but should not be forgotten when considering the evolution of any particular story. It is especially important to be aware that the collected version of a
story is often very different, indeed, from any periodical version published be-
forehand—and many of these stories had been published in *two* different periodical versions before the collection appeared. Evidence for the precise dating
of proof correction for periodical publication does not always exist, but it can
generally be assumed to have taken place, probably in the month immediately
before publication, though there are one or two instances where it would seem
that Lawrence did not see proofs at all.

"ENGLAND, MY ENGLAND"

WRITTEN

June 1915. Revisions and corrections were made for both periodical
publications. Lawrence corrected proofs for the *English Review* in August or
September 1915, but it is unlikely that he saw the proofs for the *Metropolitan*
publication.

PUBLISHED

English Review 21 (October 1915): 238–52.
Metropolitan (April 1917).

WHO'S WHO AND SUMMARY

Egbert, the central character of the story, marries *Winifred Marshall* in 1904 when he is twenty-one, and she is twenty. He comes from an old country family in the South, she from a now-prosperous but originally poor Catholic family from the North. The young couple are given a house—Crockham Cottage in Hampshire—by Winifred's father, *Godfrey.*

Egbert is well bred, cultured, and unassuming, with an affinity for nature and a nostalgic love of bygone England, though he has no trace of chauvinistic patriotism. Tall, slim, agile "like an English archer," with fair skin, fair hair, and blue eyes, everything about him suggests a lineage going back through the Vikings to the Saxons. However, he is different and ineffectual—almost irresponsible—in practical matters; he has no profession and no real ambitions, and after his marriage he comes to rely almost wholly on the financial support and patronage of his father-in-law. He spends most of his time working around the house and dabbling in literature, music, and, particularly, folk art and customs. Egbert and Winifred spend their early days together in an idyllic haze of romance and passion more or less secluded from the modern world in their ancient country cottage, which seems suffused with the primeval spirit of "savage" Saxon England. However, as their children, *Joyce, Annabel,* and *Barbara* are born to them, Egbert feels increasingly marginalized by the mother–child intimacy, and Winifred, for her part, starts to chafe at the ineffectuality of Egbert and at his refusal to take any real responsibility for anything, least of all the children; he seems to her to stand for nothing. In this, she cannot help comparing him to her father, from whose powerful influence she never really escapes and on whom she relies, really, for her family's security. Godfrey Marshall is an energetic self-made man from the North with a modest fortune that he liberally shares among his daughters and their families; robust in all practical matters and tough-minded in business, though he can be a sentimentalist in domestic matters and in his literary tastes, he is still a father "of the old English type" with the "magic prestige of paternity."

The turning point in the story (indeed, the main plot "event") occurs when Egbert's eldest daughter, Joyce, playing in the cottage garden when she is six, falls on a sickle carelessly left lying in the grass by Egbert; although her leg is eventually saved, she is lamed by the accident, and Winifred never really forgives Egbert for this, and she now increasingly devotes herself to her children and to her Catholic faith. Joyce has to have regular treatment at a nursing home in London (paid for by her grandfather), and Winifred moves to a flat there with the other children. Egbert is left behind, "ignominious" at Crockham, where the emptiness of his life eats away at him until it feels that frustration and futility are running through his veins and killing him. When the war breaks out, his whole instinct is against it; he cannot hate a nation "*en bloc,*" and he sees little to choose between German militarism and British industrialism. However, what appeared to be an admirably carefree spontaneity at the start of the story has now turned into a self-destructive recklessness, and Egbert passively allows his nihilistic drift away from his wife and family to continue as he joins up for a war he does not believe in; he betrays his instincts and accepts "his own degradation."

With this apparent death wish, Egbert's story now more clearly takes on the appearance of a symbolic allegory, a bitterly ironic elegy for "his" England. For the apocalyptic imagery through which his self-willed death on the battlefield is portrayed raises that personal death to the status of a representative destiny for a whole culture that is seen to have lost all vital energy and direction and to be bent on self-destruction.

SETTING

Egbert and Winifred's home, "Crockham Cottage," is ostensibly in Hampshire, but, in fact, it would seem to be a re-creation of Rackham House, Perceval and Madeline Lucas's house on the Meynell estate at Greatham, Pulborough, Sussex, where Lawrence and Frieda had a cottage, lent by Viola Meynell, between January and August 1915. In fact, shortly after indicating Hampshire on the first page of the story, Lawrence makes reference to "the south downs," which are in central Sussex. Godfrey Marshall also pays for Egbert and Winifred to have a flat in London, and, following Joyce's accident, the scene largely shifts there as she has to undergo treatment at a children's nursing home near Baker Street. The ending of the story takes place on a battlefield in Flanders.

BIBLIOGRAPHY 28

Goodman, Charlotte. "Henry James, DHL, and the Victimized Child." *Modern Language Studies* 10 (1979–80): 43–51.

Lee, Brian S. "The Marital Conclusions of Tennyson's 'Maud' and Lawrence's 'England, My England.' " *University of Cape Town Studies in English* 12 (1982): 19–37.

Lodge, David. *The Modes of Modern Writing.* London: Arnold; Ithaca, N.Y.: Cornell, 1977, pp. 164–76.

Lucas, Barbara. "Apropos of 'England, My England.' " *Twentieth Century* 169 (March 1961): 288–93.

Ross, Charles L. "DHL and World War I or History and the 'Forms of Reality': The Case of 'England, My England.' " In *Franklin Pierce Studies in Literature.* Edited by James F. Maybury and Marjorie A. Zerbel. Rindge, N.H.: Franklin Pierce College, 1982, pp. 11–21.

Rossman, Charles. "Myth and Misunderstanding DHL." *Bucknell Review* 22 (Fall 1976): 81–101 (83–90).

Tarinayya, M. "Lawrence's 'England, My England': An Analysis." *Journal of the School of Languages* 7 (Winter 1980–81): 70–83.

Thornton, Weldon. " 'The Flower or the Fruit': A Reading of DHL's 'England, My England.' " *DHL Review* 16 (1983): 247–58.

See also Clarke (1969): 116–20. Delavenay (1972): 431–34. Draper (1964): 129–30. Herzinger (1982): 75–76, 158–71, 186–87. Hough (1956): 172–73. Ingram (1990): 76–80. Leavis (1955): 265–68. Mohanty (1993): 43–46. Pinkney (1990): 51–53. Pritchard (1971): 106–8. Ruderman (1984): 71–89.

"TICKETS PLEASE"

WRITTEN

November 1918, as "John Thomas." Possibly revised in January 1919. Lawrence's title was changed editorially to " 'Tickets, Please!' " for its first periodical publication, and to "The Eleventh Commandment" for its second; Lawrence seems to have accepted the first title for the collected version, though whether or not he knew or approved of this and other changes to the periodical versions is not clear.

PUBLISHED

Strand (April 1919): 287–93.
Metropolitan (August 1919): 26–28, 80.

WHO'S WHO AND SUMMARY

The appropriately named *John Thomas Raynor,* a tram inspector, is a notorious womanizer who constantly flirts with the fearless young tram girls; for the many scandals he has caused, he is often more maliciously nicknamed "Coddy." *Annie Stone,* as her name suggests, is one of the more abrasive of the women conductors, and her sharp tongue has always kept John Thomas at arm's length. However, following an enjoyable evening together at a local fair, a courtship develops, and they become increasingly intimate. Indeed, Annie begins to feel seriously attached to John Thomas and to want the relationship to develop beyond a mere flirtation—she begins to want more than a mere "nocturnal presence." Once he realizes this, though, his ardor cools very quickly, and he breaks off the relationship. Annie's initial misery soon turns to a hard anger and to a vindictive determination to exact her revenge on the strutting male. Enlisting the support of other tram girls with grievances against him (*Nora Purdy, Cissy Meakin, Laura Sharp, Muriel Baggaley, Polly Birkin, Emma Houselay*), she lures John Thomas to their waiting room one evening, where a type of mock Bacchic ritual is enacted. John Thomas is asked by the women to choose one of them to marry. When he refuses, the verbal taunting of the women quickly escalates into a full-blooded and frenzied physical assault (led by Annie) in which his clothes are torn from him, and he is left badly bruised and bleeding. (This part of the story is loosely based on *The Bacchae* by Euripides where Pentheus is torn to pieces by a group of women in a Dionysian frenzy.) In desperation, he finally agrees to make a choice and, "cunning in his overthrow," he chooses the very person who has beaten him most viciously: Annie. She, in mock revulsion, refuses to have anything to do with him—but her inner response is more complex: shocked, pained, and "broken," she apparently realizes that in destroying John Thomas (and what he stands for), she has also destroyed a part of herself (again, there is a loose parallel in *The Bacchae*, where Pentheus's mother discovers that she has participated in the dismemberment of her own son).

SETTING

The story is set in the Midlands around "Bestwood," one of Lawrence's frequently used fictional names for Eastwood. The tramway of the story—"the most dangerous tram service in England"—is based on the Nottingham-to-Ripley line that opened in August 1913 and ran through Eastwood.

BIBLIOGRAPHY 29

Breen, Judith Puchner. "DHL, World War I and the Battle between the Sexes: A Reading of 'The Blind Man' and 'Tickets, Please.' " *Women's Studies* 13 (1986): 63–74.

Brooks, Cleanth, and Robert P. Warren. *Understanding Fiction.* 2d ed. New York: Appleton-Century-Croft, 1959, pp. 221–22.

Kegel-Brinkgreve, E. "The Dionysian Tramline." *Dutch Quarterly Review* 5 (1975): 180–94.

Lainoff, Seymour. "The Wartime Setting of Lawrence's 'Tickets, Please.' " *Studies in Short Fiction* 7 (Fall 1970): 649–51.

Ross, Woodburn O., and A. Dayle Wallace, eds. *Short Stories in Context.* New York: American Book, 1953, pp. 355–59.

Ryan, Kiernan. "The Revenge of the Women: Lawrence's 'Tickets, Please.' " *Literature and History* 7 (1981): 210–22.

Trilling, Lionel. *The Experience of Literature.* New York: Holt, Rinehart, and Winston, 1967, pp. 672–74.

Wheeler, Richard P. " 'Cunning in his overthrow': Lawrence's Art in 'Tickets, Please.' " *DHL Review* 10 (Fall 1977): 242–50.

Wiehe, R. E. "Lawrence's 'Tickets, Please.' " *Explicator* 20 (October 1961): Item 12.

Wood, Paul A. "Up at the Front: A Teacher's Learning Experience with Lawrence's Sexual Politics." *DHL Review* 20 (Spring 1988): 71–77.

See also Simpson (1982): 67–69, passim. Slade (1970): 103–5.

"THE BLIND MAN"

WRITTEN

November 1918.

PUBLISHED

English Review 27 (July 1920): 22–41.
Living Age (7 August 1920): 358–70.

WHO'S WHO AND SUMMARY

Isabel Pervin, a thirty-year-old Scottish woman, and *Maurice Pervin,* a twenty-nine-year-old Englishman, have been married for five years and live at the front of Maurice's farmstead, which is worked mainly by their tenant-neighbors, *the Wernhams.* One year ago, during the war, Maurice had been blinded in Flanders. Their first child had died as an infant, but Isabel is now expecting a second child. Isabel has literary interests and writes book reviews for newspapers, while Maurice enjoys doing practical work around the farm. They share their interests, however, and have lived harmoniously together since their marriage and in even greater intimacy and seclusion since Maurice was blinded—though their life is marred from time to time by Maurice's fits of depression. Isabel has invited an old friend, *Bertie Reid,* a barrister, intellectual, and man of letters, to visit them. On meeting previously, Maurice and Bertie had taken an instant dislike to each other, and the present visit is partly intended as a reconciliation between the two. Shortly after Bertie arrives, Maurice goes out into the farm. After dark, Bertie goes to look for him and finds him in a barn pulping turnips. They talk for a while, and then Maurice asks if he can touch Bertie, to get a clearer sense of what he is like. Bertie recoils from the blind man's hands but pretends not to mind; Maurice then invites him to touch his scarred eyes. Bertie feels revulsion at the idea but seems unable to refuse; as he tentatively touches the eyes, Maurice presses his fingers firmly onto the eye sockets, beginning to rock slightly at the same time. After a minute or so, Maurice releases Bertie and suggests that they have now established a deep bond of friendship; but Bertie feels profoundly intimidated by the other man's passion and merely humors him in order to be able to get away as quickly as possible. Indoors, Isabel recognizes that while Maurice seems to have been enriched by the touch of the other man, Bertie has been broken by an intimacy he did not want and cannot understand.

SETTING

The Pervins' home, the Grange, is near Oxford in the story, but it seems to be based on the vicarage at Upper Lydbrook in the Forest of Dean, Monmouthshire, where Lawrence visited Catherine and Donald Carswell in August 1918. Isabel and Maurice Pervin are modeled on the Carswells, and Bertie Reid may be a fictional re-creation of Bertrand Russell (1872–1970), with whom Lawrence had a short-lived friendship in 1915–16.

BIBLIOGRAPHY 30

Abolin, Nancy. "Lawrence's 'The Blind Man': The Reality of Touch." In *A DHL Miscellany.* Edited by Harry T. Moore. Carbondale Southern Illinois University Press, 1959, pp. 215–30.

Baldeshwiler, Eileen. "The Lyric Short Story: The Sketch of a History." *Studies in Short Fiction* 6 (Summer 1969): 443–53.

Breen, Judith Puchner. "DHL, World War I and the Battle between the Sexes: A Reading of 'The Blind Man' and 'Tickets, Please.' " *Women's Studies* 13 (1986): 63–74.

Cluysenaar, Anne. *Introduction to Literary Stylistics; A Discussion of Dominant Structures in Verse and Prose.* London: Batsford, 1976, pp. 92–99. (A stylistic analysis of "The Blind Man.")

Cushman, Keith. "Blind, Intertextual Love: 'The Blind Man' and Raymond Carver's 'Cathedral.' " In *DHL's Literary Inheritors.* Edited by Keith Cushman and Dennis Jackson. London: Macmillan; New York: St. Martin's Press, 1991, pp. 155–66.

Delany, Paul. "Who Was 'The Blind Man'?" *English Studies in Canada* 9 (March 1983): 92–99.

———. " 'We Shall Know Each Other Now': Message and Code in DHL's 'The Blind Man.' " *Contemporary Literature* 26 (1985): 26–39.

Engel, Monroe. "Knowing More Than One Imagines: Imagining More Than One Knows." *Agni* 31–32 (1990): 165–76. (Relates Raymond Carver's 'Cathedral' to 'The Blind Man.')

Fadiman, Regina. "The Poet as Choreographer: Lawrence's 'The Blind Man.' " *Journal of Narrative Technique* 2 (January 1972): 60–67.

Frakes, James R., and Isadore Traschen. *Short Fiction: A Critical Anthology.* 2d ed. Englewood Cliffs, N.J.: Prentice-Hall, 1969, pp. 163–67.

Levin, Gerald. " 'The Blind Man.' " In his *The Short Story: An Inductive Approach.* New York: Harcourt, Brace, and World, 1967, pp. 296–98.

Marks, W. S., III. "The Psychology of Regression in DHL's 'The Blind Man.' " *Literature and Psychology* 17 (Winter 1967): 177–92.

Ross, Michael L. "The Mythology of Friendship: DHL, Bertrand Russell, and 'The Blind Man.' " In *English Literature and British Philosophy: A Collection of Essays.* Edited by S. P. Rosenbaum. Chicago: University of Chicago Press, 1971, pp. 285–315.

Vowles, Richard B. "Lawrence's 'The Blind Man.' " *Explicator* 11 (December 1952): Item 14.

Warschausky, Sidney. " 'The Blind Man' and 'The Rocking-Horse Winner.' " In *Insight II: Analyses of British Literature.* Edited by John V. Hagopian and Martin Dolch. Frankfort: Hirschgraben-Verlag, 1964, pp. 221–33.

West, Ray B., Jr. "The Use of Point of View and Authority in 'The Blind Man.' " In his *Reading the Short Story.* New York: Crowell, 1968, pp. 105–17.

Wheeler, Richard P. "Intimacy and Irony in 'The Blind Man.' " *DHL Review* 9 (Summer 1976): 236–53.

See also Delavenay (1972): 435–37. Spilka (1955): 25–29, 151–53. Williams (1993): 31–36, 119–22.

"MONKEY NUTS"

WRITTEN

May 1919.

PUBLISHED

Sovereign (22 August 1922): 229–36.

WHO'S WHO AND SUMMARY

The story takes place just before the end of World War I. *Albert* and *Joe* are two soldiers on leave from the front, billeted in a country cottage to help with the harvest and other farmwork. Albert, forty years old and a corporal, is brash, breezy, and always ready with a humorous quip, while Joe, twenty-three and a private, is painfully shy and somewhat inarticulate. *Miss Stokes* is a self-confident young land-girl from a nearby farm. (Land-girls were women who contributed to the war effort by doing farmwork.) As sharp-witted and forward as Albert, she finds herself strongly drawn to Joe—toward whom she starts to make bold advances. She sends him a telegram suggesting a meeting (this is signed M. S., and when, later, Albert mischievously asks her what this stands for, she sarcastically replies "monkey nuts"—hence the title and the punch line at the end of the story); and when the three characters meet up on the way home after a visit to the circus, she sends Albert off with her punctured bicycle and confidently puts her arm around Joe's waist, insisting that he walk her home. After this, the young couple meet together regularly every evening. However, from the start, it is clear that Joe is not a willing partner in this arrangement, that, in fact, he feels confused and intimidated by Miss Stokes and resentful of her assertiveness. But his own radical lack of confidence makes him incapable of standing up for himself against her. Albert sees him becoming increasingly sulky and irritable and, discovering the cause, suggests that next time *he* meet with Miss Stokes in Joe's place. Joe agrees. Dismayed at Joe's lack of commitment to her, Miss Stokes rebuffs Albert in no uncertain manner. This leads, in the final scene, to a sort of psychological tug-of-war between Albert and Miss Stokes for the allegiance of Joe's independent spirit; and here Joe does finally seem to stand up for himself as he mockingly calls out, "Monkey nuts!" to the woman in response to her appeal to him.

SETTING

The setting here is clearly suggestive of Hermitage, five miles northeast of Newbury ("Belbury" in the story) in Berkshire, where Lawrence lived, at Chapel farm cottage, for much of the time between December 1917 and November 1919. While there, Lawrence became friendly with Cecily Lambert and her cousin, Violet Monk, who ran Grimsby farm near to Chapel farm cottage. They had already provided the inspiration for his short novel, *The Fox* (1918), and here Miss Stokes is probably based on Violet Monk.

"WINTRY PEACOCK"

WRITTEN

January 1919. Revisions and corrections, March 1920, July–August 1921.

PUBLISHED

Metropolitan (21 August 1921): 21–22, 48–49.
The New Decameron III. Oxford: Basil Blackwell, 1922, pp. 123–46.

WHO'S WHO AND SUMMARY

An unnamed *narrator* passing the Goytes' farm is asked by *Maggie Goyte* to translate a letter in French to her husband, *Alfred Goyte*. The latter, a lance corporal in the army, has been on active service in Europe; though now back in Britain following a wound to the leg, he has been in Scotland recently and is expected home on the day the story opens. As the letter is from a woman— a Belgian girl called *Elise*—Maggie Goyte strongly suspects that it is a love letter, but she cannot read French. The narrator quickly reads the letter to himself and discovers that not only is it a love letter but Elise is writing to inform Alfred of the birth of his child. The narrator tries to disguise this fact by suggesting that the baby is Elise's mother's, but Maggie shrewdly guesses the truth. She clearly has no illusions about her wayward husband and even reacts to the narrator's coded translation with laughter; but she expresses sympathy for the deceived Belgian girl. As they are talking, Maggie's pet peacock, *Joey*, makes an appearance, and there is a great show of affection between Maggie and the bird, who had come with her from her home when she married Alfred. The next day, the narrator awakes to find there has been a heavy snowfall. In the afternoon, he notices a movement in the valley and eventually finds that it is Maggie's peacock, Joey, who has apparently lost his way and become marooned in the snow. The narrator looks after the bird and next day returns it to the Goytes' farm. Alfred Goyte has since returned home (it is suggested that he was responsible for scaring the bird away), and the narrator is introduced to him and to the elder *Mr. and Mrs. Goyte,* Alfred's parents. On his way home, the narrator is overtaken by Alfred Goyte. He tells the narrator that Maggie claims to have burned his letter and asks to hear what was in it. The narrator explains both the true contents and what he told Alfred's wife. Alfred is thoroughly amused, and, after admitting to the narrator that he hates Joey and had, indeed, taken a shot at him the day before, the two men part laughing.

SETTING

''Tible'' identifies the setting as the north Derbyshire countryside around the hamlet of Ible and Middleton-by-Wirksworth, where Lawrence lived, at Mountain Cottage, between January 1918 and April 1919.

BIBLIOGRAPHY 31

Hall, James B., and Joseph Langland. *The Short Story.* New York: Macmillan, 1956, pp. 250–51.
Widmer, Kingsley. ''Birds of Passion and Birds of Marriage in DHL.'' *University of Kansas City Review* 25 (Fall 1958): 73–79.

"HADRIAN"/"YOU TOUCHED ME"

WRITTEN

June–July 1919. ''Hadrian'' was Lawrence's preferred final title and is used in the Cambridge edition of *England, My England.*

PUBLISHED

Land and Water no. 3025 (29 April 1920): 25–29.

WHO'S WHO AND SUMMARY

Ted Rockley, the head of an old pottery-manufacturing family, is dying of an alcohol-related kidney disease. *Matilda* and *Emmie Rockley* are the two of his four daughters who have not married and moved away. Matilda is two years older than her sister, physically more elegant and culturally more refined. Emmie has few accomplishments, we are told, and looks after the housekeeping. *Hadrian* is Ted Rockley's adoptive son, who left home for Canada when he was fifteen; Rockley, impatient of living in an all-female household, adopted Hadrian from a charity institution when the boy was six, Matilda sixteen, and Emmie fourteen. Hadrian comes back to Europe as a soldier during the war and returns to Pottery House after the armistice, now aged twenty-one. Despite a somewhat cold and reserved nature, Hadrian had a special rapport with Ted Rockley, and this is immediately revived on his return—shortly after his arrival, Rockley tells Matilda that, on his death, Hadrian should have his gold watch and chain and a hundred pounds. The Rockley girls always resented Hadrian's privileged status with their father and what they felt to be his sly and suspicious ways toward them; these feelings, too, resurface on his return, but now the women also suspect Hadrian of fortune hunting. One night, Matilda is restless with anxiety about her father, and she eventually goes to his bedroom to see if he is comfortable. She has forgotten, however, that her father has moved downstairs and that Hadrian now has his room; she speaks softly to the figure in the bed and then caresses his brow and head. When Hadrian speaks, she realizes her mistake and hurries from the room, shocked and as if stung by the touch of the young man. He, too, we are told, feels profoundly disturbed by the experience, as if the unwitting gesture of tenderness had awakened unknown realms of feeling and desire within him. Sometime later, he tells Rockley that he would like to marry Matilda, and the old man quickly comes to cherish the idea himself—so much so that he summons *Whittle,* his solicitor, and changes his will to make Matilda's inheritance of the family fortune conditional on her marrying Hadrian. Matilda is horrified at the suggestion that she might want to marry Hadrian, and both she and her sister are furiously indignant both at this last surge of overbearing willfulness from the father they have cared for all their lives and at what they see as the brazen fortune hunting of Hadrian. For his part, Hadrian is surprised at the suggestion that he wants Matilda simply for the inheritance, though he certainly wants that too and knows that he could not afford to marry her without it; in principle, he considers the two desires as separate—he wants Matilda *and* the money, but not *for* the money. Having rationalized his motives thus, he stubbornly persists in his proposal despite the sisters' various attempts to make him withdraw it. Finally, Matilda does agree to marry him, though her true motives are never explained, and the ending of the story remains highly ambiguous: has she finally responded to some repressed desire for Hadrian; has she bowed to the inevitable laws of patriarchal society; or has she acted simply to preserve the inheritance?

SETTING

The Pottery House of the story is based on a real house of that name in Lynn Croft, Eastwood, where, at number 97, Lawrence and his family lived between 1905 and 1911. ''Rawsley'' therefore re-creates Eastwood; and the Rockley family are modeled on the Mellor family who lived in the Pottery House—

Maud and Mabel Mellor, in particular, provided Lawrence with details for his portraits of Matilda and Emmie Rockley in the story.

BIBLIOGRAPHY 32

See Draper (1964): 124. Hough (1956): 173–74. Leavis (1955): 252–56. Lerner (1967): 206–8. Ruderman (1984): 81–83.

"SAMSON AND DELILAH"

WRITTEN

November 1916, as "The Prodigal Husband." Lawrence probably corrected proofs for the *English Review* publication in January or February 1917.

PUBLISHED

English Review 24 (March 1917): 209–24.
Lantern (June 1917).

WHO'S WHO AND SUMMARY

Mrs. Nankervis is the landlady of an inn, "The Tinners Rest," in Cornwall, where she lives alone with her daughter of sixteen, *Maryann*. There is a group of *soldiers* staying at the inn (the story takes place in the first year of World War I): a sergeant, a corporal, and two privates. A stranger arrives and settles down in the bar for the evening. This, it emerges, is *Willie Nankervis*, Mrs. Nankervis's errant husband, who has returned to reclaim the wife he abandoned after sixteen years' mining in America (Butte City is mentioned and may refer to the mining town north of Sacramento). Initially, she refuses to believe that Willie is her husband or, indeed, to accept that he has any rights with her even if he is. When he insists on staying for the night, she has him tied up and bundled outside by the soldiers (like Samson in the biblical story when he is betrayed by Delilah and delivered up to the Philistines: see Judges xvi). However, after he has worked himself free, he makes his way back to the inn and, to his surprise, finds the kitchen door open and his wife apparently waiting for him. The couple talk, and, despite Mrs. Nankervis's surface anger over his past behavior, Willie's strong physical presence insinuates itself back into her deeper feelings, and it is clear at the end that he will be allowed to stay after all.

SETTING

The story is set in southwest Cornwall, and the actual place-names of Penzance and St. Just-in-Penwith are used. "The Tinners Rest" is based on "The Tinners

Arms'' at Zennor, where Lawrence and Frieda stayed in early 1916 before moving into their cottage at Tregerthen, where they lived from March 1916 to October 1917.

BIBLIOGRAPHY 33

See Hyde (1992): 65–68. Tedlock (1963): 108–9. Widmer (1962): 148–49.

"THE PRIMROSE PATH"

WRITTEN

By the end of July 1913. First published in *England, My England* (1922).

WHO'S WHO AND SUMMARY

Daniel Sutton is thirty-five and has recently returned from Australia. He has set up a small taxi business in a Midlands town. *Daniel Berry* is his nephew, who, arriving at the railway station of the town, happens to recognize his uncle at the taxi rank. Berry had been a child the last time they met, and his uncle hardly recognizes him. Sutton eventually takes his nephew to his intended destination and afterward invites him home for dinner. As they converse through all this, Daniel Sutton's life story gradually emerges—this, particularly his relationships with women, forms the core of the story. He had always been considered the black sheep of the family, living idly—mainly for his dogs and pigeons—until he was eighteen, when he married and found a job with a sporting newspaper. He had become something of a bully, and the marriage was not a success; after seven years he had impetuously run away to Australia with another woman. This relationship did not last the sea voyage, it seems, and he claims that his lover tried to poison him so that she could go off with another man she had met on the ship. Now, he tells Berry, he is living with a young girl of twenty-one, *Elaine Greenwell,* and *Mrs. Greenwell,* her mother. On the way to his home, they stop for a drink at "The Railway Arms," where Berry's *Aunt Maud,* Sutton's estranged wife, lives with the widower publican, *George.* She is dying of consumption, and, when Sutton goes upstairs to see her, she asks him to promise, after her death, to look after their daughter, *Winnie.* He seems disturbed at this suggestion, but he gives an assurance that he will do so. Sutton seems uneasy for the rest of the evening, and he speaks roughly to Elaine when they return to his home. Witnessing his uncle's uncouth manner, here, Berry soon concludes that this arrangement, too, will not long survive Sutton's shiftless and bullying ways. (For the source of the title, ''the primrose path of dalliance'' trod by the ''puff'd and reckless libertine,'' see *Hamlet* I.iii.)

SETTING

The setting is a large town in the Midlands, and, although not mentioned by name, local details, such as the reference to Victoria Station, identify it as Nottingham. The main features of Daniel Sutton's story are closely based on the experiences of Lawrence's maternal uncle, Herbert Beardsall (b. 1871), and Daniel Berry would therefore seem to be a fictionalized version of Lawrence himself.

"THE HORSE-DEALER'S DAUGHTER"

WRITTEN

November–January 1917, as "The Miracle." Revised as "The Horse-Dealer's Daughter" in October 1921.

PUBLISHED

English Review 34 (April 1922): 308–25.

WHO'S WHO AND SUMMARY

The Pervins' horse-dealing business is in financial ruin, and the family must vacate their large house, Oldmeadow, within the next few days. Although the business had at one time prospered, it had been failing of late, and, when the head of the family, *Joe Pervin,* died, he left his three ineffectual sons, *Joe, Fred Henry,* and *Malcolm,* and his twenty-seven-year-old daughter, *Mabel,* in heavy debt. Hence the present situation. Joe, the eldest son at thirty-three, is to marry the steward of a neighboring estate and is hopeful of a job there. It is not clear what the other two sons will do, but they are all leaving later that day. Mabel has spent all of her grown life keeping the house for her father and brothers, though she has never really shared in their lives. While there was plenty of money in the household, she was able to maintain a certain pride and independence in her role, and her inner reserve and confidence had protected her from the coarseness of the immediate life around her. The period of poverty she has recently lived through, however, has been a severe humiliation to her, and, now that the family home is finally breaking up, she feels she has come to the end of her life. Her mother had died when Mabel was fourteen, and she has lived for her memory ever since; now she feels close to a final reunion. In the afternoon, she goes to the graveyard to tend her mother's grave—while there, *Jack Fergusson,* the local doctor who lives beside the church, passes by and greets her briefly. He had earlier called at Oldmeadow to see Fred Henry, his good friend, and he had shown a keen interest in Mabel; now, the sight of her face in the graveyard seems like a vision to him, and he feels suddenly relieved of all the professional cares of the day. Later that afternoon, just as the light is failing, he is returning on foot from his round of visits and from a distance sees Mabel going down to the deep pond below Oldmeadow. He sees her wade straight into the water and move out into the middle of the pond and disappear in the dusk. He races down to the pond, and, though he cannot swim, he plunges into the icy waters after her. Following a desperate struggle with the treacherous clay on the bottom of the pond, during which he almost drowns himself, he manages to pull Mabel to safety. He administers first aid and then carries her back to the house, where he strips and dries her and wraps her in blankets. When she comes to and discovers what has happened, she suddenly insists that Fergusson loves her and she begins frantically kissing and caressing him. At first, he recoils from this instinctive show of passion, but gradually it overwhelms him and draws from the depths of his being an equivalent response; his professional reserve and his surface self seem to crumble as he kisses her passionately and declares his love for her—they will marry immediately, he says at the end of the story. From the clutches of death, both characters thus experience a resurrection of their hidden selves.

SETTING

Although no name is mentioned, topographical and circumstantial details—such as the references to colliers and ironworkers—identify the setting as being a recreation of Lawrence's hometown, Eastwood. The Pervins' house, "Oldmeadow," is based on Hill Top House in Eastwood, and the Pervins themselves seem to be modeled on the family of Lawrence's friend Duncan Meakin, whose father, John Thomas, had been a horse dealer (and farmer). This family is also the model for the Mayhews in *The White Peacock,* where the house is called "The Hollies."

BIBLIOGRAPHY 34

Brooks, Cleanth, John Purser, and Robert P. Warren, eds. *An Approach to Literature.* 3d ed. New York: Appleton-Century-Crofts, 1952, pp. 186–88.

Douglas, Kenneth. "Masterpieces of Symbolism and the Modern School." In *World Masterpieces II.* Edited by Maynard Mack et al. New York: Norton, 1956, p. 2118.

Faustino, Daniel. "Psychic Rebirth and Christian Imagery in DHL's 'The Horse Dealer's Daughter.' " *Journal of Evolutionary Psychology* 9 (1989): 105–8.

Gullason, Thomas A. "Revelation and Evolution: A Neglected Dimension of the Short Story." *Studies in Short Fiction* 10 (Fall 1973): 347–56 (348–52).

Junkins, Donald. "DHL's 'The Horse Dealer's Daughter.' " *Studies in Short Fiction* 6 (Winter 1969): 210–13.

McCabe, Thomas H. "Rhythm as Form in Lawrence: 'The Horse Dealer's Daughter.' " *PMLA* 87 (January 1972): 64–68.

Meyers, Jeffrey. "DHL and Tradition: 'The Horse Dealer's Daughter.' " *Studies in Short Fiction* 26 (1989): 346–51.

O'Faolain, Sean, ed. *Short Stories: A Study of Pleasure.* Boston: Little, Brown, 1961, pp. 461–64.

Phillips, Steven R. "The Double Pattern of DHL's 'The Horse Dealer's Daughter.' " *Studies in Short Fiction* 10 (Winter 1973): 94–97.

———. "The Monomyth and Literary Criticism." *College Literature* 2 (Winter 1975): 1–16 (7–11).

Rehder, Jessie. *The Story at Work.* New York: Odyssey Press, 1963, pp. 240–41.

Ryals, Clyde de L. "DHL's 'The Horse Dealer's Daughter': An Interpretation." *Literature and Psychology* 12 (Spring 1962): 39–43.

San Juan, E., Jr. "Textual Production in DHL's 'The Horse Dealer's Daughter.' " *DLSU Graduate Journal* 12 (1987): 223–30.

Schneider, Raymond. "The Visible Metaphor." *Communications Education* 25 (1976): 121–26.

Schorer, Mark, ed. *The Story: A Critical Anthology.* New York: Prentice-Hall, 1950, pp. 326–29.

Stewart, Jack F. "Eros and Thanatos in Lawrence's 'The Horse Dealer's Daughter.' " *Studies in the Humanities* 12 (1985): 11–19.

See also Draper (1964): 124–25. Leavis (1955): 247–52.

"FANNY AND ANNIE"/"THE LAST STRAW"

WRITTEN

May 1919. "The Last Straw" was Lawrence's preferred final title for the story and is used in the Cambridge edition of *England, My England.* Proofs for the periodical publication were corrected in October 1921.

PUBLISHED

Hutchinson's Story Magazine (21 November 1921): 461–69.

WHO'S WHO AND SUMMARY

Fanny is a lady's maid returning from service in Gloucester to her ugly industrial hometown in order to marry *Harry Goodall,* a foundry worker. She is thirty, beautiful, sensitive, and distinctly superior. However, she has been jilted by her first choice of husband, a cosmopolitan, intellectual, and ambitious cousin, *Luther,* and she has come back to her "doom," her apparently lackluster first love, who seems to have waited for her faithfully for some twelve years. He is thirty-two and wholly lacking in ambition, but he is handsome and carefree and, beneath his common-seeming surface, actually quite sensitive. He still sings in the choir of the Congregational Chapel in which Fanny had first met him, and, though his singing is marred by his comical pronunciation (he has particular difficulty with his aitches—'''eaven'' and ''hangels''), he has a fine tenor voice. Fanny stays with her *Aunt Lizzie,* who runs a sweetshop and who has serious reservations about her niece's future prospects with Harry—partly because she had similarly married ''beneath her'' and had regretted it. Fanny visits Harry's family home, where his down-to-earth and outspoken mother, *Mrs. Goodall,* makes it clear to her that she thinks her son is a fool for having Fanny back after all these years. Nevertheless, Mrs. Goodall is secretly satisfied that Fanny *has* come back to her son, especially as she knows that Fanny has just inherited £200 from her Aunt Kate. *Jinny Goodall,* Harry's sharp-tongued married sister, lives nearby and appears here and later in the story partly to emphasize the clannishness of the Goodalls. At the Harvest Festival service at Morley Chapel, where Harry sings in the choir, the service is dramatically interrupted by a *Mrs. Nixon,* who angrily denounces Harry to the congregation as an irresponsible ''scamp''—her coded way, as it turns out, of accusing him of fathering the child of her youngest daughter, *Annie.* When Fanny and *Rev. Enderby* confront Harry after the service, he argues that the child is no more likely to be his than some other man's—a dubious defense against the specific accusation and one that nevertheless acknowledges his affair with the said Annie Nixon. At first it seems as if Fanny may break off the engagement after all, but she returns home with Harry, and, after some general Goodall gossip about the notorious reputation of Mrs. Nixon herself, Fanny declares her hand and makes clear her intention to stand by Harry, his stock seemingly having risen with her for *not* having been entirely unadventurous in the years of her absence.

SETTING

This story provides us with yet another fictional re-creation of Eastwood. This is shown, among other things, by the reference to Princes Street, which is the name of a street adjoining the street in Eastwood where Lawrence was born (Victoria Street). The iron foundry where Harry works may be based on Bennerley Ironworks, just south of Eastwood, though Lawrence records an experience of some ironworks on Butterley reservoir near Ripley in a letter of November 1918, a few months before writing the story (*Letters* III: 302). ''Morley Chapel'' in the story seems to be based on the Congregational Chapel at Moorgreen, a mile or so east of Eastwood.

BIBLIOGRAPHY 35

Leavis, F. R. ''Lawrence and Class.'' *Sewanee Review* 62 (1954): 535–62 (552–56). (Reprinted in Leavis [1955]: 95–100.)
Modiano, Marko. '' 'Fanny and Annie' and the War.'' *Durham University Journal* 83 (1991): 69–74.

Secor, Robert. "Language and Movement in 'Fanny and Annie.'" *Studies in Short Fiction* 6 (Summer 1969): 395–400.

"THE MORTAL COIL"

WRITTEN

October–November 1913. Rewritten October 1916. Revised November 1916.

PUBLISHED

Seven Arts 2 (July 1917): 280–305.

WHO'S WHO AND SUMMARY

Herr Baron von Friedeburg is a young army officer and the lover of *Marta Hohenest;* he is also a gambler and desperately worried about losing his commission on account of his gambling debts. An outing as a foursome has been arranged with *Teresa* and *Karl Podewils,* the friends, respectively, of Marta and Friedeburg, but Friedeburg arrives late from his gambling, and the other couple have gone on alone. Marta is angry with him for this but equally angry that he should be so concerned about his life and reputation in the army; she senses clearly and accurately that his career and social position mean more to him than his individuality and his relationship with her—indeed, that his life depends for its meaning on the rigid structure provided by the army and its associated codes of conduct. They argue but finally make up and spend the night together. Friedeburg leaves early the next morning to go on military exercises out of town. When he has gone, Teresa comes to Marta's room, and, after stoking up the stove, she climbs into Marta's bed, and they sleep. When Friedeburg returns to his lodgings later that afternoon, he finds the police there: Marta and Teresa, it emerges, have been killed by asphyxiation caused by fumes from the stove.

SETTING

This story is based on a real-life incident involving Frieda Lawrence's father, Baron Friedrich von Richthofen (1845–1915), and would seem to be set somewhere in Germany, but no precise setting is indicated.

BIBLIOGRAPHY 36

Peer, Willie van. "Toward a Pragmatic Theory of Connexity: An Analysis of the Use of the Conjunction 'and' from a Functional Perspective." In *Text Connexity, Text*

Coherence: Aspects, Methods, Results. Edited by Emel Sozer. Hamburg: Buske, 1985, pp. 363–80.

"THE THIMBLE"

WRITTEN

October 1915.

PUBLISHED

Seven Arts 1 (March 1917): 435–48.

WHO'S WHO AND SUMMARY

Mrs. Hepburn, a confident, refined, beautiful woman of twenty-seven, is await-ing the return of her soldier husband. He has been at the front in France for the past ten months since his departure immediately after their honeymoon, and he has received a wound to his face that has disfigured him. Mrs. Hepburn, too, has been through a physical trauma in the shape of pneumonia. The experience has given her a new perspective on her past life. In particular, during her re-cuperation in Scotland, she had thought very deeply about her marriage and had come to realize just how superficially she knows her husband. As she prepares herself for his return in her Mayfair flat, a sort of double vision is presented to us: on the surface, she is complacent about—even bored by—her own conven-tional good looks and about her ability to create exactly the external impression expected of a woman in her position; she is also untroubled about the prospect of meeting her husband in his "known," familiar guise. However, beneath her external calm, she has now, following her illness, become aware of a vaguely realized inner self that is, indeed, nervous and apprehensive about how it will react to the "unknown" other of her husband (and, of course, he will be phys-ically unfamiliar now, too). As she waits on a sofa in the drawing room, she abstractedly explores the fissure between the sofa arm and the cushion and eventually discovers an object that turns out to be a thimble of gold set with small jewels. It is engraved with an earl's monogram, two initials, "Z. Z.," and the date "15 Oct. 1801." Imagining a romantic past for the old thimble, Mrs. Hepburn's inner self relaxes somewhat, and just then her husband arrives. The thimble provides an initial topic of conversation as the couple awkwardly greet one another, and it then remains a point of surface contact between them as the narrative explores their complex subconscious responses. When they discuss *Mr. Hepburn's* wounding, it emerges that his trauma has led to a self-revelation similar to that of his wife: he too has become aware both of an undiscovered self and of his wife's true strangeness to him, of her essential otherness. The couple acknowledge the need for a rebirth of their love on a deeper plane than before, and they commit themselves to a ''resurrected'' life together; the story ends with Mr. Hepburn throwing the now-redundant thimble out the window.

SETTING

Mayfair, London, on the east side of Hyde Park. (The Hepburns would appear to be fictional re-creations of Lady Cynthia Asquith [1887–1960] and her husband, Herbert Asquith [1881–1947].)

''ADOLF''

WRITTEN

March 1919.

PUBLISHED

Dial 69 (September 1920): 269–76.
The New Keepsake for the Year 1921. Edited by X. M. Boulestin. London and
      Paris: Chelsea Book Club, December 1921, pp. 19–33.

WHO'S WHO AND SUMMARY

''Adolf'' is a lightly fictionalized autobiographical sketch based on Lawrence's childhood memories of rearing an orphaned wild baby rabbit brought home one morning by his miner *father*. The story describes how the *children* of the family delight in the creature and ignore their *mother*'s hardheaded warnings about becoming too attached to something that may well not survive. With the care of the children and a free run of the house, *Adolf* not only survives but thrives and begins to take mischievous liberties—especially with the contents of the tea table, much to the annoyance of the mother. Eventually, the rabbit outgrows its welcome (among other things, bringing down some lace curtains with their rail) and, showing signs of a yearning for the wild, is taken back to the woods by the father. The story finishes with the narrator's musings on the wild insolence of rabbits and on the effrontery of their white tails.

SETTING

As the story is autobiographical, it is clearly set in Eastwood, though the name is not mentioned.

BIBLIOGRAPHY 37

Marks, W. S. "DHL and His Rabbit Adolf: Three Symbolic Permutations." *Criticism*
    10 (1968): 200–216.

"REX"

WRITTEN

March 1919. Proofs corrected for *Dial,* December 1920.

PUBLISHED

Dial 70 (February 1921): 169–76.
Stories from the Dial. New York: Dial Press; London: Jonathan Cape, 1924, pp.
    37–52.

WHO'S WHO AND SUMMARY

As with "Adolf," this is an autobiographical sketch based on Lawrence's childhood memories. This time the main subject is a boisterous fox terrier puppy
given to the narrator's family for rearing as a potential show dog by the narrator's blustering *uncle,* the landlord of "The Good Omen" public house. Doted
on by the *children* of the family—and hence difficult to be disciplined properly
by the adults—*Rex,* the puppy in question, becomes something of a tearaway
both indoors and out; he and the *mother*—who does not really hold with having
animals in the house—are on permanent war alert with one another (and he
seems to win most of the battles), and out of the house he attacks chickens,
ducks, and sheep and comes close to terrorizing the people of the neighborhood,
too. However, what prevents him from being truly a menace to the mother and
father and their neighbors, what makes him ultimately obedient, is the unconditional love he bears for the children, bred by their unconditional love for him.
From the point of view of the uncle, when he comes to reclaim the dog at the
end of the story, this is precisely what has ruined him as a "real" dog: the
children have spoiled him and made him "softer than grease." As the angry
uncle leaves with Rex, the pathos of the dog's desperate protests is matched
only by the black tears and wounded hearts of the forlorn children standing
helplessly in the street watching their beloved pet disappear. After a period of
brutal treatment by the uncle, we then hear, Rex's temper becomes vicious, and
he has to be put down.

SETTING

As in "Adolf," the autobiographical nature of the story identifies its setting as
Eastwood. The public house that features in the story, "The Good Omen," is

modeled on ''The Lord Belper'' in Sneinton, Nottingham, and the uncle is based on Lawrence's maternal uncle, Herbert Beardsall (b. 1871), who kept this pub at the period of the story (and who is the model, also, for Daniel Sutton in ''The Primrose Path'').

27   The Fox

WRITTEN

November 1918–September 1920; November 1921–February 1923. There were
two different versions of this short novel, and each was published. The first was
written between November and December 1918, with revisions and corrections
in July 1919 and (proofs) September 1920. The second version, with a new
ending, was written in November 1921, with revisions and corrections in November–December 1921 and (proofs for collected version) February 1923. (For
full details of the complex history of the text's composition and transmission,
see Mehl [1992] and Ruderman [1980] in the bibliography to this chapter.)

PUBLISHED

1. a. First version: *Hutchinson's Story Magazine* 3 (8 October 1920): 477–90.
   b. Second version: published first in four installments of the *Dial*—72 (May
      1922): 471–92; 72 (June 1922): 569–87; 73 (July 1922): 75–87; 73 (Au-
      gust 1922): 184–98—and then in book form: *The Ladybird, The Fox, The
      Captain's Doll*. London: Secker, March 1923; *The Captain's Doll: Three
      Novelettes*. New York: Seltzer, April 1923.
2. *The Fox, The Captain's Doll, The Ladybird*. Edited by Dieter Mehl. Cambridge: Cambridge University Press, 1992.

WHO'S WHO AND SUMMARY

Jill Banford runs Bailey farm with her close friend and partner, *Ellen (Nellie) March.* (*Mr. Banford,* Jill's father, is a prosperous tradesman in Islington, and he has provided the capital for his daughter's farm.) The two women are both around thirty years of age; Banford is nervous and delicate, while March is more robust, with practical skills such as carpentry and joinery to give her the sense of being "the man about the place." A fox has been preying on the chickens at the farm, and one evening, as March keeps guard, the fox appears at her feet. It looks knowingly at her, and she feels spellbound, as if it had penetrated deeply into her being and had established some power over her. Over the next few months, though she does not see the fox or think of it consciously, it dominates her unconscious mind, we are told, "like a spell." Then one evening, *Henry Grenfel* appears at the farm. He is a young soldier of about twenty returning from the war (it is late 1918, and the war has just ended). He has some free time before having to report at a military camp on Salisbury Plain. Born and bred in Cornwall, he had come to live with his grandfather, the now-deceased previous owner of Bailey farm, when he was twelve, but he had run away to Canada at fifteen. He has now come back to visit his grandfather, apparently unaware of the latter's death. Though initially wary of him, Banford is soon at her ease with him and invites him to stay for something to eat; later, he is also allowed to lodge at the farm. Almost as soon as she sees him, March identifies Henry with the fox, and she feels secure and peaceful in his presence just as she did earlier with the fox. As Henry settles in at the farm, he feels himself strongly drawn to March, and he soon asks her to marry him. She is at first incredulous and suspicious of his motives, and she avoids committing herself fully, though inwardly she feels herself slowly submitting to his influence. When Banford hears of the proposal, she opposes it strongly and tries to persuade March to reject Henry—and her attitude toward him becomes sharply antagonistic. Gradually, unconsciously influenced by dreams involving the figure of the fox as well as by Henry's shooting of the real creature, March acknowledges her desire for Henry and agrees to marry him. However, when he goes away to camp, she comes under the influence of Banford again and changes her mind. When Henry receives a letter from her to this effect, he immediately requests and is granted leave from his superior, *Captain Berryman,* and he returns to the farm. He finds the women, along with Banford's father, struggling to fell a tree. He offers to finish the job, and, as he does so, the tree falls on Banford and kills her. Despite warning her to move away before he felled the tree, Henry appears to have deliberately directed the tree at Banford. March and Henry marry and make plans to leave for Canada as soon as it is practicable. But an unresolved tension remains in their relationship, and the story ends on an ambiguous note: March feels strangely drained of life, almost deathly, but she refuses to give up entirely the struggle for independence and self-responsibility that was represented by her partnership with Banford; on the other hand, Henry will not feel complete and fulfilled until she surrenders her independent spirit and commits herself to him absolutely.

SETTING

Bailey farm is modeled on Grimsby farm, run by Lawrence's friends, Cecily Lambert and her cousin Violet Monk, and situated near to Chapel Farm Cottage, Hermitage, near to Newbury in Berkshire, where Lawrence lived for much of the period from December 1917 to November 1919. (Banford and March are, in part, fictional re-creations of Cecily Lambert and Violet Monk; Henry was possibly suggested to Lawrence by Nip Lambert, Cecily's brother; see the bibliography under Ruderman [1984]: 60.) Salisbury Plain, where Henry's camp is situated, is about fifty miles west of Hermitage. "Blewbury," the market town six miles from the farm, would correspond to Newbury, and the White Horse referred to just after the start of the story (p. 9) is the chalk horse at Uffington Hill near Wantage, twelve miles northwest of Hermitage. (The setting for this story is similar to that of "Monkey Nuts.")

BIBLIOGRAPHY 38

Bergler, Edmund. "DHL's *The Fox* and the Psychoanalytic Theory on Lesbianism." *Journal of Nervous and Mental Disease* 126 (May 1958): 488–91. (Reprinted in Moore [1959]: 49–55.)

Boren, James L. "Commitment and Futility in *The Fox*." *University Review* (Kansas City) 31 (June 1965): 301–4.

Brayfield, Peg. "Lawrence's 'Male and Female Principles' and the Symbolism of *The Fox*." *Mosaic* 4, no. 3 (1971): 41–65.

Brown, Christopher. "The Eyes Have It: Vision in *The Fox*." *Wascana Review* 15, no. 2 (1980): 61–68.

Core, Deborah. " 'The Closed Door': Love between Women in the Works of DHL." *DHL Review* 11 (Summer 1978): 114–31.

Daleski, H. M. "Aphrodite of the Foam and *The Ladybird* Tales." In *DHL: A Critical Study of the Major Novels and Other Writings*. Edited by Andor Gomme. Sussex: Harvester Press; New York: Barnes and Noble, 1978, pp. 142–58. (Reprinted in his *Unities: Studies in the English Novel*. Athens: University of Georgia Press, 1985, 211–24.)

Davis, Patricia C. "Chicken Queen's Delight: DHL's *The Fox*." *Modern Fiction Studies* 19 (Winter 1973–74): 565–71. (On homoerotic aspects of Henry Grenfel.)

Devlin, Albert J. "The 'Strange and Fiery' Course of *The Fox*: DHL's Aesthetic of Composition and Revision." In *The Spirit of DHL: Centenary Studies*. Edited by Gāmini Salgādo and G. K. Das. London: Macmillan, 1988, pp. 75–91.

Doherty, Gerald. "The Third Encounter: Paradigms of Courtship in DHL's Shorter Fiction." *DHL Review* 17 (1984): 135–51.

Draper, R. P. "The Defeat of Feminism: DHL's *The Fox* and "The Woman Who Rode Away." *Studies in Short Fiction* 3 (1966): 186–98.

Ellis, David. "Introduction." *The Fox, The Captain's Doll, The Ladybird* by DHL. Edited by Dieter Mehl. Harmondsworth: Penguin, 1994, pp. xiii–xxx.

Faderman, Lillian. "Lesbian Magazine Fiction in the Early Twentieth Century." *Journal of Popular Culture* 11 (1978): 800–817. (Includes discussion of *The Fox.*)

Finney, Brian. "The Hitherto Unknown Publication of Some DHL Short Stories." *Notes and Queries* 19 (February 1972): 55–56.

Fulmer, Bryan O. "The Significance of the Death of the Fox in DHL's *The Fox.*" *Studies in Short Fiction* 5 (Spring 1968): 275–82.

Gardner, John, and Lewis Dunlap, eds. *The Forms of Fiction.* New York: Random House, 1962, pp. 521–24.

Gilbert, Sandra M. "Costumes of the Mind: Transvestism as Metaphor in Modern Literature." *Critical Inquiry* 7 (1980): 391–417. (Includes discussion of *The Fox.* Reprinted in *Writing and Sexual Difference.* Edited by Elizabeth Abel. Hemel Hempstead: Harvester, 1982.)

Good, Jan. "Toward a Resolution of Gender Identity Confusion: The Relationship of Henry and March in *The Fox.*" *DHL Review* 18 (1985–86): 217–27.

Granofsky, Ronald. "A Second Caveat: DHL's *The Fox.*" *English Studies in Canada* 15, no. 1 (1988): 49–63.

Gregor, Ian. "*The Fox:* A Caveat." *Essays in Criticism* 9 (January 1959): 10–21. (See also reply by H. Coombes, *Essays in Criticism* 9 [October 1959]: 451–53.)

Greiff, Louis K. "Bittersweet Dreaming in Lawrence's 'The Fox': A Freudian Perspective." *Studies in Short Fiction* 20 (1983): 7–16.

Gurko, Leo. "DHL's Greatest Collection of Short Stories: What Holds It Together." *Modern Fiction Studies* 18 (Summer 1972): 173–82.

Jones, Lawrence. "Physiognomy and the Sensual Will in *The Ladybird* and *The Fox.*" *DHL Review* 13 (1980): 1–29.

Levin, Gerald. "The Symbolism of Lawrence's *The Fox.*" *CLA Journal* 11 (December 1967): 135–44.

Mackenzie, Kenneth. *The Fox.* Milton Keynes: Open University, 1973.

Matterson, Stephen. "Another Source for Henry? DHL's *The Fox.*" *ANQ: A Quarterly Journal of Short Articles, Notes and Reviews* 5 (January 1992): 23–25.

Mehl, Dieter. "Introduction." *The Fox, The Captain's Doll, The Ladybird* by DHL. Edited by Dieter Mehl. Cambridge: Cambridge University Press, 1992, pp. xvii–xlvii.

Miller, Hillis. "DHL: The Fox and the Perspective Glass." *Harvard Advocate* 136 (December 1952): 14–16, 26–28.

Neider, Charles. *Short Novels of the Masters.* New York: Rinehart, 1948, pp. 40–44.

Nelson, Jane A. "The Familial Isotopy in *The Fox.*" In *The Challenge of DHL.* Edited by Michael Squires and Keith Cushman. Madison: University of Wisconsin Press, 1990, pp. 129–42.

Osborn, Marijane. "Complexities of Gender and Genre in Lawrence's *The Fox.*" *Essays in Literature* 19 (Spring 1992): 84–97.

Renner, Stanley. "Sexuality and the Unconscious: Psychosexual Drama and Conflict in *The Fox.*" *DHL Review* 21 (1989): 245–73.

Ross, Michael L. "Ladies and Foxes: DHL, David Garnett, and the Female of the Species." *DHL Review* 18 (1985–86): 229–38.

Rossi, Patrizio. "Lawrence's Two Foxes: A Comparison of the Texts." *Essays in Criticism* 22 (July 1972): 265–78.

Ruderman, Judith G. "*The Fox* and the 'Devouring Mother.' " *DHL Review* 10 (Fall 1977): 251–69.

———. "Lawrence's *The Fox* and Verga's 'The She-Wolf': Variations on the Theme of the 'Devouring Mother.' " *Modern Language Notes* 94 (1979): 153–65.

———. "Prototypes for Lawrence's *The Fox.*" *Journal of Modern Literature* 8 (1980a): 77–98.

———. "Tracking Lawrence's *Fox:* An Account of Its Composition, Evolution, and Publication." *Studies in Bibliography* 33 (1980b): 206–21.

———. "The New Adam and Eve in Lawrence's *The Fox* and Other Works." *Southern Humanities Review* 17 (1983): 225–36.

Shields, E. F. "Broken Vision in Lawrence's *The Fox.*" *Studies in Short Fiction* 9 (Fall 1972): 353–63.

Singh, A. K. "War and Lawrence: A Study of His Short Story *The Fox.*" In *Essays on DHL.* Edited by T. R. Sharma. Meerut, India: Shalabh Book House, 1987, pp. 134–38.

Sinzelle, Claude. "Skinning the Fox: A Masochist's Delight." In *DHL in the Modern World.* Edited by Peter Preston and Peter Hoare. London: Macmillan, 1989, pp. 161–79.

Springer, Mary Doyle. *Forms of the Modern Novella.* Chicago and London: University of Chicago Press, 1976, 30–32.

Stewart, Jack F. "Totem and Symbol in *The Fox* and *St. Mawr.*" *Studies in the Humanities* 16 (December 1989): 84–98.

Volkenfeld, Suzanne. " 'The Sleeping Beauty' Retold: DHL's *The Fox.*" *Studies in Short Fiction* 14 (Fall 1977): 345–53.

Whelan, P. T. "The Hunting Metaphor in *The Fox* and Other Works." *DHL Review* 21 (1989): 275–90.

See also Daleski (1965): 151–56. Draper (1964): 125–26. Draper (1970): 191–96. Goodheart (1963): 51–56. Holderness (1982): 166–74. Hough (1956): 176–77. Inniss (1971): 159–63. Leavis (1955): 256–65. Miles (1969): 39–41. Moynahan (1963): 196–209. Pritchard (1971): 140–41. Ruderman (1984): 48–70, passim. Sagar (1966): 116–17. Siegel (1991): passim. Simpson (1982): 70–73. Slade (1970): 108–10. Trebisz (1992): 54–58.

28   *The Captain's Doll*

WRITTEN

October–November 1921. Revisions and corrections, December 1921; February 1923. The novella was loosely based on the short story "The Mortal Coil," probably written in October 1913 and rewritten in October 1916 (published in *Seven Arts* [July 1917]).

PUBLISHED

1. *The Ladybird, The Fox, The Captain's Doll.* London: Secker, March 1923; *The Captain's Doll: Three Novelettes.* New York: Seltzer, April 1923.
2. *The Fox, The Captain's Doll, The Ladybird.* Edited by Dieter Mehl. Cambridge: Cambridge University Press, 1992.

WHO'S WHO AND SUMMARY

This story explores the vagaries and vacillations in the love affair between *Captain Alexander Hepburn,* a Scottish soldier in occupied Germany, and *Hannele* (Countess Johanna zu Rassentlow), an aristocratic refugee who now earns a living, with her friend, *Mitchka* (Baroness Annamaria von Prielau-Carolath), making and selling dolls and other small craft objects. Captain Hepburn's wife of seventeen years, *Evangeline,* has heard rumors of his affair, and she arrives unexpectedly from England to reclaim possession of her husband. Hannele's current "possession" of Alec is symbolized by the mannikin doll she has made of him, which, everyone agrees, is a perfect likeness. Evangeline Hepburn sees the doll when, without revealing her identity, she visits Hannele's studio to size up her opposition. She is taken aback by the intimate likeness of the doll and immediately recognizes just how far her husband's affair has gone. Later, when her identity is known to Hannele, she offers to buy the doll of her husband, while, at the same time, implicitly threatening to have Hannele and Mitchka removed by the authorities as undesirables if they should not cooperate. However, before she can carry out her threat, an accident, or what seems to be an accident, occurs: she falls out of her hotel window and is killed. Alec now withdraws from the relationship with Hannele and determines to avoid all further emotional contact for the time being. He returns to England, makes arrangements for his two children, and obtains his discharge from the army. The following year, however, he comes in search of Hannele again. In Munich, where he has last heard of her, he sees the mannikin of himself in a shop window and now feels disgusted and angered by it. This is partly because Hannele has deemed to sell it and partly because it now looks "like a deliberate satire" on him; but, as we later learn more clearly, he resents it also because it represents a woman's preconceived and finished notion of him as an object that can be wholly possessed. Insult is added to injury when he finds that the doll has been sold again and, later, that it has been used for a surreal still-life painting in which it appears with two sunflowers and a poached egg on toast! He buys the still life and leaves for Kaprun in the Austrian Tyrol, where, he has discovered, Hannele is now living, engaged to *Herr Regierungsrat von Poldi* (a middle-aged local government official). Alec at last meets up with his ex-lover once more, and they arrange an excursion to the glacier above Kaprun. In this final, long section of the novel, the two engage in a verbal duel that turns, in particular, on their opposing visions of love and marriage. Alec now feels that love is a mistake— that it leads people to make "dolls" of one another—and that marriage should be based on honor and obedience (and "the proper physical feelings"). Hannele dismisses this as a self-serving rationale for bullying and continues to argue for love. He eventually proposes to her but will marry her only if she will pledge to honor and obey him (like Boccaccio's "patient Griseldis"); she refuses a marriage on this basis and mocks his conceit and arrogance in demanding such a thing. But the story finishes with her offering to burn the still life of the doll and accepting his marriage proposal, though not unequivocally on his own terms.

SETTING

The story begins in a town in Allied-occupied Germany after the First World War; the precise location is not indicated, but it could be based on Cologne, which was occupied by British troops between December 1918 and January 1926. Later, the scene moves briefly to Munich and then, for the final phase of the story, to "Kaprun" on a lake in the Austrian Tyrol; this is based on Zell-am-See, where Lawrence stayed (at the Villa Alpensee, Thumersbach) between

20 July and 25 August 1921 (Kaprun is an actual town nearby, but not on the lake).

BIBLIOGRAPHY 39

Bordinat, Philips. "The Poetic Image in DHL's *The Captain's Doll*." *West Virginia University Bulletin: Philological Papers* 19 (July 1972): 45–49.

Daleski, H. M. "Aphrodite of the Foam and *The Ladybird* Tales." In *DHL: A Critical Study of the Major Novels and Other Writings*. Edited by Andor Gomme. Sussex: Harvester Press; New York: Barnes and Noble, 1978, pp. 142–58. (Reprinted in his *Unities: Studies in the English Novel*. Athens: University of Georgia Press, 1985, pp. 211–24.)

Dawson, Eugene W. "Love among the Mannikins: *The Captain's Doll*." *DHL Review* 1 (Summer 1968): 137–48.

Doherty, Gerald. "A 'Very Funny' Story: Figural Play in DHL's *The Captain's Doll*." *DHL Review* 18 (1985–86): 5–17.

Ellis, David. "Introduction." *The Fox, The Captain's Doll, The Ladybird* by DHL. Edited by Dieter Mehl. Harmondsworth: Penguin, 1994, pp. xiii–xxx.

Gurko, Leo. "DHL's Greatest Collection of Short Stories: What Holds It Together." *Modern Fiction Studies* 18 (Summer 1972): 173–82.

McDowell, Frederick P. W. " 'The Individual in His Pure Singleness': Theme and Symbol in *The Captain's Doll*." In *The Challenge of DHL*. Edited by Michael Squires and Keith Cushman. Madison: University of Wisconsin Press, 1990, pp. 143–58.

Martin, W. R. "Hannele's 'Surrender': A Misreading of *The Captain's Doll*." *DHL Review* 18 (1985–86): 19–23.

Mehl, Dieter. "Introduction." *The Fox, The Captain's Doll, The Ladybird* by DHL. Edited by Dieter Mehl. Cambridge: Cambridge University Press, 1992, pp. xvii–xlvii.

Mellown, Elgin W. "*The Captain's Doll*: Its Origins and Literary Allusions." *DHL Review* 9 (Summer 1976): 226–35.

Spilka, Mark. "Repossessing *The Captain's Doll*." In his *Renewing the Normative DHL: A Personal Progress*. Columbia: University of Missouri Press, 1992, pp. 248–75.

Tripathy, Akhilesh Kumar. "DHL's *Sons and Lovers* and A [*sic*] *Captain's Doll*: A Study in Thematic Link." In *Essays on DHL*. Edited by T. R. Sharma. Meerut, India: Shalabh Book House, 1987, pp. 95–103.

See also Beal (1961): 100–101. Daleski (1965): 156–58. Draper (1964): 127–29. Draper (1970): 191–96. Goodheart (1963): 134–36. Hough (1956): 177–79. Leavis (1955): 50–53, 197–224. Leavis (1976): 92–121. Panichas (1964): 109–11. Pritchard (1971): 141–43. Ruderman (1984): 60–61, passim. Slade (1970): 106–8. Stewart (1963): 571–77.

29   *The Ladybird*

WRITTEN

November–December 1921. Revisions and corrections, January 1922, February 1923. Though very different in its final form, the novel was initially based on the short story "The Thimble," written in 1915 and published in *Seven Arts* (March 1917).

PUBLISHED

1. *The Ladybird, The Fox, The Captain's Doll.* London: Secker, March 1923.
    The Captain's Doll: Three Novelettes. New York: Seltzer, April 1923.
2. *The Fox, The Captain's Doll, The Ladybird.* Edited by Dieter Mehl. Cambridge: Cambridge University Press, 1992.

WHO'S WHO AND SUMMARY

Lady Beveridge, once an influential and fashionable society figure, represents a fading spirit of tolerance and philanthropic liberalism in the wartime England of 1917. Despite having lost her sons and her brother in the war, she continues to make charitable visits to the hospital where sick and wounded enemy soldiers are interned. One day she is dismayed to come across a badly wounded old friend, the Bohemian *Count Johann Dionys Psanek,* a small, dark, inscrutable man in his mid-thirties. She had known him as a boy, and he had visited her, with his wife, as recently as 1914. She later tells her daughter, *Lady Daphne*

Apsley, about the count, as she also used to know him. Indeed, Daphne remembers that, for her seventeenth birthday, he had given her a thimble with his family crest of a ladybird on it. Lady Daphne is now twenty-five, herself only just recovering from an illness. She is tall and potentially beautiful but constantly sickly and thin, so that her doctors fear consumption. Her husband, *Major Basil Apsley,* has been reported missing in the East (though there are rumors now that he is a prisoner in Turkey), and she is still grieving the loss of her two brothers as well as of her stillborn child; life seems bleak and hopeless to her. But, the narrator tells us, the real cause of her despair is that she has been unable to find an outlet for her inherent "wild energy." Both her mother's creed of charity and benevolence and her husband's "adorable" conventionality have dammed up her true "reckless" nature. She accompanies her mother on her next visit to Count Dionys, and thereafter she finds herself constantly drawn back to him by a subtle, silent power he exerts over her. Gradually, her spirits revive, stirred by the strange esoteric knowledge that Dionys—an initiate of an old secret society—intimates to her in his suggestion that our world is inside-out, that our superficial daytime life of sight, light, and reason is only the lining of the essential world of darkness and unconscious blood-knowledge. His family name, "Psanek," means "outlaw," he tells Daphne, and it becomes clear that her outlawed recklessness and energy are beginning to find expression through her relationship with him.

The war ends, and Daphne waits for her husband with great excitement and expectation; but, when he arrives, she finds him oddly different and cold, with an essential "whiteness" about him that contrasts sharply with the "dark fire" of Psanek. To her, Basil's scar-wounded face comes to represent his scarred inner self, a pallid self that seems to carry death on its shoulder. His love for her, however, is more intense than ever. Indeed, he now literally goes on his knees before her and kisses her feet in an outpouring of "adoration-lust." Significantly, though, as he rises to his feet, Daphne gives him only her left hand while she tightly clutches Psanek's thimble in her right. Basil's adoration of Daphne soon makes her fretful and ill again; she begins to feel like a "prostitute-goddess" worshiped by a white priest with no power to enkindle her vital soul. She turns once more to Psanek and takes Basil with her to visit him. The major and the count have little in common, but Basil is fascinated by the other man, and, just before the count is due to be repatriated, he invites him to stay with them for a fortnight at Thoresway, the Beveridges' country mansion where Daphne had been born and bred (the reference to Thor is presumably not coincidental—we have been told that Daphne had inherited her wild energy from the daredevil blood of her father's soldier ancestors). Here, the final movement of the story consolidates the love triangle that has been slowly forming, with Daphne becoming the night-wife of her otherworldly demon lover, Psanek, and the daylight wife of her platonic lover, Basil. Lured to his room by his ghostly singing, Daphne embraces the "dark flame of life" of the ladybird and lapses from her superconscious, cold, white self into the unconscious blood-warmth of her true dark self, her wild ancestral energies finally released ''like a full river flowing forever inside her.'' As genuine desire is rekindled in Daphne, so the forced desire of Basil is extinguished as he acknowledges his sexless, abstract-ideal love for her.

Minor characters in the story are *Lord (Earl) Beveridge; Lady Primrose Bingham,* Basil's sister; and Daphne's maid, *Millicent.* (Lady Daphne and Basil Apsley are modeled on Lady Cynthia Asquith [1887–1960] and her husband, Herbert Asquith [1881–1947], who, like Major Apsley, was wounded in the war; he was the second son of Herbert Henry Asquith [1852–1928], British prime minister, 1908–16. The Beveridges would seem to be modeled on Cynthia Asquith's parents, Lord and Lady Elcho. Lady Cynthia acquired her title when her father, Hugo Charteris, became the eleventh earl of Wemyss in June 1914.)

SETTING

Lady Daphne's flat is in Mayfair, near Hyde Park, in London. Hurst Place and Voynich Hall, the military hospitals where the count is treated, are somewhere in the country near London. Thoresway, the Beveridges' country mansion, is ostensibly in Leicestershire but is possibly modeled on Lady Ottoline Morrell's Garsington Manor in Oxfordshire, where Lawrence visited in June 1915.

BIBLIOGRAPHY 40

Cowan, James C. ''DHL's Dualism: The Apollonian-Dionysian Polarity and *The Lady-bird.*'' In *Forms of Modern Fiction.* Edited by A. W. Friedman. Austin and London: University of Texas Press, 1975, pp. 75–99.

Daalder, Joost. ''Background and Significance of DHL's *The Ladybird.*'' *DHL Review* 15 (Spring 1982): 107–28.

Daleski, H. M. ''Aphrodite of the Foam and *The Ladybird* Tales.'' In *DHL: A Critical Study of the Major Novels and Other Writings.* Edited by Andor Gomme. Sussex: Harvester Press; New York: Barnes and Noble, 1978, pp. 142–58. (Reprinted in his *Unities: Studies in the English Novel.* Athens: University of Georgia Press, 1985, pp. 211–24.)

Davies, Rosemary Reeves. ''The Mother as Destroyer: Psychic Division in the Writings of DHL.'' *DHL Review* 13 (1980): 220–38.

Denny, N.V.E. ''*The Ladybird.*'' *Theoria* 11 (October 1958): 17–28.

Ellis, David. ''Introduction.'' *The Fox, The Captain's Doll, The Ladybird* by DHL. Edited by Dieter Mehl. Harmondsworth: Penguin, 1994, pp. xiii–xxx.

Finney, Brian. ''Two Missing Pages from 'The Ladybird.' '' *Review of English Studies* 24 (May 1973): 191–92.

Gilbert, Sandra M. ''Potent Griselda: 'The Ladybird' and the Great Mother.'' In *DHL: A Centenary Consideration.* Edited by Peter Balbert and Phillip L. Marcus. Ithaca, N.Y., and London: Cornell University Press, 1985, pp. 130–61.

Gurko, Leo. ''DHL's Greatest Collection of Short Stories: What Holds It Together.'' *Modern Fiction Studies* 18 (Summer 1972): 173–82.

Humma, John B. "*The Ladybird* and the Enabling Image." *DHL Review* 17 (1984): 219–32. (Reprinted in Humma [1990]: 16–28.)

Jones, Lawrence. "Physiognomy and the Sensual Will in *The Ladybird* and *The Fox*." *DHL Review* 13 (1980): 1–29.

Mason, R. "Persephone and the Ladybird: A Note on DHL." *London Review* 2 (Autumn 1967): 42–49.

Mehl, Dieter. "Introduction." *The Fox, The Captain's Doll, The Ladybird* by DHL. Edited by Dieter Mehl. Cambridge: Cambridge University Press, 1992, pp. xvii–xlvii.

Scott, James F. "Thimble into Ladybird: Nietzsche, Frobenius, and Bachofen in the Later Works of DHL." *Arcadia* 13 (1978): 161–76.

Steven, Laurence. "From Thimble to Ladybird: DHL's Widening Vision?" *DHL Review* 18 (1985–86): 239–53.

See also Clarke (1969): 113–15. Daleski (1965): 143–50. Draper (1970): 191–96. Hough (1956): 175–76. Hyde (1992): 223–25, passim. Leavis (1955): 56–64. Miles (1969): 41–43. Ruderman (1984): 71–89. Siegel (1991): passim. Williams (1993): 117–21. Worthen (1991a): 76–78.

30   *St. Mawr and Other Stories*

COLLECTION

Written

This title exists only in the Cambridge edition of Lawrence's works. The volume collects short fiction written in the United States and Mexico between September 1922 and March 1925. It derives from the volume *St. Mawr Together with The Princess* (London: Secker, May 1925), with the addition of other pieces from the period that were unpublished in Lawrence's lifetime: "The Overtone," "The Wilful Woman" (an untitled fragment given this name by Keith Sagar in the 1971 Penguin collection, *The Princess and Other Stories*), and the unfinished story "The Flying Fish."

Published

Edited by Brian Finney. Cambridge: Cambridge University Press, 1983.

INDIVIDUAL STORIES

Publication details of the collection are not repeated for each entry, and Brian Finney's introduction to the volume, pp. xv–xliii, should be consulted as an item of general critical relevance for all the stories.

"THE OVERTONE"

WRITTEN

It is not known for certain when this story was written. Brian Finney argues for a probable date between 4 April and 5 May 1924, with some revision possibly taking place in 1925 (see the Cambridge volume cited earlier, pp. xxi–xxix). However, Mark Kinkead-Weekes has recently established that the story was in fact written much earlier, in late January or early February 1913 (see his "Re-Dating 'The Overtone,'" forthcoming in *The D. H. Lawrence Review*).

PUBLISHED

Unpublished in Lawrence's lifetime; first posthumous publication was in the collection *The Lovely Lady*. London: Secker, January 1933.

WHO'S WHO AND SUMMARY

The story presents a poetic meditation on the death of the Great God Pan (a recurrent theme throughout Lawrence's writings), and each of the three main characters gives expression to a particular point of view on the topic (though *Elsa Laskell* provides the main center of consciousness). It is after dinner at the Renshaws' house, and *Mrs. Renshaw* is talking with her guests, *Mrs. Hankin* and the young woman Elsa Laskell, while her husband sprawls on the lounge, pretending to read. *Will Renshaw,* now fifty-two, muses over a night six months after his marriage when he felt an overwhelming urge to make love with his wife in the open air beneath the full moon on the hill above their bungalow; she, however, had denied him, perhaps through fear and mistrust of herself; and, for him, this night has stood out ever since as the beginning of the end of their sexual relationship. We then slip into Mrs. Renshaw's consciousness and hear her side of the story, partly in the form of a psalm; she, too, feels that fear and mistrust have been the cause of sexual discord between them, but she ascribes these feelings to her husband, not herself, and she blames him for constantly shying away from the sacred mystery of love in favor of a crude and insensitive pursuit of profane love. A discussion then takes place outside the house between Elsa Laskell and the two Renshaws on the subject of Pan. This clearly reflects back on what we have heard to identify Will Renshaw as a would-be sensuous Pan who has become merely a fallen Pan; and to identify Edith Renshaw as a type of spiritual Christ-figure, responsible for the death of Pan (though also for moral justice and integrity). Elsa Laskell now defines herself in terms of a balance between the two impulses of Pan and Christ, the sensual and the spiritual: she will be both nymph and woman, a pagan and a Christian. The story ends with Elsa's feeling glad to get away from the Renshaws.

SETTING

The only firm indication of the location of the Renshaw's house, where the story is set, is the reference to the River Soar, which runs along the southern boundary of Nottinghamshire into Leicestershire.

BIBLIOGRAPHY 41

Merivale, Patricia. "DHL and the Modern Pan Myth." *Texas Studies in Literature and Language* 6 (Fall 1964): 297–305. (Reprinted as Ch. 6 of her *Pan the Goat-God: His Myth in Modern Times.* Cambridge: Harvard University Press, 1969, pp. 194–219 [213–15].)

Neumarkt, Paul. "Pan and Christ: An Analysis of the *Hieros Gamos* Concept in DHL's Short Story 'The Overtone.' " *Dos Continentes* 9–10 (1971–72): 27–48.

Viinikka, Anja. *From Persephone to Pan: DHL's Mythopoeic Vision of the Integrated Personality.* Turku, Finland: Turun Yliopisto Julkaisuja, 1988, pp. 160–73.

ST. MAWR

WRITTEN

June–September 1924. Drafts: 1. Early June 1924. 2. Late June–September 1924. Proofs corrected February–March 1925.

PUBLISHED

St. Mawr Together with The Princess. London: Secker, May 1925. *St. Mawr.* New York: Knopf, June 1925.

WHO'S WHO AND SUMMARY

MAIN CHARACTERS: Lou Witt (Lady Carrington), Rico Carrington (Sir Henry Carrington), Mrs. Witt, Phoenix (Gerònimo Trujillo), Morgan Lewis, St. Mawr

After their bohemian romance across the capitals of Europe, *Lou Witt,* a "moderately rich" American of twenty-four, marries *Rico Carrington,* an Australian baronet's son with artistic pretensions. They settle in Westminster, where Rico becomes a fashionable society portrait painter. Lou's mother, *Mrs. Witt* (who "couldn't stand" Rico), along with her Mexican-Indian servant, *Phoenix,* installs herself in a nearby hotel, "being on the spot" to watch with cynical satisfaction as her daughter's marriage starts to break down.

Mr. Saintsbury, the horsey owner of the mews behind her house, shows Lou the magnificent but temperamental stallion, *St. Mawr.* She is captivated by the horse, and she experiences a form of epiphany in which an "ancient understanding" floods into her soul; she realizes she must abandon her commonplace self to seek a deeper self and reality in "another world." She buys St. Mawr and at the same time acquires the services of the horse's "attendant shadow," *Morgan Lewis,* the Welsh groom.

Mrs. Witt takes a house in Shropshire. It overlooks a churchyard, and previous suggestions of Mrs. Witt's cynicism are reinforced as we witness the pleasure she takes in watching funerals. We are introduced to the local vicar and his wife, the "delightfully worldly" *Vyners;* and, following Rico on his social round of the local gentry, we also meet the precious *Manbys* of Corrabach Hall. Mrs. Witt holds a dinner party at which the goatish looks of a local artist, *Cartwright,* spark a discussion on the Great God Pan. This is later taken up privately by Mrs. Witt and Lou when they bewail the lack of any true "Pan-quality" in the modern world: Mrs. Witt thinks she discerns something of it in Lewis; Lou senses it in Phoenix, too, but above all in St. Mawr, in whom wild life burns "straight from the source."

A riding party visits the Devil's Chair, a local viewpoint. The central event in the novel takes place here as St. Mawr suddenly "explodes," and Rico, trying "viciously" to restrain the horse, causes it to rear and fall back on top of him, breaking his ribs and crushing his ankle.

As Lou rides for help, she discovers that a dead snake had frightened St. Mawr. She then has a second vision, "a vision of evil," in which she meditates on the "reversal" of vital life in the modern world. This reversal is suggested to her by the opposition between the underlying viciousness of the superficially civilized Rico and the natural vitality and spontaneity of St. Mawr. This opposition is then dramatized further by the decision of the Vyners and the Manbys to have St. Mawr gelded—with Rico's blessing. But, before this can be done, Mrs. Witt rides with Lewis and St. Mawr across country to Oxfordshire, where she arranges for them to go to America—herself and the horse, Lou, Lewis, and Phoenix. During the ride, she proposes to Lewis, but he recognizes an underlying arrogance and willfulness in her manner and firmly rebuffs her. Recounting his traditional folk beliefs, he implicitly criticizes the mechanical rationalism of the civilization she represents and proclaims a simple faith in the mystery and vitality of the natural world—for which Mrs. Witt has no true feeling. Meanwhile, Lou has lost patience with the superficial chitchat of Corrabach hall and the flirtatious posings of *Flora Manby* and the convalescent Rico; she has returned to London to make final arrangements for her departure to America. As she muses over her past, yet another artist figure appears: the *Honourable Laura Ridley.* Everything about this character jars on Lou's nerves and reinforces her determination to flee from the hollow life of the modern wasteland.

Even in Texas, however, once the initial glamor has worn off, Lou finds life much the same as it had been in England—artificial and forced. Leaving St. Mawr and Lewis behind on the Texan ranch, she, Phoenix, and Mrs. Witt move on to the Rocky Mountains of New Mexico, where Lou goes with Phoenix to see a ranch high in the mountains. As they travel, and Lou absorbs the impact of the wild landscape, she experiences another epiphany in which she senses her quest for authenticity nearing its goal. When she sees the Las Chivas ranch, her heart goes out to it immediately—despite some ominous signs of dilapidation and Phoenix's astute recognition of its unlikely prospects as a farmstead. There then follows a poetic account of the ranch's history in which we hear of another woman's unsuccessful struggle to sustain the ranch in the face of the "invidious and relentless" forces of nature. Although the story of the woman's defeat is, in part, a cautionary one, it evokes precisely that "curious tussle of wild life" that has become so conspicuously absent for Lou in the so-called civilized world.

Lou buys the ranch and brings her mother to see it. While Lou pledges her allegiance, in semireligious terms, to the "wild spirit" that "needs" her, Mrs. Witt points out the rats and typically has the last cynical word when she draws attention to the material value of the ranch and to its name, Las Chivas, the she-goats. We thus end on an ambivalent note: has Lou actually found the Great God Pan in the wild Rocky Mountains, or has the poor little rich girl simply bought herself another illusion, a pale, goaty reflection of the real thing?

SETTING

The novel opens in London, especially around Westminster, where Lou and Rico live. The scene then shifts to "Chomesbury" in Shropshire. "Chomesbury" is based on Pontesbury, about eight miles southwest of Shrewsbury, where Lawrence visited Frederick Carter in January 1924. The excursion to the "Devil's Chair" would seem to have been inspired by a walk Lawrence took with Frederick Carter to the Stiperstones, a local viewpoint (1,762 feet above sea level) about six miles southwest of Pontesbury. ("Corrabach Hall," seven miles from "Chomesbury," is possibly based on Condover Hall, which lies six miles due east from Pontesbury; the name may also have been suggested by Castle Pulverbatch, a nearby hamlet.) We follow Mrs. Witt and Lewis on their horse ride across country on their way to Oxfordshire and return briefly to London with Lou before the next major shift of setting to America. Following brief scenes on the ship, at Havana, and then on the "Zane Grey" ranch in Texas, the final phase of the novel is set in New Mexico at the Las Chivas ranch in the Rocky Mountains. This is based on the Lawrences' Lobo ranch (later renamed Kiowa ranch) at Questa, seventeen miles from Taos, where the novel was written and where they lived between May and October 1924 and between April and September 1925 (they had also previously lived at the neighboring Del Monte ranch between December 1922 and March 1923).

BIBLIOGRAPHY 42

Barker, Anne Darling. "The Fairy Tale and *St. Mawr.*" *Forum for Modern Language Studies* 20 (1984): 76–83.

Blanchard, Lydia. "Mothers and Daughters in DHL: *The Rainbow* and Selected Shorter Works." In *Lawrence and Women.* Edited by Anne Smith. London: Vision, 1978, pp. 75–100 (91–96).

Bodenheimer, Rosemarie. "*St. Mawr, A Passage to India,* and the Question of Influence." *DHL Review* 13 (Summer 1980): 134–49.

Brown, Keith. "Welsh Red Indians: DHL and *St. Mawr.*" *Essays in Criticism* 32 (April 1982): 158–79. (Reprinted in Brown [1990]: 23–37.)

Clark, L. D. "DHL as a Southwestern Author." *Phoenix* 23 (1981): 17–21.

Craig, David, Mark Roberts, and T. W. Thomas. "Mr. Liddell and Dr. Leavis." *Essays in Criticism* 5 (January 1955): 64–80.

Doherty, Gerald. "The Greatest Show on Earth: DHL's *St. Mawr* and Antonin Artaud's Theatre of Cruelty." *DHL Review* 22 (Spring 1990): 5–21.

Engel, Monroe. "The Continuity of Lawrence's Short Novels." *Hudson Review* 11 (Summer 1958): 201–9 (206–8).

Fleishman, Avrom. "He Do the Polis in Different Voices: Lawrence's Later Style." In *DHL: A Centenary Consideration.* Edited by Peter Balbert and Phillip L. Marcus. Ithaca, N.Y., and London: Cornell University Press, 1985, pp. 162–79.

Garcia, Reloy, and James Karabatsos, eds. *A Concordance to the Short Fiction of DHL.* Lincoln: University of Nebraska Press, 1972. (Part 2: The Short Novels, pp. 291–474.)

Gidley, Mark. "Antipodes: DHL's *St. Mawr.*" *Ariel* 5 (January 1974): 25–41.

Giles, Steve. "Marxism and Form: DHL, *St. Mawr.*" In *Literary Theory at Work: Three Texts.* Edited by Douglas Tallack. London: Batsford, 1987, pp. 49–66.

Goonetilleke, D.C.R.A. *Developing Countries in British Fiction.* London and Basingstoke: Macmillan; Totowa, N.J.: Rowman and Littlefield, 1977, pp. 170–98 (174–79 and passim).

Haegert, John. "Lawrence's *St. Mawr* and the De-Creation of America." *Criticism* 34 (Winter 1992): 75–98.

Halperin, Irving. "Unity in *St. Mawr.*" *South Dakota Review* 4 (Summer 1966): 58–60.

Harris, Janice Hubbard. "The Moulting of *The Plumed Serpent:* A Study of the Relationship between the Novel and Three Contemporary Tales." *Modern Language Quarterly* 39 (June 1978): 154–68.

Highet, Gilbert. *People, Places, and Books.* New York: Oxford University Press, 1953, pp. 39–41.

Irwin, W. R. "The Survival of Pan." *PMLA* 76 (June 1961): 159–67.

James, Stuart B. "Western American Space and the Human Imagination." *Western Humanities Review* 24 (Spring 1970): 147–55.

Kaplan, Harold. *The Passive Voice: An Approach to Modern Fiction.* Athens: Ohio University Press, 1966, pp. 183–85.

Leavis, F. R. "The Novel as Dramatic Poem (LV): *St. Mawr.*" *Scrutiny* 17 (Spring 1950): 38–53. (Reprinted in Leavis [1955]: 51–53, 225–45.)

Levy, Michele Frucht. "DHL and Dostoevsky: The Thirst for Risk and the Thirst for Life." *Modern Fiction Studies* 33 (1987): 281–88.

Liddell, Robert. "Lawrence and Dr. Leavis: The Case of *St. Mawr*." *Essays in Criticism* 4 (July 1954): 321–27.

McDowell, Frederick P. W. " 'Pioneering into the Wilderness of Unopened Life': Lou Witt in America." In *The Spirit of DHL: Centenary Studies*. Edited by Gamini Salgado and G. K. Das. London: Macmillan, 1988, pp. 92–105.

Merivale, Patricia. "DHL and the Modern Pan Myth." *Texas Studies in Literature and Language* 6 (Fall 1964): 297–305. (Reprinted as Ch. 6 of her *Pan the Goat-God: His Myth in Modern Times*. Cambridge: Harvard University Press, 1969, pp. 194–219.)

Millard, Elaine. "Feminism II: Reading as a Woman: DHL, *St. Mawr*." In *Literary Theory at Work: Three Texts*. Edited by Douglas Tallack. London: Batsford, 1987, pp. 133–57.

Moynahan, Julian. "Lawrence, Woman, and the Celtic Fringe." In *Lawrence and Women*. Edited by Anne Smith. London: Vision, 1978, pp 122–35 (131–34).

Murry, John Middleton. *Love, Freedom, and Society*. London: Cape, 1957, pp. 24–28, 34–38.

Norris, Margot. *Beasts of the Modern Imagination: Darwin, Nietzsche, Kafka, Ernst, and Lawrence*. Baltimore: Johns Hopkins University Press, 1985, pp. 170–94.

Padhi, Bibhu. "Lawrence, *St. Mawr*, and Irony." *South Dakota Review* 21 (1983): 5–13.

Poirier, Richard. *A World Elsewhere: The Place of Style in American Literature*. London: Chatto and Windus, 1967, pp. 40–49.

Poole, Roger. "Psychoanalytic Theory: DHL, *St. Mawr*." In *Literary Theory at Work: Three Texts*. Edited by Douglas Tallack. London: Batsford, 1987, pp. 89–113.

Poplawski, Paul. "Language, Art, and Reality: A Stylistic Study of DHL's *St. Mawr*." Ph.D. diss., University of Wales, 1989.

Pritchard, William H. *Seeing through Everything: English Writers 1918–1940*. London: Faber and Faber, 1977, pp. 82–86.

Ragussis, Michael. "The False Myth of *St. Mawr:* Lawrence and the Subterfuge of Art." *Papers on Language and Literature* 11 (Spring 1975): 186–96.

Raina, M. L. "A Forster Parallel in Lawrence's *St. Mawr*." *Notes and Queries* 211 (March 1966): 96–97.

Rama Moorthy, Polanki. "*St. Mawr:* The Third Eye." *Aligarh Journal of English Studies* 10, no 2 (1985): 188–204.

Renner, Stanley. "The Lawrentian Power and Logic of *Equus*." In *DHL's Literary Inheritors*. Edited by Keith Cushman and Dennis Jackson. London: Macmillan, 1991, pp. 31–45. (Influence of *St. Mawr* on Peter Shaffer's play.)

Rudnick, Lois P. "DHL's New World Heroine: Mabel Dodge Luhan." *DHL Review* 14 (Spring 1981): 85–111.

Sabin, Margery. *The Dialect of the Tribe: Speech and Community in Modern Fiction*. Oxford: Oxford University Press, 1987, pp. 162–78.

Scheff, Doris. "Interpreting 'Eyes' in DHL's *St. Mawr*." *American Notes and Queries* 19 (1980): 48–51.

Scholtes, M. "*St. Mawr:* Between Degeneration and Regeneration." *Dutch Quarterly Review* 5 (1975): 253–69.

Smith, Bob L. "DHL's *St. Mawr:* Transposition of Myth." *Arizona Quarterly* 24 (Fall 1968): 197–208.

Stewart, Jack F. "Totem and Symbol in *The Fox* and *St. Mawr.*" *Studies in the Humanities* 16 (December 1989): 84–98.

Tallman, Warren. "Forest, Glacier, and Flood. The Moon. *St. Mawr:* A Canvas for Lawrence's Novellas." *Open Letter,* 3d series, no 6 (Winter 1976–77): 75–92.

Tanner, Tony. "DHL in America." In *DHL: Novelist, Poet, Prophet.* Edited by Stephen Spender. London: Weidenfeld and Nicolson, 1973, pp. 170–96.

Vickery, J. B. "Myth and Ritual in the Shorter Fiction of DHL." *Modern Fiction Studies* 5 (Spring 1959): 65–82. (Reprinted in revised form in his *The Literary Impact of the Golden Bough.* Princeton: Princeton University Press, 1973, pp. 294–325.)

Vivas, Eliseo. "Mr. Leavis on DHL." *Sewanee Review* 65 (1957): 126–27.

Wasserman, Jerry. "*St. Mawr* and the Search for Community." *Mosaic* 5 (Winter 1972): 113–23.

Wicker, Brian. *The Story-Shaped World; Fiction and Metaphysics: Some Variations on a Theme.* Notre Dame, Ind.: University of Notre Dame, 1975, pp. 124–29 and passim.

Wilde, Alan. "The Illusion of *St. Mawr:* Technique and Vision in DHL's Novel." *PMLA* 79 (March 1964): 164–70.

Winn, Harbour. "Parallel Inward Journeys: *A Passage to India* and *St. Mawr.*" *English Language Notes* 31 (December 1993): 62–66.

See also (1980–94) Clark (1980): 311–16. Harris (1984): 189–202. Hobsbaum (1981): 111–14. Humma (1990): 45–61. Ingram (1990): 103–9. MacLeod (1985/87): 157–71. Ruderman (1984): 127–41. Sagar (1985a): 246–77. Storch (1990): 123–30. Trebisz (1992): 59–62. Viinikka (1988): 173–207.

See also (to 1979) Beal (1961): 100–101. Cavitch (1969): 151–63. Cowan (1970): 81–96. Draper (1964): 131–35. Draper (1970): 250–57. Goodheart (1963): 56–62. Hough (1956): 179–86, passim. John (1974): 278–86. Kermode (1973): 111–14. Lerner (1967): 185–91. Moore (1951): 225–28. Rees (1958): 118–19. Sagar (1966): 151–59. Stewart (1963): 568–71. Tedlock (1963): 176–79. Vivas (1960): 151–65. Widmer (1961): 66–75.

"THE PRINCESS"

WRITTEN

September–October 1924. Proofs for Secker edition, April–May 1925 (Lawrence seems not to have seen the proofs of the *Calendar* printing).

PUBLISHED

In three parts: *Calendar of Modern Letters* 1 (March 1925): 2–22; 1 (April 1925): 122–32; 1 (May 1925): 226–35.

St. Mawr Together with The Princess. London: Secker, May 1925.

WHO'S WHO AND SUMMARY

Colin Urquhart is from an old Scottish family and claims royal ancestry, a claim
that makes him appear ridiculous to his relatives; indeed, we are told that he is
"just a bit mad." Handsome, cultured, and charming and a gentleman of reasonable means, he travels the world and moves in good society without ever
doing anything specific or "definitely being anything." He is, in fact, somewhat
insubstantial and unreal, and the sense of living with "a fascinating spectre" is
what "breaks" his wife after only three years of marriage. He had married
Hannah Prescott, a wealthy New England woman of twenty-two, when he was
nearly forty. She had borne him a frail child, Mary Henrietta, and had then died
suddenly when the baby was only two years old. She had called the child *Dollie,*
while Colin called her "My Princess." *The Princess,* as everyone comes to call
her, is brought up by her father and becomes almost inseparable from him;
inevitably, she inherits many of his qualities and is strongly influenced by him.
Especially, he teaches her that she really is a royal fairy princess, along with
him "the last of the royal race of old people," and that she should always keep
herself separate from other "less noble, more vulgar" people. Although she
should always be kindly and polite to others, what really matters, he tells her,
is the unchanging "green, upright demon" at the core of her royal inner self.
As a small child, then, she learns the lesson of "absolute reticence" and of the
impossibility of intimacy with others; she steps out of the childhood "picture"
her father creates of her, fully formed and finished, always to be childish and
virginal. She travels the world with her father, retaining this quality of the
sexless fairy into her thirties, while Colin Urquhart himself becomes increasingly
odd in his old age. They spend the last three years of his life in their house in
Connecticut and engage a young nurse-companion for him, *Miss Charlotte Cummins.* He dies when Dollie is thirty-eight and leaves her aimless and empty. She
begins to entertain the idea of marriage, but an *abstract* idea of both marriage
and men is all that this entails for her. She decides to travel and, with Miss
Cummins, goes to New Mexico to stay on a large ranch for the rich at the foot
of the Rockies. The Rancho del Cerro Gordo is owned by the *Wilkiesons,* who,
ten years before, had bought the ranch from *Domingo Romero,* a thirty-year-old
Mexican from an old Spanish family, who is now employed as a guide at the
ranch. Dollie becomes intrigued by the dark, strong, silent Romero, thinking she
perceives the spark of an aristocratic "demon" in his otherwise black and despairing eyes. An unspoken intimacy develops between them, but, as it does, so
Dollie's "idée fixe" of marriage begins to recede—for though she recognizes
an inner compatibility of their "demons," she senses a strong incompatibility
between their surface social selves that puts marriage out of the question. After
a month or so on the ranch, making daily riding expeditions with Romero, Miss
Cummins, and sometimes one or two other guests, Dollie asks Romero if he
could take them on a longer trip to where they might see some larger wild
animals. He offers to take her and Miss Cummins to a shack he owns in an

isolated spot farther up in the mountains. On the journey, Miss Cummins's horse is injured, and she returns to the ranch, leaving the other two to go on alone. Just before sunset, they reach the tiny cabin, set in a clearing within a primitive-seeming wooded valley. Dollie is tired and stupefied from the journey, a little uneasy to note how energetic and "full of force" Romero is. They make a fire and eat and then retire; she sleeps in the one bunk while he makes his bed on the floor. During the night, the fire goes out, and the Princess awakes, shivering in the icy cold. She feels torn by her desire for warmth—and symbolically by a desire "to be taken away from herself"—and her old obsessive desire to keep herself intact and free from the power of any other person. She calls out to Romero, and he asks her if she wants him to warm her; she answers "yes," but, as soon as he takes her in his arms, she stiffens and recoils from his animal passion and seems to scream inwardly in protest at his violation of her—even though "she had *willed* that it should happen." The next day she insists that they leave immediately, but Romero feels insulted at her attempt to deny the contact with him and angry at her insistence that she had not enjoyed his love-making; he also seems worried about what she might say to the others back at the ranch. He therefore refuses to take her back. He throws her clothes into the pool in front of the cabin, along with both their saddles, to prevent her from leaving alone, and determines to "make her" accept him as a lover. She is equally determined that he will never conquer her in this way, and, indeed, though he rapes her repeatedly, he finds that her spirit is "hard and flawless as a diamond." He may have shattered her, but he realizes finally and despairingly that she will never yield to him. By the fourth day, they both feel as though they have died in some way, and, when the Forest Service men appear in search of them, Romero goes almost willingly to his death by unnecessarily opening fire on them. After he is killed, Dollie explains his actions by saying he had gone out of his mind. Later, it seems that she has actually gone out of her mind; though she recovers her old surface self with the help of Miss Cummins, becoming once more "a virgin intact," her eyes begin to show the signs of her father's original craziness. She eventually married an elderly man, we hear, and seemed content.

SETTING

The main part of the story takes place in the Rocky Mountains above San Cristobal near Taos, New Mexico. The first fifth or so of the story briskly describes the restless movements of Colin and Dollie Urquhart in Europe and America (though India is referred to briefly, too); Florence, Rome, Paris, London, the Great Lakes, California, and Connecticut are all mentioned.

BIBLIOGRAPHY 43

Cowan, James C. "DHL's 'The Princess' as Ironic Romance." *Studies in Short Fiction* 4 (Spring 1967): 245–51.

Goonetilleke, D.C.R.A. *Developing Countries in British Fiction.* London and Basing-
        stoke: Macmillan; Totowa, N.J.: Rowman and Littlefield, 1977, pp. 179–81 and
        passim.
MacDonald, Robert H. ''Images of Negative Union: The Symbolic World of DHL's 'The
        Princess.' '' *Studies in Short Fiction* 16 (1979): 269–93.
Padhi, Bibhu. ''Lawrence's Ironic Fables and How They Matter.'' *Interpretations* 15,
        no. 1 (1983): 53–59.
Rossman, Charles. ''Myth and Misunderstanding DHL.'' *Bucknell Review* 22 (Fall 1976):
        81–101 (93–96).
Smalley, Barbara M. ''Lawrence's 'The Princess' and Horney's 'Idealized Self.' '' In
        Third Force Psychology and the Study of Literature. Edited by Bernard J. Paris.
        Rutherford, N.J.: Fairleigh Dickinson University Press, 1986, pp. 179–90.
Tanner, Tony. ''DHL in America.'' In *DHL: Novelist, Poet, Prophet.* Edited by Stephen
        Spender. London: Weidenfeld and Nicolson, 1973, pp. 170–96 (193–95).
Travis, Leigh. ''DHL: The Blood-Conscious Artist.'' *American Imago* 25 (Summer
        1968): 163–90 (174–77).
Weiner, S. Ronald. ''Irony and Symbolism in 'The Princess.' '' In *A DHL Miscellany.*
        Edited by Harry T. Moore. Carbondale: Southern Illinois University Press, 1959,
        pp. 221–38.
Widmer, Kingsley. ''Lawrence and the Fall of Modern Woman.'' *Modern Fiction Studies*
        5 (Spring 1959): 47–56 (51–55).

See also Albright (1978): 38–39. Cavitch (1969): 170–73. Clark (1980): 317–21. Cowan
(1970): 64–70. Draper (1964): 130. Hough (1956): 179–80. Nin (1932): 139–40.

''THE WILFUL WOMAN'' (FRAGMENT)

WRITTEN

September 1922.

PUBLISHED

Unpublished in Lawrence's lifetime; first posthumous publication was in the
        collection *The Princess and Other Stories.* Edited by Keith Sagar. Har-
        mondsworth: Penguin, 1971.

WHO'S WHO, SUMMARY, AND SETTING

This fragment describes the latter part of *Sybil Mond*'s journey, in November
1916, from New York via Kansas City to Lamy in New Mexico. Approaching
forty years of age and three times married, she is described as still full of
''explosive'' energy and as still possessing the obstinacy of a fourteen-year-old
girl. Her train goes through La Junta and then stops somewhere beyond Trinidad.
Here, frustrated and angered by the slow progress of the train, she insists on

leaving it and on attempting to cover the last part of the journey across country by car. She hires a sixteen-year-old boy and his ''old worn-out Dodge'' to take her. However, the boy does not really know the way over the rough terrain, and he has also forgotten to attach any headlamps to the car, so that, once night begins to fall, they are forced to abandon the journey and to return to the station at ''Wagon-Mound,'' where the ''wilful'' woman has to wait a further three hours for the next train.

"THE FLYING-FISH" (UNFINISHED)

WRITTEN

March 1925.

PUBLISHED

Unpublished in Lawrence's lifetime; first posthumous publication was in *Phoenix: The Posthumous Papers of DHL.* Edited by Edward D. McDonald. New York: Viking, 1936.

WHO'S WHO AND SUMMARY

Gethin Day is forty years old, an ex-soldier and the last remaining member of the Day family of Daybrook Hall, following the recent death of his elder sister, *Lydia.* An old prophecy says that while there is a member of the Day family at Daybrook, no calamity will befall the valley in which it stands, and Gethin knows he must now return there. The man who built Daybrook in the sixteenth century, *Sir Gilbert Day,* also wrote a sort of ''secret family bible'' of poetry, philosophy, and symbolism, *Book of Days,* and, as we follow Gethin on his journey toward England, parts of the book are referred to and provide a counterpoint to Gethin's thoughts and feelings as he travels. But probably the most memorable parts of this unfinished text are the central descriptions of the flying fish and the porpoises in the Gulf of Mexico. (Various other travelers are described on the journey, including *two Danes* with whom Gethin hires a car in Havana.)

SETTING

The story describes Gethin Day's journey by train from southern Mexico via Mexico City to Vera Cruz and then, by boat, across the Gulf of Mexico to Havana, Cuba, and thence across the Atlantic toward Britain. Lawrence made a similar journey from Mexico City to England in November and December 1923, and he made the journey from Oaxaca, in southern Mexico, to Mexico City in

February 1925. The description of "Daybrook Hall," the ancestral home of the Day family at "Crichdale" in the Midlands, is possibly modeled on Haddon Hall just north of Lathkill Dale in Derbyshire.

BIBLIOGRAPHY 44

See Cavitch (1969): 189–93. Cowan (1970): 128–37 and passim. Sagar (1966): 206–10.

31   *The Virgin and the Gipsy*

WRITTEN

Late 1925–January 1926. The novel was published only posthumously, and Lawrence never prepared it for publication. However, differences between the holograph manuscript and the published text would seem to suggest that Lawrence may have revised a now-unlocated typescript that was prepared by Secker's office shortly after the story was written.

PUBLISHED

Florence: G. Orioli, May 1930. London: Secker, October 1930. New York: Knopf, November 1930.

WHO'S WHO AND SUMMARY

The two young Saywell girls, *Yvette* and *Lucille,* return from finishing school in Switzerland to their cold and repressive rectory home, where the scandal caused by their mother's elopement with "a young and penniless man" when they were children still poisons the atmosphere with hate and envy and moral outrage. Following the flight of their undependable but flamboyant mother, *Cynthia,* the girls had been brought up in an "atmosphere of cunning self-sanctification and of unmentionability" by their father, the rector, *Arthur Saywell,* and the close relatives he had drafted for support: the pinched, envious, and sanctimoniously self-sacrificing *Aunt Cissie;* the domineering, manipulative, and physically gross *Granny,* referred to as "the Mater"; and the dingily self-effacing *Uncle Fred.* (There are also several other Aunt Saywells in the neighborhood—Aunts *Nell, Alice,* and *Lucy* later visit the rectory.)

At the start of the story, Lucille is twenty-one, and Yvette nineteen. Yvette is the "virgin" of the title and the main focus of the story once the grotesque elderly Saywells have been introduced. Referred to repeatedly as "vague" and unformed, her virgin potentiality is stressed throughout—though her vagueness also sets off echoes of her unpredictable mother. Indeed, such echoes accumulate as we witness her growing awareness of the self-enclosed sterility of the rectory and her gradual disengagement from its poisonous atmosphere. When she comes into contact with the flowing vitality of the dark gipsy and his freewheeling lifestyle, the parallels with the mother become more obvious as the latent desires of Yvette's body and inner self start to stir. *The gipsy* remains, for much of the time, a distant talismanic presence in her life, almost a symbol for her own "dark" bodily consciousness, but he comes decisively into her life and to the rescue of her integral self at the climax of the story. First, however, she must be brought to further *conscious* awareness of the unhealthy nature of the Saywell home, and this is effected largely through her friendship with the unconventional *Major Eastwood* and *Mrs. Fawcett.* This couple is not portrayed in an entirely serious manner, and their somewhat forced ("Fawcett" = "Force-it") and intellectualized allegiance to the life of spontaneous desire identifies them clearly as one of a series of self-referential and often comically playful "decoys" in Lawrence's fiction (characters who *mouth* the Lawrentian verities but do not *live* them)—note, for example, the plumbing connotation of Mrs. Fawcett's name, linking her to the sewerage imagery associated with the rectory; and the "snowy" images of blankness and lifelessness that characterize the mechanically minded Eastwood (his claim to be a "resurrected" man because of having been dug out from snow after twenty hours is mischievously undercut in context by the narratorial comment, "There was a frozen pause in the conversation"). Nonetheless, the Eastwoods do help Yvette to clarify and sharpen her resistance to the death-dealing hypocrisy of the rectory, and, in terms of plot, her meetings with them provide the motivation for her second major argument with her father, who disapproves of the Eastwoods for obvious personal, as well as moral, reasons (the first argument is provoked by Yvette's misappropriation of money from Aunt Cissie's church window fund, some of which, significantly, she gave away to *the gipsy's wife* after having her fortune told). In his attack on Yvette and the Eastwoods here, Arthur Saywell makes fully explicit the fundamental oppositions dramatized at all levels in the novel, between the forces of "saywell" social convention and the forces of spontaneous desire and passion: "I will kill you before you shall go the way of your mother," he threatens (though backing all the time with the "fear and rage and hate" of a cornered rat). Inwardly despairing at what she now recognizes as her father's true cynicism, his "base-born" disbelief in life, she more clearly discerns the need to have her "free-born" faith in life confirmed by the gipsy, against the father.

But, though she is drawn in dream and fantasy toward the gipsy, she cannot *will* an actual physical consummation with him; the floods of her deepest desires can be released only spontaneously. The symbolic enaction of such a release comes with the flood at the end of the story that sweeps away the main part of the rectory, taking Granny with it and bringing the gipsy bounding to Yvette's rescue. In the apocalyptic night that follows, the virgin and the gipsy are saved by the warmth of their naked embrace in the only standing part of the rectory (Yvette's room—always the only place of life-warmth in the house *and* positioned behind the now phallic-seeming chimney). The next morning, "the sun was shining in heaven," and all seems cleansed and fresh. The gipsy has gone, but Yvette accepts the wisdom of this; after all, she did not even know his name, something she realizes only when she receives a farewell note from him, signed, "Your obdt. servant Joe Boswell."

(Friends of Yvette and Lucille who appear in the novel but who have not been mentioned are *Bob, Ella* and *Lottie Framley;* and *Leo Wetherell,* who at one point proposes to Yvette.)

SETTING

The detailed descriptions of the landscape and the actual place-names referred to in the novel clearly identify the setting as north Derbyshire around Cromford, a possible model for "Papplewick" (though there is also a real place of this name in Nottinghamshire). Lawrence had lived in this area, at Middleton-by-Wirksworth, between May 1918 and February 1919, and had obviously come to know it very well. He had also made a tour of the region with his sister, Ada, in October 1925, just prior to composing the story, and this undoubtedly provided him with many of the immediate data for his setting, even though, as always in his work, such data are fairly thoroughly transfigured by the fictional process. Ashbourne, Bonsall, Codnor, Darley, and Tideswell are all mentioned. "Amberdale" and "Woodlinkin" would seem to correspond to Ambergate and Wirksworth, respectively, and the large "ducal house" in whose deer park Yvette and her friends pause on their motorcar trip to Bonsall Head evokes Chatsworth House, just east of Bakewell. The Saywell rectory seems, in part, to be a re-creation of the Weekley family home in Chiswick, London.

BIBLIOGRAPHY 45

Balbert, Peter. "Scorched Ego, the Novel, and the Beast: Patterns of Fourth Dimensionality in *The Virgin and the Gipsy.*" *Papers on Language and Literature* 29 (Fall 1993): 395–416.

Craig, David. "Shakespeare, Lawrence, and Sexual Freedom." In his *The Real Foundations: Literature and Social Change.* London; Chatto and Windus, 1973, pp. 17–38.

Crowder, Ashby Bland, and Lynn O'Malley Crowder. "Mythic Intent in DHL's *The Virgin and the Gipsy.*" *South Atlantic Review* 49 (1984): 61–66.

Cushman, Keith. "*The Virgin and the Gipsy* and the Lady and the Gamekeeper." In *DHL's "Lady": A New Look at "Lady Chatterley's Lover."* Edited by Michael Squires and Dennis Jackson. Athens: University of Georgia Press, 1985, pp. 154–69.

Doherty, Gerald. "The Third Encounter: Paradigms of Courtship in DHL's Shorter Fiction." *DHL Review* 17 (1984): 135–51.

Gutierrez, Donald. "Lawrence's *The Virgin and the Gipsy* as Ironic Comedy." *English Quarterly* (Waterloo, Ontario) 5 (Winter 1972–73): 61–69. (Reprinted in Gutierrez [1980]: 55–67.)

Guttenberg, Barnett. "Realism and Romance in Lawrence's *The Virgin and the Gipsy.*" *Studies in Short Fiction* 17 (1980): 99–103.

Lally, M. M. "*The Virgin and the Gipsy:* Rewriting the Pain." In *Aging and Gender in Literature: Studies in Creativity.* Edited by Anne M. Wyatt-Brown and Janice Rossen. Charlottesville: University Press of Virginia, 1993, pp. 121–37.

Meyers, Jeffrey. " 'The Voice of Water': Lawrence's *The Virgin and the Gipsy.*" *English Miscellany* 21 (1970): 199–207.

Penrith, Mary. "Some Structural Patterns in *The Virgin and the Gipsy.*" *University of Cape Town Studies in English* 6 (1976): 46–52.

Pollak, Paulina S. "Anti-Semitism in the Works of DHL: Search for and Rejection of the Faith." *Literature and Psychology* 32 (1986): 19–29.

Reed, John R. *Victorian Conventions.* Athens: Ohio University Press, 1975. (Ch. 14, "Gypsies," pp. 362–400; *The Virgin and the Gipsy,* p. 397.)

Reilly, Edward C. "A Note about Two Toads." *Notes on Contemporary Literature* 14 (1984): 7–8.

Siegel, Carol. "Floods of Female Desire in Lawrence and Eudora Welty." In *DHL's Literary Inheritors.* New York: St. Martin's Press; London: Macmillan, 1991, pp. 109–30. (Also incorporated into Siegel [1991]: 166–84.)

Springer, Mary Doyle. *Forms of the Modern Novella.* Chicago and London: University of Chicago Press, 1976, pp. 142–49.

Turner, John. "Purity and Danger in DHL's *The Virgin and the Gipsy.*" In *DHL: Centenary Essays.* Edited by Mara Kalnins. Bristol: Bristol Classical Press, 1986, pp. 139–71.

Vickery, J. B. "Myth and Ritual in the Shorter Fiction of DHL." *Modern Fiction Studies* 5 (Spring 1959): 65–82. (Reprinted in revised form in his *The Literary Impact of the Golden Bough.* Princeton: Princeton University Press, 1973, pp. 294–325.)

Watson, Garry. " 'The Fact, and the Crucial Significance, of Desire': Lawrence's *The Virgin and the Gipsy.*" *English* 34 (Summer 1985): 131–56.

Yanada, Noriyuki. "*The Virgin and the Gipsy:* Four Realms and Narrative Modes." *Language and Culture* 20 (1991): 121–46.

See also Clark (1980): 348–51. Draper (1964): 141–44. Hobsbaum (1981): 115–18. Hough (1956): 188–89. Humma (1990): 77–84. Krishnamurthi (1979): 94–114. Leavis (1955): 288–95. Moynahan (1963): 209–18. Murry (1931): 391. Pritchard (1971): 184–86. Ruderman (1984): 154–58. Slade (1970): 110–12. Tedlock (1963): 206–8. Widmer (1961): 178–87.

32   The Woman Who Rode Away and Other Stories

COLLECTION

Written

January 1924–May 1927. Collection assembled October–December 1927. Book proofs, January–February 1928.

Published

1. London: Secker, 24 May 1928. New York: Knopf, 25 May 1928.
2. Edited by Dieter Mehl and Christa Jansohn. Cambridge: Cambridge University Press, 1995. (Introduction by the editors, pp. xxi–lxv.)

All but one of the eleven stories in this collection—''None of That''—had been previously published (see later for further details on each individual story). ''The Man Who Loved Islands'' appeared only in the American first edition (Compton Mackenzie considered himself defamed by the story and prevented its publication in Britain). The stories in the volume are as follows: ''Two Blue Birds,'' *Sun*, ''The Woman Who Rode Away,'' ''Smile,'' ''The Border Line,'' ''Jimmy and the Desperate Woman,'' ''The Last Laugh,'' ''In Love,'' *Glad Ghosts*, ''None of That,'' ''The Man Who Loved Islands.'' The Cambridge edition of this collection also includes ''The Rocking-Horse Winner'' and ''The Lovely Lady,'' and these are dealt with in this chapter too.

INDIVIDUAL STORIES

Most of the stories included in the 1928 collection would have been revised by Lawrence in preparing them for the book between October 1927 and February 1928. This information is not repeated for each individual entry but should be borne in mind when considering the evolution of each story.

"TWO BLUE BIRDS"

WRITTEN

May 1926. Proofs for *Dial* publication, March 1927.

PUBLISHED

Dial 82 (April 1927): 287–301.
Great Stories of All Nations. Edited by Maxim Lieber and Blanch Colton Williams. New York: Brentano's, September 1927, pp. 425–38.

WHO'S WHO AND SUMMARY

Cameron Gee is a well-known novelist who spends most of his time working reclusively at his isolated country home. He has many debts and therefore needs to maintain a steady output of work. He is aided in this by his slavishly devoted young secretary, *Miss Wrexall.* He and his wife, *Mrs. Gee,* are both under forty and have been married for twelve years; for the past three or four years, however, they have become estranged—though still "sincerely attached" to one another—and Mrs. Gee spends most of her time in Southern Europe having affairs with other men. Even so, she still hankers after her husband, and, though she does not admit it to herself, she seems jealous of the adoring and ultra-efficient Miss Wrexall. When she does return home, she finds herself something of a stranger there, excluded from the tight working routines of her husband and his secretary. The situation has been made even more difficult for her now that Miss Wrexall has brought in her *mother* and *sister* to do all the household chores; Cameron now has an adoring surrogate family of women to look after him. Returning home one spring, Mrs. Gee decides that this overcomfortable arrangement is not, in fact, all that good for Cameron or for his work, and she decides to do something about it. One afternoon in the garden, she comes unnoticed upon Cameron dictating an article on the future of the novel to the absorbed Miss Wrexall. Mrs. Gee notices a blue tit fluttering around the feet of the secretary, and she thinks of it—presumably in relation to the scribbling secretary's devotion to her husband—as the bluebird of happiness. Then another blue tit arrives, and a squabble ensues between the two birds. This distracts

Cameron, who waves the birds away. He comments on them to Miss Wrexall, but she had not seen them; Mrs. Gee steps forward to say that she had seen them, and she picks up one of the feathers and looks meaningfully from it at the secretary and then at Cameron, with "a queer, were-wolf expression." She makes some barbed comments about the working relationship between her husband and Miss Wrexall before sauntering away again; she leaves the secretary feeling indignant over the implied insult to her "beautiful relationship" with her employer. Later, at teatime, Mrs. Gee, now with a blue dress on, invites Miss Wrexall to stay for tea in the garden with her and Cameron. The secretary goes indoors briefly and returns also wearing a blue dress; as with the blue tits earlier, a squabble ensues between the two women. Cameron makes occasional sarcastic interventions, and these suggest that he will not be prepared to sacrifice his relationship with Miss Wrexall for the sake of his marriage, and Mrs. Gee leaves, saying that "no man can expect *two* blue birds of happiness to flutter round his feet."

SETTING

The main action of the story takes place in the English country home and garden of Cameron Gee, but the precise location is not specified.

BIBLIOGRAPHY 46

Grace, William J. *Response to Literature.* New York: McGraw-Hill, 1965, pp. 146–48.
Howard, Daniel F. *A Manual to Accompany the Modern Tradition.* Boston: Little, Brown, 1968, pp. 11–12.
Widmer, Kingsley. "Birds of Passion and Birds of Marriage in DHL." *University of Kansas City Review* 25 (Fall 1958): 73–79.

SUN

WRITTEN

First version: December 1925. Proofs, September 1926. Second version: April 1928. Proofs, September 1928.

PUBLISHED

In its first version:
1. *New Coterie* 4 (Autumn 1926): 60–77.
2. *Sun.* London: E. Archer, September 1926.
3. 1928 book collection, as earlier.

In its second version:
Sun. Paris: Black Sun Press, October 1928.

WHO'S WHO AND SUMMARY

Juliet is in her late twenties and is married to *Maurice,* a New York businessman of forty. They have an infant son, *Johnny.* Their relationship has become highly fraught—"like two engines running at variance, they shattered one another"— and Juliet's health has suffered. She is advised by her doctor to take a sun cure, and, relieved to get away from Maurice, she goes to Sicily with her son, a *nurse,* and her *mother.* Here, she has a villa overlooking the sea with a large terraced vineyard for a garden. The mother does not stay long, as she and Juliet aggravate one another; and, for a while, Juliet feels just as tense and frustrated as in the city. However, as she becomes accustomed to bathing naked in the sun on a se-cluded rocky bluff above the sea, her inner tensions gradually dissolve, and she feels increasingly in harmony both with her own body and with the natural world around her. She awakens to a religious sense of the sacredness of the sun and of its powerful procreative force. Indeed, the process of her restoration to health and balance is ritualistically and sensuously described as a form of sexual inter-course between her and the sun (and the Edenic connotations of the garden thus become interfused with mythical, pagan ones). Symbolically, Juliet becomes fer-tile with new life as she reestablishes contact with the phenomenal world and with the spontaneous desires of her own body. Counterpointed with Juliet's sen-suous awakening by the sun is her instinctive sexual desire for a local *peasant laborer* whom she has sexually aroused one day when returning naked from her sunbathing. The two never speak, and their desire for one another is never actu-ally consummated in the story, but the peasant serves as a human parallel to the sun in releasing the flow of sexual desire within Juliet. He also serves as a sharp contrast to Juliet's husband, Maurice, who arrives for a holiday looking gray, monastic, and utterly "sunless"; she thinks of him later as a "blanched, etio-lated little city figure" in comparison to the peasant, whom she imagines as "an-other kind of sunshine," a warm "procreative bath, like sun." The story ends somewhat ambiguously, however, with Maurice agreeing to let Juliet remain in Sicily, free to do as she pleases, but with Juliet admitting to herself the impos-sibility of any actual relationship with the peasant and accepting the ironic in-evitability of bearing another child to Maurice. Thus, while the social forces and values represented by Maurice and the city are negated throughout the story by the natural forces represented by the sun and the peasant, they still seem to pre-vail at the end as part of the fateful "fixed wheel of circumstance."

SETTING

The story opens on the Hudson River as Juliet is saying good-bye to her husband on her way to Sicily, which provides the main setting for the story. Juliet's house and garden overlooking the sea are based on Fontana Vecchia in Taormina, Sicily, where the Lawrences lived between March 1920 and February 1922.

BIBLIOGRAPHY 47

Clark, L. D. "Lawrence's 'Maya' Drawing for 'Sun.' " *DHL Review* 15 (1982): 141–46.

Piccolo, Anthony. "Sun and Sex in the Last Stories of DHL." In *HELIOS: From Myth to Solar Energy.* Edited by M. E. Grenander. Albany: Institute for Humanistic Studies, State University of New York, 1978, pp. 166–74.

Ross, Michael L. "Lawrence's Second 'Sun.' " *DHL Review* 8 (1975): 1–18, 373–74.

Wain, John. "The Teaching of DHL." *Twentieth-Century Literature* 157 (May 1955): 464–65.

Widmer, Kingsley. "The Sacred Sun in Modern Literature." *Humanist* (Antioch) 19 (1959): 368–72.

See also Meyers (1982): 153–56. Sagar (1966): 173–75. Spilka (1955): 41–42.

"THE WOMAN WHO RODE AWAY"

WRITTEN

June 1924; revised, June–July 1924. Proofs for *Dial* publication, June 1925 (probably).

PUBLISHED

In two parts:
Dial 79 (July 1925): 1–20; 79 (August 1925): 121–36.
In two parts:
New Criterion 3 (July 1925): 529–42; 4 (January 1926): 95–124.
The Best British Short Stories of 1926, With an Irish Supplement. Edited by Edward J. O'Brien. New York: Dodd, Mead, November 1926, pp. 161–201.

WHO'S WHO AND SUMMARY

Lederman has made his fortune silver-mining in the central Mexican mountains. Originally from Holland and entirely a self-made man, he is now fifty-three years old and graying, but still as tough and tenacious as ever; and he is still devoted, above all else, to his work and to the business of making things and making money. His wife and family (two children, *Freddy* and *Margarita*) have been but sentimental extensions of his business, and he has remained, at heart, a bachelor. His wife is *the woman* of the title. She is from Berkeley, California, blond, blue-eyed, and fair-skinned and twenty years younger than her husband. She seems to have married him for the adventure of his lifestyle rather than for himself, and now, after some ten years together, she is bored and disillusioned with her life, and her nerves have begun "to go wrong." Moreover, she seems to have been strangely arrested in her development, and she is still like an unformed young girl in all but her physical appearance. When she hears stories of the mysterious Indian tribes who live in the wild hills and mountains beyond their home, she is overcome by a "foolish romanticism" that drives her to make a "crazy" plan to go in search of them. Her imagination has been fired, in particular, by talk of the Chilchui Indians, and these become the main object of her quest. The Chilchuis are the sacred tribe of all Indians and supposed descendants of Montezuma and the old Aztec or Totonac kings of preconquest Mexico; they are reputed to keep up the ancient religion and to make human sacrifices still. The woman rides off into the mountains alone. Although the trail is lonely and dangerous, she is curiously elated by the experience rather than afraid. However, her elation gives way to a vague, disheartened listlessness as she nears her destination; she feels "like a woman who has died and passed beyond," and she seems no longer to have any will or purpose of her own. Suddenly, she is confronted by three of the *Chilchui Indians* she has come in search of—they have dark faces, black eyes, and long, black hair. They question her, and she tells them she wants to meet the Chilchuis and "to know their gods." They seem gratified by this response, and, taking control of her horse, they lead her away. She feels increasingly powerless and depersonalized by their remote attitude to her; their black eyes seem to have an inhuman gleam in them, and they seem wholly uninterested in her as a woman or as an individual—when they make camp for the night, she feels merely like some animal they have caught in the hunt, and she again has a strangely exultant sense of having died. At the village of the Chilchuis, the woman is questioned about her motives for coming there by the elders of the tribe. She responds to their questions partly in the way she thinks they want her to respond, and, when they hear that she has come in search of their gods because she is tired of the white man's God, there is an excited response from them as, unknown to the woman, they believe that the sacrifice of a white woman to the sun will bring back their power over both sun and moon, a power they consider to have been usurped by the white man. There then follows a period of sacrificial preparation of the woman, during which she loses all her willpower and her old sense of self—she also becomes increasingly aware of her impending death, her own obliteration: "the quivering nervous consciousness of the highly-bred white woman was to be destroyed again." Finally, on the shortest day of the year, amid much ritual dancing and drumming, she is taken in procession farther up into the mountains, along a dried-up streambed, to the sacred cave of the tribe at the frozen source of the stream, where she is to be sacrificed. The cave has a fang or curtain of ice before it (the frozen waters that would feed the stream), and she is taken to the opening of the cave and placed on the sacrificial stone, with the whole village watching on the streambed below, which forms a natural amphitheater. As the sun goes down, it starts to penetrate the womblike darkness of the cave, and the woman sees that it will soon shine directly through the curtain of ice in front of the cave and into the innermost recesses of the cave; she realizes, too, that at this moment the priest with the knife will strike out her life and accomplish the sacrifice to achieve ''power'' and ''mastery'' for his race.

SETTING

The story is set in the mountains of the Sierre Madre near Torreon in Chihuahua State, central Mexico (Lawrence had visited a silver mine at Minas Nuevas near Navajoa in Mexico in October 1923). However, Lawrence also seems to have drawn details, here, from the more familiar landscape and indigenous culture of the New Mexican mountains above Taos. In particular, the sacrificial cave in the story seems to be based on a cave he had visited near Arroyo Seco in May 1924.

BIBLIOGRAPHY 48

Balbert, Peter. ''Snake's Eye and Obsidian Knife: Art, Ideology and 'The Woman Who Rode Away.' '' *DHL Review* 18 (Summer 1985–86): 255–73. (Reprinted in Balbert [1989]: 109–32.)

Berce, Sanda. ''The Sun-Myth: A Parable of Modern Civilization.'' *Studia University Babes-Bolyai* 33, no. 1 (1988): 56–63.

Dekker, George. ''Lilies That Fester.'' *New Left Review* 28 (November–December 1964): 75–84.

Dexter, Martin. ''DHL and Pueblo Religion: An Inquiry into Accuracy.'' *Arizona Quarterly* 9 (Fall 1953): 219–34.

Draper, R. P. ''The Defeat of Feminism: DHL's *The Fox* and 'The Woman Who Rode Away.' '' *Studies in Short Fiction* 3 (1966): 186–98.

Duryea, Polly. ''Rainwitch Ritual in Cather, Lawrence, and Momaday, and Others.'' *Journal of Ethnic Studies* 18 (Summer 1990): 59–75.

Eisenstein, Samuel A. ''DHL's 'The Woman Who Rode Away.' '' *Kyushu American Literature* (Fukuoka, Japan) 9 (1966): 1–18.

Galea, Ileana. ''DHL: The Value of Myth.'' *Cahiers Roumains d'Etudes Litteraires* 3 (1987): 72–78.

Goonetilleke, D.C.R.A. ''DHL: Primitivism?'' In his *Developing Countries in British Fiction*. London and Basingstoke: Macmillan; Totowa, N.J.: Rowman and Littlefield, 1977, pp. 170–98 (181–84 and passim).

Kinkead-Weekes, Mark. ''The Gringo Senora Who Rode Away.'' *DHL Review* 22 (Fall 1990): 251–65.

Krishnamurthy, M. G. ''DHL's 'The Woman Who Rode Away.' '' *Literary Criterion* (India) 4 (Summer 1960): 40–49.

Moore, Harry T. ''DHL.'' *Times Literary Supplement* (19 December 1963): 1038.

Padhi, Bibhu. '' 'The Woman Who Rode Away' and Lawrence's Vision of the New World.'' *University of Dayton Review* 17 (Winter 1985–86): 57–61.

Rossman, Charles. "Myth and Misunderstanding DHL." *Bucknell Review* 22 (Fall 1976): 81–101 (97–101).

Rudnick, Lois P. "DHL's New World Heroine: Mabel Dodge Luhan." *DHL Review* 14 (Spring 1981): 85–111.

Springer, Mary Doyle. *Forms of the Modern Novella.* Chicago and London: University of Chicago Press, 1976, pp. 25–32 and passim.

Steven, Laurence. " 'The Woman Who Rode Away': DHL's Cul-de-Sac." *English Studies in Canada* 10 (1984): 209–20.

Tanner, Tony. "DHL in America." In *DHL: Novelist, Poet, Prophet.* Edited by Stephen Spender. London: Weidenfeld and Nicolson, 1973, pp. 170–96 (192–93).

Travis, Leigh. "DHL: The Blood-Conscious Artist." *American Imago* 25 (Summer 1968): 163–90 (166–74).

Wasserstrom, William. "Phoenix on Turtle Island: DHL in Henry Adams' America." *Georgia Review* 32 (Spring 1978): 172–97.

Wicker, Brian. "Lawrence and the Unseen Presences." In his *The Story-Shaped World: Fiction and Metaphysics: Some Variations on a Theme.* Notre Dame, Ind.: University of Notre Dame, 1975, pp. 120–33 (127–29).

Widmer, Kingsley. "The Primitive Aesthetic: DHL." *Journal of Aesthetics and Art Criticism* 17 (1959): 348–49.

See also (1980–94) Clark (1980): 309–11. Hostettler (1985): 141–50. MacLeod (1985/87): 139–47. Mohanty (1993): 110–18. Pinkney (1990): 165–67. Ruderman (1984): 127–41. Worthen (1991a): 86–89.

See also (to 1979) Albright (1978): 62–69. Cavitch (1969): 163–69. Clark (1964): 39–41. Cowan (1970): 70–78. Draper (1964): 135–39. Eisenstein (1974): 114–25. Goodheart (1963): 133–34. Hough (1956): 138–46. John (1974): 275–78. Leavis (1955): 273–75. Millett (1970): 285–92. Pritchard (1971): 162–64. Slade (1970): 110–12. Stewart (1963): 577–80.

"SMILE"

WRITTEN

November–December 1925.

PUBLISHED

Nation and Athenaeum 39 (19 June 1926): 319–20.
New Masses (June 1926): 12, 14.

WHO'S WHO AND SUMMARY

The story centers on *Matthew,* who has been called to the deathbed of his estranged wife, *Ophelia,* who had been living in retreat at a convent in Italy.

We are told later that his wife had left him twelve times before in the ten years they had been married but had always returned; this had been the thirteenth time. By the time he arrives at the convent, his wife has died. He is taken to see her body by the *Mother Superior* and three other *nuns*. When he sees the serene composure of his wife's face, an involuntary smile appears on his face, and this incongruous display of humor infectiously spreads to the observing nuns, each of them smiling in a different way. Matthew then looks again at the "obstinate" face of his wife, and a sense of his own martyrdom at losing Ophelia replaces his humor, but he feels as if she is actually still alive and digging him in the ribs to make him smile. He tries to resist this provocation by dwelling on his imperfections in their marriage and summoning up guilt feelings, but the spirit of his wife persists in nudging him in the ribs, and he has to rush out of the room. After he has gone, the nuns look again at Ophelia and notice a "faint ironical curl" at the corners of her mouth. Outside, the Mother Superior sees Matthew loitering forlornly in the corridor, and he says, with a desperate gesture, that he has mislaid his hat—"and never was man more utterly smileless." (This story seems, rather cruelly, to be based on the actual experience of John Middleton Murry when he witnessed the death of Katherine Mansfield at the Gurdjieff Institute at Fontainebleau, France, in 1923. It is, along with the three that follow, part of a series of stories in which Murry is parodied by Lawrence. Lawrence and Murry had had a turbulent relationship since they first met in 1913; they had been wholly estranged between 1919 and late 1922–early 1923, when they reestablished contact. Later in 1923, they met once more, but old tensions soon emerged, along with a new one. Lawrence now suspected Murry of having had an affair with Frieda while she was in Europe without him between August and November 1923, and this would seem to be a large part of the motivation behind "Smile" and the other three anti-Murry stories.)

SETTING

The main setting for the story is the convent of the "Blue Sisters" somewhere in Italy. There is also a brief description of Matthew's journey there across France at the start of the story.

BIBLIOGRAPHY 49

Finney, Brian. "The Hitherto Unknown Publication of Some DHL Short Stories." *Notes and Queries* 19 (February 1972): 55–56.

See also Cowan (1970): 50–52.

"THE BORDER LINE"

WRITTEN

February 1924; February–April 1924. Lawrence wrote an entirely new ending
for the story in January 1928, when correcting the proofs for the book collection.

PUBLISHED

Hutchinson's Story Magazine (September 1924): 153–58, 234–38.
Smart Set (September 1924): 11–25.

WHO'S WHO AND SUMMARY

Katherine Farquhar, forty years old and the daughter of a German baron (von
Todtnau), is now married to *Philip Farquhar,* a Scotsman, whom she had married two years ago (in 1921) after the death in the war of her first husband, also
a Scotsman, *Alan Anstruther.* She is traveling to Baden-Baden via Strasbourg
to see her sister *Marianne* and to meet her husband. However, the journey is
also a journey of psychological self-discovery, as Katherine takes stock of her
life and of her relationship with Philip; and it develops into a psychic journey
away from her present husband and toward her previous one, Alan, whose spirit
returns to her at the ''demonish-heathen'' cathedral of Strasbourg (the border
town that thus becomes representative also of the borderline between the living
and the dead). When she meets Philip again at Baden-Baden, she now feels
humiliated to be married to him. He seems unwell, and, by the next morning,
his condition has deteriorated—he tells of a dream in which he thought Alan
was lying on him almost trying to suffocate him. Later in the day, as the couple
go to drink springwater from an old grotto, Alan appears to Katherine again,
and shortly afterward Philip has a coughing fit. When they return to the hotel,
he has blood around his chin and on his coat. The doctor diagnoses the rupture
of a minor blood vessel, and Katherine settles Philip down for the night and
sits for a while on the side of his bed—Alan sits on the other side. During the
night, she hears Philip scream and runs in to find him bleeding once more and
claiming that Alan had been lying on him again. The next night, when Philip
appeals for help from Katherine, Alan prevents her from giving it by holding
her down. By the morning, Philip is dead. (See the comment under the preceding
entry for ''Smile'' for a general comment on Lawrence's anti-Murry stories.
Here, Alan and Katherine would appear to be based loosely on Lawrence and
Frieda, and Philip on Murry.)

SETTING

We follow Katherine Farquhar on her journey from England across the Channel to Paris and thence through the Marne area of France to Soissons, through Nancy to Strasbourg, where she visits the cathedral, then into Germany, across the Rhine, and northward to Baden-Baden, which provides the setting for the final part of the story. (Lawrence and Frieda made a similar trip in February 1924.)

BIBLIOGRAPHY 50

Gutierrez, Donald. "Getting Even with John Middleton Murry." *Interpretations* 15, no. 1 (1983): 31–38.

Hudspeth, Robert N. "Duality as Theme and Technique in DHL's 'The Border Line.' " *Studies in Short Fiction* 4 (1966): 51–56.

Peek, Andrew. "Edgar Allan Poe's 'Ligeia,' Hermione Roddice and 'The Border Line': Common Romantic Contexts and a Source of Correspondence in the Fiction of Poe and Lawrence." *Journal of the DHL Society* 2, no. 2 (1980): 4–8.

See also Clark (1980): 300–302. Cowan (1970): 52–55. Hahn (1975): 284–85. Hyde (1992): 53–56. West (1950): 99–105.

"JIMMY AND THE DESPERATE WOMAN"

WRITTEN

February–April 1924.

PUBLISHED

Criterion 3 (October 1924): 15–42.

The Best British Short Stories of 1925, With an Irish Supplement. Edited by Edward J. O'Brien and John Cournos. Boston: Small, Maynard, October 1925, pp. 88–114.

WHO'S WHO AND SUMMARY

Jimmy Frith is thirty-five and the editor of a high-class literary magazine, the *Commentator.* He has been married for ten years to *Clarissa,* but they are now divorced. Riled by his ex-wife's estimation of him as "a poor little man" in need of a strong woman's support—a woman's bosom to nestle on—he determines to find a woman who will nestle on *his* bosom. Typical of a literary man, he fantasizes about "some simple uneducated girl, some Tess of the D'Urbervilles." When he enters into correspondence with a Yorkshire woman who has sent him poems for his magazine, he thinks he has found just this sort of person—someone in an apparently "tragic" situation and ready to be rescued by a heroic "Ulysses." The woman, *Mrs. Emily (Emilia) Pinnegar,* is unhappily married to a miner who keeps another woman. An ex-schoolteacher, she is now thirty-one and has an eight-year-old daughter, *Jane.* Full of romantic ideas about a wild-blooded, unsophisticated woman and about the natural spontaneity of northern mining folk—"these miners up there must be the real stuff"—Jimmy goes to see Mrs. Pinnegar in her own home. The reality, of course, is very different from what he expects: the mining environment appears "dismal and horrible" to him, and, though Mrs. Pinnegar appears deeply unhappy and resentful of her domestic situation, she is neither wild nor unsophisticated. In fact, she exhibits a cold and restrained manner and is clearly a strong and proud woman, with the word "unyielding" being repeated several times in her description. She makes Jimmy aware of his own small, shambling "physical inconspicuousness"—but he must now brazen out his self-imposed ordeal, and, "like a gambler," he asks her to come and live with him in London, along with Jane, and to marry him if she wants after her divorce. The woman mentions a few practicalities but appears to accept the offer with alacrity, almost as though it were a bargain business proposition. Jimmy is somewhat taken aback by this but nervously sustains his pseudoromantic approach by telling her that she "will mean *life*" to him, that her acceptance is "perfectly marvellous." Jimmy's encounter with Emily's energetic and intense husband, *Pinnegar,* further unnerves him. The miner's sheer physicality almost totally negates Jimmy's presence in the house, and his confident, logical, and forceful manner in addressing Jimmy—about his wife and marital relationships, about literary journals, about politics—deflates Jimmy's "Oxfordy" sense of superiority and throws his "heroic" construction of events into ironic relief for us. Inwardly, Jimmy himself knows that he cannot match the power of Pinnegar's "silent unconsciousness," and this reminder of his ineffectuality galls him and spurs him on to persevere with his fantasy "rescue" of Emily. He meets little resistance from the miner, however, who seems only too ready to be rid of his wife—though he finds it amusing that she should want to go with such "a funny fish" as Jimmy. Arrangements are thus summarily made for Emily and Jane to come to London to live with Jimmy. Though exhilarated by his "adventure," Jimmy returns home that night with strong misgivings about what he has done; hopeful of second thoughts on her part, too, he sends an anxious message to Emily giving her the opportunity of backing out of the arrangement. She, however, is clearly desperate to escape from her dismal existence, and she remains resolute in her intention of moving in with Jimmy. He is thus forced to live with the consequences of his literary fantasy, and the story ends as he collects Emily and Jane from the railway station with "a sickly grin" on his face. (See the comment under the entry for "Smile" earlier in this chapter for a general comment on Lawrence's anti-Murry stories. Here, Jimmy is clearly based on Murry, who, in 1924, married a young contributor to his journal, the *Adelphi.*)

SETTING

The story begins with Jimmy in London and then moves to "Mill Valley," a mining village ostensibly in Yorkshire near Sheffield, though bearing some resemblances to Lawrence's own Eastwood.

BIBLIOGRAPHY 51

Gutierrez, Donald. "Getting Even with John Middleton Murry." *Interpretations* 15, no. 1 (1983): 31–38.

See also Cowan (1970): 55–58.

"THE LAST LAUGH"

WRITTEN

January–February 1924; February–April 1924.

PUBLISHED

The New Decameron IV. Edited by Blair. London: Basil Blackwell, March 1925, pp. 235–61.
Ainslee's 56 (January 1926): 55–65.

WHO'S WHO AND SUMMARY

Miss James, a partially deaf artist, and *Mr. Marchbanks,* her friend, are seen departing from the house of *Lorenzo* on a snow-covered winter's night. As they walk down the street toward Miss James's house, Marchbanks claims to hear laughter, but the woman only sees and hears *him* producing a strange neighing, animal laughter. A *young policeman* approaches; he, too, has heard only the wild laughter coming from Marchbanks. The latter is convinced that the laughter is coming from a grove of trees and bushes behind some railings across the street. They all go to look, and Miss James suddenly sees a man among the holly trees and old English elms, a man whom she seems to recognize "triumphantly" as someone she always expected to see one day. Neither of the men sees him, but Marchbanks seems still to be able to hear his voice, and he runs up the street in pursuit of it. As he comes to a house, *a woman* approaches him down her garden path, saying that she had been drawn out of the house by a knock at her door, and this is despite the fact that there are no footprints in the snow leading up to the door. After a brief conversation, the woman (who is possibly a prostitute), invites Marchbanks in, and Miss James and the policeman are just in time to see the door close behind him. These two then set off down the street again, and Miss James, with strange sounds and voices swirling around her ears with the snow, comments, "He's come back!" (By this point in the story, the sudden changes wrought in the characters by the ghostly laughter and the mysterious apparition in the trees, along with giveaway references to satyrs, fauns, and groves, make it plain that the "he" referred to here is supposed to be *Pan,* the Mediterranean goat-god, returned to challenge Christianity and to revivify and renew the world.) A storm of thunder and lightning develops, and, as they approach Miss James's house, they hear a strange commotion from the church nearby—a "wild confusion" of voices, music, crashes, and laughter. Mysteriously, Miss James also perceives a springlike scent of almond blossom wafted on a breeze of warm wind. They go into her house, she up to her bedroom, and the policeman into her sitting room to warm himself. The next morning, she is in her studio looking at her paintings when she begins laughing out loud at their absurdity. This attracts the attention of the housekeeper, who thinks she has been called. When she speaks loudly, as usual, to Miss James, the latter complains, and it appears that her deafness has been cured. The housekeeper reports that the policeman is still in the sitting room and complaining of being lame. Miss James muses to herself that the world has suddenly become quite different, as if its old skin had suddenly been shed to reveal "an absolutely new blue heaven." This echoes the apparently casual and ironic remark made at the start of the story by the smiling, satyrlike Lorenzo that the snow had created "a new world." Miss James puts it all down to the return of the "being" she had seen and heard the previous night; "he" was having the last laugh after all. Marchbanks then arrives and reports that, according to the newspapers, the church next door had been wrecked by the storm. They go down to see the policeman and find that his left foot has turned into a weird clubfoot like that of some animal. Miss James hears the "low, eternal laugh" once again and turns to find Marchbanks with an agonized grin of recognition on his face. His eyes roll manically, and, with a "queer shuddering laugh," he suddenly pitches to the floor and dies as if struck by lightning. The story ends as, once again, a mysterious scent of almond blossom lingers in the air. (See the comment under the entry for "Smile" for a general comment on Lawrence's anti-Murry stories. Here, Marchbanks is the Murry figure, and Miss James is modeled on the Hon. Dorothy Brett.)

SETTING

A street in Hampstead, London, provides the main setting for the action here. The first two-thirds of the story take place outside in the street itself; the last third, in the house and studio of Miss James. The street is probably modeled on Heath Street, Hampstead, where Lawrence stayed between 14 December 1923 and 23 January 1924.

BIBLIOGRAPHY 52

Baim, Joseph. "The Second Coming of Pan: A Note on DHL's 'The Last Laugh.' " *Studies in Short Fiction* 6 (Fall 1968): 98–100.

Ghatak, T. " 'The Last Laugh': A Possible View of Lawrence's Short Story." *Parnassus* (Indian Institute of Technology, Kharagpur) 3 (July 1976): 9–14.

Gutierrez, Donald. "Getting Even with John Middleton Murry." *Interpretations* 15, no. 1 (1983): 31–38.

Merivale, Patricia. "DHL and the Modern Pan Myth." *Texas Studies in Literature and Language* 6 (Fall 1964): 297–305. (Reprinted in her *Pan the Goat-God: His Myth in Modern Times.* Cambridge: Harvard University Press, 1969, pp. 194–219.)

See also Cowan (1970): 58–61.

"IN LOVE"

WRITTEN

October 1926. Proofs for *Dial* publication, April 1927.

PUBLISHED

Dial 83 (November 1927): 391–404. (See Finney, Brian. "The Hitherto Unknown Publication of Some DHL Short Stories." *Notes and Queries* 19 [February 1972]: 55–56.)

WHO'S WHO AND SUMMARY

Joe and *Hester* are to be married in a month. Joe has recently started a small farm in Wiltshire, and Hester is going to spend the weekend with him. However, as her younger sister *Henrietta* notices before she sets off, she is somewhat worried about the arrangement. It emerges that, since they have been engaged, Joe has started to play what he thinks is the correct "part" of someone supposedly "in love," and this primarily involves being "lovey-dovey" and "spooning" after the fashion of the stars of popular film romances—such as Rudolf Valentino, for example (for an interesting inverted gloss on this story, see Lawrence's *Pansies* poem, "Film Passion"). On the first evening of Hester's stay at the farm, Joe predictably starts his spooning, but Hester fends him off by asking him to play the piano. When he is not looking, she slips out into the night and hides from him up a tree. She thinks about their relationship and decides that his very *being* in love with her proves that he does not love her *really*. After he has given up looking for her and angrily returned indoors, she decides to go and confront him directly with her grievance. At that moment, Henrietta, *Donald* (Joe's brother), and *Teddy* (Joe's cousin) arrive in a car on their way to a neighboring friend. Henrietta comes in to have a look at her sister's future home. Once inside, Hester tries to encourage her to stay. When she refuses, Hester announces that she will not stay either. Henrietta now sees that something is wrong between the couple, and she presses them to explain. This forces them to justify their behavior: Hester repeats what she had decided up the tree; Joe then admits that he had been acting "in love" only because he thought she expected it of him and because he thought she *liked* Rudolf Valentino. This misunderstanding cleared up, the couple's *real* love for one another is reaffirmed, and Hester agrees to stay alone with Joe after all.

SETTING

The main action takes place on Joe's farm in "Markbury," an English country village in Wiltshire.

GLAD GHOSTS

WRITTEN

December 1925; revised, January 1926. Proofs for *Dial* publication, June 1926 (probably). Proofs for Benn volume, September 1926.

PUBLISHED

In two parts:
Dial 81 (July 1926): 1–21; 81 (August 1926): 123–41.
Glad Ghosts. London: Ernest Benn, November 1926.

WHO'S WHO AND SUMMARY

Partly a ghost story, partly a sex story, but almost wholly in a comic vein, *Glad Ghosts* playfully sets the sensuous world against the spiritual, with the gladness of laughter as both a mediating influence and the final determining factor in the victory of Bacchus and Eros over Thanatos. This is precisely how the first-person narrator functions, too, for *Mark Morier* ("to laugh more" if we take the name to suggest the French *rire*) both cheerfully mediates the story and sexually overcomes the apparently congenital morbidity of the Lathkill family ("killers of laughter"). Morier has known the *Hon. Carlotta Fell* since they were both students at the Thwaite school of art. Despite surface differences of social class allegiance (she is a peer's daughter, and he is a "sansculotte"), they have always been close because of a shared inner allegiance to the aristocratic "Kingdom of It," to "the quick body" within "the half-dead body of this life." However, Carlotta always *acts* according the conventions of her class, and, just before the war, she marries *Lord Lathkill* (Luke Worth), whose family is reputed to be unlucky. Lathkill shows all the outward self-assurance typical of his class, but, Morier notes, he is unsure of his inner self, as though he is "already a ghost." He is dark, with fine black hair, and handsome, but he has a hollow look and "a touch of madness" in his eyes and voice. Morier meets the couple again after the war, and he sees their infant twin boys. He finds Lord Lathkill more haggard than ever and now also with a war wound to his throat, and Carlotta, too, seems to be wilting and losing her beauty. Some years pass, and Morier learns that Carlotta has given birth to another child, but then, later again, he hears of the catastrophe that has befallen the Lathkills—their twins have been killed in a motoring accident, and a few weeks later their daughter had died also, of a sudden illness: the Lathkill ill luck seems to be operating with a vengeance. The couple seem to retire from society and live reclusively with Luke's mother, the dowager *Lady Lathkill,* at the family home, Riddings, in Derbyshire.

Sometime later, on his return from Africa, Morier takes up an invitation to visit Riddings. Lady Lathkill, the elder, has developed an interest in spiritualism and the uncanny, we are told, and there are two other guests staying at the house, *Colonel Hale* and his wife, *Dorothy Hale.* Morier is offered the family's "ghost room" to sleep in. It emerges that there is a female family ghost who appears only infrequently but who, when she does appear, invariably signals an upturn in the family fortunes. Apparently, Lady Lathkill had had a message about Morier from a medium indicating that he might be the one to tempt the ghost to visit. When Morier learns that the ghost dispenses her sexual favors freely when she visits, he agrees to take the room. Everything about Riddings seems deathly, with "the obscene triumph of dead Matter"; and everybody speaks in undertones. Even Carlotta seems to have had the life drawn from her. Morier muses to himself that she needs "a living body" to restore the flow in her life. The dinner is strained, though Morier does his best to enliven the occasion. Lady Lathkill has a "witch-face" and seems to him like "an ermine in the snow, feeding on his prey." The bald, pink colonel with yellow creases under his eyes is around sixty, dejected and liverish. His youthful wife is inaccessible, black-browed and swarthy with yellow-brown eyes—"like a black she-fox": she is later referred to as a half-wild animal with a sheen of black hairs on her limbs. Over the port, the Colonel makes a long speech about his dead first wife, Lucy. He had married her when he was twenty and she was twenty-eight, and he had always been "mothered" by her; now, she continues to dominate him from beyond the grave and a year ago had insisted that he marry again, giving him precise instructions as to whom he should choose (that is, the present Mrs. Hale). However, since then, she has prevented him from consummating the marriage, and the Colonel does not know what to do. Lady Lathkill has suggested to him that this must be a preparation for his next incarnation when he will "serve Woman." But Morier suggests, in his typically blunt manner, that the Colonel should simply face down the spirit of his dead wife and tell her to go to blazes; this elicits, unusually, a loud laugh from Lord

Lathkill. Later, when the dancing begins, we hear that Lord Lathkill has been affected in some way by the Colonel's confession: he dances with Mrs. Hale with great relish—as does Morier with Carlotta. Suddenly, there is a strange icy chill in the room, and it seems that the spirit of the departed Lucy has entered. Lady Lathkill addresses her, and they hear two thuds and some drapery moving. The colonel eventually goes to bed, apparently without making his peace with Lucy. Over supper, Lord Lathkill speaks about how Morier's vitality has thrown the deathliness of the house into relief for him; his "twinkling" bodily life has shown up just how much the rest of them are bodily dead, mere corpses. He explains Lucy Hale's restlessness in terms of her late realization that she had never lived in the flesh properly; he, however, *has* realized in time. As he says this, he clasps Dorothy Hale's hand to him. At this, Carlotta begins to cry, and Lord Lathkill goes on to suggest that he and Carlotta have drifted apart sexually and that each needs to renew desire with someone else; the strong implication is that Morier should sleep with his wife, while he will sleep with Mrs. Hale.

The Colonel reenters, still troubled about the discord with Lucy. Lord Lathkill forces him to acknowledge that he only ever loved Lucy in the abstract, not with his whole body, and that this is why she is restless. The Colonel, realizing now that there can be no purely "spiritual" solution to the problem, opens his pajama jacket to expose his breast; gradually, he becomes tranquil as the ghost of his wife is laid to rest in his bodily heart. Lord Lathkill's mother reenters, and he tells her that he thinks the family ghost must be walking, as he can smell the plum blossom that supposedly accompanies her appearances. He thanks his mother for the gift of his physical body, and, as they retire, he reminds Morier to expect a visit from the "silent" ghost. Morier, indeed, passes a night of plum blossom-scented rapture and, in his mating with the ghost, experiences a "perfect knowledge" of "it." A year later, he receives a letter from Lord Lathkill reporting the birth of a "ghost-begotten" heir, blue-eyed, yellow-haired, and pugilistic, and also the birth to Dorothy and Colonel Hale of a black-haired daughter.

SETTING

The story begins in London and then moves to the Lathkill estate, "Riddings," in Middleton, Derbyshire, presumably based on the real Middleton, where Lawrence lived between May 1918 and February 1919.

"NONE OF THAT"

WRITTEN

May 1927. Unpublished prior to 1928 collection.

WHO'S WHO AND SUMMARY

The unnamed first-person *narrator* introduces us to *Luis Colmenares,* who, as a second narrator, actually tells the main story. He is a Mexican exile eking out a poor and lonely existence as an artist in Europe. Usually uncommunicative, he now seems desperate to tell his story about *Cuesta,* the bullfighter, having just seen him again, after many years, in Venice. Colmenares has black, "unseeing" eyes and an "averted" spirit, and the first narrator seems somewhat suspicious of him, commenting periodically on his "inverted passion." Colmenares refers us back to Mexico around 1913 and 1914. Cuesta is at the height of his fame as a toreador. Though short, fat, and brutish, with inhuman, yellowish eyes, he has a natural magnetism in the bullring that mesmerizes audiences. Outside the ring, women are strongly drawn to him.

Ethel Cane is a rich American woman in her mid-thirties and, in most things, the exact opposite of Cuesta—intellectual, cultured, blond, blue-eyed, fair-skinned. But she, too, has a dynamic presence—a "terrible American energy"—though of a repelling rather than an attracting kind, a power "to compel people to submit to her will." With a newfound passion for social reform, she goes to Mexico in search of "a remarkable and epoch-making husband" with whom to change the course of history. However, she finds that, in Mexico, men will not be dominated by her, while, on the other hand, though many men would gladly take her as a mistress, she is having "*none of that.*" Luis, who has known Ethel previously and who becomes her confidant in Mexico, tells us that, in fact, she recoils from physical contact and wants only "passive maleness" from a man. She asserts the preeminent power of the imagination to control material circumstances and to rise above any traumatic experience, whether suffered or committed—even rape or murder.

Ethel Cane, however, finds herself fatefully drawn to Cuesta. She finds his physical magnetism overpowering but resists and resents it because it undermines her imaginative sense of Cuesta as a mindless brute. She feels that her whole philosophy of life is threatened because she does not seem able, in this instance, to bring her body under the control of her mind, and she *will* not let her body fall for Cuesta unless her imagination is engaged at the same time; she tells Luis that if she cannot control her body in this, she will kill herself. For his part, Cuesta finds Ethel's "imagination" exactly the sort of barrier to a relationship that she sees in his body: "When he tried to look at her, she set her imagination in front of him, like a mirror they put in front of a wild dog." Neither of the characters can catch the other in their own preferred modes of relationship. In any case, Cuesta seems more interested in Ethel's money than in her self. So, although in private he soon begins to talk of her in abusive terms, he continues to call on her, if only for brief periods and never alone. This makes Ethel increasingly infatuated with him, but also increasingly frustrated and distraught over her mind–body dilemma. Eventually, she accepts one of his many invitations to visit his house late at night, and Cuesta then hands her over to his bullring gang, and she is brutally raped by them. Within three days, she is dead; she has killed herself by taking poison, and she has left Luis an ambiguous suicide note: "It is as I told you. Good-bye. But my testament holds good." She has also left Cuesta half of her fortune in a will made ten days before her death.

How one interprets this disturbing conclusion will be determined partly by one's judgment of the teller of the tale, Colmenares. In the course of recounting the bullfightlike duel between Cuesta and Ethel Cane, it becomes clear that he was deeply involved in this duel and that he, too, was engaged in a sort of duel with the woman in his ambiguous intimacy with her. We are, it seems, invited to question the nature and status of his imaginative testament when the first narrator interrupts his criticism of women's self-justifying use of the imagination, to point out that men are guilty of this, too: "To the imagination all things are pure, if you did them yourself," he says, as Colmenares looks at him with "quick, black eyes." (Lawrence based the character of Cuesta on an actual Mexican bullfighter, Rodolfo Gaona [1888–1975], who was involved in scandal when a girl was killed at one of his orgies.)

SETTING

The story is narrated from Venice, but the action takes place mainly in Mexico.

BIBLIOGRAPHY 53

Rudnick, Lois P. "DHL's New World Heroine: Mabel Dodge Luhan." *DHL Review* 14 (Spring 1981): 85–111.
Widmer, Kingsley. "Lawrence and the Fall of Modern Woman." *Modern Fiction Studies* 5 (Spring 1959): 47–56 (49–51).

See also MacLeod (1985/87): 137–38. Rees (1958): 68–69.

"THE MAN WHO LOVED ISLANDS"

WRITTEN

June–July 1926. Proofs, April 1927 (*Dial*), July 1927 (*London Mercury*).

PUBLISHED

Dial 83 (July 1927): 1–25.
London Mercury 16 (August 1927): 370–88.

WHO'S WHO AND SUMMARY

In this mock fairy tale or fable, Lawrence, as in so many of his stories, sets out to expose the inner logic of a type of idealism—here, a particularly egocentric type. Or, as his narrator in the story puts it, he sets out to show just how tiny an island needs to be "before you can presume to fill it with your own personality." For the man of the title, *Cathcart,* wants to create a brave new world—of his own making and of his own. Cathcart buys the lease of his first two islands at the age of thirty-five. He goes to live on the larger of the two. At first, it all seems quite idyllic, and he loves his island, but soon, at nights, he starts to have strange feelings about time. Having concentrated his life in one small space and thus no longer being able so easily to measure time as movement through space, he experiences a sense of the "timeless" continuity and infinity of time, as though the past is "vastly alive" all around him, and "the future not separated off." To rid himself of his ghostly nighttime visions of bygone worlds, he turns his mind to practical matters and decides to try to turn his island into "a minute world of pure perfection." He begins by spending a small fortune on it, and he populates it with a range of "*islanders*" from the mainland to create a busy but carefully controlled island community. He becomes "the Master" to his "grateful" subjects. Once things are ticking over efficiently, he begins to devote all his time to compiling a work of reference on the flowers mentioned in the ancient classics. At the end of his first year on the island, however, the bills start to flood in, and he realizes that the island has swallowed up a great deal of his capital. He is forced to plan economy measures for the next two years, but, at the end of the second year, the island has cost him thousands of pounds yet again, and now some of his employee-islanders start to leave. He makes rigid economies in the third year, but still to no avail—the island seems to "steal" from him in every direction. In the second half of the fourth year, he spends all his time on the mainland trying to sell the island, but nobody will pay the asking price. Eventually, he is forced to sell it at a loss to a hotel company that wants to make it into a "honeymoon-and-golf" island.

Cathcart now moves onto the smaller neighboring island. He takes with him only a few people, including his *housekeeper* and her daughter, *Flora*. This island is no longer "a world" for Cathcart, so much as a refuge from the world. He concentrates now—in a leisurely fashion—on his reference book, and the appropriately named Flora types it for him. Apart from this work, he no longer has to struggle or strive for anything; he feels a total lack of desire, and the days and months fly by apparently "happy," though he is not sure what this means anymore. In a momentary relapse into desire, however, he has a brief and perfunctory affair with Flora. Afterward, he recognizes the "willed" nature of her desire for him and his purely mechanical, automatic response to her; he knows it has been a grave mistake. He now feels shattered, full of self-contempt; the island is "smirched and spoiled," and he feels he has lost his place in "the rare, desireless levels of Time to which he had at last arrived." He travels on the Continent for a while but does not fit in the world anymore. He then hears from Flora that she is expecting his child, and he returns to the island, takes her to the mainland, and marries her. He waits on the island with her for the child to be born, makes all the necessary living and financial arrangements for their future, and then departs for a third island that he has recently bought.

This one is just a few acres of uninhabited rock with not even a home to live in when he arrives. He builds himself a hut and lives here alone, obtaining his only satisfaction from this sense of total isolation. He loses interest in everything and keeps no track of the time; in contrast to his original sense of infinite time on the first island, he now has no sense of time whatsoever. Space, too, becomes unreal to him, as the gray of the island and sea turns to the blankness of the white snow in winter. His mind becomes increasingly blank, and he stares "stupidly" over the whiteness and over "the waste of the lifeless sea." Total isolation develops into total desolation as, at the end of the story, the lowering elements clearly presage death for our islander.

SETTING

The islands in the story are not given precise locations, but Lawrence was inspired to write the story partly by what he knew of Compton Mackenzie's experiences after buying two Channel Islands, Herm and Jethou, in 1920, and the Shiant Islands in the Outer Hebrides in 1925. Though Lawrence had actual experience of only the Hebridean islands (he visited the Isle of Skye in August 1926, but only after first writing the story; he never visited the Channel Islands), the references, with the first island, to "men of Gaul" and to Jersey cows, the fact that most of the inhabitants have come from southern parts of England, and the apparent ease with which Cathcart travels back to London all suggest that the setting is supposed to be in the Channel Islands (some of the descriptions of the earlier islands echo descriptions of the Isle of Wight in *The Trespasser,* an island Lawrence did know quite well and very roughly in the same region as the Channel Islands). However, some of the descriptions, especially of the last island, with its harsh snowstorms, seem more suggestive of the Outer Hebrides, and it may be that Lawrence's visit to Scotland in 1926 influenced at least some of his revisions of the story.

BIBLIOGRAPHY 54

Doherty, Gerald. "The Art of Survival: Narrating the Nonnarratable in DHL's 'The Man Who Loved Islands.' " *DHL Review* 24 (Fall 1992): 117–26.

Harris, Lynn E. "The Island as a Mental Image of Withdrawal, Used in a Literary Work, DHL's 'The Man Who Loved Islands.' " In *Imagery II.* Edited by David G. Russell, David F. Marks, and John T. E. Richardson. Dunedin, New Zealand: Human Performance Associates, 1986, pp. 178–81.

Karl, Frederick R. "Lawrence's 'The Man Who Loved Islands': The Crusoe Who

Failed.'' In *A DHL Miscellany.* Edited by Harry T. Moore. Carbondale: Southern
   Illinois University Press, 1959, pp. 265–79.

Kearney, Martin. ''Spirit, Place and Psyche: Integral Integration in DHL's 'The Man
   Who Loved Islands.' '' *English Studies* 69, no. 2 (April 1988): 158–62.

Kendle, Burton S. ''DHL: The Man Who Misunderstood Gulliver.'' *English Language
   Notes* 2 (1964): 42–46.

Link, Viktor. ''DHL's 'The Man Who Loved Islands' in Light of Compton Mackenzie's
   Memoirs.'' *DHL Review* 15 (1982): 77–86.

Moynahan, Julian. ''Lawrence's 'The Man Who Loved Islands': A Modern Fable.''
   Modern Fiction Studies 5 (Spring 1959): 57–64. (Reprinted in Moynahan [1963]:
   185–96.)

Padhi, Bibhu. ''Lawrence's Ironic Fables and How They Matter.'' *Interpretations* 15,
   no. 1 (1983): 53–59.

Squires, Michael. ''Teaching a Story Rhetorically: An Approach to a Short Story by
   DHL.'' *College Composition and Communication* 24 (May 1973): 150–56.

Toyokuni, Takashi. ''A Modern Man Obsessed by Time: A Note on 'The Man Who
   Loved Islands.' '' *DHL Review* 7 (Spring 1974): 78–82.

Turner, John F. ''The Capacity to Be Alone and Its Failure in DHL's 'The Man Who
   Loved Islands.' '' *DHL Review* 16 (1983): 259–89.

Widmer, Kingsley. ''DHL and the Art of Nihilism.'' *Kenyon Review* 20 (1958): 604–16
   (610–15).

Willbern, David. ''Malice in Paradise: Isolation and Projection in 'The Man Who Loved
   Islands.' '' *DHL Review* 10 (Fall 1977): 223–41.

Wilson, Colin. *The Strength to Dream.* Boston: Houghton Mifflin, 1962, pp. 184–85.

See also Clark (1980): 356–59. Draper (1964): 140–41. Nahal (1970): 255–56 and passim.

''THE ROCKING-HORSE WINNER''

WRITTEN

February 1926.

PUBLISHED

Harper's Bazaar (July 1926): 96, 97, 122, 124, 126.
*The Ghost Book: Sixteen New Stories of the Uncanny Compiled by Lady Cynthia
   Asquith.* London: Hutchinson, September 1926, pp. 167–88.

WHO'S WHO AND SUMMARY

Paul, the ''winner'' of the title, is a young boy whose home seems to be haunted
by the ''unspoken'' phrase ''There must be more money!'' The family lives
comfortably and in some style, however, and the mother at least, we are told,

started off with all the advantages. But both the mother and the father have expensive tastes, and with this and the keeping up of appearances, there seems never to be enough money. The mother, *Hester,* blames it on bad luck, and, when Paul assumes "luck" means "money" (he has heard what he thought was the phrase "filthy lucker"), she corrects him but says that luck is what leads to money. Paul then announces that he is a lucky person because God told him so. Hester pays no real attention, and Paul is angered by this, and he goes off determined to compel her attention and to discover the clue to luck. In the nursery, when his *two sisters* are playing with their dolls, he frequently rides his rocking horse in a frenzied way and with a strange glare in his eyes that frightens his sisters. One day his mother and his uncle, *Oscar Cresswell,* come in to find him in one of his frenzies. When he finishes his ride, he declares that he had "got there." His uncle asks him the name of the horse, and Paul replies that the horse has a different name each week—last week it was Sansovino. Oscar recognizes this as a winner at Ascot, and it emerges that Paul often discusses horse racing with *Bassett,* the family's young gardener. Oscar goes to see Bassett (he had been Oscar's batman in the war and had been wounded in the left foot), and it eventually emerges that Paul and Bassett have a successful betting partnership that relies mainly on the tips Paul provides; it is a mystery to Bassett where these come from, but it becomes clear to us that they come to Paul when he "gets there" on the rocking horse. Paul has already amassed a small fortune from his winnings, and Oscar eagerly joins the little betting syndicate. Soon they have all made substantial gains, and Paul has £10,000 to his name.

He asks his uncle to arrange through a lawyer that his mother should have an anonymous birthday present of £1,000 each year for the next five years. When Hester receives the first present, she greedily asks the lawyer if she can have the whole £5,000 immediately in order to clear her debts. Through the lawyer and Oscar, Paul agrees. But after this, the house's whispering of "There must be more money!" increases drastically, as if the voice whispering it had gone mad. Paul becomes overwrought and exhausted trying to ensure that his streak of good luck continues while simultaneously trying to keep up with his studies. (His horse has now been moved into his bedroom at the top of the house.) As his luck starts to desert him, and he begins to lose money, he becomes "wild-eyed and strange, as if something were going to explode in him." He now places all his hopes on the forthcoming Derby. Two nights before the event, his parents go to a party and return late, at about one o'clock. Hester has been worried about Paul, and she rushes upstairs to see if he is safely asleep. As she approaches his room, she hears a heavy rushing and rocking sound, and, when she opens the door, she sees Paul once more surging madly on his rocking horse, his eyes ablaze. As she cries out to him, he screams out the name "Malabar" and then falls to the ground unconscious. He remains largely unconscious for the next two days, though periodically repeating the name "Malabar" and asking for Bassett. Hester asks Oscar what Malabar is, and he tells her it is the name of a horse in the Derby. He passes this information to Bassett, and they place their bets on this horse. On the third day, Paul has still not regained consciousness when Bassett asks to see him; he tells Paul that Malabar came in first at fourteen to one and that Paul has won over £70,000. Paul revives briefly at this news and now proudly repeats to his mother, "I *am* lucky!" But he dies that same night.

SETTING

Much of the story takes place in the house of Paul and his family, and its location is only vaguely indicated as being somewhere in the countryside of southern England, but probably in Surrey or Berkshire, given that Uncle Oscar can casually take Paul for a drive to his home in Hampshire and then, on another occasion, into Richmond Park (Richmond upon Thames, southwest London) for the afternoon.

BIBLIOGRAPHY 55

Works dealing primarily with the film version of the story can be found in Bibliography 95; they are not repeated here.

Amon, Frank. "DHL and the Short Story." In *The Achievement of DHL.* Edited by Frederick J. Hoffman and Harry T. Moore. Norman: University of Oklahoma Press, 1953, pp. 222–34. (Reprinted in Consolo [1969], op. cit., pp. 84–94.)

Barrett, Gerald R., and Thomas L. Erskine, eds. *From Fiction to Film: DHL's "The Rocking-Horse Winner."* Encino and Belmont, Calif.: Dickenson, 1974. (Casebook containing the text of the story, Anthony Pelissier's film script for the 1949 movie, and previously published criticism of the story by Lamson et al., San Juan, Snodgrass [all op. cit.], as well as three articles by Becker, Mellen, and Smith on the film [see Bibliography 95 on "Lawrence and Film"].)

Beauchamp, Gorman. "Lawrence's 'The Rocking-Horse Winner.' " *Explicator* 41 (January 1973): 32.

Benenson, Ben. *"The Rocking-Horse Winner"* Adapted for Stage. London: Macmillan Education, 1990.

Burroughs, William D. "No Defense for 'The Rocking-Horse Winner.' " *College English* 24 (1963): 323. (Reprinted in Consolo [1969], op. cit., pp. 55–56.)

Consolo, Dominic P., ed. *DHL: "The Rocking-Horse Winner."* Columbus, Ohio: Charles E. Merrill, 1969. (Text of story with fourteen previously published essays, cited separately here, by Amon, Burroughs, Davis, Gordon and Tate, Hepburn, Lamson et al., Lawrence, Marks, Martin, Moore, O'Connor, Tedlock, Snodgrass, Widmer, and one new essay by Frederick W. Turner, also cited separately here. "Introduction" by Consolo, pp. 1–5.)

Cowan, S. A. "Lawrence's 'The Rocking-Horse Winner.' " *Explicator* 27 (October 1968): Item 9.

Davies, Rosemary Reeves. " 'The Rocking-Horse Winner' Again: A Correction." *Stud-

ies in Short Fiction 18 (1981): 320–22. (Challenges Turner's suggestion [1967], op. cit., that the story is based on the family of Sir Charles Brooke.)

———. "Lawrence, Lady Cynthia Asquith, and 'The Rocking-Horse Winner.' " *Studies in Short Fiction* 20 (1983): 121–26.

Davis, Robert Gorham. *Instructor's Manual for "Ten Modern Masters: An Anthology of the Short Story."* New York: Harcourt, Brace, and World, 1953, p. 50. (Reprinted as "Observations on 'The Rocking-Horse Winner' " in Consolo [1969], op. cit., pp. 41–42.)

Draper, R. P. "DHL on Mother-Love." *Essays in Criticism* 8 (July 1958): 285–89.

Emmett, V. J., Jr. "Structural Irony in DHL's 'The Rocking-Horse Winner.' " *Connecticut Review* 5 (April 1972): 5–10.

Finney, Brian. "The Hitherto Unknown Publication of Some DHL Short Stories." *Notes and Queries* 19 (February 1972): 55–56.

Fitz, L. T. " 'The Rocking-Horse Winner' and *The Golden Bough*." *Studies in Short Fiction* 11 (Spring 1974): 199–200.

Fraiberg, Selma. "Two Modern Incest Heroes." *Partisan Review* 28 (1961): 646–61.

Goldberg, Michael K. "Lawrence's 'The Rocking-Horse Winner': A Dickensian Fable." *Modern Fiction Studies* 15 (Winter 1969–70): 525–36.

———. "Dickens and Lawrence: More on Rocking-Horses." *Modern Fiction Studies* 27 (Winter 1971–72): 574–75.

Goodman, Charlotte. "Henry James, DHL, and the Victimized Child." *Modern Language Studies* 10 (1979–80): 43–51.

Gordon, Carolyn, and Allen Tate. *The House of Fiction.* New York: Scribner's Sons, 1950, pp. 348–51. (2d ed., 1960, pp. 227–30. Reprinted as "Commentary on 'The Rocking-Horse Winner' " in Consolo [1969], op. cit., pp. 37–40.)

Hepburn, James G. "Disarming and Uncanny Visions: Freud's 'The Uncanny' with Regard to Form and Content in Stories by Sherwood Anderson and DHL." *Literature and Psychology* 9 (Winter 1959): 9–12. (Reprinted in Consolo [1969], op. cit., pp. 60–68.)

Holland, Norman. *The Dynamics of Literary Response.* New York: Oxford University Press, 1968, pp. 255–58.

Humma, John B. "Pan and 'The Rocking-Horse Winner.' " *Essays in Literature* (Macomber, Ill.) 5 (1978): 53–60.

Ingrasci, Hugh J. "Names as Symbolic Crowns Unifying Lawrence's 'The Rocking-Horse Winner.' " In *Festschrift in Honor of Virgil J. Vogel.* Edited by Edward Callary. DeKalb: Illinois Name Society (Papers of N. Central Names Institute), 1985, pp. 1–22.

Isaacs, Neil D. "The Autoerotic Metaphor in Joyce, Sterne, Lawrence, Stevens and Whitman." *Literature and Psychology* 15 (Spring 1965): 92–106.

Junkins, Donald. " 'The Rocking-Horse Winner': A Modern Myth." *Studies in Short Fiction* 2 (Fall 1964): 87–89.

Koban, Charles. "Allegory and the Death of the Heart in 'The Rocking-Horse Winner.' " *Studies in Short Fiction* 15 (Fall 1978): 391–96.

Lamson, Roy, Hallett Smith, Hugh Maclean, and Wallace W. Douglas. *The Critical Reader.* New York: Norton, 1949, pp. 416–21. (Rev. ed., 1962, pp. 542–47. Reprinted as "A Critical Analysis" in Consolo [1969], op. cit., pp. 47–51.)

Lawrence, Robert G. "Further Notes on DHL's Rocking-Horse." *College English* 24 (1963): 324. (Reprinted in Consolo [1969], op. cit., p. 57.)

Lesser, M. X., and John N. Morris. *Teacher's Manual to Accompany "Modern Short Stories: The Fiction of Experience."* New York: McGraw-Hill, 1964, p. 7.

Ludwig, Jack B., and W. Richard Poirier. *Instructor's Manual to Accompany "Stories: British and American."* Boston: Houghton Mifflin, 1953, pp. 27–28.

McDermott, John V. "Faith and Love: Twin Forces in 'The Rocking-Horse Winner.' " *Notes on Contemporary Literature* 18, no. 1 (1988): 6–8.

Marks, W. S., III. "The Psychology of the Uncanny in Lawrence's 'The Rocking-Horse Winner.' " *Modern Fiction Studies* 11 (Winter 1965–66): 381–92. (Reprinted in Consolo [1969], op. cit., pp. 71–83.)

Martin, W. R. "Fancy or Imagination? 'The Rocking-Horse Winner.' " *College English* 24 (1962): 64–65. (Reprinted in Consolo [1969], op. cit., pp. 52–54.)

Moore, Harry T. "Some Notes on 'The Rocking-Horse Winner.' " In Consolo (1969), op. cit., pp. 23–25. (Reprinted from Moore [1951]: 277–79.)

O'Connor, Frank. *The Lonely Voice: A Study of the Short Story.* Cleveland and New York: World, 1963, pp. 153–55. (Reprinted as "Poe and 'The Rocking-Horse Winner' " in Consolo [1969], op. cit., pp. 58–59.)

Padhi, Bibhu. "Lawrence's Ironic Fables and How They Matter." *Interpretations* 15, no. 1 (1983): 53–59.

Rohrberger, Mary. *Hawthorne and the Modern Short Story: A Study in Genre.* The Hague: Mouton, 1966, pp. 74–80.

San Juan, E., Jr. "Theme versus Imitation: DHL's 'The Rocking-Horse Winner.' " *DHL Review* 3 (Summer 1970): 136–40.

Scott, James B. "The Norton Distortion: A Dangerous Typo in 'The Rocking-Horse Winner.' " *DHL Review* 21 (Spring 1989): 175–77.

Singleton, Ralph H. *Instructor's Manual for "Two and Twenty: A Collection of Short Stories."* New York: St. Martin's Press, 1962, pp. 12–13.

Snodgrass, William DeWitt. "A Rocking-Horse: The Symbol, the Pattern, the Way to Live." *Hudson Review* 11 (Summer 1958): 191–200. (Reprinted in his *Radical Pursuit: Critical Essays and Lectures.* New York: Harper and Row, 1975; in Spilka [1963]: 117–26; and in Consolo [1969], op. cit., pp. 26–36.)

Steinmann, Martin, and Gerald Willen, eds. *Literature for Writing.* Belmont, Calif.: Wadsworth, 1963, pp. 209–10.

Tedlock, E. W., Jr. "Values and 'The Rocking-Horse Winner.' " In Consolo (1969), op. cit., pp. 69–70. (Reprinted from Tedlock [1963]: 209–10.)

Turner, Frederick W., III. "Prancing in to a Purpose: Myths, Horses, and True Selfhood in Lawrence's 'The Rocking-Horse Winner.' " In Consolo (1969), op. cit., pp. 95–106.

Turner, G. R. "Princess on a Rocking Horse." *Studies in Short Fiction* 5 (Fall 1967): 72.

Turner, John F. "The Perversion of Play in DHL's 'The Rocking-Horse Winner.' " *DHL Review* 15 (1982): 249–70.

Warschausky, Sidney. " 'The Blind Man' and 'The Rocking-Horse Winner.' " In *Insight II: Analyses of British Literature.* Edited by John V. Hagopian and Martin Dolch. Frankfort: Hirschgraben-Verlag, 1964, pp. 221–33.

Watkins, Daniel P. "Labor and Religion in DHL's 'The Rocking-Horse Winner.' " *Studies in Short Fiction* 24 (1987): 295–301.

Widmer, Kingsley. "The Triumph of the Middleclass Matriarch." In Consolo (1969), op. cit., pp. 43–44. (Reprinted from Widmer [1962]: 92–95.)

Wilson, K. "DHL's 'The Rocking-Horse Winner': Parable and Structure." *English Studies in Canada* 13, no. 4 (1987): 438–50.

See also Draper (1964): 141. Hough (1956): 188. Rees (1958): 94. Sklenicka (1991): 156–59.

"THE LOVELY LADY"

WRITTEN

February–March 1927. Revised and shortened May 1927.

PUBLISHED

The Black Cap: New Stories of Murder and Mystery Compiled by Cynthia Asquith. London: Hutchinson, October 1927, pp. 216–38. The unabridged version of the story is printed for the first time in the Cambridge edition of *The Woman Who Rode Away and Other Stories.*

WHO'S WHO AND SUMMARY

Pauline Attenborough is the "lovely lady" of the title. She is seventy-two but "wonderfully-preserved" so that in the half-light she can almost pass for thirty, though what really enables her to preserve the impression of youth is her eaglelike willpower, as her niece, *Cecilia* (Ciss), knows only too well. For with Ciss, whom she considers negligible, Pauline does not trouble to maintain her false glamor—she relaxes "the invisible wire" that connects her wrinkles with her willpower and allows Ciss to see the genuine article, haggard and weary. Cecilia is actually thirty and has lived with Pauline for the past five years since the death of her parents. Her father, brother to Pauline's deceased husband, Ronald, was only a poor Congregational minister, so that Cecilia is financially dependent on Pauline. The other member of the household is *Robert,* Pauline's son. He is thirty-two and a barrister. Cecilia loves Robert but can see no way of drawing him out of himself—he is painfully shy and lacking in confidence and, most important, under the powerful sway of his domineering mother. Moreover, Cecilia herself is quite shy and retiring and unable to bring matters to a head. Part of Robert's problem seems to be that he still lives in the shadow of his dashing elder brother, *Henry,* whom Pauline had clearly loved best of her two sons. Henry had died at the age of twenty-two after his love affair with an actress, Claudia, had been thwarted by Pauline. Cecilia feels sure that Robert has a deeply passionate nature beneath his nervous facade, but she fears that, as with Henry, his mother will never allow it to emerge—he will die even before he has had a chance to live.

Cecilia has a flat over the coach house and stables. One afternoon, she is sunbathing on the flat roof of the stable building when she hears Pauline's voice, as if from nowhere, talking about, and apparently to, her dead son, Henry. Cecilia is at first terrified at what she thinks is the voice of some ghost, but then she is intrigued to hear Pauline's voice expressing misgivings about Henry's death—indeed, expressing a clear sense of guilt at having driven him to his death. This confirms all Cecilia's suspicions about Pauline's unhealthy hold over her sons, and she becomes convinced that she has heard Pauline's true thoughts. She then notices a drainpipe near her head and realizes that this accounts for everything: Pauline has been sunbathing in the yew enclosure just beneath the stable roof, seated beside the mouth of the rainpipe, and she has been talking to herself so that her voice had been transmitted up the pipe to Cecilia. Cecilia now also realizes why Pauline will never relax in company anywhere—she talks to herself unless she remains alert and would always be in danger of revealing her secrets. On a second occasion when Cecilia is listening to Pauline in this way, she learns the truth about Robert—something else she had always suspected: he is not, in fact, the son of Pauline's husband, Ronald, but of an Italian lover of Pauline's, "Monsignor Mauro," a Jesuit priest (there have already been references to Robert's face resembling that of an Italian priest, and his hobby involves studying old legal documents from Mexico, one of which, we were told, involves the case of a man accused of seducing a nun from the Sacred Heart Convent in Oaxaca). On hearing this, Cecilia cannot resist the temptation to talk back down the drainpipe. She pretends to be Henry and tells Pauline to leave Robert alone and to allow him to marry. "He" accuses Pauline of killing him and condemns her for it. Pauline is silenced.

Later that evening, it appears that she has lost all her famous willpower, and she has shriveled up into the haggard old woman she genuinely is. When Robert sees this transformation, it works a transformation in him, too, and he suddenly seems "another man." Pauline makes her confession to Robert and reveals that her previous objection to his marrying Cecilia—consanguinity—was spurious as they are clearly not blood-related after all. Then, looking at the young couple with "real hate," she tells them to marry as soon as possible, jeering at them as "such a passionate pair of lovers!" Pauline now sinks into a terminal decline and soon dies. But, from beyond the grave, she makes one last malicious attack on Robert and Cecilia and one last ironic effort to "preserve" herself when she leaves her main fortune, as embodied in her collections of antiques, to endow a "Pauline Attenborough Museum."

SETTING

The setting for the story is Pauline Attenborough's "exquisite" Queen Anne house situated in a dale somewhere twenty-five miles out of London.

BIBLIOGRAPHY 56

Finney, Brian H. "A Newly Discovered Text of DHL's 'The Lovely Lady.'" *Yale University Library Gazette* 49 (January 1975): 245–52.
Jones, William M. "Growth of a Symbol." *University of Kansas City Review* 26 (1959): 68–73.

See also MacLeod (1985/87): 173–75. Nahal (1970): 87–89.

33   *The Escaped Cock* and Other Late Stories, 1926–29

I deal here with the late short fiction that was not collected in Lawrence's lifetime and that has not yet been published in the Cambridge edition, that is, in order of earliest composition dates: "Mercury," *The Escaped Cock (The Man Who Died)*, "Things," "The Man Who Was Through with the World," "The Undying Man," "Autobiographical Fragment"/"A Dream of Life," *Rawdon's Roof*, "Mother and Daughter," and "The Blue Moccasins."

"Things," *Rawdon's Roof*, "The Blue Moccasins," and "Mother and Daughter" were first collected posthumously in *The Lovely Lady*. London: Secker, January 1933; New York: Viking, February 1933.

"Mercury," "The Undying Man," and "Autobiographical Fragment" were first collected posthumously in *Phoenix: The Posthumous Papers of DHL*. Edited by Edward D. McDonald. New York: Viking, 1936.

"MERCURY"

WRITTEN

July 1926.

PUBLISHED

Atlantic Monthly 139 (February 1927): 197–200.
Nation and Athenaeum (5 February 1927).

WHO'S WHO AND SUMMARY

One of Lawrence's "finest descriptive pieces" (Moore 1951: 282), "Mercury" describes a typical Sunday crowd of holidaymakers who have made the ascent up "Merkur" Hill on a funicular and the flash storm that overtakes them. During the storm, as the crowd takes refuge on the veranda of a restaurant, a man's white, naked striding legs are seen hurrying past amid the thunder and lightning, flames at his heels and the upper part of his body invisible. He disappears as suddenly as he had appeared after a great bang of thunder. As the storm subsides, the crowd rush to the funicular station and find that the two men who operate the funicular have been killed by lightning: one, lying next to the votive stone of Mercury Hill, has been stripped by the lightning on the lower half of his body.

SETTING

Merkur is an actual hill in Baden-Baden, where the story was written.

THE ESCAPED COCK (THE MAN WHO DIED)

WRITTEN

The first half of the story was written in April 1927, and the second in June and July 1928. Lawrence's title for it was *The Escaped Cock,* and it was first published under that name, but it was later changed to the less risqué *The Man Who Died* for the first British and American editions, published posthumously. The proofs for the Black Sun edition of 1929 were corrected in August of that year.

PUBLISHED

1. a. Part I published as "The Escaped Cock" in *Forum* 79 (February 1928): 286–96.
   b. *The Escaped Cock.* Paris: Black Sun Press, September 1929.
   c. *The Man Who Died.* London: Secker; New York: Knopf, 1931.

WHO'S WHO AND SUMMARY

The man of the title is a type of Christ figure who finds himself reborn into the phenomenal world of the body rather than to the spiritual world of the Christian heaven. At first he resists this return to consciousness and feeling but gradually feels inspired to obey his body's instincts by the surging life of the natural world around him, realized most sharply by the zest for life exhibited by the fiery "escaped" cock whose story forms a prelude and, for a while, a counter-point, to the main story. The proud and defiant cock, with its flamboyant orange neck and red comb, is the property of *a peasant* who has tied one of its legs by a lead to prevent it from escaping; but the cock is so energetic and strong that, at the very moment that the man who died awakens from his death-sleep, the cock emits a triumphantly rending crow and breaks the lead that tethers him. Later, chased by the peasant, he almost literally bumps into the man who died, who thus helps the peasant to recapture the bird. The man is then invited to shelter at the peasant's house, where he spends time observing and admiring the vitality of the cock. The man returns repeatedly to the peasant's yard and grad-ually begins to identify with "the sharp wave of life of which the bird was the crest." Later, when he leaves to go out into the world again, he buys the cock from the peasant in order to release its hot pulsing life "into the seethe of phenomena."

We then witness *his* full return to sensuous life through his sexual initiation by the beautiful Priestess of Isis, who sees him as the lost Osiris, the pagan Egyptian deity whose body was reputedly torn apart and scattered around the world; the pagan subversion of Christ's story is completed as the man is made whole again by the Priestess within her shrine. He visits her at the shrine each night for a period throughout the spring until she conceives. She then tells him that *her mother* is plotting to betray him to the Romans. This time he will not allow his body to be betrayed and sacrificed to "the little life of jealousy and property." Having sown the seed of new life within the Priestess and cherishing her touch and the "invisible suns" she has enkindled within him, the man escapes from the slaves sent to capture him and sets sail in a small boat out into the world once more.

SETTING

The story has a generalized biblical setting.

BIBLIOGRAPHY 57

Butler, Gerald J. "*The Man Who Died* and Lawrence's Final Attitude towards Tragedy." *Recovering Literature* 6, no. 3 (1977): 1–14.

Cavitch, David. "Solipsism and Death in DHL's Late Works." *Massachusetts Review* 7 (Summer 1966): 495–508 (501–5).

Cowan, James C. "The Function of Allusions and Symbols in DHL's *The Man Who Died.*" *American Imago* 17 (Summer 1960): 241–53. (Reprinted in Cowan [1990]: 237–53.)

Fiderer, Gerald. "DHL's *The Man Who Died:* The Phallic Christ." *American Imago* 25 (Spring 1968): 91–96.

Goodheart, Eugene. "Lawrence and Christ." *Partisan Review* 31 (Winter 1964): 42–59.

Harris, Janice H. "The Many Faces of Lazarus: *The Man Who Died* and Its Context." *DHL Review* 16 (1983): 291–311.

Hays, Peter L. *The Limping Hero: Grotesques in Literature.* New York: New York University Press, 1971, pp. 35–38.

Hendrick, George. "Jesus and the Osiris-Isis Myth: Lawrence's *The Man Who Died* and Williams' *The Night of the Iguana.*" *Anglia* (Tübingen) 84 (1966): 398–406.

Highet, Gilbert. *People, Places, and Books.* New York: Oxford University Press, 1953, pp. 41–42.

Hinz, Evelyn J., and John J. Teunissen. "Savior and Cock: Allusion and Icon in Lawrence's *The Man Who Died.*" *Journal of Modern Literature* 5 (April 1976): 279–96.

Kaplan, Harold. *The Passive Voice: An Approach to Modern Fiction.* Athens: Ohio University Press, 1966, pp. 182–83.

Krook, Dorothea. "Messianic Humanism: DHL's *The Man Who Died.*" In her *Three Traditions of Moral Thought.* Cambridge: Cambridge University Press, 1959, pp. 255–92.

Kunkel, Francis L. "Lawrence's *The Man Who Died:* The Heavenly Cock." In his *Passion and the Passion: Sex and Religion in Modern Literature.* Philadelphia: Westminster Press, 1975, pp. 37–57.

Lacy, Gerald M. "Commentary." In *The Escaped Cock* by DHL. Edited by Gerald M. Lacy. Los Angeles: Black Sparrow Press, 1973, pp. 121–70.

Larsen, Elizabeth. "Lawrence's *The Man Who Died.*" *Explicator* 40, no. 4 (1982): 38–40.

Ledoux, Larry V. "Christ and Isis: The Function of the Dying and the Reviving God in *The Man Who Died.*" *DHL Review* 5 (Summer 1972): 132–48.

Lucente, Gregory L. "*Women in Love* and *The Man Who Died:* From Realism to the Mythopoeia of Passion and Rebirth." In his *The Narrative of Realism and Myth: Verga, Lawrence, Faulkner, Pavese.* Baltimore: Johns Hopkins University Press, 1981, pp. 107–23.

MacDonald, Robert H. "The Union of Fire and Water: An Examination of the Imagery of *The Man Who Died.*" *DHL Review* 10 (Spring 1977): 34–51.

Martin, Dexter. "The Beauty of Blasphemy: Suggestions for Handling *The Escaped Cock.*" *DHL News and Notes* (February 1960).

Miller, Milton. "Definitions by Comparison: Chaucer, Lawrence, and Joyce." *Essays in Criticism* 3 (1953): 369–81 (374–77).

Murry, John Middleton. "*The Escaped Cock.*" *Criterion* 10 (1930): 183–88.

Panichas, George A. "DHL's Concept of the Risen Lord." *Christian Scholar* 47 (Spring 1964): 56–65.

Perl, Jeffrey M. *The Tradition of Return: The Implicit History of Modern Literature.* Princeton: Princeton University Press, 1984.

Piccolo, Anthony. "Sun and Sex in the Last Stories of DHL." In *HELIOS: From Myth to Solar Energy.* Edited by M. E. Grenander. Albany: Institute for Humanistic Studies, State University of New York, 1978, pp. 166–74.

Rakhi. "*The Man Who Died:* A Jungian Interpretation." In *Essays on DHL.* Edited by T. R. Sharma. Meerut: Shalabh Book House, 1987, pp. 116–24.

Steinhauer, H. "Eros and Psyche: A Nietzschean Motif in Anglo-American Literature." *Modern Language Notes* 64 (April 1949): 217–28 (223–25).

Teunissen, John J. "The Serial Collaboration of DHL and Walker Percy." *Southern Humanities Review* 21 (1987): 101–15.

Thompson, Leslie M. "The Christ Who Didn't Die: Analogues to DHL's *The Man Who Died.*" *DHL Review* 8 (Spring 1975): 19–30.

Travis, Leigh. "DHL: The Blood-Conscious Artist." *American Imago* 25 (Summer 1968): 163–90 (182–85).

Troy, Mark. " '...a Wild Bit of Egyptology': Isis and *The Escaped Cock* of DHL." *Studia Neophilologica* 58 (1986): 215–24.

Viinikka, Anja. "*The Man Who Died*: D.H. Lawrence's Phallic Vision of the Restored Body." *The Journal of the D. H. Lawrence Society* (1994–95): 39–46.

Wicker, Brian. "Lawrence and the Unseen Presences." In his *The Story-Shaped World: Fiction and Metaphysics: Some Variations on a Theme.* Notre Dame, Ind.: University of Notre Dame, 1975, pp. 120–33.

Ziolkowski, Theodore. *Varieties of Literary Thematics.* Princeton: Princeton University Press, 1983, pp. 166–67.

See also (1980–94) Clark (1980): 397–405. Humma (1990): 100–109. Hyde (1992): 207–31, passim. Meyers (1982): 164–68. Mohanty (1993): 68–74. Robinson (1992): 117–19. Sagar (1985a): 278–323. Salgādo (1982): 129–33. Sklenicka (1991): 169–72. Trebisz (1992): 62–64. Worthen (1991a): 118–20.

See also (to 1979) Albright (1978): passim. Brunsdale (1978): Cavitch (1969): 201–4. Cowan (1970): passim. Draper (1964): 144–48. Eisenstein (1974): 126–48. Freeman (1960): 208–9. Goodheart (1963): 149–60. Hochman (1970): passim. Hough (1956): 246–52. Kermode (1973): 149–51. Murry (1931): 349–60. Murry (1957): 77–78, 103–4, 119–21. Nahal (1970): 216–35. Panichas (1964): 128–35. Pritchard (1971): 195–97. Sagar (1966): 216–25. Slade (1970): 112–13. Spilka (1955): 219–31. Stewart (1963): 580–82. Weiss (1962): 106–8. Zytaruk (1971): 134–43, 158–68.

"THINGS"

WRITTEN

May 1927. Proofs for *Fortnightly Review,* September 1928.

PUBLISHED

Bookman 67 (August 1928): 632–37.
Fortnightly Review (October 1928).

WHO'S WHO AND SUMMARY

This comic critique of idealism is executed by means of a superbly controlled satirical presentation of the story's two central characters, the New England idealists *Erasmus* and *Valerie Melville* (and the names are not arbitrary: in particular, "Erasmus" appropriately suggests the Dutch scholar and theologian of the Renaissance [1466–1536], while we are clearly invited to conjure with the allusion to [the part-Dutch] Herman Melville, an allusion reinforced by Erasmus being called Dick by his wife [*Moby-Dick*] and their son being called Peter [*Pierre*]).

Erasmus is twenty-seven, and Valerie is twenty-five when they are married at the start of the story. They have an income just sufficient to enable them to live comfortably without working, and this is the first of their idealistic principles—"freedom." In flight from "the Sodom and Gomorrah of industrial materialism" in America, they go in search of beauty (and a cheap place to live), moving first to Paris, where they live a drifting bohemian life dabbling in art and painting. Having explored Paris "thoroughly" and having become thoroughly bored with it, they move to Italy at the outbreak of the war; here they indulge their penchant for "Indian thought" and become Buddhists (or theosophists) for a time, dreaming of a perfect world where all greed, pain, and sorrow are eliminated. When they see that such a world shows no sign of appearing, they become disillusioned with Indian thought and turn from Buddhism to what, it emerges, they have been most interested in all along—the avid acquisition of "things" for their home: antique furniture and art objects. However, after twelve years of living this "full and beautiful life," they begin subconsciously to feel the true emptiness of their lives, and they rationalize their yearning to return to America by concluding that Europe has had its day—and that, in any case, their son, Peter, ought to be given the opportunity of seeing his homeland while still young.

The Melvilles thus take themselves back to New York—along with several vanloads of "things." But these things are all quickly consigned to a warehouse when the couple discover that, here, they can afford only a tiny apartment. The need to work begins to threaten their idealistic way of life, but the pursuit of yet another ideal staves this off once more as they move out west to the mountains—without their things—to try the simple life in harmony with wild nature. This soon proves too much like hard work, and they are relieved when a millionaire friend offers them a luxury cottage on the California coast; they move there in the renewed hope of experiencing the birth of "a new soul." The Pacific pounds this ideal to dust within nine months, and the Melvilles return to Massachusetts, to visit Valerie's parents. Here, the pressure on Erasmus to find work increases. Leaving Peter with his grandparents, therefore, the Melvilles escape once more to Europe and make for "cheap" Paris. Unfortunately, Paris is no longer cheap, and they find Europe "a complete failure" this time; moreover, Valerie begins to pine for her precious warehoused "things," and so, via her parents, an academic post is found for Erasmus at Cleveland University. Like "a cornered rat," he is reluctantly forced to accept. Once in their comfortable college home, however, the Melvilles find that they are only too happy to be conventionally and materially secure. They have found their natural element, in fact, and the story ends with our New England idealists, surrounded outside by the modern furnaces of Cleveland and inside by their antique "things," safely and happily ensconced "inside the cage" of precisely the Sodom and Gomorrah from which their surface selves had always recoiled. Rooted in a denial of any true passional commitment to life in the first place and ironically counterpointed by their obsessive accumulation of objects, the Melvilles' willful pursuit of abstract ideals is thus shown to lead inexorably to a rampant return of their repressed materialism.

SETTING

The story follows the Melvilles from home to home around the world as follows: New Haven, Paris, Florence, New York, the mountains of western United States, the coast of California, Massachusetts, Paris again, and, finally, Cleveland.

BIBLIOGRAPHY 58

Cushman, Keith. "The Serious Comedy of 'Things.' " *Etudes Lawrenciennes* 6 (1991): 83–94.
Ludwig, Jack B., and W. Richard Poirier. *Instructor's Manual to Accompany "Stories: British and American."* Boston: Houghton Mifflin, 1953, pp. 27–28.
Preston, John. "Narrative Procedure and Structure in a Short Story by DHL." *Journal of English Language and Literature* (Korea) 29 (1983): 251–56.

See also Draper (1969): 25–28.

"THE MAN WHO WAS THROUGH WITH THE WORLD" (UNFINISHED)

WRITTEN

May 1927.

PUBLISHED

Unpublished in Lawrence's lifetime. First published in *Essays in Criticism* 9 (July 1959): 213–21.

WHO'S WHO AND SUMMARY

Henry is the man of the title. Disillusioned with the world and with other people, he buys himself a piece of wild land on a mountainside and decides to live the life of a hermit (somewhat like Cathcart in the "The Man Who Loved Islands"). At first he tries to devote himself to "God" but soon finds that he has no clear sense of the sacred—at least within the framework of any of the traditional religions and their conceptions of God: "[H]e felt like an acrobat trying to hang on to a tight wire with his eyebrows." Gradually, however, a different source of the sacred seems to reveal itself as he begins to attune himself to his natural environment and to cleanse himself "from the pollution of people" by going naked in the sun (as Juliet does in the story *Sun*)—though the manuscript ends before this idea is fully developed, and Henry's intended destiny remains unclear: would it have been that of Cathcart or of Juliet or one entirely different from both?

SETTING

No specific setting is clearly indicated, but Lawrence wrote the story while living at the Villa Mirenda, Scandicci, near Florence, and the nearby sanctuary of a local hermit, San Eusabio, may have suggested the story to him.

"THE UNDYING MAN" (UNFINISHED)

WRITTEN

October 1927. This unfinished story is based on one of two stories sent to Lawrence by his friend S. S. Koteliansky. These were stories recorded by Koteliansky's mother and translated by him from the Yiddish; the present one was originally called "Maimonides and Aristotle."

PUBLISHED

Unpublished in Lawrence's lifetime. First published in *Phoenix: The Posthumous Papers of DHL.* Edited by Edward D. McDonald. New York: Viking, 1936.

WHO'S WHO AND SUMMARY

The two scholars *Rabbi Moses Maimonides* and *Aristotle,* a Greek Christian, are great friends who have always studied together. Following various experiments, they believe they have discovered the means to create an immortal man: by taking a small vein from another man and putting it with certain plants and herbs, the vein would eventually grow into a fully formed human being, and, because he had never been born, this man would never die. The two men then decide to try actually to create such an undying man. After drawing lots, it falls to Aristotle to donate his vein and thus to sacrifice his mortal life for the experiment. Before he does so, however, he has Maimonides swear never to interfere with the growth of the vein in any way. When Aristotle's vein begins to grow in a jar in Maimonedes' room and to glow red at the same time, Maimonedes begins to be afraid. Moreover, as the vein continues to grow, his Jewish conscience becomes anguished at the thought that Aristotle the Christian will live forever and become an immortal like the one and only true God of the Jewish people; he fears that this undying man may even usurp the place of the true God in the eyes of the people. The manuscript ends at this point.

SETTING

The story has a vague setting somewhere in Spain.

BIBLIOGRAPHY 59

Zytaruk, George J. " 'The Undying Man': DHL's Yiddish Story." *DHL Review* 4 (Spring 1971): 20–27.

"AUTOBIOGRAPHICAL FRAGMENT"/"A DREAM OF LIFE" (UNFINISHED)

WRITTEN

October 1927.

PUBLISHED

Unpublished in Lawrence's lifetime. First published as "Autobiographical Fragment" in *Phoenix: The Posthumous Papers of DHL*. Edited by Edward D. McDonald. New York: Viking, 1936.

The Princess and Other Stories. Edited by Keith Sagar. Harmondsworth: Penguin, 1971. In order to reflect its fictional nature, the story was renamed "A Dream of Life" by Keith Sagar for its reprinting in the collection.

WHO'S WHO AND SUMMARY

This story is, in fact, something of a mixture of autobiography and fiction: narrated in the first-person throughout, it begins as an actual autobiographical sketch about the author's impressions of the mining village of his childhood on his return there in 1927; but it then develops into a fictional fantasy where *the narrator* falls asleep on an October day, then magically awakens 1,000 years later to find his ugly mining village transformed into a type of utopia, now called Nethrupp. Everything seems golden-hued and harmonious, and the dress and lifestyle of the people are reminiscent of some ancient agrarian community—either Egyptian or Etruscan. There is an elegantly proportioned town, and the community of gentle, laughing people seems to exude a sense of physical and spiritual well-being as they sing and dance together at the end of the day, before retiring to bathe and eat and rest. The manuscript ends, unfinished, as the narrator is taken to see a man who seems to be one of the elders or leaders of the community and is told of how long he has been asleep and reassured about his butterfly-like rebirth.

SETTING

"Newthorpe," a coal-mining village on the Nottinghamshire-Derbyshire border, is clearly modeled on Lawrence's hometown, Eastwood. The narrator goes to sleep in October 1927 and wakes in 2927, 1,000 years later.

RAWDON'S ROOF

WRITTEN

November 1927. Lengthened November 1928.

PUBLISHED

London: Elkin Mathews and Marrot, March 1929. (No. 7 of the Woburn Books.) The more familiar version of the story published in *The Lovely Lady* collection of 1933 ignored Lawrence's revisions for the 1929 publication; but *that* version did not incorporate all the November 1928 revisions. Thus, we must await the Cambridge Edition version for a reliable text of the story.

WHO'S WHO AND SUMMARY

The first-person narrator, *Joe Bradley,* introduces his neighbor, *Rawdon,* as a man who has vowed never again to have a woman sleep under his roof. He is estranged from his wife and now lives alone in a rented house with his man-servant, *Joe Hawken,* a fresh-faced man of thirty-five who had come back with Rawdon—then a major—after the war. Hearing Rawdon's declaration, the narrator is more confused than ever about Rawdon's mysterious love affair with a married woman, *Janet Drummond.* She lives nearby with her husband, *Alec,* and their *two young girls.* Her husband is seldom at home—though often in debt—and it seems clear that she loves Rawdon more than her husband. However, the mystery to the narrator and other observers is that, despite their liaison being common knowledge to everyone—Rawdon sees Janet every day—neither of the lovers ever breathes a word about their relationship to anyone; it is as though "there was a hush upon it all." One November evening, Janet arrives unexpectedly at Rawdon's house; Rawdon becomes extremely nervous and begs the narrator to stay and help him out, as though he understands what Janet's visit means. Indeed, she rapidly blurts out a brief account of her husband's mistreatment of her that evening and of her decision finally to leave him for Rawdon, whom she loves; she expects to be sheltered under Rawdon's roof for the night. Rawdon, however, determined to abide by his vow, makes excuses to prevent this, and it seems clear that he has no intention of making any final commitment to Janet. She bristles at his attitude and brusquely marches out. Rawdon follows sheepishly, with his torch, to escort her home. Left alone, the narrator goes to inspect the guest room and discovers that Hawken has brought in *a woman* of his own for the night; Janet had earlier made several sarcastic comments about Hawken, and this now makes their ironic significance clear. The next day, Rawdon leaves for Tunis, and the Drummonds move away, too; Rawdon's roof remains unaltered.

SETTING

The setting here is mainly the interior of Rawdon's house, with no clear indication of its broader location beyond the suggestion of a small country town.

"MOTHER AND DAUGHTER"

WRITTEN

May 1928. Proofs, February 1929.

PUBLISHED

New Criterion 8 (April 1929): 394–419.

WHO'S WHO AND SUMMARY

Virginia Bodoin is thirty at the start of the story and a senior civil servant. *Rachel Bodoin,* her mother, is around sixty and has "a violent sort of vitality" and "a strange *muscular* energy." The two women live together now, somewhat like man and wife, though they have often lived separately before. Rachel is domineering and antagonistic toward men, and this seems to have rubbed off onto Virginia and to have been the main cause for the failure of her relationship with *Henry Lubbock,* her fiancé and lover for four years; he had left Virginia because he could no longer tolerate Rachel's attempts to "squash" and "devour" him and her witchlike influence on Virginia in encouraging her to do the same. To him, his lover had herself soon come to resemble a witch, too, the accomplice of "her tough-clawed witch of a mother." However, Virginia is not really like her mother, and, when they set up home together, tensions quickly develop as Virginia tries to live her own life. When, for example, another likely suitor is positively favored by her mother for his inexperience and pliability—

Adrian, a young colleague of Virginia's—Virginia opposes her mother's taste with a distinct touch of malice. Gradually, Rachel Bodoin realizes that Virginia is not just a continuation of her own self but also, and perhaps predominantly, her father's daughter; the "hammer" with which she had knocked *him* on the head has, it seems, now started to rebound on her. Appropriately, Virginia enters into a relationship with the fatherly, grotesque *Monsieur Arnault,* a sixty-year-old Armenian businessman whom Rachel calls "the Turkish Delight." He is described as fat and physically repulsive—"like a toad"—and he is clearly calculating in his courtship of Virginia; and yet he has "a strange potency" and presence that Virginia finds difficult to resist. To her mother's obvious disgust, Virginia agrees to marry him. What his "patriarchal and tribal" nature seems to have precipitated for Virginia is her final reaction away from the "hammering" mode of her mother—willful and domineering—and toward the opposite extreme, the submissive mode of the "harem type."

SETTING

The interior of the Bodoin's apartment in central London, around Bloomsbury, provides the main setting for this story.

BIBLIOGRAPHY 60

Blanchard, Lydia. "Mothers and Daughters in DHL: *The Rainbow* and Selected Shorter Works." In *Lawrence and Women.* Edited by Anne Smith. London: Vision, 1978, pp. 75–100 (95–97).
Felheim, Marvin, Franklin Newman, and William Steinhoff. *Study Aids for Teachers for "Modern Short Stories."* New York: Oxford University Press, 1951, pp. 27–29.
Meyers, Jeffrey. "Katherine Mansfield, Gurdjieff, and Lawrence's 'Mother and Daughter.' " *Twentieth Century Literature* 22 (December 1976): 444–53.

See also Macleod (1985/87): 175–77.

"THE BLUE MOCCASINS"

WRITTEN

June–July 1928. Proofs, October 1928. With *The Escaped Cock,* Lawrence's last completed fictional writing.

PUBLISHED

Eve: The Lady's Pictorial (Special Christmas Issue) 35 (22 November 1928): 24, 25, 27, 70, 74.
Plain Talk 4 (February 1929): 138–48.

WHO'S WHO AND SUMMARY

This story traces the rise and fall of the relationship between *Percy Barlow* and a much older woman, *Lina McLeod.* In her youth, Lina McLeod has been a fiercely independent woman. With an income from her mother, she has traveled around the world entirely on her own. Though she has made use of men as servants and subordinates, a basic tenet of her struggle for independence has been to kick over "the masculine traces" and live "manless." A souvenir and symbol of her independent travels is a pair of blue mocassins she bought in New Mexico. At the outbreak of the war, at the age of forty-five, she returns home to the family mansion in the country, Twybit Hall. She soon finds herself attracted to Percy, a young bank clerk of twenty-two. He, with "a towering respect" for her, confides in her and soon becomes wholly devoted to her. When, in 1916, he is called up for military service, they decide to marry on his first leave. When he comes home after the war, she is fifty and white-haired, and he is twenty-seven. They live happily together for a time, keeping themselves to themselves.

However, Percy soon slips into the life of the local community again, as he had done when he was a bachelor. He is made the manager of the bank, and he begins to sing in the church choir again. Handsome and friendly, he is popular with all the younger women of the town, but he is too diffident even to dream of flirting with any of them. To one woman, in particular, he seems "in some way, not wakened up": *Alice Howells,* the rector's daughter, takes it upon herself to "awaken" Percy. She is the same age as Percy and a war widow. Percy begins to find the atmosphere of the rectory more congenial than that of the "semi-cloistered" Twybit Hall. By now, Lina is fifty-seven, and Percy is thirty-four. They sleep in separate rooms and seem to have withdrawn from sexual contact. Lina had hung her blue mocassins in Percy's room, but one day she notices they are missing. He denies all knowledge of them. He has been spending much of his time recently in the church schoolroom rehearsing for a Christmas play, *The Shoes of Shagput.*

When the day of the first public performance arrives, Lina decides on an impulse to go along, without Percy's knowing. Percy is playing the role of a Moor and has his face blackened. The heroine is played by Alice Howells, and, when she appears on stage dressed as a Houri in Turkish trousers and silver veil, she is also wearing Lina's blue mocassins. Lina is furious—but so, too, is Alice Howells when she sees Lina in the audience looking so disapproving and superior, and she resolves to play her role as the seductive heroine to Percy's handsome hero that much more seductively. Toward the end of the first act, the part has her kicking off the mocassins and saying, "Away, shoes of bondage, shoes of sorrow." Lina is, understandably, almost apoplectic with rage and indignation. Now the love scenes on stage become even more risqué as Alice Howells pulls out all the stops of her seductiveness; Percy, who is unaware of Lina's presence in the hall, is "gone in sheer desire" as he clasps Alice's body close to him. Lina, finally, can take no more, and she rises to leave, but the hall is too packed, and she cannot see an easy pathway out. To sit down again would mean further loss of face, so she calmly approaches the stage and asks Percy, in a clear voice, to pass her the blue mocassins. In a daze, he meekly obeys.

At intermission, Lina goes to see Percy and, with Alice there, too, asks him to drive her home. He remonstrates with her, arguing that he cannot possibly leave now and hold up the next act. She expresses surprise that he *intends* to go on with the play, but he clearly does intend to do so. He arranges for someone else to take her home. He then asks her to leave the mocassins for Alice to use again in the next act, but she refuses. They argue over the mocassins briefly, but Lina leaves without giving way. Percy's pent-up feelings about Lina are released as he complains to Alice that Lina has always been possessive and selfish, that she has treated him like a domestic pet, a ''good doggie,'' and has never loved him passionately. She seems to have ''curdled his insides'' for good now, and, when Alice suggests that he might stay at the rectory that night, though he does not openly accept, ''his heart beat thick, and the faint, breathless smile of passion came into his eyes again.''

SETTING

The story is set around a small, unnamed English country town whose specific location is not given.

BIBLIOGRAPHY 61

Finney, Brian. ''The Hitherto Unknown Publication of Some DHL Short Stories.'' *Notes and Queries* 19 (February 1972): 55–56.
Widmer, Kingsley. ''Birds of Passion and Birds of Marriage in DHL.'' *University of Kansas City Review* 25 (Fall 1958): 73–79.

SECTION C

POETRY

This section is divided into three main parts (two chapters and a bibliography). The first provides details of the main general collections of Lawrence's poetry and of general criticism; the second provides details of the individual volumes as prepared or planned by Lawrence himself, along with their related criticism; and the third contains a master bibliography of criticism. This section differs from others in this part of the book in that, rather than providing full bibliographical details of the criticism of individual volumes, I have felt it more appropriate to provide a master bibliography of criticism devoted to Lawrence's poetry and then to provide only author-date citations, cross-referenced to this, for each of the individual entries. I have done this because there is comparatively little criticism that is wholly devoted to the individual volumes of Lawrence's poetry; and because currently there are very few comprehensive and self-contained bibliographies of the poetry criticism available (Lockwood [1987] provides perhaps the fullest listing), and thus the one presented here, though undoubtedly not complete (e.g., I make no attempt to list all known reviews), should give readers a convenient and up-to-date overview of both the nature and the amount of work done in this field. While the master bibliography is alphabetically ordered, the author-date citations given under individual entries are listed chronologically to give a sense of the historical development of the criticism in each case.

34   The Poetry of D. H. Lawrence:
General Collections and Criticism

WRITTEN

Lawrence wrote his earliest poetry in the spring of 1905 ("To Campions" and "To Guelder Roses" are the poems he later recalled having written then) and produced poetry regularly thereafter until just before his death (he completed the poems that appeared posthumously as *Last Poems* in November 1929 and prepared *Nettles* for publication in December 1929, correcting proofs for that collection in February 1930, less than a month before his death on 2 March). Nine volumes of his poems were published in his lifetime, and *Nettles* and *Last Poems* appeared shortly after his death. Lawrence can thus be said to have produced eleven complete collections of poetry during his lifetime (twelve if we count *Last Poems* as two distinct sequences, "More Pansies" and "Last Poems")—and there were, of course, many poems that remained unpublished or uncollected until sometime after his death.

The "definitive" collection of Lawrence's poetry is currently *The Complete Poems of D. H. Lawrence* (for full publication details of this and other collections referred to in this paragraph, see the following bibliography). *The Complete Poems* contains all Lawrence's published volumes of poetry, along with hitherto uncollected poems from printed and manuscript sources. It includes the posthumous collection of nine poems (seven of which had been previously unpublished in 1940), *Fire and Other Poems;* and the twenty-six poems from Lawrence's novel *The Plumed Serpent.* For the pre-1928 poetry, *The Complete Poems* derives largely from the collection Lawrence prepared between November 1927 and March 1928, *The Collected Poems of D. H. Lawrence* in two volumes. Volume 1, ''Rhyming Poems,'' derived mainly from his early poems as represented by the four previously published volumes, *Love Poems* (1913), *Amores* (1916), *New Poems* (1918), and *Bay* (1919). Volume 2, ''Unrhyming Poems,'' derived mainly from *Look! We Have Come Through!* (1917) and *Birds, Beasts and Flowers* (1923). However, most of the poems were substantially revised for the collection, and, in many ways, therefore, it can be considered as a new collection in its own right.

A two-volume text and a two-volume variorum edition of Lawrence's poetry are forthcoming in the Cambridge Edition of his works, edited by Carole Ferrier and Christopher Pollnitz (the Penguin edition of this volume will be edited by Christopher Pollnitz, and a volume of *Selected Poems* will also be published in the Penguin Lawrence Edition, edited by Holly Laird).

PUBLISHED/GENERAL CRITICISM

As suggested before, the most important general collections of Lawrence's poetry are *The Collected Poems* (1928) and *The Complete Poems* (1964), but I also list here one or two other collections. The second part of the following bibliography lists works that deal with either the whole range of Lawrence's poetry or a substantial part of it, including works that concentrate specifically on the two collections just mentioned.

BIBLIOGRAPHY 62

General Collections of Lawrence's Poetry

The Collected Poems of DHL. 2 vols. London: Secker, September 1928. New York: Jonathan Cape and Harrison Smith, July 1929.
DHL: Selected Poems. London: Secker, May 1934.
DHL: Poems. 2 vols. London and Toronto: Heinemann, April 1939.
Fire and Other Poems. San Francisco, Calif.: Grabhorn Press, November 1940.
DHL: Selected Poems. Edited by James Reeves. London: Heinemann, 1951.
DHL: The Complete Poems. 3 vols. London: Heinemann, 1957.
The Complete Poems of DHL. Collected and edited, in 2 volumes; by Vivian de Sola Pinto and Warren Roberts. London: Heinemann; New York: Viking, 1964; rev. ed., London: Heinemann, 1967; further rev., London: Heinemann, 1972. Reissued in one volume, with corrections and additions, New York: Viking Compass, 1971; and New York and Harmondsworth: Penguin, 1977. (This work should not be confused with the earlier collection previously cited, *DHL: The Complete Poems.*)
DHL: Selected Poems. Edited by Keith Sagar. Harmondsworth: Penguin, 1972.

General Criticism

As explained in the introduction to this section, only author-date citations are given here. See the master bibliography following the next chapter in this section for full details of all works cited here.

Books

Gregory (1933), Kenmare (1951), Garcia and Karabatsos (1970), Marshall (1970), Smailes (1970), Gilbert (1972), Oates (1973), Roberts (1982), Vries-Mason (1982), Murfin (1983), Mandell (1984), Davey (1985), Mackey (1986), Lockwood (1987), Laird (1988), Banerjee (1990).

Essays, Chapters, and Shorter Comment

Aldington (1926), Hughes (1931), Untermeyer (1933), Powell (1934), Blackmur (1935), Spender (1936), Southworth (1940), Kenmare (1943), Savage (1944 and 1945), Davis (1946), Rexroth (1947), Glicksberg (1948), Moore (1951), Spender (1953), Salgãdo (1955), Fisher (1956), Hough (1956), Grigson (1958), Bloom (1959), Thwaite (1959), Miller, Shapiro, and Slote (1960), Rosenthal (1960), Pinto (Spring 1961), Strickland (1961), Alvarez (1962), Auden (1963), Stewart (1963), Draper (1964), Rich (1965), Sagar (1966), Smailes (1968), Youngblood (1968), Spender (1970), Draper (1970; reviews), Inniss (1971), Sagar (1972), Bair (1973), Janik (1973), Lucie-Smith (1973), Solomon (1973), Vickery (1974), Nahal (1975), Perkins (1976), Jennings (1976), Browne (1978), Jones (1978), Pinion (1978), Rama Moorthy (1978), Mace (1979), Presley (1979), Ashworth (1981), Mitgutsch (1981), Anderson (1982), Brunsdale (1982), Gutierrez (1982), Salgãdo (1982), Gilbert (1983), Poole (1984), Rodway (1985), Sagar (1985), Vanson (1985), Chace (1987), Draper (1987), Mace (1988), Hagen (1990), Pollnitz (1990), Sagar (1992).

On "The Collected Poems of DHL"

Untermeyer (1929), Bartlett (1951), Asahi (1975), Laird (1988).

On "The Complete Poems of DHL"

Enright (1964), Rexroth (1964), Salgãdo (1965), Oates (1972).

35 The Poetry of D. H. Lawrence: Individual Volumes

Where individual poems have been the central focus of more than two or three critical essays or chapters, I have provided a separate listing of the criticism under the volume of poetry in which the poem was first collected; the poems that have received such attention are "Piano," "Fish," "Bavarian Gentians," "The Ship of Death," and, probably the most frequently studied of Lawrence's poems, "Snake."

LOVE POEMS AND OTHERS

WRITTEN

Spring 1905–October 1911 (except for "Bei Hennef," written in May 1912). Proofs, October 1912.

PUBLISHED

London: Duckworth, February 1913; New York: Kennerly, 1913.

CRITICISM

Pound (1913), Thomas (1913), Shakespear (1915), Mitra (1969), Gutierrez (1973; on "Lightning").

AMORES

WRITTEN

?Spring 1905–October 1911. Prepared for publication in January 1916. Proofs, May 1916.

PUBLISHED

London: Duckworth, July 1916; New York: Huebsch, September 1916.

CRITICISM

Tietjens (1917), Pittock (1965), Arbur (1978), Norton (1979). On "Snap-Dragon": Herzinger (1982), Heywood (1987), Ingram (1990).

LOOK! WE HAVE COME THROUGH!

WRITTEN

Most of the poems were written between 1912 and 1917, though a few were completed by 1911. Many of the poems were first written in the summer of 1912, but all were rewritten and revised for book publication in January and February 1917, and the latest poem seems to have been written in April 1917 ("Frost Flowers"). Further revision, August 1917; proof corrections, September 1917. Chatto and Windus insisted that two of the poems in Lawrence's original sequence be omitted from the published volume—"Song of a Man Who Is Loved" and "Meeting among the Mountains." In Lawrence's *Collected Poems* of 1928, he added three poems that belonged to the sequence but that had been published in other volumes of his poetry: "Bei Hennef," "Everlasting Flowers," and "Coming Awake."

PUBLISHED

London: Chatto and Windus, December 1917; New York: Huebsch, 1918.

CRITICISM

Fletcher (1918), Aiken (1919), Lowell (1919), Frieda Lawrence (1958), Potts (1967), Mitchell (1978), Murfin (1980), Herrick (1981), Rubin (1981), Meyers

(1982), Huq (1984), Raveendran (1985), Alves (1986), Gutierrez (1990; on "New Heaven and Earth").

On "Song of a Man Who Has Come Through": Hogan (1959), Levy (1964), Zanger (1965), Steinberg (1978).

NEW POEMS

WRITTEN

Mostly written by October 1911. Collected and revised for book publication in April and June 1918. Proofs, September 1918. A preface for the American edition, "Poetry of the Present," was written in August 1919.

PUBLISHED

London: Secker, October 1918; New York: Huebsch, June 1920.

"Poetry of the Present" first published in two parts in *Playboy,* nos. 4 and 5 (Fall 1919). Also published in *Voices* (October 1919) as "Verse Free and Unfree" and in *Evening Post Book Review* (19 June 1920): 1, 13.

CRITICISM

Fletcher (1920), Smailes (June 1970).

On "Piano": Richards (1929), Miller (1932), Bleich (1967), Leavis (1975), Laird (1985–86), Lecercle (1993).

BAY: A BOOK OF POEMS

WRITTEN

Some early poems written by October 1911. The rest probably written 1917–18. Collected and revised for book publication in April 1918. Proofs, September 1919.

PUBLISHED

London: Cyril W. Beaumont, November 1919.

CRITICISM

Cushman (1988), Thomas (1988; on "After the Opera").

TORTOISES

WRITTEN

September 1920.

PUBLISHED

New York: Seltzer, December 1921. Included in British edition of *Birds, Beasts and Flowers* (London: Secker, 1923).

CRITICISM

Sagar (1970), Brashear (1972).

BIRDS, BEASTS AND FLOWERS

WRITTEN

June 1920–November 1922 (except for "The American Eagle," March 1923). Prepared for publication, January–February 1923. Proofs, July–August 1923. Prefaces for 1930 illustrated edition written in November 1929.

PUBLISHED

1. New York: Seltzer, October 1923. London: Secker, November 1923 (includes *Tortoises*).
2. Illustrated Edition, with wood engravings by Blair Hughes-Stanton. London: Cresset Press, June 1930. Includes prefaces for each group of poems published for the first time (reprinted as "Notes for *Birds, Beasts and Flowers*" in *Phoenix* [1936]).

CRITICISM

Aiken (1924), Bogan (1924), Hughes (1924), Lucas (1924), Muir (1924), Squire (1924), Untermeyer (1924), Henderson (1939), Rajiva (1968), Smailes (1969), Brashear (1972), Cavitch (1974), Trail (Fall 1979), Gilbert (1979 and 1980), Heywood (1982), Meyers (1982), Perloff (1985).

On "Snake": Dalton (1962), Smith (1963), Mittleman (1966), Young (1968), Brashear (1972), Strohschoen (1977), Ebbatson (1978), Trail (1979), Tarinayya (1981), Thomas (1986), Yoshino (1986), Savita (1987).

On "Fish": Langbaum (1970), Cavitch (1974), Pollnitz (1982), Gutierrez (1985–86).

On "Hibiscus and Salvia Flower": Rodway (1982), Paulin (1989).

PANSIES

WRITTEN

November–December 1928. Revised February 1929. Proofs, May 1929. The introduction to the definitive, unexpurgated edition was first drafted in December 1928 (this version was first published only in May 1970—see under Farmer in the following bibliography) and rewritten in January 1929. A shorter foreword to the expurgated Secker edition was written in April 1929 (as indicated by the manuscript—the printed text carried the date of March 1929).

PUBLISHED

London: privately printed for subscribers only by P. R. Stephensen, August 1929. Expurgated edition: *Pansies: Poems by DHL*. London: Secker, July 1929; New York: Alfred A. Knopf, September 1929.

CRITICISM

Church (1929), Van Doren (1929), Lerner (1963), Farmer (1970), Dougherty (1983), Antrim (1984), Richards (1994).

NETTLES

WRITTEN

June–August 1929. Prepared for publication December 1929. Proofs, February 1930.

PUBLISHED

London: Faber and Faber, 13 March 1930.

CRITICISM

Rees (1930).

LAST POEMS

WRITTEN

These poems were in manuscript form on Lawrence's death and were subsequently organized into two groups and labeled "More Pansies" and "Last Poems" by the editors of the first edition. "More Pansies" written May–September 1929; "Last Poems" written October–November 1929.

PUBLISHED

Edited by Richard Aldington and Giuseppe Orioli. Florence: G. Orioli, October 1932. New York: Viking, March 1933. London: Secker, April 1933. See also *Triumph of the Machine*. London: Faber and Faber, September 1931 (separate publication of "Triumph of the Machine," later included in *Last Poems*); *The Ship of Death and Other Poems*. London: Secker, November 1933 (a selection from *Last Poems*); *The Ship of Death and Other Poems*. London: Faber and Faber, May 1941 (again a selection from *Last Poems* but different from the previous item).

CRITICISM

ffrench (1933), Richards (1933), Hassall (1959), Höltgen (1962; on "Masses and Classes"), Panichas (1964), Smailes (1968), Cipolla (1969), Fu (1970), Smailes (December 1970), Gutierrez (1971), Kirkham (1972), Janik (1975), Mace (1979), Iida (1981), Keeley (1982), Urang (1983), Sharma (1987), Katz-Roy (1992).

On "Bavarian Gentians": Cox and Dyson (1963), Harvey (1966), Sagar (1975), Ingram (1990), Forsyth (1992).

On "The Ship of Death": Honig (1967), Orrell (1971), Clark (1980), Gutierrez (1980), Parkinson (1980), Iida (1981), Sagar (1987).

BIBLIOGRAPHY 63: MASTER BIBLIOGRAPHY OF CRITICISM OF LAWRENCE'S POETRY

As elsewhere in this book, following full citation of initial publication, citations for reprintings of essays in works that are to be found in the reference bibliography of Lawrence criticism at the end of the book are given in abbreviated author-date form. Where relevant, the following abbreviations are used to indicate the individual volumes of Lawrence's poetry:

Love Poems and Others: LPO

Amores: A

Look! We Have Come Through!: LWHCT

New Poems: NP

Bay: B

Tortoises: T

Birds, Beasts and Flowers: BBF

The Collected Poems of D. H. Lawrence: CP

Pansies: P

Nettles: N

Last Poems: LP

Aiken, Conrad. "The Melodic Line." *Dial* 67 (August 1919): 97–100. (*LWHCT*)

———. *Skepticisms: Notes on Contemporary Poetry.* New York: Knopf, 1919, pp. 91–104.

———. "Disintegration in Modern Poetry." *Dial* 76 (June 1924): 535–40. (Review of *BBF*)

———. *A Reviewer's ABC: Collected Criticism of Conrad Aiken from 1916 to the Present.* Edited by Rufus A. Blanshard. New York: Meridian Books, 1958, pp. 256–68.

Aldington, Richard. "DHL as Poet." *Saturday Review of Literature* 2 (1 May 1926): pp. 749–50.

Alvarez, A. "DHL: The Single State of Man." In his *The Shaping Spirit: Studies in Modern English and American Poets.* London: Chatto and Windus; New York: Scribner's (as *Stewards of Excellence*), 1958, pp. 140–61. (Reprinted in Moore 1959: 342–59 and Spender 1973: 210–24.)

———. "The New Poetry or Beyond the Gentility Principle." In *The New Poetry.* Edited by A. Alvarez. Harmondsworth: Penguin, 1962, pp. 21–32.

Alves, Leonard. "*Look! We Have Come Through!:* DHL the Poet." *English Literature and Language* 23 (1986): 69–89.

Anderson, Emily Ann. *English Poetry 1900–1950: A Guide to Information Sources.* Detroit: Gale Research, 1982, pp. 155–70.

Antrim, Thomas M. "Lawrence's Wild Garden." *DHL Review* 17 (1984): 173–78. (*P*)

Arbur, Rosemarie. " 'Lilacs' and 'Sorrow': Whitman's Effect on the Early Poems of DHL." *Walt Whitman Review* 24 (1978): 17–21. ("Sorrow," *A*)

Asahi, Chiseki. " 'Jets of Sunlight.' " *Studies of Sonoda Women's College* (Japan) 9 (December 1974).

———. "Factors of Romanticism in DHL's 'Rhyming Poems.' " *Studies of Sonoda Women's College* (Japan) 10 (December 1975).

Ashworth, Clive. *Notes on DHL's Poems and Stories.* London: Methuen, 1981.

Auden, W. H. "Some Notes on DHL." *Nation* (26 April 1947): 482–84.

———. *The Dyer's Hand and Other Essays.* London: Faber, 1963, pp. 277–95.

Bahlke, George W. "Lawrence and Auden: The Pilgrim and the Citizen." In *The Challenge of DHL.* Edited by Michael Squires and Keith Cushman. Madison: University of Wisconsin Press, 1990, pp. 211–27.

Bair, Hebe. "Lawrence as Poet." *DHL Review* 6 (Fall 1973): 313–25.

Baker, James R. "Lawrence as Prophetic Poet." *Journal of Modern Literature* 3 (July 1974): 1219–38.

Baker, William E. *Syntax in English Poetry, 1870–1930.* Berkeley: University of California Press, 1967, passim.

Banerjee, Amitava. *DHL's Poetry: Demon Liberated: A Collection of Primary and Secondary Source Material.* London: Macmillan, 1990.

———. "The 'Marriage Poems' by Lawrence and Lowell." *Kobe College Studies* 38 (March 1993): 15–36.

Barnes, T. R. "Introduction." In *DHL: Selected Poetry and Prose.* Edited by T. R. Barnes. London: Heinemann, 1957, pp. vii–xv.

Bartlett, Phyllis. "Lawrence's *Collected Poems:* The Demon Takes Over." *PMLA* 66 (September 1951a): 583–93.

———. *Poems in Process.* New York: Oxford University Press, 1951b, pp. 181–83, 203–4.

Bayley, John. "Lawrence and Hardy: The One and the Many." *Phoenix* 23 (1982): 5–9.

Bickley, Francis. "Some Tendencies in Contemporary Poetry." In *New Paths.* Edited by C. W. Beaumont and M.T.H. Sadler. London: Beaumont, 1918, pp. 1–6.

Blackmur, R. P. "DHL and Expressive Form." In his *The Double Agent.* New York: Arrow, 1935, pp. 103–20. (Reprinted in his *Language as Gesture.* New York: Harcourt, Brace, 1952, pp. 286–300.)

Bleich, David. "The Determination of Literary Value." *Literature and Psychology* 17 (1967): 19–30. ("Piano," *NP:* response to Richards [1929], op. cit.)

Bloom, Harold. "Lawrence, Blackmur, Eliot, and the Tortoise." In *A DHL Miscellany.* Edited by Harry T. Moore. Carbondale: Southern Illinois University Press, 1959, pp. 360–69.

Bogan, Louise. "Review of *Birds, Beasts and Flowers.*" *New Republic* 39 (9 July 1924).

———. "Review of *Selected Poems* [1947]." *New Yorker* 24 (20 March 1948): 110–14. (Reprinted, as "The Poet Lawrence," in her *Selected Criticism: Prose and Poetry.* New York: Noonday, 1955; London: Peter Owen, 1958, 346–49; and, as "DHL," in *A Poet's Alphabet: Reflections on the Literary Art and Vocation.* Edited by Robert Phelps and Ruth Limmer. New York: McGraw-Hill, 1970, pp. 276–82.)

Bonds, Diane S. "Joyce Carol Oates: Testing the Lawrentian Hypothesis." In *The Challenge of DHL.* Edited by Michael Squires and Keith Cushman. Madison: University of Wisconsin Press, 1990, pp. 167–87.

Brandes, Rand. "Behind the Bestiaries: The Poetry of Lawrence and Ted Hughes." In *The Challenge of DHL.* Edited by Michael Squires and Keith Cushman. Madison: University of Wisconsin Press, 1990, pp. 248–67.

Brashear, Lucy M. "Lawrence's Companion Poems: 'Snake' and *Tortoises.*" *DHL Review* 5 (Spring 1972): 54–62. (*BBF; T*)

Browne, Michael Dennis. "Gods beyond My God: The Poetry of DHL." *Aspen Anthology,* no. 5 (1978): 17–52.

Brunsdale, Mitzi M. *The German Effect on DHL and His Works, 1985–1912.* Berne: Peter Lang, 1978, pp. 50–81, 145–49, 177–85, 192–94.

———. "DHL." In *Critical Survey of Poetry.* Vol. 4. Edited by Frank N. Magill. Englewood Cliffs, N.J.: Salem Press, 1982, pp. 1677–78.

Bump, Jerome. "Stevens and Lawrence: The Poetry of Nature and the Spirit of the Age." *Southern Review* 18 (1982): 44–61.

Cavitch, David. *DHL and the New World.* New York and London: Oxford University Press, 1969, pp. 209–18.

———. "Merging—With Fish and Others." *DHL Review* 7 (Summer 1974): 172–78. ("Fish," *BBF*)

Cecil, David. "Lawrence in His Poems." *Spectator* (4 August 1933): 163.

Chace, William M. "Lawrence and English Poetry." In *The Legacy of DHL.* Edited by Jeffrey Meyers. London: Macmillan, 1987, pp. 54–80.

Church, Richard. "Three Established Poets." *Spectator* (3 August 1929): 164–65. (*P*)

Cipolla, Elizabeth. "The *Last Poems* of DHL." *DHL Review* 2 (Summer 1969): 103–19.

Clare, John. "Form in Vers Libre." *English* 27 (1978): 450–70. (Concentrates on Eliot, Pound, and Lawrence.)

Clark, L. D. *Dark Night of the Body: DHL's "The Plumed Serpent."* Austin: University of Texas Press, 1964.

———. *The Minoan Distance: The Symbolism of Travel in DHL.* Tucson: University of Arizona Press, 1980, pp. 412–14. ("The Ship of Death," *LP*)

Clarke, Bruce. "The Melancholy Serpent: Body and Landscape in Lawrence and William Carlos Williams." In *The Challenge of DHL.* Edited by Michael Squires and Keith Cushman. Madison: University of Wisconsin Press, 1990, pp. 188–210.

Cox, C. B., and A. E. Dyson. "DHL: 'Bavarian Gentians.' " In their *Modern Poetry: Studies in Practical Criticism.* London: Edward Arnold, 1963, pp. 66–71.

Cushman, Keith. "*Bay:* The Noncombatant as War Poet." In *The Spirit of DHL: Centenary Studies.* Edited by Gāmini Salgādo and G. K. Das. London: Macmillan; New York: Barnes, 1988, pp. 181–98.

Daiches, David. *Poetry and the Modern World.* Chicago: University of Chicago Press, 1940, pp. 35, 51–53, 82–84.

Dalton, Robert O. " 'Snake': A Moment of Consciousness." *Brigham Young University Studies* 4 (Spring–Summer 1962): 243–53. (*BBF*)

Davey, Charles. *DHL: A Living Poet.* London: Brentham Press, 1985.

Davie, Donald. "On Sincerity: From Wordsworth to Ginsberg." *Encounter* 31, no. 4 (1968): 61–66.

———. "A Doggy Demos: Hardy and Lawrence." In his *Thomas Hardy and British Poetry.* London: Routledge and Kegan Paul; New York: Oxford University Press, 1973, pp. 130–51.

Davies, W. Eugene. "The Poetry of Mary Webb: An Invitation." *English Literature in Transition* 11, no. 2 (1968): 95–101. (Comparisons with Lawrence.)

Davis, E. *The Poetry of DHL.* [Cape Town, South Africa]: UNISA Study Notes, 1956. (Fifty-five-page pamphlet.)

Davis, Herbert. "The Poetic Genius of DHL." In *The New Spirit.* Edited by E. W. Martin. London: Dennis Dobson, 1946, pp. 58–65.

Deutsch, Babette. "The Burden of Mystery: Criticism of Lawrence's Poetry." In her *This Modern Poetry.* London: Faber, 1936, pp. 200–224.

DeVille, Peter. "Stylistic Observations on the Use and Appreciation of Poetry in EFL with Particular Reference to DHL." *Quaderno* 1 (1987): 151–75.

Dietrich, Carol E. " 'The Raw and the Cooked': The Role of Fruit in Modern Poetry." *Mosaic* 24 (1991): 127–44.

Dougherty, Jay. " 'Vein of Fire': Relationships among Lawrence's *Pansies.*" *DHL Review* 16 (1983): 165–81.

Draper, R. P. *DHL.* New York: Twayne, 1964, pp. 149–60.

————. "Form and Tone in the Poetry of DHL." *English Studies* 49 (December 1968): 498–508.

————. "DHL: Tragedy as Creative Crisis." In his *Lyric Tragedy.* London: Macmillan, 1985, pp. 144–61.

————. "The Poetry of DHL." In *DHL: New Studies.* Edited by Christopher Heywood. London: Macmillan; New York: St. Martin's Press, 1987, pp. 16–33.

————, ed. *DHL: The Critical Heritage.* London: Routledge and Kegan Paul, 1970, pp. 177–83 (*A*); 224–31 (*BBF*); 121–31, 137–40 (*LWHCT*); 51–57, 224–27 (*LPO*); 306–14 (*P*); 299–305 (*CP*).

Easthope, Malcolm. *Students' Guide to "Choice of Poets": Wordsworth, Blake, Lawrence, Graves, Frost.* Singapore: Graham Brash, 1986.

Ebbatson, J. R. "A Source for Lawrence's 'Snake.' " *Journal of the DHL Society* 1, no. 3 (1978): 33. (*BBF*)

Eisenstein, Samuel A. *Boarding the Ship of Death: DHL's Quester Heroes.* The Hague: Mouton, 1974, pp. 149–58.

Ellmann, Richard. "Lawrence and His Demon." *New Mexico Quarterly* 22 (Winter 1952): 385–93. (Reprinted as "Barbed Wire and Coming Through" in Hoffman and Moore [1953]: 253–67.)

Enright, D. J. "A Haste for Wisdom." *New Statesman* (30 October 1964): 653–54. (Review of the *The Complete Poems.*)

————. *Conspirators and Poets.* London: Chatto and Windus, 1966, pp. 95–101.

Fairchild, Hoxie Neale. In his *Religious Trends in English Poetry.* Vol. 5. New York: Columbia University Press, 1962, pp. 276–84.

————. In his *Religious Trends in English Poetry.* Vol. 6. New York: Columbia University Press, 1968, passim.

Farmer, David, ed. "An Unpublished Version of DHL's Introduction to *Pansies.*" *Review of English Studies,* new series, 21 (May 1970): 181–84.

————. "DHL's 'The Turning Back': The Text and Its Genesis in Correspondence." *DHL Review* 5 (Summer 1972a): 121–31. (First publication of complete poem.)

————. "Textual Alterations in *Not I But the Wind.* . . . " *Notes and Queries* 19 (September 1972b): 336.

Ferrier, Carole. "The Earlier Poetry of DHL: A Variorum Text." Ph.D. diss., University of Auckland, 1971.

————. "DHL: An Ibsen Reference." *Notes and Queries* 19 (September 1972): 335–36. (Title of "Nils Lykke" taken from Ibsen's "Lady Inger of Östrat.")

————. "DHL's Pre-1920 Poetry: A Descriptive Bibliography of Manuscripts, Typescripts, and Proofs." *DHL Review* 6 (Fall 1973): 333–59.

————. "DHL's Poetry, 1920–1928: A Descriptive Bibliography of Manuscripts, Typescripts and Proofs." *DHL Review* 12 (Fall 1979): 289–304.

Ferrier, Carole, and Egon Tiedje. "DHL's Pre-1920 Poetry: The Textual Approach: An Exchange." *DHL Review* 5 (Summer 1972): 149–57.

ffrench, Yvonne. "Review of *Last Poems.*" *London Mercury* 28 (July 1933): 262–64.

Fisher, William J. "Peace and Passivity: The Poetry of DHL." *South Atlantic Quarterly* 60 (1956): 337–48.

Fletcher, John Gould. "A Modern Evangelist." *Poetry* 12 (August 1918): 269–74. (*LWHCT*)

———. "Mr. Lawrence's *New Poems*." *Freeman* 1 (21 July 1920): 451–52.

———. "Night-Haunted Lover." *New York Herald Tribune Books* (14 July 1929): 1, 6.

Forsyth, Neil. "DHL's 'Bavarian Gentians': A Miltonic Turn toward Death." *Etudes et Lettres* 4 (October–December 1992): 83–100. (*LP*)

French, Roberts W. "Whitman and the Poetics of Lawrence." In *DHL and Tradition*. Edited by Jeffrey Meyers. London: Athlone, 1985, pp. 91–114.

———. "Lawrence and American Poetry." In *The Legacy of DHL*. Edited by Jeffrey Meyers. London: Macmillan, 1987, pp. 109–34.

Fu, Shaw-shien. "Death in Lawrence's *Last Poems*: A Study of Theme in Relation to Imagery." *Tamkang Review* (Taiwan) 1 (April 1970): 79–91.

Garcia, Leroy, and James Karabatsos, eds. *A Concordance to the Poetry of DHL*. Lincoln: University of Nebraska Press, 1970.

Garnett, Edward. "Art and the Moralists: Mr. DHL's Work." *Dial* 61 (16 November 1916): 377–81. (Reprinted in his *Friday Nights: First Series*. London: Cape, 1929, pp. 117–28.)

Gifford, Henry. "The Defect of Lawrence's Poetry." *Critical Quarterly* 3 (Summer 1961): 164–67. (Response to Pinto [Spring 1961], op. cit..)

———. "Lawrence's Poetry." *Critical Quarterly* 3 (Winter 1961): 368–69. (Response to Pinto [Autumn 1961], op. cit.)

Gilbert, Sandra M. *Acts of Attention: The Poems of DHL*. Ithaca, N.Y., and London: Cornell University Press, 1972.

———. "Hell on Earth: *Birds, Beasts and Flowers* as Subversive Narrative." *DHL Review* 12 (Fall 1979): 256–74.

———. "DHL's Uncommon Prayers." In *DHL: The Man Who Lived*. Edited by Robert B. Partlow, Jr., and Harry T. Moore. Carbondale: Southern Illinois University Press, 1980, pp. 73–93. (*BBF*)

———. "DHL." In *Dictionary of Literary Biography*. Vol. 19. *British Poets 1880–1914*. Edited by Donald E. Stanford. Detroit: Gale Research, 1983, pp. 274–88.

Glicksberg, Charles I. "The Poetry of DHL." *New Mexico Quarterly* 18 (Autumn 1948): 289–303.

Golding, Alan. "Lawrence and Recent American Poetry." In *The Challenge of DHL*. Edited by Michael Squires and Keith Cushman. Madison: University of Wisconsin Press, 1990, pp. 187–208.

Goldring, Douglas. "The Later Work of DHL." In his *Reputations: Essays in Criticism*. London: Chapman and Hall, 1920, pp. 65–78.

Gregory, Horace. *Pilgrim of the Apocalypse: A Critical Study of DHL*. New York: Viking, 1933; London: Secker, 1934, passim. (Revised as *DHL: Pilgrim of the Apocalypse: A Critical Study*. New York: Grove, 1957.)

Grigson, Geoffrey. "The Poet in DHL." *London Magazine* 5 (May 1958): 66–69.

Gutierrez, Donald. "Circles and Arcs: The Rhythm of Circularity and Centrifugality in DHL's *Last Poems*." *DHL Review* 4 (Fall 1971): 291–300. (Reprinted in Gutierrez [1980: 118–28]. See also pp. 45–49 on "Shadows" and "The Ship of Death.")

———. "The Pressures of Love: Kinesthetic Action in an Early Lawrence Poem." *Contemporary Poetry* 1 (Winter 1973): 6–20. ("Lightning," *LPO*)

———. "The Ancient Now: Past and Present in Lawrence's Poetry." *San Jose Studies* 7, no. 2 (1981): 35–43.

———. "Lawrence's Elemental Verse." *Essays in Arts and Sciences* 11 (September 1982): 69–85. (Reprinted in Gutierrez [1987]: 93–107.)

———. "The View from the Edge: DHL's 'Fish.' " *University of Dayton Review* 17 (Winter 1985–86): 63–68. (Reprinted in his *The Maze in the Mind and the World: Labyrinths in Modern Literature.* Troy, N.Y.: Whitston, 1985.) (*BBF*)

———. " 'Break On Through to the Other Side': DHL's 'New Heaven and Earth' as Apocalyptic." *Paunch* 63–64 (1990): 119–39. (*LWHCT*)

Hagen, Patricia L. "Astrology, Schema Theory, and Lawrence's Poetic Method." *DHL Review* 22 (Spring 1990): 23–37.

Hamalian, Leo. " 'A Whole Climate of Opinion': Lawrence at Black Mountain." In *The Challenge of DHL.* Edited by Michael Squires and Keith Cushman. Madison: University of Wisconsin Press, 1990, pp. 228–47. (Lawrence's influence on Charles Olson and Robert Creeley.)

———. "Beyond the Paleface: DHL and Gary Snyder." *Talisman* 7 (Fall 1991): 50–55.

Harding, D. W. "A Note on Nostalgia." *Scrutiny* 1 (1932): 8–19.

Hardy, Barbara. *The Advantage of Lyric.* Bloomington: Indiana University Press, 1977, pp. 12–16 and passim.

Harvey, R. W. "On Lawrence's 'Bavarian Gentians.' " *Wascana Review* 1 (1966): 74–86. (*LP*)

Hassall, Christopher. "Black Flowers: A New Light on the Poetics of DHL." In *A DHL Miscellany.* Edited by Harry T. Moore. Carbondale: Southern Illinois University Press, 1959, pp. 370–77. (Revised and extended as "DHL and the Etruscans." *Essays by Divers Hands,* new series, 31 [1962]: 61–78.) (*LP*)

Hehner, Barbara. " 'Kissing and Horrid Strife': Male and Female in the Early Poetry of DHL." *Four Decades of Poetry, 1890–1930* 1 (January 1976): 3–26.

Henderson, Philip. "*Birds, Beasts and Flowers.*" In his *The Poet and Society.* London: Secker and Warburg, 1939, pp. 172–201.

Herrick, Jeffrey. "The Vision of *Look! We Have Come Through!*" *DHL Review* 14 (1981): 217–37.

Herzinger, Kim. *DHL in His Time: 1908–1915.* London and Toronto: Associated University Presses, 1982, pp. 53–56. ("Snap-Dragon," *A*)

Heuser, Alan. "Creaturely Inseeing in the Poetry of G. M. Hopkins, DHL, and Ted Hughes." *Hopkins Quarterly* 12 (1985): 35–51.

Heywood, Annemarie. "Reverberations: 'Snapdragon.' " In *DHL: New Studies.* Edited by Christopher Heywood. London: Macmillan; New York: St. Martin's Press, 1987, pp. 158–81. (*A*)

Heywood, Christopher. "*Birds, Beasts and Flowers:* The Evolutionary Context and Lawrence's African Source." *DHL Review* 15 (1982): 87–105. (Reprinted in Brown [1990]: 151–63.)

Hobsbaum, Philip. *A Reader's Guide to Lawrence.* London: Thames and Hudson, 1981, pp. 8–22, 131–48.

Hoffpauir, Richard. "The Early Love Poetry of DHL." *English Studies in Canada* 15, no. 3 (1988): 326–42.

———. *The Art of Restraint: English Poetry from Hardy to Larkin.* Newark: University of Delaware, 1991, pp. 169–85.

Hogan, Robert. "Lawrence's 'Song of a Man Who Has Come Through.' " *Explicator* 17 (1959): Item 51. (*LWHCT*)

Holbrook, David. *Lost Bearings in English Poetry.* New York: Barnes and Noble, 1977, passim.

Höltgen, K. J. "DHL's Poem 'Masses and Classes.' " *Notes and Queries* 9 (November 1962): 428–29. (*LP*)

Honig, Edwin. "Lawrence: 'The Ship of Death.' " In *Master Poems of the English Language.* Edited by Oscar Williams. New York: Washington Square Press, 1967, pp. 954–57. (*LP*)

Hooker, Jeremy. "To Open the Mind." *Planet,* no. 5–6 (Summer 1971): 59–63. (Compares Lawrence and Charles Olson.)

Hooper, A. G., and C.J.D. Harvey. *Talking of Poetry.* London: Oxford University Press, 1961, pp. 149–56.

Hope, A. D. "Some Poems of DHL Reconsidered." *Phoenix* 23 (1981): 11–16.

Hough, Graham. *The Dark Sun: A Study of DHL.* London: Gerald Duckworth, 1956, pp. 191–216.

———. "Free Verse." *Proceedings of the British Academy* (1957): 157–77. (Warton lecture on English poetry, 5 June 1957.)

Hughes, Glenn. "DHL: The Passionate Psychologist." In his *Imagism and the Imagists: A Study in Modern Poetry.* Stanford, Calif. Stanford University Press; London: Oxford University Press, 1931, pp. 167–96.

Hughes, Richard. "Review of *Birds, Beasts and Flowers.*" *Nation and Athenaeum* 34 (5 January 1924): 519–20.

Huq, Shireen. "*Look! We Have Come Through!:* A Study of the Man–Woman Relationships in the Poems of DHL." *Indian P.E.N.* 46 (September–October 1984): 10–14; (November–December 1984): 7–11.

Hyde, Virginia. *The Risen Adam: DHL's Revisionist Typology.* University Park: Pennsylvania State University Press, 1992, passim.

Iida, Takeo. "DHL's 'The Ship of Death' and Other Poems in *Last Poems.*" *Studies in English Literature* (Tokyo) 58, no. 1 (September 1981): 33–47.

———. "On a Topos Called the Sun Shining at Midnight in DHL's Poetry." *DHL Review* 15 (1982): 271–90.

Ingram, Allan. "The Language of Poetry." In his *The Language of DHL.* London: Macmillan, 1990, pp. 138–58. (Mainly on "Snap-Dragon," *A,* "Bei Hennef," *LPO,* and "Bavarian Gentians," *LP.*)

Inniss, Kenneth. *DHL's Bestiary: A Study of His Use of Animal Trope and Symbol.* The Hague and Paris: Mouton, 1971; New York: Humanities Press, 1972, pp. 57–65 (*LWHCT*); 65–90 (*BBF*); 90–105 (*P* and *LP*).

Janik, Del Ivan. "Toward 'Thingness': Cézanne's Painting and Lawrence's Poetry." *Twentieth Century Literature* 19 (1973): 119–27.

———. "DHL's 'Future Religion': The Unity of *Last Poems.*" *Texas Studies in Literature and Language* 16 (Winter 1975): 739–54.

———. "Poetry in the Ecosphere." *Centennial Review* 20 (Fall 1976): 395–408 (399–402).

———. "Gary Snyder, the Public Function of Poetry, and Turtle Island." *NMAL: Notes on Modern American Literature* 3 (1979), item 24.

Jansohn, Christa. "Lawrence's 'Book of French Verse.' " *Notes and Queries* 36 (1989): 201–2.

Jeffers, Robinson. "Foreword." In *Fire and Other Poems* by DHL. San Francisco: Grabhorn Press, 1940, pp. iii–viii.

Jennings, Elizabeth. "DHL: A Vision of the Natural World." *Seven Men of Vision: An Appreciation.* London: Vision Press, 1976, pp. 45–80.

Jones, R. T. "DHL's Poetry: Art and the Apprehension of Fact." In *DHL: A Critical Study of the Major Novels and Other Writings.* Edited by Andor Gomme. New York: Barnes and Noble; Hassocks: Harvester Press, 1978, pp. 175–89.

Joost, Nicholas, and Alvin Sullivan. *DHL and "The Dial."* Carbondale and Edwardsville: Southern Illinois University Press; London and Amsterdam: Feffer and Simons, 1970, pp. 38–41, 156–78, passim.

Katz-Roy, Ginette. "The Process of 'Rotary Image-Thought' in DHL's *Last Poems.*" *Etudes Lawrenciennes* 7 (1992): 129–38.

———. " 'This May Be a Withering Tree This Europe': Bachelard, Deleuze and Guattari on DHL's Poetic Imagination." *Etudes Lawrenciennes* 9 (1993): 219–35.

Keeley, Edmund. "DHL's 'The Argonauts': Mediterranean Voyagers with Crescent Feet." *Deus Loci: The Lawrence Durrell Newsletter* 5, no. 3 (1982): 9–13. (*LP*)

Kenmare, Dallas. "Voice in the Wilderness: The Unacknowledged Lawrence." *Poetry Review* (May–June 1943): 145–48.

———. *Fire-Bird: A Study of DHL.* London: Barrie, 1951; New York: Philosophical Library, 1952.

Kirkham, Michael. "DHL's *Last Poems.*" *DHL Review* 5 (Summer 1972): 97–120.

Laird, Holly A. "The Poems of 'Piano.' " *DHL Review* 18 (1985–86): 183–99. (*NP*)

———. *Self and Sequence: The Poetry of DHL.* Charlottesville: University Press of Virginia, 1988a.

———. "Strange, Torn Edges: Reading the *Collected Poems of DHL.*" In *The Spirit of DHL: Centenary Studies.* Edited by Gāmini Salgādo and G. K. Das. London: Macmillan; New York: Barnes, 1988b, pp. 199–213.

———. "Excavating the Early Poetry of DHL." *DHL Review* 23 (Spring 1991): 111–28.

Langbaum, Robert. *The Modern Spirit: Essays on the Continuity of Nineteenth and Twentieth Century Literature.* New York: Oxford University Press, 1970, pp. 114–18. ("Fish," *BBF*)

Lawrence, Frieda. "Introduction" to *Look! We Have Come Through! A Cycle of Love Poems* by DHL. Marazion, Cornwall: Out of the Ark Press, 1958. 2d ed., Dallas: Ark Press for the Rare Books Collection of the University of Texas, 1959.

Leavis, F. R. " 'Thought' and Emotional Quality." In his *The Living Principle.* London: Chatto and Windus, 1975, pp. 71–93 (75–79). (Contrasts "Piano," *NP* with Tennyson's "Break, break, break.")

Lecercle, Jean-Jacques. "Sentimentalism and Feeling: DHL's 'Piano' and I. A. Richards' Reading of It." *Etudes Lawrenciennes* 9 (1993): 201–17. (*NP*)

Lenz, William E. "Forgotten Theory? The Poetics of Three Lawrence Poems." *Contemporary Poetry: A Journal of Criticism* 3, no. 4 (1978): 50–58.

Lerner, Laurence. "Two Views of Lawrence's Poetry: 'How Beastly the Bourgeois Is.' " *Critical Survey* 1 (Spring 1963): 87–89. (Reprinted in his *The Truthtellers* [1967]: 220–24.) (*P*)

Levy, Michele Frucht. "Lawrence, Genius but . . . Poet but . . . etc." *Publications of the Mississippi Philological Association* (1988): 95–105.

Levy, Raphael. "Lawrence's 'Song of a Man Who Has Come Through.' " *Explicator* 22 (February 1964): Item 44. (*LWHCT*)

Lockwood, M. J. *A Study of the Poems of DHL: Thinking in Poetry.* London: Macmillan; New York: St. Martin's, 1987.

Lowell, Amy. "A New English Poet." *New York Times Book Review* (20 April 1919): 205, 210–11, 215, 217. (*LWHCT*)

Lucas, F. L. "Sense and Sensibility." *New Statesman* 22 (8 March 1924): 634–35. (*BBF*)

Lucie-Smith, Edward. "The Poetry of DHL—With a Glance at Shelley." In *DHL: Novelist, Poet, Prophet.* Edited by Stephen Spender. London: Weidenfeld and Nicolson, 1973, pp. 224–33.

Mace, Hebe R. "The Achievement of Poetic Form: DHL's *Last Poems.*" *DHL Review* 12 (Fall 1979): 275–88.

———. "The Genesis of DHL's Poetic Form." In *Critical Essays on DHL.* Edited by Dennis Jackson and Fleda Brown Jackson. Boston: G. K. Hall, 1988, pp. 189–202.

Macherelli, Fabio. " 'Down the Labyrinth of the Sinister Flower': DHL's Urban Poetry." *Cahiers Victoriens et Edouardiens* 32 (October 1990): 29–39.

Mackey, Douglas A. *DHL: The Poet Who Was Not Wrong.* San Bernardino, Calif.: Burgo Press, 1986.

Mahapatra, P. K. "Cave and the Mount: Patterns of Progression and Regression in the Early Poems of DHL." *Osmania Journal of English Studies* 21 (1985): 82–95.

Mandell, Gail Porter. *The Phoenix Paradox: A Study of Renewal through Change in the "Collected Poems" and "Last Poems" of DHL.* Carbondale and Edwardsville: Southern Illinois University Press, 1984.

Marshall, Tom. *The Psychic Mariner: A Reading of the Poems of DHL.* New York: Viking, 1970.

Mason, H. A. "Wounded Surgeons." *Cambridge Quarterly* 11 (1982): 189–223. (On Leavis and Lawrence's poetry. See response by Strickland [1982] op. cit.)

Maurois, André. "DHL." In his *Poets and Prophets.* London: Cassell, 1936, pp. 173–207.

Megroz, R. L. "DHL." In his *Five Novelist Poets of Today.* London: Joiner and Steele, 1933, pp. 224–35.

Meyers, Jeffrey. *DHL and the Experience of Italy.* Philadelphia: University of Pennsylvania Press, 1982, pp. 72–93. (*BBF, LWHCT*)

Miller, James E., Jr., Karl Shapiro, and Bernice Slote. *Start with the Sun: Studies in Cosmic Poetry.* Lincoln: University of Nebraska Press, 1960, pp. 57–134, 229–38. (Lawrence as a "cosmic" poet in the tradition of Whitman, Hart Crane, and Dylan Thomas.)

Miller, W. W. *Books: An Introduction to Reading.* London: Pitman and Sons, 1932. (On "Piano," *NP*)

Mitchell, Judith. "Lawrence's 'Ballad of a Wilful Woman.' " *Explicator* 36, no. 4 (1978): 4–6. (*LWHCT*)

Mitgutsch, Waltraud. "The Image of the Female in DHL's Poetry." *Poetic Drama and Poetic Theory* (Salzburg Studies in English Literature) 27 (1981): 3–28.

Mitra, A. K. "Revisions in Lawrence's 'Wedding Morn.' " *Notes and Queries,* new series, 16 (July 1969): 260. (*LPO*)

Mittleman, Leslie B. "Lawrence's 'Snake' Not 'Sweet Georgian Brown.' " *English Literature in Transition* 9 (1966): 45–46. (Response to comments on the poem by

Neil F. Brennan in a review of *The Georgian Revolt* by Robert Ross, "Sweet Georgian Brown." *English Literature in Transition* 8 [1965]: 269–71.) (*BBF*)

Monro, Harold. *Some Contemporary Poets.* London: Leonard Parsons, 1920, pp. 193–97.

Moore, Harry T. *The Life and Works of DHL.* London: Allen and Unwin; New York: Twayne, 1951, pp. 52–78 (*A, LPO*); 87–91, 108–11 (*LWHCT*); 186–87 (*NP, B*); 198–200 (*BBF*); 297–302 (*P, N*); 302–4 (*LP*).

Morgan, James. " 'Thrice Adream': Father, Son, and Masculinity in Lawrence's 'Snake.' " *Literature and Psychology* 39 (1993): 97–111.

Morse, Stearns. "The Phoenix and the Desert Places." *Massachusetts Review* 9 (Autumn 1968): 773–84. (Lawrence and Robert Frost.)

Muir, Edwin. "Poetry in Becoming." *Freeman* 8 (2 January 1924). (*BBF*)

Murfin, Ross C. " 'Hymn to Priapus': Lawrence's Poetry of Difference." *Criticism* 22, no. 3 (1980): 214–29. (Revised version reprinted as part of Ch. 1 of next item.) (*LWHCT*)

———. *The Poetry of DHL: Texts and Contexts.* Lincoln: University of Nebraska Press, 1983.

Nahal, Chaman. "The Colour Ambience of Lawrence's Early and Later Poetry." *DHL Review* 8 (Summer 1975): 147–54.

Niven, Alastair. *DHL: The Writer and His Work.* Harlow, Essex: Longman, 1980, pp. 94–97.

Norton, David. "Lawrence's Baby Poems: A Practical Criticism Exercise." In *View of English: Victoria University Essays for English Teachers and Students.* Edited by David Norton and Roger Robinson. Wellington: Victoria University Press, 1979, pp. 19–24. (*A*)

Oates, Joyce Carol. "Candid Revelations: On *The Complete Poems of DHL.*" *American Poetry Review* 1 (November–December 1972): 11–13.

———. "The Hostile Sun: The Poetry of DHL." *Massachusetts Review* 13 (Autumn 1972): 639–56.

———. *The Hostile Sun: The Poetry of DHL.* Los Angeles: Black Sparrow Press, 1973. (Originally published in two parts as the two preceding items. Reprinted in her *New Heaven, New Earth: The Visionary Experience in Literature.* London: Gollancz, 1976, pp. 37–81.)

Olson, Charles. *DHL and the High Temptation of the Mind.* Santa Barbara, Calif.: Black Sparrow Press, 1980.

Orrell, Herbert M. "DHL: Poet of Death and Resurrection." *Cresset* 34 (March 1971): 10–13. ("The Ship of Death," *LP*)

Panichas, George A. *Adventure in Consciousness: The Meaning of DHL's Religious Quest.* The Hague: Mouton, 1964, pp. 180–207. (*LP*)

Parkinson, Thomas. "Loneliness of the Poet." In *The Anatomy of Loneliness.* Edited by Joseph Harog, J. Ralph Audy, and Yehudi Cohen. New York: International Universities Press, 1980, pp. 467–85. ("The Ship of Death," *LP*)

Pathak, R. S. "Lawrencean Poetics and the Search for Expressive Form." In *Essays on DHL.* Edited by T. R. Sharma. Meerut, India: Shalabh Book House, 1987, pp. 18–36.

Paulin, Tom. " 'Hibiscus and Salvia Flowers': The Puritan Imagination." In *DHL in the Modern World.* Edited by Peter Preston and Peter Hoare. London: Macmillan, 1989, pp. 180–92. (*BBF*)

Perkins, David. *A History of Modern Poetry from the 1890s to the High Modernist Mode.* Cambridge: Harvard University Press, 1976, pp. 439–45 and passim.

Perloff, Majorie. "Lawrence's Lyric Theater: *Birds, Beasts and Flowers.*" In *DHL: A Centenary Consideration.* Edited by Peter Balbert and Phillip L. Marcus. Ithaca, N.Y.: Cornell University Press, 1985, pp. 108–29.

Phelps, W. L. "The Poetry of DHL." In his *The Advance of English Poetry.* London: Allen and Unwin, 1919, pp. 145–48.

Pinion, F. B. *A DHL Companion: Life, Thought, and Works.* London: Macmillan, 1978; New York: Barnes and Noble, 1979, pp. 93–126.

Pinto, Vivian de Sola. "Imagists and DHL." In his *Crisis in English Poetry.* London: Hutchinson's University Library, 1951, pp. 135–40.

———. "Mr. Gifford and DHL." *Critical Quarterly* 3 (Autumn 1961): 267–70.

———. "Lawrence's Poetry." *Critical Quarterly* 4 (1962): 81.

———. "Poet without a Mask." *Critical Quarterly* 3, no. 1 (Spring 1961): 5–18. (Reprinted in Spilka [1963]: 127–41. Revised as "Introduction: DHL: Poet without a Mask." In *The Complete Poems of DHL.* Edited by Vivian de Sola Pinto and Warren Roberts. London: Heinemann, 1964, pp. 1–21 [see Bibliography 62 for details of revised editions]. See also Gifford [1961], op. cit., and Pinto's response in the preceding two items.)

———. "The Burning Bush: DHL as Religious Poet." In *Mansions of the Spirit: Essays in Literature and Religion.* Edited by George A. Panichas. New York: Hawthorne, 1967, pp. 213–35.

Pittock, Malcolm. "Lawrence the Poet." *Times Literary Supplement* (2 September 1965): 755. ("The Bride," *A*)

Pollnitz, Christopher. " 'I Didn't Know His God': The Epistemology of 'Fish.' " *DHL Review* 15 (Spring 1982): 1–50. (*BBF*)

———. " 'Raptus Virginis': The Dark God in the Poetry of DHL." In *DHL: Centenary Essays.* Edited by Mara Kalnins. Bristol: Bristol Classical Press, 1986, pp. 111–38.

———. "Craftsman before Demon: The Development of Lawrence's Verse Technique." In *Rethinking Lawrence.* Edited by Keith Brown. Milton Keynes and Philadelphia: Open University Press, 1990, pp. 133–50.

Poole, Roger. "DHL, Major Poet." *Texas Studies in Literature and Language* 26 (1984): 303–30.

Potter, Stephen. "Towards the Great Secret." *Spectator* (23 October 1964): 545.

Potts, Abbie Findlay. "Pipings of Pan: DHL." In his *The Elegiac Mode.* Ithaca, N.Y.: Cornell University Press, 1967, pp. 395–432 (410–17 on *LWHCT*).

Pound, Ezra. "Review of *Love Poems and Others* by DHL." *Poetry* 2 (July 1913): 149–51.

———. "Review of *Love Poems and Others* by DHL." *New Freewoman* (1 September 1913): 113.

Powell, Dilys. *Descent from Parnassus.* London: Cresset Press, 1934; New York: Macmillan, 1935, pp. 1–54.

Powell, S. W. "DHL as Poet." *Poetry Review* 8 (September–October 1934): 347–50.

Presley, John. "DHL and the Resources of Poetry." *Language and Style* 12 (1979): 3–12.

Press, John. "DHL." In his *Map of Modern English Verse.* London and Oxford: Oxford University Press, 1969, pp. 93–104.

Pritchard, R. E. *DHL: Body of Darkness*. London: Hutchinson University Library, 1971, pp. 47–51, 143–47.

Pritchard, William H. "English Poetry in the 1920s: Graves and Lawrence." In his *Seeing through Everything: English Writers 1918–1940.* Oxford: Oxford University Press, 1977, pp. 114–33.

Rajiva, Stanley F. "The Empathetic Vision." *Literary Half-Yearly* 9, no. 2 (1968): 49–70. (*BBF*)

Rama, Moorthy P. "The Poetry of DHL." *Commonwealth Quarterly* 2, no. 7 (1978): 69–78.

Raveendran, P. P. "The Hidden World in *Look! We Have Come Through!*" *Osmania Journal of English Studies* 21 (1985): 96–105.

Read, Herbert. "The Figure of Grammar: Whitman and Lawrence." In his *The True Voice of Feeling: Studies in English Romantic Poetry.* London: Faber and Faber, 1953, pp. 87–100.

Rees, Richard. "Lawrence and Britannia." *New Adelphi* 3 (June–August 1930): 317–19. (*N*)

Reeves, James. "Introduction." In *DHL: Selected Poems.* Edited by James Reeves. London: Heinemann, 1951, pp. vii–xviii.

Rexroth, Kenneth. "Introduction." In *DHL: Selected Poems.* New York: New Directions, 1947, pp. 1–23.

———. "Poetry, Regeneration and DHL." In his *Bird in the Bush.* New York: New Directions, 1959, pp. 177–203.

———. "Poet in a Fugitive Cause." *Nation* (23 November 1964): 382–83. (Review article on *The Complete Poems* and *Paintings of DHL.*)

Rich, Adrienne. "Reflections on DHL." *Poetry* 106 (June 1965): 218–25.

Richards, Bernard. " 'When I Went to the Film' and 'Film Passion' by DHL." *English Review* 4, no. 3 (February 1994): 19–22. (*P*)

Richards, I. A. *Science and Poetry.* London: Kegan Paul, Trench, Trubner, 1926, pp. 72–83.

———. "Poem 8." In his *Practical Criticism.* London: Kegan Paul, Trench, Trubner, 1929, pp. 105–17. (On "Piano," *NP*)

———. "Lawrence as a Poet." *New Verse* 1 (1933): 15–17. (Review of *Last Poems.* Reprinted in his *Complementarities.* Cambridge: Harvard University Press, 1976, pp. 198–200.)

Richardson, Barbara. "Philip Larkin's Early Influences." *Northwest Review* 30, no. 1 (1992): 133–40.

Roberts, F. Warren. "DHL, The Second 'Poetic Me': Some New Material." *Renaissance and Modern Studies* 14 (1970): 5–25. (Prints twelve previously unpublished poems.)

Roberts, K. R. *DHL: An Approach to His Poetry.* Huddersfield: Schofield and Sims, 1982. (School-level booklet.)

Rodway, Allan. *The Craft of Criticism.* London: Cambridge University Press, 1982, pp. 78–92. (On "Hibiscus and Salvia Flowers" and "Kangaroo," *BBF*)

———. "Phoenix Poet." *Renaissance and Modern Studies* 29 (1985): 78–85.

Roessel, David. "Pound, Lawrence, and 'The Earthly Paradise.' " *Paideuma: A Journal Devoted to Ezra Pound Scholarship* 18 (1989): 227–30.

Romilly, G. "DHL—the Poet." *Listener* 42 (22 September 1949): 493–94.

Rosenthal, M. L. *The Modern Poets: A Critical Introduction.* New York: Oxford University Press, 1960, pp. 160–68 and passim.

Rosenthal, Rae. "DHL: Satire as Sympathy." *Studies in Contemporary Satire: A Creative and Critical Journal* 11 (1984): 10–19.

Ross, Robert H. *The Georgian Revolt.* Carbondale: Southern Illinois University Press, 1965; London: Faber and Faber, 1967, pp. 89–91 and passim.

Rubin, Merle R. " 'Not I, But the Wind That Blows through Me': Shelleyan Aspects of Lawrence's Poetry." *Texas Studies in Literature and Language* 23 (1981): 102–22.

Ruggles, A. M. "The Kinship of Blake, Vachel Lindsay, and DHL." *Poet Lore* 46 (Spring 1940): 88–92.

Sagar, Keith. *The Art of DHL.* Cambridge: Cambridge University Press, 1966, pp. 119–29 (*BBF*); 231–33 (*P*): 236–40 ("More Pansies," *LP*); 239–45 (*LP*).

———. " 'Little Living Myths': A Note on Lawrence's *Tortoises.*" *DHL Review* 3 (Summer 1970): 161–67.

———. "Introduction." In *Selected Poems* by DHL. Edited by Keith Sagar. Harmondsworth: Penguin, 1972, pp. 11–17.

———. "The Genesis of 'Bavarian Gentians.' " *DHL Review* 8 (Spring 1975): 47–53. (*LP*)

———. *Ted Hughes.* London: Longman, 1977, passim.

———. *The Art of Ted Hughes.* London and New York: Cambridge University Press, 1978, pp. 38–45 and passim.

———. *DHL: Life into Art.* Harmondsworth: Penguin; New York: Penguin, 1985, pp. 194–245 (*BBF*), 324–54 (*P, N, LP*).

———. "Which 'Ship of Death'?" *DHL Review* 19 (Summer 1987): 181–84. (*LP*)

———. "Open Self and Open Poem: The Stages of DHL's Poetic Quest." *DHL Review* 24 (Spring 1992): 43–56.

Salgādo, Gāmini. "The Poetry of DHL." Ph.D. diss., University of Nottingham, 1955.

———. "Review of *The Complete Poems of DHL.*" *Critical Quarterly* 7 (Winter 1965): 389–92.

———. *A Preface to Lawrence.* London: Longman, 1982, pp. 134–49.

Savage, D. S. "DHL: A Study in Dissolution." *The Personal Principle: Studies in Modern Poetry.* London: Routledge, 1944, pp. 131–54.

———. "DHL as Poet." *Briarcliff Quarterly* 2 (July 1945): 86–95.

Savita, J. P. " 'Snake': The Poet at His Splendid Best." In *Essays on DHL.* Edited by T. R. Sharma. Meerut, India: Shalabh Book House, 1987, pp. 227–34. (*BBF*)

Seligmann, Herbert J. *DHL: An American Interpretation.* New York: Seltzer, 1924, pp. 19–28. (Poetry to *BBF*)

Shakespear, O. "The Poetry of DHL." *The Egoist* (1 May 1915): 81.

Shakir, Evelyn. " 'Secret Sin': Lawrence's Early Verse." *DHL Review* 8 (Summer 1975): 155–75.

Shapiro, Karl. "The Unemployed Magician." In *A DHL Miscellany.* Edited by Harry T. Moore. Carbondale: Southern Illinois University Press, 1959, pp. 378–95.

Sharma, Neelam. "Lawrence's *Last Poems:* An Anti-Christian Stance." In *Essays on DHL.* Edited by T. R. Sharma. Meerut, India: Shalabh Book House, 1987, pp. 202–10.

Silkin, Jon. "Narrative Distances: An Element in Lawrence's Poetry." *Critical Quarterly* 27 (Autumn 1985): 3–14.

Singhal, Surendra. "Man–Woman Relationship in the Later Poetry of DHL." In *Essays on DHL.* Edited by T. R. Sharma. Meerut, India: Shalabh Book House, 1987, pp. 211–26.

Smailes, T. A. "DHL: Poet." *Standpunte* 23 (1968a): 24–36.

———. "*More Pansies* and *Last Poems:* Variant Readings Derived from MS Roberts E 192." *DHL Review* 1 (Fall 1968b): 210–13. (See response, "A Note on Editing *The Complete Poems,*" by Vivian de Sola Pinto and Warren Roberts, on pp. 213–14 of the same issue.)

———. "Lawrence's *Birds, Beasts and Flowers.*" *Standpunte* 84 (1969): 26–40.

———. "The Evolution of a Lawrence Poem." *Standpunte* 89 (June 1970): 40–42. ("Embankment at Night, Before the War," *NP*)

———. "Lawrence's Verse: More Editorial Lapses." *Notes and Queries,* new series 17 (December 1970): 465–66. ("The Man of Tyre," *LP*)

———. *Some Comments on the Verse of DHL.* Port Elizabeth, South Africa: University of Port Elizabeth, 1970.

———, ed. "DHL: Seven Hitherto Unpublished Poems." *DHL Review* 3 (Spring 1970): 42–46.

Smith, L.E.W. " 'Snake.' " *Critical Survey* 1 (Spring 1963): 81–86. (*BBF*)

Solomon, Gerald. "The Banal, and the Poetry of DHL." *Essays in Criticism* 23 (July 1973): 254–67.

Southworth, James G. "DHL: Poet; 'A Note on High Political Ideology.' " In his *Sowing the Spring: Studies in British Poetry from Hopkins to MacNeice.* Oxford: Basil Blackwell, 1940, pp. 64–75.

Spender, Stephen. "Notes on DHL." In his *The Destructive Element.* London: Cape, 1935; Boston: Houghton, 1936, pp. 176–86.

———. "Pioneering the Instinctive Life." In his *The Creative Element: A Study of Vision, Despair and Orthodoxy among Some Modern Writers.* London: Hamish Hamilton, 1953, pp. 92–107.

———. *The Struggle of the Modern.* London: Hamilton; Berkeley: University of California Press, 1963, pp. 100–109 and passim.

———. "Form and Pressure in Poetry." *Times Literary Supplement* (23 October 1970): 1226–28.

Squire, J. C. "Review of *Birds, Beast and Flowers* by DHL." *London Mercury* 9 (January 1924): 317–18.

———. "Mr. Lawrence's Poems." In his *Sunday Mornings.* London: Heinemann, 1930, pp. 64–70.

Stavrou, Constantine. "William Blake and DHL." *University of Kansas City Review* 22 (1956): 235–40.

Stearns, Catherine. "Gender, Voice, and Myth: The Relation of Language to the Female in DHL's Poetry." *DHL Review* 17 (Fall 1984): 233–42.

Stein, Robert A. "Finding Apt Terms for Lawrence's Poetry: A Critique of Sandra Gilbert's *Acts of Attention.*" *Western Humanities Review* 28 (1974): 253–59.

Steinberg, Erwin R. " 'Song of a Man Who Has Come Through'—A Pivotal Poem." *DHL Review* 11 (Spring 1978): 50–62. (*LWHCT*)

Stewart, J.I.M. *Eight Modern Writers* (Oxford History of English Literature, vol. 12). Oxford and New York: Oxford University Press, 1963, pp. 582–92.

Stilwell, Robert L. "The Multiplying of Entities: DHL and Five Other Poets." *Sewanee Review* 76 (Summer 1968): 520–35.

Strickland, Geoffrey. "The Poems of DHL." *Times Literary Supplement* (24 March 1961): 185.

Strickland, G. R. "Leavis and Lawrence: A Reply to 'Wounded Surgeons.' " *Cambridge Quarterly* 11 (1982): 329–38. (Response to Mason [1982] op. cit.)

Strohschoen, Iris. " 'Snake' as an Example of DHL's Poetic Style." *Estudos Anglo-Americanos* 1 (1977): 59–69. (*BBF*)

Sullivan, Alvin. "DHL and *Poetry:* The Unpublished Manuscripts." *DHL Review* 9 (Summer 1976): 266–77.

Sword, H. "Orpheus and Eurydice in the Twentieth Century: Lawrence, H. D., and the Poetics of the Turn." *Twentieth Century Literature* 35 (1989): 407–28.

Tarinayya, M. "Lawrence's 'Snake': A Close Look." *Literary Criterion* 16, no. 1 (1981): 67–77. (*BBF*)

Tedlock, E. W., Jr. "A Forgotten War Poem by DHL." *Modern Language Notes* 67 (June 1952): 410–13. ("Eloi, Eloi, Lama Sabachthani?")

Thesing, William B. "DHL's Poetic Response to the City: Some Continuities with Nineteenth-Century Poets." *Modernist Studies* 4 (1982): 52–64.

Thomas, David J. "DHL's 'Snake': The Edenic Myth Inverted." *College Literature* 13 (1986): 199–206. (*BBF*)

Thomas, Edward. "More Georgian Poetry." *Bookman* 44 (April 1913): 47.

Thomas, Michael W. "Lawrence's 'After the Opera.' " *Explicator* 47, no. 1 (1988): 26–29. (*B*)

Thwaite, Anthony. *Contemporary English Poetry: An Introduction.* London: Heinemann, 1959, pp. 47–51.

Tiedje, Egon. "DHL's Early Poetry: The Composition-Dates of the Drafts in MS E 317." *DHL Review* 4 (Fall 1971): 227–52.

Tietjens, Eunice. "Review of *Amores* by DHL." *Poetry* 9 (9 February 1917): 264–66.

Trail, George Y. "The Psychological Dynamics of DHL's 'Snake.' " *American Imago* 36 (1979a): 345–56. (*BBF*)

———. "West by East: The Psycho-Geography of *Birds, Beasts and Flowers*." *DHL Review* 12 (Fall 1979b): 241–55.

Trikha, Manorama B. "DHL's Poetry: A Language Experiment." In *Essays on DHL.* Edited by T. R. Sharma. Meerut, India: Shalabh Book House, 1987, pp. 183–201.

Underhill, Hugh. "From Georgian Poetic to the 'Romantic Primitivism' of DHL and Robert Graves." *Studies in Romanticism* 22 (1983): 517–50.

Untermayer, Louis. "Strained Intensities." *Bookman* 49 (April 1924): 219–22. (*BBF*)

———. "Hot Blood's Blindfold Art." *Saturday Review of Literature* 6 (3 August 1929): 17–18. (*CP*)

———. "Poet and Man." *Saturday Review of Literature* 9 (1933): 523–24.

Urang, Sarah. *Kindled in the Flame: The Apocalyptic Scene in DHL.* Ann Arbor, Mich.: UMI Research Press, 1983, pp. 123–37. (Includes discussion of *Last Poems.*)

Van Doren, Mark. "Review of *Pansies* by DHL." *New York Herald Tribune Review of Books* (15 December 1929): 15.

Vanson, Frederic. "DHL—The Poetry." *Contemporary Review* 247 (November 1985): 257–60.

Vickery, John B. "*The Golden Bough* and Modern Poetry." *Journal of Aesthetics and Art Criticism* 15 (1957): 271–88.

———. "DHL's Poetry: Myth and Matter." *DHL Review* 7 (Spring 1974): 1–18.

Vries-Mason, Jillian de. *Perception in the Poetry of DHL.* Berne: Peter Lang, 1982.

Wallenstein, Barry. *Visions and Revisions: An Approach to Poetry.* New York: T. Y. Crowell, 1971, pp. 246–49, 253–55.

Walsh, K. R. "Three Puritan Poets: Milton, Blake, DHL." *Christian Community* 5, no. 53 (May 1936).

Whalen, Terry. "Lawrence and Larkin: The Suggestion of an Affinity." *Modernist Studies* 4 (1982): 105–22.

Wilder, Amos Niven. "The Primitivism of DHL." In his *Spiritual Aspects of the New Poetry.* New York: Harper and Brothers, 1940, pp. 153–65.

Wildi, Max. "The Birth of Expressionism in the Work of DHL." *English Studies* (Amsterdam) 19 (December 1937): 241–59.

Williams, George G. "DHL's Philosophy as Expressed in His Poetry." *Rice Institute Pamphlet* 38 (1951): 73–94.

Williams, W. E. "Introduction." In *DHL: Selected Poems.* Chosen by W. E. Williams. Harmondsworth: Penguin, 1950, pp. 7–9.

Wood, Frank. "Rilke and DHL." *Germanic Review* 15 (1940): 214–23.

Worthen, John. "Appendix II: DHL's Poetry, 1897–1913." In his *DHL: The Early Years, 1885–1912.* Cambridge: Cambridge University Press, 1991, pp. 478–94.

Yamazi, K. "On the Oriental Esthetic Stasis and the Occidental Creative Dynamics in Literature." *Cultural Science Reports* 8 (July 1959): 35–75.

Yoshino, Masaaki. "Lawrence Descending: 'Snake' and Other Poems." *Studies in English Language and Literature* 36 (1986): 1–13. (*BBF*)

Young, Archibald M. "Rhythms and Meaning in Poetry: DHL's 'Snake.' " *English* 17 (Summer 1968): 41–47. (*BBF*)

Youngblood, Sarah. "Substance and Shadow: The Self in Lawrence's Poetry." *DHL Review* 1 (Summer 1968): 114–28.

Yoxall, Henry. "Books and Pictures." *Schoolmaster* 76 (25 December 1909): 1242. (On "Dreams Old and Nascent," "Discipline," and "Baby-Movements.")

Zanger, Jules. "DHL's Three Strange Angels." *Papers on English Language and Literature* 1 (Spring 1965): 184–87. ("Song of a Man Who Has Come Through," *LWHCT*)

SECTION D

PLAYS

36   The Plays of D. H. Lawrence: General Collections and Criticism

WRITTEN

Lawrence's first play, *A Collier's Friday Night,* was written by, and probably in, November 1909. His last play, *David,* was written in the spring of 1925, with proofs corrected in January 1926 for its publication in March of that year. There were only four productions of Lawrence's plays in his lifetime, three of *The Widowing of Mrs. Holroyd* (1916, 1920, and 1926) and one of *David* (1927). Not until the 1960s, when Peter Gill mounted several acclaimed productions at the Royal Court Theatre, London, did Lawrence's plays begin to receive serious theatrical attention and recognition as skillful dramatic creations. They have been regularly staged ever since.

Lawrence's plays were not collected for publication in his lifetime, though the three next mentioned in 1.a. were published separately.

PUBLISHED

1. a. *The Plays of D. H. Lawrence.* London: Secker, July 1933. This volume collected Lawrence's three previously published plays, *The Widowing of Mrs. Holroyd, Touch and Go* (including Lawrence's preface), and *David.*
   b. *The Complete Plays of D. H. Lawrence.* London: Heinemann, 1965. New York: Viking, 1966.
2. *The Plays of D. H. Lawrence.* Edited by Hans Schwarze and John Worthen. Cambridge: Cambridge University Press, forthcoming.

BIBLIOGRAPHY 64

Brunsdale, Mitzi M. *The German Effect on DHL and His Works, 1885–1912.* Berne: Peter Lang, 1978, pp. 152–56, 215–18, 232–37.

Carlson, Susan. *Women of Grace: James's Plays and the Comedy of Manners.* Ann Arbor, Mich.: UMI Research Press, 1985, pp. 127–37. (On *The Merry-Go-Round, The Married Man,* and *The Fight for Barbara.*)

Clarke, Ian. "Lawrence and the Drama of His European Contemporaries." *Etudes Lawrenciennes* 9 (1993): 173–86.

Draper, R. P., ed. *DHL: The Critical Heritage.* London: Routledge and Kegan Paul, 1970, pp. 261–62 and passim.

Fedder, Norman. J. *The Influence of DHL on Tennessee Williams.* The Hague: Mouton, 1966.

French, Philip. "A Major Miner Dramatist." *New Statesman* (22 March 1968): 390. (Review of the DHL Season at the Royal Court Theatre, London, February–March 1968, directed by Peter Gill: *A Collier's Friday Night, The Widowing of Mrs. Holroyd, The Daughter-in-Law.* Reprinted in Jackson and Jackson [1988]: 214–16.)

Galenbeck, Susan Carlson. "A Stormy Apprenticeship: Lawrence's Three Comedies." *DHL Review* 14 (1981): 191–211. (*The Merry-Go-Round, The Married Man, The Fight for Barbara.*)

Gordon, D. J. "Lawrence as Playwright." *Nation* 202 (6 June 1966): 686–87.

Gray, Simon. "Lawrence the Dramatist." *New Society* 11 (21 March 1968): 423–24. (Review of the Lawrence Season at the Royal Court Theatre—see under French [1968]. Reprinted in Coombes [1973]: 453–57.)

Gupta, P. C. "The Plays of DHL." *University of Allahabad Studies* 2 (January 1970).

Hanson, Barry. "Royal Court Diary: Rehearsal Logbook." *Plays and Players* 15 (April 1968): 47–53, 74. (Detailed log of rehearsals for the DHL Season at the Royal Court Theatre—see under French [1968].)

Hepburn, J. G. "DHL's Plays: An Annotated Bibliography." *Book Collector* 14 (Spring 1965): 78–81.

Hobsbaum, Philip. *A Reader's Guide to DHL.* London: Thames and Hudson, 1981, pp. 149–51.

Lambert, J. W. "Plays in Performance." *Drama* 89 (Summer 1968): 19–30. (Includes review of Royal Court Theatre Lawrence Season—see under French [1968].)

Mahnken, Harry E. "The Plays of DHL: Addenda." *Modern Drama* 7 (February 1965): 431–32.

Malani, Hiran. *DHL: A Study of His Plays.* New Delhi, India: Arnold-Heinemann; Atlantic Highlands, N.J.: Humanities Press, 1982.

Moe, Christian. "Playwright Lawrence Takes the Stage in London." *DHL Review* 2 (Spring 1969): 93–97. (On the Lawrence Season at the Royal Court Theatre—see under French [1968].)

Nath, Suresh. *DHL: The Dramatist.* Ghaziabad, India: Vimal Prakashan, 1979.

———. "Symbolism in the Plays of DHL." In *Essays on DHL.* Edited by T. R. Sharma. Meerut, India: Shalabh Book House, 1987, pp. 168–82.

Nightingale, Benedict. "On the Coal Face." *Plays and Players* (May 1968): 18–19. (Review of the Royal Court Theatre Lawrence Season—see under French [1968].)

Nin, Anais. "Novelist on Stage." In *Critical Essays on DHL*. Edited by Dennis Jackson and Fleda Brown Jackson. Boston: G. K. Hall, 1988, pp. 212–14.

Niven, Alastair. *DHL: The Writer and His Work*. Harlow, Essex: Longman; New York: Scribner's, 1980, pp. 97–102.

Panter-Downes, Mollie. "Letter from London." *New Yorker* (11 May 1968): 101–2. (Review of Royal Court Theatre Lawrence Season—see under French [1968].)

Parkinson, R. N. "The Retreat from Reason or a Raid on the Inarticulate." In *The Spirit of DHL: Centenary Studies*. Edited by Gāmini Salgādo and G. K. Das. London: Macmillan, 1988, pp. 214–33.

Pinion, F. B. *A DHL Companion*. London and Basingstoke: Macmillan, 1978, pp. 265–74.

Pritchett, V. S. "Lawrence's Laughter." *New Statesman* (1 July 1966): 18–19. (Review of *The Complete Plays of DHL*.)

Sagar, Keith. "DHL: Dramatist." *DHL Review* 4 (Summer 1971): 154–82.

———. *DHL: Life into Art*. Harmondsworth: Penguin; New York: Viking, 1985, pp. 34–74.

Sagar, Keith, and Sylvia Sklar. "Major Productions of Lawrence's Plays." In *A DHL Handbook*. Edited by Keith Sagar. Manchester: Manchester University Press; New York: Barnes and Noble, 1982, pp. 283–328. (Details of thirteen major productions, with photographs and extracts from reviews.)

Salgādo, Gāmini. *A Preface to Lawrence*. London: Longman, 1982, pp. 158–59.

Scheckner, Peter. *Class, Politics, and the Individual: A Study of the Major Works of DHL*. London and Toronto: Associated University Presses, 1985, pp. 70–87. (On *The Widowing of Mrs. Holroyd, Touch and Go,* and *A Collier's Friday Night*.)

Sklar, Sylvia. *The Plays of DHL: A Biographical and Critical Study*. London: Vision, 1975.

———. "DHL." In *Dictionary of Literary Biography*. Vol. 10. *Modern British Dramatists, 1900–1950*. Edited by Stanley Weintraub. Detroit: Gale Research, 1982, pp. 288–93.

Spurling, Hilary. "Old Folk at Home." *Spectator* (22 March 1968): 378–79. (Review of Royal Court Theatre Lawrence Season—see under French [1968].)

Waterman, Arthur E. "The Plays of DHL." *Modern Drama* 2 (February 1960): 349–57. (Reprinted in Spilka [1963]: 142–50.)

Williams, Raymond. "Introduction." *Three Plays by DHL: "A Collier's Friday Night," "The Daughter-in-Law," "The Widowing of Mrs. Holroyd."* Penguin: Harmondsworth, 1969, pp. 7–14.

37   The Plays of D. H. Lawrence: Individual Plays

For each entry here, only first publication details are given: details of the collections cited in Chapter 36 are not repeated except where they represent the first publication of the play in question. The bibliographies do not repeat items from the earlier general bibliography, but it can be assumed that most of these include discussion of a range of the individual plays. In particular, Sklar (1975 and 1982), Malani (1982), Nath (1979), and Pinion (1978) include some commentary on *all* of the plays.

A COLLIER'S FRIDAY NIGHT

WRITTEN

Autumn 1909, probably in November.

PUBLISHED

First published posthumously, London: Secker, June 1934.

BIBLIOGRAPHY 65

Chatarji, Dilip. "The Dating of DHL's *A Collier's Friday Night.*" *Notes and Queries* 23 (January 1976): 11. (Reference to the death of Swinburne suggests that the play postdates April 1909.)

Jansohn, Christa. "Books, Music and Paintings in *A Collier's Friday Night.*" *Cahiers Victoriens et Edouardiens,* no. 32 (October 1990): 61–79.

Kumar, Shrawan. "DHL's Relationship: *A Collier's Friday Night.*" In *Essays on DHL.* Edited by T. R. Sharma. Meerut, India: Shalabh Book House, 1987, pp. 162–67.

O'Casey, Sean. "A Miner's Dream of Home." *New Statesman and Nation* 8 (28 July 1934): 124. (Reprinted in his *Blasts and Benedictions.* Edited by Ronald Ayling. London: Macmillan, 1967, pp. 222–25, and in Jackson and Jackson [1988]: 209–11.)

Stovel, Nora F. "DHL from Playwright to Novelist: 'Strife in Love' in *A Collier's Friday Night* and *Sons and Lovers.*" *English Studies in Canada* 13, no. 4 (1987): 451–67.

See also Modiano (1987): 47–50. Worthen (1991b): 242–46.

THE WIDOWING OF MRS. HOLROYD

WRITTEN

Autumn 1910; Autumn 1913. The first draft of the play was finished by November 1910, and Lawrence did not work on it again until August 1913, when he rewrote and revised it for publication. Proofs, October 1913.

PUBLISHED

New York: Kennerley, 1 April 1914; London; Duckworth, April 1914.

BIBLIOGRAPHY 66

Coniff, Gerald. "The Failed Marriage: Dramatization of a Lawrentian Theme in *The Widowing of Mrs. Holroyd.*" *DHL Review* 11 (Spring 1978): 21–37.

Hartmann, Geoffrey H. "Symbolism versus Character in Lawrence's First Play." In his *Easy Pieces.* New York: Columbia University Press, 1985, pp. 81–88.

Kauffmann, Stanley. "Three Cities." *New Republic* 169 (15 December 1973): 22, 33–34. (Review of production at Long Wharf Theater, New Haven, Conn.)

Stovel, Nora Foster. "DHL and 'The Dignity of Death': Tragic Recognition in 'Odour of Chrysanthemums,' *The Widowing of Mrs. Holroyd,* and *Sons and Lovers.*" *DHL Review* 16 (1983): 59–82.

Williams, Raymond. "DHL: *The Widowing of Mrs. Holroyd.*" In his *Drama from Ibsen to Brecht.* London: Chatto and Windus, 1968, pp. 257–60.

See also Cushman (1978): 62–67. Modiano (1987): 69–71. Worthen (1991b): 242–46.

THE MERRY-GO-ROUND

WRITTEN

November–December 1910.

PUBLISHED

First published posthumously in the *Virginia Quarterly Review* 17 (Winter 1941) (Christmas Supplement): 1–44.

BIBLIOGRAPHY 67

Davies, Cecil. "DHL: *The Merry-Go-Round,* A Challenge to the Theatre." *DHL Review* 16 (1983): 133–63.

See also Worthen (1991b): 242–46, 282–83.

THE MARRIED MAN

WRITTEN

April 1912.

PUBLISHED

First published posthumously in the *Virginia Quarterly Review* 16 (Autumn 1940): 523–47.

BIBLIOGRAPHY 68

See Worthen (1991b): 384–85.

THE FIGHT FOR BARBARA

WRITTEN

October 1912.

PUBLISHED

Until recently, it was thought that the play was first published posthumously as "Keeping Barbara" in *Argosy* 14 (December 1933): 68–90. However, the editors of the Cambridge edition of the plays have discovered that this version of the play (which was also the version reprinted in the 1965 *Complete Plays*) represents only about three-quarters of the original, and therefore the *complete* play will receive its first publication in the forthcoming Cambridge volume of the plays.

BIBLIOGRAPHY 69

Clarke, Ian. "*The Fight for Barbara:* Lawrence's Society Drama." In *DHL in the Modern World.* Edited by Peter Preston and Peter Hoare. London: Macmillan, 1989, pp. 47–68.

Kimpel, Ben D., and T. C. Duncan Eaves. "*The Fight for Barbara* on Stage." *DHL Review* 1 (Spring 1968): 72–74. (Review of the Mermaid Theatre [London] production, 9 August 1967.)

THE DAUGHTER-IN-LAW

WRITTEN

January 1913.

PUBLISHED

First published posthumously in *The Complete Plays of DHL.* London: Heinemann, 1965; New York: Viking, 1966.

BIBLIOGRAPHY 70

Modiano, Marko. "An Early Swedish Stage Production of DHL's *The Daughter-in-Law. DHL Review* 17 (Spring 1984): 49–59.

Sagar, Keith. "The Strange History of *The Daughter-in-Law.*" *DHL Review* 11 (Summer 1978): 175–84.

Sklar, Sylvia. "*The Daughter-in-Law* and *My Son's My Son.*" *DHL Review* 9 (Summer 1976): 254–65.

Woddis, C. "*The Daughter-in-Law.*" *Plays and Players,* no. 385 (October 1985): 32–33.

See also Modiano (1987): 71–76. Worthen (191b): 458–60.

TOUCH AND GO

WRITTEN

October 1918. Preface written June 1919.

PUBLISHED

London: C. W. Daniel, May 1920; New York: Seltzer, June, 1920.

BIBLIOGRAPHY 71

Lowell, Amy. ''A Voice in Our Wilderness: DHL's Unheeded Message 'to Blind Re-
actionaries and Fussy, Discontented Agitators.' '' *New York Times Book Review,*
Section 3 (22 August 1920): 7. (Review. Reprinted in her *Poetry and Poets:
Essays.* Boston and New York: Houghton Mifflin, 1930, pp. 175–86.)

See also Delany (1979): 381–83. Holderness (1982): 211–14. Panichas (1964): 33–35.

ALTITUDE (UNFINISHED)

WRITTEN

June 1924.

PUBLISHED

1. First published posthumously:
   a. Scene 1 only: *Laughing Horse,* no. 20 (Summer 1938): 12–35.
   b. In *The Complete Plays of DHL.* London: Heinemann, 1965; New York:
   Viking, 1966.

NOAH'S FLOOD (UNFINISHED)

WRITTEN

February–March 1925; revisions to the first two scenes were made some time
between 1926 and 1928, but most probably in 1926.

PUBLISHED

First published posthumously in *Phoenix: The Posthumous Papers of DHL.* Edited by Edward D. McDonald. New York: Viking, 1936.

DAVID

WRITTEN

March–May 1925. Proofs, January 1926.

PUBLISHED

London: Secker, March 1926; New York: Knopf, April 1926.

BIBLIOGRAPHY 72

Brunsdale, Mitzi M. "DHL's *David:* Drama as a Vehicle for Religious Prophecy."
    Themes in Drama 5 (1983): 123–37.
Gamache, Lawrence B. "Lawrence's *David:* Its Religious Impulse and Its Theatricality."
    DHL Review 15 (1982): 235–48.
Halverson, Marvin, ed. *Religious Drama I: Five Plays.* New York: Meridian Books,
    1957. (Includes *David,* pp. 165–266, along with plays by Auden, Christopher Fry,
    Dorothy Sayers, and James Schevill. Halverson comments briefly on the "poetic
    and ecstatically religious" nature of the play on p. 7.)
Laird, Holly. "Heroic Theater in *David.*" In *Critical Essays on DHL.* Edited by Dennis
    Jackson and Fleda Brown Jackson. Boston: G. K. Hall, 1988, pp. 203–9.
Panichas, George A. "DHL's Biblical Play *David.*" *Modern Drama* 6
(September 1963): 164–76. (Reprinted in Panichas [1964]: 136–50.)
Roston, Murray. "W. B. Yeats and DHL." In his *Biblical Drama in England, from the
    Middle Ages to the Present Day.* London: Faber and Faber, 1968, pp. 264–79
    (275–79).

See also Clark (1980): 342–46. Hyde (1992): 57–63, passim.

SECTION E

OTHER WORKS

38 Introduction

Lawrence is obviously best known for his major novels and stories and for certain outstanding poems and plays. But he produced a great many works in other genres, too, and, as his reputation has grown and become consolidated in the second half of this century, students and scholars have increasingly found these to be both a rich source of insight into his "mainstream" art and satisfying works of creative intelligence in their own right. Some of these works have always drawn approbation from within their specialized spheres of influence—*Studies in Classic American Literature,* for example, has been cited since its first appearance as a seminal text in that field—while others have only relatively recently been given positive evaluations, but almost all of them are now seen to be important elements in the overall legacy left by Lawrence. This is perhaps only to be expected in a period when semiotic notions of a general "textuality" are current, and canonical genre distinctions and hierarchies are increasingly questioned. But it is also a function of a certain inner logic in Lawrence's work itself, for Lawrence was nothing if not a holistic thinker who believed in the integrated unity of all human knowledge and discourse—what he called "knowing in full." He also happened to be a remarkable polymath who could draw easily on a disparate range of discourses for his own purposes.

Of course, this inevitably presents problems for the systematic bibliographer who needs to put Lawrence's works in some sort of order, if only for reference purposes. I have already made a broad, binary distinction between Lawrence's canonically defined "art" and his "other works," and this itself may be considered problematic by some. Differentiating *among* these other works is more problematic still, for few of them fall neatly into any one straightforward category, even when their titles seem to announce otherwise. Thus, although there are obviously some very broad distinctions one can readily make (between "travel" books and "psychology" books, for instance), most of Lawrence's "other works" have so much in common with one another (and with his novels, poems, and plays) that any conventional, canonical labeling risks inviting a serious misreading of them both individually and as part of the overall Lawrence text.

Yet, practically speaking, distinctions do need to be made. Therefore, having qualified my procedure, I shall nevertheless make some pragmatic distinctions in this part of the book for the sake of clarity of focus and reference. Accordingly, the following chapters are organized under these headings:

- Writings on Philosophy, Society, and Religion: *Reflections on the Death of a Porcupine and Other Essays, Apocalypse and the Writings on Revelation*
- Psychological Writings: *Psychoanalysis and the Unconscious, Fantasia of the Unconscious*, "Review of *The Social Basis of Consciousness* by Trigant Burrow"
- Writings on Literature, Art, and Censorship: *Study of Thomas Hardy and Other Essays, Studies in Classic American Literature, A Propos of "Lady Chatterley's Lover," Pornography and Obscenity*, Reviews and Introductions
- Translations
- Popular Journalism: *Assorted Articles* and Miscellaneous Pieces
- Travel Writing: *Twilight in Italy and Other Essays, Sea and Sardinia, Mornings in Mexico and Other Essays, Sketches of Etruscan Places and Other Italian Essays*
- History: *Movements in European History*
- Lawrence's Visual Art and Imagination

As I have suggested, none of the texts in these abstract subcategories can be properly understood in isolation from one another, and, in many ways, whether the initial focus be psychology, social comment, or sexuality, they can all best be seen as integral parts of a cumulative, if ever-tentative, articulation of a general philosophy of life—a philosophy that, of course, feeds dialogically into (and off) the novels, stories, poems, and plays. This, at any rate, is the assumption that has guided my choice of headings and groupings and my ordering of subcategories in this section of the book.

General collections and selections of Lawrence's "other works" are listed in the following bibliography along with a few items of general criticism of relevance to a wide range of texts. The most comprehensive and convenient collection of Lawrence's nonfictional prose is to be found in the two *Phoenix* volumes (see under McDonald, and Roberts and Moore), and, though the available Cambridge volumes of essays (dealt with later in the relevant chapters) are now more reliable and better annotated, many pieces are still easily available only in these two seminal collections—for this reason, they are referred to quite frequently throughout the coming chapters and thus cited in abbreviated form (*Phoenix* and *Phoenix II*), the full citations having been given here.

BIBLIOGRAPHY 73: LAWRENCE'S NONFICTIONAL PROSE: GENERAL COLLECTIONS AND CRITICISM

GENERAL COLLECTIONS AND SELECTIONS (IN CHRONOLOGICAL ORDER)

Phoenix: The Posthumous Papers of DHL. Edited by Edward D. McDonald. London: Heinemann; New York: Viking, 1936. (Introduction by McDonald, pp. ix–xxvii.)

Stories, Essays, and Poems: DHL. London: Dent, 1939. (Introduction by Desmond Hawkins, pp. vii–xi.)

The Portable DHL. Edited by Diana Trilling. New York: Viking, 1947. (''Travel,'' pp. 500–554; ''Essays and Critical Writing,'' pp. 604–92. Introduction by Trilling, pp. 1–32.)

DHL: Selected Essays. Harmondsworth: Penguin, 1950. (Introduction by Richard Aldington, pp. 7–10.)

The Later DHL: The Best Novels, Stories, Essays, 1925–30. Selected, with Introductions, by William York Tindall. New York: Knopf, 1952. (General introduction by Tindall, pp. v–xvii.)

DHL: Sex, Literature and Censorship: Essays. Edited by Harry T. Moore. New York: Twayne, 1953; London: Heinemann, 1955 (rev. ed.). (Introduction by Moore, pp. 9–32; rev. for the English ed., pp. 1–38.)

DHL: Selected Literary Criticism. Edited by Anthony Beal. London: Heinemann, 1955; New York: Viking, Compass, 1966. (Introduction by Beal, pp. ix–xii.)

DHL: Selected Poetry and Prose. Edited by T. R. Barnes. London: Heinemann, 1957. (Introduction by Barnes, pp. vii–xv.)

Phoenix II: Uncollected, Unpublished, and Other Prose Works by DHL. Edited by Warren Roberts and Harry T. Moore. London: Heinemann; New York: Viking, 1968. (Introduction by the editors, pp. ix–xv.)

DHL: A Selection from Phoenix. Edited by A.A.H. Inglis. Harmondsworth: Penguin, 1971.

DHL and Italy: Twilight in Italy, Sea and Sardinia, Etruscan Places. Edited by Anthony Burgess. New York: Viking; Harmondsworth: Penguin, 1972. (Introduction by Burgess, pp. vii–xiii.)

Lawrence on Hardy and Painting: ''Study of Thomas Hardy'' and ''Introduction to These Paintings.'' Edited by J. V. Davies. London: Heinemann Educational Books, 1973. (Introduction by Davies, pp. 1–9.)

DHL on Education. Edited by Joy Williams and Raymond Williams. Harmondsworth: Penguin, 1973. (Introduction by Raymond Williams, pp. 7–13.)

DHL and New Mexico. Edited by Keith Sagar. Salt Lake City, Utah: Gibbs M. Smith, 1982.

GENERAL CRITICISM

Despite a distinct surge of interest in Lawrence's nonfictional prose over the last ten years or so, few critical works deal systematically with the full range of it—hence, the relative shortness of the following list, which contains only those works that try to take a broad overview of the field. Many of the works listed in subsequent bibliographies within this section of the book do, indeed, cover a wide range of the nonfictional writings, but I have not included them here when I felt that their main focus of interest would be better contextualized elsewhere.

Of the works cited in the following list, Freeman's is the most comprehensive attempt at interrelating the artistic and "other" writings; while Pinion's overview provides the most focused and systematic treatment of the nonfictional works. Hobsbaum's survey provides a neat summary outline of the field, and it contains a few sharp insights, but it is far too slight to do real justice to the many works it tries to encompass. Tait and Edwards concentrate on assessing Lawrence specifically as an essayist, and Ellis and Mills, too, are concerned to promote a more genre-sensitive understanding of Lawrence's nonfiction. Grant's index is not a discursive overview like the others here, but it is included as an invaluable aid to criticism of the nonfictional writings as represented by the two large *Phoenix* collections. Perhaps the most scholarly and most stimulating study of Lawrence's nonfictional prose to appear in recent years, however, is that by Anne Fernihough; although it does not survey the full range of the writings covered by this section (it announces itself as primarily about Lawrence's writings on art and literature), I include it here as probably the only full-length work on Lawrence that presents a coherent picture of his thought or "ideology" through a sustained consideration of his nonfiction alone.

Edwards, Duane. " 'Inferences Made Afterwards': Lawrence and the Essay." In *Essays on the Essay: Redefining the Genre.* Edited by Alexander J. Butrym. Athens: University of Georgia Press, 1989, pp. 137–47.

Ellis, David, and Howard Mills. *DHL's Non-Fiction: Art, Thought and Genre.* Cambridge: Cambridge University Press, 1988.

Fernihough, Anne. *DHL: Aesthetics and Ideology.* Oxford: Oxford University Press, 1993.

Freeman, Mary. *DHL: A Basic Study of His Ideas.* New York: Grosset and Dunlop, 1955.

Grant, Damian. "A Thematic Index to *Phoenix* and *Phoenix II.*" In *A DHL Handbook.* Edited by Keith Sagar. Manchester: Manchester University Press, 1982, pp. 329–447.

Hobsbaum, Philip. *A Reader's Guide to DHL.* London: Thames and Hudson, 1981, pp. 87–103. ("Other Works.")

Pinion, F. B. *A DHL Companion: Life, Thought, and Works.* London: Macmillan, 1978; New York: Barnes and Noble, 1979, pp. 249–84. ("Other Writings.")

Tait, Michael S. "DHL." In *Dictionary of Literary Biography.* Vol. 98. *Modern British Essayists, First Series.* Edited by Robert Beum. Detroit: Gale Research, 1990, pp. 214–23.

39 Writings on Philosophy, Society, and Religion: *Reflections on the Death of a Porcupine and Other Essays, Apocalypse and the Writings on Revelation*

We should have no qualms whatsoever in claiming Lawrence's writings as properly and consistently philosophical in the fullest senses of that word. It would be easy to follow the historical norm in Lawrence criticism and to be tempted by some more dismissive label for the writings that do not neatly fit into the conventional categories of "art"—labels such as "prophecy" or "doctrine," for example. But the large amount and excellent quality of critical scholarship in this area—as represented by the bibliography at the end of this chapter and by Bibliography 92 in Part III—has now demonstrated beyond any doubt that, despite surface idiosyncrasies, Lawrence was, in fact, a highly systematic, knowledgeable, and, above all, original thinker who, throughout his career and across all the genres of his writing, constantly grappled—in a creative and productive way—with some of the most important intellectual matters of the modern period. In some senses, we are only just starting to catch up with Lawrence as a thinker and philosopher because it is only relatively recently that the ways of thinking and theorizing that he advocated and practiced have become academically fashionable and philosophically acceptable. One has only to consider, for example, the remarkable stimulus Lawrence's works have given recently to critics concerned with the nature of language (see Bibliography 93)—surely, one of the defining philosophical questions of our century—to appreciate this.

The most "purely" philosophical of Lawrence's writings are to be found in the two works dealt with in this chapter, but, in addition to what has already been said about the overall integrity of his writings, the long essay "Study of Thomas Hardy" should also be particularly borne in mind here. For practical reasons, I deal with it in Chapter 41, but, despite its title, it is clearly just as much (if not more) a work of philosophy as a work of literary criticism (only parts of it deal directly with the works of Hardy). Indeed, it is often considered one of Lawrence's most important philosophical statements, partly because it was his first sustained working out of his beliefs and partly because it seems to have played a pivotal role in the final composition of *The Rainbow*. Any discussion of Lawrence's philosophy, therefore, needs to take this essay and the criticism relating to it into account.

REFLECTIONS ON THE DEATH OF A PORCUPINE AND OTHER ESSAYS

WRITTEN

All the essays in the 1925 collection (i.e., "Him with His Tail in His Mouth," "Blessed Are the Powerful," ". . . Love Was Once a Little Boy," "Reflections on the Death of a Porcupine," and "Aristocracy") were written in July and August 1925, with the exception of "The Crown," written between March and October 1915 and revised for the book in August 1925 (when "Note to the Crown" was written), and "The Novel," written between May and June 1925. Other essays and fragments collected in the Cambridge volume of this title, with their composition dates, are as follows: "Love" and "Life," possibly as early as July 1916, but probably some time in 1917; "Whistling of Birds," probably February—March 1917; "The Reality of Peace," February—March 1917, with proof corrections for journal publications; "Clouds," March 1919; "Democracy," September—October 1919; "Education of the People," November—December 1918, extended June 1920; "The Proper Study," September 1923; "On Coming Home," "On Being Religious," "Books," "On Human Destiny," "On Being a Man," all October 1923–January 1924; "Climbing Down Pisgah," September 1924; "Resurrection," January 1925; "Accumulated Mail," April 1925, proofs, September 1925. Fragmentary writings: "Dostoevsky," February 1916; ". . . polite to one another . . . ," "There is no real battle . . . ," "On Being in Love" and "On Taking the Next Step," all late 1923; "Man is essentially a soul . . . ," probably some time between January and March 1925.

PUBLISHED

1. a. i. "The Crown," parts 1–3 published serially in *Signature*. I: no. 1 (4 October 1915): 3–14. II: no. 2 (18 October 1915): 1–10. III: no. 3 (4 November 1915): 1–10. The whole essay first published in the 1925 collection. The 1915 variants are printed as an appendix to the Cambridge volume of these essays.
   ii. "The Reality of Peace," published serially in four parts in *English*

Review. I: 24 (May 1917): 415–22. II: 24 (June 1917): 516–23. III: 25 (July 1917): 24–29. IV: 25 (August 1917): 125–32.

iii. "Love." *English Review* 26 (January 1918): 29–35.

iv. "Life." *English Review* 26 (February 1918): 122–26.

v. "Whistling of Birds." *Athenaeum,* no. 4641 (11 April 1919): 167–68. (Under the pseudonym of "Grantorto.")

vi. "Democracy." The first three parts of the essay, "The Average," "Identity," and "Personality," were published individually in three issues of *The Word* (The Hague): no. 12 (18 October 1919); no. 13 (25 October 1919); no. 14 (6 December 1919). The whole essay, including the fourth part, "Individualism," was first published posthumously in *Phoenix* (1936).

vii. "The Proper Study." *Adelphi* 1 (December 1923): 584–90.

viii. "On Being Religious." *Adelphi* 1 (February 1924): 791–99.

ix. "On Human Destiny." *Adelphi* 1 (March 1924): 882–91. Collected in *Assorted Articles.* London: Secker; New York: Knopf, April 1930.

x. "On Being a Man." *Vanity Fair* 22 (June 1924): 33–34. Also in *Adelphi* 2 (September 1924): 298–306. Collected in *Assorted Articles* as in viii.

xi. "Accumulated Mail." *The Borzoi 1925: Being a Sort of Record of Ten Years of Publishing.* New York: Knopf, December 1925, pp. 119–28.

xii. "Education of the People," "Books," "Climbing Down Pisgah," and "Resurrection" all first published posthumously in *Phoenix* (1936). "On Coming Home" first published posthumously in *Phoenix II* (1968).The fragmentary writings, "Dostoevsky," ". . . polite to one another . . . ," "There is no real battle . . . ," "On Being in Love," "On Taking the Next Step," and "Man is essentially a soul . . . ," were all published for the first time as appendixes to the Cambridge volume.

b. *Reflections on the Death of a Porcupine and Other Essays.* Philadelphia: Centaur Press, December 1925; London: Secker, February 1934.

2. Edited by Michael Herbert. Cambridge: Cambridge University Press, 1988.

APOCALYPSE AND THE WRITINGS ON REVELATION

WRITTEN

This volume in the Cambridge edition of Lawrence's works collects Lawrence's last major work, *Apocalypse,* written between November and December 1929 and revised in January 1930, and two related essays, "A Review of *The Book of Revelation* by Dr. John Oman," written in February 1924, and "Introduction to *The Dragon of the Apocalypse* by Frederick Carter," written in January 1930.

PUBLISHED

1. a. *Apocalypse.* Florence: Orioli, June 1931. New York: Viking, November
      1931. London: Secker, May 1932.
   b. "A Review of *The Book of Revelation* by Dr. John Oman." *Adelphi* 1
      (April 1924): 1011–13. (Under the pseudonym L. H. Davidson.)
   c. "Introduction to *The Dragon of the Apocalypse* by Frederick Carter."
      London Mercury 22 (July 1930): 217–26.
2. Edited by Mara Kalnins. Cambridge: Cambridge University Press, 1980.

BIBLIOGRAPHY 74

I list here only works that address the specific texts in question, rather than works more
generally concerned with Lawrence's ideas or philosophy; see Bibliographies 92 and 93
for related works of that nature.

Bantock, G. H. "DHL and the Nature of Freedom." In his *Freedom and Authority in
    Education.* London: Faber and Faber, 1952, pp. 133–81.
Beker, Miroslav. " 'The Crown,' 'The Reality of Peace,' and *Women in Love.*" *DHL
    Review* 2 (Fall 1969): 254–64.
Clark, L. D. "The Apocalypse of Lorenzo." *DHL Review* 3 (Summer 1970): 141–60.
Corke, Helen. *Lawrence and Apocalypse.* London: Heinemann, 1933. (Reprinted in
    Corke [1965]: 57–132.)
Davies, Rosemary Reeves. "DHL and the Media: The Impact of Trigant Burrow on
    Lawrence's Social Thinking." *Studies in the Humanities* 11, no. 2 (1984): 33–
    41.
Easson, Angus. " 'My Very Knees Are Glad': DHL and Apocalypse Again." *Aligarh
    Journal of English Studies* 10, no. 2 (1985): 205–18.
Flay, M. "Lawrence and Dostoevsky in 1915." *English Studies* 69, no. 3 (1988): 254–
    66. ("The Crown.")
Gatti, Hilary. "DHL and the Idea of Education." *English Miscellany* 21 (1970): 209–
    31.
Gutierrez, Donald. " 'New Heaven and an Old Earth,' DHL's *Apocalypse,* Apocalyptic,
    and the *Book of Revelation.*" *Review of Existential Psychology and Psychiatry*
    14, no. 1 (1977): 61–85.
Henry, Graeme. "DHL: Objectivity and Belief." *Critical Review* (Melbourne), no. 22
    (1980): 32–43.
Herbert, Michael. "Introduction." *Reflections on the Death of a Porcupine and Other
    Essays* by DHL. Edited by Michael Herbert. Cambridge: Cambridge University
    Press, 1988, pp. xix–lvii.
Hoffman, Frederick J. "From Surrealism to 'The Apocalypse': A Development in Twen-
    tieth Century Irrationalism." *English Literary History* 15 (June 1948): 147–65.
Kalnins, Mara. "Introduction." In *Apocalypse and the Writings on Revelation* by DHL.
    Edited by Mara Kalnins. Cambridge: Cambridge University Press, 1980, pp. 3–
    38.

————. "Symbolic Seeing: Lawrence and Heraclitus." In *DHL: Centenary Essays.* Edited by Mara Kalnins. Bristol: Bristol Classical Press, 1986, pp. 173–90.

Kermode, Frank. "Spenser and the Allegorists." *Proceedings of the British Academy* 48 (1962): 261–79.

Kuczkowski, Richard. "Lawrence Enters the Pantheon." *Review* 4 (1982): 159–70. (Review of the Cambridge *Apocalypse* [1980].)

Paik, Nak-chung. "Being and Thought-Adventure: An Approach to Lawrence." *Phoenix* 23 (1981): 43–100.

Panichas, G. A. "DHL and the Ancient Greeks." *English Miscellany* 16 (1965): 195–214.

————. "E. M. Forster and DHL: Their Views on Education." In *Renaissance and Modern Essays Presented to Vivian de Sola Pinto in Celebration of His Seventieth Birthday.* Edited by G. R. Hibbard. London: Routledge; New York: Barnes and Noble, 1966, pp. 193–213.

Schneider, Daniel J. "DHL and the Early Greek Philosophers." *DHL Review* 17 (Summer 1984): 97–109.

Sircar, Sanjay. "The Phallic Amoretto: Intertextuality in ' . . . Love Was Once a Little Boy.' " *DHL Review* 19 (Summer 1987): 189–93.

Steele, Bruce. "Introduction." *Study of Thomas Hardy and Other Essays* by DHL. Edited by Bruce Steele. Cambridge: Cambridge University Press, 1985, pp. xvii–liv.

Walsh, William. *The Use of the Imagination: Educational Thought and the Literary Mind.* London: Chatto and Windus, 1959. ("The Writer and the Child," pp. 163–74 [on Ursula and *The Rainbow*]; "The Writer as Teacher: The Educational Ideas of DHL," 199–228.)

Westbrook, Max. "The Practical Spirit: Sacrality and the American West." *Western American Literature* 3 (Fall 1968): 193–205. (On *Apocalypse*.)

See also Carter (1972): passim. Clark (1980): 106–10, 406–10. Cornwell (1962): 208–38. Delany (1978): 146–52, 284–91. Delavenay (1972): 327–36, passim. Goodheart (1963): 42–50. Gregory (1933): 102–8. Hyde (1992): passim. Jarrett-Kerr (1951): 13–18, 96–138. Miko (1971): 204–14 ("The Crown"), passim. Milton (1987): passim. Montgomery (1994): passim. Moore (1951): 180–82. Nixon (1986): 136–52, passim (on "The Crown"). Panichas (1964): passim. Pritchard (1971): 67–83, 197–200. Ruderman (1984): 27–32, passim (on "Education of the People"). Schneider (1986): passim. Vivas (1960). Whelan (1988): passim.

40   Psychological Writings: *Psychoanalysis and
        the Unconscious, Fantasia of the
        Unconscious,* "Review of *The Social Basis of
        Consciousness* by Trigant Burrow"

Although one might argue that all Lawrence's writings are fundamentally "psy-chological" in their very texture, and one will undoubtedly find many passages of specifically psychological discourse scattered throughout all the writings dealt with in this section, the three works dealt with in this chapter provide us with the core of his explicit theorizing about psychological matters.

Often criticized for their obscurity and for their eccentric exposition of ideas—and they are certainly not easy to read in their entirety—the two psy-chological books nevertheless represent Lawrence's fullest statement on psychology and the unconscious. Moreover, many critics have found here also the main foundations for Lawrence's general ethics and philosophy of life, as in them he develops a theory of the "pristine unconscious" that is ultimately metaphysical in conception (and largely opposed to rationalistic Freudian the-ories). For these reasons, though the two books are understandably neglected by the majority of readers, they must remain central to any fully informed study of Lawrence's art and thought. The review of Trigant Burrow's book, on the other hand, is eminently readable and, in many ways, equally important to an understanding of Lawrence's work in that it neatly clarifies the social dimension of much of his thought and confounds the common assumption that his is es-sentially an individualistic ethic of life.

WRITTEN

Psychoanalysis, January 1920. *Fantasia,* June 1921; revised October 1921 with a foreword, "An Answer to Some Critics," that was not published. "Review of *The Social Basis of Consciousness* by Trigant Burrow," August 1927.

PUBLISHED

Psychoanalysis and the Unconscious. New York: Seltzer, May 1921; London: Secker, July 1923.

Fantasia of the Unconscious. New York: Seltzer, October 1922; London: Secker, September 1923. The Secker edition of *Fantasia* did not contain the Epilogue printed in the Seltzer edition—it was directed specifically at Lawrence's American audience.

A previously unpublished version of the epilogue is printed in Harry T. Moore's *The Priest of Love.* Carbondale: Southern Illinois University Press, 1974, pp. 337–38. ''Review of *The Social Basis of Consciousness* by Trigant Burrow.'' *Bookman* 66 (November 1927): 314–17. (Collected in *Phoenix* [1936].)

BIBLIOGRAPHY 75

Davies, Rosemary Reeves. ''DHL and the Media: The Impact of Trigant Burrow on Lawrence's Social Thinking.'' *Studies in the Humanities* 11, no. 2 (1984): 33–41.

Ellis, David. ''Lawrence and the Biological Psyche.'' In *DHL: Centenary Essays.* Edited by Mara Kalnins. Bristol: Bristol Classical Press, 1986, pp. 89–109.

———. ''Poetry and Science in the Psychology Books.'' In David Ellis and Howard Mills. *DHL's Non-Fiction: Art, Thought and Genre.* Cambridge: Cambridge University Press, 1988, pp. 67–97.

Goodheart, Eugene. ''Freud and Lawrence.'' *Psychoanalysis and Psychoanalytical Review* 47 (1960): 56–64.

Gordon, David J. ''DHL's Dual Myth of Origin.'' *Sewanne Review* 89 (1981): 83–94.

Harper, Howard M., Jr. ''*Fantasia* and the Psychodynamics of *Women in Love.*'' In *The Classic British Novel.* Edited by Howard Harper, Jr., and Charles Edge. Athens: University of Georgia Press, 1972, pp. 202–19.

Hayles, Nancy Katherine. ''Evasion: The Field of the Unconscious in DHL.'' In her *The Cosmic Web: Scientific Field Models and Literary Strategies in the Twentieth Century.* Ithaca, N.Y.: Cornell University Press, 1984, pp. 85–110 (104–9).

Heywood, Christopher. '' 'Blood-Consciousness' and the Pioneers of the Reflex and Ganglionic Systems.'' In *DHL: New Studies.* Edited by Christopher Heywood. London: Macmillan; New York: St. Martin's Press, 1987, pp. 104–23.

Hinz, Evelyn J. ''The Beginning and the End: DHL's *Psychoanalysis* and *Fantasia.*'' *Dalhousie Review* 52 (1972): 251–65.

Hoffman, Frederick J. ''Lawrence's 'Quarrel' with Freud.'' *Quarterly Review of Literature* 1 (1944): 279–87.

MacDonald, Robert H. '' 'The Two Principles': A Theory of the Sexual and Psychological Symbolism of DHL's Later Fiction.'' *DHL Review* 11 (Summer 1978): 132–55.

Morrison, Claudia. ''DHL and American Literature.'' In her *Freud and the Critic: Early Use of Depth Psychology in Literary Criticism.* Chapel Hill: University of North Carolina Press, 1968, pp. 203–25.

Nielsen, Inge Padkaer, and Karsten Hvidtfelt Nielsen. ''The Modernism of DHL and the

Discourses of Decadence: Sexuality and Tradition in *The Trespasser, Fantasia of the Unconscious,* and *Aaron's Rod.*'' *Arcadia* 25, no. 3 (1990): 270–86.

Rieff, Philip. ''Introduction.'' In *Psychoanalysis and the Unconscious* and *Fantasia of the Unconscious* by DHL. New York: Viking, 1960, pp. vii–xxiii.

Roberts, Mark. ''DHL and the Failure of Energy: *Fantasia of the Unconscious; Psychoanalysis and the Unconscious.*'' In his *The Tradition of Romantic Morality.* London: Macmillan, 1973, pp. 322–48.

Schwartz, Murray M. ''DHL and Psychoanalysis: An Introduction.'' *DHL Review* 10 (Fall 1977): 215–22.

Sewell, Ernestine P. ''Herbartian Psychology in the Developing Art of DHL.'' *Publications of the Missouri Philological Association* 5 (1980): 66–71.

Vickery, John B. ''DHL and the Fantasias of Consciousness.'' In *The Spirit of DHL: Centenary Studies.* Edited by Gāmini Salgādo and G. K. Das. London: Macmillan; Totowa, N.J.: Barnes, 1988, pp. 163–80.

Wexelblatt, Robert. ''F. Scott Fitzgerald and DHL: Bicycles and Incest.'' *American Literature: A Journal of Literary History, Criticism, and Bibliography* 59 (October 1987): 378–88.

See also Clark (1980): 390–92. Cowan (1970): 15–24. Draper (1970): 184–87, 219–20. Goodheart (1963): 103–15. Howe (1977): passim. Leavis (1976): 20–28. Moore (1951): 182–86. Murry (1933): 237–45. Pritchard (1971): 125–28, 200–205. Ruderman (1984): 23–27, 29–35, passim. Schneider (1984): 21–24, 59–65. Simpson (1982): 91–96, 105–8, passim. Sklenicka (1991): 158–67. Williams (1993): 19–31.

41 Writings on Literature, Art, and Censorship: *Study of Thomas Hardy and Other Essays, Studies in Classic American Literature, A Propos of "Lady Chatterley's Lover," Pornography and Obscenity,* Reviews and Introductions

For many people, Lawrence expresses his "philosophy" in the most lively and stimulating way when he engages in a direct and focused dialogue with other writers, thinkers, or texts—as he does in most of the works dealt with here. To put this in another way, Lawrence is never more provocative and entertaining than when he is playing devil's advocate with a sufficiently challenging "interlocutor." This dialogic process seems often (if not always) to release him from a defensive tendency to repeat and labor ideas in order to protest the validity and consistency of his arguments. In his role as commentator, reviewer, polemicist, it is as if, with the main focus of attention directed away from himself, he feels able to experiment freely and unself-consciously with ideas—and such experiments often produce highly felicitous results, as witness the enduring reputation of *Studies in Classic American Literature* (itself now often considered a classic of its type) and the still-exhilarating polemical flourishes of some of the reviews and of the writings on pornography and censorship. As is commonly observed by critics, whether one finally agrees or disagrees with Lawrence's often opinionated critical polemics, one cannot fail to be impressed—and, while reading, carried along—by their sheer verve and vitality.

STUDY OF THOMAS HARDY AND OTHER ESSAYS

This volume was published for the first time in the Cambridge edition of Lawrence's works and is made up of "Study of Thomas Hardy" and other literary essays written between 1908 and 1927.

WRITTEN AND PUBLISHED

1. a. "Study of Thomas Hardy," September–December 1914. Lawrence's title
      for the essay was "Le Gai Savaire," incorrect French for "The Gay Sci-
      ence (or Skill)." First published posthumously in *Phoenix* (1936). Chapter
      3 was earlier published separately as "Six Novels of Thomas Hardy and
      the Real Tragedy." *Book Collector's Quarterly,* no. 5 (January–March
      1932): 44–61.
   b. "Art and the Individual," March 1908; revised May–September 1908.
      Early version first published posthumously in Ada Lawrence and G. Stuart
      Gelder. *Young Lorenzo: Early Life of DHL.* Florence: Orioli, January
      1932. Second version first published in the Cambridge collection.
   c. "Rachel Annand Taylor," October–November 1910. First published post-
      humously in Lawrence and Gelder (1932) as in preceding item, though
      not in the British edition (London: Secker, November 1932).
   d. "The Future of the Novel," December 1922–February 1923. First pub-
      lished with many editorial changes and under the editorial title of "Sur-
      gery for the Novel—Or a Bomb" in *Literary Digest International Book
      Review* (April 1923). The Cambridge text, based on Lawrence's manu-
      script, is the first unexpurgated version of the essay.
   e. "A Britisher Has a Word with an Editor," October–November 1923. First
      published in *Palms* 1 (Christmas 1923): 153–54. Originally entitled "A
      Britisher Has a Word with Harriett Monroe," this short piece was a reply
      to Monroe's editorial letter-article, "The Editor in England." *Poetry* 23
      (October 1923): 32–45.
   f. "Art and Morality," May–June 1925. *Calendar of Modern Letters* 2 (No-
      vember 1925): 171–77. Also in *Living Age* (26 December 1925): 681–85.
   g. "Morality and the Novel," May–June 1925. *Calendar of Modern Letters*
      2 (December 1925): 269–74. Also in *Golden Book* (13 February 1926):
      248–50.
   h. "The Novel," May–June 1925. First published in the collection *Reflec-
      tions on the Death of a Porcupine and Other Essays.* Philadelphia: Cen-
      taur Press, December 1925. London: Secker, February, 1934.
   i. "Why the Novel Matters," November 1925. Published posthumously in
      Phoenix (1936).
   j. "John Galsworthy," February 1927; revisions and corrections, March and
      August 1927. In *Scrutinies by Various Writers.* Edited by Edgell Rick-
      word. London: Wishart, March 1928. An early untitled draft of five pages
      was published in *Phoenix* (1936) as an unfinished essay under the editorial
      title of "The Individual Consciousness v. The Social Consciousness" and
      is reprinted as Appendix IV to the Cambridge volume.
2. Edited by Bruce Steele. Cambridge: Cambridge University Press, 1985.

STUDIES IN CLASSIC AMERICAN LITERATURE

WRITTEN

First versions, August 1917–June 1918. Revised August–September 1918. Proofs for periodical publications, October 1918–June 1919. Further revision and rewriting, September 1919, June 1920, November–December 1922. Proofs for book publication, May–June 1923.

PUBLISHED

1. a. i. "The Spirit of Place." *English Review* 27 (November 1918): 319–31.
   ii. "Benjamin Franklin." *English Review* 27 (December 1918): 397–408.
   iii. "Henry St. John Crèvecoeur." *English Review* 28 (January 1919): 5–18. ("Henry" changed to "Hector" for book publication.)
   iv. "Fenimore Cooper's Anglo-American Novels." *English Review* 28 (February 1919): 88–99. (Title changed for book publication to "Fenimore Cooper's White Novels.")
   v. "Fenimore Cooper's Leatherstocking Novels." *English Review* 28 (March 199): 204–19.
   vi. "Edgar Allan Poe." *English Review* 28 (April 1919): 278–91.
   vii. "Nathaniel Hawthorne." *English Review* 28 (May 1919): 404–17. (Published as "Nathaniel Hawthorne and *The Scarlet Letter*" in the book.)
   viii. "The Two Principles." *English Review* 28 (June 1919): 477–89. (Not included in the book collection but published in *The Symbolic Meaning*—see below.)
   ix. "Whitman." *Nation and Athenaeum* 29 (23 July 1921): 616–18.
   b. *Studies in Classic American Literature.* New York: Seltzer, August 1923. London: Secker, June 1924. Four essays were unpublished prior to the book collection: "Hawthorne's *Blithdale Romance*," "Dana's *Two Years before the Mast*," "Herman Melville's *Typee* and *Omoo*," and "Herman Melville's *Moby Dick*."
   c. *The Symbolic Meaning: The Uncollected Versions of "Studies in Classic American Literature."* Edited by Armin Arnold. London: Centaur Press, May 1962.

A PROPOS OF "LADY CHATTERLEY'S LOVER"

WRITTEN

April 1929 as "My Skirmish with Jolly Roger"; extended in October 1929.

PUBLISHED

1. a. "My Skirmish with Jolly Roger." Introduction to *Lady Chatterley's Lover.* Paris: Privately printed, May 1929, pp. I–VIII.
   b. *My Skirmish with Jolly Roger.* New York: Random House, July 1929.
   c. *A Propos of "Lady Chatterley's Lover."* London: Mandrake Press, June 1930.
2. *Lady Chatterley's Lover [and] A Propos of "Lady Chatterley's Lover."* Edited by Michael Squires. Cambridge: Cambridge University Press, 1993.

PORNOGRAPHY AND OBSCENITY

WRITTEN

April 1929; extended September 1929; proofs corrected October–November 1929.

PUBLISHED

1. a. *This Quarter* 2 (July–September 1929): 17–27.
   b. As no. 5 of the Criterion Miscellany, London: Faber and Faber, November 1929. (Lawrence and the then British home secretary, Lord Brentford, were both invited to submit essays on censorship by Faber and Faber; Lord Brentford's essay, "Do We Need a Censor?," was published as no. 6 of the Criterion Miscellany.)

REVIEWS AND INTRODUCTIONS

Entries here are listed in order of composition, with publication details following the date of composition. Most of these pieces are collected in *Phoenix* (1936) and *Phoenix II* (1968). Lawrence's introductions and forewords to his own works are included under the entries for those works and are not repeated here (see under the novels, *Sons and Lovers, Women in Love, Aaron's Rod, Lady Chatterley's Lover (A Propos of "Lady Chatterley's Lover")*; under the poetry volumes, *Look! We Have Come Through!, New Poems, Birds Beasts and Flowers, Collected Poems, Pansies;* under the plays, *Touch and Go;* and, in this section, under *Fantasia of the Unconscious* (Ch. 39), *Movements in European History* (Ch. 44), "The Crown" (under *Reflections on the Death of a Porucupine,* Ch. 38), "Introduction to These Paintings" (Ch. 45). Introductions to Lawrence's translations *are* listed here.

INTRODUCTIONS (INCLUDING PREFACES AND FOREWORDS)

September 1919. Foreword to *All Things Are Possible* by Leo Shestov. Translated by S.
   S. Koteliansky (and DHL—see under "Translations," Ch. 42). London: Secker
   1920.
January 1922; proofs, July 1924. Introduction to *Memoirs of the Foreign Legion* by M.
   M. (Maurice Magnus). London: Secker, October 1924; New York: Knopf, January
   1925. *See also* Norman Douglas. *DHL and Maurice Magnus: A Plea for Better
   Manners.* Florence: Privately printed, 1924; and D. H. Lawrence. "The Late Mr.
   Maurice Magnus." *New Statesman* (20 February 1926): 579. Both these items
   are included in a new edition of the *Memoirs,* edited by Keith Cushman (Santa
   Rosa, Calif.: Black Sparrow Press, 1987), along with excerpts from Magnus's
   "Dregs: Experiences of an American in the Foreign Legion."
March 1922; second version, May 1927. Introduction to *Mastro-Don Gesualdo* by Gio-
   vanni Verga. Translated by D. H. Lawrence. New York: Seltzer, October 1923;
   London: Cape, March 1925. In the first edition, there is only a short "Biographical Note" as an introduction. Jonathan Cape's "The Travellers' Library" edition
   of March 1928 contained the longer second version. A different version still is
   printed in *Phoenix* (1936).
March–April 1922 (or possibly January 1923). "A Note on Giovanni Verga." Introduction to *Little Novels of Sicily* by Giovanni Verga. Translated by D. H. Lawrence.
   New York: Seltzer, March 1925; Oxford: Blackwell, 1925. The introduction in
   the Seltzer edition, reprinted in *Phoenix II* (1968), is longer than in the Blackwell
   edition.
September 1924. "The Bad Side of Books." Foreword to *A Bibliography of the Writings
   of DHL.* Edited by Edward D. McDonald. Philadelphia: Centaur Press, June 1925.
December 1924. "Preface to *Black Swans*" (by Mollie Skinner). First published in *Phoe-
   nix II.*
May 1926. Introduction to *Max Havelaar* by Multatuli (pseudonym of E. D. Dekker).
   Translated by W. Siebenhaar. New York and London: Knopf, January 1927.
October 1926. "The Duc de Lauzun" and "The Good Man," two versions of an essay
   intended as an introduction to the duke's memoirs but never used and published
   for the first time in *Phoenix.*
September 1927. Introduction to *Cavalleria Rusticana and Other Stories* by Giovanni
   Verga. London: Cape; New York: Dial Press, 1928.
January 1928. Introduction to *The Mother* by Grazia Deledda. Translated by Mary G.
   Steegman. London: Cape, April 1928.
April 1928. Introduction to *Chariot of the Sun* by Harry Crosby. Paris: Black Sun Press,
   November 1931. This introduction was first published as "Chaos in Poetry" in
   Exchanges (December 1929).
February 1929. Introduction to *Bottom Dogs* by Edward Dahlberg. London: G. P. Put-
   nam's Sons, November 1929.
July 1929. Introduction to *The Story of Doctor Manente: Being the Tenth and Last Story
   from the Suppers of A. F. Grazzini Called Il Lasca.* Translated by D. H. Lawrence.
   Florence: G. Orioli, March 1929. London: Grey, February 1930.

January 1930. "Introduction to *The Dragon of the Apocalypse* by Frederick Carter." *London Mercury* 22 (July 1930): 217–26.

January 1930. "Introduction to *The Grand Inquisitor* by F. M. Dostoevsky." Translated by S. S. Koteliansky (and D. H. Lawrence—see under "Translations," Ch. 42). London: Elkin Mathews and Marrot, July 1930.

REVIEWS

November 1911. "Review of *Contemporary German Poetry,* edited by Jethro Bithell." *English Review* 9 (November 1911): 721–24. Reprinted in *Encounter* 33 (August 1969): 3–4.

December 1911. "Review of *The Minnesingers* by Jethro Bithell." *English Review* 10 (January 1912): 374–76.

December 1911. "Review of the *Oxford Book of German Verse,* edited by H. G. Fiedler." *English Review* 10 (January 1912): 373–74.

February 1913. "The Georgian Renaissance: A Review of *Georgian Poetry: 1911– 1912.*" *Rhythm* 2 (March 1913): xvii–xx.

May 1913. "German Books: Thomas Mann." *Blue Review* 1 (July 1913): 200–206. May 1913.

October 1922. "Review of *Fantazius Mallare* by Ben Hecht." *Laughing Horse,* no. 4 (1922). Published separately as *Letter to the "Laughing Horse."* Privately printed (Yerba Buena Press), 1936.

February 1923. "Model Americans." *Dial* 74 (May 1923): 503–10. (Review of *Americans* by Stuart Sherman.)

August 1923. "A Spiritual Record: A Review of *A Second Contemporary Verse Anthology.*" *New York Evening Post Literary Review* (29 September 1923).

February 1924. "A Review of *The Book of Revelation* by Dr. John Oman." *Adelphi* 1 (April 1924): 1011–13. (Under the pseudonym L. H. Davidson.)

October 1925. "Review of *Hadrian the Seventh* by Baron Corvo." *Adelphi* 3 (December 1925): 502–6.

October 1925. "Review of *Saïd the Fisherman* by Marmaduke Pickthall." *New York Herald Tribune Books* (27 December 1925). Also in *Adelphi* 4 (January 1927): 436–40.

November 1925. "Review of *Origins of Prohibition* by J. A. Krout." *New York Herald Tribune Books* (31 January 1926).

(Composition date unknown). "American Heroes: A Review of *In the American Grain* by William Carlos Williams." *Nation* 122 (14 April 1926): 413–14.

April 1926 (probably). "Review of *Heat* by Isa Glenn." First published in *Phoenix* (1936).

August 1926; proofs, September 1926. "Review of *The World of William Clissold* by H. G. Wells." *Calendar* 3 (November 1926): 30–35, 60.

November 1926. "Coast of Illusion: A Review of *Gifts of Fortune* by H. M. Tomlinson." *T. P. and Cassell's Weekly* 7 (1 January 1927): 339–40.

December 1926. "Review of *Pedro de Valdivia* by R. B. Cunninghame Graham." *Calendar* 3 (January 1927): 322–26.

February 1927. "Review of *Nigger Heaven* by Carl Van Vechten, *Flight* by Walter White, *Manhattan Transfer* by John Dos Passos, and *In Our Time* by Ernest Hemingway." *Calendar* 4 (April 1927): 17–21, 67–73.

April 1927. "Review of *Solitaria* by V. V. Rozanov." *Calendar* 4 (July 1927): 164–68.

May 1927. "Review of *Peep Show* by Walter Wilkinson." *Calendar* 4 (July 1927): 157–61.

August 1927. "A New Theory of Neuroses: A Review of *The Social Basis of Consciousness* by Trigant Burrow." *Bookman* 66 (November 1927): 314–17.

July 1928. "Review of *The Station* by Robert Byron, *England and the Octopus* by Clough Williams-Ellis, *Comfortless Memory* by Maurice Baring, and *Ashenden or the British Agent* by W. Somerset Maugham." *Vogue* (20 July 1928).

November 1929. "A Remarkable Russian: A Review of *Fallen Leaves* by V. V. Rozanov." *Everyman* (23 January 1930).

February 1930. "Review of *Art Nonsense and Other Essays* by Eric Gill." *Book Collector's Quarterly* 12 (October–December 1933): 1–7.

BIBLIOGRAPHY 76

Allendorf, Otmar. "The Origin of Lawrence's 'Study of Thomas Hardy.' " *Notes and Queries* 17 (December 1970): 466–67.

Arnold, Armin. *DHL and America.* London: Linden Press, 1958, pp. 28–102. (On *Studies in Classic American Literature.*)

———. *DHL and German Literature: With Two Hitherto Unknown Essays by DHL.* Montreal: Mansfield Book Mart, H. Heinemann, 1963.

———. "DHL's First Critical Essays: Two Anonymous Reviews Identified." *PMLA* 79 (March 1964): 185–88. (The two reviews are of Bithell's *The Minnesingers* and Fiedler's *Oxford Book of German Verse.*)

Axelrad, Allan M. "The Order of the Leatherstocking Tales: DHL, David Noble, and the Iron Trap of History." *American Literature: A Journal of Literary History, Criticism, and Bibliography* 54 (May 1982): 189–211.

———. "Wish Fulfillment in the Wilderness: DHL and the Leatherstocking Tales." *American Quarterly* 39 (Winter 1987): 563–85.

Beards, Richard D. "DHL and the 'Study of Thomas Hardy,' His Victorian Predecessor." *DHL Review* 2 (Fall 1969): 210–29.

Beirne, Raymond W. "Lawrence's Night-Letter on Censorship and Obscenity." *DHL Review* 7 (Fall 1974): 321–22. (Reprints Lawrence's letter to Thomas Seltzer on the attempt to ban *Women in Love* in the United States. This originally appeared under the heading "Author Berates Justice John Ford" in the *New York Times* on 11 February 1923, p. 18. It was reprinted in *Publishers Weekly* [24 February 1923]: 580.)

Bien, Peter. "The Critical Philosophy of DHL." *DHL Review* 17 (Spring 1984): 127–34.

Blanchard, Lydia. "Lawrence as Reader of Classic American Literature." In *The Challenge of DHL.* Edited by Michael Squires and Keith Cushman. Madison: University of Wisconsin Press, 1990, pp. 159–75.

Chandra, Naresh. "DHL's Criticism of Poetry." In *Essays on DHL.* Edited by T. R. Sharma. Meerut, India: Shalabh Book House, 1987, pp. 1–17.

Chowdhary, V.N.S. "DHL on the Craft of Fiction." In *Essays on DHL.* Edited by T. R. Sharma. Meerut, India: Shalabh Book House, 1987, pp. 37–46.

Clarey, JoEllyn. "DHL's *Moby Dick:* A Textual Note." *Modern Philology* 84 (1986): 191–95.

Clark, L. D. "DHL and the American Indian." *DHL Review* 9 (Fall 1976): 305–72 (308–10, 312–16).

Colacurcio, Michael J. "The Symbolic and the Symptomatic: DHL in Recent American Criticism." *American Quarterly* 27 (October 1975): 486–501. (The influence of *Studies in Classic American Literature.*)

Cowan, James C. "Lawrence's Romantic Values: *Studies in Classic American Literature.*" *Ball State University Forum* 8 (Winter 1967): 30–35.

Cura-Sazdanic, Illeana. *DHL as Critic.* Delhi: Munshiram Manoharlal, 1969.

Davies, J. V. "Introduction." *Lawrence on Hardy and Painting.* Edited by J. V. Davies. London: Heinemann, 1973, pp. 1–9.

Delavenay, Emile. "Lawrence, Otto Weininger and 'Rather Raw Philosophy.' " In *DHL: New Studies.* Edited by Christopher Heywood. London: Macmillan; New York: St. Martin's Press, 1987, pp. 137–57. ("Study of Thomas Hardy.")

Dumitriu, Geta. "Lawrence and Frobenius: A Reading of *Studies in Classic American Literature* in the Light of *Paideuma.*" *Synthesis: Bulletin du Comité National de Littérature Comparée de la République Socialiste de Roumanie* 15 (1988): 23–32.

Eliot, T. S. "American Literature and American Language." In his *To Criticize the Critic and Other Writings.* London: Faber and Faber, 1965, pp. 43–60. (Includes favorable comment on Lawrence's *Studies in Classic American Literature.*)

Foster, Richard. "Criticism as Rage: DHL." In *A DHL Miscellany.* Edited by Harry T. Moore. Carbondale: Southern Illinois University Press, 1959, pp. 312–25.

Fraser, Keith. "Norman Douglas and DHL: A Sideshow in Modern Memoirs." *DHL Review* 9 (Summer 1976): 283–95.

Gomme, Andor. "DHL." In *Critics Who Have Influenced Taste.* Edited by A. P. Ryan. London: Geoffrey Bles, 1965, pp. 95–97.

———. "Criticism and the Reading Public." In *The Modern Age* (Vol. 7 of the Pelican Guide to English Literature). 3d ed. Edited by Boris Ford. Harmondsworth: Penguin, 1973, pp. 368–94 (especially 385–92). (Originally published 1961.)

Gordon, David J. *DHL as a Literary Critic.* New Haven, Conn., and London: Yale University Press, 1966.

Grant, Douglas. "Hands Up, America!" *Review of English Literature* 4 (October 1963): 11–17.

Green, Martin. *Re-Appraisals: Some Common Sense Readings in American Literature.* New York: Norton, 1965, pp. 231–47.

Gutierrez, Donald. "Vitalism in DHL's Theory of Fiction." *Essays in Arts and Sciences* 16 (May 1987): 65–71.

Ingersoll, Earl G. "The Failure of Bloodbrotherhood in Melville's *Moby-Dick* and Lawrence's *Women in Love.*" *Midwest Quarterly* 30 (1989): 458–77.

Johnson, Lesley. *The Cultural Critics: From Matthew Arnold to Raymond Williams.* Boston: Routledge and Kegan Paul, 1979, pp. 117–22.

Journet, Debra. "DHL's Criticism of Modern Literature." *DHL Review* 17 (Spring 1984): 29–47.

Kinkead-Weekes, Mark. "The Marble and the Statue: The Exploratory Imagination of DHL." In *Imagined Worlds: Essays on Some English Novels and Novelists in*

Honour of John Butt. Edited by Maynard Mack and Ian Gregor. London: Methuen, 1968, pp. 371–418 (380–86 on ''Study of Thomas Hardy'').

———. ''Lawrence on Hardy.'' In *Thomas Hardy after Fifty Years.* Edited by Lance St John Butler. Totowa, N.J.: Rowman and Littlefield, 1977, pp. 90–103.

Klingopulos, G. D. ''Lawrence's Criticism.'' *Essays in Criticism* 7 (July 1957): 294–303.

Kumar, Arun. ''DHL's Criticism as Art.'' In *Essays on DHL.* Edited by T. R. Sharma. Meerut, India: Shalabh Book House, 1987, pp. 70–78.

Langbaum, Robert. ''Lawrence and Hardy.'' In *DHL and Tradition.* Edited by Jeffrey Meyers. London: Athlone, 1985, pp. 69–90.

Leavis, F. R. ''Genius as Critic.'' *Spectator* (24 March 1961): 412, 414. (Review of *Phoenix.*)

Lee, Brian. ''America, My America.'' In *Renaissance and Modern Essays Presented to Vivian de Sola Pinto in Celebration of His Seventieth Birthday.* Edited by G. R. Hibbard. London: Routledge; New York: Barnes and Noble, 1966, pp. 181–88.

Lodge, David. ''Literary Criticism in England in the Twentieth Century.'' In *The Twentieth Century.* Edited by Bernard Bergonzi. London: Barrie and Jenkins, 1970, pp. 362–403.

Mann, Charles W. ''DHL: Notes on Reading Hawthorne's *The Scarlet Letter.*'' *Nathaniel Hawthorne Journal* (1973): 8–25.

Meyer, William E. H., Jr. ''DHL's 'Classic' Crisis with America: A Prerequisite for International Scholarship.'' *CEA Critic* (Journal of College English Association) 53 (Winter 1991): 32–45.

Meyers, Jeffrey. ''Maurice Magnus.'' In his *DHL and the Experience of Italy.* Philadelphia: University of Pennsylvania Press, 1982, pp. 29–49.

Mills, Howard. '' 'My Best Single Piece of Writing': Lawrence's *Memoirs of Magnus.*'' *English* 35 (1986): 39–53. (Reprinted in Ellis and Mills [1988].)

Montgomery, Marion. ''Prudence and the Prophetic Poet: Reflections on Art from Hawthorne to Gill.'' *Southwest Review* 65 (1980): 141–54. (*Studies in Classic American Literature.*)

Morrison, Claudia. ''DHL and American Literature.'' In her *Freud and the Critic: Early Use of Depth Psychology in Literary Criticism.* Chapel Hill: University of North Carolina Press, 1968, pp. 203–25.

Pierle, Robert C. ''DHL's *Studies in Classic American Literature:* An Evaluation.'' *Southern Quarterly* 6 (April 1966): 333–40.

Pittock, Malcolm. ''Lawrence's 'Art and the Individual.' '' *Etudes Anglaises* 26 (July–September 1973): 312–19.

Pritchard, R. E. '' 'The Way to Freedom . . . Furtive Pride and Slinking Singleness.' '' in *DHL: A Critical Study of the Major Novels and Other Writings.* Edited by Andor H. Gomme. Hassocks: Harvester; New York: Barnes and Noble, 1978, pp. 94–119 (98–105, 109–12).

Roth, Russel. ''The Inception of a Saga: Frederick Manfred's *Buckskin Man.*'' *South Dakota Review* 7 (Winter 1969–70): 87–99. (Relates to *Studies in Classic American Literature.*)

Rowley, Stephen. ''The Death of Our Phallic Being: Melville's *Moby Dick* as a Warning Which Leads to *Women in Love.*'' *Etudes Lawrenciennes* 7 (1992): 93–105.

Rudnick, Lois P. ''DHL's New World Heroine: Mabel Dodge Luhan.'' *DHL Review* 14 (Spring 1981): 85–111 (92–95).

Salgādo, Gāmini. "DHL as Literary Critic." *London Magazine* 7 (February 1960): 49–57.

Salter, K. W. "Lawrence, Hardy and 'The Great Tradition.' " *English* 22 (Summer 1973): 60–65.

Saxena, H. S. "The Critical Writings of DHL." *Indian Journal of English Studies* 2 (1961): 130–37.

Schneider, D. J. "Richard Jefferies and DHL's 'Story of My Heart.' " *DHL Review* 21 (Spring 1989): 37–46.

Schneiderman, Leo. "Notes on DHL's *Studies in Classic American Literature.*" *Connecticut Review 1* (April 1968): 57–71.

Seavey, Ormond. "DHL and 'The First Dummy American.' " *Georgia Review* 39 (Spring 1985): 113–28.

———. "Benjamin Franklin and DHL as Conflicting Modes of Consciousness." In *Critical Essays on Benjamin Franklin.* Edited by Melvin H. Buxbaum. Boston: Hall, 1987, pp. 60–80.

Shapira, Morris. "DHL: Art Critic." *Cambridge Quarterly* 10 (1982): 189–201.

Sharma, Brahma Dutta. "DHL as a Critic of American Literature." In *Essays on DHL.* Edited by T. R. Sharma. Meerut, India: Shalabh Book House, 1987, pp. 47–56.

Sharma, K. K. *Modern Fictional Theorists: Virginia Woolf and DHL.* Gaziabad: Vimal Prakashan, 1981; Atlantic Highlands, N.J.: Humanities Press, 1982. ("DHL: 'The Novel Is the One Bright Book of Life,' " pp. 99–146; " 'Art for My Sake': DHL's Conception of Art," pp. 147–61.)

Singh, Tajindar. *The Literary Criticism of DHL.* New Delhi: Sterling; New York: Envoy, 1984.

———. "Lawrence's Claim to Recognition as a Literary Critic." *Osmania Journal of English Studies* 21 (1985): 106–18.

Sitesh, Aruna. *DHL: The Crusader as Critic.* Delhi, Bombay, Calcutta, Madras: Macmillan, 1975.

Squires, Michael. "Introduction." *Lady Chatterley's Lover [and] A Propos of "Lady Chatterley's Lover."* Cambridge: Cambridge University Press, 1993, pp. xvii–lx (lv–lx).

Stanley, Don. "DHL Wrote Gonzo Criticism." *Pacific Sun Literary Quarterly,* no. 8 (September 1976): 9. (Review of *Studies in Classic American Criticism.*)

Steele, Bruce. "Introduction." *Study of Thomas Hardy and Other Essays* by DHL. Edited by Bruce Steele. Cambridge: Cambridge University Press, 1985, pp. xvii–liv.

Swigg, Richard. *Lawrence, Hardy and American Literature.* New York: Oxford University Press, 1972, pp. 58–80, 283–308, 345–62.

Unger, Leonard. "Now, *Now,* the Bird Is on the Wing." In *Eliot's Compound Ghost: Influence and Confluence.* University Park: Pennsylvania State University Press, 1981, pp. 73–76. ("Poetry of the Present.")

Watson, Garry. "The Real Meaning of Lawrence's Advice to the Literary Critic." *University of Toronto Quarterly* 55 (Fall 1985): 1–20.

Welland, D.S.R. "Revaluations I: DHL, *Studies in Classic American Literature.*" *Bulletin of the British Association for American Studies,* no. 5 (September 1957): 3–8.

Wellek, René. "The Literary Criticism of DHL." *Sewanee Review* 91 (1983): 598–613.

West, Paul. "DHL: Mystical Critic." *Southern Review,* new series, 1 (January 1965):

210–28. (Reprinted in revised form in his *The Wine of Absurdity*. University Park and London: Pennsylvania State University, 1966, pp. 19–38.)

Westbrook, Max. "The Practical Spirit: Sacrality and the American West." *Western American Literature* 3 (Fall 1968): 193–205.

White, Richard L. "DHL the Critic: Theories of English and American Fiction." *DHL Review* 11 (Summer 1978): 156–74.

Young, Virginia Hudson. "DHL and Hester Prynne." *Publications of the Arkansas Philological Association* 13 (Spring 1987): 67–78.

See also Alcorn (1977): 78–89. Burns (1980): 2–29, passim. Clark (1980): 185–206, 247–51, 277–86. Cowan (1970): 24–33. Daleski (1965): 24–32. Delany (1978): 30–36. Delavenay (1971): 170–76. Delavenay (1972): 296–27. Draper (1970): 208–13. Gregory (1933): 89–92. Herzinger (1982): 50–53. Hochman (1970): 4–21. Howe (1977): 133–34, 136–38 and passim. Jarrett-Kerr (1951): 6–12. Miko (1971): 186–204. Montgomery (1994): 80–84, passim (on "Study of Thomas Hardy"). Moore (1951): 187–90. Murfin (1983): 77–79, 84–87. Murry (1933): 245–51. Pritchard (1971): 117–25, 132–34. Ruderman (1984): 127–41. Salgādo (1982): 150–57. Schneider (1984): 34–38. Seligmann (1924): 62–73. Widmer (1992): 121–25.

42   Translations

1. *All Things Are Possible* by Leo Shestov. Authorized translation by S. S. Koteliansky with a Foreword by D. H. Lawrence. London: Secker, April 1920. Though credited with the foreword only, Lawrence, in fact, collaborated fully with Koteliansky in the translation in August and September 1919. Proofs corrected by Lawrence December 1919.
2. Lawrence collaborated with Koteliansky in translating Ivan Bunin's story "The Gentleman from San Francisco," in June 1921. It was first published in *Dial* 72 (January 1922): 47–68. It was collected in *The Gentleman from San Francisco and Other Stories,* by Ivan Bunin. Translated by S. S. Koteliansky and Leonard Woolf. London: Hogarth Press, May 1922; New York: Seltzer, January 1923, pp. 1–40. (The British edition initially omitted to cite Lawrence as a collaborator in the story's translation. The story was probably revised further for book publication by Leonard Woolf.)
3. *Mastro-Don Gesualdo,* by Giovanni Verga, translated by Lawrence between January and March 1922 with proofs corrected in July–August 1923. Published: New York: Seltzer, October 1923; London: Cape, March 1925. Harmondsworth: Penguin, 1973. (Jonathan Cape published "The Travellers' Library" edition in March 1928 with a longer introduction by Lawrence.)
4. *Little Novels of Sicily,* by Giovanni Verga, translated by Lawrence in March and April 1922, with revisions in January 1923. Published: New York: Seltzer, March 1925; Oxford: Blackwell, 1925. London: Secker, March 1928. Reissued, with introduction and glossary by Andrew Wilkin, Har-

mondsworth: Penguin, 1973. Three of the stories were published separately prior to the book collection: "Story of the Saint Joseph's Ass" as "St. Joseph's Ass." *Adelphi* 1 (September 1923): 284–97; "Across the Sea." *Adelphi* 1 (November 1923): 466–75, 484–94; "Liberty." *Adelphi* 1 (May 1924): 1051–59.

5. *Cavalleria Rusticana and Other Stories,* by Giovanni Verga: four of the stories were translated in August and September 1922; these were revised, and the remaining stories translated between July and September 1927. Published: London: Cape; New York: Dial Press, February 1928.

6. *The Story of Doctor Manente: Being the Tenth and Last Story from the Suppers of A. F. Grazzini called Il Lasca.* Florence: G. Orioli, November 1929. London: Grey, February 1930. Translated in October and November 1928, with proof corrections and revisions between July and September 1929. The introduction was written in July and the Notes in August 1929.

7. *The Story of Doctor Manente: Being the First Story of the Second Supper of A. F. Grazzini called Il Lasca (unfinished). Sunday Telegraph Magazine,* no. 265 (25 October 1981): 62–79. Translated in July 1929 and believed lost until the manuscript came up for sale on 1 October 1981 at Sotheby's in New York.

8. *The Grand Inquisitor* by F. M. Dostoevsky. Translated by S. S. Koteliansky. With an introduction by D. H. Lawrence. London: Elkin Mathews and Marrot, July 1930. Koteliansky later stated that Lawrence collaborated in this translation. The introduction was written in January 1930.

9. *Reminiscences of Leonid Andreyev* by Maxim Gorki. Translated by Katherine Mansfield and S. S. Koteliansky. Lawrence revised Koteliansky's and Mansfield's translation in August 1923 (see Zytaruk [1970]: xxix–xxx, and [1971] in following bibliography). First published serially in 1924 in the journals *Adelphi* and *Dial. Adelphi* 1, no. 9 (February 1924): 806–20; 1, no. 10 (March 1924): 892–905; 1, no. 11 (April 1924): 983–89. *Dial* (June 1924): 481–92; (July 1924): 31–43; (August): 105–20. Published separately: New York: Crosby Gaige, 1928.

BIBLIOGRAPHY 77

Arnold, Armin. "DHL, The Russians, and Giovanni Verga." *Comparative Literature Studies* 2 (1965): 249–57.

———. "Genius with a Dictionary: Re-evaluating DHL's Translations." *Comparative Literature Studies* 5 (December 1968): 389–401.

Cecchetti, Giovanni. "Verga and DHL's Translations." *Comparative Literature* 9 (Fall 1957): 333–44.

Chomel, Luisetta. "Verga: A Note on Lawrence's Criticism." *DHL Review* 13 (1980): 275–81.

De Zordo, Ornella. "Lawrence's Translations of Lasca: A Forgotten Project." In *D. H.*

Lawrence: Critical Assessments. Vol. 4. Edited by David Ellis and Ornella De Zordo. East Sussex: Helm Information, 1992, pp. 169–78.

Hyde, G. M. *DHL and Translation.* London: Macmillan, 1981.

Mandrillo, P. "DHL as a Critic and Translator of Verga." In *Proceedings of the Ninth Congress of the Australasian Universities' Languages and Literature Association.* Edited by Marion Adams. Melbourne: University of Melbourne, 1964.

Meyers, Jeffrey. "Translations of Verga." In his *DHL and the Experience of Italy.* Philadelphia: University of Pennsylvania Press, 1982, pp. 50–71.

Nicolaj, Rina. "DHL as Interpreter and Translator of Giovanni Verga." *Etudes Lawrenciennes* 9 (1993): 107–25.

Wasiolek, Edward. "A Classic Maimed: *The Gentleman from San Francisco* Examined." *College English* 20 (1958): 25–28.

Zytaruk, George J. "Introduction." *The Quest for Rananim: DHL's Letters to S. S. Koteliansky, 1914 to 1930.* Edited by George J. Zytaruk. Montreal and London: McGill-Queen's University Press, 1970, pp. xi–xxxvi.

———. "DHL's Hand in the Translation of Maxim Gorki's "Reminiscences of Leonid Andreyev." *Yale University Library Gazette* 46 (July 1971): 29–34.

43   Popular Journalism: *Assorted Articles* and Miscellaneous Pieces

Between April 1928 and December 1929, Lawrence wrote some twenty-eight short articles intended mainly for newspaper publication. He prepared twenty-one of these for a book collection in December 1929 shortly before his death, but he did not live to see the book published (*Assorted Articles*. London: Secker; New York: Knopf, April 1930). These late journalistic essays are listed here in order of composition, with an asterisk indicating those *not* published in *Assorted Articles*. I include three slightly earlier essays that would seem to belong to this group (the first three in the list), and I omit two much earlier essays that were included in *Assorted Articles*—"On Being a Man" and "On Human Destiny"—as they have been dealt with elsewhere (see under *Reflections on the Death of a Porcupine* in Ch. 38). Where applicable, the first title given is the one used in the book collection.

*October 1926 (probably). "Return to Bestwood." First published in *Phoenix II* (1968).
January 1927. "Autobiographical Sketch" as "Myself Revealed." *Sunday Dispatch* (17 February 1929).
*April 1927. "Making Love to Music." First published in *Phoenix* (1936).
April 1928 (probably, though this may be a rewriting of an earlier version). "The 'Jeune Fille' Wants to Know" as "When She Asks Why?" *Evening News* (8 May 1928). Also as "The Bogey between the Generations." *Virginia Quarterly Review* (January 1929).
May 1928. "Laura Philippine." *T. P.'s and Cassell's Weekly* (7 July 1929).
*May 1928. "All There." First published in *Phoenix* (1936).

*May 1928. "That Women Know Best" as "Women Always Know Best." *Daily Chronicle* (29 November 1928). Published separately as *That Women Know Best,* edited by Roy Spencer. Santa Rosa, Calif.: Black Sparrow Press, 1994.

June 1928. "Insouciance" as "Over-Earnest Ladies." *Evening News* (12 July 1928).

June 1928. "Master in His Own House." *Evening News* (2 August 1928).

July 1928. "Ownership." First published in *Assorted Articles.*

July 1928. "Matriarchy" as "If Women Were Supreme." *Evening News* (5 October 1928).

*July 1928. "Autobiographical Sketch." First published in *D. H. Lawrence: A Composite Biography.* Vol. 3. Edited by Edward Nehls. Madison: University of Wisconsin Press, 1959, pp. 232–34.

August 1928. "Cocksure Women and Hensure Men." *Forum* 81 (January 1929): 50.

*August 1928. "Women Are So Cocksure." First published in *Phoenix* (1936).

August 1928. "Dull London." *Evening News* (3 September 1928).

August 1928. "Hymns in a Man's Life." *Evening News* (13 October 1928).

September 1928. "Red Trousers" as "Oh! For a New Crusade." *Evening News* (27 September 1928).

October 1928. "Is England Still a Man's Country?" *Daily Express* (29 November 1928).

November 1928. "Sex Versus Loveliness" as "Sex Locked Out." *Sunday Dispatch* (25 November 1928). Also published separately under this title, London: Privately printed, December 1928. Also under its original title, "Sex Appeal." *Vanity Fair* (July 1929).

November 1928. "Do Women Change?" as "Women Don't Change." *Sunday Dispatch* (28 August 1929). Also, in a shorter version with a different ending, in *Vanity Fair* (April 1929).

November 1928. "Enslaved by Civilization" as "The Manufacture of Good Little Boys." *Vanity Fair* 33 (September 1929): 81.

December 1928. "Give Her a Pattern" as "The Real Trouble about Women." *Daily Express* (19 June 1929). Also, as "Woman in Man's Image." *Vanity Fair* (May 1929).

*December 1928. "New Mexico." *Survey Graphic* 66 (1 May 1931): 153–55. (See also under "*Mornings in Mexico* and Other Essays" in the following chapter.)

*January or September 1929. "Nottingham and the Mining Countryside." *New Adelphi* 3 (June–August, 1930): 255–63.

February 1929. "The State of Funk." First published in *Assorted Articles.*

April 1929. "Making Pictures." *Creative Arts* 5 (July 1929): 466–71.

May 1929. "Pictures on the Walls" as "Dead Pictures on the Wall." *Vanity Fair* 3 (December 1929): 88, 108, 140.

August 1929. "The Risen Lord." *Everyman* (3 October 1929).

August 1929. ''Men Must Work and Women As Well'' as ''Men and Women.''
    Star Review 2 (November 1929): 614–26.
*October 1929. ''We Need One Another.'' *Scribner's Magazine* 87 (May 1930):
    479–84.
*October 1929. ''Nobody Loves Me.'' *Life and Letters* 5 (July 1930): 39–49.
*November 1929. ''The Real Thing.'' *Scribner's Magazine* 87 (June 1930):
    587–92.

CRITICISM

There is little criticism or commentary specifically devoted to Lawrence's popular journalism, though many critics comment in passing on these essays when
discussing Lawrence's nonfiction prose more generally. A full bibliography is
unwarranted here, therefore, but see the following items on ''Hymns in a Man's
Life'' and ''Nottingham and the Mining Countryside.''

Pinto, Vivian de Sola. ''Lawrence and the Nonconformist Hymns.'' In *A DHL
    Miscellany.* Edited by Harry T. Moore. Carbondale: Southern Illinois
    University Press, 1959, pp. 103–13.
Holderness, Graham. *DHL: History, Ideology and Fiction.* Dublin: Gill and
    Macmillan, 1982, pp. 32–39.

44   Travel Writing: *Twilight in Italy and Other Essays, Sea and Sardinia, Mornings in Mexico* and Other Essays, *Sketches of Etruscan Places and Other Italian Essays*

Not only is much of Lawrence's most beautiful descriptive writing to be found in his travel books and sketches, but here, too, one can often find sustained philosophical and religious meditations that neatly encapsulate ideas and theories that are elsewhere expressed at greater length. The travel writings represent Lawrence at his most fluent and relaxed, with his descriptions and observations appearing to emerge as freshly and spontaneously as speech—yet invariably retaining an arresting acuity of critical comment that ranges audaciously back and forth from localized detail of place and personality to generalized analysis of an entire culture and that is always preternaturally attuned to the mood and spirit of the people and places being discussed.

  Lawrence had three books of devoted travel writing published in his lifetime, along with many individual sketch-essays; he also wrote several other travel pieces that remained unpublished at his death. However, any comprehensive study of Lawrence's travel writing would need to look beyond these works not only to other scattered essays and the frequent fictional re-creations of his many journeys but also to his letters, sequences of which often constitute mini-travelogues in their own right. (See also Part I, Section D.)

BIBLIOGRAPHY 78: GENERAL CRITICISM ON LAWRENCE'S TRAVELS AND TRAVEL WRITINGS

Arnold, Armin. "In the Footsteps of DHL in Switzerland: Some New Biographical Material." *Texas Studies in Literature and Language* 3 (Summer 1961): 184–88. (On Lawrence's walk across Switzerland in September 1913.)

———. "DHL in Ascona?" In *DHL: The Man Who Lived*. Edited by Robert B. Partlow Jr., and Harry T. Moore. Carbondale: Southern Illinois University Press, 1980, pp. 195–98.

Bonadea, Barbara Bates. "DHL's View of the Italians." *English Miscellany* 24 (1973–74): 271–97.

Bose, S. C. "DHL's Travel Books and Other Writings: Parallels in Themes and Style." In *Essays on DHL*. Edited by T. R. Sharma. Meerut, India: Shalabh Book House, 1987, pp. 23–44.

Burgess, Anthony. "Introduction." *DHL and Italy: Twilight in Italy, Sea and Sardinia, Etruscan Places*. New York: Viking; Harmondsworth: Penguin, 1972, pp. vii–xiii.

Clark, L. D. "DHL and the American Indian." *DHL Review* 9 (Fall 1976): 305–72.

———. *The Minoan Distance: The Symbolism of Travel in DHL*. Tuscon: University of Arizona Press, 1980.

———. "Lawrence and Travel Literature." *English Literature in Transition 1880–1920* 27 (1984): 82–84. (Review article on Tracy [1983].)

Cook, Ian G. "Consciousness and the Novel: Fact or Fiction in the Works of DHL." In *Humanistic Geography and Literature: Essays on the Experience of Place*. Edited by Douglas C. D. Pocock. London: Croom Helm; Totowa, N.J.: Barnes and Noble, 1981, pp. 66–84.

Cowan, James C. *DHL's American Journey: A Study in Literature and Myth*. Cleveland, Ohio, and London: Press of the Case Western Reserve University, 1970.

Craig, David. "Lawrence's 'Travel Books.' " *Cambridge Review* (15 June 1957): 703–7. (Review article on the 1956 Heinemann issue of the travel books in their Phoenix edition of Lawrence's works.)

Darroch, Robert. *DHL in Australia*. Melbourne: Macmillan, 1981.

Davis, Joseph. *DHL at Thirroul*. Sydney: Collins, 1989.

Dennis, N. "Angry Visitor: The Landscape and DHL." *An Essay on Malta*. London: Murray, 1972, pp. 28–42.

Dodd, Philip, ed. *The Art of Travel: Essays in Travel Writing*. London: Frank Cass, 1982.

Edwards, Duane. "Lawrence's Travel." *Literary Review* 28 (1984): 165–72. (Review of Hamalian [1982], Meyers [1982], and Tracy [1983].)

Fasick, Laura. "Female Power, Male Comradeship, and the Rejection of the Female in Lawrence's *Twilight in Italy, Sea and Sardinia*, and *Etruscan Places*." *DHL Review* 21 (1989): 25–36.

Fay, Eliot. *Lorenzo in Search of the Sun: DHL in Italy, Mexico, and the American Southwest*. New York: Bookman, 1953; London: Vision, 1955.

Foster, Joseph. *DHL in Taos*. Albuquerque: University of New Mexico Press, 1972.

Garcia, Reloy. "The Quest for Paradise in the Novels of DHL." *DHL Review* 3 (Summer 1970): 93–114.

Gutierrez, Donald. "The Ideas of Place: DHL's Travel Books." *University of Dayton Review* 15, no. 1 (1981): 143–52.

Hamalian, Leo. *DHL in Italy.* New York: Tapligen, 1982.

Hofmann, Regina, and Michael W. Weithmann. *D. H. Lawrence and Germany: A Bibliography.* Passau, Germany: University Library of Passau, 1995. ("D. H. Lawrence and Germany: An Introduction," by Robert Burden, pp. 1–9.)

Hostettler, Maya. *DHL: Travel Books and Fiction.* Berne: Peter Lang, 1985.

Ingersoll, Earl G. "Lawrence in the Tyrol: Psychic Geography in *Women in Love* and *Mr Noon.*" *Forum for Modern Language Studies* 26 (1990): 1–12.

James, Clive. "DHL in Transit." In *DHL: Novelist, Poet, Prophet.* Edited by Stephen Spender. London: Weidenfeld and Nicolson, 1973, pp. 159–69.

Janik, Del Ivan. *The Curve of Return: DHL's Travel Books.* Victoria, B.C.: University of Victoria Press, 1981.

Kalnins, Mara. " 'Terra Incognita': Lawrence's Travel Writings." *Renaissance and Modern Studies* 29 (1985): 66–77.

Landow, George P. "Lawrence and Ruskin: The Sage as Word-Painter." In *DHL and Tradition.* Edited by Jeffrey Meyers. London: Athlone; Amherst: University of Massachusetts Press, 1985, pp. 35–50.

Meyers, Jeffrey. *DHL and the Experience of Italy.* Philadelphia: University of Pennsylvania Press, 1982.

———. "Lawrence and Travel Writers." In *The Legacy of DHL: New Essays.* Edited by Jeffrey Meyers. London: Macmillan, 1987, pp. 81–108.

Michaels-Tonks, Jennifer. *DHL: The Polarity of North and South—Germany and Italy in His Prose Works.* Bonn: Bouvier, 1976.

Moore, Harry T. *Poste Restante: A Lawrence Travel Calendar.* Berkeley and Los Angeles: University of California Press, 1956. (Introduction by Mark Schorer, pp. 1–18.)

Moynahan, Julian. "Lawrence and Sicily: The Place of Places." *Mosaic: A Journal for the Interdisciplinary Study of Literature* 19 (Spring 1986): 69–84.

Nehls, Edward. "DHL: The Spirit of Place." In *The Achievement of DHL.* Edited by Frederick J. Hoffman and Harry T. Moore. Norman: University of Oklahoma Press, 1953, pp. 268–90.

Owen, Frederick D. "DHL's Italy: Allurements and Changes." *Contemporary Review* 247 (November 1985): 261–68.

Padhi, Bibhu. "DHL's New Mexico." *Contemporary Review* 260 (April 1992): 197–201.

Parmenter, Ross. *Lawrence in Oaxaca: A Quest for the Novelist in Mexico.* Salt Lake City, Utah: Smith, 1984.

Pugh, Bridget. "Locations in Lawrence's Fiction and Travel Writings." In *A DHL Handbook.* Edited by Keith Sagar. Manchester: Manchester University Press, 1982, pp. 239–82.

Sagar, Keith. "A Lawrence Travel Calendar." In *A DHL Handbook.* Edited by Keith Sagar. Manchester: Manchester University Press, 1982, pp. 229–38.

———, ed. *DHL and New Mexico.* Salt Lake City, Utah: Gibbs M. Smith, 1982.

Schorer, Mark. "Lawrence and the Spirit of Place." In *A DHL Miscellany.* Edited by

Harry T. Moore. Carbondale: Southern Illinois University Press, 1959, pp. 280–94.

Stevens, C. J. *Lawrence at Tregerthen.* Troy, N.Y.: Whitston, 1988.

Swan, Michael. "DHL: Italy and Mexico." In his *A Small Part of Time.* London: Jonathan Cape, 1957a, pp. 279–87.

———. "Lawrence the Traveller." *London Magazine* 4 (June 1957b): 46–51.

Tanner, Tony. "DHL and America." In *DHL: Novelist, Poet, Prophet.* Edited by Stephen Spender. London: Weidenfeld and Nicolson, 1973, pp. 170–96.

Tindall, William York. "DHL and the Primitive." *Sewanee Review* 45 (April–June 1937): 198–211.

Tracy, Billy T., Jr. "The Failure of Flight: DHL's Travels." *Denver Quarterly* 12 (Spring 1977): 205–17.

———. "DHL and the Travel Book Tradition." *DHL Review* 11 (Fall 1978): 272–93.

———. *DHL and the Literature of Travel.* Ann Arbor, Mich.: UMI Research Press, 1983.

Veitch, Douglas W. *Lawrence, Greene and Lowry: The Fictional Landscape of Mexico.* Waterloo, Ontario: Wilfred Laurier University Press, 1978. ("DHL's Elusive Mexico," pp. 14–57.)

Wagner, Jeanie. "DHL's Neglected 'Italian Studies.' " *DHL Review* 13 (1980): 260–74.

See also Brunsdale (1978). Bynner (1951). Eisenstein (1974). Hobsbaum (1981): 87–90, 102–3. Merrild (1938). Niven (1980): 88–92. Pinion (1978): 256–65.

TWILIGHT IN ITALY AND OTHER ESSAYS

The Cambridge text of this title contains three main groups of essays: "Essays of Germany and the Tyrol, 1912," "Italian Essays, 1913 and 'With the Guns' 1914," and *Twilight in Italy (Italian Days).* The following entry deals first with the essays directly connected with *Twilight in Italy* and then with the other essays in this volume. The essays all derive from Lawrence's experiences in Europe (mainly Germany, Italy, the Austrian Tyrol, and Switzerland) between May 1912 and June 1913 and again between August 1913 and June 1914. For full details of the locations and the biographical background, see especially, in the following bibliography, all the entries under Eggert and also Worthen (1991). There is also a semiautobiographical account of this period of Lawrence's life in Part II of *Mr Noon,* pp. 238–92.

TWILIGHT IN ITALY

Written

September 1912–October 1913. 2. July–October 1915; January–February 1916.

Twilight in Italy had its genesis in essays first drafted and, in some cases, published between September 1912 and October 1913. An early version of "The

Crucifix across the Mountains'' was ''Christs in the Tyrol,'' first drafted, as
''Christs in the Tirol,'' in September 1912 and revised for publication (either
in September 1912 or later in the winter of 1912–13) in *Westminster Gazette*
(22 March 1913) (this essay appears in the first group of essays in the Cambridge
volume; its early version, ''Christ in the Tirol,'' is printed in an appendix).
Early versions of the three chapters ''The Spinner and the Monks,'' ''The
Lemon Gardens,'' and ''The Theatre'' were written between January and March
1913 and published as ''Italian Studies: By the Lago di Garda'' in *English
Review* 15 (September 1913): 202–34 (these appear in the second group of
essays in the Cambridge volume). ''San Gaudenzio,'' ''The Dance,'' ''Il Duro,''
and ''John'' were all first written in April 1913, and ''Italians in Exile'' and
''The Return Journey'' in October 1913. These sketches were all extensively
revised and expanded between July and October 1915. Proofs were corrected in
January and February 1916.

Published

1. *Twilight in Italy.* London: Duckworth, June 1916. New York: Huebsch, November 1916.
2. *Twilight in Italy and Other Essays.* Edited by Paul Eggert. Cambridge: Cambridge University Press, 1994.

OTHER ESSAYS

Written and Published

Essays of Germany and the Tyrol, 1912

''The English and the Germans'' (Paul Eggert's title) was written by 7 May
1912 and was previously unpublished. ''How a Spy Is Arrested'' and ''French
Sons of Germany'' were both probably written on 9 May 1912. The former was
previously unpublished; the latter was published as ''German Impressions I'' in
Westminster Gazette (3 August 1912). ''Hail in the Rhine-land'' was written
15–16 May 1912 and published as ''German Impressions II'' in *Westminster
Gazette* (9 August 1912) and *Saturday Westminster Gazette* (10 August 1912).
''A Chapel among the Mountains'' and ''A Hay-Hut among the Mountains''
were written in August 1912 and were first published posthumously in *Love
among the Haystacks.* London: Nonesuch Press, November 1930.

''With the Guns''

This piece was based on an artillery practice Lawrence had witnessed in Germany (at Irschenhausen near Munich) in August 1913. It was published under
the name of H. D. Lawrence in the *Manchester Guardian* on 18 August 1914,

p. 10, fourteen days after Britain had declared war on Germany. It was redis-covered by Carl Baron and reprinted in *Encounter* 33 (August 1969): 5–6.

BIBLIOGRAPHY 79

Churchill, Kenneth. "DHL." In his *Italy and English Literature 1764–1930.* London: Macmillan, 1980, pp. 182–98.

Eggert, Paul. "The Subjective Art of DHL: *Twilight in Italy.*" Ph.D. diss., University of Kent, 1981.

———. "DHL and the Crucifixes." *Bulletin of Research in the Humanities* 86 (Spring 1983): 67–85.

———. "Introduction." *Twilight in Italy and Other Essays.* Edited by Paul Eggert. Cambridge: Cambridge University Press, 1994, pp. xxi–lxxv. (For full details of the locations in these essays, see also Appendix II: "The Travel Routes," pp. 235–48.)

Fahey, William A. "Lawrence's San Gaudenzio Revisited." *DHL Review* 1 (Spring 1968): 51–59.

Gibbons, June. "*Twilight in Italy:* DHL and Lake Garda." *Quaderni di Lingue e Letterature* 3–4 (1978–79): 165–71.

Janik, Del Ivan. "The Two Infinites: DHL's *Twilight in Italy.*" *DHL Review* 7 (Summer 1974): 179–98.

Nichols, Ann Eljenholm. "Syntax and Style: Ambiguities in Lawrence's *Twilight in Italy.*" *College Composition and Communication* 16 (December 1965): 261–66.

"Review of *Twilight in Italy.*" *Times Literary Supplement* 15 (June 1916): 284.

See also Bell (1992): 57–61, passim. Delany (1978): 136–40. Green (1974): 343–46. Miliaras (1987): 95–163. Pinion (1978): 257–60. Pritchard (1971): 55–60. Ruderman (1984): 17–19, 128. Worthen (1991b): 391–461.

SEA AND SARDINIA

WRITTEN

February 1921. Revisions and corrections, March 1921, with further changes for publication of two sections in the *Dial* in October and November 1921 and then also for the book publication in December 1921. The book is based on Lawrence's trip, with Frieda, from Taormina in Sicily to Sardinia from 4 to 13 January 1921.

PUBLISHED

1. "Sea and Sardinia: As Far As Palermo." *Dial* 71 (October 1921): 441–51. "Sea and Sardinia: Cagliari." *Dial* 71 (November 1921): 583–92.
2. New York: Seltzer, December 1921 (With Eight Pictures in Color by Jan Juta). London: Secker, April 1923.

BIBLIOGRAPHY 80

Colum, Padraic. "Review of *Sea and Sardinia.*" *Dial* (February 1922): 193–96.

Ellis, David. "Reading Lawrence: The Case of *Sea and Sardinia.*" *DHL Review* 10 (Spring 1977): 52–63.

Gendron, Charisse. "*Sea and Sardinia:* Voyage of the Post-Romantic Imagination." *DHL Review* 15 (1982): 219–34.

Gersh, Gabriel. "In Search of DHL's *Sea and Sardinia.*" *Queen's Quarterly* 80 (Winter 1973): 581–88.

Mayne, Richard. "*Sea and Sardinia* Revisited." *New Statesman and Nation* 59 (18 June 1960): 899–900.

Mitchell, Peter Todd. "Lawrence's *Sea and Sardinia* Revisited." *Texas Quarterly* 8 (Spring 1965): 67–72.

Palmer, Paul R. "DHL and the 'Q. B.' in Sardinia." *Columbia Library Columns* 18 (November 1968): 3–9.

Sabin, Margery. "The Spectacle of Reality in *Sea and Sardinia.*" *Prose Studies* 5 (1982): 85–104.

———. *The Dialect of the Tribe: Speech and Community in Modern Fiction.* Oxford: Oxford University Press, 1987, pp. 139–62.

Weiner, S. Ronald. "The Rhetoric of Travel: The Example of *Sea and Sardinia.*" *DHL Review* 2 (Fall 1969): 230–44.

See also Cavitch (1969): 115–20. Draper (1970): 173–76. Joost and Sullivan (1970): 40–49, 141–45. Pinion (1978): 260–62.

MORNINGS IN MEXICO AND OTHER ESSAYS

I deal here with the essays published together in *Mornings in Mexico* (1927) and other essays inspired by Lawrence's experiences of America and Mexico between September 1922 and September 1925. Other essays of this period are dealt with in the section on *Reflections on the Death of a Porcupine and Other Essays* and on *Study of Thomas Hardy and Other Essays.* While these latter tend more toward philosophy and aesthetics, respectively, and the ones featured here more toward travel writing, it is important, as always with Lawrence, to consider them together as a dynamically interanimating, if discontinuous, sequence.

MORNINGS IN MEXICO

Written

April 1924–1925; book proofs corrected April 1927. "Indians and Entertainment" and "Dance of the Sprouting Corn," April 1924; "The Hopi Snake Dance," August 1924: these three essays deal with the American Southwest. The four essays dealing with Mexico come first in the text but were written within a few days of each other in December 1924, starting on the eighteenth. The final essay, "A Little Moonshine with Lemon," was written in Italy in November 1925. All the essays in the collection were published separately in journals before appearing together in book form in June 1927.

Published

1. a. "The Dance of the Sprouting Corn." *Theatre Arts Monthly* 8 (July 1924): 447–57. *Adelphi* 2 (August 1924): 298–315.
   b. "Indians and Entertainment." *New York Times Magazine* 4 (26 October 1924): 3. *Adelphi* 2 (24 November 1924): 494–507.
   c. "The Hopi Snake Dance." *Theatre Arts Monthly* 8 (December 1924): 836–60. In two parts: *Adelphi* 2 (January 1925): 685–92; 2 (February 1925): 764–778. Short version in *Living Age* (4 April 1925).
   d. "Corasmin and the Parrots." *Adelphi* 3 (December 1925): 480–89, 502–6.
   e. "Market Day" as "The Gentle Art of Marketing in Mexico." *Travel* 46 (April 1926): 7–9, 44. As "Marketing in Mexico, Saturday." *New Criterion* 4 (June 1926): 467–75.
   f. "A Little Moonshine with Lemon." *Laughing Horse,* no. 13 (April 1926): 1–3.
   g. "Walk to Huayapa" as "Sunday Stroll in Sleepy Mexico." *Travel* 48 (November 1926): 30–35, 60. *Adelphi* 4 (March 1927): 538–54.
   h. "The Mozo." *Adelphi* 4 (February 1927): 474–87. As "Sons of Montezuma." *Living Age* (1 April 1927).
2. *Mornings in Mexico.* London: Secker, June 1927. New York: Knopf, August 1927.

OTHER ESSAYS OF AMERICA AND MEXICO (MAINLY SEPTEMBER 1922–SEPTEMBER 1925)

The essays here are listed in order of composition, with first publication details following dates.

September 1920. "America, Listen to Your Own." *New Republic* 25 (15 December 1920): 68–70.

September 1922. "Indians and an Englishman." *Dial* 74 (February 1923): 144–52. *Adelphi* 1 (November 1923): 484–94.

September 1922. "Taos." *Dial* 74 (March 1923): 251–54. As "At Taos, an Englishman Looks at Mexico." *Cassell's Weekly* (11 July 1923).

October 1922. "Certain Americans and an Englishman." *New York Times Magazine* 4 (24 December): 1.

April 1923. "Au Revoir, U.S.A." *Laughing Horse,* no. 8 (December 1923): 1–3.

January 1924. "Dear Old Horse: A London Letter." *Laughing Horse,* no. 10 (May 1926): 3–6.
January 1924. "Paris Letter." *Laughing Horse,* no. 13 (April 1926): 11–14.
February 1924. "Letter from Germany." *New Statesman and Nation* (Autumn Books Supplement) (13 October 1934): 481–82.
May, June 1924. "Pan in America." *Southwest Review* 11 (January 1926): 102–15. First version, May, second version, June 1924.
August 1924. "Just Back from the Snake Dance—Tired Out." *Laughing Horse,* no. 11 (September 1924): 26–29. Early version of "The Hopi Snake Dance" (see *Mornings in Mexico* earlier).
January 1925. " 'See Mexico After' by Luis Quintanilla." First published in *Phoenix* (1936).
November 1925. "Europe versus America." *Laughing Horse,* no. 13 (April 1926): 6–9.
December 1928. "New Mexico." *Survey Graphic* 66 (1 May 1931): 153–55.

BIBLIOGRAPHY 81

Aiken, Conrad. "Mr. Lawrence's Prose." *Dial* 83 (15 October 1927) 343–46. (Reprinted in his *A Reviewer's ABC.* New York: Meridian, 1958, pp. 263–66.)
Dexter, Martin. "DHL and Pueblo Religion: An Inquiry into Accuracy." *Arizona Quarterly* 9 (Fall 1953): 219–34.
Lewis, Wyndham. "Paleface; or, 'Love? What ho! Smelling Strangeness.' " *Enemy* 2 (September 1927): 3–112. (Expanded as *Paleface: The Philosophy of the "Melting Pot."* London: Chatto and Windus, 1929.)
Niles, Blair. "The Lawrence of the 'Mornings.' " In his *Journeys in Time.* New York: Coward-McCann, 1946, pp. 292–96.
Parmenter, Ross. "Introduction." *Mornings in Mexico* by DHL. Salt Lake City: Gibbs M. Smith, 1982, pp. ix–xxxiv.
Rossman, Charles. "DHL and Mexico." In *DHL: A Centenary Consideration.* Edited by Peter Balbert and Phillip L. Marcus. Ithaca, N.Y., and London: Cornell University Press, 1985, pp. 181–209.
Walker, Ronald. *Infernal Paradise: Mexico and the Modern English Novel.* Berkeley, Los Angeles, and London: University of California Press, 1978, pp. 61–70.
Whitaker, Thomas R. "Lawrence's Western Path: *Mornings in Mexico.*" *Criticism* 3 (Summer 1961): 219–36.
Wilkinson, Clennell. "Review of *Mornings in Mexico.*" *London Mercury* (December 1927): 218–20.
Woodcock, George. "Mexico and the English Novelist." *Western Review* 21 (Fall 1956): 21–32.

See also Cavitch (1969): 175–78. Pinion (1978): 262–63. Pritchard (1971): 165–68.

SKETCHES OF ETRUSCAN PLACES AND OTHER ITALIAN ESSAYS

This volume in the Cambridge edition of Lawrence's works collects the essays of the posthumously published *Etruscan Places* along with other Italian essays written between 1919 and 1927. The information is divided accordingly into two sections.

SKETCHES OF ETRUSCAN PLACES

Written

April–June 1927. These essays are based on Lawrence's visit with Earl Brewster to Etruscan sites in April 1927. Owing to ill health, Lawrence was unable to visit all the sites he had hoped to see, and he therefore wrote only six of the twelve sketches he had originally planned. The book he had envisaged thus remained unfinished, though the six completed essays were collected posthumously as *Etruscan Places*. Four of the essays were published separately in the periodicals *Travel* in America and *World Today* in Britain.

Published

1. a. i. "Cerveteri" as "City of the Dead at Cerveteri." *Travel* 50 (November 1927): 12–16, 50. *World Today* (February 1928): 280–88.
   ii. "Tarquinia" as "Ancient Metropolis of the Etruscans." *Travel* 50 (December 1927): 20–25, 55. As "Sketches of Etruscan Places, Tarquinia." *World Today* (March 1928): 389–98.
   iii. "The Painted Tombs of Tarquinia I" as "Painted Tombs of Tarquinia." *Travel* 50 (January 1928): 28–33, 40. As "Sketches of Etruscan Places, Painted Tombs of Tarquinia." *World Today* (April 1928): 552–66.
   iv. "Volterra" as "The Wind-Swept Strongholds of Volterra." *Travel* 50 (February 1928): 31–35, 44. As "Sketches of Etruscan Places, Volterra." *World Today* (May 1928): 662–74.
   b. *Etruscan Places.* London: Secker, September 1932. New York: Viking, November 1932.
2. *Sketches of Etruscan Places and Other Italian Essays.* Edited by Simonetta de Filippis. Cambridge: Cambridge University Press, 1992.

"ITALIAN ESSAYS, 1919–1927"

The other Italian essays collected with *Etruscan Places* in the Cambridge edition, with their dates of composition and first publication details, are as follows:

1. "David" (November–December 1919; possibly April–May 1921). First published posthumously in *Phoenix* (1936).
2. "Looking Down on the City" (November–December 1919; possibly April–May 1921). First published in the Cambridge volume.
3. "Europe versus America" (November 1925). *Laughing Horse,* no. 13 (April 1926): 6–9. (Collected in *Phoenix,* 1936.)
4. "Fireworks" (June 1926). *Nation and Athenaeum* 41 (16 April 1927): 47–49. *Forum* 77 (May 1927): 648–54. (Collected in *Phoenix* as "Fireworks in Florence.")
5. "The Nightingale" (June 1926). *Forum* 78 (September 1927): 382–87. Cut version in *Spectator* (10 September 1927): 377–87.
6. "Man Is a Hunter" (October–November 1926). First published posthumously in *Phoenix* (1936).
7. "Flowery Tuscany" (February–April 1927). In three parts in *New Criterion* 6: (October 1927): 305–10; (November 1927): 403–8; (December 1927): 516–22. As "The Year in Flowery Tuscany" in *Travel* 49 (April 1929): 25–29, 56, 58, 60.
8. "Germans and English" (May 1927). First published posthumously in *Phoenix II* (1968).
9. "The Florence Museum" (possibly July 1927). First published in the Cambridge volume.

BIBLIOGRAPHY 82

Einersen, Dorrit. "Etruscan Insouciance." In *A Literary Miscellany Presented to Eric Jacobsen.* Edited by Graham D. Caie and Holger Norgaard. Copenhagen: University of Copenhagen, 1988, pp. 270–84.

Filippis, Simonetta de. "Lawrence of Etruria." In *DHL in the Modern World.* London: Macmillan, 1989, pp. 104–20.

———. "Introduction." *Sketches of Etruscan Places and Other Italian Essays.* Edited by Simonetta de Filippis. Cambridge: Cambridge University Press, 1992, pp. xxi–lxxiii (*Sketches of Etruscan Places,* xxi–liii; Italian Essays, 1919–27, liv–lxxiii).

Gutierrez, Donald. "DHL's Golden Age." *DHL Review* 9 (Fall 1976): 377–408. (Reprinted in Gutierrez [1980]: 61–117.)

Hassall, Christopher. "DHL and the Etruscans." *Essays by Divers Hands* 31 (1962): 61–78. (Enlarged version of "Black Flowers: A New Light on the Poetics of DHL," in Moore [1959]: 370–77.)

Janik, Del Ivan. "DHL's *Etruscan Places:* The Mystery of Touch." *Essays in Literature* (Western Illinois University) 3 (1976): 194–205.

Meyer, Horst E. "An Addendum to the DHL Canon." *Papers of the Bibliographical Society of America,* no. 67 (1973): 458–59. (On 1927 German translation and 1934 Italian translation of "Germans and English." See pp. lxx–lxxi of Filippis 1992.)

Morris, Tom. "On *Etruscan Places.*" *Paunch* 40–41 (April 1975): 8–39.

Tracy, Billy T. " 'Reading up the Ancient Etruscans': Lawrence's Debt to George Dennis." *Twentieth Century Literature* 23 (December 1977): 437–50. (Refers to George Dennis's *The Cities and Cemeteries of Etruria,* 1848.)

See also Cavitch (1969): 205–9. John (1974): 286–89. Kermode (1973): 125–28. Moore (1951): 288–91. Pinion (1978): 263–65. Pritchard (1971): 200–205. Sagar (1966): 210–13. Schneider (1986): 157–59.

45   History: *Movements in European History*

WRITTEN

July 1918; December 1918; January–February 1919. Revised April and May 1919. Proofs, January 1920. New chapter written (on Italian unification) and final proofs corrected, November 1920. "Epilogue" written for new 1925 edition (though unpublished there) September 1924. Between October and November 1925, Lawrence reluctantly accepted revisions for the Irish edition of 1926.

PUBLISHED

1. a. London: Oxford University Press, February 1921 (under the pseudonym of "Lawrence H. Davison").
   b. Illustrated edition (under real name). London: Oxford University Press, May 1925.
   c. New and revised edition, specially prepared for Irish Schools. Dublin and Cork: Educational Company of Ireland, September 1926. (With additional appendixes: (i) Introductory Sketch of Early Mediterranean History; (ii) Ireland and the Normans; (iii) Ireland and Foreign Countries.)
   d. New edition, with previously unpublished "Epilogue." Oxford: Oxford University Press, 1971.
2. Edited by Philip Crumpton. Cambridge: Cambridge University Press, 1989.

BIBLIOGRAPHY 83

Boulton, James T. "Introduction to the New Edition." *Movements in European History* by DHL. Oxford: Oxford University Press, 1971, pp. vii–xxiv.

Crumpton, Philip. "DHL's 'Mauled History': The Irish Edition of *Movements in European History.*" *DHL Review* 13 (Fall 1980): 105–18.

———. "DHL and the Sources of *Movements in European History.*" *Renaissance and Modern Studies* 29 (1985): 50–65.

———. "Introduction." *Movements in European History* by DHL. Edited by Philip Crumpton. Cambridge: Cambridge University Press, 1989, pp. xvii–xlvi.

Hinz, Evelyn J. "History as Education and Art: DHL's *Movements in European History.*" *Modern British Literature* 2 (Fall 1977): 139–52.

Raskin, Jonah. *The Mythology of Imperialism: Rudyard Kipling, Joseph Conrad, E. M. Forster, DHL and Joyce Cary.* New York: Random House, 1971, pp. 90, 97–98.

Salgādo, Gāmini. "Lawrence as Historian." In *The Spirit of DHL: Centenary Studies.* Edited by Gāmini Salgādo and G. K. Das. London: Macmillan; Totowa, N.J.: Barnes, 1988, pp. 234–47.

Schneider, Daniel J. "Psychology in Lawrence's *Movements in European History.*" *Rocky Mountain Review of Language and Literature* 39, no. 2 (1985): 99–106.

Scott, James F. "DHL's *Germania:* Ethnic Psychology and Cultural Crisis in the Shorter Fiction." *DHL Review* 10 (Summer 1977): 142–64 (143–44 and passim).

See also Clark (1980): 207–11. Moore (1951): 171–73. Ruderman (1984): 142–53.

46   Lawrence's Visual Art and Imagination

The visual arts exerted a strong influence on Lawrence from an early age, and, apart from his own early efforts at drawing and painting (often making copies of well-known pictures), his visits to major galleries around the world and his attendance at important exhibitions of modern art seem fundamentally to have affected his own literary aesthetics and his views on the arts generally. But perhaps most remarkable of all is the turn to original painting that he made in the last four years of his life, for, although critical opinions differ as to the success of this visual work, the mere fact of the effort and the seriousness and intensity of it surely testify to a continuing creative and explorative vitality in a man always seeking the fullest possible expression in art of the pertaining state of things in both personal and cultural terms. Prompted by the gift of some canvases from Maria Huxley, Lawrence took to the painter's task with great zest and excitement and, whatever their technical strengths or weaknesses, rapidly produced striking and sometimes startling images in paint that continue to stimulate new ways of seeing at least his own literary art, if not other visual art more generally.

Lawrence started painting his major pictures in November 1926, and twenty-five of them were exhibited at the Warren Gallery in London from 14 June 1929. In one of the more notorious, and certainly more comic, examples of stupidity in the history of censorship, however, the exhibition was raided by the police on 5 July, and thirteen pictures were taken away on the grounds of indecency (a prosecution under the Obscene Publications Act of 1857 followed on 8 August)—the criterion for indecency here apparently being the visibility of pubic hair, for which reason a pencil drawing by William Blake of Adam and Eve was also confiscated by the police. The exhibition continued until September with some early paintings of Lawrence brought in to fill the gaps, but even by 5 July the exhibition had been seen by 12,000 people, and several of the paintings had been sold. A book of reproductions was published at the same time as the exhibition with Lawrence's "Introduction to These Paintings," one of his major statements on the visual arts and on aesthetics in general. This was written in January 1929, with revisions in February and proof corrections in March. He wrote two further essays on visual art shortly afterward: "Making Pictures" (April) and "Pictures on the Wall" (May). These three essays represent Lawrence's most clearly focused attention to the visual arts (see following bibliography for publication details), but he constantly refers to them in almost all his discussions on art and aesthetics, whether in letters, essays, travel sketches, or fiction. In particular, any full discussion of his "visual imagination" would need to consider not only these late essays and the paintings that inspired them but also the early experiences of drawing, painting, and discussing of art (as recorded by Jessie Chambers and Ada Lawrence in their memoirs of Lawrence [see following bibliography] and by the catalogs of the "Young Bert" exhibition of 1972 and the "Lawrence, Art and Artists" exhibition of 1985— see under Edwards and Phillips, and Nottingham Castle Museum) and the early essay "Art and the Individual" (1908). In addition, his many passing comments on art and artists should also be considered: on the Pre-Raphaelites in his early letters and in *The White Peacock* and *Sons and Lovers;* on the Renaissance artists in "Study of Thomas Hardy" and in *The Rainbow;* on the futurists and Expressionists in the correspondence written around the time of the writing of *The Rainbow* and in the discussions on art to be found in *Women in Love,* especially those involving the futurist-modernist Loerke; on Van Gogh and Cézanne and "ways of seeing" in the group of essays on art and the novel written between 1923 and 1925 (especially "Art and Morality"), as well as related comments in his review of Trigant Burrow's *The Social Basis of Consciousness,* written in August 1927; and on the art of the ancient Etruscans in *Sketches of Etruscan Places.*

BIBLIOGRAPHY 84

LAWRENCE'S PAINTINGS AND ESSAYS

The Paintings of DHL. London: Mandrake Press, privately printed for subscribers only, June 1929. Includes "Introduction to These Paintings," pp. 7–38.

Paintings of DHL. Edited by Mervyn Levy. London: Cory, Adams, and Mackay, 1964. Includes Lawrence's "Making Pictures" and three critical essays by H. T. Moore, Jack Lindsay, and Herbert Read (see later for full details of these essays).

"Making Pictures." *Creative Art* 5 (July 1929): 466–71. Collected in *Assorted Articles.* London: Secker, April 1930, and in *Phoenix II* (1968).

"Pictures on the Walls" as "Dead Pictures on the Wall." *Vanity Fair* 3 (December 1929): 88, 108, 140. Also in *Architectural Review* (February 1930) as "Pictures on the Wall" and collected in *Assorted Articles* (as earlier) and *Phoenix II* (1968).

DHL: Ten Paintings. Redding Ridge, Conn.: Black Swan, 1982. (Includes "Making Pictures" and relevant extracts from Lawrence's letters.)

STUDIES OF LAWRENCE'S VISUAL ART AND IMAGINATION

Akers, Gary. "DHL: Painter." In *DHL: 1885–1930: A Celebration.* Edited by Andrew Cooper. Nottingham: DHL Society, 1985, pp. 97–113.

Alldritt, Keith. *The Visual Imagination of DHL.* London: Edward Arnold, 1971.

Betsky-Zweig, S. "Lawrence and Cézanne." *Dutch Quarterly Review of Anglo-American Letters* 15 (1985): 2–24. (Reprinted in *Costerus* 58 [1987]: 104–26.)

Chambers, Jessie ("E.T."). *DHL: A Personal Record.* London: Jonathan Cape, 1935; New York: Knight, 1936.

Clark, L. D. "Lawrence's 'Maya' Drawing for 'Sun.' " *DHL Review* 15 (1982): 141–46.

Coombes, H. "The Paintings of DHL." *Gemini* 2 (Spring 1959): 56–59.

Crehan, Hubert. "Lady Chatterley's Painter: The Banned Pictures of DHL." *Art News* 55 (February 1957): 38–41, 63–66.

Cushman, Keith. "Lawrence and the Brewsters as Painters." *Etudes Lawrenciennes* 7 (1992): 39–49.

Dalgarno, Emily K. "DHL: Social Ideology in Visual Art." *Mosaic* 22 (1989): 1–18.

Davies, J. V. "Introduction." *Lawrence on Hardy and Painting: "Study of Thomas Hardy" and "Introduction to These Paintings."* Edited by J. V. Davies. London: Heinemann, 1973, pp. 1–9.

Edwards, Lucy I., and David Phillips, eds. *Young Bert: An Exhibition of the Early Years of DHL.* Nottingham: Nottingham Castle Museum and Art Gallery, 1972. (Illustrated catalog of event held 8 July–29 August 1972.)

Fernihough, Anne. *DHL: Aesthetics and Ideology.* Oxford: Oxford University Press, 1993.

Foehr, Stephen. "DHL: The Forbidden Paintings." *Horizon* 23 (July 1980): 64–69.

Fortunati, Vita. "The Visual Arts and the Novel: The Contrasting Cases of Ford Madox Ford and DHL." *Etudes Lawrenciennes* 9 (1993): 129–43.

Gee, Kathleen. "A Checklist of DHL Art Work at HRHRC." *Library Chronicle of the University of Texas at Austin,* new series, 34 (1986): 60–73. (Illustrated list of holdings at the Harry Ransom Humanities Research Center at Texas.)

Gutierrez, Donald. "The Ancient Imagination of DHL." *Twentieth Century Literature* 27 (1981): 178–96.

Heywood, Christopher. "African Art and the Work of Roger Fry and DHL." *Sheffield Papers on Literature and Society,* no. 1 (1976): 102–13.

Hyde, Virginia. *The Risen Adam: DHL's Revisionist Typology.* University Park: Pennsylvania State University Press, 1992.

Ingamells, John. "Cézanne in England 1910–1930." *British Journal of Aesthetics* 5 (October 1965): 341–50 (346–47 on Lawrence).

Ingersoll, Earl G. "Staging the Gaze in DHL's *Women in Love.*" *Studies in the Novel* 26, no. 2 (Fall 1994): 268–80.

Janik, Del Ivan. "Towards 'Thingness': Cézanne's Painting and Lawrence's Poetry." *Twentieth Century Literature* 19 (1973): 119–27.

Kestner, Joseph. "Sculptural Character in Lawrence's *Women in Love.*" *Modern Fiction Studies* 21 (1975–76): 543–53.

Kushigian, Nancy. *Pictures and Fictions: Visual Modernism and the Pre-War Novels of DHL.* New York: Peter Lang, 1990.

Landow, George P. "Lawrence and Ruskin: The Sage as Word-Painter." In *DHL and Tradition.* Edited by Jeffrey Meyers. London: Athlone, 1985, pp. 35–50.

Lawrence, Ada, and G. Stuart Gelder. *The Early Life of DHL Together with Hitherto Unpublished Letters and Articles.* London: Secker, 1932.

Levy, M., C. Wilson, and J. Cohen. "The Paintings of DHL." *Studio* 164 (October 1962): 130–35.

Levy, Mervyn. "Foreword." *Paintings of DHL.* Edited by Mervyn Levy. London: Cory, Adams, and Mackay, 1964, pp. 10–14.

Lindsay, Jack. "The Impact of Modernism on Lawrence." In *The Paintings of DHL.* Edited by Mervyn Levy. London: Cory, Adams, and MacKay; New York: Viking, 1964, pp. 35–53.

Meyers, Jeffrey. *Painting and the Novel.* Manchester: Manchester University Press, 1975, pp. 46–82.

Millett, Robert W. *The Vultures and the Phoenix: A Study of the Mandrake Press Edition of the Paintings of DHL.* Philadelphia: Art Alliance Press; London and Toronto: Associated University Presses, 1983.

Mills, Howard. "Late Turner, Hardy's Tess and Lawrence's Knees." In *Tensions and Transitions.* Edited by Michael Irwin, Mark Kinkead-Weekes, and A. Robert Lee. London: Faber and Faber, 1990, pp. 137–54.

———. "Lawrence, Roger Fry and Cézanne." *DHL: The Journal of the DHL Society* (Spring 1991): 28–38.

———. " 'The World of Substance': Lawrence, Hardy, Cézanne, and Shelley." *English* 43 (Autumn 1994): 209–22.

Moore, Harry T. "DHL and His Paintings." In *Paintings of DHL.* Edited by Mervyn Levy. London: Cory, Adams, and Mackay, 1964, pp. 17–34.

Nottingham Castle Museum. *DHL and the Visual Arts.* Nottingham: Nottingham Castle Museum and Art Gallery, 1985. (Catalog of the 1985 exhibition "Lawrence, Art and Artists.")

Read, Herbert. "Lawrence as a Painter." In *Paintings of DHL.* Edited by Mervyn Levy. London: Cory, Adams, and Mackay, 1964, pp. 55–64.

Remsbury, John. " 'Real Thinking': Lawrence and Cézanne." *Cambridge Quarterly* 2 (Spring 1967): 117–47.

Remsbury, John, and Ann Remsbury. "DHL and Art." *Revista da Faculdade de Letras* (University of Lisbon) Série 3, no. 12 (1971): 5–33. (Reprinted in Gomme [1978]: 190–218.)

Richardson, John Adkins, and John I. Ades. "DHL on Cézanne: A Study in the Psychology of Critical Intuition." *Journal of Aesthetics and Art Criticism* 28 (Summer 1970): 441–53.

Russell, John. "DHL and Painting." In *DHL: Novelist, Poet, Prophet.* Edited by Stephen Spender. London: Weidenfeld and Nicolson, 1973, pp. 234–43.

Schnitzer, Deborah. *The Pictorial in Modernist Fiction from Stephen Crane to Ernest Hemingway.* Ann Arbor, Mich.: UMI Research Press, 1988, pp. 138–58.

Schvey, Henry. "Lawrence and Expressionism." In *DHL: New Studies.* Edited by Christopher Heywood. London: Macmillan, 1987, pp. 124–36.

Sepčić, Višnja. "*Women in Love* and Expressionism." *Studia Romanica et Anglica Zagrabiensia* 26 (1981): 397–443; 27 (1982): 2–64.

Shapira, Morris. "DHL: Art Critic." *Cambridge Quarterly* 10 (1982): 189–201.

Spender, Stephen. "The Erotic Art of DHL." *Vanity Fair* (January 1986): 88–93. (On Lawrence's paintings.)

Stewart, Jack F. "Expressionism in *The Rainbow.*" *Novel* 13 (1980a): 296–315.

———. "Lawrence and Gauguin." *Twentieth Century Literature* 26 (1980b): 385–401.

———. "Primitivism in *Women in Love.*" *DHL Review* 13 (Spring 1980c): 45–62.

———. "Lawrence and Van Gogh." *DHL Review* 16 (Spring 1983a): 1–24.

———. "[Review of *DHL: Ten Paintings* (1982) and Millett (1983b), op. cit.]" *DHL Review* 17 (1984): 168–72.

———. "The Vital Art of Lawrence and Van Gogh." *DHL Review* 19 (Summer 1987): 123–48.

Stroupe, John H. "Ruskin, Lawrence and Gothic Naturalism." *Forum* 11 (Spring 1970): 3–9. (The influence of Ruskin's "The Nature of Gothic.")

Torgovnick, Marianna. "Pictorial Elements in *Women in Love:* The Uses of Insinuation and Visual Rhyme." *Contemporary Literature* 21 (Summer 1980): 420–34.

———. *The Visual Arts, Pictorialism, and the Novel: James, Lawrence, and Woolf.* Princeton: Princeton University Press, 1985.

Vries-Mason, Jillian de. *Perception in the Poetry of DHL.* Berne: Peter Lang, 1982.

Williams, Linda Ruth. *Sex in the Head: Visions of Femininity and Film in DHL.* Hemel Hempstead, Hertfordshire: Harvester Wheatsheaf, 1993.

Zigal, Thomas. "DHL Making Pictures." *Library Chronicle of the University of Texas* 34 (1986): 52–59.

PART III

CRITICAL
RECEPTION

SECTION A

A GENERAL GUIDE TO LAWRENCE CRITICISM AND SCHOLARSHIP

BIBLIOGRAPHY 85: ESSENTIAL SOURCES: BIBLIOGRAPHIES AND GUIDES

PRIMARY AND MAJOR SECONDARY BIBLIOGRAPHIES

Aldington, Richard. *DHL: A Complete List of His Works, with a Critical Appreciation.* London: Heinemann, 1935.

Anderson, Emily Ann. *English Poetry 1900–1950: A Guide to Information Sources.* Detroit: Gale Research, 1982, pp. 155–70.

Bateson, F. W., and Harrison T. Meserole. *A Guide to English and American Literature.* 3d ed. London and New York: Longman, 1976, pp. 204–5.

Beards, Richard D. "The Checklist of DHL Criticism and Scholarship, 1970." *DHL Review* 4 (Spring 1971): 90–102.

———. "The Checklist of DHL Criticism and Scholarship, 1972." *DHL Review* 6 (Spring 1973): 100–108.

———. "The Checklist of DHL Criticism and Scholarship, 1973." *DHL Review* 7 (Spring 1974): 89–98.

———. "The Checklist of DHL Criticism and Scholarship, 1974." *DHL Review* 8 (Spring 1975): 99–105.

———. "The Checklist of DHL Criticism and Scholarship, 1975." *DHL Review* 9 (Spring 1976): 157–66.

———. "The Checklist of DHL Criticism and Scholarship, 1976." *DHL Review* 10 (Spring 1977): 82–88.

———. "The Checklist of DHL Criticism and Scholarship, 1977." *DHL Review* 11 (Spring 1978): 77–85.

————. "The Checklist of DHL Criticism and Scholarship, 1978." *DHL Review* 12 (Fall 1979): 332–43.

Beards, Richard D., and G. B. Crump. "DHL: Ten Years of Criticism, 1959–1968, a Checklist." *DHL Review* 1 (Fall 1968): 245–85.

Beards, Richard D., and Barbara Willens. "DHL: Criticism: September, 1968–December, 1969: A Checklist." *DHL Review* 3 (Spring 1970): 70–79. (First in a series of regular bibliographical updates published in the journal. See also under Heath, Rosenthal, and Howard.)

Beebe, Maurice, and Anthony Tommasi. "Criticism of DHL: A Selected Checklist with an Index to Studies of Separate Works." *Modern Fiction Studies* 5 (Spring 1959): 83–98.

Bell, Inglis F., and Donald Baird. *The English Novel 1578–1956: A Checklist of Twentieth-Century Criticisms.* Denver: Alan Swallow, 1958, pp. 87–93.

Burwell, Rose Marie. "A Checklist of Lawrence's Reading." *A DHL Handbook.* Edited by Keith Sagar. Manchester: Manchester University Press, 1982, pp. 59–125.

Cooke, Sheila M. *DHL: A Finding List.* 2d ed. West Bridgford, Nottingham: Nottinghamshire County Council, Leisure Services Department, 1980.

Cowan, James C. *DHL: An Annotated Bibliography of Writings about Him.* 2 vols. De Kalb: Northern Illinois University Press, 1982; 1985. (Vol. 1, covering 1909–60, has 2,061 entries; vol. 2, covering 1961–75, has 2,566 entries.)

Davies, Alistair. *An Annotated Critical Bibliography of Modernism.* Sussex: Harvester Press; Totowa, N.J.: Barnes and Noble, 1982, pp. 131–88.

Draper, R. P. "Lawrence." In *The New Cambridge Bibliography of English Literature.* Vol. 4. Edited by I. R. Willison. Cambridge: Cambridge University Press, 1972, pp. 481–503.

Ferrier, Carole. "DHL's Pre-1920 Poetry: A Descriptive Bibliography of Manuscripts, Typescripts, and Proofs." *DHL Review* 6 (Fall 1973): 333–59.

————. "DHL's Poetry, 1920–1928: A Descriptive Bibliography of Manuscripts, Typescripts and Proofs." *DHL Review* 12 (Fall 1979): 289–304.

Gertzman, Jay A. *A Descriptive Bibliography of "Lady Chatterley's Lover": With Essays toward a Publishing History of the Novel.* Westport, Conn.: Greenwood, 1989.

Heath, Alice. "The Checklist of DHL Criticism and Scholarship, 1971." *DHL Review* 5 (Spring 1972): 82–92.

Hepburn, J. G. "DHL's Plays: An Annotated Bibliography." *Book Collector* 14 (Spring 1965): 78–81.

Howard, Brad. "Checklist of DHL Criticism and Scholarship, 1989." *DHL Review* 22 (Fall 1990): 313–18.

————. "Checklist of DHL Criticism and Scholarship, 1991." *DHL Review* 24 (Fall 1992): 257–64.

Howard-Hill, T. H. *Bibliography of British Literary Bibliographies.* 2d ed., rev. and enlarged. Oxford: Clarendon Press, 1987, pp. 578–80.

Jackson, Dennis. "A Select Bibliography, 1907–79." In *A DHL Handbook.* Edited by Keith Sagar. Manchester: Manchester University Press, 1982, pp. 1–58.

Joost, Nicholas, and Alvin Sullivan. "Reviews and Advertisements in *The Dial:* A Summary." In their *DHL and "The Dial."* Carbondale and Edwardsville: Southern Illinois University Press; London and Amsterdam: Feffer and Simons, 1970, pp. 179–204. (See also the bibliography of "Reviews in *The Dial* of Lawrence's Work" in the same volume, pp. 208–9.)

Kim, Jungmai. *DHL in Korea: A Bibliographical Study, 1930–1987.* Seoul: Hanshin, 1989.

Lockwood, Margaret. "The Criticism of DHL's Poetry: A Bibliography." In her *A Study of the Poems of DHL: Thinking in Poetry.* London: Macmillan, 1987, pp. 214–30.

McDonald, Edward D. *A Bibliography of the Writings of DHL.* With a Foreword by DHL. Philadelphia: Centaur, 1925.

———. *The Writings of DHL 1925–30: A Bibliographical Supplement.* Philadelphia: Centaur, 1931.

Manly, John Matthews, and Edith Rickert. *Contemporary British Literature: Outlines for Study, Indexes, Bibliographies.* 2d ed. London: Harrap, 1928, pp. 196–99. (Studies and reviews, 1914–27. Rev. and enlarged 3d ed., *Contemporary British Literature: A Critical Survey and 232 Author-Bibliographies* by Fred B. Millett. New York: Harcourt, Brace, 1935, pp. 317–22.)

Mellown, Elgin W. *A Descriptive Catalogue of the Bibliographies of Twentieth Century British Poets, Novelists, and Dramatists.* 2d ed., rev. and enlarged. Troy, N.Y.: Whitston, 1978, pp. 202–4.

Meyers, Jeffrey. "Imaginative Portraits of DHL." *Bulletin of Bibliography* 45, no. 4 (1988): 271–73.

———. "DHL: An Iconography." *Bulletin of Bibliography* 46 (1989): 118–19.

Poplawski, Paul. *The Works of D. H. Lawrence: A Chronological Checklist.* Nottingham: D. H. Lawrence Society, 1995.

Powell, Lawrence Clark. *The Manuscripts of DHL: A Descriptive Catalogue.* Los Angeles: Los Angeles Public Library, 1937.

———. "DHL and His Critics. A Chronological Excursion in Bio-Bibliography." *Colophon* 1 (1940): 63–74. (Covers fifty-eight items, 1924–39.)

Pownall, David E. *Articles on Twentieth Century Literature: An Annotated Bibliography 1954 to 1970: An Expanded Cumulation of "Current Bibliography" in the Journal of Twentieth Century Literature. Volume One to Volume Sixteen 1955–1970.* New York: Kraus Thomson, 1974.

Ramaiah, L. S., and Radhe Shyam Sharma, eds. "Indian Responses to DHL: A Bibliographical Survey." *Osmania Journal of English Studies* 21 (1985): 119–28. (Hyderabad, India.)

Ramaiah, L. S., and Sachidananda Mohanty, eds. *DHL Studies in India: A Bibliographical Guide with a Review Essay.* Calcutta: P. Lal (Writer's Workshop), 1990.

Rice, Thomas Jackson. *DHL: A Guide to Research.* New York and London: Garland, 1983a. (Contains 2,123 entries with terminal date of 1 January 1983.)

———. *English Fiction 1900–1950: A Guide to Information Sources.* Vol. 2. *Individual Authors: Joyce to Woolf.* Detroit: Gale Research, 1983b, pp. 49–87.

Roberts, Warren. *A Bibliography of DHL.* 2d ed. Cambridge: Cambridge University Press, 1982. (Currently, the definitive primary bibliography, incorporating a useful selective secondary bibliography. Rev. ed. forthcoming. Organized into the following sections: [A] Books and Pamphlets; [B] Contributions to Books; [C] Contributions to Periodicals; [D] Translations [of Lawrence's Works]; [E] Manuscripts [descriptions and locations, compiled by Lindeth Vasey]; [F] Books and Pamphlets about DHL [243 works listed to 1981]; Appendix 1(a): Parodies of *Lady Chatterley's Lover;* Appendix 1(b): Piracies and Forgeries of *Lady Chatterley's Lover;* Appendix 2: Other Spurious Works; Appendix 3: A Periodical—

The Phoenix. Section E can be supplemented by information in Ferrier and Worthen, op. cit., and in items in the following bibliography. See also Gekowski, R. A. "Review of *A Bibliography of DHL* edited by Warren Roberts." *Modern Language Review* 79 [1984]: 170–74.)

Rosenthal, Rae, "Checklist of DHL Criticism and Scholarship, 1986–1987." *DHL Review* 20 (Fall 1988): 315–30.

———. "Checklist of DHL Criticism and Scholarship, 1988." *DHL Review* 21 (Fall 1989): 323–36.

Rosenthal, Rae, and Dennis Jackson. "Checklist of DHL Criticism and Scholarship, 1984–1985." *DHL Review* 19 (Summer 1987): 195–218.

Rosenthal, Rae, Dennis Jackson, and Brad Howard. "Checklist of DHL Criticism and Scholarship, 1979–1983." *DHL Review* 18 (Spring 1985–1986): 37–74.

Sagar, Keith. *DHL: A Calendar of His Works.* Manchester: Manchester University Press, 1979.

Spilka, Mark. "Lawrence." In *The English Novel: Select Bibliographical Guides.* Edited by A. E. Dyson. London: Oxford University Press, 1974, pp. 334–48.

Stoll, John E. *DHL: A Bibliography, 1911–1975.* Troy, N.Y.: Whitston, 1977.

Tedlock, E. W., Jr. *The Frieda Lawrence Collection of DHL Manuscripts: A Descriptive Bibliography.* Albuquerque: University of New Mexico Press, 1948.

Temple, Ruth Z., and Martin Tucker, eds. "DHL." In their *A Library of Literary Criticism (Modern British Literature).* Vol. 2. New York: Frederick Ungar, 1966, pp. 144–64.

Walker, Warren S. *Twentieth-Century Short Story Explication: Interpretations, 1900–1975, of Short Fiction since 1800.* 3d ed. London: Clive Bingley; Hamden, Conn.: Shoe String Press, 1977, pp. 450–64.

White, William. *DHL: A Checklist. Writings about DHL, 1931–50.* Detroit: Wayne State University Press, 1950.

Worthen, John. "Appendix I: DHL's Prose Works, 1906–1913." In his *DHL: The Early Years, 1885–1912.* Cambridge: Cambridge University Press, 1991, pp. 471–77.

———. "Appendix II: DHL's Poetry, 1897–1913." In his *DHL: The Early Years* as in preceding item, pp. 478–94.

COLLECTIONS, EXHIBITIONS, FIRST EDITIONS: SOME CATALOGS AND GUIDES

Barez, Reva R. "The H. Bacon Collamore Collection of DHL." *Yale University Library Gazette* 34 (1959): 16–23.

Bumpus, John, and Edward Bumpus. *DHL: An Exhibition.* London: Bumpus, 1933. (Catalog of event held April–May 1933; manuscripts, typescripts, sketches, photographs, first editions.)

Cambridge University Library. *DHL 1885–1930.* Cambridge: Cambridge University Library, 1985. (Catalog of an exhibition held September–November 1985.)

Cameron, Alan, ed. *DHL: A Life in Literature.* Nottingham: Nottingham University Library, 1985. (Catalog of Centenary Exhibition held 7 September–13 October 1985.)

Cushman, Keith, ed. *An Exhibition of First Editions and Manuscripts from the DHL Collection of J. E. Baker, Jr.* Chicago: University of Chicago, 1973. (Catalog.)

———. "A Profile of John E. Baker, Jr., and His Lawrence Collection." *DHL Review* 7 (Spring 1974): 83–88.

———. "A Profile of John Martin and His Lawrence Collection." *DHL Review* 7 (Summer 1974): 199–205.

Cutler, Bradley D., and V. Stiles. *Modern British Authors, Their First Editions.* New York: Greenburg; London, Allen and Unwin, 1930.

Edwards, Lucy I., and David Phillips, eds. *Young Bert: An Exhibition of the Early Years of DHL.* Nottingham: Nottingham Castle Museum and Art Gallery, 1972. (Illustrated catalog of event held July 8–August 29 1972.)

Fabes, Gilbert Henry. *David Herbert Lawrence: His First Editions: Points and Values.* London: W. and G. Foyle, 1933. (Reprinted, Folcroft Library Edition, 1971.)

Finney, Brian H. "A Profile of Mr. George Lazarus and His Lawrence Collection of Manuscripts and First Editions." *DHL Review* 6 (Fall 1973): 309–12.

Gotham Book Mart. *Books by and about DHL: A Bookseller's Catalogue.* New York: Gotham Book Mart, 1961.

Hoffman, F. J. *The Little Magazine: A History and a Bibliography.* Princeton: Princeton University Press, 1947. (Reprinted, New York: Kraus Reprint Corporation, 1967.)

Hoffman, L. "A Catalogue of the Frieda Lawrence Manuscripts in German at the University of Texas." *Library Chronicle of the University of Texas at Austin,* new series, 6 (1973): 87–105.

Lawrence, J. Stephan. *DHL: Supplement to Catalogue 38.* Chicago: Rare Books, 1978.

Melvin Rare Books. *A Catalogue of Valuable Books by DHL.* Edinburgh: Melvin Rare Books, 1950.

Nottingham Castle Museum. *DHL and the Visual Arts.* Nottingham: Nottingham Castle Museum and Art Gallery, 1985. (Catalog of the 1985 exhibition "Lawrence, Art and Artists.")

Nottingham University. *DHL Collection Catalogue.* Nottingham: University of Nottingham Manuscripts Department, 1979.

———. *DHL: A Phoenix in Flight. Notes to Accompany an Exhibition.* Nottingham: Nottingham University Library, 1980.

———. *DHL Collection Catalogue.* Vol. 2. Nottingham: University of Nottingham Manuscripts Department, 1983.

———. *Collection of Literary Manuscripts, Typescripts, Proofs and Related Papers of DHL.* Nottingham: University of Nottingham Department of Manuscripts and Special Collections, 1990.

Peterson, Richard F., and Alan M. Cohn. *DHL: An Exhibit.* Carbondale: Morris Library, Southern Illinois University, 1979.

Pinto, Vivian de Sola, ed. *DHL after Thirty Years, 1930–1960.* Nottingham: Curwen Press, 1960. (Catalog of exhibition held 17 June–30 July 1960.)

Rota, B. "Contemporary Collectors VII: The George Lazarus Library." *Book Collector* 4 (Winter 1955): 279–84.

Snyder, Harold Jay. *A Catalogue of English and American First Editions, 1911–32, of DHL.* New York: Privately printed, 1932.

Tannenbaum, E., ed. *DHL: An Exhibition of First Editions, Manuscripts, Paintings, Letters, and Miscellany.* Carbondale: Southern Illinois University Library, 1958. (Catalog of event held in April 1958.)

Tarr, Roger L., and Robert Sokon, eds. *A Bibliography of the DHL Collection at Illinois State University.* Bloomington, Ill.: Scarlet Ibis Press, 1979.

Texas University Humanities Research Center. *The University of New Mexico DHL Fellowship Fund Manuscript Collection.* Austin,: University of Texas Humanities Research Center, 1960. (Catalog.)

Wade, Graham. "DHL: First Editions of Novels, Poems, Verse and Essays by the Distinguished Author Are Extremely Collectable." *Book and Magazine Collector,* no. 10 (December 1984): 4–12. (Article followed by a "Complete Bibliography of DHL U.K. 1st Editions" and their price range.)

Warren Gallery. *Exhibition 12: Paintings by DHL.* London: Warren Gallery, 1929. (Catalog of event held July–September 1929.)

BIBLIOGRAPHY 86: COLLECTIONS AND OVERVIEWS

This bibliography is intended to provide a starting point for readers interested in gaining a general overview both of Lawrence's oeuvre itself and of its critical reception through time.

Andrews, W. T., ed. *Critics on DHL.* London: George Allen and Unwin, 1971. (Reviews and critical essays, 1911–60s.)

Arnold, Armin. "Appendix: A History of Lawrence's Reputation in America and Europe." In his *DHL and America.* London: Linden Press, 1958, pp. 163–223.

Baker, Ernest A. "DHL." In his *The History of the English Novel.* Vol. 10. London: Witherby, 1939, pp. 345–91.

Balbert, Peter, and Phillip L. Marcus, eds. *DHL: A Centenary Consideration.* Ithaca, N.Y., and London: Cornell University Press, 1985.

Bilan, R. P. "Leavis on Lawrence: The Problem of the Normative." *DHL Review* 11 (Spring 1978): 38–49.

———. "Leavis on Lawrence." In his *The Literary Criticism of F. R. Leavis.* Cambridge: Cambridge University Press, 1979, pp. 195–272.

Black, Michael. "The Criticism of DHL." In his *DHL: The Early Fiction: A Commentary.* London: Macmillan, 1986, pp. 1–17.

Blanchard, Lydia. "DHL." In *Critical Survey of Short Fiction.* Vol. 5. Edited by Frank N. Magill. Englewood Cliffs, N.J.: Salem Press, 1981, pp. 1788–94.

Bloom, Harold, ed. *DHL: Modern Critical Views.* New York: Chelsea House, 1986.

Brown, Keith, ed. *Rethinking Lawrence.* Milton Keynes, Pa.: Open University Press, 1990.

Brunsdale, Mitzi M. "DHL." In *Critical Survey of Poetry.* Vol. 4. Edited by Frank N. Magill. Englewood Cliffs, N.J.: Salem Press, 1982, pp. 1677–78.

Caplan, Brina. "The Phoenix Observed: Recent Critical Views of DHL." *Georgia Review* 36 (1982): 194–207. (Reviews six books, 1978–80.)

Chapman, R. T. "Lawrence, Lewis and the Comedy of Literary Reputations." *Studies in the Twentieth Century* 6 (Fall 1970): 85–95.

Coombes, Henry, ed *DHL: A Critical Anthology.* Harmondsworth: Penguin, 1973.

Draper, R. P. "A Short Guide to DHL Studies." *Critical Survey* 2 (Summer 1966): 222–26.

———. "Reputation and Influence." *DHL.* New York: Twayne, 1964; London: Macmillan, 1976, pp. 161–77.

————, ed. *DHL: The Critical Heritage*. London: Routledge and Kegan Paul, 1970.

Eggert, Paul. "Lawrence Criticism: Where Next?" *Critical Review* (Canberra, Australia) 21 (1979): 72–84.

Ellis, David, and Ornella De Zordo, eds. *DHL: Critical Assessments*. 4 vols. East Sussex: Helm Information, 1992. (An invaluable collection that makes available a huge range of criticism, from early reviews to recent essays, surveying the whole of Lawrence's output. Vol. 1: "The Contemporary Response." Vol. 2: "The Fiction [I]." Vol. 3: "The Fiction [II]." Vol. 4: "Poetry and Non-fiction; The Modern Critical Response 1938–92: General Studies.")

Friedman, Alan. "The Other Lawrence." *Partisan Review* 37, no. 2 (1970): 239–53.

Gilbert, Sandra M. "DHL." In *Dictionary of Literary Biography*. Vol. 19. *British Poets 1880–1914*. Edited by Donald E. Stanford. Detroit: Gale Research, 1983, pp. 274–88.

Goodheart, Eugene. "Lawrence and the Critics." *Chicago Review* 16 (Fall 1963): 127–37.

————. "A Representative Destiny." In his *The Utopian Vision of DHL*. Chicago and London: University of Chicago Press, 1963, pp. 160–73.

Green, Martin Burgess. *The Reputation of DHL in America*. Ann Arbor, Mich.: University Microfilms, 1966. (Reviews and criticism, 1911–56.)

Gregory, Horace. "On DHL and His Posthumous Reputation." In his *Shield of Achilles: Essays on Beliefs in Poetry*. New York: Harcourt, Brace, 1944, pp. 156–64.

Hamalian, Leo, ed. *DHL: A Collection of Criticism*. New York: McGraw-Hill, 1973.

————. "The DHL Industry." *Book Forum* 7, no. 1 (1984): 13–17.

Hayman, Ronald. "DHL." In his *Leavis*. Totowa, N.J.: Rowman and Littlefield, 1976, pp. 101–10.

Heywood, Christopher, ed. *DHL: New Studies*. London: Macmillan; New York: St. Martin's Press, 1987.

Highet, Gilbert. "Lawrence in America." In his *People, Places, and Books*. New York: Oxford University Press, 1953, pp. 37–44.

Hoffman, Frederick J., and Harry T. Moore, eds. *The Achievement of DHL*. Norman: University of Oklahoma Press, 1953. (See especially the editors' introduction, "DHL and His Critics: An Introduction," pp. 3–45.)

Hogan, Robert. "DHL and His Critics." *Essays in Criticism* 9 (October 1959): 381–87.

Hough, Graham. "The Authentic Message of Lawrence." *Sunday Times* (2 March 1980): 38.

Jackson, Dennis. "DHL in the 1970s: No More the Great Unread." *British Book News* (April 1980): 198–202.

————. " 'The Stormy Petrel of Literature Is Dead': The World Press Reports DHL's Death." *DHL Review* 14 (1981): 33–72. (Survey and selective bibliography of obituaries and related writings of 1930.)

Jackson, Dennis, and Fleda Brown Jackson, eds. *Critical Essays on DHL*. Boston: G. K. Hall, 1988. (See especially the editors' "Introduction: DHL's Critical Reception: An Overview," pp. 1–46.)

Kalnins, Mara, ed. *DHL: Centenary Essays*. Bristol: Bristol Classical Press, 1986.

Larkin, Philip. "The Sanity of Lawrence." *Times Literary Supplement* (13 June 1980): 671. (Larkin's speech opening the Lawrence exhibition at Nottingham University Library in 1980.)

Littlewood, J.C.F. "Leavis and Lawrence." *Standpunte* (South Africa) 7 (1955): 79–92.

————. "Lawrence and the Scholars." *Essays in Criticism* 33 (1983): 175–86.

MacCarthy, Fiona. "Centenary of Our Phallocrat." *London Times* (12 September 1985): 13. (Review of MacLeod and Burgess [both 1985].)

MacKillop, I. D. "F. R. Leavis: A Peculiar Relationship." *Essays in Criticism* 34 (1984): 185–92.

Meyers, Jeffrey. "Memoirs of DHL: A Genre of the Thirties." *DHL Review* 14 (1981): 1–32.

————, ed. *The Legacy of DHL: New Essays.* London: Macmillan, 1987. (See especially the editor's "Introduction," pp. 1–13.)

Millett, Fred B. "DHL." In *A History of English Literature.* Edited by William Vaughn Moody and Robert Morss Lovett. 8th ed. New York: Charles Scribner's Sons, 1964, pp. 429–31, 475–76, 497, 502.

Moore, Harry T. "The Great Unread." *Saturday Review of Literature* 21 (2 March 1940): 8.

————. "Appendix A: Books about DHL, with Some Notes on the History of His Reputation." In his *The Life and Works of DHL.* London: Allen and Unwin, 1951, pp. 333–48. (Bibliographical essay.)

————, ed. *A DHL Miscellany.* Carbondale: Southern Illinois University Press, 1959.

Niven, Alastair. "DHL (1885–1930)." In *British Writers.* Vol. 7. *Sean O'Casey to Poets of World War II.* Edited by Ian Scott Kilvert. New York: Scribner's, 1984, pp. 87–126.

Parry, Albert. "DHL through a Marxist Mirror." *Western Review* 19 (1955): 85–100.

Partlow, Robert B., Jr., and Harry T. Moore, eds. *DHL: The Man Who Lived.* Carbondale: Southern Illinois University Press, 1980.

Phillips, Jill M., ed. *DHL: A Review of the Biographies and Literary Criticism* New York: Gordon Press, 1978. (A Critically Annotated Bibliography.)

Powell, Lawrence Clark. "DHL and His Critics. A Chronological Excursion in Bio-Bibliography." *Colophon* 1 (1940): 63–74. (Covers fifty-eight items, 1924–39.)

Preston, Peter, and Peter Hoare, eds. *DHL in the Modern World.* London: Macmillan, 1989.

Quennell, Peter. "The Later Period of DHL." In *Scrutinies II.* Edited by Edgell Rickword. London: Wishart, 1931, pp. 124–37.

Rahv, Philip. "On Leavis and Lawrence." *New York Review of Books* 11 (26 September 1968): 62–68.

Reade, A. R. "The Intelligentsia and DHL." In his *Main Currents in Modern Literature.* London: Nicholson and Watson, 1935, pp. 179–96.

Roberts, Walter. "After the Prophet: The Reputation of DHL." *Month* 27 (April 1962): 237–40.

Robertson, P.J.M. "F. R. Leavis and DHL." In *The Leavises on Fiction.* New York: St. Martin's Press, 1981, pp. 76–98.

Robinson, Jeremy. "Introduction: The Myth and Legend of DHL." In his *The Passion of DHL.* Kidderminster, England: Crescent Moon, 1992, pp. 1–7.

Robson, W. W. *Modern English Literature.* London: Oxford, 1970, pp. 82–92.

Rossman, Charles. "Lawrence on the Critics' Couch: Pervert or Prophet?" *DHL Review* 3 (Summer 1970): 175–85. (Reviews Stoll [1968], Miles [1969], and Draper [1969].)

————. "Four Versions of DHL." *DHL Review* 6 (Spring 1973): 47–70. (On Yudishtar, Clarke, Cavitch [all 1969] and Hochman [1970].)

Sagar, Keith. "Beyond Lawrence." In *DHL: The Man Who Lived.* Edited by Robert B. Partlow, Jr., and Harry T. Moore. Carbondale: Southern Illinois University Press, 1980a, pp. 258–66.

———. "A Lawrence for Today: Art for Life's Sake." *Times Higher Education Supplement* (29 February 1980b): 10.

Salgādo, Gāmini, and G. K. Das, eds. *The Spirit of DHL: Centenary Studies.* London: Macmillan, 1988.

Schorer, Mark. "DHL: Then, During, Now." *Atlantic Monthly* 233 (March 1974): 84–88.

Sitesh, Aruna, ed. *DHL: An Anthology of Recent Criticism.* Delhi, India: ACE, 1990.

Sklar, Sylvia. "DHL." In *Dictionary of Literary Biography.* Vol. 10. *Modern British Dramatists, 1900–1950.* Edited by Stanley Weintraub. Detroit: Gale Research, 1982, pp. 288–93.

Smith, Anne, ed. *Lawrence and Women.* London: Vision, 1978.

Spender, Stephen, ed. *DHL: Novelist, Poet, Prophet.* London: Weidenfeld and Nicolson, 1973.

Spilka, Mark. "Post-Leavis Lawrence Critics." *Modern Language Quarterly* 25 (June 1964): 212–17. (See also, in same journal, reply by Eugene Goodheart, September 1964: 374–75; and rejoinder by Spilka in December 1964: 503–4.)

———, ed. *DHL: A Collection of Critical Essays.* Englewood Cliffs, N.J.: Prentice-Hall, 1963.

Squires, Michael, and Keith Cushman, eds. *The Challenge of DHL.* Madison: University of Wisconsin Press, 1990.

Sullivan, Alvin. "The Phoenix Riddle: Recent DHL Scholarship." *Papers on Language and Literature* 7 (Spring 1971): 203–21.

Tait, Michael S. "DHL." In *Dictionary of Literary Biography.* Vol. 98. *Modern British Essayists, First Series.* Edited by Robert Beum. Detroit: Gale Research, 1990, pp. 214–23.

Trail, George Y. "Toward a Lawrencian Poetic." *DHL Review* 5 (Spring 1972): 67–81. (Review of Garcia and Karabatsos, Smailes, Marshall [all 1970].)

Troy, William. "The DHL Myth." In his *Selected Essays.* Edited by Stanley E. Hyman. New Brunswick, N.J.: Rutgers University Press, 1967, pp. 120–33. (Originally published in *Partisan Review* 4 [January 1938]. See also in this book, "DHL as Hero," pp. 110–19 [a review of Huxley's *Letters of DHL*], originally published in *The Symposium* 4, no. 1 [1933].)

Undset, Sigrid. "DHL." In her *Men, Women and Places.* Translated by Arthure G. Chater. New York: Knopf, 1939, pp. 33–53. (Norwegian novelist's portrait of Lawrence as genius and prophet of contemporary crises of civilization.)

Ward, A. C. *The Nineteen-Twenties: Literature and Ideas in the Post-War Decade.* London: Methuen, 1930, pp. 109–15.

———. *Twentieth-Century Literature: 1901–1950.* 12th ed. London: Methuen, 1956, pp. 15, 57, 61–64, 70, 238.

Welch, Colin. "Consecrating Lawrence." *Spectator* (13 April 1985): 24.

Weldon, Thornton. "DHL." In *The English Short Story, 1880–1945: A Critical History.* Edited by Joseph M. Flora. Boston: Twayne, 1985, pp. 39–56.

West, Geoffrey. "The Significance of DHL." *Yale Review* 22 (Winter 1933): 393–95.

Widdowson, Peter, ed. *DHL.* London and New York: Longman, 1992. (See, especially, "Introduction: Post-modernising DHL," pp. 1–27.)

Widmer, Kingsley. "Notes on the Literary Institutionalization of DHL: An Anti-Review of the Current State of Lawrence Studies." *Paunch* 26 (April 1966): 5–13. (See also the subsequent three-sided debate on this article, involving Mark Spilka, Kingsley Widmer, and Arthur Efron, in *Paunch* 27: 83–96 passim.)

————. "DHL and Critical Mannerism." *Journal of Modern Literature* 3 (Fall 1973): 1044–50.

————. "Laurentian Manias: A Review of Recent Studies of DHL." *Studies in the Novel* 5 (Winter 1973): 547–58.

————. "Lawrence as Abnormal Novelist." *DHL Review* 8 (Summer 1975): 220–32.

————. "Profiling an Erotic Prophet: Recent Lawrence Biographies." *Studies in the Novel* 8 (Summer 1976): 234–43.

————. "Psychiatry and Piety on Lawrence." *Studies in the Novel* 9 (Summer 1977): 195–200. (On Leavis [1976] and Howe [1977].)

————. "DHL." In *Dictionary of Literary Biography*. Vol. 36. *British Novelists, 1890–1929: Modernists*. Edited by Thomas F. Staley. Detroit: Gale Research, 1985, pp. 115–49.

————. "Lawrence's Cultural Impact." In *The Legacy of DHL*. Edited by Jeffrey Meyers. London: Macmillan, 1987, pp. 156–74.

Wiley, Paul L. "DHL." In his *The British Novel: Conrad to the Present*. Northbrook, Ill.: AHM, 1973, pp. 71–77.

Williams, Raymond. "DHL." In his *Culture and Society: 1780–1950*. London: Chatto and Windus; New York: Columbia University Press, 1958, pp. 199–213. (Reprinted in Moore [1959] as "The Social Thinking of DHL," pp. 295–311.)

————. "DHL." In his *The English Novel from Dickens to Lawrence*. London: Chatto and Windus; New York: Oxford University Press, 1970, pp. 169–84.

BIBLIOGRAPHY 87: CHRONOLOGICAL LISTINGS OF LAWRENCE CRITICISM

This bibliography is made up of two chronologically organized lists of Lawrence criticism, the first devoted to critical books and pamphlets, and the second to essays, chapters in books, and other shorter discussions. (As the lists are also part of the sequence of chronologies in this book, they have independent headings as Chronologies 5 and 6.)

CHRONOLOGY 5: CRITICAL BOOKS AND PAMPHLETS

This chronology provides a complete list, up to 1994, of the authors of English-language books and pamphlets with Lawrence or his works as a main subject. Only names of authors are given, as full bibliographical details of their works can be found in the (alphabetically organized) master bibliography in Part IV of this book. Works are listed under the date of their first publication only; where they have been reissued in a new edition, the date of the most recent edition is given in parentheses after the author's name. Catalogs to exhibitions and pamphlets are indicated as such. Where an author has published two works in the same year, a short title is given to distinguish the works.

1922: Seltzer (publicity leaflet).

1924: Douglas. Seligmann.

1925: McDonald.

1927: Aldington.

1929: Lewis. Warren Gallery (Catalog).

1930: Aldington. Arrow. Leavis. Murry. Potter. West.

1931: McDonald. Murry.

1932: Carswell. Carter (1972). Goodman (pamphlet) (1933). Lawrence and Gelder. Luhan. Moore. Nin (1964). Snyder (catalog).

1933: Brett (1974). Bumpus and Bumpus (catalog). Corke. Fabes (catalog) (1971). Gregory (1957). Murry.

1934: Brewster and Brewster. Lawrence, Frieda (1974).

1935: Aldington. Chambers (''E.T.'') (1980).

1937: Powell.

1938: Kingsmill. Merrild (1964).

1939: Tindall.

1948: Tedlock.

1950: Aldington *(Portrait).* Aldington *(An Appreciation).* Melvin Rare Books (catalog). West (1966). White.

1951: Bynner. Corke. Jarrett-Kerr (1961). Kenmare. Moore (1964). Pinto. Wickremasinghe.

1952: Young.

1953: Fay. Hoffman and Moore.

1954: Moore (1976).

1955: Freeman. Leavis.

1956: Boadella (1978). Davis (pamphlet). Hough (*Dark Sun*). Hough (*Two Exiles*) (1960). Moore.

1957: Murry. Nehls (*Composite Biography,* three vols.: 1957, 1958, 1959).

1958: Arnold. Rees. Spilka. Tannenbaum (catalog).

1959: Moore.

1960: Drain (pamphlet). Pinto (catalog). Texas University (catalog). Vivas.

1961: Beal. Gotham Book Mart (catalog). Lawrence, Frieda. Rolph (1990).

1962: Cornwell. Weiss. Widmer.

1963: Arnold. Daiches. Goodheart. Moynahan. Roberts (1982). Spilka. Stewart (1990). Tedlock.

1964: Clark. Draper (1976). Holbrook. Panichas. Sinzelle.

1965: Corke. Daleski. Ford. Gilbert. Shaw. Tedlock.

1966: Fedder. Gordon. Green. Hanson. Harrison. Moore and Roberts. Sagar. Salgādo.

1967: Handley. Lerner.

1968: Cooke (1980). Huttar. Moynahan. Poole (pamphlet). Schorer. Stoll. Tilak.

1969: Cavitch. Clarke (*Casebook*). Clarke (*River of Dissolution*). Consolo. Cura-Sazdanic. Deva. Draper. Miko. Miles. Rothkopf. Salgādo (*Casebook*). Salgādo (*"Sea and Sardinia"*). Slade. Yudhishtar.

1970: Cowan. Draper. Farr. Garcia and Karabatsos. Hochman. Joost and Sullivan. Krishnamurthi. Marshall. Nahal. Patmore (pamphlet). Smailes. Williams.

1971: Alldritt. Andrews. Delavenay. Inniss. Kinkead-Weekes. Mailer. Martin. Miko. Millett. Pritchard. Raskin. Stoll. Tilak. Zytaruk.

1972: Bedient. Delavenay. Edwards and Phillips (catalog). Foster. Garcia. Garcia and Karabatsos. Gilbert. Prakesh, R. Prakesh, O. Pugh (1991). Swigg.

1973: Coombes. Cushman (catalog). Hamalian. Kermode. Lucas. Mackenzie. Oates (1976). Paterson. Sale. Sanders. Spender. Trease. Tripathy.

1974: Balbert. Barrett and Erskine. Eisenstein. Green. John. Squires.

1975: Callow. Corke. Feshawy. Hahn. Russell. Sitesh. Sklar.

1976: Grant. Gravil. Harris. Hillman. Holderness. Leavis. Littlewood. Michaels-Tonks. Niven. Prasad. Salgādo.

1977: Alcorn. Aylwin. Howe. Stoll. Tenenbaum.

1978: Albright. Brunsdale. Buckton. Bunnell (1993). Cushman. Delany. Gomme. Handley and Harris. Lawrence, J. S. (catalog). Murfin. Niven. Phillips. Pinion. Smith Veitch.

1979: Bennett. Nath. Nottingham University. Peterson and Cohn (catalog). Ross. Sagar. Tarr and Sokon (catalog). Worthen.

1980: Ballin. Becker. Burns. Butler (1991). Clark. Cooke. Dix. Ebbatson. Gutierrez. Kiely. Miller (*Passionate Appreciation*). Miller (*Notes*). Niven. Nottingham University (catalog). Olson. Partlow and Moore. Prasad. Spencer. Wilt.

1981: Ben-Ephraim. Bynner. Darroch. Hobsbaum. Hyde. Janik. Lucente. McEwan. Moore and Montague. Neville. Page. Sharma, K. K. Sharma, R. S.

1982: Cowan (2 vols., 1982 and 1985). Ebbatson. Hamalian. Herzinger. Holderness. Malani. Meyers. Roberts. Sagar (*DHL and New Mexico*). Sagar (*Handbook*). Salgādo. Simpson. Vries-Mason.

1983: Baker. Crick. Davis. Millett. Murfin. Nottingham University (catalog). Rice. Squires. Tracy. Urang. Van der Veen.

1984: Davies. Dervin. Harris. Mandell. Parmenter. Ruderman. Schneider. Singh. Wright.

1985: Balbert and Marcus. Burgess. Cambridge/Nottingham University Library (catalog). Cameron (catalog). Cooper and Hughes. Davey. Hardy and Harris. Hostettler. Lea. MacLeod. Meyers. New. Norris. Nottingham Castle Museum (catalog). Philippron. Sagar (*Life into Art*). Sagar (*Life*). Scheckner. Sinha. Squires and Jackson. Storer. Torgovnick.

1986: Alden. Black. Butler. Draper. Easthope. Holderness. Kalnins. Kim. Lavrin. Lebolt. Lehman. Mackey. Nixon. Schneider.

1987: Bonds. Gamache and MacNiven. Gutierrez. Harvey. Heywood. Lockwood. Meyers. Miliaras. Milton. Modiano. Murfin. Orr. Sharma. Suter. Verhoeven. Whiteley.

1988: Bloom (ed. of four essay collections). Britton. Ellis and Mills. Greenhalgh. Holderness. Jackson and Jackson. Laird. May. Salgādo and Das. Singh. Stevens. Viinikka. Whelan.

1989: Balbert. Champion. Davis. Gertzman. Kim. Messenger. Padhi. Preston and Hoare. Templeton. Worthen.

1990: Banerjee. Brown. Cowan. Edwards. Ege (pamphlet). Finney. Humma. Hyde, H. Montgomery. Hyde, G. M. Ingram. Kushigian. Meyers. Nottingham University (catalog). Pinkney. Polhemus. Ramaiah and Mohanty. Sharma. Sitesh. Squires and Cushman. Storch.

1991: Adelman. Black. Cushman and Jackson. Dorbad. Fjagesund. Kelsey. McEwan. Mensch. Ross. Siegel. Sklenicka. Spear. Squires. Tytell. Worthen (*DHL*). Worthen (*Early Years*).

1992: Asai. Bell. Black. Ellis and De Zordo. Holbrook. Hyde. Preston. Robinson. Sipple. Spilka. Trebisz. Widdowson. Widmer.

1993: Buckley and Buckley. Feinstein. Fernihough. Hilton. Mohanty. Poplawski. Walterscheid. Williams.

1994: Lewiecki-Wilson. Maddox. Montgomery. Preston.

1995: Hofmann and Weithmann (pamphlet). Poplawski. Worthen.

CHRONOLOGY 6: SELECTED ESSAYS AND SHORTER DISCUSSIONS

Given the thousands of essays and articles that have been published on Lawrence, this part of the chronology cannot avoid being highly selective, and it is intended to give only a broad, if still fairly comprehensive, overview of shorter critical discussions of Lawrence since the beginning of his writing career. The selection has been guided by the following priorities: (1) to provide citations of as many *general* overviews of Lawrence's work as possible; (2) to give an impression of the range and changing nature of critical responses to Lawrence both at any one time and over the whole period covered by the list; and (3) to include as many titles as possible that do not appear elsewhere in this book in the more specialized bibliographies. (Citations in this part of the chronology are given in full.)

1909

Yoxall, Henry. ''Books and Pictures.'' *Schoolmaster* 76 (25 December 1909): 1242. (On the poems ''Dreams Old and Nascent,'' ''Discipline'' and ''Baby-Movements.'')

1911

Cooper, Frederic T. "The Theory of Heroes and Some Recent Novels." *Bookman* (New York) 33 (April 1911): 193–96 (195).

Hunt, Violet. "A First Novel of Power." *Daily Chronicle* (10 February 1911): 6.

Monkhouse, Allan. "A Promising Novel." *Manchester Guardian* (8 February 1911): 5.

Savage, Henry. "Fiction." *Academy* 80 (18 March 1911): 328.

1912

Anonymous. "An Interesting Novel." *Morning Post* (17 June 1912): 2.

———. *"The Trespasser." Saturday Review* 113 (22 June 1912): 785–86.

———. "The Woman Who Kills." *New York Times Book Review* (17 November 1912): 677.

Selincourt, Basil de. "New Novels." *Manchester Guardian* (5 June 1912): 5.

1913

Abercrombie, Lascelles. "The Poet as Novelist." *Manchester Guardian* (2 July 1913): 7.

Alford, John. "Reviews." *Poetry and Drama* 1 (June 1913): 244–47.

Field, Louise Maunsell. "Mother Love: Mr. Lawrence's Remarkable Story of Family Life." *New York Times Book Review* (21 September 1913): 479.

Gibbon, Perceval. "A Novel of Quality." *Bookman* 44 (August 1913): 213.

Massingham, Harold. "A Novel of Note." *Daily Chronicle* (17 June 1913): 3.

Pound, Ezra. "Review of *Love Poems and Others* by DHL." *Poetry* 2 (July 1913): 149–51.

———. "Review of *Love Poems and Others* by DHL." *New Freewoman* (1 September 1913): 113.

Thomas, Edward. "More Georgian Poetry." *Bookman* 44 (April 1913): 47.

1914

Björkman, Edwin. "Introduction." In *The Widowing of Mrs. Holroyd* by DHL. London: Duckworth, 1914, pp. vii–x.

George, W. L. "DHL." *Bookman* 45 (February 1914): 244–46.

James, Henry. *Notes on Novelists.* London: ?, 1914, pp. 252–72 passim.

1915

Carswell, Catherine. [Review of *The Rainbow*.] *Glasgow Herald* (4 November 1915): 4.

Douglas, James. "Books and Bookmen." *Star* (22 October 1915): 4.

Hale, Edward Everett, Jr. "The New Realists." *Independent* 83 (30 August 1915): 297–99.

Lynd, Robert. *Daily News* (5 October 1915): 6.

Shakespear, O. "The Poetry of DHL." *Egoist* (1 May 1915): 81.

Shorter, Clement. "A Literary Letter." *Sphere* 43 (23 October 1915): 104.

Squire, J. C. (under pseudonym Solomon Eagle.) [On the suppression of *The Rainbow*.] *New Statesman* 6 (20 November 1915): 161.

Woodbridge, Homer, E. "Plays of Today and Yesterday." *Dial* 58 (16 January 1915): 46–50.

1916

Garnett, Edward. "Art and the Moralists: Mr. DHL's Work." *Dial* 61 (16 November

1916): 377–81. (Reprinted in his *Friday Nights: First Series.* London: Cape, 1929, pp. 117–28.)

Kuttner, Alfred Booth. "*Sons and Lovers:* A Freudian Appreciation." *Psychoanalytic Review* 3 (July 1916): 295–317. (Reprinted in Tedlock [1965]: 76–100, and Salgādo [1969]: 69–94.)

1917

Tietjens, Eunice. "Review of *Amores* by DHL." *Poetry* 9 (9 February 1917): 264–66.

1918

Bickley, Francis. "Some Tendencies in Contemporary Poetry." In *New Paths.* Edited by C. W. Beaumont and M.T.H. Sadler. London: Beaumont, 1918, pp. 1–6.

Fletcher, John Gould. "A Modern Evangelist." *Poetry* 12 (August 1918): 269–74.

Follett, Helen Thomas, and Wilson Follett. *Some Modern Novelists: Appreciations and Estimates.* New York: Holt, 1918, pp. 353–54.

George, W. L. *A Novelist on Novels.* London: Collins, 1918, pp. 90–101.

1919

Aiken, Conrad. "The Melodic Line." *Dial* 67 (August 1919a): 97–100.

———. *Skepticisms: Notes on Contemporary Poetry.* New York: Knopf, 1919b, pp. 91–104.

Lowell, Amy. "A New English Poet." *New York Times Book Review* (20 April 1919): 205, 210–11, 215, 217.

Phelps, William Lyon. *The Advance of English Poetry in the Twentieth Century.* London: Allen and Unwin; New York: Dodd, Mead, 1919, pp. 145–48.

Waugh, Arthur. "Mr. DHL." In his *Tradition and Change: Studies in Contemporary Literature.* London: Chapman and Hall, 1919, pp. 131–37.

1920

Fletcher, John Gould. "Mr. Lawrence's *New Poems.*" *Freeman* 1 (21 July 1920): 451–52.

Goldring, Douglas. "The Later Work of DHL." In his *Reputations: Essays in Criticism.* London: Chapman and Hall, 1920, pp. 67–78.

Lowell, Amy. "A Voice in Our Wilderness: DHL's Unheeded Message 'to Blind Reactionaries and Fussy, Discontented Agitators.' " *New York Times Book Review,* Section 3 (22 August 1920): 7. (Reprinted in her *Poetry and Poets: Essays.* Boston and New York: Houghton Mifflin, 1930, pp. 175–86.)

Monro, Harold. *Some Contemporary Poets.* London: Leonard Parsons, 1920, pp. 193–97.

1921

Buermyer, L. L. "Lawrence as Psychoanalyst." *New York Evening Post Literary Review* (16 July 1921): 6.

Colum, Mary M. "The Quality of Mr. Lawrence." *Freeman* 3 (22 June 1921): 357–58.

Deutsch, Babette. "Poets and Prefaces." *Dial* 70 (January 1921): 89–94.

Hackett, Francis. "The Unconscious." *New Republic* 27 (17 August 1921): 329–30.

Murry, John Middleton. "The Nostalgia of Mr. DHL." *Nation and Athenaeum* 29 (13 August 1921): 713–14.

Pilley, W. Charles. "A Book the Police Should Ban. Loathsome Study of Sex Depravity—Misleading Youth to Unspeakable Disaster." *John Bull* 30 (17 September 1921): 4. (On *Women in Love.*)

West, Rebecca. "Notes on Novels." *New Statesman* 17 (9 July 1921): 388–90.

1922

Eliot, T. S. "London Letter." *Dial* 73 (September 1922): 329–31.

Johnson, Reginald Brimley. "DHL." In his *Some Contemporary Novelists (Men)*. London: Leonard Parsons, 1922, pp. 121–29.

Macy, John. *The Critical Game*. New York: Boni and Liveright, 1922, pp. 325–35.

1923

Collins, Joseph. "Even Yet It Can't Be Told—The Whole Truth about DHL." In his *The Doctor Looks at Literature: Psychological Studies of Life and Letters*. New York: Doran; London: Allen and Unwin, 1923, pp. 256–288.

Shanks, Edward. "Mr. DHL: Some Characteristics." *London Mercury* 8 (May 1923): 64–75.

1924

Aiken, Conrad. "Disintegration in Modern Poetry." *Dial* 76 (June 1924): 535–40.

Bogan, Louise. "Review of *Birds, Beasts and Flowers*." *New Republic* 39 (9 July 1924).

Canby, Henry Siedel. "A Specialist in Sex." In his *Definitions: Essays in Contemporary Criticism*. Second series. New York: Harcourt, 1924, pp. 113–22.

Gould, Gerald. *The English Novel To-day*. London: John Castle, 1924, pp. 15–16, 19, 23–28.

Lucas, F. L. "Sense and Sensibility." *New Statesman* 22 (8 March 1924): 634–35.

Squire, J. C. "Review of *Birds, Beast and Flowers* by DHL." *London Mercury* 9 (January 1924): 317–18.

Untermayer, Louis. "Strained Intensities." *Bookman* 49 (April 1924): 219–22.

Watson, E. L. Grant. "On Hell and Mr. DHL." *English Review* 38 (March 1924): 386–92.

1925

Muir, Edwin. "Contemporary Writers II: Mr. DHL." *Nation and Athenaeum* 37 (4 July 1925): 425–27.

Rosenfeld, Paul. *Men Seen: Twenty-Four Modern Authors*. New York: Dial Press, 1925, pp. 45–62.

Sherman, Stuart. "DHL Cultivates His Beard." *New York Herald Tribune Books* (14 June 1925): 1–3. Reprinted in his *Critical Woodcuts*. New York and London: Scribner's, 1926, pp. 18–31.

1926

Aldington, Richard. "DHL as Poet." *Saturday Review of Literature* 2 (1 May 1926): 749–50.

Drew, Elizabeth A. *The Modern Novel: Some Aspects of Contemporary Fiction*. New York: Harcourt, Brace; London: Cape, 1926, pp. 37–38, 59–60, 69, 72, 80–82 and passim.

Hervey, Grant Madison. "The Genius of Mr. DHL." *Nation and Athenaeum* 39 (21 August 1926): 581–82.

Muir, Edwin. "DHL." In his *Transition: Essays on Contemporary Literature*. London: Hogarth Press, 1926, pp. 49–63.

Shanks, Edward. "Fiction." *London Mercury* 13 (March 1926): 549–51.

Richards, I. A. *Science and Poetry.* London: Kegan Paul, Trench, Trubner, 1926, pp. 72–83.

1927

Aiken, Conrad. "Mr. Lawrence's Prose." *Dial* 83 (October 1927): 343–46.

Eliot, T. S. "Le roman anglais contemporain." *La Nouvelle Revue Française* 28 (1 May 1927): 669–75.

Forster, E. M. *Aspects of the Novel.* New York: Harcourt, Brace, 1927, pp. 107, 158, 182, 196, 199, 207–9.

Harwood, H. C. "The Post-War Novel." *Outlook* (7 May 1927): 497.

Shanks, Edward. "Mr. DHL." In his *Second Essays on Literature.* Freeport, N.Y.: Books for Libraries Press, 1927, pp. 62–83.

Vines, Sherard. *Movements in Modern English Poetry and Prose.* Oxford: Oxford University Press, 1927, passim.

1928

Hartley, L. P. "New Fiction." *Saturday Review* 145 (2 June 1928): 706, 708.

Manly, John Matthews, and Edith Rickert. *Contemporary British Literature: Outlines for Study, Indexes, Bibliographies.* London: Harrap, 1928, pp. 196–99.

Mortimer, Raymond. "New Novels." *Nation and Athenaeum* 43 (9 June 1928): 332.

Read, Herbert. *English Prose Style.* London: Bell, 1928, pp. 68–70, 157–62.

Roberts, William Herbert. "DHL; Study of a Free Spirit in Literature." *Millgate Monthly* (May 1928). Reprinted, with an introductory note by James T. Boulton, in *Renaissance and Modern Studies* 18 (1974): 7–16.

Suckow, Ruth. "Two Temperaments." *Outlook* (New York) 149 (19 August 1928): 713.

1929

Fletcher, John Gould. "Night-Haunted Lover." *New York Herald Tribune Books* (14 July 1929): 1, 6.

Chance, Roger. "Love and Mr. Lawrence." *Fortnightly Review* 132 (October 1929): 500–511.

Church, Richard. "Three Established Poets." *Spectator* (3 August 1929): 164–65.

Dobrée, Bonamy. "DHL." In his *The Lamp and the Lute: Studies in Six Modern Authors.* Oxford: Clarendon Press, 1929, pp. 86–106.

Richards, I. A. "Poem 8." In his *Practical Criticism.* London: Kegan Paul, Trench, Trubner, 1929, pp. 105–17. (On "Piano.")

Untermayer, Louis. "Hot Blood's Blindfold Art." *Saturday Review of Literature* 6 (3 August 1929): 17–18.

Van Doren, Mark. "Review of *Pansies* by DHL." *New York Herald Tribune Review of Books* (15 December 1929): 15.

West, Rebecca. "A Letter from Abroad: DHL as Painter." *Bookman* (New York) 70 (September 1929): 89–91.

1930

Anderson, Sherwood. "A Man's Mind." *New Republic* 63 (21 May 1930): 22–23.

Fletcher, J. G. "DHL: The Obituary Judgements Re-valued." *Purpose* 2 (April–June 1930).

Forster, E. M. "DHL." *Listener* 3 (30 April 1930): 753–54.

Gwynne, Stephen. "Mr. DHL." *Fortnightly* 127 (April 1930): 553–56.

MacCarthy, Desmond. "Notes on DHL." *Life and Letters* 4 (May 1930): 384–95.

Powell, D. "DHL the Moralist." *Life and Letters* 4 (April 1930): 303–20.

Thomas, J. H. "The Perversity of DHL." *Criterion* 10 (October 1930): 5–22.

Trilling, Lionel. "DHL: A Neglected Aspect." *Symposium* 1 (July 1930): 361–70.

1931

Crossman, R.H.S. "DHL: The New Irrationalism." *Farrago* 5 (February 1931): 67–78.

Hughes, Glenn. "DHL: The Passionate Psychologist." In his *Imagism and the Imagists: A Study in Modern Poetry.* Stanford, Calif.: Stanford University Press; London: Oxford University Press, 1931, pp. 167–96.

Huxley, Aldous. "To the Puritan All Things Are Impure." In his *Music at Night and Other Essays.* London: Chatto and Windus, 1931, pp. 173–83.

Kohler, Dayton. "DHL." *Sewanee Review* 39 (January–March 1931): 25–38.

Salmon, H. L. "Lawrence and a 'Sense of the Whole.' " *New Adelphi* 2 (June 1931): 241–44.

Thompson, Alan R. "DHL: Apostle of the Dark God." *Bookman* 73 (July 1931): 492–99.

1932

Beach, Joseph Warren. "Impressionism: Lawrence." In his *The Twentieth Century Novel: Studies in Technique.* New York: Appleton-Century, 1932, pp. 366–84.

Collins, N. "The Case against DHL." In his *The Facts of Fiction.* London: Gollancz, 1932, pp. 237–48.

Connolly, Cyril. "Under Which King." *Living Age* 341 (February 1932): 533–38.

Lovett, Robert Morss, and Helen Sard Hughes. *The History of the Novel in England.* Boston: Houghton Mifflin, 1932, pp. 421–27.

Soames, Jane. "The Modern Rousseau." *Life and Letters* 8 (December 1932): 451–70.

Strachey, John. *The Coming Struggle for Power.* London: Gollancz, 1932, pp. 206–16.

1933

Anderson, Sherwood. "A Man's Song of Life." *Virginia Quarterly* 9 (January 1933): 108–14.

Chesterton, G. K. "The End of the Moderns." *London Mercury* 27 (January 1933): 228–33.

Collins, Norman. "The Case against DHL." In his *Facts in Fiction.* New York: Dutton, 1933, pp. 237–48.

Cunliffe, J. W. *English Literature in the Twentieth Century.* New York: Macmillan, 1933, 209–28.

Kunitz, Stanley J., ed. *Authors Today and Yesterday.* New York: H. W. Wilson, 1933, pp. 388–93.

Mégroz, Rodolphe Louis. "DHL." In *Post Victorians.* Edited by William Ralph Inge. London: Nicholson and Watson, 1933a, pp. 317–28.

———. *Five Novelist Poets of Today.* London: Joiner and Steele, 1933b, pp. 189–235.

Rascoe, Burton. *Prometheans: Ancient and Modern.* New York: Putnam's, 1933, pp. 221–38.

Wellek, René. "DHL." *English Post* (Prague) 1 (October 1933): 109–11.

1934

Brown, Ivor. *I Commit to the Flames.* London: Hamish Hamilton, 1934, passim (but especially pp. 78–94, "Brother Lawrence," and 95–109, "Belly and Brain").

Eliot, T. S. *After Strange Gods: A Primer of Modern Heresy.* London: Faber and Faber; New York: Harcourt, Brace, 1934, pp. 38–43, 62–67.

Lavrin, Janko. "Sex and Eros (on Rozanov, Weininger, and DHL)." *European Quarterly* 1 (1934): 88–96.

Powell, Dilys. *Descent from Parnassus.* London: Cresset Press, 1934, pp. 1–54.

Witcutt, W. P. "The Cult of DHL." *American Review* 3 (May 1934): 161–66.

1935

Collis, J. S. "An Inevitable Prophet." In his *Farewell to Argument.* London: Cassell, 1935, pp. 156–95.

Maurois, André. *Prophets and Poets.* Translated by Hamish Miles. New York: Harper, 1935, pp. 245–83.

Orage, A. R. "Twilight in Mr. DHL." In his *Selected Essays and Critical Writings.* Edited by Herbert Read and Denis Saurat. London: Allen and Unwin, 1935, pp. 65–67.

1936

Arvin, Newton. "DHL and Fascism." *New Republic* 89 (16 December 1936): 219.

Garnett, Edward. "DHL: His Posthumous Papers." *London Mercury* 35 (December 1936): 152–60.

Gurling, F. E. "DHL's Apology for the Artist." *London Mercury* 33 (April 1936): 596–603.

Henderson, P. "The Primitivism of DHL." In his *The Novel Today.* London: John Lane, 1936, pp. 60–73.

Huxley, Aldous. "DHL." In his *The Olive Tree and Other Essays.* London: Chatto and Windus, 1936, pp. 199–238.

Maurois, André. "DHL." In his *Poets and Prophets.* London: Cassell, 1936, pp. 173–201.

Quennell, Peter. "DHL and Aldous Huxley." In *The English Novelists.* Edited by D. Verschoyle. London: Chatto and Windus, 1936, pp. 247–57.

1937

Muller, Herbert J. *Modern Fiction: A Study of Values.* New York: Funk and Wagnalls, 1937, pp. 262–87.

Roberts, John H. "Huxley and Lawrence." *Virginia Quarterly Review* 13 (1937): 546–57.

Wells, Harry K. "DHL and Fascism." *New Republic* 91 (16 June 1937): 161.

Wildi, Max. "The Birth of Expressionism in the Work of DHL." *English Studies* 19 (December 1937): 241–59.

1938

Caudwell, Christopher. "DHL: A Study of the Bourgeois Artist." In his *Studies in a Dying Culture.* London: Lane, 1938, pp. 44–72. (Reprinted in his *The Concept of Freedom.* London: Lawrence and Wishart, 1965, pp. 11–30.)

Clements, Richard. "The Genius of DHL." *Central Literary Magazine* (Bucks., England) (July 1938): 272–78.

Collin, W. E. "Active Principle in the Thought of DHL." *Canadian Bookman* 20 (December 1938): 17–21.

Hoare, Dorothy. "The Novels of DHL." In her *Some Studies in the Modern Novel.* London: Chatto and Windus, 1938, pp. 97–112.

1939

Aldington, Richard. "DHL: Ten Years After." *Saturday Review of Literature* 20 (June 1939): 3–4, 14, 24.

Anderson, G. K., and Eda Lou Walton. *This Generation.* Chicago: Scott, Foresman, 1939, pp. 536–60.

Ellis, G. U. *Twilight on Parnassus.* London: Joseph, 1939, pp. 287–329.

Fraenkel, M. "The Otherness of DHL." In his *Death Is Not Enough.* London: Daniel, 1939, pp. 73–108.

Williams, C.W.S. " 'Sensuality and Substance': A Study of DHL." *Theology* 38 (1939). (Reprinted in his *The Image of the City and Other Essays.* Oxford: Oxford University Press, 1958, pp. 68–75.)

1940

Cockshut, A.O.J. *Man and Woman: A Study of Love and the Novel, 1740–1940.* New York: Oxford University Press, 1978, pp. 152–60.

Gimblett, Charles. "Protest of a Tormented Genius." *London Quarterly and Holborn Review* 165 (January 1940): 79–81.

Lawrence, Frieda. "The Small View of Lawrence." *Virginia Quarterly Review* 16 (Winter 1940): 127–29.

Nulle, S. H. "DHL and the Fascist Movement." *New Mexico Quarterly* 10 (February 1940): 3–15.

Southworth, James G. "DHL: Poet; 'A Note on High Political Ideology.' " In his *Sowing the Spring: Studies in British Poetry from Hopkins to MacNeice.* Oxford: Basil Blackwell, 1940, pp. 64–75.

Wood, Frank. "Rilke and DHL." *Germanic Review* 15 (1940): 214–23.

1941

Bates, H. E. "Lawrence and the Writers of Today." In his *The Modern Short Story: A Critical Survey.* London and New York: Nelson, 1941, pp. 194–213.

Bentley, Eric R. "DHL, John Thomas and Dionysos." *New Mexico Quarterly Review* 12 (1941): 133–43.

Miller, Henry. *The Wisdom of the Heart.* Norfolk: New Directions, 1941, pp. 1–12, 159–72.

Spender, Stephen. "Books and the War: IX. DHL Reconsidered." *Penguin New Writing* 10 (1941): 120–33.

Vivas, Eliseo. "Lawrence's Problems." *Kenyon Review* 3 (Winter 1941): 83–94.

1942

Freeman, Mary. "DHL in Valhalla." *New Mexico Quarterly* 10 (November 1942): 211–24.

Plowman, M. "The Significance of DHL." In his *The Right to Live: Essays.* London: Andrew Dakers, 1942, pp. 122–30.

1943

Church, R. *British Authors.* London: Longmans, 1943, pp. 101–4.

Kenmare, Dallas. "Voice in the Wilderness: The Unacknowledged Lawrence." *Poetry Review* (May–June 1943): 145–48.

Nicholson, Norman. *Man and Literature.* London: S.C.M. Press, 1943, pp. 64–86.

Wagenknecht, E. C. "DHL: Pilgrim of the Rainbow." In his *Cavalcade of the English Novel.* New York: Henry Holt, 1943, pp. 494–504.

1944

Bentley, Eric R. "Heroic Vitalists of the Twentieth Century." In His *A Century of Hero-Worship.* Philadelphia: Lippincott, 1944, pp. 205–53.

Coates, T. B. *Ten Modern Prophets.* London: Muller, 1944, pp. 91–99.

Hoffman, Frederick J. "Lawrence's 'Quarrel' with Freud." *Quarterly Review of Literature* 1 (1944): 279–87.

Murry, John Middleton. "On the Significance of DHL." In his *Adam and Eve: An Essay toward a New and Better Society.* London: Andrew Dakers, 1944, pp. 88–101, and passim.

1945

Miller, Henry. "Shadowy Monomania." *New Road* (1945): 113–45.

Savage, D. S. "DHL as Poet." *Briarcliff Quarterly* 2 (July 1945): 86–95.

Slochower, Harry. *No Voice Is Wholly Lost.* New York: Creative Age Press, 1945, pp. 136–43.

1946

Every, George. "DHL." In *The New Spirit.* Edited by E. Martin. London: Dennis Dobson, 1946, pp. 58–65.

Hamill, Elizabeth. *These Modern Writers.* Melbourne: Georgian House, 1946, pp. 86–99.

Mesnil, Jacques. "A Prophet: DHL." Translated by Frieda Lawrence. *Southwest Review* 31 (Summer 1946): 257–59.

Pritchett, V. S. *The Living Novel.* London: Chatto and Windus, 1946, pp. 131–38.

Routh, H. V. *English Literature and Ideas in the Twentieth Century.* London: Methuen, 1946, pp. 153–60.

Trilling, D. "Lawrence: Creator and Dissenter." *Saturday Review of Literature* 29 (7 December 1946): 17–18, 82–84.

1947

Allen, Walter. "Lawrence in Perspective." *Penguin New Writing* 29 (Autumn 1946): 104–15.

Auden, W. H. "Some Notes on DHL." *Nation* 164 (26 April 1947): 482–84.

Bartlett, N. "The Failure of DHL." *Australian Quarterly* 19 (December 1947): 87–102.

Byngham, Dion. "DHL." In *Modern British Writing.* Edited by Denys Val Baker. New York: Vanguard, 1947, pp. 326–31.

Ghiselin, B. "DHL and a New World." *Western Review* 9 (Spring 1947): 150–59.

1948

Evans, B. I. *English Literature between the Wars.* London: Methuen, 1948, pp. 49–57.

Glicksberg, Charles I. "DHL the Prophet of Surrealism." *Nineteenth Century* 143 (April
      1948): 229–37.
Hoffman, Frederick J. "From Surrealism to 'The Apocalypse': A Development in Twen-
      tieth Century Irrationalism." *English Literary History* 15 (June 1948): 147–65.
Jones, W.S.H. "DHL and the Revolt against Reason." *London Quarterly and Holborn
      Review* 173 (January 1948): 25–31.
Schorer, Mark. "Technique as Discovery." *Hudson Review* 1 (Spring 1948): 67–87.

1949

Gaunt, W. *The March of the Moderns.* London: Cape, 1949, pp. 179–86, 189–91.
Leavis, F. R. "DHL Placed." *Scrutiny* 16 (March 1949): 44–47.

1950

Bowen, Elizabeth. *Collected Impressions.* London: Longmans, 1950, 156–59.
Howe, Irving. "Sherwood Anderson and DHL." *Furioso* 5 (Fall 1950): 21–33.
Read, Herbert. "An Irregular Genius: The Significance of DHL." *World Review,* new
      series, 17 (July 1950): 50–56. (Partly a review of Aldington's biography [1950].)

1951

Auden, W. H. "Heretics." In *Literary Opinion in America.* Edited by M. D. Zabel. New
      York: Harpers, 1951, pp. 256–59.
Danby, J. F. "DHL." *Cambridge Journal* 4 (February 1951): 273–89.
Glicksberg, Charles I. "DHL and Science." *Scientific Monthly* 73 (August 1951): 99–
      104.
Greene, T. "Lawrence and the Quixotic Hero." *Sewanee Review* 59 (Fall 1951): 559–
      73.
Leavis, F. R. "Mr. Eliot and Lawrence." *Scrutiny* 18 (1951): 66–72.
Neill, S. D. *A Short History of the English Novel.* London: Jarrolds, 1951, pp. 313–25.
Scott-James, R. A. "Interior Vision: DHL." In his *Fifty Years of English Literature,
      1900–1951.* London: Longmans, Green, 1951, pp. 124–31.

1952

Bantock, G. H. "DHL and the Nature of Freedom." In his *Freedom and Authority in
      Education.* London: Faber and Faber, 1952, pp. 133–81.
Ellmann, Richard. "Lawrence and His Demon." *New Mexico Quarterly* 22 (Winter
      1952): 385–93. (Reprinted, as "Barbed Wire and Coming Through," in Hoffman
      and Moore [1953]: 253–67; and in his *along the riverrun: Selected Essays.* New
      York: Knopf, 1989.)
Schorer, Mark. "Fiction with a Great Burden." *Kenyon Review* 14 (Winter 1952): 162–
      68.
Scott, Nathan A. "DHL: Chartist of the Via Mystica." In his *Rehearsals of Discompo-
      sure: Alienation and Reconciliation in Modern Literature.* London: John Leh-
      mann, 1952, pp. 112–77.

1953

Dataller, Roger. "Elements of DHL's Prose Style." *Essays in Criticism* 3 (October
      1953): 413–24.
Jones, W.S.H. "DHL and the Revolt against Reason." In his *The Priest and the Siren.*
      London: Epworth Press, 1953, pp. 114–26.

Kettle, Arnold. *An Introduction to the English Novel.* Vol. 2. London: Hutchinson's University Library, 1953, pp. 100–120.

Miller, Milton. "Definition by Comparison: Chaucer, Lawrence, Joyce." *Essays in Criticism* 3 (October 1953): 369–81.

Spender, Stephen. "Pioneering the Instinctive Life." In his *The Creative Element: A Study of Vision, Despair and Orthodoxy among Some Modern Writers.* London: Hamish Hamilton, 1953, pp. 92–107.

1954

Adix, M. "Phoenix at Walden: Lawrence Calls on Thoreau." *Western Humanities Review* 8 (Fall 1954): 287–98.

Hough, Graham. "DHL and the Novel." *Adelphi* 30, no. 4 (1954): 365–82.

Leavis, F. R. "Lawrence and Class." *Sewanee Review* 62 (Fall 1954): 535–62.

Melchiori, Giorgio. "The Lotus and the Rose: DHL and Eliot's *Four Quartets.*" *English Miscellany* 5 (1954): 203–16.

1955

Heppenstall, Rayner. "Outsiders and Others." *Twentieth Century* 158 (November 1955): 453–59.

Kazin, Alfred. "The Painfulness of DHL." In his *The Inmost Leaf.* New York: Harcourt, 1955, pp. 98–102.

Littlewood, J.C.F. "Lawrence, Last of the English." *Theoria* 7 (1955): 79–92.

Maud, Ralph N. "DHL: True Emotion as the Ethical Control in Art." *Western Humanities Review* 9 (1955): 233–40.

Vivante, Leone. "Reflections on DHL's Insight into the Concept of Potentiality." In his *A Philosophy of Potentiality.* London: Routledge and Kegan Paul, 1955, pp. 79–115.

1956

Murry, John Middleton. "The Living Dead I: DHL." *London Magazine* 3 (May 1956): 57–63.

Price, A. Whigham. "DHL and Congregationalism." *Congregational Quarterly* 34 (July and October 1956): 242–52; 322–30.

Stavrou, Constantine W. "DHL's 'Psychology' of Sex." *Literature and Psychology* 6 (1956): 90–95.

Woodcock, George. "Mexico and the English Novelist." *Western Review* 21 (Autumn 1956): 21–32. (Lawrence, Huxley, and Greene.)

1957

Burke, Kenneth. "In Qualified Defense of Lawrence." In his *Permanence and Change: An Anatomy of Purpose.* 2d ed. Los Altos, Calif.: Hermes, 1957, pp. 250–54.

Coveney, Peter. "DHL." In his *Poor Monkey: The Child in Literature.* London: Rockliff, 1957. (Revised as *The Image of Childhood: The Individual and Society: A Study of the Theme in English Literature.* Harmondsworth: Penguin, 1967, pp. 320–36.)

McCormick, John. *Catastrophe and Imagination: An Interpretation of the Recent English and American Novel.* London and New York: Longman, Green, 1957, passim.

Pinto, Vivian de Sola. "DHL, Letter-Writer and Craftsman in Verse: Some Hitherto Unpublished Material." *Renaissance and Modern Studies* 1 (1957): 5–34.

1958

Dataller, Roger. "Mr. Lawrence and Mrs. Woolf." *Essays in Criticism* 8 (January 1958): 48–59.

Draper, R. P. "DHL on Mother-Love." *Essays in Criticism* 8 (July 1958): 285–89.

Engel, Monroe. "The Continuity of Lawrence's Short Novels." *Hudson Review* 11 (Summer 1958): 201–9.

1959

Bramley, J. A. "The Significance of DHL." *Contemporary Review* 195 (May 1959): 304–7.

Karl, Frederick R., and Marvin Magalaner. *A Reader's Guide to Great Twentieth-Century English Novels.* New York: Noonday; London: Thames and Hudson: 1959, pp. 150–204.

Magalaner, Marvin. "DHL Today." *Commonweal* 70 (12 June 1959): 275–76.

Sale, Roger. "The Narrative Technique of *The Rainbow.*" *Modern Fiction Studies* 5 (1959): 29–38.

Walsh, William. *The Use of the Imagination: Educational Thought and the Literary Mind.* London: Chatto and Windus, 1959. "The Writer and the Child," pp. 163–74 (on Ursula and *The Rainbow*); "The Writer as Teacher: The Educational Ideas of DHL," 199–228.

Widmer, Kingsley. "The Primitivistic Aesthetic: DHL." *Journal of Aesthetics and Art Criticism* 17 (March 1959): 344–53.

1960

Bramley, J. A. "The Challenge of DHL." *Hibbert Journal* 52 (April 1960): 281–87.

Garlington, Jack. "Lawrence—With Misgivings." *South Atlantic Quarterly* 59 (Summer 1960): 404–8.

Goodheart, Eugene. "Freud and Lawrence." *Psychoanalysis and Psychoanalytical Review* 47 (1960): 56–64.

Rieff, Philip. "Introduction." In *Psychoanalysis and the Unconscious* and *Fantasia of the Unconscious* by DHL. New York: Viking, 1960, pp. vii–xxiii.

1961

Baldanza, Frank. "DHL's 'Song of Songs.' " *Modern Fiction Studies* 7 (Summer 1961): 106–14.

Foster, D. W. "Lawrence, Sex and Religion." *Theology* 64 (January 1961): 8–13.

Knight, G. Wilson. "Lawrence, Joyce and Powys." *Essays in Criticism* 11 (1961): 403–17.

Peerman, D. "DHL: Devout Heretic." *Christian Century* 78 (22 February 1961): 237–41.

Turnell, M. "The Shaping of Contemporary Literature: Lawrence, Forster, Virginia Woolf." In his *Modern Literature and Christian Faith.* London: Darton, Longman, and Todd; Westminster, Md.: Newman Press, 1961, pp. 25–45.

1962

Alvarez, A. "The New Poetry or beyond the Gentility Principle." In *The New Poetry.* Edited by A. Alvarez. Harmondsworth: Penguin, 1962, pp. 21–32.

Myers, Neil. "Lawrence and the War." *Criticism* 4 (Winter 1962): 44–58.

Newman, Paul B. "DHL and *The Golden Bough.*" *Kansas Magazine* (1962): 79–86.

Sparrow, John. "Regina v. Penguin Books Ltd: An Undisclosed Element in the Case." *Encounter* 18 (February 1962): 35–43.

1963

Bodkin, Maud. *Archetypal Patterns in Poetry: Psychological Studies of Imagination.* London: Oxford University Press, 1963, pp. 289–99.

Draper, R. P. "Great Writers 4: DHL." *Time and Tide* 44 (24–30 January 1963): 23–24.

Engleberg, Edward. "Escape from the Circles of Experience: DHL's *The Rainbow* as a Modern Bildungsroman." *PMLA* 78 (March 1963): 103–13.

Hartt, Julian N. *The Lost Image of Man.* Baton Rouge: Louisiana State University Press, 1963, pp. 55–60.

Moore, Harry T. "Lawrence from All Sides." *Kenyon Review* 25 (Summer 1963): 555–58.

O'Connor, Frank. *The Lonely Voice: A Study of the Short Story.* Cleveland: World, 1963, pp. 147–55.

Spender, Stephen. *The Struggle of the Modern.* London: Hamilton; Berkeley: University of California Press, 1963, pp. 100–109 and passim.

1964

Guttmann, Allen. "DHL: The Politics of Irrationality." *Wisconsin Studies in Contemporary Literature* 5 (Summer 1964): 151–63.

Hardy, Barbara. *The Appropriate Form: An Essay on the Novel.* London: Athlone Press, 1964, pp. 132–73.

Kessler, Jascha. "DHL's Primitivism." *Texas Studies in Literature and Language* 5 (1964): 467–88.

Lindsay, Jack. "The Impact of Modernism on Lawrence." In *The Paintings of DHL.* Edited by Mervyn Levy. London: Cory, Adams, and McKay; New York: Viking, 1964, pp. 35–53.

Way, B. "Sex and Language: Obscene Words in DHL and Henry Miller." *New Left Review,* no. 27 (September–October 1964): 164–70.

Wilde, Alan. "The Illusion of *St. Mawr:* Technique and Vision in DHL's Novel." *PMLA* 79 (March 1964): 164–70.

1965

Gray, Ronald. "English Resistance to German Literature from Coleridge to DHL." In his *The German Tradition in Literature 1871–1945.* Cambridge: Cambridge University Press, 1965, pp. 327–54. (Mainly on *Women in Love.*)

Hildick, Wallace. *Word for Word: A Study of Author's Alterations.* New York: Norton, 1965, pp. 58–69.

Jordan, Sidney. "DHL's Concept of the Unconscious and Existential Thinking." *Review of Existential Psychology and Psychiatry* 5 (1965): 34–43.

Mayhall, Jane. "DHL: The Triumph of Texture." *Western Humanities Review* 19 (Spring 1965): 161–74.

Sale, Roger. "DHL, 1912–1916." *Massachusetts Review* 6 (Spring 1965): 467–80.

1966

Blissett, William. "DHL, D'Annunzio, Wagner." *Wisconsin Studies in Contemporary Literature* 7 (Winter–Spring 1966): 21–46.

Draper, R. P. "Satire as a Form of Sympathy: DHL as a Satirist." In *Renaissance and Modern Essays Presented to Vivian de Sola Pinto in Celebration of His Seventieth*

Birthday. Edited by G. R. Hibbard. London: Routledge and Kegan Paul, 1966, pp. 189–97.

Friedman, Alan. "DHL: 'The Wave Which Cannot Halt.' " In his *The Turn of the Novel.* New York: Oxford University Press, 1966, pp. 130–78.

Gordon, D. J. "Two Anti-Puritan Puritans: Bernard Shaw and DHL." *Yale Review* 56 (Autumn 1966): 76–90.

Kaplan, Harold J. *The Passive Voice: An Approach to Modern Fiction.* Athens: Ohio University Press, 1966, pp. 159–85.

Panichas, G. "E. M. Forster and DHL: Their Views on Education." In *Renaissance and Modern Essays Presented to Vivian de Sola Pinto in Celebration of His Seventieth Birthday.* Edited by G. R. Hibbard. London: Routledge; New York: Barnes and Noble, 1966, pp. 193–213.

1967

Cowan, James C. "Lawrence's Romantic Values: *Studies in Classic American Literature.*" *Ball State University Forum* 8 (Winter 1967): 30–35.

Craig, David. "Fiction and the Rising Industrial Classes." *Essays in Criticism* 17 (January 1967): 64–74.

Jacobson, P. "DHL and Modern Society." *Journal of Contemporary History* 2 (April 1967): 81–92.

Lee, R. H. "A True Relatedness: Lawrence's View of Morality." *English Studies in Africa* 10 (September 1967): 178–85.

Pinto, Vivian de Sola. "The Burning Bush: DHL as Religious Poet." In *Mansions of the Spirit: Essays in Literature and Religion.* Edited by George A. Panichas. New York: Hawthorne, 1967, pp. 213–35.

Remsbury, John. " 'Real Thinking': Lawrence and Cézanne." *Cambridge Quarterly* 2 (Spring 1967): 117–47.

Roy, Chitra. "DHL and E. M. Forster: A Study in Values." *Indian Journal of English Studies* 8 (March 1967): 46–58.

Spender, Stephen. "Writers and Politics." *Partisan Review* 34 (Summer 1967): 359–81.

Zytaruk, G. "The Phallic Vision: DHL and V. V. Rozanov." *Comparative Literature Studies* 4 (1967): 283–97.

1968

Benstock, Bernard. "Personalities and Politics: A View of the Literary Right." *DHL Review* 1 (Summer 1968): 149–69.

Elsbree, Langdon. "DHL, Homo Ludens, and the Dance." *DHL Review* 1 (Spring 1968): 1–30.

Hinz, Evelyn J. "DHL's Clothes Metaphor." *DHL Review* 1 (Summer 1968): 87–113.

Klein, Robert C. "I, Thou and You in Three Lawrencian Relationships." *Paunch,* no. 31 (April 1968): 52–70.

1969

Barry, J. "Oswald Spengler and DHL." *English Studies in Africa* 12, no. 2 (1969): 151–61.

Cowan, James C. "DHL's Quarrel with Christianity." *University of Tulsa Department of English Monographs,* no. 7: *Literature and Theology.* (1969): 32–43.

Daniel, John. "DHL—His Reputation Today." *London Review* 6 (Winter 1969/70): 25–33.

Garrett, Peter K. *Scene and Symbol from George Eliot to James Joyce.* New Haven, Conn.: Yale University Press, 1969, pp. 181–213.

Henig, Suzanne. "DHL and Virginia Woolf." *DHL Review* 2 (Fall 1969): 265–71.

Pinto, Vivian de Sola. "William Blake and DHL." In *William Blake: Essays for S. Foster Damon.* Edited by Alvin H. Rosenfeld. Providence, R.I.: Brown University Press, 1969, pp. 84–106.

Zytaruk, George J. "DHL's Reading of Russian Literature." *DHL Review* 2 (Summer 1969): 120–37.

1970

Alter, Richard. "Eliot, Lawrence, and the Jews." *Commentary* 50 (October 1970): 81–86.

Chapman, R. T. "Lawrence, Lewis and the Comedy of Literary Reputations." *Studies in the Twentieth Century,* no. 6 (Fall 1970): 85–95.

Chapple, J.A.V. *Documentary and Imaginative Literature 1880–1920.* London: Blandford Press, 1970, pp. 72–79 and passim.

Eagleton, Terry. *Exiles and Emigrés: Studies in Modern Literature.* London: Chatto and Windus; New York: Schocken, 1970, pp. 191–218.

Maes-Jelinek, Hena. *Criticism of Society in the English Novel between the Wars.* Paris: Société d'Editions "Les Belles Lettres," 1970, pp. 11–100. (Impact of World War I and subsequent events on Lawrence.)

Rahv, P. *Literature and the Sixth Sense.* London: Faber and Faber, 1970, pp. 93–94, 289–306, 437–45.

Richardson, John Adkins, and John I. Ades. "DHL on Cézanne: A Study in the Psychology of Critical Intuition." *Journal of Aesthetics and Art Criticism* 28 (Summer 1970): 441–53.

1971

Fairbanks, N. David. "Strength through Joy in the Novels of DHL." *Literature and Ideology,* no. 8 (1971): 67–78.

Phillips, Gene D. "Sexual Ideas in the Films of DHL." *Sexual Behavior* 1 (June 1971): 10–16.

Remsbury, Ann, and John Remsbury. "DHL and Art." *Revista da Faculdade de Letras* (University of Lisbon), série 3, no. 12 (1971): 5–33. (Reprinted in Gomme [1978]: 190–218.)

Rudrum, Alan. "Philosophical Implications in Lawrence's *Women in Love.*" *Dalhousie Review* 52 (1971): 240–50.

Spilka, Mark. "Lawrence Up-Tight, or the Anal Phase Once Over." *Novel: A Forum on Fiction* 4 (Spring 1971): 252–67.

———, with Colin Clarke, George Ford, and Frank Kermode. "Critical Exchange: On 'Lawrence Up-Tight': Four Tail-Pieces." *Novel: A Forum on Fiction* 5 (Fall 1971): 54–70.

1972

Cox, C. B., and A. E. Dyson. *The Twentieth-Century Mind: History, Ideas and Literature in Britain.* Vol. 1: 1900–18. London: Oxford University Press, 1972, pp. 435–40.

Harper, Howard M., Jr. "*Fantasia* and the Psychodynamics of *Women in Love.*" In *The Classic British Novel.* Edited by Howard Harper, Jr., and Charles Edge. Athens: University of Georgia Press, 1972, pp. 202–19.

Hinz, Evelyn J. "The Beginning and the End: DHL's *Psychoanalysis* and *Fantasia.*" *Dalhousie Review* 52 (1972): 251–65.

Laurenson, Diana, and Alan Swingewood. *The Sociology of Literature.* London: MacGibbon and Kee, 1972, pp. 83–88 and passim.

Lee, R. "The 'Strange Reality of Otherness': DHL's Social Attitudes." *Standpunte* 25 (June 1972): 3–10.

1973

Carey, John. "DHL's Doctrine." In *DHL: Novelist, Poet, Prophet.* Edited by Stephen Spender. London: Weidenfeld and Nicolson, 1973, pp. 122–34.

Craig, David. *The Real Foundations: Literature and Social Change.* London: Chatto and Windus, 1973; New York: Oxford University Press, 1974. ("Shakespeare, Lawrence and Sexual Freedom," pp. 17–38; "Lawrence and Democracy," pp. 143–67.)

Eagleton, Terry. "Lawrence." In *The Prose for God.* Edited by Ian Gregor and Walter Stein. London: Sheed and Ward, 1973, pp. 86–100.

Roberts, Mark. "DHL and the Failure of Energy: *Fantasia of the Unconscious; Psychoanalysis and the Unconscious.*" In his *The Tradition of Romantic Morality.* London: Macmillan, 1973, pp. 322–48.

1974

Buckley, Jerome H. *Season of Youth: The Bildungsroman from Dickens to Golding.* Cambridge: Harvard University Press, 1974, pp. 204–24.

Green, Eleanor H. "Blueprints for Utopia: The Political Ideas of Nietzsche and DHL." *Renaissance and Modern Studies* 18 (1974): 141–61.

Harris, Janice H. "DHL and Kate Millett." *Massachusetts Review* 15 (1974): 522–29.

Humma, John B. "DHL as Friedrich Nietzsche." *Philological Quarterly* 53 (1974a): 110–20.

———. "Melville's *Billy Budd* and Lawrence's 'The Prussian Officer': Old Adams and New." *Essays in Literature* (Western Illinois University) 1 (1974b): 83–88.

Kleinbard, David J. "DHL and Ontological Insecurity." *PMLA* 89 (January 1974): 154–63.

Winegarten, Renée. *Writers and Revolution: The Fatal Lure of Action.* New York: New Viewpoints, 1974, pp. 247–60.

1975

Bersani, Leo. "Lawrentian Stillness." *Yale Review* 65 (October 1975): 38–60. (Also in his *A Future for Astyanax: Character and Desire in Literature.* Boston and Toronto: Little, Brown, 1976, pp. 156–85.)

Blanchard, Lydia. "Love and Power: A Reconsideration of Sexual Politics in DHL." *Modern Fiction Studies* 21 (1975): 431–43.

Cowan, James C. "DHL's Dualism: The Apollonian-Dionysian Polarity and *The Ladybird.*" In *Forms of Modern Fiction.* Edited by A. W. Friedman. Austin and London: University of Texas Press, 1975, pp. 75–99.

Meyers, Jeffrey. *Painting and the Novel.* Manchester: Manchester University Press; New York: Barnes and Noble, 1975, pp. 46–82.

Ragussis, Michael. "The False Myth of *St. Mawr:* Lawrence and the Subterfuge of Art." *Papers on Language and Literature* 11 (Spring 1975): 186–96.

Rossman, Charles. " 'You Are the Call and I Am the Answer': DHL and Women." *DHL Review* 8 (Fall 1975): 255–328.

Worthen, John. "Sanity, Madness and *Women in Love.*" *Trivium* 10 (1975): 125–36.

1976

Bayley, John. *The Uses of Division: Unity and Disharmony in Literature.* New York: Viking, 1976, pp. 25–50.

Eagleton, Terry. *Criticism and Ideology: A Study in Marxist Literary Theory.* London: New Left Books, 1976, pp. 157–61.

Jennings, Elizabeth. "DHL: A Vision of the Natural World." *Seven Men of Vision: An Appreciation.* London: Vision Press, 1976, pp. 45–80.

Ross, C. L. "The Revision of the Second Generation in *The Rainbow.*" *Review of English Studies* 27 (1976): 277–95.

Stewart, Garrett. "Lawrence, 'Being,' and the Allotropic Style." *Novel* 9 (Spring 1976): 217–42. (Reprinted in *Towards a Poetics of Fiction: Essays from "Novel: A Forum on Fiction" 1967–76.* Edited by Mark Spilka. Bloomington: Indiana University Press, 1977, pp. 331–56.)

1977

Deleuze, Gilles, and Félix Guattari. *Anti-Oedipus: Capitalism and Schizophrenia.* Translated by Robert Hurley, Mark Seem, and Helen R. Lane. New York: Viking, 1977, passim. (Originally published in French as *L'Anti-Oedipe.* Paris: Les Editions de Minuit, 1972. Reprinted: Minneapolis: Minnesota University Press, 1983; London: Athlone Press, 1984.)

Goonetilleke, D.C.R.A. "DHL: Primitivism?" In his *Developing Countries in British Fiction.* Totowa, N.J.: Rowman and Littlefield, 1977, pp. 170–98.

Langbaum, Robert. "Reconstitution of Self: Lawrence and the Religion of Love." In his *Mysteries of Identity: A Theme in Modern Literature.* New York: Oxford University Press, 1977, pp. 251–353.

Lodge, David. "DHL." In his *The Modes of Modern Writing: Metaphor, Metonymy, and the Typology of Modern Literature.* London: Edward Arnold, 1977, pp. 160–76.

Meyers, Jeffrey. *Homosexuality and Literature: 1890–1930.* London: Athlone, 1977, pp. 131–61.

Mudrick, Marvin. *The Man in the Machine.* New York: Horizon Press, 1977, pp. 37–60 and passim.

Pritchard, William H. "DHL: 1920–1930." In his *Seeing through Everything: English Writers 1918–1940.* London: Faber and Faber, 1977, pp. 70–89.

Ross, C. L. "DHL's Use of Greek Tragedy: Euripedes and Ritual." *DHL Review* 10 (Spring 1977): 1–19.

1978

MacDonald, Robert H. " 'The Two Principles': A Theory of the Sexual and Psychological Symbolism of DHL's Later Fiction." *DHL Review* 11 (Summer 1978): 132–55.

Ragussis, Michael. "DHL: The New Vocabulary of *Women in Love:* Speech and Art Speech." In his *The Subterfuge of Art: Language and the Romantic Tradition.* Baltimore and London: Johns Hopkins University Press, 1978, pp. 172–225.

Robinson, Ian. "DHL and English Prose." In *DHL: A Critical Study of the Major Novels and Other Writings.* Edited by A. H. Gomme. Sussex: Harvester Press; New York: Barnes and Noble, 1978, pp. 13–29.

Walker, Ronald. *Infernal Paradise: Mexico and the Modern English Novel.* Berkeley, Los Angeles, and London: University of California Press, 1978, pp. 28–104.

Zoll, Allan R. "Vitalism and the Metaphysics of Love: DHL and Schopenhauer." *DHL Review* 11 (Spring 1978): 1–20.

1979

Eagleton, Mary, and David Pierce. "Pressure Points: Forster, Lawrence, Joyce, Woolf." In their *Attitudes to Class in the English Novel from Walter Scott to David Storey.* London: Thames and Hudson, 1979, pp. 93–129.

Goodman, Charlotte. "Henry James, DHL and the Victimised Child." *Modern Language Studies* 10 (1979–80): 43–51.

Hinz, Evelyn J. *"Ancient Art and Ritual* and *The Rainbow."* *Dalhousie Review* 58 (1979): 617–37.

Mace, Hebe R. "The Achievement of Poetic Form: DHL's *Last Poems."* *DHL Review* 12 (Fall 1979): 275–88.

Spanier, Sandra Whipple. "Two Foursomes in *The Blithedale Romance* and *Women in Love."* *Comparative Literature Studies* 16 (1979): 58–69.

Stewart, Jack F. "Expressionism in *The Rainbow."* *Novel* 13 (1979–80): 296–315. (Reprinted in Jackson and Jackson [1988]: 72–92.)

Stubbs, Patricia. "Mr. Lawrence and Mrs. Woolf." In her *Women and Fiction: Feminism and the Novel, 1880–1920.* New York: Barnes and Noble, 1979, pp. 225–35.

1980

Adamowski, T. H. "Self/Body/Other: Orality and Ontology in Lawrence." *DHL Review* 13 (Fall 1980): 193–208.

Cohen, Marvin R. "The Prophet and the Critic: A Study in Classic Lawrentian Literature." *Texas Studies in Literature and Language* 22 (1980): 1–21.

Henry, Graeme. "DHL: Objectivity and Belief." *Critical Review* (Melbourne) 22 (1980): 32–43.

Holmes, Colin. "A Study of DHL's Social Origins." *Literature and History* 6 (1980): 82–93.

Spivey, Ted R. "Lawrence and Faulkner: The Symbolist Novel and the Prophetic Song." In his *The Journey beyond Tragedy: A Study of Myth and Modern Fiction.* Orlando: University Presses of Florida, 1980, pp. 72–93.

Stewart, Jack F. "Lawrence and Gauguin." *Twentieth Century Literature* 26 (1980a): 385–401.

———. "Primitivism in *Women in Love."* *DHL Review* 13 (Spring 1980b): 45–62.

Wilt, Judith. *Ghosts of the Gothic: Austen, Eliot, and Lawrence.* Princeton: Princeton University Press, 1980, pp. 231–303.

Young, Richard O. " 'Where Even the Trees Come and Go': DHL and the Fourth Dimension." *DHL Review* 13 (Spring 1980): 30–44.

1981

Cook, Ian G. "Consciousness and the Novel: Fact or Fiction in the Works of DHL." In *Humanistic Geography and Literature: Essays on the Experience of Place.* Edited by Douglas C. D. Pocock. London: Croom Helm; Totowa, N.J.: Barnes and Noble, 1981, pp. 66–84.

Foster, John Burt, Jr. "Holding Forth against Nietzsche: DHL's Novels from *Women in Love* to *The Plumed Serpent*." In his *Heirs to Dionysus: A Nietzschean Current in Literary Modernism*. Princeton: Princeton University Press, 1981, pp. 189–255.

Gordon, David J. "Sex and Language in DHL." *Twentieth Century Literature* 27 (Winter 1981): 362–74.

Levine, George. "Epilogue: Lawrence, *Frankenstein*, and the Reversal of Realism." In his *The Realistic Imagination: English Fiction from "Frankenstein" to "Lady Chatterley."* Chicago: University of Chicago Press, 1981, pp. 317–28 (323–28).

McVeagh, John. *Tradefull Merchants: The Portrayal of the Capitalist in Literature*. London and Boston: Routledge and Kegan Paul, 1981, pp. 171–90.

1982

Bump, Jerome. "Stevens and Lawrence: The Poetry of Nature and the Spirit of the Age." *Southern Review* 18 (1982): 44–61.

Carter, Angela. "DHL, Scholarship Boy." *New Society* 60 (3 June 1982): 391–92.

Hayles, Nancy Katherine. "The Ambivalent Approach: DHL and the New Physics." *Mosaic* 15 (September 1982): 89–108.

Kerr, Fergus. "Russell vs. Lawrence and/or Wittgenstein." *New Blackfriars* 63 (October 1982): 430–40.

Martin, Graham. "DHL and Class." In *The Uses of Fiction: Essays in the Modern Novel in Honour of Arnold Kettle*. Milton Keynes, Pa.: Open University Press, 1982, pp. 83–97. (Reprinted in Widdowson [1992]: 35–48.)

Padhi, Bibhu. "Lawrence's Idea of Language." *Modernist Studies* 4 (1982): 65–76.

1983

Brunsdale, Mitzi M. "DHL's *David:* Drama as a Vehicle for Religious Prophecy." *Themes and Drama* 5 (1983a): 123–37.

———. "Toward a Greater Day: Lawrence, Rilke, and Immortality." *Comparative Literature Studies* 20 (1983b): 402–17.

Cianci, Giovanni. "DHL and Futurism/Vorticism." *Arbeiten aus Anglistik und Amerikanistic* 8 (1983): 41–53.

Cox, Gary D. "DHL and F. M. Dostoevsky: Mirror Images of Murderous Aggression." *Modern Fiction Studies* 29 (1983): 175–82.

Engel, Monroe. "Contrived Lives: Joyce and Lawrence." In *Modernism Reconsidered*. Edited by Robert Kiely and John Hildebidle. Cambridge and London: Harvard University Press, 1983, pp. 65–80.

Shaw, Marion. "Lawrence and Feminism." *Critical Quarterly* 25 (Autumn 1983): 23–27.

Stewart, Jack F. "Lawrence and Van Gogh." *DHL Review* 16 (Spring 1983): 1–24.

1984

Hayles, Nancy Katherine. "Evasion: The Field of the Unconscious in DHL." In her *The Cosmic Web: Scientific Field Models and Literary Strategies in the Twentieth Century*. Ithaca, N.Y.: Cornell University Press, 1984, pp. 85–110.

Martin, Graham. " 'History' and 'Myth' in DHL's Chatterley Novels." In *The British Working-Class Novel in the Twentieth Century*. Edited by Jeremy Hawthorn. London: Edward Arnold, 1984, pp. 63–74.

Schneider, Daniel. "DHL and the Early Greek Philosophers." *DHL Review* 17 (Summer 1984): 97–109.

Stearns, Catherine. "Gender, Voice, and Myth: The Relation of Language to the Female in DHL's Poetry." *DHL Review* 17 (Fall 1984): 233–42.

Stewart, Garrett. "Rites of Trespass: Lawrence." In his *Death Sentences: Styles of Dying in British Fiction.* Cambridge: Harvard University Press, 1984, pp. 215–52.

Weinstein, Philip M. *The Semantics of Desire: Changing Models of Identity from Dickens to Joyce.* Princeton: Princeton University Press, 1984, pp. 189–251. (" 'Become Who You Are': The Optative World of DHL," pp. 204–24; and see also citations under *Women in Love* and *Lady Chatterley's Lover.*)

1985

Asher, Kenneth. "Nietzsche, Lawrence and Irrationalism." *Neophilologus* 69 (1985): 1–16.

Beer, John. "DHL and English Romanticism." *Aligarh Journal of English Studies* 10, no. 2 (1985): 109–21.

Blanchard, Lydia. "Lawrence, Foucault, and the Language of Sexuality." In *DHL's "Lady": A New Look at "Lady Chatterley's Lover."* Edited by Michael Squires and Dennis Jackson. Athens: University of Georgia Press, 1985, pp. 17–35.

Heuser, Alan. "Creaturely Inseeing in the Poetry of G. M. Hopkins, DHL, and Ted Hughes." *Hopkins Quarterly* 12 (1985): 35–51.

Leavis, L. R. "The Late Nineteenth Century Novel and the Change towards the Sexual— Gissing, Hardy and Lawrence." *English Studies* 66 (1985): 36–47.

Lodge, David. "Lawrence, Dostoevsky, Bakhtin: DHL and Dialogic Fiction." *Renaissance and Modern Studies* 29 (1985): 16–32. (Reprinted, in slightly revised form, in Brown [1990]: 92–108; and in his own *After Bakhtin: Essays on Fiction and Criticism.* London and New York: Routledge, 1990, pp. 57–74.)

Pile, Stephen. " 'Dirty Bertie' Makes It to the Abbey." *Sunday Times* (17 November 1985): 7. (On the Lawrence memorial in Poets' Corner, Westminster Abbey.)

1986

Breen, Judith Puchner. "DHL, World War I and the Battle between the Sexes: A Reading of 'The Blind Man' and 'Tickets, Please.' " *Women's Studies* 13 (1986): 63–74.

Daly, Macdonald. "DHL and Walter Brierley." *DHL: The Journal of the DHL Society* 4 (1986): 22–29.

Pollak, Paulina S. "Anti-Semitism in the Works of DHL: Search for and Rejection of the Faith." *Literature and Psychology* 32 (1986): 19–29.

Rose, Jonathan. *The Edwardian Temperament 1895–1919.* Athens: Ohio University Press, 1986, pp. 80–91.

Schneider, Daniel J. "Alternatives to Logocentrism in DHL." *South Atlantic Review* 51 (May 1986): 35–47. (Reprinted in Widdowson [1992]: 160–70.)

Yanada, Noriyuki. "Nursery Rhymes Alluded to in DHL Novels." *Language and Culture* 11 (1986): 32–63.

1987

Doherty, Gerald. "White Mythologies: DHL and the Deconstructive Turn." *Criticism* 29 (Fall 1987): 477–96.

Meisel, Perry. "Hardy, Lawrence, and the Disruptions of Nature." In his *The Myth of the Modern: A Study in British Literature and Criticism after 1850.* New Haven, Conn.: Yale University Press, 1987, pp. 11–36.

Orr, John. "Lawrence: Passion and its Dissolution." In his *The Making of the Twentieth-Century Novel: Lawrence, Joyce, Faulkner and Beyond.* Basingstoke and London: Macmillan, 1987, pp. 20–43.

Sabin, Margery. *The Dialect of the Tribe: Speech and Community in Modern Fiction.* Oxford: Oxford University Press, 1987, passim: "The Life of Idiom in Joyce and Lawrence," pp. 25–42; "Near and Far Things in Lawrence's Writing of the Twenties" (*St. Mawr*), pp. 162–78; *Women in Love,* pp. 106–38; *Sea and Sardinia,* pp. 139–62.

Tallack, Douglas, ed. *Literary Theory at Work: Three Texts.* London: B. T. Batsford, 1987. (Three essays on *St. Mawr:* see under Giles, Poole, and Millard in Bibliography 42.)

1988

Bull, J. A. "The Novelist on the Margins: Hardy and Lawrence." In his *The Framework of Fiction: Socio-Cultural Approaches to the Novel.* Basingstoke and London: Macmillan, 1988, pp. 147–90.

Eggert, Paul. "DHL and Literary Collaboration." *Etudes Lawrenciennes* 3 (May 1988): 153–62.

Ellis, David. "Lawrence in His Letters." *Etudes Lawrenciennes* (May 1988): 41–49.

Pittock, Malcolm. "Where the Rainbow Ends: Some Reservations about Lawrence." *Durham University Journal* 80, no. 2 (1988): 295–304.

Schnitzer, Deborah. *The Pictorial in Modernist Fiction from Stephen Crane to Ernest Hemingway.* Ann Arbor, Mich.: UMI Research Press, 1988, pp. 138–58.

1989

Daleski, H. M. "Life as a Four-Letter Word: A Contemporary View of Lawrence and Joyce." In *DHL in the Modern World.* Edited by Peter Preston and Peter Hoare. London: Macmillan, 1989, pp. 90–103.

Dalgarno, Emily K. "DHL: Social Ideology in Visual Art." *Mosaic* 22 (1989): 1–18.

Doherty, Gerald. "The Metaphorical Imperative: From Trope to Narrative in *The Rainbow.*" *South Central Review* 6 (Spring 1989): 46–61.

Ingersoll, Earl G. "The Failure of Bloodbrotherhood in Melville's *Moby-Dick* and Lawrence's *Women in Love.*" *Midwest Quarterly* 30 (1989): 458–77.

Jewinski, Ed. "The Phallus in DHL and Jacques Lacan." *DHL Review* 21 (Spring 1989): 7–24.

Trotter, David. "Edwardian Sex Novels." *Critical Quarterly* 31 (1989): 92–106.

1990

Hamalian, Leo. "DHL and Black Writers." *Journal of Modern Literature* 16 (Spring 1990): 579–96. (Lawrence's influence on Ralph Ellison, Langston Hughes, Jean Toomer, Richard Wright, and others.)

MacKenzie, Donald. "After Apocalypse: Some Elements in Late Lawrence." In *European Literature and Theology in the Twentieth Century: Ends of Times.* Edited by David Jasper and Colin Crowder. New York: St. Martin's Press, 1990, pp. 34–55.

Nielsen, Inge Padkaer, and Karsten Hvidtfelt Nielsen. "The Modernism of DHL and the Discourses of Decadence: Sexuality and Tradition in *The Trespasser, Fantasia of the Unconscious,* and *Aaron's Rod.*" *Arcadia* 25, no. 3 (1990): 270–86.

Padhi, Bibhu. "DHL and Europe." *Contemporary Review* 257 (1990): 83–87.

Polhemus, Robert M. "The Prophet of Love and the Resurrection of the Body: DHL's *Lady Chatterley's Lover* (1928)." In his *Erotic Faith: Being in Love from Jane Austen to DHL.* Chicago: University of Chicago Press, 1990, pp. 279–306.

1991

Dollimore, Jonathan. "DHL and the Metaphysics of Sexual Difference." In his *Sexual Dissidence: Augustine to Wilde, Freud to Foucault.* Oxford: Clarendon Press, 1991, pp. 268–75.

Fjagesund, Peter. "DHL, Knut Hamsun and Pan." *English Studies* (Netherlands) 72, no. 5 (October 1991): 421–25.

Goodheart, Eugene. "Censorship and Self-Censorship in the Fiction of DHL." In *Representing Modernist Texts: Editing as Interpretation.* Edited by George Bornstein. Ann Arbor: University of Michigan Press, 1991, pp. 223–40.

Katz-Roy, Ginette. "DHL and 'That Beastly France.' " *DHL Review* 23 (1991): 143–56.

Rooks, Pamela A. "DHL's 'Individual' and Michael Polanyi's 'Personal': Fruitful Redefinitions of Subjectivity and Objectivity." *DHL Review* 23 (1991): 21–29.

Ruderman, Judith. "DHL and the 'Jewish Problem': Reflections on a Self-Confessed 'Hebrophobe.' " *DHL Review* 23 (1991): 99–109.

Stewart, Jack F. "Primordial Affinities: Lawrence, Van Gogh and the Miners." *Mosaic* 24 (Winter 1991): 92–113. (Reprinted in *DHL: The Journal of the DHL Society* [1992–93]: 22–44.)

Worthen, John. "D. H. Lawrence: Problems with Multiple Texts." In *The Theory and Practices of Text-Editing: Essays in Honour of James T. Boulton.* Edited by Ian Small and Marcus Walsh. Cambridge: Cambridge University Press, 1991, pp. 14–34.

1992

Black, Michael. "A Kind of Bristling in the Darkness: Memory and Metaphor in Lawrence." *Critical Review* (Melbourne) 32 (1992): 29–44.

Carey, John. *The Intellectuals and the Masses: Pride and Prejudice among the Literary Intelligentsia, 1880–1939.* London and Boston: Faber and Faber, 1992, pp. 35–36, 75–80 and passim.

Hyde, Virginia. "The Body and the Body Politic in Lawrence." *Review* (Blacksburg, Va.) 14 (1992): 143–53.

Katz-Roy, Ginette. "The Process of 'Rotary Image-Thought' in DHL's *Last Poems.*" *Études Lawrenciennes* 7 (1992): 129–38.

Kinkead-Weekes, Mark. "DHL and the Dance." *Dance Research* 10 (Spring 1992): 59–77. (Reprinted in *DHL: The Journal of the DHL Society* [1992–93]: 44–62.)

Semeiks, Joanna G. "Sex, Lawrence, and Videotape." *Journal of Popular Culture* 25, no. 4 (Spring 1992): 143–52.

Williams, Linda R. "The Trial of DHL." *Critical Survey* 4, no. 2 (1992): 154–61.

1993

Alldritt, Keith. "The Europeans of DHL." *Etudes Lawrenciennes* 9 (1993): 11–19.

Gervais, David. "Forster and Lawrence: Exiles in the Homeland." In his *Literary Eng-lands: Versions of "Englishness" in Modern Writing.* Cambridge: Cambridge University Press, 1993, pp. 67–101 (84–99).

Hyde, Virginia. "To 'Undiscovered Land': D. H. Lawrence's Horsewomen and Other Questers." In *Women and the Journey: The Female Travel Experience.* Edited by Bonnie Frederick and Susan H. McLeod. Pullman: Washington State University Press, 1993, pp. 171–96.

Katz-Roy, Ginette. " 'This May Be a Withering Tree This Europe': Bachelard, Deleuze and Guattari on DHL's Poetic Imagination." *Etudes Lawrenciennes* 9 (1993): 219–35.

Kim, Sung Ryol. "The Vampire Lust in DHL." *Studies in the Novel* 25, no. 4 (Winter 1993): 436–48.

Langbaum, Robert. "Lawrence and the Modernists." *Etudes Lawrenciennes* 9 (1993): 145–57.

Paccaud-Huguet, Josiane. "Narrative as a Symbolic Act: The Historicity of Lawrence's Modernity." *Etudes Lawrenciennes* 9 (1993): 75–94.

Wallace, Jeff. "Language, Nature and the Politics of Materialism: Raymond Williams and DHL." In *Raymond Williams: Politics, Education, Letters.* Edited by W. John Morgan and Peter Preston. London: Macmillan; New York: St. Martin's Press, 1993, pp. 105–28.

Zytaruk, George J. "Lawrence and Rozanov: Clarifying the Phallic Vision." *Etudes Lawrenciennes* 9 (1993): 93–103.

1994

Ellis, David. "Lawrence, Wordsworth and 'Anthropomorphic Lust.' " *Cambridge Quarterly* 23, no. 3 (1994): 230–42.

Ingersoll, Earl G. "Staging the Gaze in DHL's *Women in Love.*" *Studies in the Novel* 26, no. 2 (Fall 1994): 268–80.

Mills, Howard. " 'The World of Substance': Lawrence, Hardy, Cézanne, and Shelley." *English* 43 (Autumn 1994): 209–22.

SECTION B

VARIETIES OF LAWRENCE CRITICISM

BIBLIOGRAPHY 88: HISTORICIST APPROACHES I: HISTORY, SOCIETY, IDEOLOGY

All the works cited in this and the following bibliography attempt to contextualize or historicize Lawrence's work in some way, and the two lists should therefore be seen as complementary. However, I have divided the works, for convenience, between those that contextualize Lawrence primarily in terms of sociohistoric developments and currents of ideology and those that contextualize him in terms of traditions in literature and the arts and in terms of influence and affinity.

Of the full-length works listed in the master bibliography at the end of the book, the following are of direct relevance to a sociological and/or ideological perspective on Lawrence: Delany (1978), Delavenay (1972), Fernihough (1993), Goodheart (1963), Green (1974), Harrison (1966), Holderness (1982), Mensch (1991), Modiano (1987), Mohanty (1993), Nixon (1986), Sanders (1973), Scheckner (1985), Simpson (1982), Widmer (1962 and 1992), Sinzelle (1964), Worthen (1979 and 1991b) (and see also Alden [1986] and Raskin [1971]). All these works are important; however, for straightforward biographical material with a sociological inflection, the works of Delany, Delavenay, Sinzelle, and Worthen (1991b) are to be recommended; while for rigorous ideological contextualization, the works of Fernihough, Holderness, Mensch, Nixon, and Simpson are essential reading.

Alter, Richard. "Eliot, Lawrence, and the Jews." *Commentary* 50 (October 1970): 81–86.

———. "Eliot, Lawrence and the Jews: Two Versions of Europe." In his *Defenses of the Imagination: Jewish Writers and Modern Historical Crisis.* Philadelphia: Jewish Publication Society of America, 1978, pp. 137–51.

Armytage, W.H.G. "The Disenchanted Mechanophobes in Twentieth Century England." *Extrapolation* 9 (1968): 33–60. (Lawrence included, along with Auden, Huxley, and Orwell.)

Arvin, Newton. "DHL and Fascism." *New Republic* 89 (16 December 1936): 219. (Rejoinder to Wells [1936], op. cit.)

Atkins, John. "Lawrence's Social Landscape." *Books and Bookmen* 15 (July 1970): 24–26.

Bamlett, Steve. " 'A Way-Worn Ancestry Returning': The Function of the Representation of Peasants in the Novel." In *Peasants and Countrymen in Literature: A Symposium Organised by the English Department of the Roehampton Institute in February 1981.* London: Roehampton Institute of Higher Education, 1982, pp. 153–82.

Benstock, Bernard. "Personalities and Politics: A View of the Literary Right." *DHL Review* 1 (Summer 1968): 149–69.

Bentley, Eric R. "DHL, John Thomas and Dionysos." *New Mexico Quarterly Review* 12 (1941): 133–43.

———. "Heroic Vitalists of the Twentieth Century." In his *A Century of Hero-Worship.* Philadelphia: Lippincott, 1944, pp. 205–53.

Bentley, Michael. "Lawrence's Political Thought: Some English Contexts, 1906–19." In *DHL: New Studies.* Edited by Christopher Heywood. London: Macmillan; New York: St. Martin's Press, 1987, pp. 59–83.

Bloom, Alice. "The Larger Connection: The Communal Vision in DHL." *Yale Review* 68 (1978): 176–91.

Bloom, Clive, ed. *Literature and Culture in Modern Britain, Volume 1: 1900–1929.* London: Longman, 1993.

Breen, Judith Puchner. "DHL, World War I and the Battle between the Sexes: A Reading of 'The Blind Man' and 'Tickets, Please.' " *Women's Studies* 13 (1986): 63–74.

Bull, J. A. "The Novelist on the Margins: Hardy and Lawrence." In his *The Framework of Fiction: Socio-Cultural Approaches to the Novel.* Basingstoke and London: Macmillan, 1988, pp. 147–90.

Carey, John. "DHL's Doctrine." In *DHL: Novelist, Poet, Prophet.* Edited by Stephen Spender. London: Weidenfeld and Nicolson, 1973, pp. 122–34.

———. *The Intellectuals and the Masses: Pride and Prejudice among the Literary Intelligentsia, 1880–1939.* London and Boston: Faber and Faber, 1992, pp. 35–36, 75–80 and passim.

Caudwell, Christopher. "DHL: A Study of the Bourgeois Artist." In his *Studies in a Dying Culture.* London: Lane, 1938, pp. 44–72. (Reprinted in his *The Concept of Freedom.* London: Lawrence and Wishart, 1965, pp. 11–30.)

Chakrabarti, Anupam. "DHL: The Socio-Cultural Critic." In *Essays on DHL.* Edited by T. R. Sharma. Meerut, India: Shalabh Book House, 1987, pp. 57–69.

Chapple, J.A.V. *Documentary and Imaginative Literature 1880–1920.* London: Blandford Press, 1970, pp. 72–79 and passim.

Colmer, John. *Coleridge to Catch-22: Images of Society.* New York: St. Martin's Press, 1978, pp. 130–34, 158–61.

Craig, David. "Fiction and the Rising Industrial Classes." *Essays in Criticism* 17 (January 1967): 64–74.

———. *The Real Foundations: Literature and Social Change.* London; Chatto and Windus, 1973, pp. 17–38, 143–67. (Ch. 1 "Shakespeare, Lawrence, and Sexual Freedom"; Ch. 7, "Lawrence and Democracy.")

Dalgarno, Emily K. "DHL: Social Ideology in Visual Art." *Mosaic* 22 (1989): 1–18.

Davies, Rosemary Reeves. "DHL and the Media: The Impact of Trigant Burrow on Lawrence's Social Thinking." *Studies in the Humanities* 11, no. 2 (1984): 33–41.

Delany, Paul. "Lawrence and the Decline of the Industrial Spirit." In *The Challenge of DHL.* Edited by Michael Squires and Keith Cushman. Madison: University of Wisconsin Press, 1990, pp. 77–88.

Desouza, Eunice. "DHL: Radical or Reactionary?" *Economic Times* (16 March 1980): 7.

Dodsworth, Martin. "Lawrence, Sex and Class." *English* 24 (1985): 69–80. (Review of *Mr. Noon.*)

Eagleton, Mary, and David Pierce. "Pressure Points: Forster, Lawrence, Joyce, Woolf." In their *Attitudes to Class in the English Novel from Walter Scott to David Storey.* London: Thames and Hudson, 1979, pp. 93–129.

Eagleton, Terry. *Exiles and Emigrés: Studies in Modern Literature.* London: Chatto and Windus; New York: Schocken, 1970, pp. 191–218.

———. *Criticism and Ideology: A Study in Marxist Literary Theory.* London: New Left Books, 1976, pp. 157–61.

Efron, Arthur. "Toward a Dialectic of Sensuality and Work." *Paunch* 44–45 (May 1976): 152–70. ("Sex and Work in Marx and *The Rainbow,*" pp. 165–70.)

Eliot, T. S. *After Strange Gods: A Primer of Modern Heresy.* London: Faber and Faber; New York: Harcourt, Brace, 1934, pp. 38–43, 62–67.

Fairbanks, N. David. "Strength through Joy in the Novels of DHL." *Literature and Ideology,* no. 8 (1971): 67–78.

Freeman, Mary. "DHL in Valhalla." *New Mexico Quarterly* 10 (November 1942): 211–24.

Gervais, David. "Forster and Lawrence: Exiles in the Homeland." In his *Literary Englands: Versions of "Englishness" in Modern Writing.* Cambridge: Cambridge University Press, 1993, pp. 67–101 (84–99).

Giles, Steve. "Marxism and Form: DHL, *St. Mawr.*" In *Literary Theory at Work: Three Texts.* Edited by Douglas Tallack. London: Batsford, 1987, pp. 49–66.

Gindin, James Jack. "Society and Compassion in the Novels of DHL." *Centennial Review* 12 (1968): 355–74. (Reprinted in his *Harvest of a Quiet Eye: The Novel of Compassion.* Bloomington: Indiana University Press, 1971, pp. 205–21.)

Green, Eleanor H. "Blueprints for Utopia: The Political Ideas of Nietzsche and DHL." *Renaissance and Modern Studies* 18 (1974): 141–61.

Green, Martin. "Cottage Realism." *Month* 4 (September 1971): 85–88. (On the values of Lawrence, Raymond Williams, and Richard Hoggart.)

Griffin, A. R., and C. P. Griffin. "A Social and Economic History of Eastwood and the Nottinghamshire Mining Country." In *A DHL Handbook.* Edited by Keith Sagar. Manchester: Manchester University Press, 1982, pp. 127–63.

Griffin, C. P. "The Social Origins of DHL: Some Further Evidence." *Literature and History* 7 (1981): 223–27. (Response to Holmes [1980].)

Guttmann, Allen. "DHL: The Politics of Irrationality." *Wisconsin Studies in Contemporary Literature* 5 (Summer 1964): 151–63.

Hawthorn, Jeremy. "Lawrence and Working-Class Fiction." In *Rethinking Lawrence.* Edited by Keith Brown. Milton Keynes and Philadelphia: Open University Press, 1990, pp. 67–78.

Hicks, Granville. "DHL as Messiah." *New Republic* 88 (28 October 1936): 358–59. (See rejoinder from Wells [1936], op. cit., and ensuing correspondence.)

Holderness, Graham. "Miners and the Novel: From Bourgeois to Proletarian Fiction." In *The British Working-Class Novel in the Twentieth Century.* Edited by Jeremy Hawthorn. London: Edward Arnold, 1984, pp. 19–32. (Considers novels by Zola, Walter Brierley, Lewis Jones, Barry Hines, and, pp. 23–25, Lawrence's *Sons and Lovers* and *Lady Chatterley's Lover.*)

Holmes, Colin. "A Study of DHL's Social Origins." *Literature and History* 6 (1980): 82–93. (Reprinted in Heywood [1987]: 1–15. See also Griffin [1981].)

Hoyles, John. "DHL and the Counter-Revolution: An Essay in Socialist Aesthetics." *DHL Review* 6 (Summer 1973): 173–200.

Jacobson, P. "DHL and Modern Society." *Journal of Contemporary History* 2 (April 1967): 81–92.

Kiely, Robert. "Out on Strike: The Language and Power of the Working Class in Lawrence's Fiction." In *The Challenge of DHL.* Edited by Michael Squires and Keith Cushman. Madison: University of Wisconsin Press, 1990, pp. 89–102.

Kirkham, Michael. "DHL and Social Consciousness." *Mosaic* 12 (1978): 79–92.

Kitchin, Laurence. "The Zombie's Lair." *Listener* (4 November 1965): 701–2, 704. (Lawrence on industrialism in *Women in Love* and *Lady Chatterley's Lover.*)

———. "Colliers." *Listener* 75 (28 April 1966): 617–18. (*Sons and Lovers* and *Lady Chatterley's Lover* as "colliery novels.")

Laurenson, Diana, and Alan Swingewood. *The Sociology of Literature.* London: MacGibbon and Kee, 1972, pp. 83–88 and passim.

Leavis, F. R. "Lawrence and Class: 'The Daughters of the Vicar.' " In his *DHL: Novelist.* London: Chatto and Windus, 1955, pp. 73–95. (Originally in *Sewanee Review* 62 [Autumn 1954]: 535–62.)

Lee, R. "The 'Strange Reality of Otherness': DHL's Social Attitudes." *Standpunte* 25 (June 1972): 3–10.

Lewis, Wyndham. *Paleface: The Philosophy of the "Melting Pot."* London: Chatto and Windus, 1929. (Expanded from his article "Paleface; or, 'Love? What ho! Smelling Strangeness.' " *Enemy* 2 (September 1927): 3–112.)

McCormick, John. *Catastrophe and Imagination: An Interpretation of the Recent English and American Novel.* London and New York: Longman, Green, 1957, passim.

McVeagh, John. *Tradefull Merchants: The Portrayal of the Capitalist in Literature.* London and Boston: Routledge and Kegan Paul, 1981, pp. 171–90.

Maes-Jelinek, Hena. *Criticism of Society in the English Novel between the Wars.* Paris: Société d'Editions "Les Belles Lettres," 1970, pp. 11–100. (Considers the impact of the war and subsequent events on Lawrence.)

Martin, Graham. " 'History' and 'Myth' in DHL's Chatterley Novels." In *The British Working-Class Novel in the Twentieth Century.* Edited by Jeremy Hawthorn. London: Edward Arnold, 1984, pp. 63–74.

————. "DHL and Class." In *The Uses of Fiction: Essays in the Modern Novel in Honour of Arnold Kettle.* Milton Keynes and Philadelphia: Open University Press, 1982, pp. 83–97. (Reprinted in Widdowson [1992]: 35–48.)

Mellor, Adrian, Chris Pawling, and Colin Sparks. "Writers and the General Strike." In *The General Strike.* Edited by Margaret Morris. London: 1980, pp. 338–57.

Merlini, Madeline. "DHL and the Italian Political Scene." *Etudes Lawrenciennes* 9 (1993): 63–74.

Meyers, Jeffrey. "Fascism and the Novels of Power." In his *DHL and the Experience of Italy.* Philadelphia: University of Pennsylvania Press, 1982, pp. 105–36.

Middleton, Victoria. "In the 'Woman's Corner': The World of Lydia Lawrence." *Journal of Modern Literature* 13 (1986): 267–88.

Myers, Neil. "Lawrence and the War." *Criticism* 4 (Winter 1962): 44–58.

Nott, Kathleen. "Whose Culture?" *Listener* 47 (12 April and 19 April 1962): 631–32, 677–78. (On Leavis and Lawrence.)

Nulle, S. H. "DHL and the Fascist Movement." *New Mexico Quarterly* 10 (February 1940): 3–15.

Orr, Christopher. "Lawrence after the Deluge: The Political Ambiguity of *Aaron's Rod.*" *West Virginia Association of College English Teachers Bulletin* 1 (Fall 1974): 1–14.

Paccaud-Huguet, Josiane. "Narrative as a Symbolic Act: The Historicity of Lawrence's Modernity." *Etudes Lawrenciennes* 9 (1993): 75–94.

Page, Norman. "Hardy, Lawrence, and the Working-Class Hero." In *English Literature and the Working Class.* Edited by F. G. Tortosa and R. L. Ortega. Seville: University of Seville, 1980, pp. 39–57.

Parry, Albert. "DHL through a Marxist Mirror." *Western Review* 19 (Winter 1955): 85–100.

Pinto, Vivian de Sola. "DHL." In *The Politics of Twentieth-Century Novelists.* Edited by George Andrew Panichas. New York: Hawthorne Books, 1971, pp. 30–50.

Pollak, Paulina S. "Anti-Semitism in the Works of DHL: Search for and Rejection of the Faith." *Literature and Psychology* 32 (1986): 19–29.

Poynter, John S. "Miner and Mineowner at the Time of Lawrence's Setting for *Sons and Lovers.*" *Journal of the DHL Society* 2, no. 3 (1981): 13–23.

Pugh, Bridget. "Lawrence and Industrial Symbolism." *Renaissance and Modern Studies* 29 (1985): 33–49.

Rahv, P. *Literature and the Sixth Sense.* London: Faber and Faber, 1970, pp. 93–94, 289–306, 437–45. (On, respectively, Henry Miller and Lawrence, Leavis and Lawrence, and Harrison [1966], op. cit.).

Roberts, I. D. "DHL and Davidson School: An Institutional Viewpoint." *DHL Review* 16 (1983): 195–210.

Ruderman, Judith. "DHL and the 'Jewish Problem': Reflections on a Self-Confessed 'Hebrophobe.' " *DHL Review* 23 (1991): 99–109.

Ruthven, K. K. "On the So-Called Fascism of Some Modernist Writers." *Southern Review* (Adelaide) 5, no. 3 (September 1972): 225–30.

Rylance, Rick. "Lawrence's Politics." In *Rethinking Lawrence.* Edited by Keith Brown. Milton Keynes and Philadelphia: Open University Press, 1990, pp. 163–80.

Schorer, Mark. *Lawrence in the War Years.* Stanford, Calif.: Stanford University Press, 1968. (Fifteen-page pamphlet based on a short talk.)

Seillière, Ernest. *David Herbert Lawrence et les Récentes Idéologies Allemandes.* Paris:

Boivin, 1936. (See also reviews of this book: *Times Literary Supplement* [12 September 1936]: 724; H. W. Hausermann, *English Studies* 19 [April 1937]: 86–87.)

Shrivastava, K. C. "DHL's *Sons and Lovers* as a Proletarian Novel." In *Essays on DHL.* Edited by T. R. Sharma. Meerut, India: Shalabh Book House, 1987, pp. 104–8.

Southworth, James G. "DHL: Poet; 'A Note on High Political Ideology.' " In his *Sowing the Spring: Studies in British Poetry from Hopkins to MacNeice.* Oxford: Basil Blackwell, 1940, pp. 64–75.

Spender, Stephen. "Writers and Politics." *Partisan Review* 34 (Summer 1967): 359–81.

———. "DHL, England and the War." In *DHL: Novelist, Poet, Prophet.* Edited by Stephen Spender. London: Weidenfeld and Nicolson, 1973, pp. 71–76.

Stewart, Jack F. "Primordial Affinities: Lawrence, Van Gogh and the Miners." *Mosaic* 24 (Winter 1991): 92–113. (Reprinted in *DHL: The Journal of the DHL Society* [1992–93]: 22–44.)

Stohl, Johan H. "Man and Society: Lawrence's Subversive Vision." *Literature and Religion: Views on DHL.* Edited by Charles A. Huttar. Holland, Mich.: Hope College, 1968. (Articles independently paginated from 1.)

Storer, Ronald W. "A Day in the Life of Arthur Lawrence: 1885." In *DHL 1885–1930: A Celebration.* Edited by Andrew Cooper and Glyn Hughes. Nottingham: DHL Society, 1985a, pp. 17–30.

———. *Some Aspects of Brinsley Colliery and the Lawrence Connection.* Selston, Nottinghamshire: Ronald W. Storer, 1985b.

Strachey, John. *The Coming Struggle for Power.* London: Gollancz, 1932, pp. 206–16.

Tindall, William York. "Lawrence among the Fascists." In his *DHL and Susan His Cow.* New York: Columbia University Press, 1939, pp. 162–80.

Tomlinson, T. B. *The English Middle-Class Novel.* London: Macmillan, 1976, pp. 185–202 and passim. (Chapter on *Sons and Lovers* and *Women in Love,* pp. 185–98.)

Trotter, David. "Modernism and Empire: Reading *The Waste Land.*" *Critical Quarterly* 28 (Spring–Summer 1986): 143–53. (Discusses *Women in Love.*)

Van Herk, Aritha. "CrowB(e)ars and Kangaroos of the Future: The Post-Colonial Ga(s)p." *World Literature Written in English* 30 (Autumn 1990): 42–54. (Discusses *Kangaroo* along with three works by Faulkner, David Ireland, and Robert Kroetsch.)

Wallace, Jeff. "Language, Nature and the Politics of Materialism: Raymond Williams and DHL." In *Raymond Williams: Politics, Education, Letters.* Edited by W. John Morgan and Peter Preston. London: Macmillan; New York: St. Martin's Press, 1993, pp. 105–28.

Warner, Rex. "Cult of Power." In his *The Cult of Power: Essays.* Philadelphia: Lippincott, 1946, pp. 11–28 (15–20).

Watkins, Daniel P. "Labor and Religion in DHL's 'The Rocking-Horse Winner.' " *Studies in Short Fiction* 24 (1987): 295–301.

Watson, George. "The Politics of DHL." In his *Politics and Literature in Modern Britain.* London and Basingstoke: Macmillan, 1977, pp. 110–19.

Wells, Harry K. "A Disagreement with Mr. Hicks." *New Republic* 89 (18 November 1936): 77. (Letter in reply to Hicks [1936], op. cit., and see also Arvin [1936], Whipple [1937], and following item by Wells.)

———. "DHL and Fascism." *New Republic* 91 (16 June 1937): 161.

West, Alick. "DHL." In his *Crisis and Criticism, and Selected Literary Essays.* London: Lawrence and Wishart, 1975, pp. 259–82. (Marxist response to Caudwell.)

Whipple, T. K. "Literature in the Doldrums." *New Republic* 90 (21 April 1937): 311–14 (312–13). (On Lawrence and fascism; see reply by Wells [1937].)

Williams, Raymond. "DHL." In his *Culture and Society: 1780–1950.* London: Chatto and Windus; New York: Columbia University Press, 1958, pp. 199–213. (Reprinted in Moore [1959] as "The Social Thinking of DHL," pp. 295–311.)

———. "DHL." In his *The English Novel from Dickens to Lawrence.* London: Chatto and Windus; New York: Oxford University Press, 1970, pp. 169–84.

———. *The Country and the City.* London: Chatto and Windus; New York: Oxford University Press, 1973, pp. 264–68 and passim.

Winegarten, Renée. *Writers and Revolution: The Fatal Lure of Action.* New York: New Viewpoints, 1974, pp. 247–60.

Winnington, G. Peter. "D. H. Lawrence and Ferdinand Tönnies." *Notes and Queries* 24 (October 1977): 446–47.

Worthen, John. "Lawrence and Eastwood." In *DHL: Centenary Essays.* Edited by Mara Kalnins. Bristol: Bristol Classical Press, 1986, pp. 1–20.

BIBLIOGRAPHY 89: HISTORICIST APPROACHES II: TRADITION, INFLUENCE, AND AFFINITY

This bibliography concentrates on studies of Lawrence's cultural and artistic heritage, as well as on studies of more specific individual and intertextual influences on his art and of the possible affinities between his art and that of others. This is one of the largest fields of Lawrence criticism, and almost every other book on Lawrence would seem to be relevant to it in some way. Thus, in order to guide the reader meaningfully through related book-length studies, I subdivide author-date citations from the master bibliography into seven sections here (hopefully, these subdivisions will also be useful for correlating the other items contained in this bibliography). There are inevitably many overlaps among these subdivisions, but I have grouped works together according to what seems to me to be their predominant focus.

1. Studies that survey *general* literary and cultural influences on Lawrence are those of Cura-Sazdanic (1969), Drain (1960), Sinha (1985), and Tindall (1939). Although all these works are dated and have been superseded by Burwell (1982) (see following bibliography) in terms of raw information about Lawrence's sources, they are still interesting for their discursive accounts of *how* he was influenced by those sources. See also Drain (1962) in the following bibliography.

2. Studies that trace Lawrence's roots in *particular traditions* of thought, belief, genre, or mode are as follows: Alcorn (1977) (the nature novel), Burns (1980) (philosophy of the self and of language), Clark (1969) (Romanticism), Ebbatson (1980 and 1982) (evolutionary thought), Hyde (1992) (biblical typology), John (1974) (Romantic vitalism), Lerner (1967) (liberal humanism), Lucente (1981) (realism and myth), Montgomery (1994) (Romanticism and the visionary tradition), Siegel (1991) (women's

literary traditions), Squires (1974) (the pastoral novel), Trebisz (1992) (the novella), Whelan (1988) (myth and esoteric belief), Whiteley (1987) (realism), Wilt (1980) (the gothic tradition).

3. Studies that relate Lawrence to the literary and cultural trends specific to his own *period*—and here modernism is a major, though not exclusive, concern—are those of Cornwell (1962), Davies (1984), Herzinger (1982), Kiely (1980), Murfin (1978), Orr (1987), Pinkney (1990), Wright (1984).

4. Studies of the influence of the *visual arts* on Lawrence are represented by Alldritt (1971) (general influences), Hyde (1992) (biblical iconography), Kushigian (1990) (visual modernism), Meyers (1975) (Pre-Raphaelites, the Renaissance, futurism), Torgovnick (1985) (general theory of "pictorialism" in the novel—see also Schnitzer [1988] in the following bibliography).

5. The importance of Lawrence's *travels* to his works, the influence of different countries and their cultures, has been studied by Arnold (1958 and 1963) (America and Germany), Brunsdale (1978) (Germany), Darroch (1981) (Australia), Green (1974) (Germany), Hamalian (1982) (Italy), Hyde (1981) (Lawrence's translations of Italian and Russian authors), Meyers (1982) (Italy), Michaels-Tonks (1976) (Germany and Italy), Veitch (1978) (Mexico), and Zytaruk (1971) (Russia).

6. Closely focused studies of Lawrence's *affinities* with an individual writer, artist, or thinker seem to be a stock-in-trade of Lawrentians, and the following books, along with the other items in the following bibliography, suggest that there can be few major cultural figures left who have *not,* at some time, been closely compared to Lawrence: Bedient (1972) (G. Eliot, Forster), Delavenay (1971) (E. Carpenter), Fedder (1966) (T. Williams), Garcia (1972) (Steinbeck), Gutierrez (1987) (Wordsworth), Hough (1956, *Two Exiles*) (Byron), Lea (1985) (Murry), Lewiecki-Wilson (1994) (Joyce), Milton (1987) (Nietzsche), Murry (1957) (Schweitzer), Prasad (1976) (Hardy), Rees (1958) (Weil), Sharma (1982) (Woolf), Storch (1990) (Blake), Swigg (1972) (Hardy). A sample of other influences and affinities systematically pursued by critics as represented by the following items and in other essays and books is Sherwood Anderson, Arnold, Auden, Bennett, Bergson, Burns, Carlyle, Carver, Coleridge, Dickens, Lawrence Durrell, Ginsburg, Greene, Hamsun, Hemingway, Heraclitus, Hopkins, Hughes, Kafka, Lowry, Malraux, Mann, Melville, Miller, Charles Olson, Pound, Reich, Rilke, Ruskin, Schopenhauer, Shaw, Shelley, Tolstoy, Verga, Wagner, Welty, Whitman, Yeats, Zola.

7. Looser influence or affinity studies, where, for example, Lawrence is associated with a small group of other writers, are represented by the following books: Albright (1978), Alden (1986), Meyers (1977), Norris (1985), Paterson (1973), Polhemus (1990), Raskin (1971), Russell (1975), Sale (1973), Tenenbaum (1977), Tytell (1991).

Adix, M. "Phoenix at Walden: DHL Calls on Thoreau." *Western Humanities Review* 8 (Autumn 1954): 287–98.

Alexander, Edward. "Thomas Carlyle and DHL: A Parallel." *University of Toronto Quarterly* 37 (April 1968): 248–67.

Alexander, John C. "DHL and Teilhard de Chardin: A Study in Agreements." *DHL Review* 2 (Summer 1969): 138–56.

Alldritt, Keith. "The Europeans of DHL." *Etudes Lawrenciennes* 9 (1993): 11–19.

Alpers, Antony. *The Life of Katherine Mansfield.* New York: Viking, 1980, passim.

Ananthamurthy, U. R. "D. H. Lawrence as an Indian Writer Sees Him." *The Literary Criterion* 16 (1981): 1–17.

Arbur, Rosemarie. " 'Lilacs' and 'Sorrow': Whitman's Effect on the Early Poems of DHL." *Walt Whitman Review* 24 (1978): 17–21.

Armytage, W.H.G. "Superman and the System." *Riverside Quarterly* 3 (August 1967): 44–51. (Includes discussion of Nietzsche's influence on Lawrence.)

Arnold, Armin. "DHL and Thomas Mann." *Comparative Literature* 13 (Winter 1961): 33–38.

———. "DHL, the Russians, and Giovanni Verga." *Comparative Literature Studies* 2 (1965): 249–57.

Asher, Kenneth. "Nietzsche, Lawrence and Irrationalism." *Neophilologus* 69 (1985): 1–16.

Bahlke, George W. "Lawrence and Auden: The Pilgrim and the Citizen." In Cushman and Jackson, op. cit. (1991): 211–27.

Baier, Clair. " 'Mild like Mashed Potatoes': A Brief Note on Hans Carossa and DHL." *German Life and Letters* 32 (1979): 327–31.

Balbert, Peter. "From Hemingway to Lawrence to Mailer: Survival and Sexual Identity in *A Farewell to Arms.*" *Hemingway Review* 3 (Fall 1983): 30–43.

Ballin, Michael. "The Third Eye: The Relationship between DHL and Maurice Maeterlinck." In *The Practical Vision: Essays in English Literature in Honour of Flora Roy.* Edited by Jane Campbell and James Doyle. Waterloo, Ontario: Wilfrid Laurier University Press, 1978, pp. 87–102.

———. "DHL's Esotericism: William Blake in Lawrence's *Women in Love.*" In *DHL's "Women in Love": Contexts and Criticism.* Edited by Michael Ballin. Waterloo, Ontario: Wilfrid Laurier University, 1980, pp. 70–87.

Banerjee, A. "Yone Noguchi and DHL." *London Magazine* 26, no. 7 (October 1986): 58–62.

———. "The 'Marriage Poems' by Lawrence and Lowell." *Kobe College Studies* 38 (March 1993): 15–36.

Baron, Carl E. "Forster on Lawrence." In *E. M. Forster: A Human Exploration: Centenary Essays.* New York: New York University Press, 1979, pp. 86–95.

Barry, J. "Oswald Spengler and DHL." *English Studies in Africa* 12, no. 2 (1969): 151–61.

Bartlett, Norman. "Aldous Huxley and DHL." *Australian Quarterly* 36 (1964): 76–84.

Bayley, John. "Lawrence and the Modern English Novel." In Meyers, op. cit. (1987): 14–29.

Bazin, Nancy Topping. "The Moment of Revelation in *Martha Quest* and Comparable Moments by Two Modernists." *Modern Fiction Studies* 26 (1980): 87–98. (Lawrence and Joyce.)

Beach, Joseph Warren. "Impressionism: Lawrence." In his *The Twentieth Century Novel: Studies in Technique.* New York: Appleton-Century, 1932, pp. 366–84.

Becket, Fiona. "Building Dwelling Thinking: 'Extreme Consciousness' in Willa Cather and D. H. Lawrence." In *Willa Cather and European Cultural Influences.* Edited by Helen Dennis. Lampeter, Wales: Edwin Mellen Press, 1996.

Beer, John. "The Last Englishman: Lawrence's Appreciation of Forster." In *E. M. Forster: A Human Exploration: Centenary Essays.* New York: New York University Press, 1979, pp. 245–68.

————. "Forster, Lawrence, Virginia Woolf and Bloomsbury." *Aligarh Journal of English Studies* 5 (1980): 6–37.

————. "DHL and English Romanticism." *Aligarh Journal of English Studies* 10, no. 2 (1985): 109–21.

Bell, Michael. "DHL and Thomas Mann: Unbewusste Brüderschaft." *Etudes Lawrenciennes* 9 (1993): 185–97.

Betsky-Zweig, S. "Lawrence and Cézanne." *Dutch Quarterly Review of Anglo-American Letters* 15 (1985): 2–24.

Blanchard, Lydia. "The Savage Pilgrimage and Katherine Mansfield: A Study in Literary Influence, Anxiety, and Subversion." *Modern Language Quarterly* 47 (1986): 48–65.

————. "The Fox and the Phoenix: Tennessee Williams's Strong Misreading of Lawrence." In Cushman and Jackson, op. cit. (1991): 15–30.

Blissett, William. "DHL, D'Annunzio, Wagner." *Wisconsin Studies in Contemporary Literature* 7 (Winter–Spring 1966): 21–46.

Bobbitt, Joan. "Lawrence and Bloomsbury: The Myth of a Relationship." *Essays in Literature* (University of Denver) 1 (September 1973): 31–42.

Bonds, Diane S. "Joyce Carol Oates: Testing the Lawrentian Hypothesis." In Cushman and Jackson, op. cit. (1991): 167–87.

Bradbury, Malcolm. "Phases of Modernism: The Novel and the 1920's." In his *Possibilities: Essays on the State of the Novel.* New York: Oxford University Press, 1973, pp. 81–90.

Brandes, Rand. "Behind the Bestiaries: The Poetry of Lawrence and Ted Hughes." In Cushman and Jackson, op. cit. (1991): 248–67.

Bridgewater, Patrick. *Nietzsche in Anglosaxony.* London: Leicester University Press, 1972, pp. 104–9.

Brown, Richard. " 'Perhaps She Had Not Told Him All the Story . . . ': Observations on the Topic of Adultery in Some Modern Fiction." In *Joyce, Modernity, and Its Mediation.* Edited by Christine van Boheemen. Amsterdam: Rodopi, 1989, pp. 99–111. (Discusses *Lady Chatterley's Lover.*)

Brunsdale, Mitzi M. "Toward a Greater Day: Lawrence, Rilke, and Immortality." *Comparative Literature Studies* 20 (1983): 402–17.

Buckley, Jerome H. *Season of Youth: The Bildungsroman from Dickens to Golding.* Cambridge: Harvard University Press, 1974, pp. 204–24.

Bull, J. A. "The Novelist on the Margins: Hardy and Lawrence." In his *The Framework of Fiction: Socio-Cultural Approaches to the Novel.* Basingstoke and London: Macmillan, 1988, pp. 147–90.

Bump, Jerome. "Stevens and Lawrence: The Poetry of Nature and the Spirit of the Age." *Southern Review* 18 (1982): 44–61.

Burnett, Gary. "H. D. and Lawrence: Two Allusions." *H. D. Newsletter* 1 (Spring 1987): 32–35.

Burwell, Rose Marie. "Schopenhauer, Hardy and Lawrence: Toward a New Understanding of *Sons and Lovers.*" *Western Humanities Review* 28 (Spring 1974): 105–17.

————. "A Checklist of Lawrence's Reading." In *A DHL Handbook.* Edited by Keith Sagar. Manchester: Manchester University Press, 1982, pp. 59–125.

Calonne, David Stephen. "Euphoria in Paris: Henry Miller Meets DHL." *Library Chronicle of the University of Texas at Austin,* new series, 34 (1986): 89–98.

Cardy, Michael. "Beyond Documentation: Emile Zola and DHL." *Neohelicon* 14, no. 2 (1987): 225–31.

Cavaliero, Glen. *The Rural Tradition in the English Novel, 1900–1939.* Totowa, N.J.: Rowman and Littlefield, 1977, passim.

Cazamian, L. "DHL and Katherine Mansfield as Letter-Writers: The Lamont Lecture at Yale University." *University of Toronto Quarterly* 3 (April 1934): 286–307.

Chace, William M. "Lawrence and English Poetry." In Meyers, op. cit. (1987): 54–80.

Chambers, Jessie ("E.T."). "The Literary Formation of DHL." *European Quarterly* 1 (May 1934): 36–45. (Also in Chambers [1935]: 91–123.)

Choudhury, Sheila Lahiri. "DHL and Ford Madox Ford: A Brief Encounter." *Etudes Lawrenciennes* 9 (1993): 97–109.

Cianci, Giovanni. "DHL and Futurism/Vorticism." *Arbeiten aus Anglistik und Amerikanistic* 8 (1983): 41–53.

Clarke, Bruce. "Dora Marsden's Egoism and Modern Letters: West, Weaver, Joyce, Pound, Lawrence, Williams, Eliot." *Works and Days* 2, no. 2 (1984): 27–47.

———. "The Fall of Montezuma: Poetry and History in William Carlos Williams and DHL." *William Carlos Williams Review* 12 (1986): 1–12.

———. "The Melancholy Serpent: Body and Landscape in Lawrence and William Carlos Williams." In Cushman and Jackson, op. cit. (1991): 188–210.

Clarke, Ian. "Lawrence and the Drama of His European Contemporaries." *Etudes Lawrenciennes* 9 (1993): 173–86.

Clark, L. D. "DHL and the American Indian." *DHL Review* 9 (1976): 305–72.

———. "Making the Classic Contemporary: Lawrence's Pilgrimage Novels and American Romance." In *DHL in the Modern World.* Edited by Peter Preston and Peter Hoare. London: Macmillan, 1989, pp. 193–216.

Colmer, John. "Lawrence and Blake." In *DHL and Tradition.* Edited by Jeffrey Meyers. London: Athlone, 1985, pp. 9–20.

Conrad, Peter. "Lawrence in New Mexico." *Imagining America.* New York: Oxford University Press, 1980, pp. 159–93.

Cowan, James C. "Lawrence's Romantic Values: *Studies in Classic American Literature.*" *Ball State University Forum* 8 (Winter 1967): 30–35.

Cox, Gary D. "DHL and F. M. Dostoevsky: Mirror Images of Murderous Aggression." *Modern Fiction Studies* 29 (1983): 175–82.

Cushman, Keith. "Blind, Intertextual Love: 'The Blind Man' and Raymond Carver's 'Cathedral.' " *Etudes Lawrenciennes* 3 (1988): 125–38. (Reprinted in Cushman and Jackson, op. cit. [1991]: 155–66.)

———. "Lawrence, Compton Mackenzie, and the 'Semi-Literary Cats' of Capri." *Etudes Lawrenciennes* 9 (1993): 139–53.

Cushman, Keith, and Dennis Jackson, eds. *DHL's Literary Inheritors.* London: Macmillan, 1991. (Essays cited separately. Introduction by the editors, "Lawrence and His Inheritors," pp. 1–14.)

Daleski, H. M. "Lawrence and George Eliot: The Genesis of *The White Peacock.*" In *DHL and Tradition.* Edited by Jeffrey Meyers. London: Athlone, 1985, pp. 51–68.

———. "Life as a Four-Letter Word: A Contemporary View of Lawrence and Joyce." In *DHL in the Modern World.* Edited by Peter Preston and Peter Hoare. London: Macmillan, 1989, pp. 90–103.

Daly, Macdonald. "DHL and Walter Brierley." *DHL: The Journal of the DHL Society* 4 (1986): 22–29.

Das, G. K. "Lawrence and Forster." In *The Spirit of DHL: Centenary Studies.* Edited by Gāmini Salgādo and G. K. Das. London: Macmillan, 1988, pp. 154–62.

Dataller, Roger. "Mr. Lawrence and Mrs. Woolf." *Essays in Criticism* 8 (January 1958): 48–59.

Davie, Donald. "On Sincerity: From Wordsworth to Ginsberg." *Encounter* 31, no. 4 (1968): 61–66.

———. "A Doggy Demos: Hardy and Lawrence." In his *Thomas Hardy and British Poetry.* London: Routledge and Kegan Paul; New York: Oxford University Press, 1973, pp. 130–51.

———. "Dissent in the Present Century." *Times Literary Supplement* (3 December 1976): 1519–20.

Davies, W. Eugene. "The Poetry of Mary Webb: An Invitation." *English Literature in Transition* 11, no. 2 (1968): 95–101. (Comparisons with Lawrence.)

Davis, Philip. *Memory and Writing from Wordsworth to Lawrence.* Liverpool: Liverpool University Press, 1983, pp. 411–89.

Deakin, William. "DHL's Attack on Proust and Joyce." *Essays in Criticism* 7 (1957): 383–403.

Delany, Paul. "Lawrence and E. M. Forster: Two Rainbows." *DHL Review* 8 (Spring 1975): 54–62.

———. "Lawrence and Forster: First Skirmish with Bloomsbury." *DHL Review* 11 (Spring 1978): 63–72.

———. "Lawrence and Carlyle." In *DHL and Tradition.* Edited by Jeffrey Meyers. London: Athlone, 1985, pp. 21–34.

Delavenay, Emile. "Lawrence and the Futurists." In *The Modernists: Studies in a Literary Phenomenon: Essays in Honor of Harry T. Moore.* Edited by Lawrence B. Gamache and Ian S. MacNiven. London and Toronto: Associated University Presses, 1987a, pp. 140–62.

———. "Some Further Thoughts on Lawrence and Chamberlain." *DHL Review* 19 (Summer 1987b): 173–80. (Response to Schneider [1987].)

Digaetani, John Louis. "Situational Myths: Richard Wagner and DHL." In his *Richard Wagner and the Modern British Novel.* Rutherford, N.J.: Fairleigh Dickinson University Press; London: Associated University Presses, 1978, pp. 58–89.

Drain, Richard Leslie. "Formative Influences on the Work of DHL." Ph.D. diss., University of Cambridge, 1962.

Duryea, Polly. "Rainwitch Ritual in Cather, Lawrence, and Momaday, and Others." *Journal of Ethnic Studies* 18 (Summer 1990): 59–75.

Eggert, Paul. "Identification of Lawrence's Futurist Readings." *Notes and Queries* 29 (1982): 342–44.

Ellis, David. "Lawrence, Wordsworth and 'Anthropomorphic Lust.' " *Cambridge Quarterly* 23, no. 3 (1994): 230–42.

Empson, William. "Swinburne and DHL." *Times Literary Supplement* (20 February 1969): 185.

Engel, Monroe. "Contrived Lives: Joyce and Lawrence." In *Modernism Reconsidered.* Edited by Robert Kiely and John Hildebidle. Cambridge and London: Harvard University Press, 1983, pp. 65–80.

Faas, E. "Charles Olson and DHL: Aesthetics of the 'Primitive Abstract.' " *Boundary 2*, no. 2 (1973): 113–26.

Fenwick, Julie. "Women, Sex, and Culture in 'The Moonlight': Joyce Cary's Response to D.H. Lawrence." *Ariel* 24 (April 1993): 27–42.

Firchow, Peter E. "Rico and Julia: The Hilda Doolittle—DHL Affair Reconsidered." *Journal of Modern Literature* 8 (1980): 51–76.

Fjagesund, Peter. "DHL, Knut Hamsun and Pan." *English Studies* (Netherlands) 72, no. 5 (October 1991): 421–25.

Flay, M. "Lawrence and Dostoevsky in 1915." *English Studies* 69 (June 1988): 254–66.

Fortunati, Vita. "The Visual Arts and the Novel: The Contrasting Cases of Ford Madox Ford and DHL." *Etudes Lawrenciennes* 9 (1993): 129–43.

Foster, John Burt, Jr. "Holding Forth against Nietzsche: DHL's Novel's from *Women in Love* to *The Plumed Serpent*." In his *Heirs to Dionysus: A Nietzschean Current in Literary Modernism*. Princeton: Princeton University Press, 1981, pp. 189–255.

French, Roberts W. "Whitman and the Poetics of Lawrence." In *DHL and Tradition*. Edited by Jeffrey Meyers. London: Athlone, 1985, pp. 91–114.

———. "Lawrence and American Poetry." In Meyers, op. cit. (1987): 109–34.

Fussell, Paul. "The Places of DHL." In *Abroad: British Literary Traveling between the Wars*. New York: Oxford University Press, 1980, pp. 141–64.

Gates, Norman T. "Richard Aldington and DHL." In *Richard Aldington: Reappraisals*. Edited by Charles Doyle. Victoria, B.C.: University of Victoria Press, 1990, pp. 45–59.

Ghauri, H. R. "Yeats, Pound, Eliot, Joyce: Lawrence's Secret Sharers." *Ariel* 7 (1981–82): 54–74.

Gifford, Henry. "Anna, Lawrence and the Law." *Critical Quarterly* 1 (Autumn 1959): 203–6. (On Lawrence and Tolstoy. Response from Raymond Williams: "Lawrence and Tolstoy." *Critical Quarterly* 2 [Spring 1960]: 33–39. Rejoinder from Gifford: "Further Notes on Anna Karenina." *Critical Quarterly* 2 [Summer 1960]: 158–60. All three essays reprinted in *Russian Literature and Modern English Fiction: A Collection of Critical Essays*. Edited by Donald Davie. Chicago: University of Chicago Press, 1965, pp. 148–63.)

Gilchrist, Susan Y. "DHL and E. M. Forster: A Failed Friendship." *Etudes Lawrenciennes* 9 (1993): 127–38.

Gindin, James. "Lawrence and the Contemporary English Novel." In Meyers, op. cit. (1987): 30–53.

Glazer, Myra. "Sex and the Psyche: William Blake and DHL." *Hebrew University Studies in Language and Literature* 9, no. 2 (1981): 196–229. (Revised as "Why the Sons of God Want the Daughters of Men: On William Blake and DHL." In *William Blake and the Moderns*. Edited by Robert J. Bertholf and Annette S. Levitt. Albany: State University of New York Press, 1982, pp. 164–85.)

Goldknopf, David. "DHL and Hometown Literature: Eastwood, England." *DHL: Journal of the DHL Society* 2, no. 2 (1980): 9–12.

Goodheart, Eugene. "Lawrence and American Fiction." In Meyers, op. cit. (1987): 135–55.

Goodman, Charlotte. "Henry James, DHL and the Victimised Child." *Modern Language Studies* 10 (1979–80): 43–51.

Gordon, D. J. "Two Anti-Puritan Puritans: Bernard Shaw and DHL." *Yale Review* 56 (Autumn 1966): 76–90.

———. "DHL's Dual Myth of Origin." *Sewanee Review* 89 (1981): 83–94. (Lawrence's response to Freud and Rousseau.)

Gouirand, Jacqueline. "Viennese Modernists and DHL: A Convergence of Sensibilities." *Etudes Lawrenciennes* 9 (1993): 59–78.

Gould, Eric. "Recovering the Numinous: DHL and T. S. Eliot." In his *Mythical Intentions in Modern Literature.* Princeton: Princeton University Press, 1981, pp. 199–262.

Gransden, K. W. *E. M. Forster.* Edinburgh: Oliver and Boyd, 1962, pp. 108–18.

Gray, Ronald. "English Resistance to German Literature from Coleridge to DHL." In his *The German Tradition in Literature 1871–1945.* Cambridge: Cambridge University Press, 1965, pp. 327–54. (Mainly on *Women in Love.*)

Green, Eleanor H. "Blueprints for Utopia: The Political Ideas of Nietzsche and DHL." *Renaissance and Modern Studies* 18 (1974): 141–61.

———. "Schopenhauer and DHL on Sex and Love." *DHL Review* 8 (Fall 1975a): 329–45.

———. "The *Will zur Macht* and DHL." *Massachusetts Studies in English* 10 (Winter 1975b): 25–30.

———. "Nietzsche, Helen Corke, and DHL." *American Notes and Queries* 15 (1976): 56–59.

———. "Lawrence, Schopenhauer, and the Dual Nature of the Universe." *South Atlantic Bulletin* 62 (November 1977): 84–92.

Green, Martin. "British Decency." *Kenyon Review* 21 (Autumn 1959): 505–32. (Lawrence, Leavis, Orwell, and Kingsley Amis as exemplars of the new type of "decent" man—the rebel.)

Gregor, Ian. " 'He Wondered': The Religious Imagination of William Golding: A Tribute on His 75th Birthday." In *William Golding: The Man and His Books.* London: Faber and Faber, 1986; New York: Farrar, Straus, and Giroux, 1987, pp. 84–100.

Gutierrez, Donald. "The Ancient Imagination of DHL." *Twentieth Century Literature* 27 (1981): 178–96.

———. " 'Quick, Now, Here, Now, Always': The Flaming Rose of Lawrence and Eliot." *University of Portland Review* 34, no. 2 (1982): 3–8.

Guttenberg, Barnett. "Sherwood Anderson's Dialogue with Lawrence's Dark Gods." In Cushman and Jackson, op. cit. (1991): 46–60.

Hamalian, Leo. "DHL and Black Writers." *Journal of Modern Literature* 16 (Spring 1990): 579–96. (Lawrence's influence on Ralph Ellison, Langston Hughes, Jean Toomer, Richard Wright, and others.)

———. " 'A Whole Climate of Opinion': Lawrence at Black Mountain." In Cushman and Jackson, op. cit. (1991): 228–47. (Lawrence's influence on Charles Olson and Robert Creeley.)

Hayles, Nancy Katherine. "The Ambivalent Approach: DHL and the New Physics." *Mosaic* 15, no. 3 (1982): 89–108.

Hendrick, George. "Jesus and the Osiris-Isis Myth: Lawrence's *The Man Who Died* and Williams' *The Night of the Iguana.*" *Anglia* (Tübingen) 84 (1966): 398–406.

———. " '10' and the Phoenix." *DHL Review* 2 (Summer 1969): 162–67. (Lawrence and Tennessee Williams.)

Henig, Suzanne. "DHL and Virginia Woolf." *DHL Review* 2 (Fall 1969): 265–71.

Henzy, Karl. "Lawrence and Van Gogh in Their Letters." *DHL Review* 24 (Fall 1992): 145–60.

Heuser, Alan. "Creaturely Inseeing in the Poetry of G. M. Hopkins, DHL, and Ted Hughes." *Hopkins Quarterly* 12 (1985): 35–51.

Heywood, Christopher. "DHL's *The Lost Girl* and Its Antecedents by George Moore and Arnold Bennett." *English Studies* 47, no. 2 (1966): 131–34.

———. "African Art and the Work of Roger Fry and DHL." *Sheffield Papers on Literature and Society,* no. 1 (1976): 102–13.

———. "Olive Schreiner's Influence on George Moore and DHL." In *Aspects of South African Literature.* Edited by Christopher Heywood. London: Heinemann, 1976, pp. 42–53.

———. "Olive Schreiner's *The Story of an African Farm:* Prototype of Lawrence's Early Novels." *English Language Notes* 14 (September 1976): 44–50.

———. "*Birds, Beasts and Flowers:* The Evolutionary Context and Lawrence's African Source." *DHL Review* 15 (1982): 87–105. (Reprinted in Brown [1990]: 151–62.)

Hinchcliffe, Peter. "*The Rainbow* and *Women in Love:* From George Eliot to Thomas Hardy as Formal Models." In *DHL's "Women in Love": Contexts and Criticism.* Edited by Michael Ballin. Waterloo, Ontario: Wilfrid Laurier University, 1980, pp. 34–46.

Hinz, Evelyn J. "*Ancient Art and Ritual* and *The Rainbow.*" *Dalhousie Review* 58 (1979): 617–37.

Hinz, Evelyn J., and John J. Teunissen. " 'They Thought of *Sons and Lovers*': DHL and Thomas Wolfe." *Southern Quarterly* 29, no. 3 (Spring 1991): 77–89.

Hirai, Massako. "Forster and Lawrence: The Borderer's Vision of England." *Kobe College Studies* 38 (March 1992): 37–52.

Hooker, Jeremy. "To Open the Mind." *Planet,* nos. 5–6 (Summer 1971): 59–63. (Compares Lawrence and Charles Olson.)

Howard, Rosemary. "Lawrence and Russell." *Etudes Lawrenciennes* 9 (1993): 43–57.

Howe, Irving. "Sherwood Anderson and DHL." *Furioso* 5 (Fall 1950): 21–33.

Humma, John B. "DHL as Friedrich Nietzsche." *Philological Quarterly* 53 (1974a): 110–20.

———. "Melville's *Billy Budd* and Lawrence's "The Prussian Officer": Old Adams and New." *Essays in Literature* (Western Illinois University) 1 (1974b): 83–88.

Ingamells, John. "Cézanne in England 1910–1930." *British Journal of Aesthetics* 5 (October 1965): 341–50 (346–47).

Ingersoll, Earl G. "Virginia Woolf and DHL: Exploring the Dark." *English Studies* 71 (1990): 125–32.

Ivker, Barry. "Schopenhauer and DHL." *Xavier University Studies* 11 (1972): 22–36.

Jackson, Alan D. "DHL, 'Physical Consciousness' and Robert Burns." *Scottish Literary Journal: A Review of Studies in Scottish Language and Literature* 13 (May 1986): 65–76.

Jacquin, Bernard. "Mark Rampion: A Huxleyan Avatar of DHL." *Etudes Lawrenciennes* 7 (1992): 119–27. (Considers Huxley's *Point Counter Point* and its Rampion-version of Lawrence as inspired largely by *Women in Love* and Rupert Birkin.)

Janik, Del Ivan. "Towards 'Thingness': Cézanne's Painting and Lawrence's Poetry." *Twentieth Century Literature* 19 (1973): 119–27.

———. "A Cumbrian *Rainbow:* Melvyn Bragg's Tallentire Trilogy." In Cushman and Jackson, op. cit. (1991): 73–88.

Jarrett, James L. "DHL and Bertrand Russell." In *A DHL Miscellany.* Edited by Harry T. Moore. Carbondale: Southern Illinois University Press, 1959, pp. 168–87.

Joffe, P. H. "A Question of Complexity: The Russell–Lawrence Debate." *Theoria* 57 (1981): 17–37.

Jones, David A. "The Third Unrealized Wonder—The Reality of Relation in DHL and Martin Buber." *Religion and Life* 44 (Summer 1975): 178–87.

Jones, Lawrence. "Imagery and the 'Idiosyncratic Mode of Regard': Eliot, Hardy, and Lawrence." *Ariel* 12 (1981): 29–49.

Jones, William M. "Growth of a Symbol: The Sun in DHL and Eudora Welty." *University of Kansas City Review* 26 (1959): 68–73.

Joshi, Rita. "The Dissent Tradition: The Relation of Mark Rutherford to DHL." *English Language Notes* 22 (March 1985): 61–68.

Kaczvinsky, Donald P. " 'The True Birth of Free Man': Culture and Civilization in *Tunc-Nunquam.*" In *On Miracle Ground: Essays on the Fiction of Lawrence Durrell.* Edited by Michael H. Begnal. Lewisburg, Pa.: Bucknell University Press, 1990, pp. 140–52.

Kalnins, Mara. "Symbolic Seeing: Lawrence and Heraclitus." In *DHL: Centenary Essays.* Edited by Mara Kalnins. Bristol: Bristol Classical Press, 1986, pp. 173–90.

Kane, Richard. "From Loins of Darkness to Loins of Pork: Body Imagery in Lawrence, Eliot, and Joyce." *Recovering Literature: A Journal of Contextualist Criticism* 17 (1989–90): 5–18.

Karsten, Julie A. "Self-Realization and Intimacy: The Influence of DHL on Anais Nin." *Anais: An International Journal* 4 (1986): 36–42.

Katz-Roy, Ginette. "DHL and 'That Beastly France.' " *DHL Review* 23 (1991): 143–56.

———. " 'This May Be a Withering Tree This Europe': Bachelard, Deleuze and Guattari on DHL's Poetic Imagination." *Etudes Lawrenciennes* 9 (1993): 219–35.

Kay, Wallace G. "The Cortege of Dionysus: Lawrence and Giono." *Southern Quarterly* 4 (January 1966): 159–71.

———. "Dionysus, DHL and Jean Giono: Further Considerations." *Southern Quarterly* 6 (1968): 394–414.

Kennedy, A. *The Protean Self: Dramatic Action in Contemporary Fiction.* London: Macmillan; New York: Columbia University Press, 1974, pp. 64–66, 119–20, 123. (Lawrence, society, Joyce Cary.)

Kermode, Frank. "Spenser and the Allegorists." *Proceedings of the British Academy* 48 (1962): 261–79. (Reprinted in his *Shakespeare, Spenser, Donne: Renaissance Essays.* New York: Viking Press, 1971, pp. 261–79. This also includes discussion of *Apocalypse* and discussion of connections between *The Faerie Queene* and Lawrence, pp. 12–32.)

———. "DHL and the Apocalyptic Types." In his *Continuities.* London: Routledge and Kegan Paul, 1968, pp. 122–51. (Compares *Women in Love* with George Eliot's *Middlemarch.* Also published in *Critical Quarterly* 10 [1968]: 14–33; and, in shortened form, in Clarke, ed. [1969]: 203–18.)

Kernan, J. "Lawrence and the French." *Commonweal* 16 (26 October 1932): 617–18.

Kerr, Fergus. "Russell vs. Lawrence and/or Wittgenstein." *New Blackfriars* 63 (October 1982): 430–40.

Kinkead-Weekes, Mark. "Lawrence on Hardy." In *Thomas Hardy after Fifty Years.*

Edited by Lance St. John Butler. Totowa, N.J.: Rowman and Littlefield, 1977, pp. 90–103.

Knight, G. Wilson. "Lawrence, Joyce and Powys." *Essays in Criticism* 11 (1961): 403–17.

Knoepflmacher, U. C. "The Rival Ladies: Mrs. Ward's *Lady Connie* and Lawrence's *Lady Chatterley's Lover.*" *Victorian Studies* 4 (Winter 1960): 141–58.

Krook, Dorothea. "Messianic Humanism: DHL's *The Man Who Died.*" In her *Three Traditions of Moral Thought.* Cambridge: Cambridge University Press, 1959, pp. 255–92.

Landow, George P. "Lawrence and Ruskin: The Sage as Word-Painter." In *DHL and Tradition.* Edited by Jeffrey Meyers. London: Athlone, 1985, pp. 35–50.

Langbaum, Robert. "Lawrence and Hardy." In *DHL and Tradition.* Edited by Jeffrey Meyers. London: Athlone, 1985, pp. 69–90.

———. "Lawrence and the Modernists." *Etudes Lawrenciennes* 9 (1993): 145–57.

Larrett, William. "Lawrence and Germany: A Reluctant Guest in the Land of 'Pure Ideas.' " In *Rethinking Lawrence.* Edited by Keith Brown. Milton Keynes and Philadelphia: Open University Press, 1990, pp. 79–92.

Lavrin, Janko. "Sex and Eros (on Rozanov, Weininger, and DHL)." *European Quarterly* 1 (1934): 88–96. (Reprinted in his *Aspects of Modernism, from Wilde to Pirandello.* London: Stanley Nott, 1935, pp. 141–59.)

Leavis, F. R. "Anna Karenina." *Cambridge Quarterly* 1 (Winter 1965–66): 5–27.

Leavis, L. R. "The Late Nineteenth Century Novel and the Change towards the Sexual—Gissing, Hardy and Lawrence." *English Studies* 66 (1985): 36–47.

Lee, R. "Irony and Attitude in George Eliot and DHL." *English Studies in Africa* 16, no. 1 (1973): 15–21.

Levine, George. "Epilogue: Lawrence, *Frankenstein,* and the Reversal of Realism." In his *The Realistic Imagination: English Fiction from "Frankenstein" to "Lady Chatterley."* Chicago: University of Chicago Press, 1981, pp. 317–28 (323–28).

Levy, Michele Frucht. "DHL and Dostoevsky: The Thirst for Risk and the Thirst for Life." *Modern Fiction Studies* 33 (1987): 281–88. (*St. Mawr.*)

Lindenberger, Herbert. "Lawrence and the Romantic Tradition." In *A DHL Miscellany.* Edited by Harry T. Moore. Carbondale: Southern Illinois University Press, 1959, pp. 326–41.

Lindsay, Jack. "The Impact of Modernism on Lawrence." in *The Paintings of DHL.* Edited by Mervyn Levy. London: Cory, Adams, and McKay; New York: Viking, 1964, pp. 35–53.

Linebarger, Jim, and Lad Kirsten. "[Dylan] Thomas's 'Shall Gods Be Said to Thump the Clouds.' " *Explicator* 48 (Spring 1990): 212–16.

Lodge, David. "Lawrence, Dostoevsky, Bakhtin: DHL and Dialogic Fiction." *Renaissance and Modern Studies* 29 (1985): 16–32. (Reprinted, in slightly revised form, in Brown [1990]: 92–108; and in David Lodge. *After Bakhtin: Essays on Fiction and Criticism.* London and New York: Routledge, 1990, pp. 57–74.)

Lucie-Smith, Edward. "The Poetry of DHL—With a Glance at Shelley." In *DHL: Novelist, Poet, Prophet.* Edited by Stephen Spender. London: Weidenfeld and Nicolson, 1973, pp. 224–33.

McGuffie, Duncan. "Lawrence and Nonconformity." In *DHL 1885–1930: A Celebration.* Edited by Andrew Cooper and Glyn Hughes. Nottingham: DHL Society, 1985, pp. 31–38.

MacNiven, Ian. "Lawrence and Durrell: 'ON THE SAME TRAM.' " In Cushman and Jackson, op. cit. (1991): 61–72.

Mann, F. Maureen. "On Reading *Women in Love* in Light of Brontë's *Shirley.*" In *DHL's "Women in Love": Contexts and Criticism.* Edited by Michael Ballin. Waterloo, Ontario: Wilfrid Laurier University, 1980, pp. 47–69.

Marcus, Phillip L. "Lawrence, Yeats, and 'the Resurrection of the Body.' " In *DHL: A Centenary Consideration.* Edited by Peter Balbert and Phillip L. Marcus. Ithaca, N.Y., and London: Cornell University Press, 1985, pp. 210–36.

Markert, Lawrence W. "Symbolic Geography: DHL and Lawrence Durrell." *Deus Loci: Lawrence Durrell Newsletter* 5 (1981): 90–101.

———. " 'The Pure and Sacred Readjustment of Death': Connections between Lawrence Durrell's *Avignon Quintet* and the Writings of DHL." *Twentieth Century Literature* 33 (Winter 1987): 550–64.

Martin, Stoddard. *Wagner to "The Waste Land": A Study of the Relationship of Wagner to English Literature.* Totowa, N.J.: Barnes and Noble, 1982, pp. 168–93.

Masson, Margaret J. "DHL's Congregational Inheritance." *DHL Review* 22 (Spring 1990): 53–68.

Mather, R. "Patrick White and Lawrence: A Contrast." *Critical Review,* no. 13 (1970): 34–50.

May, Keith M. *Nietzsche and Modern Literature: Themes in Yeats, Rilke, Mann and Lawrence.* London: Macmillan, 1988.

Meisel, Perry. "Hardy, Lawrence, and the Disruptions of Nature." In his *The Myth of the Modern: A Study in British Literature and Criticism after 1850.* New Haven, Conn.: Yale University Press, 1987, pp. 11–36.

Melchiori, Giorgio. "The Lotus and the Rose: DHL and Eliot's *Four Quartets.*" *English Miscellany* 4 (1954): 203–16.

Mendel, S. "Shakespeare and DHL: Two Portraits of the Hero." *Wascana Review* 3, no. 2 (1968): 49–60.

Meyers, Jeffrey. "DHL and Katherine Mansfield." *London Magazine,* new series, 18 (May 1978a): 32–54.

———. *Katherine Mansfield: A Biography.* London: Hamilton, 1978b, pp. 78–104. ("Friendship with DHL, 1913–1923.")

———, ed. *DHL and Tradition.* London: Athlone, 1985. (seven essays cited separately. Introduction by Meyers, pp. 1–13.)

———. "Lawrence and the Travel Writers." In Meyers, op. cit. (1987): 81–108.

———, ed. *The Legacy of DHL: New Essays.* London: Macmillan, 1987.

Miller, James E., Jr., Karl Shapiro, and Bernice Slote. *Start with the Sun: Studies in Cosmic Poetry.* Lincoln: University of Nebraska Press, 1960, pp. 57–134, 229–38. (Lawrence as a "cosmic" poet in the tradition of Whitman, Hart Crane, and Dylan Thomas.)

Miller, Milton. "Definition by Comparison: Chaucer, Lawrence, Joyce." *Essays in Criticism* 3 (October 1953): 369–81.

Mills, Howard. "Late Turner, Hardy's Tess and Lawrence's Knees." In *Tensions and Transitions.* Edited by Michael Irwin, Mark Kinkead-Weekes, and A. Robert Lee. London: Faber and Faber, 1990, pp. 137–54.

———. "Lawrence, Roger Fry and Cézanne." *DHL: The Journal of the DHL Society* (Spring 1991): 28–38.

————. " 'The World of Substance': Lawrence, Hardy, Cézanne, and Shelley." *English* 43 (Autumn 1994): 209–22.

Morrison, Kristin. "Lawrence, Beardsley, Wilde: *The White Peacock* and Sexual Ambiguity." *Western Humanities Review* 30 (1936): 241–48.

Morse, Stearns. "The Phoenix and the Desert Places." *Massachusetts Review* 9 (Autumn 1968): 773–84. (Lawrence and Robert Frost.)

New, Peter. *Fiction and Purpose in "Utopia," "Rasselas," "The Mill on the Floss," and "Women in Love."* London: Macmillan; New York: St. Martin's Press, 1985.

Newman, Paul B. "DHL and *The Golden Bough.*" *Kansas Magazine* (1962): 79–86.

Newton, Frances J. "Venice, Pope, T. S. Eliot and DHL." *Notes and Queries* 5 (March 1958): 119–20.

Nielsen, Inge Padkaer, and Karsten Hvidtfelt Nielsen. "The Modernism of DHL and the Discourses of Decadence: Sexuality and Tradition in *The Trespasser, Fantasia of the Unconscious,* and *Aaron's Rod.*" *Arcadia* 25, no. 3 (1990): 270–86.

Nimitz, Cheryl. "Lawrence and Kundera—'Disturbing.' " *Recovering Literature* 17 (1989–90): 43–51.

Norton, David. "Lawrence, Wells and Bennett: Influence and Tradition." *Aumla* 54 (November 1980): 171–90.

Orrell, Herbert Meredith. "DHL, New Mexico, and the American Indian." *Cresset* 44, no. 3 (1981): 7–11.

Owen, Guy. "Erskine Caldwell and DHL." *Pembroke Magazine* 11 (1979): 18–21.

Padhi, Bibhu. "DHL and Europe." *Contemporary Review* 257 (1990): 83–87.

Panichas, G. "DHL and the Ancient Greeks." *English Miscellany* 16 (1965): 195–214.

————. "E. M. Forster and DHL: Their Views on Education." In *Renaissance and Modern Essays Presented to Vivian de Sola Pinto in Celebration of His Seventieth Birthday.* Edited by G. R. Hibbard. London: Routledge; New York: Barnes and Noble, 1966, pp. 193–213.

————. *The Reverent Discipline: Essays in Literary Criticism and Culture.* Knoxville: University of Tennessee Press, 1974. ("Notes on Eliot and Lawrence, 1915– 1924," pp. 135–56, "F. M. Dostoevsky and DHL: Their Visions of Evil," pp. 205–28. The two essays cited earlier are also reprinted here, pp. 335–50, 157– 69.)

Parkes, H. B. "DHL and Irving Babbitt." *New Adelphi* 9 (March 1935): 328–31.

Parry, Marguerite. "Mauriac and DHL." In *François Mauriac: Visions and Reappraisals.* Edited by John E. Flower and Bernard C. Swift. Oxford: Berg, 1989, pp. 181–200.

Pascal, Roy. "The Autobiographical Novel and the Autobiography." *Essays in Criticism* 9 (April 1959): 134–50. (Brontë's *Villette, Sons and Lovers,* and Joyce's *Portrait of the Artist as a Young Man.*)

Paterson, John. "Lawrence's Vital Source: Nature and Character in Thomas Hardy." In *Nature and the Victorian Imagination.* Edited by U. C. Knoepflmacher and G. B. Tennyson. Berkeley: University of California Press, 1977, pp. 455–69.

Paulin, Tom. " 'Hibiscus and Salvia Flowers': The Puritan Imagination." In *DHL in the Modern World.* Edited by Peter Preston and Peter Hoare. London: Macmillan, 1989, pp. 180–92.

Peach, Linden. "Powys, Lawrence, and a New Sensibility." *Anglo-Welsh Review* 26 (Autumn 1977): 32–41.

Peek, Andrew. "Edgar Allan Poe's 'Ligeia,' Hermione Roddice and 'The Border Line':

Common Romantic Contexts and a Source of Correspondence in the Fiction of
Poe and Lawrence.'' *Journal of the DHL Society* 2, no. 2 (1980): 4–8.

Pinto, Vivian de Sola. ''William Blake and DHL.'' In *William Blake: Essays for S. Foster
Damon.* Edited by Alvin H. Rosenfeld. Providence, R. I.: Brown University Press,
1969, pp. 84–106.

Preston, Peter. '' 'Under the Same Banner'?: DHL and Catherine Carswell's *Open the
Door!'' Etudes Lawrenciennes* 9 (1993): 111–26. (Considers the degree of affinity
between *Women in Love* and Carswell's novel.)

Price, A. Whigham. ''DHL and Congregationalism.'' *Congregational Quarterly* 34 (July
and October 1956): 242–52; 322–30.

Pritchard, William H. ''Lawrence and Lewis.'' *Agenda* 7 (Autumn–Winter 1969–70):
140–47. (See also his ''Wyndham Lewis and Lawrence.'' *Iowa Review* 2 [Sep-
tember 1971]: 91–96.)

Procter, Margaret. ''Possibilities of Completion: The Endings of *A Passage to India* and
Women in Love.'' English Literature in Transition 34, no. 3 (1991): 261–80.

Pugh, Bridget L. ''The Midlands Imagination: Arnold Bennett, George Eliot, William
Hale White and DHL.'' In *DHL in the Modern World.* Edited by Peter Preston
and Peter Hoare. London: Macmillan, 1989, pp. 139–60.

———. ''DHL: Some Russian Parallels.'' *Etudes Lawrenciennes* 9 (1993): 81–91.

Quennell, Peter. ''DHL and Aldous Huxley.'' In *The English Novelist.* Edited by Derek
Verschoyle. London: Chatto and Windus, 1936, pp. 267–78.

Quinn, Kerker. ''Blake and the New Age.'' *Virginia Quarterly Review* 13 (1937): 271–
85.

Rahman, Tariq. ''Edward Carpenter and DHL.'' *American Notes and Queries* 24 (1985):
18–20.

Remsbury, John. '' 'Real Thinking': Lawrence and Cézanne.'' *Cambridge Quarterly* 2
(Spring 1967): 117–47.

Remsbury, John, and Ann Remsbury. ''Lawrence and Art.'' In *DHL: A Critical Study
of the Major Novels and Other Writings.* Edited by Andor Gomme. Sussex: Harvester Press; New York: Barnes and Noble, 1978, pp. 190–218.

Renner, Stanley. ''The Lawrentian Power and Logic of *Equus.'' In Cushman and Jackson, op. cit. (1991): 31–45. (Influence of *St. Mawr* on Peter Shaffer's play.)

Richardson, Barbara. ''Philip Larkin's Early Influences.'' *Northwest Review* 30, no. 1
(1992): 133–40.

Richardson, John Adkins, and John I. Ades. ''DHL on Cézanne: A Study in the Psychology of Critical Intuition.'' *Journal of Aesthetics and Art Criticism* 28 (Summer 1970): 441–53.

Roberts, John H. ''Huxley and Lawrence.'' *Virginia Quarterly Review* 13 (1937): 546–
57.

Roberts, Adam. ''D. H. Lawrence and Wells's 'Future Men.' '' *Notes and Queries* 40
(March 1993): 67–68.

Roberts, Mark. ''DHL and the Failure of Energy: *Fantasia of the Unconscious; Psychoanalysis and the Unconscious.'' In his *The Tradition of Romantic Morality.* London: Macmillan, 1973, pp. 322–48.

Roberts, Warren. ''London 1908: Lawrence and Pound.'' *Helix* 13–14 (1983): 45–49.

Robinson, H. M. ''Nietzsche, Lawrence and the Somatic Conception of the Good Life.''
New Comparison: A Journal of Comparative and General Literary Studies 5
(1988): 40–56.

Roessel, David. "Pound, Lawrence, and 'The Earthly Paradise.' " *Paideuma: A Journal Devoted to Ezra Pound Scholarship* 18 (1989): 227–30.

———. " 'Like Ovid in Thrace': DHL's Identification with a Roman Poet." *Classical and Modern Literature: A Quarterly* 10 (Summer 1990): 351–57.

Rose, Jonathan. *The Edwardian Temperament 1895–1919.* Athens: Ohio University Press, 1986, pp. 80–91.

Rosenbaum, S. P. "Keynes, Lawrence and Cambridge Revisited." *Cambridge Quarterly* 11 (1982): 252–64.

Ross, C. L. "DHL's Use of Greek Tragedy: Euripedes and Ritual." *DHL Review* 10 (Spring 1977): 1–19.

Ross, Michael L. "The Mythology of Friendship: DHL, Bertrand Russell, and 'The Blind Man.' " In *English Literature and British Philosophy: A Collection of Essays.* Edited by S. P. Rosenbaum. Chicago: University of Chicago Press, 1971, pp. 285–315.

Roston, M. "W. B. Yeats and DHL." In his *Biblical Drama in England, from the Middle Ages to the Present Day.* London: Faber and Faber, 1968, pp. 264–79.

Rowley, Stephen. "The Death of Our Phallic Being: Melville's *Moby Dick* as a Warning Which Leads to *Women in Love.*" *Etudes Lawrenciennes* 7 (1992): 93–105.

———. "Colour Implications of the Poetry of T. S. Eliot and DHL." *Etudes Lawrenciennes* 9 (1993): 159–72.

Roy, Chitra. "DHL and E. M. Forster: A Study in Values." *Indian Journal of English Studies* 8 (March 1967): 46–58.

Ruggles, A. M. "The Kinship of Blake, Vachel Lindsay, and DHL." *Poet Lore* 46 (Spring 1940): 88–92.

Russell, John. "DHL and Painting." In *DHL: Novelist, Poet, Prophet.* Edited by Stephen Spender. London: Weidenfeld and Nicolson, 1973, pp. 234–43.

Ruthven, K. K. "The Savage God: Conrad and Lawrence." *Critical Quarterly* (1968): 39–54.

Sabin, Margery. "The Community of Intelligence and the Avant-Garde." *Raritan* 4 (Winter 1985): 1–25. (On James, Lawrence, Joyce, and others.)

Sagar, Keith. "DHL and Robert Louis Stevenson." *DHL Review* 24 (Fall 1992): 161–65.

Sarvan, Charles, and Liebetraut Sarvan. "DHL and Doris Lessing's *The Grass in Singing.*" *Modern Fiction Studies* 24 (1978): 533–37.

Schapiro, Barbara. "Maternal Bonds and the Boundaries of Self: DHL and Virginia Woolf." *Soundings* 69 (1986): 347–65.

Schneider, Daniel J. "DHL and *Thus Spake Zarathustra.*" *South Carolina Review* 15, no. 2 (1983a): 96–108.

———. "Schopenhauer and the Development of DHL's Psychology." *South Atlantic Review* 48 (1983b): 1–19.

———. " 'Strange Wisdom': Leo Frobenius and DHL." *DHL Review* 16 (1983c): 183–93.

———. "DHL and the Early Greek Philosophers." *DHL Review* 17 (Summer 1984): 97–109.

———. "DHL and Houston Chamberlain: Once Again." *DHL Review* 19 (Summer (1987): 157–71. (See also Delavenay [1987].)

Schnitzer, Deborah. *The Pictorial in Modernist Fiction from Stephen Crane to Ernest Hemingway.* Ann Arbor, Mich.: UMI Research Press, 1988, pp. 138–58.

Schorer, Mark. "Two Houses, Two Ways: The Florentine Villas of Lewis and Lawrence, Respectively." *New World Writing,* no. 4 (October 1953): 136–54.

Schvey, Henry. "Lawrence and Expressionism." In *DHL: New Studies.* Edited by Christopher Heywood. London: Macmillan, 1987, pp. 124–36.

Scott, James F. "DHL's *Germania:* Ethnic Psychology and Cultural Crisis in the Shorter Fiction." *DHL Review* 10 (1977): 142–64.

———. "Thimble into *Ladybird:* Nietzsche, Frobenius, and Bachofen in the Later Works of DHL." *Arcadia* 13 (1978): 161–76.

———. " 'Continental': The Germanic Dimension of *Women in Love." Literature in Wissenschaft und Unterricht* (Kiel) 12 (1979): 117–34.

Seavey, Ormond. "Benjamin Franklin and DHL as Conflicting Modes of Consciousness." In *Critical Essays on Benjamin Franklin.* Edited by Melvin H. Buxbaum. Boston: Hall, 1987, pp. 60–80.

Sepčić, Višnja. "*Women in Love* and Expressionism." *Studia Romanica et Anglica Zagrabiensia* 26 (1981): 397–443; 27 (1982): 2–64.

Sewell, Ernestine P. "Herbartian Psychology in the Developing Art of DHL." *Publications of the Missouri Philological Association* 5 (1980): 66–71.

Shrivastava, K. C., and G. D. Mehta. "The Greatness of the Novel as an Art-Form: The Views of DHL and Albert Camus." *Prajna: Banaras Hindu University Journal* 29, no. 1 (1983): 115–24.

Siegel, Carol. "Virginia Woolf's and Katherine Mansfield's Responses to DHL's Fiction." *DHL Review* 21 (1989): 291–311.

———. "Floods of Female Desire in Lawrence and Eudora Welty." In Cushman and Jackson, op. cit. (1991): 109–30. (Reprinted in Siegel [1991]: 164–84.)

Smith, G., Jr. "The Doll-Burners: DHL and Louisa Alcott." *Modern Language Quarterly* 19 (March 1958): 28–32.

Soames, Jane. "The Modern Rousseau." *Life and Letters* 8 (December 1932): 451–70.

Spanier, Sandra Whipple. "Two Foursomes in *The Blithedale Romance* and *Women in Love." Comparative Literature Studies* 16 (1979): 58–69.

Spears, Monroe K. *Dionysus and the City: Modernism in Twentieth-Century Poetry.* London and New York: Oxford University Press, 1971, passim.

Spender, Stephen. "Pioneering the Instinctive Life." In his *The Creative Element: A Study of Vision, Despair and Orthodoxy among Some Modern Writers.* London: Hamish Hamilton, 1953, pp. 92–107.

Spilka, Mark. "Lessing and Lawrence: The Battle of the Sexes." *Contemporary Literature* 16 (Spring 1975): 218–40. (Reprinted in Spilka [1992]: 121–46.)

———. "Lawrence versus Peeperkorn on Abdication; or, What Happens to a Pagan Vitalist When the Juice Runs Out?" In *DHL: The Man Who Lived.* Edited by Robert B. Partlow, Jr., and Harry T. Moore. Carbondale: Southern Illinois University Press, 1980, pp. 105–20. (Lawrence and Thomas Mann. Reprinted in Spilka [1992]: 70–95.)

———. "Hemingway and Lawrence as Abusive Husbands." In his *Renewing the Normative DHL: A Personal Progress.* Columbia and London: University of Missouri Press, 1992, pp. 193–247.

Spivey, Ted R. "Lawrence and Faulkner: The Symbolist Novel and the Prophetic Song." In his *The Journey beyond Tragedy: A Study of Myth and Modern Fiction.* Orlando: University Presses of Florida, 1980, pp. 72–93.

Squires, Michael. "Scenic Construction and Rhetorical Signals in Hardy and Lawrence." *DHL Review* 8 (1975): 125–45.

———. "Lawrence, Dickens, and the English Novel." In *The Challenge of DHL.* Edited by Michael Squires and Keith Cushman. Madison: University of Wisconsin Press, 1990, pp. 42–61.

Sreenivasan, S. "DHL and Bertrand Russell: A Study in Intellectual 'Personalities.' " *Journal of Literary Aesthetics* 1, no. 3 (1981): 85–96.

Stanford, Raney. "Thomas Hardy and Lawrence's *The White Peacock.*" *Modern Fiction Studies* 5 (1959): 19–28.

Stavrou, Constantine. "William Blake and DHL." *University of Kansas City Review* 22 (1956): 235–40.

Steinhauer, H. "Eros and Psyche: A Nietzschean Motif in Anglo-American Literature." *Modern Language Notes* 64 (1949): 217–28.

Stewart, Jack F. "Expressionism in *The Rainbow.*" *Novel* 13 (1980a): 296–315.

———. "Lawrence and Gauguin." *Twentieth Century Literature* 26 (1980b): 385–401.

———. "Primitivism in *Women in Love.*" *DHL Review* 13 (Spring 1980c): 45–62.

———. "Lawrence and Van Gogh." *DHL Review* 16 (Spring 1983): 1–24.

———. "Common Art Interests of Van Gogh and Lawrence." *Studies in the Humanities* 11, no. 2 (1984): 18–32.

———. "The Vital Art of Lawrence and Van Gogh." *DHL Review* 19 (Summer 1987): 123–48.

———. "Primordial Affinities: Lawrence, Van Gogh and the Miners." *Mosaic* 24 (Winter 1991): 92–113. (Reprinted in *DHL: The Journal of the DHL Society* [1992–93]: 22–44.)

Stoll, John E. "Common Womb Imagery in Joyce and Lawrence." *Ball State University Forum* 11 (Spring 1970): 10–24.

Stovel, Nora Foster. " 'A Great Kick at Misery': Lawrence's and Drabble's Rebellion against the Fatalism of Bennett." In Cushman and Jackson, op. cit. (1991): 131–54. (Discusses *The Lost Girl, Anna of the Five Towns,* and Margaret Drabble's *Jerusalem the Golden.*)

Strachey, John. *The Coming Struggle for Power.* London: Gollancz, 1932, pp. 206–16. (Discusses Lawrence along with Marcel Proust and Aldous Huxley as the most representative writers of the age.)

Stroupe, John H. "Ruskin, Lawrence, and Gothic Naturalism." *Ball State University Forum* 11 (Spring 1970): 3–9. (The influence of Ruskin's "The Nature of Gothic.")

Stubbs, Patricia. "Mr. Lawrence and Mrs. Woolf." In her *Women and Fiction: Feminism and the Novel, 1880–1920.* New York: Barnes and Noble, 1979, pp. 225–35.

Sword, H. "Orpheus and Eurydice in the Twentieth Century: Lawrence, H. D., and the Poetics of the Turn." *Twentieth Century Literature* 35 (1989): 407–28.

Symons, Julian. *Makers of the New: The Revolution in Literature 1912–1939.* London: Andre Deutsch, 1987, pp. 79–91.

Taylor, Anne Robinson. "Modern Primitives: Molly Bloom and James Joyce, with a Note on DHL." In her *Male Novelists and Their Female Voices: Literary Masquerades.* Troy, N.Y.: Whitston, 1981, pp. 189–228.

Tedlock, E. W., Jr. "DHL's Annotations of Ouspensky's *Tertium Organum.*" *Texas Studies in Literature and Language* 2 (Summer 1960): 206–18.

Thompson, Leslie M. "A Lawrence-Huxley Parallel: *Women in Love* and *Point Counter Point.*" *Notes and Queries* 15 (February 1968): 58–59.

Trilling, Diana. "DHL and the Movements of Modern Culture." In *DHL: Novelist, Poet, Prophet.* Edited by Stephen Spender. London: Weidenfeld and Nicolson, 1973, pp. 1–7.

Turnell, M. "The Shaping of Contemporary Literature: Lawrence, Forster, Virginia Woolf." In his *Modern Literature and Christian Faith.* London: Darton, Longman, and Todd; Westminster, Md.: Newman Press, 1961, pp. 25–45.

Turner, John, with Cornelia Rumpf-Worthen and Ruth Jenkins. "The Otto Gross-Frieda Weekley Correspondence: Transcribed, Translated, and Annotated." *DHL Review* 22 (Summer 1990): 137–227.

Ulmer, Gregory L. "DHL, Wilhelm Worringer, and the Aesthetics of Modernism." *DHL Review* 10 (Summer 1977a): 165–81.

———. "Rousseau and DHL: 'Philosophes' of the 'Gelded' Age." *Canadian Review of Comparative Literature* 4 (1977b): 68–80.

Van Herk, Aritha. "CrowB(e)ars and Kangaroos of the Future: The Post-Colonial Ga(s)p." *World Literature Written in English* 30 (Autumn 1990): 42–54. (Discusses *Kangaroo* along with three works by Faulkner, David Ireland, and Robert Kroetsch.)

Vickery, John B. *The Literary Impact of "The Golden Bough."* Princeton: Princeton University Press, 1973, pp. 294–325.

Vitoux, Pierre. "Aldous Huxley and DHL: An Attempt at Intellectual Sympathy." *Modern Language Review* 69 (July 1974): 501–22.

Wajc-Tenenbaum, R. "Aldous Huxley and DHL." *Revue des Langues Vivantes* 32 (1966): 598–610.

Walsh, K. R. "Three Puritan Poets: Milton, Blake, DHL." *Christian Community* 5, no. 53 (May 1936).

Way, B. "Sex and Language: Obscene Words in DHL and Henry Miller." *New Left Review,* no. 27 (September–October 1964): 164–70.

Weatherby, H. L. "Old-Fashioned Gods: Eliot on Lawrence and Hardy." *Sewanee Review* 75 (Spring 1967): 301–16.

Weinstein, Philip M. *The Semantics of Desire: Changing Models of Identity from Dickens to Joyce.* Princeton: Princeton University Press, 1984, pp. 189–251.

Werner, Alfred. "Lawrence and Pascin." *Kenyon Review* 23 (Spring 1961): 217–28. (Similarities between Lawrence and the painter.)

Wexelblatt, Robert. "F. Scott Fitzgerald and DHL: Bicycles and Incest." *American Literature: A Journal of Literary History, Criticism, and Bibliography* 59 (October 1987): 378–88.

Whalen, Terry. "Lawrence and Larkin: The Suggestion of an Affinity." *Modernist Studies* 4 (1982): 105–22.

Widmer, Kingsley. "The Pertinence of Modern Pastoral: The Three Versions of *Lady Chatterley's Lover.*" *Studies in the Novel* 5 (Fall 1973): 298–313.

———. "Lawrence and the Nietzschean Matrix." In *DHL and Tradition.* Edited by Jeffrey Meyers. London: Athlone, 1985, pp. 115–31.

———. "Desire and Denial: Dialectics of Passion in DHL." *DHL Review* 18 (1985–86): 139–50.

———. "Melville and the Myths of Modernism." In *A Companion to Melville Studies.* Edited by John Bryant. Westport, Conn.: Greenwood, 1986.

——. "Lawrence's Cultural Impact." In Meyers, op. cit. (1987): 156–74.

——. "Desire and Negation: The Dialectics of Passion in DHL." In *The Spirit of DHL: Centenary Studies.* Edited by Gāmini Salgādo and G. K. Das. London: Macmillan, 1988, pp. 125–43.

——. "Lawrence's American Bad-Boy Progeny: Henry Miller and Norman Mailer." In Cushman and Jackson, op. cit. (1991): 89–108.

——. *Defiant Desire: Some Dialectical Legacies of DHL.* Carbondale and Edwardsville: Southern Illinois University Press, 1992. (Five essays based on the preceding seven.)

Wildi, M. "The Birth of Expressionism in the Work of DHL." *English Studies* 19 (December 1937): 241–59.

Williams, Raymond. "Tolstoy, Lawrence, and Tragedy." *Kenyon Review* 25 (Autumn 1963): 633–50. (Reprinted as "Social and Personal Tragedy: Tolstoy and Lawrence" in his *Modern Tragedy.* London: Chatto and Windus; Stanford, Calif.: Stanford University Press, 1966, pp. 121–38.)

Wilson, Raymond J., III. "Paul Morel and Stephen Dedalus: Rebellion and Reconciliation." *Platte Valley Review* 11 (Spring 1983): 27–33.

Wood, Frank. "Rilke and DHL." *Germanic Review* 15 (1940): 214–23.

Woodcock, George. "Mexico and the English Novelist." *Western Review* 21 (Autumn 1956): 21–32. (Lawrence, Huxley, and Greene.)

Zoll, Allan R. "Vitalism and the Metaphysics of Love: DHL and Schopenhauer." *DHL Review* 11 (Spring 1978): 1–20.

Zubizarreta, John. "T. S. Eliot and D. H. Lawrence: The Relationship and Influence." *English Language Notes* 31 (September 1993).

Zytaruk, George J. "The Phallic Vision: DHL and V. V. Rozanov." *Comparative Literature Studies* 4 (1967): 283–97.

——. "DHL's Reading of Russian Literature." *DHL Review* 2 (Summer 1969): 120–37.

——. "Lawrence and Rozanov: Clarifying the Phallic Vision." *Etudes Lawrenciennes* 9 (1993): 93–103.

BIBLIOGRAPHY 90: PSYCHOANALYTICAL APPROACHES

Although selected items are repeated here, Bibliographies 5 and 75 should be consulted for further items of relevance to this bibliography.

Books on Lawrence that take a sustained psychoanalytical perspective or that contain relevant material are as follows: Albright (1978), Bedient (1972), Ben-Ephraim (1981), Boadella (1956), Cavitch (1969), Cowan (1970: especially 15–24), Cowan (1990), Dervin (1984), Goodheart (1963), Green (1974), Hochman (1970), Holbrook (1964 and 1992), Howe (1977), Lewiecki-Wilson (1994), Murry (1931), Nixon (1986), Paccaud-Huguet (1991), Pritchard (1971), Ruderman (1984), Schneider (1984), Stoll (1968 and 1971), Storch (1970), Tenenbaum (1977), Walterscheid (1993), Weiss (1962), Whelan (1988: especially 11–99), Williams (1993).

Adamowski, T. H. "Character and Consciousness: DHL, Wilhelm Reich, and Jean Paul Sartre." *University of Toronto Quarterly* 43 (1974a): 311–34.

———. "*The Rainbow* and 'Otherness.' " *DHL Review* 7 (Spring 1974b): 58–77.

———. "Intimacy at a Distance: Sexuality and Orality in *Sons and Lovers.*" *Mosaic* 13, no. 2 (1979): 71–89.

———. "Self/Body/Other: Orality and Ontology in Lawrence." *DHL Review* 13 (Fall 1980): 193–208.

———. "The Father of All Things: The Oral and the Oedipal in *Sons and Lovers.*" *Mosaic* 14, no. 4 (1981): 69–88.

Adelman, Gary. "Beyond the Pleasure Principle: An Analysis of DHL's 'The Prussian Officer.' " *Studies in Short Fiction* 1 (Fall 1963): 8–15.

Allen, C. N., and K. Curtis. "A Sociogrammatic Study of Oedipus Complex Formation: DHL's *Sons and Lovers.*" *Sociometry* 2 (1939): 37–51.

Arcana, Judith. "I Remember Mama: Mother-Blaming in *Sons and Lovers* Criticism." *DHL Review* 21 (Spring 1989): 137–51.

Beharriel, Frederic J. "Freud and Literature." *Queen's Quarterly* 65 (1958): 118–25.

Benway, Ann M. Baribault. "Oedipus Abroad: Hardy's Clym Yeobright and Lawrence's Paul Morel." *Thomas Hardy Yearbook* 13 (1986): 51–57.

Bergler, Edmund. "DHL's *The Fox* and the Psychoanalytic Theory on Lesbianism." *Journal of Nervous and Mental Disease* 126 (May 1958): 488–91. (Reprinted in Moore [1959]: 49–55.)

Bersani, Leo. "Lawrentian Stillness." *Yale Review* 65 (October 1975): 38–60. (Also in his *A Future for Astyanax: Character and Desire in Literature.* Boston and Toronto: Little, Brown, 1976, pp. 156–85.)

Bhat, Vishnu. "DHL's Sexual Ideal." *Literary Half-Yearly* 10 (January 1969): 68–73.

Blanchard, Lydia. "*Women in Love:* Mourning Becomes Narcissism." *Mosaic* 15 (1982): 105–18.

———. "Lawrence, Foucault, and the Language of Sexuality." In *DHL's "Lady": A New Look at "Lady Chatterley's Lover."* Edited by Michael Squires and Dennis Jackson. Athens: University of Georgia Press, 1985, pp. 17–35.

Bleich, David. "The Determination of Literary Value." *Literature and Psychology* 17 (1967): 19–30.

Bragan, Kenneth. "DHL and Self-Psychology." *Australian and New Zealand Journal of Psychiatry* 20, no. 1 (1986): 23–37.

Buermyer, L. L. "Lawrence as Psychoanalyst." *New York Evening Post Literary Review* (16 July 1921): 6.

Bump, Jerome. "D. H. Lawrence and Family Systems Theory." *Renascence: Essays on Value in Literature* 44 (Fall 1991): 61–80.

Burrow, Trigant. *The Social Basis of Consciousness: A Study in Organic Psychology Based upon a Synthetic and Societal Concept of the Neuroses.* New York: Harcourt, Brace, 1927.

Butler, Gerald J. "Sexual Experience in DHL's *The Rainbow.*" *Recovering Literature* 2 (1973): 1–92.

Cavitch, David. "Solipsism and Death in DHL's Late Work." *Massachusetts Review* 7 (1966): 495–508.

Chatterji, Arindam. "*Sons and Lovers:* Dynamic Sanity." *Panjab University Research Bulletin* 16 (October 1985): 3–21.

Chung, Chong-wha. "The Leadership Novels of DHL: A New Approach." *Phoenix* 23 (1981): 25–42.

Clayton, John J. "DHL: Psychic Wholeness through Rebirth." *Massachusetts Review* 25 (Summer 1984): 200–221.

Collins, Joseph. "Even Yet It Can't Be Told—The Whole Truth about DHL." In his *The Doctor Looks at Literature: Psychological Studies of Life and Letters.* New York: Doran; London: Allen and Unwin, 1923, pp. 256–88.

Conquest, Robert. "*Lady Chatterley's Lover* in the Light of Durfian Psychology." *New Statesman* (22 and 29 December, 1978): 863–64.

Cowan, James C. "DHL and the Resurrection of the Body." In *Healing Arts in Dialogue: Medicine and Literature.* Edited by Joanne Trautmann. Carbondale: Southern Illinois University Press, 1981, pp. 55–69.

———. "Phobia and Psychological Development in DHL's 'The Thorn in the Flesh.' " In *The Modernists: Studies in a Literary Phenomenon: Essays in Honor of Harry T. Moore.* Edited by Lawrence B. Gamache and Ian S. MacNiven. London and Toronto: Associated University Presses, 1987, pp. 163–70.

———, ed. *DHL Review* 10 (Fall 1977). Special Issue: "Psychoanalytic Criticism of the Short Stories." (Essays cited separately.)

———. *DHL Review* 13 (Fall 1980). Special Issue: "DHL: Psychoanalysis and Existence." (Essays cited separately.)

Cox, Gary D. "DHL and F. M. Dostoevsky: Mirror Images of Murderous Aggression." *Modern Fiction Studies* 29 (1983): 175–82.

Davies, Rosemary Reeves. "The Mother as Destroyer: Psychic Divisions in the Writings of DHL." *DHL Review* 13 (Fall 1980): 220–38.

Dawson, Eugene W. "DHL and Trigant Burrow: Pollyanalytics and Phylobiology, an Interpretive Analysis." Ph.D. diss., University of Washington, 1963.

———. "Lawrence's Pollyanalytic Esthetic for the Novel." *Paunch* 26 (1966): 60–68.

Deleuze, Gilles, and Félix Guattari. *Anti-Oedipus: Capitalism and Schizophrenia.* Translated by Robert Hurley, Mark Seem, and Helen R. Lane. New York: Viking, 1977, passim. (Originally published in French as *L'Anti-Oedipe.* Paris: Les Editions de Minuit, 1972. Reprinted Minneapolis: Minnesota University Press, 1983; London: Athlone Press, 1984.)

Dervin, Daniel. "DHL and Freud." *American Imago* 36 (1979): 93–117.

———. "Rainbow, Phoenix, and Plumed Serpent: DHL's Great Composite Symbols and Their Vicissitudes." *Psychoanalytic Review* 67 (1980): 515–41.

———. "Placing the Body in Creativity: DHL and the Occult." In *The Psychoanalytic Study of Society.* Vol. 9. Edited by Werner Muensterberger and L. Bryce Boyer. New York: Psychohistory Press, 1981a, pp. 181–220.

———. "Play, Creativity and Matricide: The Implications of Lawrence's 'Smashed Doll' Episode." *Mosaic* 14, no. 3 (1981b): 81–94.

———. "A Dialectic View of Creativity." *Psychoanalytic Review* 70 (1983): 463–91.

Doheny, J. "The Novel Is the Book of Life: DHL and a Revised Version of Polymorphous Perversity." *Paunch* 26 (1966): 40–59.

Dollimore, Jonathan. "DHL and the Metaphysics of Sexual Difference." In his *Sexual Dissidence: Augustine to Wilde, Freud to Foucault.* Oxford: Clarendon Press, 1991, pp. 268–75.

Doolittle, Hilda (H. D.). *Bid Me to Live (A Madrigal).* New York: Dial, 1960.

Durham, John. "DHL: Outline for a Psychology of Being." Ph.D. diss., Occidental College, 1967.

Efron, Arthur. "The Mind-Body Problem in Lawrence, Pepper, and Reich." *Journal of Mind and Behavior* 1 (1980): 247–70.

Ellis, David. "Lawrence and the Biological Psyche." In *DHL: Centenary Essays.* Edited by Mara Kalnins. Bristol: Bristol Classical Press, 1986, pp. 89–109.

———. "Poetry and Science in the Psychology Books." In David Ellis and Howard Mills. *DHL's Non-Fiction: Art, Thought and Genre.* Cambridge: Cambridge University Press, 1988, pp. 67–97.

Englander, Ann. " 'The Prussian Officer': The Self Divided." *Sewanee Review* 71 (October–December 1963): 605–19.

Fernihough, Anne. "The Tyranny of the Text: Lawrence, Freud and the Modernist Aesthetic." In *Modernism and the European Unconscious.* Edited by Peter Collier and Judy Davies. Cambridge: Polity Press; New York: St. Martin's Press, 1990, pp. 47–63.

———. "Analysing the Analyst: Lawrence's Clash with Freud." In her *DHL: Aesthetics and Ideology.* Oxford: Oxford University Press, 1993, pp. 61–82.

Fifield, William. "Joyce's Brother, Lawrence's Wife, Wolfe's Mother, Twain's Daughter." *Texas Quarterly* 10 (1967): 69–87.

Firchow, Peter E. "Rico and Julia: The Hilda Doolittle–DHL Affair Reconsidered." *Journal of Modern Literature* 8 (1980): 51–76.

Fraiberg, Louis. "The Unattainable Self: DHL's *Sons and Lovers.*" In *Twelve Original Essays on Great English Novels.* Edited by Charles Shapiro. Detroit: Wayne State University Press, 1960, pp. 175–201. (Reprinted in Tedlock [1965].)

Fraiberg, Selma. "Two Modern Incest Heroes." *Partisan Review* 28 (1961): 646–61. ("The Rocking-Horse Winner.")

Friedman, Alan. "The Other Lawrence." *Partisan Review* 37, no. 2 (1970): 239–53.

Galbraith, Mary. "Feeling Moments in the Work of DHL." *Paunch* 63–64 (December 1990): 15–38.

Gendzier, I. L. "The Lawrence Enigma." *American Journal of Psychiatry* 125 (1969): 1607–9.

Goodheart, Eugene. "Freud and Lawrence." *Psychoanalysis and Psychoanalytical Review* 47 (1960): 56–64.

Gordon, David J. "DHL's Dual Myth of Origin." *Sewanee Review* 89 (1981a): 83–94.

———. "Sex and Language in DHL." *Twentieth Century Literature* 27 (1981b): 362–75.

Gordon, Rosemary. "Look! He Has Come Through!: DHL, Women and Individuation." *Journal of Analytical Psychology* 23 (1978): 258–74.

Gordon, William A. "DHL and the Two Truths." In *Reconciliations: Studies in Honor of Richard Harter Fogle.* Edited by Mary Lynn Johnson and Seraphia D. Leyda. Salzburg: University of Salzburg, 1983, pp. 194–218.

Greenfield, Barbara. "In Support of Psychoanalyzing Literary Characters." *Journal of the American Academy of Psychoanalysis* 12 (1984): 127–38.

Greiff, Louis K. "Bittersweet Dreaming in Lawrence's 'The Fox': A Freudian Perspective." *Studies in Short Fiction* 20 (1983): 7–16.

Harper, Howard M., Jr. "Fantasia and the Psychodynamics of *Women in Love.*" In *The Classic British Novel.* Edited by Howard Harper, Jr., and Charles Edge. Athens: University of Georgia Press, 1972, pp. 202–19.

Harris, Lynn E. "The Island as a Mental Image of Withdrawal, Used in a Literary Work, DHL's 'The Man Who Loved Islands.' " In *Imagery II*. Edited by David G. Russell, David F. Marks, and John T. E. Richardson. Dunedin, New Zealand: Human Performance Associates, 1986, pp. 178–81.

Hayles, Nancy Katherine. "Evasion: The Field of the Unconscious in DHL." In her *The Cosmic Web: Scientific Field Models and Literary Strategies in the Twentieth Century*. Ithaca, N.Y.: Cornell University Press, 1984, pp. 85–110.

Hepburn, James G. "Disarming and Uncanny Visions: Freud's 'The Uncanny' with Regard to Form and Content in Stories by Sherwood Anderson and DHL." *Literature and Psychology* 9 (Winter 1959): 9–12. (On "The Rocking-Horse Winner.")

Heywood, Christopher. " 'Blood-Consciousness' and the Pioneers of the Reflex and Ganglionic Systems." In *DHL: New Studies*. Edited by Christopher Heywood. London: Macmillan; New York: St. Martin's Press, 1987, pp. 104–23.

Hinz, Evelyn J. "*Sons and Lovers:* The Archetypal Dimensions of Lawrence's Oedipal Tragedy." *DHL Review* 5 (Spring 1972): 26–53.

———. "The Beginning and the End: DHL's *Psychoanalysis and Fantasia.*" *Dalhousie Review* 52 (Summer 1972): 251–65.

Hirsch, Gordon D. "The Laurentian Double: Images of DHL in the Stories." *DHL Review* 10 (Fall 1977): 270–76.

Hochman, Baruch. "The Shape the Self Takes: Henry James to DHL." In *The Test of Character: From the Victorian Novel to the Modern*. Rutherford, N.J.: Fairleigh Dickinson University Press, 1983, pp. 132–56.

Hoerner, Dennis. "Connie Chatterley: A Case of Spontaneous Therapy." *Energy and Character: Journal of Bioenergetic Research* 12 (1981): 48–55.

———. "Ursula, Anton, and the 'Sons of God': Armor and Core in *The Rainbow's* Third Generation." *Paunch* 63–64 (December 1990): 173–98.

Hoffman, Frederick J. "Lawrence's 'Quarrel' with Freud." *Quarterly Review of Literature* 1 (1944): 279–87.

———. "Lawrence's Quarrel with Freud." In his *Freudianism and the Literary Mind*. 2d ed. Baton Rouge: Louisiana State University Press, 1957, pp. 151–76. (Originally published 1945.)

———. *The Mortal No: Death and the Modern Imagination*. Princeton: Princeton University Press, 1964, pp. 406–23.

Isaacs, Neil D. "The Autoerotic Metaphor in Joyce, Sterne, Lawrence, Stevens and Whitman." *Literature and Psychology* 15 (Spring 1965): 92–106. (On "The Rocking-Horse Winner.")

Jewinski, Ed. "The Phallus in DHL and Jacques Lacan." *DHL Review* 21 (Spring 1989): 7–24.

Jordan, Sidney. "DHL's Concept of the Unconscious and Existential Thinking." *Review of Existential Psychology and Psychiatry* 5 (1965): 34–43.

Kazin, Alfred. "Sons, Lovers and Mothers." *Partisan Review* 29 (Spring 1962): 373–85. (Reprinted in Tedlock [1965]: 238–50.)

Kiell, Norman. *Varieties of Sexual Experience: Psychosexuality in Literature*. New York: International Universities Press, 1976.

———, ed. *Psychoanalysis, Psychology, and Literature: A Bibliography*. 2d ed. 2 vols. Metuchen, N.J., and London: Scarecrow Press, 1982. (Supplement to the 2d ed., 1990.)

Kleinbard, David J. "Laing, Lawrence, and the Maternal Cannibal." *Psychoanalytic Review* 58 (Spring 1971): 5–13.

———. "DHL and Ontological Insecurity." *PMLA* 89 (January 1974): 154–63.

Kuczkowski, Richard J. "Lawrence's 'Esoteric' Psychology: *Psychoanalysis and the Unconscious* and *Fantasia of the Unconscious.*" Ph.D. diss., Columbia University, 1973.

Kulkarni, H. B. "Snake Imagery and the Concept of Self in Selected Works of DHL." *South Asia Review* 4 (1980): 28–36.

Kuttner, Alfred Booth. "*Sons and Lovers:* A Freudian Appreciation." *Psychoanalytic Review* 3 (July 1916): 295–317. (Reprinted in Tedlock [1965]: 76–100, and Salgādo [1969]: 69–94.)

Langbaum, Robert. *The Mysteries of Identity: A Theme in Modern Literature.* New York: Oxford University Press, 1977.

Levy, Eric P. "Lawrence's Psychology of Void and Center in *Women in Love.*" *DHL Review* 23 (Spring 1991): 5–19.

McCurdy, Harold G. "Literature and Personality: Analysis of the Novels of DHL." *Character and Personality* 8 (March, June 1940): 181–203, 311–22.

MacDonald, Robert H. " 'The Two Principles': A Theory of the Sexual and Psychological Symbolism of DHL's Later Fiction." *DHL Review* 11 (Summer 1978): 132–55.

Marks, W. S., III. "The Psychology of the Uncanny in Lawrence's 'The Rocking-Horse Winner.' " *Modern Fiction Studies* 11 (Winter 1965–66): 381–92.

———. "The Psychology in DHL's 'The Blind Man.' " *Literature and Psychology* 17 (Winter 1967): 177–92.

May, Keith M. *Out of the Maelstrom: Psychology and the Novel in the Twentieth Century.* New York: St. Martin's Press; London: Elek Books, 1977, pp. 24–61. ("The Nature of the Unconscious: Freud, Joyce and Lawrence" and "The Living Self: Integration of the Personality in Lawrence and Jung.")

Mayers, Ozzie. "The Child as Jungian Hero in DHL's *The Plumed Serpent.*" *Journal of Evolutionary Psychology* 8 (1987): 306–17.

Mehta, G. D. "The Unconscious: The Pristine Source of Man's Verbal Creativity." *Psycho-Lingua* 12 (1982): 65–68.

Mitchell, Giles R. "*Sons and Lovers* and the Oedipal Project." *DHL Review* 13 (Fall 1980): 209–19.

Mollinger, Shermaz. "The Divided Self in Nathaniel Hawthorne and DHL." *Psychoanalytic Review* 66 (1979): 79–102.

Morrison, Claudia. "DHL and American Literature." In her *Freud and the Critic: Early Use of Depth Psychology in Literary Criticism.* Chapel Hill: University of North Carolina Press, 1968, pp. 203–25.

Mortland, Donald E. "The Conclusion of *Sons and Lovers:* A Reconsideration." *Studies in the Novel* 3 (Fall 1971): 305–15.

Nakanishisi, Yoshihiro. "C. G. Jung and DHL: The Pure Soul's Pilgrimage." *Bulletin for Languages and Literatures* (Teruri University, Japan) 121 (1982): 17–35.

Ober, William B. *Boswell's Clap and Other Essays: Medical Analyses of Literary Men's Afflictions.* Carbondale: Southern Illinois University Press, 1979.

O'Connor, Frank. "DHL: *Sons and Lovers.*" In his *The Mirror in the Roadway.* London: Hamilton, 1955, 270–79.

Panken, Shirley. "Some Psychodynamics in *Sons and Lovers:* A New Look at the Oedipal Theme." *Psychoanalytic Review* 61 (1974–75): 571–89.

Pearson, S. Vere. "Psychology of the Consumptive (With Special Reference to DHL)." *Journal of State Medicine* (August 1932): 477–85.

Pollak, Paulina S. "Anti-Semitism in the Works of DHL: Search for and Rejection of the Faith." *Literature and Psychology* 32 (1986): 19–29.

Poole, Roger. "Psychoanalytic Theory: DHL, *St. Mawr.*" *Literary Theory at Work: Three Texts.* Edited by Douglas Tallack. London: Batsford, 1987, pp. 89–113.

Poole, Sara. "Horn and Ivory: Lawrence the Sandman." *Forum for Modern Language Studies* 28 (April 1992): 105–20.

Purdy, Strother B. "On the Psychology of Erotic Literature." *Literature and Psychology* 20 (1970): 23–29.

Radford, F. L., and R. R. Wilson. "Some Phases of the Jungian Moon: Jung's Influence on Modern Literature." *English Studies in Canada* 8, no. 3 (1982): 311–32.

Rees, Richard. "Miss Jessel and Lady Chatterley." In his *For Love or Money: Studies in Personality and Essence.* Carbondale: Southern Illinois University Press, 1961, pp. 115–24.

Renner, Stanley. "Sexuality and the Unconscious: Psychosexual Drama and Conflict in *The Fox.*" *DHL Review* 21 (1989): 245–73.

Rieff, Philip. "Introduction." In *Psychoanalysis and the Unconscious* and *Fantasia of the Unconscious* by DHL. New York: Viking, 1960a, pp. vii–xxiii.

———. "Two Honest Men: Freud and Lawrence." *Listener* 62 (5 May 1960b): 794–96.

———. "The Therapeutic as Mythmaker: Lawrence's True Christian Philosophy." In his *The Triumph of the Therapeutic: Uses of Faith after Freud.* New York: Harper and Row; London: Chatto and Windus, 1966, pp. 189–231.

Roberts, Mark. "DHL and the Failure of Energy: *Fantasia of the Unconscious; Psychoanalysis and the Unconscious.*" In his *The Tradition of Romantic Morality.* London: Macmillan, 1973, pp. 322–48.

Rooks, Pamela A. "DHL's 'Individual' and Michael Polanyi's 'Personal': Fruitful Redefinitions of Subjectivity and Objectivity." *DHL Review* 23 (Spring 1991): 21–29.

Rose, Shirley. "Physical Trauma in DHL's Short Fiction." *Contemporary Literature* 16 (Winter 1975): 73–83.

Ruderman, Judith G. "*The Fox* and the 'Devouring Mother.'" *DHL Review* 10 (Fall 1977): 251–69.

———. "Rekindling the 'Father-Spark': Lawrence's Ideal of Leadership in *The Lost Girl* and *The Plumed Serpent.*" *DHL Review* 13 (Fall 1980): 239–59.

Ryals, Clyde de L. "DHL's 'The Horse Dealer's Daughter': An Interpretation." *Literature and Psychology* 12 (Spring 1962): 39–43. (Jungian rebirth archetype dramatized.)

Sale, Roger. "DHL, 1912–1916." *Massachusetts Review* 6 (Spring 1965): 467–80. (Lawrence's psychological development as revealed in the early novels.)

Schapiro, Barbara. "Maternal Bonds and the Boundaries of Self: DHL and Virginia Woolf." *Soundings* 69 (1986): 347–65.

Schneider, Daniel J. "Psychology and Art in Lawrence *Kangaroo.*" *DHL Review* 14 (1981): 156–71.

Schwartz, Daniel R. "Speaking of Paul Morel: Voice, Unity, and Meaning in *Sons and Lovers.*" *Studies in the Novel* 8 (Fall 1976): 255–77.

Schwartz, Murray M. "DHL and Psychoanalysis: An Introduction." *DHL Review* 10 (Fall 1977): 215–22.

Scott, James F. "DHL's *Germania:* Ethnic Psychology and Cultural Crisis in the Shorter Fiction." *DHL Review* 10 (1977): 142–64.

Sewell, Ernestine P. "Herbartian Psychology in the Developing Art of DHL." *Publications of Missouri Philological Association* 5 (1980): 66–71.

Shuey, William A., III. "From Renunciation to Rebellion: The Female in Literature." In *The Evolving Female: Women in Psychosocial Context.* Edited by Carol Landau Heckerman. New York: Human Sciences Press, 1980, pp. 138–57.

Smalley, Barbara M. "Lawrence's 'The Princess' and Horney's 'Idealized Self.' " In *Third Force Psychology and the Study of Literature.* Edited by Bernard J. Paris. Rutherford, N.J.: Fairleigh Dickinson University Press, 1986, pp. 179–90.

Snodgrass, William DeWitt. "A Rocking-Horse: The Symbol, the Pattern, the Way to Live." *Hudson Review* 11 (Summer 1958): 191–200. (Reprinted in Consolo [1969]: 26–36 and in his *Radical Pursuit: Critical Essays and Lectures.* New York: Harper and Row, 1975.)

Sproles, Karyn Z. "DHL and the Schizoid State: Reading *Sons and Lovers* through *The White Peacock.*" *Paunch* 63–64 (December 1990): 39–70.

Stavrou, Constantine W. "DHL's 'Psychology' of Sex." *Literature and Psychology* 6 (1956): 90–95.

Stoll, John E. "Common Womb Imagery in Joyce and Lawrence." *Ball Sate University Forum* 11 (Spring 1970a): 10–24.

———. "Psychological Dissociation in the Victorian Novel." *Literature and Psychology* 20, no. 2 (1970b): 63–73.

Tabachnick, E., and N. Tabachnick. "The Second Birth of DHL." *Journal of the American Academy of Psychoanalysis* 4 (1976): 469–80.

Thornham, Susan. "Lawrence and Freud." *Durham University Journal* 39 (1977): 73–82.

Trail, George Y. "The Psychological Dynamics of DHL's 'Snake.' " *American Imago* 36 (1979a): 345–56.

———. "West by East: The Psycho-Geography of *Birds, Beasts and Flowers.*" *DHL Review* 12 (1979b): 241–55.

Travis, Leigh. "DHL: The Blood-Conscious Artist." *American Imago* 25 (1968): 163–90.

Tristram, Philippa. "Eros and Death (Lawrence, Freud and Women)." In *Lawrence and Women.* Edited by Anne Smith. London: Vision; Totowa, N.J.: Barnes and Noble, 1978, pp. 136–55.

Turner, John F. "The Perversion of Play in DHL's 'The Rocking-Horse Winner.' " *DHL Review* 15 (1982): 249–70.

Turner, John, with Cornelia Rumpf-Worthen and Ruth Jenkins. "The Otto Gross-Frieda Weekley Correspondence: Transcribed, Translated, and Annotated." *DHL Review* 22 (Summer 1990): 137–227.

Van Tassel, Daniel E. "The Search for Manhood in DHL's *Sons and Lovers.*" *Costerus* 3 (1972): 197–210.

Vause, L. Mikel. "The Death Instinct Reflected in DHL's 'Love among the Haystacks.' " *Journal of Evolutionary Psychology* 9 (1988): 187–89.

Vredenburgh, Joseph L. "Further Contributions to a Study of the Incest Object." *American Imago* 16 (Fall 1959): 263–68. (*Sons and Lovers*—Miriam and Clara as incest objects.)

Ward, Aileen. "The Psychoanalytic Theory of Poetic Form: A Content Analysis." *Literature and Psychology* 17 (1967): 30–46.

Weinstein, Philip M. *The Semantics of Desire: Changing Models of Identity from Dickens to Joyce.* Princeton: Princeton University Press, 1984, pp. 189–251. (" 'Become Who You Are': The Optative World of DHL," pp. 189–204; " 'The Trembling Instability' of *Women in Love*," pp. 204–24; "Choosing between the Quick and the Dead: Three Versions of *Lady Chatterley's Lover*," pp. 224–51.)

Weiss, Daniel. "Oedipus in Nottinghamshire." *Literature and Psychology* 7 (August 1957): 33–42.

———. "DHL's Great Circle: From *Sons and Lovers* to *Lady Chatterley's Lover*." *Psychoanalytic Review* 50 (Fall 1963): 112–38. (Revision of Ch. 4 of *Oedipus in Nottingham,* following.)

———. *Oedipus in Nottingham: DHL.* Seattle: University of Washington Press, 1962. (See also review by Edwin Berry Burgum. *American Imago* 23 [1966]: 180–83.)

———. "DHL: The Forms of Sexual Hunger." In *The Critic Agonistes: Psychology, Myth, and the Art of Fiction.* Edited by Eric Solomon and Stephen Arkin. Seattle: University of Washington Press, 1985, pp. 217–28.

Wheeler, Richard P. " 'Cunning in his overthrow': Lawrence's Art in 'Tickets, Please.' " *DHL Review* 10 (Fall 1977): 242–50.

Widmer, Kingsley. "Lawrence as Abnormal Novelist." *DHL Review* 8 (Summer 1975): 220–32.

———. "Psychiatry and Piety on Lawrence." *Studies in the Novel* 9 (Summer 1977): 195–200.

Willbern, David. "Malice in Paradise: Isolation and Projection in " 'The Man Who Loved Islands.' " *DHL Review* 10 (Fall 1977): 223–41.

Wolf, Howard R. "British Fathers and Sons, 1773–1913: From Filial Submissiveness to Creativity." *Psychoanalytic Review* 52 (Summer 1965): 53–70. (On *Sons and Lovers.*)

BIBLIOGRAPHY 91: ARCHETYPAL AND MYTH CRITICISM

Full-length studies of direct relevance to this bibliography are as follows: Carter (1932), Clark (1964), Cowan (1970 and 1990), Eisenstein (1974), Fjagesund (1991), Gutierrez (1980 and 1987), Hyde (1992), Inniss (1972), Lucente (1981: 107–23), Miles (1969), Miliaras (1987), Robinson (1992: 32–59), Ross (1991), Sharma (1981), Tindall (1930), Urang (1983), Viinikka (1988), Whelan (1988).

Anderson, Walter E. " 'The Prussian Officer': Lawrence's Version of the Fall of Man Legend." *Essays in Literature* 12 (1985): 215–23.

Ballin, Michael. "The Third Eye: The Relationship between DHL and Maurice Maeterlinck." In *The Practical Vision: Essays in English Literature in Honour of Flora*

Roy. Edited by Jane Campbell and James Doyle. Waterloo, Ontario: Wilfrid Laurier University Press, 1978, pp. 87–102.

―――. "DHL's Esotericism: William Blake in Lawrence's *Women in Love.*" In *DHL's
"Women in Love": Contexts and Criticism.* Edited by Michael Ballin. Waterloo,
Ontario: Wilfrid Laurier University, 1980a, pp. 70–87.

―――. "Lewis Spence and the Myth of Quetzalcoatl in DHL's *The Plumed Serpent.*"
DHL Review 13 (Spring 1980b): 63–78.

Berce, Sanda. "The Sun-Myth: A Parable of Modern Civilization." *Studia University
Babes-Bolyai* 33, no. 1 (1988): 56–63. (On "The Woman Who Rode Away.")

Bodkin, Maud. *Archetypal Patterns in Poetry: Psychological Studies of Imagination.*
London: Oxford University Press, 1934, pp. 289–99.

Boklund, Gunnar. "Time Must Have a Stop: Apocalyptic Thought and Expression in
the Twentieth Century." *Denver Quarterly* 2 (Summer 1967): 69–98.

Broembsen, F. von. "Mythic Identification and Spatial Inscendence: The Cosmic Vision
of DHL." *Western Humanities Review* 29 (Spring 1975): 137–54.

Brown, Keith. "Welsh Red Indians: DHL and *St. Mawr.*" *Essays in Criticism* 32 (April
1982): 158–79. (Reprinted in Brown [1990]: 23–37.)

Brunsdale, Mitzi M. "Lawrence and the Myth of Brynhild." *Western Humanities Review*
31 (Fall 1977): 342–48.

Clark, L. D. "The Symbolic Structure of *The Plumed Serpent.*" *Tulane Studies in English*
14 (1965): 75–96.

―――. "DHL and the American Indian." *DHL Review* 9 (1976): 305–72.

―――. "Making the Classic Contemporary: Lawrence's Pilgrimage Novels and American Romance." In *DHL in the Modern World.* Edited by Peter Preston and Peter
Hoare. London: Macmillan, 1989, pp. 193–216.

Cowan, James C. "The Function of Allusions and Symbols in DHL's *The Man Who
Died.*" *American Imago* 17 (Summer 1960): 241–53.

―――. "DHL's 'The Princess' as Ironic Romance." *Studies in Short Fiction* 4 (Spring
1967): 245–51.

―――. "DHL's Dualism: The Apollonian-Dionysian Polarity and *The Ladybird.*" In
Forms of Modern British Fiction. Edited by Alan Warren Friedman. Austin and
London: University of Texas Press, 1975, pp. 73–99.

Crowder, Ashby Bland, and Lynn O'Malley Crowder. "Mythic Intent in DHL's *The
Virgin and the Gipsy.*" *South Atlantic Review* 49 (1984): 61–66.

Digaetani, John Louis. "Situational Myths: Richard Wagner and DHL." In his *Richard
Wagner and the Modern British Novel.* Rutherford, N.J.: Fairleigh Dickinson
University Press; London: Associated University Presses, 1978, pp. 58–89.

Doherty, Gerald. "The Salvator Mundi Touch: Messianic Typology in DHL's *Women
in Love.*" *Ariel* 13, no. 3 (1982): 53–71.

―――. "The Third Encounter: Paradigms of Courtship in DHL's Shorter Fiction." *DHL
Review* 17 (1984): 135–51.

Eastman, Donald R. "Myth and Fate in the Characters of *Women in Love.*" *DHL Review*
9 (Summer 1976): 177–93.

Farr, Judith. "DHL's Mother as Sleeping Beauty: The 'Still Queen' of His Poems and
Fictions." *Modern Fiction Studies* 36 (Summer 1990): 195–209.

Fiderer, Gerald. "DHL's *The Man Who Died:* The Phallic Christ." *American Imago* 25
(Spring 1968): 91–96.

Fitz, L. T. " 'The Rocking-Horse Winner' and *The Golden Bough.*" *Studies in Short Fiction* 11 (Spring 1974): 199–200.

Fjagesund, Peter. "DHL, Knut Hamsun and Pan." *English Studies* (Netherlands) 72, no. 5 (October 1991): 421–25.

Galea, Ileana. "DHL: The Value of Myth." *Cahiers Roumains d'Etudes Littéraires* 3 (1987): 72–78.

Glicksberg, Charles I. "Myth in Lawrence's Fiction." In his *Modern Literary Perspectivism.* Dallas: Southern Methodist University Press, 1970, pp. 139–48 and passim.

Gorton, Mark. "Some Say in Ice: The Apocalyptic Fear of *Women in Love.*" *Foundation* 28 (1983): 56–60.

Gould, Eric. "Recovering the Numinous: DHL and T. S. Eliot." In his *Mythical Intentions in Modern Literature.* Princeton: Princeton University Press, 1981, pp. 199–262.

Gutierrez, Donald. "The Ancient Imagination of DHL." *Twentieth Century Literature* 27 (1981): 178–96.

———. " 'Quick, Now, Here, Now, Always': The Flaming Rose of Lawrence and Eliot." *University of Portland Review* 34, no. 2 (1982): 3–8.

Hendrick, George. "Jesus and the Osiris-Isis Myth: Lawrence's *The Man Who Died* and Williams' *The Night of the Iguana.*" *Anglia* (Tübingen) 84 (1966): 398–406.

Hill, Ordelle G., and Potter Woodbery. "Ursula Brangwen of *The Rainbow:* Christian Saint or Pagan Goddess?" *DHL Review* 4 (Fall 1971): 274–79.

Hinz, Evelyn J. "DHL's Clothes Metaphor." *DHL Review* 1 (Spring 1968): 87–113.

———. "Juno and *The White Peacock:* Lawrence's English Epic." *DHL Review* 3 (Summer 1970): 115–35.

———. "*The Trespasser:* Lawrence's Wagnerian Tragedy and Divine Comedy." *DHL Review* 4 (Summer 1971): 122–41.

———. "The Beginning and the End: DHL's *Psychoanalysis and Fantasia.*" *Dalhousie Review* 52 (1972a): 251–65.

———. "*Sons and Lovers:* The Archetypal Dimensions of Lawrence's Oedipal Tragedy." *DHL Review* 5 (Spring 1972b): 26–53.

———. "Hierogamy versus Wedlock: Types of Marriage Plots and Their Relationship to Genres of Prose Fiction." *PMLA* 91 (October 1976): 900–913.

———. "*Ancient Art and Ritual* and *The Rainbow.*" *Dalhousie Review* 58 (1979): 617–37.

Hinz, Evelyn J., and John J. Teunissen. "Savior and Cock: Allusion and Icon in Lawrence's *The Man Who Died.*" *Journal of Modern Literature* 5 (April 1976): 279–96.

———. "*Women in Love* and the Myth of Eros and Psyche." In *DHL: The Man Who Lived.* Edited by Robert B. Partlow, Jr., and Harry T. Moore. Carbondale: Southern Illinois University Press, 1980, pp. 207–20.

———. "War, Love, and Industrialization: The Ares/Aphrodite/Hephaestus Complex in *Lady Chatterley's Lover.*" In *DHL's "Lady": A New Look at "Lady Chatterley's Lover."* Edited by Michael Squires and Dennis Jackson. Athens: University of Georgia Press, 1985, pp. 197–221.

———. "Odysseus, Ulysses, and Ursula: The Context of Lawrence's *Rainbow.*" In *The Modernists: Studies in a Literary Phenomenon: Essays in Honor of Harry T.*

Moore. Rutherford, N.J.: Fairleigh Dickinson University Press, 1987, pp. 171–91.

Hughs, Richard. "The Brangwen Inheritance: The Archetype in DHL's *The Rainbow.*" *Greyfriar* 17 (1976): 33–40.

Humma, John B. "Pan and 'The Rocking-Horse Winner.'" *Essays in Literature* (Illinois) 5 (1978): 53–60.

Iida, Takeo. "Nature Deities: Reawakening Blood-Consciousness in the Europeans." *Etudes Lawrenciennes* 9 (1993): 27–42.

Irwin, W. R. "The Survival of Pan." *PMLA* 76 (June 1961): 159–67.

Jackson, Dennis. "The 'Old Pagan Vision': Myth and Ritual in *Lady Chatterley's Lover.*" *DHL Review* 11 (Fall 1978): 260–71. (Reprinted in revised form in Jackson and Jackson [1988]: 128–44.)

Kay, Wallace G. "Lawrence and *The Rainbow:* Apollo and Dionysus in Conflict." *Southern Quarterly* 10 (April 1972): 209–22.

———. "*Women in Love* and *The Man Who Died:* Resolving Apollo and Dionysus." *Southern Quarterly* 10 (July 1972): 325–39.

Kermode, Frank. "DHL and the Apocalyptic Types." In his *Continuities.* London: Routledge and Kegan Paul, 1968, pp. 122–51. (Also published in *Critical Quarterly* 10 [1968]: 14–33; and, in shortened form, in Clarke, ed. [1969]: 203–18.)

———. "Apocalypse and the Modern." In *Visions of Apocalypse.* Edited by Saul Friedlander, Gerald Holton, Leo Marx, and Eugene Skolnifoff. New York: Homes and Meier, 1985, pp. 84–106.

Kessler, Jascha. "Descent in Darkness: The Myth of *The Plumed Serpent.*" In *A DHL Miscellany.* Edited by Harry T. Moore. Carbondale: Southern Illinois University Press, 1959, pp. 239–61.

———. "DHL's Primitivism." *Texas Studies in Literature and Language* 5 (1964): 467–88.

Larsen, Elizabeth. "Lawrence's *The Man Who Died.*" *Explicator* 40, no. 4 (1982): 38–40.

Ledoux, Larry V. "Christ and Isis: The Function of the Dying and the Reviving God in *The Man Who Died.*" *DHL Review* 5 (Summer 1972): 132–48.

MacDonald, Robert H. "The Union of Fire and Water: An Examination of the Imagery of *The Man Who Died.*" *DHL Review* 10 (Spring 1977): 34–51.

Makolkina, Anna. "The Dance of Dionysos in H. Khodkevych and DHL." *Journal of Ukrainian Studies* 15 (1990): 31–38.

Mayers, Ozzie. "The Child as Jungian Hero in DHL's *The Plumed Serpent.*" *Journal of Evolutionary Psychology* 8 (1987): 306–17.

Merivale, Patricia. "DHL and the Modern Pan Myth." *Texas Studies in Literature and Language* 6 (Fall 1964): 297–305. (Reprinted as Ch. 6 of her *Pan the Goat-God: His Myth in Modern Times.* Cambridge: Harvard University Press, 1969, pp. 194–219.)

Miles, Thomas H. "Birkin's Electro-Mystical Body of Reality: DHL's Use of Kundalini." *DHL Review* 9 (Summer 1976): 194–212.

Miliaras, Barbara A. "The Collapse of Agrarian Order and the Death of Thomas Brangwen in DHL's *The Rainbow.*" *Etudes Lawrenciennes* 3 (1988): 65–77.

Miller, James E., Jr., Karl Shapiro, and Bernice Slote. *Start with the Sun: Studies in Cosmic Poetry.* Lincoln: University of Nebraska Press, 1960, pp. 57–134, 229–

38. (Lawrence as a "cosmic" poet in the tradition of Whitman, Hart Crane, and Dylan Thomas.)

Nakanishisi, Yoshihiro. "C. G. Jung and DHL: The Pure Soul's Pilgrimage." *Bulletin for Languages and Literatures* (Teruri University, Japan) 121 (1982): 17–35.

Neumarkt, Paul. "Pan and Christ: An Analysis of the *Hieros Gamos* Concept in DHL's Short Story 'The Overtone.' " *Dos Continentes* 9–10 (1971–72): 27–48.

Newman, Paul B. "DHL and *The Golden Bough.*" *Kansas Magazine* (1962): 79–86.

Phillips, Steven R. "The Monomyth and Literary Criticism." *College Literature* 2 (Winter 1975): 1–16. ("The Horse-Dealer's Daughter," pp. 7–11.)

Piccolo, Anthony. "Sun and Sex in the Last Stories of DHL." In *HELIOS: From Myth to Solar Energy.* Edited by M. E. Grenander. Albany: Institute for Humanistic Studies, State University of New York, 1978, pp. 166–74.

———. "Ritual Strategy: Concealed Form in the Short Stories of DHL." *Mid-Hudson Language Studies* 2 (1979): 88–99.

Radford, F. L., and R. R. Wilson. "Some Phases of the Jungian Moon: Jung's Influence on Modern Literature." *English Studies in Canada* 8, no. 3 (1982): 311–32.

Raina, M. L. "The Wheel and the Centre: An Approach to *The Rainbow.*" *Literary Criterion* (Mysore) 9 (Summer 1970): 41–55.

Rakhi. "*The Man Who Died:* A Jungian Interpretation." In *Essays on DHL.* Edited by T. R. Sharma. Meerut: Shalabh Book House, 1987, pp. 116–24.

Rieff, Philip. "A Modern Mythmaker." In *Myth and Mythmaking.* Edited by Henry A. Murray. New York: George Braziller, 1960, pp. 240–75.

———. "The Therapeutic as Mythmaker: Lawrence's True Christian Philosophy." In his *The Triumph of the Therapeutic: Uses of Faith after Freud.* New York: Harper and Row; London: Chatto and Windus, 1966, 189–231.

Ross, Charles L. "DHL's Use of Greek Tragedy: Euripedes and Ritual." *DHL Review* 10 (Spring 1977): 1–19.

Rossman, Charles. "Myth and Misunderstanding DHL." *Bucknell Review* 22 (Fall 1976): 81–101.

Ruthven, K. K. "The Savage God: Conrad and Lawrence." *Critical Quarterly* (1968): 39–54.

Ryals, Clyde de L. "DHL's 'The Horse Dealer's Daughter': An Interpretation." *Literature and Psychology* 12 (Spring 1962): 39–43. (Jungian approach.)

Sharma, Radhe Shyam. "The Symbol as Archetype: A Study of Symbolic Mode in DHL's *Women in Love.*" *Osmania Journal of English Studies* (Hyderabad) 8, no. 2 (1971): 31–53.

———. "Towards a Definition of Modern Literary Primitivism." *Osmania Journal of English Studies* 14, no. 1 (1978): 23–28. (Reprinted in Sharma [1981]: 1–44.)

Sharma, T. R. "Sun in DHL: A Hindu Archetype." In *Essays on DHL.* Edited by T. R. Sharma. Meerut: Shalabh Book House, 1987, pp. 245–59.

Smailes, T. A. "The Mythical Bases of *Women in Love.*" *DHL Review* 1 (Summer 1968): 129–36.

Smith, Bob L. "DHL's *St. Mawr:* Transposition of Myth." *Arizona Quarterly* 24 (Fall 1968): 197–208.

Spivey, Ted R. "Lawrence and Faulkner: The Symbolist Novel and the Prophetic Song." In his *The Journey beyond Tragedy: A Study of Myth and Modern Fiction.* Orlando: University Presses of Florida, 1980, pp. 72–93.

Stewart, Jack F. "Primitivism in *Women in Love*." *DHL Review* 13 (Spring 1980): 45–62.

Stoll, John E. "Common Womb Imagery in Joyce and Lawrence." *Ball State University Forum* 11 (Spring 1970): 10–24.

Tedlock, E. W., Jr. "DHL's Annotations of Ouspensky's *Tertium Organum*." *Texas Studies in Literature and Language* 2 (Summer 1960): 206–18.

Tetsumura, Haruo. "DHL's Mysticism: What the Moon Signifies." *Hiroshima Studies in English Language and Literature* 9 (1963): 51–65.

Thomas, David J. "DHL's 'Snake': The Edenic Myth Inverted." *College Literature* 13 (1986): 199–206.

Thomas, Marlin. "Somewhere under *The Rainbow:* DHL and the Typology of Hermeneutics." *Mid-Hudson Language Studies* 6 (1983): 57–65.

Troy, Mark. " '. . . a Wild Bit of Egyptology': Isis and *The Escaped Cock* of DHL." *Studia Neophilologica* 58 (1986): 215–24.

Turner, Frederick W., III. "Prancing in to a Purpose: Myths, Horses, and True Selfhood in Lawrence's 'The Rocking-Horse Winner.' " In *DHL: "The Rocking-Horse Winner."* Edited by Dominic P. Consolo. Columbus, Ohio: Charles E. Merrill, 1969, pp. 95–106.

Vickery, John B. "*The Golden Bough* and Modern Poetry." *Journal of Aesthetics and Art Criticism* 15 (1957): 271–88.

———. "Myth and Ritual in the Shorter Fiction of DHL." *Modern Fiction Studies* 5 (Spring 1959): 65–82. (Reprinted in revised form in his *The Literary Impact of the Golden Bough*. Princeton: Princeton University Press, 1973, pp. 294–325.)

———. "*The Plumed Serpent* and the Eternal Paradox." *Criticism* 5 (Spring 1963): 119–34.

———. "*Golden Bough:* Impact and Archetype." *Virginia Quarterly Review* 39 (Winter 1963): 37–57.

———. "*The Plumed Serpent* and the Reviving God." *Journal of Modern Literature* 2 (November 1972): 505–32.

———. "DHL's Poetry: Myth and Matter." *DHL Review* 7 (Spring 1974): 1–18.

———. *Myths and Texts: Strategies of Incorporation and Displacement*. Baton Rouge: Louisiana State University Press, 1983, pp. 104–31.

Widmer, Kingsley. "The Primitivistic Aesthetic: DHL." *Journal of Aesthetics and Art Criticism* 17 (March 1959a): 344–53.

———. "The Sacred Sun in Modern Literature." *Humanist* (Antioch) 19 (1959b): 368–72.

Wilder, Amos Niven. "The Primitivism of DHL." In his *Spiritual Aspects of the New Poetry*. New York: Harper and Brothers, 1940, pp. 153–65.

Zeng, Dawei. "The Functions and Limitations of Mythological Archetypal Criticism: A Comment on the Application of Mythological Archetypal Criticism to the Interpretation of DHL's Novels." *Waiguoyu* 1 (1990): 24–30.

BIBLIOGRAPHY 92: PHILOSOPHICAL AND RELIGIOUS APPROACHES

Full-length studies of relevance here can be distinguished roughly between those that focus primarily on questions of philosophy and those that engage with questions of religious faith (though there is, of course, a large area of overlap between the two groups). Those of the first category are as follows: Bell (1992), Black (1991), Burns (1980), Ebbatson (1980 and 1982), Fernihough (1993), Freeman (1955), Gordon (1966), Miko (1971), Milton (1987), Montgomery (1994), Norris (1985), Olson (1980), Schneider (1986), Tindall (1939), Verhoeven (1987), Whiteley (1987).

Books of the second category are Carter (1932), Gutierrez (1980 and 1987), Huttar (1968), Hyde (1992), Jarrett-Kerr (1951), Lewis (1929), Murfin (1978), Murry (1957), Nahal (1970), Panichas (1964), Paterson (1973), Poplawski (1993), Sipple (1992), Sitesh (1975), Wickremasinghe (1951).

Adamowski, T. H. "Character and Consciousness: DHL, Wilhelm Reich, and Jean Paul Sartre." *University of Toronto Quarterly* 43 (1974a): 311–34.

———. "*The Rainbow* and 'Otherness.' " *DHL Review* 7 (Spring 1974b): 58–77.

———. "Being Perfect: Lawrence, Sartre, and *Women in Love*." *Critical Inquiry* 2 (Winter 1975): 345–68.

———. "Self/Body/Other: Orality and Ontology in Lawrence." *DHL Review* 13 (Fall 1980): 193–208.

———. "The Natural Flowering of Life: The Ego, Sex, and Existentialism." In *DHL's "Lady": A New Look at "Lady Chatterley's Lover."* Edited by Michael Squires and Dennis Jackson. Athens: University of Georgia Press, 1985, pp. 36–57.

Adix, M. "Phoenix at Walden: DHL Calls on Thoreau." *Western Humanities Review* 8 (Autumn 1954): 287–98.

Alcorn, Marshall W., Jr. "Lawrence and the Issue of Spontaneity." *DHL Review* 15 (1982): 147–65.

Alexander, John C. "DHL and Teilhard de Chardin: A Study in Agreements." *DHL Review* 2 (Summer 1969): 138–56.

Asher, Kenneth. "Nietzsche, Lawrence and Irrationalism." *Neophilologus* 69 (1985): 1–16.

Baldanza, Frank. "DHL's 'Song of Songs.' " *Modern Fiction Studies* 7 (Summer 1961): 106–14.

Barry, J. "Oswald Spengler and DHL." *English Studies in Africa* 12, no. 2 (1969): 151–61.

Bechtel, Lawrence Reid. " 'A Question of Relationship': The Symbolic Flower of Consciousness in the Novels of DHL." *DHL Review* 19 (Fall 1987): 255–66.

Bishop, John Peale. "Distrust of Ideas." In his *Collected Essays.* Edited by Edmund Wilson. New York: Scribners, 1948, pp. 233–37.

Boklund, Gunnar. "Time Must Have a Stop: Apocalyptic Thought and Expression in the Twentieth Century." *Denver Quarterly* 2 (Summer 1967): 69–98.

Brunsdale, Mitzi M. "Toward a Greater Day: Lawrence, Rilke, and Immortality." *Comparative Literature Studies* 20 (1983): 402–17.

Carey, John. "DHL's Doctrine." In *DHL: Novelist, Poet, Prophet.* London: Weidenfeld and Nicolson, 1973, pp. 122–34.

Chaning-Pearce, Melville. "Facilis Descensus Averni." In his *The Terrible Crystal: Studies in Kierkegaard and Modern Christianity.* London: Kegan Paul, 1940; New York: Oxford University Press, 1941, pp. 179–89.

Choudhury, Sheila Lahiri. "DHL and the Prophetic Artist Tradition." *Essays and Studies* 3 (1982): 203–18.

Chung, Chong-wha. "In Search of the Dark God: Lawrence's Dualism." In *DHL in the Modern World*. Edited by Peter Preston and Peter Hoare. London: Macmillan, 1989, pp. 69–89.

Coates, T. B. *Ten Modern Prophets*. London: Muller, 1944, pp. 91–99.

Collin, W. E. "Active Principle in the Thought of DHL." *Canadian Bookman* 20 (December 1938): 17–21.

Cowan, James C. "DHL's Quarrel with Christianity." *University of Tulsa Department of English Monographs,* no. 7: *Literature and Theology* (1969): 32–43.

———. "DHL's Dualism: The Apollonian–Dionysian Polarity and *The Ladybird*." In *Forms of Modern Fiction*. Edited by A. W. Friedman. Austin and London: University of Texas Press, 1975, pp. 75–99.

Davie, Donald. "Dissent in the Present Century." *Times Literary Supplement* (3 December 1976): 1519–20.

Davies, Rosemary Reeves. "DHL and the Theme of Rebirth." *DHL Review* 14 (1981): 127–42.

Delany, Paul. "Lawrence and Carlyle." In *DHL and Tradition*. Edited by Jeffrey Meyers. London: Athlone, 1985, pp. 21–34.

Dexter, Martin. "DHL and Pueblo Religion: An Inquiry into Accuracy." *Arizona Quarterly* 9 (Fall 1953): 219–34.

Dillon, M. C. "Love in *Women in Love:* A Phenomenological Analysis." *Philosophy and Literature* 2 (Fall 1978): 190–208.

Doherty, Gerald. "The Nirvana Dimension: DHL's Quarrel with Buddhism." *DHL Review* 15 (1982): 51–67.

Eagleton, Terry. "Lawrence." In *The Prose for God*. Edited by Ian Gregor and Walter Stein. London: Sheed and Ward, 1973, pp. 86–100.

Ebbatson, Roger. "A Spark beneath the Wheel: Lawrence and Evolutionary Thought." In *DHL: New Studies*. London: Macmillan; New York: St. Martin's Press, 1987, pp. 90–103.

Ellis, David. "Lawrence, Wordsworth and 'Anthropomorphic Lust.' " *Cambridge Quarterly* 23, no. 3 (1994): 230–42.

Elsbree, Langdon. "DHL, Homo Ludens, and the Dance." *DHL Review* 1 (Spring 1968): 1–30.

———. "The Purest and Most Perfect Form of Play: Some Novelists and the Dance." *Criticism* 14 (Fall 1972): 361–72.

Engelberg, Edward. "The Displaced Cathedral in Flaubert, James, Lawrence, and Kafka." *Arcadia* (Berlin) 21, no. 3 (1986): 245–62.

Fairchild, Hoxie Neale. In his *Religious Trends in English Poetry*. Vol. 5. New York: Columbia University Press, 1962, pp. 276–84.

———. In his *Religious Trends in English Poetry*. Vol. 6. New York: Columbia University Press, 1968, passim.

Foster, D. W. "Lawrence, Sex and Religion." *Theology* 64 (January 1961): 8–13.

Foster, John Burt, Jr. "Holding Forth against Nietzsche: DHL's Novels from *Women in Love* to *The Plumed Serpent*." In his *Heirs to Dionysus: A Nietzschean Current in Literary Modernism*. Princeton: Princeton University Press, 1981, pp. 189–255.

Furbank, P. N. "The Philosophy of DHL." In *The Spirit of DHL: Centenary Studies*. Edited by Gāmini Salgādo and G. K. Das. London: Macmillan; Totowa, N.J.: Barnes, 1988, pp. 144–53.

Gamache, Lawrence B. "DHL and Religious Conflict-Dualism." *Etudes Lawrenciennes* 9 (1993): 9–25.

Gibbons, Thomas. " 'Allotropic States' and 'Fiddlebow': DHL's Occult Sources." *Notes and Queries* 35, no. 3 (1988): 338–40.

Gilbert, Sandra M. "DHL's Uncommon Prayers." In *DHL: The Man Who Lived.* Edited by Robert B. Partlow, Jr., and Harry T. Moore. Carbondale: Southern Illinois University Press, 1980, pp. 73–93. (On *Birds, Beasts and Flowers.*)

Glicksberg, Charles I. "DHL and Science." *Scientific Monthly* 73 (August 1951): 99–104.

Goodheart, Eugene. "Lawrence and Christ." *Partisan Review* 31 (Winter 1964): 42–59.

Gordon, David J. "Two Anti-Puritan Puritans: Bernard Shaw and DHL." *Yale Review* 56 (Autumn 1966): 76–90.

———. "DHL's Dual Myth of Origin." *Sewanee Review* 89 (1981): 83–94. (Lawrence's response to Freud and Rousseau.)

Gordon, William A. "DHL and the Two Truths." In *Reconciliations: Studies in Honor of Richard Harter Fogle.* Edited by Mary Lynn Johnson and Seraphia D. Leyda. Salzburg: University of Salzburg, 1983, pp. 194–218.

Gould, Eric. "Recovering the Numinous: DHL and T. S. Eliot." In his *Mythical Intentions in Modern Literature.* Princeton: Princeton University Press, 1981, pp. 199–262.

Grant, Damian. "A Thematic Index to *Phoenix and Phoenix II.*" In *A DHL Handbook.* Edited by Keith Sagar. Manchester: Manchester University Press, 1982, pp. 329–447.

Green, Eleanor H. "Blueprints for Utopia: The Political Ideas of Nietzsche and DHL." *Renaissance and Modern Studies* 18 (1974): 141–61.

———. "Schopenhauer and DHL on Sex and Love." *DHL Review* 8 (Fall 1975): 329–45.

———. "The *Will zur Macht* and DHL." *Massachusetts Studies in English* 10 (Winter 1975): 25–30.

———. "Nietzsche, Helen Corke, and DHL." *American Notes and Queries* 15 (1976): 56–59.

———. "Lawrence, Schopenhauer, and the Dual Nature of the Universe." *South Atlantic Bulletin* 62 (November 1977): 84–92.

Gregor, Ian. " 'He Wondered': The Religious Imagination of William Golding: A Tribute on His 75th Birthday." In *William Golding: The Man and His Books.* London: Faber and Faber, 1986; New York: Farrar, Straus, and Giroux, 1987, pp. 84–100.

Gutierrez, Donald. "A New Heaven and an Old Earth: DHL's *Apocalypse,* Apocalyptic and the Book of Revelation." *Review of Existential Psychology and Psychiatry* 15, no. 1 (1977): 61–85.

———. "The Ancient Imagination of DHL." *Twentieth Century Literature* 27 (1981): 178–96.

———. "Vitalism in DHL's Theory of Fiction." *Essays in Arts and Sciences* 16 (May 1987): 65–71.

Hartt, Julian N. *The Lost Image of Man.* Baton Rouge: Louisiana State University Press, 1963, pp. 55–60.

Hendrick, George. "Jesus and the Osiris–Isis Myth: Lawrence's *The Man Who Died* and Williams' *The Night of the Iguana.*" *Anglia* (Tübingen) 84 (1966): 398–406.

Henry, Graeme. "DHL: Objectivity and Belief." *Critical Review* (Melbourne) 22 (1980): 32–43.

Hoffman, Frederick J. "From Surrealism to 'The Apocalypse': A Development in Twentieth Century Irrationalism." *English Literary History* 15 (June 1948): 147–65.

Honig, Edwin. "The Ideal in Symbolic Fictions." *New Mexico Quarterly* 23 (1953): 153–68.

Hoyt, William R., III. "Re: 'DHL's Appraisal of Jesus' (A Response to William E. Phipps)." *Christian Century* 88 (14 July 1971): 861–62. (See Phipps [1971].)

Humma, John B. "DHL as Friedrich Nietzsche." *Philological Quarterly* 53 (1974): 110–20.

———. "Lawrence in Another Light: *Women in Love* and Existentialism." *Studies in the Novel* 24, no. 4 (Winter 1992): 392–409.

Iida, Takeo. "Lawrence's Pagan Gods and Christianity." *DHL Review* 23 (1991): 179–90.

———. "Nature Deities: Reawakening Blood-Consciousness in the Europeans." *Etudes Lawrenciennes* 9 (1993): 27–42.

Ivker, Barry. "Schopenhauer and DHL." *Xavier University Studies* 11 (1972): 22–36.

Jarrett, James L. "DHL and Bertrand Russell." In *A DHL Miscellany*. Edited by Harry T. Moore. Carbondale: Southern Illinois University Press, 1959, pp. 168–87.

Joad, C.E.M. *Guide to Modern Thought.* London: Faber, 1933, pp. 233, 253–60.

Joffe, P. H. "A Question of Complexity: The Russell-Lawrence Debate." *Theoria* 57 (1981): 17–37.

Jones, David A. "The Third Unrealized Wonder—The Reality of Relation in DHL and Martin Buber." *Religion and Life* 44 (Summer 1975): 178–87.

Jones, W.S.H. "DHL and the Revolt against Reason." *London and Quarterly and Holborn Review* 173 (January 1948): 25–31.

Jordan, Sidney. "DHL's Concept of the Unconscious and Existential Thinking." *Review of Existential Psychology and Psychiatry* 5 (1965): 34–43.

Joshi, Rita. "The Dissent Tradition: The Relation of Mark Rutherford to DHL." *English Language Notes* 22 (March 1985): 61–68.

Kalnins, Mara. "Introduction." In *Apocalypse and the Writings on Revelation* by DHL. Edited by Mara Kalnins. Cambridge: Cambridge University Press, 1980, pp. 3–38.

———. "Symbolic Seeing: Lawrence and Heraclitus." In *DHL: Centenary Essays.* Edited by Mara Kalnins. Bristol: Bristol Classical Press, 1986, pp. 173–90.

Katz-Roy, Ginette. " 'This May Be a Withering Tree This Europe': Bachelard, Deleuze and Guattari on DHL's Poetic Imagination." *Etudes Lawrenciennes* 9 (1993): 219–35.

Kermode, Frank. "DHL and the Apocalyptic Types." *Critical Quarterly* 10 (Spring–Summer 1968): 14–33. (Also in his *Continuities.* London: Routledge and Kegan Paul, 1968, pp. 122–51; and, in shortened form, in Clarke, ed. [1969]: 203–18.)

Kerr, Fergus. "Russell vs. Lawrence and/or Wittgenstein." *New Blackfriars* 63 (October 1982): 430–40.

Kessler, Jascha. "DHL's Primitivism." *Texas Studies in Literature and Language* 5 (1964): 467–88.

Klein, Robert C. "I, Thou and You in Three Lawrencian Relationships." *Paunch,* no. 31 (April 1968): 52–70.

Kleinbard, David J. "DHL and Ontological Insecurity." *PMLA* 89 (January 1974): 154–63.

Kort, Wesley A. *Modern Fiction and Human Time: A Study in Narrative and Belief.* Tampa: University of South Florida Press, 1985, pp. 42–57.

Krook, Dorothea. "Messianic Humanism: DHL's *The Man Who Died.*" In her *Three Traditions of Moral Thought.* Cambridge: Cambridge University Press, 1959, pp. 255–92.

Kunkel, Francis L. "*The Man Who Died:* The Heavenly Code." In his *Passion and the Passion: Sex and Religion in Modern Literature.* Philadelphia: Westminster Press, 1975, pp. 37–57.

Langbaum, Robert. "Reconstitution of Self: Lawrence and the Religion of Love." In his *Mysteries of Identity: A Theme in Modern Literature.* New York: Oxford University Press, 1977, pp. 251–353.

Lee, R. H. "A True Relatedness: Lawrence's View of Morality." *English Studies in Africa* 10 (September 1967): 178–85.

MacDonald, Robert H. " 'The Two Principles': A Theory of the Sexual and Psychological Symbolism of DHL's Later Fiction." *DHL Review* 11 (Summer 1978): 132–55.

McDowell, Frederick P. W. " 'Moments of Emergence and of a New Splendour': DHL and E. M. Forster in Their Fiction." In *DHL's "Lady": A New Look at "Lady Chatterley's Lover."* Edited by Michael Squires and Dennis Jackson. Athens: University of Georgia Press, 1985, pp. 58–90.

McGuffie, Duncan. "Lawrence and Nonconformity." In *DHL 1885–1930: A Celebration.* Edited by Andrew Cooper and Glyn Hughes. Nottingham: DHL Society, 1985, pp. 31–38.

McGuire, Errol M. "Answer to DHL: Thoreau's Vision of the Whole Man." *Thoreau Journal Quarterly* 10, no. 4 (1978): 14–24.

MacKenzie, Donald. "After Apocalypse: Some Elements in Late Lawrence." In *European Literature and Theology in the Twentieth Century: Ends of Times.* Edited by David Jasper and Colin Crowder. New York: St. Martin's Press, 1990, pp. 34–55.

Manicom, David. "An Approach to the Imagery: A Study of Selected Biblical Analogues in DHL's *The Rainbow.*" *English Studies in Canada* 11 (December 1985): 474–83.

Masson, Margaret J. "DHL's Congregational Inheritance." *DHL Review* 22 (Spring 1990): 53–68.

Maud, Ralph N. "DHL: True Emotion as the Ethical Control in Art." *Western Humanities Review* 9 (1955): 233–40.

Michie, James. "Seer in the Dark." *London Magazine* 4 (June 1957): 52–55.

Moseley, Edwin M. *Pseudonyms of Christ in the Modern World: Motifs and Methods.* Pittsburgh: University of Pittsburgh Press, 1963, pp. 69–91.

Mueller, W. R. "The Paradisal Quest." In his *The Celebration of Life.* New York: Sheed and Ward, 1972, pp. 144–68.

Murray, James G. "Screaming in Pentecost." In Huttar (1968), op. cit.

Murry, John Middleton. "On the Significance of DHL." In his *Adam and Eve: An Essay toward a New and Better Society.* London: Andrew Dakers, 1944, pp. 88–101, and passim.

Nicholson, Norman. *Man and Literature.* London: S.C.M. Press, 1943, pp. 64–86.

Noon, William T. "God and Man in Twentieth Century Fiction." *Thought* 37 (Spring 1962): 35–56. (Lawrence, Kafka, and Joyce.)

O'Connell, Adelyn. "The Concept of Person in DHL's *The Rainbow.*" In Huttar (1968), op. cit.

Paik, Nak-Chung. "Being and Thought-Adventure: An Approach to Lawrence." *Phoenix* 23 (1981): 43–100.

Panichas, G. A. "DHL's Concept of the Risen Lord." *Christian Scholar* 47 (Spring 1964): 56–65.

———. "DHL and the Ancient Greeks." *English Miscellany* 16 (1965): 195–214.

———. "F. M. Dostoevsky and DHL: Their Visions of Evil." In his *The Reverent Discipline: Essays in Literary Criticism and Culture.* Knoxville: University of Tennessee Press, 1974, pp. 205–28.

Paulin, Tom. " 'Hibiscus and Salvia Flowers': The Puritan Imagination." In *DHL in the Modern World.* Edited by Peter Preston and Peter Hoare. London: Macmillan, 1989, pp. 180–92.

Peerman, D. "DHL: Devout Heretic." *Christian Century* 78 (22 February 1961): 237–41.

Phipps, William E. "DHL's Appraisal of Jesus." *Christian Century* (28 April 1971): 521–24. (See also Hoyt [1971] for a response.)

Pinto, Vivian de Sola. "The Burning Bush: DHL as Religious Poet." In *Mansions of the Spirit: Essays in Literature and Religion.* Edited by George A. Panichas. New York: Hawthorne, 1967, pp. 213–35.

Pitre, David. "The Mystical Lawrence: Rupert Birkin's Taoist Quest." *Studies in Mystical Literature* 3 (1983): 43–64.

Plowman, M. "The Significance of DHL." In his *The Right to Live: Essays.* London: Andrew Dakers, 1942, pp. 122–30.

Price, A. Whigham. "DHL and Congregationalism." *Congregational Quarterly* 34 (July and October 1956): 242–52; 322–30.

Roberts, Mark. "DHL and the Failure of Energy: *Fantasia of the Unconscious; Psychoanalysis and the Unconscious.*" In his *The Tradition of Romantic Morality.* London: Macmillan, 1973, pp. 322–48.

Robinson, H. M. "Nietzsche, Lawrence and the Somatic Conception of the Good Life." *New Comparison: A Journal of Comparative and General Literary Studies* 5 (1988): 40–56.

Rooks, Pamela A. "DHL's 'Individual' and Michael Polanyi's 'Personal': Fruitful Redefinitions of Subjectivity and Objectivity." *DHL Review* 23 (1991): 21–29.

Rosenbaum, S. P. "The Mythology of Friendship: DHL, Bertrand Russell, and 'The Blind Man.' " In his *English Literature and British Philosophy: A Collection of Essays.* Chicago: University of Chicago Press, 1971, pp. 285–315.

Ross, C. L. "DHL's Use of Greek Tragedy: Euripedes and Ritual." *DHL Review* 10 (Spring 1977): 1–19.

Rossman, Charles. "The Gospel according to DHL: Religion in *Sons and Lovers.*" *DHL Review* 3 (Spring 1970): 31–41.

Roston, M. "W. B. Yeats and DHL." In his *Biblical Drama in England, from the Middle Ages to the Present Day.* London: Faber and Faber, 1968, pp. 264–79.

Rudrum, Alan. "Philosophical Implications in Lawrence's *Women in Love.*" *Dalhousie Review* 51 (Summer 1971): 240–50.

Ruthven, K. K. "The Savage God: Conrad and Lawrence." *Critical Quarterly* (1968): 39–54.

Salter, Leo. "DHL and Science." *Theoria* 62 (1984): 57–61.

Sawyer, Paul W. "The Religious Vision of DHL." *Crane Review* 3 (Spring 1961): 105–12.

Schneider, Daniel J. "The Symbolism of the Soul: DHL and Some Others." *DHL Review* 7 (Summer 1974): 107–26.

———. "DHL and *Thus Spoke Zarathustra.*" *South Carolina Review* 15, no. 2 (1983): 96–108.

———. "DHL and the Early Greek Philosophers." *DHL Review* 17 (Summer 1984): 97–109.

———. "Alternatives to Logocentrism in DHL." *South Atlantic Review* 51, no. 2 (May 1986): 35–47. (Reprinted in Widdowson [1992]: 160–70.)

Scott, Nathan A. "DHL: Chartist of the Via Mystica." In his *Rehearsals of Discomposure: Alienation and Reconciliation in Modern Literature.* London: John Lehmann, 1952, pp. 112–77.

Sharma, D. D. "DHL's Existential Vision." In *Essays on DHL.* Edited by T. R. Sharma. Meerut, India: Shalabh Book House, 1987, pp. 153–61.

Sipple, James B. "Laughter in the Cathedral: Religious Affirmation and Ridicule in the Writings of DHL." In *The Philosophical Reflection of Man in Literature: Selected Papers from Several Conferences Held by the International Society for Phenomenology and Literature in Cambridge, Massachusetts.* Edited by Anna-Teresa Tymieniecka. Boston: Reidel, 1982, pp. 213–44.

Smailes, T. A. "Plato's 'Great Lie of Ideals': Function in *Women in Love.*" In *Generous Converse: English Essays in Memory of Edward Davis.* Edited by Brian Green. Cape Town: Oxford University Press, 1980, pp. 133–35.

Smith, Elton. "Redemptive Snobbishness in Nietzsche, Lawrence, and Eliot." *Newsletter of the Conference on Christianity and Literature* 18, no. 3 (Spring 1969): 30–35.

Soames, Jane. "The Modern Rousseau." *Life and Letters* 8 (December 1932): 451–70.

Sreenivasan, S. "DHL and Bertrand Russell: A Study in Intellectual 'Personalities.' " *Journal of Literary Aesthetics* 1, no. 3 (1981): 85–96.

Stewart, Jack F. "Primitivism in *Women in Love.*" *DHL Review* 13 (Spring 1980): 45–62.

———. "Lawrence and Van Gogh." *DHL Review* 16 (Spring 1983): 1–24.

———. "The Vital Art of Lawrence and Van Gogh." *DHL Review* 19 (Summer 1987): 123–48.

———. "Expressionism in *The Rainbow.*" In *Critical Essays on DHL.* Edited by Dennis Jackson and Fleda Brown Jackson. Boston: G. K. Hall, 1988, pp. 72–92.

Stohl, Johan H. "Man and Society: Lawrence's Subversive Vision." In Huttar (1968), op. cit.

Sturm, Ralph D. "Lawrence: Critic of Christianity." *Catholic World* 208 (November 1968): 75–79.

Tedlock, E. W., Jr. "DHL's Annotations of Ouspensky's *Tertium Organum.*" *Texas Studies in Literature and Language* 2 (Summer 1960): 206–18.

Terry, C. J. "Aspects of DHL's Struggle with Christianity." *Dalhousie Review* 54 (Spring 1974): 112–29.

Thompson, Leslie M. "DHL and Judas." *DHL Review* 4 (Spring 1971): 1–19.

Tindall, William York. "Transcendentalism in Contemporary Literature." In *Asian Legacy and American Life.* Edited by A. E. Christy. New York: John Day, 1945, pp. 175–92.

Tischler, Nancy M. "The Rainbow and the Arch." In Huttar (1968), op. cit.

Turnell, Martin. *Modern Literature and Christian Faith.* Westminster, Md.: Newman Press; London: Darton, Longman, and Todd, 1961, pp. 25–34.

Ulmer, Gregory L. "DHL, Wilhelm Worringer, and the Aesthetics of Modernism." *DHL Review* 10 (Summer 1977a): 165–81.

———. "Rousseau and DHL: 'Philosophes' of the 'Gelded' Age." *Canadian Review of Comparative Literature* 4 (1977b): 68–80.

Vanderlip, E. C. "The Morality of DHL." In Huttar (1968), op. cit.

Vivante, Leone. "Reflections on DHL's Insight into the Concept of Potentiality." In his *A Philosophy of Potentiality.* London: Routledge and Kegan Paul, 1955, pp. 79–115.

Wallace, M. Elizabeth. "The Circling Hawk: Philosophy of Knowledge in Polanyi and Lawrence." In *The Challenge of DHL.* Edited by Michael Squires and Keith Cushman. Madison: University of Wisconsin Press, 1990, pp. 103–20.

Walsh, K. R. "Three Puritan Poets: Milton, Blake, DHL." *Christian Community* 5, no. 53 (May 1936).

Watkins, Daniel P. "Labor and Religion in DHL's 'The Rocking-Horse Winner.' " *Studies in Short Fiction* 24 (1987): 295–301.

Widmer, Kingsley. "DHL and the Art of Nihilism." *Kenyon Review* 20 (Fall 1958): 604–16.

———. "The Primitivistic Aesthetic: DHL." *Journal of Aesthetics and Art Criticism* 17 (March 1959): 344–53.

———. "Lawrence and the Nietzschean Matrix." In *DHL and Tradition.* Edited by Jeffrey Meyers. London: Athlone, 1985, pp. 115–31.

Williams, Charles. "Sensuality and Substance." *Theology* (May 1939): 352–60.

Williams, George G. "DHL's Philosophy as Expressed in His Poetry." *Rice Institute Pamphlet* 38 (April 1951): 73–94.

Williams, Hubertien H. "Lawrence's Concept of Being." In Huttar (1968), op. cit.

Wilson, Colin. "Existential Criticism." *Chicago Review* 13 (Summer 1959): 152–81.

Young, Richard O. " 'Where Even the Trees Come and Go': DHL and the Fourth Dimension." *DHL Review* 13 (Spring 1980): 30–44.

Zoll, Allan R. "Vitalism and the Metaphysics of Love: DHL and Schopenhauer." *DHL Review* 11 (Spring 1978): 1–20.

Zytaruk, G. "The Phallic Vision: DHL and V. V. Rozanov." *Comparative Literature Studies* 4 (1967): 283–97.

———. "The Doctrine of Individuality: DHL's 'Metaphysic.' " In *DHL: A Centenary Consideration.* Edited by Peter Balbert and Phillip L. Marcus. Ithaca, N.Y.: Cornell University Press, 1985, pp. 237–54.

BIBLIOGRAPHY 93: LAWRENCE AND LANGUAGE

Book-length studies that focus specifically on Lawrence's use of, or ideas on, language are as follows: Bell (1992), Bonds (1987), Burns (1980), Fernihough (1993), Humma (1990), Hyde (1981), Ingram (1990), Leavis (1976), Miko (1971), Padhi (1989).

Andrews, W. T. "DHL's Favourite Jargon." *Notes and Queries* 211 (March 1966): 97–98.

Baker, William E. *Syntax in English Poetry, 1870–1930.* Berkeley: University of California Press, 1967, passim.

Baldanza, Frank. "DHL's 'Song of Songs.' " *Modern Fiction Studies* 7 (Summer 1961): 106–14.

Barry, Peter. "Stylistics and the Logic of Intuition; or, How Not to Pick a Chrysanthemum." *Critical Quarterly* 27 (Winter 1985): 51–58. (Critique of Nash [1982], op. cit.)

Beckley, Betty. "Finding Meaning in Style: A Computerized Statistical Approach to the Linguistic Analysis of Form." *SECOL Review: Southeastern Conference on Linguistics* 9 (Summer 1985): 143–60.

Becket, Fiona, and Michael Bell, eds. "Lawrence and Language." *DHL Review* (Special Number), forthcoming, 1996.

Bersani, Leo. "Lawrentian Stillness." *Yale Review* 65 (October 1975): 38–60. (Also in his *A Future for Astyanax: Character and Desire in Literature.* Boston and Toronto: Little, Brown, 1976, pp. 156–85.)

Bickerton, Derek. "The Language of *Women in Love.*" *Review of English Studies* (Leeds) 8 (April 1967): 56–67.

Black, Michael. "A Kind of Bristling in the Darkness: Memory and Metaphor in Lawrence." *Critical Review* (Melbourne) 32 (1992): 29–44.

Blanchard, Lydia. "Lawrence, Foucault, and the Language of Sexuality." In *DHL's "Lady": A New Look at "Lady Chatterley's Lover."* Edited by Michael Squires and Dennis Jackson. Athens: University of Georgia Press, 1985, pp. 17–35.

Cluysenaar, Anne. *Introduction to Literary Stylistics; A Discussion of Dominant Structures in Verse and Prose.* London: Batsford, 1976, pp. 63–66, 92–99. (Stylistic analyses of, respectively, the poem "Gloire de Dijon," and the story "The Blind Man.")

Cohn, Dorrit. "Narrated Monologue: Definition of a Fictional Style." *Comparative Literature* 18 (Spring 1966): 97–112.

Dataller, Roger. "Elements of DHL's Prose Style." *Essays in Criticism* 3 (October 1953): 413–24.

DeVille, Peter. "Stylistic Observations on the Use and Appreciation of Poetry in EFL with Particular Reference to DHL." *Quaderno* 1 (1987): 151–75.

Ditsky, John M. " 'Dark, Darker than Fire': Thematic Parallels in Lawrence and Faulkner." *Southern Humanities Review* 8 (Fall 1974): 497–505.

Doherty, Gerald. "The Salvator Mundi Touch: Messianic Typology in DHL's *Women in Love.*" *Ariel* 13, no. 3 (1982): 53–71.

———. "The Darkest Source: DHL; Tantric Yoga, and *Women in Love.*" *Essays in Literature* 11 (1984): 211–22.

———. "White Mythologies: DHL and the Deconstructive Turn." *Criticism* 29 (Fall 1987): 477–96.

———. "The Metaphorical Imperative: From Trope to Narrative in *The Rainbow.*" *South Central Review* 6 (Spring 1989): 46–61.

———. "The Art of Leaping: Metaphor Unbound in DHL's *Women in Love.*" *Style* 26 (Spring 1992): 50–65.

Ellis, David, and Howard Mills. *DHL's Non-Fiction: Art, Thought and Genre.* Cambridge: Cambridge University Press, 1988.

Fleishman, Avrom. "He Do the Polis in Different Voices: Lawrence's Later Style." In *DHL: A Centenary Consideration.* Edited by Peter Balbert and Phillip L. Marcus. Ithaca, N.Y., and London: Cornell University Press, 1985, pp. 162–79.

Fogel, Daniel Mark. "The Sacred Poem to the Unknown in the Fiction of DHL." *DHL Review* 16 (1983): 45–57. (Stylistics.)

Fowler, Roger. "*The Lost Girl:* Discourse and Focalization." In *Rethinking Lawrence.* Edited by Keith Brown. Milton Keynes and Philadelphia: Open University Press, 1990, pp. 53–66.

Gerber, Stephen. "Character, Language and Experience in 'Water Party.' " *Paunch* 36–37 (April 1973): 3–29.

Goldberg, S. L. "*The Rainbow:* Fiddle-Bow and Sand." *Essays in Criticism* 11 (October 1961): 418–34.

Gordon, David J. "Sex and Language in DHL." *Twentieth Century Literature* 27 (Winter 1981): 362–75.

———. "DHL's Dual Myth of Origin." *Sewanee Review* 89 (1981): 83–94. (Reprinted in Jackson and Jackson [1988]: 238–45.)

Hagen, Patricia L. "The Metaphoric Foundations of Lawrence's 'Dark Knowledge.' " *Texas Studies in Literature and Language* 29 (Spring–Winter 1987): 365–76.

Hardy, Barbara. "DHL's Self-Consciousness." In *DHL and the Modern World.* Edited by Peter Preston and Peter Hoare. London: Macmillan, 1989, pp. 27–46.

Hayles, Nancy Katherine. "The Ambivalent Approach: DHL and the New Physics." *Mosaic* 15 (September 1982): 89–108.

Hodges, Karen. "Language and Litter-ature: Style as Process." *SECOL Review: Southeastern Conference on Linguistics* 6, no. 2 (1982): 98–109.

Hope, A. D. "Some Poems of DHL Reconsidered." *Phoenix* 23 (1981): 11–16. (Stylistic approach.)

Hortmann, Wilhelm. "The Nail and the Novel: Some Remarks on Style and the Unconscious in *The Rainbow.*" In *Theorie und Praxis im Erzählen des 19. und 20. Jahrhunderts: Studien zur englischen und amerikanischen Literatur zu Ehren von Willi Erzgräber.* Edited by Winfried Herget, Klaus Peter Jochum, and Ingeborg Weber. Tübingen: Narr, 1986, pp. 167–79.

Janik, Del Ivan. "Toward 'Thingness': Cézanne's Painting and Lawrence's Poetry." *Twentieth Century Literature* 19 (1973): 119–27.

Jones, Lawrence. "Imagery and the 'Idiosyncratic Mode of Regard': Eliot, Hardy, and Lawrence." *Ariel* 12 (1981): 29–49.

Katz-Roy, Ginette. "The Process of 'Rotary Image-Thought' in DHL's *Last Poems.*" *Etudes Lawrenciennes* 7 (1992): 129–38.

King, Debra W. "Just Can't Find the Words: How Expression Is Achieved." *Philosophy and Rhetoric* 24, no. 1 (1991): 54–72.

Kinkead-Weekes, Mark. "Eros and Metaphor: Sexual Relationship in the Fiction of DHL." In *Lawrence and Women.* Edited by Anne Smith. London: Vision, 1978, pp. 101–20.

Knight, G. Wilson. "Lawrence, Joyce and Powys." *Essays in Criticism* 11 (October 1961): 403–17.

Landow, George P. "Lawrence and Ruskin: The Sage as Word-Painter." In *DHL and Tradition.* Edited by Jeffrey Meyers. London: Athlone, 1985, pp. 35–50.

Leith, Richard. "Dialogue and Dialect in DHL." *Style* 14 (Summer 1980): 245–58.

Levenson, Michael. " 'The Passion of Opposition' in *Women in Love:* None, One, Two, Few, Many." *Modern Language Studies* 17 (Spring 1987): 22–36.

Lodge, David. "Metaphor and Metonymy in Modern Fiction." *Critical Quarterly* 17 (Spring 1975): 75–93 (86–88).

————. "DHL." In his *The Modes of Modern Writing: Metaphor, Metonymy, and the Typology of Modern Literature.* London: Edward Arnold, 1977, pp. 160–76.

————. "Lawrence, Dostoevsky, Bakhtin: DHL and Dialogic Fiction." *Renaissance and Modern Studies* 29 (1985): 16–32. (Reprinted, in slightly revised form, in Brown [1990]: 92–108; and in Lodge's own *After Bakhtin: Essays on Fiction and Criticism.* London and New York: Routledge, 1990, pp. 57–74.)

McIntosh, Angus. "A Four-Letter Word in *Lady Chatterley's Lover.*" In *Patterns of Language: Papers in General, Descriptive, and Applied Linguistics.* Edited by Angus McIntosh and M.A.K. Halliday. London: Longman; Bloomington: Indiana University Press, 1967, pp. 151–64. (Largely a statistical analysis of occurrences of the word "know.")

Mills, Howard W. "Stylistic Revision of *Women in Love.*" *Etudes Lawrencienne* 3 (1988): 99–108.

Monell, Siv. "On the Role of Case, Aspect and Valency in the Narrative Technique of *The Rainbow.*" In *Papers from the Second Scandinavian Symposium on Syntactic Variation, Stockholm, May 15–16, 1982.* Edited by Sven Jacobson. Stockholm: Almqvist and Wiksell, 1983, pp. 153–68.

Moore, Harry T. "The Prose of DHL." In *DHL: The Man Who Lived.* Edited by Robert B. Partlow, Jr., and Harry T. Moore. Carbondale and Edwardsville: Southern Illinois University Press, 1980, pp. 245–57.

Nash, Walter. "On a Passage from Lawrence's 'Odour of Chrysanthemums.' " In *Language and Literature: An Introductory Reader in Stylistics.* Edited by Ronald Carter. London: George Allen and Unwin, 1982, pp. 101–20.

Nassar, Eugene Paul. "Stylistic Discontinuity in DHL's *The Rainbow.*" In his *Essays Critical and Metacritical.* Rutherford, N.J.: Fairleigh Dickinson University Press, 1983, pp. 65–83.

Needham, John. "Leavis and the Post–Saussureans." *English* 24 (1984): 235–50.

Nichols, Ann Eljenholm. "Syntax and Style: Ambiguities in Lawrence's *Twilight in Italy.*" *College Composition and Communication* 16 (December 1965): 261–66.

Oltean, Stefan. "Functions of Free Indirect Discourse: The Case of a Novel." *Revue Roumaine de Linguistique* 31 (1986): 153–64.

Padhi, Bibhu. "Lawrence's Idea of Language." *Modernist Studies* 4 (1982): 65–76.

Peer, Willie van. "Toward a Pragmatic Theory of Connexity: An Analysis of the Use of the Conjunction 'and' from a Functional Perspective." In *Text Connexity, Text Coherence: Aspects, Methods, Results.* Edited by Emel Sozer. Hamburg: Buske, 1985, pp. 363–80. (On "The Mortal Coil.")

Poirier, Richard. *A World Elsewhere: The Place of Style in American Literature.* London: Chatto and Windus, 1967, pp. 37–49. (*Studies in Classic American Literature,* 37–40; *St. Mawr,* 40–49.)

Presley, John. "DHL and the Resources of Poetry." *Language and Style* 12 (1979): 3–12.

Ragussis, Michael. "The False Myth of *St. Mawr:* Lawrence and the Subterfuge of Art." *Papers on Language and Literature* 11 (Spring 1975): 186–96.

————. "DHL: The New Vocabulary of *Women in Love:* Speech and Art Speech." In his *The Subterfuge of Art: Language and the Romantic Tradition.* Baltimore and London: Johns Hopkins University Press, 1978, pp. 172–225.

Ramey, Frederick. "Words in the Service of Silence: Preverbal Language in Lawrence's *The Plumed Serpent.*" *Modern Fiction Studies* 27 (Winter 1981–82): 613–21.

Reddick, Bryan. "*Sons and Lovers:* The Omniscient Narrator." *Thoth* 7 (Spring 1966): 68–76.

———. "Point of View and Narrative Tone in *Women in Love:* The Portrayal of Interpsychic Space." *DHL Review* 7 (Summer 1974): 156–71.

Robinson, Ian. "DHL and English Prose." In *DHL: A Critical Study of the Major Novels and Other Writings.* Edited by A. H. Gomme. Sussex: Harvester Press; New York: Barnes and Noble, 1978, pp. 13–29.

Russell, John. "DHL: *The Lost Girl, Kangaroo.*" In his *Style in Modern British Fiction: Studies in Joyce, Lawrence, Forster, Lewis and Green.* Baltimore: Johns Hopkins University Press, 1975, pp. 43–88.

Sabin, Margery. "The Life of English Idiom, the Laws of French Cliché." Part I. *Raritan* 1, no. 2 (1981): 70–89; Part II: *Raritan* 1, no. 3 (1981): 70–89. (*Lady Chatterley's Lover,* "Daughters of the Vicar"; *Sons and Lovers, The Rainbow, Women in Love.*)

———. *The Dialect of the Tribe: Speech and Community in Modern Fiction.* Oxford: Oxford University Press, 1987, passim: "The Life of Idiom in Joyce and Lawrence," pp. 25–42; "Near and Far Things in Lawrence's Writing of the Twenties" (*St. Mawr*), pp. 162–78; *Women in Love,* pp. 106–38; *Sea and Sardinia,* pp. 139–62.

Sale, Roger. "The Narrative Technique of *The Rainbow.*" *Modern Fiction Studies* 5 (Spring 1959): 29–38.

Schleifer, Ronald. "Lawrence's Rhetoric of Vision: The Ending of *The Rainbow.*" *DHL Review* 13 (Summer 1980): 161–78.

Schneider, Daniel J. "Alternatives to Logocentrism in DHL." *South Atlantic Review* 51 (May 1986): 35–47. (Reprinted in Widdowson [1992]: 160–70.)

Squires, Michael. "Recurrence as a Narrative Technique in *The Rainbow.*" *Modern Fiction Studies* 21 (Summer 1975): 230–36.

Stearns, Catherine. "Gender, Voice, and Myth: The Relation of Language to the Female in DHL's Poetry." *DHL Review* 17 (Fall 1984): 233–42.

Stewart, Garrett. "Lawrence, 'Being,' and the Allotropic Style." *Novel* 9 (Spring 1976): 217–42. (Reprinted in *Towards a Poetics of Fiction: Essays from "Novel: A Forum on Fiction" 1967–76.* Edited by Mark Spilka. Bloomington: Indiana University Press, 1977, pp. 331–56.

Stewart, Jack F. "Expressionism in *The Rainbow.*" *Novel* 13 (1979–80): 296–315. (Reprinted in Jackson and Jackson [1988]: 72–92.)

———. "The Vital Art of Lawrence and Van Gogh." *DHL Review* 19 (Summer 1987): 123–48.

———. "Dialectics of Knowing in *Women in Love.*" *Twentieth Century Literature* 37 (Spring 1991): 59–75.

Trikha, Manorama B. "DHL's Poetry: A Language Experiment." In *Essays on DHL.* Edited by T. R. Sharma. Meerut, India: Shalabh Book House, 1987, pp. 183–201.

Wallace, Jeff. "Language, Nature and the Politics of Materialism: Raymond Williams and DHL." In *Raymond Williams: Politics, Education, Letters.* Edited by W. John Morgan and Peter Preston. London: Macmillan; New York: St. Martin's Press, 1993, pp. 105–28.

Wright, Terence. "Rhythm in the Novel." *Modern Language Review* 80 (January 1985): 1–15.

BIBLIOGRAPHY 94: FEMINIST CRITICISM AND STUDIES RELATED TO SEX, SEXUALITY, AND GENDER

Bibliographies 14 and 90 should be consulted for further items directly relevant to this bibliography. See also the following books cited in the master bibliography at the end of this book: Ben-Ephraim (1981), Boadella (1956), Dix (1980), Dorbad (1991), Feinstein (1993), Fernihough (1993), Green (1974), Hahn (1975), Holbrook (1964 and 1992), Kelsey (1991), Lewiecki-Wilson (1994), MacLeod (1985), Maddox (1994), Miliaras (1987), Murry (1931), Nin (1932), Nixon (1986), Patmore (1970), Polhemus (1990), Ruderman (1984), Siegel (1991), Simpson (1982), Singh (1988), Storch (1990), Williams (1993), Worthen (1991a).

Apter, T. E. "Let's Hear What the Male Chauvinist Is Saying: *The Plumed Serpent.*" In Smith, op. cit. (1978): 156–77.

Arcana, Judith. "I Remember Mama: Mother-Blaming in *Sons and Lovers* Criticism." *DHL Review* 21 (Spring 1989): 137–51.

Arnold, Armin. "DHL in Ascona?" In *DHL: The Man Who Lived.* Edited by Robert B. Partlow, Jr., and Harry T. Moore. Carbondale: Southern Illinois University Press, 1980, pp. 195–98.

Balbert, Peter. "Forging and Feminism: *Sons and Lovers* and the Phallic Imagination." *DHL Review* 11 (Summer 1978): 93–113. (Reprinted in Balbert [1989], pp. 16–55.)

———. "The Loving of Lady Chatterley: DHL and the Phallic Imagination." In *DHL: The Man Who Died.* Edited by Robert B. Partlow, Jr., and Harry T. Moore. Carbondale: Southern Illinois University Press, 1980, pp. 143–58. (Revised as part of final chapter of Balbert [1989], pp. 133–87.)

———. " 'Logic of the Soul': Prothalamic Pattern in *The Rainbow.*" *Papers on Language and Literature* 29 (1983): 309–25. (Reprinted in revised form in Balbert and Marcus [1985]: 45–66; and in Balbert [1989], pp. 56–84.)

———. "Ursula Brangwen and 'The Essential Criticism': The Female Corrective in *Women in Love.*" *Studies in the Novel* 17 (1985): 267–85. (Reprinted in Balbert [1989], pp. 85–108.)

———. "Snake's Eye and Obsidian Knife: Art, Ideology and 'The Woman Who Rode Away.' " *DHL Review* 18 (Summer 1985–86): 255–73. (Reprinted in Balbert [1989], pp. 109–32.)

———. "Silver Spoon to Devil's Fork: Diana Trilling and the Sexual Ethics of *Mr. Noon.*" *DHL Review* 20 (Summer 1988): 237–50.

———. *DHL and the Phallic Imagination: Essays on Sexual Identity and Feminist Misreading.* London: Macmillan, 1989. (Reworking of preceding five previously published essays.)

———. "From *Lady Chatterley's Lover* to *The Deer Park:* Lawrence, Mailer, and the Dialectic of Erotic Risk." *Studies in the Novel* 22 (1990): 67–81.

Barron, Janet. "Equality Puzzle: Lawrence and Feminism." In *Rethinking Lawrence.* Edited by Keith Brown. Milton Keynes, Pa.: Open University Press, 1990, pp. 12–22.

Beauvoir, Simone de. "DHL or Phallic Pride." In her *The Second Sex.* Translated by H. M. Parshley. London: Cape; New York: Knopf, 1953; Harmondsworth: Penguin, 1972, pp. 245–54. (Original French version: *Le Deuxième Sexe.* Paris: Gallimard, 1949, pp. 331–43.)

Bergler, Edmund. "DHL's *The Fox* and the Psychoanalytic Theory on Lesbianism." In *A DHL Miscellany.* Edited by Harry T. Moore. Carbondale: Southern Illinois University Press, 1959, pp. 49–55.

Bhat, Vishnu. "DHL's Sexual Ideal." *Literary Half-Yearly* 10 (January 1969): 68–73.

Black, Michael. *The Literature of Fidelity.* London: Chatto and Windus; New York: Barnes and Novel: 1975, pp. 169–211. (Ch. 11, "Sexuality in Literature: *Lady Chatterley's Lover,*" pp. 169–83. Ch. 12, "Lawrence and 'that which is perfectly ourselves,' " pp. 184–98. Ch. 13, "Tolstoy and Lawrence: Some Conclusions," pp. 199–211.)

Blanchard, Lydia. "Love and Power: A Reconsideration of Sexual Politics in DHL." *Modern Fiction Studies* 21 (1975): 431–43.

———. "Mothers and Daughters in DHL: *The Rainbow* and Selected Shorter Works." In Smith, op. cit. (1978): 75–100.

———. "The 'Real Quartet' of *Women in Love:* Lawrence on Brothers and Sisters." In *DHL: The Man Who Lived.* Edited by Robert B. Partlow, Jr., and Harry T. Moore. Carbondale: Southern Illinois University Press, 1980, pp. 199–206.

———. "Lawrence, Foucault, and the Language of Sexuality." In *DHL's "Lady": A New Look at "Lady Chatterley's Lover."* Edited by Michael Squires and Dennis Jackson. Athens: University of Georgia Press, 1985, pp. 17–35.

Bolsterli, Margaret. "Studies in Context: The Homosexual Ambience of Twentieth Century Literary Culture." *DHL Review* 6 (Spring 1973): 71–85.

Brayfield, Peg. "Lawrence's 'Male and Female Principles' and the Symbolism of *The Fox.*" *Mosaic* 4, no. 3 (1971): 41–65.

Breen, Judith Puchner. "DHL, World War I and the Battle between the Sexes: A Reading of 'The Blind Man' and 'Tickets, Please.' " *Women's Studies* 13 (1986): 63–74.

Brennan, Joseph. "Male Power in the Work of DHL." *Paunch* 63–64 (1990): 199–207.

Brookesmith, Peter. "The Future of the Individual: Ursula Brangwen and Kate Millett's *Sexual Politics.*" *Human World* (Swansea) 10 (1973): 42–65.

Brown, Keith. "After the Sexual Revolution." *Times Literary Supplement* (18 October 1985): 1171–72.

Burgan, Mary. "Androgynous Fatherhood in *Ulysses* and *Women in Love.*" *Modern Language Quarterly* 44 (June 1983): 178–97.

Capitanchik, Maurice. "DHL: The Sexual Impasse." *Books and Bookmen* 18, no. 2 (1972): 28–31.

Carter, Angela. "Lorenzo as Closet Queen." In her *Nothing Sacred: Selected Writings.* London: Virago Press, 1982, pp. 207–14. (Originally published as "The Naked Lawrence" in *New Society* 31 [13 February 1975]: 398–99.)

Christensen, Peter G. "Katherine Ann Porter's 'Flowering Judas' and DHL's *The Plumed Serpent:* Contradicting Visions of Women in the Mexican Revolution." *South Atlantic Review* 56 (1991): 35–46.

Cockshut, A.O.J. *Man and Woman: A Study of Love and the Novel, 1740–1940.* New York: Oxford University Press, 1978, pp. 152–60.

Core, Deborah. " 'The Closed Door': Love between Women in the Works of DHL." *DHL Review* 11 (Summer 1978): 114–31.

Cornwell, Ethel F. "The Sex Mysticism of DHL." In her *The "Still Point": Theme and Variations in the Writings of T. S. Eliot, Coleridge, Yeats, Henry James, Virginia Woolf and DHL.* New Brunswick, N.J.: Rutgers University Press, 1962, pp. 208–42.

Cowan, James C., ed. *DHL Review* 8 (Fall 1975). Special issue: "DHL and Women."

Davis, Patricia C. "Chicken Queen's Delight: DHL's *The Fox.*" *Modern Fiction Studies* 19 (Winter 1973–74): 565–71. (On homoerotic aspects of Henry Grenfel.)

Davis, William A., Jr. "Mountains, Metaphors, and Other Entanglements: Sexual Representation in the Prologue to *Women in Love.*" *DHL Review* 22 (Spring 1990): 69–76.

Delavenay, Emile. "DHL and Sacher-Masoch." *DHL Review* 6 (Summer 1973): 119–48.

Deleuze, Gilles, and Félix Guattari. *Anti-Oedipus: Capitalism and Schizophrenia.* Translated by Robert Hurley, Mark Seem, and Helen R. Lane. New York: Viking, 1977, passim. (Originally published in French as *L'Anti-Oedipe.* Paris: Les Editions de Minuit, 1972. Reprinted Minneapolis: Minnesota University Press, 1983; London: Athlone Press, 1984.)

D'Heurle, Adma, and Joel N. Feimer. "The Tender Connection." *Antioch Review* 37 (1979): 293–310.

Dodsworth, Martin. "Lawrence, Sex and Class." *English* 24 (1985): 69–80. (Review of *Mr Noon.*)

Doheny, John. "The Novel Is the Book of Life: DHL and a Revised Version of Polymorphous Perversity." *Paunch* 26 (April 1966): 40–59.

Doherty, Gerald. "The Throes of Aphrodite: The Sexual Dimension in DHL's *The Plumed Serpent.*" *Studies in the Humanities* 12 (December 1985): 67–78.

Dollimore, Jonathan. "The Challenge of Sexuality." In *Society and Literature 1945–1970.* Edited by Alan Sinfield. London: Methuen, 1983, pp. 51–85 (52–61, on the trial of *Lady Chatterley's Lover* and its implications).

———. "DHL and the Metaphysics of Sexual Difference." In his *Sexual Dissidence: Augustine to Wilde, Freud to Foucault.* Oxford: Clarendon Press, 1991, pp. 268–75.

Donaldson, George. " 'Men in Love'?: DHL, Rupert Birkin and Gerald Crich." In *DHL: Centenary Studies.* Edited by Mara Kalnins. Bristol: Bristol Classical Press, 1986, pp. 41–68.

Doolittle, Hilda (H. D.). *Bid Me to Live (A Madrigal).* New York: Dial, 1960.

Draper, R. P. "The Defeat of Feminism: DHL's *The Fox* and "The Woman Who Rode Away." *Studies in Short Fiction* 3 (1966): 186–98.

Eagleton, Sandra. "One Feminist's Approach to Teaching DHL." *DHL Review* 19 (Fall 1987): 325–30.

Ehrstine, John W. "The Dialectic in DHL." *Research Studies* (Washington State University) 33 (March 1965): 11–26.

Faderman, Lillian. "Lesbian Magazine Fiction in the Early Twentieth Century." *Journal of Popular Culture* 11 (1978): 800–817. (Includes discussion of *The Fox.*)

Fasick, Laura. "Female Power, Male Comradeship, and the Rejection of the Female in

Lawrence's *Twilight in Italy, Sea and Sardinia,* and *Etruscan Places.'' DHL
Review* 21 (Spring 1989): 25–36.

Fiedler, Leslie A. "The Literati of the Four-Letter Word." *Playboy* 8 (June 1961): 85,
125–28. (Reprinted in *The Twelfth Anniversary Playboy Reader.* Edited by Hugh
M. Hefner. London: Souvenir Press, 1965, pp. 193–202.)

Fraiberg, Selma. "Two Modern Incest Heroes." *Partisan Review* 28 (1961): 646–61.
("The Rocking-Horse Winner.")

Friedman, Susan Stanford. "Portrait of the Artist as a Young Woman: H. D.'s Rescrip-
tions of Joyce, Lawrence, and Pound." In *Writing the Woman Artist: Essays on
Poetics, Politics, and Portraiture.* Edited by Suzanne W. Jones. Philadelphia:
University of Pennsylvania Press, 1991, pp. 23–42.

Fusini, Nadia, and Sharon Wood. "Woman-graphy." In *The Lonely Mirror: Italian Perspectives on Feminist Theory.* Edited by Sandra Kemp and Paola Bono. London:
Routledge, 1993, pp. 38–54.

Gilbert, Sandra M. "Costumes of the Mind: Transvestism as Metaphor in Modern Lit-
erature." *Critical Inquiry* 7 (1980): 391–417. (Includes discussion of *The Fox.*
Reprinted in *Writing and Sexual Difference.* Edited by Elizabeth Abel. Hemel
Hempstead: Harvester, 1982.)

———. "Potent Griselda: 'The Ladybird' and the Great Mother." In *DHL: A Centenary
Consideration.* Edited by Peter Balbert and Phillip L. Marcus. Ithaca, N.Y., and
London: Cornell University Press, 1985, pp. 130–61.

———. "Feminism and DHL: Some Notes toward a Vindication of His Rites." *Anais*
9 (1991): 92–100.

Gilbert, Sandra M., and Susan Gubar. *No Man's Land: The Place of the Woman Writer
in the Twentieth Century.* Vol. 1: *The War of the Words.* New Haven, Conn.:
Yale University Press, 1988, pp. 37–40 and passim.

Gillis, James M. "Novelists and Sexual Perversion." In his *This Our Day: Approvals
and Disapprovals.* New York: Paulist Press, 1933, pp. 32–37.

Glazer, Myra. "Sex and the Psyche: William Blake and DHL." *Hebrew University Stud-
ies in Language and Literature* 9, no. 2 (1981): 196–229. (Revised as "Why the
Sons of God Want the Daughters of Men: On William Blake and DHL." In
William Blake and the Moderns. Edited by Robert J. Bertholf and Annette S.
Levitt. Albany: State University of New York Press, 1982, pp. 164–85.)

Good, Jan. "Toward a Resolution of Gender Identity Confusion: The Relationship of
Henry and March in *The Fox.'' DHL Review* 18 (1985–86): 217–27.

Gordon, David J. "Sex and Language in DHL." *Twentieth Century Literature* 27 (Winter
1981): 362–74.

Green, Eleanor H. "Schopenhauer and DHL on Sex and Love." *DHL Review* 8 (Fall
1975): 329–45.

Greer, Germaine. "Sex, Lies and Old Pork Pies." *Independent on Sunday* (London) (3
June 1990): 9–10.

Gutierrez, Donald. "DHL and Sex." *Liberal and Fine Arts Review* 3, nos. 1–2 (1983):
43–56.

Haegert, John W. "DHL and the Ways of Eros." *DHL Review* 11 (Fall 1978): 199–233.

———. "DHL and the Aesthetics of Transgression." *Modern Philology* 88 (1990): 2–
25.

Hampson, Carolyn. "The Morels and the Gants: Sexual Conflict as a Universal Theme."
Thomas Wolfe Review 8 (Spring 1984): 27–40.

Hardy, Barbara. "Women in DHL's Works." In *DHL: Novelist, Poet, Prophet.* Edited by Stephen Spender. London: Weidenfeld and Nicolson; New York: Harper, 1973, pp. 90–121.

Harris, Janice H. "DHL and Kate Millett." *Massachusetts Review* 15 (1974): 522–29.

———. "Sexual Antagonism in DHL's Early Leadership Fiction." *Modern Language Studies* 7 (Spring 1977): 43–52.

———. "Lawrence and the Edwardian Feminists." In *The Challenge of DHL.* Edited by Michael Squires and Keith Cushman. Madison: University of Wisconsin Press, 1990, pp. 62–76.

Heath, Jane. "Helen Corke and DHL: Sexual Identity and Literary Relations." *Feminist Studies* 11 (Summer 1985): 317–42.

Heath, Stephen. *The Sexual Fix.* London: Macmillan, 1982.

Hehner, Barbara. " 'Kissing and Horrid Strife': Male and Female in the Early Poetry of DHL." *Four Decades of Poetry, 1890–1930* 1 (January 1976): 3–26.

Heilbrun, Carolyn G. *Toward a Recognition of Androgyny.* New York and London: Norton, 1982, pp. 101–10 and passim. (Originally published New York: Knopf, 1964.)

Heldt, Lucia Henning. "Lawrence on Love: The Courtship and Marriage of Tom Brangwen and Lydia Lensky." *DHL Review* 8 (Fall 1975); 358–70.

Henig, Suzanne. "DHL and Virginia Woolf." *DHL Review* 2 (Fall 1969): 265–71.

Hinz, Evelyn J., and John J. Teunissen. "*Women in Love* and the Myth of Eros and Psyche." In *DHL: The Man Who Lived.* Edited by Robert B. Partlow, Jr., and Harry T. Moore. Carbondale: Southern Illinois University Press, 1980, pp. 207–20.

Hoffmann, C. G., and A. C. Hoffman. "Re-Echoes of the Jazz Age: Archetypal Women in the Novels of 1922." *Journal of Modern Literature* 7 (1979): 62–86. (Includes *Aaron's Rod.*)

Hugger, Ann-Grete. "The Dichotomy between Private and Public Sphere: Sex Roles in DHL's Novels." *Language and Literature* (Copenhagen) 2, no. 2 (1973): 127–36.

Hyde, Virginia. "Will Brangwen and Paradisal Vision in *The Rainbow* and *Women in Love.*" *DHL Review* 8 (Fall 1975): 346–57.

———. "The Body and the Body Politic in Lawrence." *Review* (Blacksburg, Va.) 14 (1992): 143–53.

Jewinski, Ed. "The Phallus in DHL and Jacques Lacan." *DHL Review* 21 (Spring 1989): 7–24.

Kalnins, Mara. "Lawrence's Men and Women: Complements and Opposites." In *Problems for Feminist Criticism.* Edited by Sally Minogue. London: Routledge, 1990, pp. 145–78.

Kaplan, Cora. "Radical Feminism and Literature: Rethinking Millett's *Sexual Politics.*" *Red Letters* 9 (1979): 4–16. (Reprinted in her *Sea Changes: Essays on Culture and Feminism.* London: Verso, 1986, pp. 15–30; and in *Feminist Literary Criticism.* Edited by Mary Eagleton. London and New York: Longman, 1991, pp. 157–70.)

Kinkead-Weekes, Mark. "Eros and Metaphor: Sexual Relationship in the Fiction of DHL." In Smith, op. cit. (1978): 101–20.

Knight, G. Wilson. "Lawrence, Joyce and Powys." *Essays in Criticism* 11 (1961): 403–17.

Langbaum, Robert. "Lords of Life, Kings in Exile: Identity and Sexuality in DHL." *American Scholar* 45 (Winter 1975–76): 807–15.

———. "Reconstitution of Self: Lawrence and the Religion of Love." In his *Mysteries of Identity: A Theme in Modern Literature.* New York: Oxford University Press, 1977, pp. 251–353.

Lavrin, Janko. "Sex and Eros (on Rozanov, Weininger, and DHL)." *European Quarterly* 1 (1934): 88–96.

Leavis, L. R. "The Late Nineteenth Century Novel and the Change towards the Sexual— Gissing, Hardy and Lawrence." *English Studies* 66 (1985): 36–47.

Lerner, Laurence. *Love and Marriage: Literature and Its Social Context.* New York: St. Martin's Press, 1979, pp. 153–64. (On *The Rainbow* and *Lady Chatterley's Lover.*)

———. "Lawrence and the Feminists." In *DHL: Centenary Essays.* Edited by Mara Kalnins. Bristol: Bristol Classical Press, 1986, pp. 69–88.

Light, Alison. "Feminism and the Literary Critic." *LTP: Journal of Literature, Teaching, Politics,* no. 2 (1983): 61–80. (Excerpt reprinted in *Feminist Literary Theory.* Edited by Mary Eagleton. Oxford and Cambridge, Mass.: Basil Blackwell, 1986, pp. 177–80.)

MacDonald, Robert H. " 'The Two Principles': A Theory of the Sexual and Psychological Symbolism of DHL's Later Fiction." *DHL Review* 11 (Summer 1978): 132–55.

Mahalanobis, Shanta. "Pre-War Feminism in Lawrence's *The Rainbow.*" *Journal of the Department of English* (Calcutta University) 21 (1986–87): 30–41.

Mailer, Norman. *The Prisoner of Sex.* London: Weidenfeld and Nicolson, 1971.

Malraux, André. "DHL and Eroticism." In *From the N.R.F: An Image of the Twentieth Century from the Pages of the Nouvelle Revue Française.* New York: Farrar, Straus, and Cudahy, 1958, pp. 194–98.

Meyers, Jeffrey. "DHL and Homosexuality." In *DHL: Novelist, Poet, Prophet.* Edited by Stephen Spender. London: Weidenfeld and Nicolson; New York: Harper, 1973, pp. 135–58. (Also in *London Magazine* 13 [October–November 1973]: 68–98.)

———. "DHL and Frieda Lawrence." In his *Married to Genius.* New York: Barnes and Noble, 1977a, pp. 145–73.

———. *Homosexuality and Literature: 1890–1930.* London: Athlone, 1977b, pp. 131–61. (See also reviews: J. Stokes. *Modern Language Review* 74 [1979]: 397–99; Cheryl L. Walker. *Modern Fiction Studies* 24 [1978–79]: 658–60.)

Middleton, Victoria. "Happy Birthday Mrs. Lawrence." In *DHL 1885–1930: A Celebration.* Edited by Andrew Cooper and Glyn Hughes. Nottingham: DHL Society, 1985, pp. 8–16. (Attempts to recover the "lost history" of Lawrence's mother's community involvements, especially in the Eastwood Women's Co-operative Guild.)

———. "In the 'Woman's Corner': The World of Lydia Lawrence." *Journal of Modern Literature* 13 (1986): 267–88. (The "Woman's Corner" was a regular feature in the national newspaper of the Co-operative movement—see preceding item.)

Miles, Rosalind. *The Fiction of Sex.* New York: Barnes and Noble, 1974, pp. 16–21 and passim.

Millard, Elaine. "Feminism II: Reading as a Woman: DHL, *St. Mawr.*" In *Literary*

Theory at Work: Three Texts. Edited by Douglas Tallack. London: Batsford, 1987, pp. 133–57.

Millett, Kate. *Sexual Politics.* London: Rupert Hart-Davis, 1971, pp. 237–93.

Mitgutsch, Waltraud. "The Image of the Female in DHL's Poetry." *Poetic Drama and Poetic Theory* (Salzburg Studies in English Literature) 27 (1981): 3–28.

Modiano, Marko. "D. H. Lawrence: Burning Out the Shame." *Literatur in Wissenschaft und Unterricht* 24 (September 1991): 241–51.

Moore, Harry T. "Bert Lawrence and Lady Jane." In Smith, op. cit. (1978): 178–88.

Morrison, Kristin. "Lawrence, Beardsley, Wilde: *The White Peacock* and Sexual Ambiguity." *Western Humanities Review* 30 (1976): 241–48.

Moynahan, Julian. "Lawrence, Woman, and the Celtic Fringe." In Smith, op. cit. (1978): 122–35.

Nazareth, Peter. "DHL and Sex." *Transition* 2 (October 1962): 54–57; *Transition* 3 (March 1963): 38–43.

Nielsen, Inge Padkaer, and Karsten Hvidtfelt Nielsen. "The Modernism of DHL and the Discourses of Decadence: Sexuality and Tradition in *The Trespasser, Fantasia of the Unconscious,* and *Aaron's Rod.*" *Arcadia* 25, no. 3 (1990): 270–86.

Nin, Anais. *The Novel of the Future.* New York: Macmillan, 1968, passim.

Oates, Joyce Carol. " 'At Least I Have Made a Woman of Her': Images of Women in Twentieth Century Literature." *Georgia Review* 37 (1983): 7–30. (Includes discussion of *The Rainbow, Women in Love,* and *Lady Chatterley's Lover.*)

Orr, John. "Lawrence: Passion and Its Dissolution." In his *The Making of the Twentieth-Century Novel: Lawrence, Joyce, Faulkner and Beyond.* Basingstoke and London: Macmillan, 1987, pp. 20–43.

Perez, Carlos A. "Husbands and Wives, Sons and Lovers: Intimate Conflict in the Fiction of DHL." In *The Aching Hearth: Family Violence in Life and Literature.* Edited by Sara Munson Deats and Lagretta Tallent Lenker. New York: Plenum, 1991, pp. 175–87.

Poplawski, Paul. "Lawrence against Himself: Elitism and the Mystification of Sex." In his *Promptings of Desire: Creativity and the Religious Impulse in the Works of DHL.* Westport, Conn., and London: Greenwood Press, 1993, pp. 115–35.

Pratt, Annis. "Woman and Nature in Modern Fiction." *Contemporary Literature* 13 (Fall 1972): 466–90 (481–83).

Pullin, Faith. "Lawrence's Treatment of Women in *Sons and Lovers.*" In Smith, op. cit. (1978): 49–73.

Rogers, Katherine M. *The Troublesome Helpmate: A History of Misogyny in Literature.* Seattle: University of Washington Press, 1966, pp. 237–47.

Root, Waverley Lewis. "Literary Sexism in Action: The Femininity of DHL Emphasized by Woman Writer." *Anais: An International Journal* 6 (1988): 75–76.

Ross, Charles L. "Homoerotic Feeling in *Women in Love:* Lawrence's 'Struggle for Verbal Consciousness' in the Manuscripts." In *DHL: The Man Who Lived.* Edited by Robert B. Partlow, Jr., and Harry T. Moore. Carbondale: Southern Illinois University Press, 1980, pp. 168–82.

Rossman, Charles. " 'You Are the Call and I Am the Answer': DHL and Women." *DHL Review* 8 (Fall 1975): 255–328.

———. "*The Boy in the Bush* in the Lawrence Canon." In *DHL: The Man Who Lived.* Edited by Robert B. Partlow, Jr., and Harry T. Moore. Carbondale: Southern Illinois University Press, 1980, pp. 185–94.

Ryan, Kiernan. "The Revenge of the Women: Lawrence's " 'Tickets, Please.' " *Literature and History* 7 (1981): 210–22.

Schapiro, Barbara. "Maternal Bonds and the Boundaries of Self: DHL and Virginia Woolf." *Soundings* 69 (1986): 347–65.

Scherr, Barry J. "The 'Dark Fire of Desire' in DHL's *Sons and Lovers.*" *Recovering Literature: A Journal of Contextualist Criticism* 16 (1988): 37–67.

Sedgwick, Eve Kosofsky. *Between Men: English Literature and Male Homosocial Desire.* New York: Columbia University Press, 1985, pp. 215–17.

Semeiks, Joanna G. "Sex, Lawrence, and Videotape." *Journal of Popular Culture* 25, no. 4 (Spring 1992): 143–52.

Sharma, Susheel Kumar. "Antifeminism in DHL's Short Stories." In *Essays on DHL.* Edited by T. R. Sharma. Meerut, India: Shalabh Book House, 1987, pp. 139–46.

Shaw, Marion. "Lawrence and Feminism." *Critical Quarterly* 25 (Autumn 1983): 23–27.

Shuey, William A., III. "From Renunciation to Rebellion: The Female in Literature." In *The Evolving Female: Women in Psychosocial Context.* Edited by Carol Landau Heckerman. New York: Human Sciences Press, 1980, pp. 138–57.

Siegel, Carol. "Floods of Female Desire in Lawrence and Eudora Welty." In *DHL's Literary Inheritors.* Edited by Keith Cushman and Dennis Jackson. New York: St. Martin's Press; London: Macmillan, 1991, pp. 109–30. (Reprinted in Siegel [1991]: 164–84.)

Singhal, Surendra. "Man–Woman Relationship in the Later Poetry of DHL." In *Essays on DHL.* Edited by T. R. Sharma. Meerut, India: Shalabh Book House, 1987, pp. 211–26.

Sircar, Sanjay. "The Phallic Amoretto: Intertextuality in ' . . . Love Was Once a Little Boy.' " *DHL Review* 19 (Summer 1987): 189–93.

Smith, Anne, ed. *Lawrence and Women.* London: Vision; Totowa, N.J.: Barnes and Noble, 1978a. (Nine essays cited separately—see next item and under Pullin, Blanchard, Kinkead-Weekes, Moynahan, Tristram, Apter, Moore, and Spilka.)

———. "A New Adam and a New Eve—Lawrence and Women: A Biographical Overview." (In the preceding item, Smith [1978b]: 9–48.)

Sparrow, John. "Regina v. Penguin Books Ltd: An Undisclosed Element in the Case." *Encounter* 18 (February 1962): 35–43.

Spender, Stephen. "The Erotic Art of DHL." *Vanity Fair* (January 1986): 88–93. (On Lawrence's paintings.)

Spilka, Mark. "Lawrence's Quarrel with Tenderness." *Critical Quarterly* 9 (Winter 1967): 363–77. (Reprinted in Spilka [1992], pp. 49–69, and also in Jackson and Jackson [1988]: 223–37.)

———. "Lawrence Up-Tight, or the Anal Phase Once Over." *Novel: A Forum on Fiction* 4 (Spring 1971): 252–67. (Reprinted in Spilka [1992], pp. 99–120.)

———, with Colin Clarke, George Ford, and Frank Kermode. "Critical Exchange: On 'Lawrence Up-Tight': Four Tail-Pieces" *Novel: A Forum on Fiction* 5 (Fall 1971): 54–70.

———. "Lessing and Lawrence: The Battle of the Sexes." *Contemporary Literature* 16 (Spring 1975): 218–40. (Reprinted in Spilka [1992]: 121–46.)

———. "On Lawrence's Hostility to Wilful Women: The Chatterley Solution." In Smith, op. cit. (1978): 189–211. (Reprinted in Spilka [1992], pp. 147–70.)

———. "Lawrence versus Peeperkorn on Abdication; or, What Happens to a Pagan

Vitalist When the Juice Runs Out?'' In *DHL: The Man Who Lived.* Edited by Robert B. Partlow, Jr., and Harry T. Moore. Carbondale: Southern Illinois University Press, 1980, pp. 105–20. (Reprinted in Spilka [1992], pp. 70–95.)

———. ''Lawrence and the Clitoris.'' In *The Challenge of DHL.* Edited by Michael Squires and Keith Cushman. Madison: University of Wisconsin Press, 1990, pp. 176–86. (Reprinted in Spilka [1992], pp. 171–90.)

———. *Renewing the Normative DHL: A Personal Progress.* Columbia and London: University of Missouri Press, 1992. (Includes revised versions of six of his essays cited in preceding, along with ''Hemingway and Lawrence as Abusive Husbands,'' pp. 193–247, and ''Repossessing *The Captain's Doll,''* pp. 248–75.)

Stavrou, Constantine W. ''DHL's 'Psychology' of Sex.'' *Literature and Psychology* 6 (1956): 90–95.

Stearns, Catherine. ''Gender, Voice, and Myth: The Relation of Language to the Female in DHL's Poetry.'' *DHL Review* 17 (1984): 233–42.

Stoehr, Taylor. ''Lawrence's 'Mentalized Sex.' '' *Novel* 8 (Winter 1975): 101–22.

Storch, Margaret. ''The Lacerated Male: Ambivalent Images of Women in *The White Peacock.''* *DHL Review* 21 (Spring 1989): 117–36.

Stubbs, Patricia. ''Mr. Lawrence and Mrs. Woolf.'' In her *Women and Fiction: Feminism and the Novel, 1880–1920.* Sussex: Harvester; New York: Barnes and Noble, 1979, pp. 223–35.

Stuhlman, Gunther. ''The Mystic of Sex: A First Look at DHL.'' *Anais: An International Journal* 4 (1986): 31–35.

Tax, Meredith. ''Sexual Politics.'' *Ramparts* 9 (November 1970): 50–58. (Review of Kate Millett.)

Taylor, Anne Robinson. ''Modern Primitives: Molly Bloom and James Joyce, with a Note on DHL.'' In her *Male Novelists and Their Female Voices: Literary Masquerades.* Troy, N.Y.: Whitston, 1981, pp. 189–228.

Tristram, Philippa. ''Eros and Death (Lawrence, Freud, and Women).'' In Smith, op. cit. (1978): 136–55.

Wasson, Richard. ''Class and the Vicissitudes of the Male Body in Works by DHL.'' *DHL Review* 14 (1981): 289–305.

Way, B. ''Sex and Language: Obscene Words in DHL and Henry Miller.'' *New Left Review,* no. 27 (September–October 1964): 164–70.

Welker, Robert H. ''Advocate for Eros: Notes on DHL.'' *American Scholar* 30 (1961): 191–202.

Wickham, Anna. ''The Spirit of the Lawrence Women.'' *Texas Quarterly* 9 (Autumn 1966): 31–50. (Reprinted in *The Writings of Anna Wickham.* Edited by R. D. Smith. London, 1984, pp. 355–72. See also Margaret Newlin. ''Anna Wickham: 'The sexless part which is my mind.' '' *Southern Review* 14 [1978]: 281–302.)

Widmer, Kingsley. ''Lawrence and the Fall of Modern Woman.'' *Modern Fiction Studies* 5 (1959): 44–56.

Williams, Linda Ruth. ''The Trial of DHL.'' *Critical Survey* 4, no. 2 (1992): 154–61.

Wood, Paul A. ''Up at the Front: A Teacher's Learning Experience with Lawrence's Sexual Politics.'' *DHL Review* 20 (Spring 1988): 71–77. (On ''Tickets, Please.'')

Woods, Gregory. *Articulate Flesh: Male Homo-Eroticism and Modern Poetry.* New Haven, Conn.: Yale University Press, 1987.

Woolf, Virginia. ''Notes on DHL.'' In her *The Moment and Other Essays.* London: Hogarth Press, 1947, pp. 93–98.

Zoll, Allan R. "Vitalism and the Metaphysics of Love: DHL and Schopenhauer." *DHL Review* 11 (Spring 1978): 1–20.

Zytaruk, G. "The Phallic Vision: DHL and V. V. Rozanov." *Comparative Literature Studies* 4 (1967): 283–97.

SECTION C

THE POPULAR IMAGE: LAWRENCE AND FILM

Lawrence's complex relationship to modernity—his ambivalent attitudes toward the modern world and its ambivalent attitudes toward him—is one of the reasons that he continues to exert such a fascination for contemporary readers and that critics continue to grapple with his influence and significance. This two-way ambivalence is perhaps nowhere more sharply or more pertinently defined than in the field of popular culture, where Lawrence's apparent abhorrence of mass forms of art and entertainment sits somewhat uneasily with the unrelenting circulation of popular ''versions'' of his work and personality—in the movies, television, radio, the newspapers. But, at the same time, if, in some quarters, Lawrence has come to be seen as an icon of ''high'' cultural values and as an inveterate opponent of mass popular culture, we should never forget (as I believe he never really forgot) his origins in the working classes, among the common mass of the people; and we should be alert, also, to his constant hankering for a certain type of popularity with that mass and, indeed, to his consistent exploitation of popular modes of writing and of popular media of communication (as, e.g., witness the burst of journalistic activity in his last few years). Although it has become orthodox to assume that the posthumous appropriations of Lawrence by the film and television industries would have been anathema to the author himself, one cannot help wondering if, had he lived to see the full flowering of the cinematographic and televisual arts, he would not eventually have come round to seeing film as yet one more area of artistic creativity to appropriate for himself.

This, at any rate, is a possibility that emerges quite plausibly from the following two chapters by Nigel Morris, who, while primarily aiming to provide the reader with essential basic information about Lawrence in relation to the movies and television, also develops a polemical challenge to the received wisdom in Lawrence studies that maintains that the author wholly rejected film as an authentic and creative art form.

Throughout these chapters, critical works are referred to by author and date, and full details of all such citations can be found under ''Works Cited'' at the end of the second chapter (Ch. 48). References to Lawrence's works and letters are to the editions listed in Bibliography 98 at the end of the book. Full details of all the Lawrence screen adaptations discussed here, along with listings of related critical works, can be found in Bibliography 95, which follows Chapter 48. Finally, as Lawrence's life was almost exactly contemporary with the birth and growth of the film industry, and as his responses to the same were partly conditioned by technical and institutional factors that were constantly changing during his lifetime, a chronology of the period specifically dedicated to major developments in film (and related media) has been compiled by Nigel Morris (Chronology 7) and can be found at the end of this section following the bibliography just mentioned.

47   Lawrence's Response to Film, by Nigel Morris

Lawrence's putative attitudes toward cinema and popular culture have become an inextricable part both of the critical discourse on screen adaptations of his works and of a broader debate, influentially mediated by the writings of F. R. Leavis and his followers, about cultural standards in the twentieth century as seen in terms of "high" and "low," "serious" and "popular" culture. Unfortunately, however, critics have usually been happy to accept unquestioningly the orthodoxy established by Leavis that Lawrence was unequivocally antagonistic toward popular forms of art and entertainment, and this has led inevitably to a somewhat stale and simplistic recycling of Leavisite views whenever screen adaptations of Lawrence's works are discussed, as well as whenever Lawrence is adduced as an authoritative voice in the critique of contemporary culture. Before considering the screen adaptations themselves, therefore, and the critical discourse surrounding them, it is useful to look in some detail at how Lawrence actually responded to the cinema of his day.

H. T. Moore gives voice to the received critical wisdom when he writes that Lawrence was "the most vigorous opponent of the medium . . . at least in his later years" (Moore 1973: 4). While it cannot be denied that Lawrence's attitudes toward film were, indeed, frequently negative, the evidence suggests that they were never quite so cut-and-dried as Moore would have us think. In fact, as I try to show, they were as richly varied and as richly ambivalent—at times, as self-contradictory—as were his attitudes on most other things.

To begin with, Lawrence never attacked cinema in isolation. It was always symptomatic of a deeper malaise, coupled with other machine products. Hence, Mellors, embodiment of vitality and earthy simplicity in *Lady Chatterley's*

Lover, comments on the increasing impotence of each generation, of every class: "Their spunk's gone dead—motor-cars and cinemas and aeroplanes suck the last bit out of them" (217). Mellors elsewhere associates moral decadence with motorcycles and jazz, positing a return to arts and crafts (300). Together with facile nostalgia, this failure to acknowledge *good* cinema and jazz or the positive potential of increased mobility does point unmistakably toward the blinkered prejudices of certain forms of Leavisism. But Mellors's comment is just one position in a debate of competing voices, and care should be taken before straightforwardly equating a character's remarks with the views of the author. Although on balance negative, Lawrence's own position on cinema was hardly monolithic. For instance, while he was clearly appalled by the movie actors he met on a Pacific liner in 1922 (*Letters* IV: 287, 303), within two days of disembarking he chose to see a film (*Letters* IV: 290). Only weeks later—though the deal eventually fell through—he was delighted when $10,000 was offered for the film rights to *Women in Love* (Merrild 1964: 124–28). His artist friends, Knud Merrild and Kai Götzsche, went to work in Hollywood, and Lawrence spent time there with them in 1923 (Merrild 1964: 321), even befriending a film star, Jack Holt (Moore 1973: 3).

Lawrence was certainly won over by a Western, *The Covered Wagon* (1923), an expensive and highly publicized epic. Slow-moving, deliberately paced, distinguished by impressive semidocumentary location photography, the film notably introduced to the genre the history of westward migration and the advancing frontier. While Lawrence objected to its stereotypical hero, the film, seen in London after his experiences of New Mexico, sufficiently moved him to utter repeatedly, "How like it is," and to hum "Oh, Susannah!" from the score (Brett 1933: 26–27). He and Frieda also enjoyed Douglas Fairbanks in *The Thief of Bagdad* (1924) (Brett 1933: 189)—they were apparently unaware that the film's director, Raoul Walsh, had made *Captain Blackbird* (released in 1923 as *Lost and Found on a South Sea Island*), the cast of which had so upset Lawrence aboard RMS *Tahiti*. *The Covered Wagon* and *The Thief of Bagdad* achieved enduring popular and critical reputations, confirming Lawrence's discernment: both remain available. (*The Covered Wagon* made unprecedented profits, which suggests that popularity alone did not irritate Lawrence, despite his apparent elitism.)

Achsah Brewster's memoir of Lawrence's reaction to a screening of *Ben Hur* (1926) in 1928 is frequently cited by critics as evidence of his dislike of film. According to her, Lawrence was "nauseated" by the phoniness of the movie and by the audience's apparent gullibility: "if we did not take him out immediately he would be violently sick; such falsity nauseated him; he could not bear to see other people there open-mouthed, swallowing it, believing it to be true" (Brewster and Brewster 1934: 298–99). Apart from the possibility that the effects of the film may, indeed, have made Lawrence literally dizzy (it contains a sea battle, a frenetic chariot race, and sequences in two-color technicolor), the free, indirect style of Brewster's report strongly suggests that Lawrence was indulging in calculated hyperbole here: if this represented his attitude to film in general, why in 1928 was he in a cinema at all? What might truly have sickened him was that *Ben Hur* was the most expensive film yet made: it had received years of coverage during its plagued history, and the mass interest this had created may well have piqued a poor writer struggling just to survive. Indeed, Lawrence could be forgiven for feeling resentful about the popularity of cinema, having seen Chaplin and Pickford becoming the world's highest-paid employees (with incomes of over $1 million a year each) and Valentino's slushy poems selling hundreds of thousands of copies, at a time when his own income was minuscule, and his work was vilified and banned. Lawrence's publications refer less to identifiable films than to industry personnel, audiences, technical short-comings, and the conventions of routine productions. Given his evident interest and intermittently expressed pleasure in cinema, it is wrong to assume he re-jected it outright. Rather, his doubts concerned the worst aspects of the business and frequently exemplified more general fears about mass industrialized society, which, in turn, reflected widely held attitudes of the time. When his writing either comments directly about film or becomes inflected, whether parodically or experimentally, with cinematic technique, it typically implicates broader mod-ernist concerns about industrialization, mechanization, massification, democra-tization. It is unsurprising, for example, that the proprietor of the existing cinema in *The Lost Girl,* previously "an obscure and illiterate nobody," now owns a car (85).

The commonness of Mr. May, Mr. Houghton's cinema manager in *The Lost Girl,* is repeatedly commented on (e.g., p. 95), while the daughters of "respect-able" tradesmen avoid Alvina once she becomes a cinema accompanist (117). The portrait of Mr. May, who "had acquired American qualities" (86), epito-mizes Lawrence's fears about the destruction of indigenous culture by relentless profit-seeking and suggests that he was aware of the American domination of the film industry after World War I. Anti-Americanism was widespread at the time (exacerbated by talkies, it later became a central plank of Leavisism). By 1929, the BBC was considering "the ramifications of the Transatlantic Octo-pus," fearing that "the national outlook and, with it, character is gradually becoming Americanised" (in Alvarado et al. 1985: 16). Classic serials, on radio from the 1930s, were—and remain—one response.

Yet, Lawrence was also strongly attracted by values embodied in American literature and the western landscape. Married to a German, he also had good reason to mistrust xenophobia, which he satirizes amusingly in *Lady Chatter-ley's Lover* (184). What, in fact, makes Mr. May's Americanized sensibility contemptible are his "complacent and natural unscrupulousness" in business, his hypocritical willingness to take money from colliers and work lasses in return for inferior entertainment described—through his consciousness—as "the dith-ering eyeache of a film" (*The Lost Girl* 86).

Lawrence's reactions to the "cinema people" on RMS *Tahiti* were primarily to their manners rather than occupation, though that provided further irritation by confirming deep prejudices. The women he likened to shop girls, and the men he dismissed as ''Utterly undistinguished,'' later condemning their drunkenness and perpetual infighting (*Letters* IV: 287, 303). If he, or biographers, came to compound interpersonal animosity with his attitude toward the work of these people, the confusion surely ignores his own edict to trust the art, not the artist (*Studies in Classic American Literature* 8).

Such criticism of art according to its producers' behavior—reserved for ''low'' cultural products and rarely applied to artists in ''high'' cultural forms whose genius is allowed to mitigate difficult or unpleasant behavior—manifests the same morality that led to the founding of the Hays Office in 1922 and culminated in strict self-regulation by Hollywood. This was a response partly to civic and religious pressure groups' demands for censorship, particularly concerned with cinema's celebration of sexuality, but also to a decade of scandals starting with Fatty Arbuckle's indictment for rape and murder (1920).

As early as 1896, the *May Irwin–John C. Rice Kiss,* a brief filmed extract from a harmless stage play, had caused outrage, provoking calls for censorship. Thirty years on, Lawrence blamed close-up kisses for encouraging ''secret and separate masturbation'' (*Phoenix* 326). He objected to mass stimulation of desire, subsequently unfulfilled, writing elsewhere of cinema audiences ''moaning'' from close-up kisses they could not feel (*Pansies* 444). He pointedly has Mr. May announce of the cinematograph: ''the erection will be a merely temporary one'' (*The Lost Girl* 101). His painting *Close-up (Kiss)* (1927–28) portrays a naked couple in a sexual embrace with grotesquely protruding lips, not quite touching, who otherwise demonstrate little mutual passion. The tight framing, unusual then in oil paintings, and the proportions of the canvas unmistakably confirm the cinematic allusion, reiterating Lawrence's view that films reduce feelings to mechanical formulas.

The extremity of such reactions, it should be stressed, is connected with the novelty of cinema. Audiences today are largely unaware that close-ups—not established until 1915—suggest a proximity previously exclusive to parents or lovers. Lawrence's suspicions were his idiosyncratic expression of common concerns. As occurs in Britain with any rapidly emerging medium, cinema in the 1900s prompted headlines blaming it for juvenile crime. Several fires caused by flammable film, one involving 140 deaths, together with phenomenal growth in exhibition outlets, led in Britain to the 1909 Cinematograph Act, requiring operating licenses and empowering local authorities to censor. An odor of corruption surrounded the industry generally, especially in America. (Indeed, the choice of Hollywood as a base stemmed partly from the need of filmmakers— using copies of patented equipment—to put a continent between themselves and Edison's agents and to have a quick escape route to Mexico.) Equipment fires and hellfire became easily confused, both being cited as reasons for greater control.

In *Lady Chatterley's Lover,* shortly after the narrator's rejection of popular novels, Lawrence playfully has Mrs. Bolton voice moral concerns about film that were common at the time. She condemns melodramas and romances, especially for children, but (like Miss Pinnegar in *The Lost Girl*) is prepared to allow "instructive" films (102). This distinction between instructive and entertaining films was gaining ground generally—newsreel and propaganda films had been exempted from censorship in Britain after the war, for example—and, Richard Falcon argues, it "reflected and contributed to the belief that film was a business aiming to profit from the production of entertainment, and any educational or artistic qualities of [popular] cinema were denied" (1993: 13), a belief that chimes with the convictions of Lawrence but seems also to be parodied by him by having Mrs. Bolton express it.

The much tighter controls imposed on cinema by comparison to theater stemmed from worries prompted by the fact that film audiences were predominantly urban working-class. Fear of revolution—inflamed by events in Ireland, Russia, and Greece, and the General Strike in Britain in 1926, the background against which *Lady Chatterley's Lover* and its banning should be understood—led to the outlawing in Britain of acknowledged masterpieces by Soviet directors Pudovkin and Eisenstein. But the fears were cultural as much as political, as new media heralded a democratization—or, for some, standardization—of taste. New methods of mass production in other fields raised similar fears, as we see from James Houghton's clothes sales in *The Lost Girl:* "the crowd hated excellence" and "any approach to originality," we are told, preferring "vulgar little thrills . . . machine made, and appropriate to the herd" (5).

Chanan notes that children often accompanied adult moviegoers, not for entertainment or education but because they were better at seeing and reading intertitles (1980: 255). The fact that they constituted a large part of the audience offered a popularly acceptable justification for censorship; but it also indicates just how noisy and boisterous an experience early moviegoing would have been—an infantilized experience guaranteed to alienate someone like Lawrence.

Lawrence's poem "When I went to the film" (*Pansies* [1929] in *The Complete Poems* 443–44) may not, however, be quite the facile attack on movies it is generally taken to be. Apart from Moore's observation that Shakespeare and Tolstoy are attacked equally virulently in *Pansies* (1973: 3), the past tense suggests a single and earlier experience than the habitual (if necessarily occasional) moviegoing Lawrence evidently enjoyed. The poem may well condemn synthetic pleasures and mass delusion, as well as audiences' "cuddling" with passions inflamed by the screen. But it may equally be an attempt to explain the nature of the experience, in the tradition of Coleridge's willing suspension of disbelief. Clearly, the notion of feeling "heavenly," "ecstatic," in response to feelings that are, in fact, "supremely unfelt," presents cinematic pleasure as paradoxical. Half a century passed before psychoanalytic film theory found ways of exploring that paradox by examining spectatorial identification in terms of Lacan's imaginary and symbolic and the "present absence" of the events portrayed (Metz 1975). Upon this rests an account of subject positioning, informed by the concept of interpellation (Althusser 1971), which radically challenges traditional ideas of autonomous individuality. Lawrence, almost invariably concerned in his fictional explorations with questions of character and identity, frequently anticipates important intellectual currents; a particularly apposite instance appears in *The Lost Girl* when Alvina is described as "not herself. . . . just scattered and decentralised" (66).

The poem that follows "When I went to the film" in *Pansies,* "When I went to the circus," describes "uneasy people" (444) excluded and "depressed" (445) by the elemental physicality of the experience. Here there is no "gushing" response, as there is at the movies (*Complete Poems* 444–45), and the poem repeats the point made three times in *The Lost Girl* that movies elicit only conditioned responses while live acts appeal directly to deeper, unconscious feelings. As Lawrence insists elsewhere, "Sight is the least sensual of all the senses" (*Fantasia of the Unconscious* 65), maintaining distance between perceiver and perceived rather than enabling "full baptismal immersion," as Linda Ruth Williams puts it (1993: 20).

Here, however, Lawrence is entirely contradicted by psychoanalytic film theory, which argues that narrative films frequently *do* create the illusion of total immersion, through processes of primary and secondary identification; that is, identification first with the act of seeing (the camera) and then with the characters seen. This arises from the film's appeal to the unconscious, through a process of psychic regression: from the film experienced as symbolic construct, as text, to the film experienced as imaginary, as a unified totality incorporating the spectator. The process reenacts the infant's transition through the mirror stage (a corollary of the oedipal crisis), the screen functioning as a mirror, the other, in which the spectator misrecognizes himself or herself.

Of importance here is that formal mechanisms that, in dominant cinema, center the spectator, as point of unity at which the text can be mastered and from which it appears to be narrated, were not established until around 1920. These include techniques of continuity editing, the unperceived means by which coherent narrative space and time are created from fragmented, two-dimensional images. One common technique, the shot/reverse-shot, enabling dialogues to be assembled invisibly from short takes, never became essential until sound arrived in the late 1920s. Although Lawrence could not be expected to have perceived the fact, the films he approved of were constructed quite differently from the type shown in "Houghton's Endeavour." Intrusive intertitles, rowdy audiences, melodramatic acting, the sheer difficulty of locating the focus of action in early narrative films (which showed everything in long shot, as though framed in a proscenium arch), the use of editing to link tableaux or (at its most sophisticated) to crosscut between different locations, rather than center the spectator or create meanings through juxtaposition—all these produced the distanciating effect against which Lawrence reacted.

In contrast, Lawrence was deeply conscious of communal, ritualistic aspects of theater. *Sea and Sardinia,* for example, ends with his being "charmed" by a marionette show (207–13). He finds that his eyes are "of minor importance," that it is the voice of the puppeteer that holds him, acting "direct on the blood" (211). Attending a play in *Twilight in Italy,* Lawrence observes: "This cast-off church made a good theatre. I realized how cleverly it had been constructed for the dramatic presentation of religious ceremonies" (133). This argument, that theater, unlike film, appeals to the senses rather than the mind, depends surely on the *quality* of either spectacle. If audience and stage performer are supposedly linked by organic vitality, there is little about the vaudeville turns in *The Lost Girl* to suggest edification. Conversely, early film melodrama, characterized by static camera, lack of close-ups, and natural light sources, "can be understood as the continuity, even fulfillment, of certain nineteenth-century theatrical traditions" (Cook 1985: 81). Against live performances, however hackneyed, primitive film attempting to offer comparable experiences would *inevitably* seem inferior. Lawrence did not reject later cinema outright, as art or entertainment; his remarks should be seen as rejecting mechanization and standardization— with films, identical at every screening, finished and unresponsive, serving as symptomatic examples.

"Sex versus Loveliness" (1928), "Pornography and Obscenity" (1929), and *A Propos of "Lady Chatterley's Lover"* (1930) begin to explain the danger of cinema's appeal to mental sensibilities. In a remarkably prescient, romantically inspired theory of media and ideology, Lawrence condemns films for peddling false values and meretricious images that then create preconceptions that interpose between individuals and reality, destroying insight and spontaneity. An ironic illustration exists as early as *Aaron's Rod* (1922), where the protagonist, shortly after arriving at Sir William Franks's house in Novara, finds himself "allured . . . down the corridor" ("as if in a tracking shot," according to James C. Cowan [1990: 102], although this may be anachronistic) by "two black-and-white chambermaids" to a luxuriously appointed bathroom full of all the latest conveniences. (This, Cowan ingeniously suggests, may be parodying the fashionable excesses of the comedies of Cecil B. DeMille, which made a fetish of plumbing and sanitary ware throughout middle-class America; if Cowan is right, this would confirm Lawrence to be a knowledgeable moviegoer.) Returning to his equally luxurious blue silk bedroom, Aaron feels that "he ought to have his breath taken away":

But alas, the cinema has taken our breath away so often, investing us in all the splendours of the splendidest American millionaire, or all the heroics and marvels of the Somme or the North Pole, that life has now no magnate richer than we, no hero nobler than we have been, on the film. *Connu! Connu!* Everything life has to offer is known to us, couldn't be known better, from the film. (*Aaron's Rod* 134–35)

The scene is clearly a comical one, and we do not take seriously the suggestion that Aaron *ought* to be impressed by fancy bathroom fittings and the like (one is reminded here of the satirical comedy made of plumbing references in *The Virgin and the Gipsy*); but the general point, that films have started to precondition our responses to the world, is still well taken—even if the paradoxical humor of the passage simultaneously dialogizes it by showing that Aaron does *not,* in fact, respond in a conditioned way.

For Lawrence, mechanization intervenes not only between individuals and the world but also within relationships, preventing vital, organic directness. Hence, his objections to cinematic notions of physical beauty and to popular beliefs about love. He complains—justifiably, if the notorious example of *The Birth of a Nation* (1915) is typical—"that a film heroine shall be neuter, a sexless thing of washed-out purity," that "real sex-feeling shall only be shown by the villain or villainess, low lust" (*Phoenix* 176). In "Sex versus Loveliness," he objects to standardization: "We think a lovely woman must look like Lillian Gish, a handsome man must look like Valentino" (*Phoenix II* 529). This tendency is true of all eras, of course, and hardly originated with cinema, as classical Greek statuary or the changing shape of nudes in the oil painting tradition shows. Significantly, Lawrence chooses Chaplin as a contrast, arguing that "Beauty is an *experience* . . . not a fixed pattern or an arrangement of features" (529); he does not, then, deny the potential of cinema, properly used, to create such experience. He rejects "stereotyped attributes" (529) and the elevation of surface appearance, but not specifically cinema, and uses Mrs. Langtry (a vaudeville star, not a film performer) as one example of standard good looks (530). To him, physical beauty is inseparable from sexuality, and the equation of sex in the movies with the threat of the vamp is an obscenity, a hypocrisy, relegating sex, by rights the central moral force of life, to secrecy and furtiveness. Against the vamp, the heroine was not merely virginal but unfeeling. Lawrence wants living passion, not cold perfection:

A good-looking woman becomes lovely when the fire of sex rouses pure and fine in her and flickers through her face and touches the fire in me.
    Then she becomes a lovely woman to me, then she is in the living flesh a lovely woman: not a mere photograph of one. (*Phoenix II* 530)

Accordingly, Mellors contrasts Connie with "the celluloid women of today" (*Lady Chatterley's Lover* 119).

Even before his travels, Lawrence saw Native American culture as a repository of hope for decadent civilization. In this context, it is noteworthy that, in *The Lost Girl,* Alvina feels spiritually cleansed after breaking with the Natcha-Kee-Tawaras, the "Red Indian" troupe. Her skin seems alive with "cleanliness and whiteness, luminous" (252); she exchanges dark blood-communion with Ciccio for—quite literally—surface sterility as a nurse. The language anticipates Lawrence's dismissal of movie heroines; "luminous" clinches the analogy. Then it is only a small step to reading Dr. Mitchell's "graceful, boyish attraction" and constantly reiterated "white, even teeth" as recalling those of a film star. His aversion to cucumbers, his taste for weak tea, and the self-conscious poses he strikes relate him to the insipidness and artificiality Lawrence despises in films (258–60).

That standardization is what Lawrence abhors, rather than the inherent nature of film, is confirmed by his criticism of nonvisual media. He equally attacks "the emotional idiocy" of radio, which prompts Connie to tell Clifford: "People pretend to have emotions," when really they "feel nothing" (*Lady Chatterley's Lover* 139). Earlier, she hears the loudspeaker bellowing out, "in an idiotically velveteen-genteel sort of voice, something about a series of street-cries, the very cream of genteel affectation imitating old criers" (122). Here Lawrence decries the lusty dialect of working folk being travestied in the artificiality ("velveteen" rather than "velvety") of BBC accents.

To understand Lawrence's concerns, remember that most films were shorts, often produced by studios at the rate of one a week, a feat achievable only by recycling scripts, settings, and costumes and by using the same cast and crew repeatedly, inevitably reproducing stereotyped characters and techniques, which, in turn, made few demands on spectators. Moreover, musical accompaniment was routinely drawn from a standard repertoire, used to determine the rhythm of the intertitles; emotions were not just evoked by formulaic *types* of music but signaled by specific phrases or tunes that unambiguously went with specific situations, moods, or character types. Hence, Alvina's preconception is literal rather than cynical when she sees herself at the piano "banging off the *Merry Widow Waltz*, and, in tender moments, *The Rosary*. Time after time, *The Rosary*" (*The Lost Girl* 99). Only a few prestige pictures had specially commissioned orchestral scores composed to synchronize with the action. These included the pictures Lawrence admired.

Madame Rochard in *The Lost Girl* describes pictures as "cheap" and "easy" (148–49), adjectives customarily applied to disreputable women. As Williams (1993) argues in depth, Lawrence's fears about the "nervous excitement" of cinema are aligned in his thought with modern female sexuality in its attenuation of vital bodily energy to "sex in the head." His criticisms appear tainted with misogyny, and they ironically contradict modern film theory by construing the camera's gaze as female—though without presenting this positively in terms of women's empowerment; the camera's female gaze is contrasted, rather, with that superior mode of Lawrentian knowledge reserved for males, dark blood-consciousness. The female gaze remains a threat, however. Lawrence's poem "Film Passion" deals with female fans who fetishize Valentino's objectified appearance and contrasts their adoration of his screen "shadow" with their loathing of his "substance." Anticipating almost entirely in reverse Laura Mulvey's seminal essay "Visual Pleasure and Narrative Cinema" (1975), which relates the "masculine" cinematic gaze to sadistic disavowal of castration anxieties, the poem refers to women's looking in terms of primitive magic capable of "piercing" the loins (*Collected Poems* 538). Concerns about female audiences were common in the 1920s (not coincidentally, this was the period of women's enfranchisement), when male stars were specifically marketed toward women, who attended in huge numbers (Williams 1993: 7).

Besotted female fans were just the final insult to Lawrence from the popular film audience, already despised as herdlike. In *Twilight in Italy,* he celebrates the simple dignity of a traditional popular audience as he describes a scene at the theater where peasants, including children, listen intently, "spellbound" and "absorbed" by the "mystery," "held in thrall by the sound of emotion" (138). Compare a screening in *The Lost Girl:*

The lamps go out: gurglings and kissings—and then the dither on the screen: "The Human Bird," in awful shivery letters. It's not a very good machine, and Mr May is not a very good operator. Audience distinctly critical. Lights up—and "Chot-let, penny a bar! Chot-let, penny a bar!" (110)

Elsewhere, "Alvina imagined herself leading a chorus of collier louts, in a bad atmosphere of 'Woodbines' and oranges, during the intervals when the pictures had collapsed" (100); and the narrator treats the live acts as negatively as the films.

Alvina recognizes the desirability of better attractions—"Our pictures do shake, and our films are rather ragged," she explains (117)—but Mr. Houghton procrastinates over buying a new projector and "finer lenses" (115). All this gives some indication of the poor technical quality of the early cinema Lawrence would have been exposed to, where the mechanics of the medium constantly interposed itself between audience and film, preventing concentrated absorption and exacerbating rowdy behavior. It is likely, therefore, that Lawrence's views on cinema, as in "When I went to the film," express frustration rather than contempt. He *wants* to be able to give himself up to the experience and is angered by the fatuousness of most films, by the cynicism of those who make and exhibit them (badly), and by the complacency of audiences who demand no better. Yet, when the Lawrences saw *The Passion of Christ* in Mexico during Easter 1923 (identified by Cowan as probably a 1902 production, therefore extremely primitive), and the band played the swing number "Three O'Clock in the Morning" during the Crucifixion, not even *that* discouraged them from moviegoing! (Cowan 1990: 97 and n.3).

In 1917, the Society of Motion Picture Engineers decreed the normal projection rate, sixteen frames per second, as standard. However, this was rarely respected, and speeds crept up piecemeal to twenty-four frames per second by the coming of sound in 1928, when the higher figure was accepted. Consequently, expensive, first-run theaters were equipped to project films at the speed the camera had recorded them, whereas down-market enterprises, such as Mr. Houghton's, took less care and habitually screened older (therefore cheaper) films at arbitrary speeds, accelerating movement by as much as 50 percent. Such mechanical distortion enhanced the frenetic humor of slapstick comedies but was wholly inappropriate to serious subjects. Scratches and jump-cuts occurred in spliced old films that had caught fire because, at the opposite extreme, exhausted projectionists hand-cranked so slowly that the celluloid remained too long in proximity to the lamp; and flickering was inevitable before projectors were introduced with two gate openings per frame. Hence, ''ragged dithering pictures'' accurately sums up the situation (*The Lost Girl* 143).

The Covered Wagon, made as a special, would have been restricted to superbly equipped theaters. Moreover, the marketing of such high-budget productions spared Lawrence the intrusive indignity of mass audiences. For *Birth of a Nation,* for example—hand-tinted, accompanied by an original orchestral score, and requiring considerable concentration to follow its serious subject matter throughout its full feature length—''[s]eat prices in New York, where the film premièred, were increased from the usual 10–25 cents to an astounding two dollars'' (Cook 1985: 5).

The period between the initial conception of *The Lost Girl,* in the shape of ''Elsa Culverwell'' (1912) and ''The Insurrection of Miss Houghton'' (1913), and its composition and publication in 1920 coincided exactly with the transition from ''primitive cinema'' to institutional mode of representation (IMR), to use Noel Burch's terminology (1980–81). While the values of audiences and producers may hardly have changed, Lawrence's criticisms of aesthetic and technical shortcomings were already becoming invalidated by rapid, though far from universal, advances. For example, his references in ''Art and Morality'' (1925) to ''mechanically shaken'' images and the description in *St. Mawr* (1925) of the distorted self-image, corrupted by Westerns, of the Texas cowboys—''self-conscious film heroes . . . rapidly rattling away . . . all in the flat'' (131)—simply do not accord with how up-to-date films were perceived. The IMR is defined by continuity editing and (until sound required cumbersome housings to silence the motor) increasing camera mobility, both of which create the illusion of a three-dimensional scene centered on the spectator. The transition was completed with the introduction of diegetic sound, which, demanding concentration by incorporating dialogue, works along with continuity editing to bind together the fragmented images into what, contrary to Lawrence, is perceived as continuous flow. It follows that Lawrence's pronouncements on cinema, once partially valid, are hardly adequate for later criticism. *The Lost Girl* implicitly contrasts the scattered black-and-white flickerings of primitive cinema with the glorious, centered images Lawrence's own prose can evoke (Alvina arranging flowers in church [74] provides a good example); but the potential to achieve precisely the sensuous effects that Lawrence aspired to *does* exist in contemporary cinematography, so the distinction no longer stands.

Perhaps for all his sophisticated aesthetics, Lawrence had a naively mimetic understanding of film and regarded it as a mechanical dilution of reality. Yet, his 1927 review of *Manhattan Transfer* is approving in its description of Dos Passos's consciously cinematic writing as a ''very complex film'' and anticipates by thirty years *cinéma-vérité*; he likens Dos Passos's method to a microphone and camera being placed to record the random interactions of a group of New

York residents: "It is like a movie picture with an intricacy of different stories and no close-ups and no writing in between. Mr Dos Passos leaves out the writing in between" (*Phoenix* 364–65). Kisses apart, presumably the close-up is objectionable to Lawrence as emotional manipulation. Intertitles broke identification and, Lawrence perhaps felt, insulted the spectator by closing down interpretive possibilities; they also, of course, provided third-rate filmmakers with a "cheap and easy" solution to problems of visual narration.

Lawrence himself can be described as a frequently "cinematic" writer. Linda Ruth Williams, for example, convincingly analyzes his use of shot/reverse-shot perspectives in the scene with Gerald and the horse in *Women in Love,* and she praises Russell's film for following point-of-view structures found in the original (1993: 66, 88–89). Lawrence uses women's points of view literally, in the optical sense, to advance the narrative, even if the focalization is described in, and judged by, the narrator's voice (Williams 1993: 67), a technique analogous to primary and secondary identification in film, whereby the spectator's position is split between the camera and one or more characters (though the two positions can coincide). While Lawrence is acutely conscious of the power of the male gaze—associated with Ciccio, Mellors, and the Fox, for example—it is invariably felt from the female's position.

As Williams notes, Lawrence characteristically presents male characters from a female perspective in the objectifying and distancing manner of a pinup (1993: 86). (One of the few convincing scenes in Jaeckin's *Lady Chatterley's Lover* [1981] is when Connie chances upon Mellors washing. Going beyond the book by presenting him naked, the film suggests female desire by anatomizing his body from her point of view, using shot/reverse-shot close-ups of his hands soaping his thighs and loins, a style normally reserved for objectifying females. The subversive potential of this is not sustained, however, the remainder of the film positioning the spectator, predictably, as voyeuristically male.) A moment in *The Lost Girl,* when Alvina "photographically" observes Ciccio as though "suspended" in the consulate prior to their departure (290–91), demonstrates how Lawrence's "cinematic" style is as richly ambiguous as any other aspect of his writing. On one reading, the moment is an epiphany seething with blood-consciousness and mystery, evoked by the repetition of words such as "dark," "suspended," "quivered," and "unconscious." On another, the scene satirizes life as experienced through movies: Alvina imagines her dark Latin lover come to whisk her away to exotic places, his image hanging before her in shimmering close-up, luminous, transparent, causing her (in the language of pulp romance) to quiver "as if" (not "because") "it was more than she could bear."

Lawrence's overt condemnation of the cinema, then, is contradicted by a fascination with vision. This is evident in numerous passages in his fiction that echo the experience of film spectatorship or seem aware of cinematic technique. There is every reason to assume he would have approved of the best of cinema had he lived to see it reach maturity. In "Pictures on the Walls," he advocates "pictuaries" of borrowable paintings to contain "everything except machine-made rubbish that is not worth having'' (*Phoenix II* 612). Here, his attitude toward the public and the popular is less dismissive than it appears elsewhere; and the idea of providing contemporary, ever-changing pictures, to be enjoyed rather than owned, is not so different an idea from that realized by cinema. Unfortunately, critics too often read Lawrence superficially on this question, overlooking his more positive attitudes toward visual pleasure. The contradictions and tensions that make his writing so vibrant and attractive to criticism at other times are, when it comes to film, seemingly ignored by those who seek— and inevitably find—confirmation of their own preferences.

NOTE

I should like to express thanks to the staff of the National Library of Scotland, Edinburgh, where the primary research was carried out; to the Information Service of the British Film Institute, London, for helping track down elusive bibliographic and filmographic details; to the Laver and Lee households, for their hospitality and good cheer during the research phases; and, above all, to Janice, Elliott, and Bevan, to whom these chapters are dedicated with love.

48   Screen Adaptations of Lawrence, by Nigel Morris

ADAPTATIONS/ADAPTATION: THE FILMS, THE CRITICS, THE PROBLEMS

In addition to various changing constructions of Lawrence by the literary-critical world, his popular cultural image has been strongly determined by screen adaptations of his works and by the discourses that have accompanied them (reviews and critical discussions, but also marketing materials, newspaper features, filmscripts, shooting scripts, and other published and unpublished offshoots of production and consumption). If we are to understand the past and continuing evolution of Lawrence's cultural status, then some consideration of how he and his works have been mediated by the screen seems essential.

However, critical discussion of literary adaptations tends to be laden with a confused baggage of unexamined presuppositions and prejudices concerning the very nature of adaptation, in both its theoretical and practical dimensions. Consequently, it is difficult to discuss specific adaptations and the discourses surrounding them without some informed theoretical perspective on adaptation per se. I lack room here to pursue a comprehensive discussion of the topic, but I shall try to clear the ground a little by approaching Lawrence adaptations not as somehow self-contained entities and surrogate works of literature, but as they are shaped by institutional and technical determinants of the film and television industries. This involves identifying both the typical fallacies that bedevil literary-critical interventions into screen discourse *and* the typical fallacies that bedevil the film world's pseudoliterary appropriation of print texts.

Institutional Determinants and Cultural Values

Judging literary adaptations demands acknowledgement of the economic and ideological contexts of production, exhibition, consumption, and criticism. For example, British classic serials, unlike cinema films, operate within Public Service Broadcasting (PSB) requirements to *educate, entertain,* and *inform* (in return for broadcasting rights, that is, the BBC and Independent Television [ITV] companies must serve perceived cultural needs rather than simply chase ratings). Such classic serials, trading off the status of their already institutionalized literary forebears, are invariably high-budget productions utilizing historical locations, ''great'' acting from the stage tradition, and highly visible technical and craft expertise in pursuit of both realism and aesthetic finish. Through the pleasures of mass entertainment, they ''educate'' and ''inform'' about the past and its associated cultural values, offering nostalgia and myths of national identity in the guise of history and artistic heritage. Dependence on dialogue and an apparent reverence toward their canonic origins make these programs the ''jewels in the crown'' of British broadcasting as judged from within a conservative, book-based dominant culture. While politicians and educators applaud paperback sales of the source texts, broadcasters continue making game shows and importing soaps. Tabloids, parasitical upon television for their daily copy, jingoistically hype prestige serials in return for features, interviews, photographs, and gossip, while everywhere else assaulting the values the genre supposedly upholds. Indeed, Colin McArthur speculates, classic serials, set in apparently more settled times ''in which the self-image of the society as a whole was buoyant and optimistic,'' gloss over ideological rifts in British culture. They assert national pride in contrast to the difficulties of adjusting ''to being a postcolonial power, a mediocre economic performer, a multi-racial society in which the consensus of acceptable social and political behavior is fragmenting'' (1978: 40). For Americans, too, experiencing their own uncertainties, British classic serials have offered comforting images of stability and tradition.

The journalistic cliché ''jewel in the crown'' alludes to an acclaimed classic serial of the 1980s (based on Paul Scott's *The Raj Quartet*), made by an ITV company (Granada) seeking to secure franchise renewal. The 1981 BBC *Sons and Lovers* began as an ITV project with a similar motivation. Associated Television (ATV) wished to mark the fiftieth anniversary of Lawrence's death with the first television serialization of one of his novels. Broadcasters to the English Midlands, ATV felt threatened in the forthcoming franchise review by Mercian TV, based in the East Midlands—Lawrence country. *Sons and Lovers* would give ATV cultural prestige plus an opportunity to fulfill the regional remit expected of franchise holders. After filming was delayed by a strike, ATV withdrew support without explanation, despite weeks of rehearsal. Director Stuart Burge insists the decision came because ATV knew it was now too late to influence the franchise reallocation—"in my view, their main reason for doing it in the first place" (Poole and Wyver 1984: 141).

Lucrative overseas sales of classic serials followed the success of *The Forsyte Saga* (1967) and other period dramas that in the United States ended up on National Educational Television's "Masterpiece Theatre." Expensive international coproductions ensued. The cultural prestige of television drama was boosted, establishing it as a flagship for British broadcasting. However, although classic serials had seldom contested dominant versions of history, they were now consciously profit-motivated and aimed at undifferentiated international audiences. In the case of *Sons and Lovers,* 20th Century-Fox, makers of the 1960 movie and owners of the screen rights, interfered editorially, insisting on sexually explicit scenes being reframed (Poole and Wyver: 142), presumably to avoid offending American middle-class sensibilities.

Classic serials rarely question accepted literary-critical readings in any case, but, by the 1980s, they had frozen into wholly unchallenging representations of an idealized past. (This tendency—partly an effect of efficiency drives that led to greatly reduced schedules and a consequent standardization in such things as set design and construction, lighting, camera work, and even film stock—was arguably assisted by a fear of powerful right-wing politicians on the part of broadcasters.) Alistair Cook's 1982 coffee-table book companion to "Masterpiece Theatre" neatly demonstrates the centrality of the picturesque in classic serials and their status as consumable culture. Copperplate titles and italic captions signify "literariness" in what is essentially a *pictorial* celebration of British actors, designers, and settings, while each chapter consists mainly of a potted biography of the original author or of the historical figure dramatized (in cases such as *Elizabeth R*). Production stills sit alongside oil paintings, engravings, and photographs; kings, queens, and authors are interspersed with familiar performers in role. The title of the program itself is revealing: this is television, after all, *not* theater, and "masterpiece" most commonly refers to old paintings that are associated with kings and queens—as, indeed, is Shakespeare, whose plays are performed on stage in England by the actors here seen on screen. Discourses of history, authorship, and television thus combine to propagate a tourist-brochure Britishness, with history and literature constructed as a pageant of great individuals.

The classic serial is both an adaptation of a "classic" work and a serial itself envisaged, promoted, and received as a ready-made "classic." An effortless substitute for history and literature, it supplies cultural capital that can be consumed, owned, and identified with. Suppressing the struggles inherent in interpreting and evaluating history and literature, classic serials recirculate collective values of the dominant culture, bridging "serious" art and the merely "popular" (Mortimer 1994). They celebrate "our" heritage, "our" national genius; yet, they simultaneously reinscribe the ideology of individualism by emphasizing authorship (of fictions or, through decisive leadership, of history)—an emphasis otherwise largely lacking in television, a medium organized generally by means of routine, strictly demarcated, collective production.

The economics of such organization make serials the foundation of scheduling. Hardly surprising, then, that "the classic serial . . . seems so embedded in and at the same time such an embodiment of British television" (Kerr 1982: 6). Ambiguously placed between the high cultural values of the single play (classic or commissioned for television) and the series format of popular entertainment, classic serials embody the medium's contradictions. Supposedly presenting works of art valued for their integrity, they need to maintain audience continuity and so tend to be structured, like soaps, around cliff-hangers. When, for example, the three-part BBC1 *The Rainbow* (1988) was repeated in two parts (BBC2 1993), shortly after Ken Russell's *Lady Chatterley,* episode one culminated in erotic nude scenes prefiguring the imminent lesbian lovemaking of Ursula and Winifred; while episode two began with its aftermath. The relationship is treated in the novel not only indirectly but in one uninterrupted chapter.

BBC2's 1994 *Middlemarch* was significant for attracting an unprecedented audience share and great critical acclaim following speculation that the increasingly market-oriented BBC would discontinue production of costly dramatizations if it flopped. Such competitiveness (and the surrounding controversy) itself underlines the ideological centrality of classic serials in Britain. Trollope's *The Warden* (BBC 1951) was, Paul Kerr points out, "not simply the first classic serial on television—it was the first TV serial of any kind" (1982: 14); ITV adapted *The Scarlet Letter* during its first week in 1955; BBC2 began serializing *Madame Bovary* in its first week in 1964; and Channel 4's first major commissioned drama was the Royal Shakespeare Company's *Nicholas Nickleby* in four parts. For years, the BBC gave classic serials a regular Sunday evening slot, underlining their reverential, ritualistic aspects by aligning them with another sacred British institution, the mythical viewing family. Other dramas in the same slot—such as the historical and biographical serials that followed them onto "Masterpiece Theatre" (again a Sunday evening institution), also deploying period settings and style—came to be seen as the same genre, a canon not identical to the literary Great Tradition but representing similar values.

Cinema relates to literature differently from broadcasting in terms of both technological history and economics. Early cinema, John Caughie notes, lacked sound, while early broadcasting lacked pictures (1981: 31). Movies, originating in photography, developed "a highly elaborated visual rhetoric" in which words are often superfluous; hence the uneasy relationship between realist cinema and histrionic performances and the frequent feeling that much of a literary work is lost in adaptation even when descriptions are followed to the letter. Television, conversely, an outgrowth of radio, inherits "a respect for the spoken word, the script, and the writer" together with a word-based tradition of broadcast drama. Moreover, live transmission, necessary before video was introduced, combined with inferior picture quality and the limitations of studio sets, put an emphasis on performance and dialogue that clearly allied television to theater and gave it something of the latter's cultural status. The need to fill time over several weeks, which dialogue facilitates, means television adaptations rarely step outside these conventions even today.

Feature films, hugely expensive products for commercial gain, involve tremendous financial risk in comparison to television, where costs are generally covered in advance. Only one feature film in five is profitable, and backing from investors almost always represents a major gamble on their part.

Producers learned quickly to court success with a story that had previously appealed to an audience, not only because its popularity was already apparent but also because it offered a potential ready-made audience among those who had read, or at least heard of, the original (Izod 1993: 96); hence, around 30 percent of movies from Hollywood's classic era were adaptations (Ellis 1982: 3). Adaptation from a well-known source enables the title alone to invoke an existing cultural memory, providing an immediately recognizable "narrative image" for promotional exploitation (Ellis 1992: 30). This need not be accurate, provided it arouses enough curiosity to draw potential customers. 20th Century-Fox, which released *Sons and Lovers* (1960) ahead of the trial of *Lady Chatterley's Lover,* was but one of several Hollywood majors to have taken out options on Lawrence novels at that time (Poole and Wyver 1984: 140). The notoriety of the Lawrence connection, enhanced by the racy connotations of the title, offered sufficient promise of success. Notably, five of the first seven cinematic adaptations of Lawrence—*L'Amant de Lady Chatterley* (1956), *Sons and Lovers* (1960), *Women in Love* (1970), *The Virgin and the Gipsy* (1970), and *Lady Chatterley's Lover* (1981)—had titles likely to attract the prurient, while *The Fox* (1967), like several of these, rapidly gained a reputation for its sexual content.

An associated strategy is to target films precisely at different groups. For present purposes, three distinct approaches to adaptation are discernible. First, adaptations of existing (or just commissioned) popular fiction, aimed at a wide audience; these include familiar examples such as *Jaws* (1977) and James Bond, as well as a substantial proportion of films not generally recognized as adaptations; the category might be stretched to include high-budget, all-star versions of classics, such as *The Great Gatsby* (1974). Second, adaptations of classics for a smaller, more literary "art house" market; for example, early Merchant/Ivory productions. Third, adaptations of classics developed as personal projects by auteur directors, embracing both literary and cineast audiences: Polanski's *Tess* (1979) or Scorsese's *The Age of Innocence* (1994), for example.

The first approach differs from that of British television: rather than cultural respectability or cheapness relative to original commissioned drama, the primary appeal to producers of this sort of adaptation lies in a clear, ready-made story line and in the romantic, topical, sensational, or potentially spectacular aspects of the source. The second approach comes closer to that of television in that it markets the prestige of the literary "content" of the film as inscribed by the author's name; hence, this kind of film, typified by *Jean de Florette* (1986), *Little Dorritt* (1988), and *Babette's Feast* (1987), is often associated with national culture and values opposed to those of Hollywood. John Izod explains how, as early as the 1910s, adaptations were deliberately made both to discredit those who campaigned against the alleged pernicious effects of cinema and to appeal to middle-class tastes, thereby attracting a wealthier clientele to expensive "first-run" theaters, which provided most profit when costly feature films were introduced (1993: 96). Revealingly, filmed novels still receive most Oscar nominations. The third approach bears little comparison with television, where the names of directors are virtually unknown to audiences and where adapters are not widely credited unless already famous as novelists or playwrights.

In practice, these approaches interact. For instance, Ken Russell frankly acknowledges his motivation for originating *The Rainbow* (1988): "*Women in Love* had been one of my greatest hits, so it seemed reasonable to assume that the earlier novel which featured the 'women' of the title as teenagers would prove to be equally successful" (1989: 134). Russell's implicit assertion of auteur status here, as a component in a marketable package, is tempered by commercial cynicism: "With *The Rainbow* I was back on home ground in Lawrence country. There was nude wrestling (a man and a woman this time) and stampeding animals (Shire horses this time), all that lovely scenery and the usual horny miners" (141). In addition to the novel's notoriety, the fame and controversy surrounding the director, and the sensationalized content, another significant marketable component emerges in Russell's account of his unsuccessful appeal for support to producer David Puttnam: "After all, what could be more British than D. H. Lawrence?" (144).

Technical Determinants

The sheer number and diversity of texts, literary, cinematic, televisual, ought to suggest the futility of generalizing relationships among these media, superficially united by shared tendencies toward narrative. "[N]ot the least fascinating aspect" of exploring possible connections between adaptations and literature, writes Morris Beja, "is that it is so controversial" (51). Yet, it is controversial because the terms of debate remain ill defined.

To begin with, critics frequently forget that adaptation, by definition, involves *change*. Adaptation cannot be neutral transposition between media, for elements such as theme, character, plot, and symbolism have no existence outside their activation in decoding. Meaning is produced through signification, the interplay of signs activated by the reader bringing to bear his or her own discursive formation, including knowledge of codes; it is therefore unique to each instance. That it should appear otherwise emphasizes the hold of realism, the myth of transparency of language, over habits of reading. Even if we agree with Seymour Chatman that story at least is transposable (1978: 20), the most naive reading requires application of mental schemata (culturally assimilated patterns of thought cued by textual conventions) to the frequently nonchronological, non-causal plot, from which the story is produced as a mental construct. If the narrative is constructed in the reader's mind, it has no separate existence beyond the extent to which reading is intersubjective, culturally determined; it is not *objectively* available for transposition between media.

Adapters, at the very least, have to create objective correlatives in the codes and conventions of the new medium for the meanings they construct from the original; meanings made from verbal narration in a novel require expression in film through camera work, casting, lighting, music, sound effects, and so on. Indeed, these things often involve decisions that have to be made without help from the original; a car might be mentioned casually in prose, but a film requires a particular model, age, and color, shot in a particular way in a particular time and place. Such explicitness anchors connotations, for cameras cannot present nouns devoid of adjectives, verbs without adverbs.

Interpretation in every sense, adaptation is often treated as though the aim is replication. Moreover, adaptations that overtly announce their intention to interpret—to criticize—are often treated with suspicion. For example, the *Sons and Lovers* serialization (BBCtv 1981), scripted by Trevor Griffiths, exploited the objectifying tendency of realist drama to decenter the narrative from the individual, Paul, and to foreground social-historical forces. By increasing emphasis on a minor character, Baxter Dawes, in order to stress class politics, Griffiths "restored" a voice to old Morel that he felt Lawrence's novel suppressed. The new version thus controversially challenged both Lawrence's discourse and the framework of Leavisite criticism within which it was habitually understood at the time (Poole and Wyver 1984: 146–47).

Julian Smith usefully observes that, after half a century, the movie audience for *The Virgin and the Gipsy* (1970) "has, superficially at least, travelled far beyond Lawrence's original readers in terms of *conscious* attitudes toward sensuality and personal freedom." Consequently, "Lawrence's purpose and audience . . . were quite different from those of the filmmakers"; automatically to regard differences between the original and the adaptation as evidencing failure by the filmmakers or inherent deficiencies of the medium is to discount the film's potential as "a re-vision, a seeing again of what Lawrence saw," "just one of the many possible films contained within the novella" (Smith 1973: 28).

What is adapted, in fact, George Bluestone suggests, is a paraphrase—"the novel viewed as raw material." He continues pragmatically: "Because this is possible, we often find that the film adapter has not even read the book, that he has depended instead on a paraphrase by his secretary or his screenwriter" (1957: 62). How easily this happens is confirmed in the case of *Women in Love* where Russell was appointed to direct the film only *after* script completion, never having read the original. He did eventually turn to the novel through dissatisfaction with the screenplay, but the latter still provided him with "something mysterious and haunting . . . lurking somewhere beneath the surface" (Baxter 1973: 169). He read biographies and discovered that Birkin partly resembled Lawrence, that Gerald, Gudrun, and Ursula were based on real people, and Hermione on Lady Ottoline Morrell. He researched these people to develop the characterization. Deciding that "The only comparable thing to a woman dancing to cattle in Lawrence's experience" would have been Isadora Duncan dancing to the waves on the beach, he modeled Gudrun partly on her and choreographed accordingly (Baxter 1973: 175). Birkin's monologue on eating a fig, not in the novel, was transcribed directly from one of Lawrence's poems, as it seemed to summarize what the book took thousands of words to express. Consequently, what is widely respected as an unusually successful adaptation appropriates much from other discourses surrounding Lawrence. Whatever fidelity it seems to possess derives as much from accordance with these discourses as from any direct relationship to Lawrence's text.

Adaptations exist in dialogic relationship to their sources, interpreting and substituting. They are not mere conduits. Different discourses—commerce, high culture, the director as auteur—interweave with literary discourse to create something new, analogous to the original. In *Women in Love,* Lawrence's text met the cult of Lawrence as personality when it was most potent and already the focus of popular discourses around modernity, sexuality, and censorship (as partly embodied in earlier Lawrence adaptations). It also met Russell's own iconoclastic, yet (at that time) respected, image.

The myth of exact replication is assumed unconsciously even by those commentators who seem to recognize that adaptation inevitably leads to a different text, subject to the conventions of the new medium, but who then invoke mathematical arguments to explain major differences. John Simon explains why he prefers the film *The Virgin and the Gipsy* to *Women in Love:*

Virgin is a novella of some hundred pages; *Women* on the other hand, is a novel of well over five hundred. The novella may be just about the only form of fiction that readily lends itself to cinematic adaptation: it is long enough to offer the filmmaker a sufficiency of material to use, expand, or drop; but it is not so long as to force him to cut ruthlessly and disfiguringly, nor so short as to force him into wholesale inventions and additions. (1971: 62)

This logic, reiterated by Beja (1979: 83–84), resurfaces with Neil Taylor:

The Virgin and the Gipsy is only 86 pages and became the shortest of the films (92 minutes); but while *Women in Love* the novel is more than six times longer than *The Virgin and the Gipsy* the novella, the film of *Women in Love* is only 33 minutes longer than the film of *The Virgin and the Gipsy.* Because of the conventions of the medium and the institutions in which it operates, whatever goes into the adapter's brain comes out in packages of a similar size. (1993: 106–7)

Certainly, the length of feature films evolved for no artistic reason. (The capacity of the human bladder was Alfred Hitchcock's explanation; the need for exhibitors to maximize daily screenings and allow time for profitable confectionery and drinks sales is another.) But equally, there is no theoretical reason to support mathematical formulations that posit a finite amount of information distributed evenly throughout texts, as though a standard number of ''bits'' per minute of reading time occur in literature, film, or television. Reductive in terms of different modes of narration within each medium—Chatman (1978: 64), building on the work of Gérard Genette, distinguishes five different relationships between reading-time and story-time (summary, ellipsis, scene, stretch, and pause)—they do nothing to explain, for example, the different effects of Lawrence's abstract, accretionary style in *The Rainbow* as compared with the spare simplicity of his language in ''The Rocking-Horse Winner,'' let alone explaining the complex text–film relations in each case.

While, as already suggested, it would seem to be an inescapable function of adaptations to reinterpret or deconstruct their source texts, the widespread belief that exact replication of content is the aim makes *faithfulness* a frequent criterion. But this notion, too, does not bear much critical examination.

Adaptations that assert faithfulness use direct quotations of both dialogue and decor through visual reproduction of described details such as settings and costumes. However, details lightly sketched verbally cannot be filmed realistically without background; items of ornamentation or furniture might in prose establish their owner's personality, standing, or taste, but an adaptation creates an impression of the entire room (requiring ingenuity to highlight significant objects). Roland Barthes termed this the ''effect of the real,'' an excess of objects not ''used up'' in narrative, creating the sense of a preexisting (that is, nonfictional) setting (1978: 134). This illusion depends not necessarily on what the author wrote but on assumed cultural knowledge of how a particular place and era would look. Victorian or Edwardian settings in films and classic serials tend to resemble each other because of conventionalized camera technique, lighting, film stock, and acting styles and because they use similar props, decor, and costume. Often lauded for painstaking research, they merely recirculate and reinforce a dominant image of a mythical past. Costume dramas flesh out ''factual documentaries,'' producing a collective history against which they are, in turn, judged (Poole and Wyver 1984: 47). The distortions resulting from such a circular process prompted Griffiths's complaints about how BBC production routines hijacked his attempt to present *Sons and Lovers* specifically in terms of working-class experience, with history seen as agency rather than as backdrop to a timeless personal drama. Although a period look was scrupulously reproduced, with many individually authentic details, the cumulative effect was, he felt, just too perfect, a safe, bland, middle-class version of history (Poole and Wyver 1984: 145). The titles, showing a soft watercolor being painted, reinforced this by suggesting a portrait of the artist, the individual journey of a working-class hero toward bourgeois culture. Despite Griffiths's more radical version of Lawrence's vision, then, the titles merely stressed conventional standards of taste and restraint—the norms unconsciously guiding the televisual style overall.

To produce cheap, yet convincing, representations of the frequently sketchy settings of literature, locations are increasingly employed. The interiors of Yew Tree Cottage in *The Rainbow* were filmed for the BBCtv version (1988) at the former home of Louie Burrows, once Lawrence's fiancée and, in part, the model for Ursula. This provided a period house in appropriate regional style suggesting the right social class. However, the centrality of such information in promotional materials emphasizes the obsession with "authenticity" that characterizes responses to adaptations and, again, posits an adaptable literary "content" apparently available in reality. The need for concrete analogues for the symbolic constructs of verbal discourse leads to fiction, biography, and history being treated as interchangeable and identical, further implying that they are fixed, objectively "there," hence uncontestable. A logical outcome is the critical strategy which then treats the novel's "content" as real. Moore complains of Russell's *Women in Love:* "Gerald's home, Shortlands, *actually* Lamb Close House just outside Eastwood, is given an extra story, while Hermione's Breadalby is also *far more ornate than its original,* Garsington Manor in Oxfordshire" (1973: 10; emphasis added).

A similar logic underlies the many comments on casting and performance in Lawrence adaptations, with critics invariably treating these issues independently of filmic technique, as if the characters in Lawrence's books somehow objectively exist to be straightforwardly imitated on screen. Such an approach usually relies on the critic's own visualization and often produces bathos: "The casting for *Sons and Lovers* . . . is commendable. . . . None of the actors has physical characteristics that clash with the role he or she is playing" (DeNitto 1981: 242). Moore describes Keir Dullea in *The Fox* as "one of those non-actors which Hollywood used to be so full of . . . shambling creatures with about one-and-a-half facial expressions and hick voices." He also bemoans the lack of "a flashing and vibrant figure" in *The Virgin and the Gipsy* and refers to Franco Nero—unfairly, in my opinion—as "a plump Latin non-actor" (1973: 8–9). Ignoring Hitchcock's infamous dictum "All actors are cattle"—which defined cinematic art as direction and editing—Moore adopts literary/dramatic assumptions that celebrate the static wordiness and mannered acting of many television classic serials.

Realist productions represent individual character by means of usually one actor, and this presents problems for adapting Lawrence, given his conception of character as decentered and fluid, motivated by deep, unconscious forces. The only technique commonly used in Lawrence adaptations to evoke the unconscious is the dream sequence, which, Taylor notes, is itself invariably rendered in the realist mode, making clear who is dreaming and why (1993: 110). In realist texts, moreover, concrete representation of dreams can appear absurd, as witness the ridicule poured on a sequence in *Lady Chatterley:*

It is all very peculiar, and possibly the result of eating cheese before bedtime, especially the bit when Lady Chatterley looks to the opposite bank and sees the saturnine Mellors standing expressionless with his shiny brown boots and big long shotgun. Mmm. Stallion, tunnel, shotgun, boots. . . . Why can one never find one's *Freud for Beginners* when one needs it? (Truss 1993: 33)

Pity the poor adapter: faced in Britain with prudishness, preventing direct treatment of sexuality; the lack of any established discourse to represent sexual behavior, outside pornography, romance, and low farce; and a prestige national cinema and classic serial tradition characterized by "the three Rs: realism, rationality and restraint" (Sinyard 1986: 50)—antithetical to Lawrence and Russell alike.

One adaptation that does skillfully stretch realism to suggest something of the unconscious motivation of character is *The Virgin and the Gipsy* (1970). Repeated sequences show the gipsy leading Yvette from her friends' car, later helping her off with her coat, and then, eventually, with her underclothes. Fantasy and memory become indistinguishable, so that when she sleeps with the gipsy after the flood, the rerun of the sequences preserves the book's ambiguity about which events actually happened. In the film, the Victorian dam realistically motivates the flood; but, massive and threatening against the wild, fertile landscape and architecturally resembling the rectory, it also powerfully symbolizes the sterile rationality and rigid moral controls of the Saywell society, which is finally swept away by the uncontainable natural forces symbolized by the flood.

Contrast Ursula's nightmare in BBCtv's *The Rainbow:* miners stack coffins while Uncle Tom, a cartoon capitalist in top hat and tails, dances with Winifred Inger beneath a chandelier; he next whips the miners while escorting Winifred in bridal dress against a nighttime backdrop of garishly lit mine works. The artificial coloring and discordant fairground music gradually transmuting into a harsh machine rhythm code all this as a subjective vision. Lawrence's social critique of the horrors and degradations of industrialism (convincingly rendered earlier by a documentary-like sequence conveying Ursula's perceptions) is thus reduced to the status of a naive girl's feverish vision. Consequently, the whole industrial context, rendered realistically as part of the period setting, remains thematically marginalized: canals, steam trains, trams, and motor cars all appear as picturesque museum pieces safely divorced from their origins—all part of the quaint visual pleasure of classic serials.

Further complications in the criticism of Lawrence adaptations ensue from contradictory opinions about whether Lawrence is a visual writer and about his relation to realism—both central issues for critics committed to fidelity. "Lawrence is not a great visual writer," insists Sinyard. "His most original feature is his experimentation with language and imagery to express the unconscious" (1986: 50). Tarrat, conversely, believes that "[t]he intense visual quality of some of Lawrence's scenes makes it clear where the temptation for adapters lies" (1970: 30). They agree, however, that, when his images are represented on screen, important nuances are lost, and both cite *The Fox* as an example, arguing that the film merely shows footage of an actual fox, devoid of symbolism.

Again, general conclusions from an isolated instance are hard to sustain. It would be surprising if Lawrence, a representational painter, did not possess visual acuity and did not, to some extent, think pictorially. An erstwhile imagist poet, he was well aware of the force of juxtaposition to forge concepts, and—like many films—his fiction generates strands of imagery that sustain ideas, moods, or tonalities. The failure of the symbolic fox is a failure in one film, not proof of Lawrence's unsuitability for adaptation or of film's inability to adapt him. Besides, the film of *The Fox* has its successful moments, too. The ending, for example, very neatly visualizes the liberation of March, the start of a new phase in her life, through the rain's melting of the ice that has dominated exterior scenes throughout the film. In *L'Amant de Lady Chatterley,* other visual effects successfully translate Lawrence's verbal meanings:

A graceful pan . . . establishes that Connie figures as no more than an afterthought in Clifford's plans for a son. The husband is apparently alone with the household servants as he instructs them to bring in the giant cradle he has reserved for the heir of Wragby. But as they carry the coffin-like piece of furniture into the room the camera turns slowly to the right, including Connie in the scene for the first time. Her face and stance provide a silently negative commentary on Clifford's scheme to perpetuate the Chatterley name. (Scott 1973: 43)

Describing a crib as coffinlike would appear strained in a novel, yet here the perversion of marriage into a living death is effectively conveyed.

Where film has difficulty with literary imagery, it can create its own to approximate the ideas by different means. Gontarski shows how sustained water imagery in the film *The Virgin and the Gipsy* creates a pastoral serenity reminiscent of nineteenth-century landscape painting (suggestive of the artificial harmony against which Yvette rebels); within it, "always latent is the raw libidinous power" released at the climax. Throughout the build-up, he notes, "the filmmakers have been considerably more obvious than Lawrence; that in part is due to the medium itself and to the real fact that film is usually a popular art form" (1981: 267).

The explicitness of realist film, combined with the shift to different codes and conventions, does inevitably distort—and sometimes with lamentable consequences. With *The Rainbow,* Taylor observes that, whereas Lawrence's rainbow is a personal symbol of the union of elemental forces, Russell's "is a decorative device to open and close the film symmetrically," at most a symbol of Ursula's optimism (1993: 118). Both Jaeckin's and Russell's versions of *Lady Chatterley's Lover* use scenes from *The First Lady Chatterley,* including one when she veils her face and examines her naked body in a mirror. In the novel, she is the object of her own gaze—presented from within her consciousness—whereas on film and television she becomes the object of the voyeuristic gaze of the unseen spectator, for whom her body is displayed and whose visual pleasure is redoubled by the reflection. Following the convention whereby a woman is presented for the (implied) male gaze yet given a mirror so she can be condemned for vanity, both versions become entwined in the discourses of pornography, one calculatedly, the other possibly by default.

But if film seems inferior because of its apparent inability to match the original, these and earlier examples suggest an alternative view that blames not the medium itself but the limitations of the filmmakers: an acknowledgedly great author has simply been adapted by directors of minor or uneven stature. In itself, film is as capable of subtlety as prose is, and, given a filmmaker with the appropriate vision, expertise, and production resources, Lawrence adaptations can illustrate the point as well as other films.

Russell's *Women in Love* especially, as well as being one of the few color productions to eschew the picturesque in order to emphasize the grime and dreariness of industrialism, makes virtuoso use of cinematic resources to suggest Lawrence's complex ideas. At the end of the water-party episode, Birkin and Ursula are filmed, after making love, from the same angle and in the same intertwined position as the drowned couple when they are discovered at the bottom of the drained lake. Suggesting both the mutual giving up of selfhood in sex and the potential total loss of self in the sexual relationship, the momentary visual juxtaposition cleverly condenses a significant part of the "star-equilibrium" debate in the novel. During their second lovemaking, inside Birkin's mill, there is a cut to a ninety-degree tilt shot of the couple approaching each other against a sun-drenched wheat field. Though criticized by some for resembling a shampoo commercial (Gomez 1981: 254), the unusual tilt produces a distancing effect that enables the image to be read as satirizing Ursula's romantic, domesticating vision. The final dialogue of the film reproduces the one at the end of the book, with Ursula and Birkin at the mill. However, the film adds a final reaction shot of Ursula looking toward camera, rather pleased with herself; this then freezes over the credits, effectively giving *her* the last word (Birkin has the last word in the book) but also—more important—implicitly suggesting a continuation of their dialogue and thus capturing some of the famous open-endedness of the novel.

Oliver Reed's dark appearance, contrary to Lawrence's Gerald, is appropriate within the film's scheme of light and color. Ursula and Birkin are associated with open air, sunshine, and warm, pastel colors. Gudrun and Gerald's morbid relationship develops among dismal streets, in a shaded forest, a dank subway at night, her curtained-off bedroom; both wear dark clothes; Gerald is seen begrimed with coal among his underground workers. The sisters' opening conversation, including Gudrun's cry, "*Nothing materializes!*" is moved, ominously, from the family parlor in the book, to the graveyard at the Crich wedding in the film. At the tragic climax of their relationship, when Gerald breaks away into the dazzling snow, a subjective vision shows Gudrun's silhouette, head back and laughing, eclipsing the sun. The firelit wrestling scene combines both golden hues, associated with Birkin, and dark shadows and coals for Gerald, stressing their irreconcilable brotherhood and opposition, the unsustainable unity in difference. Gerald's violence toward Gudrun during sex is partially explained by subjective inserts of his demented mother; and, as Stuart Y. McDougal describes, the scene ends with a series of fades and zooms that rhymes with the treatment of their first confrontation after she had been chasing the cattle, stressing entirely visually the figurative distance separating them (1985: 285). Against this cinematic inventiveness, it is ironic—especially given my earlier comments—that Sinyard condemns the film for its apparent lack of "fidelity" to the original:

Lawrence's symbolic flourishes often look either obvious or absurd when visualized. The crude Nature/industry, male/female contrast . . . where Gerald brutally forces his terrified mare to stand its ground as a train thunders past, seems even more ponderous when Ken Russell films it: it looks like [a high school] guide to symbolism. Gudrun's dance before the cattle in Russell's film not only looks ridiculous but reverses the meaning of the scene in the novel: Gudrun appears stupid rather than rapt, Gerald reasonable rather than stolid. (1986: 50)

"HERE'S TO OL' D. H. LAWRENCE": POPULAR CONSTRUCTIONS OF "LAWRENCE"

Each adaptation of a text, if it seems coherent, constructs a new version of the author, the personified "voice" with which the reader identifies as a necessary corollary to finding his or her own subject position (Lapsley and Westlake 1988: 127). Unless the personality of a distinctive director or screenwriter imposes itself on the adaptation, so that it is seen primarily as an addition to his or her corpus, this will become part of the developing image of the original author, itself a determinant of subsequent readings. Screen adaptations of Lawrence are no exception to this process, and each of the films or serializations touched on in this chapter has contributed to our constantly changing image of the author and his works. But to summarize the broad trajectory of Lawrence's popular reputation as partly defined by these adaptations, it will be convenient to end here by looking briefly at some lesser-known media representations of our subject.

Two hippy motorcyclists in the film *Easy Rider* (1969) sell drugs to finance an epic ride across America. Persecuted for their unconventionality, they are released from jail assisted by a sympathetic cellmate, a lawyer repeatedly arrested for drunkenness (Jack Nicholson). His first act of freedom is to propose a toast: "To ol' D. H. Lawrence."

Reputedly ad-libbed, this comic moment underscored the film's serious pretensions by offering an interpretive context for its celebration of southwestern landscape. (The bikers have visited a New Mexico commune whose emaciated, bearded leader offers prayers to organicism and cyclical continuity.) The film mistrusts authority and convention; its symbolism repeatedly asserts a life force yet refuses to take sides, preferring continuity and complementarity; and its apparently spontaneous (yet highly crafted) style and construction helped revolutionize American filmmaking. It affirms meaning beyond the transient and visible, while its informing metaphor is that of life as a journey of discovery. Glorying in the mythology of *Studies in Classic American Literature,* the film questions the meaning of America and of freedom, asserts ambiguity, and champions outsiders while recognizing their escape as being primarily from themselves. The film commemorates the proponent of the frontier myth who wrote of his soul reawakening in the desert mornings near Santa Fe.

The implied Lawrence, when his critical reputation and popularity were at their peak, is soul brother to the Woodstock counterculture: prophet, mystic, visionary, champion of free expression (linguistic and sexual), martyr repressed by uncomprehending authority, immortalized by premature death. Similar elements were implicated less romantically in the British film *The Loneliness of the Long Distance Runner* (1962) during a scene where two young rebels produce hilarity by turning down the television sound on a politician pontificating about morality—his last audible words denouncing *Lady Chatterley's Lover.*

Peter Widdowson reproduces an advertisement from a 1968 supermarket magazine for housewives (1992: 1–3). In glossy, full-page color, this offers Lawrence's works in "beautifully-grained deep green Skivertex covers" with "the look and soft feel of book-binder's calf." While the selling proposition ("[I]ntroduce me to the joys of enriching my mind and beautifying my home with the world's most beautiful books") offers a decor accessory involving a cheap, ready-made image of educated culture—the antithesis of values underpinning *Easy Rider*—the projected Lawrence is strikingly similar. "Mind expanding, and Dangerous" proclaims one bold-type subheading, echoing the language of proscribed drugs. Socially aspiring housewives are invited to buy the books of a writer "dangerous because of the *ideas* he can put into your *mind*"—ideas that include the realization that "there can be far more to the husband—wife relationship than most couples settle for"!

It is hardly unusual for the culture industry to incorporate oppositional discourses for profit (and to defuse them in the process). The contradictions here, though, are remarkable. Lawrence's youthfulness and independence are clearly in favor, yet the contemporary revolt exploited is not the whimsy of the previous year's flower power (to which Lawrence's writing was easily appropriable) but darker, more politically liberationist currents underlying *les événements* in Paris in May and the Vietnam protests. On the other hand, the very context and point of the advertisement demonstrate quite comically that Lawrence's image was, in fact, not particularly threatening any longer—that, in some ways, it now conformed quite comfortably to the ethos of the decade it had so transgressively helped inaugurate with the 1960 obscenity trial.

A quarter century later, BBC Radio 4 reported that a local district council had proposed naming streets after *Lady Chatterley's Lover:* Mellors Road, Constance Avenue, Testershall Drive, and the like (*Today,* 21 January 1994). A dissenting councilor expressed local outrage: "[T]his novel was pornographic until 1968" (*sic*). The report next considered the fashion of naming streets and buildings after black heroes such as Nelson Mandela, Bob Marley, and Marcus Garvie, rather than the usual Establishment figures, and a Labour M.P. averred that the "new" names celebrate the heroes of ordinary working people.

Apart from reconfirming the talismanic aspect of language (central to Lawrence's usage, especially in *Lady Chatterley's Lover*), the item is notable for aligning Lawrence with the demonology of popular journalism. Against an implicit norm of British culture (i.e., "Us") is set everything that its value system defines itself against (i.e., "Them"), so that Lawrence = pornography = not British = alien/black = political correctness = left wing = working class = moral degeneracy.

The difference between the Lawrence of the 1960s and that of the 1990s partly indicates shifts in popular culture generally. It also reflects that inevitable cultural process whereby any major figure is constantly re-created either in the image of the times or as one of its defining "others." What is clear, though, is that Lawrence remains a major figure, and our culture, whether "literary" or "popular," has not yet finished readjusting itself to him. Among the most frequently adapted for film and television of all serious authors, he remains a household name and a perennial embodiment of discursive conflict.

WORKS CITED

Althusser, Louis. *Lenin and Philosophy.* London: New Left Books, 1971.

Alvarado, Manuel, Robin Gutch, and Tana Wollen. *Learning the Media: An Introduction to Media Teaching.* London: Macmillan, 1987.

Baldanza, Frank. "*Sons and Lovers:* Novel to Film as a Record of Cultural Growth." *Literature/Film Quarterly* 1 (January 1973): 64–70.

Barthes, Roland. "The Realistic Effect." *Film Reader* 3 (February 1978): 131–35.

Baxter, John. *An Appalling Talent: Ken Russell.* London: Michael Joseph, 1973.

Beja, Morris. *Film and Literature.* New York: Longman, 1979.

Bluestone, George. *Novels into Film.* Baltimore: Johns Hopkins University Press, 1957.

Brett, Dorothy. *Lawrence and Brett: A Friendship.* Philadelphia: Lippincott, 1933.

Brewster, Earl, and Achsah Brewster. *D. H. Lawrence: Reminiscences and Correspondence.* London: Secker, 1934.

Burch, Nöel. "How We Got into Pictures: Notes Accompanying *Correction Please.*" *Afterimage* 8–9 (Winter 1980–81): 24–38.

Caughie, John. "Rhetoric, Pleasure and Art Television." *Screen* 22, no. 4 (1981): 9–31.

Chanan, Michael. *The Dream That Kicks: The Prehistory and Early Years of Cinema in Britain.* London: Routledge and Kegan Paul, 1980.

Chatman, Seymour. *Story and Discourse: Narrative Structure in Fiction and Film.* Ithaca, N.Y., and London: Cornell University Press, 1978.

Cook, Alistair. *Masterpieces: A Decade of Classics on Television.* London: Bodley Head, 1982.

Cook, Pam, ed. *The Cinema Book.* London: British Film Institute, 1985.

Cowan, James C. "Lawrence and the Movies: *The Lost Girl* and After." In his *D. H. Lawrence and the Trembling Balance.* University Park and London: Pennsylvania University Press, 1990, pp. 95–114.

DeNitto, Dennis. "*Sons and Lovers:* All Passion Spent." In *The English Novel and the Movies.* Edited by Michael Klein and Gillian Parker. New York: Ungar, 1981, pp. 235–47.

Ellis, John. "The Literary Adaptation: An Introduction." *Screen* 23, no. 1 (May–June 1982): 3–5.

———. *Visible Fictions.* 2d ed. London: Routledge, 1992.

Falcon, Richard. *Classified! A Teachers' Guide to Film and Video Censorship and Classification.* London: British Film Institute, 1994.

Gontarski, S. E. "An English Watercolor." In *The English Novel and the Movies.* Edited by Michael Klein and Gillian Parker. New York: Ungar, 1981, pp. 257–67.

Griffiths, Trevor. "Introduction" to *Sons and Lovers* Screenplay." Nottingham: Spokesman, 1982: pp. 7–12. (A shortened version of the same essay appeared as an article in *Radio Times* [10–16 January 1981]: 84–86.)

Izod, John. "Words Selling Pictures." In *Cinema and Fiction: New Modes of Adapting 1950–1990.* Edited by John Orr and Colin Nicholson. Edinburgh: Edinburgh University Press, 1993, pp. 95–103.

Lapsley, Robert, and Michael Westlake. *Film Theory: An Introduction.* Manchester: Manchester University Press, 1988.

Kerr, Paul. "Classic Serials: To Be Continued." *Screen 23,* no. 1 (May–June 1982): 6–19.

McArthur, Colin. *Television and History.* BFI Television Monograph no. 8. London: British Film Institute, 1978.

McDougal, Stuart Y. *Made Into Movies: From Literature to Film.* New York: Holt, Rinehart and Winston, 1985.

Mellen, Joan. "Outfoxing Lawrence: Novella into Film." *Literature/Film Quarterly* 1 (January 1973): 17–27.

Merrild, Knud. *With D. H. Lawrence in New Mexico: A Memoir of D. H. Lawrence.* London: Routledge and Kegan Paul, 1964. (Originally published as *A Poet and Two Painters: A Memoir of D. H. Lawrence.* London: Routledge, 1938.)

Metz, Christian. "The Imaginary Signifier." *Screen* 16, no. 2 (Summer 1975): 14–76.

Moore, Harry T. "D. H. Lawrence and the Flicks." *Literature/Film Quarterly* 1 (January 1973): 3–11.

Mortimer, John. "The Great British Divide." *Daily Telegraph* (8 January 1994).

Mulvey, Laura. "Visual Pleasure and Narrative Cinema." *Screen* 16, no. 3 (Autumn 1975): 6–18. (Reprinted in slightly abridged form in *Popular Television and Film.* Edited by Tony Bennett, Susan Boyd-Bowman, Colin Mercer, and Janet Woollacott. London: British Film Institute, 1981, pp. 206–15.)

Nehls, Edward, ed. *D. H. Lawrence: A Composite Biography.* Vol. 3. Madison: University of Wisconsin Press, 1959.

Poole, Mike, and John Wyver. *Powerplays: Trevor Griffiths in Television.* London: British Film Institute, 1984.

Russell, Ken. *A British Picture.* London: Heinemann, 1989.

Scott, James F. "The Emasculation of *Lady Chatterley's Lover.*" *Literature/Film Quarterly* 1 (January 1973): 37–45.

Simon, John. *Movies into Film.* New York: Dial Press, 1971.

Sinyard, Neil. *Filming Literature: The Art of Screen Adaptation.* London: Croom Helm, 1986.

Smith, Julian. "Vision and Revision: *The Virgin and the Gipsy* as Film." *Literature/ Film Quarterly* 1 (January 1973): 28–36.

Tarrat, Margaret. "An Obscene Undertaking." *Films and Filming* 17, no. 2 (November 1970): 26–30.

Taylor, Neil. "A Woman's Love: D. H. Lawrence on Film." In *Novel Images: Literature in Performance.* Edited by Peter Reynolds. London: Routledge, 1993, pp. 105–21.

Truss, Lynne. "Axles, Elbows and the Promise of Woodland Games." *Times* (7 June 1993): 33.

Widdowson, Peter, ed. *D. H. Lawrence.* London: Longman, 1992.

Williams, Linda Ruth. *Sex in the Head: Visions of Femininity and Film in D. H. Lawrence.* Hemel Hempstead: Harvester Wheatsheaf, 1993.

BIBLIOGRAPHY 95: LAWRENCE AND FILM, BY PAUL POPLAWSKI AND NIGEL MORRIS

This bibliography is divided into three parts, as follows:

1. A filmography of screen adaptations of Lawrence's works, giving full production details;
2. A listing of bibliographies, reviews, and critical studies relating to Lawrence and film generally and to individual adaptations; and
3. A listing of general background works on literature and adaptation.

FILMOGRAPHY

Only adaptations of Lawrence's works and major biographical films are listed here. For a list of more general educational and documentary films relating to Lawrence (along with a similar list of sound recordings), see Gerard (1982) under next section.

Films are listed alphabetically. Leading players are listed in most cases according to the published cast credits. The timings given are approximate and, in the case of feature films, relate to the cinema release version. References to video versions of the films are to the last known release in the U.K. (see John Elliot. *Elliot's Guide to Film on Video.* 3d ed. London: Boxtree, 1993). *NV* ("no video") at the end of an entry indicates that the film is not available on home video in either the U.K. or the United States.

Adaptations

The Boy in the Bush (Australia, 1983). Directed by Rob Stewart. Screenplay by Hugh Whitemore. Produced by Ian Warren and Geoffrey Daniels. Leading players: Ken-

neth Branagh (Jack Grant), Sigrid Thornton (Monica), Celia de Burgh (Mary),
Stephen Bisley (Esau), Jon Blake (Tom). Color. 4 × 50 mins. Portman Produc-
tions in association with Australian Broadcasting Corporation for Channel Four
London. *NV*

The Captain's Doll (U.K., 1983). Television adaptation. Directed by Claude Whatham.
Screenplay by James Saunders. Leading players: Jeremy Irons (Captain Alex Hepburn), Jane Lapotaire (Mrs. Hepburn), Gila von Weitershausen (Hannele). Color.
110 mins. BBCtv. *NV*

The Daughter-in-Law. (U.K., 1985). Television adaptation. Directed by Martyn Friend.
Produced by Carol Parks. Leading players: Sheila Hancock (Mrs. Gascoigne),
Cherie Lunghi (Minnie), David Threlfall (Luther Gascoigne), Mick Ford (Joe
Gascoigne). BBCtv.

The Fox (United States, 1967). Directed by Mark Rydell. Screenplay by Lewis John
Carlino and Howard Koch. Leading players: Sandy Dennis (Banford), Keir Dullea
(Paul [Henry in the novel]), Anne Heywood (March), Glyn Morris. Color. 110
mins. Claridge Pictures. *NV*

Kangaroo (Australia, 1986). Directed by Tim Burstall. Screenplay by Evan Jones. Produced by Ross Dimsey. Leading players: Colin Friels (Richard Somers), Judy
Davis (Harriet Somers), John Walton (Jack Callcott), Julie Nihill (Vickie Callcott), Hugh Keays-Byrne (Kangaroo), Peter Hehir (Jaz), Peter Cummins (Willie
Struthers). Color. 105 mins. Cineplex Odeon Films. Vestron Video.

Lady Chatterley's Lover (U.K./France, 1981). Directed by Just Jaeckin. Screenplay by
Just Jaeckin and Christopher Wicking based on an adaptation of the novel by
Marc Behm. Leading players: Sylvia Kristel (Connie), Nicholas Clay (Mellors),
Shane Briant (Clifford), Ann Mitchell (Mrs. Bolton). Color. 105 mins. Cannon
Pictures. RCA/Video Collection.

Lady Chatterley (U.K., 1993). Television serialization. Directed by Ken Russell. Screenplay by Ken Russell and Michael Haggiag. Leading players: Joely Richardson
(Lady Chatterley), Sean Bean (Mellors), James Wilby (Sir Clifford Chatterley),
Shirley Anne Field (Mrs. Bolton). Color. 4 × 55 mins. London Films/Global Arts
for BBCtv. BBC Enterprises Video.

L'Amant de Lady Chatterley (France, 1956). Directed by Marc Allégret. From a stage
play by Gaston Bonheur and Philippe de Rothchild. Leading players: Danielle
Darrieux (Lady Chatterley), Erno Crisi (Mellors), Leo Genn (Sir Clifford). Black
and white. 89 mins. Columbia. *NV*

(*Young Lady Chatterley* [United States, 1976] and *Young Lady Chatterley* 2 [United
States, 1984], both directed by Alan Roberts, are soft-porn movies that bear no direct
relationship to Lawrence's novel and merely exploit the notoriety of the title.)

The Plumed Serpent. There seems to have been at least one attempt to produce a film
of this novel, though nothing has ever actually materialized. *Literature/Film
Quarterly* 1 (January 1973): 11 and 29, and *DHL Review* 4 (Summer 1971) both
refer to a project with Christopher Miles as director.

The Rainbow (U.K., 1988). Directed and produced by Ken Russell. Screenplay by Ken
and Vivian Russell. Leading players: Sammi Davis (Ursula Brangwen), Paul
McGann (Anton Skrebensky), Amanda Donohoe (Winifred Inger), Christopher

Gable (Will Brangwen), David Hemmings (Uncle Henry [Uncle Tom in the novel]), Glenda Jackson (Anna Brangwen), Dudley Sutton (MacAllister), Jim Carter (head teacher). Color. 104 mins. Vestron Pictures. First Independent Video/ Sony Music Operations Video.

The Rainbow (U.K., 1988). Television serialization. Directed by Stuart Burge. Screenplay by Anne Devlin. Produced by Christopher Barr. Leading players: Imogen Stubbs (Ursula Brangwen), Tom Bell (Tom Brangwen), Kate Buffery (Winifred Inger), Jon Finch (Uncle Tom), Martin Wenner (Anton Skrebensky), Jane Gurnett (Anna Brangwen), Colin Tarrant (Will Brangwen), Clare Holman (Gudrun Brangwen). Color. 3 × 55 mins; retransmitted in 1993, 2 × 80 mins. BBCtv. *NV*

The Rocking-Horse Winner (U.K., 1949). Directed and screenplay by Anthony Pelissier. Leading players: Valerie Hobson (Hester Grahame), Hugh Sinclair (Richard Grahame), Ronald Squire (Oscar), John Howard Davies (Paul), John Mills (Bassett). Black and white. 91 mins. Two Cities Films. Video Collection.

The Rocking-Horse Winner (U.K., 1977). Adapted for television by Julian Bond. Directed by Peter Medak. Leading players: Kenneth More, Angela Thorne, Peter Cellier. Harlech Television. 30 mins.

The Rocking-Horse Winner (United States, 1977). Film version designed for educational purposes, with Kenneth More as sole performer. Color. 30 mins. Learning Corporation of America (1350 Avenue of the Americas, New York 10019).

The Rocking-Horse Winner (U.K., 1982). Adapted by Howard Schuman. Directed by Robert Bierman. Leading players: Eleanor David (Mrs. Grahame (in the story, Hester, Paul's mother)), Charles Hathorn (Paul), Charles Keating (Uncle Oscar), Gabriel Byrne (Bassett). Bierman More O'Ferrall/Paramount Pictures. 33 mins.

Sons and Lovers (U.K., 1960). Directed by Jack Cardiff. Screenplay by Gavin Lambert and T.E.B. Clarke. Produced by Jerry Wald. Leading players: Dean Stockwell (Paul Morel), Trevor Howard (Walter Morel), Wendy Hiller (Gertrude Morel), Heather Sears (Miriam), Mary Ure (Clara Dawes), William Lucas (William Morel), Donald Pleasence (Mr. Pappleworth). Black and white. 103 mins. Twentieth Century-Fox. *NV*

Sons and Lovers (U.K., 1981). Television serialization. Directed by Stuart Burge. Screenplay by Trevor Griffiths. Leading players: Karl Johnson (Paul Morel), Eileen Atkins (Gertrude Morel), Tom Bell (Walter Morel), Leonie Mellinger (Miriam Leivers), Lynn Dearth (Clara Dawes), Jack Shepherd (Baxter Dawes). Color. 6 × 70 mins. BBCtv. (For the screenplay of this production, with an introduction by Griffiths, see Griffiths [1982] in next section.) *NV*

The Trespasser (U.K., 1980). Adapted for television by Hugh Stoddart. Directed by Colin Gregg. Leading players: Alan Bates (Siegmund), Pauline Moran (Helena). Color. Colin Gregg Films for the *South Bank Show,* London Weekend Television.

The Virgin and the Gipsy (U.K., 1970). Directed by Christopher Miles. Screenplay by Alan Plater. Leading players: Joanna Shimkus (Yvette), Franco Nero (the gipsy), Maurice Denham (Yvette's father), Honor Blackman (Mrs. Fawcett), Mark Burns (Major Eastwood). Color. 92 mins. London Screenplays. *NV*

The Widowing of Mrs. Holroyd (U.K., 1961). Television adaptation. Directed by Claude Watham. Adapted by Ken Taylor. Leading players: Jimmy Ogden (Jack), Jennifer Quarmby (Minnie), Edward Judd (Charlie Holroyd), Paul Daneman (Tom Blackmore), Jennifer Wilson (Lizzie Holroyd), Marion Dawson (Mrs. Holroyd). Black and white. Granada TV Network Production (Television Playhouse Series). *NV*

The Widowing of Mrs. Holroyd (U.K., 1995). Television adaptation. Directed by Katie Mitchell. Leading players: Zoë Wanamaker (Mrs. Holroyd), Stephen Dillane (Tom Blackmore), Colin Firth (Charles Holroyd), Brenda Bruce (Grandmother), Mossie Smith (Clara), Melanie Hill (Laura), Shane Fox (Jack), Lauren Richardson (Minnie), Wayne Foskett (Rigley), Peter Needham (mine manager), Gavin Abbott and Christopher Brand (miners). BBCtv (Performance Series). *NV*

Women in Love (U.K., 1970). Directed by Ken Russell. Produced and screenplay by Larry Kramer. Leading players: Alan Bates (Birkin), Oliver Reed (Gerald), Glenda Jackson (Gudrun), Jennie Linden (Ursula), Vladek Sheybal (Loerke), Richard Heffer (Leitner), Christopher Gable (Tibby), Rachel Gurney (Laura), Eleanor Bron (Hermione). Color. 129 mins. United Artists. Warner Home Video.

Others. Granada Television *DHL Series,* 1965–67: dramatization of sixteen short stories. Produced by Margaret Morris (casting director for *The Widowing of Mrs. Holroyd* [1961], as earlier). The production team included Ken Taylor and Claude Whatham (also involved in *The Widowing* adaptation). The scripts are available in the Nottingham County Library Lawrence collection (two BBC television scripts are also available relating to dramatizations, by Simon Gray, of ''Samson and Delilah'' and ''The Princess''). See Sheila M. Cook. *DHL: A Finding List.* 2d ed. West Bridgford, Nottingham: Nottinghamshire County Council, 1980, p. 27.

Biographical Films

Coming Through (U.K., 1986). Directed by Peter Barber-Fleming. Screenplay by Alan Plater. Leading players: Kenneth Branagh (DHL), Helen Mirren (Frieda), Alison Steadman (Kate), Philip Martin Brown (David). Color. 78 mins. Central Independent Television. Video: Futuristic Entertainment.

D. H. Lawrence in Taos (United States, 1970). Documentary film, written and directed by Peter Davis. Color. 40 mins. 16mm. Contemporary Films/McGraw-Hill (McGraw Hill Films, 1221 Avenue of the Americas, New York 10020).

The Priest of Love (U.K., 1980). Directed by Christopher Miles. Screenplay by Alan Plater based on Harry T. Moore's biography of the same title (1974). Leading players: Ian McKellen (DHL), Janet Suzman (Frieda Lawrence), Ava Gardner (Mabel Dodge Luhan), Penelope Keith (the Honorable Dorothy Brett), Jorge Rivera (Tony Luhan), Mauricio Merli (Angelo Ravagli), James Faulkner (Aldous Huxley), Sir John Gielgud (Herbert G. Muskett), Sarah Miles. Color. 125 mins. (Reissued in 1985 at 135 mins.) Home Video Holdings/Channel 5 Video.

BIBLIOGRAPHIES, REVIEWS, AND CRITICAL STUDIES

General

Amette, Jacques-Pierre. "The Works of Lawrence Adapted for the Cinema." *La Nouvelle Revue Française* (February 1971): 108–9.

Clancy, Jack. "The Film and the Book: DHL and Joseph Heller on the Screen." *Meanjin* 30 (March 1971): 96–101.

Cook, Sheila M. *DHL: A Finding List.* 2d ed. Nottingham: Nottinghamshire County Council, 1980, Section E, pp. 27–29.

Cowan, James C. "Lawrence and the Movies: *The Lost Girl* and After." In his *DHL and the Trembling Balance.* University Park: Pennsylvania State University Press, 1990, pp. 95–114.

Crump, G. B. "Lawrence and the *Literature/Film Quarterly.*" *DHL Review* 6 (Fall 1973): 326–32.

Davies, Rosemary Reeves. "DHL and the Media: The Impact of Trigant Burrow on Lawrence's Social Thinking." *Studies in the Humanities* 11, no. 2 (1984): 33–41.

Denby, David, ed. *Film 70/71: An Anthology by the National Society of Film Critics.* New York: Simon and Schuster, 1971.

Gerard, David. "Films and Sound Recordings Relating to Lawrence." In *A DHL Handbook.* Edited by Keith Sagar. Manchester: Manchester University Press, 1982, pp. 449–54.

Gontarski, S. E. "Filming Lawrence." *Modernist Studies* 4 (1982): 87–95.

Jackson, Dennis. "A Select Bibliography, 1907–79." In *A DHL Handbook.* Edited by Keith Sagar. Manchester: Manchester University Press, 1982, pp. 1–58 (Section 9, "Films," pp. 57–58).

Klein, Michael, and Gillian Parker. *The English Novel and the Movies.* New York: Ungar, 1981, pp. 235–78. (Four essays, cited separately in next section under DeNitto [*Sons and Lovers*], Gomez [*Women in Love*], Gontarski [*The Virgin and the Gipsy*], and Hanlon [*L'Amant de Lady Chatterley*].)

Literature/Film Quarterly 1 (January 1973): DHL Special Number.

Moore, Harry T. "DHL and the Flicks." *Literature/Film Quarterly* 1 (January 1973): 3–11.

Phillips, Gene D. "Sexual Ideas in the Films of DHL." *Sexual Behavior* 1 (June 1971): 10–16.

Phillips, Jill M. "The Cinema and DHL." In her *DHL: A Review of the Biographies and Criticism.* New York: Gordon Press, 1978, pp. 155–57.

Pinion, F. B. *A DHL Companion.* London: Macmillan, 1978, p. 306 ("Lawrence Films").

Semeiks, Joanna G. "Sex, Lawrence, and Videotape." *Journal of Popular Culture* 25, no. 4 (Spring 1992): 143–52.

Sinyard, N. "Another Fine Mess: DHL and Thomas Hardy on Film." In his *Filming Literature: The Art of Screen Adaptation.* London: Croom Helm, 1986, pp. 45–54.

Stacy, Paul H. "Lawrence and Movies: A Postscript." *Literature/Film Quarterly* 2 (Winter 1974): 93–95. (Response to special Lawrence issue of this journal.)

Tarratt, Margaret. "An Obscene Undertaking." *Films and Filming* 17, no. 2 (November 1970): 26–30. (On five Lawrence films: *The Rocking-Horse Winner, L'Amant de Lady Chatterley, Sons and Lovers, The Fox, Women in Love.*)

Taylor, Neil. "A Woman's Love: DHL on Film." In *Novel Images: Literature in Performance.* Edited by Peter Reynolds. London: Routledge, 1993, pp. 105–21.

Williams, Linda Ruth. *Sex in the Head: Visions of Femininity and Film in DHL.* Hemel Hempstead, Hertfordshire: Harvester Wheatsheaf, 1993.

Individual Films and Television Adaptations

"The Captain's Doll" (1983)

Hutchinson, Tom. "A Man and Two Women." *Radio Times* (5–11 February 1983): 70–72.

"Coming Through" (1986)

Ross, Harris. "Lawrence Domesticated: A Review of *Coming Through.*" *DHL Review* 18 (Spring 1985–86): 75–77.

"The Fox" (1968)

Crump, G. B. "*The Fox* on Film." *DHL Review* 1 (Fall 1968): 238–44.

Fitzsimons, Carmel. "Return of the Star Who Shocked Birmingham." *Guardian* (13 October 1992). (On Anne Heywood's performance as March, which "set a record for sexual versatility.")

Gontarski, S. E. "Mark Rydell and the Filming of *The Fox:* An Interview with S. E. Gontarski." *Modernist Studies* 4 (1982): 96–104.

Kael, Pauline. "Review of *The Fox.*" In her *Going Steady.* Boston: Little, Brown, 1970, pp. 29–35.

Mellen, Joan. "Outfoxing Lawrence: Novella into Film." *Literature/Film Quarterly* 1 (January 1973): 17–27. (Reprinted in her *Women and Their Sexuality in the New Film.* New York: Horizon Press, 1973, pp. 216–28.)

Sobchack, T. "*The Fox:* The Film and the Novel." *Western Humanities Review* 23 (Winter 1969)): 73–78.

"Kangaroo" (1986)

Peek, Andrew. "Tim Burstall's *Kangaroo.*" *Westerly* 25 (1980): 39–42.

Ross, Harris. "*Kangaroo:* Australian Filmmakers Watching Lawrence Watching Australia." *DHL Review* 19 (Spring 1987): 93–101.

"Lady Chatterley's Lover"

L'Amant de Lady Chatterley (1956)

Hanlon, Lindley. "*Lady Chatterley's Lover* (1928), DHL, Marc Allegret, 1955: Sensuality and Simplification." In *The English Novel and the Movies.* Edited by Michael Klein and Gillian Parker. New York: Ungar, 1981, pp. 268–78.

Scott, James F. "The Emasculation of *Lady Chatterley's Lover.*" *Literature/Film Quarterly* 1 (January 1973): 37–45.

Lady Chatterley (1993)

Hebert, Hugh. "Gentlemen Retired Hurt." *Guardian* (June 1993): 8.

Hildred, Stafford. "It's All Bed and Bored." *Daily Star* (7 June 1993).

James, Brian. "No Way to Treat a Lady." *Radio Times* (5–11 June 1993): 26–29. (Page 27 features an interview, by Rupert Smith, with the actor who plays Mellors: "Sean Bean: A Lover's Guide.")

King, Jackie, and Nicky Pellegrino. "I Had a Joely Good Time!" *TV Quick* (5–11 June 1993).

O'Kelly, Lisa. "Bad Taste, Bad Sex, Bad Film." *Observer* (6 June 1993).

Parkin, Jill. "Ken Rustles Up Nasty Serial Sex." *Daily Express* (16 June 1993): 9.

Smith, Giles. "Horse Play." *Independent* (7 June 1993): 10.

Truss, Lynne. "Axles, Elbows and the Promise of Woodland Games." *Times* (7 June 1993): 33.

Worthen, John. "Coal Comfort, Tame Sex." *Times Literary Supplement* (2 July 1993): 19.

"The Rainbow"

Ken Russell (1988)

Crump, G. B. "Lawrence's *Rainbow* and Russell's *Rainbow.*" *DHL Review* 21 (1989): 187–201.

Fuller, G. "Next of Ken." *Film Comment* 25 (May–June 1989).

Kroll, Jack. [Review] *Newsweek* (8 May 1989).

Richards, Bernard. See next list.

Russell, Ken. *A British Picture.* London: Heinemann, 1989.

Travers, Peter. [Review] *Rolling Stone* (1 June 1989).

Stuart Burge (1988)

Dugdale, John. "Woman in Love." *Listener* (18 August 1988): 8–9.

Gerrard, Christine, and Imogen Stubbs. "The Actress and Her Roles." *English Review* 1 (February 1991): 5–10.

Harper, Howard. "The BBC Television Serialization of *The Rainbow.*" *DHL Review* 21 (1989): 202–7.

Richards, Bernard. "*The Rainbow* on Film and Television." *English Review* 1 (February 1991): 10–12.

"The Rocking-Horse Winner" (1949)

Barrett, Gerald R., and Thomas L. Erskine, eds. *From Fiction to Film: DHL's "The Rocking-Horse Winner."* Encino and Belmont, Calif.: Dickenson, 1974.

Becker, Henry, III. "*The Rocking-Horse Winner:* Film as Parable." *Literature/Film Quarterly* 1 (January 1973): 55–63. (Reprinted in Barrett and Erskine, pp. 204–13.)

Goldstein, R. M. "The Rocking-Horse Winner" *Film News* 34 (January–February 1977): 32.

Marcus, Fred. "From Story to Screen." *Media and Methods* 14 (December 1977): 56–58.

"Sons and Lovers"

(1960)

Baldanza, Frank. *"Sons and Lovers:* Novel to Film as a Record of Cultural Growth."
    Literature/Film Quarterly 1 (January 1973): 64–70.

DeNitto, Dennis. *"Sons and Lovers:* All Passion Spent." In *The English Novel and the
    Movies.* Edited by Michael Klein and Gillian Parker. New York: Ungar, 1981, pp.
    235–47.

Gillett, John. *"Sons and Lovers."* *Film Quarterly* 14 (Fall 1960): 41–42.

(1981)

Griffiths, Trevor. *"Sons and Lovers": Trevor Griffiths' Screenplay of the Novel by DHL.*
    Nottingham: Spokesman, 1982. "Introduction" by Griffiths, pp. 7–12. (A shortened
    version of this appeared as an article in *Radio Times* [10–16 January 1981]: 84–86.)

Hill, John. *Sex, Class and Realism: British Cinema 1956–1963.* London: British Film
    Institute, 1986, pp. 158–63.

Poole, Mike. "The Classic Gets Some Class." *Time Out* (30 January–5 February 1981):
    16.

———. "Sons and Good Friends." *Time Out* (27 February–5 March 1981): 58.

Poole, Mike, and John Wyver. *Powerplays: Trevor Griffiths in Television.* London: Brit-
    ish Film Institute, 1984, pp. 140–50, passim.

Twentieth Century-Fox. *DHL's "Sons and Lovers": Exhibitors' Campaign Manual.*
    (Press book of the film.) Unpublished, 1960.

"The Virgin and the Gipsy" (1970)

Alpert, Hollis. "Up the Rebels." *Saturday Review* (25 July 1970): 37.

Crump, G. B. "Gopher Prairie or Papplewick?: *The Virgin and the Gipsy* as Film." *DHL
    Review* 4 (Summer 1971): 142–53.

Gilliat, Penelope. "This England, This Past." *New Yorker* (4 July 1970).

Gontarski, S. E. "An English Watercolor." In *The English Novel and the Movies.* Edited
    by Michael Klein and Gillian Parker. New York: Ungar, 1981, pp. 257–67.

———. "Christopher Miles on His Making of *The Virgin and the Gipsy."* *Literature/
    Film Quarterly* 11 (1983): 249–56.

Kauffman, Stanley. *"The Virgin and the Gipsy."* *New Republic* (1 August 1970).

Smith, Julian. "Vision and Revision: *The Virgin and the Gipsy* as Film." *Literature/
    Film Quarterly* 1 (January 1973): 28–36.

(Further reviews of this film can be found in *Newsweek* [13 July 1970], *Time* [13 July
1970], and *Vogue* [July 1970].)

"The Widowing of Mrs. Holroyd"

Sagar, Keith, and Sylvia Sklar. "Major Productions of Lawrence's Plays." In *A DHL
    Handbook.* Edited by Keith Sagar. Manchester: Manchester University Press,
    1982, pp. 283–328 (300–301).

Times (24 March 1961): 18. [Review].

"Women in Love" (1970)

Baxter, John. *An Appalling Talent: Ken Russell.* London: Michael Joseph, 1973.

Blanchard, Margaret. "Men in Charge: A Review of *Women in Love.*" *Women: A Journal of Liberation* (Fall 1970): 31–32.

Boyum, Joy Gould. *Double Exposure: Fiction into Film.* New York: Penguin, 1985.

Crump, G. B. "*Women in Love:* Novel and Film." *DHL Review* 4 (Spring 1971): 28–41.

Farber, Stephen. "*Women in Love.*" *Hudson Review* 23 (Summer 1970): 321–26.

Gomez, Joseph A. "*Women in Love:* Novel into Film." In his *Ken Russell: The Adaptor as Creator.* London: Frederick Muller, 1976, pp. 78–95.

————. "*Women in Love* 1920, DHL; Ken Russell, 1969: Russell's Images of Lawrence's Vision." In *The English Novel and the Movies.* Edited by Michael Klein and Gillian Parker. New York: Ungar, 1981, pp. 248–56.

Hamilton, Jack. "*Women in Love.*" *Look Magazine* 34 (February 24 1970): 32–37.

Hanke, Ken. *Ken Russell's Films.* Metuchen, N.J.: Scarecrow Press, 1984.

Kael, Pauline. "Lust for 'Art.' " *New Yorker* (28 March 1970): 97–101.

Kauffman, Stanley. "*Women in Love.*" *New Republic* (18 April 1970).

Knight, Arthur. "Liberated Classics." *Saturday Review* (21 March 1970): 50.

Knoll, Robert F. "*Women in Love.*" *Film Heritage* 6 (Summer 1971): 1–6.

Reed, Rex. "Rex Reed at the Movies." *Holiday* 47 (June 1970): 21. (Reprinted in his *Big Screen, Little Screen.* New York: Macmillan, 1971, pp. 282–83.)

Russell, Ken. *A British Picture.* London: Heinemann, 1989.

Simon, John Ivan. *Movies into Film: Film Criticism 1967–70.* New York: Dial Press, 1971, 57–62.

Sirkin, Elliott. "*Women in Love.*" *Film Quarterly* 24 (Fall 1970): 43–47.

Trevelyan, John. *What the Censor Saw.* London: Michael Joseph, 1972.

United Artists. "*Women in Love:* Film Production Notes." United Artists Corporation, 1969.

Warga, Wayne. "Kramer Scripts Thinking Man's *Women in Love.*" *Los Angeles Times* (3 May 1970): *Calendar Magazine.*

Weightman, J. "Trifling with the Dead." *Encounter* 34 (January 1970): 50–53.

Zambrano, Ann Laura. "*Women in Love:* Counterpoint on Film." *Literature/Film Quarterly* 1 (January 1973): 46–54.

(Further reviews of this film can be found in *America* [25 April 1970], *Christian Century* [16 September 1970], *Commonweal* [15 May 1970], *Holiday* [June 1970], *Life* [6 March 1970], *Mademoiselle* [May 1970], *Newsweek* [6 April 1970], *Time* [13 April 1970], *Vogue* [March 1970].)

GENERAL WORKS ON LITERATURE AND ADAPTATION

The study of literature and adaptation has become a major field of academic scholarship in its own right and one that now easily rivals the Lawrence "industry" in terms of output; it would therefore be impractical to provide a full listing here. However, the following is a brief guide to some of the major bibliographies and to a range of other titles that might serve as useful points of entry into the field.

Allen, Douglas, and Michael Voysey. "Classic Serials." *Journal of the Society of Film and Television Arts* 20 (1965): 2–3.

Beja, Morris. *Film and Literature: An Introduction.* New York: Longman, 1979.

Bluestone, George. *Novels into Film.* Baltimore: Johns Hopkins University Press, 1957.

Boyum, Joy Gould. *Double Exposure: Fiction into Film.* New York: Penguin, 1985.

Chatman, Seymour. *Story and Discourse: Narrative Structure in Fiction and Film.* Ithaca, N.Y., and London: Cornell University Press, 1978.

———. *Coming to Terms: The Rhetoric of Narrative in Fiction and Film.* Ithaca, N.Y., and London: Cornell University Press, 1990.

Cohen, Keith. *Film and Fiction: The Dynamics of Exchange.* New Haven, Conn.: Yale University Press, 1979.

Daisne, John. *A Filmographic Dictionary of World Literature.* Ghent: Story-Scientia, 1971.

Ellis, John. "The Literary Adaptation: An Introduction." *Screen* 23, no. 1 (May–June 1982): 3–5.

Ferlita, Ernest, and John R. May. *Film Odyssey.* New York: Paulist Press, 1976.

Geduld, Harry M., ed. *Authors on Film.* Bloomington: Indiana University Press, 1972.

Harrington, John, ed. *Film and/as Literature.* Englewood Cliffs, N.J.: Prentice-Hall, 1977.

Hill, John. *Sex, Class and Realism: British Cinema 1956–1963.* London: British Film Institute, 1986.

Jinks, William. *The Celluloid Literature.* 2d ed. Beverly Hills, Calif.: Glencoe Press, 1974.

Kerr, Paul. "The Origins of the Mini-Series." *Broadcast* (12 March 1979).

———. "Classic Serials: To Be Continued." *Screen* 23, no. 1 (May–June 1982): 6–19.

Klein, Michael, and Gillian Parker, eds. *The English Novel and the Movies.* New York: Frederick Ungar, 1981.

Lindell, Richard L. "Literature/Film Bibliography." *Literature/Film Quarterly* 8 (1980): 269–76.

Lodge, David. "Adapting *Nice Work* for Television." In *Novel Images: Literature as Performance.* Edited by Peter Reynolds. London: Routledge, 1993, pp. 191–203.

McConnell, Frank. *Storytelling and Mythmaking.* New York and Oxford: Oxford University Press, 1979.

McDougal, Stuart Y. *Made into Movies: From Literature to Film.* New York: Holt, 1985.

Orr, John, and Colin Nicholson. *Cinema and Fiction: New Modes of Adapting 1950–1990.* Edinburgh: Edinburgh University Press, 1993.

Poole, Mike. "Englishness for Export." *Time Out* (7–13 March 1980): 13.

Reynolds, Peter, ed. *Novel Images: Literature in Performance.* London: Routledge, 1993.

Ross, Harris. *Film as Literature, Literature as Film: An Introduction to and Bibliography of Film's Relationship to Literature.* New York: Greenwood, 1987.

Screen 23, no. 1 (May–June 1982). Special issue on literary adaptation.

Simon, John. *Movies into Film.* New York: Dial Press, 1971.

Sinyard, Neil. *Filming Literature: The Art of Screen Adaptation.* London: Croom Helm, 1986.

Spiegel, Alan. *Fiction and the Camera Eye: Visual Consciousness in Film and the Modern Novel.* Charlottesville: University Press of Virginia, 1976.

Wagner, Geoffrey. *The Novel and the Cinema.* Rutherford, N.J.: Fairleigh Dickinson University Press, 1975.

Welch, Jeffrey Egan. *Literature and Film: An Annotated Bibliography, 1909–1977.* New York: Garland, 1981.

Wicks, Ulrich. "Literature/Film: A Bibliography." *Literature/Film Quarterly* 6 (1978): 135–43.

Widdowson, Peter. *Hardy in History: A Study in Literary Sociology.* London: Routledge, 1989.

Woolf, Virginia. "The Cinema." In her *Collected Essays.* 4 vols. London: Hogarth Press, 1966–67.

CHRONOLOGY 7: CINEMA AND BROADCASTING, BY NIGEL MORRIS

The technical developments listed here indicate key advances in the progress of cinema and broadcasting toward the situation that obtained by the time of Lawrence's death.

The film titles chosen to illustrate this progress inevitably represent only a tiny proportion of the hundreds of films made in this period (many of which—made on unstable stock—are lost forever). However, the selection has been designed with the following aims in mind: to include a range of films regarded as innovative either aesthetically or technically; to indicate the pace of expansion of filmmaking worldwide; to offer a flavor of how films responded to contemporary events and the output of rival companies; and to acknowledge the contributions of influential creative personnel.

The dates of films are accurate to within a year or so but cannot be said to be definitive, as different sources often rely on different dating criteria (e.g., date of completion or date of release, American release or British release).

Film-related aspects of Lawrence's life and works are briefly noted in parentheses where appropriate ("D. H. Lawrence" being abbreviated to DHL throughout).

1885	Eastman Walker Company starts selling paper roll photographic film.
1887	Rev. Hannibal Goodwill submits for patent transparent celluloid roll film: race begins to perfect movie cameras and projectors.
1888	Thomas Edison allegedly witnesses projected sound movie devised by his assistant William Kennedy Laurie Dickson. Emulsion-coated celluloid film promoted by John Carbutt. Kodak box camera introduced.
1890	Edison invents sprocketed film, removing last obstacle in development of movies.
1891	Edison demonstrates kinetoscope, employing horizontal film movement and peephole viewing device.

1893   Edison completes "Black Maria" studio and starts shooting kinetoscope films.

1894   First kinetoscope parlors in New York, Paris, and London. Disc gramophone demonstrated.

1895   Several public events recorded using various competing motion picture systems. Numerous patent applications. Demonstrations to learned societies in Belgium, Britain, France, Germany, and United States. Auguste and Louis Lumière open world's first public cinema in Paris (28 December). Marconi demonstrates wireless telegraphy. FILMS: *L'Arrivée d'un train en gare de La Ciotat* (Lumière, France): allegedly causes audiences to run from seats at sight of approaching locomotive. *L'Arroseur arrosé* (Lumière, France): brief, single-shot, staged comedy.

1896   Robert William Paul shows hand-colored film in London. Parisian religious activists form La Service des Projections Lumineuses de la Maison de la Bonne Presse, which starts promoting certain films for educational merit and denouncing immorality in sectors of industry, especially Pathé company. Lumière cinematographe opens in Bombay. FILMS: *The Irwin-Rice Kiss* (Edison, United States).

1897   140 killed in fire caused by projector in Paris cinema. Recurrence of such fires results in worldwide concerns about movie house safety. Queen Victoria's Diamond Jubilee parade in London filmed by numerous competing companies. Edison granted patent for motion picture camera. H. Insee in Berlin patents natural color process using alternating filters.

1898   First war film correspondents send footage from Cuba (Spanish-American War). Edison begins filing patents suits against rivals.

1899   Amateur movie system introduced, using substandard gauge film. Magnetic recording invented. FILMS: *L'Affaire Dreyfus* (George Méliès, France). *The Kiss in the Tunnel* (G. A. Smith, U.K.). *Shooting a Boer Spy* (Sir Robert Ashe/R. W. Paul, U.K.). *The Jeffries-Sharkey Fight* (United States).

1900   Impressive technological advances at Paris Exhibition include giant screen, 360-degree panorama using ten projectors and hand-colored 70mm film, and synchronized disc sound. R. A. Fessenden transmits human voice by radio in United States. FILMS: *Soldiers of the Cross* (Joseph Perry/Salvation Army, Australia). *Jeanne d'Arc* (Méliès, France). *The Explosion of a Motor Car* (Cecil Hepworth, U.K.). *The Last Days of Pompeii* (Paul, U.K.). *Chinese Massacring Christians* (Sigmund Lubin, United States).

1901   Queen Victoria's funeral screened worldwide. Wireless telegraphy used at sea. Edison wins patents actions against rivals. Radio signals sent between Europe and America. FILMS: *The Big Swallow* (James Williamson, U.K.). *Fire!* (Williamson, U.K.). *Jack and the Beanstalk* (Edwin S. Porter, United States). *Mrs. Nation and Her Hatchet Brigade* (Lubin, United States).

1902   Méliès' *Voyage to the Moon,* studio-made and employing extensive special effects, consolidates fiction/fantasy film tradition; contrasts with documentary (actuality or reconstruction) tendency already prevalent, which develops into realist tradition. Caruso's first recordings. Marconi sends telegraphic message from North America to King Edward VII in U.K. FILMS: *Vie et Passion de N. S. Jesus Christ* (Lucien Monguet, Ferdinand Zecca/Pathé, France). *Appointment by Telephone* (Porter, United States).

1903   Porter's *The Great Train Robbery* (made for Edison) inaugurates Western genre and is longest film yet (twelve minutes). World's first purpose-built cinema opens in Tokyo. New York–London news service begins, using Marconi wireless telegraph. FILMS: *A Message from Mars* (W. F. Brown, New Zealand). *The Great City Fire* (Warwick, U.K.). *Mary Jane's Mishap or Don't Fool with the Paraffin* (Smith, U.K.). *The Life of an American Fireman* (Porter, United States).

1904   John Fleming announces invention of radio valve.

1905   Massachusetts passes safety legislation for motion picture theaters. Pittsburgh entrepreneur converts store into permanent movie theater and calls it Nickelodeon; idea spreads rapidly, beginning move from vaudeville programs and penny arcade peepshows. Neon signs introduced. FILMS: *Revolution en Russie* (Monguet/Pathé, France). *Charles Peace* (W. R. Haggar, U.K.). *The Life of Charles Peace* (Frank Mottershaw/Sheffield, U.K.). *Mutiny on a Russian Battleship* (Alfred Collins, U.K.). *Rescued by Rover* (Lewin Fitzhamon/Hepworth, U.K.).

1906   Regular daily newsreel in London's Empire Theatre.

1907   Chicago City Council introduces first regulated film censorship against obscenity and immorality. Balham Empire is first British theater entirely devoted to movies (situated only a few minutes by bus from Croydon, where DHL lived 1908–11). Several mechanical sound synchronization systems introduced. Marconi opens public wireless service across Atlantic. News photograph transmitted by cable from Paris to London. FILMS: Cinematophone Singing Pictures (U.K.).

1908   ''Daylight projection'' experimented with for sake for morality, obviating need to darken cinemas. New York mayor orders all nickelodeons in city closed, allegedly for public safety; immediate injunction reopens them. Estimated 8,000 nickelodeons in United States. Pathé inaugurates regular newsreels. Eastman Kodak introduces slow-burning acetate film (''Safety Film''), but initial inferiority and high cost restrict it mainly to amateur use until 1940s. FILMS: *Romeo and Juliet* (Gaumont, U.K.). *A Christmas Carol* (Essanay, United States). *Julius Caesar* (Vitagraph, United States); although not first literary adaptations, these represent increasing bids for respectability and wealthier middle-class audiences.

1909   James Joyce initiates and opens Ireland's first permanent cinema. First multireel films. Film companies begin settling permanently in California. Cinematograph Films Act introduces movie theater safety regulations in U.K. and facilitates censorship. FILMS: *Le Dernier Requiem de Mozart* (E. Arnaud/Gaumont, France). *Don Juan heiratet* (Heinrich Bolten-Baeckers/Duskes, Germany). *Beatrice Cenci* (Mario Caserini, Italy). *Carmen* (Gerolamo Lo Savio/Film d'Arte Italia). *Giulio Cesare* (Giovanni Pastrone, Italy). *Macbeth* (Mario Caserini, Italy). *Otello* (Lo Savio, Italy). *Salomé Mad* (Theo Bouwmeester/Hepworth, U.K.). *Salomé Mad* (A. E. Coleby/Cricks and Martin, U.K.). *The Bride of Lammermoor, King Lear, The Life of George Washington, The Life of Moses, A Midsummer Night's Dream, Napoleon, the Man of Destiny* (all Vitagraph, United States).

1910   U.K. Cinematograph Act becomes law. Advertising campaign reintroduces "The Biograph Girl" (previously unnamed heroine of that studio's movies) as Florence Lawrence, apparently in response to enormous public interest; begins U.S. star system. (Previously, actors regarded film work as slumming and were happy to remain anonymous; this suited producers, who paid low wages.) Violent outrage over film showing black boxer Jack Johnson (first black world heavyweight champion, 1908) defeating Jim Jeffries; leads to U.S. ban. Talented director Francis Boggs murdered. Caruso broadcast live by wireless from New York Metropolitan Opera House. Marconi transatlantic wireless service extended from Ireland to London and from Nova Scotia to Canadian interior. FILMS: *Hamlet* (August Blom, Denmark). *The Idiot* (Pyotr Chardynin, Russia). *Tilly the Tomboy* series (Fitzhamon, U.K.).

1911   Picture postcards of stars sold in United States. First fan magazines published in United States. Mack Sennett starts Keystone Comedies. Many permanent studios now in southern California, including first in Hollywood. Boxers beginning to exploit fame and contacts with showmen to start careers as film stars. FILMS: *Les Hallucinations du Baron de Munchausen* (Méliès, France). *Les Misérables* (Albert Capellani, France). *Henry VIII* (Will Barker, U.K.). *Richard III* (Frank Benson, U.K.). *The Lonesdale Operator* (D. W. Griffith, United States).

1912   Famous Players in Famous Plays Company set up; distributes *Queen Elizabeth,* starring Sarah Bernhardt (Louis Mercanton, France–U.K.). Technicolor Company founded. FILMS: *Faust* (Antonin Pech, Czechoslovakia). *A la conquête du pôle* (Méliès, France). *Agent No. 13* (Alberto Eriksen, Norway). *Oliver Twist* (Thomas Bentley: first U.K. feature film). *The Prisoner of Zenda* (Porter, United States).

1913   (*Sons and Lovers:* Paul and Clara spend a few minutes in the cinematograph, hold hands for first time in dark. Narrator refers to "dithering" and "dancing" pictures [347].) British Board of Film Censors starts work. Estimates include 60,000 movie theaters worldwide; 15,700 in United States; 3,500 in U.K.; 400 in London; U.S. daily attendance 5 million. Scott's Antarctic expedition filmed. FILMS: *Tercentenary of the Rule of the House of Romanov (1613–1913)* (Nikolai Larin and Alexander Uralski, Russia). *Vampyren* (Mauritz Stiller, Sweden). *Ivanhoe* (Leedham Bantock, U.K.). Four Dickens adaptations and two films about David Garrick (U.K.). *Ivanhoe* (Herbert Brenon, United States). *The Squaw Man* (Cecil B. DeMille and Oscar Apfel, United States).

1914   First two Chaplin releases; tramp costume appears in second, *Kid Auto Races at Venice*. Vitagraph Theater on Broadway opens: first New York luxury cinema. Estimated 14,000 five-cent movie theaters in United States, selling over 30 million tickets weekly. First Kodachrome color process perfected. Extensive newsreel coverage of World War I (1914–18). FILMS: *Anna Karenina* (Vladimir Gardin, Russia). *The German Spy Peril* (Barker, U.K.). *The Virginian* (DeMille, United States).

1915   D. W. Griffith institutionalizes close-up in *Birth of a Nation* (United States). Vachel Lindsay's book *The Art of the Moving Picture* argues for centrality of cinema among arts. FILMS: *The Picture of Dorian Gray* (Vsevolod Emilievich Meyerhold, Russia). *War and Peace* (Vladimir Gardin, Russia).

1916   FILMS: *The Battle of the Somme* (Geoffrey Malins and J. B. McDowell, U.K.). *Intolerance* (Griffith, United States). Eight Chaplin releases (United States).

1917   First two-color Technicolor film. Chaplin world's highest-paid employee with yearly salary of $1 million; soon equaled by Mary Pickford. Legislation in United States frees film industry from problems with Motion Picture Patents Company (huge trust established by Edison to force smaller rivals out of business). Sixteen frames per second decreed as standard by Society of Motion Picture Engineers; widely ignored until speed standardizes at twenty-four frames per second with introduction of sound in 1928. FILMS: *The Revolutionary* (Evgeni Bauer, Russia). *Cleopatra* (J. Gordon Edwards, United States). *The Immigrant* (Chaplin, United States).

1918   Cinematograph Act introduces British censorship and regulation model into India. FILMS: *Carmen* (Ernst Lubitsch, Germany). *Dombey and Son* (Maurice Elvey, U.K.). *Shoulder Arms* (Chaplin, United States: first comedy feature). *The Squaw Man* (remake, DeMille, United States). *Engineer Prite's Project* (Lev Kuleshov, USSR).

1919   ("Tickets Please" [written 1918]: couple visit fairground cinema, intermittently plunged into darkness when projection fails: "[A] wild whooping, and a loud smacking of simulated kisses" follow, during which main characters prepare to kiss before being frustrated by sudden restoration of light [*England, My England* 38].) Cinema's most powerful creative figures— Chaplin, Pickford, Griffith, and Douglas Fairbanks—form United Artists to control distribution of their own films. First *Felix the Cat* cartoons. Soviet cinema nationalized, and film schools established, inaugurating golden age of experimental, revolutionary filmmaking. FILMS: *The Cabinet of Dr. Caligari* (Robert Wiene, Germany). Three films by Sandor (later Alexander) Korda (Hungary). *Broken Blossoms* (Griffith, United States). *Why Change Your Wife?* (DeMille, United States).

1920   (*The Lost Girl* equates cinema with commonness, Americanization, and commercial cynicism; poor technical quality of screenings stressed repeatedly, as are rowdiness and vulgar tastes of audiences; several characters compare cinema unfavorably with live acts; nevertheless, style of writing frequently suggests debt to cinema.) Hollywood producing nearly 800 films annually. Chaplin fistfight with Louis B. Mayer in Hollywood hotel dining room. Roscoe "Fatty" Arbuckle charged with murder and rape of Virginia Rappe at Hollywood party. Marconi opens first U.K. public broadcasting station. FILMS: *Erotikon* (Maurice Stiller, Sweden). *Wuthering Heights* (A. V. Bramble, U.K.). *Dr. Jekyll and Mr Hyde* (John S. Robertson, United States). *The Last of the Mohicans* (Clarence Brown and Maurice Tourneur, United States). *The Mark of Zorro* (Fred Niblo, United States).

1921   (*Women in Love* employs arguably cinematic constructions through juxtaposition of points of view.) Rudolph Valentino (former beggar, landscape gardener, dishwasher, waiter, convicted petty thief and blackmailer, taxi driver, dancer, and bit player) catapulted to stardom in *The Four Horsemen of the Apocalypse* (Rex Ingram, United States); women faint during screenings of *The Sheik* (George Melford, United States); Arab designs infiltrate fashion and interior decoration. Arbuckle acquitted; career never recovers. Formation in Paris of Club des Amis du 7me Art (Casa) by leading intellectuals and filmmakers indicates willingness outside English-speaking world to take medium seriously; manifesto includes call for truly national and purely cinematic approach, repudiates literary adaptation. French avantgarde cinema beginning fruitful interaction with artistic and literary experimentation by cubists, futurists, dadaists, and surrealists. FILMS: *Destiny* (Fritz Lang, Germany). *England Returned* (Dhiren Ganguly, India). *The Battle of Jutland* (H. Bruce Woolfe, U.K.). *The Hound of the Baskervilles* (Elvey, U.K.). *The Affairs of Anatol* (DeMille, United States). *The Kid* (Chaplin, United States). *The Prisoner of Zenda* (Rex Ingram, United States). *Hunger* (Gardin and V. I. Pudovkin, USSR).

1922   (September: DHL encounters film crew on Pacific liner. Upset by their behavior, altercates while they jeer at him. Nevertheless, visits San Francisco cinema within two days of landing. Autumn: Lawrences reportedly delighted when $10,000 offered for film rights to *Women in Love:* publisher holds out for double, but offer withdrawn. "Monkey Nuts" [written May 1919]: two soldiers visit circus toward end of World War I; although delighted by spectacle, compare it unfavorably with sensational offerings of cinema [*England, My England* 69]. *Aaron's Rod* satirizes cinema for encouraging false material desires and diminishing capacity for wonder [134–35].) Lenin advises People's Commissar for Education: "Of all the arts, for us cinema is the most important." Hollywood scandals continue with unsolved murder of director William Desmond Taylor, implicating stars Mary Miles Minter and Mabel Normand. Motion Picture Producers and Distributors of America Inc. (MPPDA) founded; President Will H. Hays responsible for visible self-regulation to disarm moral objections by pressure groups to screen representations and off-screen behavior. 16mm agreed as standard gauge for amateur filmmaking. BBC established. FILMS: *Nosferatu* (F. W. Murnau, Germany). *Nanook of the North* (Robert Flaherty, United States). *Kino Pravda* series begins (Dziga Vertov, USSR).

1923   (August: DHL spends month in Los Angeles with artist friends Knud Merrild and Kai Götzsche, who enjoy working on sets for *The Hunchback of Notre Dame* [Wallace Worsley, United States]. Visits studios, meets stars, unimpressed; bored by leading male star; struck by physical beauty ["beyond words"] of rising female star who has read *Women in Love*—but dismissed by DHL as "dumb.") Walt Disney founds studio. Valentino's romantic poems, *Day Dreams,* sell hundreds of thousands. Film actor Wallace Reid dies from morphine addiction. British Board of Film Censors and Home Office debate censorship of *Married Love* (deals with birth control in context of romantic feature film). FILMS: *Raskolnikov* (Wiene, Germany). *The Virgin Queen* (J. Stuart Blackton, U.K.). *The Covered Wagon* (James Cruze, United States). *Safety Last* (Fred Newmeyer and Sam Taylor,

United States); stars Harold Lloyd. *The Ten Commandments* (DeMille, United States).

1924   (Fairbanks in *The Thief of Bagdad* [Raoul Walsh, United States] "thrills" DHL and Frieda; DHL impressed by *The Covered Wagon.*) Hays introduces "The Formula," facilitating voluntary precensorship of controversial scripts. FILMS: *Ballet mécanique* (Fernand Léger, France). *Entr'acte* (René Clair, France). *Greed* (Erich Von Stroheim, United States). *Strike* (Sergei M. Eisenstein, USSR).

1925   ("Art and Morality" bemoans mechanical nature of movie images. *St. Mawr* presents pathetic spectacle of Texas cowboys seduced and diminished by screen image, which they try to emulate [131–32].) Film comedian Max Linder and young wife found dead in Paris hotel room; apparently suicide. Valentino arrested, charged with bigamy. Imperial Airways screen first in-flight movie. The Film Society (London) promotes film as serious artistic and political force and begins film society movement; early members include Alfred Hitchcock. FILMS: *The Gold Rush* (Chaplin, United States). *The Big Parade* (King Vidor, United States). *Battleship Potemkin* (Eisenstein, USSR).

1926   Valentino dies suddenly, aged thirty-one: perforated ulcer; near riot as thousands of women line New York streets for funeral; necrophilic cult develops amid rumors of poisoning by discarded mistress. Laurel and Hardy form permanent partnership. Pudovkin publishes *Film Technique* (USSR). U.K. claims invention of television with demonstration by John Logie Baird. NBC established, New York. FILMS: *Napoleon* (Abel Gance, France): technically and aesthetically innovative epic incorporating triple-screen sequences. *Metropolis* (Lang, Germany). *Secrets of a Soul* (Georg Wilhelm Pabst, Germany): exploration of Freudian theory. *The Lodger* (Hitchcock, U.K.: his first thriller). *Ben Hur* (Niblo, United States): most expensive film to date. *The General* (Buster Keaton, United States). *Moana of the South Seas* (Flaherty, United States): first film described as "documentary."

1927   Hays issues "Don'ts" and "Be Carefuls": bans include nudity, brothels, miscegenation, childbirth, and disrespect to church, state, and family. British International Pictures formed to challenge American monopoly. Indian Cinematograph Committee considers promoting "Empire films" to oppose American dominance. Roxy Theater, New York, opens: 5,920 seats. Fox Movietone start releasing shorts, including regular newsreels and synchronized music and speech. *The Jazz Singer* (Alan Crosland, United States) is first fully synchronized feature incorporating dialogue. BBC begins Empire service (worldwide broadcasting on shortwave). CBS founded. Baird transmits images by cable; demonstrates video disc. FILMS: *The Rose of Pushui* (Hou Yao and Li Minwei, China). *Voyage au Congo* (Marc Allégret, France). *Sword of Penitence* (Yasujiro Ozu, Japan). *Fashions for Women* (Dorothy Arzner, United States). *Flesh and the Devil* (Clarence Brown, United States): stars Greta Garbo. *The King of Kings* (DeMille, United States).

1928   (DHL sees *Ben Hur:* reportedly "nauseated." "In Love" [written 1926]: a
            young couple's engagement almost breaks down when the man starts "try-
            ing to be lovey-dovey" toward his fiancée—he mistakenly believes she
            expects him to behave like Valentino [*The Woman Who Rode Away* 151,
            160]. *Lady Chatterley's Lover:* Mellors blames cinema, among other new
            technologies, for cultural and moral decline [217, 300]; movie theater fea-
            tures prominently in passage delineating hopeless dreariness of English
            Midlands [152]; radio also attacked as banal and vacuous substitute for
            authentic experience [122, 139]. "Sex versus Loveliness" condemns cin-
            ema for promoting superficial and standardized notions of physical beauty.)
            Hollywood studios employ teams of secretaries exclusively to handle stars'
            fan mail. U.K. imposes quota on foreign films exhibited. Televisions on sale
            in United States at seventy-five dollars. Baird demonstrates color television
            and transmits images across Atlantic. FILMS: *Little Match Girl* (Jean Ren-
            oir, France). *Plane Crazy* and *Steamboat Willie* (Disney, United States):
            first Mickey Mouse cartoons. *The Lights of New York* (Bryan Foy, United
            States): first all-dialogue feature. *The Man with a Movie Camera* (Vertov,
            USSR). *October* (Eisenstein, USSR). *Storm over Asia* (Pudovkin, USSR).

1929   (*Pansies* includes several apparent attacks on movies, including "When I
            Went to the Film": condemns audiences deluding themselves into becoming
            aroused by synthetic experiences. "Film Passion" in *Nettles* explicitly sin-
            gles out female audiences for succumbing to hysteria over Valentino.) Silent
            films killed off by talkies. Kodak manufactures 16mm film. Federation of
            Workers' Film Society formed in London to bring politically radical films
            to working-class audiences. FILMS: *Un Chien Andalou* (Luis Bunuel and
            Salvador Dali, France); Bunuel and Dali immediately accepted into surre-
            alist movement after special screening in Paris. *Pandora's Box* (Pabst, Ger-
            many). *Blackmail* (Alfred Hitchcock): first U.K. talkie. *Drifters* (John
            Grierson, U.K.). *The Cocoanuts* (Joseph Santley and Robert Florey, United
            States): first Marx Brothers movie. *The Virginian* (Victor Fleming, United
            States).

1930   MPPDA ratifies "Hays Code." Sound systems standardized by international
            agreement. Fox introduce 70mm large-screen system in New York. Right-
            wing protestors wreck Parisian cinema after screening of Bunuel's *L'Age
            d'or* (subsequently banned). *All Quiet on the Western Front* (Lewis Mile-
            stone, United States) prohibited in Berlin after Nazi protests. Daily televi-
            sion broadcasts begin in Boston. FILMS: *The Blue Angel* (Josef Von
            Sternberg, Germany) and *Morocco* (Von Sternberg, United States): star,
            Marlene Dietrich. *Murder!* (Hitchcock, U.K.). *Little Caesar* (Mervyn
            LeRoy, United States).

1932   (Two years after DHL's death, Frieda engages Harry T. Moore to negotiate
            with Hollywood over adaptations. RKO official opines that, given DHL's
            image, no studio would touch his work.)

PART IV

REFERENCE BIBLIOGRAPHIES

BIBLIOGRAPHY 96: MASTER BIBLIOGRAPHY OF BOOKS AND PAMPHLETS ON LAWRENCE

This bibliography provides full details of any short name-date citations of works on Lawrence used elsewhere in this book (and, in particular, in the abbreviated listings given at the end of the specialized bibliographies). It also represents a comprehensive listing of English-language books and pamphlets on Lawrence up to 1994.

Adelman, Gary. *Snow of Fire: Symbolic Meaning in "The Rainbow" and "Women in Love."* New York and London: Garland, 1991.

Albright, Daniel. *Personality and Impersonality: Lawrence, Woolf, and Mann.* Chicago: University of Chicago Press, 1978, pp. 17–95.

Alcorn, John. *The Nature Novel from Hardy to Lawrence.* London: Macmillan; New York: Columbia University Press, 1977.

Alden, Patricia. *Social Mobility in the English Bildungsroman: Gissing, Hardy, Bennett, and Lawrence.* Ann Arbor, Mich.: UMI Research Press, 1986.

Aldington, Richard. *D. H. Lawrence: An Indiscretion.* Seattle: University of Washington Book Store, 1927.

———. *D. H. Lawrence.* London: Chatto and Windus, 1930. (Revised and enlarged as *D. H. Lawrence: An Appreciation.* Harmondsworth: Penguin Books, 1950.)

———. *D. H. Lawrence: A Complete List of His Works, With a Critical Appreciation.* London: Heinemann, 1935.

———. *Portrait of a Genius, But . . . The Life of D. H. Lawrence.* London: Heinemann, 1950.

Alldritt, Keith. *The Visual Imagination of D. H. Lawrence.* London: Edward Arnold, 1971.

Andrews, W. T., ed. *Critics on D. H. Lawrence.* London: George Allen and Unwin, 1971. (Reviews and critical essays, 1911–60s.)

Arnold, Armin. *D. H. Lawrence and America.* London: Linden Press, 1958.

———. *D. H. Lawrence and German Literature: With Two Hitherto Unknown Essays by D. H. Lawrence.* Montreal: Mansfield Book Mart, H. Heinemann, 1963.

Arrow, John. *J. C. Squire v. D. H. Lawrence.* London: E. Lahr, 1930.

Asai, Masashi. *Fullness of Being: A Study of D. H. Lawrence.* Tokyo: Liber Press, 1992.

Aylwin, A. M. *Notes on D. H. Lawrence's "The Rainbow."* London: Methuen, 1977.

Baker, Paul G. *A Reassessment of D. H. Lawrence's "Aaron's Rod."* Ann Arbor, Mich.: UMI Research Press, 1983.

Balbert, Peter. *D. H. Lawrence and the Psychology of Rhythm: The Meaning of Form in "The Rainbow."* The Hague: Mouton, 1974.

———. *D. H. Lawrence and the Phallic Imagination: Essays on Sexual Identity and Feminist Misreading.* London: Macmillan, 1989.

Balbert, Peter, and Phillip L. Marcus, eds. *D. H. Lawrence: A Centenary Consideration.* Ithaca, N.Y., and London: Cornell University Press, 1985.

Ballin, Michael G., ed. *D. H. Lawrence's "Women in Love": Contexts and Criticism.* Waterloo, Ontario: Wilfrid Laurier University Press, 1980.

Banerjee, Amitava. *D. H. Lawrence's Poetry: Demon Liberated: A Collection of Primary and Secondary Source Material.* London: Macmillan, 1990.

Barrett, Gerald R., and Thomas L. Erskine, eds. *From Fiction to Film: D. H. Lawrence's "The Rocking-Horse Winner."* Encino and Belmont, Calif.: Dickenson, 1974.

Beal, Anthony. *D. H. Lawrence.* Edinburgh: Oliver and Boyd; New York: Grove, 1961.

Becker, George J. *D. H. Lawrence.* New York: Ungar, 1980. (Selective Intro.)

Becket, Fiona. *D. H. Lawrence: The Thinker as Poet.* London and New York: Macmillan, forthcoming, 1996.

Bedient, Calvin. *Architects of the Self: George Eliot, E. M. Forster, and D. H. Lawrence.* Berkeley and London: University of California Press, 1972, pp. 98–195.

Bell, Michael. *D. H. Lawrence: Language and Being.* Cambridge: Cambridge University Press, 1992.

Ben-Ephraim, Gavriel. *The Moon's Dominion: Narrative Dichotomy and Female Dominance in Lawrence's Earlier Novels.* London and Toronto: Associated University Presses, 1981.

Bennett, Michael. *A Visitor's Guide to Eastwood and the Countryside of D. H. Lawrence.* Nottingham: Nottinghamshire County Library Service, 1979.

Black, Michael. *D. H. Lawrence: The Early Fiction: A Commentary.* London: Macmillan, 1986.

———. *D. H. Lawrence: The Early Philosophical Works: A Commentary.* London: Macmillan, 1991.

———. *D. H. Lawrence: Sons and Lovers.* Cambridge: Cambridge University Press, 1992.

Bloom, Harold, ed. *D. H. Lawrence: Modern Critical Views.* New York: Chelsea House, 1986.

———. *D. H. Lawrence's "The Rainbow."* New York: Chelsea House, 1988. (Modern Critical Interpretations.)

———. *D. H. Lawrence's "Sons and Lovers."* New York: Chelsea House, 1988. (Modern Critical Interpretations.)

———. *D. H. Lawrence's "Women in Love."* New York: Chelsea House, 1988. (Modern Critical Interpretations.)

Boadella, David. *The Spiral Flame: A Study in the Meaning of D. H. Lawrence.* Nottingham: Ritter Press, 1956. (First published serially in 1955 in the bimonthly journal *Orgonomic Functionalism* Nottingham. The Ritter Press volume seems to have been set directly from the journal with no rationalization of pagination or headings—thus, page references given in this book refer to the work's reissue as the December 1977 combined numbers 50–51 of Paunch, published in Buffalo, N.Y., 1978.)

Bonds, Diane S. *Language and the Self in D. H. Lawrence.* Ann Arbor, Mich.: UMI Research Press, 1987.

Brett, Dorothy. *Lawrence and Brett: A Friendship.* Philadelphia: Lippincott, 1933. (Reprinted, with additional material, Santa Fe: Sunstone, 1974. [Covers period 1915–26].)

Brewster, Earl, and Achsah Brewster. *D. H. Lawrence: Reminiscences and Correspondence.* London: Secker, 1934.

Britton, Derek. *"Lady Chatterley": The Making of the Novel.* London: Unwin Hyman, 1988.

Brown, Keith, ed. *Rethinking Lawrence.* Milton Keynes and Philadelphia: Open University Press, 1990.

Brunsdale, Mitzi M. *The German Effect on D. H. Lawrence and His Works, 1885–1912.* Berne: Peter Lang, 1978.

Buckley, Margaret, and Brian Buckley. *Challenge and Renewal: Lawrence and the Thematic Novel.* Kenilworth, Warwickshire: Chrysalis Press, 1993.

Buckton, Chris. *D. H. Lawrence.* London: Longman, 1978. (*Writers in Their Time* series.)

Bumpus, John, and Edward Bumpus. *D. H. Lawrence: An Exhibition.* London: Bumpus, 1933. (Catalog of event held in April–May 1933; manuscripts, typescripts, sketches, photographs, first editions.)

Bunnell, W. S. *Brodie's Notes on D. H. Lawrence's "The Rainbow."* London: Pan Books, 1978. (Revised, London: Macmillan, 1993.)

Burgess, Anthony. *Flame into Being: The Life and Work of D. H. Lawrence.* London: Heinemann; New York: Arbor House, 1985.

Burns, Aidan. *Nature and Culture in D. H. Lawrence.* London: Macmillan, 1980.

Butler, Gerald J. *This Is Carbon: A Defense of D. H. Lawrence's "The Rainbow" against His Admirers.* Seattle: Genitron Press, 1986.

Butler, Lance St. John. *York Notes on D. H. Lawrence's "Sons and Lovers."* London: Longman, 1980.

Bynner, Witter. *Journey with Genius: Recollections and Reflections concerning the D. H. Lawrences.* New York: Day, 1951; London: Nevill, 1953.

———. *Witter Bynner's Photographs of D. H. Lawrence.* Santa Fe: Great Southwest Books, 1981.

Byrne, Janet. *A Genius for Living: A Biography of Frieda Lawrence.* London: Bloomsbury, 1995.

Callow, Philip. *Son and Lover: The Younger D. H. Lawrence.* London: Bodley Head; New York: Stein and Day, 1975.

Cambridge University Library. *D. H. Lawrence 1885–1930.* Cambridge: Cambridge University Library, 1985. (Catalog of an exhibition held September–November 1985.)

Cameron, Alan, ed. *D. H. Lawrence: A Life in Literature.* Nottingham: Nottingham University Library, 1985. (Catalog of Centenary Exhibition held 7 September–13 October 1985.)

Carswell, Catherine. *The Savage Pilgrimage: A Narrative of D. H. Lawrence.* London: Chatto and Windus; New York: Harcourt, Brace, 1932.

Carter, Frederick. *D. H. Lawrence and the Body Mystical.* London: Archer, 1932. (Reprinted New York: Haskell House, 1972.)

Cavitch, David. *D. H. Lawrence and the New World.* New York and London: Oxford University Press, 1969.

Chambers, Jessie ("E.T."). *D. H. Lawrence: A Personal Record.* London: Jonathan

Cape, 1935; New York: Knight, 1936. (2d ed., with new material, London: Cass; New York: Barnes and Noble, 1965. Reprinted, Cambridge: Cambridge University Press, 1980.)

Champion, Neil. *D. H. Lawrence*. Hove, E. Sussex: Wayland, 1989. (School-level introduction.)

Clark, L. D. *Dark Night of the Body: D. H. Lawrence's "The Plumed Serpent."* Austin: University of Texas Press, 1964.

———. *The Minoan Distance: The Symbolism of Travel in D. H. Lawrence*. Tucson: University of Arizona Press, 1980.

Clarke, Colin. *River of Dissolution: D. H. Lawrence and English Romanticism*. London: Routledge and Kegan Paul, 1969.

———, ed. *D. H. Lawrence: "The Rainbow" and "Women in Love": A Casebook*. London: Macmillan, 1969; Nashville, Tenn.: Aurora, 1970.

Consolo, Dominic P., ed. *D. H. Lawrence: The Rocking-Horse Winner*. Columbus, Ohio: Charles E. Merrill, 1969.

Cooke, Sheila M. *D. H. Lawrence: A Finding List*. 2d ed. West Bridgford, Nottingham: Nottinghamshire County Council, Leisure Services Department, 1980a. (1st ed. 1968.)

———. *D. H. Lawrence and Nottinghamshire, 1885–1910*. Nottingham: Nottinghamshire County Library Service, 1980b. (Dossier of photographs, documents, background information, early works.)

Coombes, Henry, ed. *D. H. Lawrence: A Critical Anthology*. Harmondsworth: Penguin, 1973.

Cooper, Andrew, and Glyn Hughes, eds. *D. H. Lawrence 1885–1930: A Celebration*. Nottingham: D. H. Lawrence Society, 1985. (Special issue of the *Journal of the D. H. Lawrence Society*.)

Corke, Helen. *Lawrence and Apocalypse*. London: Heinemann, 1933. (Reprinted in Corke [1965], pp. 57–132.)

———. *D. H. Lawrence's "Princess": A Memory of Jessie Chambers*. London: Thames Ditton, Merle Press, 1951. (Included in Corke [1965].)

———. *D. H. Lawrence: The Croydon Years*. Austin: University of Texas Press, 1965.

———. *In Our Infancy*. Cambridge: Cambridge University Press, 1975.

Cornwell, Ethel F. *The "Still Point": Theme and Variations in the Writings of T. S. Eliot, Coleridge, Yeats, Henry James, Virginia Woolf and D. H. Lawrence*. New Brunswick, N.J.: Rutgers University Press, 1962, pp. 208–42 ("The Sex-Mysticism of D. H. Lawrence").

Cowan, James C. *D. H. Lawrence's American Journey: A Study in Literature and Myth*. Cleveland, Ohio, and London: Press of the Case Western Reserve University, 1970.

———. *D. H. Lawrence: An Annotated Bibliography of Writings about Him*. 2 vols. De Kalb: Northern Illinois University Press, 1982, 1985. (Vol. 1, covering 1909–60, has 2,061 entries; vol. 2, covering 1961–75, has 2,566 entries.)

———. *D. H. Lawrence and the Trembling Balance*. University Park: Pennsylvania State University Press, 1990.

Crick, Brian. *The Story of the "Prussian Officer" Revisions: Littlewood amongst the Lawrence Scholars*. Retford, Nottinghamshire: Brynmill Press, 1983.

Cura-Sazdanic, Illeana. *D. H. Lawrence as Critic*. Delhi: Munshiram Manoharlal, 1969.

Cushman, Keith. *D. H. Lawrence at Work: The Emergence of the "Prussian Officer" Stories*. Sussex: Harvester, 1978.

————, ed. *An Exhibition of First Editions and Manuscripts from the D. H. Lawrence Collection of J. E. Baker, Jr.* Chicago: University of Chicago, 1973. (Catalog.)

Cushman, Keith, and Dennis Jackson, eds. *D. H. Lawrence's Literary Inheritors.* London: Macmillan, 1991.

Daiches, David. *D. H. Lawrence.* Brighton, England: Privately printed at the Dolphin Press, 1963. (Pamphlet of broadcast talk.)

Daleski, H. M. *The Forked Flame: A Study of D. H. Lawrence.* London: Faber, 1965.

Darroch, Robert. *D. H. Lawrence in Australia.* Melbourne: Macmillan, 1981.

Davey, Charles. *D. H. Lawrence: A Living Poet.* London: Brentham Press, 1985.

Davies, Alistair. *Early Modernism, 1900–25: H. G. Wells, Wyndham Lewis, D. H. Lawrence, T. S. Eliot and Virginia Woolf.* Sussex: Harvester Press, 1984.

Davis, E. *The Poetry of D. H. Lawrence.* [Cape Town, South Africa]: UNISA Study Notes, 1956. (Fifty-five-page pamphlet.)

Davis, Joseph. *D. H. Lawrence at Thirroul.* Sydney: Collins, 1989.

Davis, Philip. *Memory and Writing from Wordsworth to Lawrence.* Liverpool: Liverpool University Press, 1983, pp. 411–89.

Delany, Paul. *D. H. Lawrence's Nightmare: The Writer and His Circle in the Years of the Great War.* New York: Basic Books, 1978; Sussex: Harvester, 1979.

Delavenay, Emile. *D. H. Lawrence: L'Homme and La Genèse de son Oeuvre: Les Années de Formation; 1885–1919.* 2 vols. Paris: Libraire C. Klincksieck, 1969. (Shorter English edition, translated by Katherine M. Delavenay, *D. H. Lawrence: The Man and His Work: The Formative Years: 1885–1919.* London: Heinemann; Carbondale: Southern Illinois University Press, 1972.)

————. *D. H. Lawrence and Edward Carpenter: A Study in Edwardian Transition.* London: Heinemann, 1971.

Dervin, Daniel. *A "Strange Sapience": The Creative Imagination of D. H. Lawrence.* Amherst: University of Massachusetts Press, 1984.

Deva, Som. *A Critical Study of "Sons and Lovers."* 2d ed. Beharipur, Bareilly: Literary Publication Bureau, 1969.

Dix, Carol. *D. H. Lawrence and Women.* London: Macmillan, 1980.

Dorbad, Leo J. *Sexually Balanced Relationships in the Novels of D. H. Lawrence.* New York: Peter Lang, 1991.

Douglas, Norman. *D. H. Lawrence and Maurice Magnus: A Plea for Better Manners.* Florence: Privately printed, 1924.

Drain, R. L. *Tradition and D. H. Lawrence.* Groningen: J. B. Wolters, 1960. (Inaugural lecture; pamphlet, twelve pages.)

Draper, R. P. *D. H. Lawrence.* New York: Twayne, 1964. (English Authors Series. Reprinted, London: Macmillan, 1976.)

————. *D. H. Lawrence.* London: Routledge and Kegan Paul; New York: Humanities Press, 1969. (Profiles in Literature Series.)

————. *"Sons and Lovers" by D. H. Lawrence.* Basingstoke and London: Macmillan, 1986. (Macmillan Masterguides.)

————, ed. *D. H. Lawrence: The Critical Heritage.* London: Routledge and Kegan Paul, 1970.

Easthope, Malcolm. *Students' Guide to "Choice of Poets": Wordsworth, Blake, Lawrence, Graves, Frost.* Singapore: Graham Brash, 1986.

Ebbatson, Roger. *Lawrence and the Nature Tradition: A Theme in English Fiction, 1859–1914.* Sussex: Harvester Press; Atlantic Highlands, N.J.: Humanities Press, 1980.

————. *The Evolutionary Self: Hardy, Forster, Lawrence.* Sussex: Harvester; Totowa, N.J.: Barnes and Noble, 1982, pp. 76–112.

Edwards, Duane. *"The Rainbow": A Search for New Life.* Boston: Twayne, 1990.

Edwards, Lucy I., and David Phillips, eds. *Young Bert: An Exhibition of the Early Years of D. H. Lawrence.* Nottingham: Nottingham Castle Museum and Art Gallery, 1972. (Illustrated catalog of event held 8 July–29 August 1972.)

Ege, Ufuk. *Fusion of Philosophy with Fiction in D. H. Lawrence's "Women in Love."* Lancaster: Lancaster University Central Print Unit, 1990. (Pamphlet, ten pages.)

Eggert, Paul, and John Worthen, eds. *D. H. Lawrence and Comedy.* Cambridge: Cambridge University Press, forthcoming, 1996.

Eisenstein, Samuel A. *Boarding the Ship of Death: D. H. Lawrence's Quester Heroes.* The Hague: Mouton, 1974.

Ellis, David, and Howard Mills, eds. *D. H. Lawrence's Non-Fiction: Art, Thought and Genre.* Cambridge: Cambridge University Press, 1988.

Ellis, David, and Ornella De Zordo, eds. *D. H. Lawrence: Critical Assessments.* 4 vols. East Sussex: Helm Information, 1992. (Vol. 1: "The Contemporary Response." Vol. 2: "The Fiction (I)." Vol. 3: "The Fiction (II)." Vol. 4: "Poetry and Non-fiction; The Modern Critical Response 1938–92: General Studies.")

Fabes, Gilbert Henry. *David Herbert Lawrence: His First Editions: Points and Values.* London: W. and G. Foyle, 1933. (Reprinted, Folcroft Library Edition, 1971.)

Farr, Judith, ed. *Twentieth Century Interpretations of "Sons and Lovers": A Collection of Critical Essays.* Englewood Cliffs, N.J.: Prentice-Hall, 1970.

Fay, Eliot. *Lorenzo in Search of the Sun: D. H. Lawrence in Italy, Mexico, and the American Southwest.* New York: Bookman, 1953; London: Vision, 1955.

Fedder, Norman. J. *The Influence of D. H. Lawrence on Tennessee Williams.* The Hague: Mouton, 1966.

Feinstein, Elaine. *Lawrence's Women: The Intimate Life of D. H. Lawrence.* London: HarperCollins, 1993.

Fernihough, Anne. *D. H. Lawrence: Aesthetics and Ideology.* Oxford: Oxford University Press, 1993.

Feshawy, Wagdy. *D. H. Lawrence: A Critical Study.* Cairo: Dar-al-Sakata, 1975.

Fielding, M. L. *Notes on D. H. Lawrence's "Sons and Lovers."* London: Methuen, 1975. (Study guide.)

Finney, Brian. *D. H. Lawrence: "Sons and Lovers."* Harmondsworth: Penguin, 1990. (Penguin Critical Studies series.)

Fjagesund, Peter. *The Apocalyptic World of D. H. Lawrence.* Oslo, Norway: Norwegian University Press, 1991.

Ford, George H. *Double Measure: A Study of the Novels and Stories of D. H. Lawrence.* New York: Holt, Rinehart, and Winston, 1965.

Foster, Joseph. *D. H. Lawrence in Taos.* Albuquerque: University of New Mexico Press, 1972.

Freeman, Mary. *D. H. Lawrence: A Basic Study of His Ideas.* New York: Grosset and Dunlop, 1955.

Gamache, Lawrence B., and Ian S. MacNiven, eds. *The Modernists: Studies in a Literary Phenomenon: Essays in Honor of Harry T. Moore.* London and Toronto: Associated University Presses, 1987. (Five essays on Lawrence.)

Garcia, Reloy. *Steinbeck and D. H. Lawrence: Fictive Voices and the Ethical Imperative.* Muncie, Ind.: John Steinbeck Society of America, Ball State University, 1972.

Garcia, Reloy, and J. Karabatsos, eds. *A Concordance to the Poetry of D. H. Lawrence.* Lincoln: University of Nebraska Press, 1970.

———. *A Concordance to the Short Fiction of D. H. Lawrence.* Lincoln: University of Nebraska Press, 1972.

Gertzman, Jay A. *A Descriptive Bibliography of "Lady Chatterley's Lover": With Essays toward a Publishing History of the Novel.* Westport, Conn.: Greenwood, 1989.

Gilbert, Sandra M. *D. H. Lawrence's "Sons and Lovers," "The Rainbow," "Women in Love," "The Plumed Serpent."* New York: Monarch Press, 1965.

———. *Acts of Attention: The Poems of D. H. Lawrence.* Ithaca, N.Y., and London: Cornell University Press, 1972.

Gomme, Andor, ed. *D. H. Lawrence: A Critical Study of the Major Novels and Other Writings.* Sussex: Harvester Press; New York: Barnes and Noble, 1978.

Goodheart, Eugene. *The Utopian Vision of D. H. Lawrence.* Chicago and London: University of Chicago Press, 1963.

Goodman, Richard. *Footnote to Lawrence.* London: White Owl Press, 1932. (Pamphlet. Reprinted in *Contemporary Essays* 1933. Edited by Sylva Norman. London: Matthews and Marrot, 1933, pp. 51–63.)

Gordon, David J. *D. H. Lawrence as a Literary Critic.* New Haven, Conn. and London: Yale University Press, 1966.

Gotham Book Mart. *Books by and about D. H. Lawrence: A Bookseller's Catalogue.* New York: Gotham Book Mart, 1961.

Grant, Damian. *D. H. Lawrence: "Women in Love."* London: British Council, 1976. (Notes on Literature no. 163.)

Gravil, Richard. *D. H. Lawrence: "Lady Chatterley's Lover."* London: British Council, 1976. (Notes on Literature no. 165.)

Green, Martin Burgess. *The Reputation of D. H. Lawrence in America.* Ann Arbor, Mich.: University Microfilms, 1966. (Reviews and criticism, 1911–56.)

———. *The von Richthofen Sisters: The Triumphant and the Tragic Modes of Love: Else and Frieda von Richthofen, Otto Gross, Max Weber, and D. H. Lawrence, in the Years 1870–1970.* London: Weidenfeld and Nicolson, 1974.

Greenhalgh, Michael John. *Lawrence's Uncollected Stories, 1907–13: A Critical Commentary.* Ruislip: M. J. Greenhalgh, 1988.

Gregory, Horace. *Pilgrim of the Apocalypse: A Critical Study of D. H. Lawrence.* New York: Viking, 1933; London: Secker, 1934. (Revised as *D. H. Lawrence: Pilgrim of the Apocalypse.* New York: Grove, 1957.)

Gutierrez, Donald. *Lapsing Out: Embodiments of Death and Rebirth in the Last Writings of D. H. Lawrence.* London and Toronto: Associated University Presses, 1980.

———. *Subject–Object Relations in Wordsworth and Lawrence.* Ann Arbor, Mich.: UMI Research Press, 1987.

Hahn, Emily. *Lorenzo; D. H. Lawrence and the Women Who Loved Him.* Philadelphia and New York: Lippincott, 1975.

Hamalian, Leo, ed. *D. H. Lawrence: A Collection of Criticism.* New York: McGraw-Hill, 1973.

———, ed. *D. H. Lawrence in Italy.* New York: Tapligen, 1982.

Handley, Graham. *Notes on D. H. Lawrence "Sons and Lovers."* Bath: J. Brodie, 1967.

Handley, Graham, and Paul Harris. *Selected Tales of D. H. Lawrence.* London: Pan, 1978. (Brodie's Notes.)

Hanson, Christopher. *Sons and Lovers.* Oxford: Basil Blackwell, 1966. (Notes on English Literature Series.)

Hardy, George, and Nathaniel Harris. *A D. H. Lawrence Album.* Ashbourne, Derbyshire: Moorland, 1985; New York: Franklin Watts, 1986.

Harris, Janice Hubbard. *The Short Fiction of D. H. Lawrence.* New Brunswick, N.J.: Rutgers University Press, 1984.

Harris, Nathaniel. *The Lawrences.* London: Dent, 1976.

Harrison, J. R. *The Reactionaries—Yeats, Lewis, Pound, Eliot, Lawrence: A Study of the Anti-Democratic Intelligentsia.* London: Gollancz; New York: Schocken, 1966, pp. 163–89.

Harvey, Geoffrey. *Sons and Lovers.* London: Macmillan; Atlantic Highlands, N.J.: Humanities, 1987. (Critics Debate Series.)

Herzinger, Kim. *D. H. Lawrence in His Time: 1908–1915.* London and Toronto: Associated University Presses, 1982.

Heywood, Christopher, ed. *D. H. Lawrence: New Studies.* London: Macmillan; New York: St. Martin's Press, 1987.

Hillman, Rodney. *D. H. Lawrence, "Sons and Lovers."* London: British Council, 1976. (Notes on Literature, no. 161.)

Hilton, Enid Hopkin. *More than One Life: A Nottinghamshire Childhood with D. H. Lawrence.* Stroud, Gloucestershire: Alan Sutton, 1993.

Hobsbaum, Philip. *A Reader's Guide to Lawrence.* London: Thames and Hudson, 1981.

Hochman, Baruch. *Another Ego: The Changing View of Self and Society in the Work of D. H. Lawrence.* Columbia: University of South Carolina Press, 1970.

Hoffman, Frederick J., and Harry T. Moore, eds. *The Achievement of D. H. Lawrence.* Norman: University of Oklahoma Press, 1953.

Hofmann, Regina, and Michael W. Weithmann. *D. H. Lawrence and Germany: A Bibliography.* Passau, Germany: University Library of Passau, 1995. ("D. H. Lawrence and Germany: An Introduction," by Robert Burden, pp. 1–9.)

Holbrook, David. *The Quest for Love.* London: Methuen, 1964.

———. *Where D. H. Lawrence Was Wrong about Women.* London and Toronto: Associated University Presses, 1992.

Holderness, Graham. *Who's Who in D. H. Lawrence.* London: Hamish Hamilton; New York: Taplinger, 1976.

———. *D. H. Lawrence: History, Ideology and Fiction.* Dublin: Gill and Macmillan, 1982.

———. *Women in Love.* Milton Keynes and Philadelphia: Open University Press, 1986. (Open Guides to Literature Series.)

———. *D. H. Lawrence: Life, Work, and Criticism.* Fredricton, N.B., Canada: York Press, 1988.

Hostettler, Maya. *D. H. Lawrence: Travel Books and Fiction.* Berne: Peter Lang, 1985.

Hough, Graham. *The Dark Sun: A Study of D. H. Lawrence.* London: Gerald Duckworth, 1956.

———. *Two Exiles: Lord Byron and D. H. Lawrence.* Nottingham: University of Nottingham Press, 1956. (Reprinted in his *Image and Experience: Studies in a Literary Revolution.* London: Duckworth; Lincoln: University of Nebraska Press, 1960, pp. 133–59.)

Howe, Marguerite Beede. *The Art of the Self in D. H. Lawrence.* Athens: University of Ohio Press, 1977.

Humma, John B. *Metaphor and Meaning in D. H. Lawrence's Later Novels*. Columbia: University of Missouri Press, 1990.

Huttar, Charles A., ed. *Literature and Religion: Views on D. H. Lawrence*. Holland, Mich.: Hope College, 1968.

Hyde, G. M. *D. H. Lawrence and Translation*. London: Macmillan, 1981.

———. *D. H. Lawrence*. London: Macmillan, 1990.

Hyde, H. Montgomery, ed. *The "Lady Chatterley's Lover Trial" (Regina v. Penguin Books Limited)*. London: Bodley Head, 1990.

Hyde, Virginia. *The Risen Adam: D. H. Lawrence's Revisionist Typology*. University Park: Pennsylvania State University Press, 1992.

Ingram, Allan. *The Language of D. H. Lawrence*. London: Macmillan, 1990.

Inniss, Kenneth. *D. H. Lawrence's Bestiary: A Study of His Use of Animal Trope and Symbol*. The Hague and Paris: Mouton, 1971; New York: Humanities Press, 1972.

Jackson, Dennis, and Fleda Brown Jackson, eds. *Critical Essays on D. H. Lawrence*. Boston: G. K. Hall, 1988.

Janik, Del Ivan. *The Curve of Return: D. H. Lawrence's Travel Books*. Victoria, B.C.: University of Victoria Press, 1981.

Jarrett-Kerr, Martin. *D. H. Lawrence and Human Existence*. London and New York: Rockliffe, 1951 (under pseudonym of Father William Tiverton). (Rev. ed., London: SCM Press, 1961.)

John, Brian. *Supreme Fictions: Studies in the Work of William Blake, Thomas Carlyle, W. B. Yeats, and D. H. Lawrence*. Montreal and London: McGill-Queen's University Press, 1974, pp. 231–309.

Joost, Nicholas, and Alvin Sullivan. *D. H. Lawrence and "The Dial."* Carbondale and Edwardsville: Southern Illinois University Press; London and Amsterdam: Feffer and Simons, 1970.

Kalnins, Mara, ed. *D. H. Lawrence: Centenary Essays*. Bristol: Bristol Classical Press, 1986.

Kelsey, Nigel. *D. H. Lawrence: Sexual Crisis*. London: Macmillan, 1991.

Kenmare, Dallas. *Fire-Bird. A Study of D. H. Lawrence*. London: James Barrie, 1951.

Kermode, Frank. *Lawrence*. Suffolk: Collins Fontana, 1973.

Kiely, Robert. *Beyond Egotism: The Fiction of James Joyce, Virginia Woolf and D. H. Lawrence*. Cambridge: Harvard University Press, 1980.

Kim, Jungmai. *Themes and Techniques in the Novellas of D. H. Lawrence*. Seoul, Korea: Hanshin, 1986.

———. *D. H. Lawrence in Korea: A Bibliographical Study, 1930–1987*. Seoul: Hanshin, 1989.

Kingsmill, Hugh (H. K. Lunn). *D. H. Lawrence*. London: Methuen, 1938.

Kinkead-Weekes, Mark, ed. *Twentieth Century Interpretations of "The Rainbow."* Englewood Cliffs, N.J.: Prentice-Hall, 1971.

Krishnamurthi, M. G. *D. H. Lawrence: Tale as Medium*. Mysore: Rao and Raghavan, 1970.

Kushigian, Nancy. *Pictures and Fictions: Visual Modernism and the Pre-War Novels of D. H. Lawrence*. New York: Peter Lang, 1990.

Laird, Holly A. *Self and Sequence: The Poetry of D. H. Lawrence*. Charlottesville: University Press of Virginia, 1988.

Lavrin, Nora. *D. H. Lawrence: Nottingham Connections*. Nottingham: Astra Press, 1986.

Lawrence, Frieda. *"Not I, But the Wind . . . "* Santa Fe, N. M.: Rydal Press; New York:

Viking, 1934; London: Heinemann, 1935. (Reprinted, Carbondale: Southern Illinois University Press; London: Feffer and Simons, 1974.)

———. *Frieda Lawrence: The Memoirs and Correspondence.* Edited by E. W. Tedlock,
Jr. London: Heinemann, 1961; New York: Knopf, 1964.

Lawrence, Ada, and G. Stuart Gelder. *The Early Life of D. H. Lawrence Together with
Hitherto Unpublished Letters and Articles.* London: Secker, 1932.

Lawrence, J. Stephan. *D. H. Lawrence: Supplement to Catalogue 38.* Chicago: Rare
Books, 1978.

Lea, F. A. *Lawrence and Murry: A Two-Fold Vision.* London: Brentham Press, 1985.

Leavis, F. R. *D. H. Lawrence.* Cambridge: Minority Press, 1930. (Reprinted in his *For
Continuity.* Cambridge: Minority Press, 1933.)

———. *D. H. Lawrence: Novelist.* London: Chatto and Windus, 1955.

———. *Thought, Words and Creativity: Art and Thought in D. H. Lawrence.* London:
Chatto and Windus, 1976.

Lebolt, Gladys. *D. H. Lawrence: "The True Redeemer."* Tuscaloosa, Ala.: Portals Press,
1986.

Lehman, Anthony L. *D. H. Lawrence, Idella Purnell and "Palms."* Los Angeles: George
Houlé, 1986.

Lerner, Laurence. *The Truthtellers: Jane Austen, George Eliot, D. H. Lawrence.* London:
Chatto; New York: Schocken, 1967.

Levy, Mervyn, ed. *Paintings of D. H. Lawrence.* New York: Viking; London: Cory,
Adams, and McKay, 1964. (Includes seven essays on Lawrence and art.)

Lewiecki-Wilson, Cynthia. *Writing against the Family: Gender in Lawrence and Joyce.*
Carbondale: Southern Illinois University Press, 1994.

Lewis, Wyndham. *Paleface: The Philosophy of the "Melting Pot."* London: Chatto and
Windus, 1929. (Expanded from his article "Paleface; or, 'Love? What ho! Smelling Strangeness.' " *Enemy* 2 [September 1927]: 3–112.)

Littlewood, J.C.F. *D. H. Lawrence I: 1885–1914.* Harlow, Essex: Longman, 1976. (Writers and Their Work Series.)

Lockwood, M. J. *A Study of the Poems of D. H. Lawrence: Thinking in Poetry.* London:
Macmillan; New York: St. Martin's Press, 1987.

Lucas, Robert. *Frieda Lawrence: The Story of Frieda von Richthofen and D. H.
Lawrence.* Translated from the German original by Geoffrey Skelton. London:
Secker and Warburg; New York: Viking, 1973.

Lucente, Gregory L. *The Narrative of Realism and Myth: Verga, Lawrence, Faulkner,
Pavese.* Baltimore: Johns Hopkins University Press, 1981, pp. 107–23.

Luhan, Mabel Dodge. *Lorenzo in Taos.* New York: Knopf, 1932; London: Secker, 1933.

McDonald, Edward D. *A Bibliography of the Writings of D. H. Lawrence.* With a Foreword by D. H. Lawrence. Philadelphia: Centaur, 1925.

———. *The Writings of D. H. Lawrence 1925–30: A Bibliographical Supplement.* Philadelphia: Centaur, 1931.

McEwan, Neil. *York Notes on D. H. Lawrence's "Women in Love."* London: Longman,
1991a.

———. *York Notes on D. H. Lawrence's Selected Short Stories.* London: Longman,
1991b.

Mackenzie, Kenneth. *The Fox.* Milton Keynes, England: Open University, 1973.

Mackey, Douglas A. *D. H. Lawrence: The Poet Who Was Not Wrong.* San Bernardino,
Calif.: Burgo Press, 1986.

MacLeod, Sheila. *Lawrence's Men and Women.* London: Heinemann, 1985; London: Grafton Books, 1987.

Maddox, Brenda. *The Married Man: A Life of D. H. Lawrence.* London: Sinclair-Stevenson, 1994.

Maes-Jelinek, Hena. *Criticism of Society in the English Novel between the Wars.* Paris: Société d'Editions "Les Belles Lettres," 1970, pp. 11–100.

Mailer, Norman. *The Prisoner of Sex.* London: Weidenfeld and Nicolson, 1971.

Malani, Hiran. *D. H. Lawrence: A Study of His Plays.* New Delhi, India: Arnold-Heinemann; Atlantic Highlands, N.J.: Humanities Press, 1982.

Mandell, Gail Porter. *The Phoenix Paradox: A Study of Renewal through Change in the "Collected Poems" and "Last Poems" of D. H. Lawrence.* Carbondale and Edwardsville: Southern Illinois University Press, 1984.

Marshall, Tom. *The Psychic Mariner: A Reading of the Poems of D. H. Lawrence.* New York: Viking, 1970.

Martin, Graham. *D. H. Lawrence's "The Rainbow."* Milton Keynes, England: Open University Press, 1971.

May, Keith M. *Nietzsche and Modern Literature: Themes in Yeats, Rilke, Mann and Lawrence.* London: Macmillan, 1988.

Melvin Rare Books. *A Catalogue of Valuable Books by D. H. Lawrence.* Edinburgh: Melvin Rare Books, 1950.

Mensch, Barbara. *D. H. Lawrence and the Authoritarian Personality.* London: Macmillan, 1991.

Merrild, Knud. *A Poet and Two Painters: A Memoir of D. H. Lawrence.* London: Routledge, 1938; New York: Viking, 1939. (Reprinted as *With D. H. Lawrence in New Mexico: A Memoir of D. H. Lawrence.* London: Routledge and Kegan Paul, 1964.)

Messenger, Nigel. *How to Study a D. H. Lawrence Novel.* London: Macmillan, 1989.

Meyers, Jeffrey. *D. H. Lawrence and the Experience of Italy.* Philadelphia: University of Pennsylvania Press, 1982.

———. *D. H. Lawrence: A Biography.* New York: Alfred A. Knopf, 1990.

———, ed. *D. H. Lawrence and Tradition.* London: Athlone, 1985.

———. *The Legacy of D. H. Lawrence: New Essays.* London: Macmillan, 1987.

Michaels-Tonks, Jennifer. *D. H. Lawrence: The Polarity of North and South—Germany and Italy in His Prose Works.* Bonn: Bouvier, 1976.

Miko, Stephen J. *Toward "Women in Love": The Emergence of a Lawrentian Aesthetic.* New Haven, Conn. and London: Yale University Press, 1971.

———, ed. *Twentieth Century Interpretations of "Women in Love."* Englewood Cliffs, N.J.: Prentice-Hall, 1969.

Miles, Kathleen M. *The Hellish Meaning: The Demonic Motif in the Works of D. H. Lawrence.* Carbondale: Southern Illinois University Press, 1969.

Miliaras, Barbara A. *Pillar of Flame: The Mythological Foundations of D. H. Lawrence's Sexual Philosophy.* New York, Berne, Frankfurt: Peter Lang, 1987.

Miller, Henry. *Notes on "Aaron's Rod" and Other Notes on Lawrence from the Paris Notebooks.* Edited by Seamus Cooney. Santa Barbara, Calif.: Black Sparrow Press, 1980a.

———. *The World of D. H. Lawrence: A Passionate Appreciation.* Edited with an Introduction and Notes by Evelyn J. Hinz and John J. Teunissen. Santa Barbara, Calif.: Capra Press, 1980b.

Millett, Kate. *Sexual Politics.* London: Rupert Hart-Davis, 1971, pp. 237–93.

Millett, Robert W. *The Vultures and the Phoenix: A Study of the Mandrake Press Edition of the Paintings of D. H. Lawrence.* London and Toronto: Associated University Presses, 1983.

Milton, Colin. *Lawrence and Nietzsche: A Study in Influence.* Aberdeen: Aberdeen University Press, 1987.

Modiano, Marko. *Domestic Disharmony and Industrialization in D. H. Lawrence's Early Fiction.* Uppsala, Sweden: Uppsala University, 1987.

Mohanty, Sachidananda. *Lawrence's Leadership Politics and the Defeat of Fascism.* Delhi, India: Academic Foundation, 1993.

Montgomery, Robert E. *The Visionary D. H. Lawrence: Beyond Philosophy and Art.* Cambridge: Cambridge University Press, 1994.

Moore, Harry T. *The Life and Works of D. H. Lawrence.* London: Allen and Unwin; New York: Twayne, 1951. (Revised as *D. H. Lawrence: His Life and Works.* New York: Twayne, 1964.)

———. *The Intelligent Heart: The Story of D. H. Lawrence.* New York: Farrar, Straus, and Young, 1954; London: Heinemann, 1955. (Revised as *The Priest of Love: A Life of D. H. Lawrence.* Carbondale: Southern Illinois University Press; London: Heinemann, 1974. Further revised, Harmondsworth: Penguin, 1976.)

———. *Poste Restante: A Lawrence Travel Calendar.* Berkeley and Los Angeles: University of California Press, 1956.

———, ed. *A D. H. Lawrence Miscellany.* Carbondale: Southern Illinois University Press, 1959.

Moore, Harry T., and Warren Roberts. *D. H. Lawrence and His World.* New York: Viking; London: Thames and Hudson, 1966.

Moore, Harry T., and Dale B. Montague, eds. *Frieda Lawrence and Her Circle: Letters from, to and about Frieda Lawrence.* London: Macmillan; Hamden, Conn.: Shoe String, 1981.

Moore, Olive. *Further Reflections on the Death of a Porcupine.* London: Blue Moon, 1932. (Pamphlet, thirty-four pages.)

Mori, Haruhide, ed. *A Conversation on D. H. Lawrence.* Los Angeles: Friends of the UCLA Library, 1974. (Discussion between L. C. Powell, Frieda Lawrence Ravagli, Aldous Huxley, and Dorothy G. Mitchell, held on 7 March 1952.)

Moynahan, Julian. *The Deed of Life: The Novels and Tales of D. H. Lawrence.* Princeton: Princeton University Press, 1963.

———, ed. *"Sons and Lovers": Text, Background, and Criticism.* New York: Viking Press, 1968.

Murfin, Ross C. *Swinburne, Hardy, Lawrence and the Burden of Belief.* Chicago and London: University of Chicago Press, 1978.

———. *The Poetry of D. H. Lawrence: Texts and Contexts.* Lincoln: University of Nebraska Press, 1983.

———. *"Sons and Lovers": A Novel of Division and Desire.* Boston: Twayne, 1987.

Murry, John Middleton. *D. H. Lawrence.* Cambridge: Minority Press, 1930.

———. *Son of Woman: The Story of D. H. Lawrence.* London: Cape; New York: Cape and Smith, 1931.

———. *Reminiscences of D. H. Lawrence.* London: Cape, 1933.

———. *Love, Freedom and Society: An Analytical Comparison of D. H. Lawrence and Albert Schweitzer.* London: Cape, 1957, pp. 23–123.

Nahal, Chaman. *D. H. Lawrence: An Eastern View.* South Brunswick and New York: Barnes, 1970.

Nath, Suresh. *D. H. Lawrence: The Dramatist.* Ghaziabad, India: Vimal Prakashan, 1979.

Nehls, Edward, ed *D. H. Lawrence: A Composite Biography.* 3 vols. Madison: University of Wisconsin Press, 1957, 1958, 1959.

Neville, George. *A Memoir of D. H. Lawrence.* Edited by Carl Baron. Cambridge: Cambridge University Press, 1981.

New, Peter. *Fiction and Purpose in "Utopia," "Rasselas," "The Mill on the Floss," and "Women in Love."* London: Macmillan; New York: St. Martin's Press, 1985.

Nin, Anais. *D. H. Lawrence: An Unprofessional Study.* Paris: Titus, 1932.

Niven, Alastair. *D. H. Lawrence: "The Plumed Serpent."* London: British Council, 1976. (Notes on Literature no. 164.)

———. *D. H. Lawrence: The Novels.* Cambridge: Cambridge University Press, 1978.

———. *D. H. Lawrence: The Writer and His Work.* Harlow, Essex: Longman, 1980.

Nixon, Cornelia. *Lawrence's Leadership Politics and the Turn against Women.* Berkeley, Los Angeles, and London: University of California Press, 1986.

Norris, Margot. *Beasts of the Modern Imagination: Darwin, Nietzsche, Kafka, Ernst, and Lawrence.* Baltimore: Johns Hopkins University Press, 1985.

Nottingham Castle Museum. *D. H. Lawrence and the Visual Arts.* Nottingham: Nottingham Castle Museum and Art Gallery, 1985. (Catalog of the 1985 exhibition "Lawrence, Art and Artists.")

Nottingham University. *D. H. Lawrence Collection Catalogue.* Nottingham: University of Nottingham Manuscripts Department, 1979.

———. *D. H. Lawrence: A Phoenix in Flight. Notes to Accompany an Exhibition.* Nottingham: Nottingham University Library, 1980.

———. *D. H. Lawrence Collection Catalogue.* Vol. 2. Nottingham: University of Nottingham Manuscripts Department, 1983.

———. *Collection of Literary Manuscripts, Typescripts, Proofs and Related Papers of D. H. Lawrence.* Nottingham: University of Nottingham Department of Manuscripts and Special Collections, 1990.

Oates, Joyce Carol. *The Hostile Sun: The Poetry of D. H. Lawrence.* Los Angeles: Black Sparrow Press, 1973. (Reprinted in her *New Heaven, New Earth: The Visionary Experience in Literature.* London: Gollancz, 1976, pp. 37–81.)

Olson, Charles. *D. H. Lawrence and the High Temptation of the Mind.* Santa Barbara, Calif.: Black Sparrow Press, 1980.

Orr, John. *The Making of the 20th Century Novel: Lawrence, Joyce, Faulkner and Beyond.* New York: St. Martin's Press; London: Macmillan, 1987, pp. 20–43.

Paccaud-Huguet, Josiane. *"Women in Love": de la tentation perverse à l'écriture.* Grenoble: Ellug, 1991.

Padhi, Bibhu. *D. H. Lawrence: Modes of Fictional Style.* Troy, N.Y.: Whitston, 1989.

Page, Norman, ed. *D. H. Lawrence: Interviews and Recollections.* 2 vols. London: Macmillan; Totowa, N.J.: Barnes and Noble, 1981.

Panichas, George A. *Adventure in Consciousness: The Meaning of D. H. Lawrence's Religious Quest.* The Hague: Mouton, 1964.

Parmenter, Ross. *Lawrence in Oaxaca: A Quest for the Novelist in Mexico.* Salt Lake City, Utah: Smith, 1984.

Partlow, Robert B., Jr., and Harry T. Moore, eds. *D. H. Lawrence: The Man Who Lived.* Carbondale: Southern Illinois University Press, 1980.

Paterson, John. *The Novel as Faith: The Gospel according to James, Hardy, Conrad, Joyce, Lawrence and Virginia Woolf.* Boston: Gambit, 1973, pp. 143–83.

Patmore, Derek. *D. H. Lawrence and the Dominant Male.* London: Covent Garden Press, 1970. (Seven-page pamphlet. First published in *Guardian,* 10 December 1968.)

Peterson, Richard F., and Alan M. Cohn. *D. H. Lawrence: An Exhibit.* Carbondale: Morris Library, Southern Illinois University, 1979.

Philippron, Guy. *D. H. Lawrence: The Man Struggling for Love, 1885–1912.* Belgium: Centre Permanent de Documentation et de Formation Loveral, 1985.

Phillips, Jill M., ed. *D. H. Lawrence: A Review of the Biographies and Literary Criticism* (A Critically Annotated Bibliography). New York: Gordon Press, 1978.

Pinion, F. B. *A D. H. Lawrence Companion: Life, Thought, and Works.* London: Macmillan, 1978; New York: Barnes and Noble, 1979.

Pinkney, Tony. *D. H. Lawrence.* Hemel Hempstead: Harvester Wheatsheaf, 1990. (Published in the United States as *D. H. Lawrence and Modernism.* Iowa City: University of Iowa Press, 1990.)

Pinto, Vivian de Sola. *D. H. Lawrence: Prophet of the Midlands.* Nottingham: University of Nottingham, 1951. (Twenty-four-page pamphlet of public lecture.)

———, ed. *D. H. Lawrence after Thirty Years, 1930–1960.* Nottingham: Curwen Press, 1960. (Catalog of exhibition held 17 June–30 July, 1960.)

Polhemus, Robert M. *Erotic Faith: Being in Love from Jane Austen to D. H. Lawrence.* Chicago: University of Chicago Press, 1990.

Poole, R. H. *Lawrence and Education.* Nottingham: University of Nottingham Institute of Education, 1968. (Fourteen-page pamphlet.)

Poplawski, Paul. *Promptings of Desire: Creativity and the Religious Impulse in the Works of D. H. Lawrence.* Westport, Conn.: Greenwood Press, 1993.

———. *The Works of D. H. Lawrence: A Chronological Checklist.* Nottingham: D. H. Lawrence Society, 1995.

Potter, Stephen. *D. H. Lawrence: A First Study.* London: Cape, 1930.

Powell, Lawrence Clark. *The Manuscripts of D. H. Lawrence: A Descriptive Catalogue.* Los Angeles: Los Angeles Public Library, 1937.

Prakesh, Om. *"Sons and Lovers": A Critical Study.* Bareilly: Prakesh Book Depot, 1972.

Prakesh, Ravendra. *D. H. Lawrence: "Sons and Lovers": A Critical Study.* Agra: Lakshmi Narain Agarwal, 1972.

Prasad, Madhusudan. *D. H. Lawrence: A Study of His Novels.* Bereilly, India: Prakesh Book Depot, 1980.

Prasad, Suman Prabha. *Thomas Hardy and D. H. Lawrence: A Study of the Tragic Vision in Their Novels.* New Delhi, India: Arnold-Heinemann, 1976.

Preston, Peter. *A. D. H. Lawrence Chronology.* London: Macmillan, 1994.

———, ed. *D. H. Lawrence: The Centre and the Circles.* Nottingham: University of Nottingham D. H. Lawrence Centre, 1992.

Preston, Peter, and Peter Hoare, eds. *D. H. Lawrence in the Modern World.* London: Macmillan, 1989.

Pritchard, R. E. *D. H. Lawrence: Body of Darkness.* London: Hutchinson University Library, 1971.

Pugh, Bridget. *The Country of My Heart: A Local Guide to D. H. Lawrence.* 3d ed. Nottingham: Broxtowe Borough Council, 1991.

Ramaiah, L. S., and Sachidananda Mohanty, eds. *D. H. Lawrence Studies in India: A*

Bibliographical Guide with a Review Essay. Calcutta: P. Lal (Writer's Workshop), 1990.

Raskin, Jonah. *The Mythology of Imperialism: Rudyard Kipling, Joseph Conrad, E. M. Forster, D. H. Lawrence and Joyce Cary.* New York: Random House, 1971, passim.

Rees, Richard. *Brave Men: A Study of D. H. Lawrence and Simone Weil.* London: Gollancz, 1958.

Rice, Thomas Jackson. *D. H. Lawrence: A Guide to Research.* New York and London: Garland, 1983. (Bibliography, containing 2,123 entries with terminal date of 1 January 1983.)

Roberts, K. R. *D. H. Lawrence: An Approach to His Poetry.* Huddersfield: Schofield and Sims, 1982. (School-level booklet.)

Roberts, Warren. *A Bibliography of D. H. Lawrence.* 2d ed. Cambridge: Cambridge University Press, 1982. (Currently, the definitive primary bibliography.)

Robinson, Jeremy. *The Passion of D. H. Lawrence.* Kidderminster, England: Crescent Moon, 1992.

Rolph, C. H., ed. *The Trial of Lady Chatterley: Regina v. Penguin Books Limited. The Transcript of the Trial.* London: Penguin, 1961; 1990. (With a new foreword for this thirtieth anniversary edition by Geoffrey Robinson.)

Ross, Charles L. *The Composition of "The Rainbow" and "Women in Love": A History.* Charlottesville: University Press of Virginia, 1979.

———. *"Women in Love": A Novel of Mythic Realism.* Boston: Twayne, 1991.

Rothkopf, C. Z. *"Sons and Lovers": A Critical Commentary.* New York: American R.D.M. Corporation, 1969.

Ruderman, Judith. *D. H. Lawrence and the Devouring Mother: The Search for a Patriarchal Ideal of Leadership.* Durham, N.C.: Duke University Press, 1984.

Russell, John. *Style in Modern British Fiction: Studies in Joyce, Lawrence, Forster, Lewis and Green.* Baltimore: Johns Hopkins University Press, 1975.

Sagar, Keith. *The Art of D. H. Lawrence.* Cambridge: Cambridge University Press, 1966.

———. *D. H. Lawrence: A Calendar of His Works.* Manchester: Manchester University Press, 1979.

———. *D. H. Lawrence: Life into Art.* Harmondsworth: Penguin; New York: Viking, 1985a.

———. *The Life of D. H. Lawrence.* London: Methuen, 1985b.

———, ed. *D. H. Lawrence and New Mexico.* Salt Lake City, Utah: Gibbs M. Smith, 1982a.

———, ed. *A D. H. Lawrence Handbook.* Manchester: Manchester University Press, 1982b.

Sale, Roger. *Modern Heroism: Essays on D. H. Lawrence, William Empson, and J. R. R. Tolkien.* Berkeley: University of California Press, 1973, pp. 16–106.

Salgādo, Gāmini. *D. H. Lawrence: "Sons and Lovers."* London: Edward Arnold, 1966.

———. *D. H. Lawrence: "Sea and Sardinia"; "The Rainbow."* London: British Council, 1969. (Notes on Literature no. 100.)

———. *D. H. Lawrence: "The Rainbow."* London: British Council, 1976. (Notes on Literature no. 162.)

———. *A Preface to Lawrence.* London: Longman, 1982.

———, ed. *D. H. Lawrence: "Sons and Lovers": A Casebook.* London: Macmillan, 1969.

Salgādo, Gāmini, and G. K. Das, eds. *The Spirit of D. H. Lawrence: Centenary Studies.* London: Macmillan, 1988.

Sanders, Scott. *D. H. Lawrence: The World of the Major Novels.* London: Vision, 1973.

Scheckner, Peter. *Class, Politics, and the Individual: A Study of the Major Works of D. H. Lawrence.* London and Toronto: Associated University Presses, 1985.

Schneider, Daniel J. *D. H. Lawrence: The Artist as Psychologist.* Lawrence: University Press of Kansas, 1984.

———. *The Consciousness of D. H. Lawrence: An Intellectual Biography.* Lawrence: University Press of Kansas, 1986.

Schorer, Mark. *D. H. Lawrence [An Anthology].* New York; Dell, 1968a. (Contains "The Life of D. H. Lawrence," pp. 3–106.)

———. *Lawrence in the War Years.* Stanford: Stanford University, 1968b. (Fifteen-page pamphlet based on a short talk.)

Seligmann, Herbert J. *D. H. Lawrence: An American Interpretation.* New York: Seltzer, 1924.

Seltzer, Adele. *D. H. Lawrence: The Man and His Work.* New York: Seltzer, 1922. (Publicity leaflet.)

Sharma, K. K. *Modern Fictional Theorists: Virginia Woolf and D. H. Lawrence.* Gaziabad: Vimal Prakashan, 1981; Atlantic Highlands, N.J.: Humanities Press, 1982.

Sharma, R. S. *"The Rainbow": A Study of Symbolic Mode in D. H. Lawrence's Primitivism.* Hyderabad, India: Trust, 1981.

Sharma, Shruti. *D. H. Lawrence, "Sons and Lovers," a Critical Study.* Karnal: Natraj Publishing House, 1990.

Sharma, T. R., ed. *Essays on D. H. Lawrence.* Meerut, India: Shalabh Book House, 1987.

Shaw, Rita Granger. *Notes on Lawrence's "Sons and Lovers."* Lincoln, Nebr.: Cliff's Notes, 1965.

Siegel, Carol. *Lawrence among the Women: Wavering Boundaries in Women's Literary Traditions.* Charlottesville and London: University Press of Virginia, 1991.

Simpson, Hilary. *D. H. Lawrence and Feminism.* London and Canberra: Croom Helm, 1982.

Singh, Hukum. *D. H. Lawrence (Sex, Love and Life).* Kanpur, India: Aradhana Brothers, 1988.

Singh, Tajindar. *The Literary Criticism of D. H. Lawrence.* New Delhi: Sterling; New York: Envoy, 1984.

Sinha, Radha Krishna. *Literary Influences on D. H. Lawrence.* Delhi: Chanakya, 1985.

Sinzelle, Claude M. *The Geographical Background of the Early Works of D. H. Lawrence.* Paris: Didier, 1964.

Sipple, James B. *Passionate Form: Life Process as Artistic Paradigm in the Writings of D. H. Lawrence.* New York: Peter Lang, 1992.

Sitesh, Aruna. *D. H. Lawrence: The Crusader as Critic.* Delhi, Bombay, Calcutta, Madras: Macmillan, 1975.

———, ed. *D. H. Lawrence: An Anthology of Recent Criticism.* Delhi, India: ACE, 1990.

Sklar, Sylvia. *The Plays of D. H. Lawrence: A Biographical and Critical Study.* London: Vision, 1975.

Sklenicka, Carol. *D. H. Lawrence and the Child.* Columbia and London: University of Missouri Press, 1991.

Slade, Tony. *D. H. Lawrence.* London: Evans Brothers, 1969.

Smailes, T. A. *Some Comments on the Verse of D. H. Lawrence.* Port Elizabeth, South Africa: University of Port Elizabeth, 1970.

Smith, Anne, ed. *Lawrence and Women.* London: Vision, 1978.

Snyder, Harold Jay. *A Catalogue of English and American First Editions, 1911–32, of D. H. Lawrence.* New York: Privately printed, 1932.

Spear, Hilda D. *York Notes on D. H. Lawrence's "The Rainbow."* London: Longman, 1991.

Spencer, Roy. *D. H. Lawrence Country: A Portrait of His Early Life and Background with Illustrations, Maps and Guides.* London: Cecil Woolf, 1980.

Spender, Stephen, ed. *D. H. Lawrence: Novelist, Poet, Prophet.* London: Weidenfeld and Nicolson, 1973.

Spilka, Mark. *The Love Ethic of D. H. Lawrence.* London: Dennis Dobson, 1958.

————. *Renewing the Normative D. H. Lawrence: A Personal Progress.* Columbia: University of Missouri Press, 1992.

————, ed. *D. H. Lawrence: A Collection of Critical Essays.* Englewood Cliffs, N.J.: Prentice-Hall, 1963.

Squires, Michael. *The Pastoral Novel: Studies in George Eliot, Thomas Hardy and D. H. Lawrence.* Charlottesville: University Press of Virginia, 1974.

————. *The Creation of "Lady Chatterley's Lover."* Baltimore: Johns Hopkins University Press, 1983.

————, ed. *D. H. Lawrence's Manuscripts: The Correspondence of Frieda Lawrence, Jake Zeitlin and Others.* London: Macmillan, 1991.

Squires, Michael, and Dennis Jackson, eds. *D. H. Lawrence's "Lady": A New Look at "Lady Chatterley's Lover."* Athens: University of Georgia Press, 1985.

Squires, Michael, and Keith Cushman, eds. *The Challenge of D. H. Lawrence.* Madison: University of Wisconsin Press, 1990.

Stevens, C. J. *Lawrence at Tregerthen.* Troy, N.Y.: Whitston, 1988.

Stewart, J.I.M. *Eight Modern Writers* (Oxford History of English Literature, vol. 12). Oxford and New York: Oxford University Press, 1963, pp. 484–593. (Reissued as *Writers of the Early Twentieth Century: Hardy to Lawrence.* Oxford and New York: Oxford University Press, 1990.)

Stoll, John E. *D. H. Lawrence's "Sons and Lovers": Self-Encounter and the Unknown Self.* Muncie, Ind.: Ball State University Press, 1968.

————. *The Novels of D. H. Lawrence: A Search for Integration.* Columbia: University of Missouri Press, 1971.

————. *D. H. Lawrence: A Bibliography, 1911–1975.* Troy, N.Y.: Whitston, 1977.

Storch, Margaret. *Sons and Adversaries: Women in William Blake and D. H. Lawrence.* Knoxville: University of Tennessee Press, 1990.

Storer, Ronald W. *Some Aspects of Brinsley Colliery and the Lawrence Connection.* Selston, Nottinghamshire: Ronald W. Storer, 1985.

Suter, Andreas. *Child and Childhood in the Novels of D. H. Lawrence.* Zürich: Juris Druck and Verlag Zürich, 1987.

Swigg, Richard. *Lawrence, Hardy and American Literature.* New York: Oxford University Press, 1972.

Tedlock, E. W., Jr. *The Frieda Lawrence Collection of D. H. Lawrence Manuscripts: A Descriptive Bibliography.* Albuquerque: University of New Mexico Press, 1948.

————. *D. H. Lawrence: Artist and Rebel: A Study of Lawrence's Fiction.* Albuquerque: University of New Mexico Press, 1963

————, ed. *D. H. Lawrence and "Sons and Lovers": Sources and Criticism.* New York: New York University Press; London: University of London Press, 1965.

Tannenbaum, E., ed. *D. H. Lawrence: An Exhibition of First Editions, Manuscripts, Paintings, Letters, and Miscellany.* Carbondale: Southern Illinois University Library, 1958. (Catalog of event held in April 1958.)

Tarr, Roger L., and Robert Sokon, eds. *A Bibliography of the D. H. Lawrence Collection at Illinois State University.* Bloomington, Ill.: Scarlet Ibis Press, 1979.

Templeton, Wayne. *States of Estrangement: The Novels of D. H. Lawrence, 1912–1917.* Troy, N.Y.: Whitston, 1989.

Tenenbaum, Elizabeth Brody. *The Problematic Self: Approaches to Identity in Stendhal, D. H. Lawrence, and Malraux.* Cambridge: Harvard University Press, 1977, pp. 65–112.

Texas University Humanities Research Center. *The University of New Mexico D. H. Lawrence Fellowship Fund Manuscript Collection.* Austin: University of Texas Humanities Research Center, 1960. (Catalog.)

Thornton, Weldon. *D. H. Lawrence: A Study of the Short Fiction.* New York: Twayne, 1993.

Tilak, Raghukul. *D. H. Lawrence, "Sons and Lovers."* New Delhi: Aarti Book Centre, 1968.

————. *D. H. Lawrence, "The Rainbow."* New Delhi: Aarti Book Centre, 1971.

Tindall, William York. *D. H. Lawrence and Susan His Cow.* New York: Columbia University Press, 1939.

Torgovnick, Marianna. *The Visual Arts, Pictorialism, and the Novel: James, Lawrence, and Woolf.* Princeton: Princeton University Press, 1985.

Tracy, Billy T., Jr. *D. H. Lawrence and the Literature of Travel.* Ann Arbor, Mich.: UMI Research Press, 1983.

Trease, Geoffrey. *D. H. Lawrence: The Phoenix and the Flame.* London: Macmillan; New York: Viking, 1973.

Trebisz, Małgorzata. *The Novella in England at the Turn of the XIX and XX Centuries: H. James, J. Conrad, D. H. Lawrence.* Wrocław, Poland: Wydawnictwo Uniwersytetu Wrocławskiego, 1992. ("D. H. Lawrence's Novellas," pp. 53–64; *The Fox,* pp. 54–58, *St. Mawr,* pp. 59–62, *The Man Who Died,* pp. 62–64.)

Tripathy, Biyot K. *The Major Novels of D. H. Lawrence: An Approach to His Art and Ideas.* Bhubaneshwar: Pothi, 1973.

Tytell, John. *Passionate Lives: D. H. Lawrence, F. Scott Fitzgerald, Henry Miller, Dylan Thomas, Sylvia Plath—In Love.* New York: Birch Lane Press, 1991.

Urang, Sarah. *Kindled in the Flame: The Apocalyptic Scene in D. H. Lawrence.* Ann Arbor, Mich.: UMI Research Press, 1983.

Van der Veen, Berend Klass. *The Development of D. H. Lawrence's Prose Themes, 1906–1915.* Gröningen, Netherlands: University of Gröningen, 1983.

Veitch, Douglas W. *Lawrence, Greene and Lowry: The Fictional Landscape of Mexico.* Waterloo, Ontario: Wilfrid Laurier University Press, 1978. ("D. H. Lawrence's Elusive Mexico," pp. 14–57.)

Verhoeven, W. M. *D. H. Lawrence's Duality Concept: Its Development in the Novels of the Early and Major Phase.* Groningen, The Netherlands: Phoenix, 1987.

Viinikka, Anja. *From Persephone to Pan: D. H. Lawrence's Mythopoeic Vision of the Integrated Personality.* Turku, Finland: Turun Yliopisto Julkaisuja, 1988.

Vivas, Eliseo. *D. H. Lawrence: The Failure and the Triumph of Art.* London: George Allen and Unwin, 1960.

Vries-Mason, Jillian de. *Perception in the Poetry of D. H. Lawrence.* Berne: Peter Lang, 1982.

Walterscheid, Kathryn A. *The Resurrection of the Body: Touch in D. H. Lawrence.* New York: Peter Lang, 1993.

Warren Gallery. *Exhibition 12: Paintings by D. H. Lawrence.* London: Warren Gallery, 1929. (Catalog of event held in July 1929.)

Weiss, Daniel. *Oedipus in Nottingham: D. H. Lawrence.* Seattle: University of Washington Press, 1962.

West, Anthony. *D. H. Lawrence.* London: Barker; Denver: Alan Swallow, 1950.

West, Rebecca. *D. H. Lawrence: An Elegy.* London: Secker, 1930.

Whelan, P. T. *D. H. Lawrence: Myth and Metaphysic in "The Rainbow" and "Women in Love."* Ann Arbor, Mich., and London: UMI Research Press, 1988.

White, William. *D. H. Lawrence: A Checklist. Writings about D. H. Lawrence, 1931– 50.* Detroit, Mich.: Wayne State University Press, 1950.

Whiteley, Patrick J. *Knowledge and Experimental Realism in Conrad, Lawrence, and Woolf.* Baton Rouge: Louisiana State University Press, 1987.

Wickremasinghe, Martino de Silva. *The Mysticism of D. H. Lawrence.* Colombo: M. D. Gunasena, 1951.

Widdowson, Peter, ed. *D. H. Lawrence.* London: Longman, 1992.

Widmer, Kingsley. *The Art of Perversity: D. H. Lawrence's Shorter Fictions.* Seattle: University of Washington Press, 1962.

———. *Defiant Desire: Some Dialectical Legacies of D. H. Lawrence.* Carbondale: Southern Illinois University Press, 1992.

Williams, Linda Ruth. *Sex in the Head: Visions of Femininity and Film in D. H. Lawrence.* Hemel Hempstead, Hertfordshire: Harvester Wheatsheaf, 1993.

Williams, Raymond. *The English Novel from Dickens to Lawrence.* London: Chatto, 1970, pp. 169–84.

Wilt, Judith. *Ghosts of the Gothic: Austen, Eliot, and Lawrence.* Princeton: Princeton University Press, 1980, pp. 231–303.

Worthen, John. *D. H. Lawrence and the Idea of the Novel.* London: Macmillan; Totowa, N.J.: Rowman, 1979.

———. *D. H. Lawrence: A Literary Life.* London: Macmillan, 1989.

———. *D. H. Lawrence.* London: Edward Arnold, 1991a.

———. *D. H. Lawrence: The Early Years 1885–1912.* Cambridge: Cambridge University Press, 1991b.

———. *Cold Hearts and Coronets: Lawrence, the von Richthofens and the Weekleys.* Nottingham: D. H. Lawrence Centre, 1995. (Worthen's inaugural lecture as Professor of D. H. Lawrence Studies at Nottingham.)

Wright, Anne. *Literature of Crisis, 1910–1922: "Howard's End," "Heartbreak House," "Women in Love," and "The Wasteland."* London: Macmillan; New York: St. Martin's Press, 1984.

Young, Kenneth. *D. H. Lawrence.* London, New York, Toronto: Longmans, Green, 1952. (Writers and Their Work Series.)

Yudhishtar. *Conflict in the Novels of D. H. Lawrence.* Edinburgh: Oliver and Boyd; New York: Barnes and Noble, 1969.

Zytaruk, George J. *D. H. Lawrence's Response to Russian Literature.* The Hague: Mouton, 1971.

BIBLIOGRAPHY 97: JOURNALS AND SPECIAL NUMBERS OF JOURNALS DEVOTED TO LAWRENCE

The Aligarh Journal of English Studies 10 no. 2 (1985). Special D. H. Lawrence Number.

The D. H. Lawrence Review. Edited by Dennis Jackson. Newark: University of Delaware, 1968– .

Etudes Lawrenciennes. Edited by Ginette Roy. University of Paris X—Nanterre.

Japan D. H. Lawrence Studies. Kyoto University.

Journal of the D. H. Lawrence Society. Edited by Catherine Greensmith. Nottingham: D. H. Lawrence Society, 1976– . (See also under Cooper and Hughes in preceding bibliography.)

The Laughing Horse 13 (April 1926). Special D. H. Lawrence Number. Edited by Willard Johnson.

Library Chronicle of the University of Texas at Austin, new series, 34 (1986). Special D. H. Lawrence Number.

Literature/Film Quarterly 1, no. 1 (January 1973). Special D. H. Lawrence Number. Edited by Thomas L. Erskine.

Modern Fiction Studies 5 (Spring 1959). Special D. H. Lawrence Number. Edited by Maurice Beebe.

Modernist Studies 4 (1982). "A Special Issue on D. H. Lawrence, 1885–1930."

The New Adelphi (June–August 1930). Lawrence memorial issue. Edited by John Middleton Murry.

Osmania Journal of English Studies 21 (1985). D. H. Lawrence Special Number. Edited by Adapa Ramakrishna Rao and R. S. Sharma. (Hyderabad, India.)

Paunch 26 (April 1966). Special D. H. Lawrence Number. Edited by Arthur Efron.

Paunch 63–64 (December 1990). *The Passional Secret Places of Life: New Studies in D. H. Lawrence.* Edited by Arthur Efron.

Phoenix 23 (1981). "A Special D. H. Lawrence Issue in Commemoration of the 50th Anniversary of the Writer's Death." (English Literature Society, Korea University, Seoul, Korea.)

Rananim: Journal of the D. H. Lawrence Society of Australia. 1993– .

Renaissance and Modern Studies 29 (1985). Lawrence Centennial issue. Guest editor, James T. Boulton.

Staple Magazine (Derbyshire College School of Humanities). Special Number: *Lawrence and the Real England.* Edited by Donald Measham. Matlock, Derbyshire: Arc and Throstle Press, 1985.

BIBLIOGRAPHY 98: THE WORKS OF D. H. LAWRENCE

As full bibliographical details of all Lawrence's works are given in the individual entries to the works in Part II of this book, this bibliography is designed simply for general reference purposes. Thus, only limited publication details are provided here—chiefly of the Cambridge editions—and only the major works are listed. Where a work has not yet been published in a Cambridge edition, details of first publication are given, except where a work has been referred to earlier in the book in a Penguin edition, in which case that edition is cited along with first publication details. (All references to Lawrence's works in this book are to the Cambridge editions where these are available; otherwise, they are to the Penguin editions cited here where relevant.)

A full bibliography of Lawrence's letters and of scholarship relating to them can be found in Bibliography 1 in Part I of this book, and, again, only the Cambridge edition of the letters is cited here.

The Cambridge texts of Lawrence's works are in the process of being issued in paperback under Penguin's ''Twentieth-Century Classics'' series (the ''Penguin Lawrence Edition''), with John Worthen as advisory editor. These editions will have texts and pagination normally identical to the Cambridge editions, though there will be occasional corrections to the texts and new introductions and explanatory notes, often by different scholars from those who edited the equivalent Cambridge volumes.

Aaron's Rod. Edited by Mara Kalnins. Cambridge: Cambridge University Press, 1988.

Apocalypse and the Writings on Revelation. Edited by Mara Kalnins. Cambridge: Cambridge University Press, 1980.

A Propos of "Lady Chatterley's Lover." London: Mandrake Press, 1930.

Assorted Articles. London: Secker 1930.

Birds, Beasts and Flowers. London: Secker 1923.

The Boy in the Bush [with M. L. Skinner]. Edited by Paul Eggert. Cambridge: Cambridge University Press, 1990.

The Complete Plays of D. H. Lawrence. London: Heinemann, 1965. New York: Viking, 1966.

The Complete Poems of D. H. Lawrence. Rev. ed. Edited by Vivian de Sola Pinto and Warren Roberts. London: Heinemann, 1967.

England, My England and Other Stories. Edited by Bruce Steele. Cambridge: Cambridge University Press, 1990.

Fantasia of the Unconscious. London: Secker, 1923. (*Fantasia of the Unconscious* and *Psychoanalysis and the Unconscious.* Harmondsworth: Penguin, 1971.)

The First Lady Chatterley. New York: Dial, 1944. London: Heinemann, 1972. Harmondsworth: Penguin, 1973.

The Fox, The Captain's Doll, The Ladybird. Edited by Dieter Mehl. Cambridge University Press 1992.

John Thomas and Lady Jane. London: Heinemann; New York: Viking, 1972. Harmondsworth: Penguin 1973. (First published in Italian as *La Seconda Lady Chatterley* in *Le Tre "Lady Chatterley."* Translated by Carlo Izzo. Italy: Mondadori, 1954.)

Kangaroo. Edited by Bruce Steele. Cambridge: Cambridge University Press, 1994.

Lady Chatterley's Lover. Edited by Michael Squires. Cambridge: Cambridge University Press, 1993.

Last Poems. Edited by Richard Aldington. Florence: G. Orioli, 1932.

The Letters of D. H. Lawrence. Vol. 1: September 1901–May 1913. Edited by James T. Boulton. Cambridge: Cambridge University Press, 1979.

The Letters of D. H. Lawrence. Vol. 2: June 1913–October 1916. Edited by George J. Zytaruk and James T. Boulton. Cambridge: Cambridge University Press, 1982.

The Letters of D. H. Lawrence. Vol. 3: October 1916–June 1921. Edited by James T. Boulton and Andrew Robertson. Cambridge: Cambridge University Press, 1984.

The Letters of D. H. Lawrence. Vol. 4: June 1921–March 1924. Edited by Warren Roberts, James T. Boulton, and Elizabeth Mansfield. Cambridge: Cambridge University Press, 1987.

The Letters of D. H. Lawrence. Vol. 5: March 1924–March 1927. Edited by James T. Boulton and Lindeth Vasey. Cambridge: Cambridge University Press, 1989.

The Letters of D. H. Lawrence. Vol. 6: March 1927–November 1928. Edited by James T. Boulton and Margaret H. Boulton with Gerald Lacy. Cambridge: Cambridge University Press, 1991.

The Letters of D. H. Lawrence. Vol. 7: November 1928–February 1930. Edited by Keith Sagar and James T. Boulton. Cambridge: Cambridge University Press, 1993.

The Letters of D. H. Lawrence. Vol. 8: Index. Edited by James T. Boulton. Cambridge: Cambridge University Press, forthcoming.

Look! We Have Come Through! London: Chatto and Windus, 1917.

The Lost Girl. Edited by John Worthen. Cambridge: Cambridge University Press, 1981.

Love Among the Haystacks and Other Stories. Edited by John Worthen. Cambridge: Cambridge University Press, 1990.

Mr Noon. Edited by Lindeth Vasey. Cambridge: Cambridge University Press, 1984.

Mornings in Mexico. London: Secker 1927. (*Mornings in Mexico* and *Etruscan Places.* Harmondsworth: Penguin, 1960.)

Movements in European History. Edited by Philip Crumpton. Cambridge: Cambridge University Press, 1989.

Phoenix: The Posthumous Papers of D. H. Lawrence. Edited by Edward D. McDonald. New York: Viking; London: Heinemann, 1936.

Phoenix II: Uncollected, Unpublished and Other Prose Works by D. H. Lawrence. Edited by Warren Roberts and Harry T. Moore. London: Heinemann, 1968.

The Plumed Serpent (Quetzalcoatl). Edited by L. D. Clark. Cambridge: Cambridge University Press, 1987.

Pornography and Obscenity. London: Faber and Faber, 1929.

The Princess and Other Stories. Edited by Keith Sagar. Harmondsworth: Penguin, 1971.

The Prussian Officer and Other Stories. Edited by John Worthen. Cambridge: Cambridge University Press, 1983.

Psychoanalysis and the Unconscious. London: Secker, 1923. (*Fantasia of the Unconscious* and *Psychoanalysis and the Unconscious.* Harmondsworth: Penguin, 1971.)

The Rainbow. Edited by Mark Kinkead-Weekes. Cambridge: Cambridge University Press, 1989.

Reflections on the Death of a Porcupine and Other Essays. Edited by Michael Herbert. Cambridge: Cambridge University Press, 1988.

Sea and Sardinia. London: Secker, 1923. (Harmondsworth: Penguin, 1944.)

Sketches of Etruscan Places and Other Italian Essays. Edited by Simonetta de Filippis. Cambridge: Cambridge University Press, 1992.

Sons and Lovers. Edited by Carl and Helen Baron. Cambridge: Cambridge University Press, 1992.

Sons and Lovers: A Facsimile of the Manuscript. Edited by Mark Schorer. Berkeley, Los Angeles, London: University of California Press, 1977.

St. Mawr and Other Stories. Edited by Brian Finney. Cambridge: Cambridge University Press, 1983.

Studies in Classic American Literature. London: Secker, 1924. (Harmondsworth: Penguin, 1971.)

Study of Thomas Hardy and Other Essays. Edited by Bruce Steele. Cambridge: Cambridge University Press, 1985.

The Symbolic Meaning: The Uncollected Versions of "Studies in Classic American Literature." Edited by Armin Arnold. London: T. J. Winterson, 1962.

The Trespasser. Edited by Elizabeth Mansfield. Cambridge: Cambridge University Press, 1981.

Twilight in Italy and Other Essays. Edited by Paul Eggert. Cambridge: Cambridge University Press, 1994.

The Virgin and the Gipsy. Florence: Orioli, 1930. (*St. Mawr and The Virgin and the Gipsy.* Harmondsworth: Penguin, 1950.)

The White Peacock. Edited by Andrew Robertson. Cambridge: Cambridge University Press, 1983.

The Woman Who Rode Away and Other Stories. Edited by Dieter Mehl and Christa Jansohn. Cambridge: Cambridge University Press, 1995.

Women in Love. Edited by David Farmer, Lindeth Vasey, and John Worthen. Cambridge: Cambridge University Press, 1987.

PART V

INDEXES

D. H. Lawrence: Life, Works, and Places

LIFE

D. H. Lawrence is abbreviated to DHL throughout. Citations dealing with the main elements of Lawrence's life and personality are grouped under the following headings: Characteristics; Childhood and early development; Education; Employment; Illnesses; Intellectual and artistic development; Travels; War; Writing career (and see also the entries for Frieda Lawrence; the Lawrence and Chambers families; Paintings; Popular journalism; Religion and beliefs; *Lady Chatterley's Lover*; and *Sons and Lovers*). The sections entitled WORKS and PLACES provide a comprehensive listing of Lawrence's works and places associated with his life and art.

PLACES

Lawrence and Film

The following index relates solely to Part III: Section C of this book ("The Popular Image: Lawrence and Film," pp. 589–638). It should be noted that, as a rule, items listed in Chronology 7 ("Cinema and Broadcasting," pp. 631–638)—and film titles in particular—appear here only if they are discussed in some way, or if they are referred to elsewhere in the section. Names of critics relevant to this part of the book are listed together here under the entry head "Critics," but *without* page references, as these can be found in the Name Index. (When cross-referring to the Name Index, bear in mind the above page range as some of these critics also appear elsewhere in the book.)

Names

Abel, Elizabeth, 337
Abercrombie, Lascelles, 506
Abolin, Nancy, 318
Adam, Ian, 181
Adamowski, T. H., 167, 182, 196, 253, 522, 554, 567
Adams, Elsie B., 253
Adams, Marion, 468,
Adelman, Gary, 182, 196, 292, 505, 554, 641
Ades, John I., 489, 519, 548
Adix, M., 515, 536, 567
Aiken, Conrad, 417, 480, 507–9
Akers, Gary, 488
Albright, Daniel, 156, 175, 190, 208, 215, 248, 356, 370, 397, 504, 536, 553, 641
Alcorn, John, 156, 175, 208, 227, 465, 504, 535, 641
Alcorn, Marshall W., Jr., 567
Alden, Patricia, 175, 190, 505, 529, 536, 641
Aldington, Richard, 77, 85, 97, 103, 107, 111, 259, 410, 416, 417, 445, 493, 503, 508, 512, 541, 641, 661
Alexander, John C., 232, 536, 567
Alford, John, 506
Alinei, Tamara, 167, 182
Alldritt, Keith, 156, 175, 190, 208, 227, 234, 248, 488, 504, 526, 536, 641
Allen, C. N., 167, 554

Allen, Douglas, 630
Allen, Walter, 267, 513
Allendorf, Otmar, 461
Allott, Kenneth, 103
Alpers, Antony, 103, 537
Alpert, Hollis, 628
Alter, Richard, 519, 530
Althusser, Louis, 595, 619
Alvarado, Manuel, 593, 619
Alvarez, A., 410, 417, 516
Alves, Leonard, 413, 417
Amette, Jacques-Pierre, 625
Amon, Frank, 267, 387
Ananthamurthy, U. R., 537
Anderson, Emily Ann, 410, 417, 493
Anderson, G. K., 512
Anderson, Sherwood, 388, 509, 510, 514, 536, 543, 557
Anderson, Walter E., 292, 561
Andrews, Esther, 39, 84, 86, 231
Andrews, W. T., 256, 498, 574, 641
Ansari, Iqbal A., 196, 253
Antrim, Thomas M., 415, 417
Appleman, Philip, 301
Apter, T. E., 244, 579, 586
Arbuckle, Roscoe (''Fatty''), 635, 636
Arbur, Rosemarie, 412, 417, 537
Arcana, Judith, 167, 554, 579

About the Author

PAUL POPLAWSKI is Senior Lecturer in English at Trinity College Carmarthen in Wales. He has published articles on D. H. Lawrence and his books include *Promptings of Desire: Creativity and the Religious Impulse in the Works of D. H. Lawrence* (Greenwood, 1993), *The Works of D. H. Lawrence: A Chronological Checklist* (1995), and *Language, Art and Reality in D. H. Lawrence's "St. Mawr": A Stylistic Study* (1996).

ISBN 0-313-28637-X

90000>

EAN

9 780313 286377

HARDCOVER BAR CODE